The League of American Theatres and Producers, Inc.
226 West 47th Street, New York, NY 10036
www.broadway.org
league@broadway.org

STAGE SPECS

A Technical Guide to Theatres
1999 Edition

Compiled and Edited by
ADRIENNE L. TURNER

with
BARBARA JANOWITZ
and
UNITECH PRODUCTIONS, INC.

Published by

LIVE
BROADWAY
The League of American Theatres and Producers, Inc.

STAGE SPECS™
A Technical Guide to Theatres

1999 Edition

Library of Congress Catalog Number: 90-060537

ISBN 0-9625844-1-X

CONTENTS

Acknowledgements   v

Foreword   vii

Introduction   ix

A Guide to STAGE SPECS™   x

Theatre Listings

     United States   3

     Canada   600

     Under Renovation   640

Theatre Indexes

     Alphabetical   641

     Geographical   647

     Capacity   651

Presenter's Guide

     by Name   655

     by Market   658

About the League   660

US Mileage Chart & Map   661

ACKNOWLEDGEMENTS

Stage Specs™, 1999 details the nuts and bolts in the theatres; the physical structure that allows the visual and audio creativity to reach the audience. The goal of *Stage Specs, 1999* is to succinctly present the key data necessary to bring Broadway, and all theatre, to the audiences of the US and Canada.

For many months, I have been immersed in *Stage Specs, 1999* creating and mailing the surveys, cajoling and pleading to have the data returned, entering and editing the data, and designing and laying out the pages. My sincere thanks are due to the many minds and hands that joined me on this project.

Barbara Janowitz, the League's Director of Membership Services, was dedicated to bringing this book to fruition. She acquired the resources we needed and stayed focused on the goal as she mastered the mountains of paper. She was the guiding force on the project.

Unitech, the team of Ken Keneally and Brian Lynch, have been technical supervisors to numerous theatrical productions on Broadway, off Broadway and on the road. My thanks to them for their infinite knowledge and direction of the technical details. They have brought clarity to the data and a huge benefit to the project.

Joe Vella, a graphics virtuoso, has tirelessly created the stage diagrams for the theatres and I have the strongest appreciation for his diligent, painstaking and accurate work.

Robert B. Gould and Susan E. Lee, the authors of the original Stage Specs, have my admiration for setting the standard for technical specifications of theatres.

I thank the staff of the League, the members of the League, the booking agents, general managers, PSMs, producers and technical directors who I have called upon for their assistance, advice and opinion. Thanks to Laurie Tvedt and Lizard who started us off on the right foot by passing on their wisdom acquired during their prior *Stage Specs* experience.

The '*I Couldn't Have Done It Without You*' award goes to the assistants, of various durations, who have graced *Stage Specs* with their efforts:
Jeniffer Rivera, Michael Biondi, Samantha Lazarus, Melissa Bank, Zoë Levy, Darleen Wall, Cedric Hill, Michael Weekes, Doris Mills, and Nazmin Bhatia Gordon for their calling, mailing, calling, researching, typing, typing, data checking, calling, typing, faxing and proofreading.

My highest regard and thanks to the staff of the theatres, without whom there would be no data, which is, without question the most important part of this book.

My final thanks goes to you, the user of this book, for relying on Stage Specs to assist you on your journey to your next venue, if only via these pages.

Adrienne L. Turner
Editor

FOREWORD

Almost two thirds of the Broadway industry's business takes place outside New York. Playing in as many as 150 cities each year, touring productions delight audiences of more than 16 million each season throughout the U.S. and Canada. One of the most important roles the League can play as the trade association for the North American commercial theatre industry is to facilitate the flow of information. In that spirit, we bring you, on the pages that follow, a comprehensive technical guide to 320 of those most magical of buildings: venues that provide a home for live theatrical productions.

We published the first edition of *Stage Specs* in 1990, and it's particularly exciting to note how many theatres have been renovated or expanded since then. More and more houses now have the physical capability to host the entire range of currently touring productions. The remarkable transformation of these edifices is a sure sign of the health of the touring Broadway community.

For more than a century, Broadway has captured the public's imagination as an exhilarating, enriching form of live entertainment. As this thriving industry continues to grow, we will continue to provide valuable resources to support the producers, presenters, managers, and promoters of live theatre across the continent. This book is intended as a tool for the entire performing arts community. Let's continue working together to bring the magic of live entertainment to audiences across North America.

Jed Bernstein
President
The League of American Theatres and Producers, Inc.

INTRODUCTION

When the first edition of *Stage Specs*™ was released, it was an instantaneous success and a most wanted item by all theatre professionals. Copies became dog-eared and irreplaceable. Some even became victims of kidnapping. Producers, managers, designers, road crews, all share in the need for accurate and detailed information. With the release of this 1999 edition, a long awaited (and needed) update is finally here.

UNITECH has had a very enjoyable and productive time working with Adrienne Turner and Barbara Janowitz. Their perseverance and dedication has been an inspiration to us to complete this project and get it to the members of the League and the theatre community at large. We also thank all those who took the time to fill out the requests for information and for answering all the detailed questions.

We are sure that this edition will take the spot on the shelf left open when someone "borrowed" the first edition.

Ken Keneally and Brian Lynch
UNITECH

A GUIDE TO STAGE SPECS™ 1999

This second edition of **Stage Specs™, A Technical Guide to Theatres, 1999 Edition** began with the creation of the technical survey by League staff and several production professionals. Questionnaires were sent to theatre managers and technical supervisors of over 400 American and Canadian performing arts facilities with either a history of, or potential for, hosting touring Broadway shows. Theatres with limited touring history or potential were sent a short version of the survey. Although the list of theatres included in **Stage Specs™, 1999** is inclusive, it is by no means comprehensive. Theatres that did not respond to the survey or were unable to provide the required technical information have not been included in this edition.

In the ensuing months, information was verified once again with the staff of each facility. When possible, a proof was sent to the management of the theatre to be approved prior to the publication of the guide. Facility personnel checked and proofed the material in its entirety.

While every attempt was made to certify accuracy, this book should be used only as a guideline. We recommend that in-house production personnel be contacted for show-specific information well ahead of booking an engagement, and to verify that listed data is still current. The League cannot assume responsibility for incorrect information.

If you find an error or you know of a theatre that you feel should be included in the next edition of the book but is not listed here, please let us know. It is our goal to correct any discrepancies and include missing facilities in the next edition.

ORGANIZATION OF THIS BOOK

The theatres in this book are organized alphabetically by state, city, and theatre name, with the Canadian theatres following the United States listings. This book is indexed alphabetically by theatre name (including alternate names), as well as by geography and capacity. A list of League of American Theatres and Producers presenters and a market-by-market contact guide has been included for assistance in routing and booking touring productions.

Each frequently utilized theatre is presented on two pages. The first page includes the vital statistics of the building (personnel, addresses, and telephone contacts) and a stage diagram. The second page provides detailed specifications divided into four sections: STAGE HOUSE, BACKSTAGE, SOUND and ELECTRICS. Within these sections, a number enclosed in parentheses, e.g. (3), expresses quantity. A detailed explanation of each section appears below.

Theatres with a limited touring history or those that provided less data are presented on one page, with basic information and no stage house diagram.

FACILITY INFORMATION

THEATRE NAME & ADDRESS

The theatre name shown at the top of every page is the title under which each facility wishes to be identified. Complex names, individual building names, and aliases are also listed. A complete directory of theatre names can be found in the alphabetical index. The first address indicated is the actual location of the facility followed by a separate mailing address, if applicable. The name and address of the management company is also listed, if different from the facility address.

CONTACT NUMBERS

Facility telephone numbers may include the following: *Main Administrative Phone,* usually the administration or switchboard number; *Main Administrative Fax; Stage Door Phone,* either a crew room, a telephone staffed by a doorman, or simply a backstage extension of the main switchboard; *Backstage Pay Phone;* and *Traveling Production Office Phone* and *Fax,* typically phone and fax lines dedicated to the traveling road managers. If a traveling production office number is not listed, one can often be installed on a per-show basis and a new number assigned accordingly.

E-mail and website addresses are also included when available.

THEATRE STAFF includes administrative personnel with their telephone numbers. HOUSE CREW lists technical employees of the facility who may or may not be affiliated with a particular theatrical labor union. Specific technical questions should be directed accordingly. Please note, with the exception of the administrative head and technical director, personnel are listed by function rather than job title.

UNIONS

Appropriate labor union contacts are listed. The designation of an IATSE Business Agent does not necessarily indicate that the theatre is a union house. The musical contractor may either represent the American Federation of Musicians or be an in-house contact.

SEATING CAPACITY

The theatre capacity is divided into the seating sections designated by the box office. *Pit* seating (available when the pit area is not needed for staging or an orchestra), *Standing Room*, and *Wheelchair* seating may increase the capacity, and are noted as either included or in excess of the total capacity.

BOX OFFICE

Box offices are designated as equipped with a *Computerized* ticketing system or as a *Hard Ticket Box Office*. Also shown is the *Box Office Manager* or *Treasurer* and the *Outside Ticket Agency*. A designation of *Promoter Operated* means each production must staff the box office on a per-show basis.

DIAGRAM

GENERAL

A not-to-scale graphic gives an overview of the stage house and orchestra pit dimensions as well as the rigging system rails. **Stage Specs™, 1999** does not include scaled drawings of the theatres presented; however, an attempt was made to reproduce a facsimile of theatres with irregularly-shaped stage houses. Box figures for height dimensions denote elevation from the deck, and depth from the stage to house floor. *First available line set* denotes the first line set upstage of the house curtain. Dimensions within the stage-house indicate distances to obstructions and not necessarily to the walls. SL/SR Wing space indicates distances to obstructions.

ORCHESTRA PIT

Due to the various shapes of orchestra pits found in these facilities, the side-to-side dimension of the pit is intended as a general measurement only. Additional information regarding the orchestra pit can be found in the STAGE HOUSE section on the second page of each theatre.

RIGGING RAILS

Elevated rails are shown with a dashed line; rails on the deck are represented by a solid line. A rigging rail may have a number of different labels depending on its use, including *Locking* for a counter weight system; *Fly* for a hemp system exclusively; *Pin* for an additional hemp rail; and *Gallery* for an elevated rail without a specific rigging use.

LOADING DOOR

The loading door symbols are intended to show the approximate locations only. More detailed information concerning the size and considerations of loading will be found in the text of the backstage section for each theatre. If there are multiple loading doors with varying conditions, each is numbered on the graphic diagram to match the text under LOADING DOCK. (See LOADING DOCK below.)

STAGE HOUSE

RIGGING SYSTEM

The type and operating location of the house curtain, with note of any special conditions, are listed first. The RIGGING SYSTEM details: *Type*: counter weight (single, double, or combination purchase), hemp or motorized; *Weight*: available, counter weight if operated by a locking rail and sand if-by a hemp system; *Line Sets*: quantity, spacing and lift lines per set; *Arbors*: capacity for counterweight systems; and *House* Pipes: length and travel from the stage floor to their out trim. Also noted is whether or not the line sets are moveable; block & falls on hand; chain hoists available on-site or by rental; spot wheels and hemp available for cable picks and spot lines; and any other special circumstances regarding rigging.

PERMANENT INSTALLATIONS OVER STAGE & ON DECK

The permanent installations are divided into two sections: OVER STAGE and ON DECK. OVER STAGE pertains to obstructions found in the fly system, e.g., orchestra shells, electric bridges, movie screens, traveller tracks, or any equipment the theatre does not normally remove. The numbers following the obstruction represent the distances to the upstage edge of the smoke pocket. If the obstructions are moveable (with an advance call), they are indicated with a letter M. ON DECK obstructions are permanent storage pieces or obstacles found within the stage area or wings in addition to traps and lifts located in the stage floor.

ORCHESTRA PIT

Depth of the orchestra pit from stage floor and the type of lift used, when adjustable, are described. The apron overhang measures the distance from the upstage wall of the orchestra pit to the downstage edge of the apron. Also shown is the presence of an organ lift or an orchestra pit divided into more than one section.

BACKSTAGE

LOADING DOCK

Loading door sizes, truck information, dock approaches, security, and any other special loading conditions are described in this section. If there are multiple loading doors with varying conditions, a small number on the graphic diagram will correspond to the text here. (See LOADING DOOR above.) A notation appears when *a forklift is required,* along with the appropriate contact if available. However, a *forklift supplier* may be listed even though a forklift may not be necessary to load in.

WARDROBE

The location and access to the most commonly used wardrobe area is shown. The theatre listing indicates the number of washers and dryers available or the ability to hook-up outside equipment.

DRESSING ROOMS

Dressing rooms are divided into three specific sizes: *Star,* individual rooms designated by the theatre as such; *Small,* able to accommodate one to six people; and *Chorus,* usually holding more than six people. The locations of the rooms are always shown in relation to the stage (considered to be the first floor), with "+1" denoting one floor above stage level and "-1" denoting one floor below stage level, etc. Toilets and showers, either included in the room or on the same floor, are denoted as "t" and "s". Phone jacks are noted when available. Musicians' rooms and Conductors' rooms were not considered. Office space to be used by the company stage managers is noted.

REHEARSAL & STORAGE

When possible, the sizes and locations of rehearsal & storage areas are listed, as well as any special requirements or equipment available for each. There may be additional areas where rehearsals can take place (e.g.; lobbies, basements, etc.); however, the book's listings are limited to bona fide rehearsal spaces.

SOUND

CONSOLE

The configuration of or presence of main house mixing console is specified along with the number of *inputs* and *outputs.* Additional consoles or other audio equipment may be available.

SPEAKERS

The house speakers are broken down into four basic positions: *House Cluster,* usually located over the proscenium arch; *Under Balcony* speakers; *Proscenium* speakers, located on either side of the proscenium arch; and *Portable* speakers. If there are provisions for a road truss to be hung, it is addressed in this section.

COMMUNICATIONS

Communications covers three basic areas: *intercom* contact between the stagehand positions; *Hearing-impaired Systems* used by audience members; and *Paging Systems* to the dressing rooms and backstage areas. A show monitor may or may not be included in the paging system.

ROAD CONSOLE

This section describes accommodations for a touring mixing console. Its location and cable run to the stage are approximate. Also denoted is the number of seats *required to be removed* (unusable) to accommodate a console and the ability to tie into the house speakers, consoles, and amplifiers.

ELECTRICS

ROAD SERVICE POWER

This chart encompasses all available power for touring equipment but does not include the additional power supplied to the house equipment (e.g., house dimmers). Each *Panel* is labeled with a letter; multiple panels with the same specifications have been grouped together (e.g. A-F would indicate 6 separate panels). Next follows the *Phase* of each service (symbolized by Ø, e.g. 3Ø=3 phase), *Amperage, Circuit Protection* device, most common *Use*, and approximate *Location* of the panel. Also included in this section is the recommended location of touring dimmer racks and whether a hoist is required (or provided), as well as any additional power that could be used for tour buses, generators, and the like.

FRONT OF HOUSE

This table gives an overview of the available hanging *Positions* located in the front of house (FOH). The *Pipe Width* indicates approximately how many linear feet are available for hanging instruments. A number in the *FOH Transfer Circuit* column indicates how many house circuits, if any, are readily picked-up backstage for convenient dimmer rack patch. The type of *Transfer Circuit* connectors is always listed below the chart. If there are provisions for a road truss to be hung, the applicable details are addressed in this section as are other special situations needing further explanation.

EQUIPMENT - FOH

House-owned lighting instruments normally hung in the front of house positions are listed. In some cases, the existing instruments cannot be removed, which is noted. This is not intended to be an all-inclusive inventory of equipment.

FOLLOWSPOTS

The types of house-owned followspots and their removeability are specified in this section. The number of *Booths* is noted if there is more than one. Also denoted is the number of spots per booth, the distance from the booth to the proscenium as indicated by the *throw to proscenium*, and available power indicated as the number of circuits, single or 3 Ø (Ø=phase) and the number of amps.

DIMMERS

Type of house-owned lighting console is specified in this section, as well as type and number of dimmers. Also denoted is the existence of a DMX control system, as well as the number and location of DMX stations when available.

A Note About Broadway Theatres

Due to the nature of Broadway theatres and the type of shows these houses must accommodate, what are generally regarded as fixed conditions elsewhere (e.g., quantity and spacing of line sets, amount of available road power, etc.) are constantly being changed to suit new productions. The specifications outlined in this book are a reflection of these houses at press time.

THEATRE LISTINGS

THE ALABAMA THEATRE

AT: THE ALABAMA THEATRE FOR THE PERFORMING ARTS   YEAR BUILT: **1927**   YEAR RENOVATED: **1998**

Theatre Location: 1817 3rd Avenue N., Birmingham, AL 35203
Management Company: Birmingham Landmarks Inc.
                          1811 3rd Avenue N., Birmingham, AL 35203

Main Administrative Phone: 205-252-2862
Main Administrative Fax: 205-251-3155
Website: www.alabamatheatre.com
Stage Door Phone: 205-252-2262 x120

THEATRE STAFF
General Manager   Cecil Whitmore   205-252-2262 x103
Managing Director   Linda Whitmore   205-252-2262 x101

HOUSE CREW
Technical Director   Alan Bates   205-252-2262 x115

SEATING CAPACITY

Orchestra	902
Mezzanine	313
Dress Circle	126
Balcony	859
Total:	**2,200**

STAGE DIMENSIONS (FROM SMOKE POCKET)
Stage is 28'6" deep
Width from Center Line to SL is 28'2"
Width from Center Line to SR is 28'8"
Proscenium width is 41'4"
Proscenium height is 26'
Smoke pocket to apron edge is 14'9"
Orchestra pit exists

RIGGING
Grid Height: 62'
Type: Single purchase counter weight
Weight: 5,000 lbs
Line sets: 46 sets at 6" o.c.
Arbors: 500 lb capacity
House Pipes: 46' long

LOADING DOCK
Loading door(s) are 7'10" high x 6'10" wide
Trucks load (2) at same time
Fork lift is not required and is available
No dock - unload on the street

ELECTRICS
Total power available:
  (1) 400A 3Ø SR
  (1) 100 A 3Ø SR

FOLLOWSPOTS
House Followspots:
  Lycian
Power in spot booth 60A

DIMMERS
(112) house dimmers
House has DMX control system
(1) dry run station(s) located
  FOH to SR

SOUND
House has 100A dedicated
  power located USR
FOH mixing position in
  Rear Orchestra
Sound console is available

BIRMINGHAM-JEFFERSON CONCERT HALL

AT: BIRMINGHAM-JEFFERSON CIVIC CENTER

Theatre Location: 1 Civic Center Plaza, Birmingham, AL 35202
Mailing Address: PO Box 13347, Birmingham, AL 35203-3347
Management Company: Birmingham-Jefferson Convention Complex
Birmingham, AL 35203-3347

Main Administrative Phone: 205-458-8400
Main Administrative Fax: 205-458-8437
Stage Door Phone: 205-458-8400 x6604
Backstage Pay Phone: 205-254-9850

THEATRE STAFF
Manager George Pierce 205-458-8434
Booking Phoebe Howell 205-458-8400

HOUSE CREW
Stage Manager Allen Langston 205-458-8470
Sound Steve Holmes 205-458-8411

UNIONS
IATSE Local #78 Rick Smith 205-251-1312

SEATING CAPACITY

Orchestra	1,167
Balcony	723
Gran Tier	908
Total:	**2,798**
pit (add'l)	169
wheelchair	0

BOX OFFICE
Computerized
Manager
  Sue Boyd 205-458-8515

Outside Ticket Agency
Computerized
Ticket Link
  Sid Borland 205-715-6000

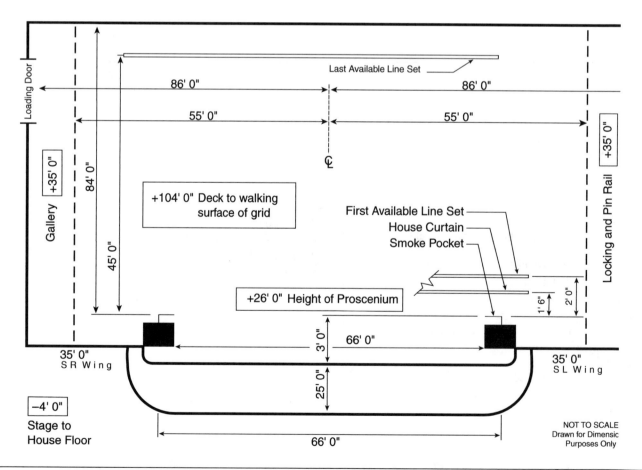

STAGE HOUSE

HOUSE CURTAIN
Operates as a traveller from SR deck

RIGGING SYSTEM
Type:	Double purchase counter weight
Weight:	80,000 lbs available
Line sets:	80 sets at 6" o.c. with 7 lift lines per set
Arbors:	1,200 lb capacity
House Pipes:	70' long with 100' of travel from deck

Line sets are not moveable
Block & Falls are not available
Chain hoists are available as a rental
(40) spot wheels and 1,000' of hemp available

PERMANENT INSTALLATIONS OVER STAGE
Orchestra shells (5) at 2'0", 9'8", 17'9", 29'9", 33'9"
Electric borders (4) at 6'6", 14'6", 22'6", 30'6"
Movie screen (1) at 12'6"
Traveller (1) at 20'0"
Cyclorama (11) at 45'0"

PERMANENT INSTALLATIONS ON DECK
None

ORCHESTRA PIT
Adjustable to 35' below stage level by hydraulic lift
Apron overhangs US wall of pit 0'0"
Pit lift is in (2) sections

BACKSTAGE

LOADING DOCK
Loading door(s):
12'0" high x 16'0" wide
Trucks load (2) at same time
Fork lift is not required
(2) Trailers can store on-site
Security at stage door

WARDROBE
Location: Green room or small
room SL
(1) Washer (1) Dryer
Washer and dryer hookups
available

DRESSING ROOMS
Star, SL, stage level, t/s, phone
jack
Small, SL, +1, t/s, phone jack
Chorus, SL, -1, t/s, phone jack

SOUND

CONSOLE
Scorpian TAC 2 FOH- HL
40 inputs, 6 main outputs,
2 matrix outputs, 8 aux
outputs

SPEAKERS
House Cluster
Speaker truss does not exist

COMMUNICATIONS
Clear Com intercom with
(2) channels
Dressing room page system

ROAD CONSOLE
Located Orchestra HL
(20) seats required to be
removed
Cable run from stage is 200'
Tie in into house system with
XLR connectors

REHEARSAL & STORAGE SPACE
Rehearsal: 130' x 90' behind
stage on stage level; piano
available
Storage: 20' x 20' located SR
in scene shop

ELECTRICS

ROAD SERVICE POWER

Panel	Phase	Amp	Circuit Protection	Use	Location
A	3	400	fuse	dimmers	SR
B-D	3	400	fuse	extra	SR

Recommended location of touring dimmer racks: SR
Hoist not required
Additional power is available for tour buses, generators, etc.

FRONT OF HOUSE (BOX BOOM VALUES ARE PER SIDE)

Position	Pipe Width	Distance to Prosc.	House Circuits	Connector Type	FOH Transfer Circuits
1st Balc Rail	115'	90'	18	20 amp new twistlock	0
1st Cove	100'	65'	35	20 amp old twistlock	35
2nd Cove	100'	85'	35	20 amp new twistlock	35
Box Boom 1		18'	16	20 amp new twistlock	16

Transfer circuits: 20 amp new twistlock located SR on jump

EQUIPMENT FOH (BOX BOOM VALUES ARE PER SIDE)
None

FOLLOWSPOTS
House Followspots:
(2) Lycian 1290 XLT
Xenon 200w; removeable
(2) Lycian 400W HMI
Long throw; removeable

Followspot Booth:
(2) spots per booth;
110' throw to prosc;
(3) 1Ø 30 amp breakers

DIMMERS
House console is ETC;
(72) Kliegl dimmers
House has programmable
DMX control system
No dry run DMX station(s)

VON BRAUN CENTER

YEAR BUILT: **1975**

Theatre Location: 700 Monroe Street, Huntsville, AL 35801

Main Administrative Phone: 256-533-1953
Main Administrative Fax: 256-551-2203
E-mail: ubcc.com
Website: www.ubcc.com

THEATRE STAFF
Director   Ron Evans   256-551-2260
Booking   Ron Evans   256-551-2260
Marketing   Sandra Steele   256-533-1953
Operations   Johnny Hunkapillan 256-551-2275

HOUSE CREW
Production Manager   David Phillips   256-551-2285

UNIONS
IATSE Local #900   David Phillips   256-551-2285

SEATING CAPACITY
Orchestra   1,484
Balcony   669
Total: **2,153**

BOX OFFICE
Computerized
Box Office Manager
  Teri Denton   256-551-2280

Outside Ticket Agency
Computerized
Ticketlink
  Sid Borland   256-327-7100

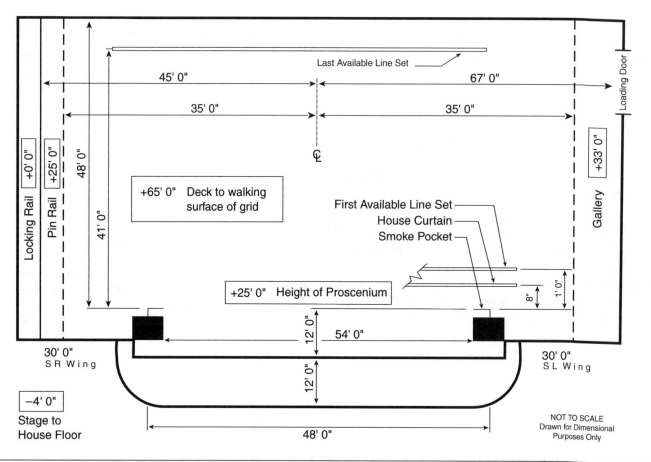

45' 0"   67' 0"
35' 0"   35' 0"

CL

Last Available Line Set

Loading Door

Locking Rail +0' 0"
Pin Rail +25' 0"

48' 0"

41' 0"

+65' 0"   Deck to walking surface of grid

Gallery +33' 0"

First Available Line Set
House Curtain
Smoke Pocket

+25' 0"   Height of Proscenium

8"   1' 0"

12' 0"   54' 0"

12' 0"

30' 0"
SR Wing

30' 0"
SL Wing

−4' 0"
Stage to
House Floor

48' 0"

NOT TO SCALE
Drawn for Dimensional
Purposes Only

STAGE HOUSE

HOUSE CURTAIN
Operates as a traveller from SR deck

RIGGING SYSTEM
Type: Combination purchase counter weight
Weight: 9,000 lbs available
Line sets: 50 sets at 6" o.c. with 6 lift lines per set
25 line sets are single purchase; 25 are double purchase
Arbors: 1,200 & 1,800 lb capacity
House Pipes: 70' long with 60' of travel from deck
Line sets are not moveable
(30) spot wheels and 2,400' of hemp available

PERMANENT INSTALLATIONS OVER STAGE (FROM SMOKE POCKET)
M=Moveable with advance call
Movie screen (1) at 3'0"; M
Travellers (2) at 12'0', 25'0"; M

PERMANENT INSTALLATIONS ON DECK
None

ORCHESTRA PIT
Adjustable to 20' below stage level by hydraulic lift

BACKSTAGE

LOADING DOCK
Loading door(s):
   18'0" high x 12'0" wide
Trucks load (2) at same time,
   side by side
Dock is at truck level
Fork lift is not required
Sound/Props cannot load in
   FOH
(4) Trailers can store on-site

WARDROBE
Location: Behind stage on stage
   level
Access: Direct from stage
No Washers No Dryers
Washer and dryer hookups
   available

DRESSING ROOMS
(2) Star, behind stage, stage
   level, t/s included, phone jack
(3) Small, behind stage, stage
   level, t/s included, phone jack
(2) Chorus, behind stage, stage
   level, t/s included, phone jack
Additional production office
   available for company mgr

SOUND

CONSOLE
Yamaha
16 inputs, 10 main outputs

SPEAKERS
House Cluster

COMMUNICATIONS
Telex intercom with
   (5) channels
Dressing room page system

ROAD CONSOLE
Located Rear HL
(8) seats required to be
   removed
Cable run from stage is 100'
Tie-in into house system with
   XLR connectors

REHEARSAL & STORAGE SPACE
Rehearsal: 28' x 49' located
   SL on stage level; piano
   available
Storage: None

ELECTRICS

ROAD SERVICE POWER

Panel	Phase	Amp	Circuit Protection	Use	Location
A	3	400	fuse	dimmers	DSR on jump
B	3	400	fuse	sound	DSR on jump

Recommended location of touring dimmer racks: DSR under power jump; add'l 50 amps available SL outside stage house 200' from stage
Hoist is required and provided

FRONT OF HOUSE (BOX BOOM VALUES ARE PER SIDE)

Position	Pipe Width	Distance to Prosc.	House Circuits	Connector Type	FOH Transfer Circuits
1st Cove	60'	30'	30'	grd 20 amp stage pin	30
Box Boom 1		20'	8	grd 20 amp stage pin	8

Transfer circuits: grd 20 amp stage pin located DSR on power jump

EQUIPMENT FOH (BOX BOOM VALUES ARE PER SIDE)
None

FOLLOWSPOTS
House Followspots:
   (2) Carbon arc Super
   Troupers; removeable

Followspot Booth:
   (2) spots per booth;
   140' throw to proscenium;
   (2) 1Ø 30 amp breakers

DIMMERS
(72) Kliegl dimmers

MOBILE CIVIC CENTER THEATRE

Theatre Location: 401 Civic Center Drive, Mobile, AL 36602

Main Administrative Phone: 334-434-7261
Main Administrative Fax: 334-208-7551
Stage Door Phone: 205-434-7185

THEATRE STAFF
General Manager	Jay Hagerman	334-434-7261
Booking	Robert J. Brazier	334-434-7261
Operations	Jimmy Smith	334-434-7261

HOUSE CREW
Stage Manager	Chris Oliver	334-434-7261
Electrics	Ross Moroney	334-434-7261
Sound	Roy D. Cook	334-434-7261

UNIONS
IATSE Local # 142	Terry Kiser	334-478-0178

SEATING CAPACITY
Orchestra	1,189
Mezzanine	280
Balcony	468
Total:	**1,937**

BOX OFFICE
Computerized
Box Office Treasurer
Rhonda Pierce 334-434-7261

Outside Ticket Agency
Ticketmaster 800-535-5151

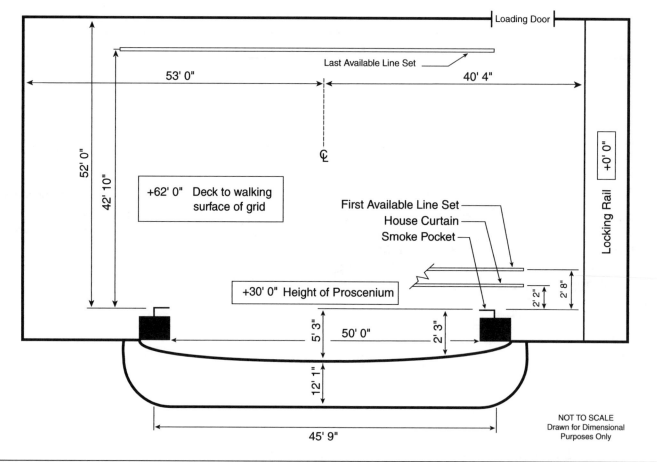

STAGE HOUSE

HOUSE CURTAIN
Operates as a guillotine or traveller from SL deck

RIGGING SYSTEM
Type: Single purchase counter weight
Weight: 13,000 lbs available
Line sets: 60 sets at 6-12" o.c. with 4 lift lines per set
Arbors: 750 lb capacity
House Pipes: 60' long with 50' of travel from deck
Line sets are not moveable
Block & Falls are not available
(6) spot wheels and 450' of hemp available
480 lbs of sand available

PERMANENT INSTALLATIONS OVER STAGE (FROM SMOKE POCKET)
Electric borders (3) at 9'0", 29'6", 48'0"
Electric raceways (3) at 4'6", 20'0", 39'0"

PERMANENT INSTALLATIONS ON DECK
Orchestra shell stores on back wall 8'0" deep

ORCHESTRA PIT
Nonadjustable at 6'3" below stage level
Apron overhangs US wall of pit

BACKSTAGE

LOADING DOCK
Loading door(s):
10'0" high x 7'10" wide
Trucks load (1) at a time
Dock (loading door sill) is at street level; Loading to stage thru separate scene shop behind stage

WARDROBE
Location: Green Room - DSL on stage level
Access: Direct from stage
Washer and dryer hookups available

DRESSING ROOMS
(9) Small, stage level, (4) SR/(5) SL, t/s included, phone jack
(2) Chorus, (1) SR/(1) SL, 2nd fl, t/s included, phone jack

SOUND

CONSOLE
Yamaha 1800 series
32 inputs, 8 main outputs

SPEAKERS
House Cluster

COMMUNICATIONS
Clear Com intercom with (2) channels

ROAD CONSOLE
Located Center HR
(12) seats required to be removed
Cable run from stage is 100'
Tie-in into house system with XLR connectors

REHEARSAL & STORAGE SPACE
Rehearsal: 48' x 68', located in adjacent arena, prior arrangement required
Storage: 32' x 84' located in scene shop behind stage

ELECTRICS

ROAD SERVICE POWER

Panel	Phase	Amp	Circuit Protection	Use	Location
A	3	600	fuse	dimmers	SR side wall
B	3	400	fuse	sound	SR side wall

Recommended location of touring dimmer racks: SR on deck

FRONT OF HOUSE (BOX BOOM VALUES ARE PER SIDE)

Position	Pipe Width	Distance to Prosc.	House Circuits	Connector Type	FOH Transfer Circuits
1st Catwalk	60'	50'	24	grd 20 amp stage pin	24
Box Boom 1		30'	12	grd 20 amp stage pin	0

Transfer circuits: grd 20 amp stage pin located on DSR proscenium wall

EQUIPMENT FOH (BOX BOOM VALUES ARE PER SIDE)

Position	Quantity	Wattage	Instrument	Removeable
1st Catwalk	12	1,000	6 x 9 Lekos	yes

FOLLOWSPOTS
House Followspots:
(2) Xenon Gladiator III; not removeable

Followspot Booth:
(3) spots per booth;
160' throw to proscenium;
(19) 1Ø 20 amp breakers

Additional followspot locations in booths HR and HL

DIMMERS
Lighting console is 250 Express
(48) Digital dimmers

EVANGELINE ATWOOD CONCERT HALL

AT: ALASKA CENTER FOR THE PERFORMING ARTS **YEAR BUILT: 1989**

Theatre Location: 621 West 6th Avenue, Anchorage, AK 99501
Management Company: Alaska Center For The Performing Arts
621 West 6th Avenue, Anchorage, AK 99501

Main Administrative Phone: 907-263-2900
Main Administrative Fax: 907-263-2927
E-mail: acpa@customcpu.com
Stage Door Phone: 907-263-2965
Backstage Pay Phone: 907-263-2950
Traveling Production Office Phone: 907-263-2957

THEATRE STAFF
President Nancy Harbour 907-263-2900
Booking Susan Dixon 907-263-2919
Marketing Ann Hale 907-263-2900

HOUSE CREW
Production Mgr Fred L. Sager 907-263-2945

UNIONS
IATSE Local #918 Lauren Miller 907-299-6960

SEATING CAPACITY

Orchestra	1,291
Mezzanine	366
Balcony	367
Total:	**2,024**
pit (add'l)	76
wheelchair (add'l)	22
standing (add'l)	0

BOX OFFICE
Computerized
Box Office Manager
Benton Bruce 907-297-2962

Outside Ticket Agency
Computerized
Softtix 907-297-2962

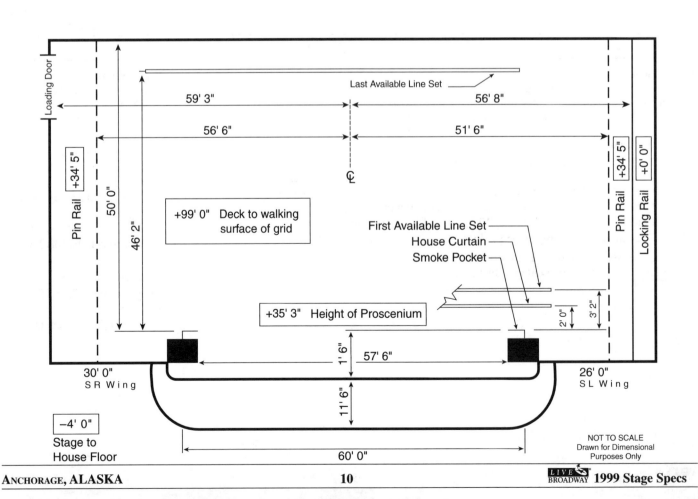

+99' 0" Deck to walking surface of grid

+35' 3" Height of Proscenium

30' 0" SR Wing

26' 0" SL Wing

−4' 0" Stage to House Floor

NOT TO SCALE
Drawn for Dimensional Purposes Only

STAGE HOUSE

HOUSE CURTAIN
Operates as a guillotine from SL deck
Operates as a traveller from SR deck

RIGGING SYSTEM
Type:	Single purchase counter weight
Weight:	49,775 lbs available
Line sets:	44 sets at 7" o.c. with 7 lift lines per set
Arbors:	1,800 lb capacity
House Pipes:	78' long with 88' of travel from deck

Line sets are moveable
Block & Falls are available
Chain hoists are available as a rental; (1) half ton
(30) spot wheels and 3,600' of hemp available

PERMANENT INSTALLATIONS OVER STAGE (FROM SMOKE POCKET)
M=Moveable with advance call
Orchestra shells (4) at 3'11",12'1", 22'11", 30'10"; M
Electric Raceways (4) at 5'8", 16'10", 28'7", 35'10"
Traveller (1) at 18'10"; M
Electric pipe (4) at 5'8", 16'10", 28'7", 35'10"
Cyclorama (1) at 43'8"; M
Fire curtain (1) at 0'6"
Electrical wench (1) at 48'0"

PERMANENT INSTALLATIONS ON DECK
Orchestra shell storage, 12' x 40' in a cove USR

ORCHESTRA PIT
Adjustable to 11' 9" below stage level by electric motor
    turnscrew
Apron overhangs US wall of pit 7'0"
Pit lift is in (1) section

BACKSTAGE

LOADING DOCK
Loading door(s):
    10'0" high x 7'6" wide
Trucks load (4) at same time
Fork lift is not required
Sound/Props can load in FOH
(2) Trailers can store on-site
Security at dock & stage door

WARDROBE
Location: SR in basement
Access: Freight elevator
(2) Washers (2) Dryers
No washer or dryer hookups

DRESSING ROOMS
(1) Star, SR, stage level, t/s
    included, phone jack
(5) Small, SR, -1, t/s
(4) Chorus, SR, -1, t/s included
Elevator access for dressing
    rooms
Additional production office
    available for company mgr

SOUND

CONSOLE
Mackie 40x8/Mackie 1604,
    located in Sound Booth
40 inputs, 8 main outputs,
    8 matrix outputs, 8 aux
    outputs
Sound Booth: 16inputs,
    8 main outputs, 4 matrix
    outputs, 4 aux outputs

SPEAKERS
House Cluster
Proscenium
Under Balcony
No speaker truss

COMMUNICATIONS
Clear Com intercom with
    (4) channels
Infrared sound system
Dressing room page system

ROAD CONSOLE
Located Center House
No seats required to be
    removed
Cable run from stage is 125'
Tie-in into house system with
    XLR connectors

REHEARSAL & STORAGE SPACE
Rehearsal:
Under construction
Storage: Under construction

ELECTRICS

ROAD SERVICE POWER
Panel	Phase	Amp	Circuit Protection	Use	Location
A	3	400	breaker	dimmers	DSR side wall
B-C	3	400	breaker	extra	DSR side wall
D	3	200	breaker	sound	DSR side wall
E	3	200	breaker	extra	DSR side wall

Recommended location of touring dimmer racks: SR
Hoist provided but not required
Additional power is available for tour buses, generators, etc.

FRONT OF HOUSE (BOX BOOM VALUES ARE PER SIDE)
Position	Pipe Width	Distance to Prosc.	House Circuits	Connector Type	FOH Transfer Circuits
1st Cove	39'	48'	16	grd 20 amp stage pin	16
2nd Cove	96'	58'	36	grd 20 amp stage pin	36
3rd Cove	44'	75'	16	grd 20 amp stage pin	16
4th Cove	100'	85'	28	grd 20 amp stage pin	28
Torm		20'	10	grd 20 amp stage pin	10

Transfer circuits: grd 20 amp stage pin located on DSR side wall
Road truss: Pipe widths of cove positions are comprised of 5' long windows

EQUIPMENT FOH (BOX BOOM VALUES ARE PER SIDE)
Position	Quantity	Wattage	Instrument	Removeable
1st Cove	36	1,000	Berkey 10°	no
2nd Cove	16	1,000	Berkey 10°	no
3rd Cove	16	1,000	Berkey 10°	no
4th Cove	28	1,000	Berkey 10°	no

FOLLOWSPOTS
House Followspots:
    (2) Xenon Super Troupers;
    not removeable

(3) Followspot Booths each
    with:
    (2) spots per booth;
    110' throw to proscenium;
    (2) 1Ø 30 amp breakers

DIMMERS
Lighting console is Colortran
    Elite;
(372) 2.4k and (33) 6k
Colortran D192 module
    dimmers
House has programmable
    DMX control system
(0) dry run DMX station(s)

SYMPHONY HALL

AT: PHOENIX CIVIC PLAZA - DOWNTOWN THEATER DIVISION

Theatre Location: 225 East Adams, Phoenix, AZ 85004
Management Company: City of Phoenix, Theater Division

Main Administrative Phone: 602-534-5600
Main Administrative Fax: 602-534-5622
Backstage Pay Phone: 602-257-9921

SEATING CAPACITY

Orchestra	1,855
Balcony	643
Total:	**2,498**
pit (add'l)	71

THEATRE STAFF

Theatre Division Mgr	Robert Allen	602-534-5611
Booking	Marilynn Leathers	602-534-5613
Operations	Diane Heppe	602-534-5623
Technical Director	Jerry Gorrell	602-262-7364

UNIONS

IATSE Local #336	Bill Hennesey	602-253-4145
Wardrobe	Betty Sites	602-887-8582

BOX OFFICE

602-262-7272

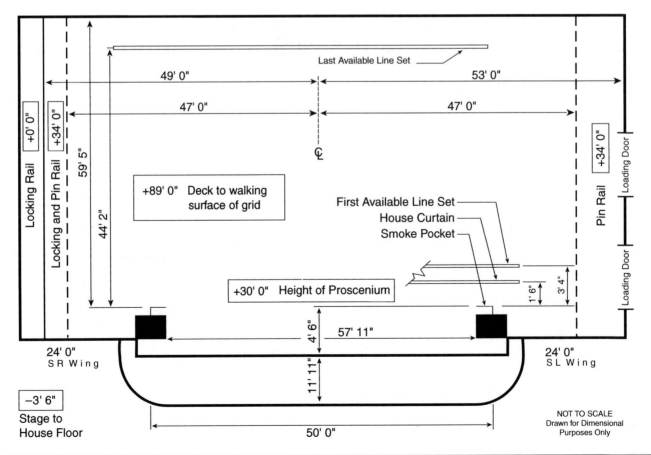

NOT TO SCALE
Drawn for Dimensional
Purposes Only

STAGE HOUSE

House Curtain
Operates as a guillotine or traveller from SR deck
Additonal curtain works as traveller from SR deck

Rigging System
Type:	Single purchase counter weight
Weight:	70,000 lbs available
Line sets:	49 sets at 6" o.c. with 5 lift lines per set
Arbors:	1,800 lb capacity
House Pipes:	66' long with 86' of travel from deck

Line sets are moveable

Permanent Installations Over Stage (from smoke pocket)
Orchestra shell (1)

Permanent Installations On Deck
Trap (12) in stage floor must be cut
Orchestra shell stores on back wall
Utility lift against SL wall

Orchestra Pit
Adjustable to 22' below stage level
Apron overhangs US wall of pit 5'4"

BACKSTAGE

Loading Dock
(2) Loading door(s) each:
   11'0" high x 9'10" wide
Trucks load (2) at same time,
   side by side
Docks (2): (1) at truck level,
   equipped with utility lift to
   basement; (1) loading door sill
   at street level
Forklift: House owns
Security at stage door

Wardrobe
Location: Dressing Room SL
(1) Washer (1) Dryer
Washer and dryer hookups
   available

Dressing Rooms
(2) Star, SL, stage level, t/s
   included, phone jack
(4) Small, SL, stage level, t/s
   included, phone jack
(2) Chorus, SL, stage level, t/s
   included, phone jack

SOUND

Console
Yamaha PM 4000
40 inputs, 8 main outputs

Speakers
House L&R
Under Balcony

Communications
RTS intercom with
   (3) channels
Infrared sound system
Dressing room page system

Road Console
Located Rear House
(6) seats required to be
   removed
Cable run from stage is 250'
Tie-in into house system
   with XLR connectors

Rehearsal & Storage Space
Rehearsal: 60' x 50' located
   SL in basement, piano
   available
Storage: None

ELECTRICS

Road Service Power

Panel	Phase	Amp	Circuit Protection	Use	Location
A-B	3	400	fuse	dimmers	SR in basement
C	3	100	fuse	sound	USL side wall

Recommended location of touring dimmer racks: DSR on deck

Front Of House (box boom values are per side)

Position	Pipe Width	Distance to Prosc.	House Circuits	Connector Type	FOH Transfer Circuits
1st Balc Rail	70'	84'	30	grd 20 amp stage pin	30
1st Cove	80'	75'	30	grd 20 amp stage pin	30
Box Boom 1		2'	6	grd 20 amp stage pin	6
Box Boom 2		50'	10	grd 20 amp stage pin	10

Transfer circuits: grd 20 amp stge pin located SR in basement

Equipment FOH (box boom values are per side)

Position	Quantity	Wattage	Instrument	Removeable
1st Balc Rail	30	1,000	Berkey 12°	no
1st Cove	54	575	ETC 19°	no
Box Boom 1	6	575	ETC 26°	no
Box Boom 2	10	575	ETC 19°	no

Followspots
House Followspots:
   (3) Xenon Super Trouper
   2k; removeable

Followspot Booth:
   (3) spots per booth;
   125' throw to proscenium;
   (3) 1Ø 30 amp breakers

Dimmers
(566) Colortran I Series
   dimmers

SCOTTSDALE CENTER FOR THE ARTS

YEAR BUILT: 1975

Theatre Location: 7380 East 2nd Street, Scottsdale, AZ 85251

Main Administrative Phone: 602-994-2787
Main Administrative Fax: 602-874-4699
E-mail: carelt@sccarts.org
Website: www.scottsdalearts.org
Stage Door Phone: 602-874-4628

THEATRE STAFF
President & CEO — Frank Jacobson — 602-874-4601
Booking — Kathy Hotchner — 602-874-4622
Marketing — Matt Lehrman — 602-874-4656
Operations — Ric Alling — 602-874-4602

HOUSE CREW
Technical Director — Ian England — 602-874-4625
Electrics — Bill Lorentz — 602-874-4628
Sound — Michael Good — 602-874-4628

UNIONS
IATSE Local #336 — Bill Hennessy — 602-253-4145
Wardrobe Local #336 — Betty Sites — 602-827-8582

SEATING CAPACITY
Main Auditorium — 773
Total: — **773**

pit (add'l) — 65
wheelchair (incl)

BOX OFFICE
Computerized
Patron Services Manager
Margarita Martinez — 602-874-4690

Outside Ticket Agency
Computerized
Ticketmaster
Carrie Jarvice — 602-438-4110

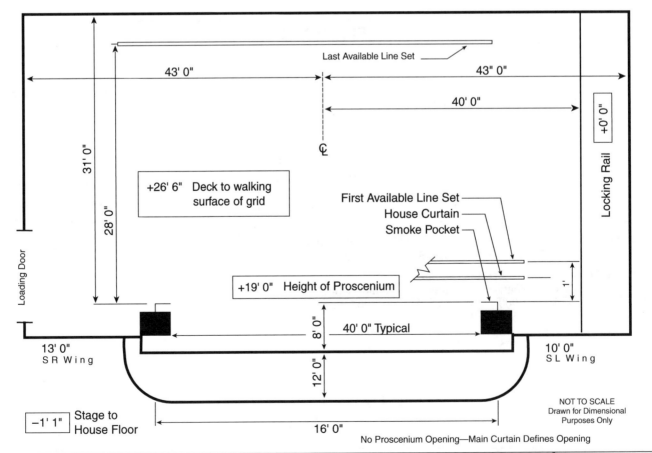

Last Available Line Set

43' 0"   43" 0"

40' 0"

31' 0"

28' 0"

+26' 6"   Deck to walking surface of grid

First Available Line Set
House Curtain
Smoke Pocket

Locking Rail   +0' 0"

1'

Loading Door

+19' 0"   Height of Proscenium

8' 0"   40' 0" Typical

12' 0"

13' 0"
SR Wing

10' 0"
SL Wing

−1' 1"   Stage to House Floor

16' 0"

NOT TO SCALE
Drawn for Dimensional
Purposes Only

No Proscenium Opening—Main Curtain Defines Opening

STAGE HOUSE

HOUSE CURTAIN
Operates as a traveler from SR deck; motorized

RIGGING SYSTEM
Type:	Double purchase counter weight
Weight:	14,000 lbs available
Line sets:	26 sets at 8" o.c. with 6 lift lines per set
Arbors:	2,000 lb capacity
House Pipes:	60' long with 20' of travel from deck

Line sets are not moveable
Block & Falls are not available
Chain hoists are available as a rental; (2) half ton
(0) spot wheels and 0' of hemp available
No overhead fly space.

PERMANENT INSTALLATIONS OVER STAGE (FROM SMOKE POCKET)
M=Moveable with advance call
Electric Raceways (4)
Movie screen (2) at 6'4"; M
Dead spaces (2)
Cyclorama (1) at 28'0"; M

PERMANENT INSTALLATIONS ON DECK
Orchestra shell storage (9) 3' x 7' x 18' tall, stored behind cyclorama

ORCHESTRA PIT
Adjustable to 14' below stage level by electric motor turnscrew
Pit lift is in (3) sections
Not a true orchestra pit: 12' adjustable for e-stage that can be used as a pit; access is cumbersome; orchestra shell units cannot leave main deck

BACKSTAGE

LOADING DOCK
Loading door(s):
  13'6" high x 12'0" wide
Trucks load (1) at a time
Dock access via long tunnel to underground location; trucks required to make a backing 90° turn into tunnel
Fork lift is not required
Sound/Props can load in FOH
Trailers cannot store on-site

WARDROBE
Location: Dressing room below stage level
Access: Stairs & elevator
(1) Washer (1) Dryer
No washer or dryer hookups

DRESSING ROOMS
(2) Star, SL, -1, t/s included
(2) Small, SL, SR, -1, t/s included
(2) Chorus, SR, -1, t/s included
Elevator access for dressing rooms
Use dressing room for company mgr office

SOUND

CONSOLE
Ramsa S52, Rear House
40 inputs, 4 matrix outputs, 8 aux outputs

SPEAKERS
House Cluster
Proscenium
Mixer matrix outputs typically drive the 4 speaker positions
No speaker truss

COMMUNICATIONS
Clear Com intercom with (1) channel
Infrared sound system
Dressing room page system

ROAD CONSOLE
Located Rear House
(4) seats required to be removed
Cable run from stage is 150'
Tie-in into house system with XLR connectors
Dry room; all "spoken word" performances need to be re-inforced

REHEARSAL & STORAGE SPACE
Rehearsal: None
Storage: In Shop which is a passage-way between loading dock and stage

ELECTRICS

ROAD SERVICE POWER

Panel	Phase	Amp	Circuit Protection	Use	Location
A	3	100	breaker	extra	SR
B	3	400	breaker	dimmers	SR deck

Dimmer rack power is half of house lighting supply
Recommended location of touring dimmer racks: USR wing
Hoist not required
Additional power is available for tour buses, generators, etc.

FRONT OF HOUSE (BOX BOOM VALUES ARE PER SIDE)

Position	Pipe Width	Distance to Prosc.	House Circuits	Connector Type	FOH Transfer Circuits
1st Cove		44'	12	grd 20 amp stage pin	0
2nd Cove		65'	42	grd 20 amp stage pin	0
3rd Cove		76'	24	grd 20 amp stage pin	0
Apron		25' - 35'	74	grd 20 amp stage pin	0

Road truss: All FOH position accessed by catwalks

EQUIPMENT FOH (BOX BOOM VALUES ARE PER SIDE)

Position	Quantity	Wattage	Instrument	Removeable
1st Cove	12	1,000	8 x 12 Leko	yes
2nd Cove	18	1,000	8 x 12 Leko	yes
3rd Cove	38	1,000	8 x 12 Leko	yes
Apron	30	1,000	Lekos	yes
Apron	12	750	Fresnels	yes

FOLLOWSPOTS
House Followspots:
  (2) Berkey Colortran; removeable

Followspot Booth:
  (2) spots per booth;
  90' throw to proscenium;
  (2) 1Ø 20 amp breakers

DIMMERS
House console is ETC Insight 108;
(300) ETC 286 series dimmers
No DMX control system
(3) dry run DMX station(s)

GRADY GAMMAGE MEMORIAL AUDITORIUM

YEAR BUILT: 1964   YEAR RENOVATED: 1997

Theatre Location:	Arizona State University, Tempe, AZ 85287-0105
Mailing Address:	ASU Public Events
	PO Box 870205, Tempe, AZ 85287-0205

Main Administrative Phone:	602-965-5062
Main Administrative Fax:	602-965-7663
Website:	www.asu.edu/ia/publicevents
Stage Door Phone:	602-965-6123

SEATING CAPACITY

Orchestra	1,641
Grand Tier	606
Balcony	682
Total:	**2,929**
wheelchair (incl.)	30
standing (add'l)	88

THEATRE STAFF

Executive Director	Colleen Jennings-Roggensack	
		602-965-5062
Booking	Bob MacLean	602-965-1749
Marketing	Celeste Winters	602-965-6726
Operations	Terri Cranmer	602-965-8255
Group Sales	Robin Cole	602-965-6678
Merchandise	Bonnie Tauss	602-965-3445

HOUSE CREW

Technical Director	Clyde Parker	602-965-1660
Sound	Harry Hale	602-965-1676

UNIONS

IATSE Local #336	Bill Hennessy	602-253-4145
Wardrobe Local #875	Betty Sites	602-827-8582
Music Local #586	Chuck Craig	602-990-3166

BOX OFFICE

Computerized
Box Office Manager
  Maria Klimaszewski   602-965-8870

Outside Ticket Agency
Computerized
Dillards
  George Conner   602-503-5555

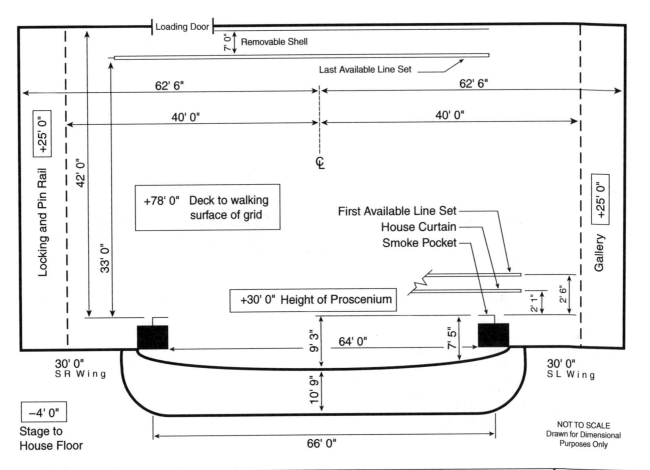

STAGE HOUSE

HOUSE CURTAIN
Operates as a guillotine from SR fly floor
Operates as a traveller from SR deck

RIGGING SYSTEM
Type:	Double purchase counter weight and hydraulic line sets
Weight:	26,000 lbs available
Line sets:	58 sets at 6" o.c. with 5 lift lines per set
Arbors:	560 lb capacity
House Pipes:	55' long with 60' of travel from deck

Line sets are moveable
Block & Falls are available
Chain hoists are not available
6,000' of hemp available

PERMANENT INSTALLATIONS OVER STAGE (FROM SMOKE POCKET)
Fire curtain (1)

PERMANENT INSTALLATIONS ON DECK
Traps in stage floor (1) 2'0" x 3'0", centered at 2'3" DS
Traps (2) 4'0" x 8'0", located split center at 3'9" US
Orchestra shell (1) 60'0" x 9'0", located US center

ORCHESTRA PIT
Adjustable to 15' below stage level by hydraulic lift
Apron overhangs US wall of pit 0'0"
Pit lift is in (1) sections

BACKSTAGE

LOADING DOCK
Loading door(s):
  11'6" high x 10'0" wide
Trucks load (2) at same time,
  (4) if using both ramps
Unload at street level and fork/
  push down curving ramp to
  loading door
Fork lift is not required
  Supplier: Nauman
  602-437-1331
Sound/Props can load in FOH
Lobby can be a work area
(2) Trailers can store on-site
Security at stage door

WARDROBE
Location: Backstage 2nd floor
Access: Elevator
(2) Washers (2) Dryers
Washer and dryer hookups
  available

DRESSING ROOMS
(2) Star, behind stage, stage
  level, t/s
(2) Small, behind stage, stage
  level, toilet on same fl
(2) Chorus, behind stage, stage
  level, t/s
Elevator access for dressing
  rooms
Additional production office
  available for company mgr

SOUND

CONSOLE
Audiotronic 600, located
  Rear House Booth
24 inputs, 8 main outputs,
  matrix outputs, 8 aux
  outputs

SPEAKERS
House Cluster
Under Balcony
No speaker truss

COMMUNICATIONS
Clear Com intercom with
  (2) channels
Infrared sound system
Dressing room page system

ROAD CONSOLE
Located Center House, rows
  13-15
(40) seats required to be
  removed
Cable run from stage is 250'
Tie-in into house system with
  XLR connectors

REHEARSAL & STORAGE SPACE
Rehearsal: None
Storage: Scene shop, 30' x
  100' behind stage

ELECTRICS

ROAD SERVICE POWER
Panel	Phase	Amp	Circuit Protection	Use	Location
A-C	3	600	breaker	dimmers	SR side wall
D-E	3	200	breaker	dimmers	SR side wall
F	3	100	breaker	dimmers	SR side wall
G	3	10	breaker	dimmers	SR side wall
H	3	200	breaker	sound	SL Proscenium wall
I	3	100	breaker	extra	Loading dock

Recommended location of touring dimmer racks: USR on deck

FRONT OF HOUSE (BOX BOOM VALUES ARE PER SIDE)
Position	Pipe Width	Distance to Prosc.	House Circuits	Connector Type	FOH Transfer Circuits
1st Balc Rail	142'	75'	48	20 amp old twistlock	24
Box Boom 1		24'	6	20 amp old twistlock	6
Box Boom 2		24'	6	20 amp old twistlock	6
Tormentor		10'	5	20 amp old twistlock	5

EQUIPMENT FOH (BOX BOOM VALUES ARE PER SIDE)
Position	Quantity	Wattage	Instrument	Removeable
1st Balc Rail	6	1,000	10 x 12 Lekos	yes
1st Box Boom	42	1,000	10 x 12 Lekos	yes

FOLLOWSPOTS
House Followspots:
  (2) 2500w Xenon Strong
  Gladiator II; removeable

Followspot Booth:
  (4) spots per booth;
  105' throw to proscenium;
  (4) 1Ø 30 amp breakers

DIMMERS
Lighting console is Colortran
  Prestige 3000;
(36) 4k, (12) 8k Century
  CCR dimmers
(48) ETC 2.4k

CENTENNIAL HALL

AT: UNIVERSITY OF ARIZONA   **YEAR BUILT: 1936   YEAR RENOVATED: 1984**

Theatre Location: 1020 E. University Boulevard, Tucson, AZ 85721
Mailing Address: 1020 E. University Blvd. PO Box 210029,
                         Tucson, AZ 85721-0029
Management Company: UA Presents
                         888 N. Euclid Ave. #203, Tucson, AZ 85721-0158

Main Administrative Phone:	520-621-3364
Main Administrative Fax:	520-621-5753
E-mail:	presents@u.arizona.edu
Website:	uapresents.arizona.edu
Stage Door Phone:	520-621-5038
Backstage Pay Phone:	520-621-9824
Traveling Production Office Phone:	520-621-3732
Traveling Production Office Fax:	520-621-1905

THEATRE STAFF

Director	Kenneth Foster	520-621-3364
Booking	Ed Brown	520-621-3731
Marketing	Mark Rasdorf	520-626-4423
Operations	Ed Brown	520-621-3731

HOUSE CREW

Technical Director	Gary Lotze	520-621-5481

UNIONS

IATSE #415	Gil Harrison	520-882-9126

SEATING CAPACITY

Orchestra	1,720
Mezzanine	736
Total	**2,456**
wheelchair (incl)	8

BOX OFFICE
  Computerized
  Box Office Manager
    Ana Maria Acuña   520-621-5532

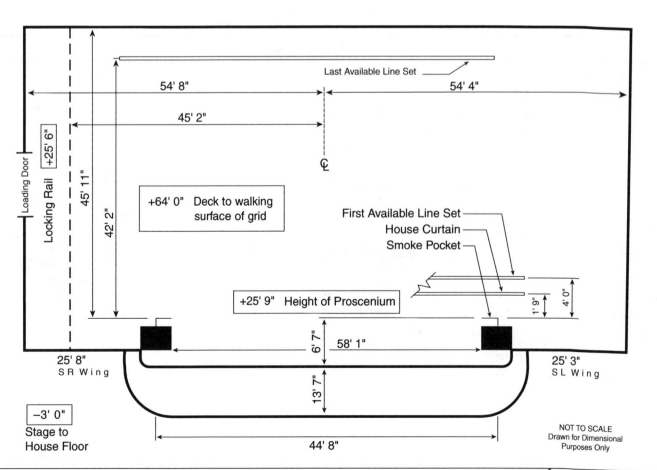

STAGE HOUSE

HOUSE CURTAIN
Operates as a guillotine from SR fly floor
Operates as a traveller from SR deck

RIGGING SYSTEM
Type:	Double purchase counter weight and Hemp System
Weight:	25,000 lbs available
Line sets:	41 sets at 6"-10" o.c. with 7 lift lines per set
Arbors:	1,800 lb capacity
House Pipes:	78' long with 62'6" of travel from deck

Line sets are moveable
Block & Falls are not available
Chain hoists are not available
(15) spot wheels and 500 of hemp available

PERMANENT INSTALLATIONS OVER STAGE (FROM SMOKE POCKET)
Orchestra shell (4) at 5'1", 13'1", 21'2", 29'1"
Electric raceways (1) at 4'0"
Fire curtain (1) at 3"

PERMANENT INSTALLATIONS ON DECK
None

ORCHESTRA PIT
Adjustable to 19' below stage level by electric motor turnscrew
Pit lift is in (1) section

BACKSTAGE

LOADING DOCK
Loading door(s):
  12' 0" wide x 10'0" high
Trucks load (1) at a time
Steep angle on truck ramp, wheel blocks available; SR stage door can also be used for loading in/out, door is 8' x 8' on street level
Sound/Props cannot load in FOH
Fork lift is not required
(1) Trailer can store on-site

WARDROBE
Location: SL Green room
Access: Stage level
(2) Washers (2) Dryers

DRESSING ROOMS
(4) Star, USL, stage level, t/s, phone jack
(2) Chorus, SL, +1, t/s, phone jack
Elevator access for dressing rooms
Additional production office available for company mgr

SOUND

CONSOLE
Soundraft Venue
40 inputs, 2 main outputs, 8 matrix outputs, 4 aux outputs

SPEAKERS
House Cluster
No speaker truss

COMMUNICATIONS
Clear Com intercom with (2) channels
Infrared sound system
Dressing room page system

ROAD CONSOLE
Located Rear Orchestra
Cable run from stage is 110'
Tie-in into house system with XLR connectors

REHEARSAL & STORAGE SPACE
Rehearsal: None
Storage: Shop area, 200 sq ft, USR, mostly road case storage

ELECTRICS

ROAD SERVICE POWER

Panel	Phase	Amp	Circuit Protection	Use	Location
A	3	600	fuse	dimmers	DSR
B	3	300	breaker	motors	DSR
C	3	300	breaker	sound	DSL

Recommended location of touring dimmer racks: DSR
Hoist not required

FRONT OF HOUSE (BOX BOOM VALUES ARE PER SIDE)

Position	Pipe Width	Distance to Prosc.	House Circuits	Connector Type	FOH Transfer Circuits
1st Cove	81'	21'	30	grd 20 amp stage pin	0
2nd Cove	120'	40'	30	grd 20 amp stage pin	0
Box Boom 1		40'	6	grd 20 amp stage pin	0

EQUIPMENT FOH (BOX BOOM VALUES ARE PER SIDE)

Position	Quantity	Wattage	Instrument	Removeable
2nd Cove	16	1,000	6 x 16	yes

2nd Cove is primary FOH positon

FOLLOWSPOTS
House Followspots:
  (3) Xenon Super Troupers; not removeable

Followspot Booth:
  (3) spots per booth;
  160' throw to proscenium;
  (4) 1Ø 100 amp breakers

DIMMERS
Lighting console is ETC Expression 3;
  (288) Strand 2.4k and ETC 2.4k dimmers
No DMX control system

MUSIC HALL

AT: TUCSON CONVENTION CENTER   **YEAR BUILT: 1971   YEAR RENOVATED: 1998**

Theatre Location: 260 South Church Avenue, Tucson, AZ 85706
Management Company: Tucson Convention Center

Main Administrative Phone: 520-791-4101
Main Administrative Fax: 520-791-5572
Website: www.ci.tucson.az.us
Stage Door Phone: 520-791-4101 x133
Backstage Pay Phone: 520-622-9924

THEATRE STAFF
Director   Daniel Huerta   520-791-4101
Booking   Clarence Boykins   520-791-4101 x112
Marketing   Clarence Boykins   520-791-4101 x112
Operations   Joe Rzonka   520-791-4101 x105
Group Sales   Clarence Boykins   520-791-4101 x112
Events Manager   Tommy Obermaier   520-791-4101
Publicity Director   Patricia Blackwell   520-791-4101

HOUSE CREW
Stagehand Supervisor David Darland   520-791-4101
Stage Manager   Wes Scott   520-791-4101

UNIONS
IATSE #415   Gill Harrison   520-882-9126
Wardrobe #415   Gill Harrison   520-882-9126

SEATING CAPACITY
Orchestra   1,489
Lower Balcony   386
Upper Balcony   402
Total: **2,277**

pit (add'l)   72

BOX OFFICE
Computerized
Box Office Treasurer
  Sammi Rothrock   520-791-4101

Outside Ticket Agency
None

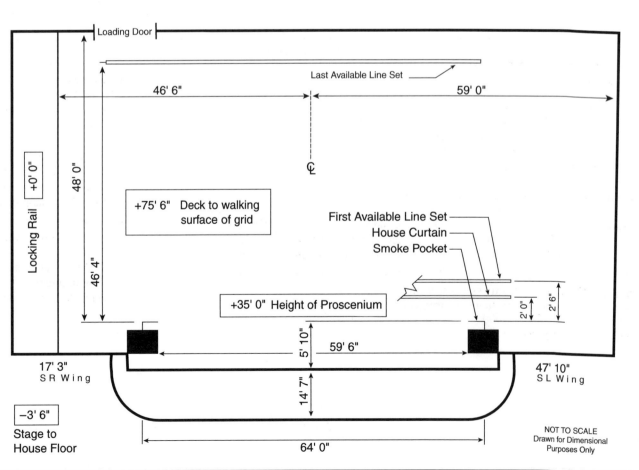

Loading Door

Last Available Line Set

46' 6"   59' 0"

℄

Locking Rail   +0' 0"

48' 0"

+75' 6"   Deck to walking
          surface of grid

46' 4"

First Available Line Set
House Curtain
Smoke Pocket

+35' 0" Height of Proscenium

2' 0"   2' 6"

5' 10"   59' 6"

17' 3"
S R Wing

47' 10"
S L Wing

14' 7"

−3' 6"
Stage to
House Floor

64' 0"

NOT TO SCALE
Drawn for Dimensional
Purposes Only

STAGE HOUSE

HOUSE CURTAIN
Operates as a guillotine or traveller from SR fly floor

RIGGING SYSTEM

Type:	Single purchase counter weight
Weight:	60,000 lbs available
Line sets:	45 sets with 1 lift line per set
House Pipes:	66' long with 72.5' of travel from deck

Line sets are not moveable
Block & Falls are not available

PERMANENT INSTALLATIONS OVER STAGE (FROM SMOKE POCKET)
M=Moveable with advance call
Orchestra shells (3) at 8'0",24'0",40'6"
Electric Borders (5) at 0'10",10'0",17'3",24'9",34'6"; M
Electric Raceways (5) at 3'6",12'6",19'6",27'0",37'6"
Movie screen (1) at 11'0"; M
Traveller (5) at grand 2'0",10'6",18'0",25'6",36'0"
Electric pipe (2) at off L & R
Dead spaces (24) various
Cyclorama (1) at 45'6"; M

PERMANENT INSTALLATIONS ON DECK
Orchestra shell storage (1) 18'0" deep, USL corner

ORCHESTRA PIT
Adjustable to 36' below stage level by hydraulic lift
Apron overhangs US wall of pit 5'10"
Pit lift is in (1) section

BACKSTAGE

LOADING DOCK
Loading door(s):
12'6" high x 10'0" wide
Trucks load (2) at same time;
side by side
Dock is at truck level
Fork lift is not required
Sound/Props can load in FOH
Lobby cannot be a work area
Many Trailers can store on-site
in an area away from public
event parking
Security by rental

WARDROBE
Location: SR Green Room on
stage level
Access: Direct from stage
No Washers No Dryers
Washer and dryer hookups
available

DRESSING ROOMS
(5) Star, SR, basement, t/s
included
(2) Chorus, SR, basement, t/s
included
Elevator access for dressing
rooms

SOUND

CONSOLE
Allen & Heath GL 4000,
located in booth
40 inputs, 8 outputs

SPEAKERS
House Cluster
Proscenium
Under Balcony
Portable
No speaker truss

COMMUNICATIONS
Clear Com intercom with
(2) channels
Hearing impaired: Comteck
204.8 Mhz
Dressing room page system

ROAD CONSOLE
Located Rear House left
No seats required to be
removed
Cable run from stage is 96'
Tie-in into house system with
XLR connectors

REHEARSAL & STORAGE SPACE
Rehearsal: 45' x 60', located
SR on stage level
Storage: None

ELECTRICS

ROAD SERVICE POWER

Panel	Phase	Amp	Circuit Protection	Use	Location
A	3	400	fuse	dimmers	SR in basement
B	3	200	fuse	sound	SR in basement
C	3	60	fuse		USR wall

Recommended location of touring dimmer racks: SR on deck
Hoist is not required

FRONT OF HOUSE (BOX BOOM VALUES ARE PER SIDE)

Position	Pipe Width	Distance to Prosc.	House Circuits	Connector Type	FOH Transfer Circuits
1st Cove	85'	16'	30	grd 20 amp stage pin	30
2nd Cove	85'	24'	30	grd 20 amp stage pin	30
3rd Cove	85'	38'	30	grd 20 amp stage pin	30
Box Boom 1		16'	8	grd 20 amp stage pin	8
Box Boom 2		24'	8	grd 20 amp stage pin	8
Box Boom 3		38'	8	grd 20 amp stage pin	8

Transfer circuits: grd 20 amp stage pin located on DSR proscenium wall

EQUIPMENT FOH (BOX BOOM VALUES ARE PER SIDE)

Position	Quantity	Wattage	Instrument	Removeable
1st Cove	30	1,000	Various Lekos	yes
2nd Cove	30	1,000	Various Lekos	yes
3rd Cove	30	1,000	Various Lekos	yes

FOLLOWSPOTS
House Followspots:
(2) Xenon Strong Super
Trouper 2k; removeable

(2) Followspot Booths:
(2) spots 1st booth/ (1) spot
2nd booth;
140' throw to proscenium;
3Ø 100 amp breakers

DIMMERS
Lighting console is Strand
LP90;
(332) CD 80 dimmers
House has programmable
DMX control system
(2) dry run DMX station(s),
SR, light booth, Center HL

WALTON ARTS CENTER

YEAR BUILT: 1992

			SEATING CAPACITY	
Theatre Location:	495 W. Dickson, Fayetteville, AR 72701		Orchestra	704
Mailing Address:	PO Box 3547, Fayetteville, AR 72702		Orchestra Pit	35
			Balcony	462
Main Administrative Phone:	501-443-9216		**Total:**	**1,201**
Main Administrative Fax:	501-443-6461			
E-mail:	comments@waltonartscenter.com			
Website:	www.waltonartscenter.com		pit (add'l)	0
Stage Door Phone:	501-443-5600		wheelchair (add'l)	0
Backstage Pay Phone:	501-442-9775		standing (add'l)	0
Traveling Production Office Phone:	501-582-3771			
Traveling Production Office Fax:	501-582-3467			

THEATRE STAFF

President & CEO	Anita Scism	501-493-9216
Events Coordinator	Jennifer Apolskis	501-443-9216

HOUSE CREW

Technical Manager	Richard Rew	501-443-5600 x233

STAGE DIMENSIONS (FROM SMOKE POCKET)
Stage is 37' deep
Width from Center Line to SL is 40'
Width from Center Line to SR is 43'
Proscenium width is 58'
Proscenium height is 24'
Smoke pocket to apron edge is 8'
Orchestra pit exists

RIGGING

Grid Height:	70'
Type:	Single purchase counter weight
Weight:	12,000 lbs
Line sets:	47 sets at 9" o.c.
Arbors:	1,800 lb capacity
House Pipes:	66' long

LOADING DOCK
Loading door(s) are 10'0" high x 8'0" wide
Trucks load (2) at same time
Fork lift is not required and is not available

ELECTRICS
Total power available:
(2) 400A 3Ø USL
(1) 100A 3Ø USL
(1) 100A 3Ø USR

FOLLOWSPOTS
House Followspots:
(2) Lycian 1275
Power in spot booth 50A

DIMMERS
(370) house dimmers
House has DMX control system
(1) dry run station(s) located
    Light Booth

SOUND
House has (2) 100A
    dedicated power located
    USL/USR
FOH mixing position in
Sound console is available

ROBINSON CENTER MUSIC HALL

Theatre Location: Markham & Broadway, Little Rock, AR 72201
Mailing Address: PO Box 3232, Little Rock, AR 72203

Main Administrative Phone: 501-376-4781
Main Administrative Fax: 501-374-2255
E-mail: evntplan@littlerock.com
Website: www.littlerock.com
Backstage Pay Phone: 501-376-9943

THEATRE STAFF
Executive Director   Barry Travis   501-370-3200
Booking   Barry Travis   501-370-3200
Operations   Mercedes Alexander   501-370-3251

HOUSE CREW
Stage Manager   Robert Oholendt   501-455-2759
Carpentry   Robert Oholendt   501-455-2759
Electrics   Robert Oholendt   501-455-2759
Sound   Warren Law   501-568-5694

UNIONS
IATSE Local #204   Robert Oholendt   501-455-1839
Wardrobe Local #204 Robert Oholendt   501-455-1839

SEATING CAPACITY
Orchestra   1,061
Mezzanine   678
Balcony   870
Total: **2,609**

wheelchair (add'l)   29

BOX OFFICE
Outside Ticket Agency
Computerized
Celebrity Attractions/Ticketmaster
   Charlton Northington 501-244-8800

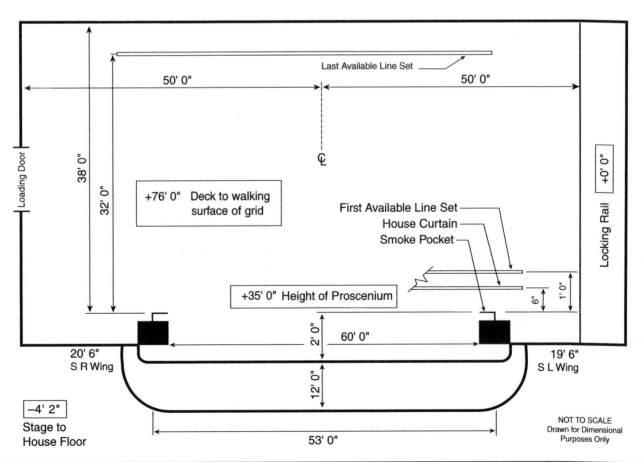

STAGE HOUSE

HOUSE CURTAIN
Operates as a guillotine or traveller from SL deck

RIGGING SYSTEM
Type:	Single purchase counter weight
Weight:	20,000 lbs available
Line sets:	58 sets at 6" o.c. with 6 lift lines per set
Arbors:	1,000 lb capacity
House Pipes:	63' long with 75' of travel from deck

Line sets are moveable
Block & Falls are available 2:1 (4); 3:2 (2)
(40) spot wheels and 1,000' of hemp available

PERMANENT INSTALLATIONS OVER STAGE (FROM SMOKE POCKET)
M=Moveable with advance call
Orchestra shells (3) at 6'6", 12'6", 17'6"; M
Electric borders (4) at 10'0", 15'0", 21'6", 30'6"; M
Electric raceways (1) at 3'0"
Traveller (4) at 1'6", 7'6", 16'0", 23'6"; M
Electric pipe (6) at 3'0", 11'6", 17'0", 18'6", 27'0", 29'6"; M
Dead spaces (3) at 10'6", 19'0", 27'6"
Fire curtain (1) at 0'3"

PERMANENT INSTALLATIONS ON DECK
Stairs (2) USL/USR
Radiators (4) US wall
Orchestra shell storage (1) US wall
Loading bridge (1) 4'0" x 40'0" located SL 60'0"

ORCHESTRA PIT
Nonadjustable at 7' below stage level

BACKSTAGE

LOADING DOCK
Loading door(s):
14'0" high x 7'0" wide
Trucks load (1) at same time
Trucks off load on hydraulic lift, 7'6" x 14'0"; raises to stage level
Fork lift is not required
Sound/Props cannot load in FOH
Trailers cannot store on-site
Security at stage door

WARDROBE
Location: Below stage
Access: Stairs SR/SL
(1) Washer (1) Dryer
Washer and dryer hookups available

DRESSING ROOMS
(1) Star, SR, stage level, t/s, phone jack
(6) Small, SR/SL, -1, t/s included, phone jack
(3) Chorus, SR/SL, -1, t/s included

SOUND

CONSOLE
Soundcraft Venue II, located Mezzanine Rear Booth
32 inputs, 24 main outputs, 4 matrix outputs, 8 aux outputs

SPEAKERS
House Cluster
Proscenium
Portable
No speaker truss

COMMUNICATIONS
Clear Com intercom
Infrared sound system
Dressing room page system

ROAD CONSOLE
Located Rear Orchestra
(24) seats required to be removed
Cable run from stage is 150'
Tie-in into house system with XLR connectors

REHEARSAL & STORAGE SPACE
Rehearsal: None
Storage: None

ELECTRICS

ROAD SERVICE POWER

Panel	Phase	Amp	Circuit Protection	Use	Location
A - B	3	400	fuse	dimmers	USL
C	3	400	fuse	sound	USL
D	3	600	fuse	extra	DSL

Recommended location of touring dimmer racks: SL
Hoist not required
Additional power is available for tour buses, generators, etc.

FRONT OF HOUSE (BOX BOOM VALUES ARE PER SIDE)

Position	Pipe Width	Distance to Prosc.	House Circuits	Connector Type	FOH Transfer Circuits
1st Balc Rail	30'	96'	0	grd 20 amp stage pin	0

Transfer circuits: grd 20 amp stage pin

EQUIPMENT FOH (BOX BOOM VALUES ARE PER SIDE)

Position	Quantity	Wattage	Instrument	Removeable
Box Boom 1	16	1,000	Lekos 6 x16	yes
Truss	9	750	Source 4 26°	yes

FOLLOWSPOTS
House Followspots:
(2) Xenon Super Troupers; not removeable
(2) Carbon Super Troupers; not removeable

Followspot Booth:
(4) spots per booth;
146' throw to proscenium;
(4) 1Ø 30 amp breakers

DIMMERS
Lighting console is Strand 430;
(129) CD80 dimmers
House has programmable DMX control system
(4) dry run DMX station(s)

WILSHIRE THEATRE

Theatre Location: 8440 Wilshire Boulevard
                                     Beverly Hills, CA 90211

Main Administrative Phone: 213-468-1700
Main Administrative Fax: 213-468-1718
Stage Door Phone: 213-653-7108
Backstage Pay Phone: 213-951-9645

THEATRE STAFF
General Manager   Martin Wiviott   213-468-1700
Marketing   Wayne McWorter   213-468-1743
Operations   Michael Tokar   213-468-1700

HOUSE CREW
Technical Director   Jack Stephens   213-468-1797
Carpentry   Tom Kolouch   213-653-8270
Electrics   Kyron Collier   213-653-7108
Sound   Jane Leslie   213-653-8231
Props   James Draper   213-653-7108

UNIONS
IATSE Local #33   Roy LaVoice   213-818-841-9233
Wardrobe Local #768   Dorothy Priest   213-818-789-8735
AFM Local #47   213-462-2162

SEATING CAPACITY
Orchestra   887
Mezzanine   197
Balcony   784
Total: **1,868**

pit (add'l)   42

BOX OFFICE
Computerized
Box Office Treasurer
  John Dobbins   213-468-1700

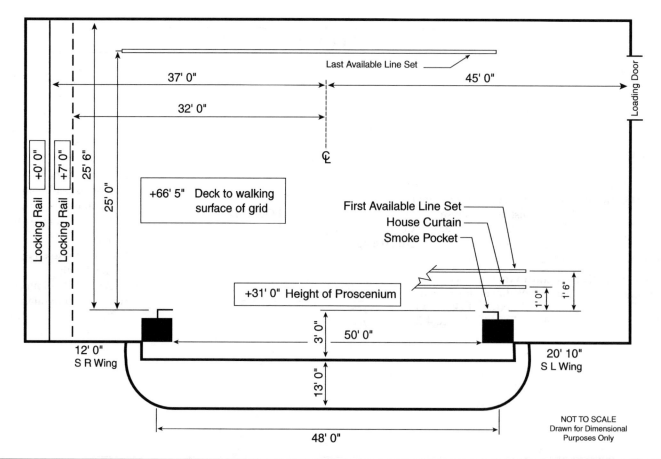

Last Available Line Set

37' 0"   45' 0"

32' 0"

Loading Door

25' 6"

25' 0"

+66' 5" Deck to walking surface of grid

First Available Line Set
House Curtain
Smoke Pocket

1' 0"   1' 6"

+31' 0" Height of Proscenium

Locking Rail +0' 0"
Locking Rail +7' 0"

3' 0"   50' 0"

12' 0"   20' 10"
S R Wing   S L Wing

13' 0"

48' 0"

NOT TO SCALE
Drawn for Dimensional
Purposes Only

STAGE HOUSE

HOUSE CURTAIN
Operates as a guillotine or traveller from SR deck

RIGGING SYSTEM
Type: Single purchase counter weight
Weight: 24,500 lbs available
Line sets: 33 sets at 6" o.c. with 5 lift lines per set
Arbors: 1,000 lb capacity
House Pipes: 52' long with 65' of travel from deck
Line sets are moveable
Block & Falls are available 2:1 (2)
(20) spot wheels and 4,000' of hemp available

PERMANENT INSTALLATIONS OVER STAGE (FROM SMOKE POCKET)
None

PERMANENT INSTALLATIONS ON DECK
Concrete ramp (1) to loading dock located on USL side wall

ORCHESTRA PIT
Nonadjustable to 7' below stage level
Apron overhangs US wall of pit 2'0"

BACKSTAGE

LOADING DOCK
Loading door(s):
    10'0" high x 5'8" wide
Trucks load (1) at same time
Dock loading door sill is at street level 2'0" above stage level; concrete ramp down to stage is available

WARDROBE
Location: SR in adjacent building
Access: Direct from loading dock
(2) Washers (2) Dryers
No washer or dryer hookups

DRESSING ROOMS
(2) Star, SR, stage level, t/s included
(2) Small, SR, stage level, toilet on same fl
(2) Chorus, SR, stage level, toilet on same fl
Additional Chorus dressing room located in adjacent building

SOUND

CONSOLE
No house console

SPEAKERS
House Cluster
Under Balcony
Holes in ceiling over house provide truss hanging position, pipe and rigging not available

COMMUNICATIONS
Infrared sound system
Dressing room page system

ROAD CONSOLE
Located Rear House
No seats required to be removed
Cable run from stage is 200'
Tie-in into house system with XLR connectors

REHEARSAL & STORAGE SPACE
Rehearsal: None
Storage: None

ELECTRICS

ROAD SERVICE POWER

Panel	Phase	Amp	Circuit Protection	Use	Location
A	3	400	breaker	dimmers	DSR in alcove
B-C	3	400	breaker	extra	DSR in alcove
D	3	200	breaker	sound	SL side wall

Recommended location of touring dimmer racks: SR on deck

FRONT OF HOUSE (BOX BOOM VALUES ARE PER SIDE)

Position	Pipe Width	Distance to Prosc.	House Circuits	Connector Type	FOH Transfer Circuits
1st Balc Rail	60'	63'	48	grd 20 amp stage pin	48
Box Boom 1		12'	10	grd 20 amp stage pin	10
Box Boom 2		32'	10	grd 20 amp stage pin	10

Transfer circuits: grd 20 amp stage pin located on DSR side wall
Road truss: Holes in ceiling over house provide truss hanging position; pipe and rigging not available

EQUIPMENT FOH (BOX BOOM VALUES ARE PER SIDE)
None

FOLLOWSPOTS
House Followspots:
    (2) Carbon Super Trouper; removeable

Followspot Booth:
    (4) spots per booth;
    160' throw to proscenium;
    (4) 3Ø 30 amp breakers

DIMMERS
None

CERRITOS CENTER FOR THE PERFORMING ARTS

YEAR BUILT: 1993

Theatre Location: 12700 Center Court Drive, Cerritos, CA 90703

Main Administrative Phone:	562-916-8510
Main Administrative Fax:	562-916-8514
Website:	www.cerritoscenter.com
Stage Door Phone:	562-916-8522
Backstage Pay Phone:	562-809-9215
Traveling Production Office Phone:	562-916-8520

SEATING CAPACITY

Orchestra & Grand	787
Gold	268
Upper	376
Total:	**1,431**
pit (add'l)	80
wheelchair (add'l)	6

THEATRE STAFF

Executive Director	Wayne Shilkret	562-916-8510
Marketing	Walter Morlock	562-916-8510
Operations	Tom Hamilton	562-916-8510
Group Sales	Jennifer Davis	562-916-8510

HOUSE CREW

Technical Admin	Tom Hamilton	562-916-8510
Stage Manager	Miles Williams	562-916-8510
Carpenter	Rogan Girard	562-916-8510
Electrician	David Thibodeau	562-916-8510
Sound	Jack Hayback	562-916-8510

UNIONS

Music	Mike Vaccaro	562-424-4958

BOX OFFICE

Computerized
Box Office Manager
  Kate Ladd   562-916-8510

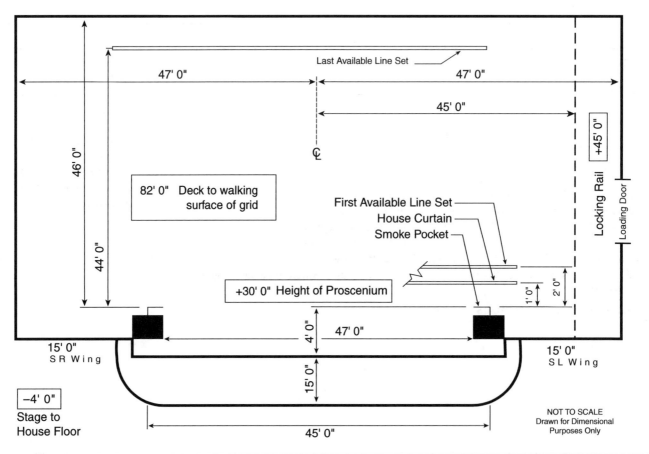

STAGE HOUSE

HOUSE CURTAIN
Operates as a guillotine or traveller from SL deck

RIGGING SYSTEM
Type: Single purchase counter weight
Weight: 15,000 lbs available
Line sets: 63 sets at 8" o.c. with 6 lift lines per set
Arbors: 1,400 lb capacity
House Pipes: 60' long with 80' of travel from deck.
Line sets are not moveable
Block & Falls are available
Chain hoists are available; (10) one ton
(30) spot wheels and 2,400' of hemp available

PERMANENT INSTALLATIONS OVER STAGE
M=Moveable with advance call
Orchestra shells (3) at 8'9",22'0",37'0"
Electric raceways (1) at 4'0"
Traveller (1) at 3'0"
Electric pipe (1) at 4'0"
Dead spaces (3) orchestra shells each occupy 2'1"
Hard portal (1) at 2'0"
Cyclorama (1); M
Fire curtain (1) at 0'0" cannot be blocked

PERMANENT INSTALLATIONS ON DECK
Jumps (above locking rail) (2), +42' & +62'
Hard legs (1 set), 30'0"h x 12'0"w; 1'8" US of smoke pocket
Loading bridge (3) at +42', +62', +77'
Adjustable proscenium (1)
Adjustable portal (1 set), 30'0"h x 12'0"w; 1'8" US of smoke pocket

ORCHESTRA PIT
Adjustable to 9' below stage level by electric motor turnscrew
Pit lift is in (1) section

BACKSTAGE

LOADING DOCK
Loading door(s):
    14'0" high x 14'0" wide
Trucks load (2) at same time
Fork lift is not required
(5) Trailers can store on-site
Security at dock & stage door

WARDROBE
Location: 2nd floor
Access: Stairs or elevator
(2) Washers (2) Dryers
Washer and dryer hookups available

DRESSING ROOMS
(1) Star, SL, 1st fl, t/s, phone jack
(7) Small, SL, 1st & 2nd fl, t/s phone jack
(2) Chorus, SL, 2nd fl, t/s
Elevator access for dressing rooms
Use dressing room for company mgr office

SOUND

CONSOLE
Yamaha PM 4000. located FOH
48 inputs

SPEAKERS
House Cluster
Proscenium
Under Balcony
Portable
Speaker truss does not exist

COMMUNICATIONS
Clear Com intercom with (1) channel
Infrared sound system
Dressing room page system

ROAD CONSOLE
Located Rear Orchestra
No seats required to be removed
Cable run from stage is 100'
Tie in into house system with XLR connectors

REHEARSAL & STORAGE SPACE
Rehearsal: None
Storage: None

ELECTRICS

ROAD SERVICE POWER

Panel	Phase	Amp	Circuit Protection Use	Location
A-C	3	400	dimmers	SR
D	3	200	sound	USR
E	3	400	sound	under stage
F	3	200	sound	FOH
G-J	3	400	extra	SR

Recommended location of touring dimmer racks: SR
Hoist provided but not required
Additional power is available for tour buses, generators, etc.

FRONT OF HOUSE (BOX BOOM VALUES ARE PER SIDE)

Position	Pipe Width	Distance to Prosc.	House Circuits	Connector Type	FOH Transfer Circuits
1st/2nd/ 3rd Cove				grd 20 amp stage pin	150
1st/2nd Balc Rails				grd 20 amp stage pin	
Tower circuits				grd 20 amp stage pin	

EQUIPMENT FOH (BOX BOOM VALUES ARE PER SIDE

Position	Quantity	Wattage	Instrument	Removeable
1st Balc Rail	12	1,000	Colortran	yes
2nd Balc Rail	12	1,000	Colortran	yes
1st Cove	18	1,000	Colortan 200	yes
2nd Cove	18	1,000	Colortran 200	yes

FOLLOWSPOTS
House Followspots:
(4) Strong Super Troupers 2k; not removeable

Followspot Booth:
(4) spots per booth;
100' throw to prosc;
(4) 2Ø 30 amp breakers

DIMMERS
Lighting console is Colortan Prestige 3000 Avolite Console;
(600) Colortran dimmers
House has DMX control system
(2) dry run DMX station(s)

ORANGE COUNTY PERFORMING ARTS CENTER

AKA: SEGERSTROM HALL   **YEAR BUILT: 1985**

Theatre Location: 600 Town Center Drive, Costa Mesa, CA 92626

Main Administrative Phone: 714-556-2121
Main Administrative Fax: 714-556-0156
E-mail: kwagemann@ocpac.org
Website: www.ocpac.org
Stage Door Phone: 714-556-2321
Backstage Pay Phone: 714-754-8505

THEATRE STAFF
President   Jerry Mandel   714-556-2121
Booking   Judy O'Dea Morr   714-556-2121
Marketing   Greg Patterson   714-556-2121
Operations   Kerry Madden   714-556-2121
Group Sales   Sandy Orrill   714-556-2121

HOUSE CREW
Production Manager Kurt Wagemann   714-556-2121
Carpentry   Robbie Foreman   714-556-2121
Electrics   Kathy Halvorson   714-556-2121
Sound   Loren Thies   714-556-2121
Props   Rob Stewart   714-556-2121

UNIONS
IATSE Local #504   Jim Buckholtz   714-774-5148

SEATING CAPACITY
Orchestra	1,178
First Tier	679
Second Tier	478
Third Tier	601
Total:	**2,936**
pit (add'l)	58

BOX OFFICE
Computerized
Box Office Treasurer
  Chris Inserra   714-556-2121

Outside Ticket Agency
Ticketmaster   714-740-2000

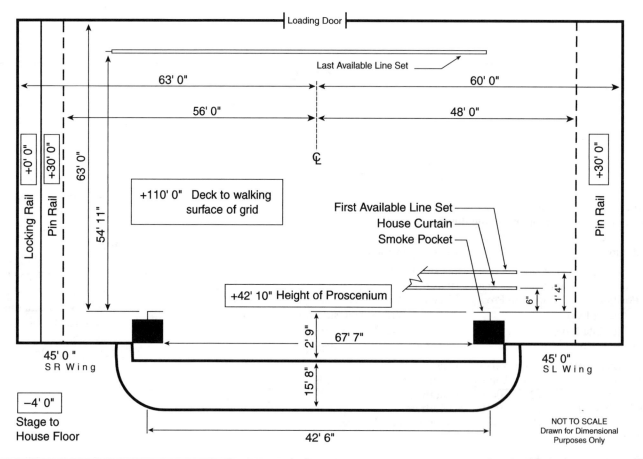

STAGE HOUSE

HOUSE CURTAIN
Operates as a guillotine or traveller from SR deck

RIGGING SYSTEM
Type:	Single purchase counter weight
Weight:	100,000 lbs available
Line sets:	92 sets at 6" o.c. with 6 lift lines per set
Arbors:	1,850 lb capacity
House Pipes:	70' long with 100' of travel from deck

Line sets are not moveable
Block & Falls are available
(50) spot wheels and 20,000' of hemp available

PERMANENT INSTALLATIONS OVER STAGE (FROM SMOKE POCKET)
M=Moveable with advance call
Orchestra shell trip (1) at 5'4"; M

PERMANENT INSTALLATIONS ON DECK
Traps in stage floor are on a sectional grid
Cable platform located DSR in wing

ORCHESTRA PIT
Adjustable to 15' below stage level by hydraulic lift
Apron overhangs US wall of pit 9'3"
Pit lift is in (2) sections

BACKSTAGE

LOADING DOCK
Loading door(s):
11'8" high x 9'11" wide
Trucks load (4) side-by-side at same time
Dock is at truck level; loading to stage thru separate loading bay behind stage house;
(1) truck bay is equipped with electric leveller
Fork lift is not required
Sound/Props can load in FOH
Lobby can be a work area
(3) Trailers can store on-site
Security at dock & stage door

WARDROBE
Location: SR in basement
Access: Freight elevator
(2) Washers (2) Dryers

DRESSING ROOMS
(5) Star, DSR, stage level, t/s included, phone jack
(5) Small, SR / SL, basement, t/s included, phone jack
(5) Chorus, SR / SL, basement, t/s included
Elevator access for dressing rooms
Additional production office available for company mgr

SOUND

CONSOLE
Yamaha PM 3000, located Rear Tier 1
32 inputs, 8 main outputs

SPEAKERS
House Cluster
Under Balcony

COMMUNICATIONS
Clear Com intercom with (2) channels
Infrared sound system
Dressing room page system

ROAD CONSOLE
Located Rear Tier 1
(6) seats required to be removed
Cable run from stage is 300'
Tie-in into house system with XLR connectors

REHEARSAL & STORAGE SPACE
Rehearsal: 70' x 50' SR located on stage level
Storage: Various sizes and locations

ELECTRICS

ROAD SERVICE POWER
Panel	Phase	Amp	Circuit Protection	Use	Location
A - E	3	400	breaker	dimmers	DSR in alcove
F	3	400	breaker	sound	DSR in alcove
G	3	100	breaker	extra	DSR procenium wall
H	3	100	breaker	extra	DSL proscenium wall
I	3	100	breaker	extra	USR back wall
J	3	100	breaker	extra	USL back wall

Recommended location of touring dimmer racks: DSR on deck
Hoist not required
Additional power is available for tour buses, generators, etc.

FRONT OF HOUSE (BOX BOOM VALUES ARE PER SIDE)
Position	Pipe Width	Distance to Prosc.	House Circuits	Connector Type	FOH Transfer Circuits
1st Balc Rail	12'	54'	4	grd 20 amp stage pin	4
2nd Balc Rail	24'	67'	11	grd 20 amp stage pin	11
3rd Balc Rail	12'	64'	4	grd 20 amp stage pin	4
4th Balc Rail	24'	84'	12	grd 20 amp stage pin	12
1st Catwalk	38'	40'	18	grd 20 amp stage pin	18
2nd Catwalk	38'	71'	36	grd 20 amp stage pin	36

Transfer circuits: grd 20 amp stage pin located DSR on deck

EQUIPMENT FOH (BOX BOOM VALUES ARE PER SIDE)
Position	Quantity	Wattage	Instrument	Removeable
1st Cove	18	1,000	8 x 13 Lekos	yes
2nd Cove	18	1,000	10 x 23 Lekos	yes

FOLLOWSPOTS
House Followspots:
(4) Xenon Super Troupers 2k; not removeable

Followspot Booth:
(4) spots per booth;
113' throw to proscenium;
(4) 3Ø 30 amp breakers

DIMMERS
House console is ETC Obsession; (582) ETC dimmers
House has programmable DMX control system
(4) dry run DMX station(s)

FLINT CENTER FOR THE PERFORMING ARTS

YEAR BUILT: 1971   YEAR RENOVATED: 1997

Theatre Location: 21250 Stevens Creek Boulevard, Cupertino, CA 95014
Mailing Address: PO Box 1897, Cupertino, CA 95015
Management Company: Domus Aurea, Inc, Santa Clara, CA

Main Administrative Phone: 408-854-8820
Main Administrative Fax: 408-864-8918
E-mail: qwert@flintcenter.com
Website: www.flintcenter.com
Backstage Pay Phone: 408-864-8919
Traveling Production Office Phone: 408-255-8264

SEATING CAPACITY

Orchestra	1,790
Mezzanine	266
Balcony	266
Suites	68
Total:	**2,390**
pit (add'l)	74
wheelchair (add'l)	16

THEATRE STAFF
General Manager   Paula Davis   408-864-8820
Asst General Manager   Anthony Kim   408-864-8820

HOUSE CREW
Production Manager   Chris Ostergard   408-864-8821
Steward   Ray Garrett   408-864-8435
Electrics   Chuck Burnett   408-864-8435

STAGE DIMENSIONS (FROM SMOKE POCKET)
Stage is 39'2" deep
Width from Center Line to SL is 25'10";
Width from Center Line to SR is 25'10"
Proscenium width is 51'9"
Proscenium height is 32'0"
Smoke pocket to apron edge is 1'4"
Orchestra pit exists

RIGGING
Grid Height: 63'2"
Type: Single purchase counter weight
Weight: 40,000 lbs
Line sets: 54 sets at 6" o.c.
Arbors: 630 lb capacity
House Pipes: 63' long

LOADING DOCK
Loading door(s) are 11'6" high x 9'9" wide
Trucks load (2) at same time
Fork lift is not required and is not available

ELECTRICS
Total power available:
(1) 200 A 3Ø SR
(1) 700 A 3Ø basement
USR 50' feeder needed

FOLLOWSPOTS
House Followspots:
(3) Strong Super Trouper 2k

DIMMERS
(340) house dimmers
(2) dry run station(s) located
FOH, Booth

SOUND
House has 200 A 3Ø of
dedicated power located
DSR
FOH mixing position is 140'
from stage, Rear Orchestra

SAROYAN THEATRE

AT: FRESNO CONVENTION CENTER   **YEAR BUILT: 1966   YEAR RENOVATED: 1997**

Theatre Location: 700 M Street, Fresno, CA 93721

Main Administrative Phone:	559-498-1511
Main Administrative Fax:	559-488-4634
Stage Door Phone:	559-498-1521
Backstage Pay Phone:	559-441-9287

SEATING CAPACITY

Orchestra	1,429
Balcony	924
Total:	**2,353**
wheelchair (add'l)	6

THEATRE STAFF

Convention Center Mgr.	Mike Sweeney	559-498-1511
Booking	Mercy Tristan	559-498-1511
Marketing	Bruce Bucz	559-498-1511
Operations	Greg Eisner	559-498-1538
Group Sales	Beverly Pierson	559-498-4000

HOUSE CREW

Senior Technician	Jeff Barrett	559-498-1538/4610
Technician	Jeff Hilton	559-498-1538/4610

UNIONS

IATSE Local #158	559-224-6236

BOX OFFICE
Computerized
Box Office Supervisor
  Beverly Pierson   559-498-4000

Outside Ticket Agency
Computerized
Bass/Advantix
  Karen Tangle   559-233-8368

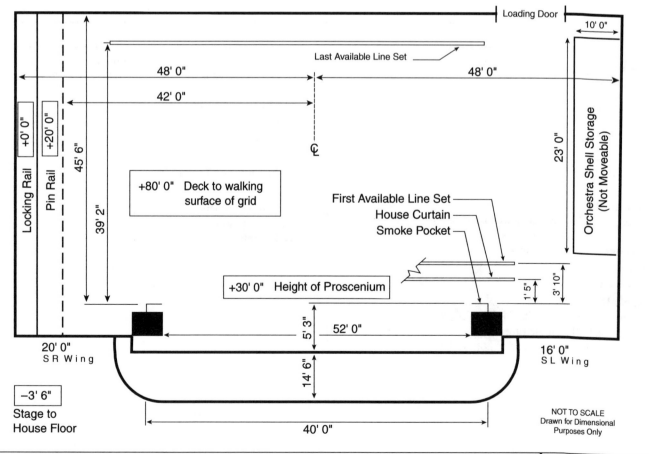

20' 0"
SR Wing

−3' 6"
Stage to
House Floor

16' 0"
SL Wing

NOT TO SCALE
Drawn for Dimensional
Purposes Only

STAGE HOUSE

HOUSE CURTAIN
Operates as a guillotine from SR deck

RIGGING SYSTEM
Type: Single purchase counter weight
Weight: 55,000 lbs available
Line sets: 55 sets at 8" o.c. with 7 lift lines per set
Arbors: 1,500 lb capacity
House Pipes: 63' long with 78' of travel from deck
Line sets are not moveable
Block & Falls are not available
Chain hoists are not available
(30) spot wheels and 1,000' of hemp available

PERMANENT INSTALLATIONS OVER STAGE (FROM SMOKE POCKET)
M=Moveable with advance call
Orchestra shell (6) at 7'9", 15'9", 23'8", 26'4", 30'3",
   35'10"
Electric borders (12) at 2'0"; M
Electric raceways (4) at 3'0", 11'5", 19'5", 28'0"
Movie screen (1); M
Traveller (2), 10'3", 24'3"; M
Cyclorama (1) at 37'9"; M
Fire curtain (1)

PERMANENT INSTALLATIONS ON DECK
Orchestra shell storage (1), at 10'0" x 23'0", USL corner

ORCHESTRA PIT
Nonadjustable at 7' below stage level
Apron overhangs US wall of pit 2'0"

BACKSTAGE

LOADING DOCK
Loading door(s):
   15'9" high x 9'0" wide
Trucks load (2) at same time
Fork lift is not required
Sound/Props cannot load in
   FOH
No trailers can store on-site

WARDROBE
Location: SR green room on
   stage level
Access: Direct from stage
No Washers No Dryers
Washer and dryer hookups
   available

DRESSING ROOMS
(2) Star, SR, stage level, t/s
   included, phone jack
(7) Small, SR, stage level, t/s
   included, (4) with phone jacks
(2) Chorus, SR, +2, t/s included
Use dressing room for company
   mgr office

SOUND

CONSOLE
Yamaha PM 916,
   located Off SL
16 inputs, 4 main outputs,
   4 matrix outputs, 2 aux
   outputs

SPEAKERS
House Cluster
Under Balcony delay

COMMUNICATIONS
Clear Com intercom with
   (2) channels
Infrared sound system
Dressing room page system

ROAD CONSOLE
Located Rear House
 Number of seats required to
   be removed varies
Cable run from stage is 150'
Tie-in into house system with
   XLR connectors

REHEARSAL & STORAGE SPACE
Rehearsal: None
Storage: 30' x 50', behind
   stage

ELECTRICS

ROAD SERVICE POWER

Panel	Phase	Amp	Circuit Protection	Use	Location
A	3	400	breaker	dimmers	USR
B	3	400	fuse	dimmers	USR
C	3	200	breaker	sound	USL
D	1	50	breaker	extra	SR side wall
E	1	50	breaker	extra	SL side wall

Recommended location of touring dimmer racks: SR on deck
Hoist not required

FRONT OF HOUSE (BOX BOOM VALUES ARE PER SIDE)

Position	Pipe Width	Distance to Prosc.	House Circuits	Connector Type	FOH Transfer Circuits
Balc Rail	60'	83	30	grd 20 amp stagepin	30
1st Cove	56'	45'	32	grd 20 amp stagepin	32
2nd Cove	80'	63'	32	grd 20 amp stagepin	32
Torm		3'	10	grd 20 amp stagepin	0

Transfer circuits: grd 20 amp stagepin, USR side wall

EQUIPMENT FOH (BOX BOOM VALUES ARE PER SIDE)

Position	Quantity	Wattage	Instrument	Removeable
1st Balc Rail	32	575	Source 4 10°	yes
1st Cove	6	575	Source 4 19°	
2nd Balc Rail	32	575	Source 4 10°	
Box Boom 1	6	1,000	Par 64 MFL	yes

FOLLOWSPOTS
House Followspots:
   (2) Xenon Super Trouper
   2k; not removeable

Followspot Booth:
   (4) spots per booth;
   150' throw to proscenium;
   (4) 1Ø 30 amp breakers

DIMMERS
House console is Strand
   Light
   Board M; (384) Strand
   CD80 dimmers
No DMX control system

WARNORS THEATRE

AKA: WARNORS CENTER FOR THE PERFORMING ARTS   **YEAR BUILT: 1928**

Theatre Location: 1400 Fulton Street, Fresno, CA 93721

Main Administrative Phone: 209-264-2848
Main Administrative Fax: 209-264-5643

THEATRE STAFF
General Manager   Samuel L. Martinez   209-264-6863
Booking   Samuel L. Martinez   209-264-6863

HOUSE CREW
Technical Director   Jason Edens   209-264-6863

UNIONS
IATSE Local #158   Larry Smith   209-224-6300

SEATING CAPACITY
Orchestra   1,420
Balcony   744
Total: **2,164**

BOX OFFICE
Computerized
Box Office Manager
Jennifer L. Bautsch   209-264-2848

Outside Ticket Agency
Computerized
Advantix/Bass
Karen Tangle   209-226-3193

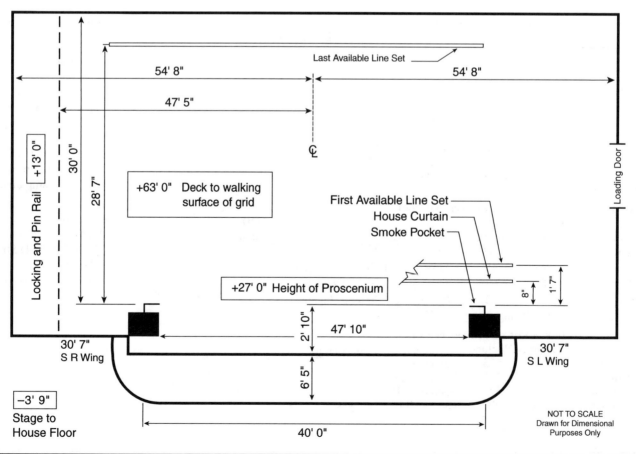

+13' 0" Locking and Pin Rail

54' 8"   54' 8"
47' 5"

Last Available Line Set

CL

30' 0"
28' 7"

+63' 0"   Deck to walking surface of grid

First Available Line Set
House Curtain
Smoke Pocket

1' 7"
8"

+27' 0" Height of Proscenium

Loading Door

2' 10"   47' 10"

30' 7"
S R Wing

30' 7"
S L Wing

6' 5"

−3' 9"
Stage to
House Floor

40' 0"

NOT TO SCALE
Drawn for Dimensional
Purposes Only

STAGE HOUSE

HOUSE CURTAIN
Operates as a guillotine from SR fly floor

RIGGING SYSTEM

Type:	Single purchase counter weight
Weight:	8,150 lbs available
Line sets:	55 sets at 8" o.c. with 3 lift lines per set
Arbors:	800 lb capacity
House Pipes:	55' long with 62' of travel from deck

Line sets are moveable
Block & Falls are not available
Chain hoists are available ; (4) one ton
(25) spot wheels and 100' of hemp available
Can rig off grid and two ad points above orchestra pit.

PERMANENT INSTALLATIONS OVER STAGE (FROM SMOKE POCKET)
M=Moveable with advance call
Movie screen (1) at 3'5"; M
Fire curtain (1)

PERMANENT INSTALLATIONS ON DECK
Loading bridge (1)

ORCHESTRA PIT
Nonadjustable to 8' below stage level
Apron overhangs US wall of pit 2'1"
Organ and piano lift DS Center

BACKSTAGE

LOADING DOCK
Loading door(s):
 15'0" high x 16'0" wide
Trucks load (2) at same time
Fork lift is not required
Sound/Props can load in FOH
Lobby can be a work area
(4) Trailers can store on-site
Security at dock & stage door

WARDROBE
Location: Basement
Access: Elevator/ Stage door
(1) Washer (1) Dryer
No washer or dryer hookups

DRESSING ROOMS
(2) Star, -1, t/s included, phone
 jack
(6) Small, -1, t/s included
(2) Chorus, SL/SR, -1, t/s
 included
Elevator access for dressing
 rooms
Use dressing room for company
 mgr office

SOUND

CONSOLE
No house console

SPEAKERS
No speaker truss

COMMUNICATIONS
No house intercom system

ROAD CONSOLE
No seats required to be
 removed
Cable run from stage is 160'

REHEARSAL & STORAGE SPACE
Rehearsal and Storage:
 Star Palace, 3000 sq ft

ELECTRICS

ROAD SERVICE POWER

Panel	Phase	Amp	Circuit Protection	Use	Location
A	1	100	breaker	sound	DSR
B	3	400	breaker	dimmers	DSR
C	3	200	breaker	extra	DSR
D	3	400	breaker	dimmers	DSR

Recommended location of touring dimmer racks: DSR
Hoist not required
Additional power is available for tour buses, generators, etc.

FRONT OF HOUSE (BOX BOOM VALUES ARE PER SIDE)

Position	Pipe Width	Distance to Prosc.	House Circuits	Connector Type	FOH Transfer Circuits
Balc Rail	60'	70'	10	Edison	10
Box Boom 1		43'	0		0

Road truss: Trussing may be hung from grid 60' above stage & by (2) points located
 above orchestra pit

EQUIPMENT FOH (BOX BOOM VALUES ARE PER SIDE)

Position	Quantity	Wattage	Instrument	Removeable
1st Balc Rail	8	1,000	Lekos	yes
Box Boom 1	10	1,000	Lekos	yes
Box Boom 2	8	1,000	Lekos	yes

In-house DMX Control

FOLLOWSPOTS
House Followspots:
 (2) Carbon Arc Super
 Troupers; removeable

Followspot Booth:
 (2) spots per booth;
 100' throw to proscenium;
 (4) 3Ø 400 amp breakers

DIMMERS
Lighting console is
 Producer III;
 (48) Genesis dimmers
House has programmable
 DMX control system
(1) dry run DMX station

TERRACE THEATER

AT: LONG BEACH CONVENTION CENTER   **YEAR BUILT: 1978**

Theatre Location: 300 East Ocean Boulevard, Long Beach, CA 90802
Management Company: SMG

Main Administrative Phone: 562-436-3636
Main Administrative Fax: 562-436-9491
Stage Door Phone: 562-499-7617
Backstage Pay Phone: 562-432-9714

SEATING CAPACITY

Orchestra	1,767
Loge	663
Balcony	508
Total:	**2,938**
pit (add'l)	83

THEATRE STAFF

General Manager	David Gordon	562-436-3636
Booking	Bobbie Jones	562-499-7577
Marketing	Lynn Komadina	562-499-7508
Operations	Rob Collins	562-499-7600

HOUSE CREW

Theatrical SM	Robert Sternberg	562-499-7616
Stage Supervisor	Tina Johnson	562-499-7617
Electrics	Elmo Martin	562-499-7617
Sound	Jack Kelly	562-499-7627

BOX OFFICE

Computerized
Box Office Treasurer
  Vickie Hanssen   562-436-3661

Outside Ticket Agency
  Ticketmaster   213-381-2000

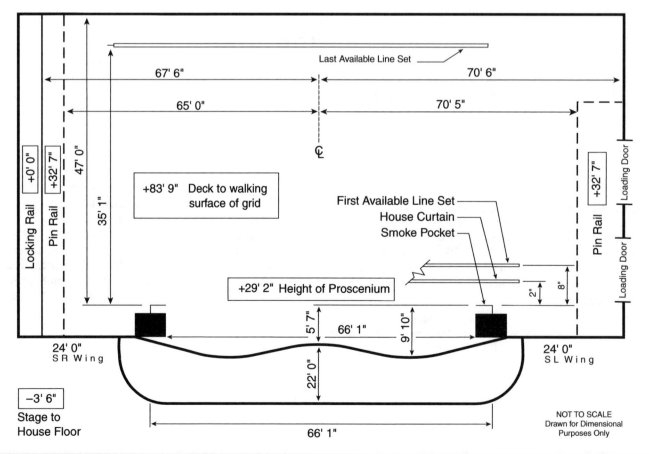

STAGE HOUSE

HOUSE CURTAIN
Operates as a guillotine from SR deck

RIGGING SYSTEM
Type:	Single purchase counter weight
Weight:	65,000 lbs available
Line sets:	58 sets at 6" o.c. with 7 lift lines per set
Arbors:	2,000 lb capacity
House Pipes:	75' long with 83' of travel from deck

Line sets are not moveable
Block & Falls are available
Chain hoists available as a rental; (4) quarter ton
(64) spot wheels available

PERMANENT INSTALLATIONS OVER STAGE (FROM SMOKE POCKET)
Orchestra shells (4) at 8'0", 18'9", 28'7", 34'11"
Electric borders (5) at 5'7", 11'2", 17'8", 24'1", 31'1"
Fire curtain at smoke pocket

PERMANENT INSTALLATIONS ON DECK
Stairs (2) at 3'0" wide, off SR, SL
Orchestra shell storage (6), 7'6" x 9'6", on back wall

ORCHESTRA PIT
Adjustable to 10' below stage level by hydraulic lift
Apron overhangs US wall of pit 6'0"
Pit lift is in (3) sections

BACKSTAGE

LOADING DOCK
Loading door(s):
  (2) 20'0" high x 10'0" wide
Trucks load (2) at same time
Very steep hill to back up on; sometimes very crowded dock area
Fork lift is not required
Sound/Props cannot load in FOH
Trailers can store on-site

WARDROBE
Location: One flight below stage
Access: Elevator from scene dock
(2) Washers (2) Dryers
Washer and dryer hookups available

DRESSING ROOMS
(3) Star, SR, t/s included, phone jack
(1) Star, SR, phone jack
(2) Small, SR, +1, t/s included, phone jack
(2) Chorus, SL, -1, t/s included
Elevator access for dressing rooms
Additional production office available for company mgr

SOUND

CONSOLE
ETC, located in booth
52 inputs, 8 main outputs, 8 matrix outputs, 8 aux outputs

SPEAKERS
House Cluster
Proscenium
Under Balcony
Portable
No speaker truss

COMMUNICATIONS
Clear Com intercom with (4) channels
Infrared sound system
Dressing room page system

ROAD CONSOLE
Located next to house console
(6) seats required to be removed
Cable run from stage is 250'
Tie-in into house system with XLR connectors

REHEARSAL & STORAGE SPACE
Rehearsal: 60' x 30', located in basement; piano, sprung floor
Storage: None

ELECTRICS

ROAD SERVICE POWER
Panel	Phase	Amp	Circuit Protection	Use	Location
A-B	3	600	breaker	dimmers	DSR
C	3	60	fuse	sound	DSR, DSL
D	3	150	fuse	extra	DSR, DSL
E	3	200	breaker	extra	Loading dock
F	3	100	breaker	extra	Loading dock

Recommended location of touring dimmer racks: SR
Hoist not required
Additional power is available for tour buses, generators, etc.

FRONT OF HOUSE (BOX BOOM VALUES ARE PER SIDE)
Position	Pipe Width	Distance to Prosc.	House Circuits	Connector Type	FOH Transfer Circuits
1st Balc Rail		108'	54	grd 20 amp stage pin	54
1st Cove		62'	50	grd 20 amp stage pin	50
Box Boom 1		66'	12	grd 20 amp stage pin	12
Box Boom 2		80'	12	grd 20 amp stage pin	12

Transfer circuits: grd 20 amp stage pin - all FOH circuits

EQUIPMENT FOH (BOX BOOM VALUES ARE PER SIDE)
Position	Quantity	Wattage	Instrument	Removeable
1st Balc Rail		1,000	6 x 22	yes
1st Cove	40	1,000	6 x 16	yes
Box Boom 1	20	1,000	6 x 8	yes
Box Boom 2	10	1,000	6 x 8	

FOLLOWSPOTS
House Followspots:
(4) Strong Gladiator II 2,500; removeable

Followspot Booth:
(4) spots per booth;
135' throw to proscenium;
(4) 3Ø 30 amp breakers

DIMMERS
Lighting console is ETC Obsession;
(144) Kleigl R 80 dimmers
House has non-programmable DMX control system

AHMANSON THEATRE

AT: MUSIC CENTER OF LOS ANGELES　　　　　　　　　**YEAR BUILT: 1967　YEAR RENOVATED: 1994**

Theatre Location:　　　　135 N Grand Avenue, Los Angeles, CA 90012
Management Company:　Center Theatre Group
　　　　　　　　　　　　135 North Grand, Los Angeles, CA 90012

Main Administrative Phone:　　　　　213-972-7401
Main Administrative Fax:　　　　　　213-972-7402
Website:　　　　　　　　　　　　　www.taperahm.com
Stage Door Phone:　　　　　　　　　213-972-7409
Backstage Pay Phone:　　　　　　　213-625-9285
Traveling Production Office Phone:　213-972-7601

THEATRE STAFF
Managing Director　　Charles Dillingham　213-972-7364
Booking　　　　　　Doug Baker　　　　　213-972-7542
Marketing　　　　　Jim Royce　　　　　213-972-7324
Group Sales　　　　Trevor O'Donnell　　213-972-7320

HOUSE CREW
Technical Director　Bob Ruby　　　　　213-972-7811
Carpentry　　　　　Bill Anderson　　　213-972-7433
Electrics　　　　　Terry Callaway　　213-972-7434
Sound　　　　　　　Robert Smith　　　213-972-7435
Props　　　　　　　Steve Rapollo　　　213-972-7439

UNIONS
IATSE Local #33　　Roy LaVoise　　　818-841-9233
Wardrobe　　　　　　Dorothy Priest　　818-789-8735

SEATING CAPACITY
Orchestra　　　　1,011
Mezzanine　　　　607
Balcony　　　　　515
Total:　　　**2,133**

BOX OFFICE
Computerized
Box Office Treasurer
　Dave Burgeson　　213-628-2772

Outside Ticket Agency
Computerized

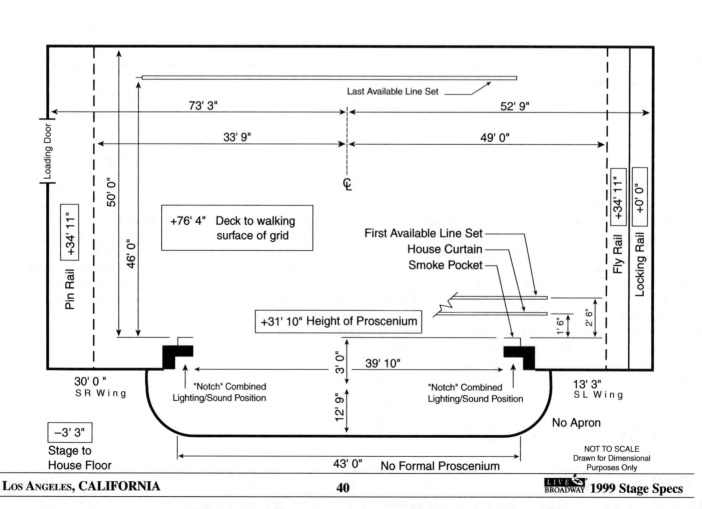

STAGE HOUSE

HOUSE CURTAIN
Operates as a guillotine from SL deck; motorized

RIGGING SYSTEM
Type:	Single purchase counter weight
Weight:	40,000 lbs available
Line sets:	92 sets with 5 lift lines per set
Arbors:	760 lb capacity
House Pipes:	50' long with 67' of travel from deck

Line sets are moveable
Block & Falls are not available
Chain hoists are not available

PERMANENT INSTALLATIONS OVER STAGE (FROM SMOKE POCKET)
None

PERMANENT INSTALLATIONS ON DECK
Trap (27) in stage floor located CS/USR
Pilasters (4) 2'0" x 3'0" located US back wall

ORCHESTRA PIT
Nonadjustable at 9'6" below stage level
Pit lift is in (2) sections

BACKSTAGE

LOADING DOCK
Loading door(s):
   8'9" high x 22'0" wide
Trucks load (3) side by side at
   same time
Fork lift is not required
Sound/Props can load in FOH
Lobby can be a work area
Security at dock & stage door

WARDROBE
Location: SL
Access: Direct from stage via
   hallway
(3) Washers (3) Dryers

DRESSING ROOMS
(3) Star, SL, stage level, t/s
   included, phone jack
(7) Small, SL, stage level, t/s on
   same fl, phone jack
(4) Chorus, SL, stage level, t/s
   included, phone jack
(3) Small, SL, +1, toilet on
   same fl, shower included,
   phone jack
Additional production office
   available for company mgr

SOUND

CONSOLE
No house console

SPEAKERS
House Cluster
Proscenium
Under Balcony

COMMUNICATIONS
Clear Com intercom with
   (4) channels
Infrared sound system
Dressing room page system

ROAD CONSOLE
Located Rear House left
(12) seats required to be
   removed
Cable run from stage is 250'
Tie-in into house system with
   XLR connectors

REHEARSAL & STORAGE SPACE
Rehearsal: None
Storage: None

ELECTRICS

ROAD SERVICE POWER

Panel	Phase	Amp	Circuit Protection	Use	Location
A-D	3	400	fuse	dimmers	SR basement
E	3	200	fuse	sound	DSR wall
F-G	3	200	fuse	extra	SR basement

Recommended location of touring dimmer racks: DSR
Hoist not required

FRONT OF HOUSE (BOX BOOM VALUES ARE PER SIDE)

Position	Pipe Width	Distance to Prosc.	House Circuits	Connector Type	FOH Transfer Circuits
Catwalk 1			18	grd 20 amp stage pin	18
Catwalk 2			24	grd 20 amp stage pin	24
Catwalk 3			24	grd 20 amp stage pin	24
Catwalk 4			24	grd 20 amp stage pin	6
Box Boom 1			11	grd 20 amp stage pin	11
Box Boom 2			7	grd 20 amp stage pin	7
Box Boom 3			7	grd 20 amp stage pin	7
Box Boom 4			7	grd 20 amp stage pin	7

Transfer circuits: grd 20 amp stage pin

EQUIPMENT FOH (BOX BOOM VALUES ARE PER SIDE)
None

FOLLOWSPOTS
House Followspots:
   (3) Xenon Super Troupers;
   removeable

Followspot Booth:
   (4) spots per booth;
   110' throw to proscenium;
   (4) 1Ø 50 amp breakers

DIMMERS
(328) Strand CD80 dimmers
   2.4k
No DMX control system
(36) dry run DMX station(s)

HENRY FONDA THEATRE

Theatre Location: 6126 Hollywood Boulevard, Los Angeles, CA 90028
Management Company: The Nederlander Organization
                                   810 Seventh Avenue, 21st floor, New York NY 10019

Main Administrative Phone: 323-468-1700
Main Administrative Fax: 323-464-1457
StageDoor Phone: 323-464-1802

THEATRE STAFF
General Manager   Martin Wiviott   323-468-1700
Booking   323-468-1710
Marketing   Wayne McWorter   323-468-1743
Operations   Michael Tokar   323-468-1700

HOUSE CREW
Technical Director   Jack Stephens   323-468-1797

UNIONS
IATSE Local #33   Roy La Voice   818-841-9233
Wardrobe Local # 768 Dorothy Priest   818-789-8735

SEATING CAPACITY
Orchestra   572
Mezzanine   291
Total: **863**

BOX OFFICE
John Dobbins   323-468-1700

Outside Ticket Agency
None

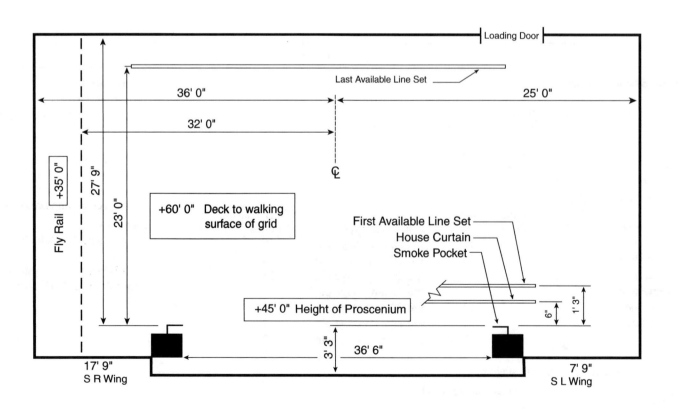

Loading Door

Last Available Line Set

36' 0"   25' 0"

32' 0"

Fly Rail +35' 0"

27' 9"

23' 0"

+60' 0" Deck to walking surface of grid

First Available Line Set
House Curtain
Smoke Pocket

1' 3"
6"

+45' 0" Height of Proscenium

3' 3"   36' 6"

17' 9"
S R Wing

7' 9"
S L Wing

NOT TO SCALE
Drawn for Dimensional
Purposes Only

STAGE HOUSE

HOUSE CURTAIN
Operates as a guillotine from SR deck

RIGGING SYSTEM

Type:	Hemp System
Weight:	1,500 lbs available
Line sets:	20 sets at 12" o.c. with 5 lift lines per set
House Pipes:	45' long with 58' of travel from deck

Line sets are moveable
Block & Falls are available 3:2 (4)
(40) spot wheels and 8,000' of hemp available

PERMANENT INSTALLATIONS OVER STAGE (FROM SMOKE POCKET)
None

PERMANENT INSTALLATIONS ON DECK
Staircase 6'0" wide located against SR side wall

ORCHESTRA PIT
None

BACKSTAGE

LOADING DOCK
Loading door(s):
12'0" high x 8'0" wide
Trucks load (1) at a time
Dock is at street level and can only be accessed by a dock extension due to limited truck space
No trailers can store on-site

WARDROBE
Location: Basement
Access: Stairs
(1) Washer (1) Dryer

DRESSING ROOMS
(11) Small, basement, t/s on same fl

SOUND

CONSOLE
No house console

SPEAKERS
None

COMMUNICATIONS
No house intercom system
Infrared sound system
Dressing room page system

ROAD CONSOLE
Located Rear Balcony
No seats required to be removed
Cable run from stage is 150'

REHEARSAL & STORAGE SPACE
Rehearsal: None
Storage: None

ELECTRICS

ROAD SERVICE POWER

Panel	Phase	Amp	Circuit Protection	Use	Location
A	3	800	fuse	dimmers	DSR proscenium wall
B	3	400	fuse	extra	DSR proscenium wall

Recommended location of touring dimmer racks: SR on jump

FRONT OF HOUSE (BOX BOOM VALUES ARE PER SIDE)

Position	Pipe Width	Distance to Prosc.	House Circuits	Connector Type	FOH Transfer Circuits
1st Balc Rail	100'	50'	36	grd 20 amp stage pin	36
Box Boom 1		50'	12	grd 20 amp stage pin	12

Transfer circuits: grd 20 amp stage pin located SR on jump

EQUIPMENT FOH (BOX BOOM VALUES ARE PER SIDE)
None

FOLLOWSPOTS
House Followspots:
None

Followspot Booth:
(2) spots per booth;
100' throw to proscenium;
(3) 1Ø 20 amp breakers

DIMMERS
None

JAMES W. DOOLITTLE THEATRE

AKA: HARTFORD THEATRE LA

Theatre Location: 1615 North Vine Street, Los Angeles, CA 90028
Management Company: UCLA Public Arts Programs
303 E Melnitz, Los Angeles, CA 90095-1427

Main Administrative Phone: 213-462-6666
Main Administrative Fax: 213-962-2936
Backstage Pay Phone: 213-468-9820

THEATRE STAFF
General Manager Cynthia Cooper 830-825-9723
HOUSE CREW
Technical Director Robert Ruotolo 213-972-0739
UNIONS
IATSE Local #33 Jim Matusak 818-841-9233
Wardrobe BA Dorothy Priest 818-789-8735

SEATING CAPACITY
Orchestra	503
Mezzanine	216
Balcony	234
Total:	**953**
pit (add'l)	74

BOX OFFICE
Box Office Treasurer
Larry Roesch 213-462-6666

Outside Ticket Agency
Ticketmaster

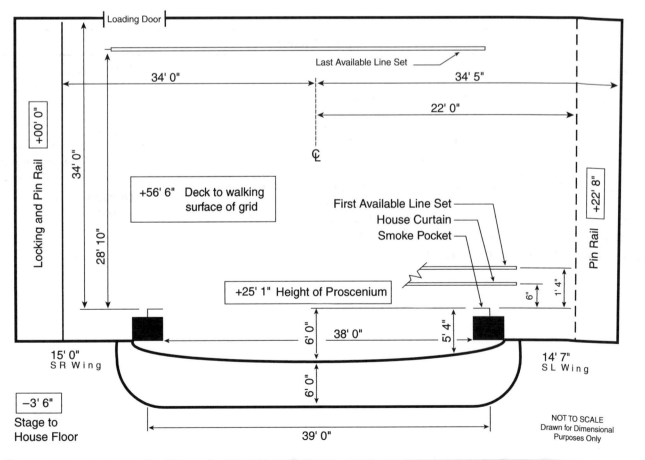

STAGE HOUSE

HOUSE CURTAIN
Operates as a guillotine from SR deck

RIGGING SYSTEM
Type: Single purchase counter weight
Weight: 10,000 lbs available
Line sets: 48 sets at 7" o.c. with 4 lift lines per set
Arbors: 500 lb capacity
House Pipes: 48' long with 50' of travel from deck
Line sets are moveable
Block & Falls are available 2:1 (2); 3:2 (1)
(60) spot wheels and 150' of hemp available
US gallery platform against back wall

PERMANENT INSTALLATIONS OVER STAGE (FROM SMOKE POCKET)
None

PERMANENT INSTALLATIONS ON DECK
None

ORCHESTRA PIT
Nonadjustable to 6' below stage level
Apron overhangs US wall of pit 6'0"

BACKSTAGE

LOADING DOCK
Loading door(s):
16'0" high x 6'6" wide
Trucks load (1) at same time
Dock loading door sill is at street level
Fork lift is not required; rental Acme Rents 213-663-3251
Sound/Props cannot load in FOH
Security at stage door

WARDROBE
Location: Basement
Access: Stairs
(1) Washer (1) Dryer

DRESSING ROOMS
(2) Star, SL, stage level, t/s included, phone jack
(6) Small, SL, 2nd / 3rd fls, t on same fl, phone jack
(1) Chorus, SL, 4th fl, t/s included, phone jack

SOUND

CONSOLE
No house console

SPEAKERS
None

COMMUNICATIONS
No house intercom system
Dressing room page system

ROAD CONSOLE
Located Rear House
(6) seats required to be removed
Cable run from stage is 200'

REHEARSAL & STORAGE SPACE
Rehearsal: None
Storage: None

ELECTRICS

ROAD SERVICE POWER

Panel	Phase	Amp	Circuit Protection	Use	Location
A-B	1	400	fuse	dimmers	DSR proscenium wall
C	1	100	breaker	sound	DSL proscenium wall

Recommended location of touring dimmer racks: SR on jump
Hoist required but not provided

FRONT OF HOUSE (BOX BOOM VALUES ARE PER SIDE)

Position	Pipe Width	Distance to Prosc.	House Circuits	Connector Type	FOH Transfer Circuits
1st Balc Rail	40'	31'	6	grd 20 amp stage pin	6
1st Cove	40'	40'	20	grd 20 amp stage pin	20
2nd Cove	40'	80'	20	grd 20 amp stage pin	20
Box Boom 1		25'	8	grd 20 amp stage pin	8

Transfer circuits: grd 20 amp stage pin located SR on jump
Road truss: Grid work extending into house with 20 circuits each side

EQUIPMENT FOH (BOX BOOM VALUES ARE PER SIDE)
None

FOLLOWSPOTS
House Followspots:
None

Followspot Booth:
(2) spots per booth;
85' throw to proscenium;
(1) 1Ø 20 amp breakers

DIMMERS
None

PANTAGES THEATRE

Theatre Location: 6233 Hollywood Blvd, Los Angeles, CA 90028
Management Company: The Nederlander Organization
810 Seventh Avenue, 21st floor, New York, NY 10019

Main Administrative Phone: 213-468-1700
Main Administrative Fax: 213-464-1457
Backstage Pay Phone: 213-464-9168

THEATRE STAFF
General Manager   Martin Wiviott   213-468-1700
Marketing   Wayne McWorter   213-468-1743
Operations   Michael Tokar   213-468-1700

HOUSE CREW
Technical Director Jack Stephens   213-468-1797
Electrics   Jeff Martel   213-468-1798
Sound   George Velmer   213-468-1796

UNIONS
IATSE Local #33   Roy Lavoice   818-841-9233
Wardrobe Local #768 Dorothy Priest   818-789-8735
AFM Local #47   213-462-2162

SEATING CAPACITY
Orchestra   1,759
Mezzanine   504
Lodge   285
Rear Balcony   125
Total: **2,673**

wheelchair (add'l)   6

BOX OFFICE
Box Office Manager
John Dobbins   213-468-1700

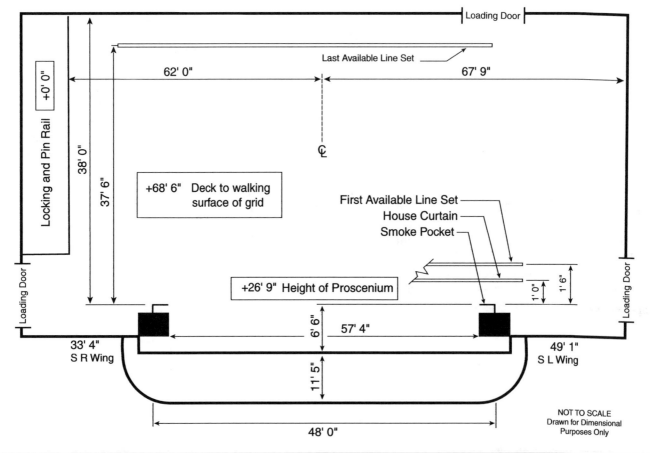

NOT TO SCALE
Drawn for Dimensional
Purposes Only

STAGE HOUSE

HOUSE CURTAIN
Operates as a guillotine from SR deck

RIGGING SYSTEM
Type:	Single purchase counter weight
Weight:	35,000 lbs available
Line sets:	75 sets at 6" o.c. with 5 lift lines per set
Arbors:	1,300 lb capacity
House Pipes:	69' long with 67' of travel from deck

Line sets are moveable

Block & Falls are available 3:2 (2)

(40) spot wheels and 2,500' of hemp available

PERMANENT INSTALLATIONS OVER STAGE (FROM SMOKE POCKET)
None

PERMANENT INSTALLATIONS ON DECK
None

ORCHESTRA PIT
Adjustable to 20' below stage level by hydraulic lift

BACKSTAGE

LOADING DOCK
Loading doors:
1) 9'6" high x 7'0" wide
2) 10'0" high x 6'0" wide
3) 6'8" high x 3'0" wide

Trucks load (3) at same time

(3) Docks, loading door sills are at street level;

Door 1 is above stage level, 45 degrees ramp or 5'x 5' elevator down to stage is available;

Doors 2 & 3 are accessed off side alleys

WARDROBE
Location: Basement

Access: Elevator

(3) Washers (3) Dryers

DRESSING ROOMS
(2) Star, SL, stage level, t/s included

(12) Small, basement, t/s on same fl

(2) Chorus, basement, t/s on same fl

SOUND

CONSOLE
Yamaha 24 channel

24 inputs, 4 main outputs

SPEAKERS
House Cluster

Proscenium

Under Balcony

COMMUNICATIONS
Clear Com intercom with (2) channels

Infrared sound system

Dressing room page system

ROAD CONSOLE
Located House Rear

No seats required to be removed

Cable run from stage is 135'

Tie-in into house system with XLR connectors

REHEARSAL & STORAGE SPACE
Rehearsal: 30' x 54' located in basement

Storage: 30' x 54' located behind stage

ELECTRICS

ROAD SERVICE POWER

Panel	Phase	Amp	Circuit Protection	Use	Location
A-B	3	1,800	fuse	dimmers	DSR proscenium wall
C	1	60	breaker	sound	DSL proscenium wall
D	3	100	fuse	sound	DSL proscenium wall
E	3	1,200	fuse	extra	DSR proscenium wall

Recommended location of touring dimmer racks: DSR on deck

FRONT OF HOUSE (BOX BOOM VALUES ARE PER SIDE)

Position	Pipe Width	Distance to Prosc.	House Circuits	Connector Type	FOH Transfer Circuits
Truss 1	50'	19'	0		0
Truss 2	70'	35'	50	grd 20 amp stage pin	50
1st Balc Rail	65'	69'	30	grd 20 amp stage pin	30
Box Boom 1		54'	8	grd 20 amp stage pin	8
Box Boom 2		75'	8	grd 20 amp stage pin	8

Transfer circuits: grd 20 amp stage pin located DSR on deck

Road truss: Truss 2 is equipped with focus track

EQUIPMENT FOH (BOX BOOM VALUES ARE PER SIDE)
None

FOLLOWSPOTS
House Followspots:
(2) Xenon Super Troupers; removeable

Followspot Booth:
(4) spots per booth;
141' throw to proscenium;
1Ø 100 amp breakers

DIMMERS
None

SHUBERT THEATRE

YEAR BUILT: 1972   YEAR RENOVATED: 1995

Theatre Location: 2020 Avenue Of The Stars, Los Angeles, CA 90067
Management Company: The Shubert Organization
                                      234 W. 44th Street, New York, NY 10036

Main Administrative Phone: 310-201-1500
Main Administrative Fax: 310-201-1585
Stage Door Phone: 310-201-1524

THEATRE STAFF
General Manager   Larry O'Connor   310-201-1500
Booking   Peter Entin   212-944-3700

HOUSE CREW
Carpentry   Milton King   310-201-1500
Electrics   Michael LeMond   310-201-1500
Sound   John Conroy   310-201-1500
Props   Dan Masoero   310-201-1500

UNIONS
IATSE Local #33   Roy Lavoise   818-841-9233
Wardrobe Local #768   Dorothy Priest   818-963-6303
Music Local #47   Stu Blumberg   310-201-1500

SEATING CAPACITY
Orchestra   1,076
Mezzanine   530
Balcony   473
Boxes   34
Total: **2,113**

wheelchair (add'l)   12

BOX OFFICE
Computerized
Box Office Treasurer
  Barbara Isley   310-201-1500

Outside Ticket Agency
Computerized
Tele-Charge
  Brian Mahoney   800-447-7400

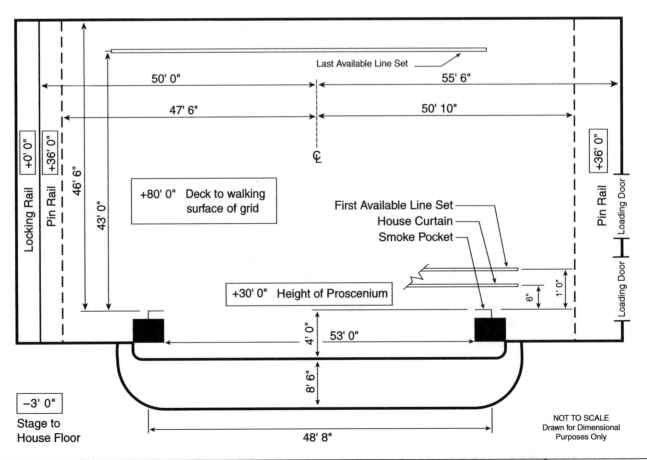

STAGE HOUSE

HOUSE CURTAIN
Operates as a guillotine from SR deck

RIGGING SYSTEM
Type:	Single purchase counter weight
Weight:	28,400 lbs available
Line sets:	70 sets at 6" o.c. with 6 lift lines per set
Arbors:	1,500 lb capacity
House Pipes:	60' long with 77' of travel from deck

Line sets are not moveable
Block & Falls are available 2:1 (2); 3:2 (1)
Chain hoists available as a rental; (2) one ton, (1) half ton
(316) spot wheels and 31,000' of hemp available

PERMANENT INSTALLATIONS OVER STAGE (FROM SMOKE POCKET)
None

PERMANENT INSTALLATIONS ON DECK
Manlift enclosure (1) located in USR corner
Interconnect panel & jump, located in USL corner
Traps in stage floor are on a sectional grid

ORCHESTRA PIT
Nonadjustable at 8' below stage level
Apron overhangs US wall of pit 8'0"

BACKSTAGE

LOADING DOCK
Loading door(s):
    (2) 10'0" high x 11'11" wide
Trucks load (2) side-by-side at same time
Dock is at truck level; short tractor and/or trailer with sliding rear axle advised; loading to stage thru separate receiving area
Fork lift is required; Supplier- A.O. Richardson Rentals 818-242-3129

WARDROBE
Location: SR on stage level
Access: Direct from stage
(3) Washers (3) Dryers
Washer and dryer hookups available

DRESSING ROOMS
(3) Star, behind stage, stage level, t/s included, phone jack
(7) Small, behind stage, stage level, t/s included, phone jack
(4) Chorus, basement, t/s included, phone jack
Elevator access for dressing rooms
Additional production office available for company mgr

SOUND

CONSOLE
No house console available

SPEAKERS
None

COMMUNICATIONS
No intercom
Infrared sound system
Dressing room page system

ROAD CONSOLE
Located Rear Orchestra
No seats required to be removed
Cable run from stage is 250'
Tie-in into house system with XLR connectors

REHEARSAL & STORAGE SPACE
Rehearsal: 45' x 60' located SR in basement, piano available; prior arrangement required
Storage: 20' x 30' located in sub-basement

ELECTRICS

ROAD SERVICE POWER

Panel	Phase	Amp	Circuit Protection	Use	Location
A - L	3	400	fuse	"multi"	USL

Recommended location of touring dimmer racks: USL wing or jump
Hoist is required but not provided.

FRONT OF HOUSE (BOX BOOM VALUES ARE PER SIDE)

Position	Pipe Width	Distance to Prosc.	House Circuits	Connector Type	FOH Transfer Circuits
Balc Rail	60'	47'	38	grd 20 amp stagepin	38
1st Cove	25'	53'	26	grd 20 amp stagepin	26
2nd Cove	50'	69'	26	grd 20 amp stagepin	26
Box Boom 1	10'	54'	23	grd 20 amp stagepin	23
Box Boom 2	12'	74'	11	grd 20 amp stagepin	11
Basket Spot		60'	0		0

Transfer circuits: 25' extension required from dimmers on floor or jump, all grd 20 amp stage pin

EQUIPMENT FOH (BOX BOOM VALUES ARE PER SIDE)
None

FOLLOWSPOTS
House Followspots:
    (3) Strong Gladiator II 2.5k Xenon; removeable

Followspot Booth:
    (3) spots per booth;
    150' throw to proscenium;
    3Ø 90 amp breakers

DIMMERS
No DMX control system

WILTERN THEATRE

Year built: 1931   Year renovated: 1985

Theatre Location: 3790 Wilshire Boulevard, Los Angeles, CA 90010
Management Company: Bill Graham Presents

Main Administrative Phone: 213-388-1400
Main Administrative Fax: 213-388-0242
Stage Door Phone: 213-388-1400
Backstage Pay Phone: 213-480-9134
Traveling Production Office Phone: 213-384-7810

Seating Capacity

Orchestra	1,288
Loge	306
Mezzanine	692
Total:	**2,286**
pit (add'l)	40

Theatre Staff
  General Manager   Rena Wasserman   213-388-1400

House Crew
  Production Manager   Reid Bartlett   213-388-1400 x24
  Electrics   Terry Klein   213-388-1400

Stage Dimensions (from smoke pocket)
  Stage is 44'2" deep;
  Width from Center Line to SL is 42'
  Width from Center Line to SR is 46'6"
  Proscenium width is 54'10"
  Proscenium height is 32'4"
  Smoke pocket to apron edge is 3'8"
  Orchestra pit exists

Rigging

Grid Height:	69'0"
Type:	Single purchase counter weight
Weight:	20,000 lbs
Line sets:	36 sets at 6-12" o.c.
Arbors:	1,280 lb capacity
House Pipes:	54' long

Loading Dock
  Loading door(s) are 12'0" high x 12'0" wide
  Trucks load (1) at a time
  Fork lift is not required and is not available

Electrics
  Total power available:
    600A 3Ø DSL

Followspots
  House Followspots:
    (4) Xenon Colortran Carbon
    Arc
  Power in spot booth
    (2) 1Ø 30A breakers

Dimmers
  (140) house dimmers
  House has DMX control system
  (2) dry run station(s) located
    DSR (Rear Orchestra)

Sound
  House has 600A of dedicated
    power located DSL
  FOH mixing position in
    Rear Orchestra right of
    center
  Sound console is available

PARAMOUNT THEATRE

YEAR BUILT: **1931**   YEAR RENOVATED: **1973**

Theatre Location: 2025 Broadway, Oakland, CA 94612
Management Company: Paramount Theatre of the Arts, Inc.

Main Administrative Phone: 510-893-2300
Main Administrative Fax: 510-893-5098
Stage Door Phone: 510-832-9710
Backstage Pay Phone: 510-832-9710

THEATRE STAFF
General Manager   Peter Botto   510-893-2300
HOUSE CREW
Stage Manager   Edward Hotchkiss   510-893-2300

SEATING CAPACITY

Orchestra	648
Orchestra Terrace	1,060
Grand Tier	324
Dress Circle	408
Balcony	552
Total:	**2,992**
pit (add'l)	48
wheelchair (add'l)	24
standing (add'l)	0

STAGE DIMENSIONS (FROM SMOKE POCKET)
Stage is 24'6" deep
Width from Center Line to SL is 44'6"
Width from Center Line to SR is 62'6"
Proscenium width is 66'0"
Proscenium height is 30'0"
Smoke pocket to apron edge is 3'0"
Orchestra pit exists

RIGGING
Grid Height: 74'
Type: Single purchase counter weight
Weight: 16,000 lbs
Line sets: 36 sets at 5"-10" o.c.
Arbors: 800 lb capacity
House Pipes: 70' long

LOADING DOCK
Loading door(s) are 8'11"high x 7'10"wide
Trucks load (2) at same time
Fork lift is not required and is not available

ELECTRICS
Total power available:
   400A 3Ø DSL proscenium
   wall
FOLLOWSPOTS
House Followspots:
   Xenon Super Trouper
Power in spot booth (3) 30A
FOH transfer circuits: 28
DIMMERS
(2/2) house dimmers
House has DMX control system
(2) dry run station(s) located
   Rear House / SL

SOUND
House has 100A 3Ø
   dedicated power located
   DSR proscenium wall
FOH mixing position in
   Rear House Left
No sound console available

MCCALLUM THEATRE FOR THE PERFORMING ARTS

AT: **BOB HOPE CULTURAL CENTER**

Theatre Location: 73-000 Waring Drive, Palm Desert , CA   92260

Main Administrative Phone: 760-346-6505
Main Administrative Fax: 760-341-9508
E-mail: info@mccallum.theatre.org
Website: http://www.mccallum.theatre.org
Stage Door Phone: 760-340-6946

THEATRE STAFF
Facilities Director   Cameron Smith   760-346-6505
Artistic Director   Charles Gioia   760-346-6505

HOUSE CREW
Production Director   Keith I. Smith   760-340-1073

SEATING CAPACITY

Orchestra	720
Mezzanine	173
Balcony	180
Boxes	56
Total:	**1,129**
standing (add'l)	12

STAGE DIMENSIONS (FROM SMOKE POCKET)
Stage is 35'0" deep
Width from Center Line to SL is 44'0"
Width from Center Line to SR is 41'0"
Proscenium width is 50'0"
Proscenium height is 30'0"
Smoke pocket to apron edge is 6'0"
Orchestra pit exists

RIGGING
Grid Height: 79'
Type: Single purchase counter weight
Weight: 49,800 lbs
Line sets: 65 sets at 6" o.c.
Arbors: 1,100 lb capacity
House Pipes: 63' long

LOADING DOCK
Loading door(s) are 24'0" high x 19"6" wide
Trucks load (4) at same time
Fork lift is not required and is available

ELECTRICS
(2) 400A SL alcove
Total power available:
   800A 3Ø 400A

FOLLOWSPOTS
House Followspots:
   Xenon Super Trouper II
Power in spot booth 100A
FOH transfer circuits per
   position:

DIMMERS
(490) house dimmers
House has DMX control system
(4) dry run station(s) located
   SL/SR

SOUND
House has 200A dedicated
   power located SL alcove
FOH mixing position in
   House Left in Boxes
Sound console is available

PASADENA CIVIC AUDITORIUM

AT: THE PASADENA CENTER   YEAR BUILT: **1931**   YEAR RENOVATED: **1997**

Theatre Location: 300 East Green St., Pasadena, CA 91103-2399
Management Company: The Pasadena Operating Company
                       300 East Green St., Pasadena, CA 91103-2399

Main Administrative Phone: 626-793-2122
Main Administrative Fax: 626-793-8014
E-mail: sherring@pasadenacenter.org
Website: www.pasadenacenter.org
Stage Door Phone: 626-578-9935
Backstage Pay Phone: 626-578-9935

THEATRE STAFF
General Manager   Richard L. Barr   626-793-2122
Booking   Richard L. Barr   626-793-2122
House Manager   Matthew Lancey   626-793-2122

HOUSE CREW
Carpentry   Vincent Collins   626-793-2122
Electrics   Albert Garcia   626-793-2122
Sound   Ray Overman   626-793-2122
Props   David G. Lindsey   626-793-2122

UNIONS
IATSE Local #33   Roy Lavoise   818-841-9233
Wardrobe   Dorothy Priest   818-789-8735

SEATING CAPACITY
Orchestra   1,922
Loge   560
Balcony   449
Total: **2,931**

pit (add'l)   98
wheelchair (add'l)   14

BOX OFFICE
Computerized
Box Office Treasurer
   William J. Anagnost   626-449-7360

Outside Ticket Agency
Computerized
Ticketmaster
   Al Richardson   213-381-2000

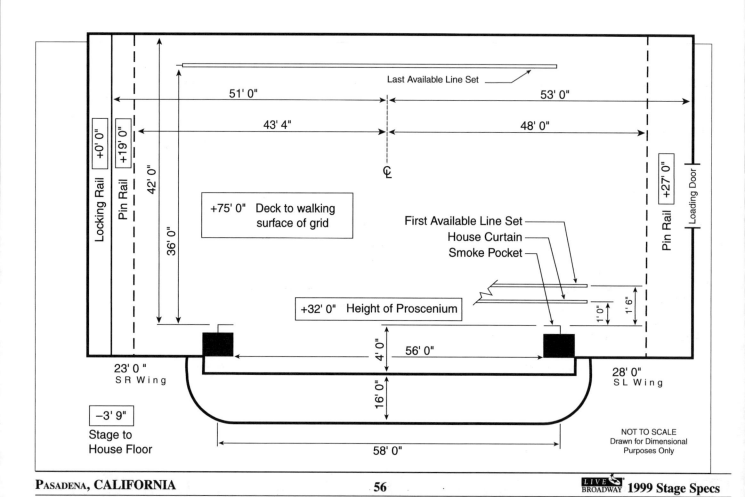

STAGE HOUSE

HOUSE CURTAIN
Operates as a guillotine or traveller from SR deck; motorized when operated as a traveller

RIGGING SYSTEM
Type: Single purchase counter weight
Weight: 45,000 lbs available
Line sets: 58 sets at 6" o.c. with 4 lift lines per set
Arbors: 1,000 lb capacity
House Pipes: 60' long with 71' of travel from deck
Line sets are moveable
Block & Falls are available 2:1 (6); 3:2 (4)
Chain hoists are not available
(60) spot wheels and 3,000' of hemp available
2,000 lbs of sand available

PERMANENT INSTALLATIONS OVER STAGE (FROM SMOKE POCKET)
M=Moveable with advance call
Orchestra shells (6) at 4'6", 13'0", 21'3", 28'0", 31'3", 36'6"
Electric raceways (4) at 3'0", 9'0", 19'0", 30'0"
Movie screen (1); M
Cyclorama (1) at 30'0", 60'0"; M
Catwalk (1) fly floors SR & SL

PERMANENT INSTALLATIONS ON DECK
Orchestra shell storage (6) 20'0" high x 3'0" wide, stores USL corner

ORCHESTRA PIT
Adjustable to 5' below stage level by hydraulic lift
Apron overhangs US wall of pit 14' 0"
Pit lift is in (3) sections
Organ & piano lift at center line

BACKSTAGE

LOADING DOCK
Loading door(s):
   10'0" high x 10'0" wide
Trucks load (2) side-by-side at same time
Dock is at street level
Forklift: House owns
Sound/Props can load in FOH
Lobby cannot be a work area
Trailers cannot store on-site

WARDROBE
Location: Basement
Access: Freight elevator
(2) Washers (2) Dryers
Washer and dryer hookups available

DRESSING ROOMS
(1) Star, SL, stage level, t/s included, phone jack
(16) Small, SR / SL, +1, t/s included
(2) Chorus, SL, -1, t/s included
Additional production office available for company mgr

SOUND

CONSOLE
Ramsa 852, located SR

SPEAKERS
Proscenium
No speaker truss

COMMUNICATIONS
Clear Com intercom with (10) channels
Infrared sound system
Dressing room page system

ROAD CONSOLE
Located Rear Orchestra right or left
No seats required to be removed
Cable run from stage is 250'
Tie-in into house system

REHEARSAL & STORAGE SPACE
Rehearsal: Gold Room - 73' x 44'6", mezzanine level of theatre, piano & sound system
Storage: None

ELECTRICS

ROAD SERVICE POWER

Panel	Phase	Amp	Circuit Protection	Use	Location
A	3	1100	fuse	dimmers	USR
B	3	400	fuse	sound	USR

Recommended location of touring dimmer racks: SR onstage or on fly floor SR
Hoist is required and provided

FRONT OF HOUSE (BOX BOOM VALUES ARE PER SIDE)

Position	Pipe Width	Distance to Prosc.	House Circuits	Connector Type	FOH Transfer Circuits
1st Balc Rail	55'	61'	20	grd 20 amp stage pin	20
Box Boom 1		45'	4	grd 20 amp stage pin	4

Transfer circuits: 28 transfer SR

EQUIPMENT FOH (BOX BOOM VALUES ARE PER SIDE)

Position	Quantity	Wattage	Instrument	Removeable
Box Boom 1		575	Source 4	yes

FOLLOWSPOTS
House Followspots:
   (2) Gladiators (Xenon); not removeable

Followspot Booth:
   (2) spots per booth;
   120' throw to proscenium;
   (5) 3Ø and 1Ø 30 amp breakers

DIMMERS
House console is 10 Scene Preset;
(60) Century dimmers
No DMX control system

SACRAMENTO COMMUNITY CENTER THEATRE

AT: CITY OF SACRAMENTO CONVENTION CENTER **YEAR BUILT: 1974   YEAR RENOVATED: 1997**

Theatre Location: 1301 L Street, Sacramento, CA 95814
Mailing Address: 1030 15th Street, Suite 100, Sacramento, CA 95814

Main Administrative Phone: 916-264-5291
Main Administrative Fax: 916-264-7687
Website: www.sacto.org/cusd/convctr
Backstage Pay Phone: 916-443-9546

THEATRE STAFF
General Manager   Michael W. Ross   916-264-5291
Booking   Pam Tobin   916-264-5291
HOUSE CREW
Stage Hand II   Carl Brownell   916-264-5133 / Fax 916-264-7538
UNIONS
IATSE Local #50   John Kelley   916-444-7654

SEATING CAPACITY
Orchestra   1,456
Grand Tier   379
Second Tier   491
Total: **2,326**

pit (add'l)   72
wheelchair (add'l)   54

BOX OFFICE
Box Office Manager
  Jeanne Sapunor   916-264-5181

Outside Ticket Agency
  None

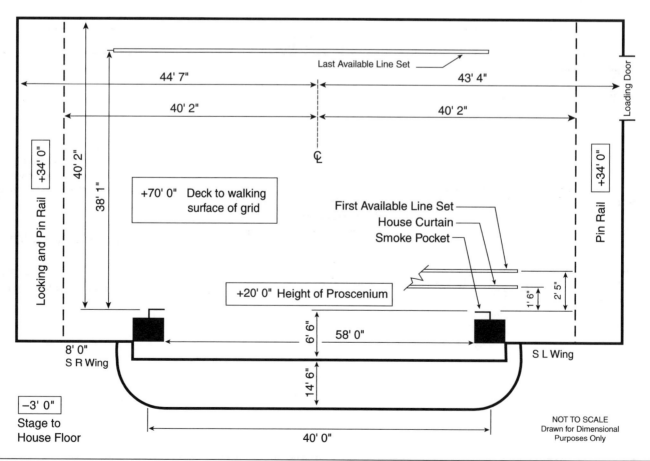

STAGE HOUSE

HOUSE CURTAIN
Operates as a guillotine or traveller from SR deck

RIGGING SYSTEM
Type: Single purchase counter weight
Weight: 16,500 lbs available
Line sets: 48 sets at 6" o.c. with 6 lift lines per set
Arbors: 1,000 lb capacity
House Pipes: 65' long with 64' of travel from deck
Line sets are moveable

PERMANENT INSTALLATIONS OVER STAGE (FROM SMOKE POCKET)
Orchestra shells (4) at 4'6", 12'6", 20'6", 28'6" (12" wide)
Movie screen (1) at 10'6"

PERMANENT INSTALLATIONS ON DECK
None

ORCHESTRA PIT
Adjustable at preset stops to 13' below stage level by hydraulic lift
Apron overhangs US wall of pit 4'0"

BACKSTAGE

LOADING DOCK
Loading door(s):
    12'6" high x 14'6" wide
Trucks load (2) side by side, at same time
Dock is at truck level; loading to stage thru separate loading bay behind stage house
Fork lift is not required
Sound/Props can load in FOH
(1 - 2) Trailers can store on-site
Security at stage door

WARDROBE
Location: SR off hallway on stage level
Access: Direct from stage
No Washers No Dryers
Washer and dryer hookups available

DRESSING ROOMS
(2) Star, SR, stage level, t/s included, phone jack
(8) Small, SR, stage level, t/s on same fl, phone jack
(2) Chorus, SR, 2nd fl, t/s included, phone jack
Use dressing room for company mgr office

SOUND

CONSOLE
Yamaha PM 2000-32
32 inputs, 20 main outputs

SPEAKERS
House Cluster
No speaker truss

COMMUNICATIONS
Clear Com intercom with (4) channels
No infrared sound system
Dressing room page system

ROAD CONSOLE
Located Rear House
No seats required to be removed
Cable run from stage is 180'
Tie-in into house system with XLR connectors

REHEARSAL & STORAGE SPACE
Rehearsal: None
Storage: None

ELECTRICS

ROAD SERVICE POWER

Panel	Phase	Amp	Circuit Protection	Use	Location
A-B	3	400	fuse	dimmers	USR
C	3	200	fuse	sound	SL

Panels A and B cannot be used if house dimmers are used
Recommended location of touring dimmer racks: USR loading dock bay
Hoist not required

FRONT OF HOUSE (BOX BOOM VALUES ARE PER SIDE)

Position	Pipe Width	Distance to Prosc.	House Circuits	Connector Type	FOH Transfer Circuits
1st Catwalk	65'	37'	32	grd 20 amp stage pin	32
2nd Catwalk	65'	68'	33	grd 20 amp stage pin	33
Box Boom 1		16'	24	grd 20 amp stage pin	24
Box Boom 2		31'	24	grd 20 amp stage pin	24

Transfer circuits: grd 20 amp stage pin located in USR loading dock bay

EQUIPMENT FOH (BOX BOOM VALUES ARE PER SIDE)
None

FOLLOWSPOTS
House Followspots:
    (4) Xenon Super Troupers; removeable

(2) Followspot Booths each:
    (2) spots per booth;
    120' throw to proscenium;
    (2) 1Ø 30 amp breakers

DIMMERS
UNDER RENOVATION
Lighting console is ETC Expression 72-194
    (62) Scurpans dimmers
No DMX control system

SAN DIEGO CIVIC THEATRE

AT: SAN DIEGO CONCOURSE

YEAR BUILT: 1965   YEAR RENOVATED: 1982

Theatre Location: 202 C Street, MS 57, San Diego, CA 92101
Management Company: San Diego Convention Center Corporation
                             111 W. Harbor Drive, San Diego, CA

Main Administrative Phone: 619-615-4100
Main Administrative Fax: 619-615-4155
Website: www.sdccc.org
Stage Door Phone: 619-615-4150
Backstage Pay Phone: 619-531-9207
Traveling Production Office Phone: 619-615-4090

THEATRE STAFF

Concourse Director	William McElrath	619-615-4100
Booking	David Drummond	619-615-4110

HOUSE CREW

Production Manager	Carolyn Satter	619-615-4151
Asst. Prod. Manager	Pete L. Seaney	619-615-4152

UNIONS

IATSE Local #122	Dan Espinoza	619-293-0555
Wardrobe	Bob Rathmell	619-220-0879

SEATING CAPACITY

Orchestra	1,136
Lower Loge & Upper Loge	196
Mezzanine	432
Dress Circle	422
Balcony	710
Total:	**2,896**
pit (add'l)	90
wheelchair (add'l)	6

BOX OFFICE

Computerized
Box Office Treasurer
  Debra McDonald   619-615-4170

Outside Ticket Agency
Ticketmaster
                       619-220-8497

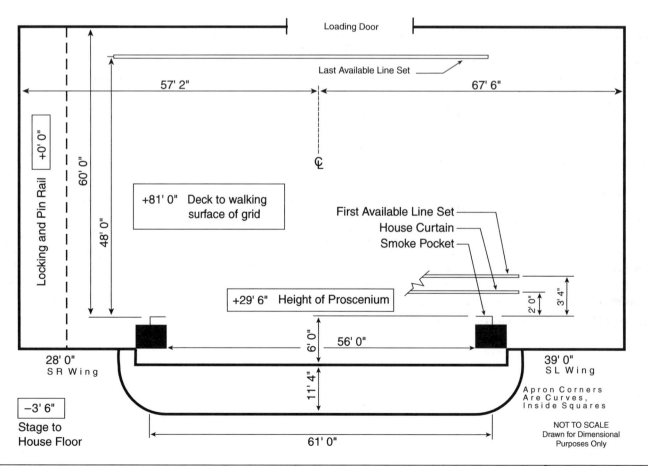

STAGE HOUSE

HOUSE CURTAIN
Operates as a guillotine or traveller from SR deck

RIGGING SYSTEM
Type:	Single purchase counter weight
Weight:	30,000 lbs available
Line sets:	64 sets at 8" o.c. with 5 lift lines per set
Arbors:	1,408 lb capacity
House Pipes:	70' long with 73' of travel from deck

Line sets are moveable
(60) spot wheels and 12,000' of hemp available

PERMANENT INSTALLATIONS OVER STAGE (FROM SMOKE POCKET)
Electric raceways (5) at 4'0", 14'7", 23'11", 33'11", 41'3"

PERMANENT INSTALLATIONS ON DECK
None

ORCHESTRA PIT
Adjustable to 30' below stage level by hydraulic lift
Apron overhangs US wall of pit 3'0"

BACKSTAGE

LOADING DOCK
Loading door(s):
    14'0" high x 23'10" wide
Trucks load (2) side-by-side at
    same time
Dock: loading door sill is at
    streel level; load bars are
    suggested as truck access is
    sloped towards dock; height
    limitation is 13'6"
Fork lift is not required
Sound/Props can load in FOH
Lobby can be a work area
Trailers cannot store on-site
Security at dock & stage door

WARDROBE
Location: Basement
Access: Freight elevator
(2) Washers (2) Dryers
Washer and dryer hookups
    available

DRESSING ROOMS
(2) Star, SL, stage level, t/s
    included, (1) phone jack
(5) Small, SL, stage level, t/s on
    same fl
(8) Chorus, SL, 2nd fl, t/s on
    same fl
Elevator access for dressing
    rooms
Use dressing room for company
    mgr office

SOUND

CONSOLE
Yamaha 1800
40 inputs, 8 main outputs

SPEAKERS
House Cluster

COMMUNICATIONS
Clear Com intercom with
    (2) channels
Infrared sound system
Dressing room page system

ROAD CONSOLE
Located Back of dress circle
(28) seats required to be
    removed
Cable run from stage is 200'
Tie-in into house system with
    XLR connectors

REHEARSAL & STORAGE SPACE
Rehearsal: 44' x 53' located
    in basement; pianos
    available
Storage:
    20' x 12' in basement
    22' x 56' behind stage

ELECTRICS

ROAD SERVICE POWER

Panel	Phase	Amp	Circuit Protection	Use	Location
A	3	400	breaker	dimmers	DSR proscenium wall
B	3	400	breaker	extra	DSR proscenium wall
C-D	3	100	breaker	extra	Loading dock
E	3	100	breaker	extra	USR basement

Recommended location of touring dimmer racks: DSR on deck
Hoist not required

FRONT OF HOUSE (BOX BOOM VALUES ARE PER SIDE)

Position	Pipe Width	Distance to Prosc.	House Circuits	Connector Type	FOH Transfer Circuits
1st Balc Rail	95'	101'	36	grd 20 amp stagepin	36
High Bay	95'	90'	28	grd 20 amp stagepin	28
Box Boom 1		46'	8	grd 20 amp stagepin	0
Box Boom 2		19'	6	grd 20 amp stagepin	0
Mezzanine Rail		90'	20	grd 20 amp stagepin	0
Torm		6'	8	grd 20 amp stage pin	0

Transfer circuits: grd 20 amp stage pin located on DSR proscenium wall

EQUIPMENT FOH (BOX BOOM VALUES ARE PER SIDE)
None

FOLLOWSPOTS
House Followspots:
    (3) Xenon Super Troupers;
    removeable

Followspot Booth:
    (4) spots per booth;
    151' throw to proscenium;
    (4) 3Ø 30 amp breakers

DIMMERS
House console is Strand 530;
    (454) 5 CD80 dimmers
House has programmable
    DMX control system
(5) dry run DMX station(s)

SPRECKELS THEATRE

AKA: THEATRICAL ENTERPRISES INC.   **YEAR BUILT: 1912**

Theatre Location: 121 Broadway, San Diego, CA 92101

Main Administrative Phone:	619-235-0494
Main Administrative Fax:	619-235-4654
E-mail:	spreckelstheatre@pacbell.com
Backstage Pay Phone:	619-237-9093
Traveling Production Office Phone:	619-239-3921

THEATRE STAFF

Theatre Manager	Dorinda Parsons	619-235-0494
Booking	Robert Stein	818-766-0660

HOUSE CREW

Technical Director	Rick Davis	619-235-0494

SEATING CAPACITY

Orchestra	628
Mezzanine	355
Balcony	435
Boxes	48
Total:	**1,466**
pit (add'l)	35
wheelchair (add'l)	8

BOX OFFICE
Computerized
Theatre Manager
  Dorinda Parsons   619-235-0494

Outside Ticket Agency
Computerized
Ticketmaster
  Jenny Rodriguez   619-298-9411

Box office is promoter operated

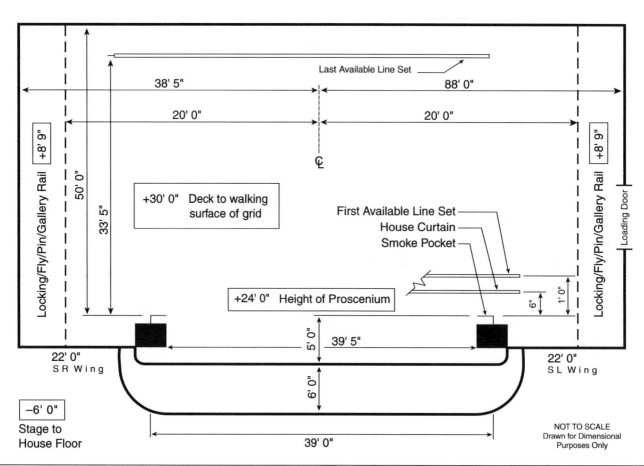

Last Available Line Set

38' 5"   88' 0"

20' 0"   20' 0"

CL

+8' 9"   +8' 9"

Locking/Fly/Pin/Gallery Rail   Locking/Fly/Pin/Gallery Rail

Loading Door

50' 0"

33' 5"

+30' 0" Deck to walking surface of grid

First Available Line Set
House Curtain
Smoke Pocket

1' 0"
6"

+24' 0" Height of Proscenium

5' 0"   39' 5"

22' 0"   22' 0"
S R Wing   S L Wing

6' 0"

−6' 0"
Stage to
House Floor

39' 0"

NOT TO SCALE
Drawn for Dimensional
Purposes Only

STAGE HOUSE

HOUSE CURTAIN
  Operates as a guillotine or traveller from SR fly floor or deck

RIGGING SYSTEM

Type:	Single purchase counter weight
Weight:	10,000 lbs available
Line sets:	35 sets at 8" o.c. with 5 lift lines per set
Arbors:	850 lb capacity
House Pipes:	60' long with 70' of travel from deck

  Line sets are moveable
  Block & Falls are available
  Chain hoists are available
  1,000' of hemp available

PERMANENT INSTALLATIONS OVER STAGE (FROM SMOKE POCKET)
  Movie screen (1) 6'0"
  Traveller (1) main curtain at 1'
  Fire curtain (1) at smoke pocket

PERMANENT INSTALLATIONS ON DECK
  None

ORCHESTRA PIT
  Nonadjustable at 6' below stage level
  Apron overhangs US wall of pit 3'0"

BACKSTAGE

LOADING DOCK
  Loading door(s):
    11'0" high x 11'0" wide
  Trucks load (2) at same time
  (2) Doors street level USR & L
  Sound/Props can load in FOH
  Trailers cannot store on-site
  Security at dock & stage door

WARDROBE
  Location: Basement
  Access: Stage & freight elevator
  (1) Washer (1) Dryer
  Washer and dryer hookups available

DRESSING ROOMS
  (2) Star, SL, stage level, toilet included, phone jack
  (13) Small, SL/SR, +1, t/s included
  (1) Chorus, SR, +1, t/s included
  Additional production office available for company mgr

SOUND

CONSOLE
  Yamaha
  12 inputs, 4 main outputs,
    4 aux outputs

SPEAKERS
  Portable
  No speaker truss

COMMUNICATIONS
  No house intercom system

ROAD CONSOLE
  Located House Center
  Number of seats required to be removed varies
  Cable run from stage is 75'
  No tie-in into house system

REHEARSAL & STORAGE SPACE
  Rehearsal: Varies
  Storage: Varies

ELECTRICS

ROAD SERVICE POWER

Panel	Phase	Amp	Circuit Protection	Use	Location
A	3	400	breaker	dimmers	DSR proscenium wall
B	3	400	breaker	extra	DSR proscenium wall

Recommended location of touring dimmer racks: DSR on deck

FRONT OF HOUSE (BOX BOOM VALUES ARE PER SIDE)

Position	Pipe Width	Distance to Prosc.	House Circuits	Connector Type	FOH Transfer Circuits
1st Balc Rail	95'	101'	36	grd 20 amp stage pin	36
1st Cove	95'	90'	28	grd 20 amp stage pin	28
Box Boom 1		46'	8	grd 20 amp stage pin	0
Torm		6'	8	grd 20 amp stage pin	0

Transfer circuits: grd 20 amp stage pin located on DSR proscenium wall

EQUIPMENT FOH (BOX BOOM VALUES ARE PER SIDE)
  None

FOLLOWSPOTS
  House Followspots:
    (2) HMI Satellite 575; removeable

  Followspot Booth:
    (2) spots per booth;
    60' throw to proscenium;
    3Ø 40 amp breakers

DIMMERS
  Lighting console is Access Pro;
    (90) Strand CD80 dimmers
  House has programmable DMX control system

CURRAN THEATRE

YEAR BUILT: 1922   YEAR RENOVATED: 1999

Theatre Location: 445 Geary Street, San Francisco, CA 94102
Management Company: Shorenstein Hays and Nederlander

Main Administrative Phone: 415-551-2075
Main Administrative Fax: 415-431-5052
Stage Door Phone: 415-441-9231
Backstage Pay Phone: 415-441-9231

THEATRE STAFF
Theatre Manager   Tess Collins   415-673-1040
Booking   David Nelson   415-551-2075
Group Sales   Eddie Budworth   415-551-2020

HOUSE CREW
Carpentry   Jim Stoye   415-673-5923
Electrics   Michael Gilmore   415-673-5923
Sound   Margot McFedries   415-675-5923
Props   Chris Delucchi   415-673-5923
Wardrobe   Anne Jones   415-673-5923

UNIONS
IATSE Local #16   F.X. Crowley   415-441-6400
Wardrobe   Anne Polland   415-861-8379
Music   Wayne Allen   415-388-8010

SEATING CAPACITY
Orchestra   684
Boxes   24
Loge   82
Mezzanine   466
Front and Rear Balcony   457
Total: **1,713**

wheelchair (add'l)   4

BOX OFFICE
Computerized
Box Office Treasurer
  Bob Dulaney   415-885-0755

Outside Ticket Agency
 Ticketmaster

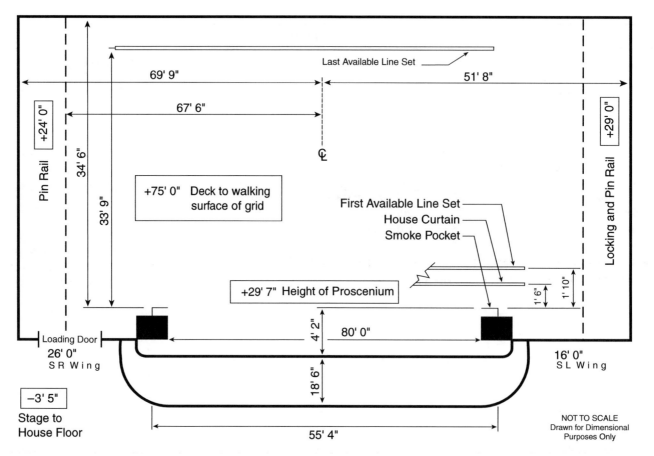

STAGE HOUSE

HOUSE CURTAIN
Operates as a guillotine from SL fly floor

RIGGING SYSTEM

Type:	Single and double purchase counter weight
Weight:	35,000 lbs available
Line sets:	55 sets at 6" o.c. with 7 lift lines per set
Arbors:	1,000 lb capacity
House Pipes:	56' long with 61-63' of travel from deck

Line sets are moveable
Block & Falls are available 2:1(1); 3:2 (2)
Chain hoists available as a rental; (1) one ton, (1) half ton
(80) hemp loft blocks and 10,000' of hemp available

PERMANENT INSTALLATIONS OVER STAGE (FROM SMOKE POCKET)
Fire curtain (1) in pocket

PERMANENT INSTALLATIONS ON DECK
Loading bridge (2), SL above locking rail
Electric jump (1), SR
Pilasters (6) at 0'14" w x 0'19" deep, back wall

ORCHESTRA PIT
Nonadjustable at 8' below stage level
Apron overhangs US wall of pit 1'3"

BACKSTAGE

LOADING DOCK
Loading door(s):
  9'9" high x 5'8" wide
Trucks load (2) at same time
Dock is at street level, alley to
  loading door, no street access
  4-6pm weekdays
Fork lift is required; Mike
  Martin Transportation
  707-762-3358
Sound/Props can load in FOH
Lobby can be a work area
Trailers cannot store on-site
Security at stage door

WARDROBE
Location: Basement
Access: SL alley, stairs/ramp
(2) Washers (2) Dryers

DRESSING ROOMS
(2) Star, SL, stage level, toilet
  and phone jack
(7) Small, SL, +1, toilet
(7) Small, SL, +2, toilet
(2) Chorus, SL, -1, toilet, (1)
  with shower
Use dressing room for company
  mgr office

SOUND

CONSOLE
No house console

SPEAKERS
Under Balcony
Speaker hang points
Max available load 2,000 lbs
  per point
No chain motors in house
2 points forward of
  proscenium

COMMUNICATIONS
 No intercom system
Infrared sound system
Dressing room page system
Show Trans

ROAD CONSOLE
Located Rear House center
  in booth
No seats required to be
  removed
Cable run from stage is 100'

REHEARSAL & STORAGE SPACE
Rehearsal: None
Storage: None

ELECTRICS

ROAD SERVICE POWER

Panel	Phase	Amp	Circuit Protection	Use	Location
A-C	3	400	breaker	dimmers	SR jump
D	3	300	fuse	hoist	SR Basement
E	1	200	fuse	winches	DSR Proscenium wall
F	1	60	fuse	sound	DSL Proscenium wall

Recommended location of touring dimmer racks: SR jump or on deck
Hoist is required and provided

FRONT OF HOUSE (BOX BOOM VALUES ARE PER SIDE)

Position	Pipe Width	Distance to Prosc.	House Circuits	Connector Type	FOH Transfer Circuits
1st Balc Rail	50'	45'	24	grd 20 amp stage pin	24
2nd Balc Rail	50'	65'	24	grd 20 amp stage pin	24
Box Boom 1		15'	12	grd 20 amp stage pin	12
Box Boom 2		30'	12	grd 20 amp stage pin	12

Transfer circuits: grd 20 amp stage pin located SR on jump
Road truss: can be hung FOH

EQUIPMENT FOH (BOX BOOM VALUES ARE PER SIDE)
None

FOLLOWSPOTS
House Followspots:
  None

Followspot Booth:
  (3) spots per booth;
  103' throw to proscenium;
  (4) 3Ø 60 amp breakers

DIMMERS
No lighting console
No dimmers
No DMX control system

GEARY THEATER

YEAR BUILT: **1910**   YEAR RENOVATED: **1996**

Theatre Location: 415 Geary Street, San Francisco, CA 94102
Mailing Address: 30 Grant Avenue, Sixth Floor, San Francisco, CA 94108
Management Company: American Conservatory Theater (mailing address)

Main Administrative Phone:	415-834-3200
Main Administrative Fax:	415-834-3360
E-mail:	actadmin@best.com
Website:	www.act.sfbay.org
Stage Door Phone:	415-439-2396
Backstage Pay Phone:	415-929-9523
Traveling Production Office Phone:	415-439-2482
Traveling Production Office Fax:	415-834-5326

SEATING CAPACITY

Center Orchestra	141
Orchestra and Boxes	364
Dress Circle	152
Balcony and Boxes	138
Second Balcony	234
Total:	**1,029**

BOX OFFICE
Computerized
Box Office Manager
Richard Bernter   415-439-2388

THEATRE STAFF

Managing Director	Heather Kitchen	415-439-2309
Producing Director	James Haire	415-439-2429
Marketing	Robert Sweibel	415-439-2424
Operations	Lesley Pierce	415-439-2491
Group Sales	Linda Graham	415-346-7805

HOUSE CREW

Tech Supervisor	Edward Raymond	415-439-2372
Carpentry	Maurice Beesley	415-439-2398
Electrics	Jim Dickson	415-439-2341
Sound	Suzanna Bailey	415-439-2341
Props	Deb Hatch	415-439-2369

UNIONS

IATSE Local #16	Rick Putz	415-441-6400
Wardrobe Local #784	Karrin Kane	415-861-8489

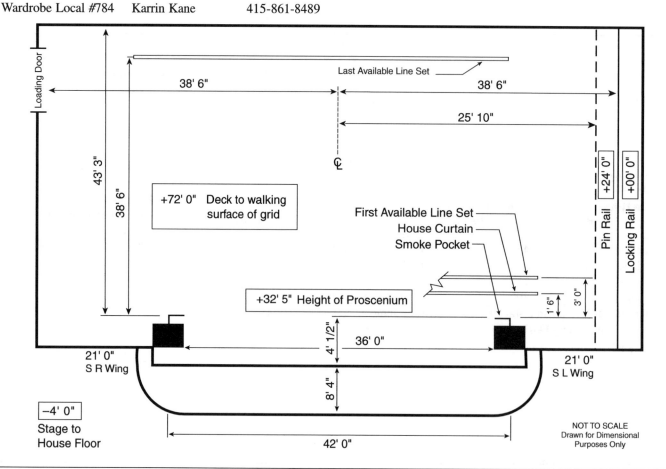

STAGE HOUSE

HOUSE CURTAIN
Operates as a guillotine or traveller from SL deck

RIGGING SYSTEM
Type: Single purchase counter weight
Weight: 48,000 lbs available
Line sets: 48 sets
House Pipes: 44' long with 72' of travel from deck
Line sets are moveable
Block & Falls are available
Chain hoists are available as a rental; (2) one ton, (2) half ton
(4) rigging points in house

PERMANENT INSTALLATIONS OVER STAGE (FROM SMOKE POCKET)
M=Moveable with advance call
Hard portal (1) at 4'1"; M
Fire curtain (1) located in smoke pocket

PERMANENT INSTALLATIONS ON DECK
Traps (40) full stage 3'4" x 6'8"
Hard legs (10) at 24'0" high x 6'0" wide located SL
Loading bridge (2)
Adjustable proscenium
Adjustable portal
Stage deck fully rakeable

ORCHESTRA PIT
Nonadjustable at 7'3" below stage level
Apron overhangs US wall of pit 4' 0"

BACKSTAGE

LOADING DOCK
Loading door(s):
   10'0" high x 14'0" wide
Trucks load (1) at same time
Need advance notice to limit parking on Mason St
Fork lift is not required
Sound/Props can load in FOH
Lobby can be a work area
Trailers cannot store on-site
Security at stage door

WARDROBE
Location: Basement
Access: Stage door
(4) Washers (2) Dryers
Washer and dryer hookups available

DRESSING ROOMS
(5) Small, t/s on same fl, phone jack
(2) Chorus, t/s on same fl, phone jack
Elevator access for dressing rooms

SOUND

CONSOLE
Mackie 2408; LCS
24 inputs, 10 main outputs, matrix outputs, 6 aux outputs
LCS:12 matrix outputs, 16 inputs

SPEAKERS
UNDER RENOVATION
Proscenium
Portable
Speaker truss is available to fly center cluster

COMMUNICATIONS
Clear Com intercom with (4) channels
Infrared sound system
Dressing room page system

ROAD CONSOLE
Located Rear Orchestra
Number of seats required to be removed varies
Cable run from stage is 150'
Tie-in into house system
Large conduit run from orchestra pit

REHEARSAL & STORAGE SPACE
Rehearsal: None
Storage: 45' x 22', located loading dock
40' x 20', located trap room

ELECTRICS

ROAD SERVICE POWER

Panel	Phase	Amp	Circuit Protection	Use	Location
A-C	3	400	fuse	dimmers	SR fly floor
D	3	125	fuse	sound	SR fly floor
E	3	400	fuse	extra	Loading dock
F	3	200	fuse	extra	Loading dock
G-J	3	60	buss duct	extra	Stage/Grid/Trap/Fly floor

Recommended location of touring dimmer racks: SR fly floor
Additional power is available for tour buses, generators, etc.

FRONT OF HOUSE (BOX BOOM VALUES ARE PER SIDE)

Position	Pipe Width	Distance to Prosc.	House Circuits	Connector Type	FOH Transfer Circuits
1st Balc Rail		60'	30	grd 20 amp stage pin	
2nd Balc Rail		90'	30	grd 20 amp stage pin	
Box Boom 1			18	grd 20 amp stage pin	
Box Boom 2			12	grd 20 amp stage pin	
Catwalk		110'	36	grd 20 amp stage pin	

Road truss: FOH Canopy has several removable panels for rigging of truss or speaker clusters - additional dimmers are available at the canopy both SR/SL (36 per side)

EQUIPMENT FOH (BOX BOOM VALUES ARE PER SIDE)

Position	Quantity	Wattage	Instrument	Removeable
1st Balc Rail	24	1,000	various	yes
2nd Balc Rail	18	1,000	various	yes
Box Boom 1	18	1,000	various	yes
Box Boom 2	6	1,000	various	yes
Back Catwalk	30	575	30° - 10° ETC	yes

Our hang changes approximately every 5 weeks

FOLLOWSPOTS
House Followspots: None

Followspot Booth: None

DIMMERS
Lighting console is Obsession; (606) ETC dimmers
House has DMX control system
Many dry run DMX station(s)

GOLDEN GATE THEATRE

YEAR BUILT: 1922 YEAR RENOVATED: 1977

Theatre Location: 1 Taylor Street, San Francisco, CA 94102
Mailing Address: 1182 Market Street, #320, San Francisco, CA 94102
Management Company: Shorenstein Hays Nederlander (mailing address as above)

Main Administrative Phone:	415-551-2075
Main Administrative Fax:	415-431-5052
E-mail:	ggthmgr@sirius.com
Website:	www.bestofbroadway-sf.com
Stage Door Phone:	415-776-8313
Backstage Pay Phone:	415-441-9909
Traveling Production Office Phone:	415-775-8850
Traveling Production Office Fax:	415-775-0245

THEATRE STAFF

General Manager	David Nelson	415-551-2075
Asst. General Manager	Pat Heagy	415-551-2075
Group Sales	Eddy Budworth	415-551-2023
House Manager	Robert Lazzara	415-775-0155/ Fax 775-5677
Asst House Manager	David Cushing	415-775-0156

HOUSE CREW

Carpentry	Joe Crowley	415-775-6066
Electrics	Scott Houghton	415-474-5949
Sound	Tim Purcell	415-474-2173
Props	Ron Hunkiewicz	415-771-2266

UNIONS

IATSE Local #16	F. X. Crowley	415-441-6400
Wardrobe Local #784	Anne Polland	415-861-8379
Music Local #6 AFM	Wayne Allen	415-775-8118

SEATING CAPACITY

Orchestra	1,153
Loge	160
Mezzanine	481
Balcony	510
Total:	**2,304**
wheelchair	24

BOX OFFICE
Computerized
Treasurer
  Keith Hockin   415-775-4997

Outside Ticket Agency
Computerized
Ticketmaster
  Kim Blalock   415-951-7900

Box office is promoter operated

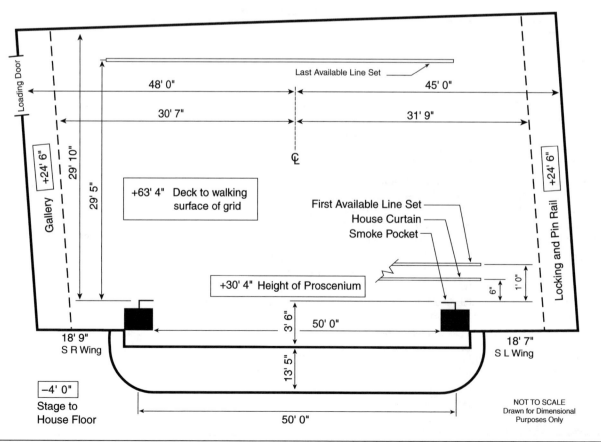

STAGE HOUSE

HOUSE CURTAIN
Operates as a guillotine from SL fly floor

RIGGING SYSTEM
Type:	Single purchase counter weight
Weight:	35,000 lbs available
Line sets:	57 sets at 6" o.c. with 5 lift lines per set
Arbors:	980 lb capacity
House Pipes:	57' long with 60' of travel from deck

Line sets are moveable
Block & Falls are available
Chain hoists available as a rental; (1) one ton
(80) spot wheels and 10,000' of hemp available

PERMANENT INSTALLATIONS OVER STAGE (FROM SMOKE POCKET)
Dead spaces (2) at 10'5", 23'0"
Fire curtain (1)

PERMANENT INSTALLATIONS ON DECK
Traps in stage floor (1) 4'8" x 5'3" located USR
Jumps (1) loading bridge 15' x 30'
Electric bridge (1) 20' x 30'
Pilasters (4) on US wall
Adjustable proscenium via house curtain
Loading bridge (1) 15' x 30'

ORCHESTRA PIT
Adjustable to 5'3" below stage level by manual lift
Apron overhangs US wall of pit 0'6"
(1) Sectional floor, no lift

BACKSTAGE

LOADING DOCK
Loading door(s):
15'7" high x 7'10" wide
Street level is 6' above stage level
Trucks load (2) side by side, at same time
Fork lift is required; Supplier: MTM 1-800-926-1600
Sound/Props can load in FOH
Lobby can be a work area
Trailers cannot store on-site
Security at dock & stage door

WARDROBE
Location: Basement
Access: Stairs & elevator which needs an operator
(2) Washers (3) Dryers
Washer and dryer hookups available

DRESSING ROOMS
(1) Star, SL, stage level, t/s included, phone jack
(22) Small, SL/SR, 2nd-6th fls, t/s on same fl
(2) Chorus, SR/SL, -1, t/s included
Elevator access for dressing rooms
Additional production office available for company mgr

SOUND

CONSOLE
No house console

SPEAKERS
House Cluster
Under Balcony
Speaker truss exists
Max available load 2,000 lbs
Pipe available; show must provide rigging

COMMUNICATIONS
No house intercom system
Infrared sound system
Dressing room page system

ROAD CONSOLE
Located Rear HL
No seats required to be removed
Cable run from stage is 150'
Tie-in into house system with XLR connectors
Tie-in located SR

REHEARSAL & STORAGE SPACE
Rehearsal: Mezzanine 100' x 30' located 2nd fl
Storage: 80' x 30', located in basement

ELECTRICS

ROAD SERVICE POWER
Panel	Phase	Amp	Circuit Protection	Use	Location
A-C	3	400	fuse	dimmers	SR fly floor
D	3	100	fuse	extra	USR back wall
E	3	100	fuse	extra	DSR proscenium wall
F	3	100	fuse	extra	Basement
G	3	100	breaker	sound	DSR proscenium wall

Recommended location of touring dimmer racks: SR fly floor
Hoist is required and provided

FRONT OF HOUSE (BOX BOOM VALUES ARE PER SIDE)
Position	Pipe Width	Distance to Prosc.	House Circuits	Connector Type	FOH Transfer Circuits
1st Balc Rail	80'	30'	64	grd 20 amp stage pin	64
Box Boom 1		25'	0	grd 20 amp stage pin	0
Box Boom 2		35'	12		12

Transfer circuits: grd 20 amp stage pin located SR on jump
Road truss: Points are available for a front truss; 200' cable run will reach a front truss from SR electric jump

EQUIPMENT FOH (BOX BOOM VALUES ARE PER SIDE)
None

FOLLOWSPOTS
House Followspots:
(3) Lycian Superstar 2.5; removeable

Followspot Booth:
(3) spots per booth;
90' throw to proscenium;
(3) 1Ø 30 amp breakers

DIMMERS
No lighting console
No DMX control system

ORPHEUM THEATRE

YEAR BUILT: 1926   YEAR RENOVATED: 1998

Theatre Location: 1192 Market Street, San Francisco, CA 94102
Mailing Address: 1182 Market Street #320, San Francisco, CA 94102
Management Company: Shorenstein Hays Nederlander
                         1182 Market Street #320, San Francisco, CA 94102

Main Administrative Phone:	415-551-2075
Main Administrative Fax:	415-431-5052
Website:	www.bestofbroadway-sf.com
Stage Door Phone:	415-551-2002
Traveling Production Office Phone:	415-551-2015
Traveling Production Office Fax:	415-551-2017

THEATRE STAFF
General Manager	David Nelson	451-551-2075
Booking	Pat Heagy	415-551-2075
House Manager	Robert Lazzara	415-551-2082
Group Sales	Eddy Budworth	415-551-2023

HOUSE CREW
Production Coordinator	Tom McCann	415-551-2075
Carpentry	George Moore	415-551-2092
Electrics	Jim (JW) Wright	415-551-2084
Sound	Jim Morris	415-551-2094
Props	Bob Corso	415-551-2093
Wardrobe	Ruth LePiane	415-551-2096

UNIONS
IATSE Local #16	F.X. Crowley	415-441-6400
Wardrobe Local #784	Anne Polland	415-861-8379
Music Local #6	Wayne Allen	415-775-8118

SEATING CAPACITY
Orchestra	1,289
Mezzanine	622
Balcony	292
Total:	**2,203**

pit (add'l)	0
wheelchair	32
standing (add'l)	0

BOX OFFICE
Computerized
Box Office Treasurer
  Carol Neilson   415-551-2026

Outside Ticket Agency
Computerized
Ticketmaster
  Kim Blalock   415-951-7900

Box office is promoter operated

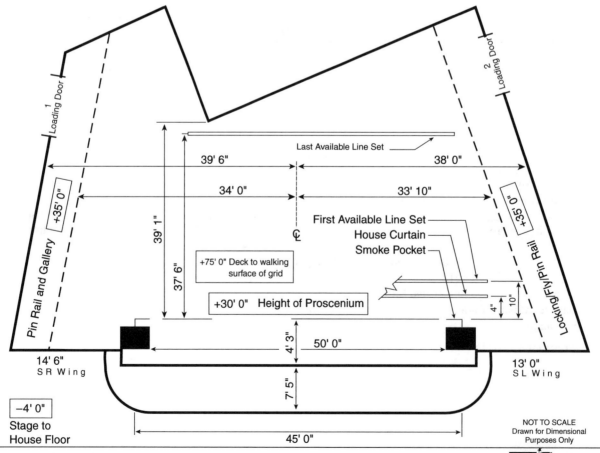

NOT TO SCALE
Drawn for Dimensional Purposes Only

STAGE HOUSE

HOUSE CURTAIN
Operates as a guillotine from SL fly floor

RIGGING SYSTEM

Type:	Single purchase counter weight
Weight:	55,000 lbs available
Line sets:	70 sets at 6" o.c. with 5 lift lines per set
Arbors:	1,500 lb capacity
House Pipes:	60' long

Line sets are not moveable
Chain hoists are availableas a rental; (5) one ton

PERMANENT INSTALLATIONS OVER STAGE (FROM SMOKE POCKET)
Fire curtain (1)
Dead spaces, (4) at 10'10", 22'10", 24'4", 34'10" (12" wide)

PERMANENT INSTALLATIONS ON DECK
Loading bridge (2) 4'0" x 4'0" located at SL above fly floor
Pilasters, multiple, irregular dimensions

ORCHESTRA PIT
Adjustble to 7' below stage level by manual lift
Apron overhangs US wall of pit 8'0"

BACKSTAGE

LOADING DOCK
Loading door(s):
  1) 12'0" high x 12'0" wide
  2) 8'0" high x 9'0" wide
Sound loads thru FOH
Main set loads thru Door 1
Props load thru Door 2
Fork lift is not required;
  Supplier is Mike Martin
  707-762-3358
Lobby can be a work area
Trailers cannot store on-site
Security at dock & stage door

WARDROBE
Location: Basement
Access: Stairs & elevator
(3) Washers (3) Dryers
No washer or dryer hookups

DRESSING ROOMS
(3) Star, SL, t/s included, phone jack
(8) Small, basement/ -1, t/s on same fl, phone jack
(2) Chorus, basement/ -1, t/s on same fl, phone jack
Elevator access for dressing rooms
Additional production office for company mgr

SOUND

CONSOLE
No house console

SPEAKERS
Speaker truss exists
Max available load 2,000 lbs
Proscenium hanging points left and right with 1 ton upper delay truss points

COMMUNICATIONS
Clear Com intercom with (4) channels
Infrared sound system
Dressing room page system

ROAD CONSOLE
Located Rear House
No seats required to be removed
Cable run from stage is 200'
Tie-in into house system with XLR connectors

REHEARSAL & STORAGE SPACE
Rehearsal: None
Storage: None

ELECTRICS

ROAD SERVICE POWER

Panel	Phase	Amp	Circuit Protection	Use	Location
A-C	3	400	breaker	dimmers	electric jump
D	3	250	breaker	sound	SL trap
E	3	100	breaker	extra	USL
F	3	200	breaker	extra	DSL
G	3	200	breaker	extra	SR
H	3	100	breaker	extra	SR
I	3	400	breaker	extra	DSL trap
J-K	3	400	breaker	extra	USC trap

Recommended location of touring dimmer racks: electric jump
Hoist is required and provided
Additional power is available for tour buses, generators, etc.

FRONT OF HOUSE (BOX BOOM VALUES ARE PER SIDE)

Position	Pipe Width	Distance to Prosc.	House Circuits	Connector Type	FOH Transfer Circuits
1st Balc Rail		42'	24	grd 20 amp stage pin	24
2nd Balc Rail		62'	24	grd 20 amp stage pin	24
Box Boom 1		35'	24	grd 20 amp stage pin	24
Box Boom 2		45'	24	grd 20 amp stage pin	24

Transfer circuits: grd 20 amp stage pin

EQUIPMENT FOH (BOX BOOM VALUES ARE PER SIDE)
None

FOLLOWSPOTS
House Followspots:
  (3) Lycian 2.5k; removeable

Followspot Booth:
  (3) spots per booth;
  120' throw to proscenium;
  (3) 1Ø 20 amp breakers
  (3) 1Ø 30 amp breakers
  (3) 3Ø 30 amp breakers

DIMMERS
No lighting console
(296) ETC Sensors dimmers
House has programmable DMX control system
(16) dry run DMX station(s) throughout theatre

SAN JOSE CENTER FOR THE PERFORMING ARTS

AT: SAN JOSE CONVENTION & CULTURAL FACILITIES   YEAR BUILT: 1972   YEAR RENOVATED: 1995

Theatre Location: 255 Almaden Boulevard, San Jose, CA 95113
Mailing Address: 408 S. Almaden Avenue, San Jose, CA 95110-2715
Management Company: City of San Jose
                         Department of Conventions, Art & Entertainment
                         408 S. Almaden Avenue, San Jose, CA 95110-2715

Main Administrative Phone: 408-277-5277
Main Administrative Fax: 408-277-3535
Website: www.sjco.com
Stage Door Phone: 408-277-4644
Backstage Pay Phone: 408-279-9130

THEATRE STAFF
General Manager   Nadine Felix   408-277-5213
Booking   Robin Merriam   408-277-2769
Marketing   Michele Mascher   408-277-3925

HOUSE CREW
Electrics   Bill Overstreet   408-277-4989

UNIONS
IATSE Local #134   Chuck Burnett   408-363-9189
Wardrobe Local #784   Anne Polland   415-861-8379
AFM Local #153   Tony Clements   408-377-3493

SEATING CAPACITY
Main Floor   1,823
Grand Tier   756
Total: **2,579**

pit (add'l)   86
wheelchair (add'l)   8

BOX OFFICE
San Jose Box Office   408-246-1160

Outside Ticket Agency
Computerized
Bass   408-288-8666

Box office is promoter operated

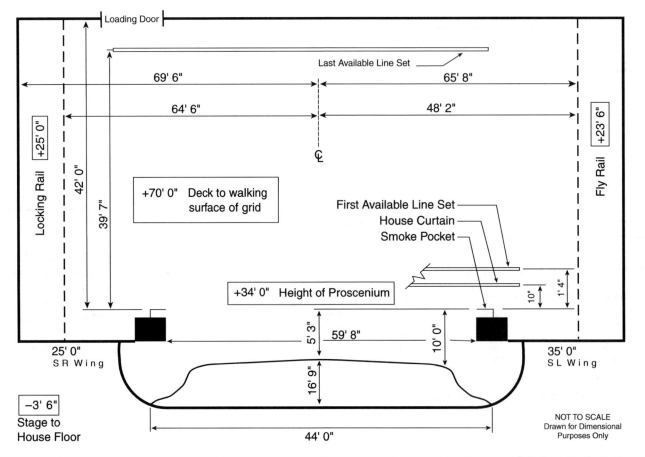

STAGE HOUSE

HOUSE CURTAIN
Operates as a guillotine from SR fly floor

RIGGING SYSTEM
Type: Combination purchase counterweight; single purchase and motorized sets

Weight: 1,700 lbs available

Line sets: 39 sets at 6" o.c. with 5 lift lines per set

Arbors: 1,000 lb capacity

House Pipes: 66' long with 62' of travel from deck

Line sets are not moveable

Block & Falls are not available

Chain hoists are not available

39 single purchase; 16 winched; 2 light bridges

PERMANENT INSTALLATIONS OVER STAGE (FROM SMOKE POCKET)
Orchestra shell (1) at 13'9"

Electric Raceways (2) located on light bridges

Traveller (1) at 8'10"

Electric bridges (2) at 3'8", 27'6"

Electric pipes (2) at 11'9", 18'8"

Dead space (1) located at shell ceiling

Fire curtain (1)

PERMANENT INSTALLATIONS ON DECK
Jumps (3)

ORCHESTRA PIT
Adjustable to 16' below stage level by hydraulic lift

Pit lift is in (2) sections

BACKSTAGE

LOADING DOCK
Loading door(s):
    10'8" high x 9'10" wide

Trucks load (1) at a time

48' trailer with sliding rear wheels or city tractor is the largest that will get to dock due to compound curve driveway

Fork lift is not required

Sound/Props can load in FOH

Trailers cannot store on-site

WARDROBE
Location: Dressing Room level SR, +1 up from stage

Access: Elevator

(2) Washers (2) Dryers

DRESSING ROOMS
(1) Star, SR, +1, t/s included

(5) Small, SR, +1, t/s included

(2) Chorus, SL, +1, t/s included

Additional production office available for company mgr

SOUND

CONSOLE
Ramsa S4424, located Rear House

24 inputs, 4 main outputs, 4 matrix outputs, 2 aux outputs

SPEAKERS
Proscenium

Under Balcony

No speaker truss

COMMUNICATIONS
CHAOS intercom with (1) channels

Infrared sound system

Dressing room page system

ROAD CONSOLE
Located Rear House

Number of seats required to be removed varies

Cable run from stage is 250'

Tie-in into house system with XLR connectors

Minimal charge to tie into house

REHEARSAL & STORAGE SPACE
Rehearsal: Rehearsal Hall, 30' x 40' located in basement, piano available

Storage: Loading Dock, 25' x 50' behind stage

ELECTRICS

ROAD SERVICE POWER

Panel	Phase	Amp	Circuit Protection	Use	Location
A	3	400	breaker	dimmers	SL
B	3	400	breaker	dimmers	SL
C	3	400	breaker	dimmers	SL
D	3	200	breaker	sound	SL
E	3	100	breaker	extra	Projection Booth

Recommended location of touring dimmer racks: off left or jump off left

Hoist required at times

FRONT OF HOUSE (BOX BOOM VALUES ARE PER SIDE)

Position	Pipe Width	Distance to Prosc.	House Circuits	Connector Type	FOH Transfer Circuits
1st Balc Rail	97'	80'	24	20 amp stage pin	0
Box Boom 1		60'	12	20 amp stage pin	0
1st Cove	48	53'	24	20 amp stage pin	0
2nd Cove	64'	65'	34	20 amp stage pin	0

Transfer circuits: Can connect and patch through board to access any of the above if using DMX 512

Road truss: FOH truss is problematic; call for details

EQUIPMENT FOH (BOX BOOM VALUES ARE PER SIDE)

Position	Quantity	Wattage	Instrument	Removeable
1st Balc Rail	24	1000	Par 64 Narrow	yes
1st Cove	4	575	Source 4, 19°	
2nd Cove	34	575	Source 4, 10°	
Box Boom 1	10	575	Source 4, 10°	

Pipe in coves is 2", otherwise 1 ½"

FOLLOWSPOTS
House Followspots:
(2) Strong Super Trouper (Carbon); not removeable

(2) matching lamps available through local rental

(2) Followspot Booths each:
(1) spot per booth;
125' throw to proscenium;
(2) 1Ø 30 amp breakers

DIMMERS
Lighting console is Obsession 1500;
(642) Sensor AF ETC dimmers

House has non-programmable DMX control system

(9) dry run DMX station(s)

HARMAN HALL

AT: CHRISTOPHER COHAN PERFORMING ARTS CENTER   **YEAR BUILT: 1996**

Theatre Location: One Grand Avenue, San Luis Obispo, CA 93407

Main Administrative Phone:	805-756-7222
Main Administrative Fax:	805-756-6088
E-mail:	cjenkins@calpoly.edu
Website:	www.pacslo.org
Stage Door Phone:	805-756-7245
Backstage Pay Phone:	805-541-9937
Traveling Production Office Fax:	805-756-7250

THEATRE STAFF

Managing Director	Ron Regier	805-756-7222

HOUSE CREW

Technical Director	Buddy Pope	805-756-7245
Technical Services Manager	Jim Chernoff	805-756-1410
House Carpenter	Tom McPherron	805-756-7248

SEATING CAPACITY

Orchestra (2 lifts)	201
Orchestra	607
Dress Circle	153
Balcony	169
Gallery	152
Total:	**1,282**
pit (add'l)	0
wheelchair (add'l)	12
standing (add'l)	0

STAGE DIMENSIONS
Measured from plasterline
Stage is 39'10" deep
Width from Center Line to SL is 48'0"
Width from Center Line to SR is 44'0"
Proscenium width is 49'10"
Proscenium height is 26'0"
Smoke pocket to apron edge is 9'9"
Orchestra pit exists

RIGGING

Grid Height:	70'
Type:	Single purchase counter weight
Weight:	50,000 lbs
Line sets:	32 sets
Arbors:	2,000 lb capacity
House Pipes:	60' long

LOADING DOCK
Loading door(s) are 15'0"high x 8'0"wide
Trucks load (3) at same time
Fork lift is required and is not available

ELECTRICS
Total power available:
(2) 800A 3Ø SL
(1) 175A 3Ø SR

FOLLOWSPOTS
House Followspots:
Strong Super Trouper
Power in spot booth

DIMMERS
(560) house dimmers
House has DMX control system

SOUND
House has 175A dedicated
power located Control
Booth
FOH mixing position in
Sound console is available

FRED KAVLI THEATRE FOR THE PERFORMING ARTS

FORMERLY: PROBST THEATRE AT: THOUSAND OAKS CIVIC ARTS PLAZA AKA: CIVIC AUDITORIUM   **YEAR BUILT: 1993**

Theatre Location: 2100 Thousand Oaks Boulevard
Thousand Oaks, CA 91362
Management Company: City of Thousand Oaks, Theatres Department

Main Administrative Phone:	805-449-2700
Main Administrative Fax:	805-449-2750
E-mail:	thmitze@ci.thousand-oaks.ca.us
Website:	www.civicartsplaza.com
Traveling Production Office Phone:	805-449-2740
Traveling Production Office Fax:	805-449-2731

SEATING CAPACITY

Orchestra	733
Founders Circle	191
Mezzanine	414
Balcony	390
Total:	**1,728**
pit (add'l)	72
wheelchair (substituted)	30
standing (add'l)	0

THEATRE STAFF

Theatres Director	Tom Mitze	805-449-2707
Booking	Tom Mitze	805-449-2707
Marketing	Kathie Harrison	805-449-2765
Operations	Mary Ann Tachco	805-449-2708

HOUSE CREW

Technical Production Manager	Gary Mintz	805-449-2706 / Fax 805-449-2750

BOX OFFICE

Computerized
Box Office Supervisor
Sharon Lauritzen   805-449-2725

Outside Ticket Agency   Computerized
Ticketmaster

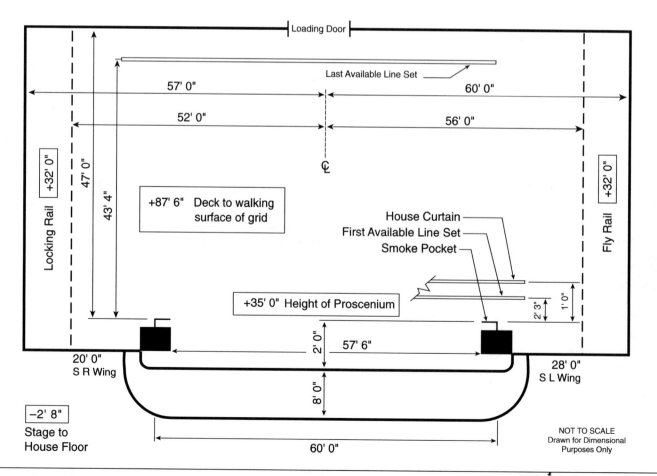

STAGE HOUSE

HOUSE CURTAIN
Operates as a guillotine from SR fly floor
Operates as a traveller from SR deck

RIGGING SYSTEM
Type: Combination purchase counterweight
Weight: 40,000 lbs available
Line sets: 70 sets at 8" o.c. with 7 lift lines per set
Arbors: 1,825 lb capacity
House Pipes: 68' long with 80' of travel from deck
Line sets are not moveable
(12) spot wheels and 1,200' of hemp available

PERMANENT INSTALLATIONS OVER STAGE (FROM SMOKE POCKET)
M=Moveable with advance call
Orchestra shell (6) at 6'0", 6'4", 15'7", 16'0", 24'11", 25'4"
Electric raceway (3) at 5'3", 6'11", 35'3"
Movie screen (1); M
Traveller (2) at 20'7", 42'7"; M
Cyclorama (1) at 43'3"
Fire curtain (1) at 0'6"
Catwalk (1) at 44'6"

PERMANENT INSTALLATIONS ON DECK
Adjustable prosecenium (1)
Adjustable portal (1) max 57'6", minimum 40'0"

ORCHESTRA PIT
Adjustable to 17' below stage level by electric motor turnscrew
Apron overhangs US wall of pit 10'0"
Pit lift is in (1) section

BACKSTAGE

LOADING DOCK
Loading door(s):
    12'0" high x 10'0" wide
Trucks load (3) at same time
Fork lift is not required
Sound/Props can load in FOH
(2) Trailers can store on-site

WARDROBE
Location: -1 below stage
Access: Freight elevator USR
(2) Washers (2) Dryers
No washer or dryer hookups

DRESSING ROOMS
(3) Star, SR, stage level, t/s included, phone jacks
(4) Small, SR, -1, t/s included
(2) Chorus, SR, -1, t/s included
Elevator access for dressing rooms
Additional production office available for company mgr

SOUND

CONSOLE
SoundCraft Vienna, located Orchestra
32 inputs, 3 main outputs, 8 matrix outputs, 8 aux outputs

SPEAKERS
House Cluster
Portable
No speaker truss

COMMUNICATIONS
Clear Com intercom with (1) channel
Infrared sound system
Dressing room page system

ROAD CONSOLE
Located Rear Orchestra
No seats required to be removed
Cable run from stage is 150'
Tie-in into house system with XLR connectors

REHEARSAL & STORAGE SPACE
Rehearsal: 45' x 25' located in basement, mirrors, barres & piano available
Storage: 30' x 20' located USC

ELECTRICS

ROAD SERVICE POWER

Panel	Phase	Amp	Circuit Protection	Use	Location
A-C	3	400	fuse	dimmers	SL
D	3	200	fuse	extra	USL
E	3	200	fuse	extra	USR
F-G	3	225	fuse	extra	Loading dock USL
H	3	200	fuse	sound	SL
I	3	60	fuse	extra	On grid

Recommended location of touring dimmer racks: SL
Hoist not required
Additional power is available for tour buses, generators, etc.

FRONT OF HOUSE (BOX BOOM VALUES ARE PER SIDE)

Position	Pipe Width	Distance to Prosc.	House Circuits	Connector Type	FOH Transfer Circuits
1st FOH	75'	75'	32	grd 20 amp stage pin	32
2nd FOH	75'	93'	32	grd 20 amp stage pin	32
Balc Rail	75'	94'	20	grd 20 amp stage pin	20
Mezzanine Rail	75'	64'	20	grd 20 amp stage pin	20
Box Boom 1	20'	30'	8	grd 20 amp stage pin	8
Orchestra Pit			12	grd 20 amp stage pin	12

Road truss: (16) one ton points - (10) over DS edge of apron and (6) over Orchestra pit

EQUIPMENT FOH (BOX BOOM VALUES ARE PER SIDE)

Position	Quantity	Wattage	Instrument	Removeable
2nd Balc Rail	10	1,000	Altman 6 x 22	yes
Mezzanine Rail	20	575	Altman Shakespeare 20	yes
1st Cove Rail	21	1,000	Century 10	no
2nd Cove Rail	21	1,000	Century 10	no
Box Boom 1	10	575	Altman Shakespeare 20	yes

FOLLOWSPOTS
House Followspots:
(2) Lyceum 2.5k; not removeable

Followspot Booth:
(2) spots per booth;
120' throw to proscenium;
(4) 1Ø 60 amp breakers

DIMMERS
Lighting console is Century Mini Light Pallette 90;
(500) Century CD80 dimmers
House has non-programmable DMX control system
(1) dry run DMX station

MACKY AUDITORIUM CONCERT HALL

YEAR BUILT: 1914   YEAR RENOVATED: 1986

Theatre Location:	17th St & University Ave., Boulder, CO 80309-0285
Mailing Address:	University of Colorado, Campus Box 285
	Boulder, CO 80309-0285

Main Administrative Phone:	303-492-8423
Main Administrative Fax:	303-492-1651
Stage Door Phone:	303-492-2741
Traveling Production Office Phone:	303-492-2473

THEATRE STAFF

Director	Kristin Anderson	303-492-8423

HOUSE CREW

Technical Director	J.P Osnes	303-492-2742
Asst Technical Director	John Hegyes	303-444-1050

SEATING CAPACITY

Orchestra I	937
Orchestra II	393
Loge I	255
Loge II	426
Opera Boxes	36
Total:	**2.047**
pit (add'l)	0
wheelchair (add'l)	5
standing (add'l)	0

STAGE DIMENSIONS (FROM SMOKE POCKET)

Stage is 27'9" deep
Width from Center Line to SL is 41'6"
Width from Center Line to SR is 26'6"
Proscenium width is 39'0"
Proscenium height is 27'0"
Smoke pocket to apron edge is 16'6"
Orchestra pit exists

RIGGING

Grid Height:	48'10"
Type:	Single purchase counter weight
Weight:	6,000 lbs
Line sets:	36 sets at 8" o.c.
Arbors:	2,000 lb capacity
House Pipes:	42'8" long

LOADING DOCK

Loading door(s) are 9'2" high x 8'0" wide
Trucks load (2) at same time
Fork lift is not required and is not available

ELECTRICS

Total power available:
(1) 600A 3Ø SL wall
(1) 200A 3Ø SL wall

FOLLOWSPOTS

House Followspots:
Ultra Arc

DIMMERS

(192) house dimmers
House has DMX control system
(3) dry run station(s) located SL
& SR

SOUND

House has 200A undedicated
power located SL
FOH mixing position in
Rows Q-T seats 1-6
Sound console is available

PIKES PEAK CENTER

YEAR BUILT: 1982

Theatre Location: 190 S. Cascade Avenue, Colorado Springs, CO 80903

Main Administrative Phone:	719-520-7453
Main Administrative Fax:	719-520-7462
E-mail:	ppcweb@co.el-paso.co.us
Website:	www.pikespeakcenter.org
Stage Door Phone:	719-520-7465
Backstage Pay Phone:	719-634-9153

THEATRE STAFF

Manager	Stephen R. Martin	719-520-7471
Booking	Cindy Ballard	719-520-7466
Operations	Willard Small	719-520-7457

HOUSE CREW

Stage Manager	Dennis Fruin	719-520-7453
Carpentry	Marc Brown	719-520-7453
Electrics	Randy Knouse	719-520-7453
Sound	Doug Wilson	719-520-7453

UNIONS

IATSE Local #62	John Young	719-520-1059

BOX OFFICE

Computerized
Box Office Manager
  Grant Jenkins   719-520-7455

Outside Ticket Agency
Computerized
  Ticketmaster   719-520-7469

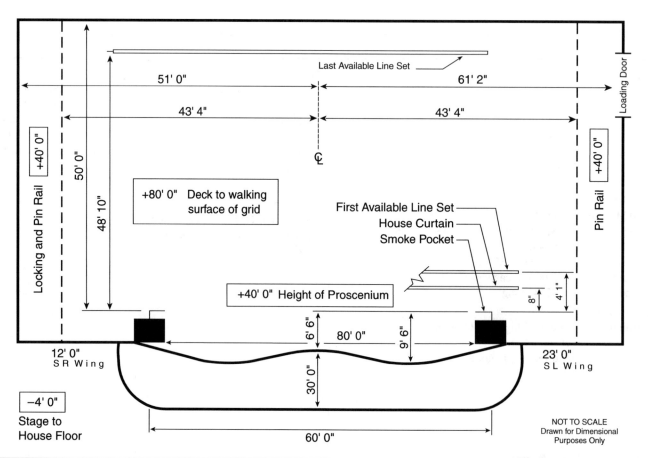

STAGE HOUSE

HOUSE CURTAIN
Operates as a traveller from SR deck

RIGGING SYSTEM
Type:	Single purchase counter weight
Weight:	60,000 lbs available
Line sets:	42 sets at 8" o.c. with 7 lift lines per set
Arbors:	2,500 lb capacity
House Pipes:	65' long with 70' of travel from deck

Line sets are not moveable
Block & Falls are not available
Chain hoists are not available
(70) spot wheels and 700' of hemp available

PERMANENT INSTALLATIONS OVER STAGE (FROM SMOKE POCKET)
Electric bridge (1) at 2'8" (15" wide)
Orchestra shell (4) at 6'4", 19'2", 31'4", 43'6"

PERMANENT INSTALLATIONS ON DECK
None

ORCHESTRA PIT
Adjustable to 17' below stage level by electric motor turnscrew
Apron overhangs US wall of pit 10'0"
Pit lift is in (2) sections

BACKSTAGE

LOADING DOCK
Loading door(s):
    12'0 high x 10'0" wide
Trucks load (2) side-by-side at same time
Fork lift is not required
Sound/Props can load in FOH
Lobby can be a work area
(2) Trailers can store on-site
Security at dock & stage door

WARDROBE
Location: Basement
Access: Freight elevator
(1) Washer (1) Dryer
Washer and dryer hookups available

DRESSING ROOMS
(3) Star, behind stage, stage level, t/s included
(3) Small, behind stage, stage level, t/s included
(2) Chorus, basement, t/s included
Elevator access for dressing rooms

SOUND

CONSOLE
Yamaha PM 2000
24 inputs, 8 main outputs

SPEAKERS
House Cluster
No speaker truss

COMMUNICATIONS
Clear Com intercom with (2) channels
Dressing room page system

ROAD CONSOLE
Located Rear Orchestra
(12) seats required to be removed
Cable run from stage is 150'
Tie-in into house system with XLR connectors

REHEARSAL & STORAGE SPACE
Rehearsal: 50' x 70' located SL on stage level
Storage: None

ELECTRICS

ROAD SERVICE POWER

Panel	Phase	Amp	Circuit Protection	Use	Location
A	3	400	fuse	dimmers	DSL side wall
B	3	400	fuse	sound	DSL side wall
C-D	3	400	fuse	extra	DSL side

Recommended location of touring dimmer racks: SL on deck
Hoist not required
Additional power is available for tour buses, generators, etc.

FRONT OF HOUSE (BOX BOOM VALUES ARE PER SIDE)

Position	Pipe Width	Distance to Prosc.	House Circuits	Connector Type	FOH Transfer Circuits
Balc Rail	65'	90'	12	grd 20 amp stagepin	12
1st Cove	65'	50'	31	grd 20 amp stagepin	31
2nd Cove	65'	80	40	grd 20 amp stagepin	40
Box Boom 1			4	grd 20 amp stagepin	4

Transfer circuits: grd 20 amp stage pin located on DSL side wall

EQUIPMENT FOH (BOX BOOM VALUES ARE PER SIDE)
None

FOLLOWSPOTS
House Followspots:
    (2) Xenon Super Troupers; removeable

Followspot Booth:
    (4) spots per booth;
    150' throw to proscenium;
    (6) 3Ø 30 amp breakers

DIMMERS
Lighting console is Lighting Palette II;
    (470) dimmers
No DMX control system

AUDITORIUM THEATRE

AT: DENVER PERFORMING ARTS COMPLEX   **YEAR BUILT: 1908   YEAR RENOVATED: 1954**

Theatre Location: 910 14th Street, Denver, CO 80204
Mailing Address: Denver Performing Arts Complex
                         950 13th Street, Denver, CO 80204
Management Company: Denver Theatres and Arenas
                         1380 Lawrence Street, Suite 790, Denver, CO 80204

Main Administrative Phone: 303-640-2862
Main Administrative Fax: 303-640-2397
Stage Door Phone: 303-640-5009
Backstage Pay Phone: 303-623-9886

THEATRE STAFF
General Manager   Rodney Smith   303-640-5142
Booking   Roberta McFarland   303-640-2637
Marketing   Frankie Hood   303-640-2637

HOUSE CREW
Technical Director   Rodney J. Smith   303-640-5142
Carpentry   Tony Paxton   303-640-7953
Electrics   David Wilson   303-640-7953
Sound   Phil Allen   303-640-7953
Props   Deborah Guess   303-640-7953

UNIONS
IATSE Local #7   James Taylor   303-534-2423
Wardrobe Local #719 Cindy Corey   303-237-7897
Music In-house   James Harvey   303-458-1018

SEATING CAPACITY
Total: **2,065**

BOX OFFICE
Computerized
Client Contracted; No In house

Outside Ticket Agency
Computerized
Ticketmaster   303-830-8400

Box office is promoter operated

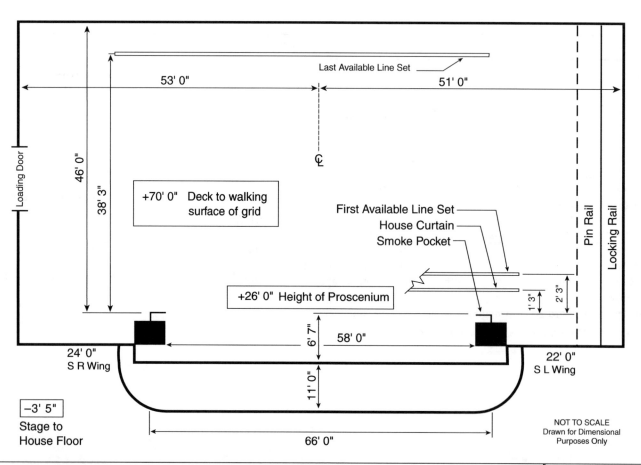

STAGE HOUSE

House Curtain
Operates as a guillotine from SL deck

Rigging System
Type:	Single purchase counter weight
Weight:	12,500 lbs available
Line sets:	70 sets at 6" o.c. with 6 lift lines per set
Arbors:	800 lb capacity
House Pipes:	63' long with 63' of travel from deck

Line sets are moveable
Block & Falls are not available
Chain hoists available
(40) spot wheels and 10,000' of hemp available
Stage Set

Permanent Installations Over Stage (from smoke pocket)
Dead spaces (6) at 1'4"-2'0", 7'5"-8'0", 12'11"-13'7", 18'5"-19'7", 29'11"-30'7", 33'11"-34'7"
Fire curtain (1) 0'0"

Permanent Installations On Deck
None

Orchestra Pit
Nonadjustable to 5'5" below stage level
Apron overhangs US wall of pit 0'0"
Pit is filled with platforms to house level when additional seating is needed; without platforms pit is 2'0" below house level with 2'6" removeable wall from house level; 6'x11' piano lift center - also goes to lower dressing rooms

BACKSTAGE

Loading Dock
Loading door(s):
  12'0" high x 10'0" wide
Trucks load (2) at same time
Dock is at street level; ramp or fork down
Fork lift is not required House owns
Sound/Props can load in FOH
Lobby can be a work area

Wardrobe
Location:Stage -1
Access: Elevator & stairs
(2) Washers (2) Dryers
No washer or dryer hookups

Dressing Rooms
(2) Star, SL, stage level, t/s included, phone jack
(4) Small, SL, +1, t/s included
(7) Small, SL, -1, t/s included, (2) phone jacks
(8) Small, SR, -1, t/s included, (3) phone jacks
(2) Chorus, -1 (pit level), t/s included
Elevator access for dressing rooms
Use dressing room for company mgr office

SOUND

Console
Yamaha PM 3500-52, Rear Orchestra center
52 inputs, 8 main outputs, 8 matrix outputs, 12 aux outputs

Speakers
Proscenium
Under Balcony
Portable
Front fills
No speaker truss

Communications
Clear Com intercom with (4) channels
Infrared sound system
Dressing room page system

Road Console
Located Rear Orchestra
No seats required to be removed
Cable run from stage is 150'
Tie-in into house system with XLR connectors

Rehearsal & Storage Space
(6) Storage or Rehearsal areas; 35' x 37' up stage with a 10' x 12' door; phone jacks available, upright or grand piano available; prior arrangement required

ELECTRICS

Road Service Power

Panel	Phase	Amp	Circuit Protection	Use	Location
A-C	3	400	breaker	dimmers	DSL
D	3	200	breaker	sound	DSR
E-F	3	400	breaker	dimmers	DSR
G		100	breaker	extra	SR

Recommended location of touring dimmer racks: DSL
Hoist not required
Additional power is available for tour buses, generators, etc.

Front Of House (box boom values are per side)

Position	Pipe Width	Distance to Prosc.	House Circuits	Connector Type	FOH Transfer Circuits
1st Balc Rail	118'	71'		grd 20 amp stage pin	30
Cove	58'	50'		grd 20 amp stage pin	40
Box Boom 1	1'-7'	65'		grd 20 amp stage pin	12

Transfer circuits: grd 20 amp stage pin

Equipment FOH (box boom values are per side)

Position	Quantity	Wattage	Instrument	Removeable
Cove	30	1,000	ERS	yes

Followspots
House Followspots:
  (3) Strong Xenon Super Troopers 2k; removeable
  (2) Lycian Super Arc 350; removeable

  (3) Followspot Booths:
  FOH Center
  120' throw to proscenium;
  (4)1Ø 40 amp breakers

  FOH SL and FOH SR
  100' throw to proscenium;
  (1)1Ø 20 amp breakers

Dimmers
Lighting console is 1- LP 90, 1-LBX;
  (3) Strand CD 80 dimmers
No DMX control system
(0) dry run DMX station(s)

TEMPLE HOYNE BUELL THEATRE

AT: DENVER PERFORMING ARTS COMPLEX   **YEAR BUILT: 1991**

Theatre Location: 1323 Champa Street, Denver, CO 80204
Mailing Address: Denver Performing Arts Complex
                         950 13th Street, Denver, CO 80204
Management Company: Denver Theatres and Arenas
                         1380 Lawrence Street, Suite 790, Denver, CO 80204

SEATING CAPACITY	
Orchestra	1,767
Mezzanine	256
Balcony	741
Boxes	74
Total:	**2,838**
pit (add'l)	50
wheelchair (incl.)	
standing	0

Main Administrative Phone: 303-640-2862
Main Administrative Fax: 303-640-2637
Stage Door Phone: 303-640-5041
Backstage Pay Phone: 303-623-9886

THEATRE STAFF
General Manager   Rodney J. Smith   303-640-5142
Booking   Roberta McFarland   303-640-2637
Marketing   Frankie Hood   303-640-2637
Operations   Anthony Tenorio   303-640-7115

HOUSE CREW
Technical Director   Rodney J. Smith   303-640-5142
Carpentry   David Lambert   303-640-5033
Electrics   Steve Diedel   303-640-5034
Sound   Barry Fisch   303-640-5034
Props   Alan Price   303-640-5032

UNIONS
IATSE Local #7   James Taylor   303-534-2423
Wardrobe Local #719 Cindy Corey   303-237-7897

BOX OFFICE
Outside Ticket Agency
Computerized
Ticketmaster
  Sally Brown   303-830-8400

Box office is promoter operated

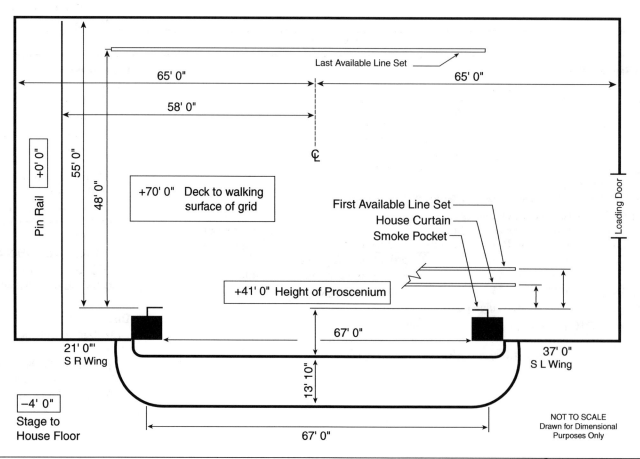

STAGE HOUSE

HOUSE CURTAIN
Operates as a guillotine from SR deck

RIGGING SYSTEM
Type:	Single purchase counter weight
Line sets:	90 sets at 6" o.c. with 7 lift lines per set
Arbors:	1,500 lb capacity
House Pipes:	63' long with 69' of travel from deck

Line sets are moveable
Block & Falls are available
Chain hoists are available; (10) one ton
(100) spot wheel; hemp is available
Large stage size, easy working grid

PERMANENT INSTALLATIONS OVER STAGE (FROM SMOKE POCKET)
Dead spaces (6) between 17'-18', 19'-20', 33'-34', 34'-35', 54'-55', 72'-73'
Catwalk at upstage wall, not an obstruction

PERMANENT INSTALLATIONS ON DECK
Traps in stage floor (30) on a sectional grid
Jumps (above locking rail) (1) 33' H x 7' W x 48' L, SR
Electric jump (1) 33' H x 14' W x 48' L, SL
Loading bridge (1) 60' H x 9' W x 48' L, SR

ORCHESTRA PIT
Adjustable to 11' below stage level by hydraulic lift
Apron overhangs US wall of pit 4'0"
Pit lift is in (1) section
Two orchestra pit sizes: small - maximum 35 musicians; large - maximum 70 musicians

BACKSTAGE

LOADING DOCK
Loading door(s): 30'0" high x 28'0" wide
Trucks load (4) at same time
(2) Docks available; other trucks load at street level
Fork lift is not required Evert Management 303-640-2862
Sound/Props cannot load in FOH
(2) Trailers can store on-site
Security at stage door

WARDROBE
Location: Street level
Access: Elevator
(2) Washers (2) Dryers
Washer and dryer hookups available

DRESSING ROOMS
(2) Star, SR, stage level, t/s included, phone jack
(6) Small, upstage, stage level, t/s included, phone jack
(6) Chorus, upstage, +1, t/s included, phone jack
(1) each quick change, green room, conductor's, musicians, wig room, wardrobe
Elevator access for dressing rooms
Additional production office available for company mgr

SOUND

CONSOLE
Ramsa 900 Series; mobile
32 inputs, 3 main outputs, 4 matrix outputs, 6 aux outputs

SPEAKERS
House Cluster
Monitors

COMMUNICATIONS
Clear Com intercom with (4) channels
Infrared sound system
Dressing room page system

ROAD CONSOLE
Located Rear House right
(16) seats required to be removed
Cable run from stage is 250'
Tie-in into house system with XLR connectors

REHEARSAL & STORAGE SPACE
Rehearsal: None
Storage: Dock, 25' x 25' HL; 2nd fl, large room; Basement, large room

ELECTRICS

ROAD SERVICE POWER

Panel	Phase	Amp	Circuit Protection Use	Location
A-C	3	400		SL
D-F	3	400		SL fly
G-H	3	400		USR
I	3	200	sound	Trap room
J	3	200	sound	DSL

Recommended location of touring dimmer racks: SL
Hoist not required
Additional power is available for tour buses, generators, etc.

FRONT OF HOUSE (BOX BOOM VALUES ARE PER SIDE)

Position	Pipe Width	Distance to Prosc.	House Circuits	Connector Type	FOH Transfer Circuits
1st Balc Rail	80'	73'	35	grd 20 amp stage pin	
2nd Balc Rail	104'	84'	35	grd 20 amp stage pin	
1st Cove	63'	61'	36	grd 20 amp stage pin	
2nd Cove	100'	94'	36	grd 20 amp stage pin	

Transfer circuits: grd 20 amp stage pin

EQUIPMENT FOH (BOX BOOM VALUES ARE PER SIDE)
All inventory in house is available and removeable

FOLLOWSPOTS
House Followspots: (4) Gladiator II; removeable

Followspot Booth: (4) spots per booth; 125' throw to proscenium; (4) 3Ø 30 amp breakers

Also, Projector Power 125' throw to proscenium; (1) 3Ø 50 amp breaker

DIMMERS
Lighting console is LP90; (3) CD 80 Strand Century (96) 2.4k dimmers
No DMX control system
No dry run DMX station(s)

LINCOLN CENTER

YEAR BUILT: 1978

Theatre Location: 417 W. Magnolia, Fort Collins, CO 80521
Management Company: City of Fort Collins

Main Administrative Phone: 970-221-6735
Main Administrative Fax: 970-484-0424
E-mail: dsiever@c1.fortcollins.co.us
Website: c1.fortcollins.co.us
Traveling Production Office Phone: 970-224-6149
Traveling Production Office Fax: 970-416-2174

THEATRE STAFF
Director David T. Siever 970-221-6735

HOUSE CREW
Technical Production
   Coordinator Jon Whatley 970-221-6735

SEATING CAPACITY
Center	806
Sides	374
Total:	**1,180**
pit (add'l)	0
wheelchair (add'l)	20
standing (add'l)	0

STAGE DIMENSIONS (FROM SMOKE POCKET)
Stage is 40'0" deep
Width from Center Line to SL is 30'0"
Width from Center Line to SR is 30'0"
Proscenium width is 60'0"
Proscenium height is 19'6"
Smoke pocket to apron edge is 6'0"
Orchestra pit exists

RIGGING
Grid Height:	No grid
Type:	Single purchase counter weight
Weight:	5,000 lbs
Line sets:	29 sets at 9" o.c.
Arbors:	800 lb capacity
House Pipes:	76' long

LOADING DOCK
Loading door(s) are 14'0" high x 6'0" wide
Trucks load (2) at same time
Fork lift is not required and is not available

ELECTRICS
Total power available:
  (3) 500A 3Ø USL

FOLLOWSPOTS
House Followspots:
  Xenon Super Trouper
Power in spot booth (1) 20A
FOH transfer circuits: 32

DIMMERS
(186) house dimmers
House has DMX control system
(1) dry run station(s) located DSL

SOUND
House has 100A 3Ø dedicated power located USL
FOH mixing position in House Center
Sound console is available

THE BUSHNELL

Theatre Location: 166 Capitol Avenue, Hartford, CT 06106-1621

Main Administrative Phone:	860-987-6000
Main Administrative Fax:	860-987-6070
Stage Door Phone:	860-987-6064
Backstage Pay Phone:	860-728-9418

THEATRE STAFF

Executive Director	Douglas C. Evans	860-987-6023
Booking	Pamela Menhenett	860-987-6057
Marketing	Tod Kallenbach	860-987-6018
Operations	Erika Haynes	860-987-6031
Group Sales	Laura DiLorenzo	860-987-6056

HOUSE CREW

Technical Coordinator	Allen Sale	860-987-6039
Stage Manager	Mike Sivo	860-549-6955
Carpentry	Mike Sivo	860-549-6955
Electrics	Tom Burns	860-987-6062
Sound	Peter Tozer	860-987-6061
Props	Howard Clarke	860-549-6955

UNIONS

IATSE Local #84	Alan Paterson	860-527-4613
Music Local #400		
Musical Contractor:	Paul Landerman	860-289-0221
Business Agent:	Joseph Messina	860-563-1606

SEATING CAPACITY

Orchestra	1,114
Mezzanine	994
Balcony	652
Total:	**2,760**

pit (add'l)	77
wheelchair (add'l)	8
standing (add'l)	0

BOX OFFICE

Computerized
Box Office Manager
  Margaret Rush   860-987-6050

Outside Ticket Agency
Computerized
  Tele-charge   800-233-3123

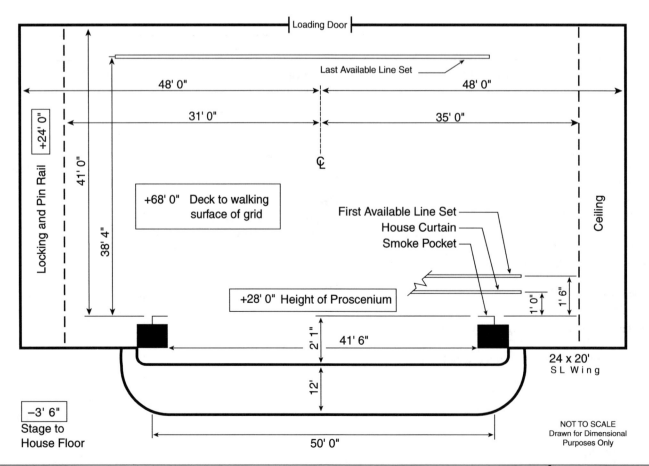

Loading Door

Last Available Line Set

48' 0"   48' 0"

31' 0"   35' 0"

℄

+24' 0"

41' 0"

Locking and Pin Rail

38' 4"

+68' 0" Deck to walking surface of grid

First Available Line Set
House Curtain
Smoke Pocket

Ceiling

1' 0"   1' 6"

+28' 0" Height of Proscenium

2' 1"   41' 6"

12'

24 x 20'
S L Wing

−3' 6"
Stage to
House Floor

50' 0"

NOT TO SCALE
Drawn for Dimensional
Purposes Only

STAGE HOUSE

HOUSE CURTAIN
Operates as a guillotine from SR fly floor

RIGGING SYSTEM

Type:	Double purchase counter weight
Weight:	52,000 lbs available
Line sets:	53 sets at 8" o.c. with 6 lift lines per set
Arbors:	2,000 lb capacity
House Pipes:	60' long

Line sets are moveable
Block & Falls are available
Chain hoists available as a rental; (1) one ton
(50) spot wheels and hemp available as needed

PERMANENT INSTALLATIONS OVER STAGE (FROM SMOKE POCKET)
None

PERMANENT INSTALLATIONS ON DECK
None

ORCHESTRA PIT
Adjustable to 14' below stage level by hydraulic lift
Apron overhangs US wall of pit 2'1"
Pit lift is in (1) section

BACKSTAGE

LOADING DOCK
Loading door(s):
9'0" high x 8'0" wide
Trucks load (3) at same time
Fork lift is not required
Sound/Props can load in FOH
Lobby can be a work area
(2) Trailers can store on-site
Security at dock & stage door

WARDROBE
Location: Basement
Access: Stairs & Freight elevator
(2) Washers (2) Dryers
Washer and dryer hookups available

DRESSING ROOMS
(1) Star, SR, stage level, toilet
(10) Small, SR, 2nd/ 3rd fl, t/s on same fl
(3) Chorus, SR, 4th fl/ -1, t/s on same fl
Elevator access for dressing rooms
Use dressing room for company mgr office

SOUND

CONSOLE
Yamaha PM 1800, located HL
24 inputs, 2 main outputs, 4 matrix outputs, 6 aux outputs

SPEAKERS
House Cluster
Proscenium
Under Balcony
No speaker truss

COMMUNICATIONS
Clear Com intercom with (2) channels
Infrared sound system
Dressing room page system

ROAD CONSOLE
Located Rear House
(12) seats required to be removed
Cable run from stage is 100'
Tie-in into house system with XLR connectors

REHEARSAL & STORAGE SPACE
Rehearsal: Community Room located in Annex; Seaverns Room located FOH; piano & equipment available
Storage: None

ELECTRICS

ROAD SERVICE POWER

Panel	Phase	Amp	Circuit Protection Use	Location
A-D	3	400	Sound	DSL
E	3	400	Sound	Annex- USL
F-G	3	200	Sound	Annex-SR, loading dock
H	3	200	Sound	SR

Sound power is transformer isolated
Location of touring dimmer racks: SL wing; Hoist not required; Addl power is available

FRONT OF HOUSE (BOX BOOM VALUES ARE PER SIDE)

Position	Pipe Width	Distance to Prosc.	House Circuits	Connector Type	FOH Transfer Circuits
1st Balc Rail		85'	32	grd 20 amp stage pin	32
1st Cove			8	grd 20 amp stage pin	8
Box Boom1		42'	12	grd 20 amp stage pin	12

Transfer circuits: All 72 FOH circuits can be picked up DSL at transfer panel;
All connectors are 20 amp male stage pin panel mount plugs
Road truss: FOH trusses can be hung from existing points in welded in place for Phantom and Show Boat

EQUIPMENT FOH (BOX BOOM VALUES ARE PER SIDE)

Position	Quantity	Wattage	Instrument	Removeable
1st Balc Rail	16	575	Source 4 26°	yes
1st Cove	4	575	Source 4 10°	yes
Box Boom 1	8	575	Source 4 19°	yes

All Cove position 10 units are equipped with iris

FOLLOWSPOTS
House Followspots:
(3) Strong Super Trouper 2k; removeable

Followspot Booth:
(3) spots per booth;
175' throw to proscenium;
(3) 1Ø 30 amp breakers

DIMMERS
Lighting console is ETC Insight 108;
(288) ETC Sensor 2.4k dimmers
House has programmable DMX control system
(1) dry run DMX station

FOXWOODS CASINO: THE FOX THEATRE

Theatre Location: Foxwoods Resort Casino, Route 2, PO Box 3777
                      Mashantucket, CT 06339

Main Administrative Phone: 860-312-3000
Main Administrative Fax: 860-312-4045

THEATRE STAFF
Production Manager   Richard Kelusak   860-312-4337
Booking   Sue Ellen Carija   860-312-4253

HOUSE CREW
Technical Director   Bill van Ingen   860-312-4061
Sound   Dave Albro   860-312-4064
Electrics   Gerard Mills   860-312-4396

SEATING CAPACITY

Banquets	108
Tables	484
Theater	937
Tribal Opera Box	24
Tribal Box Seats	16
Total:	**1,471**

STAGE DIMENSIONS (FROM SMOKE POCKET)
Stage is 34' deep
Width from Center Line to SL is 55'3"
Width from Center Line to SR is 50'
Proscenium width is 58'
Proscenium height is 20'3"
Smoke pocket to apron edge is 3'8"
Orchestra pit exists

RIGGING
Type: Single purchase counter weight
Weight: 35,000 lbs
Line sets: 7 sets
Arbors: 1,200 lb capacity
House Pipes: 66' long

LOADING DOCK
Loading door(s) are 10'0" high x 8'0" wide
Trucks load (1) at a time
Fork lift is not required and is not available

ELECTRICS
Total power available:
   (2) 400A 3Ø USL
   (2) 400A 3Ø USR

FOLLOWSPOTS
House Followspots:
   (3) Super Trouper Xenon 2k

DIMMERS
(432) house dimmers
House has DMX control system
Dry run stations located all
   through house

SOUND
House has 800A undedicated
   power located USR & USL
FOH mixing position in
   Rear Orchestra
Sound console is available

THE SHUBERT PERFORMING ARTS CENTER

YEAR BUILT: 1914   YEAR RENOVATED: 1997

Theatre Location: 247 College Street, New Haven, CT 06510

Main Administrative Phone:	203-624-1825
Main Administrative Fax:	203-789-2286
E-mail:	shubert@shubert.com
Website:	www.shubert.com
Stage Door Phone:	203-492-3728
Backstage Pay Phone:	203-785-9951
Traveling Production Office Phone:	203-492-3883
Traveling Production Office Fax:	203-492-3879

THEATRE STAFF

President & CEO	Caroline Werth	203-624-1825
Booking	Brigitte Blachere	203-624-1825
Marketing	Robert Resnikoff	203-624-1825
Operations	Sheri Kaplan	203-624-1825
Group Sales	Susan Jacobson	203-624-1825

HOUSE CREW

General Manager	John Fisher	203-624-1825
Carpentry	Edward Mangini	203-624-1825
Electrics	David Reilly	203-624-1825
Sound	Thomas Quagliano	203-624-1825
Props	Nicholas Laudano	203-624-1825

UNIONS

IATSE Local #74	Edward Mangini	203-773-9139
Wardrobe Local #74	Donna Maher	203-773-9139
Music	William Whitaker	203-624-1825

SEATING CAPACITY

Orchestra	669
Mezzanine	512
Boxes	72
Balcony	396
Total:	**1,649**

BOX OFFICE

Computerized
Box Office Manager
  Susan Jacobson   203-624-1825

Outside Ticket Agency
Computerized
  Advantix   800-228-6622

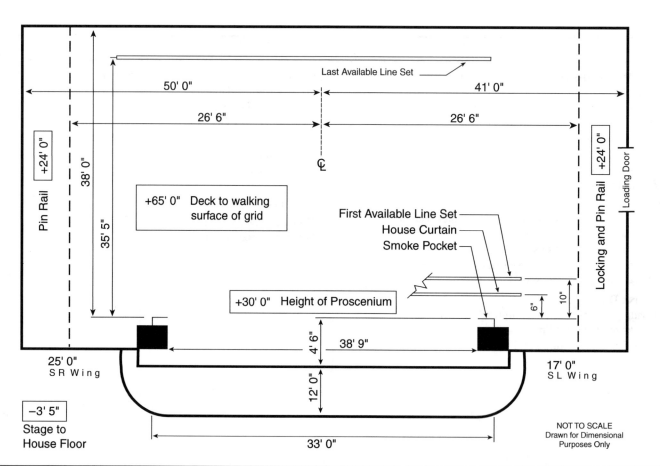

50' 0"
26' 6"   26' 6"
41' 0"
Last Available Line Set
₵
Pin Rail   +24' 0"
38' 0"
35' 5"
+65' 0" Deck to walking surface of grid
First Available Line Set
House Curtain
Smoke Pocket
Locking and Pin Rail   +24' 0"
Loading Door
6"   10"
+30' 0" Height of Proscenium
4' 6"   38' 9"
25' 0"
S R Wing
12' 0"
17' 0"
S L Wing
−3' 5"
Stage to House Floor
33' 0"
NOT TO SCALE
Drawn for Dimensional Purposes Only

STAGE HOUSE

HOUSE CURTAIN
Operates as a guillotine from SL deck

RIGGING SYSTEM
Type:	Combination purchase counter weight
Weight:	28,000 lbs available
Line sets:	48 sets at 9" o.c. with 5 lift lines per set
Arbors:	1,400 lb capacity
House Pipes:	50' long with 59' of travel from deck

Line sets are moveable
Block & Falls are available
Chain hoists are not available
(30) spot wheels and 6,000' of hemp available
Line sets #1-35 are single purchase and #36-48 are double purchase

PERMANENT INSTALLATIONS OVER STAGE (FROM SMOKE POCKET)
None

PERMANENT INSTALLATIONS ON DECK
Traps in stage floor are on a sectional grid

ORCHESTRA PIT
Nonadjustable at 7' below stage level
Apron overhangs US wall of pit 6'0"

BACKSTAGE

LOADING DOCK
Loading door(s):
10'0" high x 8'0" wide
Trucks load (1) at same time
Dock (loading door sill) is at street level accessed by an alley; trucks can load thru front of house as well
Fork lift is not required
Sound/Props can load in FOH
Lobby cannot be a work area
Trailers cannot store on-site
Security at stage door

WARDROBE
Location: Basement
Access: Elevator
(2) Washers (2) Dryer2

DRESSING ROOMS
(4) Star, basement, t/s included, phone jack
(2) Small, basement, toilet on same fl, phone jack
(4) Chorus, basement, toilet on same fl, phone jack
Elevator access for dressing rooms
Additional production office available for company mgr

SOUND

CONSOLE
Soundcraft 400B, located Rear Orchestra HL
16 inputs, 2 main outputs, 4 aux outputs

SPEAKERS
House Cluster
Proscenium
Under Balcony
Under Mezzanine
Balc fill / Side box fills
Lip speakers
No speaker truss

COMMUNICATIONS
Clear Com intercom with (2) channels
Infrared sound system
Dressing room page system

ROAD CONSOLE
Located Rear Orchestra
No seats required to be removed
Cable run from stage is 150'
Tie-in into house system with XLR connectors

REHEARSAL & STORAGE SPACE
Rehearsal: None
Storage: 45' x 25' located in trap room

ELECTRICS

ROAD SERVICE POWER

Panel	Phase	Amp	Circuit Protection	Use	Location
A-D	3	400	fuse	dimmers	SR side wall
E	3	100	breaker	sound	SR side wall

Recommended location of touring dimmer racks: SR
Hoist not required

FRONT OF HOUSE (BOX BOOM VALUES ARE PER SIDE)

Position	Pipe Width	Distance to Prosc.	House Circuits	Connector Type	FOH Transfer Circuits
1st Balc Rail	16'	40'	6	grd 20 amp stage pin	6
2nd Balc Rail	40'	50'	30	grd 20 amp stage pin	30
Box Boom 1		8'	8	grd 20 amp stage pin	8
Box Boom 2		70'	8	grd 20 amp stage pin	8

Transfer circuits: 20 amp stage pin transfer panel - SR wall

EQUIPMENT FOH (BOX BOOM VALUES ARE PER SIDE)

Position	Quantity	Wattage	Instrument	Removeable
2nd Balc Rail	30	575	Source 4 19°	yes
Box Boom 1	8	1,000	6 x 12 Leko	yes
Box Boom 2	8	575	Source 4 19°	yes

FOLLOWSPOTS
House Followspots:
(2) Xenon Super Troupers 2k; removeable

Followspot Booth:
(2) spots per booth;
70' throw to proscenium;
(3) 3Ø 20 amp breakers

DIMMERS
Lighting console is Obsession II;
(282) Strand CD80 dimmers
No dry run DMX station(s)

PALACE THEATRE

AT: STAMFORD CENTER FOR THE ARTS   **YEAR BUILT: 1927   YEAR RENOVATED: 1997**

Theatre Location: 61 Atlantic Street, Stamford, CT 06901
Management Company: Stamford Center for the Arts
                              307 Atlantic Street, Stamford, CT 06901

Main Administrative Phone: 203-358-2305
Main Administrative Fax: 203-358-2313
Website: www.onlyatsca.com
Stage Door Phone: 203-316-0810
Backstage Pay Phone: 203-327-8015
Traveling Production Office Phone: 203-316-0832
Traveling Production Office Fax: 203-316-0836

THEATRE STAFF
Executive Director   George Moredock   203-358-2305
Booking   George Moredock   203-358-2305
Marketing   Dawn Tucker   203-358-2305
Operations   John Huddlestone   203-325-9696
Group Sales   Nancy Coffin   203-358-2305

HOUSE CREW
Production Manager   Rich Franzino   203-462-5069 / Fax 203-356-7921
Carpentry   Randy Thomas   203-964-0133
Electrics   Daniel Kirsch   203-964-0133
Sound   Bill Gagliano   203-964-0133
Props   Tim Whitney   203-964-0133

UNIONS
IATSE Local #133   Randy Thomas   203-964-0133

SEATING CAPACITY
Orchestra	794
Balcony	786
Total:	**1,580**

wheelchair (add'l)	4
standing (add'l)	45

BOX OFFICE
Box Office Manager
   Linda Axelson   203-325-4466

Outside Ticket Agency
None

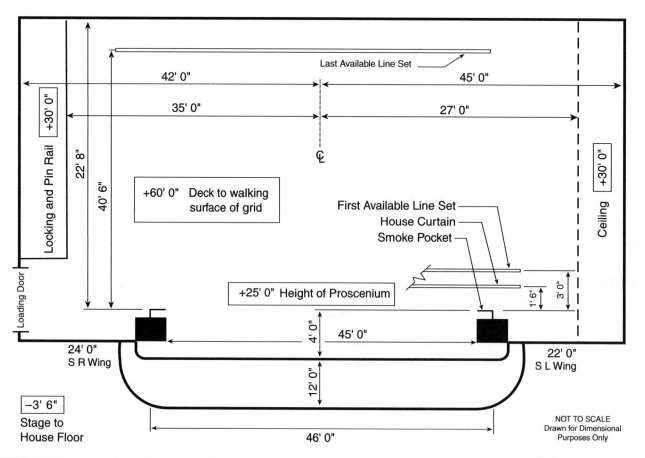

+60' 0"   Deck to walking surface of grid

+25' 0" Height of Proscenium

Last Available Line Set

First Available Line Set
House Curtain
Smoke Pocket

Locking and Pin Rail   +30' 0"

Ceiling   +30' 0"

Loading Door

42' 0"   45' 0"
35' 0"   27' 0"
22' 8"
40' 6"

4' 0"   45' 0"
12' 0"
46' 0"

24' 0" S R Wing
22' 0" S L Wing

1' 6"   3' 0"

−3' 6"
Stage to House Floor

NOT TO SCALE
Drawn for Dimensional Purposes Only

STAGE HOUSE

HOUSE CURTAIN
Operates as a guillotine from SR deck

RIGGING SYSTEM

Type:	Single purchase counter weight
Weight:	32,000 lbs available
Line sets:	40 sets at 6" o.c. with 5 lift lines per set
Arbors:	1,000 lb capacity
House Pipes:	52' long with 50' of travel from deck

Line sets are moveable; No line sets from 23'0" to 27'6"
Block & Falls are not available
Chain hoists are not available
(40) spot wheels and 3,000' of hemp available

PERMANENT INSTALLATIONS OVER STAGE (FROM SMOKE POCKET)
Orchestra shell (2) at 9'6", 18'6"
Dead spaces (1) at 23'0" to 27'6"
Fire curtain (1) at 0'0"

PERMANENT INSTALLATIONS ON DECK
Electric jump (2) 10'0" x 40'0" located +30 SL/SR
Pilasters (5) 2'0" x 2'0" located on back wall

ORCHESTRA PIT
Nonadjustable at 8' below stage level
Apron overhangs US wall of pit 9'0"

BACKSTAGE

LOADING DOCK
Loading door(s):
10'6" high x 8'4" wide
Trucks load (1) at same time
Dock is ground level in municipal parking lot; must clear usage with the city
Fork lift is not required
Sound/Props cannot load in FOH
Trailers cannot store on-site
Security at dock & stage door

WARDROBE
Location: Basement
Access: Stairs & elevator
(2) Washers (2) Dryers
No washer or dryer hookups

DRESSING ROOMS
(2) Star, SL, -1, t/s included, phone jack
Chorus, SL, -1, t/s included
Chorus, SR, -1, t/s included
Elevator access for dressing rooms
Additional production office available for company mgr

SOUND

CONSOLE
Mackie SR 32-4, located Rear House right
32 inputs, 2 main outputs, 6 aux outputs

SPEAKERS
House Cluster
Proscenium
Portable
No speaker truss

COMMUNICATIONS
Clear Com intercom with (2) channels
Infrared sound system
Dressing room page system

ROAD CONSOLE
Located Rear House right
No seats required to be removed
Cable run from stage is 200'
Tie-in into house system with XLR connectors

REHEARSAL & STORAGE SPACE
Rehearsal: None
Storage: None

ELECTRICS

ROAD SERVICE POWER

Panel	Phase	Amp	Circuit Protection	Use	Location
A	3	600	breaker	dimmers	DSL
B	3	200	breaker	sound	DSL

Recommended location of touring dimmer racks: SL wing
Hoist not required

FRONT OF HOUSE (BOX BOOM VALUES ARE PER SIDE)

Position	Pipe Width	Distance to Prosc.	House Circuits	Connector Type	FOH Transfer Circuits
Rear Balc Rail		90'	36	grd 20 amp stage pin	36
Box Boom 1		25'	24	grd 20 amp stage pin	24
Box Boom 2		55'	12	grd 20 amp stage pin	12
DS Pro Truss		3'	24	grd 20 amp stage pin	24

Transfer circuits: DMX interface

EQUIPMENT FOH (BOX BOOM VALUES ARE PER SIDE)

Position	Quantity	Wattage	Instrument	Removeable
Rear Balc Rail	30	1,000	6 x 22 Lekos	yes
Box Boom 1	16	1,000	6 x 12 Lekos (8), 6 x 16 (8)	yes
Box Boom 2	8	1,000	6 x 16 Lekos	yes

FOLLOWSPOTS
House Followspots:
(2) Explorer medium throw 1200w; removeable

Followspot Booth:
(2) spots per booth;
90' throw to proscenium;
1Ø 100 amp breakers

DIMMERS
House has lighting console (288) ETC L-86 and Strand CD80 dimmers
DMX control system

TRUGLIA THEATRE

AT: STAMFORD CENTER FOR THE ARTS IN THE RICH FORUM BUILDING   **YEAR BUILT: 1991**

Theatre Location: Rich Forum, 307 Atlantic Street, Stamford, CT 06901
Management Company: Stamford Center for the Arts

Main Administrative Phone:	203-358-2305
Main Administrative Fax:	203-358-2313
Website:	www.onlyatsca.com
Stage Door Phone:	203-358-2305
Backstage Pay Phone:	203-357-8672
Traveling Production Office Phone:	203-363-2733
Traveling Production Office Fax:	203-425-8142

SEATING CAPACITY
Orchestra	392
First Balcony	159
Second Balcony	160
Total:	**711**
pit (add'l)	46
wheelchair (add'l)	24
standing (add'l)	30

THEATRE STAFF
Executive Director	George Moredock	203-358-0205
Booking	George Moredock	203-358-0205
Marketing	Dawn Tucker	203-358-2305
Operations	John Hiddlestone	203-358-2305
Group Sales	Nancy Coffin	203-358-2305

HOUSE CREW
Production Manager	Rich Franzino	203-462-5069 / Fax 203-356-7921
Carpentry	Randy Thomas	203-425-8133
Electrics	Daniel Kirsch	203-425-8133
Sound	Bill Gagliano	203-425-8133
Props	Tim Whitney	203-425-8133

UNIONS
IATSE Local #133	Randy Thomas	203-964-0133

BOX OFFICE
Box Office Manager
  Linda Axelson   203-325-4466

Outside Ticket Agency
None

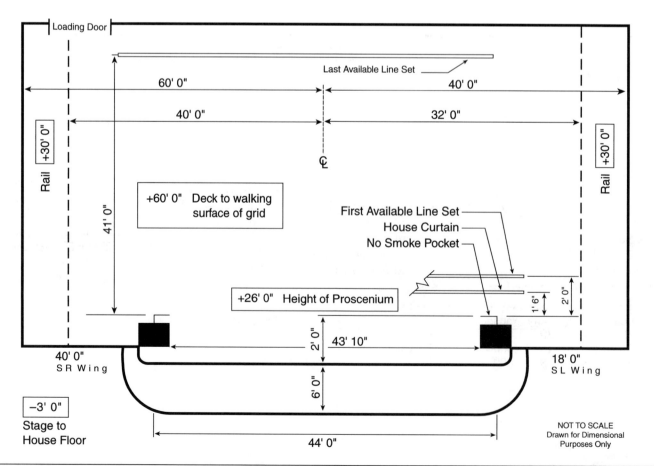

STAGE HOUSE

HOUSE CURTAIN
Operates as a guillotine

RIGGING SYSTEM
Type:	Single purchase counter weight
Weight:	25,000 lbs available
Line sets:	53 sets at 9" o.c. with 6 lift lines per set
Arbors:	1,000 lb capacity
House Pipes:	52' long with 50' of travel from deck

Line sets are moveable
Block & Falls are not available
Chain hoists are not available
Jumps 30' high SL + SR

PERMANENT INSTALLATIONS OVER STAGE (FROM SMOKE POCKET)
M=Moveable with advance call
Electric borders (6) at 2'0", 8'0", 14'9", 2'6", 27'6", 32'9"; M
Movie screen (1) at 7'3"
Electric pipe (7)
Cyclorama (1) at 41'0"

PERMANENT INSTALLATIONS ON DECK
Trap (1) 40'0" x 20'0" trap
Jumps (2) 30'0" high SL/ SR
Electric Jump (2) SL/ SR
Loading bridge (2)

ORCHESTRA PIT
Adjustable to 8' below stage level by electric motor turnscrew
Apron overhangs US wall of pit 6'0"
Pit lift is in (1) section

BACKSTAGE

LOADING DOCK
Loading door(s):
   9'0" high x 8'0" wide
Trucks load (1) at same time
Fork lift is not required
Sound/Props cannot load in FOH
Trailers cannot store on-site
Security at dock & stage door

WARDROBE
Location: Stage level
Access: Behind dressing rooms
(2) Washers (2) Dryers

DRESSING ROOMS
(1) Star, SR, stage level, t/s included, phone jack
(2) Small, SL, stage level, t/s included, phone jack
(2) Chorus, SL, stage level, t/s included
(2) Chorus, SR, stage level, t/s included
Additional production office available for company mgr

SOUND

CONSOLE
Delta 200 Soundcraft, located Booth Orchestra HR
24 inputs, LR main outputs, 4 aux outputs

SPEAKERS
House Cluster
Proscenium
Portable
Lobby
No speaker truss

COMMUNICATIONS
HME intercom with (2) channels
Infrared sound system
Dressing room page system

ROAD CONSOLE
Located Orchestra HR
(4) seats required to be removed
Cable run from stage is 150'
Tie-in into house system with XLR connectors

REHEARSAL & STORAGE SPACE
Rehearsal: None
Storage: None

ELECTRICS

ROAD SERVICE POWER

Panel	Phase	Amp	Circuit Protection	Use	Location
A-B	3	400	fuse	dimmers	Dimmer room 50' off DSR
C	3	100	fuse	dimmers	Dimmer room 50' off DSR
D	3	100	fuse	sound	USR wall

Recommended location of touring dimmer racks: DSR
Hoist not required

FRONT OF HOUSE (BOX BOOM VALUES ARE PER SIDE)

Position	Pipe Width	Distance to Prosc.	House Circuits	Connector Type	FOH Transfer Circuits
1st Balc Rail	55'	38'	21	grd 20 amp stage pin	
2nd Balc Rail	55'	38'	6	grd 20 amp stage pin	
1st Cove	55'	55'	24	grd 20 amp stage pin	
2nd Cove	55'	70'	24	grd 20 amp stage pin	
Box Boom 1		48'	12	grd 20 amp stage pin	
Apron Boom			8	grd 20 amp stage pin	

Transfer circuits: DMX interface

EQUIPMENT FOH (BOX BOOM VALUES ARE PER SIDE)

Position	Quantity	Wattage	Instrument	Removeable
2nd Balc Rail	20	1,000	6 x 16 360Q	yes
1st Cove	20	1,000	6 x 12 Altman KL	yes
2nd Cove	20	1,000	6 x 20 Altman KL	yes
Box Boom 1	6	1,000	6 x 16 360Q	

FOLLOWSPOTS
House Followspots:
   (1) Altman Med throw Explorer; removeable

Followspot Booth:
   (2) spots per booth;
   96' throw to proscenium;
   (1) 3Ø 100 amp breakers

DIMMERS
House lighting console is Obsession 600 ver 2.4;
(418) Colortran ENR 2.4k dimmers

THE PLAYHOUSE THEATRE

YEAR BUILT: 1913

Theatre Location: 10th & Market Street, DuPont Building
Wilmington, DE 19801

Main Administrative Phone:	302-774-2215
Main Administrative Fax:	302-594-1437
Website:	www.dupont.com/playhousetheater
Backstage Pay Phone:	302-652-9514

THEATRE STAFF

General Manager	Patricia L. Dill	302-774-2215
Booking	Patricia L. Dill	302-774-2215
Marketing	Sara Lu Schwartz	302-594-3111
Group Sales	Nancy U. McEwen	302-594-3280

HOUSE CREW

Technical Director	Terry A. Gray	302-594-3139
Carpentry	David Neel	302-594-3273
Electrics	Susan Miller	302-594-3269
Props	Yvonne King	

UNIONS

IATSE Local #284	Jarvis B. Wilsher	302-652-4626
Wardrobe Local #284	Jarvis B. Wilsher	302-652-4626
AFM Local #21	Harvey Price	302-429-5812

SEATING CAPACITY

Orchestra & Box Seats	608
Mezzanine	448
Balcony	195
Total:	**1,251**
wheelchair (add'l)	12
standing (add'l)	20

BOX OFFICE

Computerized
Treasurer
 Barbara E. Slavin   302-594-3166

Outside Ticket Agency
 None

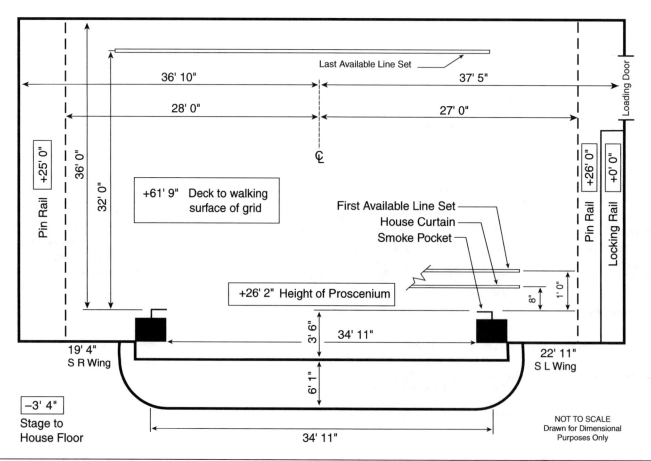

+61' 9" Deck to walking surface of grid

+26' 2" Height of Proscenium

Last Available Line Set

First Available Line Set
House Curtain
Smoke Pocket

Pin Rail +25' 0"

36' 0"
32' 0"

36' 10"   37' 5"
28' 0"   27' 0"

Loading Door

Pin Rail +26' 0"
Locking Rail +0' 0"

8"   1' 0"

3' 6"   34' 11"

19' 4"
S R Wing

6' 1"

22' 11"
S L Wing

−3' 4"
Stage to
House Floor

34' 11"

NOT TO SCALE
Drawn for Dimensional
Purposes Only

STAGE HOUSE

HOUSE CURTAIN
Operates as a guillotine from SL deck

RIGGING SYSTEM
Type: Single or double purchase counter weight
Weight: 45,000 lbs available
Line sets: 60 sets at 6" o.c. with 6 lift lines per set
Arbors: 1,000 lb capacity
House Pipes: 52' long with 56' of travel from deck
Line sets are moveable
Block & Falls are not available
Chain hoists are not available
(50) spot wheels and 1,500' of hemp available

PERMANENT INSTALLATIONS OVER STAGE (FROM SMOKE POCKET)
None

PERMANENT INSTALLATIONS ON DECK
Traps in stage floor (1) 6'0" by 9'0", USR
Stairs to orchestra from stage-portables
Radiators upstage back wall
Loading bridge just below grid steel

ORCHESTRA PIT
Nonadjustable at 7' below stage level

BACKSTAGE

LOADING DOCK
Loading door(s):
    10'0" high x 6'0" wide
Dock is approximately 150'
    from load-in door
Sound/Props can load in FOH
Trailers cannot store on-site;
    parking 3 miles away
Security at dock & stage door

WARDROBE
Location: Basement
Access: Trap in door
(2) Washers (2) Dryers
No washer or dryer hookups

DRESSING ROOMS
(7) Star, SR, +1, t/s included,
    phone jack
(2) Chorus, SR, +2, t/s included
(2) Chorus, SR, -2, t included
Additional production office
    available for company mgr

SOUND

CONSOLE
Yamaha
16 inputs, 4 main outputs

SPEAKERS
House Cluster
Proscenium
Under Balcony

COMMUNICATIONS
Clear Com intercom with
    (1) channel
Infrared sound system
Dressing room page system

ROAD CONSOLE
Located Rear House
No seats required to be
    removed
Cable run from stage is 130'
Tie-in into house system with
    XLR connectors

REHEARSAL & STORAGE SPACE
Rehearsal: Large room
    adjacent to hotel; piano
    available
Storage: 15' x 20', located in
    basement

ELECTRICS

ROAD SERVICE POWER

Panel	Phase	Amp	Circuit Protection	Use	Location
A-C	3	400	fuse	dimmers	DSL in basement
D	3	400	fuse	extra	DSR in basement
E	3	100	fuse	sound	DSL in basement

Recommended location of touring dimmer racks: DSL

FRONT OF HOUSE (BOX BOOM VALUES ARE PER SIDE)

Position	Pipe Width	Distance to Prosc.	House Circuits	Connector Type	FOH Transfer Circuits
1st Balc Rail	44'	33'	20	grd 20 amp stage pin	20
Box Boom 1		28'	10	grd 20 amp stage pin	10

EQUIPMENT FOH (BOX BOOM VALUES ARE PER SIDE)
None

FOLLOWSPOTS
House Followspots:
    (3) Xenon Super Troupers;
    removeable

Followspot Booth:
    (3) spots per booth;
    65' throw to proscenium;
    (3) 3Ø 30 amp breakers

DIMMERS
No house lighting console
No dimmers

EISENHOWER THEATER

AT: THE JOHN F. KENNEDY CENTER FOR THE PERFORMING ARTS   **YEAR BUILT: 1971   YEAR RENOVATED: 1997**

Theatre Location: 2700 F Street, NW, Washington, DC 20566

Main Administrative Phone:	202-416-8000
Main Administrative Fax:	202-416-8205
E-mail:	*name*@mail.kennedy-center.org
Website:	www.kennedy-center.org
Stage Door Phone:	202-416-8240
Backstage Pay Phone:	202-785-3363
Traveling Production Office Phone:	202-416-8241/43 / Fax: 416-8256

SEATING CAPACITY

Orchestra	772
Box Tier	64
Balcony	306
Total:	**1,142**
pit (add'l)	42
wheelchair (add'l)	
standing (add'l)	12

THEATRE STAFF

Theatre Manager	Edwin Blacker	202-416-8250 / Fax:416-8257
Booking	Elizabeth Thomas	202-416-8032
Marketing	Joanne Steller	202-416-8530
Group Sales	Karen McFadden	202-416-8400

HOUSE CREW

Director of Production	Mickey Berra	202-416-8704
Production Operations	Deirdre Lavrakas	202-416-8761
Production Project Mgr	Neil Fleitell	202-416-8239
Carpentry	Jerry Ryan	202-416-8251
Electrics	Mike Cassidy	202-416-8245
Sound	Ken Persson	202-416-8246
Props	Larry Barrett	202-416-8253

UNIONS

IATSE Local #22	J. Walter Cahill	301-593-4650
Wardrobe Local #772	Margaret Angus	703-979-1232
Music In-house	Jamie van der Vink	202-416-8215
Wigs Local #798	Kathy Waszkelewkz	301-610-7332

BOX OFFICE
Computerized
Box Office Manager
 Martha Locke Latta   202-416-8384

Outside Ticket Agency
None

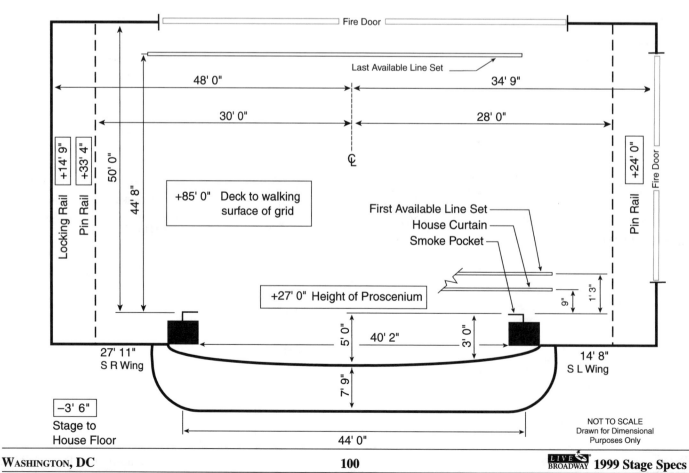

STAGE HOUSE

House Curtain
Operates as a guillotine from SR fly floor; motorized

Rigging System
Type:	Double purchase counter weight
Weight:	80,000 lbs available
Line sets:	76 sets at 6-12" o.c. with 5 lift lines per set
Arbors:	1,200 lb capacity
House Pipes:	45' long with 82' of travel from deck

Line sets are moveable
Block & Falls are available 2:1 (4); 3:3(1)
Chain hoists are available; (10) one ton, (14) half ton
(100) spot wheels and 16,000' of hemp available
60 spot blocks

Permanent Installations Over Stage (from smoke pocket)
None

Permanent Installations On Deck
Traps in stage floor are on a sectional grid
Loading bridge (2)

Orchestra Pit
Nonadjustable at 6' below stage level
Apron overhangs US wall of pit 6'6"

BACKSTAGE

Loading Dock
Loading door(s):
15'0" high x 13'9" wide
Trucks load (2) at same time
Loading door sill is at street level; loading to stage thru separate shop behind stage house; additional dock is below stage accessed by elevator (smaller trucks only)
Fork lift is not required; House owns
Sound/Props cannot load in FOH
Trailers cannot store on-site
Security at dock & stage door

Wardrobe
Location: Basement
Access: Direct from loadinng dock
(1) Washer (1) Dryer

Dressing Rooms
(1) Star, SR, same floor, toilet included
(10) Small, SR, -1, t/s included
(2) Chorus, SR, -1, t/s included
Elevator access for dressing rooms
Additional production office available for company mgr

SOUND

Console
Soundcraft Europa
36 inputs, 3 main outputs, 8 matrix outputs, 12 aux outputs

Speakers
House Cluster
Proscenium
Under Balcony
Portable
Speaker truss does not exist

Communications
Clear Com intercom with (12) channels
Infrared sound system
Dressing room page system

Road Console
Located Rear Orchestra
No seats required to be removed
Cable run from stage is 125'
Tie-in into house system with connectors

Rehearsal & Storage Space
Rehearsal: ERR 45' x 44'
2nd fl, sprung floor, piano, mirror;prior arrangement required
Storage: Backstage off SL; Backstage US

ELECTRICS

Road Service Power
Panel	Phase	Amp	Circuit Protection	Use	Location
A - F	3	400	fuse	dimmers	DSL Alcove
G	1	200	breaker	dimmers	DSL Alcove
H	3	100	breaker	sound	DSR Alcove
I	3	200	breaker	extra	Under stage

Recommended location of touring dimmer racks: Off SL
Hoist not required

Front Of House (box boom values are per side)
Position	Pipe Width	Distance to Prosc.	House Circuits	Connector Type	FOH Transfer Circuits
Truss	40'	20'	24	grd 20 amp stage pin	0
1st Balc Rail	70'	60'	36	grd 20 amp stage pin	0
Box Boom 1		34	12	grd 20 amp stage pin	0
Box Boom 2		60	12	grd 20 amp stage pin	0

Road truss: All FOH is dimmer per circuit, can be transfered to road control via response network controller

Equipment FOH (box boom values are per side)
Position	Quantity	Wattage	Instrument	Removeable
1st Balc Rail	24	575	Source 4 10°	yes
Box Boom 1	24	575	Source 4 19°	yes
Box Boom 2	36	575	Source 4 10°	yes

Followspots
House Followspots:
(4) Xenon Super Troupers; removeable

(2) Followspot Booths each with:
(2) spots per booth;
90' throw to proscenium;
(4) 1Ø 30 amp breakers

Dimmers
Lighting console is Obsession;
(654) Sensor 2.4kw dimmers
House has programmable DMX control system
(12) dry run DMX station(s)

NATIONAL THEATRE

YEAR BUILT: 1835 YEAR RENOVATED: 1984

Theatre Location: 1321 Pennsylvania Ave. NW, Washington, D.C. 20004
Management Company: The Shubert Organization
234 W. 44th Street, New York, NY 10036

Main Administrative Phone: 202-628-6161
Main Administrative Fax: 202-638-4830
Website: www.nationaltheatre.org
Stage Door Phone: 202-628-6165
Backstage Pay Phone: 202-638-9515

SEATING CAPACITY

Orchestra	821
Mezzanine	466
Balcony	346
Boxes	36
Total:	**1,669**
pit (add'l)	30
standing (add'l)	20

THEATRE STAFF

General Manager	Harry Teter	202-737-5987
Booking	Peter Entin	212-944-3700
Group Sales	LuAnne Origer	202-628-6166

HOUSE CREW

Carpentry	Hank Reynolds	202-628-6165 x40
Electrics	Fred Tepper	202-628-6165 x33
Sound	Chuck Clay	202-628-6165 x33
Props	Ricardo Whitson	202-628-6165 x29

UNIONS

IATSE Local #22	Walter Cahill	301-593-4650
Wardrobe Local #772	Margaret Angus	703-974-1232
Music Local #161-710	Ed Walters	301-279-9316

BOX OFFICE
Computerized
Box Office Treasurer
John Loomis   202-628-6165

Outside Ticket Agency
Computerized
Tele-charge   800-447-7400

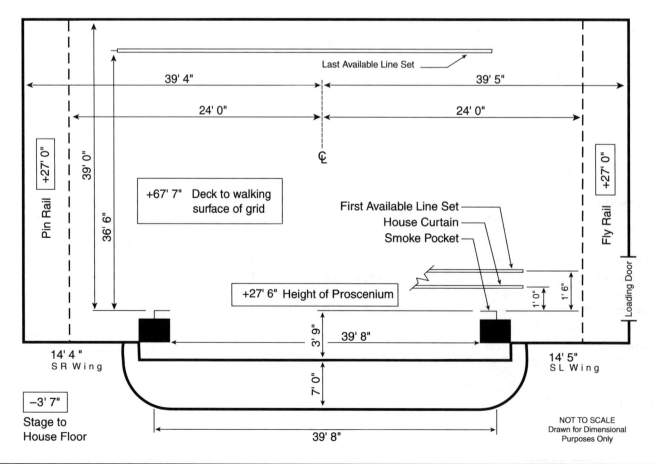

STAGE HOUSE

HOUSE CURTAIN
Operates as a guillotine from SL fly floor

RIGGING SYSTEM
Type:	Hemp System
Weight:	15,000 lbs available
Line sets:	68 sets at 5" o.c. with 5 lift lines per set
House Pipes:	48' long with 67' of travel from deck

Line sets are moveable
Block & Falls are available 2:1 (13); 3:2 (5)
Chain hoists are available as a rental; (2) one ton
(100) spot wheels and 5,000' of hemp available

PERMANENT INSTALLATIONS OVER STAGE (FROM SMOKE POCKET)
None

PERMANENT INSTALLATIONS ON DECK
Electric jump - SR, 14'2" x 37'0" @ + 31'0" on fly floor
Pilaster - US
Stairs - SR (crossover)

ORCHESTRA PIT
Nonadjustable at 7' below stage level
Apron overhangs US wall of pit 3'6"

BACKSTAGE

LOADING DOCK
Loading door(s):
9'0" high x 9'0" wide
Trucks load (2) max, at same time, with prior approval
Covered dock; theatre dock is at truck level; up ramp to stage house
Fork lift is not required; Supplier is Potomac Industrial Trucks (301) 336-1700
Sound/Props cannot load in FOH
Trailers cannot store on-site
Security at dock & stage door

WARDROBE
Location: Basement backstage
Access: Next to elevator
(2) Washers (2) Dryers
Washer and dryer hookups available

DRESSING ROOMS
(2) Star, SL, stage level, t/s included, phone jack
(11) Small, SL, +1,+2, t/s included
(8) Chorus, SL, +1,+2, t/s included
Elevator access for dressing rooms
Additional production office available for company mgr

SOUND

CONSOLE
No house console

SPEAKERS
Speaker truss exists
Max allowable load 1,500 lbs

COMMUNICATIONS
Infrared sound system
Dressing room page system

ROAD CONSOLE
Located Rear Orchestra right
(12) seats required to be removed
Cable run from stage is 150'
Tie-in into house system

REHEARSAL & STORAGE SPACE
Rehearsal: 38' x 18', low ceiling, mirror & piano
Storage: None

ELECTRICS

ROAD SERVICE POWER

Panel	Phase	Amp	Circuit Protection	Use	Location
A	3	400	fuse	dimmers	SR on jump
B-F	3	400	fuse	extra	SR on jump
G	3	100	breaker	sound	SR on side wall
H	3	100	fuse	sound	SL on side wall

Recommended location of touring dimmer racks: Fly floor Right
Hoist required and provided

FRONT OF HOUSE (BOX BOOM VALUES ARE PER SIDE)

Position	Pipe Width	Distance to Prosc.	House Circuits	Connector Type	FOH Transfer Circuits
Mezzanine Rail	50'	36'7"	40	grd 20 amp stage pin	40
1st Balc Rail	50'	45'9"	39	grd 20 amp stage pin	39
Box Boom 1		42'3"	12	grd 20 amp stage pin	12
Box Boom 2		42'3"	12	grd 20 amp stage pin	12

Transfer circuits: grd 20 amp stage pin
Road truss: 40' truss over orchestra

EQUIPMENT FOH (BOX BOOM VALUES ARE PER SIDE)
None
Circuits only supplied

FOLLOWSPOTS
House Followspots:
None

Followspot Booth:
(4) spots per booth;
95' throw to proscenium;
(4) 3Ø 30 amp breakers

DIMMERS
No lighting console
No dimmers
No DMX control system

OPERA HOUSE

AT: THE JOHN F. KENNEDY CENTER FOR THE PERFORMING ARTS   **YEAR BUILT: 1971   YEAR RENOVATED: 1984**

Theatre Location: 2700 F Street, N.W., Washington, D.C. 20566-0001

Main Administrative Phone: 202-416-8000
Main Administrative Fax: 202-416-8205
E-mail: *name*@mail.kennedy-center.org
Website: www.kennedy-center.org
Stage Door Phone: 202-416-8159
Backstage Pay Phone: 202-785-0845
Traveling Production Office Phone: 202-416-8160
Traveling Production Office Fax: 202-416-8163

THEATRE STAFF

Theatre Manager	Richard W. Kidwell	202-416-8181
Booking	Elizabeth Thomas	202-416-8032
Marketing	Joanne Steller	202-416-8530
Operations	Carol Mangano	202-416-8480
Group Sales	Karen McFadden	202-416-8400

HOUSE CREW

Director of Production	Mickey Berra	202-416-8704
Production Operations	Deirdre Lavrakas	202-416-8761
Production Project Mgr	Neil Fleitell	202-416-8239
Carpentry	Buddy Reed	202-785-0845
Electrics	George Kerig	202-785-0845
Sound	Dennis Roe	202-785-0845

UNIONS

IATSE Local #22	J. Walter Cahill	301-593-4650
Wardrobe Local #772	Margaret Angus	703-979-1232
Music In-house	Jamie van der Vink	202-416-8215
Wigs	Kathy Waszkelewkz	301-610-7332

SEATING CAPACITY

Orchestra	1,214
Boxes	96
First Tier	434
Second tier	402
Total:	**2,146**
pit (add'l)	160
standing (add'l)	40

BOX OFFICE
Computerized
Box Office Manager
   Martha Locke Latta   202-416-8384

Outside Ticket Agency
   None

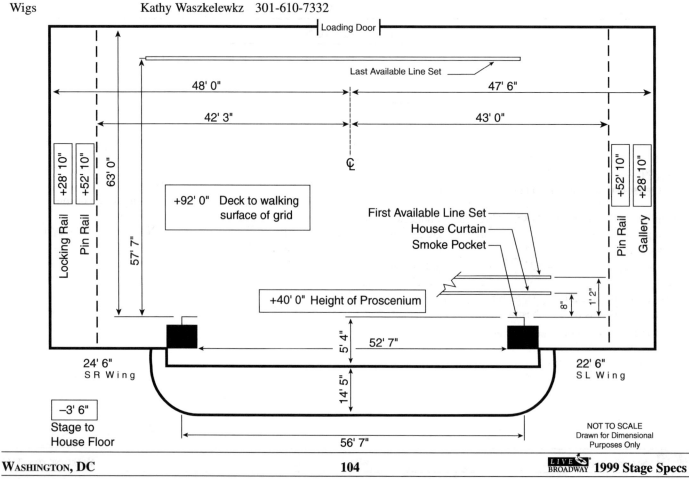

STAGE HOUSE

HOUSE CURTAIN
Operates as a guillotine from SR deck

RIGGING SYSTEM
Type:	Double purchase counter weight
Weight:	100,000 lbs available
Line sets:	106 sets at 6" o.c. with 6 lift lines per set
Arbors:	3,000 lb capacity
House Pipes:	60' long with 87' of travel from deck

Line sets are not moveable
Block & Falls are available 2:1 (3)
(125) spot wheels and 24,000' of hemp available

PERMANENT INSTALLATIONS OVER STAGE (FROM SMOKE POCKET)
Electric bridge (1) at 3'6" (30" wide)

PERMANENT INSTALLATIONS ON DECK
Traps in stage floor are on a sectional grid

ORCHESTRA PIT
Adjustable to 13' below stage level by hydraulic lift
Apron overhangs US wall of pit 3'3"

BACKSTAGE

LOADING DOCK
Loading door(s):
  14'4" high x 9'7"wide
Trucks load (2) at same time
Dock (2) are at street level, loading to stage thru separate loading bay behind stage house
Fork lift is required; house owns
Sound/Props cannot load in FOH
Security at dock & stage door

WARDROBE
Location: Basement
Access: Freight elevator
(2) Washers (2) Dryers

DRESSING ROOMS
(2) Star, SR / SL, stage, t/s included, phone jack
(12) Small, SL, basement, t/s on same fl, phone jack
(7) Chorus, SL, basement, t/s on same fl, phone jack
(2) Chorus, basement, t/s on same fl, phone jack
Elevator access for dressing rooms
Additional production office available for company mgr

SOUND

CONSOLE
Yamaha 1532
32 inputs, 8 main outputs

SPEAKERS
House Cluster
Proscenium
Under Balcony
Speaker truss is equipped with house speakers & can accomodate road equipment
Max allowable load 1,000 lbs

COMMUNICATIONS
Clear Com intercom with (8) channels
Infrared sound system
Dressing room page system

ROAD CONSOLE
Located Rear House
No seats required to be removed
Cable run from stage is 250'
Tie-in into house system with XLR connectors

REHEARSAL & STORAGE SPACE
Rehearsal: 70' x 40' located SR on 2nd floor Pianos available
Storage: Located US behind stage house

ELECTRICS

ROAD SERVICE POWER

Panel	Phase	Amp	Circuit Protection	Use	Location
A	3	800	breaker	dimmers	DSR in alcove
B	3	800	breaker	extra	DSR in alcove
C	3	100	breaker	sound	Rear of HR

Recommended location of touring dimmer racks: DSR on deck
Hoist not required

FRONT OF HOUSE (BOX BOOM VALUES ARE PER SIDE)

Position	Pipe Width	Distance to Prosc.	House Circuits	Connector Type	FOH Transfer Circuits
1st Balc Rail	24'	85'	12	grd 20 amp stage pin	12
1st Cove	50'	100'	40	grd 20 amp stage pin	40
Box Boom 1		20'	10	grd 20 amp stage pin	10
Box Boom 2		30'	10	grd 20 amp stage pin	10

Transfer circuits: Transfer circuits: grd 20 amp stage pin located DSR in alcove

EQUIPMENT FOH (BOX BOOM VALUES ARE PER SIDE)

Position	Quantity	Wattage	Instrument	Removeable
1st Balc Rail	40	1,000	8 x 13 Lekos	yes
1st Cove	12	1,000	10 x 23 Lekos	yes
Box Boom 1	10	1,000	8 x 13 Lekos	yes
Box Boom 2	10	1,000	8 x 13 Lekos	yes

FOLLOWSPOTS
House Followspots:
  (3) Xenon Super Troupers

Followspot Booth:
  (3) spots per booth;
  125' throw to proscenium;
  3Ø 200 amp breakers

DIMMERS
House console is Obsession; ETC dimmers
House has programmable DMX control system
(8) dry run DMX station(s).

WARNER THEATRE

YEAR BUILT: 1924   YEAR RENOVATED: 1992

Theatre Location: 513 13th Street, Washington, DC 20004
Management Company: Warner Theatre Operating Group
                         1299 Pennsylvania Avenue NW, Suite111
                         Washington, DC 20004-2405

Main Administrative Phone:	202-626-8250
Main Administrative Fax:	202-783-0204
E-mail:	wtog@erols.com
Website:	www.warnertheatre.com
Stage Door Phone:	202-626-8281
Traveling Production Office Phone:	202-626-8282
Traveling Production Office Fax:	202-626-8283

THEATRE STAFF

General Manager	Jane Podgurski	202-626-8251
Booking	Barrett Newman	202-626-8255
Marketing	Christine Newman	202-626-8271
Operations	Mark J. Grabowski	202-626-8260
Group Sales		202-626-8257

HOUSE CREW

Production Manager	Ronald Avey	202-626-8265
Carpentry	Jerry King	202-626-8265
Electrics	Gary Pair	
Sound	D.C. Valentine/Jake Williams	

UNIONS

IATSE Local #22	J. Walter Cahill	301-593-4650
Wardrobe Local #722	Margarite Angus	202-825-3055
AFM	Clarence Knight	301-283-3833

SEATING CAPACITY

Orchestra	988
Mid Balcony	440
Upper Balcony	370
Total:	**1,798**
pit (add'l)	33
wheelchair (add'l)	16

BOX OFFICE

Computerized
Box Office Manager
   Winfrey Brown   202-626-8256

Outside Ticket Agency
Computerized
Ticketmaster
   Winfrey Brown   202-626-8256

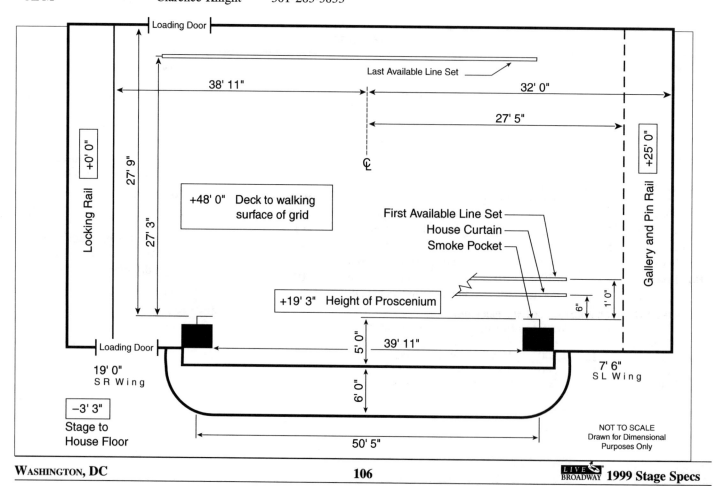

STAGE HOUSE

HOUSE CURTAIN
Operates as a guillotine from SR fly floor or deck

RIGGING SYSTEM
Type:	Single purchase counter weight
Weight:	40,000 lbs available
Line sets:	53 sets at 6" o.c. with 5 lift lines per set
Arbors:	1,000 lb capacity
House Pipes:	52' long with 43' of travel from deck

Line sets are moveable
Chain hoists are available as a rental; (1) one ton
(10) spot wheels and 1,000' of hemp available
No FOH rigging points

PERMANENT INSTALLATIONS OVER STAGE (FROM SMOKE POCKET)
None

PERMANENT INSTALLATIONS ON DECK
Jump (1), 15'0" x 12'0"
Electric jump (1) at 25'0 x 16'0" located at SL
Stairs (1) 3' wide located at SL, 6'0" to US edge of pocket
Columns (2), 2'0" x 2'0", 8'0" and 15'0" to US pocket
Loading bridge (1) full US to DS, 19'0" to US pocket

ORCHESTRA PIT
Adjustable to 8' below stage level by platform decking
Apron overhangs US wall of pit 6'0"
Pit lift is in (9) sections

BACKSTAGE

LOADING DOCK
Loading door(s):
8'3" high x 6'0" wide
Trucks load in (1) at a time, (2) for load-out
Load-in w/nose in 1st only, no truck parking, load-out 2 trucks w/ nose in 1st then tail in 1st; all ground level loading area, dead case storage available in the dock
Fork lift is not required
Sound/Props can load in FOH
Trailers cannot store on-site
Security at dock & stage door

WARDROBE
Location: 2 levels below dock
Access: Stairs & elevator
(2) Washers (2) Dryers
No washer or dryer hookups

DRESSING ROOMS
(2) Star, SR, stage level, t/s included, phone jack
(4) Small, SR, stage level, +1, t/s on same fl, phone jack
(3) Chorus, -2, t/s included, phone jack
Elevator access for dressing rooms
Additional production office available for company mgr

SOUND

CONSOLE
Ramsa WR5852, located FOH
52 channel inputs, 18 main outputs

SPEAKERS
House Cluster
Under Balcony
Portable
No speaker truss

COMMUNICATIONS
Telex intercom with (2) channels
Infrared sound system
Dressing room page system

ROAD CONSOLE
Located Rear House
No seats required to be removed
Cable run from stage is 120'
Tie-in into house system

REHEARSAL & STORAGE SPACE
Rehearsal: None
Stage is the only rehearsal space, some orchestra rehearsals can be done in main lobby
Storage:
Loading dock, 15' x 25'
Wardrobe, 15' x 15'

ELECTRICS

ROAD SERVICE POWER
Panel	Phase	Amp	Circuit Protection	Use	Location
A	3	400	fuse	extra	USR
B	3	200	fuse	extra	USL
C	3	100	fuse	extra	DS off R
D	3	600	fuse	dimmers	dimmer gallery

Recommended location of touring dimmer racks: Jump SL
Hoist is required and provided
Additional power is available for tour buses, generators, etc.

FRONT OF HOUSE (BOX BOOM VALUES ARE PER SIDE)
None

EQUIPMENT FOH (BOX BOOM VALUES ARE PER SIDE)
Position	Quantity	Wattage	Instrument	Removeable
1st Balc Rail	16	1,000	Leko	no
1st Perch SL	28	1,000	Leko	no
Box Boom 1	12	1,000	Leko	no
Box Boom 2	12	1,000	Leko	no

FOLLOWSPOTS
House Followspots:
(3) Xenon Super Trouper; removeable
Voyager 400 HTI2; not removeable

Followspot Booth:
(3) spots per booth;
110' throw to proscenium;
(3) 1Ø 20 amp breakers

DIMMERS
Lighting console is Colortran Compact Elite;
(300) Colortran ENR dimmers
House has programmable DMX control system and AMX

RUTH ECKERD HALL

AT: RICHARD B. BAUMGARDNER CENTER FOR THE PERFORMING ARTS   **YEAR BUILT: 1984**

Theatre Location: 1111 McMullen Booth Road, Clearwater, FL 33759
Management Company: PACT, Inc.

Main Administrative Phone:	727-791-7060
Main Administrative Fax:	727-724-5976
Backstage Pay Phone:	727-791-9025

SEATING CAPACITY

Orchestra	2,112
Total:	**2,112**
pit (add'l)	61

THEATRE STAFF

Executive Director	Robert Freedman	727-712-2704
General Manager/CFO	Bill Ross	727-712-2762
Booking	Bob Rossi	727-712-7060
Marketing	Lex Poppens	727-712-7060
Group Sales	Glenda Young	727-712-7060

HOUSE CREW

Technical Director	Jeffrey L. Hartzog	727-712-2710
Electrics	Dustin Adams	727-791-7060
Sound	Bill Camillo	727-791-7060

UNIONS

IATSE Local #321	Paul Paleveda	727-877-2788
Wardrobe Local #321	Paul Paleveda	727-877-2788
Music In House	Bob Rossi	727-712-7060 x309

BOX OFFICE
  Hard Ticket
  Box Office Administrator
    Susan Crockett   727-712-2757

  Outside Ticket Agency
  Ticketmaster   800-755-6244

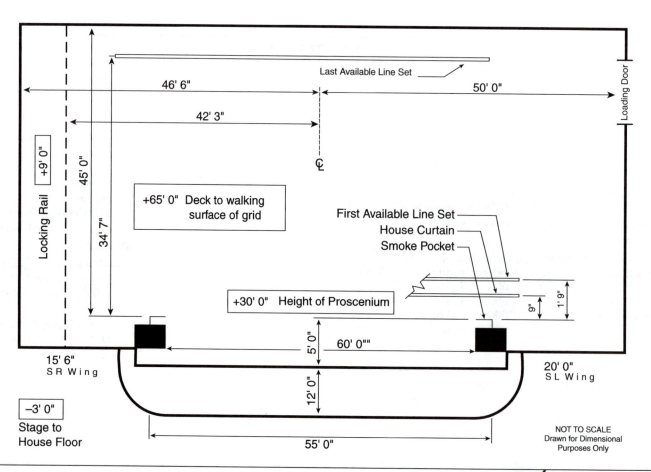

STAGE HOUSE

HOUSE CURTAIN
Operates as a guillotine from SL deck

RIGGING SYSTEM
Type: Double purchase counter weight
Weight: 40,000 lbs available
Line sets: 55 sets at 7" o.c. with 8 lift lines per set
Arbors: 1,500 lb capacity
House Pipes: 74' long with 60' of travel from deck
Line sets are moveable
Block & Falls are available 3: 2 (2)
Chain hoists are available as rental, (2) one ton
(20) spot wheels and 4,000' of hemp available

PERMANENT INSTALLATIONS OVER STAGE (FROM SMOKE POCKET)
M=Moveable with advance call
Orchestra shells (1) flown against back wall 8'0" deep
Electric Raceways (6) at 3'9", 9'4", 13'5", 19'3", 25'8", 32'8"
Traveller (1) at 16'4"; M
Cyclorama (1) at 34'5"
Fire curtain (1) at 0'4"
House curtain (1) at 1'11"

PERMANENT INSTALLATIONS ON DECK
Stairs (2), DS corners of stage to audience
Orchestra shell storage (1), 60'x 8', against US wall - flown
Loading bridge (2) SR, 51' & 59' above stage
Adjustable Tymparium, 30' raised - 20' lowered
Adjustable portal, 1 each side, 8' portal panel on each side reduces proscenium to 44'6"

ORCHESTRA PIT
Adjustable to 20' below stage level by hydraulic lift
Apron overhangs US wall of pit 8'0"
Pit lift is in (1) section

BACKSTAGE

LOADING DOCK
Loading door(s): 12'0" high x 12'0" wide
Trucks load (2) at same time
Dock is at truck level and is equipped with levelling plates; loading to stage thru separate loading area
Fork lift is not required
Sound/Props cannot load in FOH
(6) Trailers can store on-site
Security at dock & stage door

WARDROBE
Location: Hall US on stage level
Access: Via dressing rooms
(1) Washer (1) Dryer
Washer and dryer hookups available

DRESSING ROOMS
(1) Star, SR, stage level, t/s included, phone jack
(5) Small, SR & SL, stage level, t/s included, phone jack
(2) Chorus rooms, SR & SL, stage level, t/s included
(2) Chorus rooms, SR & SL, stage level, t/s same fl
Additional production office available for company mgr

SOUND

CONSOLE
Soundtrac - Megas Stage, located House Left
40 inputs, 8 main outputs, 8 matrix outputs, 6 aux outputs

SPEAKERS
House Cluster
Proscenium
Portable
No speaker truss

COMMUNICATIONS
Clear Com intercom with (2) channels
FM hearing augmentation
Dressing room page system

ROAD CONSOLE
Located Rear House
(9) seats required to be removed
Cable run from stage is 250'
Tie-in into house system with XLR connectors

REHEARSAL & STORAGE SPACE
Rehearsal: 35' x 20', behind stage on 2nd floor, piano, mirrors, ballet barres
Storage: 50' x 30', under stage, pit lowered

ELECTRICS

ROAD SERVICE POWER

Panel	Phase	Amp	Circuit Protection	Use	Location
A	3	400	fuse	dimmers	SL side wall
B	3	400	fuse	extra	SL side wall
C	3	100	fuse	sound	SL loading dock
D	3	400	fuse	extra	SR upstage wall

Recommended location of touring dimmer racks: SL on deck
Hoist not required
Additional 100 amps are available located in loading area approx. 70' from stage

FRONT OF HOUSE (BOX BOOM VALUES ARE PER SIDE)

Position	Pipe Width	Distance to Prosc.	House Circuits	Connector Type	FOH Transfer Circuits
1st Cove	60'	65'	40	grd 20 amp stage pin	40
Box Boom 1		24'	12	grd 20 amp stage pin	12

Transfer circuits: grd 20 amp stage pin located on SL side wall
Road truss: Full rigging capabilities above fly system.

EQUIPMENT FOH (BOX BOOM VALUES ARE PER SIDE)

Position	Quantity	Wattage	Instrument	Removeable
1st Cove	6	1,000	6 x 22 Lekos	yes
Box Boom 1	40	750	6 x 16 Lekos	yes
Box Boom 1	6	750	6 x 12 Lekos	yes

FOLLOWSPOTS
House Followspots:
(2) Colortran Xenon 2k; not removeable
(2) Kupo Xenon 1k; not removeable

Followspot Booth:
(1) spots per booth;
120' throw to proscenium;
(2) 3Ø 60 amp breakers

DIMMERS
House console is Colortran Encore 48 / 96;
(276) Strand dimmers
House has programmable DMX control system
(1) dry run DMX station(s).

CORAL SPRINGS CITY CENTRE

YEAR BUILT: **1990**   YEAR RENOVATED: **1996**

Theatre Location: 2855 Coral Springs Dr., Coral Springs, FL 33065
Management Company: Professional Facilities Management
220 Weybosset St., Providence, RI 02901

Main Administrative Phone: 954-344-5999
Main Administrative Fax: 954-344-5980

THEATRE STAFF
General Manager   Kelley Shanley   954-344-5999

HOUSE CREW
Technical Manager   Chris Young   954-346-1264

SEATING CAPACITY

Orchestra	930
Lower Balcony	286
Upper Balcony	222
Total:	**1,438**
wheelchair (add'l)	18

STAGE DIMENSIONS (FROM SMOKE POCKET)
Stage is 25'6" deep
Width from Center Line to SL is 39'0"
Width from Center Line to SR is 32'0"
Proscenium width is 48'0"
Proscenium height is 24'0"
Smoke pocket to apron edge is 3'6"
Orchestra pit exists

RIGGING

Grid Height:	52'
Type:	Single purchase counter weight
Weight:	10,000 lbs
Line sets:	24 sets at 8" o.c.
Arbors:	1,500 lb capacity
House Pipes:	50' long

LOADING DOCK
Loading door(s) are 9'6" high x 9'6" wide
Trucks load (1) at a time
Fork lift is not required and is not available

ELECTRICS
Total power available:
(2) 100A 3Ø SR
200A 3Ø SR
400A 3Ø SR

FOLLOWSPOTS
House Followspots:
Ultra Arc
Power in spot booth

DIMMERS
(96) house dimmers
House has DMX control system

SOUND
House has 100A dedicated
power located SR
FOH mixing position in
Rear Orchestra
Sound console is available

BROWARD CENTER FOR THE PERFORMING ARTS

AKA: AU-RENE THEATRE

YEAR BUILT: 1991

Theatre Location: 201 Southwest Fifth Avenue, Fort Lauderdale, FL 33312
Management Company: Performing Arts Center Authority
(address as above)

Main Administrative Phone:	954-522-5334
Main Administrative Fax:	954-462-3541
Website:	www.curtainup.org
Stage Door Phone:	954-468-3323
Backstage Pay Phone:	954-467-1134
Traveling Production Office Phone:	954-468-3291
Traveling Production Office Fax:	954-468-3310

THEATRE STAFF
President	Mark Nerenhausen	954-468-3299
General Manager	Bill Hammond	954-468-3295
Marketing	Linda Potenza	954-468-2692
Operations	Judy Joseph	954-468-3312

HOUSE CREW
Technical Director	Shelly Bradshaw	954-468-3313
Production Assistant	Lorin Fleisher	954-468-3317

UNIONS
IATSE Local #646	Alice Rennie	954-463-6175
Wardrobe Local #646	Alice Rennie	954-463-6175

SEATING CAPACITY
Lower Orchestra	705
Upper Orchestra	688
Mezzanine	553
Balcony	628
Total:	**2,574**
pit (add'l)	114
wheelchair (incl.)	52
standing (add'l)	32

BOX OFFICE
Computerized
Treasurer
  Alison Peters   954-468-3338

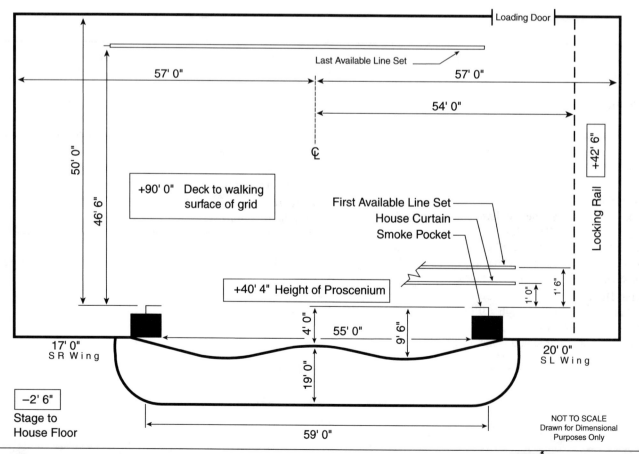

Loading Door

Last Available Line Set

57' 0"   57' 0"

54' 0"

+42' 6"

50' 0"

46' 6"

Locking Rail

+90' 0" Deck to walking surface of grid

First Available Line Set
House Curtain
Smoke Pocket

+40' 4" Height of Proscenium

1' 0" 1' 6"

4' 0" 55' 0" 9' 6"

17' 0"
SR Wing

20' 0"
SL Wing

19' 0"

−2' 6"
Stage to
House Floor

59' 0"

NOT TO SCALE
Drawn for Dimensional
Purposes Only

STAGE HOUSE

HOUSE CURTAIN
Operates as a guillotine from SR deck

RIGGING SYSTEM
Type:	Single purchase counter weight
Weight:	60,000 lbs available
Line sets:	87 sets at 6" o.c. with 6 lift lines per set
Arbors:	1,200 lb capacity
House Pipes:	63' long with 87' of travel from deck

Line sets are moveable
Block & Falls are not available
Chain hoists are available as a rental; (4) one ton
(30) spot wheels and 6000' of hemp available

PERMANENT INSTALLATIONS OVER STAGE (FROM SMOKE POCKET)
M=Moveable with advance call
Orchestra shell (3) at 5'4", 14'4", 20'3"
Electric raceways (1) 2'6"; M
Hard portal (1) at 1'2"

PERMANENT INSTALLATIONS ON DECK
Traps (1) in stage floor 4'6" x 2'6"
Hard legs (1) 10'0" x 40'0"
Orchestra shell storage (1) 94'0" x 10'0"
Loading bridge (1) 50'0" x 6'0"

ORCHESTRA PIT
Adjustable to 9' below stage level by Llambda scissor lift
Apron overhangs US wall of pit 7'0"
Pit lift is in (1) section

BACKSTAGE

LOADING DOCK
Loading door(s):
  8'0" high x 12'0" wide
Trucks load (2) at same time
Fork lift is not required
Sound/Props can load in FOH
Lobby can be a work area
(5) Trailers can store on-site
Security at stage door

WARDROBE
Location: Backstage
Access: Security or loading
  dock
(2) Washers (2) Dryers
Washer and dryer hookups
  available

DRESSING ROOMS
(2) Star, SR, stage level, t/s,
  phone jack
(4) Small, SR, stage level, t/s,
  phone jack
(6) Chorus, SR, stage level, t/s
Additional production office
  available for company mgr

SOUND

CONSOLE
Ramsa WRS 852, located
  booth or house
42 inputs, 8 matrix outputs,
  10 aux outputs

SPEAKERS
House Cluster
Proscenium
Under Balcony
Portable and Floor monitor
Speaker truss exists
Max available load 2,000 lbs
Holes in ceiling over house
  provide additional hanging
  positions

COMMUNICATIONS
Clear Com intercom with
  (4) channels
Infrared sound system
Dressing room page system

ROAD CONSOLE
Located Center Orchestra in
  sound control room
(12) seats required to be
  removed
Cable run from stage is 175'

REHEARSAL & STORAGE SPACE
(3) Rehearsal: New River,
  74'x54', 2nd fl, mirrors,
  barres, sprung floor;
  Einstein, 36'x18', 1st fl;
  Green Room, 38'8" x
  16'10", 1st fl, mirrors,
  barres, wood floor
Storage: None

ELECTRICS

ROAD SERVICE POWER
Panel	Phase	Amp	Circuit Protection	Use	Location
A	3	400	breaker	dimmers	DSL
B	3	400	breaker	dimmers	USL
C	3	100	breaker	sound	DSR
D	3	100	breaker	dimmers	DSL
E	3	100	breaker	dimmers	USR
F	3	100	breaker	dimmers	USL

Recommended location of touring dimmer racks: DSL; Hoist not required
Additional power is available for tour buses, generators, etc

FRONT OF HOUSE (BOX BOOM VALUES ARE PER SIDE)
Position	Pipe Width	Distance to Prosc.	House Circuits	Connector Type	FOH Transfer Circuits
Mezz Rail		92'	33	grd 20 amp stage pin	
1st Cove	94'	65'	52	grd 20 amp stage pin	
2nd Cove	94'	18'	39	grd 20 amp stage pin	
Box Boom 1		66'	12	grd 20 amp stage pin	
Prosc Boom		55'	12	grd 20 amp stage pin	

EQUIPMENT FOH (BOX BOOM VALUES ARE PER SIDE)
Position	Quantity	Wattage	Instrument	Removeable
Mezz Rail	36	1,000	5-10°, 5-15°, 36-20° Colortran	yes
Far Cat	46	1,000	5° Colortran	yes
Box Boom 1	20	1,000	20-20°, 6-40° Colortran	yes
Prosc Torm	9	1,000	3-20°, 6-40° Colortran	yes

FOLLOWSPOTS
House Followspots:
  (4) Xenon Super Trouper
  2k; not removeable

Followspot Booth:
  (4) spots per booth;
  190', 55° angle throw to
  proscenium;
  3Ø 30 amp breakers

DIMMERS
Lighting console is ETC
  Impression 2x;
  (546) Colortran dimmers
House has programmable
  DMX control system
Plugging stations DSL

PARKER PLAYHOUSE

YEAR BUILT: **1967**   RENOVATION ONGOING

Theatre Location: 707 NE 8th Street, Ft. Lauderdale, FL 33304
Mailing Address: PO Box 4603, Ft. Lauderdale, FL 33338
Management Company: PTG - Florida, Inc.
                                    100 South Beseigne Blvd. Suite 1200, Miami, FL 33131

Main Administrative Phone: 954-764-1441
Main Administrative Fax: 954-463-5180
Stage Door Phone: 954-764-1476
Backstage Pay Phone: 954-522-9423

THEATRE STAFF
General Manager   John Poland   305-379-2700
Marketing   Alexai Perez   305-379-2700
Group Sales   Ron Legler   800-647-6877
Theatre Manager   954-764-1441

HOUSE CREW
Technical Director   Casey Clark   561-416-2027
Carpentry   Anthony Bertolami   954-763-7002 x7049
Electrics   Open   954-763-7002
Sound   Hugh Foote   954-763-7002
Props   Constance Jonas   954-763-7002
Wardrobe   Joanne Wenger   954-763-7002

UNIONS
IATSE Local #646   Alice Rennie   954-463-6175
Music   Bob Persi   954-434-2856

SEATING CAPACITY
Orchestra   1,181
Total: **1,181**

wheelchair (add'l)   29

BOX OFFICE
Computerized
Box Office Manager
   Arthur Prosser 954-763-7002 x7036

Outside Ticket Agency
Computerized
Ticketmaster

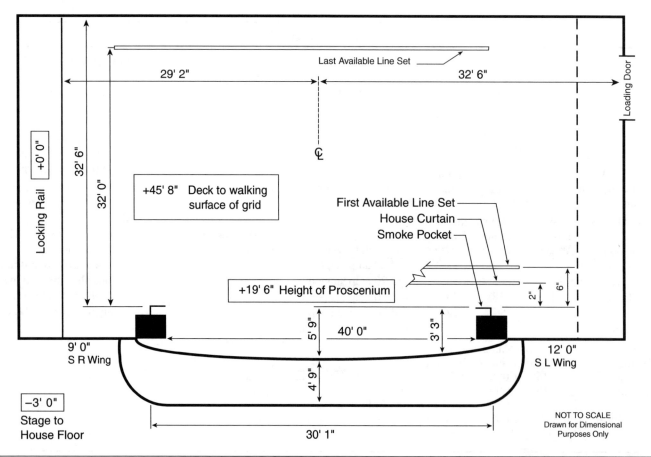

FORT LAUDERDALE, FLORIDA   114   LIVE BROADWAY 1999 Stage Specs

STAGE HOUSE

HOUSE CURTAIN
Operates as a guillotine from SR deck

RIGGING SYSTEM
Type:	Single purchase counter weight Hemp
Weight:	16,000 lbs available
Line sets:	61 sets at 6" o.c. with 5 lift lines per set
Arbors:	1,000 lb capacity
House Pipes:	40' long with 44'6" of travel from deck

Line sets are moveable
Block & Falls are available
Chain hoists are not available
(20) spot wheels

PERMANENT INSTALLATIONS OVER STAGE (FROM SMOKE POCKET)
Electric raceways (1) at 2'0"
Cyclorama (1) at 32'0"
Fire Curtain (1) at 3'0"

PERMANENT INSTALLATIONS ON DECK
None

ORCHESTRA PIT
Nonadjustable at 6' below stage level
Apron overhangs US wall of pit 2'3"
Pit can be covered upon request; no audience pit seating available

BACKSTAGE

LOADING DOCK
Loading door(s):
  11'9" high x 9'10" wide
Trucks load (2) at same time
Ramps are required, dock is at stage & ground level; 18'0" height restriction in dock
Fork lift is not required
Sound/Props can load in FOH
Lobby cannot be a work area
Trailers can store on-site

WARDROBE
Location: Stage level, USR, behind stage
Access: Direct from stage
(1) Washers (2) Dryers
No washer or dryer hookups

DRESSING ROOMS
(2) Star, SR, stage level, t/s included, phone jack
(2) Star, SL, stage level, t on same fl, phone jack
(3) Small, SR, +1, t/s on same fl
(4) Small, SL, +1, t/s on same fl
Use dressing room for company mgr office

SOUND

CONSOLE
Mackie SR 32 X4, located Rear Center

SPEAKERS
House Cluster
Portable
No speaker truss
No organ grilles

COMMUNICATIONS
Clear Com intercom with (1) channel
Infrared sound system
Dressing room page system

ROAD CONSOLE
Located Rear Center
No seats required to be removed
Cable run from stage is 250'
Tie-in into house system

REHEARSAL & STORAGE SPACE
Rehearsal: None
Storage: 23' x 30', SL

ELECTRICS

ROAD SERVICE POWER

Panel	Phase	Amp	Circuit Protection	Use	Location
A	3	600	breaker	dimmers	DSR
B	3	400	breaker	sound	DSL

SR in green room
Hoist not required

FRONT OF HOUSE (BOX BOOM VALUES ARE PER SIDE)

Position	Pipe Width	Distance to Prosc.	House Circuits	Connector Type	FOH Transfer Circuits
1st Cove		35'	42	grd 20 amp stage pin	42

EQUIPMENT FOH (BOX BOOM VALUES ARE PER SIDE)

Position	Quantity	Wattage	Instrument	Removeable
1st Cove	18	1,000	Berkey Colortran 20°	yes
2nd Cove	20	1,000	Berkey Colortran 12°	yes

FOLLOWSPOTS
House Followspots:
  (2) Strong Xenon Troupers 2k; removeable

Followspot Booth:
  (2) spots per booth;
  100' throw to proscenium;
  (2) circuits

DIMMERS
Lighting console is ETC Expression 250;
(192) Sensor dimmers
House has programmable DMX control system
(2) dry run DMX station(s)

BARBARA B. MANN PERFORMING ARTS HALL

AT: EDISON COMMUNITY COLLEGE　　　　　　　　**YEAR BUILT: 1985　YEAR RENOVATED: 1998**

Theatre Location:　　　8099 College Pkwy. SW, Ft. Myers, FL 33919
Management Company: Professional Facilities Management (c/o PPAC)
　　　　　　　　　　　220 Weybosset St., Providence, RI

Main Administrative Phone:　　　　941-489-3033
Main Administrative Fax:　　　　　941-481-4620
E-mail:　　　　　　　　　　　　　bbmann@coconet.com
Website:　　　　　　　　　　　　www.bbmannpah.com
Backstage Pay Phone:　　　　　　941-433-9968

THEATRE STAFF

General Manager	Mary Bensel	941-489-3033
Booking	Norbert Mongeon	401-421-2997
Marketing	Julia Mays	941-489-3033
Operations	Eva Calhoun	941-489-3033
Group Sales	Lana Waltzer	941-489-3033

HOUSE CREW

Technical Director	Kevin Pepperal	941-489-3033

SEATING CAPACITY

Orchestra	822
Loges	42
Mezzanine	258
Balcony	631
Total:	**1,753**
pit (add'l)	44
wheelchair (add'l)	18

BOX OFFICE

Computerized
Box Office Manager
　Joseph Hansen　　941-481-4849

Outside Ticket Agency
Computerized
Ticketmaster

Box office is promoter operated

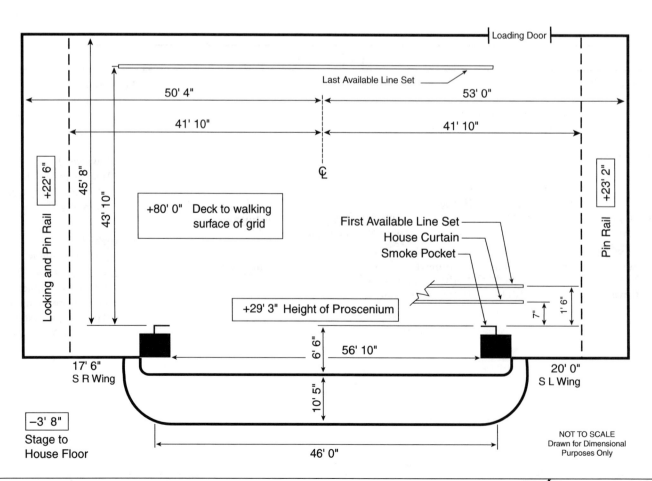

STAGE HOUSE

HOUSE CURTAIN
Operates as a guillotine or traveller from SR deck

RIGGING SYSTEM
Type:	Single purchase counter weight
Weight:	13,500 lbs available
Line sets:	59 sets at 8" o.c. with 7 lift lines per set
Arbors:	1,200 lb capacity
House Pipes:	65' long with 72' of travel from deck

Line sets are moveable
Block & Falls are not available
Chain hoists are available as a rental
(75) spot wheels and 4,000' of hemp available

PERMANENT INSTALLATIONS OVER STAGE (FROM SMOKE POCKET)
M=Moveable with advance call
Orchestra shells (4) 7'6", 17'6", 27'5", 36'4"; M
Electric Raceways (5) 2'10", 12'10", 22'9", 32'9", 42'7"; M
Movie screen (1) 45'0"; M
Cyclorama (2) 35'8', 36'4"; M
Fire curtain (1) 0'4"

PERMANENT INSTALLATIONS ON DECK
Orchestra shell stores on SL wall 10'0" deep

ORCHESTRA PIT
Nonadjustable at 8'2" below stage level
Apron overhangs US wall of pit 7'6"

BACKSTAGE

LOADING DOCK
Loading door(s):
   10'0" high x 10'0"wide
Trucks load (1) at a time
Sound/Props cannot load in
   FOH
(20) Trailers can store on-site
Security at dock & stage door

WARDROBE
Location:SL, behind stage,
   stage level
Access: Direct from stage
(2) Washers (2) Dryers
No washer or dryer hookups

DRESSING ROOMS
(3) Star, SR, stage level, t/s,
   phone jack
(2) Chorus, SR/ SL, stage level,
   t/s
Additional production office
   available for company mgr

SOUND

CONSOLE
Crest Century GT FOH
40 inputs, 3 main outputs,
   6 matrix outputs, 8 aux
   outputs

SPEAKERS
House Cluster
Proscenium
Upper Balcony
Speaker truss does not exist

COMMUNICATIONS
Clear Com & Telex intercom
   with (2) channels
Infrared sound system
Dressing room page system

ROAD CONSOLE
Located Rear House right
No seats required to be
   removed
Cable run from stage is 200'
Tie-in into house system with
   XLR or ¼" connectors

REHEARSAL & STORAGE SPACE
Rehearsal: None
Storage: None

ELECTRICS

ROAD SERVICE POWER

Panel	Phase	Amp	Circuit Protection	Use	Location
A-B	3	400	breaker	dimmers	USL side wall
C	3	100	breaker	extra	USL side wall
D	3	100	breaker	sound	DSL side wall
E	3	400	breaker	extra	USL back wall
F	3	200	breaker	sound	DSL side wall

Recommended location of touring dimmer racks: SL on deck
Hoist not required

FRONT OF HOUSE (BOX BOOM VALUES ARE PER SIDE)

Position	Pipe Width	Distance to Prosc.	House Circuits	Connector Type	FOH Transfer Circuits
1st Balc Rail	10'	50'	6	grd 20 amp stage pin	6
1st Cove	60'	36'	30	grd 20 amp stage pin	30
2nd Cove	60'	63'	30	grd 20 amp stage pin	30
Box Boom 1	3'	30'	8	grd 20 amp stage pin	8
Box Boom 2	3'	40'	8	grd 20 amp stage pin	8

Transfer circuits: grd 20 amp stage pin

EQUIPMENT FOH (BOX BOOM VALUES ARE PER SIDE

Position	Quantity	Wattage	Instrument	Removeable
1st Cove	30	1,000	Kliegl 6x16	yes
2nd Cove	30	1,000	Kliegl 8x13	yes
Box Boom 1	12	1,000	Kliegl 6x12 & 16	yes
Box Boom 2	8	1,000	Kliegl 8x13	yes

1st Balc Rail instruments will obstruct view

FOLLOWSPOTS
House Followspots:
   (2) Xenon Super Troupers
2k; removeable

Followspot Booth:
   (2) spots per booth;
   150' throw to prosc;
   (2) 1Ø 30 amp breakers

DIMMERS
Lighting console is ETC
   Expression 2X;
   (270) K-96 2.4k dimmers
House has programmable
   DMX control system
(1) dry run DMX station

FLORIDA THEATRE

YEAR BUILT: 1928   YEAR RENOVATED: 1994

Theatre Location: 128 East Forsyth Street Suite 300
Jacksonville, FL 32202

Main Administrative Phone:	904-355-5661
Main Administrative Fax:	904-358-1874
E-mail:	stillcool@ftjax.com
Website:	www.ftjax.com
Stage Door Phone:	904-355-1501
Backstage Pay Phone:	904-354-9673
Traveling Production Office Phone:	904-358-3329
Traveling Production Office Fax:	904-358-3412

SEATING CAPACITY

Orchestra	998
Balcony	916
Total:	**1,914**
wheelchair (add'l)	8

BOX OFFICE
Computerized
Box Office Manager
    Lynda Lee   904-355-2787

Outside Ticket Agency
Computerized
    Ticketmaster   904-353-3309

THEATRE STAFF

Executive Director	J. Erik Hart	904-355-5661
Marketing	Mike Maxwell	904-355-5661
Operations	Saundra Floyd	904-355-5661
Group Sales	Lynda Lee	904-355-2787

HOUSE CREW

Technical Director	Saul Lucio	904-355-1501
Sound	Tom Sholar	904-355-1501

UNIONS

IATSE Local #115	Keith Klemmt	904-731-7163
Wardrobe Local #115	Keith Klemmt	904-731-7163
Music Local #444	Mary Frank	904-398-9735

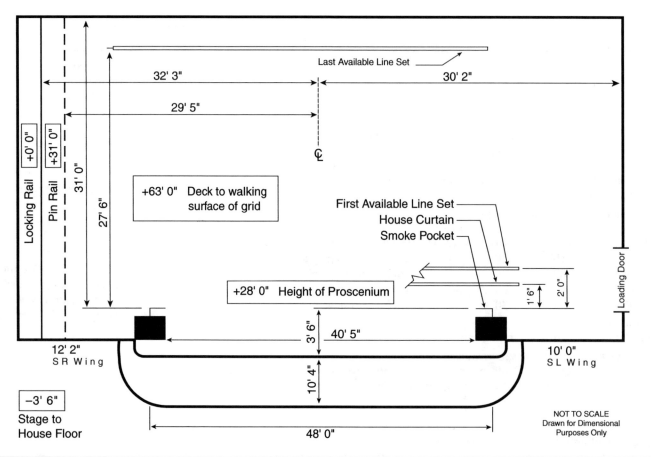

STAGE HOUSE

House Curtain
Operates as a guillotine from SR deck

Rigging System
Type:	Single purchase counter weight
Weight:	25,000 lbs available
Line sets:	50 sets at 6" o.c. with 4 lift lines per set
Arbors:	750 lb capacity
House Pipes:	43' long with 60' of travel from deck

Line sets are not moveable
Block & Falls are available
(20) spot wheels and 4,000' of hemp available

Permanent Installations Over Stage (from smoke pocket)
Orchestra shells (3) at 3'0", 9'0", 18'0"
Electric Raceways (1) at 3'6"
Movie screen (1) at 4'6"

Permanent Installations On Deck
Chimney flue (1) 4'0" x 10'0" located USL corner

Orchestra Pit
Adjustable to 5'6" below stage level by hydraulic lift
Apron overhangs US wall of pit 10'4" at center line
Pit lift is in (2) sections

BACKSTAGE

Loading Dock
Loading door(s):
  9'0" high x 8'0" wide
Trucks load (2) at same time
Street level with ramp access to stage loading doors SL
Fork lift is not required
Sound/Props cannot load in FOH
(2) Trailers can store on-site
Security at dock & stage door

Wardrobe
Location: Basement
Access: Thru SR green door
(1) Washer (1) Dryer
No washer or dryer hookups

Dressing Rooms
(1) Star, SR,+1, t/s included, phone jack
(2) Small,SR, +1, t/s included, phone jack
(2) Chorus, SR, +2/+3, t/s included
Additional production office available for company mgr

SOUND

Console
Yamaha PM 4000, located Orchestra
40 inputs, 8 main outputs, 8 matrix outputs, 12 aux outputs

Speakers
House Cluster
Proscenium
Under Balcony
Portable
No speaker truss
4 DS rigging points, 17' & 21' from center

Communications
Clear Com intercom with (2) channels
Dressing room page system

Road Console
Located Orchestra
No scats required to be removed
Cable run from stage is 120'
Tie-in into house system with XLR connectors

Rehearsal & Storage Space
Rehearsal: None
Storage: None

ELECTRICS

Road Service Power

Panel	Phase	Amp	Circuit Protection	Use	Location
A	3	600	breaker	dimmers	SL Wall
B	3	200	breaker	sound	SL Wall

Recommended location of touring dimmer racks: USL
Hoist is not required or provided
Additional power is available for tour buses, generators, etc.

Front Of House (box boom values are per side)

Position	Pipe Width	Distance to Prosc.	House Circuits	Connector Type	FOH Transfer Circuits
1st Cove	45'	54'	30	grd 20 amp stage pin	0
Box Boom 1		45'	10	grd 20 amp stage pin	0
Balc Rail	40'	48'	22	grd 20 amp stage pin	0

Road truss: 2 DS lighting points with 1-ton motors and control (13' 6" from center), 4 DS audio point 17' + 21' from center).

Equipment FOH (box boom values are per side)

Position	Quantity	Wattage	Instrument	Removeable
1st Cove Rail	9	575	Altman Shakespeare	yes
Box Boom 1	30	575	Altman Shakespeare	yes

Followspots
House Followspots:
  (4) Lycian 1290 XLT
  Xenon 2k; not removeable

Followspot Booth:
  (4) spots per booth;
  123' throw to proscenium;
  (4) 3Ø 30 amp breakers

Dimmers
Lighting console is Strand LP90
Compact and Leprecon LP 2000
(274) Strand CD80 dimmers
House has non-programmable DMX control system
(3) dry run DMX station(s)

MORAN THEATER

AT: TIMES-UNION CENTER FOR THE PERFORMING ARTS FORMERLY: JACKSONVILLE CIVIC AUDITORIUM YEAR RENOVATED: 1997

Theatre Location: 300 West Water Street, Jacksonville, FL 32202
Management Company: SMG
                       1000 Water Street, Jacksonville, FL 32204

Main Administrative Phone: 904-633-6110
Main Administrative Fax: 904-633-6190
Stage door phone: 904-633-6112
Traveling Production Office Phone: 904-630-4095
Traveling Production Office Fax: 904-630-4096

THEATRE STAFF
  Director   Robin Timothy   904-633-6110
  Booking   J.E. DeSpain   904-633-6194
  Marketing   Tiare Bevan   904-630-3958
  Operations   Tony Wise   904-630-3958

HOUSE CREW
  Technical Stage Mgr   Lyle E. Klemmt   904-633-6192 / Fax 630-4092
UNIONS
  IATSE Local #115   K. Keith Klemmt   904-731-7163
  Wardrobe Local #115   K. Keith Klemmt   904-731-7163

SEATING CAPACITY
1st Orchestra	698
2nd Orchestra	1,018
Loge	464
Balcony	604
Boxes	40
Total:	**2,824**
pit (add'l)	110

BOX OFFICE
  Computerized
  Box Office Manager
    Sandy Avery   904-630-3974

  Outside Ticket Agency
  Ticket Master   904-353-3309

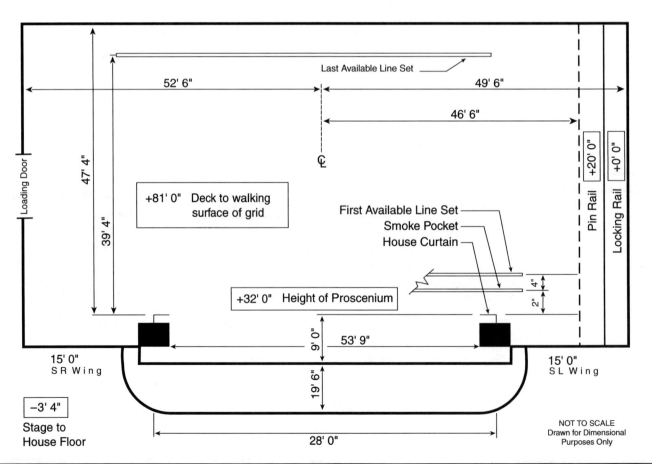

STAGE HOUSE

House Curtain
Operates as a guillotine from SL deck

Rigging System
Type:	Single purchase counter weight
Weight:	20,000 lbs available
Line sets:	60 sets at 6-9"o.c. with 5 lift lines per set
Arbors:	640-1,300 lb capacity
House Pipes:	64' long with 75' of travel from deck

Line sets are moveable
Block & Falls are available 2:1 (2)
(40) spot wheels and 2,500' of hemp available

Permanent Installations Over Stage (from smoke pocket)
Electric racewoys (1) at 4'0"

Permanent Installations On Deck
Obstruction DSL: AV Box located DSL 3'8" from smoke pocket

Orchestra Pit
Adjustable to 13' below stage level by hydraulic lift
Apron overhangs US wall of pit 0'0"
Pit lift is in (2) sections

BACKSTAGE

Loading Dock
Loading door(s):
  11'8" high x 11'6" wide
Trucks load (3) at same time
20' from loading door to theatre
Fork lift is not required
(2) Trailers can store on-site
Security at dock & stage door

Wardrobe
Location: Basement
Access: Elevator/Stairs
(1) Washer (1) Dryer
Washer and dryer hookups available

Dressing Rooms
(2) Star, SR, stage level, t/s included
(2) Small, SR, stage level, t/s included
(2) Chorus, SR, stage level, t/s included
Additional production office available for company mgr

SOUND

Console
Crest, located FOH
40 inputs, 8 main outputs

Speakers
House Cluster
Proscenium
Under Balcony
Portable
No speaker truss

Communications
Clear Com intercom with
  (4) channels
Infrared sound system
Dressing room page system

Road Console
Located Mid-Orchestra
No seats required to be removed
Cable run from stage is 150'
Tie-in into house system with XLR connectors

Rehearsal & Storage Space
Rehearsal: None
Storage: 60' x 20', loading dock 60' x 40', in basement

ELECTRICS

Road Service Power

Panel	Phase	Amp	Circuit Protection	Use	Location
A-E	3	400	breaker	dimmers	DSL
F	3	200	breaker	sound	DSL
G	3	200	breaker	extra	SR
H	3	100	breaker	extra	USL
I	3	100	breaker	extra	USR

Recommended location of touring dimmer racks: DSL
Hoist not required
Additional power is available for tour buses, generators, etc.

Front Of House (box boom values are per side)
None
Transfer circuits: DMX input

Equipment FOH (box boom values are per side)
Position	Quantity	Wattage	Instrument	Removeable
1st Balc Rail	40		Source 4	yes
1st Cove	36		Source 4	yes
2nd Cove	24		Source 4	yes
Box Boom 1	10		Source 4	yes

Followspots
House Followspots:
  (4) Strong Xenon 2k ;
  removeable

Followspot Booth:
  (4) spots per booth;
  150' throw to proscenium;
  (4) 1Ø 30 amp breakers

Dimmers
Lighting console is
  Obsession 600;
(350) Sensor dimmers
House has programmable DMX control system
(3) dry run DMX station(s)

YOUKEY THEATRE AT THE LAKELAND CENTER

YEAR BUILT: 1974   YEAR RENOVATED: 1996

Theatre Location: 700 West Lemon Street, Lakeland, FL 33801
Mailing Address: PO Box 1810, Lakeland, FL 33802-1810

Main Administrative Phone: 941-834-8100
Main Administrative Fax: 941-834-8101
E-mail: ajohn@city.lakeland.net
Website: www.thelakelandcenter.com
Stage Door Phone: 941-834-3254

SEATING CAPACITY

Orchestra	1,290
Mezzanine	454
Balcony	442
Total:	**2,186**
pit (add'l)	40
wheelchair (add'l)	30
standing (add'l)	0

THEATRE STAFF

Director	Allen Johnson	941-834-8100
Assistant Director	Tony Delgado	941-834-8144

HOUSE CREW

Technical Supv.	Barry Sears	941-834-8142
Engineering Supv	Avon Frier	941-834-8149

STAGE DIMENSIONS (FROM SMOKE POCKET)

Stage is 45'0" deep;
Width from Center Line to SL is 54'2"
Width from Center Line to SR is 42'0"
Proscenium width is 56'0"
Proscenium height is 25'0"
Smoke pocket to apron edge is 3'5"
Orchestra pit exists

RIGGING

Grid Height: 61'8"
Type: Single purchase counter weight
Weight: 12,000 lbs
Line sets: 54 sets at 8" o.c.
Arbors: 1,450 lb capacity
House Pipes: 63' with 57' of travel long

LOADING DOCK

Loading door(s) are 14'0" high x 12'0" wide,
Trucks load (2) at same time
Fork lift is not required and is available

ELECTRICS

Total power available:
  (1) 600A 3Ø SR proscenium wall

FOLLOWSPOTS

House Followspots:
  Xenon Super Trouper; Capital Quartz
Power in spot booth
  (8) 1Ø 20A breakers
FOH transfer circuits per position: 0

DIMMERS

No house dimmers
House has DMX control system

SOUND

House has 200A of dedicated power located SR
FOH mixing position in Rear House
Sound console is available

GUSMAN CENTER FOR THE PERFORMING ARTS

AKA: OLYMPIA THEATER   YEAR BUILT: **1926**

		SEATING CAPACITY	
Theatre Location:	174 E. Flagler Street, Miami, FL 33131-1104		
Mailing Address:	25 SE Second Avenue, #415	Orchestra	880
	Miami, FL 33131-1104	Mezzanine	163
Management Company:	City of Miami- Department of Off-Street Parking	Balcony	666
	190 NE Third Street, Miami , FL 33132	**Total:**	**1,709**

Main Administrative Phone: 305-374-2444
Main Administrative Fax: 305-374-0303

THEATRE STAFF
Director of Theater Operations Jeannie Piazza-Zungia 305-374-2444
Booking   Jeannie Piazza-Zungia 305-374-2444

HOUSE CREW
Technical Director   Jerry Kinsey   305-374-9561

STAGE DIMENSIONS (FROM SMOKE POCKET)
Stage is 28'0" deep
Width from Center Line to SL is 32'5"
Width from Center Line to SR is 36'5"
Proscenium width is 41'4"
Proscenium height is 28'0"
Smoke pocket to apron edge is 12'0"
Orchestra pit exists

RIGGING
Grid Height:	68'
Type:	Combination purchase counter weight
Weight:	8,200 lbs
Line sets:	31 sets at 12" o.c.
Arbors:	800 lb capacity
House Pipes:	48'4" long

LOADING DOCK
Trucks load (1) at a time
Fork lift is not required and is not available
Street with 180' alley with 90° turn

ELECTRICS
Total power available:
(1) 600A 3Ø SR

FOLLOWSPOTS
House Followspots:
Berkey Colortran 2k
No power in spot booth
FOH transfer circuits : 40

DIMMERS
(350) house dimmers
House has DMX control system
(6) dry run station(s) located
throughout house

SOUND
House has 200A dedicated
power located DSR
FOH mixing position in
Rear House
Sound console is available

THE JACKIE GLEASON THEATER OF PERFORMING ARTS

AKA: TOPA

YEAR BUILT: 1951   YEAR RENOVATED: 1990

Theatre Location: 1700 Washington Avenue, Miami Beach, FL 33139
Mailing Address: 1901 Convention Center Drive, Miami Beach, FL 33139

Main Administrative Phone: 305-673-7311
Main Administrative Fax: 305-673-7435
Website: www.ci.miami-beach.fl.us
Stage Door Phone: 305-673-7319
Backstage Pay Phone: 305-538-9323
Traveling Production Office Phone: 305-673-7308
Traveling Production Office Fax: 305-673-7329

THEATRE STAFF
General Manager	Douglas Tober	305-673-7311
Booking	Robert Papke	305-673-7311
Marketing	Robert Papke	305-673-7311

HOUSE CREW
Technical Director	Dick Helfritz	305-535-0263
Stage Manager	Jim Dalton	305-673-7319
Carpentry	Harry McCabe	305-673-7322
Electrics	Bill Schwendell	305-673-7322
Sound	Rob Rick	305-673-7325
Props	Tom Furman	305-673-7322

UNIONS
IATSE Local #545	Dan Bonfiglio	305-895-0025
Wardrobe Local #853	Bernice Rose	305-931-6664
Music	Bob Percy	305-434-2856

SEATING CAPACITY
Orchestra	1,857
Pit	52
Wheelchair	34
Mezzanine	762
Total:	**2,705**
pit (add'l)	52
wheelchair (add'l)	34

BOX OFFICE
Computerized
Box Office Manager
  Joy Martin   305-673-7336

Outside Ticket Agency
Computerized
Ticketmaster   305-358-5885
Vanessa Binns-Posada

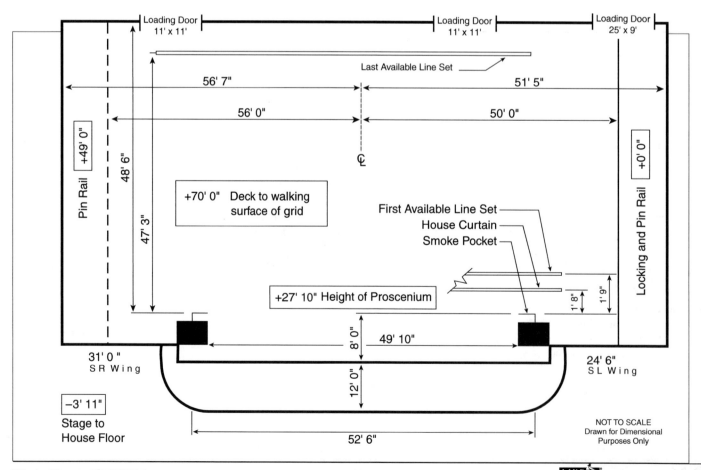

STAGE HOUSE

HOUSE CURTAIN
Operates as a guillotine from SL deck

RIGGING SYSTEM
Type:	Single purchase counter weight
Weight:	30,000 lbs. available
Line sets:	86 sets at 6" o.c. with 7 lift lines per set
Arbors:	1,650 lb. capacity
House Pipes:	63' long with 64' of travel from deck.

Line sets are moveable
Block & Falls are available
Chain hoists are not available
(200) spot wheels and 200' of hemp available

PERMANENT INSTALLATIONS OVER STAGE (FROM SMOKE POCKET)
M=Moveable with advance call
Orchestra shell (3) at 4'3", 12'3", 20'9"; M
Electric bridge (1); M
Dead spaces (4) 15'3", 15'9", 32'3", 32'9"
Cyclorama (1); M
Fire curtain (1)
Catwalk (2)

PERMANENT INSTALLATIONS ON DECK
Trap (1) 5'0" x 9'5" (phantom), at 24'2"
Loading bridge (2) located SL 50' and 60'

ORCHESTRA PIT
Adjustable to 9'6" below stage level by scissor lift
Apron overhangs US wall of pit 6'4"
Pit lift is in 1 section

BACKSTAGE

LOADING DOCK
Loading door(s):
　12'0" high x 8'0" wide
Trucks load (4) at stame time
Forklift: house owns
Dock SR requires 90° turn of
　pieces as they leave truck
Sound/Props can load in FOH
Lobby can be a work area
Security at stage door

WARDROBE
Location: USR behind stage on
　SL
Access: Direct from stage
(1) Washer (1) Dryer
No washer or dryer hookups

DRESSING ROOMS
(4) Star, SR, stage level, t/s
(5) Small, SR, stage level, t/s
(4) Chorus, SR, stage level/ +3,
　t/s

SOUND

CONSOLE
DDA Q Series, located
　Center House
32 inputs, 4 main outputs,
　8 aux outputs

SPEAKERS
House Cluster
Proscenium
Under Balcony
No speaker truss

COMMUNICATIONS
Clear Com intercom with
　(2) channels
Infrared sound system
Dressing room page system

ROAD CONSOLE
Located Rear House
(12-18) seats required to be
　removed
Cable run from stage is 250'
Tie-in into house system with
　XLR connectors

REHEARSAL & STORAGE SPACE
Rehearsal: 48' x 65', stage
　level, mirror, piano
Storage: 20' x 67' located US
　scene dock

ELECTRICS

ROAD SERVICE POWER
Panel	Phase	Amp	Circuit Protection	Use	Location
A	3	100	breaker	sound	DSR
B-D	3	600	breaker	dimmers	DSL

Recommended location of touring dimmer racks: DSL
Separate dedicated isolated transformer for sound
Hoist not required
Additional power available for tour buses, generators, etc.

FRONT OF HOUSE (BOX BOOM VALUES ARE PER SIDE)
Position	Pipe Width	Distance to Prosc.	House Circuits	Connector Type	FOH Transfer Circuits
1st Balc Rail	40'	98'	20	grd 20 amp stage pin	20
1st Cove	70'	55'	34	grd 20 amp stage pin	34
2nd Cove	70'	76'	18	grd 20 amp stage pin	18
Bridge		33'	12	grd 20 amp stage pin	12
Box Boom 1		43'	18	grd 20 amp stage pin	18
Box Boom 2		53'	18	grd 20 amp stage pin	18

Transfer circuits: DMX soft patch or DSL stage pin hard patch

EQUIPMENT FOH (BOX BOOM VALUES ARE PER SIDE
Position	Quantity	Wattage	Instrument	Removeable
1st Balc Rail	20	1,000	Colortran 10°	yes
1st Cove	12	1,000	Colortran 10°	yes
2nd Cove	32	1,000	Colortran 12°	yes
Box Boom 1	36	1,000	Colortran 12°	yes

FOLLOWSPOTS
House Followspots:
　(3) Strong Xenon Super
　Troupers; removeable

Followspot Booth:
　(3) spots per booth;
　103' throw to proscenium;
　(4) 3Ø 50 amp breakers

DIMMERS
Lighting console is ETC;
　(500) LMI L86 dimmers
House has programmable
　DMX control system
(2) dry run DMX station(s),
　DSL, lighting booth Rear
　House

PHILHARMONIC CENTER OF THE ARTS

AKA: FRANCIS PEW HAYES HALL   **YEAR BUILT: 1989**

Theatre Location: 5833 Pelican Bay Boulevard, Naples, FL 34108

Main Administrative Phone:	941-597-1111
Main Administrative Fax:	941-597-8163
E-mail:	prod@naplesphilcenter.org
Website:	www.naplesphilcenter.org
Backstage Pay Phone:	941-597-9949

THEATRE STAFF

Booking	Maureen Shallcross	941-597-0605
Marketing	Beth Kalvin	941-597-0673
Operations	Maureen Shallcross	941-597-0605
Group Sales	Claudia Polzin	941-597-0670

HOUSE CREW

Carpentry	Jim Capuzziello	941-597-0681
Electrics	Bob Mooney	941-597-0626
Sound	Brett Musick	941-597-0657

UNIONS

IATSE Local #647	Jim Kattner	941-498-9090

SEATING CAPACITY

Orchestra	1,006
Box	192
Total:	**1,198**

BOX OFFICE
Computerized
Director of Customer Services
Ron Smith   941-597-0667

Outside Ticket Agency
None

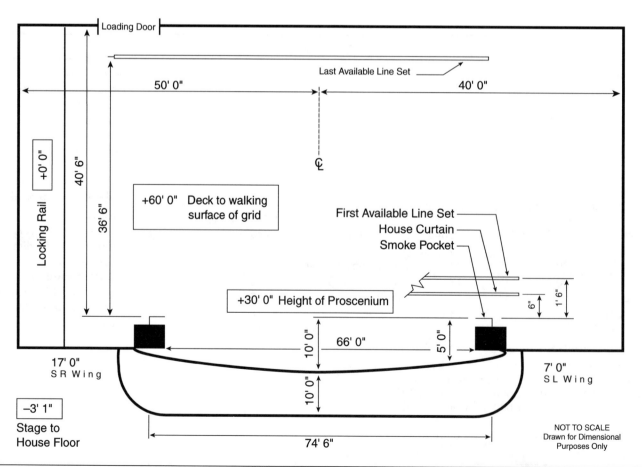

STAGE HOUSE

HOUSE CURTAIN
Operates as a guillotine from SR deck
Guy wires SR & SL

RIGGING SYSTEM
Type: Single purchase counter weight
Weight: 19,000 lbs available
Line sets: 53 sets at 6" o.c. with 6 lift lines per set
Arbors: 1,100 lb capacity
House Pipes: 63' long with 55' of travel from deck
Line sets are moveable
Block & Falls are available

PERMANENT INSTALLATIONS OVER STAGE (FROM SMOKE POCKET)
M=Moveable with advance call
Orchestra shells (6) at 3'9", 9'9", 15'9", 21'9", 27'9", 33'9"
Movie screen (1) at 1'0"; M
Organ Facade Cover (1)

PERMANENT INSTALLATIONS ON DECK
Orchestra shell storage (1) 12'0" x 18'0"

ORCHESTRA PIT
Adjustable to 9' below stage level by electric motor
     turnscrew
Apron overhangs US wall of pit 10'0"
Pit lift is in (1) section

BACKSTAGE

LOADING DOCK
Loading door(s):
     16'0" wide x 13'6" high
Trucks load (2) at same time
Unloading 2 trucks simulta-
     neously takes careful
     manuveuring
Fork lift is not required
Sound/Props cannot load in
     FOH
(3) Trailers can store on-site

WARDROBE
Location: USL
Access: Easy hallway access to
     loading dock or stage
(2) Washers   (2) Dryers
Washer and dryer hookups
     available

DRESSING ROOMS
(4) Star, USR, stage level, t/s
     included, phone jack
(2) Chorus, USR, stage level, t/s
     included, phone jack
Additional production office
     available for company mgr

REHEARSAL & STORAGE SPACE
Rehearsal: 50' x 50' in adjacent
     black box theatre; piano
     available; prior arrangements
     required.
Storage: transient space in shop
     off loading dock

SOUND

CONSOLE
Yamaha PM 3500, located
     Rear House
52 inputs, 1 stereo main
     outputs, 4 stereo, 4 mono
     matrix outputs, 8 aux
     outputs

SPEAKERS
House Cluster
Portable
No speaker truss

COMMUNICATIONS
Clear Com intercom with
     (2) channels
FM hearing augmentation
Dressing room page system
Dressing room program &
     hearing impaired program
     are the same feed unless
     otherwise requested

ROAD CONSOLE
Located Rear House
(20) seats required to be
     removed
Cable run from stage is 180'
Tie-in into house system with
     XLR connectors

ELECTRICS

ROAD SERVICE POWER

Panel	Phase	Amp	Circuit Protection	Use	Location
A-C	3	400	fuse	dimmer	DSL in alcove
D	3	100	fuse	sound	DSR in alcove

Recommended location of touring dimmer racks: Stage left
Hoist not required
Additional power is available for tour buses, generators, etc.

FRONT OF HOUSE (BOX BOOM VALUES ARE PER SIDE)

Position	Pipe Width	Distance to Prosc.	House Circuits	Connector Type	FOH Transfer Circuits
1st Cove	80'	40'	40	20 amp stage pin	0
2nd Cove	66'	62'	38	20 amp stage pin	0

Transfer circuits: Can be patched into touring equipment using an ETC response system

EQUIPMENT FOH (BOX BOOM VALUES ARE PER SIDE)

Position	Quantity	Wattage	Instrument	Removeable
1st Cove Rail	30	575	Source 4 19°	yes
2nd Cove Rail	36	1,000	8 x 13 Lekos	yes
1st Cove Rail Ends	10	575	Source 4 19°	yes

1st Cove Rail Ends are 10 per side
FOH units can be patched into touring equipment using an ETC response system

FOLLOWSPOTS

House Followspots:
     (3) Strong Xenon Super
     Troupers 2000; removeable

Followspot Booth:
     (4) spots per booth;
     120' throw to proscenium;
     (4) 1Ø 20 amp breakers

DIMMERS
House console is ETC
     Obsession 600; (336) Lee
     Courtran dimmers
House has programmable
     DMX control system
(5) dry run DMX station(s)

BOB CARR PERFORMING ARTS CENTER

AT: CENTROPLEX

YEAR BUILT: 1926   YEAR RENOVATED: 1994

Theatre Location: 401 West Livingston Street, Orlando, FL 32801
Mailing Address: 600 West Amela Street, Orlando, FL 32801

Main Administrative Phone: 407-849-2582
Main Administrative Fax: 407-843-0758
E-mail: jkay@ci.orlando.fl.us
Backstage Pay Phone: 407-420-9604

THEATRE STAFF
Manager   Janet Kay   407-849-2582
Booking   Robin Hanolan   407-849-2000
Marketing   Craig O'Neil   407-849-2000

HOUSE CREW
Carpentry   Emil Ellis   407-849-2586
Electrics   Gary Ronkin
Sound   Gary Armstrong
Props   John Romaine
Wardrobe   Mary Amlund

UNIONS
IATSE Local #631   Brian Lawlor   407-422-2747
Wardrobe Local #631   Brian Lawlor   407-422-2747

SEATING CAPACITY
Orchestra   1,794
Balcony   646
Total: **2,440**

wheelchair (add'l)   26

BOX OFFICE
Box Office Manager
  Ann Johnson   407-849-2000

Outside Ticket Agency
Computerized
Ticketmaster
  Donna Dowless   407-839-0900

Box office is promoter operated

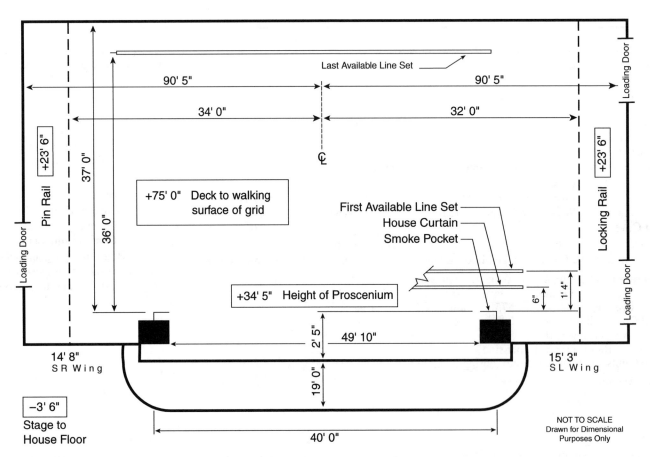

NOT TO SCALE
Drawn for Dimensional
Purposes Only

STAGE HOUSE

HOUSE CURTAIN
Operates as a guillotine from SL fly floor

RIGGING SYSTEM
Type: Double purchase counter weight
Weight: 30,000 lbs available
Line sets: 71 sets at 6" o.c. with 5 lift lines per set
Arbors: 2,000 lb capacity
House Pipes: 55' long with 73' of travel from deck
Line sets are moveable
Block & Falls are available
Chain hoists are available
(100) spot wheels and 5,000' of hemp available
Rigging points available above orchestra pit, DS of proscenium

PERMANENT INSTALLATIONS OVER STAGE (FROM SMOKE POCKET)
M=Moveable with advance call
Orchestra shell (3) at 6'2", 15'8", 25'2"; M

PERMANENT INSTALLATIONS ON DECK
Orchestra shell storage (1) 30'd x 50'w located at 29'0" SR of proscenium

ORCHESTRA PIT
Adjustable to 10' below stage level by hydraulic lift
Apron overhangs US wall of pit 4'0"
Pit lift is in (1) section

BACKSTAGE

LOADING DOCK
Loading door(s):
  12'0" high x 8'0"wide
Trucks load (4) at same time
SL door used as primary dock,
  SR dock requires 90° turn as items leave truck
Fork lift is not required
Sound/Props can load in FOH
Lobby can be a work area
Security at stage door

WARDROBE
Location: 2nd floor
  Dressing room level
Access: Elevator
(2) Washers (2) Dryers
Washer and dryer hookups available

DRESSING ROOMS
(4) Star, behind stage, 2nd fl, t/s, phone jack
(4) Small, behind stage, 2nd fl, t/s
(2) Chorus, behind stage, 2nd fl, t/s
Elevator access for dressing rooms
Additional production office available for company mgr

SOUND

CONSOLE
Mackie SR408, located FOH booth
40 inputs, 3 main outputs, 4 matrix outputs, 8 aux outputs

SPEAKERS
House Cluster
Proscenium
Under Balcony
EAW sub system fills room with no problem
No speaker truss

COMMUNICATIONS
Clear Com intercom with (1) channel
Infrared sound system
Dressing room page system

ROAD CONSOLE
Located FOH, in front of booth
No seats required to be removed
Cable run from stage is 250'
Tie-in into house system with XLR connectors

REHEARSAL & STORAGE SPACE
Rehearsal or Storage:
  40' x 40' located USR on stage level; used for rehearsal or storage

ELECTRICS

ROAD SERVICE POWER

Panel	Phase	Amp	Circuit Protection	Use	Location
A	3	200	fuse	extra	USR
B	3	200	breaker	extra	USR
C-D	3	400	breaker	dimmers	USR
E	3	400	fuse	dimmers	USR
F	3	200	fuse	extra	DSR
G	3	200	fuse	sound	DSL

Recommended location of touring dimmer racks: SR
Hoist not required
Additional power is available for tour buses, generators, etc.

FRONT OF HOUSE (BOX BOOM VALUES ARE PER SIDE)

Position	Pipe Width	Distance to Prosc.	House Circuits	Connector Type	FOH Transfer Circuits
Balc Rail		100'	0		0
2nd Rail		90'	14	20 amp new twistlock	
1st Rail		65'	46	20 amp new twistlock	
Box Boom 1		25'	8	20 amp new twistlock	0

Transfer circuits: 20 amp three pin transfer location offstage R; (56) transfer circuits

EQUIPMENT FOH (BOX BOOM VALUES ARE PER SIDE)

Position	Quantity	Wattage	Instrument		Removeable
1st Rail	68	1,000	20/20	48/12	yes

2nd Rail & Balc Rail not user friendly

FOLLOWSPOTS
House Followspots:
  (3) Strong Super Troupers; removeable

Followspot Booth:
  (1) spot per booth;
  110' throw to proscenium;
  (1) 1Ø 30 amp breakers

DIMMERS
Lighting console is Obsession 600;
(266) Strand CD80 dimmers
House has non-programmable DMX control system
(2) dry run DMX station(s)

TUPPERWARE CENTER THEATRE

AKA: TUPPERWARE CONVENTION CENTER AT: TUPPERWARE HEADQUARTERS

YEAR BUILT: 1976 YEAR RENOVATED: 1998

Theatre Location:	14901 S Orange Blossom Trail, Orlando, FL 32837
Mailing Address:	PO Box 2353, Orlando, FL 32802-2353
Management Company:	In House and Outside Promotions
	PO Box 2353, Orlando, FL 32802-2353

SEATING CAPACITY

Orchestra	2,000
Total:	**2,000**

Main Administrative Phone:	407-847-1918
Main Administrative Fax:	407-847-1813
E-mail:	jeff_hunter@tupmail.com
Stage Door Phone:	407-847-1918 x2816
Backstage Pay Phone:	407-870-5338

BOX OFFICE

Box Office Manager
Michael Long   407-826-4404

Outside Ticket Agency
Ticketmaster   407-839-3900

THEATRE STAFF

General Manager	Jeff Hunter	407-826-4475
Booking	Diane Dykes	407-826-4475

HOUSE CREW

Tech Services Sprvr	David Costner	407-847-1803

UNIONS

IATSE Local #631	Brian Lawlor	407-422-2747

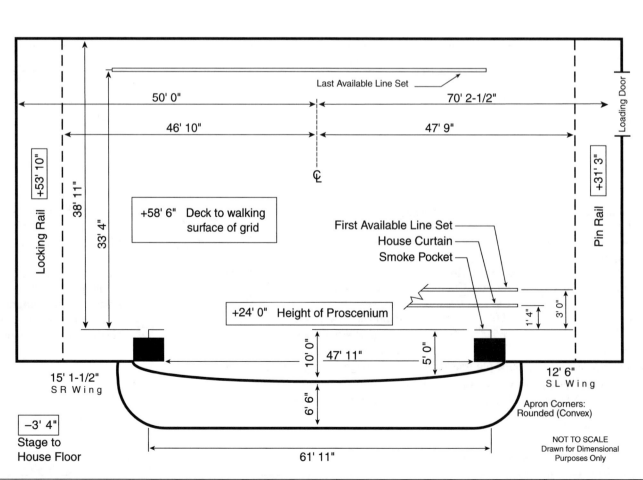

STAGE HOUSE

HOUSE CURTAIN
Operates as a guillotine or traveller from SR deck

RIGGING SYSTEM
Type:	Single purchase counter weight
Weight:	100,000 lbs available
Line sets:	38 sets at 8" o.c. with 7 lift lines per set
Arbors:	1,600 lb capacity
House Pipes:	63'5" long with 57'1" of travel from deck

Line sets are not moveable
(24) spot wheels and 2,000' of hemp available

PERMANENT INSTALLATIONS OVER STAGE (FROM SMOKE POCKET)
M=Moveable with advance call
Electric raceways (7) at
   3'8", 4'4", 11'0", 11'8", 16'4", 17'0", 28'8"
Movie screen (1) at 0'8"
Traveller (1); M
Electric pipe (7) at
   3'8", 4'4", 11'0", 11'8", 16'4", 17'0", 28'8"; M
Scoop bar (1) deadhung on back wall
Dead spaces (9) at 2'8", 5'4", 10'8", 12'4", 26'8", 28'0",
   29'4", 30'0", 32'8"
Cyclorama (1) at 32'8"; M
Fire curtain (1) located in smoke pocket

PERMANENT INSTALLATIONS ON DECK
Traps (1) in stage floor 8' x 8'
Columns (6) 5@ 2' x 1'4"; 1@ 32"x 39 1/2"
Patch bay/Dimmer bay (2) 9'6 1/2" x 12'0"

ORCHESTRA PIT
Adjustable to 3'6" below stage level by manual lift
Apron overhangs US wall of pit 6' 0"
Pit lift is in (14) sections; Pit is 4'x8', platforms on 2'x4' legs

BACKSTAGE

LOADING DOCK
Loading door(s):
   13'0" high x 13'0" wide
Trucks load (1) at a time
Loading door is at stage level,
   dock space exists with
   permanent ramp if needed
Fork lift is not required
Sound/Props can load in FOH
Lobby can be a work area
(15) Trailers can store on-site
Security at dock & stage door

WARDROBE
Location: In dressing rooms;
   W/D in kitchen of attached
   facility
Access: Stairs / hallway to
   kitchen or outside access
(2) Washers (2) Dryers
Washer and dryer hookups
   available

DRESSING ROOMS
(1) Star, SR, +1/+2, t/s included,
   phone jack
(3) Small, SR, +1, t/s included
(2) Chorus, SR, +1, t/s included
Additional production office
   available for company mgr

SOUND

CONSOLE
PM 4000, located Back wall
   FOH
40 inputs, 8 main outputs,
   8 matrix outputs, 8 aux
   outputs

SPEAKERS
House Cluster
Proscenium
Portable
Side filler
No speaker truss
Max available load 750 lbs

COMMUNICATIONS
Clear Com intercom with
   (2) channels
Infrared sound system
Dressing room page system

ROAD CONSOLE
Located Sound Booth, Rear
   House
No seats required to be
   removed
Cable run from stage is 250'
Tie-in into house system with
   XLR connectors

REHEARSAL & STORAGE SPACE
Rehearsal: None
Storage: None

ELECTRICS

ROAD SERVICE POWER
Panel	Phase	Amp	Circuit Protection	Use	Location
A	3	400	fuse	dimmers	DSL
B	3	200	fuse	dimmers	DSL
C	3	100	fuse	motors	USC
D	3	100	fuse	sound	DSR
E	3	30	fuse	extra	USC
F	1	30	fuse	extra	dock

Recommended location of touring dimmer racks: SL
Hoist not required
Additional power is available for tour buses, generators, etc.

FRONT OF HOUSE (BOX BOOM VALUES ARE PER SIDE)
Position	Pipe Width	Distance to Prosc.	House Circuits	Connector Type	FOH Transfer Circuits
1st Cove	80'	26'	30	grd 20 amp stage pin	0
2nd Cove	80'	75'	16	grd 20 amp stage pin	0
Box Boom 1		26'	4	grd 20 amp stage pin	0
Proscenium		1'9"	12	grd 20 amp stage pin	0

Road truss: Max weight per point 750 lbs; can hang truss DS of proscenium

EQUIPMENT FOH (BOX BOOM VALUES ARE PER SIDE)
Position	Quantity	Wattage	Instrument	Removeable
1st Cove	34	1,000	par cans	yes
2nd Cove	31	1,000	par cans	yes
1st Box Boom	12	575	par cans	yes
Spot Booth	10	1,000	6 x 22	

FOLLOWSPOTS
House Followspots:
   (2) Super Trouper Xenon
   2k; removeable

Followspot Booth:
   (2) spots per booth;
   75' throw to proscenium;
   (3) 3Ø 20 amp breakers

DIMMERS
Lighting console is available
(80) dimmers
House has programmable
   DMX control system
(1) dry run DMX station,
   DSL

ROYAL POINCIANA PLAYHOUSE

YEAR BUILT: 1958   YEAR RENOVATED: 1997

Theatre Location: 70 Royal Poinciana Plaza, Palm Beach, FL 33480
Mailing Address: PO Box 231, Palm Beach, FL 33480
Management Company: PTG Florida, Inc.
100 S Biscayne Blvd, Suite 1200, Miami, FL 33131

Main Administrative Phone: 561-833-0705
Main Administrative Fax: 561-655-6552
Stage Door Phone: 561-820-9129
Backstage Pay Phone: 561-833-9148

THEATRE STAFF
Theatre Manager | Nancy McDaniel | 561-833-0705
Marketing | Yarni Yavitz | 305-379-2700
General Manager | John Poland | 305-379-2700
Group Sales | Ron Legler | 800-647-6877

HOUSE CREW
Technical Director | Casey Clark | 561-416-2027
Carpentry | Phillip Burney | 561-833-0705
Electrics | Terry McKenzie | 561-833-0705
Sound | Michael Ray | 561-833-0705
Props | Robert Lebs | 561-833-0705
Wardrobe | Faye Eldridge | 561-833-0705

UNIONS
IATSE Local #623 | John Dermoody | 561-694-7774
Music In-House | Bob Persi | 954-434-2856

SEATING CAPACITY
Orchestra | 878
Total: | **878**

pit (add'l) | 21
wheelchair (add'l) | 20

BOX OFFICE
Computerized
Box Office Manager
Susan Kent | 561-659-3310

Outside Ticket Agency
Computerized
Ticketmaster | 800-749-8669

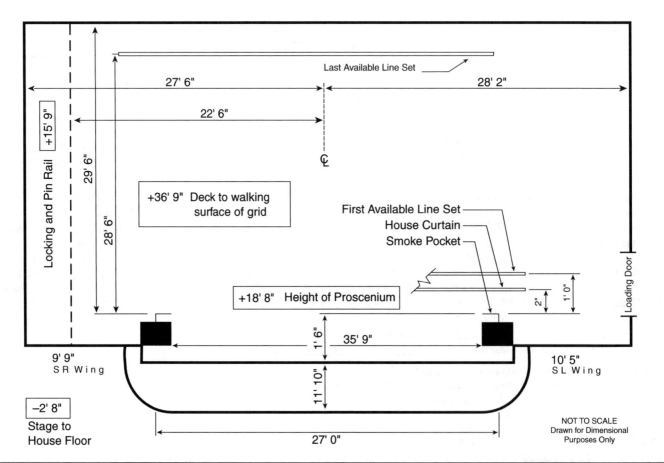

STAGE HOUSE

HOUSE CURTAIN
Operates as a guillotine from SR deck

RIGGING SYSTEM
Type: Double purchase counter weight
Weight: 10,000 lbs available
Line sets: 24 sets with 5 lift lines per set
Arbors: 750 lb capacity
House Pipes: 48' long with 35'9" travel from deck
Line sets are moveable
Block & Falls are available
Chain hoists are not available
(20) spot wheels available

PERMANENT INSTALLATIONS OVER STAGE (FROM SMOKE POCKET)
Fire curtain (1) at 0'3"

PERMANENT INSTALLATIONS ON DECK
None

ORCHESTRA PIT
Nonadjustable at 4'6" below stage level
Apron overhangs US wall of pit 0'0"
Orchestra pit remains covered to auditorium floor level with one row of seating on cover, unless otherwise arranged

BACKSTAGE

LOADING DOCK
Loading door(s):
   16'0" high x 12'0" wide
Trucks load (2) at same time
Ramps are required; dock and stage are at ground level.
Fork lift is not required
Sound/Props can load in FOH
Trailers cannot store on-site

WARDROBE
Location: Upper level, 2nd floor
Access: Motorized winch is provided
(2) Washers (2) Dryers
No washer or dryer hookups

DRESSING ROOMS
(4) Star, SL / SR, stage level, t/s included, phone jack
(8) Small, SL / SR, +1, t/s on same fl
Use dressing room for company mgr office

SOUND

CONSOLE
Yamaha PM 1800, located HR
24 inputs, 8 main outputs, 8 aux outputs

SPEAKERS
House Cluster
No speaker truss

COMMUNICATIONS
Clear Com intercom with (1) channel
Infrared sound system
Dressing room page system

ROAD CONSOLE
Located mid HR
No seats required to be removed
Cable run from stage is 150'
Tie-in into house system with XLR connectors

REHEARSAL & STORAGE SPACE
Rehearsal: None
Storage: SR, 25' x 33'
     SL, 24' x 39';
     SL 8' x 30' loft

ELECTRICS

ROAD SERVICE POWER

Panel	Phase	Amp	Circuit Protection	Use	Location
A	3	600	breaker	dimmers	SL storage
B	1	100	breaker	dimmers	sub panels
C	1	100	breaker	sound	sub panels

Recommended location of touring dimmer racks: SL storage under loft
Hoist not required

FRONT OF HOUSE (BOX BOOM VALUES ARE PER SIDE)

Position	Pipe Width	Distance to Prosc.	House Circuits	Connector Type	FOH Transfer Circuits
1st Cove	50'	32'	48	grd 20 amp stage pin	48
Box Boom		32'	0	grd 20 amp stage pin	0

Transfer circuits: grd 20 amp stage pin

EQUIPMENT FOH (BOX BOOM VALUES ARE PER SIDE)

Position	Quantity	Wattage	Instrument	Removeable
1st Cove		1,000	6 x 16 Altman	yes

FOLLOWSPOTS
House Followspots:
   None

Followspot Booth:
  (1) spot per booth;
  32' throw to proscenium;
  (2) 1Ø 20 amp breakers

DIMMERS
Lighting console is 72 Channel, 25c Preset
No DMX control system

SAENGER THEATRE

YEAR BUILT: 1925   **YEAR RENOVATED: 1981**

Theatre Location: 118 South Palafox Place, Pensacola, FL 32501
Mailing Address: PO Box 13666, Pensacola, FL 32591
Management Company: Ogden Entertainment

Main Administrative Phone: 850-444-7699
Main Administrative Fax: 850-444-7684

THEATRE STAFF
  General Manager   Douglas Lee   850-444-7699
HOUSE CREW
  Operations Manager   James Kerrigan   850-444-7699

SEATING CAPACITY

Orchestra Front	784
Orchestra Terrace	300
Grand Tier (1st Balcony)	161
Dress Circle (2nd Balcony)	312
Family Circle (3rd Balcony)	245
Total:	**1,802**
pit (add'l)	0
wheelchair (add'l)	10
standing (add'l)	0

STAGE DIMENSIONS (FROM SMOKE POCKET)
  Stage is 34'0" deep
  Width from Center Line to SL is 34'0"
  Width from Center Line to SR is 37'0"
  Proscenium width is 43'3"
  Proscenium height is 25'6"
  Smoke pocket to apron edge is 3'0"
  Orchestra pit exists

RIGGING
  Grid Height: 62'
  Type: Single purchase counter weight
  Weight: 22,000 lbs
  Line sets: 30 sets at 8" o.c.
  Arbors: 750 lb capacity
  House Pipes: 56' long

LOADING DOCK
  Loading door(s) are 9'11" high x 7'11" wide
  Trucks load (1) at a   time
  Fork lift is not required and is not available

ELECTRICS
  Total power available:
    (1) 600A 3Ø DSR
    (1) 200A 3Ø DSL

FOLLOWSPOTS
  House Followspots:
    None
  Power in spot booth 100A
  FOH transfer circuits: 33

DIMMERS
  (156) house dimmers
  No DMX control system

SOUND
  House has 200A undedicated
    power located Off SL
  FOH mixing position in
    Rear Orchestra
  Sound console is available

MAHAFFEY THEATER FOR THE PERFORMING ARTS

AT: BAYFRONT CENTER

YEAR BUILT: 1963   YEAR RENOVATED: 1988

Theatre Location: 400 First Street S., St. Petersburg, FL 33701

Main Administrative Phone:	813-892-5798
Main Administrative Fax:	813-892-5858
E-mail:	lebruns@stpete.org
Website:	www.stpete.org
Stage Door Phone:	813-892-5745
Backstage Pay Phone:	813-894-9317
Traveling Production Office Phone:	813-892-5746
Traveling Production Office Fax:	813-892-5747

SEATING CAPACITY

Orchestra	658
Loge	371
Dress Circle	738
Balcony	621
Boxes	120
Total:	**1,908**
pit (add'l)	88

THEATRE STAFF

Building Manager	Jeff Foreman	813-892-5798
Booking	Lorri Bruns	813-892-5798
Marketing	Lorri Bruns	813-892-5798
Operations	Roland Ribblet	813-892-5798

HOUSE CREW

Production Manager	Todd A. Beatty	813-892-5889

UNIONS

IATSE Local #552	Mark Normington	813-821-6965
Wardrobe Local #552	Mark Normington	813-821-6965

BOX OFFICE

Computerized
Box Office Manager
  Lamar Vernon   813-892-5702

Outside Ticket Agency
Computerized
Ticketmaster
  Sheri Dye   813-286-2100

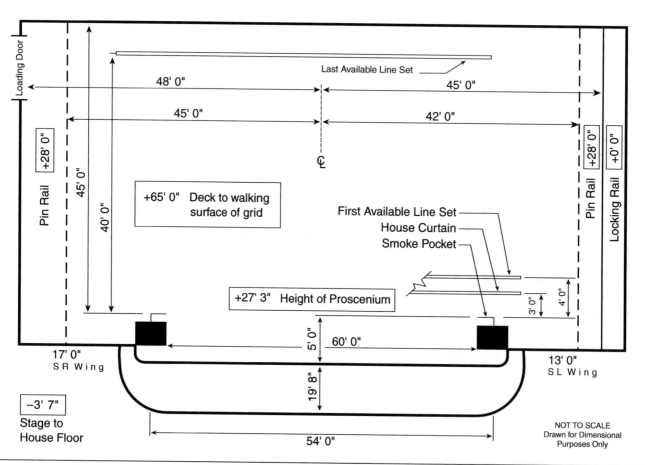

Loading Door

Last Available Line Set

48' 0"   45' 0"

45' 0"   42' 0"

Pin Rail +28' 0"   Pin Rail +28' 0"   +0' 0"

45' 0"

40' 0"

+65' 0" Deck to walking surface of grid

CL

First Available Line Set
House Curtain
Smoke Pocket

Locking Rail

3' 0"   4' 0"

+27' 3" Height of Proscenium

5' 0"   60' 0"

17' 0"
SR Wing

13' 0"
SL Wing

19' 8"

−3' 7"

Stage to
House Floor

54' 0"

NOT TO SCALE
Drawn for Dimensional
Purposes Only

STAGE HOUSE

HOUSE CURTAIN
Operates as a guillotine or traveller from SL deck

RIGGING SYSTEM
Type:	Single purchase counter weight
Weight:	60,000 lbs. available
Line sets:	67 sets at 6" o.c.
Arbors:	1,200 lb. capacity
House Pipes:	64'8" long with 52' of travel from deck.

Line sets are moveable
Block & Falls are available
Chain hoists are not available
(30) spot wheels and 6,000' of hemp available

PERMANENT INSTALLATIONS OVER STAGE (FROM SMOKE POCKET)
M=Moveable with advance call
Orchestra shell (1) at 10'6" - 12'0"
Electric raceways (4) at 4'6" 1st electric - electric winch
Electric bridge (1) at 22'0"; M
Cyclorama (1) at 40'6"
Main curtain (1) at 3'0"
3rd Electric raceway (1) at 24'0"

PERMANENT INSTALLATIONS ON DECK
Electric jump (1) at 4'6" 1st electric
Orchestra shell storage (5) at upstage of 40'6 - 45'
Adjustable proscenium (2), SL and SR, 44' - 60' wide

ORCHESTRA PIT
Adjustable to 14' below stage level by hydraulic lift
Apron overhangs US wall of pit 8'0"
Pit lift is in (2) sections
All FOH equipment can be lowered on pit lifts for easier load-ins

BACKSTAGE

LOADING DOCK
Loading door(s):
  10'0" high x 16'0" wide
Trucks load (2) at same time
Dock is SL, truck may need to provide ramps for exact level to dock
Fork lift is not required
Sound/Props cannot load in FOH
Lobby can be a work area
Many trailers can store on-site
Security at stage door

WARDROBE
Location: Backstage
Access: Dock to hallway,
  - ½ down, 50' from truck
(2) Washers (2) Dryers
Washer and dryer hookups available

DRESSING ROOMS
(3) Star, SL, stage level, t/s included, phone jack
(2) Small, SL, stage level, t/s included, phone jack
(3) Chorus, SL, stage level, t/s included, phone jack
Additional production office available for company mgr

SOUND

CONSOLE
Soundcraft 8000, located Orchestra
40 inputs, 2 main outputs, 8 matrix outputs, 8 aux outputs

SPEAKERS
House Cluster
Proscenium
Under Balcony
Other box seating & balcony delays (Bose)
No speaker truss

COMMUNICATIONS
RTS intercom with (2) channels
FM System - phonic ear
Dressing room page system

ROAD CONSOLE
Located Orchestra
Cable run from stage is 150'
Tie-in into house system with XLR connectors

REHEARSAL & STORAGE SPACE
Rehearsal: Various sizes and locations
Storage: Off SR 35' x 47'
Dock 30' x 26', off SR

ELECTRICS

ROAD SERVICE POWER
Panel	Phase	Amp	Circuit Protection	Use	Location
A-B	3	400	fuse	dimmers	DSR
C	3	400	fuse	extra	DSR
D	3	200	fuse	sound	USL
E	3	200	fuse	extra	Dock

All road power has option of building ground or cold water pipe
Recommended location of touring dimmer racks: off DSR
Hoist not required
Additional power is available for tour buses, generators, etc.

FRONT OF HOUSE (BOX BOOM VALUES ARE PER SIDE)
Position	Pipe Width	Distance to Prosc.	House Circuits	Connector Type	FOH Transfer Circuits
1st Cove	90'	21'	18	grd 20 amp stage pin	18
2nd Cove	90'	50'	22	grd 20 amp stage pin	22
3rd Cove	90'	65'	18	grd 20 amp stage pin	18
1st Balc Rail	50'	80'	15	grd 20 amp stage pin	15
Box Boom 1		9'	8	grd 20 amp stage pin	

Transfer circuits: grd 20 amp stage pin
Road truss: Hanging of truss DS of proscenium is not possible without a lot of work

EQUIPMENT FOH (BOX BOOM VALUES ARE PER SIDE
Position	Quantity	Wattage	Instrument	Removeable
1st Cove	15	1,000	6 x 12 & Zoom	yes
2nd Cove	18	1,000	6 x 12	yes
3rd Cove	16	1,000	5	yes
1st Balc Rail	31	1,000	6 x 12 5	yes
Box Boom 1	4	1,000	6 x 9	yes

FOLLOWSPOTS
House Followspots:
(2) Strong Super Trouper; removeable

Followspot Booth:
(2) spots per booth;
80' throw to proscenium;
(4) 1Ø 30 amp breakers

DIMMERS
House console is Colortran 3000;
(296) Colortran dimmers
House has DMX control system
(7) dry run DMX station(s)

VAN WEZEL PERFORMING ARTS HALL

YEAR BUILT: 1970

Theatre Location: 777 N. Tamiami Trail, Sarasota, FL 34236
Management Company: City of Sarasota

Main Administrative Phone: 941-955-7676
Main Administrative Fax: 941-951-1449
E-mail: vanwezel@gte.net
Website: ww.vanwezel.org
Backstage Pay Phone: 941-365-9608

THEATRE STAFF
Executive Director   William A. Mitchell   941-955-7676
Booking   William A Mitchell   941-955-7676
Marketing   Ilene Denton   941-953-7584
Operations   Heidi Hancock   941-955-7676

HOUSE CREW
Technical Director   Jerry Jagielski   941-955-7676

UNIONS
IATSE Local #823   Bryan Slattery   941-955-5844

SEATING CAPACITY
A	914
B	543
C	250
Total:	**1,707**
pit (add'l)	54
wheelchair	5+

BOX OFFICE
Computerized
  Loreda Williams
  941-955-7676 x 225

Outside Ticket Agency
None

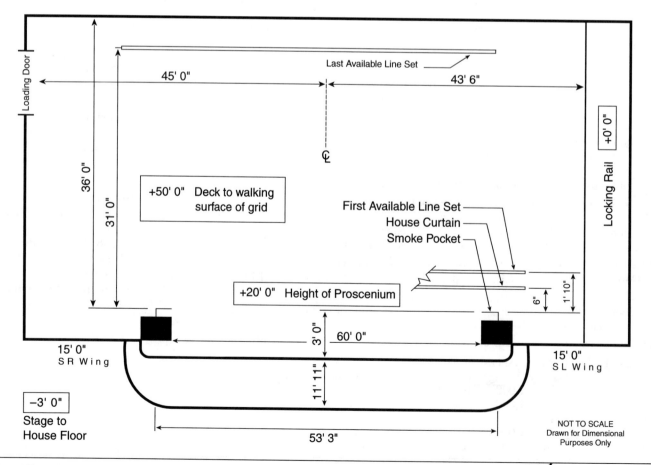

STAGE HOUSE

HOUSE CURTAIN
Operates as a guillotine or traveller from SL deck

RIGGING SYSTEM
Type:	Single purchase counter weight
Weight:	10,000 lbs available
Line sets:	30 sets at 6" o.c. with 5 lift lines per set
Arbors:	700 lb capacity
House Pipes:	52' long with 49' of travel from deck

Line sets are not moveable
Block & Falls are available 2:1 (2)
Chain hoists are not available
(7) spot wheels and 1,400' of hemp available

PERMANENT INSTALLATIONS OVER STAGE (FROM SMOKE POCKET)
M=Moveable with advance call
Hardteaser (1) at 2'2"
Hard torm legs (1) at 3'4"
Electric bridge (1) at 3'10" (22" wide); M
Movie screen (1) at 7'10"; M

PERMANENT INSTALLATIONS ON DECK
Orchestra shell (1) stores on back wall - 1'0" deep

ORCHESTRA PIT
Adjustable to 12' below stage level by hydraulic lift
Apron overhangs US wall of pit 4' 4"

BACKSTAGE

LOADING DOCK
Loading door(s):
  9'6" high x 11'0'' wide
Trucks load (1) at same time
Dock is at truck level; loading
  to stage thru separate loading
  bay behind stage house
Fork lift is not required
Sound/Props cannot load in
  FOH
(5) Trailers can store on-site
Security at dock & stage door

WARDROBE
Location: Basement
Access: Orchestra pit elevator
(1) Washer (1) Dryer
No washer or dryer hookups

DRESSING ROOMS
(5) Star, stage level, SL, t/s
  included
(4) Small, SL/SR, -1, t/s
  included
(2) Chorus, SL/SR, -1, t/s
  included
Additional production office
  available for company mgr

SOUND

CONSOLE
Yamaha PM 1532
32 inputs, 0 main outputs,
  4 matrix outputs, 4 aux
  outputs

SPEAKERS
House Cluster

COMMUNICATIONS
Telex intercom with
  (4) channels
Infrared sound system
Dressing room page system

ROAD CONSOLE
Located HL, rows 11-12
(12) seats required to be
  removed
Cable run from stage is 75'
Tie-in into house system with
  XLR connectors

REHEARSAL & STORAGE SPACE
Rehearsal: None
Storage: None

ELECTRICS

ROAD SERVICE POWER

Panel	Phase	Amp	Circuit Protection	Use	Location
A	3	400	breaker	dimmers	SR side wall
B	3	300	breaker	dimmers	SR side wall
C	3	200	breaker	dimmers	SR side wall
D-E	3	100	breaker	sound	SR side wall

Recommended location of touring dimmer racks: SR on deck
Hoist not required

FRONT OF HOUSE (BOX BOOM VALUES ARE PER SIDE)

Position	Pipe Width	Distance to Prosc.	House Circuits	Connector Type	FOH Transfer Circuits
1st Cove	30'	75'	24	20 amp old twistlock	0
Box Boom 1		55'	12	20 amp old twistlock	0

EQUIPMENT FOH (BOX BOOM VALUES ARE PER SIDE)

Position	Quantity	Wattage	Instrument	Removeable
1st Cove	12	1,000	10 x 22 Lekos	yes
Box Boom 1	10	1,000	Berkey 10°	yes

FOLLOWSPOTS
House Followspots:
  (2) Xenon Super Troupers;
  removeable

Followspot Booth:
  (2) spots per booth;
  70' throw to proscenium;
  (4) 30 amp breakers

DIMMERS
Lighting console is
  Idea 225-cue;
  (190) LMI dimmers
House has programmable
  DMX control system
(1) dry run DMX station

TALLAHASSEE LEON COUNTY CIVIC CENTER

AKA: LEON COUNTY CIVIC CENTER

YEAR BUILT: 1981   YEAR RENOVATED: 1998

Theatre Location: 505 West Pensacola Street, Tallahassee, FL 32301-1619
Mailing Address: PO Box 10604, Tallahassee, FL 32302

Main Administrative Phone:	850-487-1691
Main Administrative Fax:	850-222-6947
Website:	www.tlccc.org
Backstage Pay Phone:	850-599-9042
Traveling Production Office Phone:	850-681-3669
Traveling Production Office Fax:	850-681-1043

THEATRE STAFF

Director	Ron Spencer	850-487-1691
Booking	Ron Spencer	850-487-1691
Marketing	Laura Diehl	850-487-1691
Operations	George Varn	850-487-1691

HOUSE CREW

Production Coord.	Kristin L. Vandenberg	850-487-1691
Electrics	Bob New	850-487-1691
Sound	Dave Cooperson	850-487-1691

SEATING CAPACITY

Floor	150
Riser	264
Orchestra	1,060
1st Balcony	740
2nd Balcony	276
Total:	**2,490**
wheelchair (add'l)	26

BOX OFFICE
Computerized
Box Office Manager
  Sharon Turner   850-222-0400

Outside Ticket Agency
Computerized
  Ticketmaster

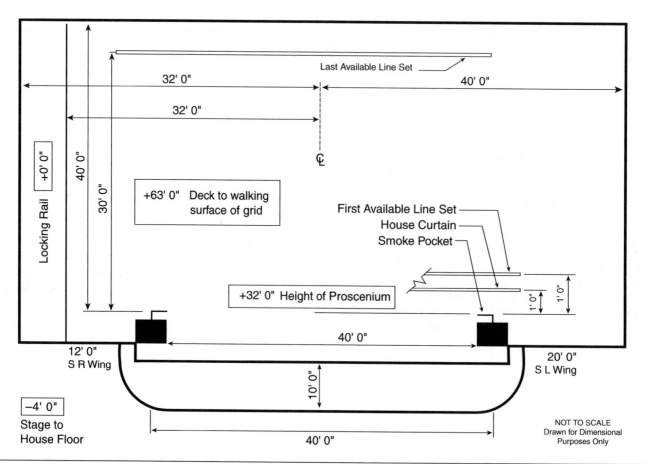

STAGE HOUSE

HOUSE CURTAIN
Operates as a guillotine from SR house floor

RIGGING SYSTEM
Type:	Single purchase counter weight
Weight:	9,000 lbs available
Line sets:	16 sets at 12" o.c. with 6 lift lines per set
Arbors:	750 lb capacity
House Pipes:	60' long with 60' of travel from deck

Line sets are moveable
Block & Falls are available
Chain hoists are available as a rental; (10) one ton
1,000' of hemp available
Rig to arena high steel @ 83' from deck

PERMANENT INSTALLATIONS OVER STAGE (FROM SMOKE POCKET)
None

PERMANENT INSTALLATIONS ON DECK
None

ORCHESTRA PIT
Pit width adjusts based on requirements of stage apron
Pit is on house floor

BACKSTAGE

LOADING DOCK
Loading door(s):
15'0" high x 15'0" wide
Trucks load (3) at same time
Loading for addl trucks possible
thru (3) 13'6" high x 10'0"
wide doors, 40' from main
load-in door
Fork lift is required: House
owns
Sound/Props cannot load in
FOH
(10) Trailers can store on-site
Security on request

WARDROBE
Location: 150' USC hallway
parallel to DS edge of stage
Access: 20' from loading door
(1) Washer (1) Dryer
Washer and dryer hookups
available

DRESSING ROOMS
(3) Small, USC, stage level, t/s
included, phone jack
(4) Chorus, USC stage level, t/s
included
Additional production office
available for company mgr

SOUND

CONSOLE
No house console

SPEAKERS
Speaker truss exists
Flexible, anything can be
done

COMMUNICATIONS
Clear Com intercom with
(2) channels
Infrared sound system

ROAD CONSOLE
Located HR
No seats required to be
removed
Cable run from stage is 60'
Tie-in into house system with
XLR connectors

REHEARSAL & STORAGE SPACE
Rehearsal: None
Storage: Arena floor,
90' x 100', behind stage

ELECTRICS

ROAD SERVICE POWER

Panel	Phase	Amp	Circuit Protection	Use	Location
A	3	600	fuse	dimmers	USL
B	3	200	fuse	extra	USL
C	3	400	fuse	sound	USL
D	3	200	fuse	extra	USL
E	3	200	fuse	extra	FOH

Recommended location of touring dimmer racks: SL house floor
Hoist not required
Additional power is available for tour buses, generators, etc.

FRONT OF HOUSE (BOX BOOM VALUES ARE PER SIDE)
None
Road truss: 60' triangle truss hung 30' DS of stage for FOH lighting instruments; cable
& dimmers available thru rental company

EQUIPMENT FOH (BOX BOOM VALUES ARE PER SIDE)
None

FOLLOWSPOTS
House Followspots:
(2) Xenon Gladiator II
(5) Xenon Super Troupers
(2) 400 Super Arcs;
removeable

Followspot Booth: None
Alternate location: Catwalk

DIMMERS
No lighting console
No dimmers
No DMX control system

TAMPA BAY PERFORMING ARTS CENTER

AKA: CAROL MORSANI HALL

YEAR BUILT: 1987

Theatre Location: 1010 North MacInnes Place, Tampa, FL 33602
Mailing Address: PO Box 518, Tampa, FL 33601-0518

Main Administrative Phone:	813-222-1000
Main Administrative Fax:	813-222-1057
Website:	www.tampacenter.com
Stage Door Phone:	813-222-1070
Backstage Pay Phone:	813-229-9551
Traveling Production Office Phone:	813-222-1071
Traveling Production Office Fax:	813-222-1079

THEATRE STAFF

President	Judith Lisi	813-222-1000
Booking	Judith Lisi	813-222-1000
Marketing	Carol Edgerly	813-222-1055
Operations	Lorrin Shepard	813-222-1010

HOUSE CREW

Production Manager	Michael Chamoun	813-222-1020
		mike.chamoun@tbpac.org
Carpentry	Scott Cline	813-222-1023
Electrics	Greg Cap	813-222-1090
Electrics	William Davis	813-222-1090
Sound	Terry McCann	813-222-1026

UNIONS

IATSE Local #321	Paul Paleveda	813-877-2788
Wardrobe Local #321	Paul Paleveda	813-877-2788
Music	Ralph Wilder	407-293-5225

SEATING CAPACITY

Orchestra	1,325
Mezzanine	438
Balcony	393
Gallery	344
Total:	**2,500**
wheelchair (incl.)	57

BOX OFFICE
Computerized
Box Office Manager
 Tony Walters   813-222-1067

Outside Ticket Agency
Computerized
Ticketmaster
 Tony Walters   813-222-1067

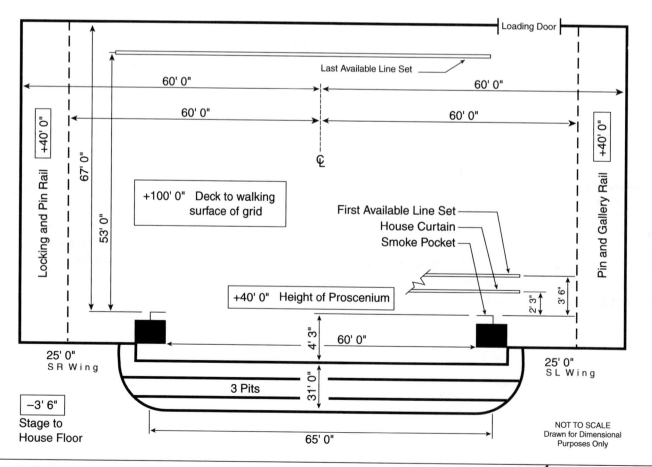

STAGE HOUSE

House Curtain

Operates as a guillotine from SR deck

Rigging System

Type:	Single purchase counter weight
Weight:	10,000 lbs available
Line sets:	109 sets at 6" o.c. with 7 lift lines per set
Arbors:	2,000 lb capacity
House Pipes:	72' long with 95' of travel from deck

Line sets are not moveable

Block & Falls are not available

Chain hoists are available

(50) spot wheels and 15,000' of hemp available

Permanent Installations Over Stage (from smoke pocket)

M=Moveable with advance call

Hard portal (1) at 2'8"; M

Cyclorama (1) at 45'6"; M

Fire curtain (1) 40 ton wood wall, doubles as acoustic wall

Catwalk (1) 40' high runs along wall SL / US / SR

Electric raceways (1) at 6'0"; M

Permanent Installations On Deck

Hard legs (1), 1'10" to smoke pocket

Pilasters (2)

Columns (2) 3'0" square, 57'0" US, 30' SL + SR

Loading bridge (2) SR wall 95'0" + 105'0"

Adjustable proscenium (1)

Adjustable portal (1)

Orchestra Pit

Adjustable to 21' below stage level by electric motor turnscrew

Apron overhangs US wall of pit 10'0"

Pit lift is in (3) sections

BACKSTAGE

Loading Dock

Loading door(s):
14'0" high x 20'0" wide

Trucks load (4) at same time

Loading to stage thru separate loading area behind stage house, doors 32'0" high x 13'6" wide

Fork lift is not required

Sound/Props can load in FOH

Lobby can be a work area

Security at stage door

Wardrobe

Location: Dressing room hallway USR

Access: USR door - same level as stage

(2) Washers (2) Dryers

Dressing Rooms

(1) Star, SR, stage level, t/s included, phone jack

(6) Small, SR, stage level, t/s included

(3) Chorus, SR, stage level, t/s included

(4) Chorus, SR, stage level, t/s included, phone jack

Additional production office available for company mgr

SOUND

Console

Yamaha PM 4000, located Rear & Orchestra

40 inputs, 8 main outputs, 8 matrix outputs, 8 aux outputs

Speakers

House Cluster

Proscenium

Portable

No speaker truss

Communications

RTS intercom with (2) channels

Infrared sound system

Dressing room page system

Road Console

Located Rear Orchestra

No seats required to be removed

Cable run from stage is 200'

Tie-in into house system with XLR connectors

Rehearsal & Storage Space

Rehearsal: 52' x'75' - USR stage level, must reserve / rental

Storage: 30' x 100' - loading area behind stage, area shared by a second theatre

ELECTRICS

Road Service Power

Panel	Phase	Amp	Circuit Protection	Use	Location
A-C	3	400	fuse	dimmers	SL
D	3	200	breaker	sound	SL
E	3	60	fuse	extra	SL

Recommended location of touring dimmer racks: SL

Hoist not required   Additional power is available for tour buses, generators, etc.

Front Of House (box boom values are per side)

Position	Pipe Width	Distance to Prosc.	House Circuits	Connector Type	FOH Transfer Circuits
1st Balc Rail		100'	6	grd 20 amp stage pin	6
2nd Balc Rail		115'	24	grd 20 amp stage pin	16
3rd Balc Rail		125'	16	grd 20 amp stage pin	6
Box Boom 1			10	grd 20 amp stage pin	10
Box Boom 2			12	grd 20 amp stage pin	12
Reverb		150'	18	grd 20 amp stage pin	8

Transfer circuits: Stage pin connectors SL   Road truss: Grid beams on 11' centers

Equipment FOH (box boom values are per side)

Position	Quantity	Wattage	Instrument	Removeable
1st Balc Rail	24	1,000	6 x 9 Leko	yes
2nd Balc Rail	6	1,000	8 x 14/24 Leko	yes
3rd Balc Rail	16	1,000	10 x 5 Leko	yes
Box Boom1	24	1,000	8 x 14/24	yes
Box Boom 2	20	1,000	8 x 14/24	yes
Reverb	18	1,000	10 x 5° Lekos	yes

Followspots

House Followspots:
(4) Strong Xenon Super Trouper; not removeable

Followspot Booth:
(4) spots per booth;
150' throw to proscenium;
(4) 1Ø 30 amp breakers

Dimmers

Lighting console is Strand 550;
(761) CD80 AMX dimmers

No DMX control system

RAYMOND F. KRAVIS CENTER FOR THE PERFORMING ARTS

AKA: KRAVIS CENTER   **YEAR BUILT: 1992**

Theatre Location: 701 Okeechobee Blvd, West Palm Beach, FL 33401

Main Administrative Phone:	561-833-8300
Main Administrative Fax:	561-833-3901
E-mail:	lessig@kravis.org
Website:	www.kravis.org
Stage Door Phone:	561-833-7952
Traveling Production Office Phone:	561-838-9101
Traveling Production Office Fax:	561-838-9502

SEATING CAPACITY

Orchestra	998
Grand Tier	324
Loge	293
Mezzanine	293
Balcony	281
Total:	**2,189**

BOX OFFICE
Computerized
Box Office Manager
  Maria Quesada   561-651-4240

THEATRE STAFF

CEO	Judith Sheperd	561-833-8300
Booking	Lee Bell	561-833-8300
Marketing	Ilene Arrons	561-833-8300

HOUSE CREW

Technical Director	Tim Lessig	561-651-4249
Stage Manager	Marie Cormier	561-651-4245
Production Supv	Walter Scott	561-651-4205
Production Supv	John Woram	561-651-4314

UNIONS

IATSE Local #623	John Dermody	561-694-7774

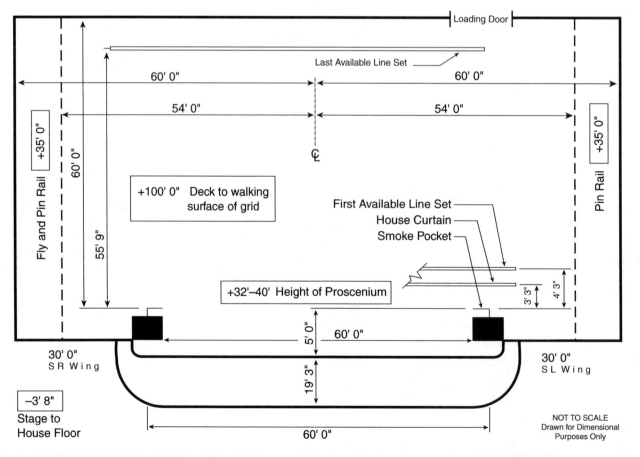

STAGE HOUSE

HOUSE CURTAIN
Operates as a guillotine from SR fly floor or deck; motorized

RIGGING SYSTEM
Type:	Single purchase counter weight
Weight:	120,000 lbs available
Line sets:	91 sets at 6" o.c. with 7 lift lines per set
Arbors:	1,500 lb capacity
House Pipes:	76' 3" long with 93' of travel from deck

Line sets are not moveable
Block & Falls are not available
Chain hoists are not available
(100) spot wheels and 6,000' of hemp available

PERMANENT INSTALLATIONS OVER STAGE (FROM SMOKE POCKET)
M=Moveable with advance call
Orchestra shells (4) at 8'9", 21'9", 34'9", 47'9"; M

PERMANENT INSTALLATIONS ON DECK
None

ORCHESTRA PIT
Adjustable to 10' below stage level by electric motor turnscrew
Apron overhangs US wall of pit 10'0"
Pit lift is in (2) sections

BACKSTAGE

LOADING DOCK
Loading door(s):
   12'0" high x 8'0" wide
Trucks load (3) at same time
Fork lift is not required
Sound/Props cannot load in FOH
(1) Trailer can store on-site
Security at dock & stage door

WARDROBE
Location: Basement
Access: Elevator/Stairs
(2) Washers (2) Dryers
Washer and dryer hookups available

DRESSING ROOMS
(4) Small, SL/SR, stage level, t/s included, phone jack
(3) Small, basement, t/s included, phone jack
(8) Chorus, basement, t/s included
(1) Chorus, basement, t/s included, phone jack
Elevator access for dressing rooms
Use dressing room for company mgr office

SOUND

CONSOLE
Soundcraft Vienna
24 inputs, 8 main outputs, 8 matrix outputs, 8 aux outputs

SPEAKERS
House Cluster
Proscenium
Portable
No speaker truss

COMMUNICATIONS
Clear Com intercom with (8) channels

ROAD CONSOLE
Located Front of House
No seats required to be removed
Cable run from stage is 200'
Tie-in into house system with XLR connectors

REHEARSAL & STORAGE SPACE
Rehearsal: None
Storage: Receiving area, 2100 sq ft, US

ELECTRICS

ROAD SERVICE POWER

Panel	Phase	Amp	Circuit Protection	Use	Location
A-C	3	400	fuse	dimmers	USL
D	3	100	fuse	extra	SL
E	3	200	fuse	extra	SL
F	3	200	fuse	sound	SL
G-H	3	100	fuse	extra	USL - Grid
I-J	3	100	fuse	extra	forestage grid
K	3	200		extra	receiving area

Recommended location of touring dimmer racks: SL
Hoist not required
Additional power is available for tour buses, generators, etc.

FRONT OF HOUSE (BOX BOOM VALUES ARE PER SIDE)

Position	Pipe Width	Distance to Prosc.	House Circuits	Connector Type	FOH Transfer Circuits
Far Catwalk		112'	22	grd 20 amp stage pin	11
Mid Catwalk		64'	32	grd 20 amp stage pin	32
Near Catwalk		54'	34	grd 20 amp stage pin	26
Left Tech Ledge		46'	6	grd 20 amp stage pin	
Right Tech Ledge		46'	6	grd 20 amp stage pin	

EQUIPMENT FOH (BOX BOOM VALUES ARE PER SIDE)

Position	Quantity	Wattage	Instrument	Removeable
1st Balc Rail	18	1,000	10 Ellipsoidal	yes
2nd Balc Rail	18	1,000	10 Ellipsoidal	yes
3rd Balc Rail	16	1,000	20/40 Zoom	yes
1st Cove	30	1,000	6 x 16 Lekos	yes
2nd Cove	34	1,000	6 x 16 Lekos	yes
3rd Cove	25	1,000	5 Ellipsoidal	yes
Box Boom 1	36	1,000	6 x 16 Lekos	yes
4th Tech Ledge	20	1,000	10 Ellipsoidal	yes

FOLLOWSPOTS
House Followspots:
   (4) Strong Super Trouper; not removeable

Followspot Booth:
   (4) spots per booth;
   111' throw to proscenium;
   (4) 1Ø 50 amp breakers

DIMMERS
Lighting console is ETC Obsession II;
(694) CD 80 dimmers
House has programmable DMX control system

THE CLASSIC CENTER THEATRE

YEAR BUILT: 1996

Theatre Location: 300 N. Thomas Street, Athens, GA 30601

Main Administrative Phone: 706-208-0900
Main Administrative Fax: 706-548-0870
E-mail: ccbook@classiccenter.com
Website: www.classiccenter.com

THEATRE STAFF
Executive Director   Paul Cramer   706-208-0900
Booking   Kris Bakowski   706-357-4414

HOUSE CREW
Technical Director   Neil Gluckman   404-284-7618
Maintenance Engineer   Broach Howard   706-357-4405

SEATING CAPACITY

Orchestra	568
Parterre	563
Loge	358
Mezzanine	476
Boxes	88
Total:	**2,053**
pit (add'l)	75
wheelchair (add'l)	40

STAGE DIMENSIONS (FROM SMOKE POCKET)
Stage is 41'0" deep
Width from Center Line to SL is 48'0"
Width from Center Line to SR is 45'0"
Proscenium width is 54'0"
Proscenium height is 32'0"
Smoke pocket to apron edge is 4'0"
Orchestra pit exists

RIGGING
Grid Height: 78'
Type: Single purchase counter weight
Line sets: 47 sets at 6" o.c.
Arbors: 3,000 lb capacity
House Pipes: 60' long

LOADING DOCK
Loading door(s) are 12'5" high x 10'2" wide
Trucks load (2) at same time
Fork lift is not required and is available

ELECTRICS
Total power available:
(2) 400A 3Ø DSL
(1) 100A 3Ø DSL

FOLLOWSPOTS
House Followspots:
Xenon Strong Super Trouper
Power in spot booth 60A

DIMMERS
(210) house dimmers
House has DMX control system
(4) dry run station(s) located
SR / SL / Mid House

SOUND
House has 200A dedicated
power located DSL
FOH mixing position in
between Orchestra &
Parterre
Sound console is available

ATLANTA CIVIC CENTER THEATER

AT: ATLANTA CIVIC CENTER   **YEAR BUILT: 1969   YEAR RENOVATED: 1995**

Theatre Location: 395 Piedmont Avenue, NE, Atlanta, GA 30308
Management Company: City of Atlanta

Main Administrative Phone: 404-523-6275
Main Administrative Fax: 404-525-4634
E-mail: demetriusparker@mindspring.com
Website: www.atlanta.org/civicctr.htm
Stage Door Phone: 404-522-6371
Backstage Pay Phone: 404-525-9605
Traveling Production Office Phone: 404-523-6275
Traveling Production Office Fax: 404-525-4634

THEATRE STAFF
Director   Ann Marie Moraitakis   404-523-6275
Booking   Joyce Whisenant   404-523-6275
Marketing   Ann Marie Moraitakis   404-523-6275
Operations   Cliff Bacon   404-523-6275

HOUSE CREW
Production Manager   Rebecah Jones   404-658-6308
Carpentry   Chico Atcheson   404-523-6275
Electrics   Darryl Hilton   404-523-6275
Sound   Coits Weaver   404-523-6275
Steward   George Stanley   404-523-6275

UNIONS
IATSE #927   Larry Boyter   404-870-9910

SEATING CAPACITY
Orchestra   2,496
Boxes   250
Loge   704
Dress Circle   667
Balcony   474
Total: **4,591**

BOX OFFICE
Outside Ticket Agency
Computerized
Ticketmaster
  Karen Swope   404-249-8300

Box office is promoter operated

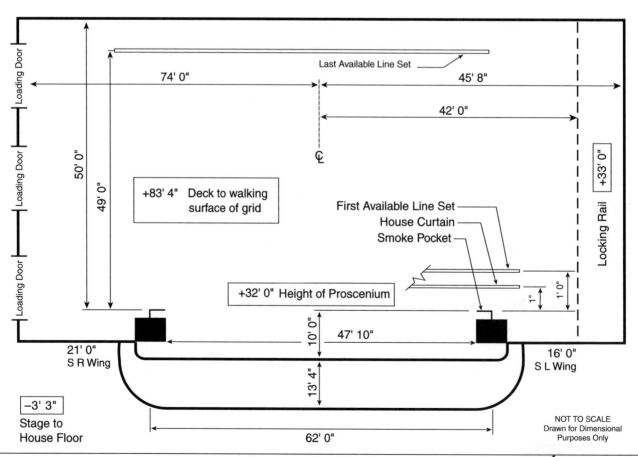

STAGE HOUSE

HOUSE CURTAIN
Operates as a guillotine or traveller from SL fly floor or deck

RIGGING SYSTEM
Type:	Double purchase counter weight; Hemp
Weight:	40,000 lbs available
Line sets:	60 sets at 6" o.c. with 7 lift lines per set
Arbors:	2,000 lb capacity
House Pipes:	60' long with 80' of travel from deck

Line sets are moveable
Chain hoists are not available
(11) spot wheels

PERMANENT INSTALLATIONS OVER STAGE (FROM SMOKE POCKET)
M=Moveable with advance call
Orchestra shells; M
Orchestra shell arms; M
Electric Raceways (9) at 5'2", 8'7", 11'5", 15'4", 19'1", 27'2", 29'11", 35'0", 39'3"; M
Electric bridge (3) over auditorium with electric raceways
Electric pipe on raceways (9)
Catwalk (5) not over stage but in FOH

PERMANENT INSTALLATIONS ON DECK
Jumps (above locking rail) (1), 49' x 5', SL
Electric jump (1), 6'x 9', SL
Columns (2) 20'0", SR
Loading bridge (3), 3' x 60', SL
Pilasters (3), 1'6" x 2'6", US wall

ORCHESTRA PIT
Adjustable to 18' below stage level by electric motor turnscrew
Apron overhangs US wall of pit 5'0"; Pit lift in (4) sections

BACKSTAGE

LOADING DOCK
Loading door(s):
    (3) 20'0" high x 12'0" wide
Trucks load (3) side by side at same time
(3) Docks: One is at street level accessed by ramp; Docks 2/ 3 are at truck level
Fork lift is required; house owns
Sound/Props cannot load in FOH
(21) Trailers can store on-site
Security at dock & stage door

WARDROBE
Location: Backstage
Access: Stage entrance
(2) Washers (2) Dryers
Washer and dryer hookups available

DRESSING ROOMS
(2) Star, behind stage on stage level,t/s
(6) Small, behind stage on stage level, t/s on same fl
(4) Chorus, behind stage, +2, t/s
Additional production office available for company mgr

SOUND

CONSOLE
GL.4-24 Channels, located Backstage Left
24 inputs, 2 main outputs, 2 matrix outputs, 8 aux outputs

SPEAKERS
House Cluster
Under Balcony
Stage Monitors
No speaker truss

COMMUNICATIONS
Technical Projects intercom, 8 stations, (9) channels
Infrared sound system
Dressing room page system

ROAD CONSOLE
None
Tie-in into house system with XLR connectors

REHEARSAL & STORAGE SPACE
Rehearsal: None
Storage: None

ELECTRICS

ROAD SERVICE POWER

Panel	Phase	Amp	Circuit Protection	Use	Location
A-B	3	400	fuse	dimmers	SR back wall
C-D	3	400	fuse	dimmers	SL back wall
E	3	200	fuse	sound	SL back wall
F-G	3	400	fuse	extra	SL dimmer room
H	3	60	fuse	extra	SR tunnel

Recommended location of touring dimmer racks: SL
Hoist is required and provided
Additional power is available for tour buses, generators, etc

FRONT OF HOUSE (BOX BOOM VALUES ARE PER SIDE)

Position	Pipe Width	Distance to Prosc.	House Circuits	Connector Type	FOH Transfer Circuits
1st Cove	33'	60'	18	grd 20 amp stage pin	30
2nd Cove	93'	77'	30	grd 20 amp stage pin	27

Transfer circuits: (57) FOH ¼" brass single prong plugs extendable 3' from patch bay

EQUIPMENT FOH (BOX BOOM VALUES ARE PER SIDE)

Position	Quantity	Wattage	Instrument	Removeable
2nd Cove	21	575	6 x16 Lekos/Source4 26°	yes

Portable Balcony Rail (4) available as 10' sections without circuits

FOLLOWSPOTS
House Followspots:
    (2) Xenon Super Troupers; removeable
    (2) Carbon Arc Super Troupers; removeable
    (2) Voyager Follow Spot 400w; removeable

Followspot Booth:
    (4) spots per booth;
    210' throw to proscenium;
    (4) 3Ø 200 amp breakers

DIMMERS
Lighting console is ETC Insight 2;
(52) CLI 10k dimmers

FOX THEATRE

Year built: 1929

Theatre Location: 600 Peachtree Street NE, Atlanta, GA 30365

Main Administrative Phone:	404-881-2100
Main Administrative Fax:	404-872-2972
Stage Door Phone:	404-881-2047
Backstage Pay Phone:	404-881-9042
Traveling Production Office Phone:	404-881-2066
Traveling Production Office Fax:	404-881-9042

Theatre Staff
General Manager	Edgar Neiss	404-881-2114
Booking	Edgar Neiss	404-881-2114
Operations	Wendy Riggs	404-881-2062
Group Sales	Martha Beesley	404-881-2012

House Crew
Production Mgr	Sam Ritchie	404-881-2065
Carpentry	Tim Hartwig	404-881-2100
Electrics	Scott Kepley	404-881-2100
Sound	Jess McCurry	404-881-2074
Props	Pat Noon	404-881-2100

Unions
IATSE Local #927	Larry Boyter	404-870-9911
Wardrobe	Sue Cochran	770-949-7546

Seating Capacity
Orchestra	2,620
Loge	436
First Dress Circle	846
Second Dress Circle	376
Gallery	240
Total:	**4,518**
pit (add'l)	164

Box Office
Computerized
Box Office Manager
  Patricia Tucker   404-881-2010

Outside Ticket Agency
Computerized
  Ticketmaster   404-249-8300

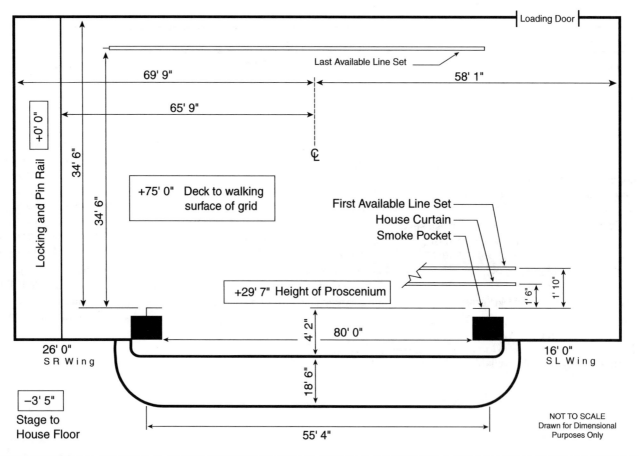

STAGE HOUSE

HOUSE CURTAIN
Operates as a guillotine or traveller from SR deck; motorized

RIGGING SYSTEM
Type: Single purchase counter weight
Weight: 25,000 lbs available
Line sets: 63 sets at 4-12" o.c. with 5 lift lines per set
Arbors: 1,000 lb capacity
House Pipes: 70' long with 67' of travel from deck
Line sets are not moveable
Block & Falls are available 2:1, 3:1
Chain hoists are available

PERMANENT INSTALLATIONS OVER STAGE (FROM SMOKE POCKET)
None

PERMANENT INSTALLATIONS ON DECK
None

ORCHESTRA PIT
Adjustable to 10'3" below stage level by electric motor turnscrew
Apron overhangs US wall of pit 0'0"
Pit lift is in (1) section
Pit organ lift at center

BACKSTAGE

LOADING DOCK
Loading door(s):
    14'10" high x 8'7" wide
Trucks load (2) back to back at same time
Dock is 4'1" above street level
    Forklift via Atlanta Fork Lift
    404-373-1606
Sound/Props can load in FOH
Lobby can be a work area
Security at stage door

WARDROBE
Location: Basement SR
Access: Lift trap in stage floor and elevators SL/SR
(3) Washers (3) Dryers
No washer or dryer hookups

DRESSING ROOMS
(2) Star, SR, 3rd fl, t/s included
(5) Small, SR, 1st/2nd/4th/5th fl, t/s on same fl
(11) Chorus, SR, 1st/2nd/4th/ 5th fl t/s on same fl
Additional production office available for company mgr

SOUND

CONSOLE
Yamaha PM 4000 48, located Rear House
48 inputs, 8 main outputs, 8 aux outputs

SPEAKERS
House Cluster
Proscenium
Under Balcony
Center Cluster and Under Balcony speakers are permanent, proscenium system is easily removable
No speaker truss

COMMUNICATIONS
HME intercom with (2) channels
Phonic ear RF system
Dressing room page system

ROAD CONSOLE
Located Rear House
No seats required to be removed
Cable run from stage is 250'
Tie-in into house system with XLR connectors

REHEARSAL & STORAGE SPACE
Rehearsal: Medium size room, 6th floor, barres
Storage: 20' x 20' off stage left

ELECTRICS

ROAD SERVICE POWER

Panel	Phase	Amp	Circuit Protection	Use	Location
A	3	800	breaker	dimmers	DSR in basement
B	3	400	fuse	dimmers	DSR in basement
C	3	125	fuse	sound	DSL or DSR in basement
D	3	60	fuse	extra	USR rear wall
E	3	30	fuse	extra	USR rear wall
F	3	400	fuse	extra	SL side wall

Recommended location of touring dimmer racks: SR
Hoist not required
Additional power is available for tour buses, generators, etc.

FRONT OF HOUSE (BOX BOOM VALUES ARE PER SIDE)

Position	Pipe Width	Distance to Prosc.	House Circuits	Connector Type	FOH Transfer Circuits
1st Balc Rail	46'	62'	35	grd 20 amp stage pin	35
1st Cove	50'	65'	12	grd 20 amp stage pin	12
Box Boom 1		72'	12	grd 20 amp stage pin	12

Transfer circuits: grd 20 amp stage pin on DSR wall

EQUIPMENT FOH (BOX BOOM VALUES ARE PER SIDE)

Position	Quantity	Wattage	Instrument	Removeable
1st Balc Rail	12	575	Source 4 20°	yes
1st Cove	9	1,000	Altman 6x22	yes
Box Boom 1	15	575	Source 4 19°	yes

FOLLOWSPOTS
House Followspots:
    (4) Lycian 1290 XLT Xenon 2k; removeable

Followspot Booth:
    (4) spots per booth;
    165' throw to proscenium;
    (4) 3Ø 60 amp breakers

DIMMERS
Lighting console is ETC Obsession 600;
(240) AVAB dimmers
House has non-program-mable DMX control system
No dry run DMX station(s)

WILLIAM BELL AUDITORIUM

AT: AUGUSTA RICHMOND COUNTY CIVIC CENTER COMPLEX   **YEAR BUILT: 1940   YEAR RENOVATED: 1990**

Theatre Location:	712 Telfair Street, Augusta, GA 30906	
Mailing Address:	601 Seventh Street, PO Box 2306, Augusta, GA 30903	
Management Company:	Leisure Management International	
	11 Greenway Plaza, Suite 3000, Houston, TX 77046	

SEATING CAPACITY

Orchestra	1,172
Balcony	1,518
Total:	**2,690**
wheelchair (add'l)	12

Main Administrative Phone:	706-722-3521
Main Administrative Fax:	706-724-7545
E-mail:	jgreen@arccc.com
Stage Door Phone:	706-823-6672
Backstage Pay Phone:	706-722-9422
Traveling Production Office Phone:	706-823-6394
Traveling Production Office Fax:	706-823-6395

BOX OFFICE
Computerized
Box Office Manager
   Loretta Rau   706-722-3521 x542

Outside Ticket Agency
Computerized
   Ticketmaster
   Kim Brandt   800-735-1318

THEATRE STAFF

General Manager	Pat Cumiskey	706-722-3521 x514
Booking	Linda Roberts	706-722-3521 x511
Marketing	Christine Loftin	706-722-3521 x502
Operations	George Croft	706-722-3521 x508

UNIONS

IATSE Local #629	Pat Land	803-279-1523
Wardrobe Local #629	Pat Land	803-279-1523

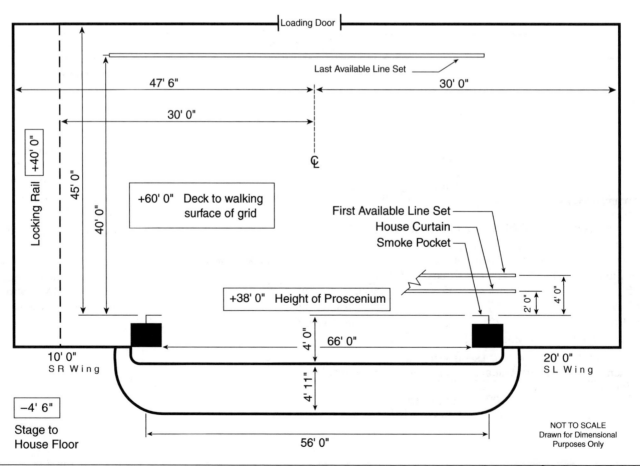

STAGE HOUSE

HOUSE CURTAIN
Operates as a guillotine or traveller from SR deck

RIGGING SYSTEM
Type:	Single purchase counter weight
Weight:	14,000 lbs available
Line sets:	40 sets with 2 lift lines per set
Arbors:	950 lb capacity
House Pipes:	70' long with 54'4" of travel from deck

Line sets are moveable
Block & Falls are not available
Chain hoists available as a rental; (2) one ton, (2) half ton
600' of hemp available

PERMANENT INSTALLATIONS OVER STAGE (FROM SMOKE POCKET)
M=Moveable with advance call
Traveller (1) - track stays, traveller can be dropped
Electric bridge (1)
Electric pipe (1); motorized
Dead spaces (4)
Cyclorama (1) flat blue; M
Fire curtain (1)
Catwalk (1)

PERMANENT INSTALLATIONS ON DECK
Jumps (1)
Electric bridge (1) 40' x 4'
Loading bridge (1) 40' x 4' located SR - US/DS
House Cove (1)

ORCHESTRA PIT
Nonadjustable at 7' below stage level
Apron overhangs US wall of pit 1'6"
Pit lift is in (12) sections

BACKSTAGE

LOADING DOCK
Loading door(s):
   10'0" high x 8'0" wide
Trucks load (1) at same time
See enclosed loading dock height for semi or large trucks; others could require forklift
Fork lift required: House owns
Sound/Props cannot load in FOH
Many trailers can store on-site
Security at dock & stage door

WARDROBE
Location: Loading dock storage or hallway to dressing rooms
Access: Loading dock
(1) Washer (1) Dryer
Washer and dryer hookups available

DRESSING ROOMS
(1) Star, SR, +1, t/s on same fl
(2) Small, SR, +1, t/s on same fl, phone jack
(7) Chorus, SR, +2,/+3, t/s on same fl
Additional production office available for company mgr

SOUND

CONSOLE
Yamaha PMA 1800, located SL or 1st Balcony
24 inputs, 2 main outputs, 4 matrix outputs, 6 aux outputs

SPEAKERS
House Cluster
Portable
Speaker truss exists

COMMUNICATIONS
Telex intercom with (3) channels
Dressing room page system

ROAD CONSOLE
Located Rear House center
(12) seats required to be removed
Cable run from stage is 200'
Tie-in into house system with XLR connectors

REHEARSAL & STORAGE SPACE
Rehearsal: None
Storage: (2) areas
   Loading dock, 19' x 42'
   Off SL, 27' x 31'

ELECTRICS

ROAD SERVICE POWER

Panel	Phase	Amp	Circuit Protection	Use	Location
A	3	600	breaker	sound	stage L&R on backwall

Recommended location of touring dimmer racks: Rear House Center
Hoist not required
Additional power is available for tour buses, generators, etc.
110 AC outlets on wall around stage area 20A

FRONT OF HOUSE (BOX BOOM VALUES ARE PER SIDE)

Position	Pipe Width	Distance to Prosc.	House Circuits	Connector Type	FOH Transfer Circuits
1st Cove	70'	30'	40	grd 20 amp stage pin	40

Transfer circuits: 40 from stage to house cove - pin plugs
Road truss: Can rig from grid or hang from pipes

EQUIPMENT FOH (BOX BOOM VALUES ARE PER SIDE)

Position	Quantity	Wattage	Instrument	Removeable
1st Cove	1		Fresnels/Lekos	yes

This cove is FOH approximately 40' from stage and 50' up

FOLLOWSPOTS
House Followspots:
   (2) Xenon Super Troupers

(2) Followspot Booths each:
   (2) spots per booth;
   140' throw to proscenium;
   (2) 3Ø 30 amp breakers

DIMMERS
Lighting console is ETC Insight;
   (288) LMI dimmers
House has programmable DMX control system
(1) dry run DMX station DSR

JOHNNY MERCER THEATRE

AT: SAVANNAH CIVIC CENTER

Theatre Location: Montgomery at Liberty, Savannah, GA 31498
Mailing Address: PO Box 726, Savannah , GA 31402
Management Company: City of Savannah (mailing address as above)

Main Administrative Phone: 912-651-6550
Main Administrative Fax: 912-651-6552
Stage Door Phone: 912-651-6550 x105

THEATRE STAFF
Director   Cynthia Brinson   912-651-6550
Booking   Cynthia Brinson   912-651-6550

HOUSE CREW
Building Super Alan Longwater   912-651-6550

UNIONS
IATSE Local #320 Micheal Mounihan   912-352-9676

SEATING CAPACITY
Orchestra   1,582
Mezzanine   264
Balcony   678
Total: **2,524**

BOX OFFICE
Computerized
Box Office Treasurer
 Richard Dotson   912-651-6554

Outside Ticket Agency
Charge-by-phone   912-651-6556

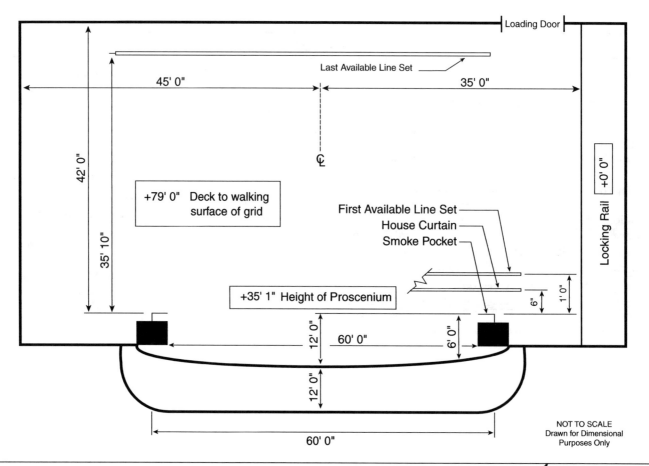

STAGE HOUSE

HOUSE CURTAIN
Operates as a guillotine or traveller from SL deck

RIGGING SYSTEM
Type:	Single purchase counter weight
Weight:	38,000 lbs available
Line sets:	51 sets with 7 lift lines per set
Arbors:	1,200 lb capacity
House Pipes:	70' long with 70' of travel from deck

Line sets are not moveable

PERMANENT INSTALLATIONS OVER STAGE (FROM SMOKE POCKET)
Electric Battons (3) at 3'10", 14'10", 30'10"

PERMANENT INSTALLATIONS ON DECK
None

ORCHESTRA PIT
Adjustable to 18' below stage level by hydraulic lift
Apron overhangs US wall of pit 6'0"

BACKSTAGE

LOADING DOCK
Loading door(s):
   22'0" high x 16'0" wide
Trucks load (2) at same time
Dock is 1'0" above truck level
Forklift: House owns

WARDROBE
Location: DSL on stage level
Access: Direct from stage
Washer and dryer hookups
   available

DRESSING ROOMS
(4) Star, SR, stage level, t/s
   included
(4) Star, SL, stage level, t/s
   included

SOUND

CONSOLE
Allen & Heath GL 4000 32
   Channel

SPEAKERS
House Cluster

COMMUNICATIONS
Clear Com intercom
Infrared sound system
Dressing room page system

ROAD CONSOLE
Located Rear House
No seats required to be
   removed
Cable run from stage is 125'
Tie-in into house system with
   XLR connectors

REHEARSAL & STORAGE SPACE
Rehearsal: None
Storage: 120' x 40' located
   USL behind stage

ELECTRICS

ROAD SERVICE POWER

Panel	Phase	Amp	Circuit Protection	Use	Location
A	3	400	fuse	dimmers	DSL procenium wall
B	3	200	fuse	sound	DSR procenium wall

Recommended location of touring dimmer racks: SL on deck
Additional power is available for tour buses, generators, etc.

FRONT OF HOUSE (BOX BOOM VALUES ARE PER SIDE)

Position	Pipe Width	Distance to Prosc.	House Circuits	Connector Type	FOH Transfer Circuits
1st Balc Rail	16'	35'	16	20 amp new twistlock	0
2nd Balc Rail	70'	60'	16	20 amp new twistlock	0
Box Boom 1		12'	6	grd 20 amp stage pin	0

EQUIPMENT FOH (BOX BOOM VALUES ARE PER SIDE)
None

FOLLOWSPOTS
House Followspots:
   (2) Xenon Super Troopers
2k

Followspot Booth:
   (3) spots per booth;
   150' throw to proscenium;
   (8)1Ø 20 amp breakers

DIMMERS
Lighting console is
   ETC Express with monitor

NEAL S. BLAISDELL CENTER CONCERT HALL

YEAR BUILT: 1965   YEAR RENOVATED: 1994

Theatre Location: 777 Ward Avenue, Honolulu, HI 96814
Management Company: Department of Enterprise Services
                     City and County of Honolulu

Main Administrative Phone: 808-527-5400
Main Administrative Fax: 808-527-5499
E-mail: aud@co.honolulu.hi.us
Website: www.co.honolulu.hi.us/depts/aud
Backstage Pay Phone: 808-596-9823

THEATRE STAFF
  Director   Alvin Au   808-527-5400
  Booking   Shirley Andrade   808-527-5424
  Operations   John C. Fuhrmann   808-527-5418
HOUSE CREW
  Production Manager   Mary E. Lewis   808-527-5443
UNIONS
  IATSE Local #665   Al Burns   808-596-0227

SEATING CAPACITY
  Orchestra   1,311
  Balcony   706
  Total: **2,017**

  pit (add'l)   192
  wheelchair (add'l)   14
  standing (add'l)   75

BOX OFFICE
  Computerized
  Box Office Manager
    Victoria Ignacio   808-591-2211

  Outside Ticket Agency
  Computerized
    The Connection

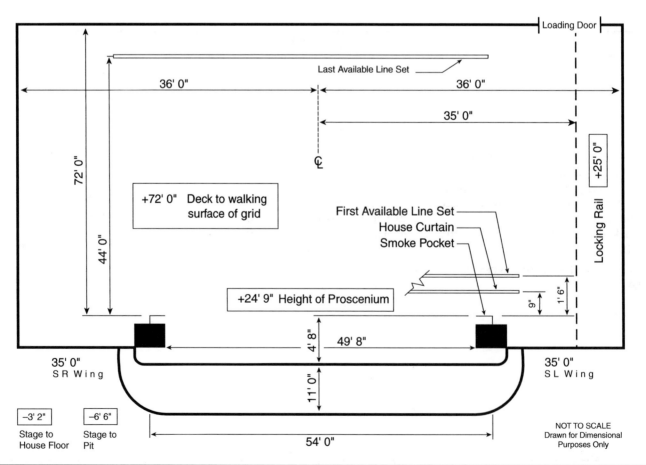

STAGE HOUSE

HOUSE CURTAIN
Operates as a guillotine or traveller from SL deck

RIGGING SYSTEM
Type:	Combination purchase counter weight
Weight:	41,000 lbs available
Line sets:	47 sets at 9" o.c. with 5 lift lines per set
Arbors:	2,376 lb capacity
House Pipes:	68' long with 65' of travel from deck

Line sets are moveable
Block & Falls are not available
Chain hoists available as a rental; (4) half ton
400' of hemp available

PERMANENT INSTALLATIONS OVER STAGE (FROM SMOKE POCKET)
M=Moveable with advance call
Orchestra shells (5) at 5'10", 13'4", 21'9", 29'10", 38'0"; M
Traveller (2) 17'11", 28'4"; M
Cyclorama (1); M

PERMANENT INSTALLATIONS ON DECK
Stairs (1) spiral to rail, USL corner

ORCHESTRA PIT
Adjustable to 6'6" below stage level by hydraulic lift
Apron overhangs US wall of pit 0'0"
Pit lift is in (1) section

BACKSTAGE

LOADING DOCK
Loading door(s):
   12'0" high x 10'0" wide
Trucks load (6) at same time
Dock (loading door sill) is at street level
Fork lift is required; house owns
Sound/Props cannot load in FOH
(4) Trailers can store on-site

WARDROBE
Location: SL on stage level
Access: Direct from stage
(1) Washer (1) Dryer
Washer and dryer hookups available

DRESSING ROOMS
(3) Star, SR, stage level, t/s included
(8) Small, SR, stage level, t/s on same fl
(2) Chorus, SR, +1, t/s on same fl
Elevator access for dressing rooms
Additional production office available for company mgr

SOUND

CONSOLE
Electro Voice BK1632, located Light Booth
16 inputs, 2 main outputs

SPEAKERS
House Cluster
Portable
No speaker truss

COMMUNICATIONS
Clear Com intercom with (2) channels
Infrared sound system
Dressing room page system

ROAD CONSOLE
Located Front of balcony
(12-16) seats required to be removed
Cable run from stage is 137'
Tie-in into house system with XLR connectors

REHEARSAL & STORAGE SPACE
Rehearsal: None
Storage: Cage, 20' x 30', left of loading door

ELECTRICS

ROAD SERVICE POWER

Panel	Phase	Amp	Circuit Protection	Use	Location
A	3	600	breaker	dimmers	USR
B	3	60	breaker	extra	USR
C	3	60	breaker	extra	SL
D	3	100	breaker	sound	USR
E	3	100	breaker	extra	

Recommended location of touring dimmer racks: USR
Hoist not required

FRONT OF HOUSE (BOX BOOM VALUES ARE PER SIDE)

Position	Pipe Width	Distance to Prosc.	House Circuits	Connector Type	FOH Transfer Circuits
1st Cove		33'	12	grd 20 amp stage pin	0
2nd Cove		45'	12	grd 20 amp stage pin	0
3rd Cove		56'	36	grd 20 amp stage pin	0
4th Cove		68'	36	grd 20 amp stage pin	0
1st Balc Rail		88'	0	grd 20 amp stage pin	0

EQUIPMENT FOH (BOX BOOM VALUES ARE PER SIDE)

Position	Quantity	Wattage	Instrument	Removeable
1st Cove Rail	6	1,000	Lekos	yes
2nd Cove Rail	28	1,000	Lekos	yes
3rd Cove Rail	21	1,000	Lekos	yes
4th Cove Rail	21	1,000	Lekos	yes

FOLLOWSPOTS
House Followspots:
   (3) Strong Xenon Super Troupers; not removeable

Followspot Booth:
   (3) spots per booth;
   135' throw to proscenium;
   (3) 1Ø 20 amp breakers

DIMMERS
Lighting console is ETC Obsession;
   (360) ETC high rise sensor dimmers
House has programmable DMX control system
(1) dry run DMX station

MORRISON CENTER FOR THE PERFORMING ARTS

AKA: THE VELMA V. MORRISON CENTER FOR THE PERFORMING ARTS **AT:** BOISE STATE UNIVERSITY   **YEAR BUILT: 1984**

Theatre Location:	2201 Campus Lane, Boise, ID 83725
Mailing Address:	Boise State University
	1910 University Drive, Boise, ID 83725

Main Administrative Phone:		208-426-1609
Main Administrative Fax:		208-426-3021
Website:		www.mc.idbsu.edu
Traveling Production Office Phone:		208-426-3810

THEATRE STAFF

Executive Director	Frank Heise	208-426-4020
Operations	T. J. Clark	208-426-1629

HOUSE CREW

Events Coordinator	Brent A. Karlberg	208-426-1272
Sound	David Jensen	208-426-3508

UNIONS

Non-Union Hall

SEATING CAPACITY

Orchestra	1,287
Mezzanine	743
Total:	**2,030**
pit (add'l)	60

BOX OFFICE
Computerized
Box Office Manager

Arline Eidam	208-426-4103

Outside Ticket Agency
Computerized

Select-A-Seat	208-426-1110

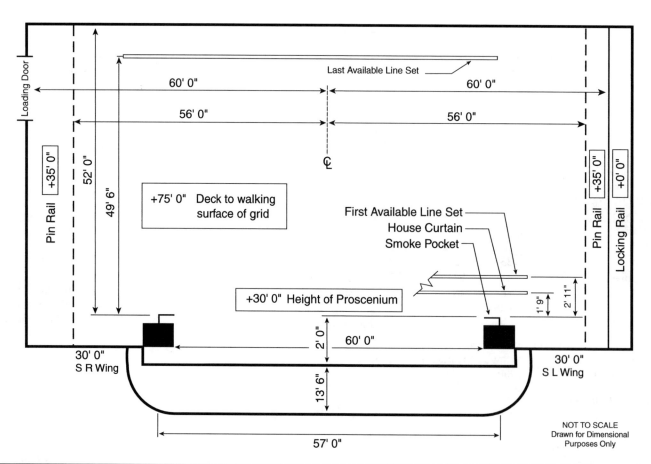

+75' 0" Deck to walking surface of grid

+30' 0" Height of Proscenium

Last Available Line Set

First Available Line Set
House Curtain
Smoke Pocket

60' 0"   60' 0"
56' 0"   56' 0"

52' 0"
49' 6"

30' 0" S R Wing
30' 0" S L Wing

60' 0"
2' 0"
13' 6"
57' 0"

Pin Rail +35' 0"
Pin Rail +35' 0"
Locking Rail +0' 0"

Loading Door

2' 11"
1' 9"

NOT TO SCALE
Drawn for Dimensional
Purposes Only

STAGE HOUSE

HOUSE CURTAIN
Operates as a guillotine from SL deck
Operates as a traveller from SR deck

RIGGING SYSTEM
Type:	Single purchase counter weight
Weight:	40,000 lbs available
Line sets:	54 sets at 7" o.c. with 7 lift lines per set
Arbors:	1,200 lb capacity
House Pipes:	57' long with 73' of travel from deck

Line sets are not moveable
Block & Falls are available
Chain hoists are not available
(10) spot wheels and 1,000' of hemp available

PERMANENT INSTALLATIONS OVER STAGE (FROM SMOKE POCKET)
M=Moveable with advance call
Orchestra shells (2) at 6'0", 16'0"
Movie screen (1) at 1'2"; M
Traveller (2) at 1'9", 33'8"; M
Electric pipe (4) at 5'3", 14'0", 24'6", 36'3"

PERMANENT INSTALLATIONS ON DECK
None

ORCHESTRA PIT
Adjustable to 9' below stage level by hydraulic lift
Apron overhangs US wall of pit 12'0"
Pit lift is in (1) section

BACKSTAGE

LOADING DOCK
Loading door(s):
  12'0" high x 10'0" wide
Trucks load (2) at same time
Dock is at truck level; equipped
  with levelling ramp for (1)
  truck
Fork lift is not required
Sound/Props cannot load in
  FOH
Lobby cannot be a work area
(2) Trailers can store on-site
Security on request

WARDROBE
Location: Third floor
Access: Freight elevator & stairs
(1) Washer (1) Dryer
Washer and dryer hookups
  available

DRESSING ROOMS
(1) Star, SR, stage level, t/s
  included
(2) Star, SR, +1, t/s included
(2) Small, SR, stage level, t/s
  included
(2) Chorus, SR, +1, t/s included
Use dressing rooms or Green
  room as office for company
  mgr

SOUND

CONSOLE
DDA Q-2, located HL
40 mic inputs, 3 main
  outputs, 8 stereo matrix
  outputs, 8 aux outputs

SPEAKERS
House Cluster
Proscenium
Portable
Delayed stereo surround fills
No speaker truss
Limited rig, per show basis

COMMUNICATIONS
Clear Com intercom with
  (2) channels
FM sound system
Dressing room page system

ROAD CONSOLE
Located HR
(27) seats required to be
  removed
Cable run from stage is 75'
Tie-in into house system with
  XLR connectors
House does have SPL limits

REHEARSAL & STORAGE SPACE
Rehearsal: None
Storage: Shop, 30' x 50', SR
  behind stage

ELECTRICS

ROAD SERVICE POWER

Panel	Phase	Amp	Circuit Protection	Use	Location
A-B	3	400	fuse	dimmers	SR
C	3	200	fuse	dimmers	SR
D	3	60	breaker	sound	SL
E	3	60	breaker	hoist	SR
F	3	60	breaker	extra	Parking lot
G	3	100	fuse	extra	Loading dock
H	3	60	fuse	extra	Loading dock
I	3	60	breaker	extra	Projection booth

Recommended location of touring dimmer racks: SR
Hoist not required
Additional power is available for tour buses, generators, etc.

FRONT OF HOUSE (BOX BOOM VALUES ARE PER SIDE)

Position	Pipe Width	Distance to Prosc.	House Circuits	Connector Type	FOH Transfer Circuits
1st Catwalk	65'	6'	15	grd 20 amp stage pin	13
2nd Catwalk	75'	37'	25	grd 20 amp stage pin	18
3rd Catwalk	75'	47'	23	grd 20 amp stage pin	15
Box Boom 1		35'	6	grd 20 amp stage pin	6
Torm		15'	6	grd 20 amp stage pin	6

Transfer circuits: grd 20 amp stage pin

EQUIPMENT FOH (BOX BOOM VALUES ARE PER SIDE)
None

FOLLOWSPOTS
House Followspots:
  (2) Super Troupers 200
  DIV; not removeable

Followspot Booth:
  (2) spots per booth;
  143' throw to proscenium;
  (2) 3Ø 60 amp breakers

DIMMERS
Lighting console is ETC
  Obsession II;
  (271) ETC Sensor dimmers
House has programmable
  DMX control system
(4) dry run DMX station(s)
  at SL/SR/Catwalks

PARAMOUNT ARTS CENTRE

YEAR BUILT: **1931**   YEAR RENOVATED: **1978**

Theatre Location: 23 East Galena Blvd., Aurora, IL 60506

Main Administrative Phone: 630-896-7676
Main Administrative Fax: 630-892-1084
Website: www.paramountarts.com
Stage Door Phone: 630-896-6810

THEATRE STAFF
Executive Director   Janet R. Bean   630-844-0390

HOUSE CREW
Technical Director   Dennis Bentley   630-896-7676
Carpentry   Manny Gonzales   630-896-6810
Electrics   R.T. Lorenz   630-896-6810

SEATING CAPACITY

Main Floor section 1	1,027
Main Floor section 2	662
Balcony	199
Total:	**1,888**
pit (add'l)	0
wheelchair (add'l)	0
standing (add'l)	0

STAGE DIMENSIONS (FROM SMOKE POCKET)
Stage is 38'4" deep
Width from Center Line to SL is 30'0"
Width from Center Line to SR is 41'0"
Proscenium width is 48'2"
Proscenium height is 30'0"
Smoke pocket to apron edge is 13'0"
Orchestra pit exists

RIGGING
Grid Height: 65'
Type: Single purchase counter weight
Weight: 20,000 lbs
Line sets: 30 sets
Arbors: 1,000 lb capacity
House Pipes: 54' long

LOADING DOCK
Loading door(s) are 12'0" high x 10'0" wide
Trucks load (2) at same time
Fork lift is not required

ELECTRICS
Total power available:
(2) 600A 3Ø SR proscenium
   wall
(3) 200A 3Ø SR proscenium
   wall

FOLLOWSPOTS
House Followspots:
   Super Trouper Carbon Arc
Power in spot booth (2) 50A

DIMMERS
(189) house dimmers
House has DMX control system
(3) dry run station(s) located
   SL, Mid house, Booth

SOUND
House has 200A 3Ø,
   dedicated power located
   SR
FOH mixing position in
   Center Orchestra
Sound console is available

ASSEMBLY HALL

AT: **UNIVERSITY OF ILLINOIS**   **YEAR BUILT: 1963   YEAR RENOVATED: 1998**

Theatre Location:	1800 S. First Street, Champaign, IL 61820
Mailing Address:	University of Illinois Assembly Hall
	PO Box 1790, Champaign, IL 61824-1790

Main Administrative Phone:	217-333-2923
Main Administrative Fax:	217-244-8888
Website:	www.assembly.uiuc.edu
Stage Door Phone:	217-333-2277
Traveling Production Office Phone:	217-244-8260
Traveling Production Office Fax:	217-244-8261

THEATRE STAFF

Director	Kevin Ullestad	217-333-2923
Booking	Kevin Ullestad	217-333-2923
Marketing	Gary O'Brien	217-333-2923
Operations	Fred Rhodes	217-333-2923
Group Sales	Rose VanCour	217-333-2923

HOUSE CREW

Technical Director	Bill Beebe	217-333-2923
Carpenter	Jeff Reimer	217-333-2923
Electrician	John Page	217-333-2923
Sound	Doug Pugh	217-333-2923

UNIONS

IATSE Local #482	Kevin McGuire	217-384-6437
Musicians In-House		

SEATING CAPACITY

Orchestra	871
Mezzanine	632
Balcony	2,143
Total:	**3,646**

BOX OFFICE
Computerized
Box Office Manager
  Linda Schwieter   217-333-5000

Outside Ticket Agency
None

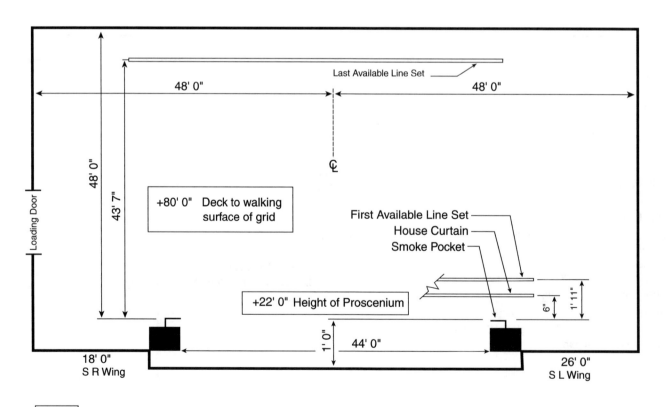

Last Available Line Set

48' 0"   48' 0"

+80' 0"   Deck to walking surface of grid

48' 0"

43' 7"

Loading Door

First Available Line Set
House Curtain
Smoke Pocket

1' 11"
6"

+22' 0" Height of Proscenium

1' 0"   44' 0"

18' 0"
S R Wing

26' 0"
S L Wing

−4' 6"
Stage to
House Floor

NOT TO SCALE
Drawn for Dimensional
Purposes Only

STAGE HOUSE

House Curtain
Operates as a traveller from SR deck

Rigging System
Type:	Electronic Winch System
Line sets:	30 sets at 6-12" o.c. with 4 lift lines per set
Arbors:	1,500 lb capacity
House Pipes:	52' long with 65' of travel from deck

Line sets are not moveable
Block & Falls are not available
Chain hoists are available; (4) half ton
(20) spot wheels and 3,000' of hemp available

Permanent Installations Over Stage
Dead spaces (5) at 7'6", 9'2" (20" wide), 17'0" (28" wide), 23'6" (18" wide), 33'3" (24" wide)

Permanent Installations On Deck
Stage floor is made up of portable 4' x 8' modules; 12 traps can be cut into any module

Orchestra Pit
Nonadjustable at 4'6" below stage level
Pit is not permanent and can vary in size

BACKSTAGE

Loading Dock
Loading door(s):
    13'10" high x 12'0" wide
Trucks load (3) at same time
Docks are covered, accessed by underground tunnel
Forklift: 2 In-house
Sound/Props cannot load in FOH
Lobby cannot be a work area
(20) Trailers can store on-site
Security at dock & stage door

Wardrobe
Location: SR on stage level
Access: Direct from stage
(3) Washers (3) Dryers
Washer and dryer hookups available

Dressing Rooms
(2) Small/Star, SR, stage level, t/s, phone jack
(2) Small/Star, SR, stage level, t/s, phone jack
(2) Chorus, SR, stage level, t/s, phone jack
(2) Chorus, SR, stage level, t/s, phone jack
Additional production office available for company mgr

SOUND

Console
Yamaha PM 1800, located Center House
32 inputs, 1 Stereo main outputs, 4 matrix outputs, 6 aux outputs

Speakers
House Cluster
Proscenium
Portable
Catwalk
Speaker truss exists
Max allowable load 1,200 lbs

Communications
Clear Com intercom with (42) channels
Dressing room page system

Road Console
Located Center Orchestra
No seats required to be removed
Cable run from stage is 150'
Tie in into house system with XLR connectors

Rehearsal & Storage Space
Rehearsal: None
Storage: Loading dock area 80' x 40'

ELECTRICS

Road Service Power
Panel	Phase	Amp	Circuit Protection	Use	Location
A	3	800	breaker	dimmers	SR side wall
B	3	800	breaker	sound	SR side wall
C	3	400	breaker	extra	SR side wall
D	3	225	breaker	extra	SR side wall
E	3	70	fuse	sound	SL side wall

Recommended location of touring dimmer racks: SR next to deck
Hoist not required
Additional power is available for tour buses, generators, etc.

Front Of House (box boom values are per side)
Position	Pipe Width	Distance to Prosc.	House Circuits	Connector Type	FOH Transfer Circuits
Bridge	54'	100'	12	grd 15 amp stage pin	
1st Balc Rail	54'	60'	3	grd 15 amp stage pin	

Transfer circuits: 12 Circuits with stage plug connectors
Dimmers are permanently patched to circuits

Equipment FOH (box boom values are per side)
Position	Quantity	Wattage	Instrument	Removeable
1st Balc Rail	12	575	Source 4 5°	no
1st Boom Box	32	575	Source 4 19°	yes

Followspots
House Followspots:
    (12) Strong Super Trouper Carbon Arcs; not removeable

Followspot Booth:
    (2) spots per booth;
    125' throw to proscenium;
    (2) 1Ø 50 amp breakers

Dimmers
Lighting console is ETC Expression 2x;
(81) 6x & (100) 1k Kliegl dimmers
House has programmable DMX control system
No dry run DMX station(s)

ARIE CROWN THEATER

AT: LAKESIDE CENTER/MCCORMICK PLACE   **YEAR BUILT: 1960   YEAR RENOVATED: 1997**

Theatre Location: 2301 S. Lake Shore Dr, Chicago, IL 60616

Main Administrative Phone: 312-791-6516
Main Administrative Fax: 312-791-6100
Stage Door Phone: 312-791-6095
Backstage Pay Phone: 312-326-9023

THEATRE STAFF
Theater Director   Jacqueline Huels   312-791-6516
Booking   Jacqueline Huels   312-791-6516
Theater Coordinator   Francine Swanson   312-791-6516

HOUSE CREW
Technical Director   Russell Schraut, Jr.   312-791-6023
Carpentry   James A. Kiddle   312-791-6139
Electrics   Russell Schraut, Jr.   312-791-6023
Sound   Byran K. Walton   312-791-6099
Props   Albert B. Gaines   312-791-6024
Fly   Clark C. Morris   312-791-6230

UNIONS
IATSE Local #2   Robert Ingersoll   312-236-3457
Wardrobe Local #769   Hugh Pruitt   312-332-2244

SEATING CAPACITY
Orchestra   2,374
Box Seats   54
Balcony   1,821
Total: **4,249**

pit (add'l)   80
wheelchair (remove 69 seats)   54

BOX OFFICE
Computerized
Box Office Treasurer
Jim Buhle   312-791-6516

Outside Ticket Agency
Computerized
Ticketmaster   312-559-1950

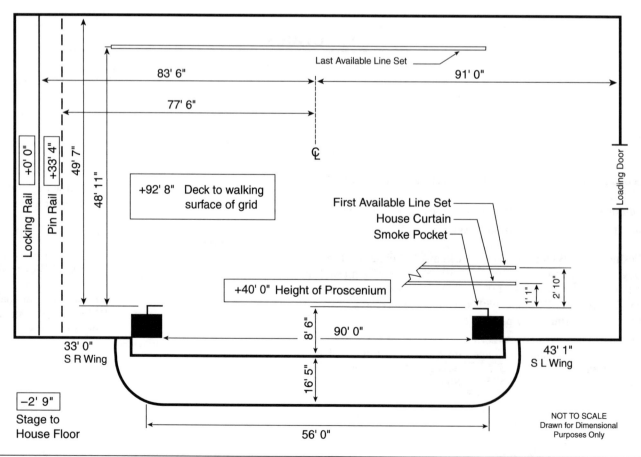

Last Available Line Set

83' 6"   91' 0"

77' 6"

Locking Rail +0' 0"

Pin Rail +33' 4"

49' 7"

48' 11"

+92' 8" Deck to walking surface of grid

First Available Line Set
House Curtain
Smoke Pocket

Loading Door

+40' 0" Height of Proscenium

1' 1"   2' 10"

8' 6"   90' 0"

33' 0"
S R Wing

43' 1"
S L Wing

16' 5"

−2' 9"
Stage to
House Floor

56' 0"

NOT TO SCALE
Drawn for Dimensional
Purposes Only

STAGE HOUSE

HOUSE CURTAIN
Operates as a traveller from SR deck; motorized

RIGGING SYSTEM
Type:	Single purchase counter weight
Weight:	50,000 lbs available
Line sets:	60 sets at 8" o.c. with 9 lift lines per set
Arbors:	3,400 lb capacity
House Pipes:	108' long with 89' of travel from deck

Line sets are moveable
Block & Falls are available 23:2 (1)
(30) spot wheels and 6,000' of hemp available

PERMANENT INSTALLATIONS OVER STAGE (FROM SMOKE POCKET)
Electric raceways (12) at 5'0", 8'4", 11'8", 15'0", 21'0", 23'8", 27'0", 33'0", 40'4", 43'0", 44'10", 47'8"
Travellers (7) at 2'6", 9'0", 16'4", 23'0", 29'0", 35'0", 41'8"
Cyclorama (1) at 50'4"
Scrim (1) at 47'0"

PERMANENT INSTALLATIONS ON DECK
None

ORCHESTRA PIT
Adjustable to 10' below stage level by hydraulic lift

BACKSTAGE

LOADING DOCK
Loading door(s):
  7'4" high x 16'0" wide
Trucks load (2) at same time
Dock is at truck level; loading to stage thru separate loading bay

WARDROBE
Location: SL in the dressing corridor
Access: Direct from loading bay
(1) Washer (1) Dryer

DRESSING ROOMS
(1) Star, SL on stage level, t/s included
(10) Small, SL on stage level, t/s included
(2) Chorus, SL on stage level, t/s included

REHEARSAL & STORAGE SPACE
Rehearsal: 25' x 35' located behind stage on 2nd fl, piano available
Storage: (2) areas - Large storage bay located off SL; USC alcove

SOUND

CONSOLE
Crest
40 inputs, 8 main outputs, 8 aux outputs

SPEAKERS
House Cluster
Under Balcony
Continuous orchestra lip
Over balcony speakers
Side & backwalk speakers
No speaker truss

COMMUNICATIONS
Clear Com intercom with (4) channels
Infrared sound system
Dressing room page system

ROAD CONSOLE
Located Rear House in cross aisle
No seats required to be rcmovcd
Cable run from stage is 225'
Tie-in into house system with XLR connectors

ELECTRICS

ROAD SERVICE POWER

Panel	Phase	Amp	Circuit Protection	Use	Location
A-C	3	60	fuse	extra	USR side wall
D-E	3	100	fuse	extra	USR side wall
F-I	3	400	fuse	dimmers	USR side wall
J	3	100	fuse	sound	DSR proscenium wall
K	3	100	fuse	sound	DSL proscenium wall

Location of touring dimmer racks: SR on deck; Additional power is available

FRONT OF HOUSE (BOX BOOM VALUES ARE PER SIDE)

Position	Pipe Width	Distance to Prosc.	House Circuits	Connector Type	FOH Transfer Circuits
1st Balc Rail	75'	109'	30	grd 20 amp stage pin	0
Cloud Bridge	70'	86'	54	grd 20 amp stage pin	0
Box Boom 1		38'	4	grd 20 amp stage pin	0
Box Boom 2		56'	4	grd 20 amp stage pin	0
Box Boom 3		74'	4	grd 20 amp stage pin	0
Mast	Vertical	100'	12	grd 20 amp stage pin	0
Torm	Vertical		12	grd 20 amp stage pin	

Road truss: At 5'7" and 24'5" DS of plaster line

EQUIPMENT FOH (BOX BOOM VALUES ARE PER SIDE)

Position	Quantity	Wattage	Instrument	Removeable
1st Balc Rail	48	575	Source 4 19°/ 10°	yes
Cloud Bridge	20	575	Source 4 10°	yes
Box Boom 1	5	575	Source 4 26°	yes
Box Boom 2	5	575	Source 4 9°	yes
Box Boom 3	5	575	Source 4 19°	yes
Mast	5	575	Source 4 10°	yes
Torm	8	575	Source 4 19°	yes

FOLLOWSPOTS
House Followspots:
  (3) Strong Xenon Gladiators; not removeable

Followspot Booth:
  (3) spots per booth; 174'0" throw to proscenium;
  (3) 3Ø 30 amp breakers

DIMMERS
Lighting console is ETC Expression; ETC Concept; (984) ETC Sensor dimmers
House has non-programmable DMX control system
(19) dry run DMX station(s), DSR, DSL, Pin rail, USR, Center Mix, light booth, SR/SL torms, et al

AUDITORIUM THEATRE

YEAR BUILT: 1889   YEAR RENOVATED: 1998

Theatre Location: 50 East Congress Parkway, Chicago, IL 60605
Management Company: Auditorium Theatre Council
                          50 East Congress Parkway, Chicago, IL 60605

Main Administrative Phone: 312-922-2110
Main Administrative Fax: 312-341-9668
Website: www.auditoriumtheatre.org
Stage Door Phone: 312-431-2381
Backstage Pay Phone: 312-939-9100

SEATING CAPACITY

Orchestra	1,325
Boxes	184
First Balcony	1,324
Second Balcony	460
Gallery	368
Total:	**3,661**
wheelchair	varies

THEATRE STAFF

Executive Director	Jan Kallish	312-431-2395
Marketing	Cheryl Sloane	312-431-2370
Group Sales	Ray Sisco	312-922-2110

HOUSE CREW

Technical Director	Pat McLaughlin	312-431-2335
Carpentry	Rick Conrad	312-431-2335
Electrics	Dabney Forest	312-431-2335
Sound	Robert Tyler	312-431-2335
Props	Pat McLaughlin	312-431-2335

UNIONS

IATSE Local #2	Robert Ingersoll	312-236-3457
Wardrobe Local #769	Hugh Pruett	773-477-4952

BOX OFFICE

Computerized
Director Ticket Services
  Bill Pope   312-431-2342

Outside Ticket Agency
Computerized
Ticket Master
  Jean Blasco   312-559-1920

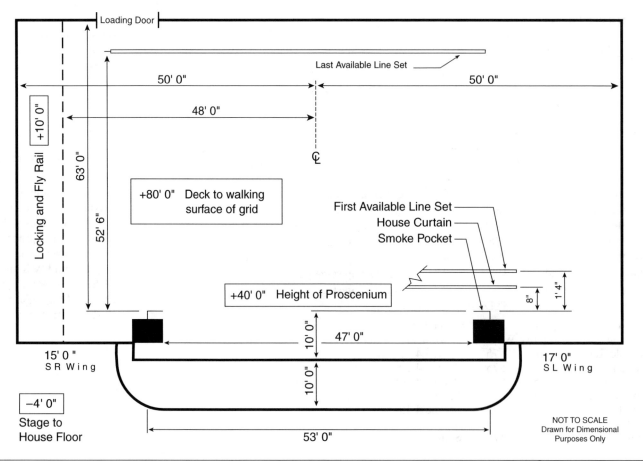

Loading Door

Last Available Line Set

50' 0"   50' 0"

48' 0"

℄

Locking and Fly Rail   +10' 0"

63' 0"

52' 6"

+80' 0"   Deck to walking surface of grid

First Available Line Set
House Curtain
Smoke Pocket

1' 4"

8"

+40' 0"   Height of Proscenium

10' 0"

47' 0"

15' 0"
SR Wing

17' 0"
SL Wing

10' 0"

−4' 0"
Stage to House Floor

53' 0"

NOT TO SCALE
Drawn for Dimensional
Purposes Only

STAGE HOUSE

HOUSE CURTAIN
Operates as a guillotine from SL fly floor

RIGGING SYSTEM

Type:	Single purchase counter weight
Weight:	20,000 lbs available
Line sets:	99 sets with 1 lift line per set
Arbors:	1,500 lb capacity
House Pipes:	63' long

Line sets are moveable
Block & Falls are not available
Chain hoists are not available
(0) spot wheels and 10,000' of hemp available

PERMANENT INSTALLATIONS OVER STAGE (FROM SMOKE POCKET)
None

PERMANENT INSTALLATIONS ON DECK
None

ORCHESTRA PIT
Nonadjustable at 7' below stage level
Apron overhangs US wall of pit 7'0"
Pit has electric organ SR corner

BACKSTAGE

LOADING DOCK
Loading door(s):
  12'0" high x 10'0" wide
Trucks load (2) at same time
Dock at street level
Sound/Props cannot load in
  FOH
Trailers cannot store on-site
Security at dock & stage door

WARDROBE
Location: Storage room
  2nd floor
(2) Washers (2) Dryers
No washer or dryer hookups

DRESSING ROOMS
(1) Star, SR, stage level, t/s
  included
(4) Small, SR, stage level / +2,
  t/s on same fl
(6) Chorus, SR, +2/+3, t/s on
  same fl
Use dressing room for company
  mgr office

SOUND

CONSOLE
No house console

SPEAKERS
House Cluster
Proscenium
No speaker truss

COMMUNICATIONS
Intercom with (8) channels
Infrared sound system
Dressing room page system

ROAD CONSOLE
Located Center House
No seats required to be
  removed
Cable run from stage is 120'

REHEARSAL & STORAGE SPACE
Rehearsal: None
Storage: 40' x 40' in base-
  ment

ELECTRICS

ROAD SERVICE POWER

Panel	Phase	Amp	Circuit Protection	Use	Location
A	3	400	fuse	dimmers	SR
B-C	3	200	fuse	extra	SR
D	3	100	fuse	extra	SR
E	3	100	fuse	sound	SL

Recommended location of touring dimmer racks: SR

FRONT OF HOUSE (BOX BOOM VALUES ARE PER SIDE)

Position	Pipe Width	Distance to Prosc.	House Circuits	Connector Type	FOH Transfer Circuits
1st Balc Rail	50'	100'	35	grd 20 amp stage pin	0
1st Cove	50'	160'	6	grd 20 amp stage pin	0
Box Boom 1		30'	6	grd 20 amp stage pin	0

EQUIPMENT FOH (BOX BOOM VALUES ARE PER SIDE)

Position	Quantity	Wattage	Instrument	Removeable
1st Cove	6	2,000	6 x 22 Lekos	yes
Box Boom 1	12	2,000	6 x 22 Lekos	yes

FOLLOWSPOTS
House Followspots:
  (2) Ultra Arc; removeable

Followspot Booth:
  (2) spots per booth;
  160' throw to proscenium;
  1Ø 20 amp breakers

DIMMERS
No lighting console
(435) Century Strand
dimmers

BRIAR STREET THEATER

YEAR BUILT: 1985   YEAR RENOVATED: 1997

Theatre Location: 3133 North Halsted, Chicago, IL 60657
Mailing Address: 3133 North Halsted, Chicago, IL 60657
Management Company: Fox Theatricals
                                     212 East Ohio, Chicago , IL 60611

Main Administrative Phone: 773-348-5996
Main Administrative Fax: 773-348-4162

THEATRE STAFF
Theatre Manager   Phil Eickhoff   773-348-5996
HOUSE CREW
  Independent per show

SEATING CAPACITY
Main Floor   575
Balcony   50
Total: **625**

STAGE DIMENSIONS
  No smoke pocket
  Stage is 20'0" deep
  Width from Center Line to SL is 35'0"
  Width from Center Line to SR is 30'0"
  Proscenium width is 36'0"
  No orchestra pit

RIGGING
  Grid Height: 23'
  Type: 4 Hand Winch Electrics

LOADING DOCK
  Loading door(s) are 10'0" high x 8'0" wide
  Trucks load (1) at a time
  Fork lift is not required

ELECTRICS
  Total power available:
    (1) 400A 3Ø back wall
FOLLOWSPOTS
  Power in spot booth 40 amp 1Ø
DIMMERS
  (92) house dimmers
  House has DMX control system
  (1) dry run station(s) located
    control booth

SOUND
  House has 100 amp
    undedicated power located
    Back Wall
  No sound console available

CHICAGO THEATRE

YEAR BUILT: 1921   YEAR RENOVATED: 1986

Theatre Location: 175 N. State Street, Chicago, IL 60601
Management Company: Chicago Alameda Theatre Enterprises
                    (address as above)

Main Administrative Phone: 312-263-1138
Main Administrative Fax: 312-263-9505
Stage Door Phone: 312-263-3889

THEATRE STAFF
 Theatre Manager   Michelle Bjelke   312-263-1138
 Assistant Manager   Jennifer Albert   312-263-1138

HOUSE CREW
 Carpentry   Don La Pointe   312-263-1359
 Sound   Mike Haack   312-263-1359
 Props   Chuck Lorang   312-263-1359
 Fly   Pat Farley   312-263-1359

UNIONS
 IATSE Local #2   Bob Ingersoll   312-236-3457
 Wardrobe Local #769   Hugh Pruett   312-332-2244

SEATING CAPACITY

Main Floor	1,874
Boxes	208
Balcony	1,362
Total:	**3,444**
pit (add'l)	90
wheelchair (incl)	
standing	0

BOX OFFICE
 Computerized
 Box Office Manager
  Bob Siegel   312-263-6536

 Outside Ticket Agency
 Computerized
 Ticketmaster
  Jean Blasco   312-559-1950
                      312-559-1212

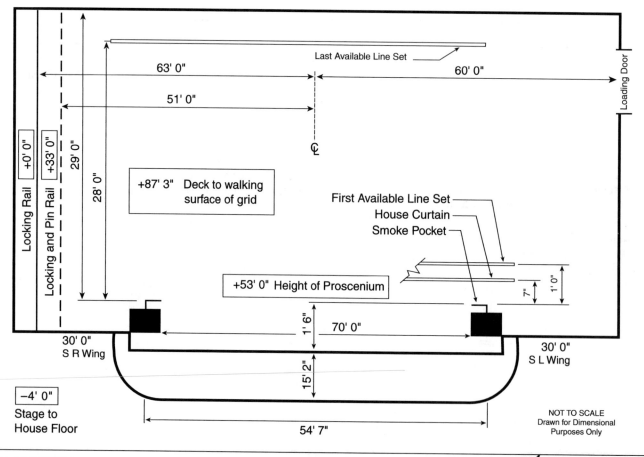

NOT TO SCALE
Drawn for Dimensional
Purposes Only

STAGE HOUSE

HOUSE CURTAIN
Operates as a guillotine or traveller from SR deck

RIGGING SYSTEM
Type:	Single purchase counter weight and Hemp house
Weight:	20,000 lbs available
Line sets:	59 sets at 6" o.c. with 5 lift lines per set
Arbors:	700 lb capacity
House Pipes:	75' long with 80' of travel from deck

Line sets are moveable
Block & Falls are not available
Chain hoists are available; (6) one ton
(50) spot wheels and 6000' of hemp available

PERMANENT INSTALLATIONS OVER STAGE (FROM SMOKE POCKET)
Movie screen (1) at 8'0"
Traveller, (2) one located DS, one not rigged
Fire curtain (1) at smoke pocket

PERMANENT INSTALLATIONS ON DECK
Traps (2) in stage floor, 9'x9' & 6'x6'; 20'0" and 26'0"

ORCHESTRA PIT
Adjustable to 6' below stage level by hydraulic lift
Apron overhangs US wall of pit 1' 6"
Pit lift is in (30) sections

BACKSTAGE

LOADING DOCK
Loading door(s):
  9'6" high x 8'2" wide
Trucks load (6) at same time
Street level dock
Sound/Props can load in FOH
Lobby cannot be a work area
Trailers cannot store on-site
Security at stage door

WARDROBE
Location: Below stage
(2) Washers (2) Dryers
Washer and dryer hookups available

DRESSING ROOMS
(2) Star, SR/SL, stage level/ +1, t/s, phone jack
(6) Small, SL,SR, stage level, +2, t/s
(2) Chorus, SR, +1, t/s
Additional production office available for company mgr

SOUND

CONSOLE
No house console

SPEAKERS
No speaker truss

COMMUNICATIONS
Clear Com intercom with (1) channel
Infrared sound system
Dressing room page system

ROAD CONSOLE
Located Rear House left of center
No seats required to be removed
Cable run from stage is 250'

REHEARSAL & STORAGE SPACE
Rehearsal: None
Storage: 20' x 20' above stage, motor to lift;
30' x 30' above stage, motor to lift

ELECTRICS

ROAD SERVICE POWER

Panel	Phase	Amp	Circuit Protection	Use	Location
A-B	3	600	breaker	dimmers	DSR
C	3	200	breaker	sound	DSR
D	3	200	breaker	extra	DSL
E	3	60	breaker	winches	DSR

Recommended location of touring dimmer racks: anywhere
Hoist is provided
Additional power is available for tour buses, generators, etc.

FRONT OF HOUSE (BOX BOOM VALUES ARE PER SIDE)
None

EQUIPMENT FOH (BOX BOOM VALUES ARE PER SIDE)
None

FOLLOWSPOTS
House Followspots:
  (2) Xenon Supers 2k
  (2) Ultra Archs 750w

Followspot Booth:
  (2) spots per booth;

DIMMERS
No lighting console
CD 80 Strand dimmers
House has DMX control system

CIVIC OPERA HOUSE

YEAR BUILT: 1929   YEAR RENOVATED: 1996

Theatre Location: 20 North Wacker Drive, Chicago, IL 60606
Management Company: Lyric Opera of Chicago
                                     20 North Wacker Drive, Suite 860, Chicago, IL 60606

Main Administrative Phone:	312-419-0033
Main Administrative Fax:	312-419-0061
Stage Door Phone:	312-332-2244 x346
Traveling Production Office Phone:	312-345-0616
Traveling Production Office Fax:	312-345-0618

SEATING CAPACITY

Orchestra (Main Level)	1,712
Mezzanine Box Second Floor	248
Dress Circle	430
First Balcony	416
Upper Balcony	757
Total:	**3,563**
pit (add'l)	82

THEATRE STAFF

Theatre Manager	Kenneth Shaw	312-419-0033
Booking	Kenneth Shaw	312-419-0033

HOUSE CREW

Technical Director	Drew Landmesser	312-332-2244 x305
Carpentry	Bill Beaton	312-332-2244 x370
Electrics	Jim Hart	312-332-2244 x380
Sound	Todd Snick	312-332-2244 x373
Props	Tom Gilbert	312-332-2244 x375

UNIONS

IATSE Local #2	Bob Ingersoll	312-236-3457
Wardrobe Local #769	Hugh Pruett	312-332-2244
Music	Everett Zlatoff-Mirsky	
	Chicago Perf. Arts	708-365-5445

BOX OFFICE
Computerized
Box Office Treasurer
   James McShane 312-332-2244 x394

Outside Ticket Agency
Computerized
Ticketmaster
   Jean Blasco   312-902-1500

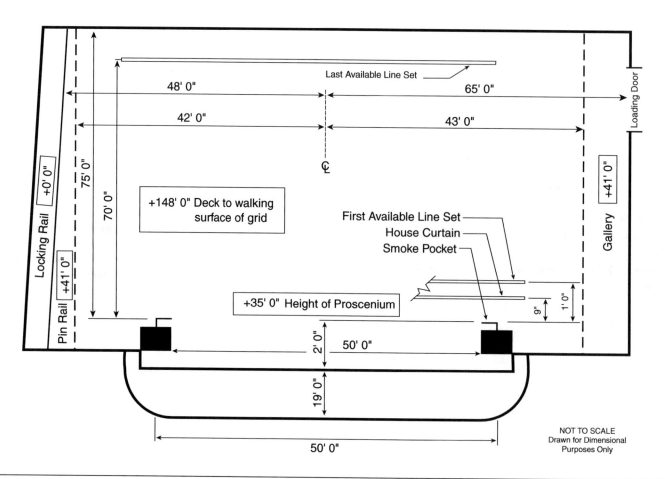

NOT TO SCALE
Drawn for Dimensional
Purposes Only

STAGE HOUSE

HOUSE CURTAIN
Operates as a guillotine from SR deck

RIGGING SYSTEM
Type:	Single purchase counter weight
Line sets:	103 sets at o.c. with 5 lift lines per set
Arbors:	2,000 lb capacity
House Pipes:	70' long with 139' of travel from deck

Line sets are not moveable
Block & Falls available

PERMANENT INSTALLATIONS OVER STAGE (FROM SMOKE POCKET)
Bridge
Electrics

PERMANENT INSTALLATIONS ON DECK
Trap (1) in stage floor, 10'0" x 10'0" on center, 20'4" US of plaster line

ORCHESTRA PIT
Nonadjustable at 8'5" below stage level
Apron overhangs US wall of pit 10'4"

BACKSTAGE

LOADING DOCK
Trucks load (2) at same time
Ramp US left at Wacker Drive, 45' max trailer length; Truck lift at Washington St., 53' max trailer with city tractor; 48' max trailer with overland tractor
Forklift: House owns

WARDROBE
Location: 5th Floor
(2) Washers (2) Dryers

DRESSING ROOMS
(9) Star, 1st fl, t/s included
(1) Small, 2nd mezz, t/s included
(1) Chorus, stage level, t/s included
(2) Chorus, 3rd fl, t/s included
(3) Chorus, 4th fl, (2) with t/s included
(3) Chorus, 5th fl, t/s included

SOUND

CONSOLE
Data not provided

SPEAKERS
Data not provided

COMMUNICATIONS
Wired intercom system available
Dressing room page system

ROAD CONSOLE
Data not provided

REHEARSAL & STORAGE SPACE
Rehearsal: (3) All with resilient floors:
60'x78', 2nd fl;
30' x 70', 3rd fl, mirrors;
30' x 70', 5th fl, mirrors
Storage: None

ELECTRICS

ROAD SERVICE POWER

Panel	Phase	Amp	Circuit Protection	Use	Location
A	3	200	fuse	sound	DSL
B	3	100	fuse	extra	USL
C	3	100	fuse	extra	USL
D	3	200	fuse	extra	

Recommended location of touring dimmer racks:

FRONT OF HOUSE (BOX BOOM VALUES ARE PER SIDE)
None

EQUIPMENT FOH (BOX BOOM VALUES ARE PER SIDE)
None

FOLLOWSPOTS
House Followspots:
None

Followspot Booth:
None

DIMMERS
No lighting
No dimmers
No DMX console

FORD CENTER FOR THE PERFORMING ARTS, ORIENTAL THEATRE

FORMERLY: ORIENTAL THEATRE

YEAR BUILT: 1926   YEAR RENOVATED: 1998

Theatre Location: 24 West Randolph Street, Chicago, IL 60601
Management Company: Livent, Inc.
                        165 Avenue Road, Toronto, ON M5R 3S4 CANADA

Main Administrative Phone: 312-782-2004
Main Administrative Fax: 312-782-2005
Website: www.livent.com

SEATING CAPACITY

Orchestra	990
Mezzanine	227
Balcony	1,032
Total	**2,249**
wheelchair (add'l)	32

THEATRE STAFF

General Mgr	Dulcie Gilmore	312-706-1848
Booking	Dulcie Gilmore	312-706-1848
Marketing	Eileen Lacario	312-706-1875
Operations	Rory Rice	312-706-1840
Group Sales	Eileen LaCario	312-706-1875

HOUSE CREW

Technical Director	Peter W. Lamb	416-324-5476
Carpentry	Tom Boucher	312-706-1867
Electrics	Jodi Durham	312-706-1867
Sound	Dennis Gilbert	312-706-1867
Props	Bud Sweet	312-706-1867

UNIONS

IATSE Local #2	Robert Ingersoll	312-236-3457
Wardrobe Local #764	Hugh Pruett	773-477-4952

BOX OFFICE
  Computerized
  Ticketing Mgr
    Phil Lombard   312-782-2004

  Outside Ticket Agency
  Computerized
    Ticketmaster   312-902-1400

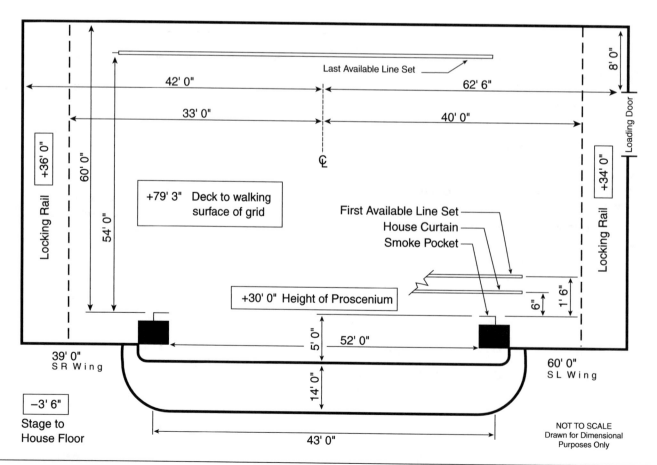

STAGE HOUSE

HOUSE CURTAIN
No house curtain

RIGGING SYSTEM
Type: Single purchase counter weight
Weight: 67,000 lbs available
Line sets: 90 sets at 7" o.c. with 7 lift lines per set
Arbors: 1,500 lb capacity
House Pipes: 64'7" long with 71' of travel from deck
Line sets are moveable
Block & Falls are available
Chain hoists are not available
(50) spot wheels and 5,000' of hemp available

PERMANENT INSTALLATIONS OVER STAGE (FROM SMOKE POCKET)
Fire curtain (1) in smoke pocket
Catwalk (1) located between L & R fly floors US wall

PERMANENT INSTALLATIONS ON DECK
Traps (60) in stage floor 4'0" x 8'0", located centered on stage
Jumps (1) 16'0" x 60'0" located SL at +34' elevation
Jump automation (2) 5'0" x 60'0" long located SR at 56'0" elevation
Loading bridge (1) 5'0" x 60'0" located SR 73'0" above stage level

ORCHESTRA PIT
Nonadjustable at 9' below stage level
Apron overhangs US wall of pit 9' 0"
No pit lift

BACKSTAGE

LOADING DOCK
Loading door(s):
     12'0" high x 12'0" wide
Trucks load (1) at a time
Laneway SL, right angle load-in
Fork lift is not required
Sound/Props can load in FOH
Lobby can be a work area
Trailers cannot store on-site
Security at stage door

WARDROBE
Location: 1st basement
Access: SL elevator
(4) Washers (4) Dryers
No washer or dryer hookups

DRESSING ROOMS
(6) Small, SL, -1, t/s included, phone jack
(5) Small, US, -1, t/s included, phone jack
(2) Chorus, SL, -1, t/s included
Elevator access for dressing rooms
Additional production office available for company mgr

SOUND

CONSOLE
No house console

SPEAKERS
None
Fore stage grid - points available

COMMUNICATIONS
No house intercom system; wire & connectors to production locations
Infrared sound system
Dressing room page system

ROAD CONSOLE
Located Rear Orchestra center
No seats required to be removed
Cable run from stage is 300'
Runs through cable tray to mix position from trap room

REHEARSAL & STORAGE SPACE
Rehearsal: Main rehearsal hall, 57'7" x 41'10" located 2nd basement (Sprung floor)
Dance rehearsal hall, 38'6" x 33'10" located 1st basement, sprung floor
Storage: None

ELECTRICS

ROAD SERVICE POWER

Panel	Phase	Amp	Circuit Protection	Use	Location
A-M	3	400	breaker	dimmers	SL jump
N	3	400	breaker	sound	Sound rack room
O	3	400	breaker	extra	USC trap level
P-Q	3	100	breaker	extra	USL/USR
R-S	3	100	breaker	extra	DSL/DSR
T	3	100	breaker	extra	Forestage grid

Recommended location of touring dimmer racks: SL dimmer jump
Hoist required and provided.

FRONT OF HOUSE (BOX BOOM VALUES ARE PER SIDE)
UNDER RENOVATION
Transfer circuits: Balcony Rail circuits appear at dimmer jump SL
Road truss: Pre-cut rigging holes & points available to forestage grid

EQUIPMENT FOH (BOX BOOM VALUES ARE PER SIDE)
None

FOLLOWSPOTS
House Followspots:
     UNDER RENOVATION

Followspot Booth:
     UNDER RENOVATION

DIMMERS
No lighting console
No dimmers
No DMX control system

THE PALACE THEATRE

Theatre Location: 159 West Randolph, Chicago, IL 60611
Management Company: Fox Theatrical, 212 E. Ohio, Chicago, IL 60611

Main Administrative Phone: 312-573-1173
Main Administrative Fax: 312-573-1177

THEATRE STAFF
Fox Theatricals   312-573-1173
HOUSE CREW
Technical   Phil Eickhoff   312-573-1173

SEATING CAPACITY	
Orchestra	1,086
Mezzanine	224
Balcony	1,026
Total:	**2,336**
pit (add'l)	50
wheelchair (add'l)	0
standing (add'l)	0

STAGE DIMENSIONS (FROM SMOKE POCKET)
Stage is 45'0" deep
Width from Center Line to SL is 55'0"
Width from Center Line to SR is 58'0"
Proscenium width is 56'0"
Proscenium height is 28'0"
Smoke pocket to apron edge is 3'0"
Orchestra pit exists

RIGGING
Grid Height: 80'
Type: Single purchase counter weight

LOADING DOCK
Loading door(s) are 10'0"high x 8'0"wide
Trucks load (3) at same time
Fork lift is required

ELECTRICS
UNDER RENOVATION
Total power available:
    (4) 400A 1Ø
    (1) 400A 3Ø
FOLLOWSPOTS
None
DIMMERS
No house dimmers

SOUND
House has 200A dedicated
    power
FOH mixing position in
    House Center
No sound console available

ROYAL GEORGE THEATRE

YEAR BUILT: 1986

Theatre Location:	1641 N. Halsted Street, Chicago, IL 60614
Management Company:	The Royal Group
	1633 N. Halsted Street #400, Chicago, IL 60614

Main Administrative Phone:	312-944-5626
Main Administrative Fax:	312-944-5627
E-mail:	royalgrp@aol.com
Backstage Pay Phone:	312-337-9650
Traveling Production Office Phone:	312-988-7691

SEATING CAPACITY

Main Floor	264
Balcony	188
Total:	**452**

pit (add'l)	0
wheelchair (add'l)	0
standing (add'l)	0

THEATRE STAFF

General Manager	James Jensen	312-944-5626
Executive Officer	Robert Perkins	312-944-5626

HOUSE CREW

Technical Director	Christopher Fitzgerald	312-988-7236

STAGE DIMENSIONS (FROM SMOKE POCKET)
Stage is 22'5" deep
Width from Center Line to SL is 29'6"
Width from Center Line to SR is 47'4"
Proscenium width is 37'1"
Proscenium height is 20'9"
Smoke pocket to apron edge is 7'4"
Orchestra pit exists

RIGGING
Grid Height: 21' to bottom of Catwalks

LOADING DOCK
Loading door(s) are 9'8" high x 7'8" wide
Trucks load (1) at a time

ELECTRICS
Total power available:
(1) 400A 3Ø
(4) 100A 3Ø

FOLLOWSPOTS
House Followspots:
None
Power in spot booth (3) 20A

DIMMERS
(48) house dimmers
No DMX control system

SOUND
House has 60A dedicated
power located SL
FOH mixing position in
Rear House
No sound console available

SHUBERT THEATRE

YEAR BUILT: 1906

Theatre Location: 22 W. Monroe, Chicago, IL 60603
Management Company: Nederlander of Chicago, Inc.

Main Administrative Phone: 312-977-1701
Main Administrative Fax: 312-977-1740
Stage Door Phone: 312-977-1701
Backstage Pay Phone: 312-263-9183
Traveling Production Office Fax: 312-977-1745

THEATRE STAFF
General Manager   Suzanne Bizer   312-977-1701
Marketing   Jill Hurwitz   312-977-1701
Group Sales   Gemma Mulvihill   312-977-1710

HOUSE CREW
Carpentry   Jim Kernan   312-977-1713
Sound   Ray Schmitz   312-977-1713
Props   Bill Kehoe   312-977-1713

UNIONS
IATSE Local #2   Bob Ingersoll   312-236-3457
Wardrobe Local #769   Hugh Pruett   312-332-2244
Music   Anita Smith   847-823-6900

SEATING CAPACITY
Orchestra   798
Loge   295
Mezzanine   498
Balcony   393
Boxes   24
Total: **2,008**

wheelchair (incl'd)

BOX OFFICE
Computerized
Treasurer
   Liam O'Connell   312-977-1701

Outside Ticket Agency
Computerized
Ticketmaster
   Jean Blasco   312-559-1950

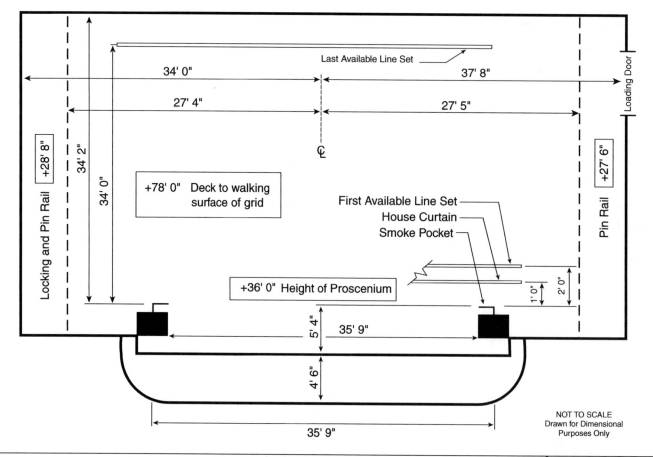

Last Available Line Set

34' 0"   37' 8"
27' 4"   27' 5"

℄

Loading Door

Locking and Pin Rail   +28' 8"
34' 2"
34' 0"

+78' 0"   Deck to walking surface of grid

First Available Line Set
House Curtain
Smoke Pocket

Pin Rail   +27' 6"

1' 0"   2' 0"

+36' 0" Height of Proscenium

5' 4"   35' 9"

4' 6"

35' 9"

NOT TO SCALE
Drawn for Dimensional
Purposes Only

STAGE HOUSE

HOUSE CURTAIN
Operates as a guillotine from SR deck

RIGGING SYSTEM
Type:	Single purchase counter weight
Weight:	18,600 lbs available
Line sets:	60 sets at 6" o.c. with 5 lift lines per set
Arbors:	750 lb capacity
House Pipes:	50' long with 62'-68' of travel from deck

Line sets are moveable
(55) spot wheels and 14,000' of hemp available

PERMANENT INSTALLATIONS OVER STAGE (FROM SMOKE POCKET)
None

PERMANENT INSTALLATIONS ON DECK
Trap (1) in stage floor USL to basement; additional floor traps must be cut

ORCHESTRA PIT
Nonadjustable at 7' below stage level
Apron overhangs US wall of pit 6'8"

BACKSTAGE

LOADING DOCK
Loading door(s):
  12'0" high x 7'0" wide
Trucks load (2) side by side at same time
Dock (loading door sill) is at street level; trucks also unload in west alley
Fork lift required; contact house
Trailers can store on-site

WARDROBE
Location: SR in basement
Access: Trap in stage floor USL
(1) Washer (2) Dryers

DRESSING ROOMS
(2) Star, SR, basement, t/s included
(9) Small, basement, t/s on same fl
(1) Chorus, basement, t/s on same fl

SOUND

CONSOLE
No house console

SPEAKERS
Under Balcony
All speakers wired to patch panel in DSR basement
Speaker truss exists
Max available load 2,000 lbs per point

COMMUNICATIONS
Intercom available
Infrared sound system
Dressing room page system

ROAD CONSOLE
Located Rear House left
(16) seats required to be removed
Cable run from stage is 150'

REHEARSAL & STORAGE SPACE
Rehearsal: None
Storage: None

ELECTRICS

ROAD SERVICE POWER

Panel	Phase	Amp	Circuit Protection	Use	Location
A-C	3	1200	fuse	dimmers	SR on jump
D	3	20	breaker	extra	DSR on jump
E	3	40	breaker	sound	DSR in basement

Recommended location of touring dimmer racks: SR on jump (47'0" from deck)
Hoist is required and provided

FRONT OF HOUSE (BOX BOOM VALUES ARE PER SIDE)

Position	Pipe Width	Distance to Prosc.	House Circuits	Connector Type	FOH Transfer Circuits
1st Balc Rail	42'	47'	17	grd 20 amp stage pin	17
2nd Balc Rail	75'	64'	36	grd 20 amp stage pin	36
Box Boom 1		22'	8	grd 20 amp stage pin	8

Transfer circuits: grd 20 amp stage pin located SR on jump 47' from deck
Road truss: Truss position has chain motors and power; pipe and rigging unavailable

EQUIPMENT FOH (BOX BOOM VALUES ARE PER SIDE)
None

FOLLOWSPOTS
House Followspots: (2)

Followspot Booth:
  (3) spots per booth;
  101' throw to proscenium;
  (3) 3Ø 30 amp breakers

DIMMERS
No lighting console
No dimmers
No DMX

BRADEN AUDITORIUM

AT: ILLINOIS STATE UNIVERSITY, BONE STUDENT CENTER   YEAR BUILT: 1972

			SEATING CAPACITY	
Theatre Location:	Illinois State University, Normal, IL 61790-2640		Orchestra	1,402
Mailing Address:	Illinois State University, Campus Box 2640		Mezzanine	1,006
	Normal, IL 61970-2640		Balcony	1,050
			Total:	**3,457**
Main Administrative Phone:		309-438-2222		
Main Administrative Fax:		309-438-5167	wheelchair (add'l)	26
Stage Door Phone:		309-438-2228		
Backstage Pay Phone:		309-454-9163		
Traveling Production Office Phone:		309-438-3328		

THEATRE STAFF

Theatre Manager	Cassandra Carter	309-438-2222
Booking	Cassandra Carter	309-438-2222

HOUSE CREW

Technical Director	Andy Gordon	309-438-2228
Asst Technical Director	Chuck Fudge	309-438-2228
Stage Manager	Cory Monk	309-438-2228

STAGE DIMENSIONS (FROM SMOKE POCKET)
Stage is 48'0" deep
Width from Center Line to SL is 74'0"
Width from Center Line to SR is 70'0"
Proscenium width is 16'8"
Proscenium height is 28'0"
Smoke pocket to apron edge is 16'0"
Orchestra pit exists

RIGGING

Grid Height:	72'
Type:	Single purchase counter weight
Weight:	20,000 lbs
Line sets:	43 sets at 6"-30" o.c.
Arbors:	3,500 lb capacity
House Pipes:	84' long

LOADING DOCK
Loading door(s) are 15'0" high x 10'0" wide
Trucks load (2) at same time
Fork lift is not required and is not available

ELECTRICS
Total power available:
  (2) 400A 3Ø SR plaster wall
  (1) 200A 3Ø SR plaster wall
  (1) 100A 3Ø SR plaster wall

FOLLOWSPOTS
House Followspots:
  Lycian 1290
Power in spot booth
  (4) 30amp 1Ø

DIMMERS
(532) house dimmers
House has DMX control system
(2) dry run station(s) located SR

SOUND
House has 200 amp 3Ø
  dedicated power located
  SR
FOH mixing position in
  Center Orchestra
Sound console is available

PEORIA CIVIC CENTER THEATRE

YEAR BUILT: 1982

Theatre Location: 201 SW Jefferson Street, Peoria, IL 61602
Management Company: SMG
701 Market Street, Suite 4400, Philadelphia, PA 19106

Main Administrative Phone: 309-673-8900
Main Administrative Fax: 309-673-9223
Website: www.peoriaciviccenter.com
Stage Door Phone: 309-680-3644

THEATRE STAFF
General Manager   Donald Q. Welch   309-673-8900
Booking   Debbie Ritschel   309-673-8900
Group Sales   Sharon Young   309-673-8900

HOUSE CREW
Theatre Manager   Griff Garmers   309-680-3640
Sound   Dave Ferrell   309-680-3675

UNIONS
IATSE Local #193   Don Bentley   309-673-7596

SEATING CAPACITY
Orchestra   1,451
First Balcony   378
Second Balcony   348
Total: **2,177**

pit (add'l)   67

BOX OFFICE
Computerized
  Michelle Camper   309-673-8900

Outside Ticket Agency
  Ticketmaster   309-676-8700
                     800-643-1034

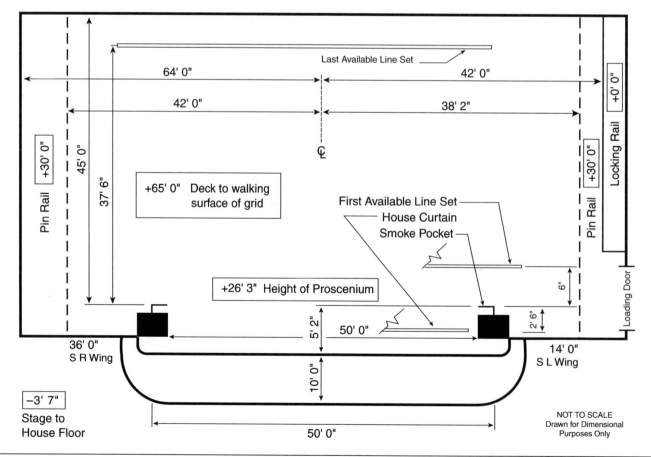

STAGE HOUSE

HOUSE CURTAIN
Operates as a guillotine from SR deck

RIGGING SYSTEM
Type: Single purchase counter weight
Weight: 48,000 lbs available
Line sets: 41 sets at 6-12" o.c. with 6 lift lines per set
Arbors: 1,200 lb capacity
House Pipes: 60' long with 63' of travel from deck
Line sets are moveable
Block & Falls are available 3:2 (2)
(32) spot wheels and 3,000' of hemp available

PERMANENT INSTALLATIONS OVER STAGE (FROM SMOKE POCKET)
Electric raceways (5) at 1'0", 9'6", 18'0", 26'6", 30'0"
Orchestra shells (5) at 5'0", 13'6", 22'0", 31'6", 36'0"

PERMANENT INSTALLATIONS ON DECK
Jumps (2) above locking rail SR/SL
Orchestra shells storage 4'0" x 20'0", USR
Adjustable portal (1) 50', at fire curtain

ORCHESTRA PIT
Adjustable to 7'11" below stage level
Apron overhangs US wall of pit 10'0"

BACKSTAGE

LOADING DOCK
Loading door(s):
16'0" high x 12'0" wide
Trucks load (2) side by side at same time
Dock is at street level; one truck bay equipped with scissor lift
Fork lift is not required
Sound/Props can load in FOH
Lobby can be a work area
(15) Trailers can store on-site
Security at dock & stage door

WARDROBE
Location: SR on 3rd floor
Access: Elevator
(1) Washer (1) Dryer

DRESSING ROOMS
(1) Star, SR, stage level, t/s included, phone jack
(3) Small, SR & SL, on 3rd floor, t/s included, phone jack
(6) Chorus, SR & SL, t/s included, phone jack
Elevator access for dressing rooms
Use dressing room for company mgr office

SOUND

CONSOLE
Soundcraft
40 inputs, 3 main outputs, 14 x 8 matrix outputs, 8 aux outputs

SPEAKERS
House Cluster

COMMUNICATIONS
Clear Com intercom with (2) channels
Sennheiser infra-red system
Dressing room page system

ROAD CONSOLE
Located Rear House
No seats required to be removed
Cable run from stage is 150'
Tie-in into house system with XLR connectors

REHEARSAL & STORAGE SPACE
Rehearsal: 25' x 50' located SL on 3rd floor, piano available
Storage: 30' x 45' located SR 57' x 32' located SL on loading dock

ELECTRICS

ROAD SERVICE POWER

Panel	Phase	Amp	Circuit Protection	Use	Location
A-C	3	400	fuse	dimmers	DSR Alcove
D	3	100	breaker	extra	SL loading dock
E	3	100	breaker	sound	DSL side wall

Additional 400 amps are available USR side wall approx 60' from stage
Recommended location of touring dimmer racks: SR on deck
Hoist not required

FRONT OF HOUSE (BOX BOOM VALUES ARE PER SIDE)

Position	Pipe Width	Distance to Prosc.	House Circuits	Connector Type	FOH Transfer Circuits
1st Balc Rail	60'	114'	25	grd 20 amp stage pin	25
1st Cove	60'	55'	30	grd 20 amp stage pin	30
Box Boom 1		55'	12	grd 20 amp stage pin	12
Term 1		6'	6	grd 20 amp stage pin	6
Term 2		10'	12	grd 20 amp stage pin	12

Transfer circuits: grd 20 amp stage pin located DSR in alcove
Additional circuits: (16) 1st Balcony Rear, (12) 2nd Balcony Rear; chain motor rigging possible, but must be attached to well beams not grid work; well beams located on 11'0" centers starting 5'6" right and left of center

EQUIPMENT FOH (BOX BOOM VALUES ARE PER SIDE)

Position	Quantity	Wattage	Instrument	Removeable
1st Balc Rail	30	575	Source 4 5°	yes
1st Cove	25	575	Source 4 10°	yes
Box Boom 1	24	575	Source 4 19°	yes

FOLLOWSPOTS
House Followspots:
(1) Super Trouper Xenon; removeable
(2) Xenon Troupers; removeable

Followspot Booth:
(4) spots per booth;
114' throw to proscenium;
3Ø 200 amp breakers

DIMMERS
Lighting console is Expression 2x;
(480) ETC Sensor dimmers
House has programmable DMX control system
(2) dry run DMX station(s)

ROSEMONT THEATRE

YEAR BUILT: 1995

Theatre Location: 5400 River Road, Rosemont, IL 60018

Main Administrative Phone: 847-671-5100
Main Administrative Fax: 847-671-6405
E-mail: Rostheatre@aol.com
Traveling Production Office Phone: 847-671-6430
Traveling Production Office Fax: 847-671-6433

SEATING CAPACITY

100 Level	2,200
200 Level	2,100
Total:	**4,300**
pit (add'l)	90
wheelchair (add'l)	16

THEATRE STAFF

General Manager	Ron Stern	847-671-5100 x108
Booking	Ron Stern	847-671-5100
Marketing	Chris Dieball	847-671-5100 x112
Operations	Ken Lennstrom	847-671-5100 x110
Group Sales	Jeff Shapiro	

HOUSE CREW

Technical Director	Chris Iovino	847-671-5100 x111
Carpentry	Ray Yukich	
Electrics	Tom Hermann	
Sound	Chris Iovino	
Props	Sam Yazdani	

UNIONS

IATSE Local #2	Bob Ingersoll	312-236-3457
Wardrobe Local #769	Hugh Pruett	312-332-2244
Music AFM	Arny Roth	773-935-0566

BOX OFFICE

Computerized
Box Office Manager
   Don Caumeyn   847-671-5100 x103

Outside Ticket Agency
Computerized
Ticketmaster
   Chris Werner   312-559-1950

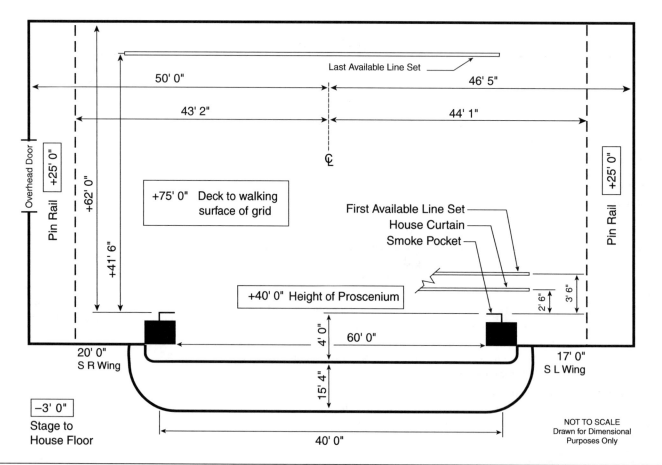

Last Available Line Set

50' 0"
46' 5"
43' 2"
44' 1"

CL

Overhead Door

Pin Rail +25' 0"

+62' 0"

+75' 0" Deck to walking surface of grid

+41' 6"

First Available Line Set
House Curtain
Smoke Pocket

Pin Rail +25' 0"

+40' 0" Height of Proscenium

2' 6"
3' 6"

4' 0"

60' 0"

20' 0"
S R Wing

17' 0"
S L Wing

15' 4"

−3' 0"
Stage to
House Floor

40' 0"

NOT TO SCALE
Drawn for Dimensional
Purposes Only

STAGE HOUSE

HOUSE CURTAIN
Operates as a guillotine or traveller from SL deck; motorized

RIGGING SYSTEM
Type:	Single purchase counter weight
Weight:	90,000 lbs available
Line sets:	66 sets at 6" o.c. with 5 lift lines per set
Arbors:	1,800 lb capacity
House Pipes:	78' long with 65' of travel from deck

Line sets are moveable
Block & Falls are not available
Chain hoists available as a rental; (4) one ton, (8) half ton
(50) spot wheels and 3,000' of hemp available
Full compliment of steel for chain hoist

PERMANENT INSTALLATIONS OVER STAGE (FROM SMOKE POCKET)
Electric raceways (3) at 4'6", 18'6", 34'5"
Fire curtain (1)

PERMANENT INSTALLATIONS ON DECK
None

ORCHESTRA PIT
Adjustable to 13' below stage level by electric motor turnscrew
Apron overhangs US wall of pit 0'0"
Pit lift is in (1) section

BACKSTAGE

LOADING DOCK
Loading door(s):
  12'0" high x 10'0" wide
Trucks load (3) at same time
Fork lift is not required
Sound/Props cannot load in FOH
Trailers can store on-site
Security at dock & stage door

WARDROBE
Location: Basement
Access: Dock w/ freight elevator
(2) Washers (2) Dryers
Washer and dryer hookups available

DRESSING ROOMS
(8) Small, SL, stage level, t/s included, phone jack
(2) Chorus, SL, -1, t/s included, phone jack
Elevator access for dressing rooms
Additional production office available for company mgr

SOUND

CONSOLE
Yamaha PM 4000
48 inputs, 8 matrix outputs, 8 aux outputs

SPEAKERS
House Cluster
Under Balcony

COMMUNICATIONS
Clear Com intercom with (4) channels
Infrared sound system
Dressing room page system

ROAD CONSOLE
Located House left of center
No seats required to be removed
Cable run from stage is 275'
Tie-in into house system with XLR connectors

REHEARSAL & STORAGE SPACE
Rehearsal: Lobby - large, removable mirrors and rehearsal piano
Storage: Loading dock & basement, use freight elevator

ELECTRICS

ROAD SERVICE POWER

Panel	Phase	Amp	Circuit Protection Use	Location
A	3	800	dimmers	Loading dock SR
B	3	200	dimmers	Loading dock SR
C	3	100	dimmers	Loading dock SR
D	3	100	dimmers	Loading dock SR
E	3	200	sound	SR dock or SL
F	3	200	extra	portable at dock

Recommended location of touring dimmer racks: Loading dock SR
Hoist not required
Additional power is available for tour buses, generators, etc.

FRONT OF HOUSE (BOX BOOM VALUES ARE PER SIDE)

Position	Pipe Width	Distance to Prosc.	House Circuits	Connector Type	FOH Transfer Circuits
1st Catwalk		49'	29	grd 20 amp stage pin	0
2nd Catwalk		57'	51	grd 20 amp stage pin	0
3rd Catwalk		71'	15	grd 20 amp stage pin	0
4th Catwalk		91	15	grd 20 amp stage pin	0

Road truss: Ample available rigging DS of proscenium

EQUIPMENT FOH (BOX BOOM VALUES ARE PER SIDE)
Small complement of lighting instruments

FOLLOWSPOTS
House Followspots:
  (4) Lycian 1275 Super 1.2k

Followspot Booth:
  87' throw to proscenium;

DIMMERS
House has lighting console (654) CD80 2.4k dimmers
House has programmable DMX control system
(4) dry run DMX station(s), (2) SR, (2) on dock near power

SANGAMON AUDITORIUM

AT: UNIVERSITY OF ILLINOIS AT SPRINGFIELD   **YEAR BUILT: 1981**

Theatre Location: Public Affairs Center, Springfield, IL 62794-9243
Mailing Address: P.O. Box 19243, Springfield, IL 62794-9243

Main Administrative Phone: 217-206-6150
Main Administrative Fax: 217-206-7279
E-mail: kennedy.john@uis.edu
Website: www.uis.edu/~onstage
Backstage Pay Phone: 217-529-9703
Traveling Production Office Phone: 217-206-7247
Traveling Production Office Fax: 217-206-6045

THEATRE STAFF
Director   John Dale Kennedy   217-206-6150
Booking   John Dale Kennedy   217-206-6150
Marketing   Debi D. Edwards   217-206-6150
Group Sales   James P. Stephenson 217-206-6160

HOUSE CREW
Technical Director Scott M. Wilson   217-206-6150
Carpentry   John F. Sefick   217-206-6150
Electrics   John F. Sefick   217-206-6150
Sound   Noel Garlits   217-206-6150
Props   John F. Sefick   217-206-6150

UNIONS
IATSE Local #138   Richard Goyne   217-496-2945
Music   In-House

SEATING CAPACITY
Orchestra   425
Loge   595
Mezzanine   564
Balcony   368
Total: **1,952**

pit (add'l)   66
wheelchair (incl.)   27

BOX OFFICE
Computerized
Ticket Manager
  James P. Stephenson   217-206-6160
                        800-207-6960

Outside Ticket Agency
  None

Box office is promoter operated

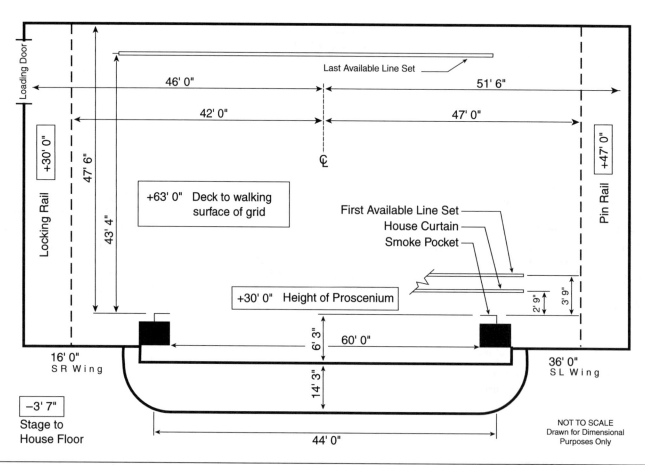

STAGE HOUSE

HOUSE CURTAIN
Operates as a guillotine or traveller from SR fly floor or deck

RIGGING SYSTEM
Type:	Combination purchase counter weight
Weight:	70,000 lbs available
Line sets:	55 sets at 6-8" o.c. with 6 lift lines per set
Arbors:	700 lb capacity
House Pipes:	63' long with 63' of travel from deck

Line sets are moveable
(10) spot wheels and 1,200' of hemp available

PERMANENT INSTALLATIONS OVER STAGE (FROM SMOKE POCKET)
Orchestra shell (2) at 7'7", 20'0"

PERMANENT INSTALLATIONS ON DECK
Orchestra shell stores in SL wing - 18'0" deep

ORCHESTRA PIT
Adjustable to 18' below stage level by hydraulic lift
Apron overhangs US wall of pit 5'0"

BACKSTAGE

LOADING DOCK
Loading door(s):
10'8" high x 8'0" wide
Trucks load (2) side by side at same time
Fork lift is not required
Sound/Props cannot load in FOH
(2+) Trailers can store on-site

WARDROBE
Location: basement
Access: freight elevator
(1) Washer (1) Dryer
No washer or dryer hookups

DRESSING ROOMS
(2) Star, SR, stage level, t/s included, phone jack
(2) Small, SR, -1, t/s included, phone jack
(2) Chorus, SR, -1, t/s included
Elevator access for dressing rooms

SOUND

CONSOLE
Tascam M2600
24 inputs, 2 main outputs, 4 stereo submix matrix outputs, 6 - 1 stereo aux outputs

SPEAKERS
House Cluster
Proscenium
No speaker truss
Fly points in front of proscenium

COMMUNICATIONS
Clear Com intercom with (2) channels
Infrared sound system
Dressing room page system

ROAD CONSOLE
Located Center
(12) seats required to be removed
Cable run from stage is 160'
Tie-in into house system with XLR connectors
42" max height at FOH position

REHEARSAL & STORAGE SPACE
Rehearsal: 60' x 60' in basement, prior arrangement required
Storage: 12' x 60' in basement

ELECTRICS

ROAD SERVICE POWER

Panel	Phase	Amp	Circuit Protection	Use	Location
A	3	400	breaker	dimmers	USR back wall
B-C	3	400	breaker	extra	USR back wall
D	3	100	breaker	sound	DSL proscenium wall

Recommended location of touring dimmer racks: SR on deck
Hoist not required
Additional power is available for tour buses, generators, etc.

FRONT OF HOUSE (BOX BOOM VALUES ARE PER SIDE)

Position	Pipe Width	Distance to Prosc.	House Circuits	Connector Type	FOH Transfer Circuits
1st Cove	60'	31'	14	grd 20 amp stage pin	14
2nd Cove	60'	48'	24	grd 20 amp stage pin	24
3rd Cove	60'	67'	27	grd 20 amp stage pin	27
Box Boom 1		16'	15	grd 20 amp stage pin	15

Transfer circuits: grd 20 amp stage pin located in USR back wall

EQUIPMENT FOH (BOX BOOM VALUES ARE PER SIDE)

Position	Quantity	Wattage	Instrument	Removeable
2nd Cove	20	1,000	6" Lekos	yes
3rd Cove	20	1,000	8" Lekos	yes

FOLLOWSPOTS
House Followspots:
(3) Lycian Superstar long throws; not removeable

Followspot Booth:
(8) spots per booth;
140' throw to proscenium;
(8) 1Ø 50 amp breakers

DIMMERS
Lighting console is AVAB;
(300) AVAB dimmers
No DMX control system
(1) dry run DMX station(s)

TRYON FESTIVAL THEATRE

AT: KRANNERT CENTEER FOR THE PERFORMING ARTS   YEAR BUILT: **1969**   YEAR RENOVATED: **1995**

Theatre Location:	University of Illinois, Urbana, IL 61801	
Mailing Address:	500 S. Goodwin Avenue, Urbana, IL 61801	

Main Administrative Phone:	217-333-6700
Main Administrative Fax:	217-244-0810
E-mail:	krantix.uluc.edu
Website:	www.kcpa.uluc.edu
Traveling Production Office Phone:	217-333-9728
Traveling Production Office Fax:	217-244-0810

SEATING CAPACITY

Orchestra	671
Balcony	258
Total:	**929**
pit (add'l)	40
wheelchair (add'l)	4
standing (add'l)	0

THEATRE STAFF

Director	Mike Ross	217-333-6700

HOUSE CREW

Director of Events	Mark Collmer	217-333-9278
Events Tech.Director	Thomas Blake	217-333-7489
Lighting Director	Michael Williams	217-333-9719

STAGE DIMENSIONS (FROM SMOKE POCKET)

Stage is 35' deep
Width from Center Line to SL is 59'2"
Width from Center Line to SR is 69'6"
Proscenium width is 40'
Proscenium height is 25'10"
Smoke pocket to apron edge is 2'6"
Orchestra pit exists

RIGGING

Grid Height:	90'
Type:	Double purchase counter weight; motorized
Weight:	15,500 lbs
Line sets:	24 sets at 12-24" o.c.
Arbors:	1,760 lb capacity
House Pipes:	50' long

LOADING DOCK

Loading door(s) are 13'4" high x 14'6" wide
Trucks load (2) at same time
Fork lift is not required and is available

ELECTRICS

Total power available:
   400A 3Ø off SR

FOLLOWSPOTS

House Followspots:
   Lycian Superstars
Power in spot booth (4) 20A 1Ø

DIMMERS

(254) house dimmers
House has DMX control system
(3) dry run station(s) located
   SL/ SR / House Center line

SOUND

House has 400A 3Ø dedicated power located USR
FOH mixing position in Rear House Right
Sound console is available

INDIANA UNIVERSITY AUDITORIUM

YEAR BUILT: 1941 UNDER RENOVATION: 1999

Theatre Location: 1200 East Seventh Street, Bloomington, IN 47405

Main Administrative Phone: 812-855-9528
Main Administrative Fax: 812-855-4244
E-mail: comments@indiana.edu
Website: www.iuauditorium.com
Stage Door Phone: 812-334-9166
Traveling Production Office Phone: 812-855-8221
Traveling Production Office Fax: 812-855-9166

THEATRE STAFF
General Manager   Bryan L. Rives   812-855-9528
Booking   Doug Booher   812-855-0170
Group Sales   Marge Ison   812-855-1103

HOUSE CREW
Stage Manager   Don Erwin   812-855-5259
Electrics   Don Oard   812-855-5259

UNIONS
IATSE Local #618   Mark Sarris   812-331-7472
Wardrobe Local #893 Mary Ann Jacobs   812-876-1558
Music Local #3   Al Cobine   812-332-1183

SEATING CAPACITY
Orchestra   1,800
Mezzanine   250
Balcony   1,166
Total (estimated):   **3,216**

wheelchair   incl.

BOX OFFICE
Computerized
Box Office Manager
  Marge Ison   812-855-1103

Outside Ticket Agency
Computerized
Ticketmaster
  Marge Ison   812-855-1103

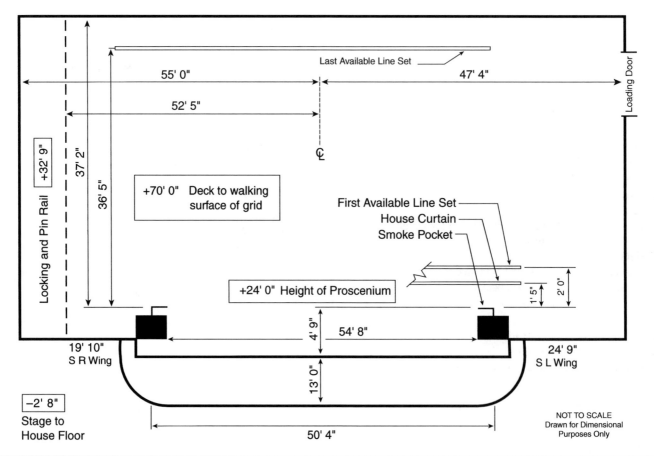

Last Available Line Set

55' 0"   47' 4"

52' 5"

Loading Door

+32' 9"

37' 2"

36' 5"

CL

Locking and Pin Rail

+70' 0" Deck to walking surface of grid

First Available Line Set
House Curtain
Smoke Pocket

1' 5"   2' 0"

+24' 0" Height of Proscenium

4' 9"   54' 8"

19' 10"
S R Wing

24' 9"
S L Wing

13' 0"

−2' 8"
Stage to
House Floor

50' 4"

NOT TO SCALE
Drawn for Dimensional
Purposes Only

STAGE HOUSE

HOUSE CURTAIN
Operates as a guillotine or traveller from SR deck

RIGGING SYSTEM
Type: Single purchase counter weight
Weight: 11,000 lbs available
Line sets: 37 sets at 6-12" o.c. with 5 lift lines
                   per set
Arbors: 1,000 lb capacity
House Pipes: 70' long with 62' of travel from deck
Line sets are not moveable
Block & Falls are available 2:1 (1)
(40) spot wheels

PERMANENT INSTALLATIONS OVER STAGE (FROM SMOKE POCKET)
M=Moveable with advance call
Orchestra shells (5); M
Electric borders (5)
Movie screen (1)
UNDER RENOVATION

PERMANENT INSTALLATIONS ON DECK
None

ORCHESTRA PIT
UNDER RENOVATION
Adjustable by hydraulic lift
Apron overhangs US wall of pit 0'0"
Pit lift is in (1) section

BACKSTAGE

LOADING DOCK
Loading door(s):
   15'8" high x 6'6" wide
Trucks load (1) at same time
Fork lift is not required
Sound/Props cannot load in
   FOH
Trailers cannot store on-site
Security at dock & stage door

WARDROBE
Location: Basement (under
   stage)
Access: Stairs/Freight elevator
(1) Washer (1) Dryer

DRESSING ROOMS
(2) Star, SR, stage level, t/s
   included, phone jack
(8) Small, SR, +2, t/s included,
   phone jack
(2) Chorus, SR, - 1, t/s included,
   phone jack
Use dressing room for company
   mgr office

SOUND

UNDER RENOVATION

REHEARSAL & STORAGE SPACE
Rehearsal: Stage
   Other rooms within
   walking distance on
   campus available with
   advance notice
Storage: Dock
   More space may be
   available after renovation

ELECTRICS

ROAD SERVICE POWER
   UNDER RENOVATION

FRONT OF HOUSE (BOX BOOM VALUES ARE PER SIDE)
   UNDER RENOVATION

EQUIPMENT FOH (BOX BOOM VALUES ARE PER SIDE)
   UNDER RENOVATION

FOLLOWSPOTS
   House Followspots:
      (2) Xenon Super Trouper;
   removeable

   Followspot Booth:
      (3) spots per booth;
      180' throw to proscenium;

DIMMERS
   UNDER RENOVATION

EMBASSY THEATRE

YEAR BUILT: 1928   YEAR RENOVATED: 1996

Theatre Location: 121 West Jefferson Blvd, Ft. Wayne, IN 46802
Mailing Address: 125 West Jefferson Blvd, Ft. Wayne, IN 46802
Management Company: Embassy Theatre Foundation
                            125 West Jefferson Blvd, Ft. Wayne, IN 46802

Main Administrative Phone: 219-424-6287
Main Administrative Fax: 219-424-4806
E-mail: embassy2@fortwayne.infi.net
Website: www.ft-wayne.in.us/arts/embassy
Stage Door Phone: 219-424-6287

THEATRE STAFF
Executive Director   Doris G. Stovall   219-424-6287
Booking   Ken Retzlaff   219-424-6287

HOUSE CREW
Tech/Theatre Mgr   Ken Retzlaff   219-424-6287

UNIONS
IATSE Local #146   Butch Barile   219-487-0073
Wardrobe Local #146   Butch Barile   219-487-0073
Music Local #58   Dan Ross   219-744-1700

SEATING CAPACITY
Main Floor	1355
Loge	412
Middle Balcony	460
Upper Balcony	198
Total:	**2,425**
pit (add'l)	64
wheelchair (add'l)	12

BOX OFFICE
Computerized
Box Office Manager
  Amy Adams   219-424-5665

Outside Ticket Agency
Ticketmaster

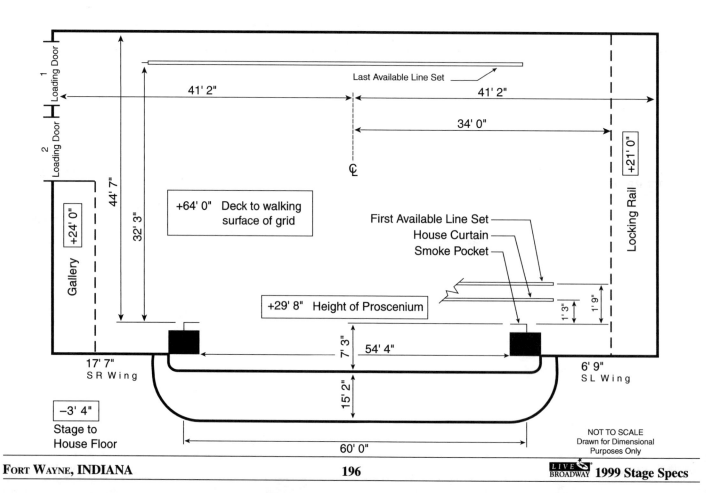

NOT TO SCALE
Drawn for Dimensional
Purposes Only

STAGE HOUSE

HOUSE CURTAIN
Operates as a traveller from SR deck

RIGGING SYSTEM
Type:	Double purchase counter weight
Weight:	15,700 lbs available
Line sets:	58 sets at 6" o.c. with 5 lift lines per set
Arbors:	900 lb capacity
House Pipes:	58' long with 55' of travel from deck

Line sets are not moveable
Block & Falls are not available
Chain hoists available as a rental; (1) half ton

PERMANENT INSTALLATIONS OVER STAGE (FROM SMOKE POCKET)
M=Moveable with advance call
Orchestra shell (4) at 7'9", 19'3", 30'9"; M
Electric borders (1) at 0'9"
Electric raceways (4) at 2'9", 6'9", 14'3", 20'9"
Movie screen (1) at 10'3"; M
Traveller (2) 1'3", 6'3"
Deadhang pipes (3) 8'9", 9'9", 10'9"

PERMANENT INSTALLATIONS ON DECK
Traps (1), 7'0" x 4'8" located wing SR
Orchestra shell storage (6) at SL

ORCHESTRA PIT
Adjustable to 15' below stage level by electric motor
turnscrew
Apron overhangs US wall of pit 3' 0"
Pit lift is in (2) sections
Organ lift SR

BACKSTAGE

LOADING DOCK
Loading door(s):
1) 11'1" high x 9'10" wide
2) 8'1" high x 7'8" wide
Trucks load (2) at same time
Door #1- Ramp to lift 12,000 lb
capacity; lift down to deck
Door #2 - Double ramp to deck
Sound/Props can load in FOH
Lobby can be a work area
Trailers can store on street

WARDROBE
Location: Dressing room area
Access: Chain hoist/trap door
(1) Washer (1) Dryer
Washer and dryer hookups
available

DRESSING ROOMS
(7) Small, SL,-1, shower
included, toilet on same fl
(1) Small, SL, stage level, t/s
included, phone jack
(2) Chorus, SR, -1, shower
included, toilet on same fl
Additional production office
available for company mgr

SOUND

CONSOLE
No house console

SPEAKERS
This info is subject to
change- project pending
Proscenium
No speaker truss

COMMUNICATIONS
Clear Com intercom with
(2) channels
Dressing room page system

ROAD CONSOLE
Located Rear SR
Number of seats required to
be removed varies
Cable run from stage is 125'
Tie-in into house system with
XLR connectors

REHEARSAL & STORAGE SPACE
Rehearsal: None
Storage: Loading Dock

ELECTRICS

ROAD SERVICE POWER
Panel	Phase	Amp	Circuit Protection	Use	Location
A	3	600	fuse	dimmers	DSR wing
B	3	400	fuse	extra	USR wing
C	3	100	fuse	sound	USR wing

Recommended location of touring dimmer racks: SR on deck
Hoist not required

FRONT OF HOUSE (BOX BOOM VALUES ARE PER SIDE)
Position	Pipe Width	Distance to Prosc.	House Circuits	Connector Type	FOH Transfer Circuits
1st Balc Rail	60'	50'	48	grd 20 amp stagepin	48

Road truss: Capable of 500 lbs per point, 20' from smoke pocket

EQUIPMENT FOH (BOX BOOM VALUES ARE PER SIDE)
Position	Quantity	Wattage	Instrument	Removeable
1st Balc Rail	8	500	Curtain warmers (Lekos)	yes

FOLLOWSPOTS
House Followspots:
(2) Xenon Super Trouper;
not removeable

Followspot Booth:
(2) spots per booth;
110' throw to proscenium;
3Ø 120 amp breakers

DIMMERS
Lighting console is Strand
Light
Board M;
(48) CD80 dimmers
House has programmable
AMX control system

SCOTTISH RITE AUDITORIUM

Theatre Location: 417 West Berry Street, Fort Wayne, IN 46815
Management Company: Scottish Rite of Freemasonry

Main Administrative Phone: 219-423-2593
Stage Door Phone: 219-422-9113

SEATING CAPACITY

Orchestra	2,147
Total:	**2,147**
pit (add'l)	50

THEATRE STAFF

Executive Secretary	David D. Platt	219-423-2593
Booking	David D. Platt	219-423-2593

HOUSE CREW

Technical Director	Noel Sell	219-461-1288
Sound	James Fuzy	219-456-9830

STAGE DIMENSIONS (FROM SMOKE POCKET)
Stage is 32'2" deep
Width from Center Line to SL is 40'0"
Width from Center Line to SR is 32'5"
Proscenium width is 65'0"
Proscenium height is 35'0"
Smoke pocket to apron edge is 4'5"
Orchestra pit exists

RIGGING

Grid Height:	75'0"
Type:	Single purchase counter weight
Weight:	20,000 lbs
Line sets:	58 sets at 6" o.c.
Arbors:	600 lb capacity
House Pipes:	60' long

LOADING DOCK
Loading door(s) are 8'0" high x 7'10" wide
Trucks load (2) at same time

ELECTRICS
Total power available:
  (1) 400A 1Ø fused

FOLLOWSPOTS
House Followspots:
  (1) Carbon Arc Super Trouper
Power in spot booth
  (1) 20A 1Ø

DIMMERS
No house dimmers

SOUND
FOH mixing position in
  Rear House
Sound console is available

CLOWES MEMORIAL HALL

AT: BUTLER UNIVERSITY   YEAR BUILT: 1961   RENOVATION ONGOING

Theatre Location: 4600 Sunset Avenue, Indianapolis, IN 46208

Main Administrative Phone: 317-940-9697
Main Administrative Fax: 317-940-9820
E-mail: clowes@butler.edu
Website: www.cloweshall.org
Backstage Pay Phone: 317-940-0131
Traveling Production Office Phone: 317-940-8703
Traveling Production Office Fax: 317-940-9997

THEATRE STAFF

Executive Director	Elise J. Kushigian	317-940-9620
Booking	Elise J. Kushigian	317-940-9620
Marketing	Samantha Cross	317-640-9341
Operations	Michael Jonson	317-940-9603
House Manager	Shawn L. Jones	317-940-6414

HOUSE CREW

Carpentry	George Whitehouse	317-940-9615
Electrics	John Lucas	317-940-6423
Sound	Dainis Ozers	317-940-9612
Fly	James Winegard	317-940-9622

UNIONS

IATSE Local #30	Kim Nicely	317-638-3226
Wardrobe Local #893	Joanne Sanders	317-632-9147
Music	In-house	

SEATING CAPACITY

Orchestra	1,228
First Terrace & Boxes	307
Second Terrace & Boxes	289
Third Terrace & Boxes	282
Total:	**2,106**

pit (add'l)	76

BOX OFFICE

Computerized
Box Office Manager
  Sheila Sharp   317-940-9611

Outside Ticket Agency
Computerized
Ticketmaster
  David Barnes   317-990-4790

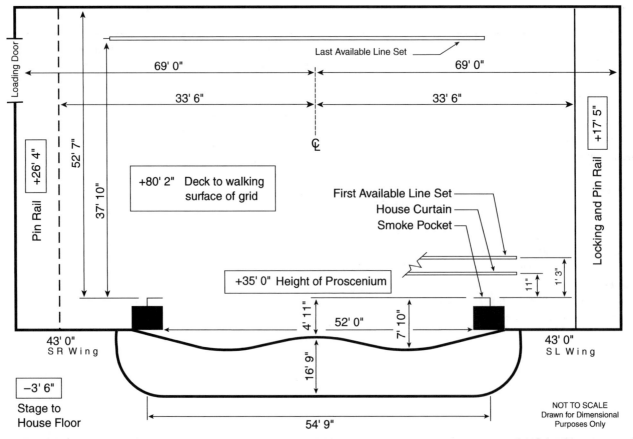

Loading Door

Pin Rail +26' 4"

52' 7"

37' 10"

69' 0"   69' 0"

33' 6"   33' 6"

CL

Last Available Line Set

+80' 2" Deck to walking surface of grid

First Available Line Set
House Curtain
Smoke Pocket

+35' 0" Height of Proscenium

+17' 5"

Locking and Pin Rail

11"   1' 3"

4' 11"   52' 0"   7' 10"

16' 9"

43' 0"
SR Wing

43' 0"
SL Wing

−3' 6"

Stage to
House Floor

54' 9"

NOT TO SCALE
Drawn for Dimensional
Purposes Only

STAGE HOUSE

HOUSE CURTAIN
Operates as a guillotine from SL fly floor

RIGGING SYSTEM
Type:	Double purchase counter weight
Weight:	24,000 lbs available
Line sets:	60 sets at 6" o.c. with 7 lift lines per set
Arbors:	2,200 lb capacity
House Pipes:	65' long with 75' of travel from deck

Line sets are moveable
Block & Falls are available
Chain hoists available
(75) spot wheels and 10,000' of hemp available

PERMANENT INSTALLATIONS OVER STAGE (FROM SMOKE POCKET)
M=Moveable with advance call
Electric pipe at 0'9", 10'0", 17'6", 25'10", 34'5"; M
Orchestra shell (13) at 1'3"M, 4'6", 9'0"M, 10'6"M, 13'0", 17'0"M, 18'9"M, 22'2", 25'2"M, 26'7"M, 32'6"M, 33'1"M, 36'6"

PERMANENT INSTALLATIONS ON DECK
Masonry chimney (1) 3'0" x 5'0" at 37'0" located in SR wings

ORCHESTRA PIT
Adjustable to 20' below stage level by hydraulic lift
Pit lift is in (1) section
Moveable seating doubles pit size

BACKSTAGE

LOADING DOCK
Loading door(s):
  10'4" high x 9'3" wide
Trucks load (1) at a time
Fork lift is not required
Sound/Props can load in FOH
Lobby can be a work area
(4) Trailers can store on-site
Security at dock & stage door

WARDROBE
Location: Green Room in basement
Access: Orchestra pit elevator
(2) Washers (2) Dryers
Washer and dryer hookups available

DRESSING ROOMS
(6) Star, basement, t/s included, phone jack
(2) Chorus, basement, t/s included
Additional production office available for company mgr

SOUND

CONSOLE
Midas XL 200, located Terrace 2
32 inputs, 12 aux outputs

SPEAKERS
House Cluster
Proscenium
Portable
No speaker truss

COMMUNICATIONS
Clear Com intercom with (4) channels
Infrared sound system
Dressing room page system

ROAD CONSOLE
Located Rear House right
(30) seats required to be removed
Cable run from stage is 120'
Tie-in into house system with XLR connectors

REHEARSAL & STORAGE SPACE
Rehearsal: Located on campus, prior arrangement required
Storage: None

ELECTRICS

ROAD SERVICE POWER

Panel	Phase	Amp	Circuit Protection	Use	Location
A	3	800	breaker	electrics	SR
B	3	400	breaker	extra	SR
C	3	200	breaker	extra	SR
D	3	100	breaker	extra	SL

Recommended location of touring dimmer racks: SR
Hoist not required
Additional power is available for tour buses, generators, etc.

FRONT OF HOUSE (BOX BOOM VALUES ARE PER SIDE)

Position	Pipe Width	Distance to Prosc.	House Circuits	Connector Type	FOH Transfer Circuits
2nd Balc Rail	4'8"	95'	8	grd 30 amp stage pin	0
1st Cove	45'	80'	26	ungrd 20 amp stage pin	0
2nd Cove	50'	55'	4	ungrd 20 amp stage pin	0
Box Boom 1	30'	45'	10	ungrd 20 amp stage pin	0

Transfer circuits: 20 & 30 amp stage pin

EQUIPMENT FOH (BOX BOOM VALUES ARE PER SIDE)

Position	Quantity	Wattage	Instrument	Removeable
1st Cove	26	575	Source 4 10°	yes
Torms	16	575	Source 4 19°/26°	yes

FOLLOWSPOTS
House Followspots:
  (2) Xenon Super Troupers; removeable

Followspot Booth:
  (3) spots per booth;
  130' throw to proscenium;
  (2) 3Ø 30 amp breakers

DIMMERS
Lighting console is ETC Expression;
(168) 10k, 5k, 2.4k dimmers
House has programmable DMX control system
(1) dry run DMX station(s)

MURAT THEATRE

AT: MURAT CENTRE

YEAR BUILT: 1909   YEAR RENOVATED: 1996

Theatre Location: 502 N New Jersey Street, Indianapolis, IN 46205
Management Company: SFX/Sunshine Promotions
                      10089 Allisonville Road, Fishers, IN 46038

Main Administrative Phone:	317-231-0000
Main Administrative Fax:	317-231-9410
Backstage Pay Phone:	317-632-0614
Traveling Production Office A:	317-231-0263/65
Traveling Production Office B:	317-231-0264/66

SEATING CAPACITY

Total: 2,517

wheelchair (add'l)   20

BOX OFFICE
Computerized
Box Office Manager
  Amy Nettles   317-231-0000 x210

Outside Ticket Agency
Computerized
Ticketmaster
  David Barnes   317-263-2222

THEATRE STAFF

General Manager	Tim Roberts	317-231-0000 x202
Booking	Tim Roberts	317-231-0000 x201
Marketing	Amy Anderson	317-231-0000 x201
Group Sales	Misty Eaton	317-231-0000 x206

HOUSE CREW

Technical Director	Albert West	317-231-0000 x225/ Fax 231-0267
Stage Manager	Don McGuire	317-267-9925
Carpentry	Don McGuire	317-267-9925

UNIONS

IATSE Local # 30	Kim Nicely	317-638-3226
Wardrobe Local # 893	Joann Sanders	317-632-9147

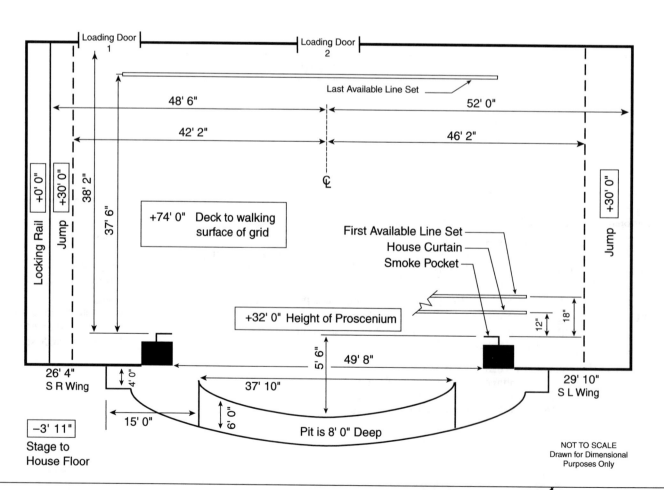

Loading Door 1
Loading Door 2

Last Available Line Set

48' 6"   52' 0"
42' 2"   46' 2"

38' 2"
37' 6"

CL

+74' 0"   Deck to walking surface of grid

Locking Rail   +0' 0"
Jump   +30' 0"
Jump   +30' 0"

First Available Line Set
House Curtain
Smoke Pocket

+32' 0" Height of Proscenium

12"   18"

5' 6"   49' 8"

26' 4"
S R Wing

29' 10"
S L Wing

4' 0"

15' 0"   37' 10"

6' 0"

−3' 11"
Stage to
House Floor

Pit is 8' 0" Deep

NOT TO SCALE
Drawn for Dimensional
Purposes Only

STAGE HOUSE

HOUSE CURTAIN
Operates as a guillotine or traveller from SR deck

RIGGING SYSTEM
Type: Single purchase counter weight
Weight: 70,000 lbs available
Line sets: 69 sets at 6" o.c. with 7 lift lines per set
Arbors: 1,400 lb capacity
House Pipes: 63' long with 68' of travel from deck
Line sets are moveable
Block & Falls are not available
Chain hoists available as a rental; (2) one ton
(14) spot wheels and 3,000' of hemp available

PERMANENT INSTALLATIONS OVER STAGE (FROM SMOKE POCKET)
Fire curtain (1)

PERMANENT INSTALLATIONS ON DECK
Trap (1) in stage floor 4'0" x 8'0", located 27'8" US at 23'2" left of center
Jumps (1) 38'0" x 5'10" +30'0"
Electric jump (1) 38'0" x 5'10" +30'0"
Loading bridge (1) 38'0" x 5'10" +65'0"

ORCHESTRA PIT
Nonadjustable at 8' below stage level
Apron overhangs US wall of pit 13'10"
Can cover pit at stage height

BACKSTAGE

LOADING DOCK
Loading door(s):
1) 12'0" high x 9'0"wide USR
2) 8'8" high x 7'7" wide USC
Trucks load (2) at same time
Dock door 1 is 3'6" off lot
Dock door 2 is 2'6" off lot
Fork lift is not required
Sound/Props can load in FOH
(4) Trailers can store on-site
Security at stage door

WARDROBE
Location: Sub basement
Access: Small freight elevator
(2) Washers (2) Dryers
Washer and dryer hookups available

DRESSING ROOMS
(2) Small, SL, stage level, t/s included
(4) Small, Subfloor, t/s included
(2) Star, SL, -1, t/s included
(3) Chorus, SL, -1, t/s on subfloor
Elevator access for dressing rooms on subfloor
Additional production office available for company mgr

SOUND

CONSOLE
Yamaha M2000,
40 inputs, 2 main outputs,
4 matrix outputs, 6 aux outputs

SPEAKERS
House Cluster
Under Balcony
Other floor

COMMUNICATIONS
Clear Com intercom with (4) channels
Infrared sound system

ROAD CONSOLE
Located Rear Orchestra
No seats required to be removed
Cable run from stage is 105'
Tie-in into house system with XLR connectors

REHEARSAL & STORAGE SPACE
Rehearsal: Egyptian Room, 55' x 29' stage for rental
Storage: Basement, various dimensions

ELECTRICS

ROAD SERVICE POWER

Panel	Phase	Amp	Circuit Protection	Use	Location
A	3	200	fuse	sound	USL corner
B-D	3	400	fuse	dimmers	Mid SL

Recommended location of touring dimmer racks: USL
Hoist not required
Additional power is available for tour buses, generators, etc.

FRONT OF HOUSE (BOX BOOM VALUES ARE PER SIDE)

Position	Pipe Width	Distance to Prosc.	House Circuits	Connector Type	FOH Transfer Circuits
1st Balc Rail		49'	18	grd 20 amp stage pin	
1st Cove			24	grd 20 amp stage pin	
Box Boom 1		55'	16	grd 20 amp stage pin	
Box Boom 2		20'	16	grd 20 amp stage pin	

Transfer circuits: DMX

EQUIPMENT FOH (BOX BOOM VALUES ARE PER SIDE)

Position	Quantity	Wattage	Instrument	Removeable
1st Balc Rail	20	1,000	Lekos	yes
1st Cove		1,000	Lekos	yes
Box Boom 1	28	1,000	Source 4 10°	yes

FOLLOWSPOTS
House Followspots:
Strong Super Trouper II Xenon Spots; not removeable
Spares: Lycian Superstar 1.2; removeable

Followspot Booth:
(4) spots per booth;
114' throw to proscenium;
(4) 1Ø 30 amp breakers

DIMMERS
Lighting console is ETC Insight 2;
(256) ETC Sensor Racks dimmers
House has DMX control system
(3) dry run DMX station(s)

EMENS AUDITORIUM

YEAR BUILT: 1963   YEAR RENOVATED: 1990

Theatre Location: Ball State University, Muncie, IN 47306

Main Administrative Phone: 765-285-1542
Main Administrative Fax: 765-285-3719
Stage Door Phone: 765-285-1719
Traveling Production Office Phone: 765-285-2043

THEATRE STAFF
  General Manager   Robert E. Myers   765-285-1542
  Booking   Robert E. Myers   765-285-1542

HOUSE CREW
  Stage Manager   Keven Byrne   765-285-1719
  Carpentry   Barry Rowland   765-285-1719
  Electrics   Floyd Paulsen   765-285-1719
  Sound   Barry Rowland   765-285-1719

UNIONS
  IATSE Local #292   Alan Rowland   765-289-9062

SEATING CAPACITY
  Orchestra   2,536
  Balcony   1,039
  Total: **3,375**

BOX OFFICE
  Computerized
  Office Manager
    Pam Milhollin   765-285-8156

  Outside Ticket Agency
  Computerized
  Ticketmaster

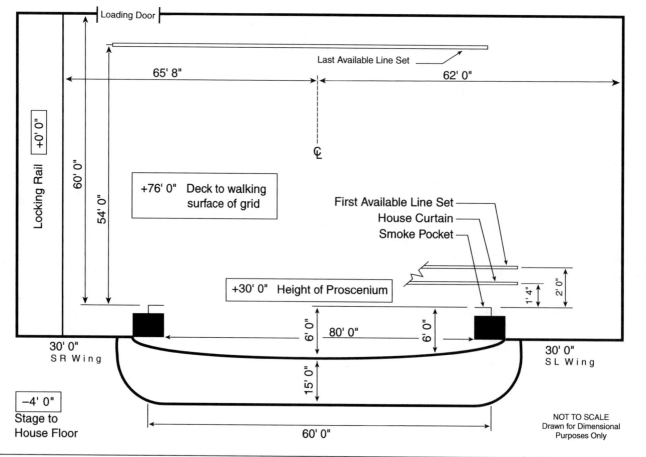

Loading Door

Last Available Line Set

65' 8"   62' 0"

Locking Rail   +0' 0"

60' 0"

54' 0"

+76' 0"   Deck to walking surface of grid

First Available Line Set
House Curtain
Smoke Pocket

1' 4"   2' 0"

+30' 0"   Height of Proscenium

6' 0"   80' 0"   6' 0"

30' 0"
S R Wing

30' 0"
S L Wing

15' 0"

−4' 0"
Stage to
House Floor

60' 0"

NOT TO SCALE
Drawn for Dimensional
Purposes Only

STAGE HOUSE

HOUSE CURTAIN
Operates as a guillotine from SR deck

RIGGING SYSTEM
Type:	Single purchase counter weight; Hemp System
Weight:	20,000 lbs available
Line sets:	60 sets at 8" o.c. with 8 lift lines per set
Arbors:	2,000 lb capacity
House Pipes:	92' long with 70' of travel from deck

Line sets are not moveable
Block & Falls are not available
Chain hoists are not available
(12) spot wheels and 1,000' of hemp available

PERMANENT INSTALLATIONS OVER STAGE (FROM SMOKE POCKET)
Orchestra shell (4) at 2'8", 10'0", 16'8", 20'0"
Electric raceways (8) at 1'4", 4'0", 6'0", 12'0", 18'0", 20'8", 24'8", 32'4"
Cyclorama (1) at 34'4"
Fire curtain

PERMANENT INSTALLATIONS ON DECK
Orchestra shell storage (1) USL
Loading bridge (1) SR

ORCHESTRA PIT
Adjustable to 14' below stage level by hydraulic lift
Pit lift is in (1) section

BACKSTAGE

LOADING DOCK
Loading door(s):
   10'0" high x 10'0" wide
Trucks load (2) at same time
Fork lift is not required
Sound/Props cannot load in FOH
(1) Trailer can store on-site
Security at stage door

WARDROBE
Location: Basement SL
Access: Stairs
(1) Washer (1) Dryer
Washer and dryer hookups available

DRESSING ROOMS
(2) Star, SL, stage level, t/s included
(1) Star, SR, stage level, t/s included
(2) Chorus, -1, t/s included
Elevator access for dressing rooms
Additional production office available for company mgr

SOUND

CONSOLE
Yamaha PM 3500, located Balcony
48 inputs, 8 main outputs, 8 matrix outputs

SPEAKERS
House Cluster
Proscenium

COMMUNICATIONS
Clear Com intercom with (2) channels
Infrared sound system
Dressing room page system

ROAD CONSOLE
Located Rear House
(18) seats required to be removed
Cable run from stage is 150'
Tie-in into house system with XLR connectors

REHEARSAL & STORAGE SPACE
Rehearsal: None
Storage: 30' x 30' located in basement

ELECTRICS

ROAD SERVICE POWER

Panel	Phase	Amp	Circuit Protection	Use	Location
A	3	400	fuse	dimmers	USR
B	3	200	fuse	sound	USR
C	3	800	fuse	dimmers	basement
D	2	200	breaker	motors	USR

Recommended location of touring dimmer racks: SR
Hoist is not required
Additional power is available for tour buses, generators, etc.

FRONT OF HOUSE (BOX BOOM VALUES ARE PER SIDE)

Position	Pipe Width	Distance to Prosc.	House Circuits	Connector Type	FOH Transfer Circuits
1st Cove	70'	75'	48	grd 20 amp stage pin	48

Transfer circuits: 48 transfer circuits DSR
Road truss: Grid over stage

EQUIPMENT FOH (BOX BOOM VALUES ARE PER SIDE)

Position	Quantity	Wattage	Instrument	Removeable
1st Cove	48	various	Century/Strand/ ETC	yes

FOLLOWSPOTS
House Followspots:
   (4) Super Trouper 1.6k; removeable

(3) Followspot Booths each with:
   (2) spots per booth;
   160' throw to proscenium;
   1Ø 20 amp breakers

DIMMERS
Lighting console is Strand LP90;
   (456) CD80 dimmers
House has DMX control system
(4) dry run DMX station(s), SR

STEPHENS AUDITORIUM

AT: IOWA STATE UNIVERSITY

YEAR BUILT: 1969

Theatre Location: Iowa State University, Ames, IA 50011
Mailing Address: Iowa State Center, Iowa State University
Suite 4, Scheman Bldg.
Ames, IA 50011
Management Company: Ogden Entertainment, Inc.

Main Administrative Phone:	515-294-3347
Main Administrative Fax:	515-294-3349
E-mail:	center@center.iastate.edu
Website:	www.center.iastate.edu
Stage Door Phone:	515-294-8123
Backstage Pay Phone:	515-294-8071
Traveling Production Office Phone:	515-294-5140
Traveling Production Office Fax:	515-294-6566

THEATRE STAFF

Executive Director	Mark North	515-294-3347
Director of Performing Arts	Paul Ferrone	515-294-3347

HOUSE CREW

Technical Director	Steve Harder	515-294-8123

SEATING CAPACITY

Main Floor	1,584
First Balcony w/Loge	467
Second Balcony w/Loge	354
Third Balcony	204
Total:	**2,609**
pit (add'l)	112
wheelchair (add'l)	26

STAGE DIMENSIONS (FROM SMOKE POCKET)

Stage is 50' deep
Width from Center Line to SL is DS 55' US 28'
Width from Center Line to SR is DS 55' US 28'
Proscenium width is 70'
Proscenium height is 30'
Smoke pocket to apron edge is 9'0"
Orchestra pit exists

RIGGING

Grid Height:	69'
Type:	Single purchase counter weight
Weight:	12,000 lbs
Line sets:	55 sets at 6" o.c.
Arbors:	1,200 lb capacity
House Pipes:	60' long

LOADING DOCK

Loading door(s) are 20'0" high x 12'0" wide
Trucks load (2) at same time
Fork lift is not required and is not available

ELECTRICS

(1) 600A 3Ø DSR in basement
(1) 400A 3Ø DSR in basement'
(1) 125A 3Ø SL sidewall
(1) 60A 3Ø US in basement

FOLLOWSPOTS

House Followspots:
Strong Xenon Super Trouper 2k
Power in spot booth 100A 1Ø

DIMMERS

No house dimmers
House has DMX control system
(1) dry run station(s) located DSR

SOUND

House has 125A 3Ø dedicated power located SL sidewall
FOH mixing position in House Center
Sound console is available

ADLER THEATRE

AT: RiverCenter

Year built: 1930   Year renovated: 1986

Theatre Location: 136 East Third Street, Davenport, IA 52801
Management Company: Compass Facility Management
                    600 5th Street, Suite 301
                    PO Box 625
                    Ames, IA 50010

Main Administrative Phone: 319-326-8500
Main Administrative Fax: 319-326-8505

THEATRE STAFF
General Manager   Robert Johnson   319-326-8500
Booking   John Kothenbeutel   319-326-8500
Marketing   John Kothenbeutel   319-326-8500
Operations   Rick Palmer   319-326-8500
Group Sales   Shari Baker   319-326-8500

UNIONS
IATSE Local #85   Chris Tilton

SEATING CAPACITY
Orchestra   1,232
Balcony   1,120
Total: **2,352**

pit (add'l)   90
wheelchair (add'l)   11

BOX OFFICE
Computerized
Box Office Manager
  Nancy Powers   319-326-8552

Outside Ticket Agency
  Ticketmaster   800-869-1414

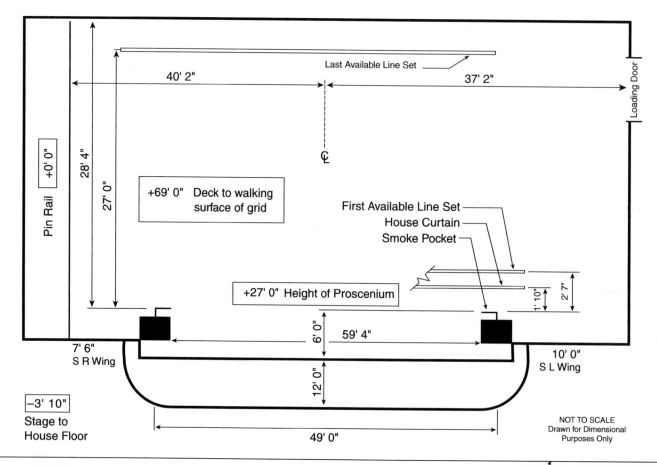

40' 2"   Last Available Line Set   37' 2"

Loading Door

Pin Rail +0' 0"

28' 4"

27' 0"

+69' 0" Deck to walking surface of grid

CL

First Available Line Set
House Curtain
Smoke Pocket

1' 10"   2' 7"

+27' 0" Height of Proscenium

6' 0"   59' 4"

7' 6"
S R Wing

10' 0"
S L Wing

12' 0"

−3' 10"
Stage to
House Floor

49' 0"

NOT TO SCALE
Drawn for Dimensional
Purposes Only

STAGE HOUSE

HOUSE CURTAIN
Operates as a traveller from SR deck

RIGGING SYSTEM
Type:	Single purchase counter weight
Weight:	6,500 lbs available
Line sets:	21 sets at 6"-10" o.c. with 5 lift lines per set
Arbors:	550 lb capacity
House Pipes:	70' long with 65' of travel from deck

Line sets are moveable
Block & Falls are available
Chain hoists available as a rental; (2) one ton, (1) half ton
(10) spot wheels and 140' of hemp available

PERMANENT INSTALLATIONS OVER STAGE (FROM SMOKE POCKET)
Electric bridges (3) at 3'5", 11'6", 21'7"
Orchestra shell (3) at 5'9", 14'0", 23'4"
Traveller (2) at 8'3", 25'3"
Movie screen (1) at 9'2"

PERMANENT INSTALLATIONS ON DECK
None

ORCHESTRA PIT
Adjustable to 12' below stage level by electric motor turnscrew
Apron overhangs US wall of pit 6'0"
Pit lift is in (2) sections

BACKSTAGE

LOADING DOCK
Loading door(s):
  8'10" high x 8'0" wide
Trucks load (1) at a time
Loading door sill is at street level 5'0" above stage level and is equipped with 8' high x 8' wide x 16' long freight elevator; loading doors accessed via an alley

WARDROBE
Location: Basement
Access: Elevator
(1) Washer (1) Dryer

DRESSING ROOMS
(2) Star, SR/SL, stage level, t/s included
(2) Small, SL, 2nd fl, t/s included
(3) Chorus, SL, 2nd fl, t/s included

SOUND

CONSOLE
Tascam
24 inputs, 8 main outputs

SPEAKERS
House Cluster
Under Balcony

COMMUNICATIONS
Clear Com intercom with (2) channels
No hearing impaired system
Dressing room page system

ROAD CONSOLE
Located Rear House
(12) seats required to be removed
Cable run from stage is 90'
Tie-in into house system with XLR connectors

REHEARSAL & STORAGE SPACE
Rehearsal: None
Storage: 50' x 20' located in basement

ELECTRICS

ROAD SERVICE POWER

Panel	Phase	Amp	Circuit Protection	Use	Location
A	3	400	fuse	dimmers	DSL side wall
B	3	200	fuse	sound	DSL side wall

Recommended location of touring dimmer racks: SL on deck
Additional power is available for tour buses, generators, etc.

FRONT OF HOUSE (BOX BOOM VALUES ARE PER SIDE)

Position	Pipe Width	Distance to Prosc.	House Circuits	Connector Type	FOH Transfer Circuits
1st Balc Rail	80'	55'	18	grd 20 amp stage pin	18
1st Cove	100'	60'	18	grd 20 amp stage pin	18
2nd Cove	100'	75'	24	grd 20 amp stage pin	24
Box Boom 1		40'	12	grd 20 amp stage pin	12
Torm		20'	6	grd 20 amp stage pin	6

Transfer circuits: grd 20 amp stage pin located on SL side wall

EQUIPMENT FOH (BOX BOOM VALUES ARE PER SIDE)

Position	Quantity	Wattage	Instrument	Removeable
2nd Cove	24	1,000	6 x 12 Lekos	yes

FOLLOWSPOTS
House Followspots:
(2) Ultra Arc IIs; removeable

Followspot Booth:
(10) spots per booth;
130 throw to proscenium;
(12) 1Ø 20 amp breakers

DIMMERS
No lighting console
No dimmers
No DMX control system

CIVIC CENTER OF GREATER DES MOINES

YEAR BUILT: 1979   YEAR RENOVATED: 1993

Theatre Location: 221 Walnut Street, Des Moines, IA 50309-2104

Main Administrative Phone: 515-243-0766
Main Administrative Fax: 515-243-1179
Website: www.civiccenter.org
Stage Door Phone: 515-243-0766

THEATRE STAFF
General Manager   Jeff Chelesvig   515-243-0766
Marketing   Terri McIlhon   515-243-0766
Operations   Ken Schumacher   515-243-0766
Group Sales   Cami Ahlers   515-243-0766

HOUSE CREW
Technical Director   Greg Anderson   515-243-0766
Electrics   Al Dyer   515-243-0766
Sound   Don Adcock   515-243-0766

UNIONS
IATSE Local #67   Mike Vivone   515-249-3450
Music   Harold Jansen   515-226-2811

SEATING CAPACITY
Orchestra   2,653
Total: **2,653**

pit (add'l)   82
standing (add'l)   20

BOX OFFICE
Computerized
Box Office Manager
Marvin Mason Jr.   515-243-0766

Outside Ticket Agency
Computerized
Tickemaster
Jim Toncar   515-243-5505

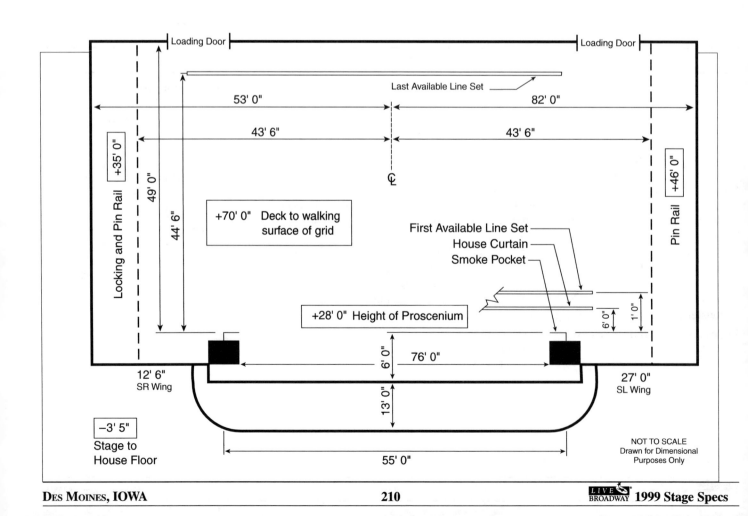

- Loading Door
- Loading Door
- Last Available Line Set
- 53' 0"
- 82' 0"
- 43' 6"
- 43' 6"
- Locking and Pin Rail +35' 0"
- 49' 0"
- 44' 6"
- +70' 0" Deck to walking surface of grid
- First Available Line Set
- House Curtain
- Smoke Pocket
- Pin Rail +46' 0"
- +28' 0" Height of Proscenium
- 6' 0"
- 1' 0"
- 6' 0"
- 76' 0"
- 12' 6" SR Wing
- 27' 0" SL Wing
- 13' 0"
- −3' 5" Stage to House Floor
- 55' 0"
- NOT TO SCALE
  Drawn for Dimensional Purposes Only

STAGE HOUSE

HOUSE CURTAIN
Operates as a guillotine from SR deck

RIGGING SYSTEM
Type: Single purchase counter weight; Hemp System
Weight: 30,000 lbs available
Line sets: 59 sets at 6-12" o.c. with 6 lift lines per set
Arbors: 1,000 lb capacity
House Pipes: 66' long with 68' of travel from deck
Line sets are moveable
Block & Falls are available
Chain hoists available as a rental
(50) spot wheels and 5,000' of hemp available

PERMANENT INSTALLATIONS OVER STAGE (FROM SMOKE POCKET)
M=Moveable with advance call
Orchestra shells (2) at 7'0", 20'6"; M
Movie screen (1) at 46'0"; M
Dead spaces (2) at 40'0" [18"w], 47'6" [18"w]; M

PERMANENT INSTALLATIONS ON DECK
None

ORCHESTRA PIT
Adjustable to 9' below stage level by electric motor turnscrew
Apron overhangs US wall of pit 12'0"
Pit lift is in (2) sections

BACKSTAGE

LOADING DOCK
Loading door(s) are in a separate receiving area:
1) 8'6" high x 5'9" wide
2) 9'6" high x 7'11" wide
Both doors at truck level; Door 2 has electric leveler;
Trucks load (2) side by side at same time
From receiving area to stage add'l (2) rollup doors, huge
Fork lift is not required
Sound/Props cannot load FOH
Lobby cannot be a work area
(1) Trailer can store on-site if tractor removed
Security at stage door

WARDROBE
Location: Basement
Access: Freight elevator
(2) Washers (2) Dryers
Washer /dryer hookup available

DRESSING ROOMS
(2) Star, SR, stage, t/s included, phn jack
(4) Small, SL/SR, -1, t/s, phn jack
(2) Chorus, CS, -1, t/s, phn jack
(2) Orchestra, -1, t/s, phn jack
Elevator access for dressing rms
Use dressing room for company mgr office

SOUND

CONSOLE
Yamaha PM 4,000-40-8-2, located Rear House
40 inputs, 2 main outputs, 8 matrix outputs, 2aux outputs

SPEAKERS
Proscenium
Portable
No speaker truss but 8 rigging points available
Max available load 2,000 lbs

COMMUNICATIONS
Clear Com intercom with (2) channels
Infrared sound system
Dressing room page system

ROAD CONSOLE
Located Center Orchestra
No seats required to be removed
Cable run from stage is 200'
Tie-in into house system with XLR connectors

REHEARSAL & STORAGE SPACE
Rehearsal: None
Storage: None

ELECTRICS

ROAD SERVICE POWER

Panel	Phase	Amp	Circuit Protection	Use	Location
A	3	400	breaker	dimmers	DSR on jump
B	3	400	breaker	dimmers	DSR on jump
C	3	200	breaker	sound	USL back wall

Recommended location of touring dimmer racks: SR on deck
Hoist is not required
Additional power is available for tour buses, generators, etc.

FRONT OF HOUSE (BOX BOOM VALUES ARE PER SIDE)

Position	Pipe Width	Distance to Prosc.	House Circuits	Connector Type	FOH Transfer Circuits
1st Cove	76'	70'	36	grd 20 amp stage pin	36
2nd Cove	80'	94'	42	grd 20 amp stage pin	42
Box Boom 1		60'	9	grd 20 amp stage pin	9

Transfer circuits: grd 20 amp stage pin; Addressable or DMX control

EQUIPMENT FOH (BOX BOOM VALUES ARE PER SIDE)

Position	Quantity	Wattage	Instrument	Removeable
1st Cove	12	1,000	Altman 12° Lekos	yes
1st Cove	24	600	Source 4 19°	yes
2nd Cove	36	600	Source 4 10°	yes
Box Boom 2	9	600	Source 4 19°	yes

Box Boom 1 generally not usable due to proximity to stage side masking

FOLLOWSPOTS
House Followspots:
(4) Strong Super Troupers Xenon 2k; removeable

Followspot Booth:
(4) spots per booth;
159' throw to proscenium;
(4) 50 amp breakers

DIMMERS
Lighting console is Century Strand M;
(575) Century Strand CD80 dimmers
House has programmable DMX control system
(1) dry run DMX station(s), DSR

HANCHER AUDITORIUM

AT: UNIVERSITY OF IOWA

YEAR BUILT: 1972   YEAR RENOVATED: 1994

Theatre Location: 231 Hancher Auditorium
                      University of Iowa, Iowa City, IA 52242-1794

Main Administrative Phone:	319-335-1130
Main Administrative Fax:	319-335-1180
E-mail:	brian-anstedt@uiowa.edu
Website:	www.uiowa.edu/~hancher
Stage Door Phone:	319-335-1150
Backstage Pay Phone:	319-335-0196
Traveling Production Office Phone:	319-335-1155

THEATRE STAFF

Director	Wallace Chapell	319-335-1130
Booking	Wallace Chapell	319-335-1130
Marketing	Judith Hurtig	319-335-1130
Associate Director	Charles Swanson	319-335-1130
House Manager	Connie Tipsword	319-335-1130

HOUSE CREW

Technical Director	Brian Anstedt	319-335-1130
Stage Manager	Stephanie Miller-Lamb	319-335-1130
Electrics	Brian Anstedt	319-335-1130
Sound	Gary Sanborn	319-335-1130

UNIONS

IATSE Local #690	Meg Sump	319-339-0432

SEATING CAPACITY

Orchestra	1,114
Balcony	1,419
Total:	**2,533**
pit (incl)	103
wheelchair (add'l)	34

BOX OFFICE
Computerized
Box Manager
  Richard Gross   319-335-1160

Outside Ticket Agency
None

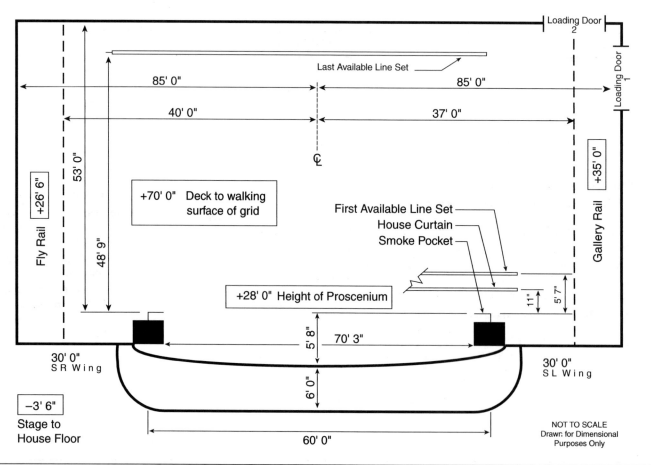

STAGE HOUSE

HOUSE CURTAIN
Operates as a guillotine from SR deck; motorized

RIGGING SYSTEM

Type:	Double purchase counter weight
Weight:	20,000 lbs available
Line sets:	48 sets at 7" o.c. with 6 lift lines per set
Arbors:	1,000 lb capacity
House Pipes:	70' long with 60' of travel from deck

Line sets are moveable
Block & Falls are available
(15) spot wheels and 3,000' of hemp available

PERMANENT INSTALLATIONS OVER STAGE (FROM SMOKE POCKET)
M=Moveable with advance call
Orchestra shells (3) at 9'5", 24'6", 39'9"
Traveller (1) at 48'9"; M
Electric bridge (4) at 4'6", 16'6", 26'2", 36'3"
Hard portal (2) at 2'4", 2'11"
Cyclorama (1) at 47'4"; M
Fire curtain (1)

PERMANENT INSTALLATIONS ON DECK
Orchestra shell (9) each 15' x 15', located off SR - US 30'
Electric bridge (4) at 20", located at 4'6", 16'6", 26' 2", 36'3"
Loading bridge (1) 4' x 53', located SR
Adjustable portal (2), located at 2'4", 2'11"

ORCHESTRA PIT
Adjustable to 12' below stage level by hydraulic lift
Apron overhangs US wall of pit 7'0"
Pit lift is in (2) sections

BACKSTAGE

LOADING DOCK
Loading door(s):
    (1) 7'10" high x 11'6" wide
    (2) 9'0" high x 8'0" wide
Trucks load (1) at a time
Fork lift is not required
(1) Trailer can store on-site
Sound/Props cannot load in FOH
Security at dock & stage door

WARDROBE
Location: Backstage Hall
Access: Stage Door
(2) Washers (2) Dryers
Washer and dryer hookups available

DRESSING ROOMS
(6) Star, USR, stage level, t/s included, phone jack
(2) Chorus, USR, stage level, t/s included, phone jack
Additional production office available for company mgr

SOUND

CONSOLE
Ramsa WR-S 852, located Rear House
52 inputs, 8 main outputs
Monitor Console, Allen-Heath SR-M 248

SPEAKERS
House Cluster
Proscenium
Under Balcony
Portable

COMMUNICATIONS
Clear Com intercom with (4) channels
Infrared sound system
Dressing room page system
No speaker truss

ROAD CONSOLE
Located Rear House
No seats required to be removed
Cable run from stage is 100'
Tie-in into house system with XLR connectors

REHEARSAL & STORAGE SPACE
Rehearsal: None
Storage: 30' located SL wing, upright piano;
30' located SR wing

ELECTRICS

ROAD SERVICE POWER

Panel	Phase	Amp	Circuit Protection Use	Location
A	3	800	dimmers	DSR
B	3	70	sound	DSL
C	1	200	projection	Projection Booth

Recommended location of touring dimmer racks: SR

FRONT OF HOUSE (BOX BOOM VALUES ARE PER SIDE)

Position	Pipe Width	Distance to Prosc.	House Circuits	Connector Type	FOH Transfer Circuits
1st Balc Rail	95'	60'	16	grd 20 amp stage pin	16
1st Cove	50'	70'	20	grd 20 amp stage pin	20
2nd Cove	50'	90'	20	grd 20 amp stage pin	20
Box Boom 1		10'	6	grd 20 amp stage pin	6
Box Boom 2		20'	9	grd 20 amp stage pin	9
Box Boom 3		30'	12	grd 20 amp stage pin	12

Transfer circuits: grd 20 amp stage pin

EQUIPMENT FOH (BOX BOOM VALUES ARE PER SIDE)

Position	Quantity	Wattage	Instrument	Removeable
1st Balc Rail	20	575	Source 4 36°	yes
1st Cove	3	575	Source 4 10°	
2nd Cove	20	575	Source 4 5°	
Box Boom 1	6	1,000	6 x 16 Lekos	yes
Box Boom 2	9	1,000	6 x 22 Lekos	yes
Box Boom 3	12	1,000	6 x 22 Lekos	yes

FOLLOWSPOTS
House Followspots:
    (3) Xenon Super Troupers; not removeable

(3) Followspot Booths each with:
(1) spots per booth;
90' throw to proscenium;
(1) 1Ø 20 amp breakers

DIMMERS
Lighting console is ETC Expression 2x;
(460) ETC Sensor dimmers
House has programmable DMX control system
(2) dry run DMX station(s)

SIOUX CITY MUNICIPAL AUDITORIUM

YEAR BUILT: 1950   YEAR RENOVATED: 1991

Theatre Location:	401 Gordon Ave, Sioux City, IA 51101	
Mailing Address:	PO Box 3183, Sioux City, IA 51102	

Main Administrative Phone:	712-279-4800
Main Administrative Fax:	712-279-4900
E-mail:	ccat@pionet.net
Website:	www.siouxlan.com/ccat
Stage Door Phone:	712-279-4910
Traveling Production Office Phone:	712-279-4913
Traveling Production Office Fax:	712-279-4901

SEATING CAPACITY

Mezzanine	1,811
First Balcony	816
Floor	1,470
Raised Section	548
Total:	**4,645**
standing (add'l)	1,355

THEATRE STAFF

Executive Director	Dennis Gann	712-279-4800
Bookings Manager	Cheryl Swanson	712-279-4814

HOUSE CREW

Facility Manager	Walt Johnson	712-279-4905
Superintendent	Tim Wells	712-279-4810

STAGE DIMENSIONS (FROM SMOKE POCKET)
Stage is 37'4" deep
Width from Center Line to SL is 48'5"
Width from Center Line to SR is 48'3"
Proscenium width is 79'6"
Proscenium height is 35'0"
Orchestra pit exists

RIGGING

Grid Height:	65'
Type:	Double purchase counter weight
Weight:	12,000 lbs
Line sets:	41 sets at 10" o.c.
Arbors:	2,000 lb capacity
House Pipes:	84' long

LOADING DOCK
Loading door(s) are 8'9" high x 8'1" wide
Trucks load (2) at same time
Fork lift is required and is available

ELECTRICS
(1) 400A USL
(1) 400A USR
(1) 200A USC

FOLLOWSPOTS
House Followspots:
   Lycian Arc 2k
Power in spot booth 220 volt

DIMMERS
No house dimmers
No DMX control system

SOUND
House has 400A dedicated
   power located Rear House
FOH mixing position in
   Rear Orchestra
Sound console is available

LIED CENTER

AT: UNIVERSITY OF KANSAS   **YEAR BUILT: 1993**

Theatre Location: KU West Campus, Lawrence, KS 66045

Main Administrative Phone: 785-864-3469
Main Administrative Fax: 785-864-5031
E-mail: opman@falcon.cc.ukans.edu
Website: www.ukans.edu/ulied
Stage Door Phone: 785-864-2796
Traveling Production Office Phone: 785-864-2791
Traveling Production Office Fax: 785-864-5020

THEATRE STAFF
Director   Jacqueline Z. Davis   785-864-3469
Booking   Jacqueline Z. Davis   785-864-3469
Marketing   Karen Christilles   785-864-2794
Operations   Fred Pawlicki   785-864-3469

HOUSE CREW
Technical Director   Lee A. Saylor   785-864-2796

UNIONS
IATSE Local #498   Bill Reed   913-384-1368
Wardrobe Local #810

SEATING CAPACITY
Orchestra   1,102
First Balcony   508
Second Balcony   334
Total: **1,944**

pit (add'l)   74

BOX OFFICE
Computerized
Box Office Manager
  Michelle Traband   785-864-2781

Outside Ticket Agency
Computerized
Ticketmaster
  Louis Tabone   816-753-6286

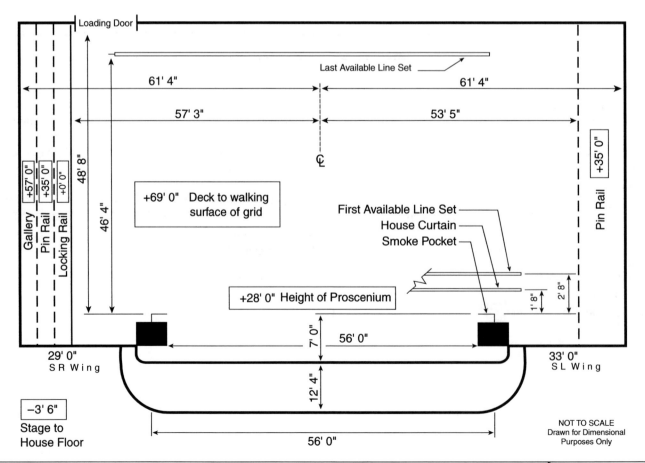

STAGE HOUSE

HOUSE CURTAIN
Operates as a guillotine or traveller from SR deck

RIGGING SYSTEM
Type: Single purchase counter weight
Weight: 46,000 lbs available
Line sets: 43 sets at 8" o.c. with 8 lift lines per set
Arbors: 1,200 lb capacity
House Pipes: 80' long with 69' of travel from deck
Line sets are not moveable
Block & Falls are not available
Chain hoists are not available
(14) spot wheels and 1,400' of hemp available
No points DS of procenium

PERMANENT INSTALLATIONS OVER STAGE (FROM SMOKE POCKET)
M=Moveable with advance call
Orchestra shell (3) at 4'0", 13'4", 23'4"
Movie screen (1) at 8'0"; M
Traveler (3) at 1'4", 18'8", 42'8"; M

PERMANENT INSTALLATIONS ON DECK
Orchestra shell (7) stored USL 9'0" wide x 21'0" deep

ORCHESTRA PIT
Adjustable to 8' below stage level by Gala lift
Apron overhangs US wall of pit 7'0"
Pit lift is in (1) section

BACKSTAGE

LOADING DOCK
Loading door(s):
 10'0" high x 8'0" wide
Trucks load (2) at same time
Fork lift is not required
Sound/Props cannot load in
 FOH
(8) Trailers can store on-site
Security at stage door

WARDROBE
Location: off dock
(2) Washers (2) Dryers
Washer and dryer hookups
 available

DRESSING ROOMS
(4) Small, behind stage, stage
 level, t/s included
(3) Chorus, behind stage, stage
 level, t/s included
Elevator access for dressing
 rooms
Additional production office
 available for company mgr

SOUND

CONSOLE
Soundcraft Vienna, located
 Booth or Cross aisle
32 inputs, 3 main outputs,
 8 matrix outputs, 8 aux
 outputs

SPEAKERS
House Cluster
Proscenium
Under Balcony
Portable
Surround
No speaker truss

COMMUNICATIONS
Clear Com intercom with
 (8) channels
Infrared sound system
Dressing room page system

ROAD CONSOLE
Located Center Orchestra
(18) seats required to be
 removed
Cable run from stage is 125'
Tie-in into house system with
 XLR connectors

REHEARSAL & STORAGE SPACE
Rehearsal: Dance studio
 25' x 43', behind stage,
 piano, mirrors & barre
Storage: Shop 700 sq ft,
 off dock

ELECTRICS

ROAD SERVICE POWER

Panel	Phase	Amp	Circuit Protection	Use	Location
A-C	3	400	fuse	dimmers	SL
D	3	200	fuse	sound	DSL
E	3	200	fuse	sound	DSR
F	3	200	fuse	extra	dock
G	3	60	fuse	extra	dock

Location of touring dimmer racks: SL; Hoist not required; Additional power is available

FRONT OF HOUSE (BOX BOOM VALUES ARE PER SIDE)

Position	Pipe Width	Distance to Prosc.	House Circuits	Connector Type	FOH Transfer Circuits
1st Cove	60'	45'	34	grd 20 amp stage pin	30
2nd Cove	60'	66'	29	grd 20 amp stage pin	28
Box Boom 1		6'	20	grd 20 amp stage pin	0
Box Boom 2		13'	24	grd 20 amp stage pin	0
Box Boom 3		22'	20	grd 20 amp stage pin	20
Box Boom 4		46'	20	grd 20 amp stage pin	8

Transfer circuits: grd 20 amp stage pin
Road truss: no truss hanging points available DS of prosceniuim

EQUIPMENT FOH (BOX BOOM VALUES ARE PER SIDE)

Position	Quantity	Wattage	Instrument	Removeable
1st Cove	28	1,000	20 Colortran	yes
2nd Cove	17	1,000	14-5 , 14-10 Colortran	yes
Box Boom 3	12	1,000	20 Colortran	yes

FOLLOWSPOTS
House Followspots:
 (2) Strong Super Trouper
 2,000; removeable

(3) Followspot Booths:
 (1) spot in booth;
 85' throw to proscenium;
 (1) 1Ø 60 amp breakers

 (4) spots in booth;
 85' throw to proscenium;
 (2) 1Ø 60 amp breakers

 (1) spot in booth;
 85' throw to proscenium;
 (1) 1Ø 60 amp breakers

DIMMERS
Lighting console is Colortran
 Prestige 3000 Plus;
 (400) Colortran ENR
 dimmers
House has programmable
 DMX control system
(2) dry run DMX station(s)

MCCAIN AUDITORIUM

Theatre Location:	Kansas City University, Manhattan, KS 66506-4711	
Mailing Address:	207 McCain Auditorium-Kansas City University	
	Manhattan, KS 66506-4711	

Main Administrative Phone:	785-532-6425
Main Administrative Fax:	785-532-5870
E-mail:	mccain@ksu.edu
Website:	ksu.edu/mccain/
Stage Door Phone:	785-532-2361
Traveling Production Office Phone:	785-532-7029
Traveling Production Office Fax:	785-532-7030

SEATING CAPACITY

Orchestra	921
Lower Balcony	409
Upper Balcony	422
Total:	**1,752**
pit (add'l)	45
wheelchair (add'l)	8
standing (add'l)	0

THEATRE STAFF

Director	Richard P. Martin	785-532-6425
Asst Director	David L. Frain	785-532-6425

HOUSE CREW

Public Programming	Terri L. Lee	785-532-6427

STAGE DIMENSIONS (FROM SMOKE POCKET)
Stage is 34'6" deep
Width from Center Line to SL is 65'0"
Width from Center Line to SR is 65'0"
Proscenium width is 60'0"
Proscenium height is 22'0"
Smoke pocket to apron edge is 5'6"
Orchestra pit exists

RIGGING

Grid Height:	66'
Type:	Double purchase counter weight
Weight:	11,965 lbs
Line sets:	36 sets at 9" o.c.
Arbors:	2,100 lb capacity
House Pipes:	60' long

LOADING DOCK
Loading door(s) are 10'0" high x 8'0" wide
Trucks load (3) at same time
Fork lift is not required and is available

ELECTRICS
Total power available:
(3) 400A 3Ø USL

FOLLOWSPOTS
House Followspots:
(2) Xenon Super Trouper
Power in spot booth 20A

DIMMERS
(338) house dimmers
House has DMX control system
(1) dry run station located USL

SOUND
House has 400A undedicated
power located USL
FOH mixing position in
Rear Orchestra
Sound console is available

TOPEKA PERFORMING ARTS CENTER

AKA: TPAC   **YEAR BUILT: 1939   YEAR RENOVATED: 1991**

Theatre Location: 214 South East, Topeka, KS 66603

Main Administrative Phone:	785-234-2787
Main Administrative Fax:	785-234-2307
Website:	www.tpactix.org
Traveling Production Office Phone:	785-234-1510
Traveling Production Office Fax:	785-234-2925

THEATRE STAFF
Executive Director   Harold Hansen   785-234-2787

HOUSE CREW
                       Blair Adams   785-234-2787

SEATING CAPACITY

Floor	1,366
Balcony	1,256
Total:	**2,622**
pit (add'l)	38
wheelchair (add'l)	26

STAGE DIMENSIONS (FROM SMOKE POCKET)
Stage is 32'0" deep
Width from Center Line to SL is 42'6"
Width from Center Line to SR is 42'6"
Proscenium width is 49'10"
Proscenium height is 25'0"
Smoke pocket to apron edge is 1'8"
Orchestra pit exists

RIGGING

Grid Height:	47'
Type:	Single purchase counter weight
Weight:	2,500 lbs
Line sets:	41 sets at 6" o.c.
Arbors:	1,000 lb capacity
House Pipes:	50' long

LOADING DOCK
Loading door(s) are 10'0" high x 8'0" wide
Trucks load (1) at a time
Fork lift is not required and is available

ELECTRICS
Total power available:
(1) 600A 3Ø USR
(1) 200A 3Ø USR

FOLLOWSPOTS
House Followspots:
(2) Super Troupers
(2) Lycian
Power in spot booth (1) 20A

DIMMERS
(278) house dimmers
House has DMX control system

SOUND
House has 200A dedicated
  power located USR
FOH mixing position in
  Rear House
Sound console is available

THE OPERA HOUSE IN LEXINGTON

AKA: LEXINGTON OPERA HOUSE AT: LEXINGTON CENTER   **YEAR BUILT: 1886 YEAR RENOVATED: 1976**

Theatre Location: 401 West Short Street, Lexington, KY 40507
Mailing Address: 430 West Vine Street, Lexington, KY 40507
Management Company: Lexington Center Corp
     430 West Vine Street, Lexington, KY 40507

Main Administrative Phone: 606-233-4567 x3286
Main Administrative Fax: 606-253-2718
Stage Door Phone: 606-233-4567 x3760
Traveling Production Office Phone: 606-233-4843

THEATRE STAFF
Director for Performing Arts   Richard F. Pardy   606-233-4567 x3285
Booking   Richard F. Pardy   606-233-4567 x3285
Operations   Amy Salmons   606-233-4567 x3286

HOUSE CREW
Technical Coordinator   Craig King   606-233-4567 x3151

UNIONS
IATSE Local #346   Don Burton   606-233-4567 x3245
Music AFM   Dick Baker   606-223-4292

SEATING CAPACITY
Orchestra   445
Mezzanine   303
Balcony   206
Boxes   24
Total: **978**

pit (add'l)   62
wheelchair (incl.)   4

BOX OFFICE
Computerized
Box Office Manager
   Jeff Bojanowski 606-233-456 x3730

Outside Ticket Agency
Charge-A-Tick   606-233-3535

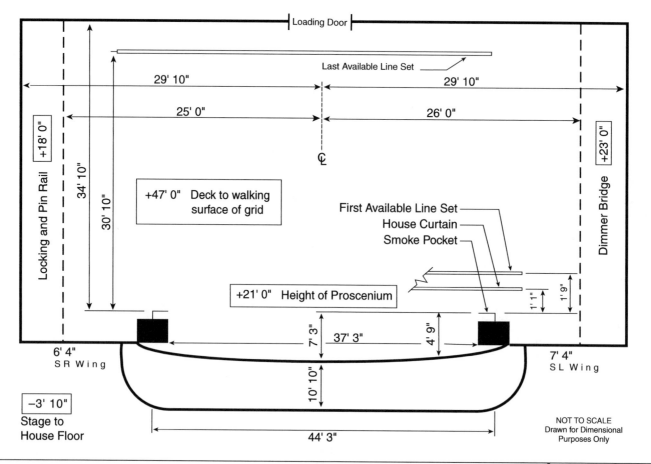

STAGE HOUSE

HOUSE CURTAIN
Operates as a guillotine from SR fly floor
Operates as a traveler from SR deck

RIGGING SYSTEM
Type:	Double purchase counter weight
Weight:	22,000 lbs. available
Line sets:	40 sets at 8" o.c. with 6 lift lines per set
Arbors:	900 and 1,400 lb. capacity
House Pipes:	47'6" long with 43' of travel from deck

Line sets are moveable
Block & Falls are available
Chain hoists are not available
(12) spot wheels and 500' of hemp available
Grid is stamped metal floor - Rigging points at cable wells only

PERMANENT INSTALLATIONS OVER STAGE (FROM SMOKE POCKET)
Electric Raceways (1) at 3'3"
Dead Spaces (2) at 15'0", 27'0"
Cyclorama (1) at 27'0"
Fire curtain (1) at smoke pocket

PERMANENT INSTALLATIONS ON DECK
Traps (2) in stage floor 4' x 4' located DSC
Column (1) at 5' x 5' at far UL corner of stage

ORCHESTRA PIT
Adjustable to 8'6" below stage level by hydraulic lift
Apron overhangs US wall of pit 0'0"
Pit lift is in (1) section

BACKSTAGE

LOADING DOCK
Loading door(s):
    14'7" high x 10'9" wide
Trucks load (1) at a time
Dock is below truck level;
    Ramp down from truck and
    90° turn into building
(2) Roll up doors, on stage,
    DSL/ DSR allow large set
    pieces to move off stage
Fork lift is not required
Sound/Props cannot load in
    FOH
    Trailers cannot store on-site

WARDROBE
Location: Basement or off SR
Access: Freight elevator to
    basement off SR
(1) Washer (1) Dryer
Washer and dryer hookups
    available

DRESSING ROOMS
(2) Star, -1, t/s included, phone
    jack
(2) Chorus, -1, t/s included,
    phone jack
Elevator access for dressing
    rooms
Additional production office
    available for company mgr

SOUND

CONSOLE
Yamaha PM 3500 & Yamaha
    Pro Mix; located Rear HL
48 inputs, 2 main outputs,
    8 matrix outputs,
    8 aux outputs

SPEAKERS
House Cluster
Proscenium
Under Balcony
Portable
No speaker truss

COMMUNICATIONS
Clear-com intercom with
    (1) channel
FM sound system,
    not infrared
Dressing room page system

ROAD CONSOLE
Located Rear Orchestra left
    No seats required to be
    removed
Cable run from stage is 150'
Tie in into house system
    with XLR connectors

REHEARSAL & STORAGE SPACE
Rehearsal: 20' x 38' located
    on 2nd floor with mirror,
    barre, piano available; 25'
    x 45' on 3rd floor, piano
    available
Storage: 30' x 50' off SR

ELECTRICS

ROAD SERVICE POWER

Panel	Phase	Amp	Circuit Protection	Use	Location
A	3	600	fuse	dimmers	SL side wall of stage
B	3	400	fuse	dimmers	SL in room adj. to stage
C	3	100	breaker	sound	DSR side wall of stage
D	3	60	breaker	extra	DSR side wall of stage
E	3	60	breaker	extra	USR wall of stage

Recommended location of touring dimmer racks: Off SL
Hoist is not required
Additional power is available for tour buses, generators, etc.

FRONT OF HOUSE (BOX BOOM VALUES ARE PER SIDE)

Position	Pipe Width	Distance to Prosc.	House Circuits	Connector Type	FOH Transfer Circuits
1st Balc Rail	63'	56'	35	20 amp new twistlock	35
1st Cove	47'	61'	36	20 amp new twistlock	36

Transfer circuits: ungrd 20 amp stage pin plug located SL on jump

EQUIPMENT FOH (BOX BOOM VALUES ARE PER SIDE

Position	Quantity	Wattage	Instrument	Removeable
Balc Rail	25	750	6 x 16 Lekos	yes
1st Cove	16	1,000	8 x13 Lekos	no
1st Cove	6	750	6 x 22 Lekos	no

Box boom positions are non-existent; Box Boom lights can hang at end of Balcony Rail

FOLLOWSPOTS
House Followspots:
    (2) Strong Xenon Troupers;
    removeable

Followspot Booth:
    (1) spot per booth;
    70' throw to proscenium;
    (2) 3Ø 30 amp breakers

DIMMERS
Lighting console is ETC
    Obsession 600; (288) ETC
    Sensor AF dimmers
House has programmable
    DMX control system
(2) dry run DMX station(s)

BROWN THEATRE

FORMERLY: MACAULEY THEATRE   **AKA:W.L. LYONS BROWN THEATRE**   **YEAR BUILT: 1924**   **YEAR RENOVATED: 1998**

Theatre Location: 315 West Broadway, Louisville, KY 40202
Management Company: Kentucky Center for the Arts
                   501 West Main Street, Louisville, KY 40202

Main Administrative Phone: 502-562-0188
Main Administrative Fax: 502-581-9213
Backstage Pay Phone: 502-584-9587

THEATRE STAFF

Theatre Manager	Jonathan Sprouse	502-562-0188
Booking	Beverly Sartin	502-562-0143
Marketing	Barbara Griffee	502-562-0153
Operations	Joe Mossey	502-562-0103
Group Sales	Sandie Fulks	502-562-0108

UNIONS

IATSE #17	Rick Madison	502-587-7936

SEATING CAPACITY

Orchestra	840
Balcony	561
Total:	**1,401**
wheelchair (add'l)	10

BOX OFFICE

Computerized
Director of Ticketing Sales
   Mindy Johnson   502-562-0193

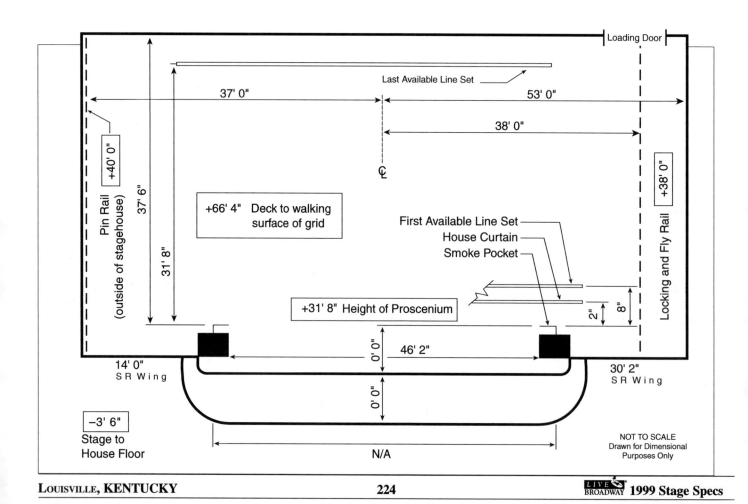

STAGE HOUSE

HOUSE CURTAIN
Operates as a guillotine from SL fly floor or deck

RIGGING SYSTEM
Type:	Single purchase counter weight
Weight:	20,000 lbs available
Line sets:	51 sets at 0" o.c. with 4 lift lines per set
Arbors:	1,200 lb capacity
House Pipes:	63' long with 57'6" of travel from deck

Line sets are not moveable
Block & Falls are available 2:1 (1)
Chain hoists available as a rental; (1) one ton
(20) spot wheels and 4,000' of hemp available
Previously a hemp house/ plenty of rigging

PERMANENT INSTALLATIONS OVER STAGE (FROM SMOKE POCKET)
M=Moveable with advance call
Orchestra shells (5) at 6'0",13'4",20'8",28'0",32'8"; M
Electric Raceways (5) at 4'0', 11'4", 18'0", 24'5", 31'4"
Fire curtain (1)

PERMANENT INSTALLATIONS ON DECK
Traps in stage floor (2), 2'0" x 4'0"; located at 15'0" CS & 21'0" SR

ORCHESTRA PIT
Adjustable to to 8 below stage level by manual lift
Apron overhangs US wall of pit 2'0"
Pit lift is in (8) sections

BACKSTAGE

LOADING DOCK
Loading door(s):
  10'0" high x 9'6" wide
Trucks load (2) back to back at same time
Fork lift is not required
Sound/Props can load in FOH
Lobby cannot be a work area
Security at dock & stage door

WARDROBE
Location: Basement under stage
Access: Stairs upstage left
(2) Washers (2) Dryers
No washer or dryer hookups

DRESSING ROOMS
(2) Star, SR, t/s, phone jack
(3) Small, SR, +1, t/s
(2) Chorus, SR, +2/+3, t/s
Use dressing room for company mgr office

SOUND

CONSOLE
Soundcraft 200B

SPEAKERS
House Cluster
Under Balcony
Portable
No speaker truss
No points DS of proscenium

COMMUNICATIONS
Clear Com intercom with (2) channels
Dressing room page system

ROAD CONSOLE
Located Center House right at back wall
No seats required to be removed
Cable run from stage is 125'
Tie-in into house system with XLR connectors

REHEARSAL & STORAGE SPACE
Rehearsal: None
Storage: None

ELECTRICS

ROAD SERVICE POWER

Panel	Phase	Amp	Circuit Protection	Use	Location
A	3	600	fuse	dimmers	USR
B	3	400	fuse	sound	USR
C	3	100	fuse	extra	USR
D	3	200	fuse	extra	PSL

Recommended location of touring dimmer racks: USR
Hoist not required

FRONT OF HOUSE (BOX BOOM VALUES ARE PER SIDE)

Position	Pipe Width	Distance to Prosc.	House Circuits	Connector Type	FOH Transfer Circuits
Balcony		42'	20	grd 20 amp stage pin	USR
1st Cove		47'	28	grd 20 amp stage pin	USR
2nd Cove		67'	12	grd 20 amp stage pin	USR
Box Boom1		53'-58'	8	grd 20 amp stage pin	USR

Transfer circuits: grd 20 amp stage pin

EQUIPMENT FOH (BOX BOOM VALUES ARE PER SIDE)

Position	Quantity	Wattage	Instrument	Removeable
1st Balc Rail	12	575	Source 4 36°	yes
1st Cove	4	575	Source 4 10°	yes
2nd Cove	12	575	Source 4 10°	yes
Box Boom 1	8	575	Source 4 19°	yes

FOLLOWSPOTS
House Followspots:
  (2) Strong Troupers; not removeable

Followspot Booth:
  (2) spots per booth;
  70'0" throw to proscenium;
  (2) 1Ø 100 amp breakers

DIMMERS
House has lighting console
House has own dimmers
House has programmable DMX control system
(0) dry run DMX station(s)

KENTUCKY CENTER FOR THE PERFORMING ARTS

AKA: WHITNEY HALL

YEAR BUILT: 1983

Theatre Location: 501 W. Main Street
5 Riverfront Plaza, Louisville, KY 40202

Main Administrative Phone: 502-562-0100
Main Administrative Fax: 502-562-0105

THEATRE STAFF

President	Michael Hardy	502-532-0146
	Beverly Sartin	502-532-0143
Marketing	Marilyn Settergren	502-562-0153
Operations	Joe Massey	502-562-0103
Group Sales	Sandie Fulks	502-562-0108

HOUSE CREW

Production Mgr	Dennis Murray	502-562-0102
Electrics	Terry Schwartz	502-562-0135

UNIONS

IATSE Local #17	J. Ricky Madison	502-587-7436
Wardrobe	Sue Stepnik	502-336-7789
Music	Sam Harris	
	Harris Entertainment	502-267-0148

SEATING CAPACITY

Orchestra	1,360
Grand Tier	475
Balcony	447
Boxes	124
Total:	**2,406**
pit (add'l)	73

BOX OFFICE

Computerized
Director, Ticketing Services
     Mindy Johnson   502-562-0193

Outside Ticket Agency
     None

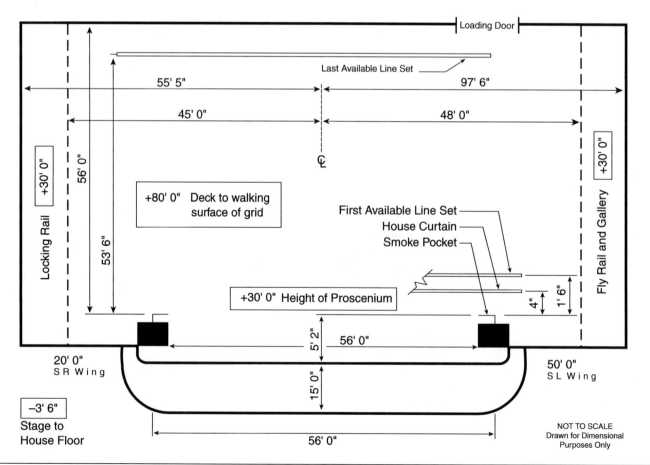

STAGE HOUSE

HOUSE CURTAIN
Operates as a guillotine from SR fly floor

RIGGING SYSTEM
Type:	Single purchase counter weight with (80) manual and (17) motorized line sets
Weight:	20,000 lbs. available
Line sets:	80 sets at 6" o.c. with 9 lift lines per set
Arbors:	2,000 lb. capacity
House Pipes:	84' long with 76' of travel from deck.

Line sets are not moveable
Block & Falls are available
Chain hoists available as rental
(30+) spot wheels and 2,000' of hemp available

PERMANENT INSTALLATIONS OVER STAGE (FROM SMOKE POCKET)
Orchestra shells (4) 10'8", 20'8", 30'3", 40'3"
Orchestra shell arms (2) fastened to proscenium wall
Electric Borders (5) at 5'6", 15'8", 25'8", 35'8", 45'8"
Electric Raceways (7) at 4'3", 14'2", 24'2", 31'2", 34'3", 44'2", 51'9"
Electric bridge (7) at 4'3", 14'2", 24'2", 31'2", 34'3", 44'2", 51'9"
Dead spaces (5) at 9'2", 19'2', 29'3", 38'9", 48'8", no pipe
Fire curtain (1) at 0'0"

PERMANENT INSTALLATIONS ON DECK
Orchestra shell storage, 17'0" x 20'0", far SL storage wing
Loading bridge (2), does not intrude into storage space

ORCHESTRA PIT
Adjustable to 20' below stage level by hydraulic lift
Apron overhangs US wall of pit 8'0"
Pit lift is in (2) sections

BACKSTAGE

LOADING DOCK
Loading door(s): 12'8" high x 15'10" wide
Trucks load (2) at same time
Truck access slopes away from dock, tough to park 2nd truck; (1) truck at a time is faster
Fork lift is not required
Sound/Props cannot load in FOH
(1) Trailer can store on-site
Security at dock & stage door

WARDROBE
Location: SR down ramp from stage
Access: Direct from dressing rooms or stage
(2) Washers (2) Dryers
Washer and dryer hookups available

DRESSING ROOMS
(4) Star, SR, stage level, t/s included
(4) Small, SR, stage level, t/s included
(3) Chorus, SR, stage level, t/s included
Elevator access for dressing rooms
Additional production office available for company mgr

SOUND

CONSOLE
Soundcraft 8000, located Booth Quad 8
10 inputs, 2 main outputs, 4x12 matrix outputs, 4 aux outputs

SPEAKERS
House Cluster
Proscenium
Under Balcony
Portable
No speaker truss

COMMUNICATIONS
Clear Com intercom with (2) channels
Infrared sound system
Dressing room page system

ROAD CONSOLE
Located Rear Orchestra
(20) seats required to be removed
Cable run from stage is 150'
Tie in into house system with XLR connectors

REHEARSAL & STORAGE SPACE
Rehearsal: LR Hall, 42' x 75', +2, mirror; SR Hall, 26' x 36', stage level; 4 hr minimum must be booked in advance
Storage: (2) Hallways each 5' x 100', stage level & -1

ELECTRICS

ROAD SERVICE POWER

Panel	Phase	Amp	Circuit Protection	Use	Location
A-B	3	600	fuse	dimmers	USR
C-D	3	600	fuse	extra	DSL
E	3	100	fuse	sound	DSL
F	3	60	fuse	sound	DSL

Recommended location of touring dimmer racks: USR
Hoist not required and not provided
Additional power is available for tour buses, generators, etc.

FRONT OF HOUSE (BOX BOOM VALUES ARE PER SIDE)

Position	Pipe Width	Distance to Prosc.	House Circuits	Connector Type	FOH Transfer Circuits
Balcony Rail	60'	80'	45	grd 20 amp stage pin	45
1st Cove	60'	30'	40	grd 20 amp stage pin	40
2nd Cove	60'	80'	51	grd 20 amp stage pin	51
Box Boom 1			10	grd 20 amp stage pin	10
Box Boom 2			10	grd 20 amp stage pin	10

Transfer circuits: grd 20 amp stage pin

EQUIPMENT FOH (BOX BOOM VALUES ARE PER SIDE)

Position	Quantity	Wattage	Instrument	Removeable
1st Balc Rail	27	1,000	12	no
1st Cove	28	1,000	10 + 12	no
2nd Cove	42	1,000	10	no
Box Boom 1	24	1,000	15 - 35 Lekos	no
Box Boom 2	24	1,000	15 - 35 Lekos	no

Please use FOH instruments whenever possible; ETC-Ethernet is available

FOLLOWSPOTS
House Followspots: (3) Colortran Colorarc 2000; removeable
Followspot Booth: (3) spots per booth; 105' throw to proscenium; (3) 1Ø 30 amp breakers

DIMMERS
Lighting console is ETC Obsession; (900) ED1 dimmers
House has programmable DMX control system
(2) dry run DMX station(s)

LOUISVILLE PALACE THEATRE

YEAR BUILT: 1928   YEAR RENOVATED: 1994

Theatre Location: 625 4th Street, Louisville, KY 40202
Management Company: Theatre Management Group
                    515 Post Oak Boulevard, Suite 310, Houston, TX 77027

Main Administrative Phone: 502-583-4555
Main Administrative Fax: 502-583-9955
Website: www.broadwayseries.com
Traveling Production Office Phone: 502-540-5096
Traveling Production Office Fax: 502-540-5098

THEATRE STAFF
General Manager   Terry Hennessey   502-583-4555
Booking   Terry Hennessey   502-583-4555
Marketing   Leslie Broecker   502-584-7469
Group Sales   Corissa Schremser   502-584-7469

HOUSE CREW
Stage Manager   Judie Coleman   502-583-4555

UNIONS
IATSE Local #17   Rick Madison   502-587-7936

SEATING CAPACITY
Orchestra   1685
Balcony   938
Total: **2,623**

pit (add'l)   96

BOX OFFICE
Box Office Manager
  Debbie Benningfield 502-583-4555

Outside Ticket Agency
Computerized
Ticket Master
  Jennifer Newkirk   502-361-0066

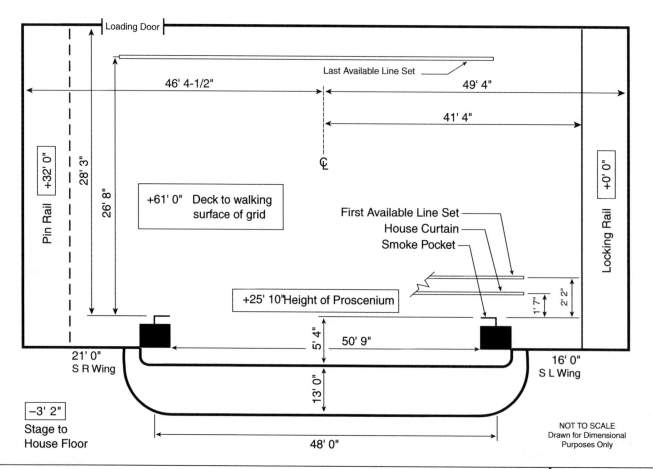

STAGE HOUSE

HOUSE CURTAIN
Operates as a guillotine or traveller from SL deck

RIGGING SYSTEM
Type:	Single purchase counter weight
Weight:	30,000 lbs available
Line sets:	41 sets at 7" o.c. with lift lines per set
Arbors:	1,200 lb capacity
House Pipes:	64' long with 56' of travel from deck

Line sets are moveable
Block & Falls are available
Chain hoists are not available
(32) spot wheels and 3,600' of hemp available

PERMANENT INSTALLATIONS OVER STAGE (FROM SMOKE POCKET)
M=Moveable with advance call
Movie screen (1) at 2'2"; M

PERMANENT INSTALLATIONS ON DECK
Trap (1) in stage floor 5' x 8", 21' US edge of smoke pocket

ORCHESTRA PIT
Adjustable to 9' below stage level by electric motor
   turnscrew
Apron overhangs US wall of pit 0'4"
Pit lift is in (1) section

BACKSTAGE

LOADING DOCK
Loading door(s):
   9'11" high x 8'5" wide
Trucks load (3) at same time
Load trucks to grade: stage floor
   30' below grade;
     House provides 14' split ramp;
   6,000 lb capacity
Forklift is not required
   Forklift supplier: Bove Finn
   502-968-5438
Sound/Props can load in FOH
Lobby can be a work area
(3) Trailers can store on-site
Security at dock & stage door

WARDROBE
Location: Lower level
Access: Trap or stairs
(2) Washers (1) Dryer
Washer and dryer hookups
   available

DRESSING ROOMS
(2) Small, -1, t/s on same fl,
   phone jack
(2) Small, -1, t/s included
(2) Small, SR, +2, t on same fl
(1) Small, SR, stage level, t/s
   included, phone jack
(1) Small, -1, t/s on same fl
(2) Chorus, -1, t/s on same fl,
   phone jack
Use dressing room for company
   mgr office

SOUND

CONSOLE
PM-3000/M-2000, located
   Rear or Center FOH
40 inputs, 2 main outputs,
   8 matrix outputs, 8 aux
   outputs
40 inputs, 2main outputs,
   4 matrix outputs, 4 aux
   outputs

SPEAKERS
House Cluster
Proscenium
Under Balcony
Portable
Upper Balcony
No speaker truss

COMMUNICATIONS
Clear Com intercom with
   (2) channels
Infrared sound system

ROAD CONSOLE
Located Rear House
(18) seats required to be
   removed
Cable run from stage is 200'
Tie-in into house system with
   XLR connectors

REHEARSAL & STORAGE SPACE
Rehearsal: None
Storage: 8'14" behind rail off
   stage

ELECTRICS

ROAD SERVICE POWER

Panel	Phase	Amp	Circuit Protection	Use	Location
A	3	600	fuse	dimmers	DL
B	3	200	fuse	sound	DR
C-E	3	60	fuse	extra	Back outside wall

Recommended location of touring dimmer racks: Off SL behind rail
Hoist not required
Additional power is available for tour buses, generators, etc.

FRONT OF HOUSE (BOX BOOM VALUES ARE PER SIDE)

Position	Pipe Width	Distance to Prosc.	House Circuits	Connector Type	FOH Transfer Circuits
1st Balc Rail	40'	60'	30	grd 20 amp stage pin	30
Box Boom 1		80'	24	grd 20 amp stage pin	24

Transfer circuits: grd 20 amp stage pin

EQUIPMENT FOH (BOX BOOM VALUES ARE PER SIDE)

Position	Quantity	Wattage	Instrument	Removeable
1st Balc Rail	8	1,000	Berkey 12°	yes
Box Boom 1	12	1,000	Berkey 10°/12°	yes

FOLLOWSPOTS
House Followspots:
   (2) Satellite II 1200w;
   removeable

Followspot Booth:
   (4) spots per booth;
   144' throw to proscenium;
   (4) 1Ø 20 amp breakers

DIMMERS
Lighting console is NSI;
   (96) ETC Sensor dimmers
House has programmable
   DMX control system
(2) dry run DMX station(s)

CENTROPLEX THEATRE FOR THE PERFORMING ARTS

Theatre Location: 275 South River Road, Baton Rouge, LA 70806

Main Administrative Phone: 504-389-3080
Main Administrative Fax: 504-389-4954
Stage Door Phone: 504-389-4953
Backstage Pay Phone: 504-387-9649

THEATRE STAFF
Executive Director   Will Wilton   504-389-3030
Booking   Vaughn Barbarin   504-389-3030
HOUSE CREW
Technical Director   Curtis Appleby   504-389-3030
UNIONS
IATSE Local #540   Hayes Taylor   504-273-8933

SEATING CAPACITY
Orchestra   1,190
Balcony   707
Total: **1,897**

BOX OFFICE
Computerized
Box Office Manager
  Jennifer Doerfle   504-389-4949

Outside Ticket Agency
Computerized
  Ticketmaster   504-336-5000

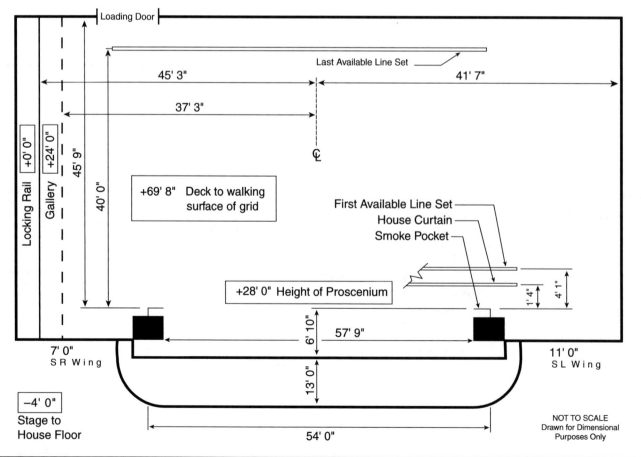

STAGE HOUSE

HOUSE CURTAIN
Operates as a guillotine from SR deck

RIGGING SYSTEM
Type:	Single purchase counter weight
Weight:	32,000 lbs available
Line sets:	34 sets at 8" o.c. with 7 lift lines per set
Arbors:	1,000 lb capacity
House Pipes:	68' long with 67' of travel from deck

Line sets are not moveable
(6) spot wheels available

PERMANENT INSTALLATIONS OVER STAGE
Orchestra shells (4) at 7'0", 17'0", 27'0", 36'0"
Hard teaser (1) at 22'0"

PERMANENT INSTALLATIONS ON DECK
Orchestra shell stores on DSL wall 8'0" deep
Air conditioning ducts (2) located 26'0" above deck against SR & SL side walls; extending out from wall 6'0"

ORCHESTRA PIT
Adjustable to 12' below stage level by hydraulic lift

BACKSTAGE

LOADING DOCK
Loading door(s):
  9'0" high x 8'2" wide
Trucks load (2) side by side at same time
Dock is at truck level; loading to stage thru separate receiving area
Forklift: House owns

WARDROBE
Location: SR Green Room or USC Scene Shop
Access: Direct from stage
Washer and dryer available

DRESSING ROOMS
(3) Star, SR, stage level, t/s included
(2) Chorus, SR, 2nd fl, t/s included

SOUND

CONSOLE
Rams & C900
20 inputs, 3 main outputs

SPEAKERS
Proscenium
1st Catwalk

COMMUNICATIONS
Telex intercom with
  (2) channels
Infrared sound system
Dressing room page system

ROAD CONSOLE
Located Rear House
(24) seats required to be removed
Cable run from stage is 120'
Tie in into house system with XLR connectors

REHEARSAL & STORAGE SPACE
Rehearsal: 30' x 25' located SL on 2nd floor, by prior arrangement
Storage: 52' x 28' located in USC Scene Shop

ELECTRICS

ROAD SERVICE POWER

Panel	Phase	Amp	Circuit Protection	Use	Location
A	3	400	breaker	extra	DSR in alcove
B	3	400	breaker	extra	DSR in alcove

Recommended location of touring dimmer racks: DSR on deck
Additional 200 amps available USC in scene shop 70' from stage

FRONT OF HOUSE (BOX BOOM VALUES ARE PER SIDE)

Position	Pipe Width	Distance to Prosc.	House Circuits	Connector Type	FOH Transfer Circuits
1st Balc Rail	65'	69'	25	grd 20 amp stage pin	25
3rd Catwalk	60'	60'	16	grd 20 amp stage pin	12
4th Catwalk	60'	75'	16	grd 20 amp stage pin	12
Box Boom 1		12'	16	grd 20 amp stage pin	16
Box Boom 2		35'	16	grd 20 amp stage pin	16

Transfer circuits: grd 20 amp stage pin located DSR

EQUIPMENT FOH (BOX BOOM VALUES ARE PER SIDE)

Position	Quantity	Wattage	Instrument	Removeable
	12	2,000	Strand 12 x 12 ellipsoidals	
	12	1,000	Strand 10 x 12 ellipsoidals	

FOLLOWSPOTS
House Followspots:
  (2) Lycian 1290 XLT; not removeable
Followspot Booth:
  (2) spots per booth;
  95' throw to proscenium;
  30 amp breakers

DIMMERS
No lighting console
No dimmers
No DMX control system

HEYMANN PERFORMING ARTS CENTER

Theatre Location: 1373 South College Road, Lafayette, LA 70503

Main Administrative Phone:		318-291-5540
Main Administrative Fax:		318-291-5580
Stage Door Phone:		318-291-5540
Backstage Pay Phone:		318-235-9378
Traveling Production Office Phone:		318-237-9207

THEATRE STAFF

General Manager	Frank Bradshaw	318-291-5540
Booking	Sue Anderson	318-291-5540

HOUSE CREW

Technical Director	Blane Toce	318-291-5540
Stage Manager	Rick Waldrip	318-291-5540

UNIONS

IATSE Local #260	George Hollier	318-439-1014

SEATING CAPACITY

Orchestra	1,230
First Balcony	572
Second Balcony	428
Total:	**2,230**

BOX OFFICE

Computerized
Box Office Manager

Elnora Plumbar	318-291-5540

Outside Ticket Agency

In-house	318-291-5555

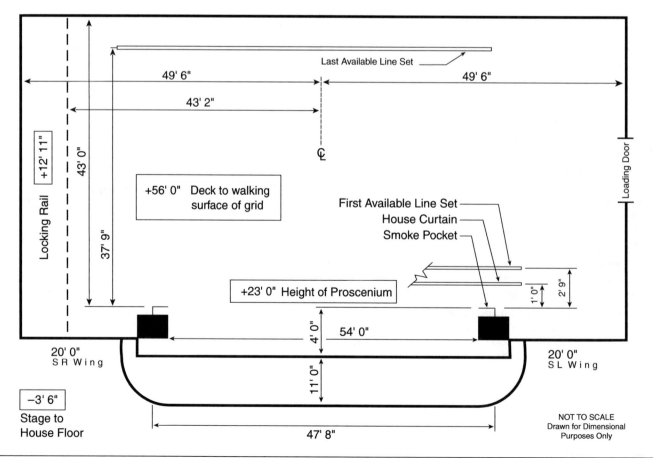

STAGE HOUSE

HOUSE CURTAIN
Operates as a traveller from SR deck

RIGGING SYSTEM

Type:	Single and double purchase counter weight
Weight:	20,000 lbs. available
Line sets:	38 sets at 4-12" o.c. with 6 lift lines per set
Arbors:	2,000 lb capacity
House Pipes:	70' long with 52' of travel from deck

Line sets are not moveable
200' of hemp available

PERMANENT INSTALLATIONS OVER STAGE (FROM SMOKE POCKET)
Electric border (3) at 6'6", 16'6", 22'5"

PERMANENT INSTALLATIONS ON DECK
None

ORCHESTRA PIT
Nonadjustable at 6' below stage level
Apron overhangs US wall of pit 0'8"
Pit conversion available

BACKSTAGE

LOADING DOCK
Loading door(s):
   12'0" high x 12'0" wide
Trucks load (1) at a time
Fork lift not required; House owns
Sound/Props cannot load in FOH
No trailers can store on-site

WARDROBE
Location: SR on stage level
Access: Direct from stage
(1) Washer (1) Dryer

DRESSING ROOMS
(2) Star, SR, stage level, t/s included, phone jack
(4) Small, SL, stage level, t/s included, phone jack
(2) Chorus, SR, stage level, t/s included, phone jack
Additional production office available for company mgr

SOUND

CONSOLE
Yamaha PM 1800
32 inputs, 8 main outputs

SPEAKERS
House Cluster
Under Balcony

COMMUNICATIONS
Clear Com intercom with (2) channels
Infrared sound system
Dressing room page system

ROAD CONSOLE
Located Rear House
(10) seats required to be removed
Cable run from stage is 200'
Tie-in into house system with XLR connectors

REHEARSAL & STORAGE SPACE
Rehearsal: None
Storage: 40' x 40' located SL by scene dock

ELECTRICS

ROAD SERVICE POWER

Panel	Phase	Amp	Circuit Protection	Use	Location
A	3	600	breaker	dimmers	DSR side wall
B	3	100	breaker	sound	SR side wall
C	3	200	breaker	extra	USL behind stage
D	3	200	breaker	extra	USL behind stage

Recommended location of touring dimmer racks: SR on deck
Additional 200 amps are available SL on loading dock approximately 81' from stage

FRONT OF HOUSE (BOX BOOM VALUES ARE PER SIDE)

Position	Pipe Width	Distance to Prosc.	House Circuits	Connector Type	FOH Transfer Circuits
1st Cove	64'	52'	24	20 amp old twistlock	24
Box Boom 1		40'	8	20 amp old twistlock	8

Transfer circuits: grd 20 amp stage pin located on SR side wall

EQUIPMENT FOH (BOX BOOM VALUES ARE PER SIDE

Position	Quantity	Wattage	Instrument	Removeable
1st Cove	6	1,000	Source 4	yes
Box Boom 1	24	1,000	Source 4	yes
Box Boom 2	6	1,000	Source 4	yes

FOLLOWSPOTS
House Followspots:
   (3) Lycian long throws ; removeable

Followspot Booth:
   (2) spots per booth;
   126' throw to prosc;
   (4) 1Ø 30 amp breakers

DIMMERS
None

MONROE CIVIC CENTER THEATRE

AT: MONROE CIVIC CENTER

Theatre Location: 401 Lea Joyner Expressway, Monroe, LA 71201
Management Company: Leisure Management International

Main Administrative Phone: 318-329-2225
Main Administrative Fax: 318-329-2548
E-mail: cvcll@ci.monroe.la.us
Backstage Pay Phone: 318-322-8095
Traveling Production Office Phone: 318-329-2813
Traveling Production Office Fax: 318-329-2814

THEATRE STAFF
General Manager   David Greenbaum   318-329-2555

HOUSE CREW
Technical Director   Wayne Gentry   318-329-2343

SEATING CAPACITY

Orchestra	1,317
1st Balcony	448
2nd Balcony	408
Total:	**2,173**
pit (add'l)	0
wheelchair (add'l)	24
standing (add'l)	0

STAGE DIMENSIONS (FROM SMOKE POCKET)
Stage is 56'0" deep
Width from Center Line to SL is 28'0"
Width from Center Line to SR is 28'0"
Proscenium width is 56'0"
Proscenium height is 25'0"
Smoke pocket to apron edge is 4'0"
Orchestra pit exists

RIGGING
Grid Height: 63'
Type: Single purchase counter weight
Weight: 11,000 lbs
Line sets: 54 sets at 8" o.c.
Arbors: 1,200 lb capacity
House Pipes: 56' long

LOADING DOCK
Loading door(s) are 14'0"high x 12'0"wide
Trucks load (2) at same time
Fork lift is required and is available

ELECTRICS
Total power available:
   (1) 600A 3Ø SR

FOLLOWSPOTS
House Followspots:
   Lycian
Power in spot booth (4) 20A
FOH transfer circuits: 9

DIMMERS
(56) house dimmers
No DMX control system

SOUND
House has 600A 3Ø
   undedicated power located
   SR
FOH mixing position in
   Rear Orchestra
Sound console is available

SAENGER THEATRE

AT: SAENGER PERFORMING ARTS CENTER

Theatre Location: 143 North Rampart Street, New Orleans, LA 70112

Main Administrative Phone:	504-525-1052
Main Administrative Fax:	504-569-1533
Stage Door Phone:	504-523-9511
Backstage Pay Phone:	504-523-8317

THEATRE STAFF

Booking	Dale M. Harris	504-525-1052
Marketing	Angie Gates	504-569-1544
Operations	E.P. Miller	504-569-1542
Group Sales	Darrell Haley	504-569-1520

HOUSE CREW

Technical Director	Fred Kittler	504-569-1548
Carpentry	Charlie Noble	504-486-5769
Electrics	Lucien Lustremau	504-523-9511
Props	Glen Gandolini	504-486-5769

UNIONS

IATSE Local #39	Albert J. Kraus, Jr.	504-486-5769
Wardrobe	Roy Young	504-837-2718

SEATING CAPACITY

Orchestra	1,674
Balconies	1,067
Total:	**2,741**
pit (add'l)	52

BOX OFFICE

Box Office Treasurer
Patricia Laduit   504-569-1520

Outside Ticket Agency
Ticketmaster   800-488-5252

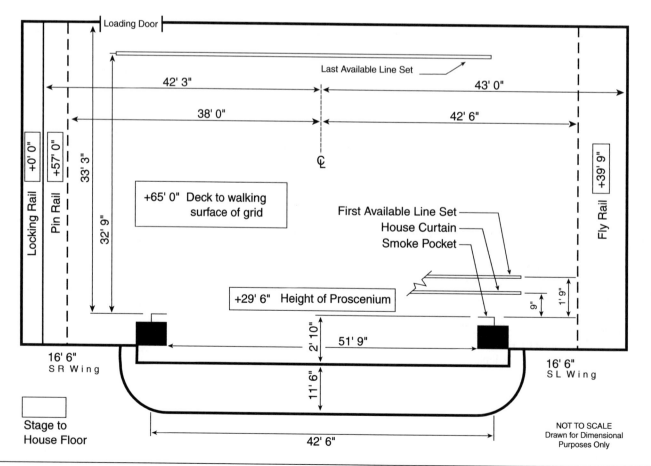

STAGE HOUSE

HOUSE CURTAIN
Operates as a guillotine from SR deck

RIGGING SYSTEM

Type:	Single purchase counter weight
Weight:	26,000 lbs available
Line sets:	57 sets at 6" o.c. with lift lines per set
Arbors:	750 lb capacity
House Pipes:	47' long with 57' of travel from deck

Line sets are moveable
(30) spot wheels and 4,000' of hemp available

PERMANENT INSTALLATIONS OVER STAGE (FROM SMOKE POCKET)
None

PERMANENT INSTALLATIONS ON DECK
Traps (3) in stage floor 3'0" x 4'0" located USL

ORCHESTRA PIT
Adjustable to 12' below stage level by electric motor turnscrew
Apron overhangs US wall of pit 0'0"
Pit lift is in (1) section

BACKSTAGE

LOADING DOCK
Loading door(s):
9'10" high x 8'0" wide
Trucks load (3) side by side at same time
Fork lift is required; Clarklift, Inc. (504) 888-4870

WARDROBE
Location: Basement
Access: Trap in stage floor USL
(2) Washers (2) Dryers

DRESSING ROOMS
(1) Star, SR, stage, t/s included, phone jack
(10) Small, +2/+3/+4, t/s on same fl
(3) Chorus, +2/+3/+4, t/s on same fl
Additional production office available for company mgr

SOUND

CONSOLE
No house console

SPEAKERS
House Cluster
Proscenium
Under Balcony

COMMUNICATIONS
Clear Com intercom with (2) channels
Dressing room page system

ROAD CONSOLE
Located Rear House
(39) seats required to be removed
Cable run from stage is 150'
Tie-in into house system with XLR connectors

REHEARSAL & STORAGE SPACE
Rehearsal: None
Storage: None

ELECTRICS

ROAD SERVICE POWER

Panel	Phase	Amp	Circuit Protection	Use	Location
A-D	3	400	fuse	dimmers	SR in basement
E-F	3	200	fuse	sound	SR in basement
G	3	100	fuse	hoist	SR in basement
H	3	100	fuse	extra	SR in basement

Recommended location of touring dimmer racks: SR or in basement
Hoist provided

FRONT OF HOUSE (BOX BOOM VALUES ARE PER SIDE)

Position	Pipe Width	Distance to Prosc.	House Circuits	Connector Type	FOH Transfer Circuits
1st Balc Rail	52'	75'	24	grd 20 amp stage pin	24
Box Boom 1		12'	12	grd 20 amp stage pin	12
Box Boom 2		27'	10	grd 20 amp stage pin	10

Transfer circuits: grd 20 amp stage pins located on DSR proscenium wall

EQUIPMENT FOH (BOX BOOM VALUES ARE PER SIDE)
None

FOLLOWSPOTS
House Followspots:
(2) Xenon Super Trouper; not removeable

Followspot Booth:
(3) spots per booth;
170' throw to proscenium;
(3) 3Ø 50 amp breakers

DIMMERS
No lighting console
No dimmers
No DMX control system

STRAND THEATRE OF SHREVEPORT

YEAR BUILT: 1925   YEAR RENOVATED: 1984

Theatre Location: 619 Louisiana Avenue, Shreveport, LA 71101
Mailing Address: PO Box 1547, Shreveport, LA 71165-1547

Main Administrative Phone: 318-226-1481
Main Administrative Fax: 318-424-5434
E-mail: strand@thestrandtheatre.com
Website: www.thestrandtheatre.com
Stage Door Phone: 318-222-9047
Backstage Pay Phone: 318-222-9047
Traveling Production Office Phone: 318-227-8580
Traveling Production Office Fax: 318-227-8584

THEATRE STAFF
Executive Director   Penne Mobley   318-226-1481
Booking   Penne Mobley   318-226-1481
HOUSE CREW
Production Coordinator Stephen Palmer   318-226-1481
UNIONS
IATSE Local #298   318-227-1914

SEATING CAPACITY
Orchestra   832
Boxes   56
Loge   170
Mid Balcony   294
Upper Balcony   284
Total: **1,636**

BOX OFFICE
Computerized
Box Office Treasurer
  Gail Battle   318-226-8555

Outside Ticket Agency
  None

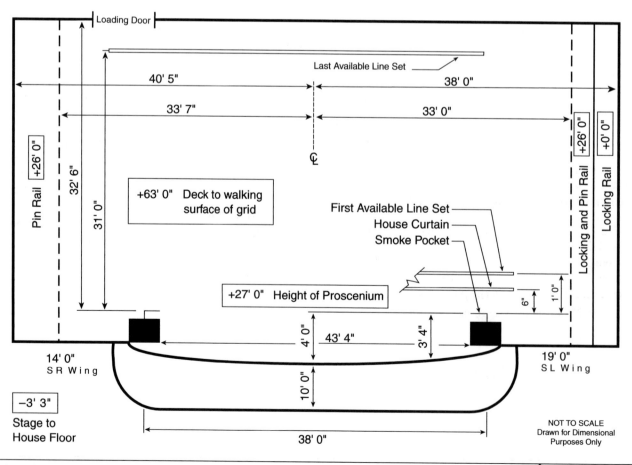

Loading Door

Last Available Line Set

40' 5"   38' 0"

33' 7"   33' 0"

CL

Pin Rail +26' 0"

+26' 0"
+0' 0"

Locking and Pin Rail
Locking Rail

32' 6"

31' 0"

+63' 0" Deck to walking surface of grid

First Available Line Set
House Curtain
Smoke Pocket

+27' 0" Height of Proscenium

1' 0"
6"

4' 0"   43' 4"   3' 4"

14' 0"
SR Wing

19' 0"
SL Wing

10' 0"

−3' 3"
Stage to
House Floor

38' 0"

NOT TO SCALE
Drawn for Dimensional
Purposes Only

STAGE HOUSE

HOUSE CURTAIN
Operates as a guillotine from SR deck

RIGGING SYSTEM
Type: Single purchase counter weight
Weight: 18,000 lbs available
Line sets: 35 sets at 6" o.c. with 6 lift lines per set
Arbors: 2,700 lb capacity
House Pipes: 52' long with 54' of travel from deck
Line sets are moveable
Block & Falls are available 3:2 (1)
(8) spot wheels and 5,000' of hemp available

PERMANENT INSTALLATIONS OVER STAGE (FROM SMOKE POCKET)
Electric raceways (4) at 3'6", 12'0", 18'6", 25'0"
Orchestra shell (3) at 8'0", 15'6", 24'0"
Traveller (1) at 15'0"

PERMANENT INSTALLATIONS ON DECK
None

ORCHESTRA PIT
Adjustable to 10'0" below stage level by hydraulic lift
Apron overhangs US wall of pit 13'0"

BACKSTAGE

LOADING DOCK
Loading door(s):
  10'0" high x 8'0" wide
Trucks load (1) at a time
Dock is at truck level and is accessed by an alley; draw bridge extends the dock outward for right angle truck access
Fork lift is not required
Sound/Props cannot load in FOH
Lobby can be a work area
(6) Trailers can store on-site
Security at dock & stage door

WARDROBE
Location: Basement
Access: Orchestra pit elevator
No Washers No Dryers
Washer and dryer hookups available

DRESSING ROOMS
(2) Star, SR, stage level, t/s included, phone jack
(2) Small, SR, stage level, t/s on same fl
(3) Chorus, SR, basement, t/s included

SOUND

CONSOLE
Soundcraft 800B
24 inputs, 8 main outputs

SPEAKERS
House Cluster
Under Balcony

COMMUNICATIONS
HME intercom with
  (2) channels
Dressing room page system

ROAD CONSOLE
Located Rear HR
(24) seats required to be removed
Cable run from stage is 150'
Tie-in into house system with XLR connectors

REHEARSAL & STORAGE SPACE
Rehearsal: None
Storage: 20' x 25' located in basement

ELECTRICS

ROAD SERVICE POWER

Panel	Phase	Amp	Circuit Protection	Use	Location
A-B	3	400	fuse	dimmers	USR back wall
C	3	100	fuse	sound	DSR proscenium wall

Recommended location of touring dimmer racks: SR on deck
Hoist not required

FRONT OF HOUSE (BOX BOOM VALUES ARE PER SIDE)

Position	Pipe Width	Distance to Prosc.	House Circuits	Connector Type	FOH Transfer Circuits
1st Balc Rail	18'	43'	12	grd 20 amp stage pin	0
1st Cove	35'	94'	20	grd 20 amp stage pin	0

Balcony rail does not have pipe; instruments must bolt to existing hardware

EQUIPMENT FOH (BOX BOOM VALUES ARE PER SIDE)

Position	Quantity	Wattage	Instrument	Removeable
1st Cove	18	1,000	10° Lekos	yes

FOLLOWSPOTS
House Followspots:
  (2) Xenon Colortran Color ARC 2000s; removeable

Followspot Booth:
  (3) spots per booth;
  98' throw to proscenium;
  (2) 1Ø 30 amp breakers
  (2) 1Ø 15 amp breakers

DIMMERS
Lighting console is Colortran Prestige 2000
  (20) Colortran dimmers
No DMX control system

LYRIC OPERA HOUSE

YEAR BUILT: 1894   YEAR RENOVATED: 1987

Theatre Location: 140 West Mount Royal Avenue,
Baltimore, MD 21201-5795

Mailing Address: 110 West Mount Royal Ave,
Baltimore, MD 21201-5795

Management Company: Lyric, Inc. (mailing address as above)

Main Administrative Phone: 410-685-5086
Main Administrative Fax: 410-332-8234
E-mail: rpomory@ix.netcom.com
Stage Door Phone: 410-685-5086 x14
Backstage Pay Phone: 410-539-9709/10

THEATRE STAFF
President   Robert M. Pomory   410-685-0117
Manager   John T. Kroneberger   410-685-5087 x11
Booking   Robert M. Pomory   410-685-0117

HOUSE CREW
Carpentry   George Tivvis   410-837-3730
Electrics   Steven Wallace   410-837-3730
Sound   John Sabo   410-837-3730
Props   Mark Pringle   410-837-3730
Fly   John Tivvis   410-837-3730

UNIONS
IATSE Local #19   Thomas G. Weeks   410-879-2762
Wardrobe Local #913   Carol Grimsley   410-795-1254
Musical Contractor   John Melick   410-377-7771

SEATING CAPACITY
Orchestra	973
Boxes	208
Dress Circle	192
Grand Tier	348
Balcony	816
Total:	**2,537**

BOX OFFICE
Computerized
Box Office   410-685-5086 x26

Outside Ticket Agency
Computerized
Ticketmaster
  Linda Craig   410-796-2456

Box office is promoter operated

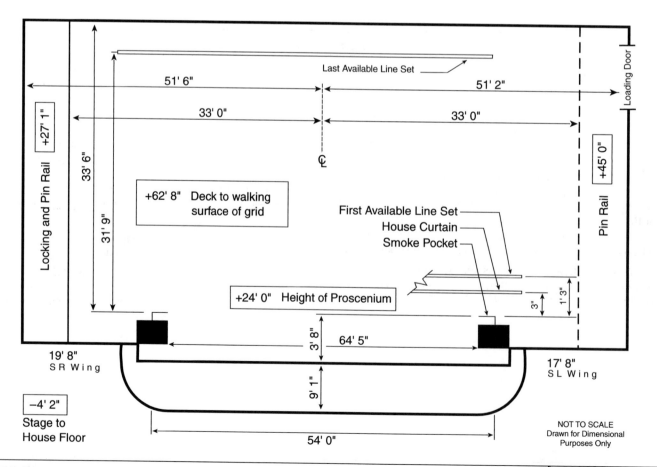

Last Available Line Set

51' 6"   51' 2"
33' 0"   33' 0"

+27' 1" Locking and Pin Rail

33' 6"
31' 9"

+62' 8" Deck to walking surface of grid

First Available Line Set
House Curtain
Smoke Pocket

+45' 0" Pin Rail

3"   1' 3"

+24' 0" Height of Proscenium

3' 8"   64' 5"

19' 8"
S R Wing

17' 8"
S L Wing

9' 1"

−4' 2"
Stage to
House Floor

54' 0"

NOT TO SCALE
Drawn for Dimensional
Purposes Only

Loading Door

STAGE HOUSE

HOUSE CURTAIN
Operates as a guillotine or traveller from SR deck

RIGGING SYSTEM
Type:	Hemp system
Weight:	10,000 lbs available
Line sets:	44 sets at 8" o.c. with 5 lift lines per set
House Pipes:	50' long with 61' of travel from deck

Line sets are not moveable
Block & Falls are available
Chain hoists are not available
(90) spot wheels and 18,000' of hemp available

PERMANENT INSTALLATIONS OVER STAGE (FROM SMOKE POCKET)
Dead Space (1) at 15'0" (37" wide)

PERMANENT INSTALLATIONS ON DECK
Pilasters (2), 5'3" wide x 2'7" deep, located 21'8" SR & SL of center
Columns (2), 4'0" & 20'0" - 18" square in SR wing

ORCHESTRA PIT
Nonadjustable at 8' below stage level
Apron overhangs US wall of pit 8'9"

BACKSTAGE

LOADING DOCK
Loading door(s):
  16'3" high x 20'0" wide
Trucks load (1) at a time
Loading dock address:
100 W. Mount Royal Avenue
Dock is at truck level; Freight elevator is 10' h x 10' w x 32' long with 16,000 lb capacity
Fork lift is not required
Sound/Props cannot load in FOH
Trailers cannot store on-site
Security at stage door

WARDROBE
Location: Basement
Access: Freight elevator
(2) Washers (2) Dryers
Washer and dryer hookups available

DRESSING ROOMS
(2) Star, SL, +1, t/s included, phone jack
(6) Small, SL, +1, t/s included, phone jack
(2) Chorus, SR, -1, t/s included
Additional production office available for company mgr

SOUND

CONSOLE
Yamaha 32 channel

SPEAKERS
House Cluster
Under Balcony

COMMUNICATIONS
Clear Com intercom with (2) channels
AM hearing impaired system

ROAD CONSOLE
Located HL in box AA
(6) seats required to be removed
Cable run from stage is 150'
Tie in into house system with XLR connectors

REHEARSAL & STORAGE SPACE
Rehearsal: 77' x 37', SL on stage level; equipment available
Storage: Basement, 12' x 20'

ELECTRICS

ROAD SERVICE POWER

Panel	Phase	Amp	Circuit Protection	Use	Location
A	3	600	breaker	dimmers	SR in basement
B	3	600	breaker	dimmers	SL in basement

Recommended location of touring dimmer racks: SL in basement

FRONT OF HOUSE (BOX BOOM VALUES ARE PER SIDE)

Position	Pipe Width	Distance to Prosc.	House Circuits	Connector Type	FOH Transfer Circuits
Bridge	65'	46'	36'	grd 20 amp stage pin	36
Box Boom 1		21'	0		0
Box Boom 2		29'	0		0
Box Boom 3		38'	0		0

Transfer circuits: grd 20 amp stage pin located DSL & DSR in basement

EQUIPMENT FOH (BOX BOOM VALUES ARE PER SIDE)
None

FOLLOWSPOTS
House Followspots:
(3) Carbon arc Super Troupers; removeable

Followspot Booth:
(3) spots per booth;
120' throw to proscenium;
(3) 1Ø 30 amp breakers

DIMMERS
None

MORRIS A. MECHANIC THEATRE

YEAR BUILT: 1967   YEAR RENOVATED: 1977

Theatre Location: 25 Hopkins Plaza, Baltimore, MD 21201
Management Company: Baltimore Center for the Performing Arts
                         1 N. Charles St., Baltimore, MD 21201

Main Administrative Phone: 410-625-4230
Main Administrative Fax: 410-625-4250
Website: www.themechanic.org
Stage Door Phone: 410-625-4219
Traveling Production Office Phone: 410-625-4213
Traveling Production Office Fax: 410-625-4213

THEATRE STAFF
General Manager	Haynes Knight	410-625-4230
Booking	Haynes Knight	410-625-4230
Marketing	Marilyn Waranch	410-625-4230
Operations	Bob Hayes	410-625-4230
Group Sales	Mary Fremgen	410-625-4230

HOUSE CREW
Carpentry	George Weeks	410-539-4145
Electrics	William Wallace II	410-539-4145
Sound	Steve Kicas	410-539-4145
Props	James Bloom	410-539-4145

UNIONS
IATSE Local #19	Thomas G. Weeks	410-879-2762
Wardrobe Local #913	Carole Grimsley	410-795-1254
Music In-house	Ray Moore	410-833-7308

SEATING CAPACITY
Orchestra	778
Dress Circle	110
Mezzanine	676
Total:	**1,564**

pit (add'l)	43
wheelchair (add'l)	6

BOX OFFICE
Computerized
Treasurer
  John Griffin   410-625-4230

Outside Ticket Agency
Computerized
  Ticketmaster   410-752-1200

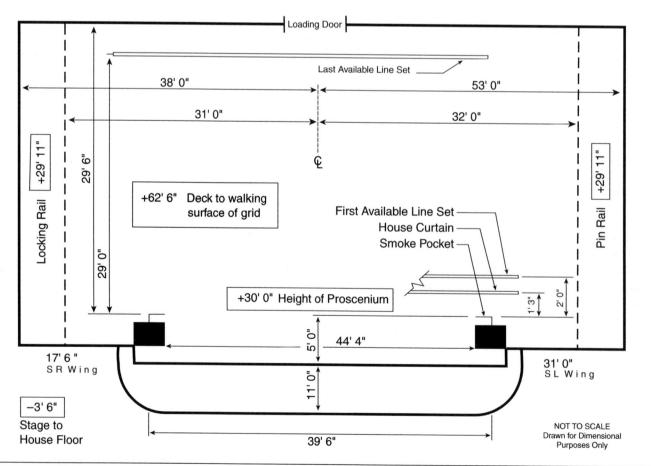

STAGE HOUSE

HOUSE CURTAIN
Operates as a guillotine from SL deck

RIGGING SYSTEM
Type:	Double purchase counter weight; Hemp System
Weight:	60,000 lbs available
Line sets:	68 sets at 6" o.c. with 7 lift lines per set
Arbors:	1,600 lb capacity
House Pipes:	58' long with 62' of travel from deck

Line sets are moveable

(50) spot wheels and 6,000' of hemp available

PERMANENT INSTALLATIONS OVER STAGE (FROM SMOKE POCKET)
House curtain (1) 2'0"

PERMANENT INSTALLATIONS ON DECK
Traps (60) in stage floor are on a sectional grid

ORCHESTRA PIT
Nonadjustable at 8' below stage level
Apron overhangs US wall of pit 2' 6"

BACKSTAGE

LOADING DOCK
Loading door(s):
   10'0" high x 25'0" wide
Trucks load (2) back to back at same time
Fork lift is required; Clark Lift (410) 355-1000
Sound/Props can load in FOH
Lobby can be a work area
Security at stage door

WARDROBE
Location: SL on stage level
Access: direct from stage
(2) Washers (2) Dryers
Washer and dryer hookups available

DRESSING ROOMS
(1) Star, SL, stage level, t/s included, phone jack
(5) Small, SL, stage level, t/s included, phone jack
(3) Chorus, SL, stage level, t/s
Additional production office available for company mgr

SOUND

CONSOLE
Yamaha 1516
16 inputs, 8 main outputs

SPEAKERS
House Cluster
Proscenium
Under Balcony
Truss speakers
Speaker truss exists
Max available load 1,000 lbs

COMMUNICATIONS
Clear Com intercom with (2) channels
Infrared sound system
Dressing room page system

ROAD CONSOLE
Located Rear House
Number of seats required to be removed varies
Cable run from stage is 175'
Tie-in into house system with XLR connectors

REHEARSAL & STORAGE SPACE
Rehearsal: None
Storage: under stage; trap room

ELECTRICS

ROAD SERVICE POWER

Panel	Phase	Amp	Circuit Protection	Use	Location
A-B	3	800	breaker	dimmers	USL back wall
C	3	40	breaker	extra	USR back wall
D	3	30	breaker	sound	DSL procenium wall

Recommended location of touring dimmer racks: SL
Hoist not required

FRONT OF HOUSE (BOX BOOM VALUES ARE PER SIDE)

Position	Pipe Width	Distance to Prosc.	House Circuits	Connector Type	FOH Transfer Circuits
1st Balcony Rail	65'	45'	44	grd 20 amp stage pin	44
1st Catwalk	100'	59'	24	grd 20 amp stage pin	24
2nd Catwalk	100'	74'	30	grd 20 amp stage pin	30
Box Boom 1		18'	10	grd 20 amp stage pin	10
Box Boom 2		28'	10	grd 20 amp stage pin	10

Transfer circuits: grd 20 amp stage pin, located on USL back wall

EQUIPMENT FOH (BOX BOOM VALUES ARE PER SIDE)
None

FOLLOWSPOTS
House Followspots:
   (2) Xenon Super Troupers; removeable

Followspot Booth:
   (3) spots per booth;
   110' throw to proscenium;
   (3) 3Ø 35 amp breakers

DIMMERS
No lighting console
No dimmers
No DMX control system

THE COLONIAL THEATRE

YEAR BUILT: 1900   YEAR RENOVATED: 1996

Theatre Location: 106 Boylston Street, Boston, MA 02116
Management Company: American Artists, Inc.
                                       120 Boylston Street Suite 502, Boston, MA 02116

Main Administrative Phone: 617-426-9366
Stage Door Phone: 617-426-9366 x418
Backstage Pay Phone: 617-426-9123
Traveling Production Office Phone: 617-880-2434
Traveling Production Office Fax: 617-880-2435

THEATRE STAFF
President   Jon B. Platt   617-451-2345
General Manager   Sondra R. Katz   617-451-2345
Booking   Jon B. Platt   617-734-0043
Operations   Janis Lippman   617-451-2345
Group Sales   Regan Byrne   617-451-2345
House Manager   Polly Balzano   617-880-2414

HOUSE CREW
Carpentry   Chris Welling   617-880-2428
Electrics   Bob Bayard   617-880-2433
Props   Floyd Jones   617-880-2430

UNIONS
IATSE Local #11   Jeff Flanders   617-426-5595
Wardrobe   Carol Colantroni 617-776-5838
Music   Rich Hammett   617-773-6422

SEATING CAPACITY
Orchestra   743
Boxes   32
Loge   15
Mezzanine   556
Balcony   359
Total: **1,705**

pit (add'l)   10
wheelchair (add'l)   11

BOX OFFICE
Computerized
Box Office Treasurer
   A. Greer Bono   617-426-9366 x413

Outside Ticket Agency
Computerized
Ticketmaster
   Michael Norton   617-244-8400

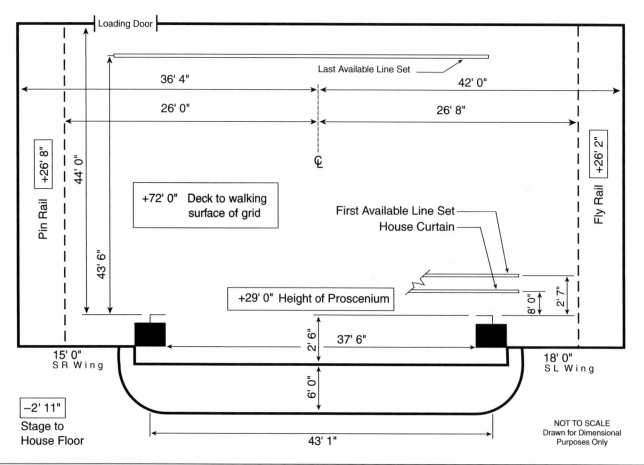

STAGE HOUSE

HOUSE CURTAIN
Operates as a guillotine from SL fly floor

RIGGING SYSTEM
Type: Single purchase counter weight and Hemp System
Weight: 25,000 lbs available
Line sets: 76 sets at 6" o.c. with 5 lift lines per set
House Pipes: 50' long with 72' of travel from deck
Line sets are moveable
Block & Falls are available 2:1(4); 3:2(1)
Chain hoists are available
(26) spot wheels and 32,000' of hemp available

PERMANENT INSTALLATIONS OVER STAGE (FROM SMOKE POCKET)
None

PERMANENT INSTALLATIONS ON DECK
Traps in stage floor (1), 8'1" x 9'6"
Jumps (2)
Electric Jump (2), SR
Radiators, side and back wall

ORCHESTRA PIT
Nonadjustable at 7'4" below stage level
Apron overhangs US wall of pit 4' 7"
Pit lift is in (10) sections

BACKSTAGE

LOADING DOCK
Loading door(s):
23'6" high x 7'0" wide
Trucks load (1) at a time
Fork lift use depends on size of set pieces
Elevated Platform
Trailers cannot store on site
Sound Props cannot load FOH
Security at stage door

WARDROBE
Location: Basement
Access: Stairs
(2) Washers (2) Dryers
Washer and dryer hookups available

DRESSING ROOMS
(3) Star, SL, stage level, t/s, phone jacks
(14) Small, SL, +2 t/s, phone jack
(2) Chorus, SL, -1, t/s, phone jack
Elevator access for dressing rooms
Additonal production office available for company mgr

SOUND

CONSOLE
No house console

SPEAKERS
Various auditorium speakers

COMMUNICATIONS
No house intercom
Infrared sound system
Dressing room page system

ROAD CONSOLE
Located Rear House
Number of seats required to be removed varies
Cable run from stage is 150'
Tie-in into house system with XLR connectors

REHEARSAL & STORAGE SPACE
Rehearsal: Ladies Lounge, FOH, mirrors, piano available
Storage: Scene dock, 24' x 20', SL Under stage 32' x 60', basement, elevator needed

ELECTRICS

ROAD SERVICE POWER

Panel	Phase	Amp	Circuit Protection	Use	Location
A	3	900	fuse	dimmers	SR
B	3	200	fuse	sound	SR in basement

Recommended location of touring dimmer racks: SR on deck or SR jump at +31'1"
Hoist is required but not provided.

FRONT OF HOUSE (BOX BOOM VALUES ARE PER SIDE)

Position	Pipe Width	Distance to Prosc.	House Circuits	Connector Type	FOH Transfer Circuits
Balc Rail		48'	36	20 amp stage pin	36
Box Boom 1		36'	12	20 amp stage pin	12

EQUIPMENT FOH (BOX BOOM VALUES ARE PER SIDE)
None

FOLLOWSPOTS
House Followspots:
Available for rental

Followspot Booth:
(3) spots per booth;
125' throw to proscenium;
(4) 3Ø 200 amp breakers

DIMMERS
No lighting console
(5) ED Brand dimmers
No DMX control system

SHUBERT THEATRE

Theatre Location: 265 Tremont Street, Boston, MA 02116

Main Administrative Phone: 617-482-9393
Main Administrative Fax: 617-426-0124
Stage Door Phone: 617-482-9393 x110

THEATRE STAFF
President/CEO   Josiah Spaulding, Jr.   617-482-9393 x286
Vice President/COO   William C. Taylor   617-482-9393 x214
Director Theatre Svc   Joyce Spinney   617-482-9393 x213
Theatre Manager   Michael Szczepkowski 617-482-9393 x107

HOUSE CREW
Carpentry   Norman White   617-482-9393 x111
Electrics   Ken Monteiro   617-482-9393 x113
Sound   James McCartney   617-482-9393 x113
Props   Michele Cooney-Higgins 617-482-9393 x112
Fly   Lenny Pilot   617-482-9393 x111

UNIONS
IATSE Local #11   Jeff Flanders   617-426-5595
Wardrobe Local #775   Carol Colantouni   617-776-5838
Music Local #9-535   Fred Buda   617-438-2152

SEATING CAPACITY
Orchestra   703
Boxes   32
Mezzanine   439
First Balcony   364
Total: **1,538**

pit (add'l)   66
wheelchair (incl.)

BOX OFFICE
Computerized
Box Office Treasurer
  Tim White   617-482-9393 x109

Outside Ticket Agency
Computerized
  Tele-charge   800-447-7400

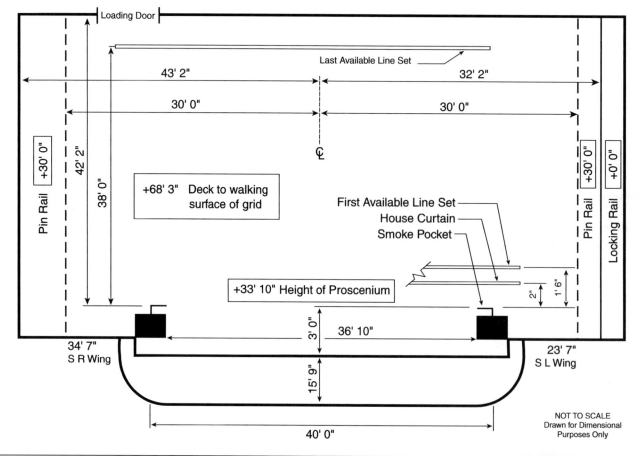

NOT TO SCALE
Drawn for Dimensional
Purposes Only

STAGE HOUSE

HOUSE CURTAIN
Operates as a guillotine from SL fly floor

RIGGING SYSTEM
Type:	Single purchase counter weight
Weight:	25,000 lbs available
Line sets:	64 sets at 4-12" o.c. with 4 lift lines per set
Arbors:	550 lb capacity
House Pipes:	42' long with 65' of travel from deck

Line sets are not moveable
Block & Falls are available 2:1 (3); 3:2 (3)
(50) spot wheels and 10,000' of hemp available
1,200 lbs of sand available

PERMANENT INSTALLATIONS OVER STAGE (FROM SMOKE POCKET)
None

PERMANENT INSTALLATIONS ON DECK
None

ORCHESTRA PIT
Nonadjustable at 8' below stage level
Apron overhangs US wall of pit 8'0"

BACKSTAGE

LOADING DOCK
Loading door(s):
   10'0" high x 8'0" wide
Trucks load (2) back to back at same time
Dock (loading door sill) is at street level
Trailers cannot store on-site

WARDROBE
Location: Basement
Access: Trap in prop room
(2) Washers (2) Dryers
No washer or dryer hookups

DRESSING ROOMS
(2) Star, SL, stage level, t/s on same fl
(9) Small, SL, 2nd floor, t/s on same fl
(3) Chorus, basement, t/s included

SOUND

CONSOLE
Soundcraft 500

SPEAKERS
Speaker truss exists
Max available load 2,000 lbs per point

COMMUNICATIONS
Intercom with (2) channels
FM sound system
Dressing room page system
Lobby video monitor

ROAD CONSOLE
Located Rear House
(16) seats required to be removed
Cable run from stage is 150'

REHEARSAL & STORAGE SPACE
Rehearsal: None
Storage: None

ELECTRICS

ROAD SERVICE POWER

Panel	Phase	Amp	Circuit Protection	Use	Location
A-B	3	400	breaker	dimmers	SR above prop room
C	3	100	breaker	sound	DSR proscenium wall
D-G	3	400	breaker	extra	SR above prop room

Recommended location of touring dimmer racks: SR above prop room
Hoist is required and provided

FRONT OF HOUSE (BOX BOOM VALUES ARE PER SIDE)

Position	Pipe Width	Distance to Prosc.	House Circuits	Connector Type	FOH Transfer Circuits
1st Balc Rail	45'	48'	36	grd 20 amp stage pin	36
2nd Balc Rail	45'	64'	36	grd 20 amp stage pin	36
Box Boom 1		10'	12	grd 20 amp stage pin	12
Box Boom 2		20'	12	grd 20 amp stage pin	12
Box Boom 3		30'	12	grd 20 amp stage pin	12
Box Boom 4		80'	12	grd 20 amp stage pin	12

Transfer circuits: grd 20 amp stage pin located SR above prop room

EQUIPMENT FOH (BOX BOOM VALUES ARE PER SIDE)
None

FOLLOWSPOTS
House Followspots:
   None

Followspot Booth:
   (3) spots per booth;
   92' throw to proscenium;
   3Ø 100 amp breakers

DIMMERS
None

WANG CENTER FOR THE PERFORMING ARTS

Theatre Location: 270 Tremont Street, Boston, MA 02116

Main Administrative Phone: 617-482-9393
Main Administrative Fax: 617-482-1436
Stage Door Phone: 617-482-9393 x110

THEATRE STAFF
  President/CEO   Josiah Spaulding, Jr.   617-482-9393 x286
  Vice President/COO   William C. Taylor   617-482-9393 x214
  Director Theater Svcs Joyce Spinney   617-482-9393 x213

HOUSE CREW
  Carpentry   Russell Jones   617-482-9393 x262
  Electrics   James Paulson   617-482-9393 x261
  Sound   Paul Coughlin   617-482-9393 x240

UNIONS
  IATSE Local #11   Jeff Flanders   617-426-5595
  Wardrobe Local #775   Carol Colantuoni   617-776-5838
  Music Local #9-535   Fred Buda   617-438-2152

SEATING CAPACITY
  Orchestra   1,607
  Orchestra Boxes   101
  Dress Circle   151
  Mezzanine   217
  First Balcony   824
  Second Balcony   711
  Total: **3,611**

  pit (add'l)   6

BOX OFFICE
  Computerized
  Box Office Treasurer
    Raffaella De Gruttola
    617-482-9393 x253

  Outside Ticket Agency
    Tele-charge   800-447-7400

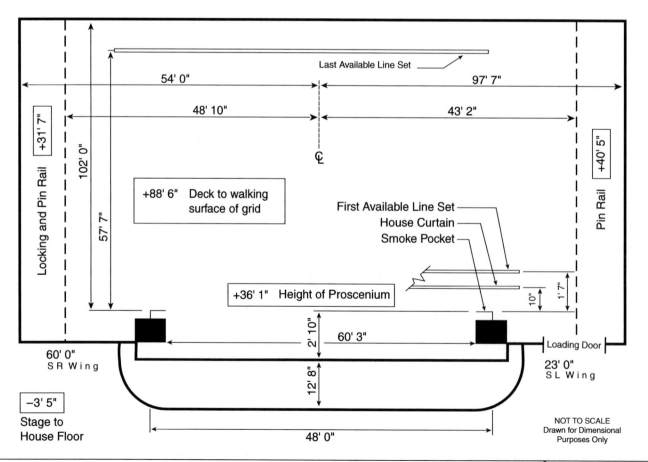

STAGE HOUSE

HOUSE CURTAIN
Operates as a guillotine from SR deck

RIGGING SYSTEM
Type:	Single purchase counter weight
Weight:	67,000 lbs available
Line sets:	79 sets at 12" o.c. with 7 lift lines per set
Arbors:	1,800 lb capacity
House Pipes:	80' long with 86' of travel from deck

Line sets are not moveable
Block & Falls are available 2:1 (2)
(120) spot wheels and 10,000 of hemp available

PERMANENT INSTALLATIONS OVER STAGE (FROM SMOKE POCKET)
Dead space (1) at 25'7" (2' wide)
Trap - in grid for rigging 8'0" x 16'0"

PERMANENT INSTALLATIONS ON DECK
Columns (2) each 2'0" square at 86'6" located 8'0" SL of center & at 60'0" located 38'0" SR of center

ORCHESTRA PIT
Nonadjustable at 7' below stage level
Apron overhangs US wall of pit 14'6"

BACKSTAGE

LOADING DOCK
Loading door(s):
10'0" high x 12'0" wide
Trucks load (2) side by side at same time
Fork lift is not required
Sound/Props can load in FOH
Trailers cannot store on-site
Security at dock & stage door

WARDROBE
Location: SR in Basement
Access: Freight Elevator
(1) Washer (1) Dryer

DRESSING ROOMS
(2) Star, SL, -1, t/s included, phone jack
(4) Small, SL, -1, t/s included, phone jack
(8) Chorus, -1, t/s included, phone jack
Elevator access for dressing rooms
Additional production office available for company mgr

SOUND

CONSOLE
Soundcraft 500
24 inputs, 8 main outputs

SPEAKERS
House Cluster
Proscenium
Under Balcony

COMMUNICATIONS
No house intercom system
Infrared sound system
Dressing room page system

ROAD CONSOLE
Located Rear HR
(24) seats required to be removed
Cable run from stage is 225'
Tie-in into house system with XLR connectors

REHEARSAL & STORAGE SPACE
Rehearsal: 40' x 60' located in basement
Storage: 40' x 60' located US behind stage house

ELECTRICS

ROAD SERVICE POWER

Panel	Phase	Amp	Circuit Protection	Use	Location
A	3	1600	breaker	dimmers	DSL
B	3	100	breaker	sound	USL
C	3	100	breaker	extra	DSR
D	3	100	breaker	extra	USL

Recommended location of touring dimmer racks: DSR on deck
Hoist not required

FRONT OF HOUSE (BOX BOOM VALUES ARE PER SIDE)

Position	Pipe Width	Distance to Prosc.	House Circuits	Connector Type	FOH Transfer Circuits
1st Balc Rail	90'	60'	38	grd 20 amp stage pin	38
Box Boom 1		65'	15	grd 20 amp stage pin	15
Torm		8'	15	grd 20 amp stage pin	15

Transfer circuits: grd 20 amp stage pin located on DSL proscenium wall

EQUIPMENT FOH (BOX BOOM VALUES ARE PER SIDE)
None

FOLLOWSPOTS
House Followspots:
None

Followspot Booth:
(3) spots per booth;
250' throw to proscenium;
(3) 3Ø 60 amp breakers

DIMMERS
None

WILBUR THEATRE

AKA: THE TREMONT STREET THEATRE   **YEAR BUILT: 1914**

Theatre Location: 246 Tremont Street, Boston, MA 02116
Management Company: American Artists
                         120 Boylston Street, 5th Floor, Boston, MA 02116

Main Administrative Phone: 617-423-4008
Main Administrative Fax: 617-695-1606
Website: www.broadwayinboston.com
Stage Door Phone: 617-423-4008 x15
Backstage Pay Phone: 617-451-0035

THEATRE STAFF
President   Jon Platt   617-451-2345
Marketing   Regan Byrne   617-451-2345
Operations   Janis Lippman   617-451-2345
Group Sales   Ann Sheehan   617-482-8616
General Manager   Sondra Katz   617-451-2345
House Manager   Caryn Freedman   617-423-4008 x19

HOUSE CREW
Carpentry   Jacki Cocchi   617-423-4008 x21
Electrics   Steve Saffan   617-423-4008 x21
Props   Robert McEvoy   617-423-4008 x21

UNIONS
IATSE Local #11   Jeff Flanders   617-426-5595
Wardrobe Local #775   Carol Colantouni   617-357-1962

SEATING CAPACITY
Orchestra   508
Boxes   12
Mezzanine   245
Rear Mezzanine   131
Balcony   327
Total: **1,223**

BOX OFFICE
Computerized
Box Office Treasurer
   Diane Campbell   617-423-4008 x14

Outside Ticket Agency
Computerized
   Ticketmaster   617-931-2787

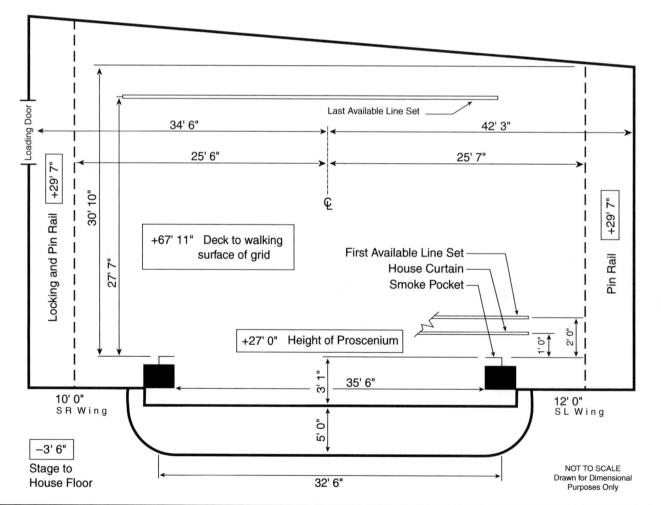

STAGE HOUSE

HOUSE CURTAIN
Operates as a guillotine from SR fly floor or deck

RIGGING SYSTEM
Type:	Single purchase counter weight
Weight:	11,000 lbs available
Line sets:	29 sets at 9" o.c. with 4 lift lines per set
Arbors:	400 lb capacity
House Pipes:	42' long with 60' of travel from deck

Line sets are not moveable
Block & Falls are available 2:1 (2)
(40) spot wheels and 3,600' of hemp available
600 lbs of sand available

PERMANENT INSTALLATIONS OVER STAGE (FROM SMOKE POCKET)
Beam (1) between 19'4" and 20'10" - line sets 24 and 25

PERMANENT INSTALLATIONS ON DECK
Traps in stage floor are on a sectional grid

ORCHESTRA PIT
Nonadjustable at 5' below stage level
Apron overhangs US wall of pit

BACKSTAGE

LOADING DOCK
Loading door(s):
16'0" high x 8'0" wide
Trucks load (1) at a time
Dock (loading door sill) is at street level 18" below stage level; ramp (1) up to stage is available

WARDROBE
Location: Basement
Access: Trap in stage floor USC
(1) Washers (2) Dryers
Washer and dryer hookups available

DRESSING ROOMS
(2) Star, SL, stage level, toilet included
(1) Star, SL, 2nd fl, toilet included
(4) Small, SL, 3rd fl, toilet included
(2) Small, SL, 2nd fl, toilet included
Showers (2) available in basement

SOUND

CONSOLE
No house console

SPEAKERS
No speaker truss

COMMUNICATIONS
No intercom system
Infrared sound system

ROAD CONSOLE
Located Rear HL
(6) seats required to be removed
Cable run from stage is 100'

REHEARSAL & STORAGE SPACE
Rehearsal: None
Storage: None

ELECTRICS

ROAD SERVICE POWER
Panel	Phase	Amp	Circuit Protection	Use	Location
A	3	800	breaker	dimmers	USL side wall

Recommended location of touring dimmer racks: SL on deck

FRONT OF HOUSE (BOX BOOM VALUES ARE PER SIDE)
Position	Pipe Width	Distance to Prosc.	House Circuits	Connector Type	FOH Transfer Circuits
1st Balc Rail	37'	36'	24	grd 20 amp stage pin	24
Box Boom 1		13'	12	grd 20 amp stage pin	12
Box Boom 2		40'	5	grd 20 amp stage pin	5

Transfer circuits: grd 20 amp stage pin located on USL side wall

EQUIPMENT FOH (BOX BOOM VALUES ARE PER SIDE)
None

FOLLOWSPOTS
House Followspots:
None

Followspot Booth:
(3) spots per booth;
100' throw to proscenium;
(3) 1Ø 20 amp breakers

DIMMERS
No lighting console
No dimmers
No DMX

LOWELL MEMORIAL AUDITORIUM

Year built: 1922   Year renovated: 1984

Theatre Location: 50 E. Merrimack Street, Lowell, MA 01852-1205
Management Company: Mill City Management , Inc.

Main Administrative Phone: 978-937-8688
Main Administrative Fax: 978-452-7342
E-mail: lma.@tinc.net
Website: www.lowellaud.com

Seating Capacity

Floor	792
Parquet - Lower Balcony	706
Upper Balcony	1,346
Total:	**2,844**
wheelchair (add'l)	24

Theatre Staff

Executive Director	Thomas McKay	978-937-8688
Director of Events	Tin Coulouras	978-937-8688

House Crew

Technical Director	Richie Voutselas	508-394-2400

Stage Dimensions (from smoke pocket)
Stage is 33' deep
Width from Center Line to SL is 29'
Width from Center Line to SR is 29'
Proscenium width is 56'6"
Proscenium height is 34'
No orchestra pit

Rigging
Grid Height: 32'
Type: Hemp; Motorized grid

Loading Dock
Loading door(s) are 6'6" high x 12'2" wide
Trucks load (1) at a time
Fork lift is not required and is not available

Electrics
Total power available:
  (1) 400A 3Ø SR
  (1) 200A 3Ø SR

Followspots
House Followspots:
  Satellite

Dimmers
No house dimmers

Sound
House has 200A 3Ø dedicated power located SR
Sound console is available

MACOMB CENTER FOR THE PERFORMING ARTS

AT: MACOMB COMMUNITY COLLEGE   YEAR BUILT: 1982

Theatre Location: 44575 Garfield Road, Clinton Township, MI 48038

Main Administrative Phone: 810-286-2141
Main Administrative Fax: 810-286-2272
Stage Door Phone:Backstage Pay Phone: 810-286-9870
Traveling Production Office Phone: 810-286-2055

THEATRE STAFF
Executive Director   Bill Biddle   810-286-2141

HOUSE CREW
Production Manager   Larry Carrico   810-286-2055
Technical   George Hommowun   810-286-2055

SEATING CAPACITY	
Main Floor	705
Balcony	512
Total:	**1,217**
pit (add'l)	34
wheelchair (add'l)	18
standing (add'l)	0

STAGE DIMENSIONS (FROM SMOKE POCKET)
Stage is 39'6" deep
Width from Center Line to SL is 68'0"
Width from Center Line to SR is 68'0"
Proscenium width is 48'6"
Proscenium height is 26'0"
Smoke pocket to apron edge is 4'0"
Orchestra pit exists

RIGGING
Grid Height:	68'
Type:	Single purchase counter weight
Weight:	31,200 lbs
Line sets:	52 sets at 7" o.c.
Arbors:	1,200 lb capacity
House Pipes:	63' long

LOADING DOCK
Loading door(s) are 8'11" high x 9'9" wide
Trucks load (2) at same time
Fork lift is not required and is not available

ELECTRICS
Total power available:
  (1) 100A 3Ø DSR
  (2) 400A 3Ø SR wall

FOLLOWSPOTS
House Followspots:
  Xenon Super Trouper
Power in spot booth 60A
FOH transfer circuits per
  position: varies

DIMMERS
(176) house dimmers
No DMX control system

SOUND
House has 100A dedicated
  power located DSR
FOH mixing position in
  Rear Orchestra
Sound console is available

DETROIT OPERA HOUSE

YEAR BUILT: 1922   YEAR RENOVATED: 1996

Theatre Location: 1526 Broadway, Detroit, MI 48226

Main Administrative Phone:	313-237-3250
Main Administrative Fax:	313-237-3251
E-mail:	dohmgr@motopera.org
Website:	www.motopera.org
Stage Door Phone:	313-237-3257
Traveling Production Office Phone:	313-237-3258
Traveling Production Office Fax:	313-237-3259/61

THEATRE STAFF

Facility Manager	Bret Batterson	313-237-3250
Booking	Brett Batterson	313-237-3250
Group Sales	Kim Mogielski	313-874-7464
House Manager	Kerry Painter	

HOUSE CREW

Technical Director	Vladmir Vukovic	313-237-3266
Carpentry	John Kinsora	313-237-3265
Electrics	Robert Mesinar	313-237-3264
Sound	Steve Kemp	313-237-3276
Props	Alan Bigelow	313-237-3263
Wardrobe	Mary Ellen Shindel	313-874-3282

UNIONS

IATSE Local #38	Tim Magee	313-368-0825
Wardrobe Local #786	Bev Lombard	810-771-3870
AFM Local #5	Dianne Bredesen	313-665-8235

SEATING CAPACITY

Orchestra	1,337
Boxes	182
Balcony 1	217
Total:	**2,736**
pit (add'l)	92
wheelchair (incl.)	varies

BOX OFFICE
Computerized
Box Office Manager
  Kim Mogielski   313-874-7464

Outside Ticket Agency
Computerized
Ticketmaster
  Kim Mogielski   313-874-7464

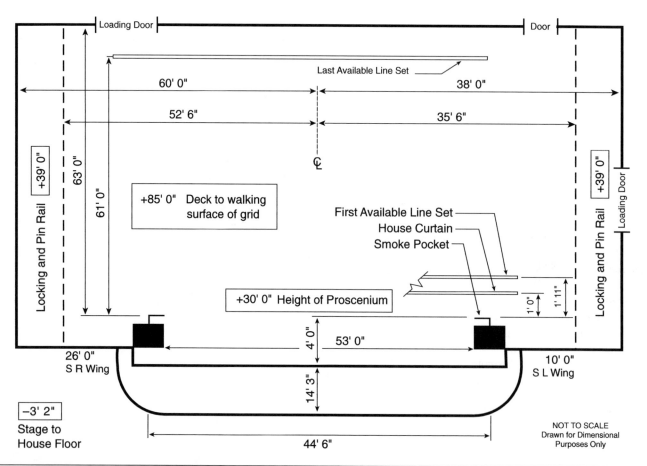

Loading Door   Door

Last Available Line Set

60' 0"   38' 0"

52' 6"   35' 6"

CL

63' 0"

61' 0"

+39' 0"

+39' 0"

Locking and Pin Rail

Locking and Pin Rail

Loading Door

+85' 0"   Deck to walking surface of grid

First Available Line Set
House Curtain
Smoke Pocket

1' 0"   1' 11"

+30' 0" Height of Proscenium

4' 0"   53' 0"

26' 0"
S R Wing

10' 0"
S L Wing

−3' 2"
Stage to
House Floor

14' 3"

44' 6"

NOT TO SCALE
Drawn for Dimensional
Purposes Only

STAGE HOUSE

HOUSE CURTAIN
Operates as a guillotine from SL deck
Curtain has center split for "page bows"

RIGGING SYSTEM

Type:	Single purchase counter weight
Weight:	90,000 lbs available
Line sets:	89 sets at 8" o.c. with 6 lift lines per set
Arbors:	1,950 lb capacity
House Pipes:	63' long with 82' of travel from deck

Line sets are not moveable
Block & Falls are not available
Chain hoists available as a rental; (8) one ton, (1) half ton
(100) spot wheels and 4,000' of hemp available
Roof mounted loft blocks

PERMANENT INSTALLATIONS OVER STAGE
None

PERMANENT INSTALLATIONS ON DECK
Traps in stage floor (2) 8'0" x 8'0"
Jumps (above locking rail) (2) at SL & SR
Loading Bridge (1) SL

ORCHESTRA PIT
Adjustable to 9'6" below stage level by Gala lift
Apron overhangs US wall of pit 16'0"
Pit lift is in (2) sections

BACKSTAGE

LOADING DOCK
Loading door(s):
Trucks load (2) 53' trailers at same time
Dock, covered & fenced loading dock; approach from Witherell St. & Madison Ave.
Fork lift is not required
Sound/Props can load in FOH
Lobby cannot be a work area
Trailers cannot store on-site
Security at stage door

WARDROBE
Location: Basement under stage
Access: Freight elevator provides direct access
(2) Washers (2) Dryers
No washer or dryer hookups

DRESSING ROOMS
(3) Star, SL, stage level, t/s included, phone jack
(3) Chorus, SR/ SL, -1/+2, t/s
(3) Small, SR, +1, t/s
Elevator access for dressing rooms
Additional production office available for company mgr

SOUND

CONSOLE
DDA CS3
32 inputs, 3 main outputs, 4 matrix outputs, 6 aux outputs

SPEAKERS
Portable
Speaker systems are primarily for on stage monitors
No speaker truss

COMMUNICATIONS
Clear Com intercom with (4) channels
Infrared sound system
Dressing room page system

ROAD CONSOLE
Located Center at row 23
(22) seats required to be removed
Cable run from stage is 150'

REHEARSAL & STORAGE SPACE
Reahearsal: 65' x 45', 3rd floor, mirrors, piano
Storage: Upstage bustel, 53' x 38', rear of stage

ELECTRICS

ROAD SERVICE POWER

Panel	Phase	Amp	Circuit Protection	Use	Location
A-C	3	400	breaker	dimmers	USR
D-E	3	200	breaker	extra	DSR
F	3	200	breaker	extra	DSL
G	3	200	breaker	extra	USR
H	3	200	breaker	extra	USL
I	3	200	breaker	sound	DSR/ DSL

Sound power DSR/ DSL are common feed; Add'l power is available buses, generators
Location of touring dimmer racks: SR; Hoist provided but not required

FRONT OF HOUSE (BOX BOOM VALUES ARE PER SIDE)

Position	Pipe Width	Distance to Prosc.	House Circuits	Connector Type	FOH Transfer Circuits
1st Cove		120'	30	grd 20 amp stage pin	30
Box Boom 1		45'	12	grd 20 amp stage pin	12
Box Boom 2		65'	24	grd 20 amp stage pin	24
1st Balc Rail		40'	12	grd 20 amp stage pin	12
Truss		50'	48	grd 20 amp stage pin	48

Transfer circuits: grd 20 amp stage pin; Box Boom 1 doubles as rail circuits
Road truss: 6 FOH points for truss; 65' trim to clear fspot booth

EQUIPMENT FOH (BOX BOOM VALUES ARE PER SIDE)

Position	Quantity	Wattage	Instrument	Removeable
1st Balc Rail	20	575	Source 4	yes
1st Cove Rail	varies	575	Source 4 5°/ 10°	yes
Box Boom 1	16	575	Source 4 10°	yes

FOLLOWSPOTS
House Followspots:
(3) Robert Triat 2500w HMI; removeable

Followspot Booth:
(3) spots per booth;
120' throw to proscenium;
(3) 1Ø 30 amp breakers

DIMMERS
Lighting console is Obsession;
(192) Sensor dimmers
House has programmable DMX control system
(12) dry run DMX station(s)

FISHER THEATRE

AT: FISHER BUILDING

YEAR BUILT: 1928   YEAR RENOVATED: 1960

Theatre Location: 3011 West Grand Boulevard, Detroit, MI 48202
Management Company: J.H. Theatrical

Main Administrative Phone: 313-872-1000
Main Administrative Fax: 313-872-0632
Website: www.fisherdetroit.com
Stage Door Phone: 313-872-3370
Backstage Pay Phone: 313-872-9293

SEATING CAPACITY
Orchestra	994
Mezzanine	226
Loge	384
Balcony	485
Total:	**2,089**

standing (add'l)

THEATRE STAFF
Theatre Manager	James Luzenski	313-872-1156
Booking	Alan Lichtenstein	313-832-5900
Group Sales	Amy Yokin	313-871-1132

HOUSE CREW
Carpentry	Albert Ashbaugh	313-872-3367
Electrics	Robert Kynaston	313-872-3369
Sound	J.B. Rablovsky	313-871-0006
Props	Joe Achatz	313-872-3368

UNIONS
IATSE Local #38	Tim McGee	313-368-0825
Wardrobe	Beverly Llombert	810-771-3870
Music	Max Leib	407-498-9857

BOX OFFICE
Computerized
Box Office Treasurer
   Marc Roland   313-872-1113

Outside Ticket Agency
Computerized
   Ticketmaster   248-645-6666

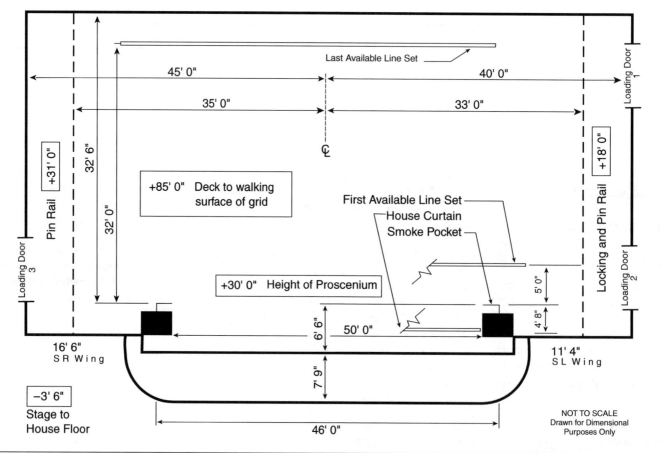

+85' 0"   Deck to walking surface of grid

+30' 0"   Height of Proscenium

Last Available Line Set

First Available Line Set
House Curtain
Smoke Pocket

45' 0"   40' 0"
35' 0"   33' 0"

+31' 0" Pin Rail
+18' 0" Locking and Pin Rail

32' 6"
32' 0"

Loading Door 3
Loading Door 1
Loading Door 2

5' 0"
4' 8"

6' 6"
50' 0"
7' 9"
46' 0"

16' 6" SR Wing
11' 4" SL Wing

−3' 6"
Stage to House Floor

NOT TO SCALE
Drawn for Dimensional
Purposes Only

STAGE HOUSE

HOUSE CURTAIN
Operates as a guillotine from SL fly floor or deck

RIGGING SYSTEM
Type:	Single purchase counter weight
Weight:	24,000 lbs available
Line sets:	63 sets at 6" o.c. with 5 lift lines per set
Arbors:	600 lb capacity; 1 ton motor for arbors
House Pipes:	55'6" long with 71'0" of travel from deck

Line sets are moveable
Block & Falls are available
Chain hoists are not available
(200) spot wheels and 12,000' of hemp available

PERMANENT INSTALLATIONS OVER STAGE (FROM SMOKE POCKET)
None

PERMANENT INSTALLATIONS ON DECK
Trap (1) in stage floor 6'7" x 6'0" located DS, edge is 10'0" US
Jump (2) SL & SR fly floor, full depth of stage
Loading bridge (1) 3'6" width above floor, full depth of stage
Adjustable portal (1) 10' x 28' velour legs, on hemp set

ORCHESTRA PIT
Nonadjustable at 7' below stage level
Apron overhangs US wall of pit 3'6"

BACKSTAGE

LOADING DOCK
Loading door(s):
  1) 9'6" high x 8'0" wide
  2) 9'0" high x 8'0" wide
  3) 8'0" high x 8'0" wide
Trucks load (2) at same time
Stage is at street level
Fork lift is required; Supplier - Brockman (313) 584-4550
Sound/Props cannot load in FOH
Trailers cannot store on-site
Security at dock

WARDROBE
Location: Basement under stage
Access: SR/SL stairs and elevator SL
(2) Washers (2) Dryers
No washer or dryer hookups

DRESSING ROOMS
(3) Star, SL,+1, t/s included, phone jack
(12) Small, SL, +2/+3/+4, t/s on same fl, phone jack
(1) Chorus, -1, t/s on same fl
Elevator access for dressing rooms
Additional production office available for company mgr

SOUND

CONSOLE
No house console

SPEAKERS
House Cluster
Proscenium
No speaker truss
Max available load 750 lbs

COMMUNICATIONS
No intercom system
Infrared sound system
Dressing room page system

ROAD CONSOLE
Located Rear House
(12) seats required to be removed
Cable run from stage is 200'
Tie-in into house system

REHEARSAL & STORAGE SPACE
Rehearsal: None
Storage: None

ELECTRICS

ROAD SERVICE POWER

Panel	Phase	Amp	Circuit Protection	Use	Location
A-D	3	400	breaker	dimmers	Off SL
E	3	200	breaker	extra	Off SR

Sound power SR smoke pocket 200 amps 3 phase
Recommended location of touring dimmer racks: Off SL
Hoist not required

FRONT OF HOUSE (BOX BOOM VALUES ARE PER SIDE)

Position	Pipe Width	Distance to Prosc.	House Circuits	Connector Type	FOH Transfer Circuits
Rail	50'	70'	32	ungrd 20 amp stage pin	32
Ceiling Cove	50'	70'	20	ungrd 20 amp stage pin	20
Box Boom1	50'	10'	6	ungrd 20 amp stage pin	6
Box Boom2	50'	30'	6	ungrd 20 amp stage pin	6
Pro Boom 1			6	ungrd 20 amp stage pin	6
Pro Boom 2			6	ungrd 20 amp stage pin	6

Transfer circuits: ungrd 20 amp stage pin

EQUIPMENT FOH (BOX BOOM VALUES ARE PER SIDE)
None

FOLLOWSPOTS
House Followspots:
  (3) Strong Carbon Supers; removeable

Followspot Booth:
  (3) spots per booth;
  143' throw to proscenium;
  (4) 1Ø 30 amp breakers

DIMMERS
No lighting console
No DMX control system

FOX THEATRE

YEAR BUILT: 1928   **YEAR RENOVATED: 1988**

Theatre Location: 2211 Woodward Avenue, Detroit, MI 48201
Management Company: Olympia Entertainment, Inc. (address as above)

Main Administrative Phone:	313-596-3200
Main Administrative Fax:	313-596-3220
Stage Door Phone:	313-596-3240
Backstage Pay Phone:	313-964-7578
Traveling Production Office Phone:	313-596-3230
Traveling Production Office Fax:	313-596-3231

THEATRE STAFF

General Manager	Allan C. Vella	313-596-3205
Booking	Greg Young	313-596-3258
Marketing	Bill Lee	313-596-3286
Operations	Greg Bellamy	313-596-3212
Group Sales	Scott Myers	313-965-3395

HOUSE CREW

Technical Director	Randy Mauck	313-596-3232
Carpentry	Phil Kennedy	313-596-3233
Electrics	Brian Boucher	313-596-3238
Sound	Steve Iyvani	313-596-3237
Props	Frank Beesley	313-596-3233

UNIONS

IATSE Local #38	Tim Magee	313-368-0825
Wardrobe Local #786	Beverly Llombard	313-771-3870
AFM Local #5	Johnny Trudell	313-538-5257

SEATING CAPACITY

Main Floor	2,871
Mezzanine	370
Galleries	1,438
Total:	**4,679**
pit (add'l)	152
wheelchair (add'l)	29

BOX OFFICE
Computerized
Box Office Manager
  Jose Martinez   313-596-3280

Outside Ticket Agency
Computerized
Ticketmaster
  Jerry Schmidt   248-433-0000

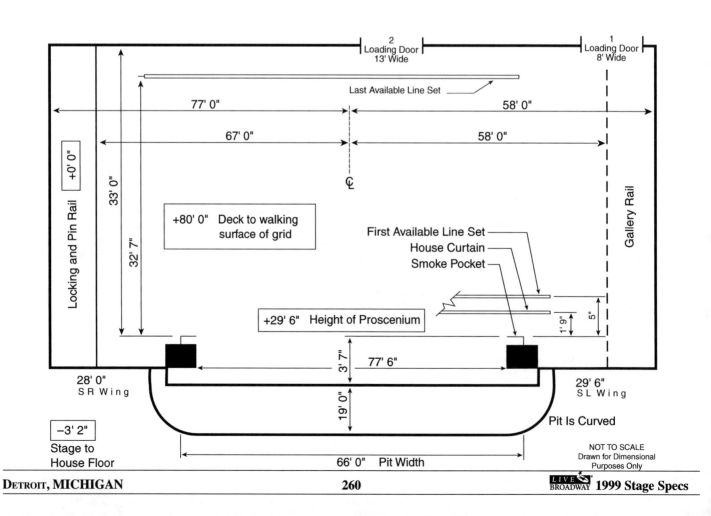

STAGE HOUSE

HOUSE CURTAIN
Operates as a traveller from SR deck
Can fly, but it tends to hang up

RIGGING SYSTEM
Type: Single purchase counter weight
Weight: 10,000 lbs available
Line sets: 51 sets at 6" o.c. with 7 lift lines per set
Arbors: 1,500 lb capacity
House Pipes: 86' long with 77' of travel from deck
Line sets are moveable
Block & Falls are not available
Chain hoists are not available
(100) spot wheels and 3,000' of hemp available

PERMANENT INSTALLATIONS OVER STAGE (FROM SMOKE POCKET)
M=Moveable with advance call
(1) Movie screen at 3'9"
(1) Traveller at 1'0"
(1) Cyclorama; M
Fire curtain (1) at 0'0" to 0'9"

PERMANENT INSTALLATIONS ON DECK
Stairs (1), 8'0" x 12'0", USR corner
Radiators (4), on back wall
Loading bridge (1), 24'0" x 4'0", SR wall + 70'0"
Adjustable proscenium (1), between 22'0" & 29'6", 2'0"
down of fire curtain

ORCHESTRA PIT
Adjustable to 12' below stage level by electric motor
turnscrew
Apron overhangs US wall of pit 0'3"
Pit lift is in (1) section
Pit has organ lift USC

BACKSTAGE

LOADING DOCK
Loading door(s):
1) 13'0" high x 8'0" wide
2) 20'0" high x 13'0" wide
Trucks load (3-5) at same time
Ramp or fork from street level;
in loading door and down 18'
ramp into shed; two doors
from shed to stage
Fork lift is not required but
house can arrange
Sound/Props can load in FOH
Lobby can be a work area
(3) Trailers can store on-site
Security at dock & stage door

WARDROBE
Location: Basement SL
Access: Elevator
(2) Washers (2) Dryers
Washer and dryer hookups
available

DRESSING ROOMS
(1) Star suite, SL, +2, t/s
included, phone jack
(2) Star, SL, +3, t/s included,
phone jack
(12) Small, SL, +4/+5/+6, t/s
included, phone jack
Elevator access for dressing
rooms
Additional production office
available for company mgr

SOUND

CONSOLE
House console exists; Mix in
house
40 inputs, 8 main outputs,
8 matrix outputs, 8 aux
outputs

SPEAKERS
House Cluster
Proscenium
Portable, wherever needed
No speaker truss

COMMUNICATIONS
Clear Com intercom with
(2) channels
Radio listening device
Dressing room page system

ROAD CONSOLE
Located HL off center aisle
Number of seats required to
be removed varies
Cable run from stage is 175'
Tie-in into house system with
XLR connectors

REHEARSAL & STORAGE SPACE
Rehearsal: Several rooms can
be used for orchestra
rehearsals
Storage: Shed, 40' x 60',
behind stage, not always
available

ELECTRICS

ROAD SERVICE POWER

Panel	Phase	Amp	Circuit Protection	Use	Location
A	3	600	fuse	dimmers	USR
B	3	400	fuse	dimmers	USR
C-D	3	600	fuse	dimmers/extra	DSR
E	3	200	fuse	sound	DSR/DSL
F	3	60	fuse	motors	DR
G	3	100	fuse	extra	UL
G	3	100	fuse	spot/projector	spot booth

Recommended location of touring dimmer racks: SR
Hoist is provided

FRONT OF HOUSE (BOX BOOM VALUES ARE PER SIDE)

Position	Pipe Width	Distance to Prosc.	House Circuits	Connector Type	FOH Transfer Circuits
1st Balc Rail	60'	75'	28	grd 20 amp stage pin	30
Box Boom 1	6'	90'	18	grd 20 amp stage pin	18

Transfer circuits: grd 20 amp stage pin
Road truss: Several front truss configurations can be accomodated using existing holes;
No new holes can be made due to decorative plaster

EQUIPMENT FOH (BOX BOOM VALUES ARE PER SIDE)

Position	Quantity	Wattage	Instrument	Removeable
1st Balc Rail	40	575	Source 4 19°	yes
Box Boom 1	30	1,000	Altman 10°	yes

FOLLOWSPOTS
House Followspots:
(3) Strong Xenon Super
Troupers 2k; removeable

Followspot Booth:
(3) spots per booth;
165' throw to proscenium;
(4) 3Ø 30 amp breakers

DIMMERS
Lighting console is Strand
Light board 'M';
(192) CD-80 dimmers
House has programmable
DMX control system
(1) dry run DMX station(s)

MASONIC TEMPLE THEATRE

YEAR BUILT: 1922

Theatre Location: Second Blvd at Temple Avenue, Detroit, MI 48201
Mailing Address: 500 Temple Avenue, Detroit, MI 48201
Management Company: Nedmas, Inc,
A Nederlander Company

Main Administrative Phone: 313-832-5900
Main Administrative Fax: 313-832-1047
Website: www.nederlanderdetroit.com
Stage Door Phone: 313-832-6677

THEATRE STAFF
Dir Theater Oper. Alan N. Lichtenstein 313-832-5900
Booking Alan N. Lichtenstein 313-832-5900

HOUSE CREW
Stage Manager William Kozemchick 313-832-6677
Electrics Dave Brock 313-832-6677
Props Tom Brock 313-832-6677

UNIONS
IATSE Local #38 Tim McGee 313-368-0825
Wardrobe Bev Lombard

SEATING CAPACITY
Main Floor/Front Balcony 3,518
Rear Balcony 886
Total: **4,404**

pit (add'l) 40

BOX OFFICE
Computerized
Box Office Manager
Jim Phelan 313-832-2232

Outside Ticket Agency
Ticketmaster 248-645-6666

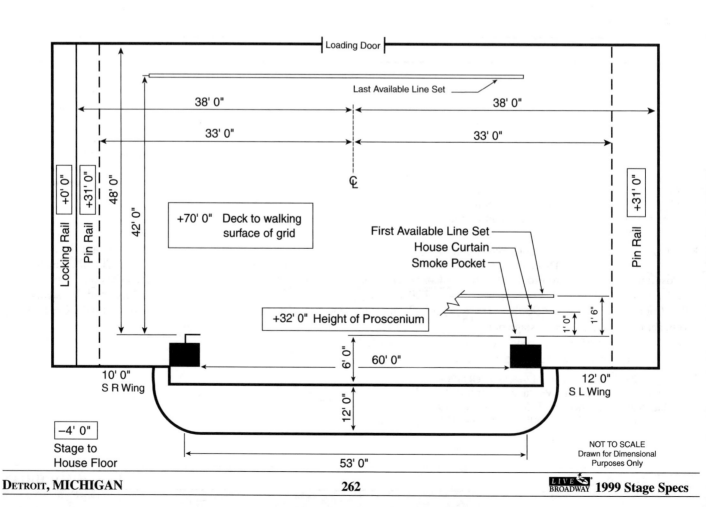

STAGE HOUSE

HOUSE CURTAIN
Operates as a guillotine from SR deck

RIGGING SYSTEM
Type:	Single purchase counter weight
Weight:	77,000 lbs available
Line sets:	94 sets at 6" o.c. with 5 lift lines per set
Arbors:	1,400 lb capacity
House Pipes:	61' long with 68' of travel from deck

Line sets are moveable
Block & Falls are not available
Chain hoists are not available
(80) spot wheels and 1,000' of hemp available

PERMANENT INSTALLATIONS OVER STAGE (FROM SMOKE POCKET)
None

PERMANENT INSTALLATIONS ON DECK
None

ORCHESTRA PIT
Nonadjustable at 7' below stage level
Apron overhangs US wall of pit 3'0"
Pit lift is in (1) section

BACKSTAGE

LOADING DOCK
Loading door(s):
 9'0 high x 10'0 wide
Trucks load (1) at same time
Dock is at truck level

WARDROBE
Location: SL on 2nd fl - green room
Access: Freight elevator
(2) Washers (2) Dryers
No washer or dryer hookups

DRESSING ROOMS
(2) Star, SL, stage level, t/s included
(15) Small, SR, +1/+2/+3/+4, t/s on same fl
(2) Small, SL, +1/+2, t/s on same fl
(2) Chorus, SL, +2, t/s on same fl

SOUND

CONSOLE
Altec, located Center House
24 inputs, 8 main outputs

SPEAKERS
None

COMMUNICATIONS
No intercom system
Radio frequency hearing impaired system

ROAD CONSOLE
Located Rear House
(15) seats required to be removed
Cable run from stage is 200'
 Tie-in into house system with XLR connectors

REHEARSAL & STORAGE SPACE
Rehearsal: 150' x 100', 5th floor
Storage: 70' x 50', boiler room

ELECTRICS

ROAD SERVICE POWER

Panel	Phase	Amp	Circuit Protection	Use	Location
A-C	3	400	fuse	dimmers	USR back wall
D	3	200	fuse	sound	DSL side wall
E	3	200	fuse	extra	USL jump
F	3	400	fuse	extra	USL jump

Recommended location of touring dimmer racks: SR on jump
Hoist required but not provided

FRONT OF HOUSE (BOX BOOM VALUES ARE PER SIDE)

Position	Pipe Width	Distance to Prosc.	House Circuits	Connector Type	FOH Transfer Circuits
1st Balc Rail	45'	95	24	grd 20 amp stage pin	24
Box Boom 1		20	0		0

Transfer circuits: grd 20 amp stage pin located SR on jump
Road truss: Holes in ceiling over house provide additional hanging positions

EQUIPMENT FOH (BOX BOOM VALUES ARE PER SIDE)
None

FOLLOWSPOTS
House Followspots:
 (4) Carbon arc Super Troupers; removeable

Followspot Booth:
 (3) spots per booth;
 110' throw to proscenium;
 (4) 1Ø 20 amp breakers

DIMMERS
No lighting console
No dimmers

MUSIC HALL CENTER FOR THE PERFORMING ARTS

Theatre Location: 350 Madison Avenue, Detroit, MI 48226

Main Administrative Phone: 313-963-7622
Main Administrative Fax: 313-963-2462
Stage Door Phone: 313-962-4255

THEATRE STAFF
President & COO   Margaret A. Tallet   313-962-4301
Booking   Karen Wright   313-962-4304

HOUSE CREW
Carpentry   Jack P. Brock   313-962-4254
Electrics   Thomas Bryant   313-962-4254

SEATING CAPACITY

Orchestra	749
Mezzanine	576
Balcony	336
Total:	**1,706**

STAGE DIMENSIONS (FROM SMOKE POCKET)
Width from Center Line to SL is 30'0"
Width from Center Line to SR is 31'0"
Proscenium width is 41'9"
Proscenium height is 80'0"
Smoke pocket to apron edge is 4'0"
Orchestra pit exists

LOADING DOCK
Loading door(s) are 10'0" high x 8'0" wide
Trucks load (1) at same time
Dock is at truck level

ELECTRICS
Total power available:
  (3) 400A 3Ø USL back wall
  (1) 200A 3Ø SL basement

FOLLOWSPOTS
House Followspots:
  Strong Super Trouper
Power in spot booth 200A 1Ø

DIMMERS
No house dimmers

SOUND
FOH mixing position in
  Rear House
Sound console is available

WHARTON CENTER FOR PERFORMING ARTS

AT: MICHIGAN STATE UNIVERSITY   **YEAR BUILT: 1982**

Theatre Location: Michigan State University, East Lansing, MI 48824

Main Administrative Phone:	517-353-1982
Main Administrative Fax:	517-353-5329
E-mail:	wrightw@pilot.msu.edu
Website:	web.msu.edu/wharton
Stage Door Phone:	517-353-1982 x110
Traveling Production Office Phone:	517-353-9776

THEATRE STAFF

Executive Director	William Wright	517-353-1982
Booking	William Wright	517-353-1982
Marketing	Kevin Shaw	517-353-1982
Group Sales	Lori Lancour	517-353-1982

HOUSE CREW

Technical Director	Richard French	517-353-1982
Stage Manager	Leonard Sklar	517-353-1982

SEATING CAPACITY

Orchestra	1,626
Balcony	755
Total:	**2,381**
pit (add'l)	119

BOX OFFICE

Computerized	517-355-6686

Outside Ticket Agency
None

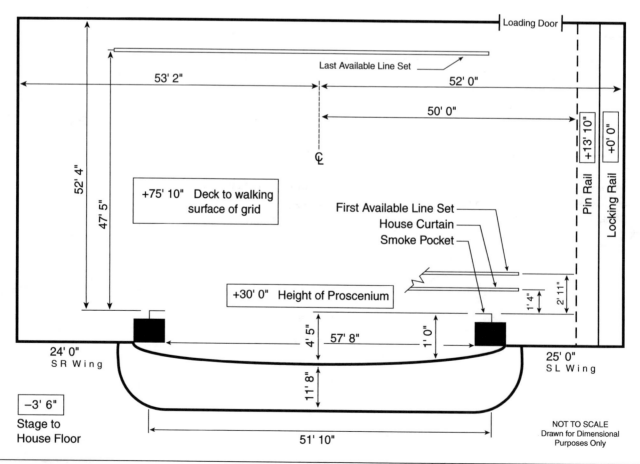

+75' 10" Deck to walking surface of grid

+30' 0" Height of Proscenium

53' 2"   52' 0"

50' 0"

52' 4"

47' 5"

First Available Line Set
House Curtain
Smoke Pocket

Last Available Line Set

Loading Door

Pin Rail +13' 10"

Locking Rail +0' 0"

1' 4"   2' 11"

4' 5"   57' 8"   1' 0"

24' 0"
S R Wing

25' 0"
S L Wing

11' 8"

−3' 6"
Stage to
House Floor

51' 10"

NOT TO SCALE
Drawn for Dimensional
Purposes Only

STAGE HOUSE

HOUSE CURTAIN
Operates as a guillotine or traveller from SL deck
Motorized when operated as a guillotine

RIGGING SYSTEM
Type:	Single purchase counter weight
Weight:	25,000 lbs available
Line sets:	59 sets at 8" o.c. with 9 lift lines per set
Arbors:	1,500 lb capacity
House Pipes:	84' long with 73' of travel from deck

Line sets are not moveable
(15) spot wheels and 3,000' of hemp available

PERMANENT INSTALLATIONS OVER STAGE (FROM SMOKE POCKET)
Electric raceways (5) at 2'11",8'0",19'5",31'5",40'0"
Orchestra shell (1) at 4'9"
Movie screen (1) at 13'5"

PERMANENT INSTALLATIONS ON DECK
None

ORCHESTRA PIT
Adjustable to 11' below stage level by hydraulic lift
Apron overhangs US wall of pit 0'0"
Pit lift is in (2) sections

BACKSTAGE

LOADING DOCK
Loading door(s):
9'10" high x 9'10" wide
Trucks load (3) at same time, side by side
Dock is at truck level
Fork lift is not required
Sound/Props cannot load in FOH
Trailers can store on-site
Security at dock & stage door

WARDROBE
Location: Laundry Room SR on 2nd floor
Access: Freight elevator
(1) Washer (1) Dryer

DRESSING ROOMS
(3) Star, stage level, SR, t/s included, phone jack
(5) Small, SR, 2nd fl, t/s included, phone jack
(10) Chorus, SR, 2nd fl, t/s included, phone jack

SOUND

CONSOLE
Yamaha PM 1,000
24 inputs, 4 outputs

SPEAKERS
House Cluster
Under Balcony
No speaker truss

COMMUNICATIONS
Clear Com intercom with
(1) channel
FM hearing augmentation
Dressing room page system

ROAD CONSOLE
Located Rear HL
(12) seats required to be removed
Cable run from stage is 85'
Tie-in into house system with XLR connectors

REHEARSAL & STORAGE SPACE
Rehearsal: 34'x 68' on 3rd floor; piano available
Storage: None

ELECTRICS

ROAD SERVICE POWER

Panel	Phase	Amp	Circuit Protection	Use	Location
A	3	600	fuse	dimmers	USR side wall
B	3	200	fuse	sound	USR back wall

Recommended location of touring dimmer racks: USR on deck
Hoist not required

FRONT OF HOUSE (BOX BOOM VALUES ARE PER SIDE)

Position	Pipe Width	Distance to Prosc.	House Circuits	Connector Type	FOH Transfer Circuits
1st Cove	60'	67'	28	grd 20 amp stage pin	28
2nd Cove	98'	35'	48	grd 20 amp stage pin	48
Box Boom 1		75'	18	grd 20 amp stage pin	18

Transfer circuits: grd 20 amp stage pin located on USR wall

EQUIPMENT FOH (BOX BOOM VALUES ARE PER SIDE)
None

FOLLOWSPOTS
House Followspots:
(2) Xenon Super Troupers; removeable

Followspot Booth:
(6) spots per booth;
135' throw to proscenium;
(3) 1Ø 30 amp breakers

DIMMERS
Lighting console is ETC Expression;
(319) ETC dimmers
House has programmable DMX control system

DEVOS HALL

AT: GRAND CENTER

Theatre Location: 245 Monroe Avenue NW, Grand Rapids, MI 49503
Management Company: City of Grand Rapids

Main Administrative Phone: 616-456-3922
Main Administrative Fax: 616-456-3995

THEATRE STAFF
Operations Manager   Tim Male   616-742-6505
Operations Director   Jim Watt   616-742-6188
Booking   Lynne Ike   616-742-6504
Marketing   Kevin Scheibler 616-742-6500
Group Sales   Brent Garvin   616-742-6503

HOUSE CREW
Stage Manager   Sandy Thomley   616-742-6508 / Fax 616-742-6590
Carpentry   Dick Claypool
Electrics   Matt Taylor
Sound   Don Stover

UNIONS
IATSE Local #26   Michael David   616-742-5526

SEATING CAPACITY	
Orchestra	808
Loge	102
Mezzanine	865
Dress Circle	71
Balcony	524
Total:	**2,370**
pit (add'l)	76

BOX OFFICE
Box Office
  Leslie Tiff   616-742-6520

Outside Ticket Agency
  Ticketmaster   616-456-3333

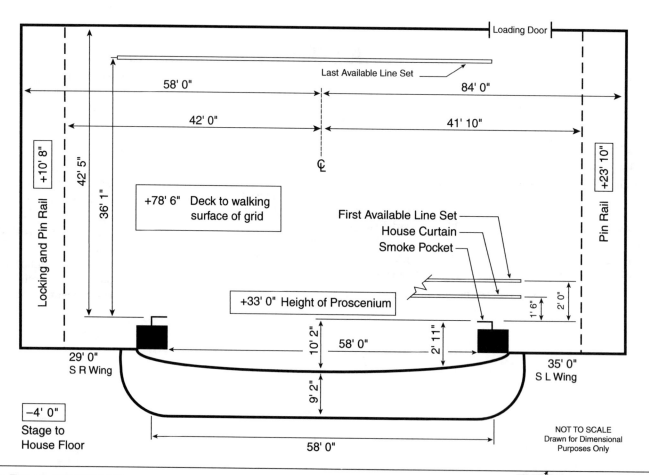

NOT TO SCALE
Drawn for Dimensional
Purposes Only

STAGE HOUSE

HOUSE CURTAIN
Operates as a guillotine from SR fly floor
Operates as a traveller from SR deck

RIGGING SYSTEM
Type:	Double purchase counter weight
Weight:	42,000 lbs available
Line sets:	40 sets at 8" o.c. with 5 lift lines per set
Arbors:	1,800 lb capacity
House Pipes:	62' long with 72' of travel from deck

Line sets are moveable
(65) spot wheels and 13,000' of hemp available

PERMANENT INSTALLATIONS OVER STAGE (FROM SMOKE POCKET)
Orchestra shell (1) at 6'0" (24" wide)
Electric bridge (2) at 4'2", 29'9" (24") wide

PERMANENT INSTALLATIONS ON DECK
Orchestra shell store on back wall 5'6" deep
Air conditioning duct (1) at 3'0" square on back wall located 30'0" SR of center

ORCHESTRA PIT
Adjustable to 9' below stage level by electric motor turnscrew
Apron overhangs US wall of pit 12'9"

BACKSTAGE

LOADING DOCK
Loading door(s):
   14'0" high x 20'0" wide
Trucks load (2) side by side at same time
Dock is at truck level; loading to stage thru separate scene shop behind stage
Fork lift is required

WARDROBE
Location: Basement
Access: Orchestra pit elevator
(2) Washers (2) Dryers
Washer and dryer hookups available

DRESSING ROOMS
(3) Star, SR, stage level, t/s included, phone jack
(4) Small, SR, 2nd fl, t/s included, phone jack
(3) Chorus, SR, basement, t/s included, phone jack

SOUND

CONSOLE
Yamaha 916
16 inputs, 6 main outputs

SPEAKERS
House Cluster
Proscenium
Under Balcony

COMMUNICATIONS
Clear Com intercom with
   (2) channels
Infrared sound system
Dressing room page system

ROAD CONSOLE
Located Rear House
(15) seats required to be removed
Cable run from stage is 200'
Tie-in into house system with XLR connectors

REHEARSAL & STORAGE SPACE
Rehearsal: 32' x 48' located USL on stage level, piano available
Storage: None

ELECTRICS

ROAD SERVICE POWER

Panel	Phase	Amp	Circuit Protection	Use	Location
A	3	500	breaker	dimmers	DSL proscenium wall
B	3	200	fuse	sound	USC back wall
C	3	100	breaker	extra	DSR

Panel B service is a portable transformer
Recommended location of touring dimmer racks: SL on deck
Hoist not required

FRONT OF HOUSE (BOX BOOM VALUES ARE PER SIDE)

Position	Pipe Width	Distance to Prosc.	House Circuits	Connector Type	FOH Transfer Circuits
1st Cove	60'	55'	32	grd 20 amp stage pin	32
Box Boom 1		50'	12	grd 20 amp stage pin	12

Transfer circuits: grd 20 amp stage pin located onn DSL proscenium wall

EQUIPMENT FOH (BOX BOOM VALUES ARE PER SIDE)

Position	Quantity	Wattage	Instrument	Removeable
1st Cove	10	1,000	10 x 23 Lekos	yes
Box Boom 1	34	1,000	8 x 13 Lekos	yes

FOLLOWSPOTS
House Followspots:
   (2) Xenon Super Troupers ; removeable
   (2) Xenon Troupers; removeable

Followspot Booth:
   (2) spots per booth;
   134' throw to proscenium;
   (4) 1Ø 30 amp breakers

DIMMERS
Lighting console is ETC Expression;
   (192) ETC dimmers
No DMX control system

JAMES W. MILLER AUDITORIUM

AT: WESTERN MICHIGAN UNIVERSITY   **YEAR BUILT: 1968**

Theatre Location: Western Michigan University, Kalamazoo, MI 49008

Main Administrative Phone:	616-387-2311
Main Administrative Fax:	616-387-2317
E-mail:	richard.snyder@wmich.edu
	mark.evert@wmich.edu
Website:	www.wmich.edu/miller
Stage Door Phone:	616-387-2318
Backstage Pay Phone:	616-385-9243
Traveling Production Office Phone:	616-387-2321
Traveling Production Office Fax:	616-387-2348

THEATRE STAFF

Director	Richard Snyder	616-387-2313
Booking	Richard Snyder	616-387-2313
Marketing	Khia Guidinger	616-387-8085
Operations	Elaine Williams	616-387-2315
Group Sales	Corina Jensen	616-387-2299

HOUSE CREW

Technical Director	Mark Evert	616-387-2316/ Fax 616-387-2559
Carpentry	Guy Barks	616-387-2307
Electrics	Jon Flegel	616-387-2371
Sound	David Clemens	616-387-2319

SEATING CAPACITY

Orchestra	1,385
Grand Tier	1,213
Balcony	899
Total:	**3,497**
pit (add'l)	80
wheelchair (incl)	10

BOX OFFICE

Computerized
Ticket Office Manger
 Mimi Asefa   616-387-2309

Outside Ticket Agency
Computerized
TicketsPlus
 Steve Demots   616-222-4115

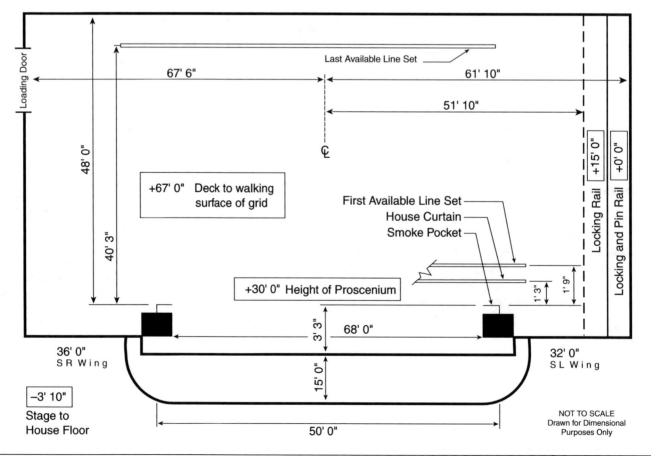

STAGE HOUSE

HOUSE CURTAIN

Operates as a traveller from SL deck; variable speed motorized

RIGGING SYSTEM

Type:	Single purchase counter weight
Weight:	50,000 lbs available
Line sets:	51 sets at 8" o.c. with 8 lift lines per set
Arbors:	2,000 lb capacity
House Pipes:	84' long with 66' of travel from deck

Block & Falls are available

(50) spot wheels and 2,000' of hemp available

PERMANENT INSTALLATIONS OVER STAGE (FROM SMOKE POCKET)

Orchestra shells (4) at 6'2", 14'8", 21'8", 29'9"

Electric Raceways (7) at 4'0", 6'6", 11'1", 17'11", 26'2", 31'6", 33'11"; have full travel

Movie screen (1) at 9'2"

Traveller (1) at 7'3"

Fire curtain (1) at 0'0"

PERMANENT INSTALLATIONS ON DECK

Jump (1) above locking rail 15' high x 10' wide x 50' long, starts at smoke pocket

Orchestra shell storage (3) at US winches, US last 5' center and right

Loading bridge (1) 10' x 50'

ORCHESTRA PIT

Adjustable to 13' below stage level by hydraulic lift

Apron overhangs US wall of pit 0'0"

Pit lift is in (1) section

First two rows of seats removable to extend pit area another 10'; this portion is not adjustable in respect to elevation

BACKSTAGE

LOADING DOCK

Loading door(s):
15'9" high x 12'0" wide

Trucks load (2) at same time

Fork lift is not required

Sound/Props can load in FOH

Lobby can be a work area

(1) Trailer can store on-site

Security at stage door

WARDROBE

Location: SL Green Room on stage level

Access: Direct from stage

(2) Washers (2) Dryers

Washer and dryer hookups available

DRESSING ROOMS

(2) Star, SL, stage level, t/s included

(4) Small, SL, stage level, t/s included

(2) Chorus, SL or SR, stage level, t/s included, phone jack

Additional production office available for company mgr

REHEARSAL & STORAGE SPACE

Rehearsal: (2) large rooms but not true rehearsal areas

Storage: Musicians Room, 800 sq ft., in basement, orchestra lift access, equipment available

SOUND

CONSOLE

Quantum 26, located Rear House

26 inputs, 2 main outputs, matrix outputs, 4 aux outputs

SPEAKERS

House Cluster

Under Balcony

Balcony Fill

Under Balcony Fill

Dressing Room Page

No speaker truss

Rigging to grid only, no house positions

COMMUNICATIONS

Technical Proj. intercom with (2) channels

Dressing room page system

ROAD CONSOLE

Located Rear Orchestra, 2 areas left/ right of center

No seats required to be removed

Cable run from stage is 100'

Tie in into house system with XLR connectors

ELECTRICS

ROAD SERVICE POWER

Panel	Phase	Amp	Circuit Protection	Use	Location
A	3	1600	fuse	dimmers	DR corner
B	3	400	fuse	dimmers	DR w parallel DL proscenium
C	3	200	fuse	sound	DR proscenium
D	3	125	fuse	extra	UR of center rear wall

Recommended location of touring dimmer racks: SR

Hoist not required

Additional power is available for tour buses, generators, etc.

FRONT OF HOUSE (BOX BOOM VALUES ARE PER SIDE)

Position	Pipe Width	Distance to Prosc.	House Circuits	Connector Type	FOH Transfer Circuits
1st Cove	69'	50'	25	grd 20 amp stage pin	
2nd Cove	150'	75'	38	grd 20 amp stage pin	
Box Boom 1	2'6"	45'	12	grd 20 amp stage pin	
Box Boom 2	2'6"	45'	12	grd 20 amp stage pin	

Transfer circuits: Break out connectors or DMX; 24 additional circuits are available to coves from curtain warmer position 25' from 1st Cove and 50' from 2nd Cove

Road truss: No Front or House Truss points

EQUIPMENT FOH (BOX BOOM VALUES ARE PER SIDE)

Position	Quantity	Wattage	Instrument	Removeable
1st Cove	72	1,000	40 - 20 / 6 - 10	yes
2nd Cove	46	1,000	48 - 16 / 24 -10	yes
Box Boom 1	32	1,000	16	yes

FOLLOWSPOTS

House Followspots:
(3) Super Trouper Carbon
(2) Super Trouper Xenon Conversion

Followspot Booth:
(6) spots per booth;
150' throw to proscenium;
(8) 120/ 240 watt, 25A / 30A breakers

DIMMERS

House console is Strand LP 90; 475 Strand CD 80AE dimmers

House has programmable DMX control system

(1) dry run DMX station

DULUTH ENTERTAINMENT CONVENTION CENTER

YEAR BUILT: 1966

Theatre Location: 350 Harbor Drive, Duluth, MN 55802

Main Administrative Phone:	218-722-5573
Main Administrative Fax:	218-722-4247
E-mail:	decc@decc.duluth.mn.us
Website:	www.decc.org
Stage Door Phone:	218-772-5573
Traveling Production Office Phone:	218-720-3258
Traveling Production Office Fax:	218-720-3316

THEATRE STAFF

Executive Director	Dan Russell	218-722-5573
Booking	Craig Samborski	218-722-5573
Marketing	Craig Samborski	218-722-5573

HOUSE CREW

Technical Svc Manager	Joe Tavnowski	218-722-5573

UNIONS

IATSE Local #32	Floyd Turcott	218-624-7203

SEATING CAPACITY

Orchestra	1556
Balcony	811
Total:	**2,367**
pit (add'l)	60

BOX OFFICE
Computerized
Box Office Manager
  Kay Bauers   218-722-5573 x137

Outside Ticket Agency
Computerized
Ticketmaster
  Kay Bauers   218-722-5573 x137

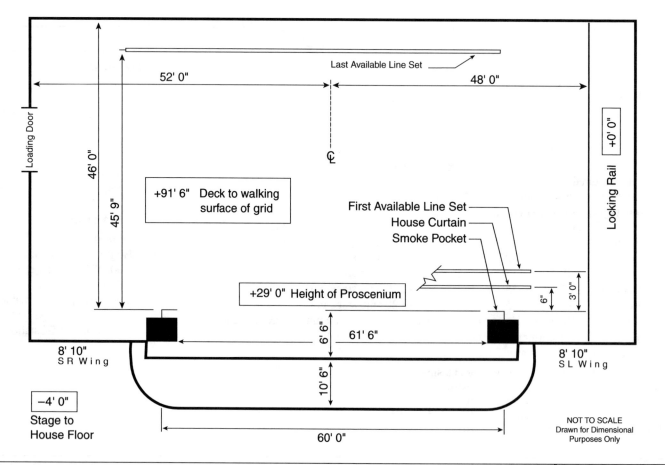

STAGE HOUSE

HOUSE CURTAIN
Operates as a guillotine or traveller from SL deck

RIGGING SYSTEM
Type: Single purchase counter weight
Weight: 18,000 lbs available
Line sets: 50 sets at 6-12" o.c. with 7 lift lines
                 per set
Arbors: 1,500 lb capacity
House Pipes: 70' long with 80' of travel from deck
Line sets are not moveable
3,000' of hemp available

PERMANENT INSTALLATIONS OVER STAGE (FROM SMOKE POCKET)
Electric borders (4) at 5'0",12'6",21'0",30'0"
Orchestra shells (4) at 7'6",16'0",26'0"33'0"

PERMANENT INSTALLATIONS ON DECK
None

ORCHESTRA PIT
Adjustable to 14' below stage level by hydraulic lift
Apron overhangs US wall of pit 0'0"
Pit lift is in (1) section

BACKSTAGE

LOADING DOCK
Loading door(s):
  9'0" high x 12'0" wide
Trucks load (2) side by side at
  same time
Dock is at truck level

WARDROBE
Location: Behind stage on stage
  level
Access: Direct from stage
No Washers No Dryers
Washer and dryer hookups
  available

DRESSING ROOMS
(3) Star, USR, stage level, t/s,
  (1) with phone jack
(2) Small, USL, stage level, t/s
(2) Chorus, behind stage on
  stage level, t/s
Use dressing room for company
  mgr office

SOUND

CONSOLE
Soundcraft
24 inputs, 12 main outputs

SPEAKERS
House Cluster
Proscenium
No speaker truss

COMMUNICATIONS
Clear Com intercom with
  (2) channels
Dressing room page system

ROAD CONSOLE
Located Rear House
No seats required to be
  removed
Cable run from stage is 100'
Tie-in into house system with
  XLR connectors

REHEARSAL & STORAGE SPACE
Rehearsal: 15' x 30' located
  USL on stage level
Storage: None

ELECTRICS

ROAD SERVICE POWER

Panel	Phase	Amp	Circuit Protection	Use	Location
A	3	600	fuse	dimmers	DSL proscenium wall

Recommended location of touring dimmer racks: SL on deck
Additional power is available for tour buses, generators, etc.

FRONT OF HOUSE (BOX BOOM VALUES ARE PER SIDE)

Position	Pipe Width	Distance to Prosc.	House Circuits	Connector Type	FOH Transfer Circuits
1st Balc Rail	85'	70'	16	grd 20 amp stage pin	16
1st Cove	85'	75'	24	grd 20 amp stage pin	24

Transfer circuits: grd 20 amp stage pin located on USL back wall

EQUIPMENT FOH (BOX BOOM VALUES ARE PER SIDE)
None

FOLLOWSPOTS
House Followspots:
  (2) Xenon Super Troupers;
  removeable

Followspot Booth:
  (2) spots per booth;
  170' throw to proscenium;
  1Ø 30 amp breakers

DIMMERS
Lighting console is Strand
  Light board "M";
  (52) Strand dimmers
House has programmable
  DMX control system

HISTORIC STATE THEATRE

YEAR BUILT: **1921**   YEAR RENOVATED: **1991**

Theatre Location: 805 Hennepin Ave., Minneapolis, MN 55403
Management Company: Historic Theatre Group, Ltd.

Main Administrative Phone: 612-373-5600
Main Administrative Fax: 612-339-4146
E-mail: htg@orpheum.com

THEATRE STAFF
General Manager   Fred Krohn   612-373-5600
Booking   Larry D. Kline   612-373-5605
Marketing   Lisa Krohn   612-373-5603
Group Sales   Gail Nelson   612-373-5673

HOUSE CREW
Operations Manager Mark Kroening   612-339-3863
Carpentry   Mike Ortenblad   612-373-5611
Electrics   Diane Galvin   612-373-5611
Sound   Steve Olson   612-373-5611
Props   Vince Fish   612-373-5611

UNIONS
IATSE Local #13   Matt Rice   612-379-7564
Wardrobe Local #781 Joy Oberg   612-426-3968
Music Local #3073   Steve Lund   612-595-2645

SEATING CAPACITY
Orchestra   1,294
Balcony-Loge   179
Second Balcony   411
Third Balcony   251
Total: **2,135**

pit (add'l)   30
wheelchair (add'l)   10

BOX OFFICE
Computerized
Box Office Manager
   Joe Duca   612-373-5637

Outside Ticket Agency
Computerized
   Ticketmaster   612-989-5151

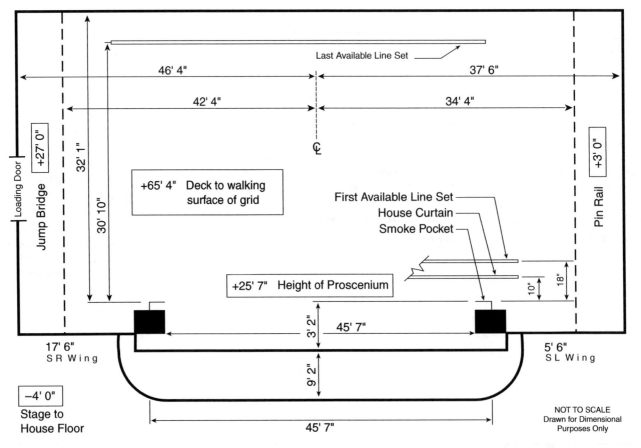

17' 6"
SR Wing

5' 6"
SL Wing

−4' 0"
Stage to
House Floor

NOT TO SCALE
Drawn for Dimensional
Purposes Only

STAGE HOUSE

House Curtain
Operates as a guillotine or traveller from SL deck

Rigging System
Type:	Single purchase counter weight
Weight:	40,000 lbs available
Line sets:	60 sets at 6" o.c. with 6 lift lines per set
Arbors:	1,500 lb capacity
House Pipes:	57' long with 63' of travel from deck

Line sets are not moveable
Block & Falls are not available
Chain hoists available as a rental; (3) one ton
(100) spot wheels and 7,500' of hemp available
10 permanent points in house

Permanent Installations Over Stage (from smoke pocket)
M=Moveable with advance call
Movie screen (1) at 7'0"; M

Permanent Installations On Deck
Stairs (3) lip of the stage free standing
Loading bridge, SL

Orchestra Pit
Adjustable to 8'0" below stage level by manual lift
Apron overhangs US wall of pit 10'3"
Pit lift is in (1) section

BACKSTAGE

Loading Dock
Loading door(s):
8'10" high x 6'9" wide
Trucks load (2) at same time
Dock on street level; elevator to basement door 7'4"; compartment size 8'1" x 5'4";
Fork lift is not required
Sound/Props cannot load in FOH
Trailers cannot store on-site
Security at stage door

Wardrobe
Location: Basement
Access: Stage door down elevator
(2) Washers (2) Dryers
No washer or dryer hookups

Dressing Rooms
(1) Star, SR, stage level, t/s included, phone jack
(2) Star, SR/SL, -1, t/s included, phone jack
(6) Small, -1, t/s on same fl
(2) Chorus, -1, t/s included
Elevator access for dressing rooms

SOUND

Console
(3) Yamaha PM 4000, located Rear House
64 inputs, 6 main outputs, 8 matrix outputs, 12 aux outputs

Speakers
House Cluster
Proscenium
Under Balcony
Portable
Positions available for speaker truss

Communications
Clear Com intercom with (2) channels
Infrared sound system
Dressing room page system

Road Console
Located Rear House left of center
No seats required to be removed
Cable run from stage is 250'
Tie-in into house system with XLR connectors

Rehearsal & Storage Space
Rehearsal: None
Storage: Commons, 1,420 sq ft, located in basement

ELECTRICS

Road Service Power

Panel	Phase	Amp	Circuit Protection	Use	Location
A	3	600	breaker	dimmers	USR
B	3	400	breaker	dimmers	DSR
C	3	200	breaker	sound	USL / USR
D	3	60	breaker	extra	DSR

Recommended location of touring dimmer racks: USR

Front Of House (box boom values are per side)

Position	Pipe Width	Distance to Prosc.	House Circuits	Connector Type	FOH Transfer Circuits
1st Cove	45'	59'	24	grd 20 amp stage pin	24
Box Boom 1		64'	12	grd 20 amp stage pin	12
Box Boom 2		70'	12	grd 20 amp stage pin	12
Box Boom 3		62'	12	grd 20 amp stage pin	12
Box Boom 4		67'	12	grd 20 amp stage pin	12

Transfer circuits: grd 20 amp stage pin

Equipment FOH (box boom values are per side)

Position	Quantity	Wattage	Instrument	Removeable
1st Cove	24	1,000	6 x 16 Leko	yes
Box Boom 1	24	1,000	6 x 22/6 x16 Leko	yes

Followspots
House Followspots:
(3) Strong Xenon Super Troupers; removeable

Followspot Booth:
(3) spots per booth;
124' throw to proscenium;
3Ø 60 amp breakers

Dimmers
Lighting console is ETC Expression;
(200) ETC dimmers
House has programmable DMX control system

ORPHEUM THEATRE

YEAR BUILT: **1921**   YEAR RENOVATED: **1993**

Theatre Location: 910 Hennepin Avenue, Minneapolis, MN 55403
Mailing Address: 805 Hennepin Avenue, Minneapolis, MN 55403
Management Company: Historic Theatre Group
                                     805 Hennepin Avenue, Minneapolis, MN 55403

Main Administrative Phone: 612-373-5600
Main Administrative Fax: 612-339-4146
E-mail: htg@orpheum.com
Website: www.orpheum.com
Backstage Pay Phone: 612-338-9534

THEATRE STAFF
General Manager   Fred Krohn   612-373-5600
Booking   Jess Ford   612-373-5605
Marketing   Lisa Krohn   612-373-5606
Group Sales   Gail Nelson   612-373-5673

HOUSE CREW
Operations Manager   David Marietta   612-338-5604
Carpentry   Mike Ortenblad   612-338-5604
Electrics   Tom Rost   612-338-5604
Sound   Spencer Washowski 612-338-5604
Props   Jean Harvath   612-338-5604

UNIONS
IATSE Local #13   Matt Rice   612-379-7564
Wardrobe Local #781   Joy Oberg   612-426-3968
Music Local #3073   Steve Lund   612-224-3122

SEATING CAPACITY
Main Floor (Orchestra)	1,499
First Balcony	249
Second Balcony	408
Third Balcony	324
Boxes	46
Total:	**2,526**
pit (add'l)	50
wheelchair (add'l)	42

BOX OFFICE
Computerized
Box Office Manager
  Joe Duca   612-373-5637

Outside Ticket Agency
Computerized
Ticketmaster   612-989-5151

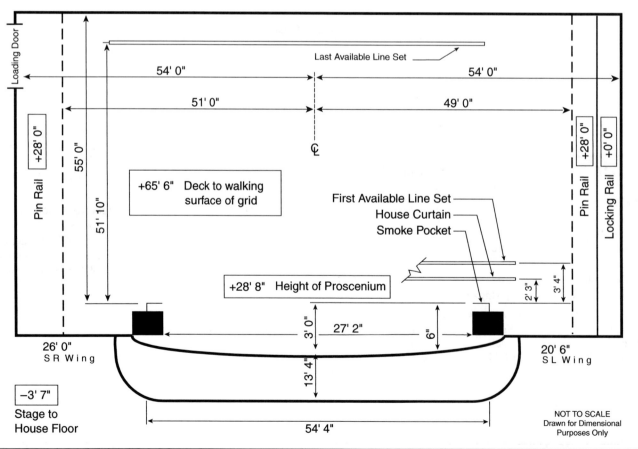

54' 0"   54' 0"

51' 0"   49' 0"

Last Available Line Set

₵

Loading Door

Pin Rail   +28' 0"

55' 0"

51' 10"

+65' 6"   Deck to walking surface of grid

First Available Line Set
House Curtain
Smoke Pocket

Pin Rail   +28' 0"

Locking Rail   +0' 0"

2' 3"   3' 4"

+28' 8"   Height of Proscenium

3' 0"   27' 2"   6"

26' 0"
SR Wing

13' 4"

20' 6"
SL Wing

−3' 7"
Stage to
House Floor

54' 4"

NOT TO SCALE
Drawn for Dimensional
Purposes Only

STAGE HOUSE

HOUSE CURTAIN
Operates as a guillotine or traveller from SL deck

RIGGING SYSTEM
Type:	Single purchase counter weight
Weight:	40,000 lbs available
Line sets:	96 sets at 6" o.c. with 7 lift lines per set
Arbors:	1,200 lb capacity
House Pipes:	70' long with 63' of travel from deck

Line sets are moveable
Block & Falls are not available
Chain hoists are available as a rental; (5) one ton
(200) spot wheels and 2,000' of hemp available

PERMANENT INSTALLATIONS OVER STAGE (FROM SMOKE POCKET)
Fire curtain (1) at 3'3"
Catwalk (1), Elevation 28', at SL-SR, Back Wall

PERMANENT INSTALLATIONS ON DECK
Loading bridge (1)

ORCHESTRA PIT
Adjustable to 9'2" below stage level by manual lift
Apron overhangs US wall of pit 5'8"
Pit lift is in (1) section

BACKSTAGE

LOADING DOCK
Loading door(s):
 7'10" high x 9'11" wide
Trucks load (2) at same time
Fork lift is not required
Sound/Props can load in FOH
Lobby can be a work area
(2) Trailers can store on-site
Security at stage door

WARDROBE
Location: Basement
Access: Freight Elevator
(2) Washers (2) Dryers
Washer and dryer hookups
 available

DRESSING ROOMS
(5) Star, SR, stage level, t/s
 included, phone jack
(4) Chorus, -1, t/s included
Elevator access for dressing
 rooms
Additional production office
 available for company mgr

SOUND

CONSOLE
Yamaha PM 1800
32 inputs, 4 main outputs,
 4 aux outputs

SPEAKERS
House Cluster
Under Balcony
Orchestra Level
No speaker truss
Max available load 1,200 lbs
Points available for rigging

COMMUNICATIONS
Clearcom intercom with
 (2) channels
FM hearing impaired system
Dressing room page system

ROAD CONSOLE
Located Center House
No seats required to be
 removed
Cable run from stage is 113'
Tie-in into house system with
 XLR connectors

REHEARSAL & STORAGE SPACE
Rehearsal: None
Storage: None

ELECTRICS

ROAD SERVICE POWER

Panel	Phase	Amp	Circuit Protection	Use	Location
A-D	3∅	400	fuse	dimmers	SR wall
E-F	3∅	400	fuse	dimmers	USR wall
G	3∅	200	fuse	sound	DSL
H	3∅	200	fuse	sound	DSR

Recommended location of touring dimmer racks: SR
Additional power is available for tour buses, generators, etc.

FRONT OF HOUSE (BOX BOOM VALUES ARE PER SIDE)

Position	Pipe Width	Distance to Prosc.	House Circuits	Connector Type	FOH Transfer Circuits
1st Balc Rail			24	grd 20 amp stage pin	24
1st Cove		150'	36	grd 20 amp stage pin	36
Box Boom 1			12	grd 20 amp stage pin	12
Box Boom 2			12	grd 20 amp stage pin	12

EQUIPMENT FOH (BOX BOOM VALUES ARE PER SIDE)
None

FOLLOWSPOTS
House Followspots:
 (3) Super Trouper 2k;
 removeable

Followspot Booth:
 (4) spots per booth;
 134' throw to proscenium;
 (4) 1∅ 30 amp breakers

DIMMERS
House console is Expression;
 (286) ETC dimmers
House has programmable
 DMX control system
(2) dry run DMX station(s)

SHELDON PERFORMING ARTS THEATRE

AKA: **T.B. SHELDON AUDITORIUM THEATRE**   YEAR BUILT: **1904** YEAR RENOVATED: **1989**

		SEATING CAPACITY	
Theatre Location:	Third Street at East Avenue, Red Wing, MN 55066	Orchestra	286
Mailing Address:	PO Box 34, Red Wing, MN 55066	Balcony	189
		Total:	**475**
Main Administrative Phone:	651-385-3667		
Main Administrative Fax:	651-385-3663	pit (add'l)	22
E-mail:	sheldon@pressenter.com	wheelchair (add'l)	6
		standing (add'l)	0

THEATRE STAFF

Executive Director	Sean Dowse	651-385-3664
Events Manager	Barbara Von Haaren	651-385-3662

HOUSE CREW

Technical Director	John Harlow	651-385-3662

STAGE DIMENSIONS (FROM SMOKE POCKET)
Stage is 33'4" deep
Width from Center Line to SL is 25'10"
Width from Center Line to SR is 29'5"
Proscenium width is 32'0"
Proscenium height is 15'0"
Smoke pocket to apron edge is 4'6"
Orchestra pit exists

RIGGING

Grid Height:	40'
Type:	Single purchase counter weight
Weight:	4,800 lbs
Line sets:	30 sets at 6" o.c.
Arbors:	1,000 lb capacity
House Pipes:	36' long

LOADING DOCK
Loading door(s) are 10'6"high x 5'10"wide
Trucks load (1) at a time
Fork lift is not required and is not available

ELECTRICS
Total power available:
  (3) 600A 3Ø

FOLLOWSPOTS
House Followspots:
  Ultra Arc
  Marc 300
Power in spot booth (3) 20A 1Ø

DIMMERS
(192) house dimmers
No DMX control system

SOUND
House has (2) 20A dedicated
  power located DSL
FOH mixing position in
  BalconyHouse Right
Sound console is available

THE FITZGERALD THEATER

FOMERLY: THE WORLD THEATRE

YEAR BUILT: 1910   YEAR RENOVATED: 1986

Theatre Location: 10 East Exchange Street, Saint Paul, MN 55101

Main Administrative Phone: 651-290-1200
Main Administrative Fax: 651-290-1195
E-mail: fitzgerald@mpr.org
Website: www.mpr.org/www/fitztheater
Traveling Production Office Phone: 651-290-1215

THEATRE STAFF
  Operations   Brian Sanderson   651-290-1229
HOUSE CREW
  Production Manager   Thomas Campbell   651-290-1215

SEATING CAPACITY
  Main   348
  1st Balcony   352
  2nd Balcony   254
  Box Seats   24
  Temporary Stack Chairs   30
  Total: **1,008**

  pit (add'l)   32
  wheelchair (add'l)   18
  standing (add'l)   14

BOX OFFICE
  Computerized
  Box Office Manager
    Katie Burger   651-290-1217

  Outside Ticket Agency
  Ticketmaster

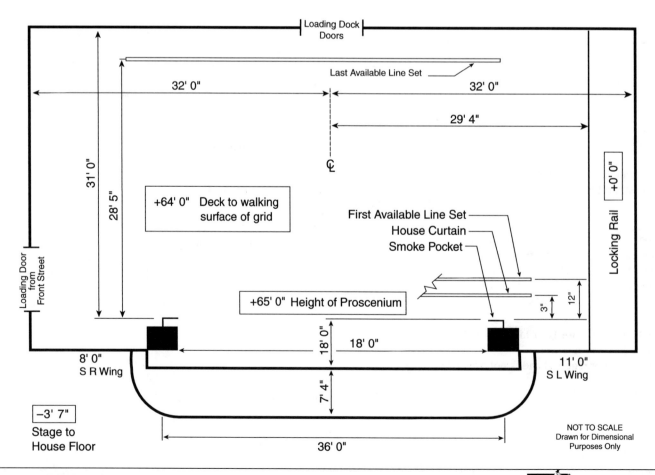

STAGE HOUSE

HOUSE CURTAIN
Operates as a guillotine or traveller from SL deck

RIGGING SYSTEM
Type:	Single purchase counter weight
Weight:	10,000 lbs available
Line sets:	31 sets at 6" o.c. with 4 lift lines per set
Arbors:	1,936 lb capacity
House Pipes:	44' long with 58' of travel from deck

Line sets are moveable
Block & Falls are not available
Chain hoists available as a rental; (1) half ton
1,000' of hemp available
1/2-ton chain hoist

PERMANENT INSTALLATIONS OVER STAGE (FROM SMOKE POCKET)
M=Moveable with advance call
Orchestra shells (4) at 6'5", 14'5", 22'2", 26'7"
Electric Raceways (1) at 1'9"
Movie screen (1) at 9'1"; M
Cyclorama (1) at 26'0"; M
Fire curtain (1) at -0'3"

PERMANENT INSTALLATIONS ON DECK
Jumps (above locking rail) (1)
Orchestra shell storage (4), 6'0" x 6'0"; M

ORCHESTRA PIT
Nonadjustable
Apron overhangs US wall of pit 6'6"

BACKSTAGE

LOADING DOCK
Loading door(s):
9'0" high x 9'6" wide
Trucks load (2) at same time
Heavy duty platforms used to extend loading dock to allow for unloading 2 trucks at a time
Fork lift is not required
Sound/Props can load in FOH
Trailers cannot store on-site

WARDROBE
Location: Basement
Access: Use stage trap and 1/2-ton chain hoist
No Washers No Dryers
Washer and dryer hookups available

DRESSING ROOMS
(3) Small, SR, stage level/+1/+2
(2) Chorus, SR, +1/+2
Showers on 3rd fl; restrooms in basement
Use dressing room for company mgr office

SOUND

CONSOLE
Soundcraft Series 5, located HR 1st Balcony
40+ 4 stereo inputs, 3 main outputs, 10 matrix outputs, 12 aux outputs

SPEAKERS
House Cluster
Proscenium
Under Balcony
No speaker truss

COMMUNICATIONS
Clear Com intercom with (2) channels
Dressing room page system

ROAD CONSOLE
Located Rear House
(12) seats required to be removed
Cable run from stage is 80'
Tie-in into house system with XLR connectors

REHEARSAL & STORAGE SPACE
Rehearsal: 16'0" x 32'0", located in basement, phone available; can also be used as Chorus dressing room
Storage: 12'0" x 34'0", located in basement

ELECTRICS

ROAD SERVICE POWER

Panel	Phase	Amp	Circuit Protection	Use	Location
A	3	400	fuse	dimmers	on stage DSR
B	3	200	fuse	extra	Loading dock

Recommended location of touring dimmer racks: On stage DSR
Hoist not required

FRONT OF HOUSE (BOX BOOM VALUES ARE PER SIDE)

Position	Pipe Width	Distance to Prosc.	House Circuits	Connector Type	FOH Transfer Circuits
1st Cove	36'	46'	24	grd 20 amp stage pin	24
2nd Cove	36'	62'	21	grd 20 amp stage pin	21
Box Boom 1	10'	24'	6	grd 20 amp stage pin	6
Box Boom 2	10'	32'	6	grd 20 amp stage pin	6

EQUIPMENT FOH (BOX BOOM VALUES ARE PER SIDE)

Position	Quantity	Wattage	Instrument	Removeable
1st Balc Rail	8	1,000	Altman 360Q 6x16	yes
2nd Balc Rail	3	1,000	Altman 360Q 6x16	yes
1st Cove	8	1,000	CCT 8° ERS	yes
2nd Cove	18	1,000	CCT 10° Zoom ERS	yes
Box Boom 1	4/3	1,000	Altman 360Q 6x12/6x16	yes
Box Boom 2	6	1,000	Altman 360Q 6x16	yes

FOLLOWSPOTS
House Followspots:
(1) Lyceum Super Arc/HTI 400 Lamp; removeable
Ultra Arc/ HTI 400 Lamp1; removeable

Followspot Booth:
78' throw to proscenium;
(2) 1Ø 20 amp breakers

DIMMERS
Lighting console is Mini-Light Pallet or Mantrix 2s;
(174) CD 80 dimmers
No DMX control system
No dry run DMX station(s)

ORDWAY MUSIC THEATRE MAIN HALL

YEAR BUILT: 1985

Theatre Location: 345 Washington Street, St Paul, MN 55102-1495

Main Administrative Phone: 651-282-3000
Main Administrative Fax: 651-224-5319
E-mail: productionmgr@ordway.org
Website: www.ordway.org
Stage Door Phone: 651-282-3070

THEATRE STAFF

President	Kevin McCollum	651-282-3000
Booking	Bob Alwine	651-282-3002
Booking	Robb Wolfe	651-282-3143
Marketing	Lynn Von Eschen	651-282-3010
Operations	Mary McColl	651-282-3040
Group Sales	Peter Wright	651-282-3113

HOUSE CREW

Production Mgr	Albert Webster	651-282-3041
Stage Manager	Janet Huyck	651-282-3042
Carpentry	Dave Colby	651-282-3047
Electrics	Bill Henley	651-282-3046
Sound	Jim Pfitzinger	651-282-3045
Props	Mike Mackin	651-282-3044

UNIONS

IATSE Local #20	Dave Colby	651-282-3047
Wardrobe Local #781	Joy Oberg	651-426-3968

SEATING CAPACITY

Orchestra	706
Mezzanine	578
Balcony	349
Gallery	274
Total:	**1,907**

wheelchair (add'l)	3
standing (add'l)	52

BOX OFFICE
Computerized
Box Office Manager
Jon Rennie   651-282-3080

Outside Ticket Agency
None

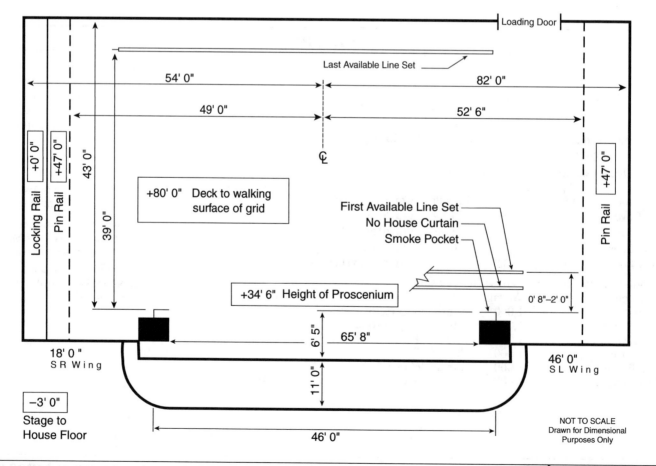

18' 0"
SR Wing

−3' 0"
Stage to
House Floor

46' 0"
SL Wing

NOT TO SCALE
Drawn for Dimensional
Purposes Only

STAGE HOUSE

HOUSE CURTAIN
Operates as a guillotine from SR fly rail
Often not installed

RIGGING SYSTEM
Type:	Single purchase counter weight
Weight:	30,000 lbs available
Line sets:	67 sets at 6" o.c. with 6-8 lift lines per set
Arbors:	1,200 lb capacity
House Pipes:	63' & 86' long with 69' of travel from deck

Line sets are moveable
Block & Falls are not available
Chain hoists available; (2) half ton
(110) spot wheels and 8,000' of hemp available

PERMANENT INSTALLATIONS OVER STAGE (FROM SMOKE POCKET)
Orchestra shells (1) at 11'0"
Electric bridge (2) at 4'6", 33'6"
Fire curtain (1) at 0'0"

PERMANENT INSTALLATIONS ON DECK
Traps; contact house
Jumps (2)
Orchestra shell storage, US of deck
Adjustable proscenium

ORCHESTRA PIT
Nonadjustable at 8' below stage level by electric motor turnscrew
Apron overhangs US wall of pit 7' 0"
Pit is replaced by seating when not used, pit has various configurations, but only one is used by Broadway musical theatre, call to discuss

BACKSTAGE

LOADING DOCK
Loading door(s):
16'0" high x 12'0" wide
Trucks load (2) at same time
Fork lift is not required
Sound/Props cannot load in FOH
Trailers cannot store on-site
Security at dock & stage door

WARDROBE
Location: Basement/2nd floor
Access: Freight elevator
(2-3) Washers (2-3) Dryers
Washer and dryer hookups available

DRESSING ROOMS
(2) Star, SL, stage level, t/s included, phone jack
(6) Small, SL, stage level, t/s included
(2) Chorus, SL, -1, t/s included
Elevator access for dressing rooms
Use dressing room for company mgr office

SOUND

CONSOLE
Gamble EX-56
64 inputs, 16 matrix outputs, 10 aux outputs

SPEAKERS
House Cluster
Proscenium

COMMUNICATIONS
Clear Com intercom with (4) channels
Dressing room page/ stage monitor system

ROAD CONSOLE
Located Rear Mezzanine HL
(10-16) seats required to be removed
Cable run from stage is 200'
Tie-in into house system with XLR connectors

REHEARSAL & STORAGE SPACE
Rehearsal: Large - 56' x 56' located 2nd floor, must be reserved in advance, equipment available
Small - 37' x 28' located on 2nd floor, must be reserved in advance, equipment available
Storage: Hallways only

ELECTRICS

ROAD SERVICE POWER

Panel	Phase	Amp	Circuit Protection	Use	Location
A	3	100	breaker	hoist	DSL
B-E	3	400	breaker	dimmers	DSL
F	3	200	breaker	extra	DSL
G	3	400	breaker	extra	DSL
H	3	100	breaker	extra	USL
I	3	200	breaker	sound	DSR
J	3	100	breaker	sound	DSR

(2) 30 amp circuits at FOH sound console position;
(4) 20 amp stage circuits, (sound) 2 each side
Recommended location of touring dimmer racks: SL
Hoist provided but not required
Additional power is available for tour buses, generators, etc.

FRONT OF HOUSE (BOX BOOM VALUES ARE PER SIDE)

Position	Pipe Width	Distance to Prosc.	House Circuits	Connector Type	FOH Transfer Circuits
1st Balc Rail	27'	95'	9	grd 20 amp stage pin	0
1st Cove	64'	58'	36	grd 20 amp stage pin	0
2nd Cove	72'	80'	38	grd 20 amp stage pin	0
3rd Cove	74'	100'	34	grd 20 amp stage pin	0
Box Boom 1		14'	8	grd 20 amp stage pin	0
Box Boom 2		24'	6	grd 20 amp stage pin	0

EQUIPMENT FOH (BOX BOOM VALUES ARE PER SIDE)
Contact House Electrics

FOLLOWSPOTS
House Followspots:
(3) Lycian 2.5k HMI; not removeable

Followspot Booth:
(1) spot per booth;
120' throw to proscenium;
(1) 3Ø 30 amp breakers

DIMMERS
Lighting console available
(816) DMX Protocol, AMX Protocol dimmers

JACKSON MUNICIPAL AUDITORIUM

AKA: THALIA MARIA HALL

YEAR BUILT: **1968**   YEAR RENOVATED: **1998**

Theatre Location: 255 E. Pascagoula Street, Jackson, MS 39205

Main Administrative Phone:	960-960-1537
Main Administrative Fax:	960-960-1583
Stage Door Phone:	960-960-1538

THEATRE STAFF

Manager	Maxine Dilday	960-960-1537
Office Coordinator	Vicki Green	960-960-1537

HOUSE CREW

Stage Manager	C.B. Carroll	960-960-1538

UNIONS

IATSE Local #589	Jill Lucas	601-960-1538

SEATING CAPACITY

Main Floor	1,610
Loge	154
Lower Balcony	192
Upper Balcony	394
Total:	**2,350**
wheelchair (add'l)	12

STAGE DIMENSIONS (FROM SMOKE POCKET)
  Stage is 40'0" deep
  Width from Center Line to SL is 50'0"
  Width from Center Line to SR is 55'0"
  Proscenium width is 60'0"
  Proscenium height is 30'0"
  Smoke pocket to apron edge is 12'0"
  Orchestra pit exists

RIGGING

Grid Height:	70'
Type:	Single purchase counter weight
Weight:	30,000 lbs
Line sets:	54 sets at 6" o.c.
Arbors:	800 lb capacity
House Pipes:	60' long

LOADING DOCK
  Loading door(s) are 12'0" high x 12'0" wide
  Trucks load (1) at a time
  Fork lift is not required and is not available

ELECTRICS
  Total power available:
    (3) 400A 3Ø SR

FOLLOWSPOTS
  House Followspots:
    Carbon Arc
    Super Trouper
  Power in spot booth 100A
  FOH transfer circuits: 24

DIMMERS
  (288) house dimmers
  House has DMX control system
  (1) dry run station located SR

SOUND
  House has 400A dedicated
    power located SR
  FOH mixing position in
    Rear House Center
  No sound console available

MUNICIPAL AUDITORIUM MUSIC HALL

AT: KANSAS CITY CONVENTION & ENTERTAINMENT CENTERS   **YEAR BUILT: 1936   YEAR RENOVATED: 1995**

Theatre Location: 301 West 13th Street, Kansas City, MO 64105
Management Company: Kansas City Convention Center

Main Administrative Phone: 816-871-3700
Main Administrative Fax: 816-871-3710
Stage Door Phone: 816-871-3700

THEATRE STAFF
Manager   Bill Langley   816-871-3700
Booking   Grace Okonta   816-871-3700
Marketing   Grace Okonta   816-871-3700
Operations   Dean Barrett   816-871-3700
Group Sales   Joie Meyers   816-871-3700

HOUSE CREW
Stage Manager   Bill Brown   816-871-3700
Technical Service Supv   Curt Futvoye   816-871-3700

UNIONS
IATSE Local #31   Gary Thomas   816-842-5167
Wardrobe Local #31   Gary Thomas   816-842-5167
Music Local #34-627   Dick Albrecht   816-221-6934

SEATING CAPACITY
Orchestra   1,191
Boxes and Loges   282
Balcony   918
Total: **2,391**

wheelchair (add'l)   10

BOX OFFICE
Computerized
Box Office Manager
  Joie Meyers   816-871-3700

Outside Ticket Agency
Computerized
  Ticketmaster

Box office is promoter operated

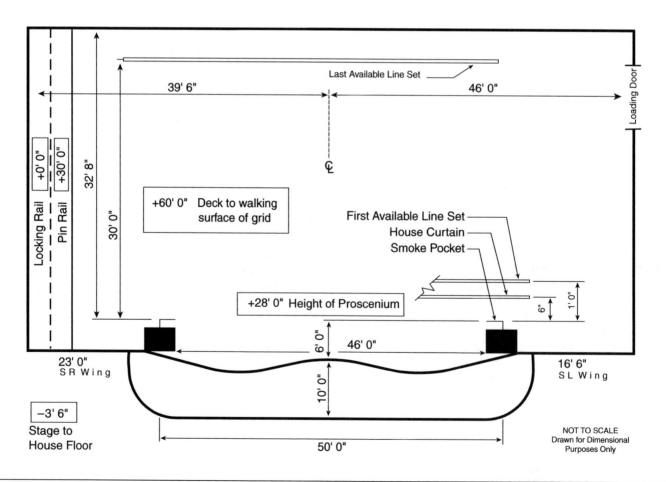

STAGE HOUSE

HOUSE CURTAIN
Operates as a guillotine from SR deck

RIGGING SYSTEM
Type: Single purchase counter weight
Weight: 12,000 lbs available
Line sets: 56 sets at 6" o.c. with 4 lift lines per set
Arbors: 590 lb capacity
House Pipes: 50' long with 58' of travel from deck
Line sets are moveable
Block & Falls are not available
Chain hoists are not available
(25) spot wheels and 25' of hemp available

PERMANENT INSTALLATIONS OVER STAGE (FROM SMOKE POCKET)
None

PERMANENT INSTALLATIONS ON DECK
None

ORCHESTRA PIT
Nonadjustable at 8'2" below stage level
Apron overhangs US wall of pit 0'0"
Pit lift is in (1) section
Organ lift in pit

BACKSTAGE

LOADING DOCK
Loading door(s):
   8'0" high x 20'0" wide
Trucks load (2) at same time
Unload on street, down ramp
   40' to elevator (8' x 24'), up 3
   floors to stage
Sound/Props cannot load in
   FOH
Trailers can store on-site

WARDROBE
Location: Behind stage on stage
   level
Access: Off elevator down
   hallway
(1) Washer (1) Dryer
Washer and dryer hookups
   available

DRESSING ROOMS
(4) Star, SR, stage level, +1, t/s
   included, phone jack
(9) Small, SR, stage level, +1,
   t/s included, phone jack
(3) Chorus, SR, stage level, +1,
   t/s on same fl
Elevator access for dressing
   rooms
Use dressing room for company
   mgr office

SOUND

CONSOLE
Yamaha 2904, located DSR
24 inputs, 4 main outputs,
   1 matrix outputs, 4 aux
   outputs

SPEAKERS
House Cluster
Proscenium
Under Balcony
Monitors backstage
No speaker truss
Can be rented

COMMUNICATIONS
Clear Com intercom with
   (8) channels
Infrared sound system
Dressing room page system

ROAD CONSOLE
Located Rear House
No seats required to be
   removed
Cable run from stage is 100'
Tie-in into house system with
   XLR connectors

REHEARSAL & STORAGE SPACE
Rehearsal: None
Storage: 50' x 40' located in
   basement

ELECTRICS

ROAD SERVICE POWER

Panel	Phase	Amp	Circuit Protection	Use	Location
A-B	3	600	fuse	dimmers	SL
C	3	600	fuse	dimmers	DSR

Recommended location of touring dimmer racks: SR or SL
Hoist not required
Additional power is available for tour buses, generators, etc.

FRONT OF HOUSE (BOX BOOM VALUES ARE PER SIDE)

Position	Pipe Width	Distance to Prosc.	House Circuits	Connector Type	FOH Transfer Circuits
1st Balc Rail	42'	76'	24	grd 20 amp stage pin	24
1st Cove		63'	14	grd 20 amp stage pin	0
2nd Cove		71'	14	grd 20 amp stage pin	0
3rd Cove		79'	14	grd 20 amp stage pin	0
Box Boom1		55'	6	grd 20 amp stage pin	12

Transfer circuits: grd 20 amp stage pin

EQUIPMENT FOH (BOX BOOM VALUES ARE PER SIDE)

Position	Quantity	Wattage	Instrument	Removeable
1st Balc Rail	12	1,000	8" Altman	yes
Box Boom 1	12	1,000	6 x 16 Altman	yes

FOLLOWSPOTS
House Followspots:
   (2) Super Trouper Xenon
   2k; removeable
   (1) Lycian Xenon 2k;
   removeable

Followspot Booth:
   (3) spots per booth;
   150' throw to proscenium;
   (2) 3Ø 100 amp breakers

DIMMERS
Lighting console is Obsession ETC;
(224) Strand CD80
   dimmers
House has programmable
   DMX control system

STARLIGHT THEATRE

YEAR BUILT: 1950   YEAR RENOVATED: 1983

Theatre Location: 4600 Starlight Road, Kansas City, MO 64132
Management Company: Starlight Theatre Association
                        4600 Starlight Road, Kansas City, MO 64132

Main Administrative Phone:	816-333-9481
Main Administrative Fax:	816-361-6398
E-mail:	starlight@kcstarlight.com
Website:	www.kcstarlight.com
Stage Door Phone:	816-333-9481
Backstage Pay Phone:	816-363-9869
Traveling Production Office Phone:	816-333-9481
Traveling Production Office Fax:	816-361-6398

SEATING CAPACITY
Orchestra	7,860
Total:	**7,860**

wheelchair	varies
standing (add'l)	

BOX OFFICE
  Computerized
  Ticket Systems Manager
    Mark Hickman   800-776-1730

  Outside Ticket Agency
  Computerized
    Ticket Control
    Scott Hughes   913-721-1581

  Box office is promoter operated

THEATRE STAFF
Producer/Exec VP	Robert M. Rohlf	816-333-9481
Booking	Robert M. Rohlf	816-333-9481
Marketing	George Guastello	816-333-9481
Operations	Dan Rieke	816-333-9481
Group Sales	Aimee Reed	816-333-9481

HOUSE CREW
Prod. Coordinator	Christy Lagoski	816-333-9481
Carpentry	Gil Vinzant	816-333-9481
Electrics	Greg Brown	816-333-9481
Sound	Herb Lagoski	816-333-9481
Props	Jay Lewis	816-333-9481

UNIONS
IATSE Local #31	Gary Thomas	816-842-5167
Music	Ronnie Hawthorne	913-342-7535

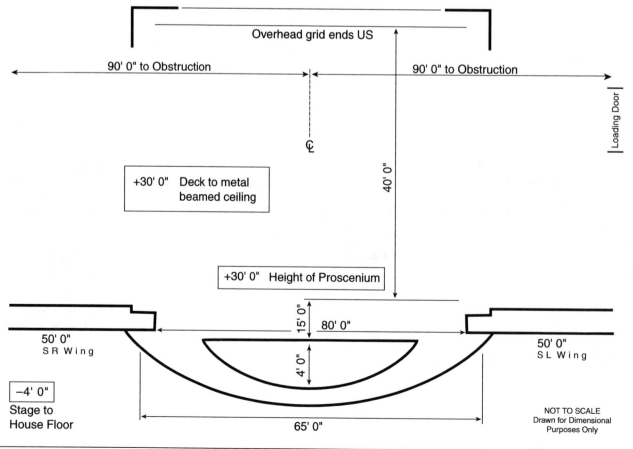

STAGE HOUSE

HOUSE CURTAIN
No house curtain available

RIGGING SYSTEM
None - Outdoor Venue
No rigging system available; stage is covered by a system of steel beams protected by tarps

PERMANENT INSTALLATIONS OVER STAGE (FROM SMOKE POCKET)
None

PERMANENT INSTALLATIONS ON DECK
None

ORCHESTRA PIT
Nonadjustable to 10' below stage level
Apron overhangs US wall of pit 14'0"
Entrance to pit SR/ SL is also underneath crossover

BACKSTAGE

LOADING DOCK
Loading door(s):
(No doors; Outdoor venue)
Unlimited trucks can load at same time
Stage level is at street level; trucks can drive directly onto stage area
(5) Trailers can store on-site
Security at dock & stage door

WARDROBE
Location: SL in adjacent covered pavilion
Access: Direct from stage
(2) Washers (2) Dryers
No washer or dryer hookups

DRESSING ROOMS
(2) Star, SL, stage level, t/s included, phone jack
(1) Small, SL, stage level, toilet included, shower on same fl, phone jack
Additional production office available for company mgr

SOUND

CONSOLE
No house console

SPEAKERS
House Cluster
Proscenium
Front fills, 2 on stage monitors
Speaker truss exists
Max available load 4,000 lbs
No pipe and rigging available

COMMUNICATIONS
Clear Com intercom with (4) channels
Infrared sound system
Dressing room page system

ROAD CONSOLE
Located Center HR
No seats required to be removed
Cable run from stage is 150'
Tie-in into house system with XLR connectors

REHEARSAL & STORAGE SPACE
Rehearsal: (2) 40'x 80' located in adjacent covered pavilions
Storage: 60' x 100' located in adjacent shop building

ELECTRICS

ROAD SERVICE POWER

Panel	Phase	Amp	Circuit Protection	Use	Location
A	3	600	breaker	dimmers	DSL in Alcove
B	3	400	breaker	sound	DSL in Alcove
C	3	200	breaker	extra	DSL in Alcove
D	1	100	breaker	extra	DSL in Alcove

Recommended location of touring dimmer racks: SL on deck or DSL in alcove
Hoist not required
Additional power is available for tour buses, generators, etc.

FRONT OF HOUSE (BOX BOOM VALUES ARE PER SIDE)

Position	Pipe Width	Distance to Prosc.	House Circuits	Connector Type	FOH Transfer Circuits
Booth Rail	80'	385'	5	ungrd 50 amp crouse-hinds	0

Road truss: Towers (2) located house right and left in Box Boom positions contain 16 circuits each w/ ungrd 50 amp crouse-hinds connectors

EQUIPMENT FOH (BOX BOOM VALUES ARE PER SIDE)
None

FOLLOWSPOTS
House Followspots:
(4) Xenon Super Troupers; not removeable

Followspot Booth:
(4) spots per booth;
385' throw to proscenium;
(5) 3Ø 120 amp breakers

DIMMERS
Lighting console is Strand Palette Mini Lt;
(144) 6,000 / 2.4k dimmers
House has non-programmable DMX control system

FOX THEATRE

AKA: THE FABULOUS FOX   **YEAR BUILT: 1929   YEAR RENOVATED: 1995**

Theatre Location: 527 North Grand Boulevard, St. Louis, MO 63103

Main Administrative Phone: 314-534-1678
Main Administrative Fax: 314-534-4153
Website: www.fabulousfox.com
Backstage Pay Phone: 314-534-9455
Traveling Production Office Phone: 314-534-0104
Traveling Production Office Fax: 314-531-8524

THEATRE STAFF
Executive Director   David Fay   314-534-1678
Booking   Mike Isaacson   314-534-1678
Marketing   Jana Scharnhorst   314-534-1678
Operations   Richard Baker   314-534-1678
Group Sales   Karen Shye   314-534-1678
Planning/Developing   Mike Isaacson   314-534-1678

HOUSE CREW
Production Manager   John Wolf   314-534-1678
Carpentry   Marty McMannus   314-534-1678
Electrics   Tom Pehle   314-534-1678
Sound   Frank Palliser   314-534-1678
Props   Paul Deluca   314-534-1678

UNIONS
IATSE Local #6   Jack Beckman   314-621-5077
Wardrobe   Lee Berger   314-487-5217
Music Local #2-197   Bob Ceccarini   314-227-2031

SEATING CAPACITY
Orchestra   2,279
Mezzanine   358
Balcony   708
Middle Balcony   586
Upper Balcony   169
Total: **4,100**

pit (add'l)   178
wheelchair (add'l)   27
standing (add'l)   44

BOX OFFICE
Computerized
General Manager
  Larry McDonnell   314-534-1678

Outside Ticket Agency
Metrotix
  Larry McDonnell   314-534-1678

Box office is promoter operated

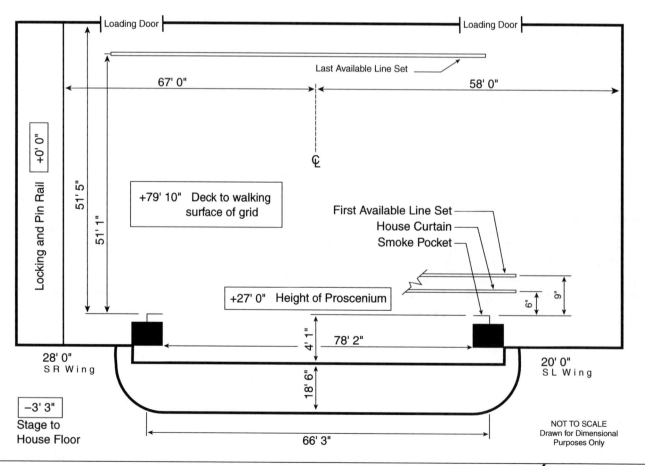

STAGE HOUSE

HOUSE CURTAIN
Operates as a guillotine from SR deck

RIGGING SYSTEM
Type: Single purchase counter weight
Weight: 30,000 lbs available
Line sets: 85 sets at 6" o.c. with 7 lift lines per set
Arbors: 1,100 lb capacity
House Pipes: 77' long with 72' of travel from deck
Line sets are moveable
Block & Falls are available 3:2 (1)
Chain hoists available as a rental; (4) one ton
(50) spot wheels and 4,000' of hemp available

PERMANENT INSTALLATIONS OVER STAGE (FROM SMOKE POCKET)
M=Moveable with advance call
Electric Raceways (5) at 1'9", 9'10", 18'0, 26'0, 27'5"; M
Dead Spaces (2) at 31'4", 34'6"
Fire Curtain (1) at 0'10"

PERMANENT INSTALLATIONS ON DECK
Columns (2) 30'0" SL, SR

ORCHESTRA PIT
Adjustable to 10' below stage level by electric motor turnscrew
Apron overhangs US wall of pit 0' 0"
Pit lift is in (2) sections
Organ lift at center line

BACKSTAGE

LOADING DOCK
Loading door(s):
(2) 14'0" high x 12'0"wide
Open parking lot allows many trucks to load at same time
Both doors at street level; SL Door 39" above stage floor, SR Door 18" above stage floor; ramps down to stage
Fork lift is required; Forklifts of St. Louis, 314-426-4040
Sound/Props can load in FOH
Lobby can be a work area
(2) Trailers can store on-site
Security at stage door

WARDROBE
Location: SL Basement
Access: Elevator
(2) Washers (2) Dryers
Washer and dryer hookups available

DRESSING ROOMS
(2) Star, SL, +1, t/s on same fl, phone jack
(9) Small, SL, +2/+4/+5, t/s on same fl
(1) Chorus, SL, +2, t/s on same fl, phone jack
Elevator access for dressing rooms
Additional production office available for company mgr

SOUND

CONSOLE
Yamaha PM 1800, located House Left
40 inputs, 6 main outputs, 4 matrix outputs, 4 aux outputs

SPEAKERS
House Cluster
Proscenium
No speaker truss

COMMUNICATIONS
Clear Com intercom with (2) channels
Infrared sound system
Dressing room page system

ROAD CONSOLE
Located House Left
No seats required to be removed
Cable run from stage is 150'
Tie-in into house system with XLR connectors

REHEARSAL & STORAGE SPACE
Rehearsal: None
Storage: None

ELECTRICS

ROAD SERVICE POWER

Panel	Phase	Amp	Circuit Protection	Use	Location
A	3	800	fuse	dimmers	DSR Basement
B	3	400	fuse	dimmers	DSR Basement
C	3	200	fuse	extra	DSR Basement
D	1	400	fuse	sound	DSR Basement
E	1	200	fuse	sound	DSL

Recommended location of touring dimmer racks: SR
Hoist not required
Additional power is available for tour buses, generators, etc.

FRONT OF HOUSE (BOX BOOM VALUES ARE PER SIDE)

Position	Pipe Width	Distance to Prosc.	House Circuits	Connector Type	FOH Transfer Circuits
Truss	50'	18'	24	grd 20 amp stage pin	24
Balc Rail	40'	75'	14	grd 20 amp stage pin	14
Box Boom		80'			

EQUIPMENT FOH (BOX BOOM VALUES ARE PER SIDE)
None

FOLLOWSPOTS
House Followspots:
(4) Xenon Super Troupers; removeable

Followspot Booth:
(4) spots per booth;
162' throw to proscenium;
(2) 3Ø 80 amp breakers
(1) 1Ø 60 amp breakers

DIMMERS
Lighting console is EDI Omega;
(144) ETC Sensor dimmers
House has programmable DMX control system

THE MUNY

AKA: MUNICIPAL THEATRE ASSOCIATION OF ST. LOUIS

YEAR BUILT: 1919

Theatre Location: Forest Park, St. Louis, MO 63112

Main Administrative Phone:	314-361-1900
Main Administrative Fax:	314-361-0009
E-mail:	generalmanagement@muny.com
Website:	www.muny.com
Stage Door Phone:	314-361-1900

THEATRE STAFF

General Mgr. & CEO	Dennis M. Reagan	314-361-1900
Booking	Dennis M. Reagan	314-361-1900
Marketing	Laura Peters	314-361-1900
Operations	Sean Smith	314-361-1900
Group Sales	Kelly Mazzacavallo	314-361-1900

HOUSE CREW

Technical Director	George Spies	314-361-1900
Stage Manager	Joe Schulte	314-361-1900
Carpentry	Dan Roach	314-361-1900
Electrics	Dan Murphy	314-361-1900
Sound	Gene Greer	314-361-1900
Props	Dick McCarthy	314-361-1900

UNIONS

IATSE Local #6	Jack Beckman	314-621-5077
Wardrobe Local #805	Lee Burgherr	314-487-5217
Music Local #2-197	Bob Ceccarini	314-361-1900

SEATING CAPACITY

Boxes	1,000
Terrace A	2,934
Terrace B	3,777
Terrace C	2,342
Total:	**10,053**
pit (add'l)	124
wheelchair (add'l)	27

BOX OFFICE

Computerized
Box Office Treasurer
George Walsh   314-361-1900

Outside Ticket Agency
Computerized
MetroTix
Mark Reifsteck   314-534-1678

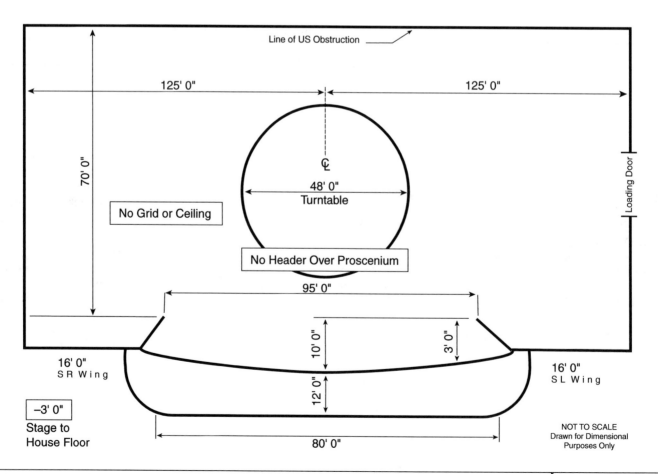

Line of US Obstruction

125' 0"   125' 0"

70' 0"

No Grid or Ceiling

CL

48' 0"
Turntable

No Header Over Proscenium

95' 0"

10' 0"   3' 0"

16' 0"
S R Wing

16' 0"
S L Wing

12' 0"

−3' 0"
Stage to
House Floor

80' 0"

Loading Door

NOT TO SCALE
Drawn for Dimensional
Purposes Only

STAGE HOUSE

HOUSE CURTAIN
No house curtain available

RIGGING SYSTEM
No rigging system available
Stage is open to the elements
Electric hard traveller panels (2) sets located at 9'0", 14'0"
    from proscenium operate from SR & SL

PERMANENT INSTALLATIONS OVER STAGE (FROM SMOKE POCKET)
None

PERMANENT INSTALLATIONS ON DECK
Hard legs (3 sets) at 3'0", 13'0", 17'0"
Electric bridges located FOH
Tree islands (2) at 42'0", located 8'0" SR & SL of center
Motorized turntable 48'0" diameter, located CS

ORCHESTRA PIT
Nonadjustable at 5' below stage level

BACKSTAGE

LOADING DOCK
Loading door(s):
    14'0" high x 11'0" wide
Trucks load (1) at a time; back
    in to stage level
Fork lift is required call George
    Spies, Technical Director
Sound/Props can load in FOH
Lobby cannot be a work area
(3) Trailers can store on-site
Security at dock & stage door

WARDROBE
Location: USL on stage level
Access: Direct from stage
(2) Washers (2) Dryers
Washer and dryer hookups
    available

DRESSING ROOMS
All rooms have toilet included,
    shower on same fl, phone jack
(3) Star, SL, stage level
(7) Small, SL, stage level
(2) Chorus, SL, stage level
Use dressing room for company
    mgr office

SOUND

CONSOLE
(2) Soundcraft Europas,
    located House Center
40 inputs, 8 groups main
    outputs, 8 matrix outputs,
    12 aux outputs

SPEAKERS
Proscenium

COMMUNICATIONS
Clear Com intercom with
    (4) channels
FM hearing system
Dressing room page system

ROAD CONSOLE
Located Center House
(38) seats required to be
    removed
Cable run from stage is 150'
Tie-in into house system
    with XLR connectors

REHEARSAL & STORAGE SPACE
Rehearsal: Music Rm 28' x
    50' in adjacent building,
    equipment available
    (2) additional outdoor
    rehearsal spaces
Storage: None

ELECTRICS

ROAD SERVICE POWER

Panel	Phase	Amp	Circuit Protection	Use	Location
A-B	3	400	breaker	dimmers	SL
C	3	200	breaker	sound	SL

Recommended location of touring dimmer racks: SL
Hoist provided
Additional power is available for tour buses, generators, etc.

FRONT OF HOUSE (BOX BOOM VALUES ARE PER SIDE)

Position	Pipe Width	Distance to Prosc.	House Circuits	Connector Type	FOH Transfer Circuits
Bridge	150'	40'	50	grd 20 amp stage pin	0

EQUIPMENT FOH (BOX BOOM VALUES ARE PER SIDE)

Position	Quantity	Wattage	Instrument	Removeable
1st Balc Rail	50	1,000	Pars & Lekos	yes

FOLLOWSPOTS
House Followspots:
    (3) Xenon 3000; not
    removeable

Followspot Booth:
    (3) spots per booth;
    286' throw to proscenium;
    (3) 3Ø 35 amp breakers

DIMMERS
House has lighting console;
    (156) Century CD80 pack
    dimmers
House has rented DMX
    control system

HAMMONS HALL

AT: SOUTHWEST MISSOURI STATE UNIVERSITY   **YEAR BUILT: 1992   YEAR RENOVATED: 1997**

AKA: JUANITA K. HAMMONS HALL FOR THE PERFORMING ARTS

Theatre Location: 525 S. John Q. Hammons Pkwy, Springfield, MO 65806
Mailing Address: 901 S. National, Springfield, MO 65804
Management Company: Southwest Missouri State University
                                        (mailing address as above)

Main Administrative Phone: 417-836-6776
Main Administrative Fax: 417-836-6891
Website: www.hhpa.smsu.edu
Stage Door Phone: 417-836-8427

THEATRE STAFF
Executive Director   Enoch Morris   417-836-6776
Booking   Jennifer Brymer   417-836-6771
Marketing   Deb Gallion   417-836-6767
Operations   Ed Carson   417-836-8427
Group Sales   Chris Williams   417-836-8468

HOUSE CREW
Technical Director   Tom Kile   417-836-8533

SEATING CAPACITY
Orchestra   1,160
Mezzanine   681
Petite   337
Boxes   42
Total: **2,220**

pit (add'l)   76
wheelchair (incl.)   11

BOX OFFICE
Computerized
Asst. Box Office Manager
   Angela Deke   417-836-6756

Outside Ticket Agency
None

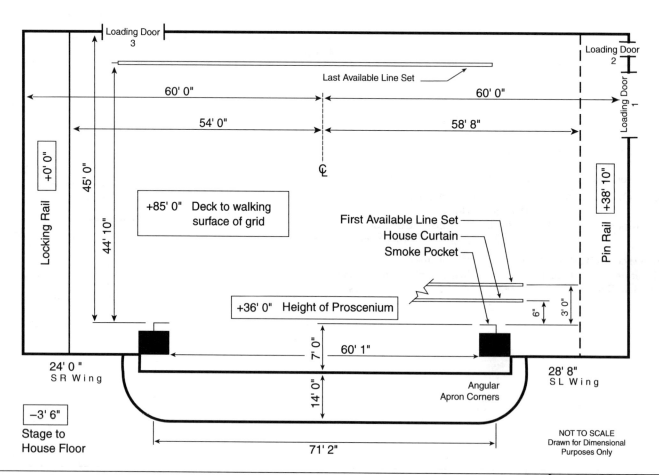

STAGE HOUSE

HOUSE CURTAIN
Operates as a guillotine or traveller from SR fly floor

RIGGING SYSTEM

Type:	Single purchase counter weight
Weight:	40,000 lbs available
Line sets:	59 sets at 7" o.c. with 7 lift lines per set
Arbors:	1,500 lb capacity
House Pipes:	78' long with 89' of travel from deck

Line sets are moveable
Block & Falls are not available
Chain hoists are not available
(32) spot wheels and 3,000' of hemp available

PERMANENT INSTALLATIONS OVER STAGE (FROM SMOKE POCKET)
M=Moveable with advance call
Orchestra shell (1) at 46'0" stores in recessed part of DS
Orchestra shell (ceiling) (2) at 3'9" and 11'11" fly to 75'0"
Traveler (2) variable; M
Electric pipe (4) at 6'7", 16'7", 26'6", 37'0"
Cyclorama (2); M

PERMANENT INSTALLATIONS ON DECK
Trap (4) in stage floor 4'0" x 8'0" - 7'0" US of plaster, 5'6"
   SL + SR of C, offstage pair 15'6" SR +SL of C
Electric jump (16) - (6) on grid, (5) ea SR & SL galleries
Orchestra shell storage (1) 46' 0" US, stores in recessed part
   of US
Loading bridge (2) 5'0" x 45'0", SR 1 @ 45'0", 1 @ 85'0"
   above deck

ORCHESTRA PIT
Adjustable to 9'10' below stage level by hydraulic lift
Apron overhangs US wall of pit 8'3"
Pit lift is in (1) section

BACKSTAGE

LOADING DOCK
Loading door(s):
   1) 12'0" high x 12'0" wide
   2) 6'10" high x 3'6"wide
   3) 6'10" high x 5'10"wide
Trucks load (2) at same time
Fork lift is not required
Sound/Props can load in FOH
Lobby cannot be work area
(8) Trailers can store on-site
Security at dock & stage door

WARDROBE
Location: Off loading dock
Access: Through backstage or
   loading dock
(2) Washers (3) Dryers
Washer and dryer hookups
   available

DRESSING ROOMS
(3) Star, behind stage, stage
   level, t/s included, phone jack
(3) Small, behind stage, stage
   level, t/s included, phone jack
(13) Chorus, SL, SR, -1, t/s
   included phone jack
Elevator access for dressing
   rooms
Use dressing room for company
   mgr office

SOUND

CONSOLE
Yamaha, located Booth
32 inputs, 11 main outputs,
   4 matrix outputs, 6 aux
   outputs

SPEAKERS
House Cluster
Under Balcony
Other Balcony top
No speaker truss

COMMUNICATIONS
Clear Com intercom with
   (2) channels
Fm hearing augmentation
Dressing room page system

ROAD CONSOLE
Located Rear Orchestra,
   right of center
(5) seats required to be
   removed
Cable run from stage is 150'
Tie-in into house system with
   XLR connectors

REHEARSAL & STORAGE SPACE
Rehearsal: None
Storage: 28' x 45', off SL
   between dock & stage

ELECTRICS

ROAD SERVICE POWER

Panel	Phase	Amp	Circuit Protection	Use	Location
A-B	3	400	breaker	dimmers	SL
C	3	200	fuse	sound	SR
D-E	3	60	breaker	extra	loading dock door

Location for touring dimmer racks: SL; Hoist not required; Additional power available

FRONT OF HOUSE (BOX BOOM VALUES ARE PER SIDE)

Position	Pipe Width	Distance to Prosc.	House Circuits	Connector Type	FOH Transfer Circuits
1st Balc Rail	47'6"	83'	19	grd 20 amp stagepin	19
2nd Balc Rail	30'	90'	6	grd 20 amp stagepin	6
1st Catwalk	90'	74'	35	grd 20 amp stagepin	35
2nd Catwalk	78'	35'	35	grd 20 amp stagepin	35
3rd Catwalk	90'	4'	35	grd 20 amp stagepin	35
Box Booms		12'&48'	12	grd 20 amp stagepin	12

Transfer circuits: grd 20 amp stage pin;Road truss: Catwalks full length from HR to HL

EQUIPMENT FOH (BOX BOOM VALUES ARE PER SIDE)

Position	Quantity	Wattage	Instrument	Removeable
1st Balc Rail	4	1,000	6 x 16	yes
2nd Balc Rail	11	1,000	10 x 23	yes
1st Cove	32	1,000	10 x 23	yes
2nd Cove	32	1,000	8 x 13	yes
3rd Cove			various	yes
Box Boom 1	24	1,000	6 x 16	yes
Box Boom 2	24	1,000	8 x 13	yes

FOLLOWSPOTS
House Followspots:
   (3) Xenon Super Trouper
   2k; removeable

Followspot Booth:
   (3) spots per booth;
   120' throw to proscenium;
   (4) 3Ø 30 amp breakers

DIMMERS
Lighting console is Strand M
   Light Pallette 90;
   (395) CD80 dimmers
House has programmable
   control system thru lighting
   board
(5) dry run DMX station(s)

ALBERTA BAIR THEATER

Theatre Location: 2801 Third Avenue North, Billings, MT 59101

Main Administrative Phone: 406-256-8915
Main Administrative Fax: 406-256-5060

THEATRE STAFF
Executive Director   Bill Fisher   406-256-8915
Booking   Bill Fisher   406-256-8915
Marketing   Corby Skinner   406-256-8915

HOUSE CREW
Technical Director   Thomas Lund   406-259-7400
House Manager   Jennifer Bingham   406-256-6057

SEATING CAPACITY
Orchestra   758
Loge   204
Balcony   456
Total: **1,418**

wheelchair   5

BOX OFFICE
Computerized
Ticket Office Manager
Jennifer Bingham   406-256-6057

Outside Ticket Agency
None

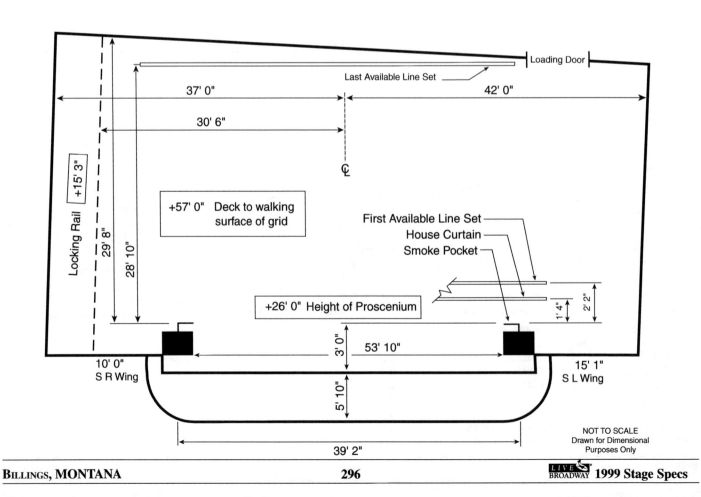

37' 0"

30' 6"

Last Available Line Set

Loading Door

42' 0"

Locking Rail +15' 3"

29' 8"

28' 10"

+57' 0" Deck to walking surface of grid

+26' 0" Height of Proscenium

First Available Line Set
House Curtain
Smoke Pocket

1' 4"   2' 2"

3' 0"

53' 10"

10' 0"
S R Wing

15' 1"
S L Wing

5' 10"

39' 2"

NOT TO SCALE
Drawn for Dimensional
Purposes Only

STAGE HOUSE

HOUSE CURTAIN
Operates as a guillotine or traveller from SL deck

RIGGING SYSTEM

Type:	Single purchase counter weight
Weight:	7,850 lbs available
Line sets:	38 sets at 8" o.c. with 5 lift lines per set
Arbors:	1,000 lb capacity
House Pipes:	60' long with 55' of travel from deck

Line sets are not moveable
Block & Falls are available 3:2 (2)
(7) spot wheels and 110' of hemp available

PERMANENT INSTALLATIONS OVER STAGE (FROM SMOKE POCKET)
Electric raceways (4) at 3'11", 10'10", 18'10", 24'10"
Electric border (1) at 26'2"
Orchestra shell (3) at 11'6", 25'6", 30'2"

PERMANENT INSTALLATIONS ON DECK
Column (1) in SR wing - 16" wide x 24" deep
Concrete column located on DSL proscenium wall

ORCHESTRA PIT
Adjustable to 11' below stage level by hydraulic lift
Apron overhangs US wall of pit 12'3"

BACKSTAGE

LOADING DOCK
Loading door(s):
12'0" high x 5'10" wide
Trucks load (2 back to back) at same time
Dock (loading door sill) is at street level
Forklift: American Rent-All
406-245-6663

WARDROBE
Location: Green room in basement
Access: Orchestra pit elevator
(1) Washers (1) Dryers

DRESSING ROOMS
(2) Star, SR, basement, t/s
(1) Small, SL, basement, t/s
(2) Chorus, basement, t/s

SOUND

CONSOLE
Altec
12 inputs, 4 main outputs

SPEAKERS
House Cluster

COMMUNICATIONS
Clear Com intercom with
(2) channels
Comtek BSA 72

ROAD CONSOLE
Located Rear House
(15) seats required to be removed
Cable run from stage is 100'
Tie-in into house system with XLR connectors

REHEARSAL & STORAGE SPACE
Rehearsal: None
Storage:

ELECTRICS

ROAD SERVICE POWER

Panel	Phase	Amp	Circuit Protection	Use	Location
A	3	400	breaker	dimmers	SL side wall
B	3	400	breaker	sound	SL side wall
C	3	400	breaker	extra	SL side wall

Recommended location of touring dimmer racks: USL on deck

FRONT OF HOUSE (BOX BOOM VALUES ARE PER SIDE)

Position	Pipe Width	Distance to Prosc.	House Circuits	Connector Type	FOH Transfer Circuits
Bridge	54'	48'	38	grd 20 amp stage pin	19
Box Boom 1		32'	8	grd 20 amp stage pin	4

Transfer circuits: grd 20 amp stage pin

EQUIPMENT FOH (BOX BOOM VALUES ARE PER SIDE)

Position	Quantity	Wattage	Instrument	Removeable
Bridge	4	1,000	6 x 16 Lekos	no
Box Boom 1	38	1,000	6 x 16 Lekos	no
Box Boom 1	2	1,000	6 x 16 Lekos	no

FOLLOWSPOTS
House Followspots:
(2) Xenon Super Troupers; not removeable

Followspot Booth: No booth
Spots operated from
platform at
rear of balcony
100' throw to proscenium;
(2) 1Ø 50 amp breakers

DIMMERS
No lighting console
No dimmers
No DMX control system

LIED CENTER FOR PERFORMING ARTS

AT: UNIVERSITY OF NEBRASKA   **YEAR BUILT: 1990**

Theatre Location: 301 N 12th Street, Lincoln, NE 68588-0151
Mailing Address: PO Box 880151, Lincoln, NE 68588-0151

Main Administrative Phone: 402-472-4700
Main Administrative Fax: 402-472-4730
Stage Door Phone: 402-472-7724

THEATRE STAFF
Executive Director   Charles Bethea   402-472-4700
Marketing   Norah George   402-472-4707
Operations   Bob Vaughn   402-472-4702

HOUSE CREW
Technical Director   Dan Stratman   402-472-4692
Stage Manager   Ted Tipton   402-472-4699
Electrics   John Himmelberger   402-472-7738
Sound   Kim Cummings   402-472-7735

UNIONS
IATSE Local #151   Paul Young   402-466-2731

SEATING CAPACITY
Orchestra   1,255
Balcony   955
Total: **2,210**

pit (add'l)   66
wheelchair (add'l)   10

BOX OFFICE
Computerized
Box Office Manager
   Eileen Brewster   402-472-5430

Outside Ticket Agency
None

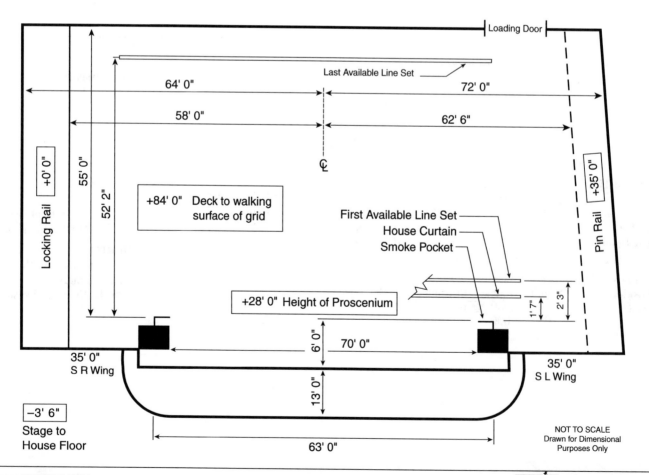

STAGE HOUSE

HOUSE CURTAIN
Operates as a guillotine from SR deck; motorized

RIGGING SYSTEM
Type:	Single purchase counter weight
Weight:	12,000 lbs available
Line sets:	68 sets at 6" o.c. with 7 lift lines per set
Arbors:	1,200 lb capacity
House Pipes:	76' long with 77' of travel from deck

Line sets are not moveable
Block & Falls are not available
Chain hoists are not available
(6) spot wheels and 2,000' of hemp available

PERMANENT INSTALLATIONS OVER STAGE (FROM SMOKE POCKET)
Orchestra shells (3) at 8'8", 24'4", 40'0"
Movie screen (1) at 16'0"
Traveller (2) at 29'2", 46'10"
Electric bridge (1) at 4'0" to 6'6"
Hard torms (1) at 3'2"
Fire curtain (1) at 0'0" - 0'7"

PERMANENT INSTALLATIONS ON DECK
Hard legs (1) 21'0"W x 36'0"H on tracks, 3'2" US
Orchestra shells storage (1) 10'0"W x 22'0"L x 30'0"H
  extreme USL of stage
Electric bridge (1) 2'6"W x 80'0"L, 4'0" - 6'6"

ORCHESTRA PIT
Adjustable to 8' below stage level by hydraulic lift
Apron overhangs US wall of pit 12'0"
Pit lift is in (1) section
Pit lift also used as apron & seating; DS edge of pit curved
  13' on center to 0' L & R

BACKSTAGE

LOADING DOCK
Loading door(s):
  9'0" high x 2'8" wide
Trucks load (2) at same time
Fork lift is not required
Fork lift not permitted on stage
Sound/Props cannot load in
  FOH
(2) Trailers can store on-site
Security at stage door

WARDROBE
(2) Washers (2) Dryers
Washer and dryer hookups
  available

DRESSING ROOMS
(4) Star, SR, stage level,
  t/s included, phone jack
(2) Chorus, SL, stage level,
  t/s included, phone jack
(4) Small, SL/SR, basement,
  t/s included
(4) Chorus, SL/SR, basement,
  t/s included
Elevator access to dressing
  rooms
Use dressing rooms for company mgr office

SOUND

CONSOLE
TAC Scorpion, located Booth
  FOH 40 inputs
Rear house: 12 inputs, 2main
  outputs, 1 aux outputs

SPEAKERS
House Cluster
Portable
Balcony Fill
No speaker truss

COMMUNICATIONS
Clear Com intercom with
  (1) channel
FM system
Dressing room page system

ROAD CONSOLE
Located Rear Orchestra
(12) Seats required to be
  removed
Cable run from stage is 200'
Tie-in into house system with
  XLR connectors

REHEARSAL & STORAGE SPACE
Rehearsal: (2) areas each
  with mirrors, barres, piano
Warm up 25' x 35' in
  basement;
  Carson Theatre 50' x 70'
  off SL
Storage: (2) @ 35' x 50', off
  dock & off SL, equip rental

ELECTRICS

ROAD SERVICE POWER

Panel	Phase	Amp	Circuit Protection	Use	Location
A - C	3	400	breaker	dimmers	SL
D	3	200	breaker	sound	SL
E	3	200	breaker	sound	SR

Location of touring dimmer racks SL: Hoist not required: Addl power available

FRONT OF HOUSE (BOX BOOM VALUES ARE PER SIDE)

Position	Pipe Width	Distance to Prosc.	House Circuits	Connector Type	FOH Transfer Circuits
Catwalk 1		70'	26	grd 20 amp stage pin	8
Catwalk 2		85'	26	grd 20 amp stage pin	8
Catwalk 3		100'	12	grd 20 amp stage pin	3
1st Balc Rail		75'	15	grd 20 amp stage pin	6
Box Boom 1		10'	12	grd 20 amp stage pin	3
Box Boom 2		25'	15	grd 20 amp stage pin	12
Box Boom 3		45'	6	grd 20 amp stage pin	0

Transfer circuits: grd 20 amp stage pin

EQUIPMENT FOH (BOX BOOM VALUES ARE PER SIDE)

Position	Quantity	Wattage	Instrument	Removeable
Canopy	15	575	15 - 40 Zoom	yes
1st Balc Rail	12	575	15 - 40 Zoom	yes
1st Cove	10	575	12 ERS	yes
2nd Cove	20	575	8 x 18 ERS	yes
3rd Cove	16	575	10 x 23 ERS	yes
Box Boom 1	9	575	(3) 12° (6) Zoom	yes
Box Boom 2	9	575	(6) 12° (3) Zoom	yes
Box Boom 3	6	575	(3) 12° (3) 8 x 13	yes

FOLLOWSPOTS
House Followspots:
  (3) Strong Super Trouper
  Xenon; not removeable

(3) Followspot Booths each
  with:
  (1) spot per booth;
  150' throw to proscenium;
  (3) 1Ø 30 amp breakers

DIMMERS
Lighting console is Strand
  520 or ETC Express 72/
  144;
(540) Strand CD-80
  dimmers
House has DMX control
  system;
  AMX house with DMX to
  AMX converter
(3) dry run DMX station(s)

ORPHEUM THEATER

Theatre Location: 409 South 16th Street, PO Box 719, Omaha, NE 68101
Management Company: City of Omaha

Main Administrative Phone:	402-444-5045
Main Administrative Fax:	402-444-4739
Stage Door Phone:	402-444-5045
Backstage Pay Phone:	402-342-9596

THEATRE STAFF

Theatre Manager	Larry Lahaie	402-444-4750
Booking	Susan Busskohl	402-444-4750
Group Sales	Marlene Belik	402-444-4750
Marketing	Stan Benis	402-444-4686

HOUSE CREW

Technical Supervisor	Al Brown	402-444-4750
Stage Manager	Jeff Brown	402-444-5045
Sound	Greg Toman	402-444-5045

UNIONS

IATSE Local #42	Robert Willis	402-733-7442
Wardrobe Local # 831	Joann Smith	402-733-8630
Musical Contractor		
Local #70-558	Shorty Vess	402-341-7352

SEATING CAPACITY

Orchestra	1,326
Boxes	20
Mezzanine	346
Balcony	1,135
Total:	**2,807**
pit (add'l)	60

BOX OFFICE
Computerized
Box Office Treasurer
  Jeff Tracy   402-444-4744

Outside Ticket Agency
None

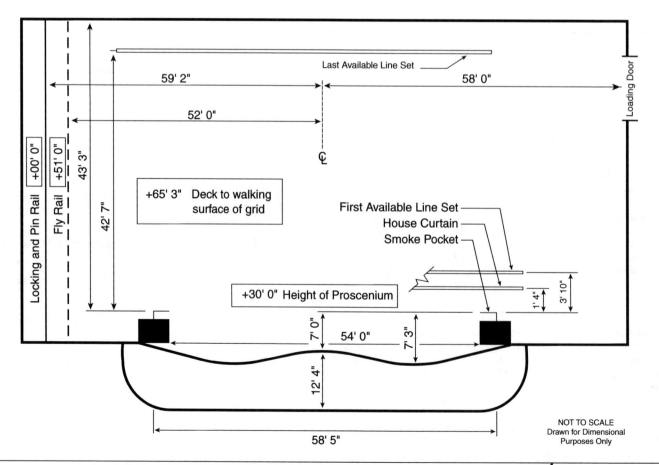

NOT TO SCALE
Drawn for Dimensional
Purposes Only

STAGE HOUSE

HOUSE CURTAIN
Operates as a guillotine from SR fly floor

RIGGING SYSTEM
Type:	Single purchase counter weight
Weight:	17,500 lbs available
Line sets:	32 sets at 6" o.c. with 7 lift lines per set
Arbors:	400 and 1400 lb capacity
House Pipes:	70' long with 59' of travel from deck

Line sets are not moveable
Block & Falls are not available
Chain hoists are not available
(20) spot wheels and 500' of hemp available

PERMANENT INSTALLATIONS OVER STAGE (FROM SMOKE POCKET)
None

PERMANENT INSTALLATIONS ON DECK
Columns (2) 5' wide x 3' deep at 33' located 37'0", USR & USL of center

ORCHESTRA PIT
Adjustable to 12'11" below stage level by hydraulic lift
Apron overhangs US wall of pit 6'7"

BACKSTAGE

LOADING DOCK
Loading door(s):
 10'0" high x 12'0" wide
Trucks load (1) at a time
If portable dock is built can load
 (4) trucks at same time
Fork lift is not required;
 Supplier is City of Omaha
 402-444-4750

WARDROBE
Location: Basement
Access: Direct from stage
(2) Washers (2) Dryers
Washer & dryer hookups available

DRESSING ROOMS
(2) Star, -1, shower included, toilet on same fl
(2) Small, -1, toilet included, shower on same fl
(1) Chorus, -1, t/s included

SOUND

CONSOLE
Yamaha PM 700
12 inputs, 4 main outputs

SPEAKERS
House Cluster
Under Balcony
No speaker truss

COMMUNICATIONS
Clear Com intercom with
 (1) channel
No hearing impaired system
Dressing room page system

ROAD CONSOLE
Located Booth or Rear
 Orchestra
(12) seats required to be
 removed
Cable run from stage is 120'
Tie-in into house system with
 XLR connectors

REHEARSAL & STORAGE SPACE
Rehearsal: None
Storage: None

ELECTRICS

ROAD SERVICE POWER

Panel	Phase	Amp	Circuit Protection	Use	Location
A-C	3	400	breaker	dimmers	SR

Hoist not required or provided

FRONT OF HOUSE (BOX BOOM VALUES ARE PER SIDE)

Position	Pipe Width	Distance to Prosc.	House Circuits	Connector Type	FOH Transfer Circuits
1st Balc Rail	93'	50'	30	grd 20 amp stage pin	30
Box Boom 1		45'	12	grd 20 amp stage pin	12

Transfer circuits: grd 20 amp stage pin located on DSR proscenium wall

EQUIPMENT FOH (BOX BOOM VALUES ARE PER SIDE)

Position	Quantity	Wattage	Instrument	Removeable
1st Balc Rail	12	1,000	Various Lekos	yes
Box Boom 1	12	1,000	Various Lekos	no

FOLLOWSPOTS
House Followspots:
 (3) Strong Xenon Super
 Troupers 2k; removeable

Followspot Booth:
 (3) spots per booth;
 135' throw to proscenium;
 (4) 1Ø 20 amp breakers

 Additional followspot
 location in balcony

DIMMERS
No lighting console
No dimmers
No dry run DMX station(s)

CASHMAN THEATRE

AT: **CASHMAN FIELD CENTER**

YEAR BUILT: 1983   YEAR RENOVATED: 1995

Theatre Location:	850 Las Vegas Blvd North, Las Vegas, NV 89101
Management Company:	Las Vegas Convention and Visitors Authority
	3150 Paradise Road, Las Vegas, NV 89109

Main Administrative Phone:	702-386-7100
Main Administrative Fax:	702-386-7126

THEATRE STAFF

Facility Director	Barry Strafacci	702-386-7100

HOUSE CREW

Technical Director	Terry Weaver	702-386-7100
Stage Manager	Fred Cundiff	702-386-7100

SEATING CAPACITY

Orchestra	244
Mezzanine	1,142
Balcony	556
Total:	**1,942**
wheelchair (add'l)	12

BOX OFFICE

Box office is promoter operated

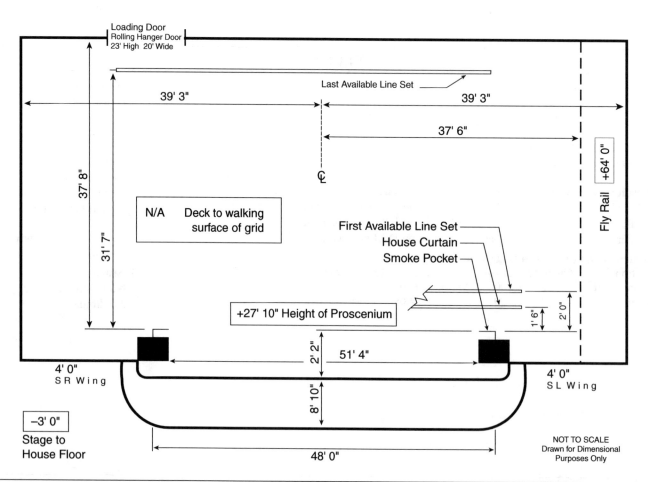

Loading Door
Rolling Hanger Door
23' High 20' Wide

Last Available Line Set

39' 3"   39' 3"

37' 6"

37' 8"

Fly Rail +64' 0"

31' 7"

N/A   Deck to walking surface of grid

First Available Line Set
House Curtain
Smoke Pocket

+27' 10" Height of Proscenium

1' 6"   2' 0"

2' 2"   51' 4"

4' 0"
SR Wing

4' 0"
SL Wing

8' 10"

−3' 0"
Stage to
House Floor

48' 0"

NOT TO SCALE
Drawn for Dimensional
Purposes Only

STAGE HOUSE

HOUSE CURTAIN
Operates as a guillotine or traveller from SL deck

RIGGING SYSTEM
Type:	Single purchase counter weight
Weight:	10,000 lbs available
Line sets:	40 sets at 6" o.c. with 7 lift lines per set
Arbors:	1,500 lb capacity
House Pipes:	66' long with 30' of travel from deck

Line sets are not moveable
Block & Falls are not available
Chain hoists are not available
(0) spot wheels and no hemp available
No grid, no pin rail, loading bridge weight limit is 1,000 lbs per foot

PERMANENT INSTALLATIONS OVER STAGE (FROM SMOKE POCKET)
M=Moveable with advance call
Electric borders (3) at 3'2", 10'0", 23'5"; M
Traveller (1) at 14'6"; M
Electric pipe (4) at 4', 13'2", 22'4", 25'6"; M
Cyclorama (2) at 29'3", 31'7"; M
Fire curtain (1)
Catwalk (1) over seating

PERMANENT INSTALLATIONS ON DECK
Trap (1) in stage floor
Loading bridge (1) 3'0 W x 31'L

ORCHESTRA PIT
Adjustable to 12' below stage level by manual lift
Apron overhangs US wall of pit 8'10"
Pit lift is in (1) section
Baby grand piano available, lowered to pit by fork lift or other means

BACKSTAGE

LOADING DOCK
Loading door(s):
23'0" high x 20'0"wide
Trucks load (1) at same time at stage door, (8) at same time if adjacent hall is leased
Stage level loading
Fork lift is required: Supplier is Lvcva (fee) 702-386-7100
Unlimited trailers can store on-site

WARDROBE
Location: 2nd floor
Access: Elevator
(1) Washer (1) Dryer
Washer and dryer hookups available

DRESSING ROOMS
(2) Star, SR, stage level, t/s included, phone jack
(9) Small, SL, stage level +1/+2, t/s included, phone jack
(2) Chorus, +2, t/s included, phone jack
Elevator access for dressing rooms
Additional production office available for company mgr

SOUND

CONSOLE
Yamaha 2404, located Balcony
24 inputs, 4 main outputs, 1 matrix outputs, 4 aux outputs

SPEAKERS
Proscenium
Portable
No speaker truss

COMMUNICATIONS
Clear Com intercom with (8) channels
Infrared sound system
Dressing room page system

ROAD CONSOLE
Location varies
Number of seats required to be removed varies
(13) patches SR, (13) SL, (26) in basement

REHEARSAL & STORAGE SPACE
Rehearsal: can be leased
Storage:(2) Adjacent exhibit halls can be leased,
'A', 50,000-100,000 sq ft
'B' for use as storage, addl wardrobe or dressing rms

ELECTRICS

ROAD SERVICE POWER

Panel	Phase	Amp	Circuit Protection	Use	Location
A	3	800	fuse	sound	USR
B	3	400	fuse		USL

Main dimmer rack is located on 4th floor
Recommended location of touring dimmer racks: (2) disconnects provided on stage
Additional power is available for tour buses, generators, etc.

FRONT OF HOUSE (BOX BOOM VALUES ARE PER SIDE)

Position	Pipe Width	Distance to Prosc.	House Circuits	Connector Type	FOH Transfer Circuits
House Truss		35'	36	grd 20 amp stage pin	
Proscenium Truss		0'	24	grd 20 amp stage pin	
Box Boom 1			10		

Transfer circuits: uses multi cables

EQUIPMENT FOH (BOX BOOM VALUES ARE PER SIDE)

Position	Quantity	Wattage	Instrument	Removeable
1st Balc Rail	12			
House Truss	30	750	16" Lekos	
Proscenium Truss	22	750	12" Lekos	
Box Boom 1	16	750	16" Lekos	

Cyclorama , 6 double 1000 cyc lights, removeable

FOLLOWSPOTS
House Followspots:
(4) Super Trouper; not removeable

(2) Followspot Booths:
(1) spot per booth;
98' throw to proscenium;
(198) 1Ø 20 amp breakers

DIMMERS
Lighting console is ETC Expression Comp BD;
(24) sub masters Soft Patch dimmers

PIONEER CENTER FOR THE PERFORMING ARTS

YEAR BUILT: 1968

Theatre Location: 100 South Virginia Street, Reno, NV 89501
Management Company: Reno Performing Arts Center Association

Main Administrative Phone:		702-686-6610
Main Administrative Fax:		702-686-6630
Backstage Pay Phone:		702-323-9830
Traveling Production Office Phone:		702-686-6638
Traveling Production Office Fax:		702-686-6639

THEATRE STAFF

Executive Director	John Skelton	702-686-6610
Booking	Christine Orr	702-686-6619
Operations	Tim Welch	702-686-6618

HOUSE CREW

Technical Director	Kai Howard	702-686-6620

SEATING CAPACITY

Balcony	514
Orchestra	986
Total:	**1,500**
pit (add'l)	30
wheelchair (add'l)	12

BOX OFFICE
Computerized
Guest Services Director
  Ken Potts   702-686-6616

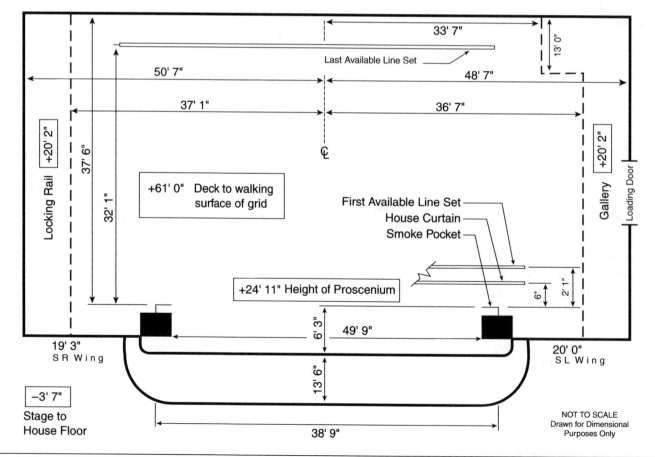

+61' 0" Deck to walking surface of grid

+24' 11" Height of Proscenium

33' 7"
13' 0"
Last Available Line Set
50' 7"
48' 7"
37' 1"
36' 7"
CL
Locking Rail +20' 2"
Gallery +20' 2"
Loading Door
37' 6"
32' 1"
First Available Line Set
House Curtain
Smoke Pocket
6"
2' 1"
6' 3"
49' 9"
19' 3"
SR Wing
20' 0"
SL Wing
13' 6"
−3' 7"
Stage to
House Floor
38' 9"

NOT TO SCALE
Drawn for Dimensional
Purposes Only

STAGE HOUSE

HOUSE CURTAIN
Operates as a guillotine or traveller from SR fly floor or deck

RIGGING SYSTEM
Type:	Double purchase counter weight
Weight:	20,000 lbs available
Line sets:	40 sets, o.c. varies, with 5 lift lines per set
Arbors:	varies
House Pipes:	varies

Line sets are moveable
Block & Falls are not available
Chain hoists are not available
(60) spot wheels and 900' of hemp available

PERMANENT INSTALLATIONS OVER STAGE (FROM SMOKE POCKET)
Electric borders (3) at 15'7", 21'4", 27'5"
Electric raceways (1) at 3'6"
Dead spaces (1) at 24' 0" (for 6")

PERMANENT INSTALLATIONS ON DECK
Stairs (2), 7'7" x 5'5" SR; 7'7" x 5'5" SL; at 30'8" to upstage edge (SR) and 0'0" (SL)

ORCHESTRA PIT
Adjustable to below stage level
Apron overhangs US wall of pit 3'8"
Pit lift is in (18) sections
Pit is made of wenger scaffold

BACKSTAGE

LOADING DOCK
Loading door(s):
   11'10" high x 9'10" wide
Trucks load (1) at a time
Loading is down freight elevator
   9'2" wide x 21' long x 12' high; does go to truck height
Fork lift is not required
Sound/Props cannot load in FOH
Trailers cannot store on-site

WARDROBE
Location: Backstage left
(2) Washers (2) Dryers
Washer and dryer hookups available

DRESSING ROOMS
(2) Star, SR, stage level, t/s included, phone jack
(1) Small, SR, stage level, t/s included
(1) Small, SR, stage level, t/s on same fl, phone jack
(2) Chorus, behind stage, t/s included
Elevator access for dressing rooms
Use dressing room for company mgr office

SOUND

CONSOLE
Yamaha PM 1200, located Rear House right
32 inputs, stereo L & E main outputs, 4 aux outputs

SPEAKERS
No house system
Portable
No speaker truss

COMMUNICATIONS
Clear Com intercom with (2) channels

ROAD CONSOLE
Located Rear House right
(6) seats required to be removed

REHEARSAL & STORAGE SPACE
Rehearsal: None
Storage: 52'5" x 28'10", located stage left

ELECTRICS

ROAD SERVICE POWER

Panel	Phase	Amp	Circuit Protection	Use	Location
A	3	800	yes	dimmers	SR
B	3	100	yes	sound	shop off SL

Recommended location of touring dimmer racks: SR
Hoist not required

FRONT OF HOUSE (BOX BOOM VALUES ARE PER SIDE)

Position	Pipe Width	Distance to Prosc.	House Circuits	Connector Type	FOH Transfer Circuits
Balc Rail		56'	18	grd 20 amp stage pin	
1st Cove		55'	18	grd 20 amp stage pin	

Transfer circuits: all FOH circuits can be picked up at DSR with 5 pin DMX -512

EQUIPMENT FOH (BOX BOOM VALUES ARE PER SIDE)

Position	Quantity	Wattage	Instrument	Removeable
1st Cove	28	575	Altman Shakespeare	yes

FOLLOWSPOTS
House Followspots:
   (2) Super Trouper II; removeable

Followspot Booth:
   (2) spots per booth;
   95' throw to proscenium;
   (2) 1Ø 30 amp breakers

DIMMERS
Lighting console is Expression 2x;
(160) Kliegl K96 dimmers
House has programmable DMX control system
(2) dry run DMX station(s), located DSR, 1st Cove

TAJ MAHAL

AKA: XANADU SHOWROOM

		SEATING CAPACITY	
Theatre Location:	1000 Boardwalk, Atlantic City, NJ 08401	**Total:**	**1,194**

Main Administrative Phone: 609-449-5100
Main Administrative Fax: 609-449-5137
E-mail: entertainment@trumptaj.com
Website: ww.trumptaj.com

THEATRE STAFF

Entertainment Manager	John Totaro	609-449-5110
Vice Pres Entertainment	Stephanie Nielson	609-449-5140

HOUSE CREW

Bob Anderson	609-449-5125
Bill Quirk	609-449-5198

STAGE DIMENSIONS (FROM SMOKE POCKET)

Stage is 48'0" deep
Width from Center Line to SL is 44'0"
Width from Center Line to SR is 44'0"
Proscenium width is 42'0"
Proscenium height is 26'0"
Smoke pocket to apron edge is 10'0"
No orchestra pit

RIGGING

Grid Height:	73'
Type:	Single purchase counter weight
Weight:	40,000 lbs
Line sets:	13 sets at 36" o.c.
Arbors:	500 lb capacity
House Pipes:	60' long

LOADING DOCK

Loading door(s) are 10'0"high x 16'0"wide
Trucks load (2) at same time
Fork lift is not required and is available

ELECTRICS

Total power available:
   800A 3Ø SR
   400A 3Ø SR

FOLLOWSPOTS

House Followspots:
   Strong Super Trouper
Power in spot booth 60A

DIMMERS

(254) house dimmers
House has DMX control system
(3) dry run station(s) located
   SR, Light Booth

SOUND

House has 200A dedicated
   power located SL
Sound console is available

BLOCKBUSTER - SONY MUSIC ENTERTAINMENT CENTRE

YEAR BUILT: 1995

Theatre Location: 1 Harbour Blvd., Camden, NJ 08103

Main Administrative Phone:	609-365-1300	
Main Administrative Fax:	609-365-1062	
Website:	ww.ecentre.com	
Traveling Production Office Phone:	609-635-0700	
Traveling Production Office Fax:	609-635-9886	

SEATING CAPACITY
Total: **6,590**

wheelchair (add'l)   120

THEATRE STAFF
Executive Director   Alan DeZon   609-365-1300

HOUSE CREW
Director of Operations   Curt Voss   609-365-1300
Carpentry   Chuck Ogle   609-365-1300 x721
Electrics   Tim Johnson   609-365-1300

STAGE DIMENSIONS (FROM SMOKE POCKET)
Stage is 60'0" deep
Width from Center Line to SL is 50'0"
Width from Center Line to SR is 50'0"
Proscenium width is 100'0"
Proscenium height is 46'6"
Orchestra pit exists

RIGGING
Grid Height:	67'
Type:	Single purchase counter weight
Weight:	13,000 lbs
Line sets:	68 sets at 6-8" o.c.
Arbors:	2,000 lb capacity
House Pipes:	70' long

LOADING DOCK
Loading door(s) are 12'0" high x 20'0" wide
Trucks load (8) at same time
Fork lift is not required and is available

ELECTRICS
Total power available:
  (2) 600A 3Ø SL
  (1) 400A 3Ø USR
  (1) 200A 3Ø USR

FOLLOWSPOTS
House Followspots:
  Lycian Arc 2k
No power in spot booth
FOH transfer circuits: DMX

DIMMERS
(384) house dimmers
House has DMX control system
(24) dry run station(s) located
  FOH, Catwalks, SL, SR, Grid

SOUND
House has (1) 400A, (1)
  200A dedicated power
  located USR
FOH mixing position in
  Center Orchestra
No sound console available

JOHN HARMS CENTER FOR THE ARTS

YEAR BUILT: 1926   YEAR RENOVATED: 1998

Theatre Location: 30 N. Van Brunt Street, Englewood, NJ 07631

Main Administrative Phone:	201-567-5797
Main Administrative Fax:	201-567-7357
Stage Door Phone:	201-894-9687
Backstage Pay Phone:	201-894-9687

SEATING CAPACITY

Orchestra- Permanent Seats	754
Orchestra- Temporary Seats	56
Loge	243
Balcony	324
Total:	**7,383**
wheelchair (add'l)	6

THEATRE STAFF

General Manager	Daiza Falco	201-567-5797 x 11
Executive Director	David Rodriguez	201-567-5797 x 20

HOUSE CREW

Director of Operations	Gerry Bakal	201-507-5797 x 12

STAGE DIMENSIONS (FROM SMOKE POCKET)

Stage is 29'8" deep
Width from Center Line to SL is 29'8"
Width from Center Line to SR is 31'8"
Proscenium width is 33'4"
Proscenium height is 23'0"
Smoke pocket to apron edge is 3'0"
Orchestra pit exists

RIGGING

Grid Height:	43'
Type:	Single purchase counter weight
Weight:	20,800 lbs
Line sets:	26 sets at 6-18" o.c.
Arbors:	800 lb capacity
House Pipes:	42'

LOADING DOCK

Loading door(s) are 10'0' high x 8'0" wide
Trucks load (1) at a time
Fork lift is not required and is not available

ELECTRICS

UNDER RENOVATION
Total power available:
1200A 3Ø

FOLLOWSPOTS

House Followspots:
Strong Super Trouper
Power in spot booth (4) 20A

DIMMERS

(275) house dimmers
House has DMX control system
(20) dry run station(s) located
catwalk

SOUND

House has 200A
dedicated power located
SL / SR
FOH mixing position in
Rear Orchestra Center
Sound console is available

STATE THEATRE NEW BRUNSWICK

AT: NEW BRUNSWICK CULTURAL CENTER

YEAR BUILT: **1921**   YEAR RENOVATED: **1988**

Theatre Location: 11 Livingston Avenue, New Brunswick, NJ 08901

Main Administrative Phone:	732-247-7200
Main Administrative Fax:	732-247-4005
E-mail:	infor@statetheatre.com
Website:	www.statetheatre.com
Backstage Pay Phone:	732-246-9609
Traveling Production Office Phone:	732-745-5650
Traveling Production Office Fax:	732-745-5651

SEATING CAPACITY

Premium	756
A	328
B	552
C	157
Total:	**1,793**
pit (add'l)	flexible
wheelchair (add'l)	15
standing (add'l)	0

THEATRE STAFF

Theatre Manager	David Hartkern	732-247-7200 x518
President	David Fleming	732-247-7200 x511

HOUSE CREW

Director Operations	Vantony A. Jenkins	732-247-7200 x529
Carpentry	Mike Sivetz	732-247-7200 x528
Electrics	Craig Werner	732-247-7200 x526

STAGE DIMENSIONS (FROM SMOKE POCKET)
Stage is 37'8" deep
Width from Center Line to SL is 48'4"
Width from Center Line to SR is 38'4"
Proscenium width is 45'9"
Proscenium height is 28'7"
Smoke pocket to apron edge is 12'0"
Orchestra pit exists

RIGGING

Grid Height:	55'
Type:	Single purchase counter weight
Weight:	4,800 lbs
Line sets:	34 sets
House Pipes:	50' long

LOADING DOCK
Loading door(s) are 15'0"high x 12'0"wide
Trucks load (2) at same time
Fork lift is not required and is not available

ELECTRICS
Total power available:
(1) 600A 3Ø SR
(1) 150A 3Ø SR

FOLLOWSPOTS
House Followspots:
Xenon Super Trouper
No power in spot booth

DIMMERS
(300) house dimmers
House has DMX control system
(2) dry run station(s) located SR

SOUND
House has 100A dedicated
power located SR
FOH mixing position in
Rear House Center
Sound console is available

PRUDENTIAL HALL

AT: NEW JERSEY PERFORMING ARTS CENTER **YEAR BUILT: 1997**

Theatre Location: 1 Center Street, Newark, NJ 07102
Management Company: New Jersey Performing Arts Center (address as above)

Main Administrative Phone: 973-642-8989
Main Administrative Fax: 973-648-6724
Website: www.njpac.org
Stage Door Phone: 973-642-8989 x 3177
Backstage Pay Phone: 973-622-8829
Traveling Production Office Phone: 973-297-5865
Traveling Production Office Fax: 973-353-8010

THEATRE STAFF
President & CEO   Lawrence P. Goldman 973-642-8989 x5846
Booking   Stephanie S. Hughley 973-642-8989 x3106
Operations   Audrey Winkler   973-642-8989 x5869
Group Sales   Schary Cole   973-642-8989 x5873

HOUSE CREW
Production Manager   Ross S. Richards   973-642-8989 x3862
Carpentry   Charlie Buli   973-642-8989 x5860
Electrics   Jim Eisner   973-642-8989 x5856
Sound   Kevin Mochel   973-642-8989 x5878

UNIONS
IATSE Local #21   Bill Lynch   201-379-9265
Wardrobe Local #21   Bill Lynch   201-379-9265

SEATING CAPACITY
Grand Tier Orchestra & Boxes	1,162
First Tier & Boxes	378
Second Tier & Boxes	363
Third Tier & Boxes	345
Fourth Tier & Boxes	594
Total:	**2,842**
pit (incl.)	100
wheelchair (add'l)	12

BOX OFFICE
Computerized
Director of Ticket Sales
   Linda Forlini   973-642-8989 x5840

Outside Ticket Agency
None

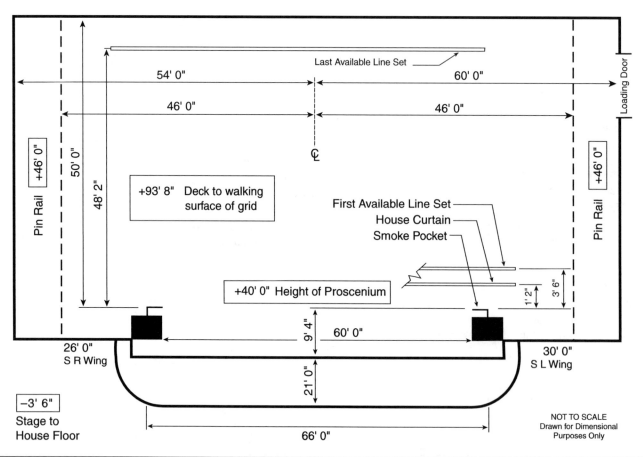

54' 0"   60' 0"
46' 0"   46' 0"
Last Available Line Set
Loading Door
Pin Rail +46' 0"   Pin Rail +46' 0"
50' 0"
48' 2"
+93' 8" Deck to walking surface of grid
First Available Line Set
House Curtain
Smoke Pocket
+40' 0" Height of Proscenium
1' 2"
3' 6"
9' 4"   60' 0"
26' 0" S R Wing   30' 0" S L Wing
21' 0"
−3' 6"
Stage to House Floor
66' 0"

NOT TO SCALE
Drawn for Dimensional
Purposes Only

STAGE HOUSE

HOUSE CURTAIN
Operates as a guillotine from SR deck

RIGGING SYSTEM
Type:	Single purchase counter weight system
Weight:	100,000 lbs available
Line sets:	78 sets at 6" o.c. with 6 lift lines per set
Arbors:	2,000 lb capacity
House Pipes:	73'6" long with 88' of travel from deck

Block & Falls are available / 3,000' of hemp available

Chain hoists available as a rental; (4) one ton

Tab pipes, 47' SL & SR of CL, under fly galleries; motorized ladders, 40' SL & SR adjustable 5'-50' from PL

PERMANENT INSTALLATIONS OVER STAGE (FROM SMOKE POCKET)
M=Moveable with advance call

Orchestra shells (1) at 50'0" stored, 0'6" deployed

Electric Raceways (1) at 1st Electric, 5'2"

Traveller (2) at 20'2", 27'8"; M

Electric pipe (5) at 14'8", 22'2", 30'2", 38'8", 43'8"; M

Hard portal (1), 1'10" US, 62'0" W x 24'0" H

Cyclorama (1) at 41'8"; M

Fire curtain (1) at 0'0"

Ductwork, 50'0" at 30'0" H, SL & SR

PERMANENT INSTALLATIONS ON DECK
Electric jump 73'6"

Hard legs (2), 10' W x 44'H, 6' soft legs; lineset 3, 2'4" US

Stairs (2) DSL,DSR

Loading bridge (2)

Adjustable portal (1)

Orchestra Tower storage (1), 60'0" x 15'0", starts 50'0" US

ORCHESTRA PIT
Adjustable by Gala Spiral Lifts: Apron overhangs US wall of pit 9'4": Pit lift is in (2) sections

BACKSTAGE

LOADING DOCK
Loading door(s): 18'6" high x 11'8" wide

Trucks load (3) side by side at same time

Fork lift is not required

Sound/Props cannot load in FOH

Trailers can store on-site

Security at dock & stage door

WARDROBE
Location: Wardrobe SR of theatre, Laundry in basement

(2) Washers (2) Dryers

No washer or dryer hookups

DRESSING ROOMS
Elevator access for dressing rooms

Additional production office available for company mgr

SOUND

CONSOLE
Soundcraft Vienna II, located Orchestra level

40 inputs, 8 main outputs, 8 matrix outputs, 8 aux outputs

SPEAKERS
Portable

No speaker truss

COMMUNICATIONS
Clear Com intercom with (4) channels

Infrared sound system

Dressing room page system

ROAD CONSOLE
Located Orchestra

Cable run from stage is 250'

Tie-in into house system with XLR connectors

REHEARSAL & STORAGE SPACE
Rehearsal: Rehearsal Hall 60' x 50', 3rd level, mirrors, sprung floor, barres, baby grand Community Room 22' x 32', 3rd level, mirrors, barres, upright piano

Storage: Loading Dock 50' x 32' SL, Dollies, J-bars

ELECTRICS

ROAD SERVICE POWER
Panel	Phase	Amp	Circuit Protection	Use	Location
A-E	3	400	breaker	dimmers	mid SL, stage level
F-I	3	100	breaker	extra	DSL, DSR
J-M	3	100	breaker	extra	USL, USR
N	3	100	breaker	extra	Trap room
O	3	400	breaker	extra	Loading dock
P-Q	3	200	breaker	sound	USL, USR
R	3	100	breaker	sound	Loading dock

Location of touring dimmer racks SL: Hoist not required: Addl power available

FRONT OF HOUSE (BOX BOOM VALUES ARE PER SIDE)
Position	Pipe Width	Distance to Prosc.	House Circuits	Connector Type	FOH Transfer Circuits
2nd Balc Rail	40'	94.5'	27	grd 20 amp stage pin	27
3rd Balc Rail	40'	104'	8	grd 20 amp stage pin	8
Far Catwalk	60'	110'	56	grd 20 amp stage pin	56
Near Catwalk	40'	100'	32	grd 20 amp stage pin	32
Upper box rails	16'	55'	8	grd 20 amp stage pin	8
Mid box rails	16'	45'	8	grd 20 amp stage pin	8
Low box rails	16'	32'	8	grd 20 amp stage pin	8
Proscenium torm		10'	12	grd 20 amp stage pin	12

EQUIPMENT FOH (BOX BOOM VALUES ARE PER SIDE)
Position	Quantity	Wattage	Instrument	Removeable
2nd Balc Rail	8	575	Source4 10°	yes
Hi Balc Rail	12	575	Source4 10°	yes
Mid Balc Rail	8	575	Source4 10°	yes
Low Balc Rail	8	575	Source4 10°	yes
Far Catwalk	24	575	Source4 5°	yes

FOLLOWSPOTS
House Followspots: (4) Xenon Super Trouper II 2k; not removeable

Followspot Booth: (4) spots per booth; 165' throw to proscenium; (4) 3Ø 30 amp breakers

DIMMERS
House console is ETC Obsession 1500; (665) ETC Sensor dimmers

No DMX control system

(2) dry run DMX station(s)

POPEJOY HALL

AT: UNIVERSITY OF NEW MEXICO, CENTER FOR THE ARTS

YEAR BUILT: 1965   YEAR RENOVATED: 1996

Theatre Location:	Cornell & Redondo
	Albuquerque, NM 87131-3176
Mailing Address:	Popejoy Hall, University of New Mexico,
	Albuquerque, NM 87131-3176
Management Company:	UNM Public Events (mailing address as above)

Main Administrative Phone:	505-277-3824
Main Administrative Fax:	505-277-7353
Website:	www.popejoyhall.com
Stage Door Phone:	505-277-9415
Traveling Production Office Phone:	505-277-7832

THEATRE STAFF

Director	Tom Tkach	505-277-3824
Booking	Tom Tkach	505-277-3824

UNIONS

IATSE Local #423	Michael Hanrahan, Sr.	505-883-6055
Wardrobe Local #483	Kim Cunnington	505-821-7608
Music Local #418	Brent Stephens	505-881-9590

SEATING CAPACITY

Orchestra	1,116
Mezzanine	236
Balcony	598
Total:	**1,950**

pit (add'l)	94
wheelchair (incl)	32

BOX OFFICE
Outside Ticket Agency
Computerized
Pro-Tix

Tom Reynolds	505-925-5634

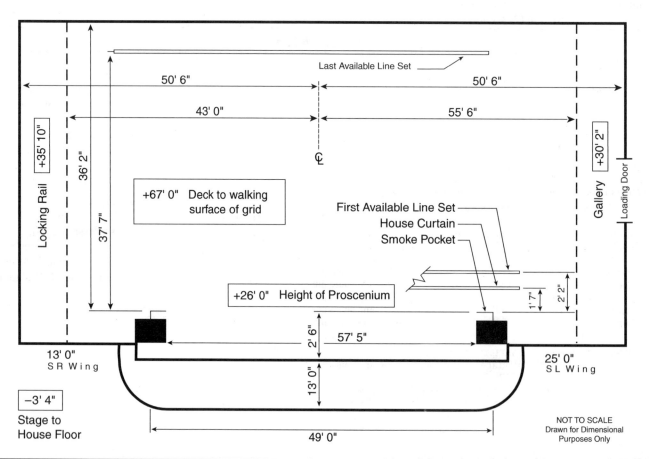

STAGE HOUSE

HOUSE CURTAIN
Operates as a guillotine or traveller from SR fly floor or deck

RIGGING SYSTEM

Type:	Single purchase counter weight
Weight:	15,000 lbs available
Line sets:	47 sets at 6" o.c. with 7 lift lines per set
House Pipes:	64' long with 64' of travel from deck

Line sets are moveable
Block & Falls are available
Chain hoists available as a rental; (10) one ton (6) half ton
(10) spot wheels and 600' of hemp available

PERMANENT INSTALLATIONS OVER STAGE (FROM SMOKE POCKET)
M=Moveable with advance call
Orchestra shell (4) Ceiling pieces at 4'2", 11'9", 19'2", 26'9"; M
Electric pipe (1) 1st electric at 3'6"
Fire curtain (1) at 0'3" from plaster line

PERMANENT INSTALLATIONS ON DECK
Adjustable portal (2), 32' high x 12' wide, DS of pocket

ORCHESTRA PIT
Adjustable to 16' below stage level by hydraulic lift
Apron overhangs US wall of pit 6'0"
Pit lift is in (1) section

BACKSTAGE

LOADING DOCK
Loading door(s):
  9'11" high x 7'10 wide
Trucks load (3) at same time
Fork lift is not required
Sound/Props cannot load in FOH
(3) Trailers can store on-site
Security at stage door

WARDROBE
Location: Downstairs level
Access: Orchestra pit
(1) Washer (1) Dryer
Washer and dryer hookups available

DRESSING ROOMS
(2) Star, SR, stage level, t/s included, phone jack
(4) Small, SR, stage level/ +1/ -1, t/s included, phone jack
(3) Chorus, SR, +1 / -1, t/s included, phone jack
Use dressing room for company mgr office

SOUND

CONSOLE
Midas XL 200
  SR 24 inputs
  SL 24 inputs

SPEAKERS
Proscenium
No speaker truss

COMMUNICATIONS
Clear Com intercom with (2) channels
Infrared sound system
Dressing room page system

ROAD CONSOLE
Located Rear Orchestra
(11) seats required to be removed
Cable run from stage is 230'
Tie-in into house system

REHEARSAL & STORAGE SPACE
Rehearsal: None
Storage: Trap Room, 10' x 101', on lower level

ELECTRICS

ROAD SERVICE POWER

Panel	Phase	Amp	Circuit Protection	Use	Location
A	3	400	breaker	dimmers	DSL
B	3	400	breaker	sound	DSL
C	3	600	breaker	extra	DSL

Total service fused @ 800 amps
Recommended location of touring dimmer racks: DSL
Hoist not required
Additional power is available for tour buses, generators, etc.

FRONT OF HOUSE (BOX BOOM VALUES ARE PER SIDE)

Position	Pipe Width	Distance to Prosc.	House Circuits	Connector Type	FOH Transfer Circuits
1st Cove		46'9"	80	twist lock	
2nd Cove		50'8"	10	twist lock	
1st Balc Rail		77'6"	12	twist lock	
Box Boom 1		36'0"	20	twist lock	

Transfer circuits: DMX512

EQUIPMENT FOH (BOX BOOM VALUES ARE PER SIDE)

Position	Quantity	Wattage	Instrument	Removeable
1st Balc Rail	34	1,000	Altman 6x16	yes
1st Cove	12	1,000	Altman KL8 Zoom	yes
2nd Cove	24	1,000	10" Ellipsoidals	
Box Boom 1	8	1,000	Altman Zoom	yes

FOLLOWSPOTS
House Followspots:
  (2) Lycians HP1209
  (2) Super Trouper Xenon

Followspot Booth:
  (1) spot per booth;
  138' throw to proscenium;

DIMMERS
Lighting console is Strand 550D / 430 / LBX;
House has own dimmers
House has programmable DMX control system

PAN AMERICAN CENTER

AT: NEW MEXICO STATE UNIVERSITY   YEAR BUILT: 1968

		SEATING CAPACITY	
Theatre Location:	Corner of University & Payne, Las Cruces, NM 88003	**Total:**	**3,000**
Mailing Address:	NMSR Special Events, Box 30001, Dept. 3SE		
	Las Cruces, NM 88003		

Main Administrative Phone:	505-646-4413
Main Administrative Fax:	505-646-3605
E-mail:	wlofdahl@nmsu.edu
Website:	ccsu.nmsu.edu/spevents
Traveling Production Office Phone:	505-646-1871

THEATRE STAFF

Director Special Events Will Lofdahl   505-646-4413

HOUSE CREW

Operations Manager   Gary Rachele   505-646-5437

STAGE DIMENSIONS (FROM SMOKE POCKET)
Stage is 40' deep
Width from Center Line to SL is 30'
Width from Center Line to SR is 30'
Proscenium width is 40'
Proscenium height is 24'
Adjustable portable staging
No orchestra pit

RIGGING

Grid Height:	58'
Type:	Tomcat truss system (chain motors)
Line sets:	6 sets

LOADING DOCK
Loading door(s) are 7'6" high x 9'0" wide
Trucks load (6) at same time
Fork lift is required and is available

ELECTRICS
Total power available:
(1) 600A 3Ø USL
(1) 400A 3Ø USL
(1) 400A 3Ø USR
(1) 200A 3Ø DSL

FOLLOWSPOTS
House Followspots:
Xenon Super Troupers

DIMMERS
No house dimmers

SOUND
No backstage power available
No sound console available

PALACE THEATRE

AT: PALACE PERFORMING ARTS CENTER   **YEAR BUILT: 1931**

Theatre Location: 19 Clinton Avenue, Albany, NY 12207
Management Company: Palace Performing Arts Center

Main Administrative Phone: 518-465-3334
Main Administrative Fax: 518-427-0151
E-mail: palaceth@aol.com
Stage Door Phone: 518-465-3379

THEATRE STAFF
Business Manager   Aleks Stojanovic   518-465-3334
Executive Director   Robert Goepfert   518-465-0681

HOUSE CREW
IATSE B.A   Dick Rider   518-427-1580

SEATING CAPACITY

Downstairs	1,547
Loge & Balcony	1,260
Total:	**2,870**

pit (add'l)	0
wheelchair (add'l)	0
standing (add'l)	0

STAGE DIMENSIONS (FROM SMOKE POCKET)
Stage is 23'9" deep
Width from Center Line to SL is 35'0"
Width from Center Line to SR is 35'0"
Proscenium width is 64'0"
Proscenium height is 43'0"
Smoke pocket to apron edge is 3'0"
Orchestra pit exists

RIGGING
Grid Height: 86'
Type: Double purchase counter weight
Weight: 8,000 lbs
Line sets: 30 sets at 6" o.c.
Arbors: 600 lb capacity
House Pipes: 70' long

LOADING DOCK
Loading door(s) are 8'0" high x 6'0" wide
Trucks load (1) at a time
Fork lift is not required and is not available

ELECTRICS
Total power available:
    (2) 400A 3Ø SR

FOLLOWSPOTS
House Followspots:
    Strong Super Trouper
Power in spot booth from main
electrics

DIMMERS
No house dimmers
No DMX control system

SOUND
No backstage power available
FOH mixing position in
    Center Orchestra
No sound console available

BROOME COUNTY FORUM THEATRE

AKA: THE FORUM AT: BROOME CENTER FOR THE PERFORMING ARTS

YEAR BUILT: 1919   YEAR RENOVATED: 1996

Theatre Location: 236 Washington Street, Binghamton, NY 13901
Management Company: Broome County Parks and Recreation
                    P.O. Box 1766, Binghamton, NY 13902

Main Administrative Phone:	607-778-2480
Main Administrative Fax:	607-778-6540
Stage Door Phone:	607-778-8967
Traveling Production Office Phone:	607-778-2977
Traveling Production Office Fax:	607-778-6110

THEATRE STAFF
Forum Manager	Christine Springer	607-778-2480

HOUSE CREW
Forum Manager	Christine Springer	607-778-2480
IATSE Local #54 BA	Harold Hingos	607-656-8533

SEATING CAPACITY

Orchestra	991
Mezzanine	135
Balcony	393
Total:	**1,519**
pit (add'l)	40
wheelchair (add'l)	8

STAGE DIMENSIONS (FROM SMOKE POCKET)
Stage is 31'0" deep
Width from Center Line to SL is 34'0"
Width from Center Line to SR is 30'0"
Proscenium width is 38'6"
Proscenium height is 24'6"
Smoke pocket to apron edge is 4'0"
Orchestra pit exists

RIGGING
Grid Height:	60'
Type:	Single purchase counter weight
Weight:	15,000 lbs
Line sets:	48 sets at 5" o.c.
Arbors:	1,000 lb capacity
House Pipes:	50' long

LOADING DOCK
Loading door(s) are 11'3" high x 6'8" wide
Trucks load (2) at same time
Fork lift is not required and is not available

ELECTRICS
Total power available:
  (1) 600A 3Ø DSR
  (1) 400A 3Ø DSR

FOLLOWSPOTS
House Followspots:
  Carbon Arc
No power in spot booth

DIMMERS
(192) house dimmers
House has DMX control system
(3) dry run station(s) located SR

SOUND
House has 400 amp dedicated power located DSR basement
FOH mixing position in Rear House Right
No sound console available

BROOKLYN ACADEMY OF MUSIC: MAJESTIC THEATER

Theatre Location: 651 Fulton Street, Brooklyn, NY 11217
Mailing Address: 30 Lafayette Avenue, Brooklyn, NY 11217

Main Administrative Phone: 718-636-4100
Main Administrative Fax: 718-636-4126
Stage Door Phone: 718-636-4150/4188

SEATING CAPACITY
Benches 652
Gallery Stools 241
Total: **893**

THEATRE STAFF
General Manager Alice Bernstein 718-636-4195
Asst General Manager Robin Ford 718-636-4195

HOUSE CREW
Production Manager Coleman Rupp 718-636-4146

STAGE DIMENSIONS (FROM SMOKE POCKET)
Stage is 37'8" deep
Width from Center Line to SL is 31'3"
Width from Center Line to SR is 29'0"
Proscenium width is 37'11"
Proscenium height is 29'0"

RIGGING
Grid Height: 64'2"
Type: Hydraulic counter weight system
Line sets: 32 sets at 12" o.c.
Arbors: 1,200 lb capacity
House Pipes: 49' long

LOADING DOCK
Loading door(s) are 16'0" high x 8'0" wide
Trucks load (1) at a time
Fork lift is required and is not available
Dock is at 212 Ashland Place; stage is 5' above street level

ELECTRICS
Data not provided

FOLLOWSPOTS
House Followspots:
(2) Satellite 575 w HMI

DIMMERS
(168) house dimmers
House has DMX control system

SOUND
Sound console is available

BROOKLYN ACADEMY OF MUSIC: OPERA HOUSE

Theatre Location: 30 Lafayette Avenue, Brooklyn, NY 11217

Main Administrative Phone: 718-636-4146
Main Administrative Fax: 718-636-1486
Traveling Production Office Phone: 718-636-4147

THEATRE STAFF
General Manager   Alice Bernstein   718-636-4195
Asst General Manager   Robin Ford   718-636-4195

HOUSE CREW
Production Manager   Coleman Rupp   718-636-4146

UNIONS
IATSE Local #1   Tony DePaulo   212-333-2500
Wardrobe Local #764   Ray Polgar   212-221-1717
AFM Local #802   Bill Dennison   212-245-4802

SEATING CAPACITY

Orchestra	934
Mezzanine	619
Balcony	530
Boxes	72
Total:	**2,155**
pit (add'l)	76

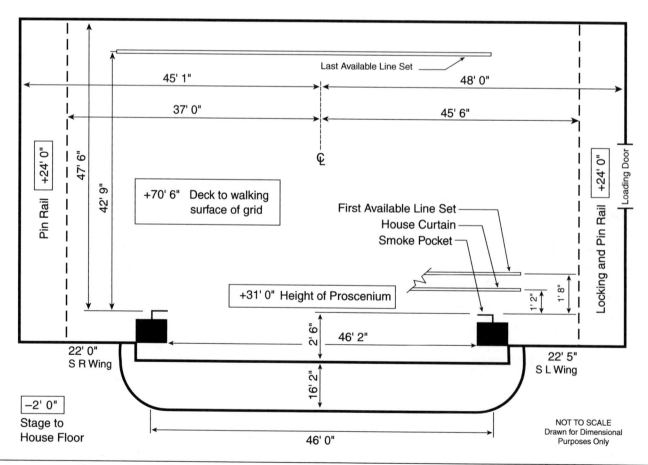

Last Available Line Set

45' 1"   48' 0"

37' 0"   45' 6"

C̶L

Pin Rail +24' 0"

47' 6"

42' 9"

+70' 6" Deck to walking surface of grid

First Available Line Set
House Curtain
Smoke Pocket

Locking and Pin Rail +24' 0"

Loading Door

1' 2"   1' 8"

+31' 0" Height of Proscenium

2' 6"   46' 2"

22' 0"
S R Wing

22' 5"
S L Wing

16' 2"

−2' 0"
Stage to
House Floor

46' 0"

NOT TO SCALE
Drawn for Dimensional
Purposes Only

STAGE HOUSE

HOUSE CURTAIN

Operates as a guillotine from fly floor; center split

RIGGING SYSTEM

Type:	Single or double purchase counter weight
Weight:	600 lbs available
Line sets:	79 sets at 6" o.c.
Arbors:	1,100 lb capacity
	600 lbs for double purchase
House Pipes:	66' long with 62' of travel from deck

Line sets are not moveable

Chain hoists available as a rental; (9) one ton

PERMANENT INSTALLATIONS OVER STAGE (FROM SMOKE POCKET)

M=Moveable with advance call

Orchestra shells (1)

Electric borders (5) at 3'0", 10'0", 18'0", 24'0", 33'0"

Traveller (1); M

Ceiling sections (4) at 5'0", 11'0", 19'0", 25'0"

PERMANENT INSTALLATIONS ON DECK

None

ORCHESTRA PIT

Adjustable to 11' below stage level by hydraulic lift

Pit lift is in (2) sections

BACKSTAGE

LOADING DOCK

Loading door(s):
13'0" high x 6'2" wide

Dock is at 319 Ashland Place;
Door is 3'8" above stage
floor; ramp available

Fork lift is required

Sound/Props cannot load in
FOH

Lobby cannot be a work area

Trailers cannot store on-site

Security at stage door

WARDROBE

Location: (2) on 4th fl; laundry
on 1st fl

Access: Elevator and Stairs

(2) Washers (2) Dryers

DRESSING ROOMS

Elevator access for dressing
rooms

Additional production office
available for company mgr

SOUND

CONSOLE

Yamaha PM 3000, located
Orchestra HL

40 inputs, 8 main outputs

SPEAKERS

House Cluster

Proscenium

Under Balcony

Portable

Mezzanine

Additional stage speakers

Speaker truss exists

COMMUNICATIONS

Clear Com intercom with
(4) channels

Dressing room page system

ELECTRICS

ROAD SERVICE POWER

Panel	Phase	Amp	Circuit Protection	Use	Location
A	3	600	fuse	dimmers	DSL
B-C	3	400	fuse	extra	DSL
D	3	200	fuse	sound	DSL

Recommended location of touring dimmer racks: DSL

Hoist not required

Additional power is available for tour buses, generators, etc.

FRONT OF HOUSE (BOX BOOM VALUES ARE PER SIDE)

Position	Pipe Width	Distance to Prosc.	House Circuits	Connector Type	FOH Transfer Circuits
1st Balc Rail		60'	23		
2nd Balc Rail		85'	5		
Mezz Rail		50'	16		
Box Boom 1			9		
Box Boom 2			4		

Road truss: 3 Hoist points at 15' DS of 0'0" for truss

EQUIPMENT FOH (BOX BOOM VALUES ARE PER SIDE)

Position	Quantity	Wattage	Instrument	Removeable
1st Balc Rail	10	1,000	Q axial	yes
2nd Balc Rail	24	1,000	Q axial	yes
Box Boom 1	12		ETC Source4	
Box Boom 2	12			

FOLLOWSPOTS

House Followspots:
(2) Super Troupers

Followspot Booth:
(2) spots per booth

DIMMERS

(472) 2.4k 6ks ETC Sensor
dimmers

House has programmable
DMX control system

SHEA'S PERFORMING ARTS CENTER

YEAR BUILT: 1926   YEAR RENOVATED: 1998

Theatre Location: 646 Main Street, Buffalo, NY 14202
Management Company: Shea's O'Connell Preservation Guild, Inc.

Main Administrative Phone: 716-847-1410
Main Administrative Fax: 716-847-1644
E-mail: sheas@buffnet.net
Website: www.sheas.org
Stage Door Phone: 716-847-0054

THEATRE STAFF
President & CEO   Patrick Fagan   716-847-1410 x123
Booking   Patrick Fagan   716-847-1410 x123
Marketing   Meghan McQuestion   716-847-1420 x122
Group Sales   Kate Scaglione   716-847-1410 x132

HOUSE CREW
Dir. of Tech. Services   Chris Dimitroff   716-847-1410 x166
Carpentry   Gerald Orzechowski
Electrics   Peter Gill
Sound   Joseph Abad   716-822-2770

UNIONS
IATSE Local #10   Joseph Abad   716-822-2770
Wardrobe Local #783   Mary Jo Witherall   716-827-1766
AFM Local #92   Lon Gormley   716-881-6422

SEATING CAPACITY
Orchestra   1,694
Loge   358
Balcony   1,131
Total   **3,183**

BOX OFFICE
Computerized
Director of Patron Services
  Scott Saxon   716-847-1410 x131

Outside Ticket Agency
Computerized
Ticketmaster
  Carol Bracato   716-847-1614

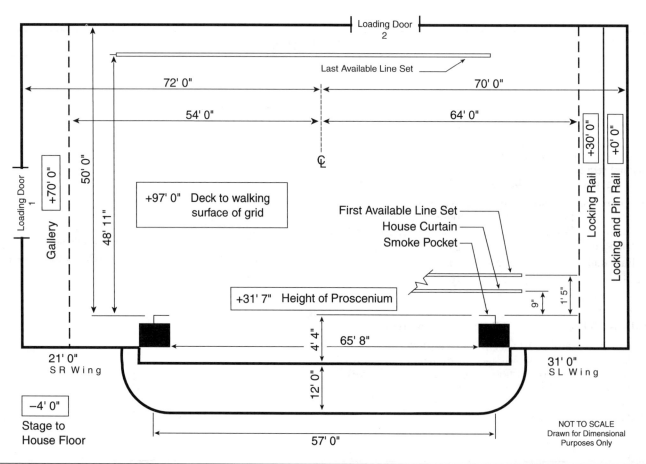

STAGE HOUSE

HOUSE CURTAIN
Operates as a guillotine from SL deck

RIGGING SYSTEM
Type: Single purchase counter weight
Weight: 25,000 lbs available
Line sets: 82 sets at 6" o.c. with 7 lift lines per set
Arbors: 2,000 lb capacity
House Pipes: 68' long with 92' of travel from deck
Line sets are moveable
Block & Falls are available
Chain hoists are not available
(80) spot wheels

PERMANENT INSTALLATIONS OVER STAGE (FROM SMOKE POCKET)
M=Moveable with advance call
Movie Screen (1) at 10'5"; M

PERMANENT INSTALLATIONS ON DECK
None

ORCHESTRA PIT
Adjustable to 7'4" below stage level by electric motor turnscrew
Apron overhangs US wall of pit 3'0"
Pit lift is in (1) section
Organ lift SL

BACKSTAGE

LOADING DOCK
Loading door(s):
1) 7'8" high x 8'0" wide
2) 11'0" high x 9'0" wide
Trucks load (4) at same time
Dock at 2'8" over deck level, ramp down inside stage house, staging dock with levelers
Fork lift is not required
Sound/Props can load in FOH
Lobby can be a work area
(3) Trailers can store on-site
Security at stage door

WARDROBE
Location: 2nd floor
Access: Stairs and Elevator
(3) Washers (3) Dryers
No washer or dryer hookups

DRESSING ROOMS
(3) Star, US,+1, t/s included, phone jack
(2) Small, US, +1, t/s included, phone jack
(6) Small, US, +2, t/s included, phone jack
(6) Chorus, US, +3, t/s on same fl, phone jack
Elevator access for dressing rooms
Additional production office available for company mgr

SOUND

CONSOLE
Soundcraft 800 B, located Center Rear
32 inputs, 8 main outputs, 8 matrix outputs, 8 aux outputs

SPEAKERS
House Cluster
Proscenium
Under Balcony
Base of proscenium
No speaker truss

COMMUNICATIONS
Clear Com intercom with (2) channels
Infrared sound system
Dressing room page system

ROAD CONSOLE
Located Rear Center
No seats required to remove
Cable run from stage is 150'
Tie-in into house system with XLR connectors

REHEARSAL & STORAGE SPACE
Rehearsal: None
Storage: None

ELECTRICS

ROAD SERVICE POWER

Panel	Phase	Amp	Circuit Protection	Use	Location
A	3	200	fuse	sound	USL
B-D	3	400	fuse	dimmers	DSL
E-F	3	400	fuse	extra	DSL
G	3	400	fuse	extra	DSR

Recommended location of touring dimmer racks: DSL
Hoist not required
Additional power is available for tour buses, generators, etc.

FRONT OF HOUSE (BOX BOOM VALUES ARE PER SIDE)

Position	Pipe Width	Distance to Prosc.	House Circuits	Connector Type	FOH Transfer Circuits
Rail	102'	54'	36	grd 20 amp stage pin	36
Box Boom 1		66'	12	grd 20 amp stage pin	12
House Boom		80'	18	grd 20 amp stage pin	18
Truss			36	grd 20 amp stage pin	36

EQUIPMENT FOH (BOX BOOM VALUES ARE PER SIDE)

Position	Quantity	Wattage	Instrument	Removeable
Balc Rail	50	1,000	Source 4 19°	

Variety of Source 4 instruments from 10° - 36°

FOLLOWSPOTS
House Followspots:
(3) Xenon Super Trouper 2000; not removeable

Followspot Booth:
(3) spots per booth;
144' throw to proscenium;
1Ø 100 amp breakers

DIMMERS
Lighting console is ETC Expression;
(244) ETC Sensor 2.4k dimmers
House has programmable DMX control system

CLEMENS CENTER POWERS THEATRE

AT: SAMUEL L. CLEMENS PERFORMING ARTS & COMMUNITY CENTER   YEAR RENOVATED: 1999

Theatre Location: 116 E. Gray Street, Elmira, NY 14902
Mailing Address: PO Box 1046, Elmira, NY 14902

Main Administrative Phone: 607-733-5639
Main Administrative Fax: 607-737-1162
Website: www.clemenscenter.com
Traveling Production Office Phone: 607-732-2365
Traveling Production Office Fax: 607-732-2435

THEATRE STAFF
Executive Director   Thomas Weidmann   607-733-5639
Dir. of Presenting   Jennifer Verity   607-733-5639
Crew contact   David Bailey   607-733-7159

SEATING CAPACITY
Orchestra   1,050
Balcony   551
Total: **1,608**

wheelchair (add'l)   7

STAGE DIMENSIONS (FROM SMOKE POCKET)
Stage is 32'6" deep
Width from Center Line to SL is 48'3"
Width from Center Line to SR is 36'6"
Proscenium width is 48'0"
Proscenium height is 27'0"
Smoke pocket to apron edge is 3'0"
Orchestra pit exists

RIGGING
Grid Height: 55'
Type: Single purchase counter weight
Line sets: 26 sets at 8-12" o.c.
Arbors: 2,150 lb capacity
House Pipes: 52' long

LOADING DOCK
Loading door(s) are 12'0" high x 7'0" wide
Trucks load (3) at same time
Fork lift is not required and is not available

ELECTRICS
Total power available:
(1) 400A 3Ø SR
(1) 200A 1Ø SL

FOLLOWSPOTS
House Followspots:
Xenon Super Trouper
Power in spot booth (4) 20A

DIMMERS
(48) house dimmers
House has DMX control system
(1) dry run station(s) located SR

SOUND
House has 200A 1Ø dedicated power located SL
FOH mixing position in Rear Orchestra
No sound console available

AMBASSADOR THEATRE

Theatre Location:	219 West 49th Street, New York, NY 10019	
Management Company:	The Shubert Organization, Inc.	
	234 West 44th Street, New York, NY 10036	
Main Administrative Phone:		212-944-3700
Main Administrative Fax:		212-944-4136
Website:		www.telecharge.com
Stage Door Phone:		212-944-3804
Backstage Pay Phone:		212-245-9570

THEATRE STAFF

Chairman	Gerald Schoenfeld	212-944-3700
President	Philip J. Smith	212-944-3700
Executive Vice President	Robert Wankel	212-944-3700
VP Theatre Operations	Peter Entin	212-944-3700
Director of Sales Development	Jack Thomas	212-239-6288
Theatre Manager	Peter Kulok	212-944-3846

HOUSE CREW

Carpentry	William Ngai	212-944-3804
Electrics	Vincent Jacobi	212-944-3804
Props	Dennis Smalls	212-944-3804

UNIONS

IATSE Local #1	Tony DePaulo	212-333-2500
Wardrobe Local #764	Ray Polgar	212-221-1717
Music Local #802	Bill Dennison	212-245-4802

SEATING CAPACITY

Orchestra	565
Boxes	8
Front Mezzanine	264
Rear Mezzanine	251
Total:	**1,088**
pit	37
wheelchair	4
standing (add'l)	25

BOX OFFICE

Computerized
Head Treasurer
  Tom Poulos   212-944-3844

Outside Ticket Agency
Computerized
  Tele-Charge   212-239-6200

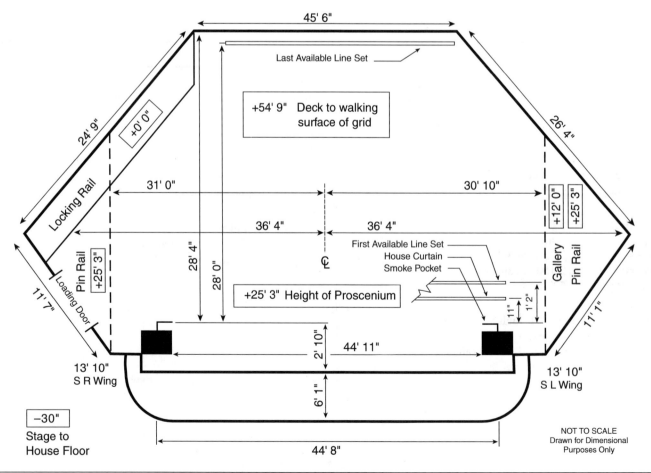

- 45' 6"
- Last Available Line Set
- +54' 9" Deck to walking surface of grid
- 24' 9"
- +0' 0"
- 26' 4"
- Locking Rail
- 31' 0"
- 30' 10"
- +12' 0"
- +25' 3"
- 36' 4"
- 36' 4"
- First Available Line Set
- House Curtain
- Smoke Pocket
- 28' 4"
- 28' 0"
- CL
- Gallery Pin Rail
- Pin Rail
- +25' 3"
- Loading Door
- +25' 3" Height of Proscenium
- 11"
- 1' 2"
- 11' 7"
- 2' 10"
- 44' 11"
- 13' 10" S R Wing
- 13' 10" S L Wing
- 11' 1"
- 6' 1"
- −30" Stage to House Floor
- 44' 8"
- NOT TO SCALE Drawn for Dimensional Purposes Only

STAGE HOUSE

House Curtain
Operates as a guillotine from SR deck

Rigging System
Type:	Single purchase counter weight
Weight:	16,000 lbs available
Line sets:	36 sets at 6" o.c. with 4 lift lines per set
Arbors:	450 & 600 lb capacity
House Pipes:	44' long with 54' of travel from deck

Line sets are moveable
Block & Falls are available 2:1 (2)
(50) spot wheels and 10,000' of hemp available

Permanent Installations Over Stage (from smoke pocket)
None

Permanent Installations On Deck
Electric jump (1) 12'x8', located 12' off SL
Electric bridge (1) over SL

Orchestra Pit
Nonadjustable at 8' below stage level
Apron overhangs US wall of pit 6'6"

BACKSTAGE

Loading Dock
Loading door(s):
9'8" high x 5'2" wide
Trucks load (1) at a time
Dock loading door sill is at
street level
Fork lift is not required
Sound/Props can load in FOH
Lobby cannot be a work area
Trailers cannot store on-site
Security at stage door

Wardrobe
Location: Basement
Access: Alley off SL
(1) Washer (1) Dryer
Washer and dryer hookups
available

Dressing Rooms
(2) Star, behind stage, 2nd fl,
t included, s on same fl
(2) Star, behind stage, 3rd fl,
t included, s on same fl
(4) Small, behind stage, (2) 4th
fl/(2) 5th fl, t included, s on
same fl

SOUND

Console
No house console

Speakers
Speaker truss exists
Max available load 1,000 lbs
Pipe and rigging available

Communications
Theater Technology intercom
with (4) channels
Infrared sound system
Dressing room page system

Road Console
Located Rear HR
(5) seats required to be
removed
Cable run from stage is 200'
Tie-in into house system

Rehearsal & Storage Space
Rehearsal: None
Storage: None

ELECTRICS

Road Service Power

Panel	Phase	Amp	Circuit Protection	Use	Location
A-F	1	400	fuse	dimmers	DSL side wall
G	1	200	breaker	sound	SL on jump
H	1	200	breaker	sound	SL on jump

Recommended location of touring dimmer racks: DSL on jump
Hoist required but not provided.

Front Of House (box boom values are per side)

Position	Pipe Width	Distance to Prosc.	House Circuits	Connector Type	FOH Transfer Circuits
Truss Electric	40'	25'	22	grd 20 amp stage pin	22
1st Balc Rail	66'	31'	30	grd 20 amp stage pin	30
Box Boom 1		20'	8	grd 20 amp stage pin	8
Box Boom 2		31'	8	grd 20 amp stage pin	8

Transfer circuits: grd 20 amp stage pin located DSL on jump

Equipment FOH (box boom values are per side)
None

Followspots
House Followspots:
None

Followspot Booth:
(3) spots per booth;
77' throw to proscenium;
1Ø 100 amp breakers

Dimmers
No lighting console
No dimmers
No DMX control system

BELASCO THEATRE

Theatre Location: 111 West 44th Street, New York, NY 10036
Management Company: The Shubert Organization, Inc.
234 West 44th Street, New York, NY 10036

Main Administrative Phone: 212-944-3700
Main Administrative Fax: 212-944-4136
Website: www.telecharge.com
Stage Door Phone: 212-944-4103
Backstage Pay Phone: 212-730-9344

SEATING CAPACITY

Orchestra	507
Mezzanine	285
Balcony	201
Total:	**993**
pit	25
wheelchair	2
standing (add'l)	25

THEATRE STAFF

Chairman	Gerald Schoenfeld	212-944-3700
President	Philip J. Smith	212-944-3700
Executive Vic e President	Robert Wankel	212-944-3700
VP Theatre Operations	Peter Entin	212-944-3700
Director of Sales Development	Jack Thomas	212-239-6288
Theatre Manager	Joe Traina	212-944-3852

HOUSE CREW

Carpentry	Richard Fernandez	212-944-4103
Electrics	Leslie Ann Kilian	212-944-4103
Props	Philip Feller	212-944-4103

UNIONS

IATSE Local #1	Tony DePaulo	212-333-2500
Wardrobe Local #764	Ray Polgar	212-221-1717
Music Local #802	Bill Dennison	212-245-4802

BOX OFFICE
Computerized
Head Treasurer
Howard Fox 212-944-3850

Outside Ticket Agency
Computerized
Tele-Charge 212-239-6200

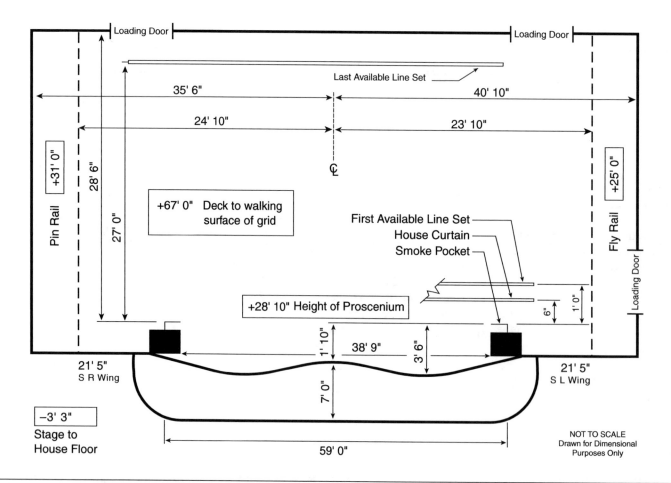

STAGE HOUSE

House Curtain
Operates as a guillotine from SL deck

Rigging System
Type:	Hemp System
Weight:	4,000 lbs available
	2,000 lbs of sand available
Line sets:	50 sets at 6" o.c. with 5 lift lines per set
House Pipes:	44' long with 66' of travel from deck

Line sets are moveable
Block & Falls are available 2:1 (4); 3:2 (3)
(50) spot wheels and 5,000' of hemp available

Permanent Installations Over Stage (from smoke pocket)
None

Permanent Installations On Deck
Lift in stage floor 15'0" x 25'0" located CS (not operational)
Stairs to basement located on DSR proscenium wall

Orchestra Pit
Nonadjustable at 8' below stage level

BACKSTAGE

Loading Dock
Loading door(s):
  (2) @ 15'7" high x 5'11" wide
Trucks load (1) at a time
Docks (2) - Door 1 is 24" above street level; Door 2 is 8" above stage level, loading to stage thru separate scene dock behind stage house; doors are accessed by an alley; no ramps available
Fork lift is not required
Sound/Props can load in FOH
Lobby can be a work area
Security at stage door

Wardrobe
Location: Dressing Room
Access: Stairs
(1) Washer (1) Dryer

Dressing Rooms
(1) Star, stage level, SR, t/s included
(9) Small, SR, (3) 2nd fl/(3) 3rd fl/(3) 4th fl, t/s on same fl
(3) Chorus, SR, 2nd/3rd/4th fl, t/s on same fl
Use dressing room for company mgr office

SOUND

Console
No house console

Speakers
Holes in ceiling over house provide truss hanging position
Pipe and rigging not available

Communications
No house intercom system
Infrared sound system

Road Console
Cable run from stage is 150'

Rehearsal & Storage Space
Rehearsal: None
Storage: None

ELECTRICS

Road Service Power

Panel	Phase	Amp	Circuit Protection	Use	Location
A-F	3	400	fuse	dimmers	SR on deck

Recommended location of touring dimmer racks: USR on deck
Hoist is required but not provided.

Front Of House (box boom values are per side)
None

Equipment FOH (box boom values are per side)
None

Followspots
House Followspots:
  None

Followspot Booth:
  (2) spots per booth;
  70' throw to proscenium;
  1Ø 60 amp breakers

Dimmers
No lighting console
No dimmers
No DMX control system

BOOTH THEATRE

Theatre Location: 222 West 45th Street, New York, NY 10036
Management Company: The Shubert Organization, Inc.
                                          234 West 44th Street, New York, NY 10036

Main Administrative Phone: 212-944-3700
Main Administrative Fax: 212-944-4136
Website: www.telecharge.com
Stage Door Phone: 212-944-3825
Backstage Pay Phone: 212-391-8886

THEATRE STAFF
Chairman	Gerald Schoenfeld	212-944-3700
President	Philip J. Smith	212-944-3700
Executive Vice President	Robert Wankel	212-944-3700
VP Theatre Operations	Peter Entin	212-944-3700
Director of Sales Development	Jack Thomas	212-239-6288
Theatre Manager	Rene Savich	212-944-3805

HOUSE CREW
Carpentry	Thomas Manoy	212-944-3825
Electrics	Ronnie Burns, Sr.	212-944-3825
Props	Arnold Treco	212-944-3825

UNIONS
IATSE Local #1	Tony DePaulo	212-333-2500
Wardrobe Local #764	Ray Polgar	212-221-1717
Music Local #802	Bill Dennison	212-245-4802

SEATING CAPACITY
Orchestra	503
Boxes	12
Mezzanine	252
Total:	**767**

pit (add'l)	14
wheelchair (add'l)	2
standing (add'l)	20

BOX OFFICE
Computerized
Head Treasurer
   Ed Whittaker   212-944-3853

Outside Ticket Agency
Computerized
   Tele-Charge   212-239-6200

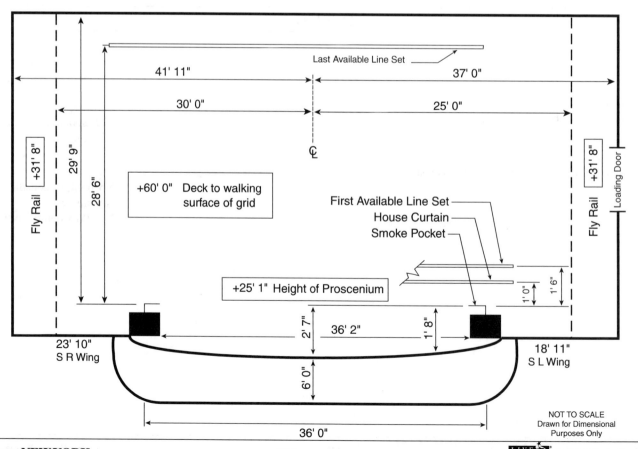

Last Available Line Set

41' 11"   37' 0"

30' 0"   25' 0"

CL

Fly Rail +31' 8"

29' 9"

28' 6"

+60' 0" Deck to walking surface of grid

First Available Line Set
House Curtain
Smoke Pocket

+25' 1" Height of Proscenium

2' 7"   36' 2"   1' 8"

1' 0"   1' 6"

Fly Rail +31' 8"

Loading Door

23' 10"
S R Wing

18' 11"
S L Wing

6' 0"

36' 0"

NOT TO SCALE
Drawn for Dimensional
Purposes Only

STAGE HOUSE

HOUSE CURTAIN
Operates as a guillotine from SR deck

RIGGING SYSTEM
Type:	Hemp System
Weight:	1,600 lbs available
Line sets:	32 sets at 6" o.c. with 5 lift lines per set
House Pipes:	42' long with 59' of travel from deck

Line sets are moveable
Block & Falls are available 2:1 (2); 3:2 (4)
(180) spot wheels and 36,000' of hemp available

PERMANENT INSTALLATIONS OVER STAGE (FROM SMOKE POCKET)
None

PERMANENT INSTALLATIONS ON DECK
Traps in stage floor are on a sectional grid

ORCHESTRA PIT
Nonadjustable at 7' below stage level
Apron overhangs US wall of pit 3'6"

BACKSTAGE

LOADING DOCK
Loading door(s):
   10'0" high x 7'6" wide
Trucks load (1) at a time
Loading door sill is at street
   level 2'0" below stage level;
   ramp up to stage is available
Fork lift is not required
Sound/Props can load in FOH
Lobby can be a work area
Security at stage door

WARDROBE
Location: Dressing Room
Access: Stairs
(1) Washer (1) Dryer

DRESSING ROOMS
(9) Small, SR, (3) 2nd fl/(3) 3rd
   fl/(3) 4th fl, toilet on same fl
Shower available in basement
Use dressing room for company
   mgr office

SOUND

CONSOLE
No house console

SPEAKERS
None

COMMUNICATIONS
No house intercom system
Infrared sound system

ROAD CONSOLE
Located Rear House
No seats required to be
   removed
Cable run from stage is 70'

REHEARSAL & STORAGE SPACE
Rehearsal: None
Storage: None

ELECTRICS

ROAD SERVICE POWER

Panel	Phase	Amp	Circuit Protection	Use	Location
A-F	3	400	fuse	dimmers	SR on jump
G	3	100	fuse	sound	SR side wall
H	3	400	fuse	extra	SR side wall

Recommended location of touring dimmer racks: SR on jump
Hoist is required and provided

FRONT OF HOUSE (BOX BOOM VALUES ARE PER SIDE)

Position	Pipe Width	Distance to Prosc.	House Circuits	Connector Type	FOH Transfer Circuits
Truss	40'	28'	36'	ungrd 20 amp stage pin	36
1st Balc Rail	46'	26'	32'	ungrd 20 amp stage pin	32
Box Boom 1		8'	7	ungrd 20 amp stage pin	7
Box Boom 2		13'	7	ungrd 20 amp stage pin	7
Box Boom 3		18'	7	ungrd 20 amp stage pin	7

Transfer circuits: ungrd 20 amp stage pin located SR on 1st & 2nd jumps

EQUIPMENT FOH (BOX BOOM VALUES ARE PER SIDE)
None

FOLLOWSPOTS
House Followspots:
   None

Followspot Booth:
   (3) spots per booth;
   62' throw to proscenium;
   3Ø 400 amp breakers

DIMMERS
No lighting console
No dimmers
No DMX control system

BROADHURST THEATRE

Theatre Location: 235 West 44th Street, New York, NY 10019
Management Company: The Shubert Organization, Inc.
                                     234 West 44th Street, New York, NY 10036

Main Administrative Phone: 212-944-3700
Main Administrative Fax: 212-944-4136
Website: www.telecharge.com
Stage Door Phone: 212-944-4115
Backstage Pay Phone: 212-730-9035

THEATRE STAFF
Chairman   Gerald Schoenfeld   212-944-3700
President   Philip J. Smith   212-944-3700
Executive Vice President   Robert Wankel   212-944-3700
VP Theatre Operations   Peter Entin   212-944-3700
Director of Sales Development Jack Thomas   212-239-6288
Theatre Manager   Hugh Barnett   212-944-3858

HOUSE CREW
Carpentry   Eustaquio Verdejo   212-944-4115
Electrics   Bruce Burden   212-944-4115
Props   Fred Ricci   212-944-4115

UNIONS
IATSE Local #1   Tony DePaulo   212-333-2500
Wardrobe Local #764   Ray Polgar   212-221-1717
Music Local #802   Bill Dennison   212-245-4802

SEATING CAPACITY
Orchestra   703
Boxes   24
Mezzanine   429
Total: **1,156**

pit (add'l)   30
wheelchair   4
standing (add'l)   27

BOX OFFICE
Computerized
Head Treasurer
  Cliff Cobb   212-944-3856

Outside Ticket Agency
Computerized
  Tele-Charge   212-239-6200

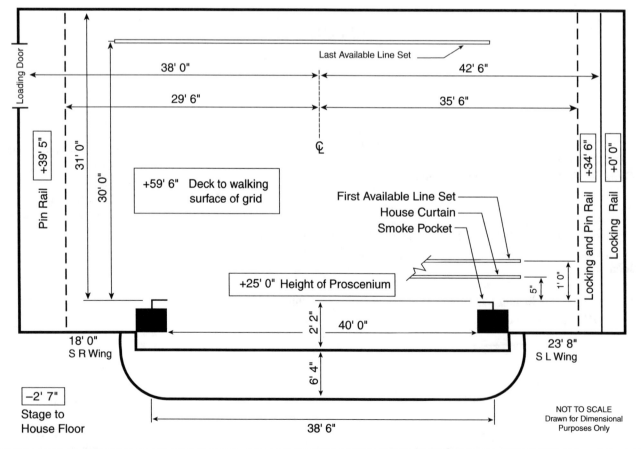

STAGE HOUSE

HOUSE CURTAIN
Operates as a guillotine from SL deck

RIGGING SYSTEM
Type:	Single purchase counter weight
Weight:	4,000 lbs available
Line sets:	52 sets at 6" o.c. with 4 lift lines per set
Arbors:	600 lb capacity
House Pipes:	42' long with 59' of travel from deck

Line sets are moveable
Block & Falls are not available
Chain hoists are not available
(40) spot wheels and 5,000' of hemp available

PERMANENT INSTALLATIONS OVER STAGE (FROM SMOKE POCKET)
None

PERMANENT INSTALLATIONS ON DECK
Trap (1) in stage floor located in SR wings
Pilasters (2) each 18" x 36" square against back wall located 20'0" SR & SL of Center
Sound jump located on DSL proscenium wall

ORCHESTRA PIT
Nonadjustable at 7' below stage level
Apron overhangs US wall of pit 5'10"

BACKSTAGE

LOADING DOCK
Loading door(s):
   10'0" high x 7'8" wide
Trucks load (1) at same time
Dock (loading door sill) is at street level
Fork lift is not required
Sound/Props can load in FOH
Lobby can be a work area
Security at stage door

WARDROBE
Location: Basement
Access: Trap in stage floor SR
(2) Washers (2) Dryers

DRESSING ROOMS
(3) Star, SR, (1) stage level/(2) basement, t/s included
(9) Small, SR, (3) 2nd fl/(3) 3rd fl/(3) 4th fl, t/s on same fl
(1) Chorus, SR, 5th fl, t/s included
Use dressing room for company mgr office

SOUND

CONSOLE
No house console

SPEAKERS
Speaker truss exists
Max available load 500 lbs per point

COMMUNICATIONS
No house intercom system
Infrared sound system
Dressing room page system

ROAD CONSOLE
Located Rear House
(14) seats required to be removed
Cable run from stage is 75'

REHEARSAL & STORAGE SPACE
Rehearsal: None
Storage: None

ELECTRICS

ROAD SERVICE POWER

Panel	Phase	Amp	Circuit Protection	Use	Location
A-F	3	400	fuse	dimmers	SR on jump
G	3	100	breaker	sound	SL on jump
H	3	600	fuse	extra	SR in basement
I	3	200	fuse	extra	SR in basement
J	3	200	fuse	extra	SR in basement

Recommended location of touring dimmer racks: SR on jump
Hoist is required and provided

FRONT OF HOUSE (BOX BOOM VALUES ARE PER SIDE)

Position	Pipe Width	Distance to Prosc.	House Circuits	Connector Type	FOH Transfer Circuits
Truss	40'	20'	30	grd 20 amp stage pin	30
1st Balc Rail	30'	30'	27	grd 20 amp stage pin	27
Box Boom 1		12'	15	grd 20 amp stage pin	15
Box Boom 2		18'	0		0
Box Boom 3		26'	9	grd 20 amp stage pin	9

Transfer circuits: grd 20 amp stage pin located SR on jump

EQUIPMENT FOH (BOX BOOM VALUES ARE PER SIDE)
None

FOLLOWSPOTS
House Followspots:
   None

Followspot Booth:
   (3) spots per booth;
   70' throw to proscenium;
   3Ø 100 amp breakers

   (2) Follow spot perches
   Box Boom 3 L & R

DIMMERS
No lighting console
No dimmers
No DMX control system

BROADWAY THEATRE

AKA: B.F. MOSS'S COLONY THEATRE

Theatre Location: 1681 Broadway, New York, NY 10019
Management Company: The Shubert Organization, Inc.
234 West 44th Street, New York, NY 10036

Main Administrative Phone: 212-944-3700
Main Administrative Fax: 212-944-4136
Website: www.telecharge.com
Stage Door Phone: 212-944-3808
Backstage Pay Phone: 212-974-9587

THEATRE STAFF

Chairman	Gerald Schoenfeld	212-944-3700
President	Philip J. Smith	212-944-3700
Executive Vice President	Robert Wankel	212-944-3700
VP Theatre Operations	Peter Entin	212-944-3700
Director of Sales Development	Jack Thomas	212-239-6288
House Manager	Michael Harris	212-944-3858

HOUSE CREW

Carpentry	Charles Rasmusson	212-581-8625
Electrics	George Milne	212-944-3808
Props	Richard Dalcortivo	212-944-3808

UNIONS

IATSE Local #1	Tony DePaulo	212-333-2500
Wardrobe Local #764	Ray Polgar	212-221-1717
Music Local #802	Bill Dennison	212-245-4802

SEATING CAPACITY

Orchestra	906
Boxes	24
Front Mezzanine	250
Rear Mezzanine	584
Total:	**1,764**
wheelchair (incl)	2

BOX OFFICE

Computerized
Treasurer
  Leonard Bonis   212-944-3859

Outside Ticket Agency
Computerized
Tele-charge   212-239-6200

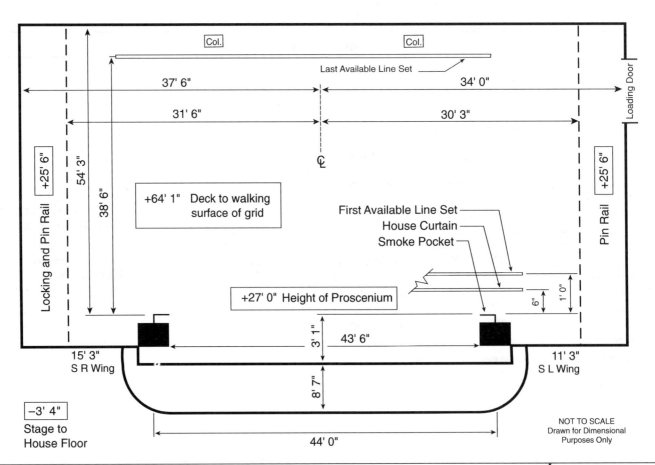

37' 6"	34' 0"
31' 6"	30' 3"

Col.   Col.

Last Available Line Set

Loading Door

+25' 6"   +25' 6"

Locking and Pin Rail   Pin Rail

54' 3"

38' 6"

+64' 1"   Deck to walking surface of grid

First Available Line Set
House Curtain
Smoke Pocket

6"   1' 0"

+27' 0" Height of Proscenium

3' 1"   43' 6"

15' 3"
S R Wing

11' 3"
S L Wing

8' 7"

−3' 4"
Stage to
House Floor

44' 0"

NOT TO SCALE
Drawn for Dimensional
Purposes Only

STAGE HOUSE

HOUSE CURTAIN
Operates as a guillotine from SR deck
Operates from House electric bridge

RIGGING SYSTEM
Type:	Single purchase counter weight
Weight:	25,000 lbs available
Line sets:	74 sets at 6" o.c. with 4 lift lines per set
Arbors:	700 lb capacity
House Pipes:	45' long with 56' of travel from deck

Line sets are moveable
Block & Falls are available 2:1 (2)
(150) spot wheels
Chain hoists for electric jump

PERMANENT INSTALLATIONS OVER STAGE (FROM SMOKE POCKET)
None

PERMANENT INSTALLATIONS ON DECK
Columns (2), 2'0" x 2'0", 39'0" US
Loading bridge (1)

ORCHESTRA PIT
Nonadjustable at 7' below stage level
Apron overhangs upstage wall of pit 5'10"

BACKSTAGE

LOADING DOCK
Loading door(s):
   15'6" high x 10'8" wide
Trucks load (1) at a time
Dock (loading door sill) is at
   street level 3'0" below stage
   level accessed by a built in
   ramp inside stage house
Fork lift is not required
Sound/Props can load in FOH
Lobby cannot be a work area
Trailers cannot store on-site
Security at stage door

WARDROBE
Location: Basement
Access: Trap in stage floor USL
(1) Washer (1) Dryer

DRESSING ROOMS
(7) Star, SR/SL, stage level/ +1,
   t/s included, phone jack
(1) Star, SL, +1, t/s on same fl,
   phone jack
(8) Small, SL, +2/+4, t/s on
   same fl, (5) w/ phone jack
(2) Chorus, SL, +3, t/s included,
   phone jack
Use dressing room for company
   mgr office

SOUND

CONSOLE
No house console

SPEAKERS
Speaker truss exists

COMMUNICATIONS
No house intercom system
Infrared sound system
Dressing room page system

ROAD CONSOLE
Located Rear Orchestra right
   of center
No seats required to be
   removed
Cable run from stage is 150'
House is wired extensively
   for mics to mix, mix to
   amps, 150 ground AC,
   antenna, video, communications and speakers
   (4pin twist)

REHEARSAL & STORAGE SPACE
Rehearsal: None
Storage:
   625 sq ft in basement,
   (2) 80 sq ft, +4

ELECTRICS

ROAD SERVICE POWER

Panel	Phase	Amp	Circuit Protection	Use	Location
A-F	3	400	fuse	extra	SL loft
G-J	3	400	fuse	extra	USR
K	3	150	fuse	sound	DSL room

Recommended location of touring dimmer racks: Loft SL
Hoist provided but not required

FRONT OF HOUSE (BOX BOOM VALUES ARE PER SIDE)

Position	Pipe Width	Distance to Prosc.	House Circuits	Connector Type	FOH Transfer Circuits
Truss	42'	45'	48	grd 20 amp stage pin	
Balc Rail	50'	30'	36	grd 20 amp stage pin	
Box Boom 1		18'	12	grd 20 amp stage pin	12
Box Boom 2		24'	12	grd 20 amp stage pin	12
Box Boom 3		30'	12	grd 20 amp stage pin	12

Transfer circuits: grd 20 amp stage pin

EQUIPMENT FOH (BOX BOOM VALUES ARE PER SIDE)
None

FOLLOWSPOTS
House Followspots:
   None

Followspot Booth:
   (3) spots per booth;
   120' throw to proscenium;
   3Ø 100 amp breakers

DIMMERS
No lighting console
No dimmers
No DMX control system

BROOKS ATKINSON THEATRE

Theatre Location:	256 West 47th Street, New York, NY 10036	
Management Company:	The Nederlander Organization	
	810 7th Avenue, 21st Floor, New York, NY 10019	
	212-262-2400 / Fax 212-262-5558	

Main Theatre Phone:	212-719-4099
Main Theatre Fax:	212-398-6164
Stage Door Phone:	212-719-4099
Backstage Pay Phone:	212-221-8955

THEATRE STAFF

Chairman Emeritus	James M. Nederlander	212-262-2400
Chairman	James L. Nederlander	212-262-2400
President	Robert E. Nederlander	212-262-2400
Exec Vice President	Nick Scandalios	212-262-2400
Director of Operations	Jim Boese	212-262-2400
Nederlander Group Sales	Laurel Kramer	212-765-8058
House Manager	Barbara Carrellas	212-719-4391

HOUSE CREW

Carpentry	Thomas A. Lavaia	212-221-8955
Electrics	Kevin A. McGarty	212-221-8955
Props	Terry Taylor	212-221-8955

UNIONS

IATSE Local #1	Tony DePaulo	212-333-2500
Wardrobe Local #764	Ray Polgar	212-221-1717
Music Local #802	Bill Dennison	212-245-4802

SEATING CAPACITY

Orchestra	574
Boxes	24
Front Mezzanine	156
Rear Mezzanine	290
Total:	**1,044**
pit (add'l)	27
wheelchair (add'l)	2
standing (add'l)	29

BOX OFFICE

Computerized
Treasurer

Ilene J. Towell	212-719-4092

Outside Ticket Agency
Computerized

TicketMaster	212-713-6300

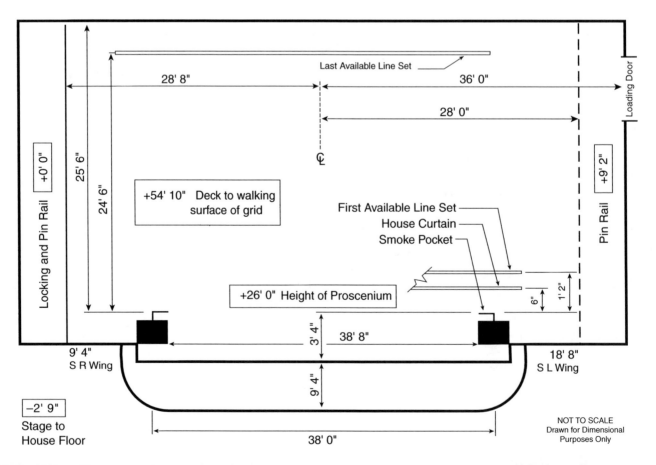

STAGE HOUSE

House Curtain
Operates as a guillotine from SL deck

Rigging System
Type:	Single purchase counter weight
Weight:	15,000 lbs available
Line sets:	43 sets at 4" o.c. with 4 lift lines per set
Arbors:	550 lb capacity
House Pipes:	40' long with 57' of travel from deck
Line sets are moveable	
(25) spot wheels and 2,000' of hemp available	

Permanent Installations Over Stage (from smoke pocket)
Ducts US at +26'

Permanent Installations On Deck
Traps in stage floor are on a sectional grid
Electric jump (1) located on DSL proscenium wall 9'0" high

Orchestra Pit
Nonadjustable at 6' below stage level
Apron overhangs US wall of pit 1'0"

BACKSTAGE

Loading Dock
Loading door(s):
    8'0" high x 6'8" wide
Dock (loading door sill) is at
    street level 12" below stage
    level accessed by concrete
    ramp up to stage
Trucks load (1) at a time
Fork lift is not required
Sound/Props can load in FOH
Lobby can be a work area
Trailers cannot store on-site
Security at stage door

Wardrobe
Location: SR on 3rd floor
Access: Stairs
(1) Washer (1) Dryer

Dressing Rooms
All with t/s on same fl
(3) Star, (2) SR/(1) stage level
(1) Small, SR, 2nd fl
(2) Small, SR, 3rd fl
(2) Small, SL, 2nd fl
(2) Small, SL, 3rd fl
(1) Chorus, SR, 4rd fl
(1) Chorus, SL, 4th fl
Use dressing room for company
    mgr office

SOUND

Console
No house console

Speakers
None
No speaker truss
Rigging points exist

Communications
No house intercom system
Infrared sound system
Dressing room page system

Road Console
Located Rear House
No seats required to be
    removed
Cable run from stage is 100'

Rehearsal & Storage Space
Rehearsal: None
Storage: None

ELECTRICS

Road Service Power

Panel	Phase	Amp	Circuit Protection	Use	Location
A-F	3	400	fuse	dimmers	SL side wall

Recommended location of touring dimmer racks: SL on jump
Hoist is required and provided

Front Of House (box boom values are per side)

Position	Pipe Width	Distance to Prosc.	House Circuits	Connector Type	FOH Transfer Circuits
1st Balc Rail	40'	30'	24	grd 20 amp stage pin	24
Box Boom 1		11'	4	grd 20 amp stage pin	4
Box Boom 2		18'	4	grd 20 amp stage pin	4
Box Boom 3		25'	5	grd 20 amp stage pin	5
Booth Rail	35'	65'	30	grd 20 amp stage pin	30

Transfer circuits: grd 20 amp stage pin SL in basement & on jump

Equipment FOH (box boom values are per side)
None

Followspots
House Followspots:
    None

Followspot Booth:
    (3) spots per booth;
    70' throw to proscenium

Dimmers
No lighting console
No dimmers
No DMX control system

CITY CENTER

Year built: 1923

Theatre Location: 131 West 55th Street, New York, NY 10019
Mailing Address: 130 West 56th Street, New York, NY 10019
Management Company: City Center 55th Street Theatre Foundation
130 West 56th Street, New York, NY 10019

Main Administrative Phone: 212-247-0430
Main Administrative Fax: 212-246-9778
Website: www.citycenter.org
Backstage Pay Phone: 212-974-9833

Theatre Staff
Executive Director	Judith Daykin	212-247-0430
Managing Director	Lois Framhein	212-247-0430
Marketing	Ina Clark	212-247-0430
Operations	Eugene Lowery	212-247-0430

House Crew
Production Manager	Theresa Von Klug	212-240-0430
Carpentry	Frank Illo	212-247-0430
Electrics	Eric Schultz	212-247-0430
Props	Michael Murray	212-247-0430

Unions
IATSE Local #1	Ronny Lynch	212-333-2500
Wardrobe Local #764	Ray Polgar	212-221-1717
Music Local #802	Bill Dennison	212-245-4802

Seating Capacity
Orchestra	768
Grand Tier & Mezzanine	1,220
Gallery	765
Total:	**2,753**

pit (incl)	69
wheelchair (add'l)	25
standing (add'l)	

Box Office
Computerized
Box Office Treasurer
  Ron Ferreira   212-581-1212

Outside Ticket Agency
Computerized
City Center City Tix
  Eric Wiehardt   212-581-1212

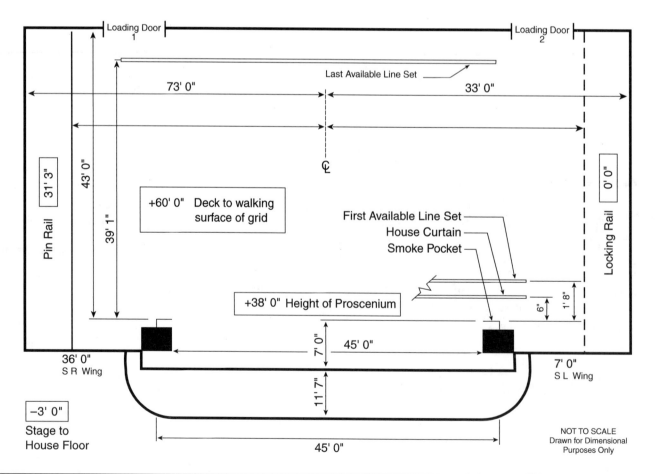

Loading Door 1 — Loading Door 2
Last Available Line Set
73' 0"   33' 0"
43' 0"
Pin Rail 31' 3"
39' 1"
+60' 0" Deck to walking surface of grid
CL
First Available Line Set
House Curtain
Smoke Pocket
Locking Rail 0' 0"
+38' 0" Height of Proscenium
1' 8"
6"
7' 0"
45' 0"
36' 0" S R Wing
7' 0" S L Wing
11' 7"
−3' 0" Stage to House Floor
45' 0"

NOT TO SCALE
Drawn for Dimensional
Purposes Only

STAGE HOUSE

HOUSE CURTAIN
Operates as a guillotine

RIGGING SYSTEM
Type: Single purchase counter weight;
    Hemp System
Weight: 50,000 lbs available
Line sets: 90 sets at 6" o.c. with 4 lift lines per set
Arbors: 600 lb capacity
House Pipes: 51' long with 58' of travel from deck
Line sets are moveable
Block & Falls are available
Chain hoists are not available
(20) spot wheels and 1,000 of hemp available
Electrics require two line sets

PERMANENT INSTALLATIONS OVER STAGE (FROM SMOKE POCKET)
Fire curtain (1) at 0'0"

PERMANENT INSTALLATIONS ON DECK
Adjustable portal (1) at 2'4"

ORCHESTRA PIT
Adjustable to 11'5" below stage level by electric motor
    turnscrew
Apron overhangs US wall of pit 11'5"
Pit lift is in (1) section

BACKSTAGE

LOADING DOCK
Loading door(s):
    1) 9'6"high x 5'6"wide
    2) 12'0"high x 8'0" wide
Trucks load (2) 40' at same time
40'0" inclined indoor alley;
    arched opening 5'6" above
    sidewalk
Sound/Props cannot load in
    FOH
Lobby cannot be a work area
(2) Trailers can store on-site
Security at stage door

WARDROBE
Location: Dressing room tower
Access: Elevator from back-
    stage
(2) Washers (2) Dryers
Washer and dryer hookups
    available

DRESSING ROOMS
(12) Small, SL,+1/+2/+3/+4,
    t/s included, phone jack
(1) Chorus, SL, +2, t/s included
(1) Chorus, SL, +5, t/s
Elevator access for dressing
    rooms
Use dressing room for company
    mgr office

SOUND

CONSOLE
Yamaha PM 3000 w/XL88
    Matrix, located Rear House
24 inputs, 8 main outputs,
    16 matrix outputs, 8 aux
    outputs

SPEAKERS
House Cluster
Proscenium
Under Balcony
No speaker truss

COMMUNICATIONS
Clear Com intercom with
    (2) channels
Infrared sound system
Dressing room page system

ROAD CONSOLE
Location varies
Number of seats required to
    be removed varies
Tie-in into house system with
    XLR connectors

REHEARSAL & STORAGE SPACE
Rehearsal: reservations req'd
    Studio #3, 36' x 47', 3rd fl,
    mirrors, piano, barres, t/s;
    Studio #4, 43' x 62', 4th fl,
    mirrors, piano, barres, t/s;3.
    Studio #5, 43' x 62', 5th fl
Storage: Various locations
    available

ELECTRICS

ROAD SERVICE POWER

Panel	Phase	Amp	Circuit Protection Use	Location
A	3	400	fuse	DSR
B	3	400	fuse	DSR

Recommended location of touring dimmer racks: SR
Hoist not required

FRONT OF HOUSE (BOX BOOM VALUES ARE PER SIDE)

Position	Pipe Width	Distance to Prosc.	House Circuits	Connector Type	FOH Transfer Circuits
Balc Rail		55'		grd 20 amp stage pin	30
Mezz Rail		32'		grd 20 amp stage pin	30
Boxes		38'		grd 20 amp stage pin	12

Transfer circuits: grd 20 amp stage pin

EQUIPMENT FOH (BOX BOOM VALUES ARE PER SIDE)

Position	Quantity	Wattage	Instrument	Removeable
1st Balc Rail	30	1,500	8" Fresnel	yes
2nd Balc Rail	2	575	Source 4 19°	yes
Box Boom 1	4	575	Source 4 19°	yes
Box Boom 1	24	575	Source 4 26°	yes

FOLLOWSPOTS
House Followspots:
    (3) Colortran Color Arc
    2000; removeable

Followspot Booth:
    (3) spots per booth;
    114' throw to proscenium;
    3Ø 400 amp breakers

DIMMERS
House console is ETC
    Obsession 600;
    (594) Colortran D-192
    2.4kw dimmers
No DMX control system
(6) dry run DMX station(s)

CORT THEATRE

Theatre Location: 138 West 48th Street, New York, NY 10036
Management Company: The Shubert Organization, Inc.
                        234 West 44th Street, New York, NY 10036

Main Administrative Phone:	212-944-3700
Main Administrative Fax:	212-944-4136
Website:	www.telecharge.com
Stage Door Phone:	212-944-3783
Backstage Pay Phone:	212-997-9776

THEATRE STAFF

Chairman	Gerald Schoenfeld	212-944-3700
President	Philip J. Smith	212-944-3700
Executive Vice President	Robert Wankel	212-944-3700
VP Theatre Operations	Peter Entin	212-944-3700
Director of Sales Development	Jack Thomas	212-239-6288
Theatre Manager	Jay Kingwill	212-944-3864

HOUSE CREW

Carpentry	Edward Diaz	212-944-3783
Electrics	Lee Iwanski	212-944-3783
Props	James P. Keane	212-944-3783

UNIONS

IATSE Local #1	Tony DePaulo	212-333-2500
Wardrobe Local #764	Ray Polgar	212-221-1717
Music Local #802	Bill Dennison	212-245-4802

SEATING CAPACITY

Orchestra	504
Boxes	32
Mezzanine	264
Balcony	283
Total:	**1,083**
pit (add'l)	31
wheelchair (add'l)	2
standing (add'l)	20

BOX OFFICE

Computerized
Head Treasurer
   Tom Hinton   212-944-3862

Outside Ticket Agency
Computerized
   Tele-Charge   212-239-6200

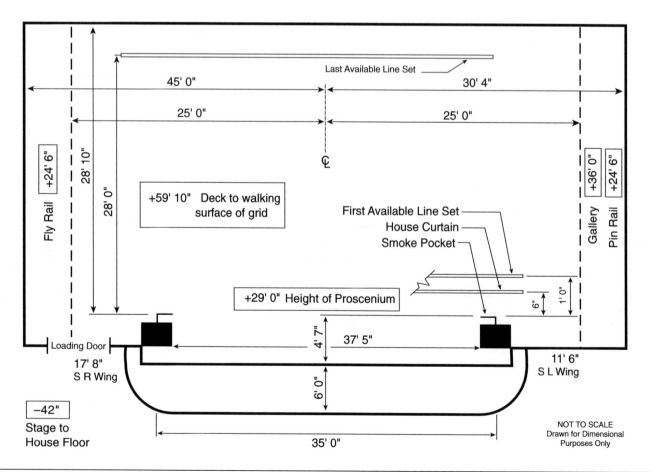

STAGE HOUSE

House Curtain
Operates as a guillotine from SR deck

Rigging System
Type: Hemp System
Weight: 2,500 lbs available
Line sets: 30 sets at 6" o.c. with 4 lift lines per set
House Pipes: 40' long with 58' of travel from deck
Line sets are moveable
Block & Falls are available 2:1 (2); 3:2 (1)
(60) spot wheels and 10,000' of hemp available

Permanent Installations Over Stage (from smoke pocket)
None

Permanent Installations On Deck
Traps in stage floor are on a sectional grid
Steam pipes against back wall
Stairway (1) 3'0" x 9'9" located in USL corner

Orchestra Pit
Nonadjustable at 15' below stage level
Apron overhangs US wall of pit 1'6"

BACKSTAGE

Loading Dock
Loading door(s):
     16'0" high x 10'10" wide
Trucks load (1) at a time
Dock (loading door sill) is at street level accessed by a 5'0" wide alley
Fork lift is not required
Sound/Props can load in FOH
Lobby can be a work area
Trailers cannot store on-site
Security at stage door

Wardrobe
Location: Basement
Access: Trap in stage floor
(1) Washer (1) Dryer

Dressing Rooms
(4) Star, SL, stage level, t/s on same fl
(7) Small, SL, 4th fl, t/s on same fl
Use dressing room for company mgr office

SOUND

Console
No house console

Speakers
Holes in ceiling over house provide truss hanging position
Pipe and rigging unavailable

Communications
No house intercom system
Infrared sound system

Road Console
Located Rear Balcony or Mezzanine
(10) seats required to be removed
Cable run from stage is 200'

Rehearsal & Storage Space
Rehearsal: None
Storage: None

ELECTRICS

Road Service Power

Panel	Phase	Amp	Circuit Protection	Use	Location
A-F	3	400	fuse	dimmers	SL on jump
G	3	100	breaker	sound	DSR on jump
H	3	100	breaker	extra	SR side wall
I	3	100	breaker	extra	Basement
J	3	100	breaker	extra	SL side wall

Recommended location of touring dimmer racks: SL on jump
Hoist is required and provided

Front Of House (box boom values are per side)

Position	Pipe Width	Distance to Prosc.	House Circuits	Connector Type	FOH Transfer Circuits
2nd Balc Rail	55'	35'	36	grd 20 amp stage pin	36
1st Cove	30'	55'	20	grd 20 amp stage pin	20
Right Cove	10'	55'	10	grd 20 amp stage pin	10
Left Cove	10'	55'	10	grd 20 amp stage pin	10
Box Boom 1		10'	12	grd 20 amp stage pin	12
Box Boom 2		20'	12	grd 20 amp stage pin	12

Transfer circuits: grd 20 amp stage pin located SL on jump

Equipment FOH (box boom values are per side)
None

Followspots
House Followspots:
     None

Followspot Booth:
     None

Dimmers
No lighting console
No dimmers
No DMX control system

ETHEL BARRYMORE THEATRE

Theatre Location: 243 West 47th Street, New York, NY 10019
Management Company: The Shubert Organization, Inc.
234 West 44th Street, New York, NY 10036

Main Administrative Phone: 212-944-3700
Main Administrative Fax: 212-944-4136
Website: www.telecharge.com
Stage Door Phone: 212-944-3797
Backstage Pay Phone: 212-974-9534

SEATING CAPACITY

Orchestra	620
Boxes	24
Front Mezzanine	196
Rear Mezzanine	256
Total:	**1,096**
pit	53
wheelchair	2

THEATRE STAFF

Chairman	Gerald Schoenfeld	212-944-3700
President	Philip J. Smith	212-944-3700
Executive Vice President	Robert Wankel	212-944-3700
VP Theatre Operations	Peter Entin	212-944-3700
Director of Sales Development	Jack Thomas	212-239-6288
Theatre Manager	Daniel Landon	212-944-3849

HOUSE CREW

Carpentry	Brian McGarty	212-944-3797
Electrics	Steven Altman	212-944-3797
Props	Patricia Avery	212-944-3797

UNIONS

IATSE Local #1	Tony DePaulo	212-333-2500
Wardrobe Local #764	Ray Polgar	212-221-1717
Music Local #802	Bill Dennison	212-245-4802

BOX OFFICE

Computerized
Head Treasurer
Bill Friendly 212-944-3847

Outside Ticket Agency
Computerized
Tele-Charge 212-239-6200

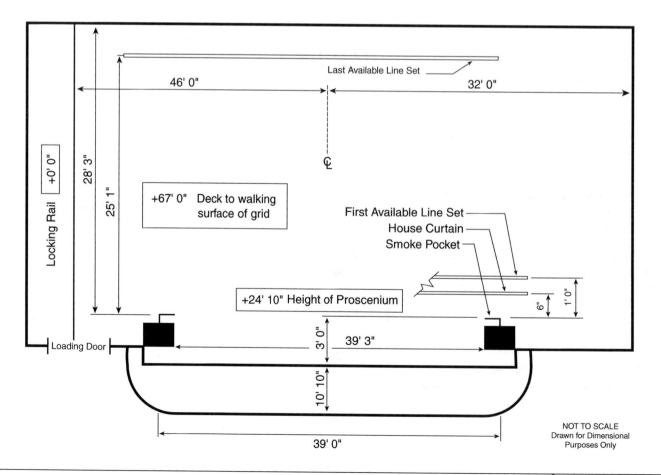

Last Available Line Set
46' 0"   32' 0"
Locking Rail +0' 0"
28' 3"
25' 1"
+67' 0" Deck to walking surface of grid
First Available Line Set
House Curtain
Smoke Pocket
+24' 10" Height of Proscenium
Loading Door
3' 0"   39' 3"
6"   1' 0"
10' 10"
39' 0"

NOT TO SCALE
Drawn for Dimensional
Purposes Only

STAGE HOUSE

HOUSE CURTAIN
Operates as a guillotine from SR deck

RIGGING SYSTEM

Type:	Single purchase counter weight
Weight:	6,000 lbs available
Line sets:	40 sets at 6" o.c. with 4 lift lines per set
Arbors:	750 lb capacity
House Pipes:	46' long with 60' of travel from deck

Line sets are moveable
(20) spot wheels and 3,000' of hemp available

PERMANENT INSTALLATIONS OVER STAGE (FROM SMOKE POCKET)
None

PERMANENT INSTALLATIONS ON DECK
Traps in stage floor are on a sectional grid
Pilasters (4) each 32" square against back wall

ORCHESTRA PIT
Nonadjustable at 6' below stage level
Apron overhangs US wall of pit 1'6"

BACKSTAGE

LOADING DOCK
Loading door(s):
7'10" high x 5'8" wide
Trucks load (1) at same time
Dock loading door sill is at street level

WARDROBE
Location: Basement
Access: Trap in stage floor
(1) Washer (1) Dryer

DRESSING ROOMS
(1) Star, stage level, SL, t/s included
(10) Small, SL, (2) 2nd fl/(4) 3rd fl/(4) 4th fl, t/s on same fl
(1) Chorus, SL, 2nd fl, t/s included

SOUND

CONSOLE
No house console

SPEAKERS
No speaker truss

COMMUNICATIONS
No house intercom system
Infrared sound system

ROAD CONSOLE
Located Rear HL
(8) seats required to be removed
Cable run from stage is 150'

REHEARSAL & STORAGE SPACE
Rehearsal: None
Storage: None

ELECTRICS

ROAD SERVICE POWER

Panel	Phase	Amp	Circuit Protection	Use	Location
A-F	3	400	fuse	dimmers	USR back wall
G	3	100	breaker	sound	DSR proscenium wall

Recommended location of touring dimmer racks: SR on deck
Hoist is required and provided

FRONT OF HOUSE (BOX BOOM VALUES ARE PER SIDE)

Position	Pipe Width	Distance to Prosc.	House Circuits	Connector Type	FOH Transfer Circuits
Truss	43'	25'	44	grd 20 amp stage pin	44
1st Balc Rail	40'	40'	44	grd 20 amp stage pin	44
Box Boom 1		15'	22	grd 20 amp stage pin	22
Box Boom 2		40'	22	grd 20 amp stage pin	22
Front Light Booth		80'	11	grd 20 amp stage pin	11

Transfer circuits: grd 20 amp stage pin

EQUIPMENT FOH (BOX BOOM VALUES ARE PER SIDE)
None

FOLLOWSPOTS
House Followspots:
None

Followspot Booth:
(3) spots per booth;
80' throw to proscenium;
(4) 2Ø 100 amp breakers

DIMMERS
No lighting console
No dimmers
No DMX control system

EUGENE O'NEILL THEATRE

YEAR BUILT: 1925   YEAR RENOVATED: 1994

Theatre Location: 230 West 49th Street, New York, NY 10019
Management Company: Jujamcyn Theaters
                            246 West 44th Street, New York, NY 10036

Main Administrative Phone: 212-840-8181
Main Administrative Fax: 212-944-0708
E-mail: jujamcyn@jujamcyn.com
Stage Door Phone: 212-664-9603
Backstage Pay Phone: 212-664-9068

SEATING CAPACITY
Orchestra   710
Mezzanine   366
Boxes   32
Total: **1,108**

pit (incl)
wheelchair (incl)
standing (add'l)   28

THEATRE STAFF
Chairman   James H. Binger   212-840-8181
President   Rocco Landesman   212-840-8181
Producing Director/VP   Paul Libin   212-840-8181
Creative Director   Jack Viertel   212-840-8181
General Manager   Howard Rogut   212-840-8181
Director of Operations   Jennifer Hershey   212-840-8181
Theatre Manager   Laurel Ann Wilson   212-840-8181

HOUSE CREW
Carpentry   Daniel Dour   212-664-9603
Electrics   Albert Sayers   212-664-9603
Props   Christopher H. Beck   212-664-9603

UNIONS
IATSE Local #1   Tony DePaulo   212-333-2500
Wardrobe Local #764   Ray Polgar   212-221-1717
Music Local #802   Bill Dennison   212-245-4802

BOX OFFICE
Computerized
Box Office Treasurer
   Gail Yerkovich   212-840-8181

Outside Ticket Agency
Computerized
Tele-charge
   Vince Rieger   212-944-4160

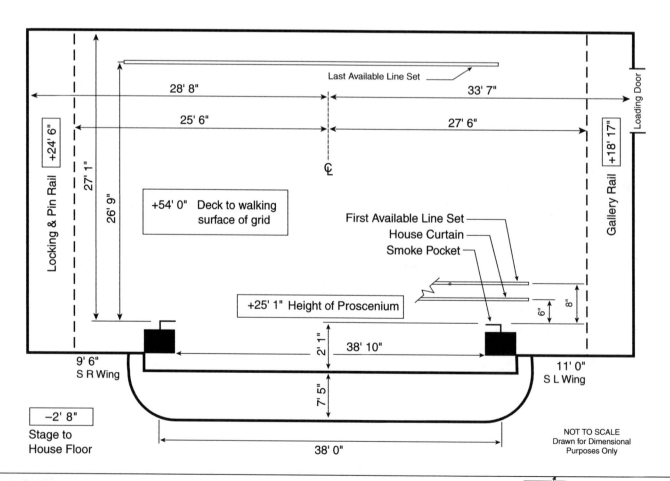

STAGE HOUSE

HOUSE CURTAIN
Operates as a guillotine from SR deck

RIGGING SYSTEM
Type:	Single purchase counter weight
Weight:	18,000 lbs available
Line sets:	59 sets at 6" o.c. with 4 lift lines per set
Arbors:	540 - 740 lb capacity
House Pipes:	42' long with 53' of travel from deck

Line sets are moveable
Block & Falls are available 2:1(1); 3:2 (1)
(100) spot wheels and 5,000' of hemp available

PERMANENT INSTALLATIONS OVER STAGE (FROM SMOKE POCKET)
None

PERMANENT INSTALLATIONS ON DECK
Traps in stage floor 19'6" x 36'0" located CS

ORCHESTRA PIT
Nonadjustable at 11' below stage level
Apron overhangs US wall of pit 9'2"

BACKSTAGE

LOADING DOCK
Loading door(s):
  7'10" high x 5'10" wide
Trucks load 1 at a time
Dock (loading door sill) is at
  street level
Fork lift is not required
Sound/Props can load in FOH
Lobby can be a work area
No trailers can store on-site
Security at stage door

WARDROBE
Location: Basement
Access: Trap in stage floor USR
(1) Washer (1) Dryer

DRESSING ROOMS
(2) Star, SR, stage level/+2
  toilet included, phone jack
(1) Star, SL, +1,
  toilet included, phone jack
(8) Small, SL, on various levels,
  t/s on same fl
(3) Chorus, SL, on various
  levels, t/s on same fl
Use dressing room for company
  mgr office

SOUND

CONSOLE
No house console

SPEAKERS
None
Holes in ceiling over house
  provide truss hanging
  position
Pipe and rigging unavailable

COMMUNICATIONS
No house intercom system
Infrared sound system

ROAD CONSOLE
Located Center HL
(3) seats required to be
  removed
Cable run from stage is 100'

REHEARSAL & STORAGE SPACE
Rehearsal: None
Storage: None

ELECTRICS

ROAD SERVICE POWER

Panel	Phase	Amp	Circuit Protection	Use	Location
A-F	3	400	fuse	dimmers	SL jump
G	3	200	fuse	dimmers	Basement SL

Recommended location of touring dimmer racks: SL jump
Hoist is required but not provided

FRONT OF HOUSE (BOX BOOM VALUES ARE PER SIDE)

Position	Pipe Width	Distance to Prosc.	House Circuits	Connector Type	FOH Transfer Circuits
Balc Rail	31'	36'	26	grd 20 amp stage pin	26
Box Boom 1		32'	8	grd 20 amp stage pin	8
Box Boom 2		45'	11	grd 20 amp stage pin	11

Transfer circuits: grd 20 amp stage pin
Road truss: Hole in place for lighting and sound trusses.

EQUIPMENT FOH (BOX BOOM VALUES ARE PER SIDE)
None

FOLLOWSPOTS
House Followspots:
  None

Followspot Booth:
  (3) spots per booth;
  70' throw to proscenium;
  (2) 1Ø 30 amp breakers

DIMMERS
No lighting console
No dimmers
No DMX control system

FORD CENTER FOR THE PERFORMING ARTS

YEAR BUILT: 1997

Theatre Location: 213 West 42nd Street, New York, NY 10036
Management Company: Livent (U.S.) Inc.

Main Administrative Phone:	212-556-4700
Main Administrative Fax:	212-556-4779
Website:	www.livent.com
Stage Door Phone:	212-556-4750

THEATRE STAFF

General Manager	Dan Fallon	212-556-4760
Booking	Lisa Waterworth	212-556-4765
Marketing	Keith Hurd	212-556-4727
Operations	Dan Fallon	212-556-4760
Group Sales	Christy Warner	212-556-4741

HOUSE CREW

Technical Director		
Production Manager	Peter Lamb	212-416-324-5476
PSM (Ragtime)	Tom Capps	212-556-4787
Carpentry	Jim Harris	212-556-4792
Electrics	Art Friedlander	212-556-4783
Sound	John Gibson	212-556-4794
Props	Joe Harris	212-556-4791

UNIONS

IATSE Local #1	Tony DePaulo	212-333-2500
Wardrobe Local #764	Ray Polgar	212-221-1717
Music Local #802	Bill Dennison	212-245-4802

SEATING CAPACITY

Orchestra	1,100
Dress Circle	371
Balcony	350
Total:	**1,821**
pit	80
wheelchair	16
standing (add'l)	0

BOX OFFICE

Computerized
Director of Ticketing
  Peter Attanasio   212-556-4734

Outside Ticket Agency
Computerized
Ticketmaster

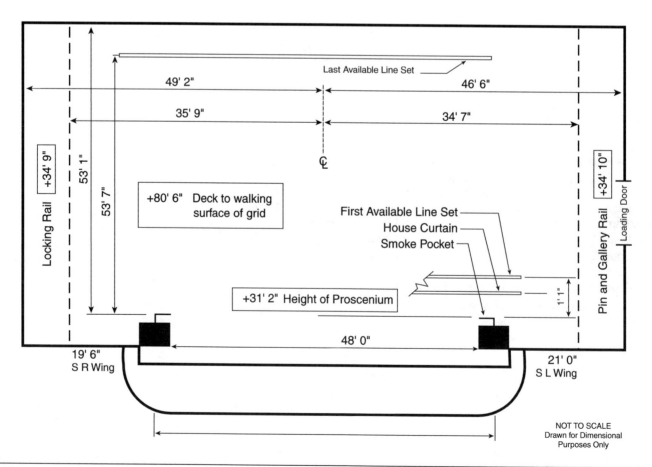

STAGE HOUSE

HOUSE CURTAIN
No house curtain

RIGGING SYSTEM
Type:	Single purchase counter weight
Weight:	70,000 lbs available
Line sets:	90 sets at 7" o.c. with 7 lift lines per set
Arbors:	1,500 lb capacity
House Pipes:	65'6" long

(100) spot wheels and 10,000' of hemp available
FOH grid +49'6", 25'6" up and down stage

PERMANENT INSTALLATIONS OVER STAGE (FROM SMOKE POCKET)
Fire curtain, deluge system

PERMANENT INSTALLATIONS ON DECK
Traps are on a sectional grid
Jumps (above locking rail) (4) at +34'9" 13'3" wide, +53'5", +65'5", "77'5", SR
Electric jump (2) at +34'10", "49'9", SL
Loading bridge (2) at +65'5", +75'5", SR

ORCHESTRA PIT
Nonadjustable at 9'6" below stage level

BACKSTAGE

LOADING DOCK
Loading door(s):
  10'0" high x 10'0" wide
Trucks load (2), with street permits, at same time
Load street level on W. 43rd St; Loading door USL wall 6" lip to stage level
Fork lift is required
Sound/Props can load in FOH
Lobby can be used as a work area
Trailers cannot store on-site
Security at stage door

WARDROBE
Location: Basement
Access: Stairs / Elevator from stage door
(4) Washers (5) Dryers
No washer or dryer hookups

DRESSING ROOMS
(6) Star, SL, -1, t/s included, phone jack
(5) Small, SL, t/s included, phone jack
(3) Chorus, SL, t/s included, phone jack
Elevator access for dressing rooms
Additional production office available for company mgr

SOUND

CONSOLE
None

SPEAKERS
Portable

COMMUNICATIONS
No house intercom system; lines to production areas
Infrared sound system
Dressing room page system

ROAD CONSOLE
No seats required to be removed
Cable run from stage is 300'
There are house utility and audio lines throughout

REHEARSAL & STORAGE SPACE
Rehearsal: 54' x 50', FOH, 4th fl, 7' grand piano, mirrors, linoleum surface sprung floor 35'x29', FOH 4th fl, barre, mirrors, linoleum surface sprung floor
Storage: None

ELECTRICS

ROAD SERVICE POWER

Panel	Phase	Amp	Circuit Protection	Use	Location
A-L	3	400	fuse	dimmers	SL on jump
M-P	3	100	fuse	extra	DSL/USL/USR/DSR
Q-R	3	400	fuse	sound	trap room
S	3	100	fuse	extra	US grid
T	3	100	fuse	extra	FOH grid
U	3	100	fuse	sound	FOH rear orch

Recommended location of touring dimmer racks: SL on jump +49'9"

FRONT OF HOUSE (BOX BOOM VALUES ARE PER SIDE)

Position	Pipe Width	Distance to Prosc.	House Circuits	Connector Type	FOH Transfer Circuits
1st Cove			40	grd 20 amp stage pin	40
1st Balc Rail			30	grd 20 amp stage pin	30
2nd Balc Rail			16	grd 20 amp stage pin	16
Box Boom 1			26	grd 20 amp stage pin	26
Box Boom 2			3	grd 20 amp stage pin	3
Box Boom 3			3	grd 20 amp stage pin	3

Road truss: (30) rigging points and ceiling holes exist

EQUIPMENT FOH (BOX BOOM VALUES ARE PER SIDE)
None

FOLLOWSPOTS
House Followspots:
None

Followspot Booth:
(4) spots per booth; throw to proscenium;
(6) 1Ø & 3Ø 60 amp breakers

DIMMERS
No lighting console
House has non-programmable DMX control system

GERSHWIN THEATRE

AKA: URIS THEATRE   **YEAR BUILT: 1972**

Theatre Location: 222 West 51st Street, New York, NY 10019
Management Company: The Nederlander Organization
                            810 7th Avenue, 21st Floor, New York, NY 10019
                            212-262-2400 / Fax 212-262-5558

Main Theatre Phone: 212-586-6510
Main Theatre Fax: 212-956-1751
Stage Door Phone: 212-664-8473

THEATRE STAFF
Chairman Emeritus   James M. Nederlander   212-262-2400
Chairman   James L. Nederlander   212-262-2400
President   Robert E. Nederlander 212-262-2400
Exec Vice President   Nick Scandalios   212-262-2400
Director of Operations   Jim Boese   212-262-2400
Nederlander Group Sales   Laurel Kramer   212-765-8058
House Manager   Richard D. Kaye   212-315-1333

HOUSE CREW
Carpentry   John Riggins   212-664-8473
Electrics   Henry L. Brisen   212-664-8473
Props   Stephen McDonald   212-664-8473

UNIONS
IATSE Local #1   Tony DePaulo   212-333-2500
Wardrobe Local #764   Ray Polgar   212-221-1717
Music Local #802   Bill Dennison   212-245-4802

SEATING CAPACITY
Orchestra   1,298
Front Mezzanine   275
Mid Mezzanine   154
Rear Mezzanine   206
Total: **1,933**

pit (add'l)   36
wheelchair (incl)   4

BOX OFFICE
Computerized
Treasurer
  Gary Kenny   212-586-7299

Outside Ticket Agency
Computerized
  TicketMaster   212-713-6300

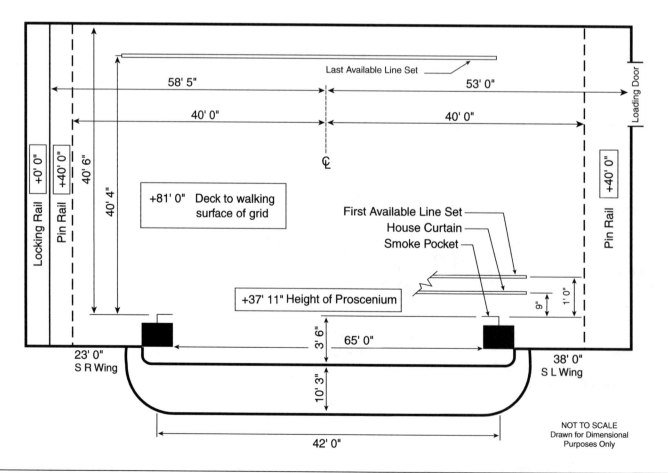

NOT TO SCALE
Drawn for Dimensional
Purposes Only

STAGE HOUSE

HOUSE CURTAIN
Operates as a guillotine from SR deck

RIGGING SYSTEM
Type:	Single purchase counter weight
Weight:	24,000 lbs available
Line sets:	74 sets at 6" o.c. with 6 lift lines per set
Arbors:	1,200 lb capacity
House Pipes:	50' long with 72' of travel from deck

Line sets are moveable
Block & Falls are available 2:1 (2)
Chain hoists are not available
(200) spot wheels and 20,000' of hemp available

PERMANENT INSTALLATIONS OVER STAGE (FROM SMOKE POCKET)
None

PERMANENT INSTALLATIONS ON DECK
Traps in stage floor are on a sectional grid
Pilasters (4) on US wall
Radiators along US wall
Electric bridge (1) 16' wide x 42' long SL
Loading bridge (1) 3' wide x 42'long SR

ORCHESTRA PIT
Nonadjustable at 7'3" below stage level
Apron overhangs US wall of pit 6'0"

BACKSTAGE

LOADING DOCK
Loading door(s):
18'0" high x 13'0" wide
Trucks load (1) at a time
Load from street then bring
scenery up 2 floors on freight
elevator which is 14'0" high x
13'0" wide x 43'0" long
Fork lift is not required
Sound/Props can load in FOH
Lobby can be a work area
Trailers cannot store on-site
Security at stage door

WARDROBE
Location: Trap level
Access: Stage elevator
(2) Washers (1) Dryer
Washer and dryer hookups
available

DRESSING ROOMS
(2) Star, SL/SR, stage level,
t/s included, phone jack
(3) Small, SR, stage level,
t/s included, phone jack
(5) Small, SR/SL, +1,
t/s included, phone jack
(2) Chorus, SR/SL, -1,
t/s included
Elevator access for dressing
rooms
Additional production office
available for company mgr

SOUND

CONSOLE
No house console

SPEAKERS
None
Speaker truss exists
Pipe and rigging available

COMMUNICATIONS
Norcon intercom with
(1) channel
Infrared sound system
Dressing room page system

ROAD CONSOLE
Located Rear Orchestra
Cable run from stage is 200'

REHEARSAL & STORAGE SPACE
Rehearsal: 60' x 60' located
on 4th fl, SR
Storage: None

ELECTRICS

ROAD SERVICE POWER

Panel	Phase	Amp	Circuit Protection	Use	Location
A-D	3	200	fuse	sound	SL on 3rd floor
E-H	3	400	fuse	dimmers	SL on 3rd floor
I-M	3	400	fuse	dimmers	SL/SR on 5th floor
N-O	3	400	fuse	extra	SL/SL trap
P	3	200	fuse	extra	4th floor SL
Q	3	100	breaker	extra	SL trap

Recommended location of touring dimmer racks: 5th floor SL
Hoist required but not provided

FRONT OF HOUSE (BOX BOOM VALUES ARE PER SIDE)

Position	Pipe Width	Distance to Prosc.	House Circuits	Connector Type	FOH Transfer Circuits
1st Balc Rail	100'	66'	30	grd 20 amp stage pin	30
1st Cove	80'	75'	16	grd 20 amp stage pin	16
Box Boom 1		30'	18	grd 20 amp stage pin	18
Truss	65'	70'	0	grd 20 amp stage pin	0
Booth	15'	115'	6	grd 20 amp stage pin	6

Transfer circuits: grd 20 amp stage pin
Road truss: Open front grid & house truss available

EQUIPMENT FOH (BOX BOOM VALUES ARE PER SIDE)
None

FOLLOWSPOTS
House Followspots:
(2) Super Troupers Carbon
Arc; removeable

Followspot Booth:
(3) spots per booth;
115' throw to proscenium;
(3) 1Ø 30 amp breakers/
3Ø 100 amp breaker

DIMMERS
No lighting console
No dimmers
No DMX control system

HELEN HAYES THEATRE

AKA: LITTLE THEATRE

YEAR BUILT: 1911   YEAR RENOVATED: 1985

Theatre Location: 240 West 44th Street, New York, NY 10036
Management Company: Little Theatre Group
                                       240 West 44th Street, New York, NY 10036

Main Administrative Phone: 212-944-9457
Main Administrative Fax: 212-302-3584
Stage Door Phone: 212-302-3297
Backstage Pay Phone: 212-730-7197

THEATRE STAFF
General Manager   Paul Morer   212-944-9457
House Manager   Alan Markinson   212-944-9457

HOUSE CREW
Carpentry   Ron Mooney   212-944-9457
Electrics   Jeremy Johnson   212-944-9457
Props   Roger Keller   212-944-9457

UNIONS
IATSE Local #1   Tony DePaulo   212-333-2500
Wardrobe Local #764   Ray Polgar   212-221-1717
Music Local #802   Bill Dennison   212-245-4802

SEATING CAPACITY
Orchestra   379
Balcony   218
Total: **597**

BOX OFFICE
Computerized
Treasurer
  David Heveran   212-944-9457

Outside Ticket Agency
Computerized
Tele-charge   212-239-6200

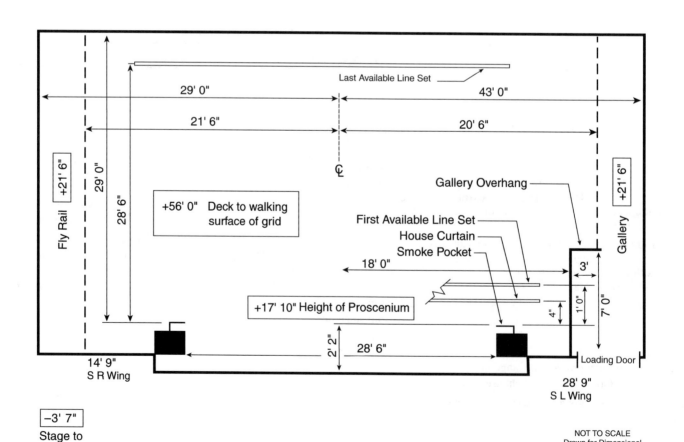

STAGE HOUSE

House Curtain
Operates as a guillotine from SR deck

Rigging System
Type: Hemp System
Weight: 2,000 lbs available
Line sets: 25 sets at 6" o.c. with 4 lift lines per set
House Pipes: 30' long with 55' of travel from deck
Line sets are moveable
Block & Falls are available 2:1 (2); 3:2 (1)
(30) spot wheels and 1,000' of hemp available

Permanent Installations Over Stage (from smoke pocket)
Catwalk US of house curtain from SR to SL galleries (18" wide)

Permanent Installations On Deck
Trap (1) in stage floor located CS
Electric jump located on DSL proscenium wall

Orchestra Pit
Orchestra pit permanently covered

BACKSTAGE

Loading Dock
Loading door(s):
   9'0" high x 6'0" wide
Trucks load (1) at a time
Dock (loading door sill) is at street level 12" below stage level access by an alley; ramp (1) up to stage is available
Fork lift is not required
Sound/Props can load in FOH
Lobby can be a work area
Trailers cannot store on-site
Security at stage door

Wardrobe
Location: Basement
Access: Direct from stage
(1) Washer (1) Dryer

Dressing Rooms
(2) Star, basement, t/s on same fl
(6) Small, basement, t/s on same fl
Use dressing room for company mgr office

SOUND

Console
No house console

Speakers
Truss over house provides hanging position

Communications
No house intercom system

Road Console
Located Rear House
(6) seats required to be removed
Cable run from stage is 100'

Rehearsal & Storage Space
Rehearsal: None
Storage: None

ELECTRICS

Road Service Power

Panel	Phase	Amp	Circuit Protection	Use	Location
A	3	400	fuse	dimmers/sound	USL side wall

Recommended location of touring dimmer racks: USL on deck
100' feeder cable required from dimmer racks to panel A

Front Of House (box boom values are per side)

Position	Pipe Width	Distance to Prosc.	House Circuits	Connector Type	FOH Transfer Circuits
1st Balc Rail	35'	30'	8	grd 20 amp stage pin	8
1st Cove	30'	48'	12	grd 20 amp stage pin	12
Box Boom 1		18'	5	grd 20 amp stage pin	5

Transfer circuits: grd 20 amp stage pin located DSL on bridge
Trusses (2) dead hung over house, no circuits, are available

Equipment FOH (box boom values are per side)
None

Followspots
House Followspots:
   None

Followspot Booth:
   None

Dimmers
No lighting console
No dimmers
No DMX control system

IMPERIAL THEATRE

Theatre Location: 249 West 45th Street, New York, NY 10036
Management Company: The Shubert Organization, Inc
234 West 44th Street, New York, NY 10036

Main Administrative Phone: 212-944-3700
Main Administrative Fax: 212-944-4136
Website: www.telecharge.com
Stage Door Phone: 212-944-3834
Backstage Pay Phone: 212-997-8843

THEATRE STAFF
Chairman   Gerald Schoenfeld   212-944-3700
President   Philip J. Smith   212-944-3700
Executive Vice President   Robert Wankel   212-944-3700
VP Theatre Operations   Peter Entin   212-944-3700
Director of Sales Development Jack Thomas   212-239-6288
Theatre Manager   Joseph Pullara   212-944-3870

HOUSE CREW
Carpentry   Walter Bullard, Jr.   212-944-3834
Electrics   John A. Cooper   212-944-3834
Props   James Satterwhite   212-944-3834

UNIONS
IATSE Local #1   Tony DePaulo   212-333-2500
Wardrobe Local #764   Ray Polgar   212-221-1717
Music Local #802   Bill Dennison   212-245-4802

SEATING CAPACITY
Orchestra   738
Boxes   19
Front Mezzanine   283
Rear Mezzanine   377
Total: **1,417**

pit (add'l)   42
wheelchair (add'l)   2

BOX OFFICE
Computerized
Head Treasurer
Jim Giebler   212-944-3868

Outside Ticket Agency
Computerized
Tele-Charge   212-239-6200

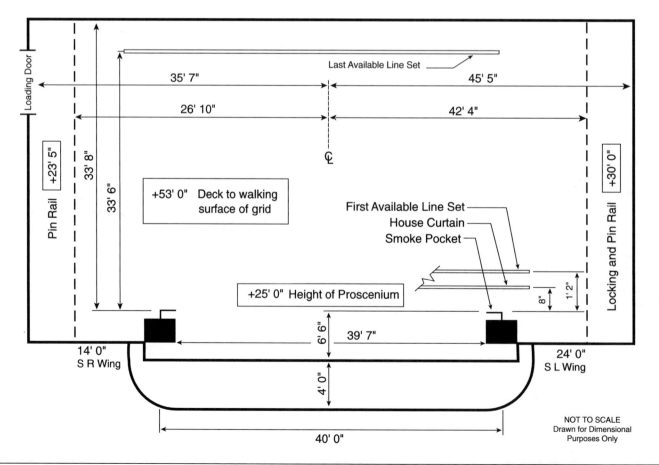

STAGE HOUSE

HOUSE CURTAIN
Operates as a guillotine from SR deck

RIGGING SYSTEM
Type:	Single purchase counter weight
Weight:	20,000 lbs available
Line sets:	70 sets at 6" o.c. with 4 lift lines per set
Arbors:	700 lb capacity
House Pipes:	45' long with 53' of travel from deck

Line sets are moveable
Block & Falls are available
Chain hoists are available as a rental; (1) one ton
(40) spot wheels and 3,000' of hemp available

PERMANENT INSTALLATIONS OVER STAGE (FROM SMOKE POCKET)
None

PERMANENT INSTALLATIONS ON DECK
Electric jump (1) 9' wide x 30' long located SR
Loading bridge (1) 5' wide x 30' long located SL
Jump (1) 5' wide x 30' long located SL

ORCHESTRA PIT
Nonadjustable at 9' below stage level
Apron overhangs US wall of pit 10'6"

BACKSTAGE

LOADING DOCK
Loading door(s):
  7'8" high x 5'11" wide
Loading door is on street level
Trucks load (1) at a time
Fork lift is not required
Sound/Props can load in FOH
Lobby cannot be a work area
Trailers cannot store on-site
Security at dock

WARDROBE
Location: Basement
Access: Trap in stage floor
(2) Washers (2) Dryers

DRESSING ROOMS
(1) Star, SR, stage level,
  toilet included, phone jack
(10) Small, SR,
  (3) 2nd fl/(3) 3rd fl/ (4) 4th fl
  toilet on same fl
(1) Chorus, SR, 5th fl,
  t/s included
(1) Chorus, SR, 5th fl, t/s
Additional showers located in
  basement
Use dressing room for company
  mgr office

SOUND

CONSOLE
No house console

SPEAKERS
None
Speaker truss exists
Max available load 1,000 lbs

COMMUNICATIONS
Infrared sound system
Dressing room page system

ROAD CONSOLE
Located Rear House
No seats required to be
  removed
Cable run from stage is 200'

REHEARSAL & STORAGE SPACE
Rehearsal: None
Storage: None

ELECTRICS

ROAD SERVICE POWER

Panel	Phase	Amp	Circuit Protection	Use	Location
A-F	3	400	fuse	dimmers	SR 5th floor jump
G	3	100	fuse	sound	DSR on jump

Recommended location of touring dimmer racks: SR 5th floor jump
Hoist is required and provided

FRONT OF HOUSE (BOX BOOM VALUES ARE PER SIDE)

Position	Pipe Width	Distance to Prosc.	House Circuits	Connector Type	FOH Transfer Circuits
Truss	40'	60'	0		0
1st Balc Rail	30'	60'	36	grd 15 amp stage pin	36
Box Boom 1		10'	12	grd 15 amp stage pin	12
Box Boom 2		20'	12	grd 15 amp stage pin	12

Transfer circuits: grd 15 amp stage pin

EQUIPMENT FOH (BOX BOOM VALUES ARE PER SIDE)
None

FOLLOWSPOTS
House Followspots:
  None

Followspot Booth:
  (3) spots per booth;
  70' throw to proscenium;
  3Ø 100 amp breakers

DIMMERS
No lighting console
No dimmers
No DMX control system

JOHN GOLDEN THEATRE

AKA: THEATRE MASQUE

Theatre Location:	252 West 54th Street, New York, NY 10036	
Management Company:	The Shubert Organization, Inc.	
	234 West 44th Street, New York, NY 10036	

Main Administrative Phone:	212-944-3700
Main Administrative Fax:	212-944-4136
Website:	www.telecharge.com
Stage Door Phone:	212-944-3810
Backstage Pay Phone:	212-764-0199

SEATING CAPACITY

Orchestra	468
Front Mezzanine	110
Rear Mezzanine	227
Total:	**805**
pit	12
wheelchair	2

THEATRE STAFF

Chairman	Gerald Schoenfeld	212-944-3700
President	Philip J. Smith	212-944-3700
Executive Vice President	Robert Wankel	212-944-3700
VP Theatre Operations	Peter Entin	212-944-3700
Director of Sales Development	Jack Thomas	212-239-6288
House Manager	Carolyne Jones	212-944-3867

HOUSE CREW

Carpentry	Charles Zarobinski	212-944-3810
Electrics	Sylvia Yoshioka	212-944-3810
Props	Michael Supple	212-944-3810

UNIONS

IATSE Local #1	Tony DePaulo	212-333-2500
Wardrobe Local #764	Ray Polgar	212-221-1717
Music Local #802	Bill Dennison	212-245-4802

BOX OFFICE

Computerized
Treasurer
  Bill Carrick   212-944-3865

Outside Ticket Agency
Computerized
Tele-charge   212-239-6200

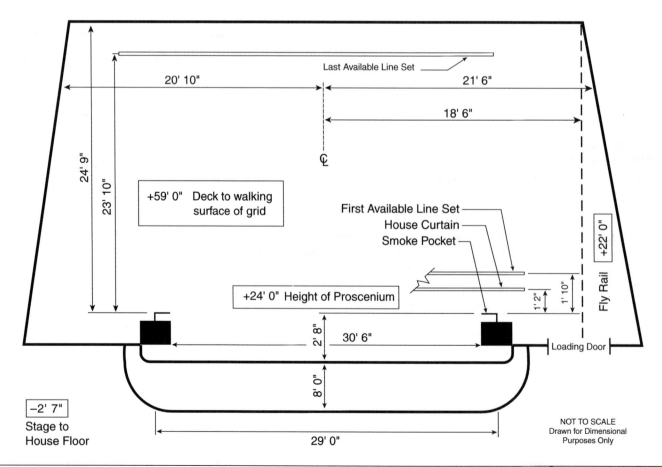

STAGE HOUSE

HOUSE CURTAIN
Operates as a guillotine from SR deck

RIGGING SYSTEM
Type:	Hemp System
Weight:	2,000 lbs of sand available
Line sets:	35 sets at 6" o.c. with 4 or 5 lift lines per set
House Pipes:	32' long with 58' of travel from deck

Line sets are moveable

Block & Falls are available 2:1 (2); 3:2 (2)

Chain hoists are not available

(80) spot wheels and 40 short lines and 25 long lines

PERMANENT INSTALLATIONS OVER STAGE (FROM SMOKE POCKET)
None

PERMANENT INSTALLATIONS ON DECK
Trap (1) 8'0"L x 5'4"W USL approx 1' from back wall

ORCHESTRA PIT
Nonadjustable at 9' below stage level

BACKSTAGE

LOADING DOCK
Loading door(s):
  9'0" high x 5'7" wide

Trucks load (1) at a time

Dock (loading door sill) is at street level. Ramp to load in door

Fork lift is not required

Sound/Props can load in FOH

Lobby can be a work area

Trailers cannot store on-site

Security at stage door

WARDROBE
Location: Basement

Access: Direct from stage

(1) Washer (1) Dryer

DRESSING ROOMS
(11) Small, SL, 1st/ 2nd/ 3rd/ 4th/ 5th fls, toilet on same fl, showers on 5th fl

Use dressing room for company mgr office

SOUND

CONSOLE
No house console

SPEAKERS
Holes in ceiling over house provide truss hanging position

Pipe and rigging unavailable

COMMUNICATIONS
No house intercom system

ROAD CONSOLE
Located Rear House

(6) seats required to be removed

Cable run from stage is 100'

REHEARSAL & STORAGE SPACE
Rehearsal: None

Storage: None

ELECTRICS

ROAD SERVICE POWER

Panel	Phase	Amp	Circuit Protection	Use	Location
A-F	3	400	fuse	dimmers/extra	SR in basement

(1) set of reducers to 200A for sound are available

Recommended location of touring dimmer racks: Basement

Hoist required but not provided

FRONT OF HOUSE (BOX BOOM VALUES ARE PER SIDE)

Position	Pipe Width	Distance to Prosc.	House Circuits	Connector Type	FOH Transfer Circuits
Booth	12'	100'	12	grd 20 amp stage pin	
1st Balc Rail	35'	35'	33	grd 20 amp stage pin	
Box Boom 1	21'		20	grd 20 amp stage pin	
Apron Boom	10'-30'		6	grd 20 amp stage pin	

Transfer circuits: grd 20 amp stage pin

Road truss: Main chandelier makes it impractical to install

EQUIPMENT FOH (BOX BOOM VALUES ARE PER SIDE)
None

FOLLOWSPOTS
House Followspots:
  None

Followspot Booth:
  (2) spots per booth;
  100' throw to proscenium;
  (2) 2Ø 20 amp breakers

DIMMERS
No lighting console

No dimmers

No DMX control system

LONGACRE THEATRE

Theatre Location:	220 West 48th Street, New York, NY 10036	
Management Company:	The Shubert Organization, Inc.	
	234 West 44th Street, New York, NY 10036	

Main Administrative Phone:	212-944-3700
Main Administrative Fax:	212-944-4136
Website:	www.telecharge.com
Stage Door Phone:	212-944-4132
Backstage Pay Phone:	212-974-9462

THEATRE STAFF
Chairman	Gerald Schoenfeld	212-944-3700
President	Philip J. Smith	212-944-3700
Executive Vice President	Robert Wankel	212-944-3700
VP Theatre Operations	Peter Entin	212-944-3700
Director of Sales Development	Jack Thomas	212-239-6288
Theatre Manager	David Conte	212-944-3878

HOUSE CREW
Carpentry	Timothy McWilliams	212-944-4132
Electrics	Paul F. Dean, Jr.	212-944-4132
Props	Lonnie Gaddy	212-944-4132

UNIONS
IATSE Local #1	Tony DePaulo	212-333-2500
Wardrobe Local #764	Ray Polgar	212-221-1717
Music Local #802	Bill Dennison	212-245-4802

SEATING CAPACITY
Orchestra	506
Boxes	16
Mezzanine	314
Balcony	243
Total:	**1,079**
pit (add'l)	16
wheelchair (add'l)	2

BOX OFFICE
Computerized
Treasurer
James Murphy	212-944-3871

Outside Ticket Agency
Computerized
Tele-charge	212-239-6200

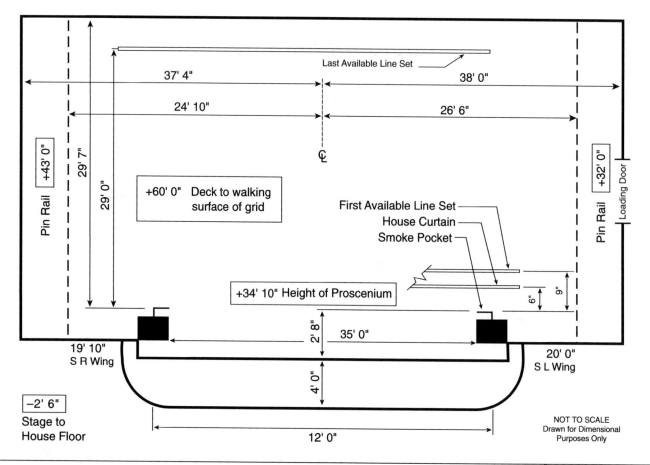

STAGE HOUSE

HOUSE CURTAIN
Operates as a guillotine from SL deck

RIGGING SYSTEM
Type:	Hemp System
Weight:	4,000 lbs available
Line sets:	35 sets with 5 lift lines per set
House Pipes:	42' long with 58' of travel from deck

Line sets are moveable
Block & Falls are available 2:1 (3); 3:2 (2)
(50) spot wheels and 2,500' of hemp available
Chain hoists for electric jump

PERMANENT INSTALLATIONS OVER STAGE (FROM SMOKE POCKET)
None

PERMANENT INSTALLATIONS ON DECK
None

ORCHESTRA PIT
Nonadjustable at 6' below stage level
Apron overhangs upstage wall of pit 1'5"

BACKSTAGE

LOADING DOCK
Loading door(s):
    10'6" high x 7'10" wide
Trucks load (1) at a time
Dock (loading door sill) is 5'0"
    above street level; ramp (1) up
    to loading door is available
Fork lift is not required
Sound/Props can load in FOH
Lobby can be a work area
Trailers cannot store on-site
Security at stage door

WARDROBE
Location: SR Dressing room on
    3rd fl
Access: Stairs
(1) Washer (1) Dryer

DRESSING ROOMS
(4) Star, SR, 2nd fl, toilet
    included
(9) Small, SR, stage level/ 2nd
    fl, 3rd fl, toilet included
Showers located in basement
Use dressing room for company
    mgr office

SOUND

CONSOLE
No house console

SPEAKERS
None
Speaker truss exists
Max available load 4,000 lbs
Pipe and rigging available

COMMUNICATIONS
No house intercom system
Infrared sound system
Dressing room page system

ROAD CONSOLE
Located Rear Mezzanine
(5) seats required to be
    removed
Cable run from stage is 250'

REHEARSAL & STORAGE SPACE
Rehearsal: None
Storage: None

ELECTRICS

ROAD SERVICE POWER

Panel	Phase	Amp	Circuit Protection	Use	Location
A	3	800	fuse	extra	SL in basement
B	3	1000	fuse	extra	SR on jump
C	3	100	fuse	dimmers	SL
D	3	100	fuse	dimmers	SR
E	3	200	fuse	sound	SL in basement

Recommended location of touring dimmer racks: SR on jump
Hoist required and provided
Additional power is available for tour buses, generators, etc

FRONT OF HOUSE (BOX BOOM VALUES ARE PER SIDE)

Position	Pipe Width	Distance to Prosc.	House Circuits	Connector Type	FOH Transfer Circuits
Goal Post		52'	0	grd 20 amp stage pin	0
2nd Balc Rail		55'	29	grd 20 amp stage pin	29
Box Boom 1		38'	12	grd 20 amp stage pin	12
Box Boom 2		38'	12	grd 20 amp stage pin	12

Transfer circuits: grd 20 amp stage pin located SR on jump

EQUIPMENT FOH (BOX BOOM VALUES ARE PER SIDE)
None

FOLLOWSPOTS
House Followspots:
    None

Followspot Booth:
    (2) spots per booth;
    66' throw to proscenium;
    (3) 2Ø 60 amp breakers

DIMMERS
No lighting console
No dimmers
No DMX control system

LUNT-FONTANNE THEATRE

Theatre Location: 205 West 46th Street, New York, NY 10036
Management Company: The Nederlander Organization
810 7th Avenue, 21st Floor, New York, NY 10019
212-262-2400 / Fax 212-262-5558

Main Theatre Phone: 212-575-9200
Main Theatre Fax: 212-262-5558
Stage Door Phone: 212-997-8816
Backstage Pay Phone: 212-997-8816

THEATRE STAFF
Chairman Emeritus   James M. Nederlander   212-262-2400
Chairman   James L. Nederlander   212-262-2400
President   Robert E. Nederlander   212-262-2400
Exec Vice President   Nick Scandalios   212-262-2400
Director of Operations   Jim Boese   212-262-2400
Nederlander Group Sales   Laurel Kramer   212-765-8058
House Manager   Kip Makkonen   212-575-9732

HOUSE CREW
Carpentry   Joe Hughes   212-997-8816
Electrics   Richard Tattersall   212-997-8816
Props   Dennis Sabella   212-997-8816

UNIONS
IATSE Local #1   Tony DePaulo   212-333-2500
Wardrobe Local #764   Ray Polgar   212-221-1717
Music Local #802   Bill Dennison   212-245-4802

SEATING CAPACITY
Orchestra	868
Front Mezzanine	168
Rear Mezzanine	436
Boxes	20
Total:	**1,492**

BOX OFFICE
Computerized
Treasurer
   Joe Olcese   212-575-9200

Outside Ticket Agency
Computerized
   TicketMaster   212-713-6300

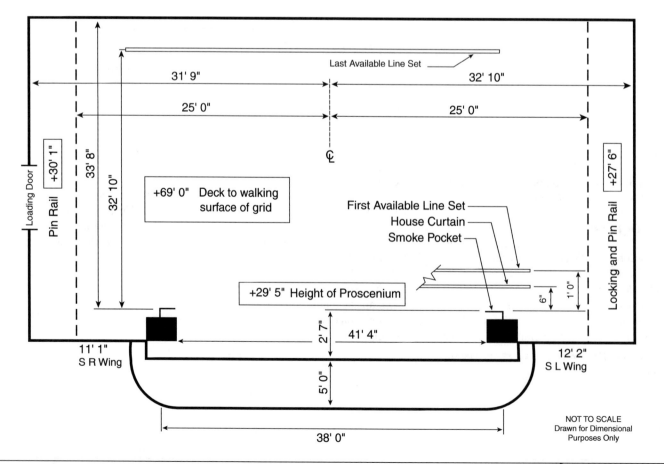

STAGE HOUSE

HOUSE CURTAIN
Operates as a guillotine from SR deck

RIGGING SYSTEM
Type:	Single purchase counter weight
Weight:	20,000 lbs available
Line sets:	74 sets at 6" o.c. with 4 lift lines per set
Arbors:	720 lb capacity
House Pipes:	42' long with 65' of travel from deck

Line sets are moveable
Block & Falls are available 2:1 (4); 3:2 (2)
Chain hoists are not available
(20) spot wheels and 4,000' of hemp available

PERMANENT INSTALLATIONS OVER STAGE (FROM SMOKE POCKET)
None

PERMANENT INSTALLATIONS ON DECK
Traps are on a sectional grid and must be cut
Pilasters (4) against back wall
Radiators (1)

ORCHESTRA PIT
Nonadjustable at 8' below stage level
Apron overhangs US wall of pit 4'0"

BACKSTAGE

LOADING DOCK
Loading door(s):
  11'0" high x 6'0" wide
Trucks load (1) at a time
Dock (loading door sill) is 15"
  above street level; ramp up to
  loading door is available
Fork lift is not required
Sound/Props can load in
  through FOH
Lobby can be a work area
Trailers cannot store on-site
Security at stage door

WARDROBE
Location: Basement
Access: Trap at back door
(2) Washers (2) Dryers
Washer and dryer hookups
  available

DRESSING ROOMS
(3) Star, SR, 1st/2nd fl, t/s
  included, phone jack
(9) Small, SR, 3rd/ 4th/ 5th fl, t/
  s on same fl
(1) Chorus, SL, t/s included
Use dressing room for company
  mgr office

SOUND

CONSOLE
No house console

SPEAKERS
No speaker truss
Holes in ceiling over house
  provide truss hanging
  position
Pipe and rigging unavailable

COMMUNICATIONS
No intercom system
Infrared sound system

ROAD CONSOLE
Located Rear House
(12) seats required to be
  removed
Cable run from stage is 150'

REHEARSAL & STORAGE SPACE
Rehearsal: None
Storage: None

ELECTRICS

ROAD SERVICE POWER

Panel	Phase	Amp	Circuit Protection	Use	Location
A-H	3	400	fuse	dimmers	DS on proscenium
I	3	400	fuse	extra	Basement
J	3	200	fuse	extra	Basement
K	3	100	fuse	extra	Basement
L	3	200	fuse	sound	Basement DS of proscenium

Recommended location of touring dimmer racks: over proscenium wall
Hoist required but not provided
Additional panel USL/ DSR available

FRONT OF HOUSE (BOX BOOM VALUES ARE PER SIDE)

Position	Pipe Width	Distance to Prosc.	House Circuits	Connector Type	FOH Transfer Circuits
1st Balc Rail	60'	25'	20	grd 20 amp stage pin	20
FOH Truss	45'	35'	0	grd 60 amp pin	1
1st Cove	35'	35'	30	grd 20 amp stage pin	30
Box Boom 1		18'	8	grd 20 amp stage pin	8
Box Boom 2		25'	0	grd 20 amp stage pin	0

Transfer circuits: grd 20 amp stage pin

EQUIPMENT FOH (BOX BOOM VALUES ARE PER SIDE)
None

FOLLOWSPOTS
House Followspots:
  None

Followspot Booth:
  (3) spots per booth;
  80' throw to proscenium;
  3Ø 100 amp

DIMMERS
No lighting console
No dimmers
No DMX control system

LYCEUM THEATRE

Theatre Location: 149 West 45th Street, New York, NY 10036
Management Company: The Shubert Organization, Inc.
                                234 West 44th Street, New York, NY 10036

Main Administrative Phone: 212-944-3700
Main Administrative Fax: 212-944-4136
Website: www.telecharge.com
Stage Door Phone: 212-944-3782
Backstage Pay Phone: 212-997-9472

THEATRE STAFF
Chairman   Gerald Schoenfeld   212-944-3700
President   Philip J. Smith   212-944-3700
Executive Vice President   Robert Wankel   212-944-3700
VP Theatre Operations   Peter Entin   212-944-3700
Director of Sales Development Jack Thomas   212-239-6288
Theatre Manager   Warren McClane   212-944-3876

HOUSE CREW
Carpentry   George Dummitt   212-944-3782
Electrics   Charles DeVerna   212-944-3782
Props   Timothy Higgins   212-944-3782

UNIONS
IATSE Local #1   Tony DePaulo   212-333-2500
Wardrobe Local #764   Ray Polgar   212-221-1717
Music Local #802   Bill Dennison   212-245-4802

SEATING CAPACITY
Orchestra	400
Boxes	16
Mezzanine	287
Balcony	210
Total:	**913**
pit (add'l)	11
wheelchair	2

BOX OFFICE
Computerized
Head Treasurer
    Diane Heatherington   212-944-3874

Outside Ticket Agency
Computerized
    Tele-Charge   212-239-6200

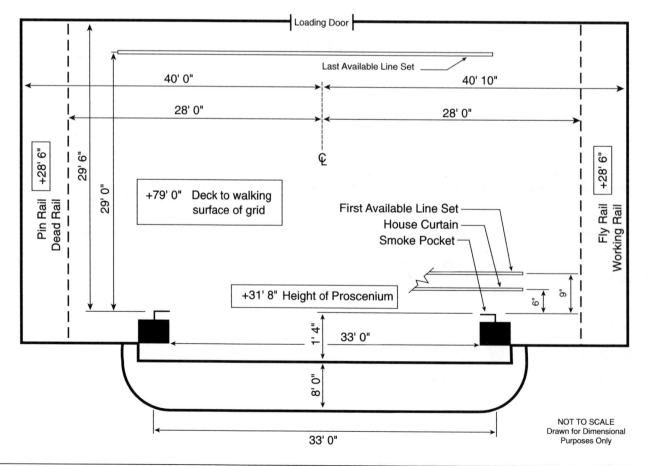

STAGE HOUSE

House Curtain
Operates as a guillotine from SR deck

Rigging System
Type: Hemp System
Weight: 2,500 lbs available
Line sets: 40 sets at 6" o.c. with 5 lift lines per set
House Pipes: 35' long with 78' of travel from deck
Line sets are moveable
Block & Falls are available 2:1 (2); 3:2 (2)
Chain hoists are available
Motorized capstan generally rented for load-in and load-out

Permanent Installations Over Stage (from smoke pocket)
None

Permanent Installations On Deck
Traps (1), approx 3'6" x 7'6", approx 12'0" USR of smoke pocket
Stair rails, approx 5'6" from SL/SR walls

Orchestra Pit
Nonadjustable at 7' below stage level
Apron overhangs US wall of pit 3'0"

BACKSTAGE

Loading Dock
Loading door(s):
   10'0" high x 3'9" wide
Trucks load (1) at a time
Loading path is up 4 stairs from street (ramps provided) through long corridor 9'4" x 3'7"
Fork lift is not required
Sound/Props can load in through FOH
Lobby can be a work area
Trailers cannot store on-site
Security at stage door

Wardrobe
Location: Basement
Access: Stairs to basement; may use block & fall
(1) Washer (1) Dryer

Dressing Rooms
(3) Small, SR, toilet included
(4) Small, SL, (1) stage level, (3) all up flight (s) of stairs, toilet included
(2) Chorus, backstage, 2nd / 3rd fl, t/s on same fl
(6) Small, backstage, 2nd / 3rd fl, t/s on same fl

SOUND

Console
No house console

Speakers
No speaker truss

Communications
Infrared sound system

Road Console
Board can be in booth 200' control run, box run 100', stage 50'

Rehearsal & Storage Space
Rehearsal: None
Storage: None

ELECTRICS

Road Service Power

Panel	Phase	Amp	Circuit Protection	Use	Location
A-F	3	400	fuse	dimmers	Basement
G	3	100	breakcr	sound	DSL
H	3	150	breaker	extra	DSL

Ground for sound must be water pipe or conduit
Recommended location of touring dimmer racks: SL
Hoist is required but not provided

Front Of House (box boom values are per side)

Position	Pipe Width	Distance to Prosc.	House Circuits	Connector Type	FOH Transfer Circuits
1st Cove	24'	75'	24	grd 20 amp stage pin	24
Upper Rail	50'	65'	42	ungrd 15 amp stage pin	42
Lower Rail	40'	30'	0		0
Box Boom 1	20'	20'	0		0
Box Boom 2	20'	30'	6	ungrd 15 amp stage pin	6
Prosc. Booms	30'	30'	0		0

Transfer circuits: ungrd 20 amp stage pin located in basement & SL side
Road truss: All FOH pick ups except booms are in basement

Equipment FOH (box boom values are per side)
None

Followspots
House Followspots:
   None

Followspot Booth:
   (3) spots per booth;
   70' throw to proscenium;
   3Ø 50 amp breakers

Dimmers
No lighting console
No dimmers
No DMX control system

MAJESTIC THEATRE

Theatre Location:	245 West 44th Street, New York, NY 10036	
Management Company:	The Shubert Organization, Inc.	
	234 West 44th Street, New York, NY 10036	

Main Administrative Phone:	212-944-3700
Main Administrative Fax:	212-944-4136
Website:	www.telecharge.com
Stage Door Phone:	212-944-4131
Backstage Pay Phone:	212-764-1750

THEATRE STAFF

Chairman	Gerald Schoenfeld	212-944-3700
President	Philip J. Smith	212-944-3700
Executive Vice President	Robert Wankel	212-944-3700
VP Theatre Operations	Peter Entin	212-944-3700
Director of Sales Development	Jack Thomas	212-239-6288
Theatre Manager	Spofford Beadle	212-944-3879

HOUSE CREW

Carpentry	Richard Miller, Jr.	212-944-4131
Electrics	James Billings	212-944-4131
Props	Randal McAndrews	212-944-4131

UNIONS

IATSE Local #1	Tony DePaulo	212-333-2500
Wardrobe Local #764	Ray Polgar	212-221-1717
Music Local #802	Bill Dennison	212-245-4802

SEATING CAPACITY

Orchestra	885
Boxes	32
Front Mezzanine	292
Rear Mezzanine	436
Total:	**1,645**
wheelchair	5
standing (add'l)	36

BOX OFFICE

Computerized
Head Treasurer
  Dick Cobb   212-944-3877

Outside Ticket Agency
Computerized
  Tele-Charge   212-239-6200

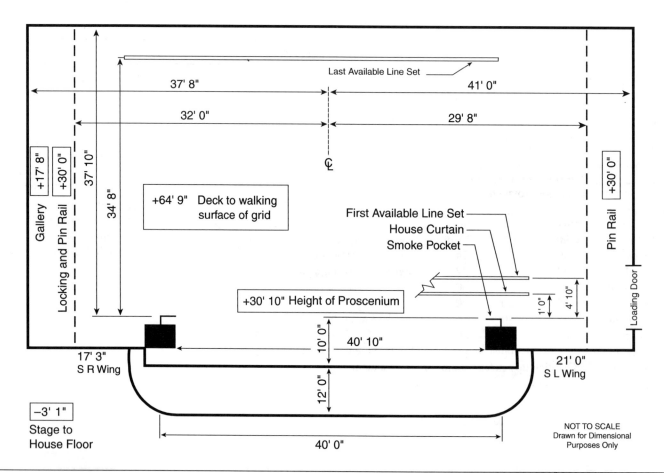

STAGE HOUSE

HOUSE CURTAIN
Operates as a guillotine from SR deck

RIGGING SYSTEM
Type:	Single purchase counter weight
Weight:	27,000 lbs available
Line sets:	70 sets at 6" o.c. with 4 lift lines per set
Arbors:	550 lb capacity
House Pipes:	42' long with 60' of travel from deck

Line sets are moveable
Block & Falls are available 2:1 (3); 3:2 (1)
(100) spot wheels and 3,000' of hemp available

PERMANENT INSTALLATIONS OVER STAGE (FROM SMOKE POCKET)
None

PERMANENT INSTALLATIONS ON DECK
Jump (1) located on DSR proscenium wall 8'8" high
Traps in stage floor are on a sectional grid

ORCHESTRA PIT
Nonadjustable at 14' below stage level
Apron overhangs US wall of pit 3'0"

BACKSTAGE

LOADING DOCK
Loading door(s):
  8'10" high x 6'4" wide
Trucks load (1) at a time
Dock (loading door sill) is 12"
  above street level; ramp (1) up
  to loading door is available
Fork lift is not required
Sound/Props can load in FOH
Lobby can be a work area
Trailers cannot store on site
Security at stage door

WARDROBE
Location: Basement
Access: Elevator
No Washers No Dryers
Washer and dryer hookups
  available

DRESSING ROOMS
(2) Star, SR, 2nd fl, t/s included
(16) Small, all toilet included
  SR, (2) 3rd fl, (2) 4th fl
  SL, (3) 2nd, (3) 3rd, (3) 4th,
  (3) 5th fl
Use dressing room for company
  mgr office

SOUND

CONSOLE
No house console

SPEAKERS
None
Speaker truss exists
Max available load 1,000 lbs
  per point

COMMUNICATIONS
Intercom system
Hearing impaired system
Dressing room page system

ROAD CONSOLE
Located Rear House
(16) seats required to be
  removed
Cable run from stage is 200'

REHEARSAL & STORAGE SPACE
Rehearsal: None
Storage: None

ELECTRICS

ROAD SERVICE POWER

Panel	Phase	Amp	Circuit Protection	Use	Location
A-F	3	400	fuse	dimmers	SR on jump
G	3	100	breaker	sound	SR organ loft
H	3	100	breaker	extra	SL side wall
I	3	100	breaker	extra	USR back wall
J	3	100	breaker	extra	USL
K	3	100	breaker	extra	Outside lights

Recommended location of touring dimmer racks: SR on jump

FRONT OF HOUSE (BOX BOOM VALUES ARE PER SIDE)

Position	Pipe Width	Distance to Prosc.	House Circuits	Connector Type	FOH Transfer Circuits
Truss	27'	25'	20	grd 20 amp stage pin	20
1st Balc Rail	40'	30'	40	grd 20 amp stage pin	40
Box Boom 1		15'	20	grd 20 amp stage pin	20
Box Boom 2		25'	20	grd 20 amp stage pin	20

Transfer circuits: grd 20 amp stage pin located SR on jump

EQUIPMENT FOH (BOX BOOM VALUES ARE PER SIDE)
None

FOLLOWSPOTS
House Followspots:
  None

Followspot Booth:
  (3) spots per booth;
  75' throw to proscenium;
  3Ø 100 amp breakers

DIMMERS
No lighting console
No dimmers
No DMX control system

MARQUIS THEATRE

YEAR BUILT: 1988

Theatre Location: 1535 Broadway, New York, NY 10036
Mailing Address: 211 West 45th Street, New York, NY 10036
Management Company: The Nederlander Organization
810 7th Avenue, 21st Floor, New York, NY 10019
212-262-2400 / Fax 212-262-5558

Main Theatre Phone: 212-382-0100
Main Theatre Fax: 212-997-1242
Stage Door Phone: 212-764-0182
Backstage Pay Phone: 212-764-0178

THEATRE STAFF
Chairman Emeritus James M. Nederlander 212-262-2400
Chairman James L. Nederlander 212-262-2400
President Robert E. Nederlander 212-262-2400
Exec Vice President Nick Scandalios 212-262-2400
Director of Operations Jim Boese 212-262-2400
Nederlander Group Sales Laurel Kramer 212-765-8058
Theatre Manager David R. Calhoun 212-730-2079

HOUSE CREW
Carpentry Joe Valentino, Jr. 212-764-0177
Electrics Anthony Ferrara 212-764-0177
Sound Richie Carney 212-764-0177
Props Ron Wiegel 212-764-0177

UNIONS
IATSE Local #1 Tony DePaulo 212-333-2500
Wardrobe Local #764 Ray Polgar 212-221-1717
Music Local #802 Bill Dennison 212-245-4802

SEATING CAPACITY
Orchestra 993
Boxes 4
Front Mezzanine 355
Rear Mezzanine 230
Total: **1,582**

wheelchair (add'l) 8

BOX OFFICE
Computerized
Treasurer
Richard Waxman 212-382-0100

Outside Ticket Agency
Computerized
TicketMaster 212-307-4100

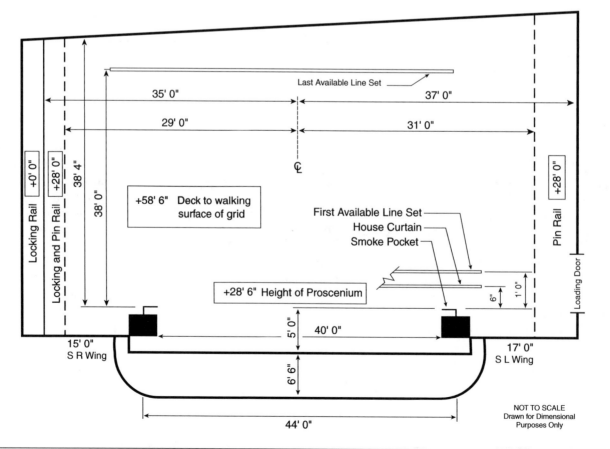

STAGE HOUSE

HOUSE CURTAIN
Operates as a guillotine from SR deck

RIGGING SYSTEM
Type:	Single purchase counter weight
Weight:	50,000 lbs available
Line sets:	60 sets at 6" o.c. with 5 lift lines per set
Arbors:	1,400 lb capacity
House Pipes:	42' long with 54' of travel from deck

Line sets are moveable
(50) spot wheels and 10,000' of hemp available
US gallery against back wall

PERMANENT INSTALLATIONS OVER STAGE (FROM SMOKE POCKET)
None

PERMANENT INSTALLATIONS ON DECK
Column (1) 2'0" square at 39'0" located USC
Traps in stage floor are on a sectional grid

ORCHESTRA PIT
Nonadjustable at 9' below stage level
Apron overhangs US wall of pit 4'0"

BACKSTAGE

LOADING DOCK
Loading door(s):
7'0" high x 7'0" wide
Trucks load (1) at a time
Dock (loading door sill) is at street level one floor below stage level and is equipped with 7'6" high x 8'0" wide x 22'0" long freight elevator
Fork lift is not required
Sound/Props can load in FOH
Lobby can be a work area
Trailers cannot store on-site
Security at stage door

WARDROBE
Location: DSL on stage level
Access: Direct from stage
(2) Washers (2) Dryers

DRESSING ROOMS
(2) Star, SL, stage level, t/s included
(8) Small, SL, (7) 2nd fl / (1) 3rd fl, t/s included
(3) Chorus, SL, (1) 2nd fl / (2) 3rd fl, t/s included
Use dressing room for company mgr office

SOUND

CONSOLE
No house console

SPEAKERS
Various auditorium speakers
Special ceiling cove over house provides cluster hanging position

COMMUNICATIONS
No intercom system
Infrared sound system
Dressing room page system

ROAD CONSOLE
Located Rear House
No seats required to be removed
Cable run from stage is 125'
Tie-in into house system with XLR connectors

REHEARSAL & STORAGE SPACE
Rehearsal: None
Storage: None

ELECTRICS

ROAD SERVICE POWER

Panel	Phase	Amp	Circuit Protection	Use	Location
A-F	3	600	fuse	dimmers	SL on jump
G	3	400	fuse	extra	SL side wall
H	3	200	fuse	sound	SL Sound Room
I	3	100	fuse	extra	SR light booth

Recommended location of touring dimmer racks: SL on jump
Hoist is required and provided

FRONT OF HOUSE (BOX BOOM VALUES ARE PER SIDE)

Position	Pipe Width	Distance to Prosc.	House Circuits	Connector Type	FOH Transfer Circuits
1st Balc Rail	50'	55'	35	grd 20 amp stage pin	35
1st Catwalk	50'	50'	40	grd 20 amp stage pin	40
2nd Catwalk	65'	75'	40	grd 20 amp stage pin	40
Box Boom 1		20'	18	grd 20 amp stage pin	18
Torm		10'	18	grd 20 amp stage pin	18

Transfer circuits: grd 20 amp stage pin located SL on jump

EQUIPMENT FOH (BOX BOOM VALUES ARE PER SIDE)
None

FOLLOWSPOTS
House Followspots:
None

Followspot Booth:
(3) spots per booth;
85' throw to proscenium;
3Ø 100 amp breakers

DIMMERS
No lighting console
No dimmers
No DMX control system

MARTIN BECK THEATRE

YEAR BUILT: 1924   YEAR RENOVATED: 1996

Theatre Location: 302 West 45th Street, New York, NY 10036
Management Company: Jujamcyn Theaters
                           246 West 44th Street, New York, NY 10036

Main Administrative Phone: 212-840-8181
Main Administrative Fax: 212-944-0708
E-mail: jujamcyn@jujamcyn.com
Stage Door Phone: 212-245-9770
Backstage Pay Phone: 212-664-8554

SEATING CAPACITY
 Orchestra   743
 Mezzanine   666
 Boxes   28
 Total: **1,437**

 pit (incl)
 wheelchair (incl)
 standing (add'l)   20

THEATRE STAFF
 Chairman   James H. Binger   212-840-8181
 President   Rocco Landesman   212-840-8181
 Producing Director/VP   Paul Libin   212-840-8181
 Creative Director   Jack Viertel   212-840-8181
 General Manager   Howard Rogut   212-840-8181
 Director of Operations   Jennifer Hershey   212-840-8181
 Theatre Manager   George A. Elmer   212-840-8181

HOUSE CREW
 Carpentry   Joseph J. Maher, Jr.   212-245-9770
 Electrics   Dermot J. Lynch   212-245-9770
 Props   Fred L. Becker, Jr.   212-245-9770

UNIONS
 IATSE Local #1   Tony DePaulo   212-333-2500
 Wardrobe Local #764   Ray Polgar   212-221-1717
 Music Local #802   Bill Dennison   212-245-4802

BOX OFFICE
 Computerized
 Box Office Treasurer
   Michael Rutigliano   212-840-8181

 Outside Ticket Agency
 Computerized
 Tele-charge
   Vince Rieger   212-944-4160

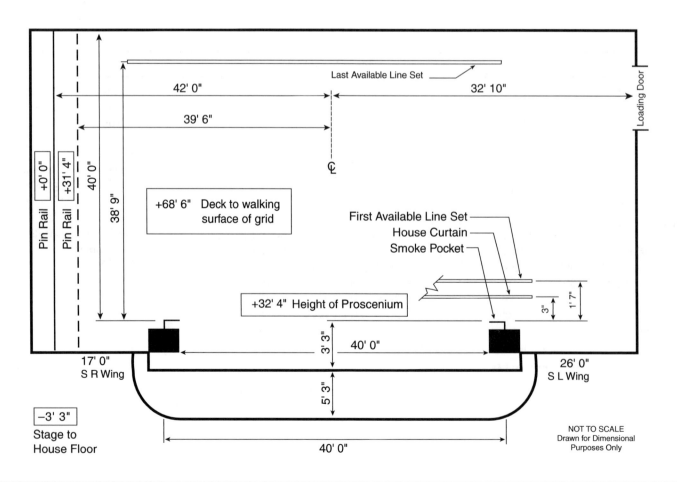

STAGE HOUSE

HOUSE CURTAIN
Operates as a guillotine from SR deck

RIGGING SYSTEM
Type:	Single purchase counter weight
Weight:	45,000 lbs available
Line sets:	83 sets at 4" o.c. with 4 lift lines per set
Arbors:	425 lb capacity
House Pipes:	42' long with 68'6" of travel from deck

Line sets are moveable
Block & Falls are available 2:1 (2); 3:2 (2)
Chain hoists are available as a rental
(100) spot wheels and 50' of hemp available

PERMANENT INSTALLATIONS OVER STAGE (FROM SMOKE POCKET)
Electric Bridge at 21'4" from deck SR
Fire Curtain located 6" DS of curtain
Catwalk located SL of small jump

PERMANENT INSTALLATIONS ON DECK
Trap (90) in stage floor
Jumps (3) located on fly floor, Electric loading bridge
Columns (1) SL
Electric bridges (1) 21'6"h x 3'0"w x 40'0"long
Loading bridge (1) 64'0"h x 3'0"w x 40'0"long

ORCHESTRA PIT
Nonadjustable at 8'7" below stage level
Apron overhangs US wall of pit 6'9"
Pit lift is in (8) sections

BACKSTAGE

LOADING DOCK
Loading door(s):
  12'4" high x 11'0" wide
Trucks load (1) at a time
Dock (loading door sill) is 12" above street level; (1) ramp up to loading door is available
Fork lift is not required
Sound/Props can load in FOH
Lobby can be a work area
Trailers cannot store on-site
Security at stage door

WARDROBE
Location: SR in basement
Access: Trap in stage floor USL
(1) Washer (1) Dryer

DRESSING ROOMS
(3) Star, SR, +1/ +2, t/s included, phone jack
(2) Small, SL, +1, toilet on same fl, phone jack
(4) Small, SL, +2, t/s on same fl, phone jack
(5) Small, SL, +3, t/s on same fl
(5) Small, SL, +4, t/s on same fl
(3) Chorus, SL, +2/ +3, t/s on same fl, phone jack
Use dressing room for company mgr office

SOUND

CONSOLE
No house console

SPEAKERS
Speaker truss exists
Pipe and rigging available

COMMUNICATIONS
No house intercom system
Infrared sound system

ROAD CONSOLE
Located Rear HL
No seats required to be removed
Cable run from stage is 150'
No permanent in-house equipment

REHEARSAL & STORAGE SPACE
Rehearsal: None
Storage: None

ELECTRICS

ROAD SERVICE POWER
Panel	Phase	Amp	Circuit Protection	Use	Location
A-F	3	400	fuse	dimmers	SR in basement
G	3	100	fuse	sound	SR in basement
H	3	60	fuse	extra	SR in basement

Recommended location of touring dimmer racks: SR in basement
Hoist required but not provided

FRONT OF HOUSE (BOX BOOM VALUES ARE PER SIDE)
Position	Pipe Width	Distance to Prosc.	House Circuits	Connector Type	FOH Transfer Circuits
Truss	40'	28'	0		0
Prosc Boom			0		0
Balc Rail	56'	32'	36	grd 20 amp stage pin	36
Box Boom 1			12	grd 20 amp stage pin	12
Box Boom 2			16	grd 20 amp stage pin	16

Transfer circuits: grd 20 amp stage pin

EQUIPMENT FOH (BOX BOOM VALUES ARE PER SIDE)
None

FOLLOWSPOTS
House Followspots:
  None

(1) Followspot Booth:
  (1) spot per booth;
  88'6" throw to proscenium;
  3Ø 100 amp breakers

(2) followspot towers

DIMMERS
No lighting console
No dimmers
No DMX control system

MINSKOFF THEATRE

YEAR BUILT: 1972   YEAR RENOVATED: 1993

Theatre Location: 200 West 45th Street, New York, NY 10036
Management Company: The Nederlander Organization
810 7th Avenue, 21st Floor, New York, NY 10019
212-262-2400 / Fax 212-262-5558

Main Theatre Phone: 212-869-0550
Main Theatre Fax: 212- 944-8644
Stage Door Phone: 212-840-9797
Backstage Pay Phone: 212-840-9797

THEATRE STAFF
Chairman Emeritus James M. Nederlander 212-262-2400
Chairman James L. Nederlander 212-262-2400
President Robert E. Nederlander 212-262-2400
Exec Vice President Nick Scandalios 212-262-2400
Director of Operations Jim Boese 212-262-2400
Nederlander Group Sales Laurel Kramer 212-765-8058
House Manager David J. Vaughn 212-869-0555

HOUSE CREW
Carpentry Gary Bender 212-840-9797
Electrics Michael Lynch 212-840-9797
Props Frank Lavaia 212-840-9797

UNIONS
IATSE Local #1 Tony DePaulo 212-333-2500
Wardrobe Local #764 Ray Polgar 212-221-1717
Music Local #802 Bill Dennison 212-245-4802

SEATING CAPACITY
Orchestra 1,101
Front Mezzanine 302
Rear Mezzanine 307
Total: **1,710**

BOX OFFICE
Computerized
Treasurer
Nicholas Loiacono 212-869-0550

Outside Ticket Agency
Computerized
TicketMaster 212-713-6300

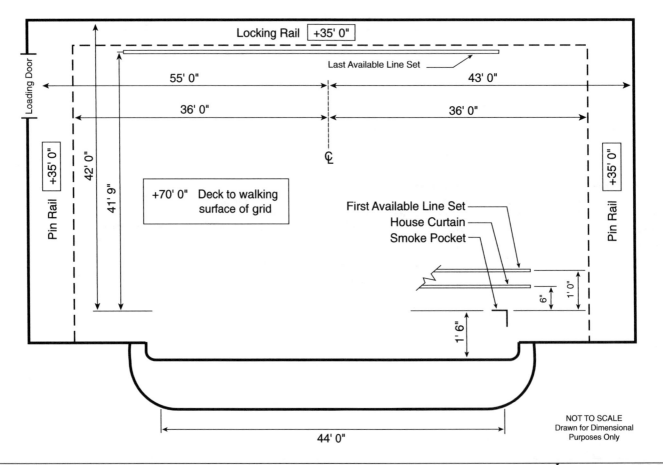

STAGE HOUSE

HOUSE CURTAIN
Operates as a guillotine from SL fly floor

RIGGING SYSTEM

Type:	Single purchase counter weight
Weight:	70,000 lbs available
Line sets:	70 sets at 6" o.c. with 4 lift lines per set
Arbors:	1,400 lb capacity
House Pipes:	44' long with 68' of travel from deck

Line sets are moveable
Block & Falls are available 2:1 (2); 3:2 (1)
(40) spot wheels and 4,000' of hemp available

PERMANENT INSTALLATIONS OVER STAGE (FROM SMOKE POCKET)
Lock rail on US wall

PERMANENT INSTALLATIONS ON DECK
None

ORCHESTRA PIT
Nonadjustable at 9' below stage level
Apron overhangs US wall of pit 10'0"

BACKSTAGE

LOADING DOCK
Loading door(s):
15'8" high x 12'0" wide
Trucks load (1) at a time
Dock (loading door sill) is at street level; stage is 3 floors above dock and is equipped with 6'0" high x 8'0" wide freight elevator
Fork lift is not required
Sound/Props can load in through FOH
Lobby can be a work area
Trailers cannot store on-site
Security at stage door

WARDROBE
Location: SL on stage leel
Access: Direct from stage
(2) Washers (2) Dryers

DRESSING ROOMS
(6) Star, SL, stage level, t/s included
(8) Small, (4) SR, (4) SL, half fl below stage, t/s included
(2) Chorus, SL, 3rd fl, t/s included

SOUND

CONSOLE
No house console

SPEAKERS
No speaker truss
Catwalk over house provides speaker hanging position

COMMUNICATIONS
Aztec intercom with (1) channel
Infrared sound system
Dressing room page system

ROAD CONSOLE
Located Rear House
(16) seats required to be removed
Cable run from stage is 140'

REHEARSAL & STORAGE SPACE
Rehearsal: None
Storage: None

ELECTRICS

ROAD SERVICE POWER

Panel	Phase	Amp	Circuit Protection	Use	Location
A-F	3	400	fuse	dimmers	SL on jump
G	3	100	fuse	sound	SL side wall
H	3	400	fuse	extra	SL on jump
I	3	400	fuse	extra	SL on jump
J	3	400	fuse	extra	SL on jump
K	3	100	breaker	extra	SR side wall
J	3	100		sound	DSL on jump

Recommended location of touring dimmer racks: SL on deck or jump
Hoist is required but not provided

FRONT OF HOUSE (BOX BOOM VALUES ARE PER SIDE)

Position	Pipe Width	Distance to Prosc.	House Circuits	Connector Type	FOH Transfer Circuits
1st Balc Rail	40'	63'	42	grd 20 amp stage pin	42
1st Cove	60	57'	52	grd 20 amp stage pin	52
2nd Cove	60'	79'	52	grd 20 amp stage pin	52
Box Boom 1		12'	19	grd 20 amp stage pin	19
Box Boom 2		28'	19	grd 20 amp stage pin	19

Transfer circuits: grd 20 amp stage pin located SL on jump
Road truss: Holes in ceiling over house provides additional hanging positions; pipe and rigging unavailable

EQUIPMENT FOH (BOX BOOM VALUES ARE PER SIDE)

None

FOLLOWSPOTS
House Followspots:
None

Followspot Booth:
(5) spots per booth;
96' throw to proscenium;
(3) 3Ø 60 amp breakers
Additional lfollowspot locations on side walls, 68' throw

DIMMERS
No lighting console
No dimmers
No DMX control system

MUSIC BOX THEATRE

Theatre Location: 239 West 45th Street, New York, NY 10036
Management Company: The Shubert Organization, Inc.
234 West 44th Street, New York, NY 10036

Main Administrative Phone: 212-944-3700
Main Administrative Fax: 212-944-4136
Website: www.telecharge.com
Stage Door Phone: 212-944-4130
Backstage Pay Phone: 212-997-8870

SEATING CAPACITY

Orchestra	539
Boxes	16
Mezzanine	455
Total	**1,010**
pit(add'l)	35
standing (add'l)	16
wheelchair	4

THEATRE STAFF

Chairman	Gerald Schoenfeld	212-944-3700
President	Philip J. Smith	212-944-3700
Executive Vice President	Robert Wankel	212-944-3700
VP Theatre Operations	Peter Entin	212-944-3700
Director of Sales Development	Jack Thomas	212-239-6288
Theatre Manager	Sherman Gross	212-768-7220

HOUSE CREW

Carpentry	Dennis Maher	212-944-4130
Electrics	Richard T. Beck	212-944-4130
Props	Kim Garnett	212-944-4130

UNIONS

IATSE #1	Tony DePaulo	212-333-2500
Wardrobe #764	Ray Polgar	212-221-1717
Music #802	Bill Dennison	212-245-4802

BOX OFFICE
Computerized
Head Treasurer
Bob Kelly 212-944-3892

Outside Ticket Agency
Computerized
Tele-Charge 212-239-6200

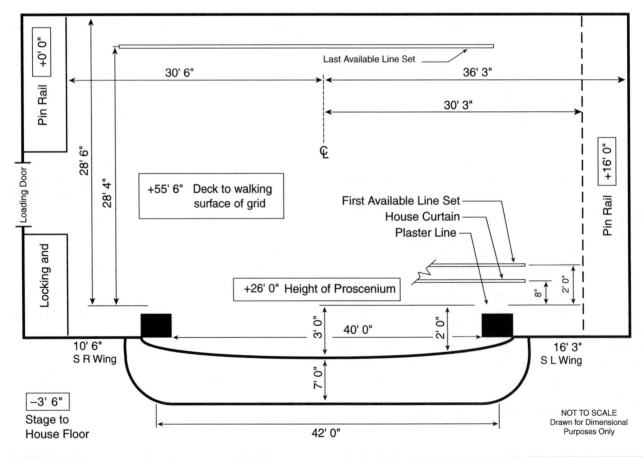

STAGE HOUSE

HOUSE CURTAIN
Operates as a guillotine from SR deck

RIGGING SYSTEM

Type:	Single purchase counter weight
Weight:	7,000 lbs available
Line sets:	60 sets at 6" o.c. with 5 lift lines per set
Arbors:	400 lb capacity
House Pipes:	42' long with 48' of travel from deck

Line sets are moveable
Block & Falls are available 2:1 (1); 3:2 (1)
(50) spot wheels and 10,000' of hemp available

PERMANENT INSTALLATIONS OVER STAGE (FROM SMOKE POCKET)
None

PERMANENT INSTALLATIONS ON DECK
Traps in stage floor are on a sectional grid

ORCHESTRA PIT
Nonadjustable at 10' below stage level
Apron overhangs US wall of pit 6'0"

BACKSTAGE

LOADING DOCK
Loading door(s):
    8'0" high x 6'6" wide
Trucks load (1) at same time
Dock (loading door sill) is 4"
    above street level ramp (1) up
    to loading door is available
Fork lift is not required
Sound/Props can load in FOH
Lobby can be a work area
Trailers cannot store on-site
Security at stage door

WARDROBE
Location: SL in basement
Access: Trap in stage floor SR
(1) Washers (1) Dryers

DRESSING ROOMS
(2) Star, on 2nd fl, t/s included
(1) Star, on 3rd fl, toilet
    included
(7) Small, (2) on 1st, (2) on 2nd,
    (3) on 3rd, toilet included
(6) Small, on 4th fl, t/s on
    same fl
(1) Chorus, 4th fl, t/s on same fl
Use dressing room for company
    mgr office

SOUND

CONSOLE
No house console

SPEAKERS
None
Holes in ceiling over house
    provide truss hanging
    position
Pipe and rigging not avail-
    able

COMMUNICATIONS
Infrared sound system

ROAD CONSOLE
Located Rear House or Box
    positions
No seats required to be
    removed
Cable run from stage is 120'

REHEARSAL & STORAGE SPACE
Rehearsal: None
Storage: None

ELECTRICS

ROAD SERVICE POWER

Panel	Phase	Amp	Circuit Protection	Use	Location
A - B	3	400	fuse	dimmers	SL side wall
C	3	400	fuse	extra	SL side wall
D	3	400	fuse	sound	SL side wall
E	3	200	fuse	extra	Basement

Recommended location of touring dimmer racks: SL on jump
Hoist is required but not provided

FRONT OF HOUSE (BOX BOOM VALUES ARE PER SIDE)

Position	Pipe Width	Distance to Prosc.	House Circuits	Connector Type	FOH Transfer Circuits
1st Balc Rail	35'	27'	30	ungrd 15 amp stage pin	30
Cove Wings		40'	8	ungrd 15 amp stage pin	8
Booth Rail	14'	70'	12	grd 20 amp stage pin	12

Transfer circuits: ungrd 15 amp stage pin located on DSL proscenium wall
Cove Wings are similar to Box Boom positions

EQUIPMENT FOH (BOX BOOM VALUES ARE PER SIDE)
None

FOLLOWSPOTS
House Followspots:
    None

Followspot Booth:
    (2) spots per booth;
    70' throw to proscenium;
    1Ø 20 amp breakers

DIMMERS
No lighting console
No dimmers
No DMX control system

NEDERLANDER THEATER

AKA: BILLY ROSE / TRAFALGAR

Theatre Location: 208 West 41st Street, New York, NY 10036
Management Company: The Nederlander Organization
                           810 7th Avenue, 21st floor, New York, NY 10019
                           212-262-2400 / Fax 212-262-5558

Main Theatre Phone: 212-921-8000
Main Theatre Fax: 212-840-0675
Stage Door Phone: 212-221-9770
Backstage Pay Phone: 212-221-9770

THEATRE STAFF

Chairman Emeritus	James M. Nederlander	212-262-2400
Chairman	James L. Nederlander	212-262-2400
President	Robert E. Nederlander	212-262-2400
Exec Vice President	Nick Scandalios	212-262-2400
Director of Operations	Jim Boese	212-262-2400
Nederlander Group Sales	Laurel Kramer	212-765-8058
House Manager	Louise Angelino	212-921-8704

HOUSE CREW

Carpentry	Joe Ferreri	212-221-9770
Electrics	Brian Lynch	212-221-9770
Props	Billy Wright	212-221-9770

UNIONS

IATSE Local #1	Tony DePaulo	212-333-2500
Wardrobe Local #764	Ray Polgar	212-221-1717
Music Local #802	Bill Dennison	212-245-4802

SEATING CAPACITY

Orchestra	596
Boxes	24
Front Mezzanine	198
Rear Mezzanine	364
Total:	**1,182**
pit (add'l)	24
standing (add'l)	22

BOX OFFICE

Computerized
Head Treasurer
  John Campise   212-921-8703

Outside Ticket Agency
Computerized
  TicketMaster   212-713-6300

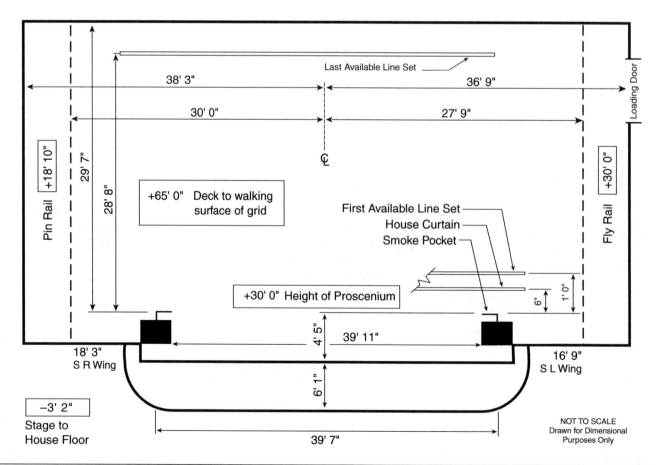

Last Available Line Set

38' 3"   36' 9"
30' 0"   27' 9"

CL

Pin Rail +18' 10"   Fly Rail +30' 0"

29' 7"
28' 8"

+65' 0" Deck to walking surface of grid

First Available Line Set
House Curtain
Smoke Pocket

6"   1' 0"

+30' 0" Height of Proscenium

4' 5"   39' 11"

18' 3"
S R Wing   16' 9"
S L Wing

6' 1"

Loading Door

−3' 2"
Stage to
House Floor

39' 7"

NOT TO SCALE
Drawn for Dimensional
Purposes Only

STAGE HOUSE

HOUSE CURTAIN
Operates as a guillotine from SL deck

RIGGING SYSTEM
Type:	Hemp System
Weight:	4,000 lbs of sand available
Line sets:	15 sets with 5 lift lines per set

Line sets are moveable
Block & Falls are available 2:1 (2); 3:2 (2)
Chain hoists are not available
(50) spot wheels and of hemp available

PERMANENT INSTALLATIONS OVER STAGE (FROM SMOKE POCKET)
None

PERMANENT INSTALLATIONS ON DECK
None

ORCHESTRA PIT
Non-adjustable at 7' below stage level
Apron overhangs US wall of pit 2'4"

BACKSTAGE

LOADING DOCK
Loading door(s):
   10'8" high x 10'7" wide
Trucks load (1) at a time
Dock (loading door sill) is
   2'10" above street level; ramp
   (1) up to loading door must be
   supplied
Fork lift is not required
Sound/Props can load in FOH
Lobby can be a work area
Trailers cannot store on-site
Security at stage door

WARDROBE
Location: Basement
Access: Trap in USL stage floor
(2) Washers (1) Dryer
No washer or dryer hookups

DRESSING ROOMS
(2) Small, SR, stage level, (1) t/s
   included
(6) Small, SR, +1/+2, (1) t/s
   included
(2) Chorus, SR, +3//+4, t/s
   included
Use dressing room for company
   mgr office

SOUND

CONSOLE
No house console

SPEAKERS
None

COMMUNICATIONS
No intercom system
Infrared sound system
No dressing room page
   system

ROAD CONSOLE
Located Rear Orchestra
(10) seats required to be
   removed
Cable run from stage is 100'

REHEARSAL & STORAGE SPACE
Rehearsal: None
Storage: None

ELECTRICS

ROAD SERVICE POWER

Panel	Phase	Amp	Circuit Protection	Use	Location
A-G	3	400	fuse	dimmers	USR
H	3	200	fuse	sound	USR
I-K	3	200	fuse	extra	USR

Recommended location of touring dimmer racks: SR on dimmer rack platform
Hoist is required but not provided

FRONT OF HOUSE (BOX BOOM VALUES ARE PER SIDE)

Position	Pipe Width	Distance to Prosc.	House Circuits	Connector Type	FOH Transfer Circuits
1st Balc Rail	16'	29'	0		0
Box Boom 1			0		0
Box Boom 2		42'	0		0

EQUIPMENT FOH (BOX BOOM VALUES ARE PER SIDE)
None

FOLLOWSPOTS
House Followspots:
   None

Followspot Booth:
   (3) spots per booth;
   77' throw to proscenium;
   (3) 150 amp breakers

DIMMERS
No lighting console
(6) Strand Century dimmers
No DMX control system

NEIL SIMON THEATRE

AKA: ALVIN THEATRE

Theatre Location: 250 West 52nd Street, New York, NY 10019
Management Company: The Nederlander Organization
                       810 7th Avenue, 21st Floor, New York, NY 10019
                       212-262-2400/ Fax 212-262-5558

Main Theatre Phone: 212-757-8646
Main Theatre Fax: 212-262-0771
Stage Door Phone: 212-974-9445
Backstage Pay Phone: 212-974-9445

THEATRE STAFF
Chairman Emeritus   James M. Nederlander 212-262-2400
Chairman   James L. Nederlander 212-262-2400
President   Robert E. Nederlander 212-262-2400
Exec Vice President   Nick Scandalios   212-262-2400
Director of Operations Jim Boese   212-262-2400
Nederlander Group Sales Laurel Kramer   212-765-8058
Theatre Manager   Dixon Rosario   212-757-8646

HOUSE CREW
Carpentry   Thomas P. Green   212-974-9445
Electrics   James Travers   212-974-9445
Props   Bill Yoscary   212-245-5304

UNIONS
IATSE Local #1   Tony DePaulo   212-333-2500
Wardrobe Local #764   Ray Polgar   212-221-1717
Music Local #802   Bill Dennison   212-245-4802

SEATING CAPACITY
Orchestra   669
Boxes   20
Front Mezzanine   190
Rear Mezzanine   437
Total: **1,316**

standing (add'l)   28

BOX OFFICE
Computerized
Head Treasurer
  Richard Aubrey   212-245-2998

Outside Ticket Agency
Computerized
  TicketMaster   212-713-6300

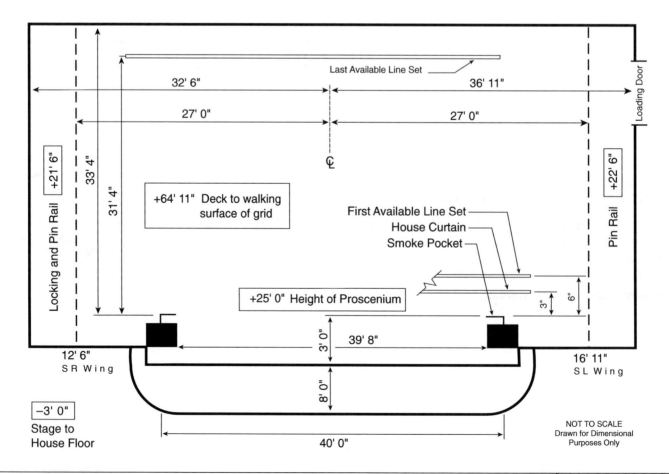

STAGE HOUSE

HOUSE CURTAIN
Operates as a guillotine from SL deck

RIGGING SYSTEM

Type:	Single purchase counter weight
Weight:	50,000 lbs available
Line sets:	61 sets at 6" o.c. with 4 lift lines per set
Arbors:	550 lb capacity
House Pipes:	42' long with 64' of travel from deck

Line sets are moveable
Block & Falls are available 2:1 (1); 3:2 (1)
Chain hoists available as a rental; (1) one ton
(100) spot wheels and 10,000' of hemp available

PERMANENT INSTALLATIONS OVER STAGE (FROM SMOKE POCKET)
None

PERMANENT INSTALLATIONS ON DECK
Traps (1) 5'5" x 4'0"
Jumps (1)
Electric jump (2) , 10'0" x 20'0" SL
Radiators, US wall 0'6" off wall
Loading bridge (1) 33'4" x 4'0"

ORCHESTRA PIT
Adjustable to 6' below stage level
Apron overhangs US wall of pit 1'5"
Pit lift is in (20) sections

BACKSTAGE

LOADING DOCK
Loading door(s):
  8'8" high x 6'3" wide
Trucks load (1) at a time
Ramp from street level to
  sidewalk needed
Fork lift is required
Sound/Props can load in FOH
Lobby can be a work area
Trailers cannot store on-site
Security at dock & stage door

WARDROBE
Location: Basement
Access: Trap in stage floor USL
(2) Washers (1) Dryers
Washer and dryer hookups
  available

DRESSING ROOMS
(1) Star, SR, stage level, t/s
  included, phone jack
(1) Chorus, SR, +1, t/s included
(1) Small, SL, +1, t/s included,
  phone jack
(7) Small, SL, +1/+2/+3, t
  included
Elevator access for dressing
  rooms
Sound/Props can load in FOH
Lobby can be a work area
Trailers cannot store on-site

SOUND

CONSOLE
No house console

SPEAKERS
Speaker truss exists
Max available load is 680 lbs
  per point

COMMUNICATIONS
No house intercom system
Infrared sound system

ROAD CONSOLE
Located Rear House
Number of seats required to
  be removed varies
Cable run from stage is 250'

REHEARSAL & STORAGE SPACE
Rehearsal: None
Storage: None

ELECTRICS

ROAD SERVICE POWER

Panel	Phase	Amp	Circuit Protection	Use	Location
A-D	3	400	fuse	dimmers	SL on jump
E	3	100	fuse	sound	SL on jump

Recommended location of touring dimmer racks: SL on jump
Hoist required but not provided

FRONT OF HOUSE (BOX BOOM VALUES ARE PER SIDE)

Position	Pipe Width	Distance to Prosc.	House Circuits	Connector Type	FOH Transfer Circuits
Truss	40'	30'	0		0
1st Balc Rail	50'	27'	0		0
Box Boom 1	28'	26'	0		0

EQUIPMENT FOH (BOX BOOM VALUES ARE PER SIDE)
None

FOLLOWSPOTS
House Followspots:
None

Followspot Booth:
  (3) spots per booth;
  90' throw to proscenium;
  (1) 2Ø 60 amp breakers

DIMMERS
No lighting console
No dimmers
No DMX control system

THE PALACE THEATRE

YEAR BUILT: 1913   YEAR RENOVATED: 1991

Theatre Location: 1564 Broadway, New York, NY 10036
Mailing Address: 160 West 47th Street, New York, NY 10036
Management Company: The Nederlander Organization
     810 7th Avenue, 21st Floor, New York, NY 10019
     212-262-2400 / Fax 212-262-5558

Main Theatre Phone: 212-730-8200
Main Theatre Fax: 212-730-7932
Stage Door Phone: 212-221-9057

THEATRE STAFF
Chairman Emeritus   James M. Nederlander 212-262-2400
Chairman   James L. Nederlander 212-262-2400
President   Robert E. Nederlander 212-262-2400
Exec Vice President   Nick Scandalios 212-262-2400
Director of Operations   Jim Boese 212-262-2400
Nederlander Group Sales   Laurel Kramer 212-765-8058
Theatre Manager   Stephen A. Marquard 212-730-0021

HOUSE CREW
Carpentry   Thomas Phillips 212-221-9057
Electrics   Francis E. Webber 212-221-9057
Props   Stephen Camus 212-221-9057

UNIONS
IATSE Local #1   Tony DePaulo 212-333-2500
Wardrobe Local #764   Ray Polgar 212-221-1717
Music Local #802   Bill Dennison 212-245-4802

SEATING CAPACITY	
Orchestra	830
Front Mezzanine	384
Front Mezzanine Box	19
Rear Mezzanine	184
Balcony	301
Balcony Box	22
Total:	**1,740**
wheelchair (incl.)	8
standing (add'l)	32

BOX OFFICE
Computerized
Treasurer
  Cissy Caspare   212-730-8200

Outside Ticket Agency
Computerized
  TicketMaster   212-713-6300

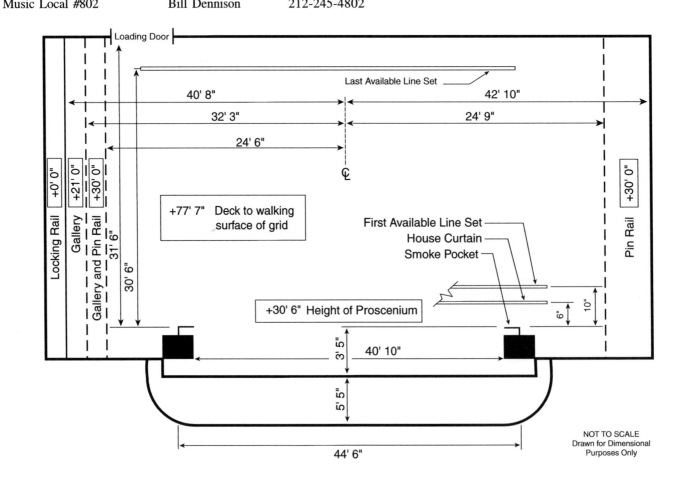

Loading Door

40' 8"   42' 10"

32' 3"   24' 9"

24' 6"

Last Available Line Set

℄

+77' 7" Deck to walking surface of grid

Locking Rail +0' 0"
Gallery +21' 0"
Gallery and Pin Rail +30' 0"
31' 6"
30' 6"

Pin Rail +30' 0"

First Available Line Set
House Curtain
Smoke Pocket

6"   10"

+30' 6" Height of Proscenium

3' 5"   40' 10"

5' 5"

44' 6"

NOT TO SCALE
Drawn for Dimensional
Purposes Only

STAGE HOUSE

HOUSE CURTAIN
Operates as a guillotine from SR deck

RIGGING SYSTEM

Type:	Single purchase counter weight
Weight:	30,000 lbs available
Line sets:	63 sets at 6" o.c. with 5 lift lines per set
Arbors:	650 lb capacity
House Pipes:	45' long with 75' of travel from deck

Line sets are moveable
Block & Falls are available
Chain hoists are not available
(60) spot wheels and 12,000' of hemp available

PERMANENT INSTALLATIONS OVER STAGE (FROM SMOKE POCKET)
None

PERMANENT INSTALLATIONS ON DECK
Traps (1) USR

ORCHESTRA PIT
Nonadjustable at 7' below stage level
Apron overhangs US wall of pit 4'6"

BACKSTAGE

LOADING DOCK
Loading door(s):
7'9" high x 6'6" wide
Trucks load (1) at a time
Dock (loading door sill) is at street level 18" above stage level; ramp (1) down to stage is available
Fork lift is not required
Sound/Props can load in FOH
Lobby can be a work area
Trailers cannot store on-site
Security at stage door

WARDROBE
Location: Basement
Access: Freight elevator
No Washers No Dryers
Washer and dryer hookups available

DRESSING ROOMS
(2) Star, SL, basement/3rd fl, t/s included
(9) Small, SL, (2) basement, (1) 4th fl, (3) 5th fl, (3) 6th fl, t/s on same fl
(4) Chorus, (1) SR & (1) SL basement, (1) SL 4th fl, (1) 7th fl, t/s on same fl
Elevator access for dressing rooms
Use dressing rooms for company mgr office

SOUND

CONSOLE
No house console

SPEAKERS
None
No speaker truss
2.5 ton chain hoist for center speaker cluster is available

COMMUNICATIONS
No house intercom system
Infrared sound system

ROAD CONSOLE
Located Rear HL
No seats required to be removed
Cable run from stage is 125'

REHEARSAL & STORAGE SPACE
Rehearsal: None
Storage: None

ELECTRICS

ROAD SERVICE POWER

Panel	Phase	Amp	Circuit Protection	Use	Location
A	3	(2) 600	fuse	dimmers	SR on bridge
B	3	(4) 400	fuse	dimmers	SR on bridge
C	3	(2) 200	fuse	dimmers	SR on bridge
D	3	600	fuse	extra	SR on bridge
E	3	(2) 400	fuse	extra	SR on bridge
F	3	200	fuse	extra	SR on bridge
G	3	600	fuse	extra	SR basement
H	3	(2) 400	fuse	extra	SR basement
I	3	200	fuse	extra	SR basement
J	3	200	fuse	sound	Rear of house in basement
K	3	100	fuse	extra	SR back wall

Panel A, B, & C are serviced by 1600, 800 & 800 amps, respectively
Recommended location of touring dimmer racks: SR on bridge   Hoist required but not provided

FRONT OF HOUSE (BOX BOOM VALUES ARE PER SIDE)

Position	Pipe Width	Distance to Prosc.	House Circuits	Connector Type	FOH Transfer Circuits
Truss	36'	24'	0		0
1st Balc Rail	58'	35'	30	grd 20 amp stage pin	30
Box Boom 1		15'	12	grd 20 amp stage pin	12
Box Boom 2		21'	0		0

Transfer circuits: grd 15 amp stage pin located SR on bridge; circuits for Box Boom 2 can be jumpered from Box Boom 1
Road truss: 150' cable run from FOH truss to SR bridge dimmers

EQUIPMENT FOH (BOX BOOM VALUES ARE PER SIDE)
None

FOLLOWSPOTS
House Followspots:
None

Followspot Booth:
(3) spots per booth;
88' throw to proscenium;
3Ø 300 amp breakers

DIMMERS
No lighting console
No dimmers
No DMX control system

PLYMOUTH THEATRE

Theatre Location:	236 West 45th Street, New York, NY 10036	
Management Company:	The Shubert Organization, Inc.	
	234 West 44th Street, New York, NY 10036	

Main Administrative Phone:	212-944-3700
Main Administrative Fax:	212-944-4136
Website:	www.telecharge.com
Stage Door Phone:	212-944-4128
Backstage Pay Phone:	212-391-8878

SEATING CAPACITY

Orchestra	621
Boxes	24
Mezzanine	392
Total:	**1,037**
pit (add'l)	42
wheelchair (add'l)	2
standing (add'l)	23

THEATRE STAFF

Chairman	Gerald Schoenfeld	212-944-3700
President	Philip J. Smith	212-944-3700
Executive Vice President	Robert Wankel	212-944-3700
VP Theatre Operations	Peter Entin	212-944-3700
Director of Sales Development	Jack Thomas	212-239-6288
Theatre Manager	Joan Baron	212-944-3882

HOUSE CREW

Carpentry	James Williams	212-944-4128
Electrics	Neil Hannon	212-944-4128
Props	Karen Caton	212-944-4128

UNIONS

IATSE Local #1	Tony DePaulo	212-333-2500
Wardrobe Local #764	Ray Polgar	212-221-1717
Music Local #802	Bill Dennison	212-245-4802

BOX OFFICE

Computerized
Head Treasurer
  Barry Bond   212-944-3880

Outside Ticket Agency
Computerized
  Tele-Charge   212-239-6200

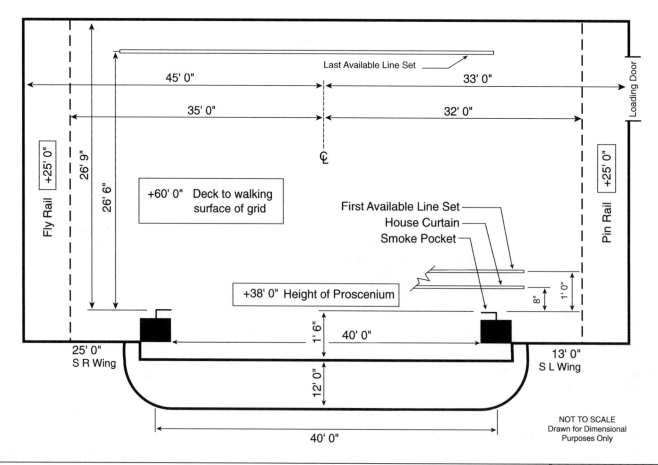

STAGE HOUSE

HOUSE CURTAIN
Operates as a guillotine from SR deck

RIGGING SYSTEM
Type: Hemp System
Weight: 6,000 lbs available
Line sets: 28 sets at 6" o.c. with 4 lift lines per set
House Pipes: 42' long with 59' of travel from deck
Line sets are moveable
Block & Falls are available 2:1 (3); 3:2 (3)
(150) spot wheels and 1,000' of hemp available

PERMANENT INSTALLATIONS OVER STAGE (FROM SMOKE POCKET)
None

PERMANENT INSTALLATIONS ON DECK
Traps in stage floor are on a secitional grid

ORCHESTRA PIT
Nonadjustable at 8' below stage level

BACKSTAGE

LOADING DOCK
Loading door(s):
   14'0" high x 8'0" wide
Trucks load (1) at a time
Dock (loading door sill) is at
   street level
Fork lift is not required
Sound/Props can load in FOH
Lobby can be a work area
Trailers cannot store on-site
Security at stage door

WARDROBE
Location: Basement
Access: Trap in stage floor
(1) Washers (1) Dryers

DRESSING ROOMS
(1) Star, SL, on 2nd fl, t/s
   included
(6) Small, SL, on 2nd fl, toilet
   on same fl
(2) Chorus, SL, on 3rd & 4th
   fls, t/s on same fl
Use dressing room for company
   mgr office

SOUND

CONSOLE
No house console

SPEAKERS
None
Speaker truss
Max available load 1,000 lbs
   per point

COMMUNICATIONS
No house intercom system
Infrared sound system
Dressing room page system

ROAD CONSOLE
Located Rear Balcony
No seats required to be
   removed
Cable run from stage is 175'

REHEARSAL & STORAGE SPACE
Rehearsal: None
Storage: None

ELECTRICS

ROAD SERVICE POWER

Panel	Phase	Amp	Circuit Protection	Use	Location
A - F	3	400	fuse	dimmers	SL on jump
G	3	30	breakcr	sound	SR on jump
H	3	100	breaker	extra	USR back wall
I	3	60	breaker	extra	USL back wall

Recommended location of touring dimmer racks: SL on jump
Hoist is required and provided

FRONT OF HOUSE (BOX BOOM VALUES ARE PER SIDE)

Position	Pipe Width	Distance to Prosc.	House Circuits	Connector Type	FOH Transfer Circuits
Truss	40'	31'	30	grd 20 amp stagepin	30
1st Balc Rail	50'	30'	30	grd 20 amp stagepin	30
Box Boom 1		10'	12	grd 20 amp stagepin	12
Box Boom 2		20'	12	grd 20 amp stagepin	12

Transfer circuits: grd 20 amp stage pin located SL on jump

EQUIPMENT FOH (BOX BOOM VALUES ARE PER SIDE)
None

FOLLOWSPOTS
House Followspots:
   None

Followspot Booth:
   (3) spots per booth;
   62' throw to proscenium;
   3Ø 100 amp breakers

DIMMERS
No lighting console
No dimmers
No DMX control system

RICHARD RODGERS THEATRE

AKA: CHANIN'S 46TH STREET THEATRE   **YEAR BUILT: 1926**

Theatre Location: 226 West 46th Street, New York, NY 10036
Management Company: The Nederlander Organization
     810 7th Avenue, 21st Floor, New York, NY 10019
     212-262-2400 / Fax 212-262-5558

Main Theatre Phone:	212-221-1211
Main Theatre Fax:	212-764-6479
Stage Door Phone:	212-997-9416
Backstage Pay Phone:	212-997-9416

THEATRE STAFF

Chairman Emeritus	James M. Nederlander	212-262-2400
Chairman	James L. Nederlander	212-262-2400
President	Robert E. Nederlander	212-262-2400
Exec Vice President	Nick Scandalios	212-262-2400
Director of Operations	Jim Boese	212-262-2400
Nederlander Group Sales	Laurel Kramer	212-765-8058
House Manager	Felice Rose	212-221-1848

HOUSE CREW

Carpentry	Kevin Camus	212-997-9416
Electrics	Stephen Carver	212-997-9416
Props	Stephen DeVerna	212-997-9416

UNIONS

IATSE Local #1	Tony DePaulo	212-333-2500
Wardrobe Local #764	Ray Polgar	212-221-1717
Music Local #802	Bill Dennison	212-245-4802

SEATING CAPACITY

Orchestra	816
Boxes	32
Front Mezzanine	252
Rear Mezzanine	268
Total:	**1,368**
pit (add'l)	32
standing (add'l)	14

BOX OFFICE

Box Office Treasurer
     Fred Santore   212-221-1211

Outside Ticket Agency
Computerized
     TicketMaster   212-713-6300

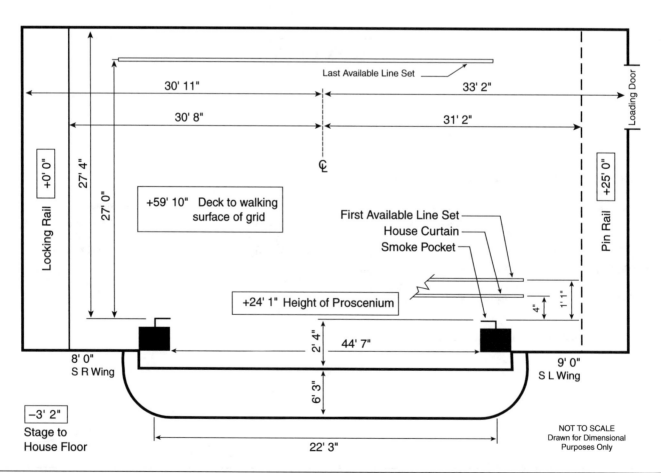

STAGE HOUSE

HOUSE CURTAIN
Operates as a guillotine from SR deck

RIGGING SYSTEM
Type:	Single purchase counter weight
Weight:	15,000 lbs available
Line sets:	69 sets at 4" o.c. with 4 lift lines per set
Arbors:	450 lb capacity
House Pipes:	42' long with 56' of travel from deck

Line sets are moveable
Block & Falls are available 2:1 (1); 3:2 (1)
Chain hoists available as a rental
(50) spot wheels and 2,400' of hemp available

PERMANENT INSTALLATIONS OVER STAGE (FROM SMOKE POCKET)
None

PERMANENT INSTALLATIONS ON DECK
Traps (66), various sizes
Electric jump (1), 16' x 14'6"
Pilasters (3), 3' x 1' x 60'
Radiators (2), 2'6" x 8'6"
Loading bridge (1), 4' x 28' x 60'

ORCHESTRA PIT
Nonadjustable at 8' below stage level
Apron overhangs US wall of pit 3'9"

BACKSTAGE

LOADING DOCK
Loading door(s):
  10'2" high x 6'3" wide
Trucks load (1) at a time
Dock is 4' above street level;
  ramp to loading door is
  available
Fork lift is not required
Sound/Props can load in FOH
Lobby can be a work area
Trailers cannot store on-site
Security at stage door

WARDROBE
Location: Basement
Access: Trap & stairs
(2) Washers (2) Dryers
No washer or dryer hookups

DRESSING ROOMS
(1) Star, stage level, SR,
  toilet included, phone jack
(2) Small, various fls, SR, toilet
  included, phone jack
(1) Chorus, SR, toilet included,
  phone jack
(4) Small, various fls, SL,
  shower included, phone jack
(1) Chorus, SL, shower included, phone jack
Use dressing room for company
  mgr office

SOUND

CONSOLE
No house console

SPEAKERS
No speaker truss

COMMUNICATIONS
No house intercom system
Infrared sound system

ROAD CONSOLE
Located Rear House
(8) seats required to be
  removed
Cable run from stage is 150'

REHEARSAL & STORAGE SPACE
Rehearsal: None
Storage: None

ELECTRICS

ROAD SERVICE POWER
Panel	Phase	Amp	Circuit Protection	Use	Location
A-H	3	400	fuse	dimmers	SL
I	3	100	breaker	extra	SL
J	3	100	breaker	extra	USR

Recommended location of touring dimmer racks: SL on jump
Hoist required but not provided
Additional power is available for tour buses, generators, etc.

FRONT OF HOUSE (BOX BOOM VALUES ARE PER SIDE)
Position	Pipe Width	Distance to Prosc.	House Circuits	Connector Type	FOH Transfer Circuits
Balc Rail	53'	42'	24	grd 20 amp stage pin	24
Box Boom 1		20'	23	grd 20 amp stage pin	23
Box Boom 2		38'		grd 20 amp stage pin	
Truss	40'		24	grd 20 amp stage pin	24

Transfer circuits: ungrd 15 amp stage pin located SL on jump
Road truss: Need to supply break-outs on either end for truss position; transfer circuits
  pick-up on SL jump

EQUIPMENT FOH (BOX BOOM VALUES ARE PER SIDE)
None

FOLLOWSPOTS
House Followspots:
  None

Followspot Booth:
  (3) spots per booth;
  90' throw to proscenium;
  (12) 3Ø 20 amp breakers

DIMMERS
No lighting console
No dimmers
No DMX control system

ROYALE THEATRE

Theatre Location: 242 West 45th Street, New York, NY 10036
Management Company: The Shubert Organization, Inc.
234 West 44th Street, New York, NY 10036

Main Administrative Phone: 212-944-3700
Main Administrative Fax: 212-944-4136
Website: www.telecharge.com
Stage Door Phone: 212-944-4116
Backstage Pay Phone: 212-391-8879

THEATRE STAFF
Chairman Gerald Schoenfeld 212-944-3700
President Philip J. Smith 212-944-3700
Executive Vice President Robert Wankel 212-944-3700
VP Theatre Operations Peter Entin 212-944-3700
Director of Sales Development Jack Thomas 212-239-6288
Theatre Manager Bill Liberman 212-944-3885

HOUSE CREW
Carpentry Michael VanPraagh 212-944-4116
Electrics Herbert Messing 212-944-4116
Props Ron Vitelli, Jr. 212-944-4116

UNIONS
IATSE Local #1 Tony DePaulo 212-333-2500
Wardrobe Local #764 Ray Polgar 212-221-1717
Music Local #802 Bill Dennison 212-245-4802

SEATING CAPACITY
Orchestra 612
Boxes 16
Front Mezzanine 168
Rear Mezzanine 252
Total **1,048**

pit (add'l) 30
wheelchair 2
standing (add'l) 35

BOX OFFICE
Computerized
Head Treasurer
Roy Franklyn 212-944-3883

Outside Ticket Agency
Computerized
Tele-Charge 212-239-6200

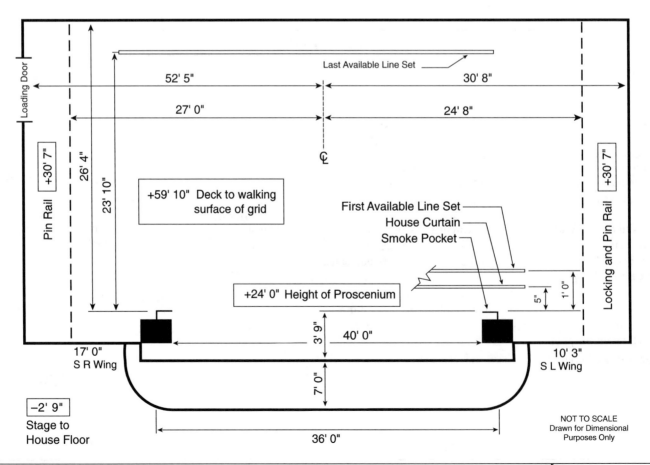

STAGE HOUSE

HOUSE CURTAIN
Operates as a guillotine from SL deck

RIGGING SYSTEM
Type:	Single purchase counter weight
Weight:	12,000 lbs available
Line sets:	57 sets at 4" o.c. with 4 lift lines per set
Arbors:	500 lb capacity
House Pipes:	42' long with 53'6" of travel from deck

Line sets are moveable
Block & Falls are available 2:1 (3); 3:2 (1)
Chain hoists are not available
(75) spot wheels and 5,700' of hemp available

PERMANENT INSTALLATIONS OVER STAGE (FROM SMOKE POCKET)
None

PERMANENT INSTALLATIONS ON DECK
Electric jump (1), SR
Pilasters (4), various sizes
Radiators, on US wall

ORCHESTRA PIT
Nonadjustable at 8' below stage level
Apron overhangs US wall of pit 1'6"
Pit lift is in (10) sections

BACKSTAGE

LOADING DOCK
Loading door(s):
   8'8" high x 5'10" wide
Trucks load (1) at a time
Must off-load from street,
   obtain permit
Fork lift is not required
Sound/Props can load in
   through FOH
Trailers cannot store on-site
Security at dock & stage door

WARDROBE
Location: SR on 2nd floor
Access: Stairs
(1) Washer (1) Dryer

DRESSING ROOMS
(1) Star, SL, stage level, toilet
   included, phone jack
(4) Small, SL, +1, +2, t/s on
   same fl, phone jack
(4) Small, SR, +1, +2, toilet on
   same fl
(1) Chorus, SR, +2, toilet on
   same fl
Use dressing room for company
   mgr office

SOUND

CONSOLE
No house console

SPEAKERS
Speaker truss exists
Max available load 2,000 lbs
   per point
Truss can accomodate road
   equipment

COMMUNICATIONS
No house intercom system
Infrared sound system
Dressing room page system

ROAD CONSOLE
Located Rear House
(12) seats required to be
   removed
Cable run from stage is 75'

REHEARSAL & STORAGE SPACE
Rehearsal: None
Storage: None

ELECTRICS

ROAD SERVICE POWER

Panel	Phase	Amp	Circuit Protection	Use	Location
A - F	3	400	fuse	dimmers	DSR stage level
G	3	100	fuse	extra	SR basement

Recommended location of touring dimmer racks: SR jump
Hoist is required and provided

FRONT OF HOUSE (BOX BOOM VALUES ARE PER SIDE)

Position	Pipe Width	Distance to Prosc.	House Circuits	Connector Type	FOH Transfer Circuits
Truss	42'	30'	0		0
1st Balc Rail	70'	33'	36	grd 20 amp stage pin	36
Box Boom 1		10'	12	grd 20 amp stage pin	12
Box Boom 2		25'	20	grd 20 amp stage pin	20

Transfer circuits: grd 20 amp stage pin located SR under jump

EQUIPMENT FOH (BOX BOOM VALUES ARE PER SIDE)
None

FOLLOWSPOTS
House Followspots:
   None

Followspot Booth:
   (3) spots per booth;
   80' throw to proscenium;
   3Ø 100 amp breakers

DIMMERS
No lighting console
No dimmers
No DMX control system

ST. JAMES THEATRE

YEAR BUILT: 1927   YEAR RENOVATED: 1999

Theatre Location: 246 West 44th Street, New York, NY 10036
Management Company: Jujamcyn Theaters
                      246 West 44th Street, New York, NY 10036

Main Administrative Phone: 212-840-8181
Main Administrative Fax: 212-944-0708
E-mail: jujamcyn@jujamcyn.com
Stage Door Phone: 212-730-9506
Backstage Pay Phone: 212-730-9347

THEATRE STAFF
Chairman   James H. Binger   212-840-8181
President   Rocco Landesman   212-840-8181
Producing Director/VP   Paul Libin   212-840-8181
Creative Director   Jack Viertel   212-840-8181
General Manager   Howard Rogut   212-840-8181
Director of Operations Jennifer Hershey   212-840-8181
Theatre Manager   Daniel G. Adamian   212-840-8181

HOUSE CREW
Carpentry   Timothy McDonough   212-730-9506
Electrics   Timothy F. Donovan 212-730-9506
Props   Barnett Epstein   212-730-9506

UNIONS
IATSE Local #1   Tony DePaulo   212-333-2500
Wardrobe Local #764   Ray Polgar   212-221-1717
Music Local #802   Bill Dennison   212-245-4802

SEATING CAPACITY
Orchestra   705
Mezzanine   656
Balcony   326
Boxes   20
Total: **1,707**

pit (add'l)   26
wheelchair (incl)
standing (add'l)   20

BOX OFFICE
Computerized
Box Office Treasurer
  Vincent Sclafani   212-840-8181

Outside Ticket Agency
Computerized
Tele-charge
  Vince Rieger   212-944-4160

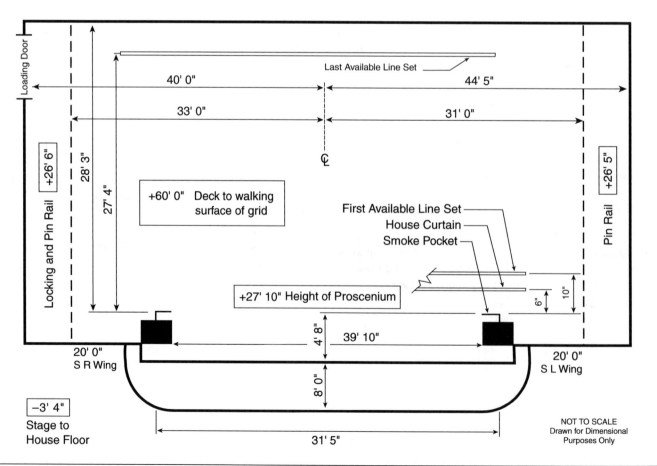

STAGE HOUSE

HOUSE CURTAIN
Operates as a guillotine from SR deck

RIGGING SYSTEM

Type:	Single purchase counter weight
Weight:	20,000 lbs available
Line sets:	59 sets at 6" o.c. with 4 lift lines per set
Arbors:	550 lb capacity
House Pipes:	42' long with 59' of travel from deck

Line sets are moveable
Block & Falls are not available
Chain hoists are available as a rental
(50) spot wheels and 5,000' of hemp available

PERMANENT INSTALLATIONS OVER STAGE (FROM SMOKE POCKET)
None

PERMANENT INSTALLATIONS ON DECK
None

ORCHESTRA PIT
Nonadjustable at 7' below stage level
Apron overhangs US wall of pit 3'4"

BACKSTAGE

LOADING DOCK
Loading door(s):
  8'5" high x 6'6" wide
Trucks load (1) at a time
Dock (loading door sill) is 10"
  above street level; ramp (1) up
  to loading door is available
Fork lift is not required
Sound/Props can load in FOH
Lobby can be a work area
Trailers cannot store on-site
Security at stage door

WARDROBE
Location: Basement
Access: Trap in stage floor USL
(1) Washer (1) Dryer
Washer and dryer hookups
  available

DRESSING ROOMS
(3) Star, SL, stage level, +1, t/s
  included, phone jack
(1) Chorus, SL, -1, t/s included,
  phone jack
(5) Small, SL, +2/+4, toilet on
  same fl, phone jack
(4) Small, SL, +3/+5, shower on
  same fl, (1) phone jack
(2) Small, SL, +6, toilet on same
  fl, (1) phone jack

SOUND

CONSOLE
No house console

SPEAKERS
Speaker truss exists
Sound truss 4' over pit

COMMUNICATIONS
No intercom system
Infrared sound system

ROAD CONSOLE
Located Rear House
No seats required to be
  removed
Cable run from stage is 150'

REHEARSAL & STORAGE SPACE
Rehearsal: None
Storage: None

ELECTRICS

ROAD SERVICE POWER

Panel	Phase	Amp	Circuit Protection	Use	Location
A-F	3	400	fuse	dimmers	Basement
G	3	200	fuse	sound	Basement
H	3	400	fuse	extra	Basement
I-K	3	400	fuse	dimmers	Basement

Recommended location of touring dimmer racks: Basement & platform (below fly floor)
Hoist required but not provided
Additional power is available for tour buses, generators, etc.

FRONT OF HOUSE (BOX BOOM VALUES ARE PER SIDE)

Position	Pipe Width	Distance to Prosc.	House Circuits	Connector Type	FOH Transfer Circuits
1st Balc Rail	50'	38'	30	ungrd 20 amp stage pin	30
2nd Balc Rail	24'	65'	16	ungrd 20 amp stage pin	16
Box Boom 1		24'	16	grd 20 amp stage pin	16
Box Boom 2		36'	16	grd 20 amp stage pin	16

Transfer circuits: ungrd 20 amp stage pin and grd 20 amp stage pin
Road truss: Electric truss, focusing truss & sound truss

EQUIPMENT FOH (BOX BOOM VALUES ARE PER SIDE)
None

FOLLOWSPOTS
House Followspots:
  None

Followspot Booth:
  (3) spots per booth;
  99' throw to proscenium;
  3Ø 100 amp breakers

DIMMERS
No lighting console
No dimmers
No DMX control system

SHUBERT THEATRE

Theatre Location:	225 West 44th Street, New York, NY 10036	
Management Company:	The Shubert Organization, Inc.	
	234 West 44th Street, New York, NY 10036	

Main Administrative Phone:	212-944-3700
Main Administrative Fax:	212-944-4136
Website:	www.telecharge.com
Stage Door Phone:	212-944-3898
Backstage Pay Phone:	212-764-0184

THEATRE STAFF

Chairman	Gerald Schoenfeld	212-944-3700
President	Philip J. Smith	212-944-3700
Executive Vice President	Robert Wankel	212-944-3700
VP Theatre Operations	Peter Entin	212-944-3700
Director of Sales Development	Jack Thomas	212-239-6288
Theatre Manager	Brian Gaynair	212-944-3888

HOUSE CREW

Carpentry	Sander Gossard	212-944-3898
Electrics	John Caggiano	212-944-3898
Props	Robert Miller	212-944-3898

UNIONS

IATSE Local #1	Tony DePaulo	212-333-2500
Wardrobe Local #764	Ray Polgar	212-221-1717
Music Local #802	Bill Dennison	212-245-4802

SEATING CAPACITY

Orchestra	672
Boxes	16
Mezzanine	410
Balcony	351
Total:	**1,449**
pit (add'l)	55
wheelchair (incl)	5
standing (add'l)	26

BOX OFFICE

Computerized
Head Treasurer
  Dick Wolff   212-944-3886

Outside Ticket Agency
Computerized
  Tele-Charge   212-239-6200

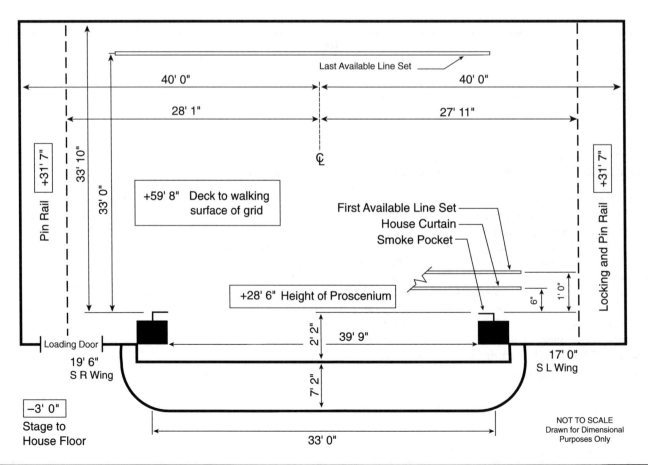

+59' 8" Deck to walking surface of grid

+28' 6" Height of Proscenium

First Available Line Set
House Curtain
Smoke Pocket

Last Available Line Set

40' 0"   40' 0"
28' 1"   27' 11"
33' 10"
33' 0"

Pin Rail +31' 7"

Locking and Pin Rail +31' 7"

Loading Door
19' 6"
S R Wing

17' 0"
S L Wing

2' 2"   39' 9"

7' 2"

6"   1' 0"

−3' 0"
Stage to
House Floor

33' 0"

NOT TO SCALE
Drawn for Dimensional
Purposes Only

STAGE HOUSE

HOUSE CURTAIN
Operates as a guillotine from SL deck

RIGGING SYSTEM
Type: Single purchase counter weight
Weight: 40,000 lbs available
Line sets: 57 sets at 6" o.c. with 4 lift lines per set
Arbors: 860/1240 lb capacity
House Pipes: 45' long with 57' of travel from deck
Line sets are moveable
Block & Falls are available 2:1 (1); 3:2 (1)
Chain hoists are not available
(50) spot wheels and 2,000' of hemp available
Head block / idler automation ready

PERMANENT INSTALLATIONS OVER STAGE (FROM SMOKE POCKET)
None

PERMANENT INSTALLATIONS ON DECK
Jump (1), + 44'6" SL
Electric jump, + 41'4" SR
Electric bridges (1), + 31'7" SR
Loading bridge (1), + 55'6" SL

ORCHESTRA PIT
Nonadjustable at 8' below stage level
Apron overhangs US wall of pit 4'6"

BACKSTAGE

LOADING DOCK
Loading door(s):
    7'3" high x 7'5" wide
Trucks load (1) at a time
Dock (loading door sill) is 12"
    above street level accessed by
    an alley; ramp to loading door
    is available
Fork lift is not required
Sound/Props can load in
    through FOH
Lobby can be a work area
Trailers cannot store on-site
Security at stage door

WARDROBE
Location: Basement
Access: Stairs
(1) Washer (1) Dryer

DRESSING ROOMS
(1) Star, SL, stage level, t/s
    included, phone jack
(9) Small, SL, (3) +1, (3) +2,
    (1) +3, toilet included, phone
    jack
(2) Chorus, SR/SL, +1/ -1, t/s
    included
Use dressing room for company
    mgr office

SOUND

CONSOLE
No house console

SPEAKERS
None

COMMUNICATIONS
No house intercom system
Infrared sound system
Dressing room page system

ROAD CONSOLE
Located Rear House
Seats required to be removed
Cable run from stage is 100'

REHEARSAL & STORAGE SPACE
Rehearsal: None
Storage: None

ELECTRICS

ROAD SERVICE POWER

Panel	Phase	Amp	Circuit Protection	Use	Location
A - F	3	400	fuse	dimmers	SR on bridge
G	3	100	fuse	sound	DSR proscenium
H	3	600		extra	Trap room SL
I	3	600		extra	Automation jump over SL fly

Recommended location of touring dimmer racks: SR on bridge
Hoist required but not provided

FRONT OF HOUSE (BOX BOOM VALUES ARE PER SIDE)

Position	Pipe Width	Distance to Prosc.	House Circuits	Connector Type	FOH Transfer Circuits
1st Balc Rail	40'	32'	18	grd 20 amp stage pin	18
2nd Balc Rail	40'	32'	30	grd 20 amp stage pin	30
Box Boom 1		6'	6	grd 20 amp stage pin	6
Box Boom 2		20'	6	grd 20 amp stage pin	6

EQUIPMENT FOH (BOX BOOM VALUES ARE PER SIDE)
None

FOLLOWSPOTS
House Followspots:
    None

Followspot Booth:
    (3) spots per booth;
    75' throw to proscenium;
    3Ø 100 amp breakers

DIMMERS
No lighting console
No dimmers
No DMX control system

THE THEATER AT MADISON SQUARE GARDEN

FORMERLY: PARAMOUNT THEATER AT: MADISON SQUARE GARDEN   **YEAR BUILT: 1968   YEAR RENOVATED: 1991**

Theatre Location: 7th Ave (between W. 31st St & W. 33rd St),
                            New York, NY 10001
Mailing Address: 4 Pennsylvania Avenue, New York, NY 10001

Main Administrative Phone: 212-465-6000
Main Administrative Fax: 212-465-6198
Website: www.thegarden.com

THEATRE STAFF
Director of Operations   Tony Overton   212-465-6175
Booking   Joel Peresman   212-465-6620
Operations   Jim Arnemann   212-465-6713
Special Events   Avery Bank   212-465-6710

HOUSE CREW
Vice Pres Production   Shannon Curran   212-465-6055

UNIONS
IATSE Local #1   Tony DePaulo   212-333-2500
Wardrobe Local #764   Ray Polgar   212-221-1717
Music Local #802   Bill Dennison   212-245-4802

SEATING CAPACITY	
100's	936
200's	2,755
300's	1,299
Boxes	120
Total:	**5,610**

BOX OFFICE
Computerized
VP Box Office
  Bob Beatty   212-465-6030

Outside Ticket Agency
None

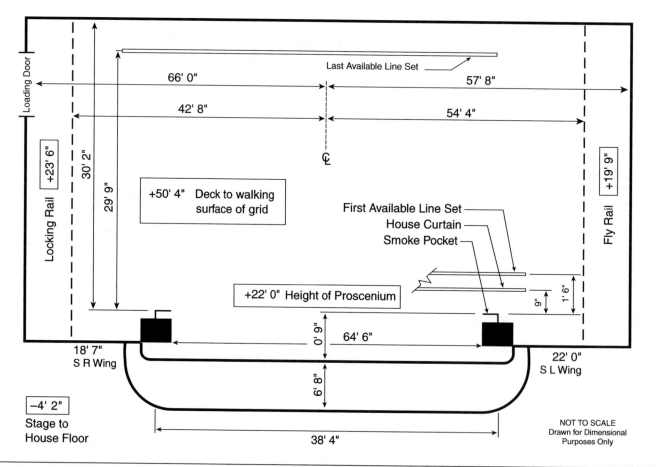

STAGE HOUSE

HOUSE CURTAIN
Operates as a guillotine from SL fly floor; motorized
Operates as a traveller from SL deck; motorized

RIGGING SYSTEM

Type:	Single purchase counter weight
Weight:	70,000 lbs available
Line sets:	40 sets with 6 lift lines per set
Arbors:	2,100 lb capacity
House Pipes:	72' long with 48' of travel from deck

Line sets are moveable
Block & Falls are available
Chain hoists are not available
(40) spot wheels and 2,000' of hemp available

PERMANENT INSTALLATIONS OVER STAGE (FROM SMOKE POCKET)
M=Moveable with advance call
Electric pipe (1); M
Deluge curtain
Traveller (3)

PERMANENT INSTALLATIONS ON DECK
Jumps (2)
Electric jump 11'0" x 13'0" platform DSR +10'0"
Electric bridges (1) motorized electric pipe 6'0" DS of 0'0"
Loading bride (2)

ORCHESTRA PIT
Can create on floor in front of stage

BACKSTAGE

LOADING DOCK
Loading door(s):
    8'0" high x 7'5" wide
Trucks load (2) at same time
No loading dock; trucks unload at street level - 4'10" below grade of house deck; fork lifts on site
Fork lift is required & provided
Sound/Props can load in FOH
Lobby can be a work area
Trailers cannot store on-site
Security at dock & stage door

WARDROBE
Location: SL, +1 above stage
Access: Stairs USL/ freight elevator SL

DRESSING ROOMS
(2) Star, t/s included, phone jack
(7) Small, t/s included, phone jack
(2) Chorus, t/s included, phone jack
Elevator access for dressing rooms

SOUND

CONSOLE
Yamaha, located
    House bunker (16' x 8)
24 inputs, 8 main outputs, 8 matrix outputs, 6 aux outputs

SPEAKERS
House Cluster
Proscenium
Portable
Delays throughout theatre
No speaker truss

COMMUNICATIONS
Clear Com intercom with (48) channels
Infrared sound system
Dressing room page system

ROAD CONSOLE
Located Rear of section 200 or bunker
Number of seats required to be removed varies
Cable run from stage is 350'
Tie-in into house system with XLR connectors

REHEARSAL & STORAGE SPACE
Rehearsal: None
Storage: None

ELECTRICS

ROAD SERVICE POWER

Panel	Phase	Amp	Circuit Protection	Use	Location
A-E	3	400	breaker	dimmers	SR above control room
F	3	600	breaker	dimmers	SR control room
G	3	400	breaker	dimmers	SR control room
H	3	200	breaker	sound	SR/L of transfer switch
I-J	3	100	breaker	extra	SL
K-M	3	400	breaker	extra	Catwalk
N	3	60	breaker	extra	Catwalk
O	3	100	breaker	extra	Ramp storage room

Recommended location of touring dimmer racks: SR above electric control room

FRONT OF HOUSE (BOX BOOM VALUES ARE PER SIDE)
Pipe and grid available

EQUIPMENT FOH (BOX BOOM VALUES ARE PER SIDE)
None

FOLLOWSPOTS
House Followspots:
    (4) Strong-Lumex (on catwalk); removeable

Followspot Booth:
    None

DIMMERS
Lighting console is Insight 2X;
House has dimmers
House has DMX control system

VIRGINIA THEATRE

YEAR BUILT: 1925   YEAR RENOVATED: 1995

Theatre Location: 245 West 52nd Street, New York, NY 10019
Management Company: Jujamcyn Theaters
                         246 West 44th Street, New York, NY 10036

Main Administrative Phone: 212-840-8181
Main Administrative Fax: 212-944-0708
E-mail: jujamcyn@jujamcyn.com
Stage Door Phone: 212-974-9853
Backstage Pay Phone: 212-974-9853

THEATRE STAFF
Chairman   James H. Binger   212-840-8181
President   Rocco Landesman   212-840-8181
Producing Director/VP   Paul Libin   212-840-8181
Creative Director   Jack Viertel   212-840-8181
General Manager   Howard Rogut   212-840-8181
Director of Operations   Jennifer Hershey   212-840-8181
Theatre Manager   Howard Rogut   212-840-8181

HOUSE CREW
Carpentry   David N. Anderson   212-974-9853
Electrics   Donald Beck   212-974-9853
Props   Scott Mulrain   212-974-9853

UNIONS
IATSE Local #1   Tony DePaulo   212-333-2500
Wardrobe Local #764   Ray Polgar   212-221-1717
Music Local #802   Bill Dennison   212-245-4802

SEATING CAPACITY
Orchestra   790
Mezzanine   485
Total: **1,275**

pit (incl)
wheelchair (incl)
standing (add'l)   15

BOX OFFICE
Computerized
Box Office Treasurer
  Robert D. Wolff   212-840-8181

Outside Ticket Agency
Computerized
Tele-charge
  Vince Rieger   212-944-4160

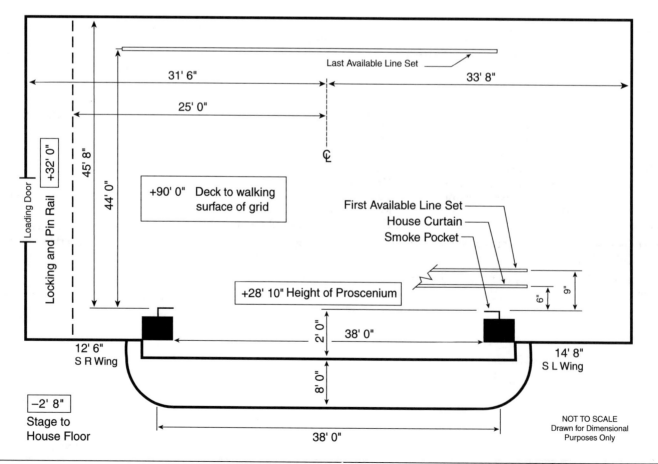

Last Available Line Set

31' 6"   33' 8"

25' 0"

+90' 0" Deck to walking
         surface of grid

+32' 0"
45' 8"
44' 0"

Loading Door
Locking and Pin Rail

First Available Line Set
House Curtain
Smoke Pocket

9"
6"

+28' 10" Height of Proscenium

2' 0"
38' 0"

12' 6"
S R Wing

14' 8"
S L Wing

8' 0"

−2' 8"
Stage to
House Floor

38' 0"

NOT TO SCALE
Drawn for Dimensional
Purposes Only

STAGE HOUSE

HOUSE CURTAIN
Operates as a guillotine from SR deck

RIGGING SYSTEM

Type:	Single purchase counter weight
Weight:	15,000 lbs available
Line sets:	65 sets at 5" o.c. with 4 lift lines per set
Arbors:	450 lb capacity
House Pipes:	40' long with 73' of travel from deck

Line sets are moveable
Block & Falls are available 2:1 (2)
Chain hoists are available as a rental
(50) spot wheels and 10,000' of hemp available

PERMANENT INSTALLATIONS OVER STAGE (FROM SMOKE POCKET)
None

PERMANENT INSTALLATIONS ON DECK
Traps, 44'0"w x 29'3"deep
Electric jump/automation, 3 tier; 8'0"w x 16'0" deep

ORCHESTRA PIT
Nonadjustable at 10' below stage level
Apron overhangs US wall of pit 5'0"

BACKSTAGE

LOADING DOCK
Loading door(s):
9'0" high x 7'0" wide
Trucks load (1) at a time
Dock (loading door sill) is 2'0"
above street level; stage is
4'0" above loading door sill;
(1) ramp up to loading door
and stage is available
Fork lift is not required
Sound/Props can load in FOH
Lobby can be a work area
Trailers cannot store on-site
Security at stage door

WARDROBE
Location: Basement
Access: Trap in stage floor USC
(1) Washer (1) Dryer

DRESSING ROOMS
(1) Star, SR, stage level, t/s
included, phone jack
(2) Small, SR, +1, toilet on
same fl, phone jack
(3) Small, SR, (1) +1, (2) +4,
toilet on same fl
(1) Small, SR, +4, t/s included,
phone jack
(4) Small, SR, (3) +2, (1) +3, t/s
on same fl
Additional production office
available for company mgr

SOUND

CONSOLE
No house console

SPEAKERS
Speaker truss exists

COMMUNICATIONS
No house intercom system
Infrared sound system

ROAD CONSOLE
Located Rear HR
(13) seats required to be
removed
Cable run from stage is 125'

REHEARSAL & STORAGE SPACE
Rehearsal: None
Storage: None

ELECTRICS

ROAD SERVICE POWER

Panel	Phase	Amp	Circuit Protection	Use	Location
A-F	3	400	fuse	dimmers	USL floor
G-II	3	200	fuse	extra	Basement SR
I	1	200	fuse	sound	Basement SL

Recommended location of touring dimmer racks: USL on electric jump
Hoist required but not provided

FRONT OF HOUSE (BOX BOOM VALUES ARE PER SIDE)

Position	Pipe Width	Distance to Prosc.	House Circuits	Connector Type	FOH Transfer Circuits
Balc Rail	35'	30'	48	grd 20 amp stage pin	48
Box Boom 1	20'	10'	16	grd 20 amp stage pin	16
Box Boom 2	5'	15'	12	grd 20 amp stage pin	12
Box Boom 3	18'	30'	16	grd 20 amp stage pin	16
Truss	40'	25'	36	grd 20 amp stage pin	36
Booth	25'	40'	12	grd 20 amp stage pin	12

Transfer circuits: grd 20 amp stage pin
FOH truss: 2 house trusses, (1) electric, (1) sound; house has motors on each truss;
focus track for electric truss

EQUIPMENT FOH (BOX BOOM VALUES ARE PER SIDE)
None

FOLLOWSPOTS
House Followspots:
None

Followspot Booth:
(3) spots per booth;
100' throw to proscenium;
1Ø 100 amp breakers

DIMMERS
No lighting console
No dimmers
No DMX control system
(2) dry run DMX station(s)

VIVIAN BEAUMONT THEATER

AT: LINCOLN CENTER

YEAR BUILT: 1965

Theatre Location: 150 West 65th Street, New York, NY 10023

Main Administrative Phone: 212-501-3100
Main Administrative Fax: 212-873-0761
E-mail: (last name)@lct.org
Website: www.lct.org
Stage Door Phone: 212-362-7600
Backstage Pay Phone: 212-874-9258

THEATRE STAFF
General Manager   Steven C. Callahan   212-501-3223
Production Manager   Jeff Hamlin   212-501-3210
Marketing   Thomas Cott   212-501-3217
Operations   Alex Mustelier   212-501-3213

HOUSE CREW
Carpentry   Walter Murphy   212-501-3263
Electrics   Patrick Merryman   212-501-3264
Props   George T. Green, Jr.   212-501-3102

UNIONS
IATSE Local #1   Tony DePaulo   212-333-2500
Wardrobe Local #764   Ray Polgar   212-221-1717
Music Local #802   Bill Dennison   212-245-4802

SEATING CAPACITY
Orchestra   712
Loge   361
Total: **1,073**

wheelchair (add'l)   2

BOX OFFICE
Computerized
Box Office Treasurer
Fred Bonis   212-501-3257

Outside Ticket Agency
Computerized
Telecharge   212-239-6200

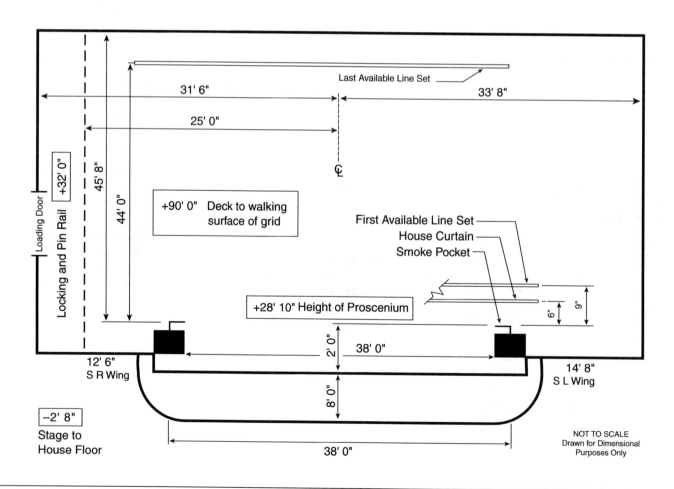

STAGE HOUSE

HOUSE CURTAIN
Operates from SR deck
No house curtain proper; must be installed for each show

RIGGING SYSTEM

Type:	Single purchase counter weight
Weight:	50,000 lbs available
Line sets:	90 sets at 6" o.c. with 7 lift lines per set
Arbors:	1,000 lb capacity
House Pipes:	66' long with 85' of travel from deck

Line sets (81) are moveable; 9 fixed
Block & Falls are available 2:1 (2); 3:2 (3)
(30) spot wheels and 5,000' of hemp available

PERMANENT INSTALLATIONS OVER STAGE (FROM SMOKE POCKET)
None

PERMANENT INSTALLATIONS ON DECK
None

ORCHESTRA PIT
Thrust stage area is custom configured for every production

STAGE DIAGRAM
Not a typical proscenium theatre. Apron is a bell curve shape and the fire curtain follows the curve of the apron. Measurements given are approximate. Contact house for ground plan.

BACKSTAGE

LOADING DOCK
Loading door(s):
  14'4" high x 25'0" wide
Trucks load (1) at same time
Dock is at street level
Fork lift is not required
Supplier is Island Forklifts, Inc.
  516-696-2500
Sound/Props can load in FOH
Lobby can be a work area
Trailers cannot store on-site
Security at stage door

WARDROBE
Location: Dressing room area
  on first level
Access: Direct from stage
(2) Washers (2) Dryers
No washer or dryer hookups

DRESSING ROOMS
(1) Chorus, SR, -1, t/s included
(2) Star, SR/SL, t/s included,
  phone jack
(18) Small, SL/SR, t/s included,
  phone jack
Elevator access for dressing
  rooms
Additional production office
  available for company mgr

SOUND

CONSOLE
No house console

SPEAKERS
No speaker truss

COMMUNICATIONS
No house intercom
Infrared sound system

ROAD CONSOLE
Located Rear House
Number of seats required to
  be removed varies
Cable run from stage is 250'
Tie in into house system with
  XLR connectors

REHEARSAL & STORAGE SPACE
Rehearsal: (3) located under
  stage
  Large, 70' x 39', , mirrors
  & piano; Small, 42' x 19';
  Ballet, 26' x 42', mirrors,
  barres & piano
Storage: None

ELECTRICS

ROAD SERVICE POWER

Panel	Phase	Amp	Circuit Protection	Use	Location
A-H	3	400	fuse	dimmers	DSL
I-L	3	200	fusc	dimmers	DSL
M	3	200	fuse	sound	DSR
N	3	400	fuse	extra	USR
O	3	200	fuse	extra	Dock

Recommended location of touring dimmer racks: DSL
Hoist not required
Additional power is available for tour buses, generators, etc.

FRONT OF HOUSE (BOX BOOM VALUES ARE PER SIDE)

Position	Pipe Width	Distance to Prosc.	House Circuits	Connector Type	FOH Transfer Circuits
Balc Rail	160'	52'	0		0
Catwalk 1	60'	36'	0		0
Catwalk 2	112'	52'	0		0
Catwalk 3	140'	56'	0		0
Box Boom 1	32'	50'	0		0
Box Boom 2	32'	50'	0		0
Box Boom 3	32'	50'	0		0
Box Boom 4	32'	50'	0		0

Road truss: Can set motor points anywhere in FOH grid

EQUIPMENT FOH (BOX BOOM VALUES ARE PER SIDE)
None

FOLLOWSPOTS
House Followspots:
  None

Followspot Booth: None
  Followspot position on
  Catwalk 3

DIMMERS
No lighting console
No dimmers
No DMX control system

WALTER KERR THEATRE

AKA: RITZ THEATRE

YEAR BUILT: 1921   YEAR RENOVATED: 1990

Theatre Location: 219 West 48th Street, New York, NY 10036
Management Company: Jujamcyn Theaters
                                      246 West 44th Street, New York, NY 10036

Main Administrative Phone: 212-840-8181
Main Administrative Fax: 212-944-0708
E-mail: jujamcyn@jujamcyn.com
Stage Door Phone: 212-664-9154
Backstage Pay Phone: 212-664-9154

THEATRE STAFF
Chairman   James H. Binger   212-840-8181
President   Rocco Landesman   212-840-8181
Producing Director/VP Paul Libin   212-840-8181
Creative Director   Jack Viertel   212-840-8181
General Manager   Howard Rogut   212-840-8181
Director of Operations   Jennifer Hershey   212-840-8181
Theatre Manager   Susan Elrod   212-840-8181

HOUSE CREW
Carpentry   George A. Fullum   212-664-9154
Electrics   Vincent J. Valvo   212-664-9154
Props   James F. Caulfield   212-664-9154

UNIONS
IATSE Local #1   Tony DePaulo   212-333-2500
Wardrobe Local #764   Ray Polgar   212-221-1717
Music Local #802   Bill Dennison   212-245-4802

SEATING CAPACITY
Orchestra   543
Mezzanine   322
Balcony   66
Boxes   16
Total: **947**

pit (incl.)
wheelchair (incl.)
standing (add'l)   13

BOX OFFICE
Computerized
Treasurer
   Carmine LaMendola   212-840-8181

Outside Ticket Agency
Computerized
Tele-charge
   Vince Rieger   212-944-4160

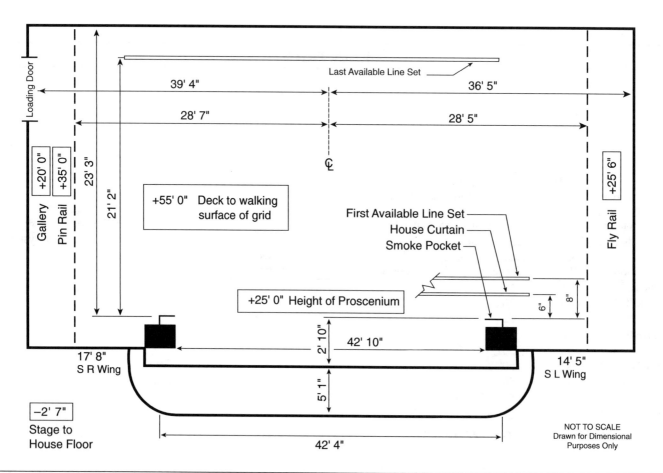

STAGE HOUSE

HOUSE CURTAIN
Operates as a guillotine from SL deck

RIGGING SYSTEM
Type: Hemp System
Weight: 1,500 lbs available
Line sets: 25 sets at 6" o.c. with 5 lift lines per set
House Pipes: 42' long with 54' of travel from deck
Line sets are moveable
Block & Falls are available 3:2 (2)
Chain hoists are not available
(40) spot wheels and 8,000' of hemp available

PERMANENT INSTALLATIONS OVER STAGE (FROM SMOKE POCKET)
None

PERMANENT INSTALLATIONS ON DECK
None

ORCHESTRA PIT
Nonadjustable at 7' below stage level
Apron overhangs US wall of pit 1'6"

BACKSTAGE

LOADING DOCK
Loading door(s):
   10'0" high x 8'8" wide
Trucks load (1) at a time
Dock (loading door sill) is at
   street level
Fork lift is not required
Sound/Props can load in FOH
Lobby can be a work area
Trailers cannot store on-site
Security at stage door

WARDROBE
Location: Basement
Access: Trap in stage floor USL
(1) Washer (1) Dryer
No washer or dryer hookups

DRESSING ROOMS
(1) Star, SL, stage level, t/s
   included, phone jack
(6) Small, SL, (2) on 2nd fl, (2)
   on 3rd fl, (2) on 4th fl, toilet
   on same fl, phone jack
(3) Chorus, SL, 2nd, 3rd & 4th
   fls, toilet on same fl, phone
   jack
Additional showers in basement
Use dressing room for company
   mgr office

SOUND

CONSOLE
No house console

SPEAKERS
Holes in ceiling over house
   provide truss hanging
   position
Pipe and rigging unavailable

COMMUNICATIONS
No house intercom system
Infrared sound system

ROAD CONSOLE
Located Rear House
(8) seats required to be
   removed
Cable run from stage is 100'

REHEARSAL & STORAGE SPACE
Rehearsal: None
Storage: None

ELECTRICS

ROAD SERVICE POWER

Panel	Phase	Amp	Circuit Protection	Use	Location
A-F	3	400	fuse	dimmers	SR jump
G	3	100	fuse	sound	SR wall
H	3	30	breaker	extra	USR back wall

Recommended location of touring dimmer racks: SR on jump
Hoist required but not provided

FRONT OF HOUSE (BOX BOOM VALUES ARE PER SIDE)

Position	Pipe Width	Distance to Prosc.	House Circuits	Connector Type	FOH Transfer Circuits
1st Balc Rail	60'	27'	32	grd 20 amp stage pin	32
2nd Balc Rail	60'	54'	32	grd 20 amp stage pin	32
Box Boom 1		30'	12	grd 20 amp stage pin	12
Box Boom 2		38'	12	grd 20 amp stage pin	12

Transfer circuits: grd 20 amp stage pin located SR on jump
Road truss: Holes in ceiling over house provide truss hanging position; pipe and rigging
   unavailable

EQUIPMENT FOH (BOX BOOM VALUES ARE PER SIDE)
None

FOLLOWSPOTS
House Followspots:
   None

Followspot Booth: No booth
   Followspot from balcony
   56' throw to proscenium;
   Power drawn from 2nd
   Balc Rail

DIMMERS
No lighting console
No dimmers
No DMX control system

WINTER GARDEN THEATRE

Theatre Location: 1634 Broadway, New York, NY 10019
Management Company: The Shubert Organization, Inc.
234 West 44th Street, New York, NY 10036

Main Administrative Phone: 212-944-3700
Main Administrative Fax: 212-944-4136
Website: www.telecharge.com
Stage Door Phone: 212-944-3899
Backstage Pay Phone: 212-664-9608

THEATRE STAFF
Chairman Gerald Schoenfeld 212-944-3700
President Philip J. Smith 212-944-3700
Executive Vice President Robert Wankel 212-944-3700
VP Theatre Operations Peter Entin 212-944-3700
Director of Sales Development Jack Thomas 212-239-6288
Theatre Manager Manuel Levine 212-944-3891

HOUSE CREW
Carpentry Frank Lofgren 212-944-3899
Electrics John A. Kievit, Jr. 212-944-3899
Props Reggie Carter 212-944-3899

UNIONS
IATSE Local #1 Tony DePaulo 212-333-2500
Wardrobe Local #764 Ray Polgar 212-221-1717
Music Local #802 Bill Dennison 212-245-4802

SEATING CAPACITY
Orchestra 989
Boxes 52
Mezzanine 472
Total: **1,513**

pit (add'l) 60
wheelchair (add'l) 3

BOX OFFICE
Computerized
Head Treasurer
Leonard Cobb 212-944-3889

Outside Ticket Agency
Computerized
Tele-Charge 212-239-6200

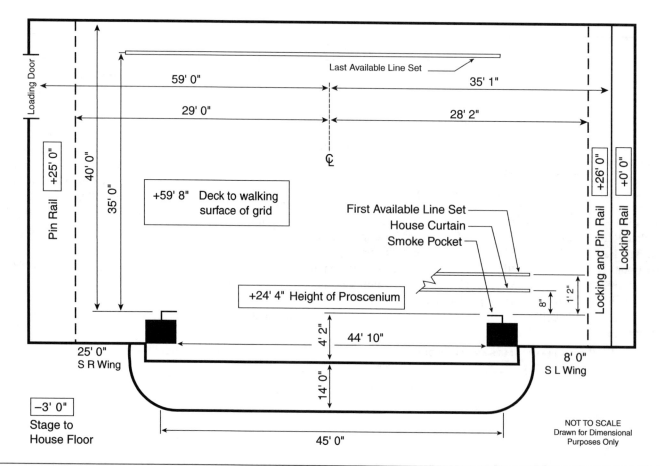

STAGE HOUSE

HOUSE CURTAIN
Operates as a guillotine from SL deck

RIGGING SYSTEM
Type:	Single purchase counter weight
Weight:	18,000 lbs available
Line sets:	75 sets at 6" o.c. with 4 lift lines per set
Arbors:	500-700 lb capacity
House Pipes:	42' long with 55' of travel from deck

Line sets are moveable
Block & Falls are available 2:1 (2); 3:2 (1)
(30) spot wheels and 6,000' of hemp available
US gallery platform against back wall

PERMANENT INSTALLATIONS OVER STAGE (FROM SMOKE POCKET)
Catwalk +25'0" x30", US wall

PERMANENT INSTALLATIONS ON DECK
None

ORCHESTRA PIT
Nonadjustable at 11' below stage level

BACKSTAGE

LOADING DOCK
Loading door(s):
9'10" high x 8'6" wide
Trucks load (1) at a time
Dock (loading door sill) is at
street level 4'0" below stage
level; ramp (1) up to stage
available
Fork lift is not required
Sound/Props can load in FOH
Lobby can be a work area
Trailers cannot store on-site
Security at stage door

WARDROBE
Location: SR on 4th floor
Access: Stairs
(2) Washers (2) Dryers

DRESSING ROOMS
(3) Star, (1) on stage level, (2)
on 3rd fl, toilet included
(12) Small, SR, (3) on 2nd , (1)
on 3rd, (8) on 4th fls, toilet on
same fl
(3) Chorus, SR, on 3rd & 4th
fls, t/s included
Use dressing room for company
mgr office

SOUND

CONSOLE
No house console

SPEAKERS
None

COMMUNICATIONS
No house intercom system
Infrared sound system
Dressing room page system

ROAD CONSOLE
Located Rear House
Seats required to be removed
Cable run from stage is 200'
Tie-in into house system

REHEARSAL & STORAGE SPACE
Rehearsal:None
Storage: None

ELECTRICS

ROAD SERVICE POWER

Panel	Phase	Amp	Circuit Protection	Use	Location
A - F	3	400	fuse	dimmers	USL back wall
G	3	100	fuse	sound	DSR side wall
H	3	100	fuse	extra	USR back wall

Panel A - F is serviced by 800 amps
Recommended location of touring dimmer racks: SL on jump
Hoist is required and provided

FRONT OF HOUSE (BOX BOOM VALUES ARE PER SIDE)

Position	Pipe Width	Distance to Prosc.	House Circuits	Connector Type	FOH Transfer Circuits
1st Balc Rail	50'	60'	30	grd 20 amp stage pin	30
Box Boom 1		25'	10	grd 20 amp stage pin	10
Box Boom 2		35'	10	grd 20 amp stage pin	10

Transfer circuits: grd 20 amp stage pin located SL on jump
Road truss: Holes in ceiling over house provide truss hanging position; pipe and rigging
available

EQUIPMENT FOH (BOX BOOM VALUES ARE PER SIDE)
None

FOLLOWSPOTS
House Followspots:
None

Followspot Booth:
(3) spots per booth;
100' throw to proscenium;
(5) 1Ø 20 amp breakers

DIMMERS
No lighting console
No dimmers
No DMX control system

AUDITORIUM CENTER

YEAR BUILT: 1928   YEAR RENOVATED: 1996

Theatre Location: 875 E. Main Street, Rochester, NY 14605
Management Company: Rochester Broadway Theatre League
100 East Avenue, Rochester, NY

Stage Door Phone: 716-232-9755

THEATRE STAFF

Chief Operations Officer	John Parkhurst	716-325-7760
Booking	Rodney Larson	716-461-4359
Marketing	Larry Ross	716-325-7760
Operations	Troy Smith	716-325-7760
Group Sales	Michelle Glosser	716-325-7760
House Manager	Sally Shannon	716-325-7760

HOUSE CREW

Stage Manager	Gary Zaccaria	716-987-5898
Carpentry	Bill Kablach	716-987-5898
Electrics	Bob Frattare	716-987-5898
Sound	Don Zaccaria	716-987-5898

UNIONS

IATSE Local #25

Tom Mason	716-987-5898
Chris Mauro	716-385-4822
Ray Ricker	716-671-6647

SEATING CAPACITY

Orchestra	1,381
Boxes	32
Balcony	930
Loge	184
Total:	**2,527**

pit (add'l)	20
wheelchair (add'l)	6

BOX OFFICE

Computerized
Sales Manager
Linda Glosser   716-325-7760

Outside Ticket Agency
Ticketmaster
Linda Glosser   716-856-8501

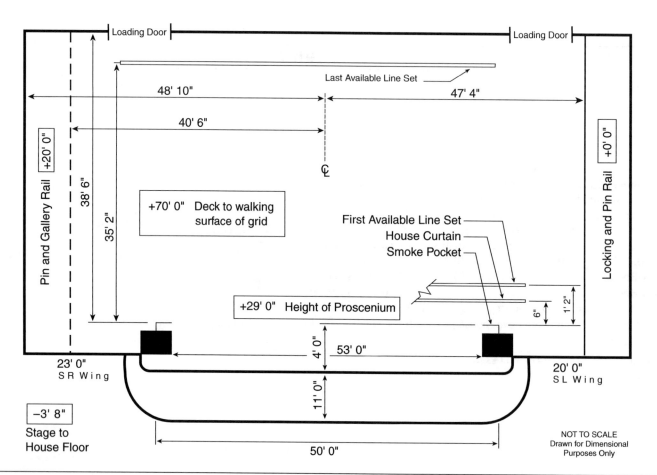

Loading Door — Loading Door

Last Available Line Set

48' 10"   47' 4"

40' 6"

Pin and Gallery Rail +20' 0"

Locking and Pin Rail +0' 0"

38' 6"

35' 2"

+70' 0" Deck to walking surface of grid

First Available Line Set
House Curtain
Smoke Pocket

1' 2"
6"

+29' 0" Height of Proscenium

4' 0"   53' 0"

23' 0"
SR Wing

20' 0"
SL Wing

11' 0"

−3' 8"
Stage to
House Floor

50' 0"

NOT TO SCALE
Drawn for Dimensional
Purposes Only

STAGE HOUSE

HOUSE CURTAIN
Operates as a guillotine from SL deck

RIGGING SYSTEM
Type: Single purchase counter weight
Weight: 20,000 lbs available
Line sets: 70 sets at 6" o.c. with 5 lift lines per set
Arbors: 1,000 lb capacity
House Pipes: 63' long with 69' of travel from deck
Line sets are moveable
Block & Falls are not available
Chain hoists available as a rental
(36) spot wheels and 1,500' of hemp available

PERMANENT INSTALLATIONS OVER STAGE (FROM SMOKE POCKET)
M=Moveable with advance call
Act curtain (1) 0'6", M

PERMANENT INSTALLATIONS ON DECK
Trap (1) in stage floor , 4'0" x 10'0" located CS
Loading bridge (1) located SL

ORCHESTRA PIT
Nonadjustable at 5' below stage level
Apron overhangs US wall of pit 1'6"
Pit lift is Center Line in (1) section

BACKSTAGE

LOADING DOCK
(2) Loading door(s) each:
11'6" high x 9'1" wide
Trucks load (4) at same time
Trucks unload into parking lot
and ramp cases onto stage
Fork lift is not required
Sound/Props cannot load in
FOH
Lobby cannot be a work area
(2) Trailers can store on-site
Security at stage door

WARDROBE
Location: Downstairs
Access: SL via ramp
(2) Washers (2) Dryers
Washer and dryer hookups
available

DRESSING ROOMS
(2) Star, SL, stage level, t/s,
phone jacks
(5) Small, SL, stage level, t/s,
phone jacks
Small, SL, stage level, t/s,
phone jacks
(3) Chorus, SL, stage level, t/s
Additional production office
available for company mgr

REHEARSAL & STORAGE SPACE
SL Hallway - 8 x 40
SL - 80' x 30', carpeted floor,
high ceiling

SOUND

CONSOLE
House console is available

SPEAKERS
No speaker truss

COMMUNICATIONS
No intercom system
Infrared sound system
Dressing room page system

ROAD CONSOLE
Located Center House
No seats required to be
removed
Cable run from stage is 110'
Tie in into house system

ELECTRICS

ROAD SERVICE POWER

Panel	Phase	Amp	Circuit Protection	Use	Location
A-B	3	600	fuse	extra	SL basement
C-D	3	400	fuse	extra	SL basement
E	3	100	fuse	sound	SL basement
F	3	400	fuse	house	SL basement

Recommended location of touring dimmer racks: SL wing or hallway
Hoist not required

FRONT OF HOUSE (BOX BOOM VALUES ARE PER SIDE)

Position	Pipe Width	Distance to Prosc.	House Circuits	Connector Type	FOH Transfer Circuits
Balc Rail	28'	55'	16	grd 20 amp stage pin	0
Box Boom		50'	0	grd 20 amp stage pin	0
Side Boom		30'	0	grd 20 amp stage pin	0

Transfer circuits: grd 20 amp stage pin

EQUIPMENT FOH (BOX BOOM VALUES ARE PER SIDE)
None

FOLLOWSPOTS
House Followspots:
(3) Xenon Super Trouper
2k; removeable
(2) Lycian 400w;
removeable

Followspot Booth:
(3) spots per booth;
175' throw to proscenium;
(4) 3Ø 100 amp breakers

DIMMERS
House has programmable
DMX control system
(1) dry run DMX station

PROCTOR'S THEATRE

YEAR BUILT: 1926   RENOVATION ONGOING

Theatre Location: 432 State Street , Schenectady, NY   12305
Management Company: Arts Center and Theatre of Schenectady

Main Administrative Phone: 518-382-3884
Main Administrative Fax: 518-346-2468
Backstage Pay Phone: 518-382-9270

THEATRE STAFF

General Manager	Fred Daniels	518-382-3884
Director	Gloria Lamere	518-382-3884
Marketing	Fred Daniels	518-382-3884
Operations	Bob Warlock	518-382-3884
Group Sales	Donna Foy	518-382-3884

HOUSE CREW

Production Director	Dan Sheehan	518-382-3884
Carpentry	Martin Petersen	518-381-9091
Electrics	James Petersen	518-381-9091

UNIONS

IATSE Local #14	Richard Rider	518-427-1580
Wardrobe Local #14	Gail Farley	518-427-1580
Music Local # 85-133	John Hines	518-458-2208

SEATING CAPACITY

Orchestra	1,553
Boxes	40
Dress Circle	163
Balcony	944
Total:	**2,700**
pit (add'l)	56

BOX OFFICE

Computerized
  Box Office Manager
  Deb Niedbalski   518-382-3884

Outside Ticket Agency
Computerized
  In house   518-346-6204

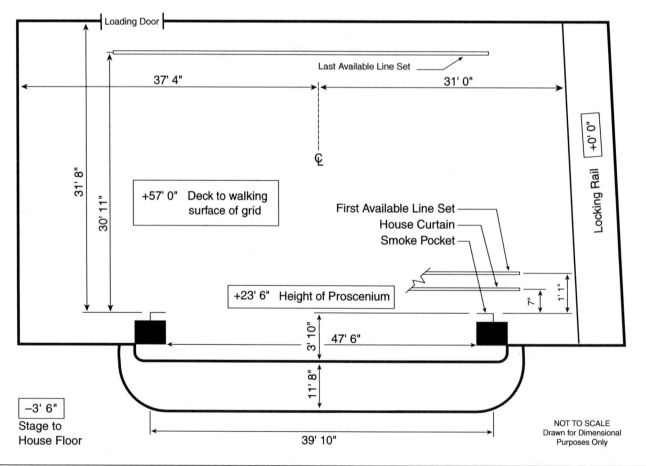

Loading Door

Last Available Line Set

37' 4"   31' 0"

+0' 0"

Locking Rail

CL

31' 8"

30' 11"

+57' 0" Deck to walking
         surface of grid

First Available Line Set
House Curtain
Smoke Pocket

7"   1' 1"

+23' 6" Height of Proscenium

3' 10"   47' 6"

11' 8"

−3' 6"
Stage to
House Floor

39' 10"

NOT TO SCALE
Drawn for Dimensional
Purposes Only

STAGE HOUSE

HOUSE CURTAIN
Operates as a guillotine or traveller from SL deck

RIGGING SYSTEM
Type:	Single purchase counter weight
Weight:	12,000 lbs available
Line sets:	50 sets at 6" o.c. with 4 lift lines per set
Arbors:	700 lb capacity
House Pipes:	50' long with 55' of travel from deck

Line sets are moveable
Block & Falls are available 3:2 (2)
Chain hoists available as a rental; (1) one ton
(40) spot wheels and 3,000' of hemp available

PERMANENT INSTALLATIONS OVER STAGE (FROM SMOKE POCKET)
M=Moveable with advance call
Movie screen (1) at 7'5"; M
Main rug lineset #1 (1) at 1'2"; M

PERMANENT INSTALLATIONS ON DECK
Electric jump (1) 6'0" x 10'0" located DSL (DS of proscenium)
Loading bridge (1) located SL

ORCHESTRA PIT
Adjustable to 15' below stage level by hydraulic lift
Apron overhangs US wall of pit 2'0"
Pit lift is in (2) sections

BACKSTAGE

LOADING DOCK
Loading door(s):
  9'5" high x 7'7" wide
Trucks load (2) at same time
Fork lift is required; Pengate Handling
Sound/Props can load in FOH
Lobby can be a work area
(4) Trailers can store on-site

WARDROBE
Location: USR
Access: Hallway off loading door
(2) Washers (2) Dryers

DRESSING ROOMS
(1) Star, SR, 2nd fl, t/s included
(16) Small, SR, +2/+3, t/s included
Additional production office available for company mgr

SOUND

CONSOLE
Yamaha PM 3000, located Rear Orchestra
40 inputs, 3 main outputs, 8 matrix outputs, 16 aux outputs

SPEAKERS
House Cluster
Proscenium
Under Balcony
No speaker truss

COMMUNICATIONS
Clear Com intercom with (2) channels
RF Frequency 72.9 MHz
Dressing room page system

ROAD CONSOLE
Located FOH
No seats required to be removed
Cable run from stage is 175'
Tie-in into house system with XLR connectors

REHEARSAL & STORAGE SPACE
Rehearsal: None
Storage: Crossover - 50'w x 20'd located US of stage house

ELECTRICS

ROAD SERVICE POWER
Panel	Phase	Amp	Circuit Protection	Use	Location
A	3	600	fuse	dimmers	DSL
B	3	200	fuse	sound	DSL
C	3	100	fuse	extra	USL

Recommended location of touring dimmer racks: DSL
Hoist is provided
Additional power is available for tour buses, generators, etc.

FRONT OF HOUSE (BOX BOOM VALUES ARE PER SIDE)
Position	Pipe Width	Distance to Prosc.	House Circuits	Connector Type	FOH Transfer Circuits
Balc Rail	48'	60'	48	grd 20 amp stage pin	48
Box Boom		60'	12	grd 20 amp stage pin	12

Transfer circuits: grd 20 amp stage pin

EQUIPMENT FOH (BOX BOOM VALUES ARE PER SIDE)
Equipment available upon request

FOLLOWSPOTS
House Followspots:
  (3) Xenon Super Troupers

Followspot Booth:
  (3) spots per booth;
  120' throw to proscenium;
  (3) 1Ø 30 amp breakers

DIMMERS
Lighting console is ETC Express 72/144;
  (96) LMI L86 dimmers
House has non-programmable DMX control system
(2) dry run DMX station(s), DSL, FOH

CROUSE-HINDS CONCERT THEATRE

AT: ON CENTER COMPLEX

YEAR BUILT: **1976**   YEAR RENOVATED: **1988**

Theatre Location:	411 Montgomery St, Syracuse, NY 13202
Mailing Address:	800 South State Street, Syracuse, NY 13202
Management Company:	ON Center
	800 South State Street, Syracuse, NY 13202

Main Administrative Phone:	315-435-8000
Main Administrative Fax:	315-435-8099
E-mail:	sales@oncenter.org
Website:	www.oncenter.org
Stage Door Phone:	315-435-2463
Traveling Production Office Phone:	315-435-3588
Traveling Production Office Fax:	315-435-3642

THEATRE STAFF

Executive Director	Jerry Gallagher	315-435-8000
Marketing	Jerry Keohane	315-435-8000
Operations	John Paddock	315-435-8000
Director of Events	Mary Thompson	315-435-8000

HOUSE CREW

Technical Director	Scott W. Uhrig	315-435-8036

UNIONS

IATSE Local #9	Bob Merola	315-474-1904
Wardrobe Local #9	Bob Merola	315-474-1904

SEATING CAPACITY

Orchestra	1,035
Mezzanine	349
Mezzanine Boxes	48
Balcony	482
Balcony Boxes	84
Total:	**2,025**
pit (add'l)	92

BOX OFFICE
Computerized
Manager
  Mike Spaulding   315-435-8105

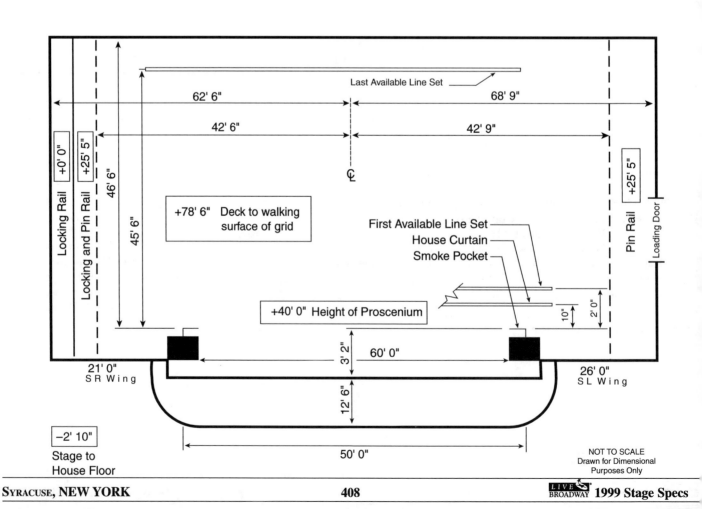

STAGE HOUSE

HOUSE CURTAIN
Operates as a guillotine from SR deck; motorized

RIGGING SYSTEM
Type: Single purchase counter weight
Weight: 70,000 lbs available
Line sets: 80 sets at 6' o.c. with 6 lift lines per set
Arbors: 1,500 lb capacity
House Pipes: 64' long with 73' of travel from deck
Line sets are not moveable
Block & Falls are available
Chain hoists available as a rental; (4) one ton
(20) spot wheels and 200' of hemp available

PERMANENT INSTALLATIONS OVER STAGE (FROM SMOKE POCKET)
Orchestra shells (4) at 6'2", 17'8", 29'2", 40'8"
Electric raceways & borders, (6) at 3'2", 9'8", 16'8", 21' 2", 32'2", 38'8"
Travellers (2) at 11'8", 22'8"

PERMANENT INSTALLATIONS ON DECK
Elevator to grid 3'0" x 5'0" located in USR corner
Orchestra shell stores on SL wall - 14'3" deep

ORCHESTRA PIT
Adjustable to 12' below stage level by hydraulic lift
Apron overhangs US wall of pit 10'0"
Pit lift is in (2) sections

BACKSTAGE

LOADING DOCK
Loading door(s):
9'0" high x 10'0" wide
Trucks load (1) at a time
Dock is at truck level: loading to stage thru separate shop area; truck height limitation is 13'4"
Forklift is not required; House owns
Security at dock & stage door

WARDROBE
Location: SR 1 floor below stage
Access: Freight elevator
(1) Washer (1) Dryer
Washer and dryer hookups available

DRESSING ROOMS
All - t/s included, phone jack
(1) Star, USR, stage level
(4) Small, SL, stage level
(3) Small, SL, -1
(3) Small, SL, -2
(3) Chorus, SR, -1
Elevator (freight) access for dressing rooms
Additional production office available for company mgr

SOUND

CONSOLE
Ward-Beck
16 inputs, 4 aux outputs

SPEAKERS
House Cluster
Truss Speakers
Speaker truss is equipped with house speakers and cannot accomodate road equipment

COMMUNICATIONS
Telex intercom with (1) channel
Infrared sound system
Dressing room page system (partial)

ROAD CONSOLE
Located Rear House center
(16) seats required to be removed
Cable run from stage is 250'
Tie-in into house system with XLR connectors

REHEARSAL & STORAGE SPACE
Rehearsal: 40' x 24' located -2 below stage, piano available, prior arrangement equired
Storage: None

ELECTRICS

ROAD SERVICE POWER

Panel	Phase	Amp	Circuit Protection	Use	Location
A-B	3	400	fuse	dimmers	DSL proscenium wall
C	3	200	fuse	sound	DSL proscenium wall
D-F	3	200	fuse	extra	DSL proscenium wall

Recommended location of touring dimmer racks: DSL on deck
Hoist not required
Additonal 400 amps are available in an adjacent theatre approximately 150'

FRONT OF HOUSE (BOX BOOM VALUES ARE PER SIDE)

Position	Pipe Width	Distance to Prosc.	House Circuits	Connector Type	FOH Transfer Circuits
1st Cove	40'	68'	52	grd 20 amp stage pin	20
1st Balc Rail		76'	4	grd 20 amp stage pin	0
2nd Balc Rail		72'	4	grd 20 amp stage pin	0
Box Boom 1			14	grd 20 amp stage pin	8
Box Boom 2			10	grd 20 amp stage pin	2
Box Boom 3			10	grd 20 amp stage pin	0

Transfer circuits: grd 20 amp stage pin located on DSL proscenium wall

EQUIPMENT FOH (BOX BOOM VALUES ARE PER SIDE)

Position	Quantity	Wattage	Instrument	Removeable
1st Cove	44	1,000	Altman 10°	yes
2nd Balc Rail	4	1,000	Altman 6x12	yes
Box Boom 1	18	1,000	Altman 6x12/6x16	yes
Box Boom 2	4	1,000	Altman 6x16	yes

FOLLOWSPOTS
House Followspots:
(2) Xenon Super Troupers; not removeable

Followspot Booth:
(3) spots per booth;
120' throw to proscenium;
3Ø 50 amp breakers

DIMMERS
Lighting console is Colortron Prestige 3000;
(400) Colortron Dimension 192 dimmers

SYRACUSE AREA LANDMARK THEATRE

AKA: **LANDMARK THEATRE**   YEAR BUILT: **1927**

Theatre Location: 362 S. Salina Street, Syracuse, NY 13201
Mailing Address: PO Box 1400, Syracuse , NY 13202

Main Administrative Phone: 315-475-7979
Main Administrative Fax: 315-475-7993
Traveling Production Office Fax: 315-476-5743

THEATRE STAFF

Facilities Manager	Dennis Snow	315-475-7479
Booking	Dennis Snow	315-475-7479

HOUSE CREW

Operations Manager	Ben Sheedy	315-475-7074

SEATING CAPACITY

Orchestra	1,832
Loge	280
1st Balcony	542
2nd Balcony	232
Total:	**2,922**
pit (add'l)	36
wheelchair (add'l)	20

STAGE DIMENSIONS (FROM SMOKE POCKET)
Stage is 28'0" deep
Width from Center Line to SL is 40'0"
Width from Center Line to SR is 36'0"
Proscenium width is 51'6"
Proscenium height is 29'0"
Smoke pocket to apron edge is 5'0"
Orchestra pit exists

RIGGING

Grid Height:	63'6"
Type:	Single purchase counter weight
Weight:	8,000 lbs
Line sets:	42 sets at 4" o.c.
Arbors:	552 lb capacity
House Pipes:	53" long

LOADING DOCK
Loading door(s) are 9'11" high x 5'5" wide
Trucks load (2) at same time
Fork lift is not required

ELECTRICS
Total power available:
  (1) 400A 3Ø SR wing

FOLLOWSPOTS
House Followspots:
  Arc Super Trouper
Power in spot booth 100A

DIMMERS
(12) house dimmers
No DMX control system
(0) dry run station(s)

SOUND
House has 200A dedicated
  power located SR wing
FOH mixing position in
  Rear Orchestra
No sound console available

STANLEY PERFORMING ARTS CENTER

YEAR BUILT: 1928   RENOVATION ONGOING

Theatre Location: 259 Genesee Street, Utica, NY 13501
Management Company: The Central New York Community Arts Council, Inc.
                         259 Genesee Street, Utica, NY 13501

Main Administrative Phone:	315-724-5919
Main Administrative Fax:	315-724-3854
E-mail:	artfaust@msn.com
Stage Door Phone:	315-724-6470
Traveling Production Office Phone:	315-724-7561
Traveling Production Office Fax:	315-724-6271

THEATRE STAFF

Manager	John Faust	315-724-5919
Booking	John Faust	315-724-5919
Operations	David Storms	315-724-5919
Group Sales	Jacqueline Carbone	315-724-5919

UNIONS

IATSE Local #128	Dennis Brenon Sr.	315-735-3293
Music	Evelyn Murphy	315-732-5146
	Utica Symphony Orchestra	

SEATING CAPACITY

Orchestra	1,653
Loge	264
Balcony	1,028
Total:	**2,945**

pit (add'l)	60
wheelchair (add'l)	38
standing	0

BOX OFFICE
Computerized
Ticket Office Manager
  Jacqueline Carbone   315-724-5919

Outside Ticket Agency
Computerized
Ticketmaster
  Carol Brucato   716-847-1614

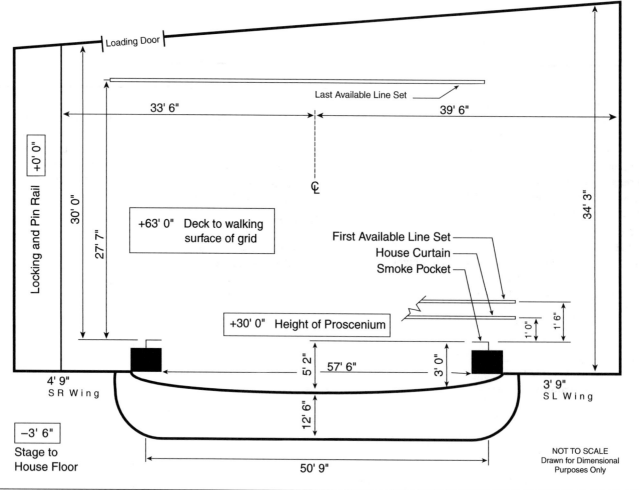

Loading Door

33' 6"   39' 6"

Last Available Line Set

Locking and Pin Rail   +0' 0"

30' 0"

27' 7"

CL

+63' 0"   Deck to walking
            surface of grid

34' 3"

First Available Line Set
House Curtain
Smoke Pocket

+30' 0"   Height of Proscenium

1' 0"   1' 6"

5' 2"   57' 6"   3' 0"

4' 9"
SR Wing

3' 9"
SL Wing

12' 6"

−3' 6"
Stage to
House Floor

50' 9"

NOT TO SCALE
Drawn for Dimensional
Purposes Only

STAGE HOUSE

HOUSE CURTAIN
Operates as a guillotine from SR deck

RIGGING SYSTEM
Type:	Single purchase counter weight
Weight:	7,470 lbs available
Line sets:	38 sets at 7" o.c. with 5 lift lines per set
Arbors:	500 lb capacity
House Pipes:	64' long with 53' of travel from deck

Line sets are moveable
Block & Falls are available 2:1 (2)
Chain hoists are not available
(8) spot wheels and 240' of hemp available

PERMANENT INSTALLATIONS OVER STAGE (FROM SMOKE POCKET)
Orchestra shells (2) at 16'10", 15'0"
Electric Borders (4) at 3'3", 11'11", 18'6", 24'1"
Movie screen (1) at 8'6"
Hard portal (1) at 1'6"
Fire curtain (1) at smoke pocket

PERMANENT INSTALLATIONS ON DECK
Traps in stage floor (12) are on a sectional grid in center of stage
Adjustable portal (1)

ORCHESTRA PIT
Adjustable to 7' below stage level by electric motor turnscrew
Apron overhangs US wall of pit 0'0"
Pit lift is in (1) section

BACKSTAGE

LOADING DOCK
Loading door(s):
  9'0" high x 8'0" wide
Trucks load (1) at a time
Dock (loading door sill) is at street level 13'0" above stage level; rigging is available to lower scenery to stage (2,000 lb capacity)
Fork lift is not required, but is useful RigAll 315-732-4138
Sound/Props cannot load in FOH
(2) Trailers can store on-site

WARDROBE
Location: Basement
Access: Trap in SR stage floor
(1) Washer (1) Dryer
Washer and dryer hookups available

DRESSING ROOMS
(1) Star, SL, stage level, t/s included, phone jack
(6) Small, SL, +2/+3, t/s included
(1) Chorus, SL, +3, t/s included
Use dressing room for company mgr office

SOUND

CONSOLE
No house console

SPEAKERS
No speaker truss

COMMUNICATIONS
No intercom system

ROAD CONSOLE
Located Rear House right
(10) seats required to be removed
Cable run from stage is 130'

REHEARSAL & STORAGE SPACE
Rehearsal: None
Storage: None

ELECTRICS

ROAD SERVICE POWER

Panel	Phase	Amp	Circuit Protection	Use	Location
A	3	400	fuse	dimmers	US back wall
B	3	200	fuse	sound	DSR alcove
C	3	60	fuse	dimmers	DSR alcove

Recommended location of touring dimmer racks: DSR alcove

FRONT OF HOUSE (BOX BOOM VALUES ARE PER SIDE)

Position	Pipe Width	Distance to Prosc.	House Circuits	Connector Type	FOH Transfer Circuits
1st Balc Rail	25'	53'	0		0

Road truss: Truss may be hung from ceiling 55' above orchestra floor; 4 points available at 750 lbs per point

EQUIPMENT FOH (BOX BOOM VALUES ARE PER SIDE)
None

FOLLOWSPOTS
House Followspots:
  (2) Orbitors Long Throw; removeable
  (1) Phoebus Ultra Arc Short Throw; removeable

Followspot Booth:
  (4) spots per booth;
  155' throw to proscenium;
  2Ø 30 amp breakers

DIMMERS
House has SCR dimmers
House has programmable DMX control system
(2) dry run DMX station(s)

EISENHOWER HALL THEATRE

AT: US MILITARY ACADEMY WEST POINT AKA: IKE HALL   **YEAR BUILT: 1974**

Theatre Location: Building 655 US Miltary Academy
                            West Point, NY 10996-1593

Main Administrative Phone: 914-938-2782
Main Administrative Fax: 914-446-5302
E-mail: vw0304@exmail.army.mil
Stage Door Phone: 914-938-3483
Traveling Production Office Phone: 914-938-3483
Traveling Production Office Fax: 914-446-5302

THEATRE STAFF
Cultural Arts Director   William Yost   914-938-2782
Booking   William Yost   914-938-2782
House Manager   Gary Keegan   914-938-4159
Production Arts   Keith Powell   914-938-2782

HOUSE CREW
Technical Director   Fred Goldsmith   914-938-3483
Electrics   Eric Halvorson   914-938-3483
Sound   William Montgomery 914-938-3483

UNIONS
IATSE Local #311   Mike Brennan   914-692-4358

SEATING CAPACITY
Orchestra   2,875
First Balcony   730
Second Balcony   730
Total: **4,335**

pit (add'l)   130

BOX OFFICE
Computerized
Box Office Treasurer
  Gary Keegan   914-938-4159

Outside Ticket Agency
Computerized
  Ticketmaster   914-454-3338

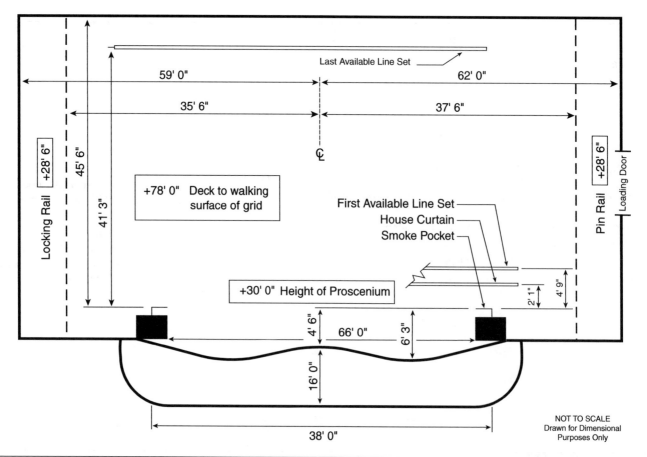

STAGE HOUSE

HOUSE CURTAIN
Operates as a guillotine from SR deck

RIGGING SYSTEM
Type:	Double purchase counter weight
Weight:	32,000 lbs available
Line sets:	59 sets at 6" o.c. with 6 lift lines per set
Arbors:	1,500 lb capacity
House Pipes:	58' long with 75' of travel from deck

Line sets are not moveable
Block & Falls are available
Chain hoists are not available
(80) spot wheels and 1,000' of hemp available

PERMANENT INSTALLATIONS OVER STAGE (FROM SMOKE POCKET)
Orchestra shell (5) at 5'8", 8'9", 15'7", 23'1", 31'7"
Movie screen (1) at 3'1"
Hard portal (1) tormenter
Catwalk (1) located 33' in the air, pin rail to racking rail 40' to plaster line

PERMANENT INSTALLATIONS ON DECK
Traps (48) in stage floor 3' x 6' lines up with 1st line set 24 US, 36' wide
Hard legs - tormentor 33', 3 side panels 5' wide
Stairs located SR and SL to the house
Orchestra shell storage (1) 6' wide located SL
Loading bridge (2) 3' wide, (1) at +58' up, (1) at +68' up
Adjustable proscenium - tormentor

ORCHESTRA PIT
Nonadjustable at 9' below stage level
Apron overhangs US wall of pit 3'6"

BACKSTAGE

LOADING DOCK
Loading door(s):
14'9" high x 19'0" wide
Trucks load (4) side by side at same time
(4) Trailers can store on-site

WARDROBE
Location: USR stage level
Access: Direct to stage
(1) Washer (1) Dryer
No washer or dryer hookups

DRESSING ROOMS
(2) Star, SR, stage , t/s, phone jack
(2) Chorus, SR, stage, t/s
(1) Chorus, SR, +1, t/s
(1) Chorus, SR, +2, t/s
(1) Chorus, SR, -1, t/s
Use dressing room for company mgr office

SOUND

CONSOLE
Euphonics CS 2000, located Sound Booth
48 inputs, 5 main outputs, 8 aux outputs

SPEAKERS
House Cluster

COMMUNICATIONS
Clear Com intercom with (8) channels
Dressing room page system

ROAD CONSOLE
Located Center house
No seats required to be removed
Cable run from stage is 150'
Tie-in into house system with XLR connectors

REHEARSAL & STORAGE SPACE
Rehearsal: None
Storage: None

ELECTRICS

ROAD SERVICE POWER

Panel	Phase	Amp	Circuit Protection	Use	Location
A-B	3	400	fuse	dimmers	DSL
C	3	400	fuse	sound	DSL
D	3	400	fuse	extra	DSL

Recommended location of touring dimmer racks: SL
Additional power is available for tour buses, generators, etc.

FRONT OF HOUSE (BOX BOOM VALUES ARE PER SIDE)

Position	Pipe Width	Distance to Prosc.	House Circuits	Connector Type	FOH Transfer Circuits
1st Cove	88'	66'	28	20 amp new twistlock	24
2nd Cove	100'	100'	28	20 amp new twistlock	24

Transfer circuits: grd 20 amp stage pin
Road truss: stage grid 78' from stage floor, all steel grid, clear floor stores pipe for hanging motors

EQUIPMENT FOH (BOX BOOM VALUES ARE PER SIDE)

Position	Quantity	Wattage	Instrument	Removeable
1st Cove	40	1,000	8 x 12 Lekos	yes
2nd Cove	40	1,000	10 x 15 Lekos	yes

FOLLOWSPOTS
House Followspots:
(4) Lycian Long Throw; removeable

Followspot Booth:
(1) spot per booth;
200 throw to proscenium;
(4) 1Ø 20 amp breakers

DIMMERS
Lighting console is Obsession 1500;
(484) Colortran 19° dimmers
House has DMX control system

WESTBURY MUSIC FAIR

Theatre Location:	960 Brush Hollow Road, Westbury, NY 11590	

SEATING CAPACITY

Orchestra	2,742
Total:	**2,742**

Main Administrative Phone:	516-333-7228
Main Administrative Fax:	516-333-7991
Stage Door Phone:	516-333-7228
Backstage Pay Phone:	516-334-9850
Traveling Production Office Phone:	516-333-7228
Traveling Production Office Fax:	516-333-7991

pit (add'l)	0
wheelchair (add'l)	0
standing (add'l)	0

THEATRE STAFF

Theatre Manager	Adam Citron	516-333-7228
Booking	Jason Stone	516-333-7228

HOUSE CREW

Production Manager	Laura Kurtz	516-333-7228 x116
Props	Michael Cassidy	516-333-7228
Shop Steward	Tom Fager	516-333-7228

STAGE DIMENSIONS (FROM SMOKE POCKET)
24' diameter turntable
Orchestra pit exists

RIGGING

Grid Height:	15'
Type:	Hemp System
Line sets:	24 sets at 6" o.c.
House Pipes:	4' long

LOADING DOCK
Loading door(s) are 8'0" high x 8'0" wide
Trucks load (2) at same time
Fork lift is not required and is not available

ELECTRICS
Total power available:
(1) 100A 3Ø Rear House
(1) 100A 3Ø Main service rm

FOLLOWSPOTS
House Followspots:
None
Power in spot booth (2) 400A
3Ø disconnects

DIMMERS
(72) house dimmers
House has DMX control system

SOUND
100A 3Ø dedicated power
FOH mixing position is
50' from stage
Sound console is available

BLUMENTHAL CENTER: BELK THEATER

AT: NORTH CAROLINA BLUMENTHAL PERFORMING ARTS CENTER AKA: CHARLOTTE PAC   YEAR BUILT: 1992   YEAR RENOVATED: 1992

Theatre Location: 130 North Tryon Street, Charlotte, NC 28202
Mailing Address: PO Box 37322, Charlotte, NC 28237-37322

Main Administrative Phone: 704-333-4686
Main Administrative Fax: 704-376-2289
Website: www.performingartsctr.org
Stage Door Phone: 704-379-1257
Backstage Pay Phone: 704-331-9232
Traveling Production Office Phone: 704-379-1254
Traveling Production Office Fax: 704-379-1259

THEATRE STAFF
President   Judith Allen   704-333-4686
Booking   Carol May   704-348-5815
Marketing   Carol May   704-348-5815
Operations   Robyn Williams   704-379-1263

HOUSE CREW
Technical Director   Karl Hoffman   704-379-1232
Electrics   Craig Taylor   704-379-1234
Sound   Rossi Craft   704-379-1256

UNIONS
IATSE Local #322   Bruce Grier   704-367-9435
Wardrobe Local #322   Bruce Grier   704-367-9435

SEATING CAPACITY
Orchestra   883
Grand Tier   463
Mezzanine   325
Balcony   426
Total: **2,097**

BOX OFFICE
Computerized
Manager of Sales
Warren Shanahan   704-379-1222

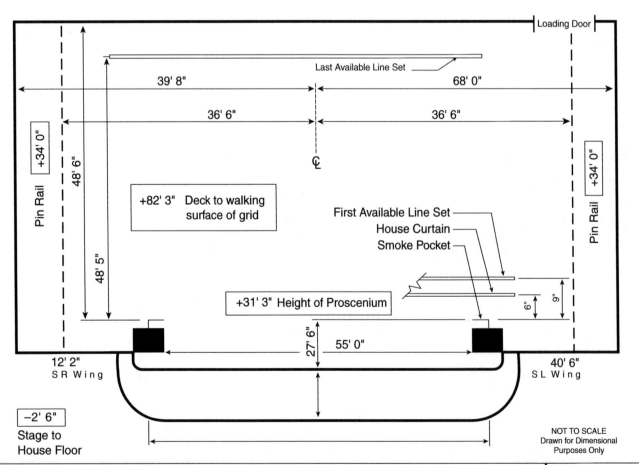

Loading Door

Last Available Line Set

39' 8"   68' 0"

36' 6"   36' 6"

C L

Pin Rail   +34' 0"   Pin Rail   +34' 0"

48' 6"

+82' 3"   Deck to walking
          surface of grid

First Available Line Set
House Curtain
Smoke Pocket

48' 5"

6"   9"

+31' 3" Height of Proscenium

27' 6"   55' 0"

12' 2"
SR Wing   40' 6"
                 SL Wing

−2' 6"
Stage to
House Floor

NOT TO SCALE
Drawn for Dimensional
Purposes Only

STAGE HOUSE

HOUSE CURTAIN
Operates as a guillotine from SR fly floor
Operates as a traveller from SR deck

RIGGING SYSTEM
Type: Single purchase counter weight
Weight: 90,000 lbs available
Line sets: 85 sets at 6" o.c. with 7 lift lines per set
Arbors: 1,500 lb capacity
House Pipes: 62' long with 79' of travel from deck
Line sets are not moveable
Block & Falls are not available
Chain hoists are not available

PERMANENT INSTALLATIONS OVER STAGE (FROM SMOKE POCKET)
Orchestra shell (1) at 5'3"
Electric raceways (1) 4'3"
Fire curtain (1) at 0'3"

PERMANENT INSTALLATIONS ON DECK
Jumps (3) at +34'0" high located at loading gallery +50'0") high
Orchestra shell storage (1) at US of 48'3"
Loading bridge (3) at 50'0", 61'9", 73'6"
Adjustable proscenium (1) 45'0" - 57'0"

ORCHESTRA PIT
Adjustable by electric motor turnscrew
Apron overhangs US wall of pit 8'0"
Pit lift is in (2) sections

BACKSTAGE

LOADING DOCK
Loading door(s):
(2) 15'0" high x 12'0" wide
Trucks load (3) at same time
Fork lift is not required
Sound/Props cannot load in FOH
(1) Trailer can store on-site
Security at dock & stage door

WARDROBE
Location: -1 below stage
Access: Loading elevator
(2) Washers   (2) Dryers
Washer and dryer hookups available

DRESSING ROOMS
(1) Star, US, stage level, t/s included, phone jack
(3) Small, US, stage level, t/s included, phone jack
(3) Small, US, stage level, t/s
(3) Chorus, -1, t/s on same fl
Elevator access for dressing rooms
Additional production office available for company mgr

SOUND

CONSOLE
Soundcraft 8000, located Orchestra
32 inputs, 4 main outputs, 8 matrix outputs, 8 aux outputs

SPEAKERS
House Cluster
Proscenium
Under Balcony
No speaker truss

COMMUNICATIONS
Clear Com intercom with (4) channels
Infrared sound system
Dressing room page system

ROAD CONSOLE
Located Rear Orchestra
(18) seats required to be removed
Cable run from stage is 250'
Tie-in into house system with XLR connectors

REHEARSAL & STORAGE SPACE
Rehearsal: Studio Theater, 50' x 50', stage level, prior rental arrangement required, equipment available
Storage: None

ELECTRICS

ROAD SERVICE POWER

Panel	Phase	Amp	Circuit Protection	Use	Location
A-C	3	400	breaker	extra	SL wall
D	3	200	breaker	sound	SL wall
E	3	400	breaker	extra	UR
F	3	200	breaker	sound	UR
G	3	400	breaker	extra	Loading area
H	3	400	breaker	extra	Studio Theater

Recommended location of touring dimmer racks: SL wing
Hoist not required
Additional power is available for tour buses, generators, etc.

FRONT OF HOUSE (BOX BOOM VALUES ARE PER SIDE)

Position	Pipe Width	Distance to Prosc.	House Circuits	Connector Type	FOH Transfer Circuits
Mezz Rail		94'	12	grd 20 amp stage pin	12
Tech Box			18	grd 20 amp stage pin	9
Box Boom 1			16	grd 20 amp stage pin	8
2nd Cove		98'	72	grd 20 amp stage pin	36

EQUIPMENT FOH (BOX BOOM VALUES ARE PER SIDE)

Position	Quantity	Wattage	Instrument	Removeable
2nd Cove	24	1,000	5 ellipsoidal	yes

FOLLOWSPOTS
House Followspots:
(3) Xenon Super Trouper 2k; not removeable

Followspot Booth:
(4) spots per booth;
132' throw to proscenium;
(4) 3Ø 30 amp breakers

DIMMERS
Lighting console is ETC Concept 500;
(480) ETC L-86 dimmers
House has programmable DMX control system
(1) dry run DMX station daisy chained through all FOH positions

OVENS AUDITORIUM

YEAR BUILT: 1955

Theatre Location: 2700 E. Independence Blvd., Charlotte, NC 28205

Main Administrative Phone: 704-372-3600
Main Administrative Fax: 704-335-3118
Stage Door Phone: 704-335-3156
Backstage Pay Phone: 704-374-9875
Traveling Production Office Phone: 704-335-3147
Traveling Production Office Fax: 704-335-3172

THEATRE STAFF
Building Manager Carole J. Thompson 704-372-3600
Booking Carole J. Thompson 704-372-3600
Marketing Ereka Crawford 704-357-4731
Operations Jeff McManus 704-335-3155
Group Sales Diatra Fullwood 704-357-4722

HOUSE CREW
Stage Manager Jeff McManus 704-335-3155
Electrics Bo Pich 704-335-3157

UNIONS
IATSE Local #322 Bruce Grier 704-367-9435
Wardrobe Local #322 Bruce Grier 704-367-9435

SEATING CAPACITY
Orchestra 1,544
Mezzanine 585
Balcony 474
Total: **2,603**

wheelchair (add'l) 6

BOX OFFICE
Computerized
Box Office Manager
  Stephen Heninger 704-335-3248

Outside Ticket Agency
Computerized
  Ticketmaster 704-527-7300

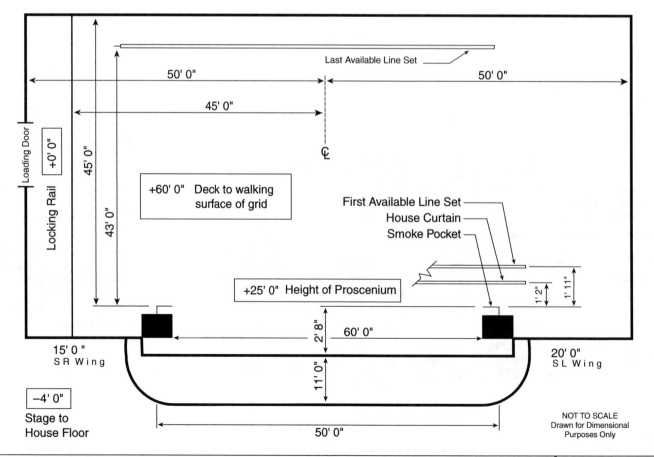

STAGE HOUSE

HOUSE CURTAIN
Operates as a guillotine or traveller from SR deck

RIGGING SYSTEM
Type:	Combination purchase counter weight Multi Line II
Weight:	18,000 lbs available
Line sets:	60 sets at 6" o.c. with 6 lift lines per set
Arbors:	1,100 lb capacity
House Pipes:	70' long with 56' of travel from deck

Line sets are moveable
Block & Falls are available; Chain hoists are not available
(50) spot wheels and 10,000' of hemp available
Channeled Grid- line sets 29-41 are operated from a jump rail as a double purchase

PERMANENT INSTALLATIONS OVER STAGE (FROM SMOKE POCKET)
M=Moveable with advance call
Orchestra shells (6) at 2'10", 9'9", 15'9", 20'6", 28'9", 34'0"; M
Electric Borders (6) at 5'9", 13'9", 18'3", 25'0", 32'6", 38'6"; M
Electric Raceways (2) at 6'3" & 14'3"
Traveller (3) at 3'7", 9'3" & 30'3"; M

PERMANENT INSTALLATIONS ON DECK
Jumps (above locking rail) (1), 9'6" x 5'0", SR side wall, 14'6" high
Electric jump (1), 10'x8' DSR proscenium wall 8'6" high
Stairs (1)
Loading bridge (1)

ORCHESTRA PIT
Adjustable to 12' below stage level by hydraulic lift
Apron overhangs US wall of pit 10'0"; Pit lift is (1) section

BACKSTAGE

LOADING DOCK
Loading door(s):
   10'6" high x 9'4" wide
Trucks load (3) side-by-side at same time
Straight, easy load in
Forklift: House owns
Sound/Props can load in FOH
Lobby can be a work area
(10+) Trailers can store on-site

WARDROBE
Location: Upstairs or downstairs
Access: Stairwells or by orchestra pit elevator
(2) Washers (2) Dryers
Washer and dryer hookups available

DRESSING ROOMS
(5) Star, SL, stage level, t/s included
(2) Chorus, behind stage, stage level, t/s included
Use dressing room for company mgr office

SOUND

CONSOLE
Ramsa, located DSR
16 inputs, 2 main outputs, 0 matrix outputs, 4 aux outputs

SPEAKERS
House Cluster
Road show under balcony may be hung from balcony rail
No speaker truss
Max available load 2,000 lbs
Must stack or hang in proscenium opening

COMMUNICATIONS
Clear Com intercom with (1) channel
RF sound system
Dressing room page system

ROAD CONSOLE
Located Rear Orchestra
No seats required to be removed
Cable run from stage is 150'
Tie-in into house system with XLR connectors

REHEARSAL & STORAGE SPACE
Rehearsal: None
Storage: 50' x 40' located SR in loading area

ELECTRICS

ROAD SERVICE POWER
Panel	Phase	Amp	Circuit Protection	Use	Location
A	3	600	breaker	electrics	DSR
B	3	600	fuse	electrics	USR
C	3	400	fuse	sound	DSL
D	3	200	fuse	extra	SR Dock

Recommended location of touring dimmer racks: stage right
Hoist not required
Additional power is available for tour buses, generators, etc.

FRONT OF HOUSE (BOX BOOM VALUES ARE PER SIDE)
Position	Pipe Width	Distance to Prosc.	House Circuits	Connector Type	FOH Transfer Circuits
1st Balc Rail	60'	80'0"	20	grd 20 amp stage pin	20
1st Cove	80'		12	grd 20 amp stage pin	20
Box Boom 1	45'		26	grd 20 amp stage pin	26

Transfer circuits: grd 20 amp stage pin
Road truss: No FOH rigging points exist

EQUIPMENT FOH (BOX BOOM VALUES ARE PER SIDE)
Position	Quantity	Wattage	Instrument	Removeable
1st Balc Rail	24	1,000	20° Leko	yes
1st Cove	20	1,000	20° Leko	yes
Box Boom 1	20	1,000	20° Leko	yes

24 Cove instruments are on 12 circuits

FOLLOWSPOTS
House Followspots:
   (3) Xenon Super Trouper 2k; not removeable

Followspot Booth:
None

DIMMERS
Lighting console is analog-Strand Light Pallette;
(199) Strand 702.4 dimmers
House has programmable DMX control system
(0) dry run DMX station(s)

AYCOCK AUDITORIUM

AT: UNIVERSITY OF NORTH CAROLINA AT GREENSBORO   **YEAR BUILT: 1927   YEAR RENOVATED: 1997**

			SEATING CAPACITY	
Theatre Location:	Tate & Spring Garden St., Greensboro, NC 27402-6170		Front Orchestra	297
Mailing Address:	University of North Carolina at Greensboro		Mid. Orchestra	385
	PO Box 26170, Greensboro, NC 27402-6170		Rear Orchestra	425
Main Administrative Phone:		336-334-5353	Mezzanine	242
Main Administrative Fax:		336-334-5634	2nd Balcony	438
E-mail:		1_collin@dawson.uncg.edu	3rd Balcony	556
Website:		euc.uncg.edu/ucls/aycock.html	**Total:**	**2,543**
Stage Door Phone:		336-334-4721		
Traveling Production Office Phone:		336-334-4721	wheelchair (add'l)	12

THEATRE STAFF

Director	Lyman Collins	336-334-5353

HOUSE CREW

Asst. Director for		
Event Production	Jan Hullihan	336-334-5353

STAGE DIMENSIONS
Measured from curtain line, no smoke pocket
Stage is 37'6" deep
Width from Center Line to SL is 31'10"
Width from Center Line to SR is 31'4"
Proscenium width is 39'8"
Proscenium height is 32'2"
Smoke pocket to apron edge is 6'0"
Orchestra pit exists

RIGGING
Grid Height:	57'
Type:	Combination purchase counter weight; Motorized
Weight:	12,000 lbs
Line sets:	36 sets at 8" o.c.
Arbors:	1,250 lb capacity
House Pipes:	48' long

LOADING DOCK
Loading door(s) are 9'8" high x 7'0" wide
Trucks load (1) at a time
Fork lift is not required and is available

ELECTRICS
Total power available:
(1) 350A 3Ø DSL at
proscenium wall

FOLLOWSPOTS
House Followspots:
Strong Super Trouper
No power in spot booth
FOH transfer circuits per
position: 0

DIMMERS
(40) house dimmers
House has DMX control system
(0) dry run station(s)
No light booth

SOUND
House has (1) 100 amp 3Ø
dedicated power located
DSR proscenium wall
FOH mixing position in
Rear Orchestra
Sound console is available

WAR MEMORIAL AUDITORIUM

Theatre Location: 1921 West Lee Street, Greensboro, NC 27403
Mailing Address: PO Box 5447, Greensboro, NC 27435

Main Administrative Phone: 336-373-7400
Main Administrative Fax: 336-373-2170
Website: www.greensborocoliseum.com
Stage door phone: 336-218-5326
Traveling Production Office Phone: 336-373-7419

THEATRE STAFF
Managing Director   Matthew G. Brown   336-373-7406
Booking   Scott E. Johnson   336-373-7449
Marketing   Kerry Andrews   336-373-7432
Group Sales   Joni Moffit   336-373-2632

HOUSE CREW
Production Manager   Mike Perdue   336-373-7457
Prod. Technician   Scott Polkinhorn   336-373-7453

UNIONS
IATSE Local #574   Bill Daves   336-724-6401
Wardrobe Local #574   Nell Daves   336-724-6401

SEATING CAPACITY
Orchestra   1,550
Mezzanine   226
Balcony   600
Total: **2,376**

wheelchair (incl.)   18

BOX OFFICE
Computerized
Box Office Manager
  Kris Meroth   336-373-7482

Outside Ticket Agency
Computerized
Ticketmaster
  Kris Meroth   336-373-7482

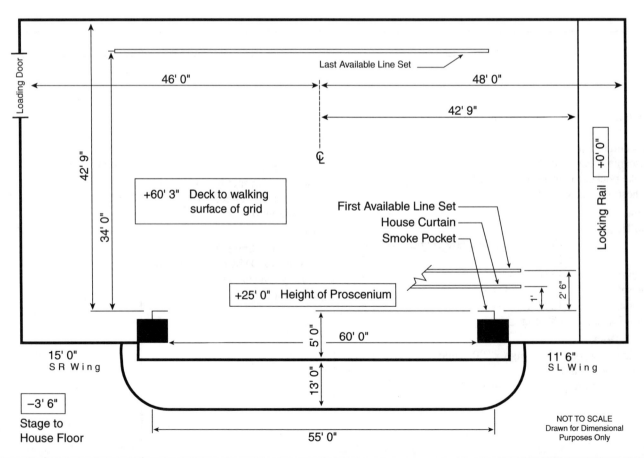

STAGE HOUSE

HOUSE CURTAIN
Operates as a guillotine or traveller from SL deck
2nd house curtain is motorized

RIGGING SYSTEM
Type:	Single purchase counter weight
Weight:	20,000 lbs available
Line sets:	54 sets at 6" o.c. with 6 lift lines per set
Arbors:	1,200 lb capacity
House Pipes:	65'9" long with 52' of travel from deck

Line sets are not moveable
Block & Falls are not available
Chain hoists are available as a rental; (4) half ton
(60) spot wheels and of hemp available

PERMANENT INSTALLATIONS OVER STAGE (FROM SMOKE POCKET)
Orchestra shell/clouds (3) at 12'3", 2'6"
Orchestra shell (1) at 14'0" to 28'0" x 6'6" onstage
Cyclorama (1) at 38'0"
Fire curtain (1)

PERMANENT INSTALLATIONS ON DECK
Orchestra shell storage
Loading bridge (1) at grid level

ORCHESTRA PIT
Adjustable to 14' below stage level by hydraulic lift
Apron overhangs US wall of pit 13'0"
Pit lift is in (1) section
Basement storage below the stage

BACKSTAGE

LOADING DOCK
Loading door(s):
   10'0" high x 18'0" wide
Trucks load (1) at a time
Fork lift is not required
Sound/Props can load in FOH
Lobby can be a work area
(8) Trailers can store on-site
Security at dock & stage door

WARDROBE
Location: Upstage
Access: Back hallway, direct
   from stage
(2) Washers (2) Dryers
Washer and dryer hookups
   available

DRESSING ROOMS
(1) Star, SL, stage level, t/s on
   same fl, phone jack
(4) Small, SL, stage level, t/s on
   same fl, phone jack
(4) Chorus, SL/SR, stage, t/s on
   same floor, phone jack
Additional production office
   available for company mgr

SOUND

CONSOLE
Yamaha, located House
   Booth
16 inputs, 2 main outputs,
   4 matrix outputs, 4 aux
   outputs

SPEAKERS
House Cluster
Proscenium
Under Balcony
No speaker truss

COMMUNICATIONS
Clear Com intercom with
   (1) channel
FM impaired system
Dressing room page system

ROAD CONSOLE
Located Rear House
No seats required to be
   removed
Cable run from stage is 120'
Tie-in into house system with
   XLR connectors

REHEARSAL & STORAGE SPACE
Rehearsal: None
Storage: 26'0" x 30'0", USR
   by dock

ELECTRICS

ROAD SERVICE POWER

Panel	Phase	Amp	Circuit Protection	Use	Location
A	3	600	fuse	dimmer	DSR
B	3	100	fuse	sound	DSR

Recommended location of touring dimmer racks: DSR
Hoist not required
Additional power is available for tour buses, generators, etc.

FRONT OF HOUSE (BOX BOOM VALUES ARE PER SIDE)

Position	Pipe Width	Distance to Prosc.	House Circuits	Connector Type	FOH Transfer Circuits
1st Balc Rail	50'	80'	25	ungrd 30 amp stage pin	0
1st Cove	70'	80'	12	20 amp new twistlock	0
Box Boom 1		70'	4	20 amp new twistlock	0

Road truss: No points available DS of the proscenium

EQUIPMENT FOH (BOX BOOM VALUES ARE PER SIDE)

Position	Quantity	Wattage	Instrument	Removeable
1st Cove	2	575	ETC 10°	yes
Box Boom 1	12	500	9 x 12	yes

FOLLOWSPOTS
House Followspots:
   (2) Xenon Super Troupers
   1600; not removeable

Followspot Booth:
   (2) spots per booth;
   152' throw to proscenium;
   (2) 1Ø 20 amp breakers

DIMMERS
House console is Hub 3-
   scene preset;
   (15) Hub dimmers
No DMX control system

RALEIGH MEMORIAL AUDITORIUM

AT: RALEIGH CONVENTION & CONFERENCE CENTER COMPLEX

YEAR BUILT: 1932   YEAR RENOVATED: 1990

Theatre Location: 2 East South Street, Raleigh, NC 27601
Management Company: Raleigh Convention & Conference Center
                                      500 Fayetteville Street Mall, Raleigh, NC 27601

Main Administrative Phone: 919-831-6011
Main Administrative Fax: 919-831-6013
Website: www.ral-conventioncenter.org

THEATRE STAFF
Director   Roger Krupa   919-831-6011
Booking Agent   Holly Hamilton   919-831-6011
Marketing Director   Jim Lavery   919-831-6011
Operations Director Coy Poole   919-831-6011

HOUSE CREW
Stage Manager   Micky Barbour   919-831-6238

UNIONS
IATSE Local #603   Lee Howley   919-217-5417

SEATING CAPACITY
Orchestra   2,277
Total: **2,277**

pit (add'l)   45

BOX OFFICE
Computerized
Box Office Manager
  Sylvia Barrett   919-831-6011

Outside Ticket Agency
Computerized
Ticketmaster
  Teresa Copper   919-856-2100

Box office is promoter operated

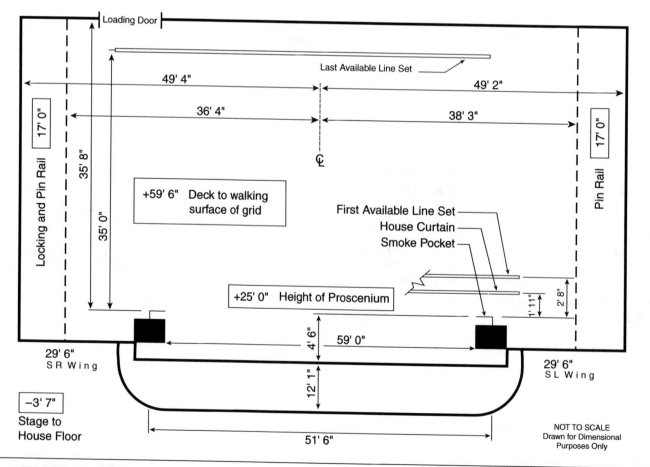

STAGE HOUSE

HOUSE CURTAIN
Operates as a traveller from SR deck

RIGGING SYSTEM
Type:	Double purchase counter weight
Weight:	80,000 lbs available
Line sets:	46 sets at 9" o.c. with 6 lift lines per set
Arbors:	4,000 lb capacity
House Pipes:	67' long with 54' of travel from deck

Line sets are not moveable
Block & Falls are available
Chain hoists are available; (8) one ton
(40) spot wheels and 60000 of hemp available

PERMANENT INSTALLATIONS OVER STAGE (FROM SMOKE POCKET)
Electric raceways (5) at 3'5", 10'5", 17'7", 23'9", 30'9"
Orchestra shell (4) at 5'5", 12'3", 19'1", 24'11"

PERMANENT INSTALLATIONS ON DECK
None

ORCHESTRA PIT
Adjustable to 22' below stage level by hydraulic lift

BACKSTAGE

LOADING DOCK
Loading door(s):
   26'0" high x 10'0" wide
Trucks load (2) side by side at
   same time
Fork lift: House provides &
   rents
Sound/Props can load in FOH
Lobby can be a work area
Trailers can store on-site
Security at dock & stage door

WARDROBE
Location: Basement
Access: Orchestra pit elevator
(2) Washers (3) Dryers
Washer and dryer hookups
   available

DRESSING ROOMS
(2) Star, SR/ SL, stage level, t/s
   included, phone jack
(11) Small, SR(5)/ SL(6), stage
   level, t/s on same fl
(2) Chorus, SL, stage level, t/s
   included
Elevator access for dressing
   rooms
Additional production office
   available for company mgr

SOUND

CONSOLE
Soundcraft 500B
16 inputs

SPEAKERS
House Cluster
Proscenium
Under Balcony
Speaker truss exists
Dead hung

COMMUNICATIONS
Clear Com intercom with
   (4) channels
Infrared sound system
Dressing room page system

ROAD CONSOLE
Located House left or center
(16) seats required to be
   removed
Cable run from stage is 90'
Tie-in into house system with
   XLR connectors

REHEARSAL & STORAGE SPACE
Rehearsal: 40' x 60' located
   in basement, piano, by
   prior arrangement
Storage: 20' x 60' located
   behind stage

ELECTRICS

ROAD SERVICE POWER
Panel	Phase	Amp	Circuit Protection	Use	Location
A	3	800	fuse	dimmers	DSL
B	3	100	breaker	sound	DSR
C	3	400	fuse	dimmers	DSL

Recommended location of touring dimmer racks: SL on deck
Additional power is available for tour buses, generators, etc.

FRONT OF HOUSE (BOX BOOM VALUES ARE PER SIDE)
Position	Pipe Width	Distance to Prosc.	House Circuits	Connector Type	FOH Transfer Circuits
2nd Catwalk	120'	45'	64	grd 20 amp stage pin	0
Box Boom 1		45'	8	grd 20 amp stage pin	0

Transfer circuits: grd 20 amp stage pin

EQUIPMENT FOH (BOX BOOM VALUES ARE PER SIDE)
Position	Quantity	Wattage	Instrument	Removeable
Cove	32	1,000	12° Colortran	yes
Cove	20	1,000	10° Colortran	yes
2nd Balc Rail	12	1,000	6 x 12 Strand/Century	yes
1st Cove Rail	6	750	6 x 12 Strand/Century	yes
2nd Cove Rail	8	750	6 x 9 Strand/Century	yes
Box Boom 1	56	1,000	30° Colortran	yes

FOLLOWSPOTS
House Followspots:
   (3) Xenon Super Troupers

Followspot Booth:
   (3) spots per booth;
   175' throw to proscenium;
   (4-6) 3Ø 20 amp breakers

DIMMERS
Lighting console is Colortran
   Master 60XL;
   (272) ENR dimmers
House has programmable
   DMX control system
(9) dry run DMX station(s)

STEVENS CENTER

YEAR BUILT: **1929**   YEAR RENOVATED: **1983**

Theatre Location:	405 West Fourth Street, Winston-Salem, NC 27101

Main Administrative Phone: 336-723-6320
Main Administrative Fax: 336-722-7240
Website: www.ncarte/edu/stevenscenter
Stage Door Phone: 336-721-0712

THEATRE STAFF
Executive Director   Steve Davis   336-723-6320

HOUSE CREW
Production Manager   Paul Valoris   336-721-0712

SEATING CAPACITY

Orchestra	852
Balcony	528
Total:	**1,380**
pit (add'l)	0
wheelchair (add'l)	8
standing (add'l)	0

STAGE DIMENSIONS (FROM SMOKE POCKET)
Stage is 34'6" deep
Width from Center Line to SL is 40'6"
Width from Center Line to SR is 37'0"
Proscenium width is 42'0"
Proscenium height is 30'0"
Smoke pocket to apron edge is 8'0"
Orchestra pit exists

RIGGING
Grid Height: 67'
Type: Single purchase counter weight
Line sets: 43 sets at 6-9" o.c.
Arbors: 1,000 lb capacity
House Pipes: 52' long

LOADING DOCK
Loading door(s) are 9'6" high x 9'6" wide
Trucks load (1) at a time
Fork lift is required and is not available

ELECTRICS
Total power available:
   (2) 400A 3Ø SL wall
   (1) 200A 3Ø SL wall

FOLLOWSPOTS
House Followspots:
   Lycian 1267
Power in spot booth (2) 20A
FOH transfer circuits per
   position: 0

DIMMERS
(96) house dimmers
House has DMX control system
(1) dry run station(s) located SL

SOUND
House has 400A / 200A
   undedicated power located
   SL on wall
FOH mixing position in
   Rear House Right
Sound console is available

CHESTER FRITZ AUDITORIUM

YEAR BUILT: 1972

Theatre Location: University Ave. & Yale Drive, Grand Forks, ND 58202
Mailing Address: P.O. Box 9028, Grand Forks, ND 58202

Main Administrative Phone: 701-777-3076
Main Administrative Fax: 701-777-4710
Stage Door Phone: 701-777-2194
Backstage Pay Phone: 701-772-9797
Traveling Production Office Phone: 701-777-5012
Traveling Production Office Fax: 701-777-4027

SEATING CAPACITY

Main Floor	1138
Mezzanine	594
Balcony	594
Total:	**2,326**
pit (add'l)	80
wheelchair (add'l)	8

THEATRE STAFF

Director   Wallace Bloom   701-777-3076
Program Manager   Truman Reed   701-777-3077

HOUSE CREW

Technical Director   Lyle Siedschlaw   701-777-2194

STAGE DIMENSIONS (FROM SMOKE POCKET)
Stage is 38'1" deep
Width from Center Line to SL is 30'0"
Width from Center Line to SR is 3'0"
Proscenium width is 60'0"
Proscenium height is 29'9"
Orchestra pit exists

RIGGING
Grid Height: 68'
Type: Single purchase counter weight
Weight: 20,000 lbs
Line sets: 51 sets at 8" o.c.
Arbors: 1,740 lb capacity
House Pipes: 74' long

LOADING DOCK
Loading door(s) are 12'9" high x 10'0" wide
Trucks load (1) at a time
Fork lift is not required and is available

ELECTRICS
Total power available:
(1) 400A 3Ø SR
(2) 200A 3Ø SR
(2) 100A 3Ø SR

FOLLOWSPOTS
House Followspots:
(4) Lycian 400
Power in spot booth (6) 20A

DIMMERS
UNDER RENOVATION

SOUND
UNDER RENOVATION
House has 200A for sound
FOH mixing position in
House Right
Sound console is available

PROCTOR & GAMBLE HALL

AT: ARONOFF CENTER FOR THE ARTS   **YEAR BUILT: 1995**

Theatre Location: 650 Walnut Street, Cincinnati, OH 45202
Management Company: Cincinnati Arts Association (address as above)

Main Administrative Phone:	513-721-3344
Main Administrative Fax:	513-977-4150
Stage D oor Phone:	513-977-4128
Traveling Production Office Phone:	513-977-4070
Traveling Production Office Fax:	513-977-4069

SEATING CAPACITY

Orchestra	1,279
Loge	543
Balcony	777
Boxes	56
Total:	**2,655**
pit (add'l)	64

THEATRE STAFF

Events Manager	Patricia Margulies	513-977-4124
Booking	Linda Davis	513-977-4123
Marketing	Patti Swofford	513-977-4102
Operations	Janet Taylor	513-977-4120
Group Sales	Morella Raleigh	513-977-4181

HOUSE CREW

Technical Director	Bob Haas	513-977-4172
Carpentry	Terry Sheidan	513-977-4171
Electrics	Thomas E. Lane	513-977-4146
Sound	Tom Dignan Jr.	513-977-4146

UNIONS

IATSE Local #5	Dave M. Eviston	513-721-1302
Wardrobe Local #864	Peter Diamond	513-861-5300
Music Local #1	Gene Frye	513-241-0900

BOX OFFICE

Computerized
Box Office Manager
   John J. Harig   513-977-4156

Outside Ticket Agency
Computerized
Ticketmaster
   Dennis Scanlon   513-721-6100

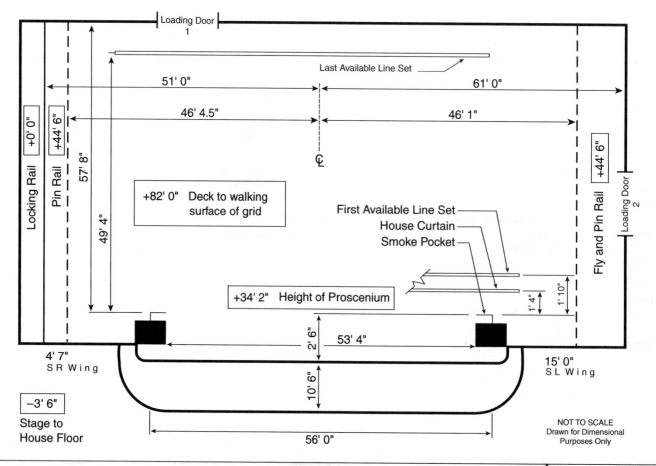

STAGE HOUSE

HOUSE CURTAIN
Operates as a guillotine or traveller from SR
fly floor or deck

RIGGING SYSTEM
Type: Single purchase counter weight
Weight: 100,000 lbs available
Line sets: 87 sets at 6" o.c. with 7 lift lines per set
Arbors: 2,200 lb capacity
House Pipes: 67' long with 78' of travel from deck
Line sets are moveable
Block & Falls are available
Chain hoists are not available
(70) spot wheels and 10,000' of hemp available

PERMANENT INSTALLATIONS OVER STAGE (FROM SMOKE POCKET)
M=Moveable with advance call
Traveller (1) at 47'5" from plaster; M

PERMANENT INSTALLATIONS ON DECK
Jumps (1) 0'6" x 56'0"
Electric jump (1) 21'0" x 40'5"
Loading bridge (2) 46-4.5 SR of CL; + 81'0", +71'0"

ORCHESTRA PIT
Adjustable by electric motor turnscrew
Apron overhangs US wall of pit 6'0"
Pit lift is in (1) section

BACKSTAGE

LOADING DOCK
Loading door(s):
    1) 10'4" high x 9'0" wide
    2) 8'0" high x 8'0" wide
Trucks load (2) at same time
Two interior bays capable of 48'
    trailer within dock doors
Fork lift is not required
Sound/Props cannot load in
    FOH
Lobby can be a work area
(2) Trailers can store on-site
Security at dock & stage door

WARDROBE
Location: -1 below stage
Access: Stage door
(2) Washers   (2) Dryers
Washer and dryer hookups
    available

DRESSING ROOMS
(3) Star, SR, stage level, t/s
    included, phone jack
(4) Small, SR, stage level, t/s
    included, phone jack
(4) Chorus, SR/SL, -1, t/s
    included
Elevator access for dressing
    rooms
Additional production office
    available for company mgr

SOUND

CONSOLE
Crest Century
40 inputs, 8 main outputs,
    8 matrix outputs, 8 aux
    outputs

SPEAKERS
House Cluster
Proscenium
Under Balcony
(2) rollout towers SR/SL
No speaker truss

COMMUNICATIONS
Clear Com intercom with
    (2) channels
Infrared sound system
Dressing room page system

ROAD CONSOLE
Located Rear Orchestra
(32) seats required to be
    removed
Cable run from stage is 150'
Tie-in into house system
    with XLR connectors

REHEARSAL & STORAGE SPACE
Rehearsal: 50' x 36' located
    in basement; piano
    available
Storage: Off dock, 19' x 57'
    Basement, 50' x 50', fit in
    freight elevator 10' x 10'

ELECTRICS

ROAD SERVICE POWER

Panel	Phase	Amp	Circuit Protection	Use	Location
A-D	3	400	fuse	dimmers	SL
E	1	400	fuse	sound	SR
F	3	100	breaker	extra	grid
G-J	3	100		extra	dock/bsmt/jumps/FOH

(16) 3-phase 100A Busways located throughout facility
Location of touring dimmer racks SL:Hoist not required: Addl power available

FRONT OF HOUSE (BOX BOOM VALUES ARE PER SIDE)

Position	Pipe Width	Distance to Prosc.	House Circuits	Connector Type	FOH Transfer Circuits
1st Catwalk		11'6"	30	grd 20 amp stage pin	30
2nd Catwalk		25'6"	30	grd 20 amp stage pin	30
3rd Catwalk		39'	30	grd 20 amp stage pin	30
1st Balc Rail		76'	26	grd 20 amp stage pin	26
2nd Balc Rail		81'	12	grd 20 amp stage pin	12
Box Boom 1			60	grd 20 amp stage pin	60

Transfer circuits: FOH circuits transfer through ETC Network Response Unit DMX
Road truss: FOH Truss hang please call; ceiling panels are removable; plans on request

EQUIPMENT FOH (BOX BOOM VALUES ARE PER SIDE)

Position	Quantity	Wattage	Instrument	Removeable
1st Balc Rail	12	575	ETC Source 4 19°	yes
2nd Balc Rail	26	575	ETC Source 4 10°	yes
2nd Cove	18	575	ETC Source 4 10°	yes
3rd Cove	18	575	ETC Source 4 10°	yes
Box Boom 1	58	575	ETC Source 4 36°, 26°, 19°, 10°	yes

FOLLOWSPOTS
House Followspots:
    (4) StrongSuper Trouper
    Xenon 2k; removeable

Followspot Booth:
    (4) spots per booth;
    127' throw to proscenium;
    (4) 3Ø 30 amp breakers

DIMMERS
Lighting console is ETC
    Obsession 600;
    (538) Colortran dimmers
House has programmable
    DMX control system
(40) dry run DMX station(s)

ALLEN THEATRE

AT: PLAYHOUSE SQUARE CENTER   **YEAR RENOVATED: 1982**

Theatre Location: 1511 Euclid Avenue, Cleveland , OH 44115
Management Company: Playhouse Square Foundation
                         1511 Euclid Avenue, Cleveland, OH 44115

Main Administrative Phone: 216-771-4444
Main Administrative Fax: 216-771-0217
Website: http://www.playhouse.com

THEATRE STAFF
Director Programming   Gina Vernaci   216-771-4444
Marketing   Jim Szakacs   216-771-4444
HOUSE CREW
Technical Director   Bob Rody   216-771-4444
UNIONS
IATSE Local #27   Dale Short   216-621-9537

SEATING CAPACITY
Orchestra   1,458
Loge   234
Mezzanine   346
Balcony   414
Total: **2,452**

pit (add'l)   52

BOX OFFICE
Computerized
Box Office Treasurer
  Susan Schlund   216-771-4444

Outside Ticket Agency
Computerized
  Advantix   216-241-6000

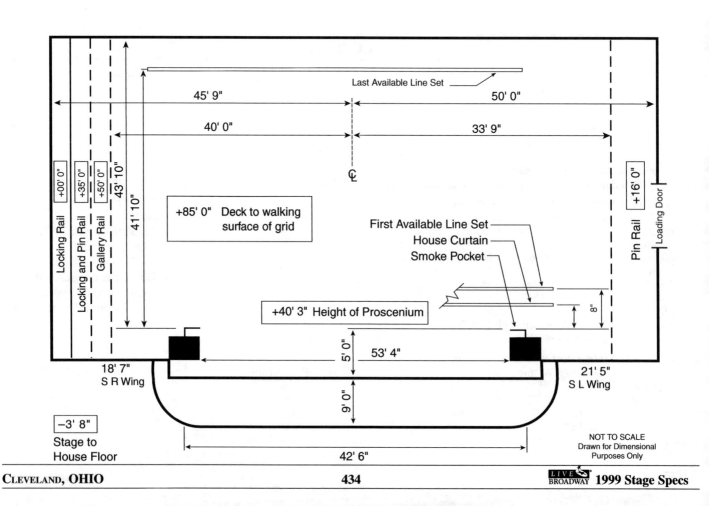

STAGE HOUSE

HOUSE CURTAIN
Operates as a guillotine from SR deck

RIGGING SYSTEM
Type:	Single purchase counter weight
Weight:	8,000 lbs available
Line sets:	60 sets at 8" o.c. with 7 lift lines per set
Arbors:	2,000 lb capacity
House Pipes:	62' long

Line sets are moveable
Block & Falls are available
Chain hoists are not available
(40) spot wheels and 2,500' of hemp available

PERMANENT INSTALLATIONS OVER STAGE (FROM SMOKE POCKET)
Catwalk (1) 46' US

PERMANENT INSTALLATIONS ON DECK
Traps (58) on a sectional grid
Jumps (2) 5'4" x 48'0", SR +35' up & +50' up
Electric jump (1), 18' x 48', +35' SL
Loading bridge (1) 5'4" x 48', +80' SR
Edge of pipes on SL are 3'6" from onstage edge of SL jump

ORCHESTRA PIT
Adjustable to 8'6" below stage level by Gala spiralift
Apron overhangs US wall of pit 8'4"
Pit lift is in (1) section

BACKSTAGE

LOADING DOCK
Loading door(s):
  (2) 7'11" x 8'0"
Trucks load (2) at same time
Fork lift is not required
Sound/Props can load in FOH
Lobby cannot be a work area
Trailers can store on-site
Security at dock & stage door

WARDROBE
Location: Stage -1
Access: Loading dock
(2) Washers (2) Dryers
Washer and dryer hookups
  available

DRESSING ROOMS
(5) Small, SR, +1, t/s included,
  phone jack
(4) Small, SR, +1, t/s included
(4) Chorus, -1, (2) t/s included
Ekevator Access for Dressing
  Rooms
Additional production office
  available for company mgr

SOUND

CONSOLE
Century Series Crest GT,
  located FOH
48 inputs, 20 outputs, L/ R
  main outputs, 4 matrix
  outputs, 8 aux outputs

SPEAKERS
House Cluster
Proscenium
Under Balcony
Portable
Center cluster
No speaker truss

COMMUNICATIONS
Clear Com intercom with
  (4) channels
Infrared sound system
Dressing room page system

ROAD CONSOLE
Located FOH
No seats required to be
  removed
Cable run from stage is 250'
Tie-in into house system with
  XLR connectors

REHEARSAL & STORAGE SPACE
Rehearsal: Possible at
  adjacent "State Theatre"
Storage: Trap room, 30' x 30'
  located in basement
Dock, 55' x 40' located in
  basement

ELECTRICS

ROAD SERVICE POWER
Panel	Phase	Amp	Circuit Protection Use	Location
A - G	3	400	fuse	SL jump
H	3	400	fuse	SL jump
I	3	200	fuse	USL wall

Recommended location of touring dimmer racks: SL jump 35'
Hoist provided
Additional power is available for tour buses, generators, etc.

FRONT OF HOUSE (BOX BOOM VALUES ARE PER SIDE)
Position	Pipe Width	Distance to Prosc.	House Circuits	Connector Type	FOH Transfer Circuits
Box Boom 1		44'	18	grd 20 amp stage pin	
Box Boom 2		60'	18	grd 20 amp stage pin	
1st Balc Rail		71'	25	grd 20 amp stage pin	
2nd Balc Rail		74'		grd 20 amp stage pin	
Perch SL & SR		84'	30	grd 20 amp stage pin	

Road truss: FOH house transfer entails use of house dimmers, configured through
  Ethernet

EQUIPMENT FOH (BOX BOOM VALUES ARE PER SIDE)
Position	Quantity	Wattage	Instrument	Removeable
Box Boom 1	20	1,000	Altman	yes
Perch Right	10	575	Source 4 10°	
Perch Left	20	575	Source 4 10°	yes

FOLLOWSPOTS
House Followspots:
  (3) Strong Super Troupers
  2k; removeable

Followspot Booth:
  159' throw to proscenium;
  (3) 3Ø 50 amp breakers

DIMMERS
Lighting console is Strand
  CD 520I;
  (186) Strand CD80
  dimmers
House has programmable
  DMX control system
(17) dry run DMX station(s)

MUSIC HALL

Theatre Location:	East 6th Street & St. Clair Avenue, Cleveland , OH 44114	
Mailing Address:	500 Lakeside Avenue, Cleveland , OH 44114	
Management Company:	City of Cleveland Marketing	
Main Administrative Phone:		216-348-2211
Main Administrative Fax:		216-348-2236
Stage Door Phone:		216-348-2277

SEATING CAPACITY

Dress Circle	610
Parquet	1,030
Loge	197
Balcony	1,091
Total:	**3,000**
pit (add'l)	0
wheelchair (add'l)	0
standing (add'l)	0

THEATRE STAFF

Convention Sales Mgr	Tony Scott	216-348-2211

HOUSE CREW

Stage Manager	Phil Smith	216-348-2236
Carpenter	Mike Taylor	216-348-2236
Electrician	Jerry Mobley	216-348-2235

STAGE DIMENSIONS (FROM SMOKE POCKET)

Stage is 43' deep
Width from Center Line to SL is 51'
Width from Center Line to SR is 51'
Proscenium height is 27'3"
Smoke pocket to apron edge is 2'6"
Orchestra pit exists

RIGGING

Grid Height:	93'
Type:	Single purchase counter weight
Weight:	2,600 lbs
Line sets:	51 sets at 6" o.c.
Arbors:	510 lb capacity
House Pipes:	72' long

LOADING DOCK

Loading door(s) are 13'8" high x 10'0" wide
Trucks load (1) at a time
Fork lift is not required and is available

ELECTRICS

Total power available:
(1) 1400A 3Ø USL/USR
(1) 1000A 1Ø USR

FOLLOWSPOTS

House Followspots:
Super Trouper Xenon
Power in spot booth (3) 30A 1Ø

DIMMERS

No house dimmers
No DMX control system
No dry run station(s)

SOUND

House has (1) 20A 1Ø
dedicated power located
USR/ USL
FOH mixing position in
Rear House Right
No sound console available

OHIO THEATRE

AT: PLAYHOUSE SQUARE CENTER   **YEAR RENOVATED: 1982**

Theatre Location: 1511 Euclid Avenue, Cleveland, OH 44115
Management Company: Playhouse Square Foundation
                          1511 Euclid Avenue, Cleveland, OH 44115

Main Administrative Phone: 216-771-4444
Main Administrative Fax: 216-771-0217
Website: www.playhousesquare.com
Backstage Pay Phone: 216-241-9480

THEATRE STAFF
Director Programming   Gina Vernaci   216-771-4444
Marketing   Jim Szakacs   216-771-4444
HOUSE CREW
Technical Director   Bob Rody   216-771-4444
UNIONS
IATSE Local #27   Dale Short   216-621-9537

SEATING CAPACITY
Orchestra   613
Mezzanine   176
Balcony   216
Total: **1,005**

pit (add'l)   30

BOX OFFICE
Computerized
Box Office Treasurer
  Susan Schlund   216-771-4444

Outside Ticket Agency
Computerized
  Advantix   216-241-6000

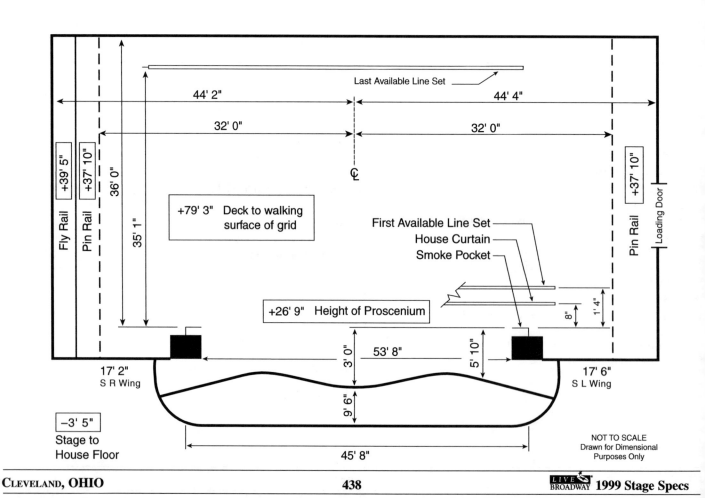

+79' 3" Deck to walking surface of grid

Last Available Line Set

44' 2"   44' 4"
32' 0"   32' 0"

First Available Line Set
House Curtain
Smoke Pocket

+26' 9" Height of Proscenium

53' 8"

17' 2" S R Wing   17' 6" S L Wing

−3' 5"
Stage to House Floor

45' 8"

NOT TO SCALE
Drawn for Dimensional
Purposes Only

STAGE HOUSE

House Curtain
Operates as a guillotine from SL deck

Rigging System
Type:	Single purchase counter weight
Weight:	25,000 lbs available
Line sets:	51 sets at 8" o.c. with 5 lift lines per set
Arbors:	675 lb capacity
House Pipes:	48' long with 57' of travel from deck

Line sets are not moveable
(30) spot wheels and 2,400' of hemp available

Permanent Installations Over Stage (from smoke pocket)
None

Permanent Installations On Deck
Traps in stage floor are on a sectional grid and must be cut

Orchestra Pit
Nonadjustable at 8' below stage level
Apron overhangs US wall of pit 3' 1"

BACKSTAGE

Loading Dock
Loading door(s):
9'0" high x 8'0" wide
Trucks load (1) at a time
Dock is at truck level below stage house; floor lift, 23'2" x 5'6", travels from dock up to stage level
Fork lift is not required
No trailers can store on-site
Security at stage door

Wardrobe
Location: SL on 3rd floor
Access: Stairs
(2) Washers (2) Dryers
No washer or dryer hookups

Dressing Rooms
(2) Star, SL, stage level, t/s included
(1) Small, SL, 2nd fl, t/s included
(2) Chorus, SL, 4th/ 5th fl, t/s included
Use dressing room for company mgr office

SOUND

Console
Yamaha 1800, located Rear House
32 inputs, 8 main outputs, 4 matrix outputs, 6 aux outputs

Speakers
House Cluster
Proscenium
Under Balcony
Portable
No speaker truss

Communications
Clear Com intercom with (2) channels
Infrared sound system
Dressing room page system

Road Console
Located Rear House
(12) seats required to be removed
Cable run from stage is 100'
Tie-in into house system with XLR connectors
XLR mic in ¼ line in XLR outputs

Rehearsal & Storage Space
Rehearsal: 48' x 50' located at State Theatre; prior arrangement required
Storage: None

ELECTRICS

Road Service Power

Panel	Phase	Amp	Circuit Protection	Use	Location
A	3	400	fuse	dimmers	SL back wall
B	3	200	fuse	sound	SR back wall

Recommended location of touring dimmer racks: SL on deck
Hoist not required

Front Of House (box boom values are per side)

Position	Pipe Width	Distance to Prosc.	House Circuits	Connector Type	FOH Transfer Circuits
1st Balc Rail	60'	44'	12	grd 20 amp stage pin	0
1st Cove	61'	51'	24	grd 20 amp stage pin	0
2nd Cove	61'	70'	24	grd 20 amp stage pin	0
Box Boom 1		7'	6	grd 20 amp stage pin	0
Box Boom 2		23'	6	grd 20 amp stage pin	0

Equipment FOH (box boom values are per side)
None

Followspots
House Followspots:
(2) Lycian Short Throws; removeable
Followspot Booth:
(2) spots per booth;
100' throw to proscenium;
(6) 3Ø 100 amp breakers

Dimmers
House console is Strand 430;
324 CD (80) dimmers
No DMX control system

PALACE THEATRE

YEAR BUILT: 1922   YEAR RENOVATED: 1988

Theatre Location: 1615 Euclid Avenue, Cleveland, OH 44115
Management Company: Playhouse Square Foundation
                            1501 Euclid Avenue Suite 200, Cleveland, OH 44115

Main Administrative Phone: 216-771-4444
Main Administrative Fax: 216-771-7136
Website: www.playhousesquare.com
StageDoor Phone: 216-771-4444 x3667
Backstage Pay Phone: 216-241-9615

THEATRE STAFF
Director Programming   Gina Vernaci   216-771-4444
Marketing   Jim Szakacs   216-771-4444
Operations   John Hemsath   216-771-4444

HOUSE CREW
Technical Director   Bob Rody   216-771-4444
Tech Supervisor   Joe Korcuska   216-771-4444

UNIONS
IATSE Local #27   Dale Short   216-621-9537

SEATING CAPACITY
Orchestra   1,563
Mezzanine   510
Balcony   593
Total: 2,666

pit (add'l)   50

BOX OFFICE
Computerized
Box Office Treasurer
  Susan Schlund   216-771-4444

Outside Ticket Agency
Computerized
  Advantix   216-241-6000

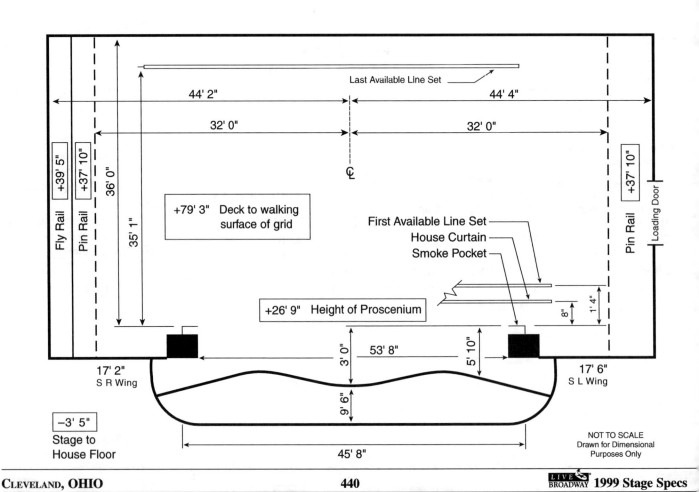

Last Available Line Set

44' 2"   44' 4"
32' 0"   32' 0"

CL

Fly Rail +39' 5"
Pin Rail +37' 10"   Pin Rail +37' 10"
Loading Door

36' 0"
35' 1"

+79' 3" Deck to walking surface of grid

First Available Line Set
House Curtain
Smoke Pocket

+26' 9" Height of Proscenium

8"   1' 4"

3' 0"   53' 8"   5' 10"

17' 2"   17' 6"
S R Wing   S L Wing

9' 6"

−3' 5"
Stage to
House Floor

45' 8"

NOT TO SCALE
Drawn for Dimensional
Purposes Only

STAGE HOUSE

HOUSE CURTAIN
Operates as a guillotine from SR deck

RIGGING SYSTEM
Type:	Single purchase counter weight
Weight:	32,000 lbs available
Line sets:	42 sets at 8" o.c. with 5 lift lines per set
Arbors:	1,500 lb capacity
House Pipes:	56' long with 71' of travel from deck

Line sets are not moveable
(25) spot wheels and 2,400' of hemp available

PERMANENT INSTALLATIONS OVER STAGE (FROM SMOKE POCKET)
Movie screen (1) at 5'6"
Dead spaces (1) at 17'2" x 19'2"

PERMANENT INSTALLATIONS ON DECK
Pilasters (4) against back wall

ORCHESTRA PIT
Adjustable to 8' below stage level by hydraulic lift
Apron overhangs US wall of pit 2'6"

BACKSTAGE

LOADING DOCK
Loading door(s):
7'9" high x 7'10" wide
Trucks load (1) at a time
Dock is at truck level and is equipped with a portable dock for right angle loading into stage house

WARDROBE
Location: Basement
Access: Freight elevator
(2) Washers (2) Dryers

DRESSING ROOMS
(2) Star, SR, stage level, t/s included, phone jack
(7) Small, SR, 2nd, 3rd & 4th fls, t/s included, phone jack
(2) Chorus, SR, 4th fl, t/s included, phone jack
(5) more rooms available - approximately 12'x12'

SOUND

CONSOLE
Yamaha 1800, located Rear House
32 inputs, 6 main outputs, 2 aux outputs

SPEAKERS
House Cluster
Proscenium
Under Balcony
No speaker truss

COMMUNICATIONS
Clear Com intercom with (4) channels
Infrared sound system
Dressing room page system

ROAD CONSOLE
Located Rear House
No seats required to be removed
Cable run from stage is 140'
Tie-in into house system with XLR connectors

REHEARSAL & STORAGE AREAS
Rehearsal: (2) @ 48' x 60' located adjacent to theatre; piano available; prior arrangements required
Storage: various sizes located in basement

ELECTRICS

ROAD SERVICE POWER

Panel	Phase	Amp	Circuit Protection	Use	Location
A-B	3	600	breaker	dimmers	SL on jump
C-D	3	600	breaker	extra	SL on jump
E	3	100	breaker	sound	DSL side wall
F	3	200	breaker	winches	USR back wall
G	3	200	breaker	extra	DSL side wall

Feeder hookup on jump is accessible via freight elevator DSL side wall
Recommended location of touring dimmer racks: SL on jump
Hoist not required

FRONT OF HOUSE (BOX BOOM VALUES ARE PER SIDE)

Position	Pipe Width	Distance to Prosc.	House Circuits	Connector Type	FOH Transfer Circuits
1st Balc Rail	77'	46'	36	grd 20 amp stage pin	36
SR Perch	32'	68'6"	24	grd 20 amp stage pin	20
SL Perch	32'	68'6"	24	grd 20 amp stage pin	20
Box Boom 1		32'	12	grd 20 amp stage pin	6

Transfer circuits: grd 20 amp stage pin located SL on jump; perches have (4) 8'0" sections of stacked pipe

EQUIPMENT FOH (BOX BOOM VALUES ARE PER SIDE)

Position	Quantity	Wattage	Instrument	Removeable
Perch	12	1,000	6 x 22 Lekos	yes
Box Boom 1	18	1,000	6 x 16 Lekos	yes

FOLLOWSPOTS
House Followspots:
(3) Strong Super Trouper 2k; not removeable

Followspot Booth:
(3) spots per booth;
136' throw to proscenium;
(3) 3Ø 100 amp breakers

DIMMERS
Lighting console is Light Board M;
(366) 2.4k Strand CD80 dimmers
No DMX control system
No dry run DMX station(s)

STATE THEATRE

Year built: 1922   Year renovated: 1984

Theatre Location: 1519 Euclid Avenue, Cleveland, OH 44115
Management Company: Playhouse Square Foundation
                                   1501 Euclid Avenue Suite 200, Cleveland, OH 44115

Main Administrative Phone: 216-241-6000
Main Administrative Fax: 216-771-0217
Website: www.playhousesquare.com
Backstage Pay Phone: 216-696-9833

Theatre Staff
  Director Programming   Gina Vernanci   216-771-4444
  Marketing   Jim Szakacs   216-771-4444
House Crew
  Technical Director   Bob Rody   216-771-4444
  Technical Supervisor   Joe Korcuska   216-771-4444
Unions
  IATSE Local #27   Dale Short   216-621-9537

Seating Capacity
  Orchestra   1,641
  Mezzanine   879
  Balcony   578
  Total: **3,098**

  pit (add'l)   100

Box Office
  Computerized
  Box Office Treasurer
    Susan Schlund   216-771-4444

  Outside Ticket Agency
  Computerized
    Advantix   216-241-6000

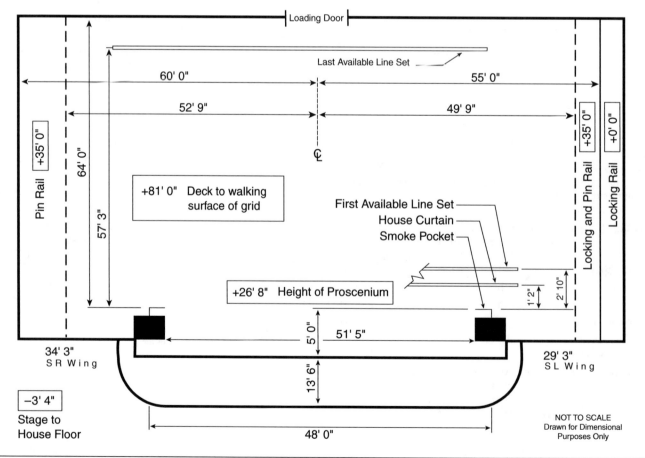

Loading Door

Last Available Line Set

60' 0"   55' 0"
52' 9"   49' 9"

CL

+81' 0" Deck to walking surface of grid

Pin Rail +35' 0"
64' 0"
57' 3"

+35' 0"
+0' 0"
Locking and Pin Rail
Locking Rail

First Available Line Set
House Curtain
Smoke Pocket

+26' 8" Height of Proscenium

1' 2"
2' 10"

5' 0"
51' 5"

34' 3"
S R Wing

29' 3"
S L Wing

13' 6"

−3' 4"
Stage to
House Floor

48' 0"

NOT TO SCALE
Drawn for Dimensional
Purposes Only

STAGE HOUSE

House Curtain
Operates as a guillotine from SR deck

Rigging System
Type:	Single or double purchase counter weight
Weight:	60,000 lbs available
Line sets:	82 sets at 8" o.c. with 7 lift lines per set
Arbors:	1,500 lb capacity
House Pipes:	63' long with 79' of travel from deck

Line sets are not moveable

Block & Falls are available

Chain hoists are not available

(70) spot wheels and 6,000' of hemp available

Permanent Installations Over Stage (from smoke pocket)
None

Permanent Installations On Deck
None

Orchestra Pit
Adjustable to 8'6" below stage level

Apron overhangs US wall of pit 12'0"

BACKSTAGE

Loading Dock
Loading door(s):
8'0" high x 8'0" wide

Trucks load (2) at same time

Fork lift is not required
Supplier: 216-587-0400

Sound/Props can load in FOH

Lobby can be a work area

Trailers cannot store on-site

Security at dock & stage door

Wardrobe
Location: Basement

Access: Freight elevator

(2) Washers (2) Dryers

No washer or dryer hookups

Dressing Rooms
(2) Star, SR, stage level, t/s included

(5) Small, SR, stage level, t/s included

(4) Chorus, basement, t/s included

Additional production office available for company mgr

SOUND

Console
Yamaha PM 1800, located Rear House

32 inputs, 6 main outputs, 2 aux outputs

Speakers
House Cluster

Proscenium

Under Balcony

Portable

No speaker truss

Communications
Clear Com intercom with (2) channels

Infrared sound system

Dressing room page system

Road Console
Located Rear House

No seats required to be removed

Cable run from stage is 165'

Tie-in into house system with XLR connectors

Rehearsal & Storage Space
Rehearsal: (2)@ 48' x 60', located +1; dance deck & flooring, mirrors & piano

Storage: None

ELECTRICS

Road Service Power

Panel	Phase	Amp	Circuit Protection	Use	Location
A-B	3	400	fuse	dimmers	DSR side wall
C-D	3	400	fuse	extra	DSR side wall
E	3	100	fuse	sound	SR side wall

Recommended location of touring dimmer racks: SR on deck

Hoist not required

Front Of House (box boom values are per side)

Position	Pipe Width	Distance to Prosc.	House Circuits	Connector Type	FOH Transfer Circuits
1st Balc Rail	90'	59'	36	grd 20 amp stage pin	36
Right Cove	24'	75'	12	grd 20 amp stage pin	12
Left Cove	24'	75'	12	grd 20 amp stage pin	12
Box Boom 1		50'	12	grd 20 amp stage pin	12
Torm		8'	12	grd 20 amp stage pin	12

Transfer circuits: grd 20 amp stage pin located on DSR wall

Road truss: Right & left Cove positions have (4) 8'0" sections of stacked pipe under spot perches

Equipment FOH (box boom values are per side)
None

Followspots
House Followspots:
(3) Strong Xenon 2k; not removeable

Followspot Booths:
(3) spots per booth;
145' throw to proscenium;
(3) 3Ø 60 amp breakers

Dimmers
Lighting console is Strand Light Palette;

(468) Strand CD80 dimmers

No DMX control system

CAPITOL THEATRE

AT: RIFFE CENTER   **YEAR BUILT: 1989**

Theatre Location:	77 South High Street, Columbus, OH 43215
Mailing Address:	55 East State Street, Columbus, OH 43215
Management Company:	CAPA
	55 East State Street, Columbus, OH 43215

Main Administrative Phone:	614-460-7211
Main Administrative Fax:	614-460-7216
E-mail:	*first initial last name*@capa.com
Website:	www.capa.com
Stage Door Phone:	614-460-7213

THEATRE STAFF

President	Douglas Kridler	614-469-1045
Marketing	Rosa Stolz	614-469-1045
Operations	Jennifer Kallaher	614-460-7211
Group Sales	Debby Rosenthal	614-469-1045

HOUSE CREW

Technical Director	John Dory	614-460-7213

UNIONS

IATSE Local #12	Richard Tisdale	614-221-3753
Wardrobe Local #747	Denise Armstrong	614-875-3316
AFM Local #103	Vaughn Weister	614-261-9826

SEATING CAPACITY

Orchestra	566
Mezzanine	285
Total:	**851**

wheelchair (add'l)	6

BOX OFFICE

Computerized
Dir. of Ticketing
  Rich Corsi   614-469-0939

Outside Ticket Agency
Computerized
  TicketMaster   614-347-4400

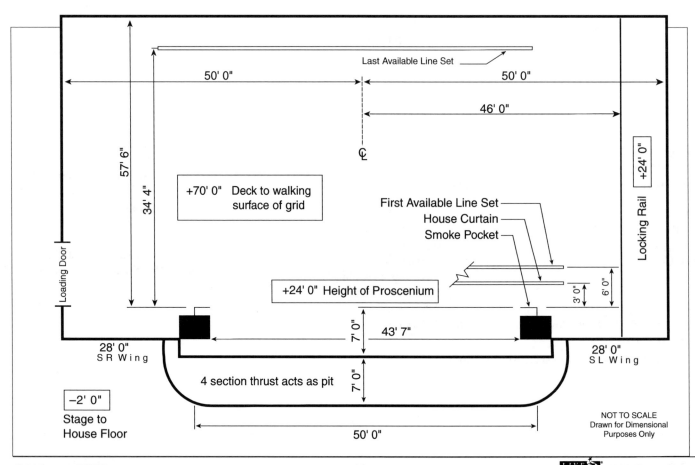

50' 0"   50' 0"

Last Available Line Set

46' 0"

57' 6"

34' 4"

+70' 0" Deck to walking surface of grid

C̵L

+24' 0"

Locking Rail

First Available Line Set
House Curtain
Smoke Pocket

+24' 0" Height of Proscenium

3' 0"   6' 0"

Loading Door

28' 0"
SR Wing

7' 0"   43' 7"

7' 0"

28' 0"
SL Wing

4 section thrust acts as pit

−2' 0"

Stage to
House Floor

50' 0"

NOT TO SCALE
Drawn for Dimensional
Purposes Only

STAGE HOUSE

HOUSE CURTAIN
Operates as a guillotine or traveller from SL fly floor or deck

RIGGING SYSTEM
Type: Single purchase counter weight and motorized Hemp system
Weight: 30,000 lbs available
Line sets: 43 sets at 6" o.c. with 6 lift lines per set
Arbors: 2,400 lb capacity
House Pipes: 65' long with 65' of travel from deck
Line sets are not moveable
Block & Falls are available
Chain hoists are not available
(10) spot wheels and 500 of hemp available
Motorized electric US & DS

PERMANENT INSTALLATIONS OVER STAGE (FROM SMOKE POCKET)
M=Moveable with advance call
Orchestra shell (3) at 6'6", 14'6", 22'6"
Electric raceways (2) at 3'6" - 4'10", 26'0" - 27'4"
Traveler (2) at 19'2", 30'6"; M
Hard portal (1) at 1'0" header , 1'6" legs
Cyclorama (1); M

PERMANENT INSTALLATIONS ON DECK
Traps (20) @ 5'0" x 5'0" located DS

ORCHESTRA PIT
Adjustable to 20' below stage level by electric motor turnscrew
Apron overhangs US wall of pit 7'0"
Pit lift is in (4) sections
Vom entrances from pit/trap area to thrust SR & SL
4 section thrust also acts as pit

BACKSTAGE

LOADING DOCK
Loading door(s):
8'6" high x 6'0" wide
Trucks load (2) at same time
Narrow alley approaches dock; freight elevator to theatre on 3rd fl; truck lift to bring trailer to 3rd fl
Fork lift is not required
Sound/Props cannot load in FOH
Security at dock

WARDROBE
Location: 5th floor
Access: Freight elevator
(2) Washers (2) Dryers
No washer or dryer hookups

DRESSING ROOMS
(2) Star, SR, stage level, t/s
(4) Small, SR, stage level, t/s
(2) Chorus, 24p, SR, -1, t/s
Elevator access for dressing rooms
Use dressing room for company mgr office

SOUND

CONSOLE
Soundcraft 500, located House Center
32 inputs, 2 main outputs, 4 aux outputs

SPEAKERS
House Cluster
Proscenium
Portable
Other
No speaker truss

COMMUNICATIONS
Clear Com intercom with (4) channels
Infrared sound system
Dressing room page system

ROAD CONSOLE
Located House mix
No seats required to be removed
Cable run from stage is 50'
Tie-in into house system with XLR connectors

REHEARSAL & STORAGE SPACE
Rehearsal: (2) on 4th fl, 19'x37' and 16' x 32', piano available
Storage: US, 2,200 sq ft

ELECTRICS

ROAD SERVICE POWER

Panel	Phase	Amp	Circuit Protection	Use	Location
A	3	600	fuse	sound	SR

Recommended location of touring dimmer racks: SR
Hoist not required
Additional power is available for tour buses, generators, etc.

FRONT OF HOUSE (BOX BOOM VALUES ARE PER SIDE)

Position	Pipe Width	Distance to Prosc.	House Circuits	Connector Type	FOH Transfer Circuits
1st Beam	100'	40	26	grd 20 amp stage pin	
2nd Beam	100'	60	42	grd 20 amp stage pin	
3rd Beam	100'	80	38	grd 20 amp stage pin	
4th Beam	100'	100	38	grd 20 amp stage pin	
Box Boom 1		various	43	grd 20 amp stage pin	
Rings		50	92	grd 20 amp stage pin	

Transfer circuits: Onstage & FOH trusses can be hung

EQUIPMENT FOH (BOX BOOM VALUES ARE PER SIDE)

Position	Quantity	Wattage	Instrument	Removeable
1st Beam	40	1000	KL6	yes
2nd Beam	40	1000	KL6	yes
3rd Beam	20	1000	KL6	yes
4th Beam	30	1000	KL6	yes
Box Boom 1	40	1000	KL6	yes

Beams curve toward stage at ends

FOLLOWSPOTS
House Followspots:
(2) Super Trouper 1.6k

Followspot Booth:
(2) spots per booth;
100' throw to proscenium;
(2) 1Ø 60 amp breakers

DIMMERS
Lighting console is Obsession II;
(648) Colortran 192 dimmers
House has programmable DMX control system
(4) dry run DMX station(s), (3) in booth, (1) SR

OHIO THEATRE

YEAR BUILT: 1928   YEAR RENOVATED: 1984

Theatre Location: 55 East State Street, Columbus, OH 43215
Management Company: Columbus Assoc. for the Performing Arts (CAPA)

Main Administrative Phone: 614-469-1045
Main Administrative Fax: 614-461-0429
E-mail: *first initial last name*@capa.com
Website: www.capa.com
Stage Door Phone: 614-469-1045 x24
Backstage Pay Phone: 614-225-9995

THEATRE STAFF
President   Douglas Kridler   614-469-1045
Booking   Douglas Kridler   614-469-1045
Marketing   Rosa Stolz   614-469-1045
Operations   John Bateman   614-469-1045
Group Sales   Debby Rosenthal   614-469-1045

HOUSE CREW
Stage Manager   Andrew Duke   614-228-2279
Sound   Jack Kamer   614-469-1045

UNIONS
IATSE Local #12   Richard Tisdale   614-221-3753
Wardrobe Local #747   Denise Armstrong   614-875-4828
AFM Local #103   Jerry Kaye   614-889-5060

SEATING CAPACITY
Orchestra   1,362
Loge   324
Mid. Balcony   607
Rear Balcony   486
Total: **2,779**

BOX OFFICE
Computerized
Director of Ticketing
   Rich Corsi   614-469-0939

Outside Ticket Agency
Computerized
   Ticketmaster   614-847-4400

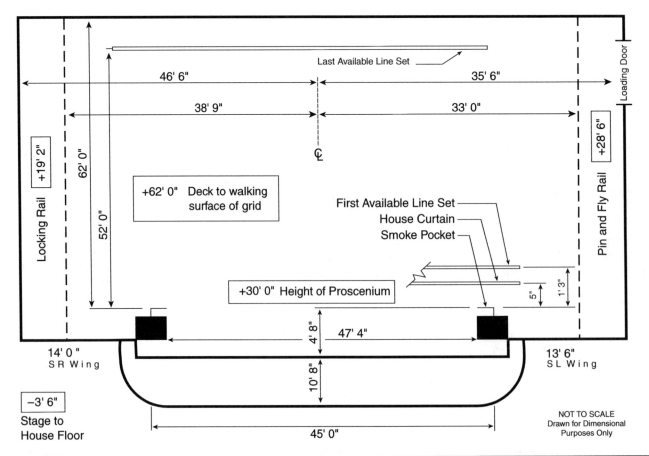

STAGE HOUSE

HOUSE CURTAIN
Operates as a guillotine from SL deck

RIGGING SYSTEM
Type:	Double purchase counter weight
Weight:	62,000 lbs available
Line sets:	55 sets at 7" o.c. with 6 lift lines per set
Arbors:	2,400 lb capacity
House Pipes:	65' long with 59' of travel from deck

Line sets are moveable
Block & Falls are not available
Chain hoists available as a rental; (3) half ton
(25) spot wheels and 1,000' of hemp available

PERMANENT INSTALLATIONS OVER STAGE (FROM SMOKE POCKET)
M=Moveable with advance call
Orchestra shells (5) at 4'0", 11'5", 18'9", 26'0", 33'4"
Electric Borders (1) at 40'0"; M
Electric Raceways (5) at 3'4", 9'9", 17'5", 24'6", 32'0"
Movie screen (1) at 6'3"; M
Traveller (1) at 2'2"
Fire curtain (1) at 0'4"

PERMANENT INSTALLATIONS ON DECK
Columns (1), 2'0" x 2'0"; 12'4" to US edge of smoke pocket
Orchestra shell storage (5), 40'0" x 10'0"; 52'0" to US edge of smoke pocket
Lift (2), 8'0" x 40'0"; 10'6" to US edge of smoke pocket

ORCHESTRA PIT
Adjustable to 8' below stage level by electric motor turnscrew
Apron overhangs US wall of pit 13'7"
Pit lift is in (2) sections; Organ lift SR

BACKSTAGE

LOADING DOCK
Loading door(s):
 11'8" high x 8'5" wide
Trucks load (2) at same time
Column at center of alley makes 2nd truck tough to manuveur
Fork lift is not required
Sound/Props cannot load in FOH
Lobby cannot be a work area
Trailers cannot store on-site
Security at stage door

WARDROBE
Location: Lower level
Access: Elevators
(2) Washers (2) Dryers
No washer or dryer hookups

DRESSING ROOMS
(1) Star, SL, +1, t/s included, phone jack
(9) Small, SL, -1 / +2 / +3 / +4, t/s included, phone jack
(1) Chorus, SL, -1, t/s included, phone jack
Elevator access for dressing rooms
Additional production office available for company mgr

SOUND

CONSOLE
Yamaha PM 2000, located Upper Balcony
24 inputs, 8 main outputs, 8 matrix outputs, 6 aux outputs

SPEAKERS
House Cluster
Proscenium
Under Balcony
No speaker truss

COMMUNICATIONS
Clear Com intercom with (2) channels
Infrared sound system
Dressing room page system

ROAD CONSOLE
Located Rear Orchestra
(4) seats required to be removed
Cable run from stage is 250'
Tie-in into house system with XLR connectors

REHEARSAL & STORAGE SPACE
Rehearsal:Prior arrangement
66' x 41', lower level, piano
25' x 35', lower level, mirrors, dance floor
43' x 40', lower level, mirrors, dance floor
Storage: None

ELECTRICS

ROAD SERVICE POWER

Panel	Phase	Amp	Circuit Protection	Use	Location
A	3	400	fuse	dimmers	SR
B	3	400	fuse	extra	SR
C	3	400	fuse	sound	SL
D	3	200	breaker	sound	SL

Recommended location of touring dimmer racks: SR
Hoist not required

FRONT OF HOUSE (BOX BOOM VALUES ARE PER SIDE)

Position	Pipe Width	Distance to Prosc.	House Circuits	Connector Type	FOH Transfer Circuits
Balc Rail	54'	48'	17	grd 20 amp stage pin	17
Box Boom 1		20'	10	grd 20 amp stage pin	10
Box Boom 2		60'	4	grd 20 amp stage pin	4
Box Boom 3		80'	4	grd 20 amp stage pin	4

Transfer circuits: grd 20 amp stage pin

EQUIPMENT FOH (BOX BOOM VALUES ARE PER SIDE)
None

FOLLOWSPOTS
House Followspots:
 (2) Xenon Converted Super Troupers 2k; not removeable

Followspot Booth:
 (2) spots per booth;
 169' throw to proscenium;
 (3) 1Ø 20 amp breakers

DIMMERS
Lighting console is Obsession;
(384) CD 80 dimmers
No DMX control system

PALACE THEATRE

YEAR BUILT: 1927   **YEAR RENOVATED:** 1987

Theatre Location: 34 West Broad Street, Columbus, OH 43215
Mailing Address: 55 East State Street, Columbus, OH 43215
Management Company: Columbus Association for the Performing Arts (CAPA)
                                      (mailing address as above)

Main Administrative Phone: 614-469-1331
E-mail: *first initial last name*@capa.com
Website: www.capa.com
Stage Door Phone: 614-469-1331
Backstage Pay Phone: 614-469-1032

THEATRE STAFF
President   Douglas Kridler   614-469-1045
Booking   Douglas Kridler   614-469-1045
Marketing   Rosa Stolz   614-469-1045
Operations   Mike Bilger   614-469-1045
Group Sales   Debby Rosenthal   614-469-1045

HOUSE CREW
Stage Manager   Richard Steele   614-469-1540

UNIONS
IATSE Local #12   Richard Tisdale   614-221-3753
Wardrobe Local #747   Denise Armstrong   614-875-4828
AFM Local #103   Jerry Kaye   614-889-5060

SEATING CAPACITY
Orchestra	1,596
Boxes	24
Mezzanine	760
Balcony	447
Total:	**2,827**
pit (add'l)	32

BOX OFFICE
Computerized
Director of Ticketing
  Rich Corsi   614-469-0939

Outside Ticket Agency
Computerized
Ticketmaster   614-847-4400

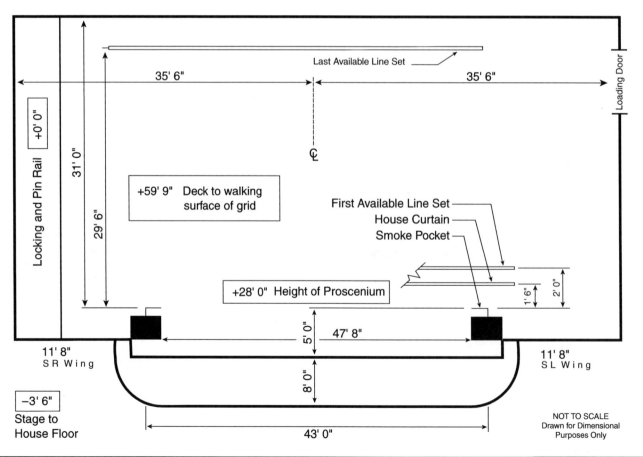

Last Available Line Set

35' 6"   35' 6"

Loading Door

Locking and Pin Rail   +0' 0"

31' 0"

29' 6"

+59' 9" Deck to walking surface of grid

First Available Line Set
House Curtain
Smoke Pocket

1' 6"   2' 0"

+28' 0" Height of Proscenium

5' 0"   47' 8"

11' 8"
SR Wing

11' 8"
SL Wing

8' 0"

−3' 6"
Stage to
House Floor

43' 0"

NOT TO SCALE
Drawn for Dimensional
Purposes Only

STAGE HOUSE

HOUSE CURTAIN
Operates as a guillotine or traveller from SR deck

RIGGING SYSTEM
Type:	Single purchase counter weight
Weight:	19,500 lbs available
Line sets:	48 sets at 6" o.c. with 4 lift lines per set
Arbors:	950 lb capacity
House Pipes:	55' long with 55' of travel from deck

Line sets are moveable
Block & Falls are available
Chain hoists are not available
(30) spot wheels and 6,000' of hemp available

PERMANENT INSTALLATIONS OVER STAGE (FROM SMOKE POCKET)
M=Moveable with advance call
Movie screen (1); M
Traveller (1)
Fire curtain (1) at proscenium

PERMANENT INSTALLATIONS ON DECK
Loading bridge (1) DS to US + 55'0", 29'6" US of smoke pocket

ORCHESTRA PIT
Nonadjustable at 6'3" below stage level
Apron overhangs US wall of pit 4'6"
Pit lift is in (11) sections

BACKSTAGE

LOADING DOCK
Loading door(s):
10'0" high x 7'9" wide
Trucks load (2) at same time
Ramp or forklift from truck to alley then onto stage
Forklift depends on load;
Clark Lift 614-228-6200
Sound/Props can load in FOH
Trailers cannot store on-site
Security at dock & stage door

WARDROBE
Location: Under stage
Access: USR ramp
(1) Washer (1) Dryer
Washer and dryer hookups available

DRESSING ROOMS
(1) Star, SL, 2nd fl, t/s
(11) Small, SL, 3rd-7th fls, t/s included
(2) Chorus, 6th-7th fls, t/s included
Elevator access for dressing rooms
Additional production office available for company mgr

SOUND

CONSOLE
EV, located HR
32 inputs, 6 main outputs, 4 aux outputs

SPEAKERS
Proscenium
No speaker truss

COMMUNICATIONS
Telex intercom with (1) channel
FM sound system

ROAD CONSOLE
Located Rear House
No seats required to be removed
Cable run from stage is 150'
Tie-in into house system with XLR connectors

REHEARSAL & STORAGE SPACE
Rehearsal: None
Storage: 10 x 30 USL street level

ELECTRICS

ROAD SERVICE POWER

Panel	Phase	Amp	Circuit Protection	Use	Location
A	3	600	breaker	dimmers	DSR
B	3	400	breaker	dimmers	DSR
C	3	200	fuse	motors	DSR
D	3	200	fuse	sound	DSL

Recommended location of touring dimmer racks: SR
Hoist not required

FRONT OF HOUSE (BOX BOOM VALUES ARE PER SIDE)

Position	Pipe Width	Distance to Prosc.	House Circuits	Connector Type	FOH Transfer Circuits
1st Balc Rail	80'	57'	12	grd 20 amp stage pin	12
Box Boom 1		55'	12	grd 20 amp stage pin	12
Box Boom 2		55'	12	grd 20 amp stage pin	12

EQUIPMENT FOH (BOX BOOM VALUES ARE PER SIDE)

Position	Quantity	Wattage	Instrument	Removeable
Box Boom 1	12	1,000	6 x 16 Lekos	yes

FOLLOWSPOTS
House Followspots:
(2) Xenon Super Troupers; removeable

Followspot Booth:
(2) spots per booth;
170' throw to proscenium;
(3) 3Ø 30 amp breakers

DIMMERS
Lighting console is Obsession 2;
(288) ETC Sensor dimmers
House has programmable DMX control system
(2) dry run DMX station(s)

SOUTHERN THEATRE

YEAR BUILT: 1896   YEAR RENOVATED: 1993

Theatre Location: 21 East Main Street, Columbus, OH 43215
Mailing Address: 55 East State Street, Columbus, OH 43215
Management Company: CAPA (Columbus Assn. for the Performing Arts)
                         55 East State Street, Columbus, OH 43215

Main Administrative Phone: 614-340-1896
Main Administrative Fax: 614-340-1897
E-mail: *first initial last name*@capa.com
Website: www.capa.com

THEATRE STAFF
President   Douglas Kridler   614-469-1045
Marketing   Rosa Stolz   614-469-1045
Operations   John Bateman   614-340-1396
Group Sales   Debby Rosenthal   614-469-1045

HOUSE CREW
Stage Manager   Jason Gay   614-340-1998

UNIONS
IATSE Local #12   Richard Tisdale   614-221-3753
Wardrobe Local #747   Denise Armstrong   614-875-3316
AFM Local #103   Vaughn Weister   614-261-9826

SEATING CAPACITY
Huntington Circle   158
Orchestra   226
Loge   180
Balcony   123
Second Balcony   206
Boxes   16
Total: **909**

pit (add'l)   24

BOX OFFICE
Computerized
Director of Ticketing
  Rich Corsi   614-469-0939

Outside Ticket Agency
Computerized
  Ticketmaster   614-847-4400

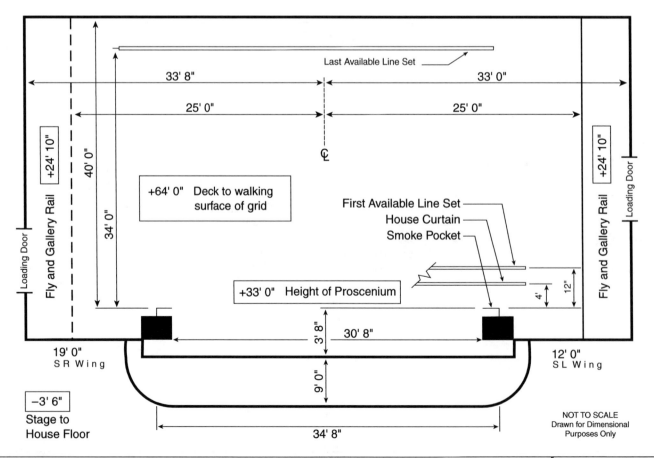

STAGE HOUSE

HOUSE CURTAIN
Operates as a guillotine from SL deck

RIGGING SYSTEM
Type: Single purchase counter weight
Weight: 40,000 lbs available
Line sets: 50 sets at 6" o.c. with 5 lift lines per set
Arbors: 1,000 lb capacity
House Pipes: 48' long with 61' of travel from deck
Line sets are moveable
Block & Falls are not available
Chain hoists are not available
(20) spot wheels and 2,000' of hemp available

PERMANENT INSTALLATIONS OVER STAGE (FROM SMOKE POCKET)
Orchestra shell (4) at 4'11", 13'5", 21'11", 30'5"
Fire curtain (1)
Catwalk (1) at 35'4"

PERMANENT INSTALLATIONS ON DECK
Stairs (1) 3' x 3', DSR
Loading bridge (2)

ORCHESTRA PIT
Adjustable to 13'3" below stage level by electric motor
   turnscrew
Apron overhangs US wall of pit 9' 0"
Pit lift is in (1) section
Upper part of proscenium is radius

BACKSTAGE

LOADING DOCK
Loading door(s):
   10'0" high x 10'0" wide
Trucks load (2) at same time
Restricted in and out during
   rush hours
Fork lift is not required
Sound/Props cannot load in
   FOH
Trailers cannot store on-site

WARDROBE
Location: Lower level
Access: Elevator
(1) Washer (2) Dryer
(1) Washer hookup

DRESSING ROOMS
(1) Star, SL, stage level,
   t/s included, phone jack
(2) Small, -1, t/s included,
   phone jack
(4) Small, -1, t/s on same fl,
   phone jack
(2) Chorus, -1, t/s on same fl,
   phone jack
Elevator access for dressing
   rooms
Additional production office
   available for company mgr

SOUND

CONSOLE
Yamaha 3500, located HL
48 inputs, 2 main outputs,
   8 matrix outputs, 8 aux
   outputs

SPEAKERS
Proscenium
Under Balcony
Portable
No speaker truss

COMMUNICATIONS
Clear Com intercom with
   (2) channels
RF sound system
Dressing room page system

ROAD CONSOLE
Located Rear Box HL
(6) seats required to be
   removed
Cable run from stage is 125'
Tie-in into house system with
   XLR connectors

REHEARSAL & STORAGE SPACE
Rehearsal: None
Storage: None

ELECTRICS

ROAD SERVICE POWER

Panel	Phase	Amp	Circuit Protection	Use	Location
A-B	3	400	breaker	dimmers	SR
C	3	200	breaker	sound	DSL Jump

Recommended location of touring dimmer racks: USR Deck
Hoist not required

FRONT OF HOUSE (BOX BOOM VALUES ARE PER SIDE)

Position	Pipe Width	Distance to Prosc.	House Circuits	Connector Type	FOH Transfer Circuits
House Arch	68'	45'	28	grd 20 amp stage pin	0
Balc Rail		50'	18	grd 20 amp stage pin	0
Booth Bridge	68'	35'	32	grd 20 amp stage pin	0

EQUIPMENT FOH (BOX BOOM VALUES ARE PER SIDE)

Quantity	Wattage	Instrument
13	1,000	Altman
4	575	Source 4 5°
12	575	Source 4 10°
12	575	Source 4 19°
32	575	Source 4 26°
44	575	Source 4 36°

FOLLOWSPOTS
House Followspots:
   (2) Lycian Super Arc 400

Followspot Booth:
   (4) spots per booth;
   85' throw to proscenium;
   (4) 3Ø 20 amp breakers

DIMMERS
Lighting console is Obsession II;
   (400) Sensor AR dimmers
House has programmable
   DMX control system
(12) dry run DMX station(s)
   located SR Gallery, House
   Arch, Booth Bridge

ERVIN J. NUTTER CENTER

AKA: NUTTER CENTER **AT:** ERVIN J. NUTTER CENTER ENTERTAINMENT & SPORTS COMPLEX   YEAR BUILT: **1940**

Theatre Location: 3640 Colonel Glenn Highway, Dayton, OH 45435
Management Company: Wright State University
                        3640 Colonel Glenn Highway, Suite 430
                        Dayton, OH 45435

SEATING CAPACITY		
Total:		**12,192**

Main Administrative Phone: 937-775-3498
Main Administrative Fax: 937-775-2070
Website: www.nuttercenter.com
Stage Door Phone: 937-775-4713

THEATRE STAFF

Executive Director   John Siehl   937-775-3498
Asst Executive Director L. Clapper   937-775-4785

HOUSE CREW

Operations Manager   John Cox   937-775-4672

STAGE DIMENSIONS (FROM SMOKE POCKET)
Portable stage & Orchestra Pit

RIGGING
Rigging system rental available

LOADING DOCK
Loading door(s) are 12'0" high x 12'0" wide
Trucks load (3) at same time
Fork lift is not required and is available

ELECTRICS
Total power available:
  (2) 600A 3Ø behind stage
  (1) 400A 3Ø behind stage
  (1) 200A 3Ø behind stage
  (1) 480A 3Ø behind stage

FOLLOWSPOTS
House Followspots:
  Lycian

DIMMERS
No house dimmers
No DMX control system

SOUND
House has dedicated power
  located USC
FOH mixing is Portable
Sound console is available

MONTGOMERY COUNTY'S MEMORIAL HALL

AKA: MEMORIAL HALL

YEAR BUILT: 1910   YEAR RENOVATED: 1990

Theatre Location: 125 East 1 St., Dayton, OH 45422
Management Company: Montgomery County
                             451 West 3 St., Dayton, OH 45422

Main Administrative Phone: 937-225-5898
Main Administrative Fax: 937-225-4922
E-mail: memorialhall@hcst.net
Website: www.memorialhalldayton.com
Stage Door Phone: 937-226-0427

THEATRE STAFF
Director	Carol Cleavenger	937-225-5898
Booking	Kelly Loftus	937-225-5898
Marketing	Kelly Loftus	937-225-5898
Operations	Kelly Loftus	937-225-5898
Group Sales	Kelly Loftus	937-225-5898
Performance Coord.	Travis Price	937-225-5898

HOUSE CREW
Production Coordinator	Pat Keough	937-225-5898
Carpentry	Paul Wilms	937-225-5898
Electrics	Mike Duff	937-225-5898
Sound	Keith Thomas	937-225-5898

UNIONS
IATSE Local #66	Ken Rice	937-223-2642

SEATING CAPACITY
Orchestra	1,467
Loge	380
Balcony	654
Total:	**2,501**

wheelchair (add'l)	6

BOX OFFICE
Hard Ticket Box Office
Marketing Director
  Kelly Loftus   937-225-5898

Outside Ticket Agency
Computerized
Ticketmaster
  Dennis Scanlon   513-721-6100

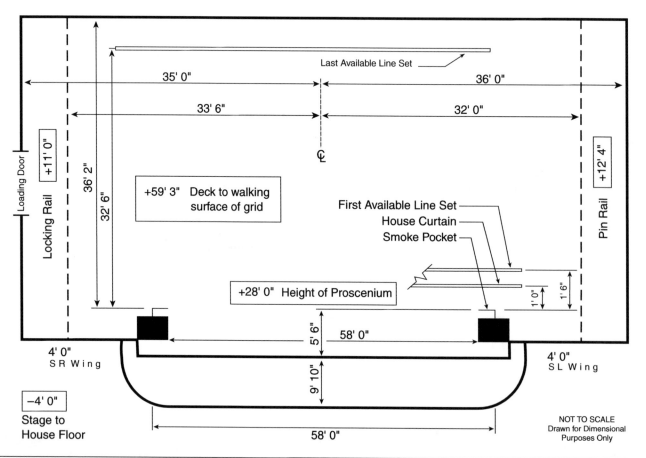

STAGE HOUSE

HOUSE CURTAIN
Operates as a traveller from SL deck

RIGGING SYSTEM
Type:	Combination purchase counter weight
Weight:	36,800 lbs available
Line sets:	46 sets at 6" o.c. with 7 lift lines per set
Arbors:	800 lb capacity
House Pipes:	58' long with 54' of travel from deck

Line sets are not moveable
Block & Falls are not available
Chain hoists are not available
(20) spot wheels and 3,000' of hemp available

PERMANENT INSTALLATIONS OVER STAGE (FROM SMOKE POCKET)
Electric borders (4) 9'6", 16'6", 23'6", 29'6"
Orchestra shell (4) 6'6", 13'0", 20'6", 26'6"
Traveller (2) 18'6", 25'0"

PERMANENT INSTALLATIONS ON DECK
None

ORCHESTRA PIT
Nonadjustable at 5' below stage level
Apron overhangs US wall of pit 1'0"

BACKSTAGE

LOADING DOCK
Loading door(s):
   10'0" high x 10'0" wide
Trucks load (1) at same time
Dock is at truck level 14'0"
   below the stage, equipped
   with freight elevator: 10' h x
   10' w x 20' long

WARDROBE
Location: SL in basement
Access: Freight Elevator
(1) Washer (0) Dryers

DRESSING ROOMS
(2) Star, SR / SL, stage level, t/s
   on same fl, phone jack
(8) Small, basement, t/s on same
   fl
(2) Chorus, SR / SL, +2, t/s on
   same fl
Additional production office
   available for company mgr

SOUND

CONSOLE
Soundcraft Delta
32 inputs, 8 main outputs

SPEAKERS
House Cluster
Under Balcony

COMMUNICATIONS
Clear Com intercom with
   (2) channels
Infrared sound system
Dressing room page system

ROAD CONSOLE
Located Rear House
(8) seats required to be
   removed
Cable run from stage is 225'
Tie-in into house system with
   XLR connectors

REHEARSAL & STORAGE SPACE
Rehearsal: None
Storage: 100' x 100' in
   basement

ELECTRICS

ROAD SERVICE POWER

Panel	Phase	Amp	Circuit Protection	Use	Location
A	3	800	fuse	dimmers	DSL
B	3	800	fuse	dimmers	DSL
C	3	800	fuse	extra	DSL
D	3	100	fuse	sound	SL

Recommended location of touring dimmer racks: SL on deck
Hoist not required

FRONT OF HOUSE (BOX BOOM VALUES ARE PER SIDE)

Position	Pipe Width	Distance to Prosc.	House Circuits	Connector Type	FOH Transfer Circuits
1st Balc Rail	40'	60'	15	grd 20 amp stage pin	15
1st Cove	35'	60'	6	grd 20 amp stage pin	6
2nd Cove	60'	25'	15	grd 20 amp stage pin	15
Box Boom 1		60'	6	grd 20 amp stage pin	6

Transfer circuits: grd 20 amp stage pin, located DSL side wall

EQUIPMENT FOH (BOX BOOM VALUES ARE PER SIDE)
None

FOLLOWSPOTS
House Followspots:
   (2) Xenon Super Troupers;
   removeable

Followspot Booth:
   (4) spots per booth;
   95' throw to proscenium;
   1Ø 400 amp breakers

DIMMERS
Lighting console is ETC 250;
   (188) Strand Century
   CD80 dimmers
House has programmable
   DMX control system
(2) dry run DMX station(s)

VICTORIA THEATRE

YEAR BUILT: 1868   YEAR RENOVATED: 1991

Theatre Location: 138 North Main Street, Dayton, OH 45402-1776
Management Company: Victoria Theatre Association (address as above)

Main Administrative Phone: 937-228-7591
Main Administrative Fax: 937-449-5068
Website: www.victoriatheatre.com
Stage Door Phone: 937-449-5063
Backstage Pay Phone: 937-445-9112

THEATRE STAFF
President   Mark Light   937-228-7591 x3012
Booking   Dione Kennedy   937-228-7591 x3014
Marketing   Katherine Pridemore   937-228-7591 x3056
Operations   Joann Brown   937-228-7591 x3075

HOUSE CREW
Production Manager   John Dorsey   937-228-7591 x3075
Carpentry   Nelson D'Aloia   937-228-7591 x3075
Electrics   Jim Clemmer   937-228-7591 x3047
Sound   Chuck Young   937-228-7591 x3049
Props   Todd Knopp   937-228-7591 x3046

UNIONS
IATSE Local #66   Ken Rice   937-223-2642
Wardrobe Local #866   Mary Hughes   937-223-2542

SEATING CAPACITY
Orchestra   633
Balcony   494
Opera Boxes (2)   12
Total :   **1,139**

BOX OFFICE
Computerized
Senior Ticket Agent
  Katie Sibbing   937-228-7591 x3045

Outside Ticket Agency
None

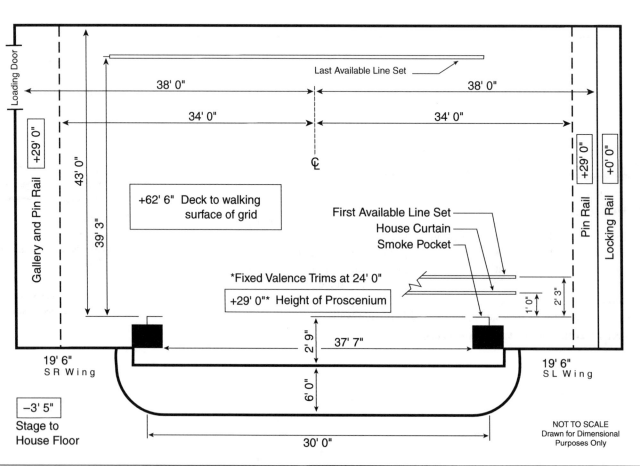

STAGE HOUSE

HOUSE CURTAIN
Operates as a guillotine from SR deck

RIGGING SYSTEM
Type:	Single purchase counter weight
Weight:	60,000 lbs available
Line sets:	75 sets at 6" o.c. with 6 lift lines per set
Arbors:	1,000 lb capacity
House Pipes:	54' long with 57' of travel from deck

Line sets moveable

(60) spot wheels and 5,000' of hemp available

24 quarter ton cable winches on tracks 12 each SR & SL

PERMANENT INSTALLATIONS OVER STAGE (FROM SMOKE POCKET)
M=Moveable with advance call

Movie screen (1) stores US on line 75; M

Cyclorama (1) no permanent position; M

Fire curtain (1) within smoke pocket

Catwalk (3) located on perimeter of stage

PERMANENT INSTALLATIONS ON DECK
Jumps (4) located SL, US, SR

Stairs (2) 3'0" wide located front of stage to orchestra (can move)

Radiators (1) set, 43'0" US on back wall

Loading bridge (4)

ORCHESTRA PIT
Adjustable to 9'2" below stage level by electric motor turnscrew

Apron overhangs US wall of pit 7'6"

Pit lift is in (1) section

Stage apron is straight line, pit elevator has convex curve on DS edge, pit elevator is 30'0" wide and 6'6" deep at Center Line and 3'6"deep at sides

BACKSTAGE

LOADING DOCK
Loading door(s):
10'9"high x 8'7"wide

Trucks load (1) at a time

Trucks park on one way street against traffic; overhead cable for electric transit system prevents parking trucks (2) abreast; truck ramp available for 2' rise from street to stage

Fork lift is not required

Sound/Props can load in FOH

Trailers cannot store on-site

Security at stage door

WARDROBE
Location: Downstairs in dressing room corridor

Access: Pit elevator & large lobby passenger elevator

(1) Washer (1) Dryer

Washer and dryer hookups available

DRESSING ROOMS
Elevator access for dressing rooms

Use dressing room for company mgr office

and open areas

SOUND

CONSOLE
Yamaha PM - 3500/40, located Rear House

40 + 4 stereo inputs, 8 main outputs, 8 matrix outputs, 8 aux outputs

SPEAKERS
Proscenium

Under Balcony

Portable

No speaker truss

Touring towers and stacks must be placed DS of prosc on floor or riser

COMMUNICATIONS
Clear Com intercom with (2) channels

Infrared sound system

Dressing room page system

ROAD CONSOLE
Located Rear House

No seats required to be removed

Cable run from stage is 220'

Tie-in into house system with connectors

REHEARSAL & STORAGE SPACE
Rehearsal: Studios on-site or in adjacent building; separate rental arrangements required

Storage: Basement corridors

ELECTRICS

ROAD SERVICE POWER

Panel	Phase	Amp	Circuit Protection	Use	Location
A-C	3	400	fuse	dimmers	SR wall
D	3	100	fuse	sound	DSL wall

Recommended location of touring dimmer racks: off SR

Hoist not required

FRONT OF HOUSE (BOX BOOM VALUES ARE PER SIDE)

Position	Pipe Width	Distance to Prosc.	House Circuits	Connector Type	FOH Transfer Circuits
1st Balc Rail	70'	30'6"	14	grd 20 amp stage pin	14
2nd Balc Rail	44'	86'3"	24	grd 20 amp stage pin	24
1st Cove		62'10"	24	grd 20 amp stage pin	24
Box Boom 1		34'6"	18	grd 20 amp stage pin	18

Transfer circuits: ETC/EMI response interface; optical isolation unit also available

EQUIPMENT FOH (BOX BOOM VALUES ARE PER SIDE)

Position	Quantity	Wattage	Instrument	Removeable
1st Balc Rail	24	575	Source 4 26°	no
2nd Balc Rail	14	575	Source 4 19°	no
1st Cove Rail	24	575	Source 4 10°	no
Box Boom 1	28	575	Source 4 19°	no

FOLLOWSPOTS
House Followspots:
(2) Strong Xenon Super Trouper 2k; not removeable

Followspot Booth:
(3) spots per booth;
88' throw to proscenium;
(3) 3Ø 30 amp breakers

DIMMERS
Lighting console is ETC Expression;
(432) LMI LM-64 dimmers

House has programmable DMX control system

(1) dry run DMX station, DSR

CROUSE PERFORMANCE HALL

AT: VETERANS MEMORIAL CIVIC AND CONVENTION CENTER　　　　**YEAR BUILT: 1984**

Theatre Location:　　　7 Town Square, Lima, OH 45801

Main Administrative Phone:　　　419-224-5222
Main Administrative Fax:　　　419-224-6964
E-mail:　　　vmccc@alpha.wcoil.com
Website:　　　www.metroevents.com/vmccc

SEATING CAPACITY	
Main Floor	1,250
Balcony	447
Total:	**1,697**
pit (add'l)	86
wheelchair (add'l)	26

THEATRE STAFF

Manager	Jane Riggs	419-224-5222
Booking	Jane Riggs	419-224-5222
Crew Contact	Brian Keegan	419-224-5222

STAGE DIMENSIONS (FROM SMOKE POCKET)

Stage is 42'0" deep
Width from Center Line to SL is 56'0"
Width from Center Line to SR is 48'0"
Proscenium width is 60'0"
Proscenium height is 26'0"
Smoke pocket to apron edge is 7'0"
Orchestra pit exists

RIGGING

Grid Height:	55'
Type:	Single purchase counter weight
Weight:	4,000 lbs
Line sets:	41 sets distance o.c varies
Arbors:	1,200 lb capacity
House Pipes:	64' long

LOADING DOCK

Loading door(s) are 8'0" high x 8'0" wide
Trucks load (1) at a time
Fork lift is not required and is available

ELECTRICS

Total power available:
　(2) 400A 3Ø SR
　(1) 100A 1Ø off SL

FOLLOWSPOTS

House Followspots:
　Xenon Super Trouper
Power in spot booth
FOH transfer circuits : 42

DIMMERS

(177) house dimmers
House has DMX control system
No dry run station(s)

SOUND

House has 100A undedicated
　power located off SL
FOH mixing position in
　Rear House Center
Sound console is available

STRANAHAN THEATER AND GREAT HALL

FORMERLY: TOLEDO MASONIC AUDITORIUM

YEAR BUILT: 1969

Theatre Location: 4645 Heatherdowns Blvd., Toledo, OH 43614
Management Company: V/Gladieux Enterprises
2630 West Laskey Road, Toledo, OH 43613

Main Administrative Phone:	419-381-8851
Main Administrative Fax:	419-381-9525
Stage Door Phone:	419-381-9357
Backstage Pay Phone:	419-381-9357

THEATRE STAFF

General Manager	Penny Marks	419-381-8851
Booking	Penny Marks	419-381-8851
Marketing	Sally Oberski	419-381-8851
Group Sales	Cheryl Byrne	419-381-8851

HOUSE CREW

Technical Director	Manny Littin	419-381-8851

UNIONS

IATSE Local #24	Jim Sergura	419-693-2589
Music	Keith McWatters	419-241-1271

SEATING CAPACITY

Orchestra	1,590
Balcony	747
Total:	**2,337**
pit (add'l)	87

BOX OFFICE
Computerized
Box office Manager
Cheryl Byrne   419-381-8851

Outside Ticket Agency
Computerized
Ticketmaster   419-474-1333

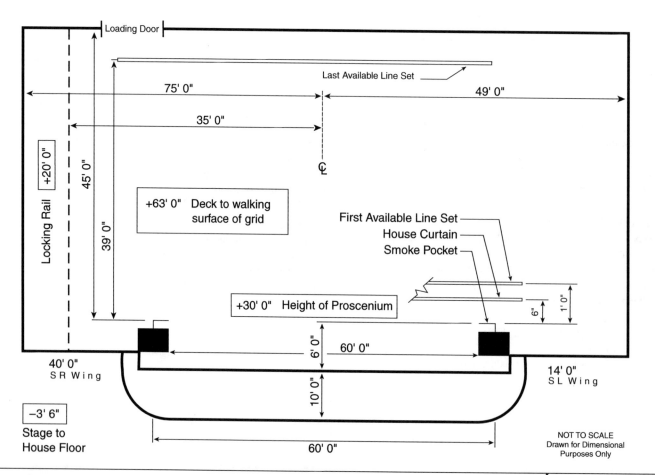

Loading Door

75' 0"

49' 0"

Last Available Line Set

35' 0"

45' 0"

+20' 0"

Locking Rail

39' 0"

+63' 0" Deck to walking surface of grid

First Available Line Set
House Curtain
Smoke Pocket

1' 0"
6"
6"

+30' 0" Height of Proscenium

6' 0"

60' 0"

40' 0"
S R Wing

14' 0"
S L Wing

10' 0"

−3' 6"
Stage to House Floor

60' 0"

NOT TO SCALE
Drawn for Dimensional Purposes Only

STAGE HOUSE

HOUSE CURTAIN

Operates as a guillotine from SR fly floor

Operates as a traveller from SR deck

RIGGING SYSTEM

Type:	Double purchase counter weight
Weight:	60,000 lbs available
Line sets:	56 sets at 6" o.c. with 7 lift lines per set
Arbors:	1,500 lb capacity
House Pipes:	72' long with 63' of travel from deck

Line sets are not moveable

Block & Falls are available

Chain hoists are not available

(25) spot wheels and 1,000' of hemp available

Electric pipes fly travel to 5'7"under grid

PERMANENT INSTALLATIONS OVER STAGE (FROM SMOKE POCKET)

M=Moveable with advance call

Orchestra shells (5) at 9'8", 12'6", 16'9", 230", 30'8"

Electric borders (6) at 1'9", 11'0", 16'0", 22'0", 29'0", 35'8"; M

Traveller (5) at 6'0", 10'0", 15'0", 20'0", 26'0"; M

Electric bridge (1) at 1'9"

Scoop bar (1) at 20'0"; M

Cyclorama (1) at 39'8" (white)

Fire curtain (1)

PERMANENT INSTALLATIONS ON DECK

Orchestra shell (1 set) 20'0" x 20'0" located SR storage area

Electric bridge (1) 2'0" x 65'0"

Loading bridge (1) 20'0" above SR floor

ORCHESTRA PIT

Adjustable to 12' below stage level by hydraulic lift

Apron overhangs US wall of pit 6'0"; Pit lift in (1) section

BACKSTAGE

LOADING DOCK

Loading door(s):
10'0" high x 10'0" wide

Trucks load (2) at same time

Best to load (1) truck at a time

Fork lift is not required

Sound/Props cannot load in FOH

(unlimited) Trailers can store on-site

Security at dock & stage door

WARDROBE

Location: Basement

Access: from SL via orchestra pit, or house elevator or ramp to basement

(1) Washer (1) Dryer

Washer and dryer hookups available

DRESSING ROOMS

(2) Star, SL, stage level, t/s included, phone jack

(2) Star, SL, stage level, t/s included

(2) Chorus, basement, t/s included

(7) Small, basement, t/s included

Elevator access for dressing rooms

Additional production office available for company mgr

SOUND

CONSOLE

Yamaha 3200, located Rear Console

32 inputs, 2 matrix outputs, 8 aux outputs

SPEAKERS

House Cluster

Proscenium

Under Balcony

No speaker truss

COMMUNICATIONS

Clear Com intercom with (2) channels

Infrared sound system

Dressing room page system

ROAD CONSOLE

Located Rear House

(5) seats required to be removed

Cable run from stage is 130'

Tie-in into house system with XLR connectors

REHEARSAL & STORAGE SPACE

Rehearsal: Green Room, 30' x 30' in basement; piano available

Storage: (4) areas
Basement 30' x 30';
Basement 15' x 30';
SL 10' x 45'; SR 25' x 45'

ELECTRICS

ROAD SERVICE POWER

Panel	Phase	Amp	Circuit Protection	Use	Location
A-B	3	600	fuse	dimmers	SR
C	3	100	breaker	sound	SL
D		100		extra	outside for bus

Recommended location of touring dimmer racks: SR

Hoist not required

Additional power is available for tour buses, generators, etc.

FRONT OF HOUSE (BOX BOOM VALUES ARE PER SIDE)

Position	Pipe Width	Distance to Prosc.	House Circuits	Connector Type	FOH Transfer Circuits
1st Cove		64'	15	grd 20 amp stage pin	15
2nd Cove		76'	24	grd 20 amp stage pin	24
Box Boom 1		64'	4	grd 20 amp stage pin	4

Transfer circuits: grd 20 amp stage pin

Road truss: Nothing can fly DS of proscenium opening

EQUIPMENT FOH (BOX BOOM VALUES ARE PER SIDE)

Position	Quantity	Wattage	Instrument	Removeable
1st Cove Rail	15	575	Kleigl Lekos	yes
2nd Cove Rail	21	1,000	Altman Lekos	yes
1st Box Boom	6	1,000	Kleigl Lekos	yes

FOLLOWSPOTS

House Followspots:
(2) Strong Super Trouper Xenon; removeable
(1) Strong Super Trouper Carbon; removeable

Followspot Booth:
(3) spots per booth;
135' throw to proscenium;
(6) 1Ø 30 amp breakers

DIMMERS

House has lighting console
(45) dimmers - no memory

ROSE STATE PERFORMING ARTS THEATER

YEAR BUILT: 1998 UNDER RENOVATION: 1999

Theatre Location: 6420 SE 15th Street, Midwest City, OK 73110

Main Administrative Phone: 405-297-2725
Main Administrative Fax: 405-297-3890

THEATRE STAFF
Facility Manager   James Brown   405-733-7964
Booking   Richard Charney   405-733-7963
Marketing   Kim Jones   405-391-3727
Operations   Larry Payne   405-733-7434

HOUSE CREW
Technical Director   Steve Estes   405-733-7970
Carpentry   Brent Winters   405-843-3028
Electrics   Heidi Hamilton   405-524-0309
Sound   John Crawford   405-690-6510

UNIONS
IATSE Local #112   Kevin McKinney   405-848-8140
Wardrobe Local #112   Gina Crawford   405-682-6283

SEATING CAPACITY
Orchestra	622
Mezzanine	314
Balcony	223
Upper Balcony	222
Boxes	24
Total:	**1,405**
pit (add'l)	20
wheelchair (incl.)	14

BOX OFFICE
Box Office Manager
  David Couser   405-297-3050

Outside Ticket Agency
None

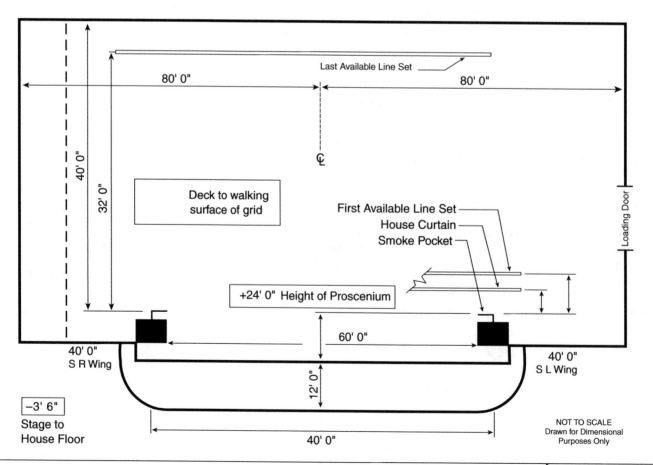

+24' 0" Height of Proscenium

Deck to walking surface of grid

First Available Line Set
House Curtain
Smoke Pocket

Last Available Line Set

−3' 6"
Stage to
House Floor

40' 0"
S R Wing

40' 0"
S L Wing

Loading Door

NOT TO SCALE
Drawn for Dimensional
Purposes Only

STAGE HOUSE

HOUSE CURTAIN
Operates as a guillotine from SR fly floor
Operates as a traveller from SR deck

RIGGING SYSTEM

Type:	Combination purchase counter weight system
Weight:	70,000 lbs available
Line sets:	25 sets at 9" o.c. with 7 lift lines per set
Arbors:	3,432 lb capacity
House Pipes:	65' long with 56' of travel from deck

Line sets are moveable
Block & Falls are not available
Chain hoists are not available
2,700' of hemp available

PERMANENT INSTALLATIONS OVER STAGE (FROM SMOKE POCKET)
M=Moveable with advance call
STAGE UNDER RENOVATION
Orchestra shell (3)
Electric raceway (4)
Traveller (2); M
Cyclorama (1) at 3'9"; M
A/C duct US

PERMANENT INSTALLATIONS ON DECK
Loading bridge (2)
Orchestra shell storage (9) 5'0" x 15'0" off SR
Bleachers (2) 36'0" x 8'0" (1) stored in each wing

ORCHESTRA PIT
Adjustable to 14'6" below stage level by hydraulic lift
Apron overhangs US wall of pit 10'0"
Pit lift is in (1) section

BACKSTAGE

LOADING DOCK
Loading door(s):
  11'3" high x 12'0" wide
Trucks load (2) at same time
Fork lift is not required
Sound/Props cannot load in FOH
Lobby cannot be a work area
Trailers can store on-site
Security at stage door

WARDROBE
Location: Behind stage
(1) Washer (1) Dryer
No washer or dryer hookups

DRESSING ROOMS
(2) Star, SR, +1, t/s included, phone jack
(2) Chorus, USL, stage level, t/s included
(2) Small, SL, stage level, t/s included
Elevator access for dressing rooms
Additional production office available for company mgr

SOUND

CONSOLE
Crest, located Sound Booth
24 inputs, 24 main outputs, 2 matrix outputs

SPEAKERS
House Cluster
Under Balcony
Speaker truss exists
Max available load 2,000 lbs
No pipe or rigging available

COMMUNICATIONS
Clear Com intercom with (6) channels
Dressing room page system

ROAD CONSOLE
Located Rear Orchestra left
Number of seats required to be removed varies
Cable run from stage is 130'
Tie-in into house system with XLR connectors

REHEARSAL & STORAGE SPACE
Rehearsal: Lecture Room - 20' x 40' SL, grand piano & upright piano
Storage: (3)
  Loading bay 70' x 12' USR;
  Lecture Rm 40' x 20' USR;
  40' x 40' USC

ELECTRICS

ROAD SERVICE POWER

Panel	Phase	Amp	Circuit Protection	Use	Location
A	3	400	fuse	dimmers	USR
B	3	200	fuse	sound	USR
C	3	800	fuse	extra	Electrics room

Recommended location of touring dimmer racks: SR
Hoist not required
Additional power is available for tour buses, generators, etc.

FRONT OF HOUSE (BOX BOOM VALUES ARE PER SIDE)

Position	Pipe Width	Distance to Prosc.	House Circuits	Connector Type	FOH Transfer Circuits
2nd Cove	65'	25'	30	grd 20 amp stage pin	0
Box Boom 1		25'	12	grd 20 amp stage pin	0
Box Boom 2		16'	18	grd 20 amp stage pin	0

Transfer circuits: FOH is DMX compatible and could patch into compatible console
Road truss: Trusses can hang anywhere from grid; FOH only from #1/ #2 Catwalk

EQUIPMENT FOH (BOX BOOM VALUES ARE PER SIDE)

Position	Quantity	Wattage	Instrument	Removeable
Box Boom 1 High	4		Lekos	
Box Boom 1 Low	8		Lekos	

FOLLOWSPOTS
House Followspots:
  (4) Xenon Super Troupers

Followspot Booth:
  UNDER RENOVATION

DIMMERS
House console is ETC;
  (191) ETC 2.4k dimmers
House has programmable DMX control system
(1) dry run DMX station(s) located Center Orchestra

CHAPMAN MUSIC HALL

AT: TULSA PERFORMING ARTS CENTER

YEAR BUILT: 1977   YEAR RENOVATED: 1998

Theatre Location: 110 East Second Street, Tulsa, OK 74103

Main Administrative Phone:	918-596-7122
Main Administrative Fax:	918-596-7144
Website:	www.tulsapac.com
Stage Door Phone:	918-596-7122
Backstage Pay Phone:	918-584-9309
Traveling Production Office Phone:	918-596-7125

THEATRE STAFF

Director	John E. Scott	918-596-7122
Marketing	Nancy Hermann	918-596-7122

HOUSE CREW

Technical Director	Warren Houtz	918-596-7122
Carpentry	Patrick Sharp	918-596-7122
Electrics	John Raney	918-596-7122
Sound	John Jack	918-596-7122

UNIONS

IATSE Local#354	Steve Brown	918-496-7722
Wardrobe Local #904	Marcia Holland	918-369-9041
Musical Contractor	Richard Cox	918-743-0515

SEATING CAPACITY

Orchestra	1,381
Mezzanine	618
Balcony	368
Total:	**2,367**
pit (add'l)	62
wheelchair (incl)	34

BOX OFFICE

Computerized
Manager
    Steven Fendt   918-596-7110

Outside Ticket Agency
Computerized
Carson Attractions
    Dena Dildine   918-584-2000

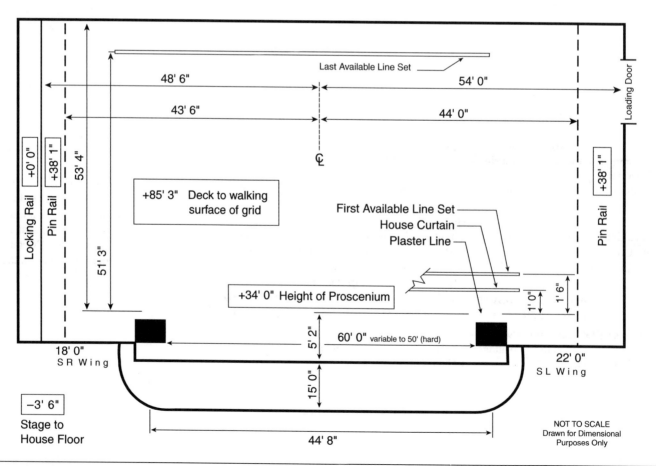

+85' 3" Deck to walking surface of grid

+34' 0" Height of Proscenium

Last Available Line Set

First Available Line Set
House Curtain
Plaster Line

48' 6"   54' 0"
43' 6"   44' 0"
53' 4"
51' 3"
+0' 0" Locking Rail
+38' 1" Pin Rail
+38' 1" Pin Rail
Loading Door
60' 0" variable to 50' (hard)
5' 2"
15' 0"
1' 0"   1' 6"
18' 0" SR Wing
22' 0" SL Wing
−3' 6" Stage to House Floor
44' 8"

NOT TO SCALE
Drawn for Dimensional
Purposes Only

STAGE HOUSE

HOUSE CURTAIN
Operates as a guillotine from SR deck

RIGGING SYSTEM

Type:	Single purchase counter weight
Weight:	24,000 lbs available
Line sets:	80 sets at 9" o.c. with 7 lift lines per set
Arbors:	1,500 lb capacity
House Pipes:	75' long with 83' of travel from deck

Line sets are not moveable
Block & Falls are available 2:1 (3); 3:2 (2)
Chain hoists available as a rental; (2) one ton
(38) spot wheels and 6,000' of hemp available

PERMANENT INSTALLATIONS OVER STAGE (FROM SMOKE POCKET)
Orchestra shells (4) at 5'3",15'9",25'10",36'1"
Movie screen (1) at 27'4"
Traveller (1) at 37'3"

PERMANENT INSTALLATIONS ON DECK
Traps (8) in stage floor at 4'0" x 8'0" located CS
Adjustable proscenium (1) at 50''-60' w x 24'-34'h

ORCHESTRA PIT
Adjustable to 11'6" below stage level by hydraulic lift
Apron overhangs US wall of pit 5'0"
Pit lift is in (1) section

BACKSTAGE

LOADING DOCK
Loading door(s):
  11'10" high x 12'2" wide
Trucks load (1) at a time
Dock is at truck level; loading
  to stage thru separate loading
  bay area
Security at stage door

WARDROBE
Location: Basement
Access: Freight elevator
(3) Washers (3) Dryers
No additional washer or dryer
  hookups

DRESSING ROOMS
(4) Star, SL -1, t/s
(5) Small, SL -1, t/s
(4) Chorus,SL , -1, t/s
Additional production office
  available for company mgr

SOUND

CONSOLE
Harrison Systems HM-5
32 inputs, 40 main outputs,
  4 aux outputs

SPEAKERS
House Cluster
Proscenium
No speaker truss

COMMUNICATIONS
Clear Com intercom with
  (2) channels
Infrared sound system
Dressing room page system

ROAD CONSOLE
Located Rear House
No seats required to be
  removed
Cable run from stage is 250'
Tie-in into house system with
  XLR connectors

REHEARSAL & STORAGE SPACE
Rehearsal:
  52' x 52' located 3 floors
  below stage, piano available, prior rental arrangement required
Storage: Various sizes &
  locations

ELECTRICS

ROAD SERVICE POWER

Panel	Phase	Amp	Circuit Protection	Use	Location
A	3	400	fuse	dimmers	DSL side wall
B	3	400	fuse	extra	DSL side wall
C	3	400	fuse	extra	DSL side wall
D	3	400	fuse	sound	USL loading bay

Additional 400 amps are available in adjacent theatre 240' from stage
Recommended location of touring dimmer racks: SL on deck

FRONT OF HOUSE (BOX BOOM VALUES ARE PER SIDE)

Position	Pipe Width	Distance to Prosc.	House Circuits	Connector Type	FOH Transfer Circuits
Bridge	65'	7'	40	grd 20 amp stage pin	40
1st Cove	75'	67'	35	grd 20 amp stage pin	35
2nd Cove	65'	90'	24	grd 20 amp stage pin	24
Balc Rail	58'	75'	36	grd 20 amp stage pin	36
Torm		10'	0		0
Box Boom 1		45'	8	grd 20 amp stage pin	8

Transfer circuits: grd 20 amp stage pin located on DSL side wall

EQUIPMENT FOH (BOX BOOM VALUES ARE PER SIDE)

Position	Quantity	Wattage	Instrument	Removeable
1st Cove	16	575	Source 4	yes
2nd Cove	24	575	Source 4	yes
Balc Rail	18	575	Source 4 10°	yes
Box Boom 1	18	575	Source 4	yes

FOLLOWSPOTS
House Followspots:
  (4) Xenon Strong Gladiator
  II; removeable

Followspot Booth:
  (4) spots per booth;
  135' throw to proscenium;
  (4) 1Ø 40 amp breakers

DIMMERS
Lighting console is Strand
  550i;
(783) Strand 2.4/6k
  dimmers
House has programmable
  DMX control system
Variable number of dry run
  DMX station(s)

HULT CENTER FOR THE PERFORMING ARTS

AKA: SILVA CONCERT HALL   **YEAR BUILT: 1982**

Theatre Location: One Eugene Center, Eugene, OR 97401

Main Administrative Phone: 541-682-5087
Main Administrative Fax: 541-682-5426
E-mail: rich.a.scheeland@ci.eugene.or.us
Website: www.ci.eugene.or.us./hult
Stage Door Phone: 541-682-5597
Backstage Pay Phone: 541-485-9691
Traveling Production Office Phone: 541-682-5184
Traveling Production Office Fax: 541-682-6840

THEATRE STAFF
Acting Co-Director   Richard Scheel   541-682-5087
Acting Co-Director   Laura Niles   541-682-5087
Booking   Erick Hoffman   541-682-8380
Marketing   Erick Hoffman   541-682-8380

HOUSE CREW
Stage Supervisor   Jerry Glenn   541-682-2747

UNIONS
IATSE Local #675   Pam Sherman   541-344-6306
Wardrobe Local #675 Pam Sherman   541-344-6306
Music AFM   Alan Tarpinian   541-484-0951

SEATING CAPACITY
Orchestra   1,283
Mezzanine   488
Boxes   66
Lower Balcony   346
Upper Balcony   244
Total: **2,427**

pit (add'l)   60
wheelchair (incl)

BOX OFFICE
Computerized
Box Office Manager
  Marcia James Gluz   541-682-2859

Outside Ticket Agency
  None

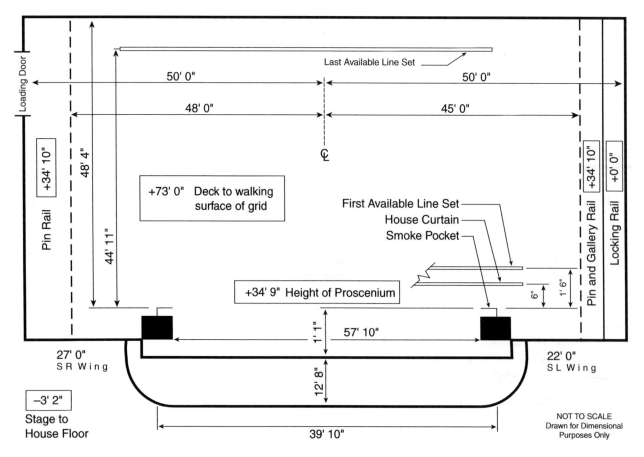

STAGE HOUSE

HOUSE CURTAIN
Operates as a guillotine from SR deck

RIGGING SYSTEM
Type:	Single purchase counter weight
Weight:	48,000 lbs available
Line sets:	84 sets at 6" o.c. with 6 lift lines per set
Arbors:	1,200 lb capacity
House Pipes:	63' long with 72' of travel from deck.

Line sets are not moveable
Block & Falls are not available
Chain hoists are available as rental; (4) one ton, (2) half ton
(8) spot wheels and 800' of hemp available

PERMANENT INSTALLATIONS OVER STAGE (FROM SMOKE POCKET)
M=Moveable with advance call
Orchestra shell (6) at 2'6", 6'0", 14'0", 23'0", 3'0", 40'6"; M
Electric raceways (1) at 3'6"
Traveller (2) at 9'6", 32'0"; M
Electric bridge (1) at 3'6"
Electric pipe (4) at 11'6", 19'6", 27'6", 35'6"; M
Strep light (5) at 5'6", 13'0", 21'6", 30'0", 39'6"; M
Dead spaces (8) at 3'0", 4'0", 11'0", 20'0", 27'0", 28'0", 35'0", 43'0"
Cyclorama (2) at 34'0", 44'6"; M
Fire curtain (1) at 0'6"

PERMANENT INSTALLATIONS ON DECK
Orchestra shell storage (1) off SR

ORCHESTRA PIT
Adjustable to 10' below stage level by hydraulic lift
Apron overhangs US wall of pit 12'0"
Pit lift is in (1) section

BACKSTAGE

LOADING DOCK
Loading door(s):
24'0" high x 12'0" wide
Trucks load (2) at same time
Fork lift is not required
Sound/Props cannot load in FOH
(2) Trailers can store on-site
Security at dock & stage door

WARDROBE
Location: By dressing rooms
Access: Freight elevator from dock
(1) Washer (2) Dryers
Washer and dryer hookups available

DRESSING ROOMS
(2) Star, SR, -1, t/s included, phone jack
(4) Small, SR, -1, t/s on same fl
(2) Chorus, SR, -1, t/s on same fl
Elevator access for dressing rooms
Additional production office available for company mgr

SOUND

CONSOLE
Yamaha 3500 FOH
40 inputs, 8 main outputs, 8 matrix outputs, 8 aux outputs

SPEAKERS
House Cluster
Proscenium
Monitor Wedge
No speaker truss
Max allowable load 1,200 lbs max, (1) point per side

COMMUNICATIONS
RTS intercom with (2) channels
Infrared sound system
Dressing room page system

ROAD CONSOLE
Located Center House
Cable run from stage is 150'
Tie-in into house system with XLR connectors

REHEARSAL & STORAGE SPACE
Rehearsal: Studio 1, 50' x 60' under lobby, prior arrangement required, piano, mirrors, barres
Storage: None

ELECTRICS

ROAD SERVICE POWER

Panel	Phase	Amp	Circuit Protection	Use	Location
A-C	3	400	fuse	dimmers	DSR
D	3	100	fuse	sound	USR
E	3	60	fuse	sound	USL

Recommended location of touring dimmer racks: SR
Hoist not required
Additional power is available for tour buses, generators, etc.

FRONT OF HOUSE (BOX BOOM VALUES ARE PER SIDE)

Position	Pipe Width	Distance to Prosc.	House Circuits	Connector Type	FOH Transfer Circuits
1st Cove	50'	48'	10	grd 20 amp stage pin	8
2nd Cove	60'	84'	2	grd 20 amp stage pin	0
Box Boom 1		8'	8		6

Transfer circuits: grd 20 amp stage pin
Road truss: Balcony Rail extremely limited; 6 units max; temporary position must be installed

EQUIPMENT FOH (BOX BOOM VALUES ARE PER SIDE)

Position	Quantity	Wattage	Instrument	Removeable
1st Cove	8	1,000	213 Series 10°	yes
2nd Cove	34	1,000	213 Series 5°	
Box Boom 1	8	575	Source 4 19°/ 26°	yes

FOLLOWSPOTS
House Followspots:
(4) Xenon Super Trouper

Followspot Booth:
(1) spot per booth;
140' throw to proscenium;
(4) 1Ø 20 amp breakers

DIMMERS
House has programmable DMX control system
(1) dry run DMX station

ARLENE SCHNITZER CONCERT HALL

AT: PORTLAND CENTER FOR THE PERFORMING ARTS   **YEAR BUILT: 1928   YEAR RENOVATED: 1984**

| Theatre Location: | 1037 SW Broadway, Portland, OR 97205 |
| Mailing Address: | 1111 SW Broadway, Portland, OR 97205 |

Main Administrative Phone:	503-248-4335
Main Administrative Fax:	503-274-7490
Stage Door Phone:	503-274-6563
Traveling Production Office Phone:	503-274-6569

THEATRE STAFF

Director	Harriet Sherburne	503-274-6565
Booking	Lori Leyba	503-274-6558
Operations	Don Scorby	503-274-6576
Events Services	Patricia Iron	503-274-6554

HOUSE CREW

Stage Supervisor	Steve Crick	503-796-6506

UNIONS

IATSE Local #28	John DiSciullo	503-295-2828
Wardrobe Local #28	John DiSciullo	503-295-2828

SEATING CAPACITY

Orchestra	1,504
Dress Circle	168
Mezzanine	384
Lower Balcony	364
Upper Balcony	356
Total:	**2,776**
pit (add'l)	32
wheelchair	12

BOX OFFICE

Computerized
| Peggy Shaeffer | 503-796-6513 |

Outside Ticket Agency
Computerized
Fastix / Ticketmaster
| Tom Keenan | 503-224-0368 |
| Tom Lasley | 503-243-4655 |

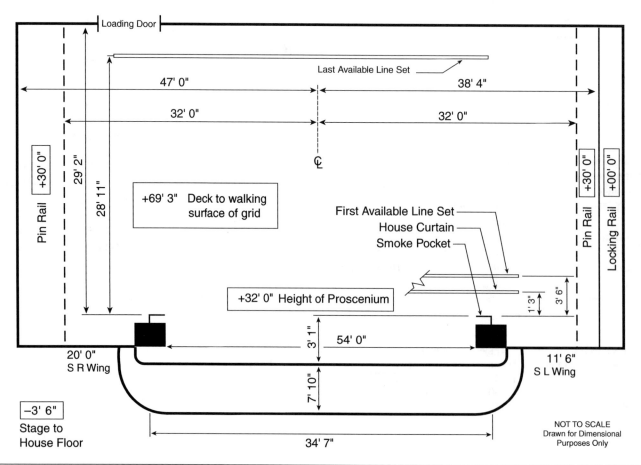

NOT TO SCALE
Drawn for Dimensional
Purposes Only

STAGE HOUSE

HOUSE CURTAIN
Operates as a guillotine or traveller from SL deck

RIGGING SYSTEM
Type:	Single purchase counter weight
Weight:	12,000 lbs available
Line sets:	30 sets with 7 lift lines per set
Arbors:	1,200 lb capacity
House Pipes:	61'0" long with 68'0" of travel from deck

Line sets are not moveable
Block & Falls are not available
Chain hoists are not available.
(42) spot wheels available

PERMANENT INSTALLATIONS OVER STAGE
M=Moveable with advance call
Orchestra shells (3) at 7'2", 16'4", 25'6"
Orchestra shell arms (3) at 6'0", 15'2", 24'4"
Electric Borders (3) at 4'7", 12'11", 22'7"; M
Electric Raceways (2) at 3'5", 11'11"
Movie screen (1) at 10'11"; M
Traveller (1) at 9'11"

PERMANENT INSTALLATIONS ON DECK
Orchestra shell storage (6) at 11'0" W x 4'0" D x 16'0" H, off SR

ORCHESTRA PIT
Adjustable to 8' below stage level by hydraulic lift
Apron overhangs US wall of pit 3'0"
Pit lift is in (1) section

BACKSTAGE

LOADING DOCK
Loading door(s):
  9'8" high x 8'0" wide
Trucks load (1) at a time
Dock comments: 6'0" x 11'0" H, street level loading door; inner ramp down 28" to stage
Fork lift is required
Sound/Props can load in FOH
Lobby cannot be a work area
Security at stage door

WARDROBE
Location: May use a dressing room; washer and dryer are across the street in another building
2 Washer(s) 2 Dryer(s)
No washer or dryer hookups available

DRESSING ROOMS
(2) Star, SL, stage level, t/s included
(7) Small, SL, +1/ +2/ +3/ +4, t/s
(2) Chorus, SL/SR, +1.5, t/s
Elevator access for dressing rooms
Additional production office available

SOUND

CONSOLE
Langley Recall, located Balcony Cockpit
40 inputs, 10 x 8 matrix outputs, 12 aux outputs

SPEAKERS
House Cluster
Under Balcony
14 Monitor cabinets, 2 Way
No speaker truss

COMMUNICATIONS
HME intercom with (4) channels
Infrared sound system
Dressing room page system

ROAD CONSOLE
Located Rear Orchestra
(13) seats required to be removed
Cable run from stage is 200'

REHEARSAL & STORAGE SPACE
Rehearsal: None
Storage: Loading Dock, 8'0" x 16'0", USR

ELECTRICS

ROAD SERVICE POWER
Panel	Phase	Amp	Circuit Protection	Use	Location
A	3	800	fuse	dimmers	SL or SR
B	3	250	fuse	sound	SR
C	3	50	fuse	sound	SR

Recommended location of touring dimmer racks: SL on deck
Hoist not required

FRONT OF HOUSE (ALL VALUES ARE PER SIDE)
Position	Pipe Width	Distance to Prosc.	House Circuits	Connector Type	FOH Transfer Circuits
Ceiling slot (2)	24'	115'	6	grd 20 amp stage pin	6
1st Balc Rail	60'	50'	12	grd 20 amp stage pin	12
Eye Lash (2)	24'	95'	6	grd 20 amp stage pin	6
Box Boom 1		65'	8	grd 20 amp stage pin	8
Box Boom 2		85'	8	grd 20 amp stage pin	8
Apron Cove (2)	24'	76'	6	grd 20 amp stage pin	6

Transfer circuits: grd 20 amp stage pin

EQUIPMENT FOH (ALL VALUES ARE PER SIDE)
Position	Quantity	Wattage	Instrument	Removeable
Ceiling slot	6	1,000	Strand 5°	no
1st Balc Rail	6	1,000	Strand 8 x 13	yes
Eye Lash	6	1,000	Altman 20°	no
Box Boom 1	12	1,000	Altman 20°	no
Box Boom 2	12	1,000	Altman 12°	no
Apron Cove	6	1,000	Altman 20°	no

FOLLOWSPOTS
House Followspots:
(2) Strong Xenon Super Trouper 1,600; removeable

Followspot Booth:
(4) spots per booth;
150' throw to proscenium;
(4) 1Ø 30 amp breakers

DIMMERS
Lighting console is ETC Obsession II 750;
(212) ETC Sensor dimmers
House has programmable DMX control system
(3) dry run DMX station(s)

PORTLAND CIVIC AUDITORIUM

AT: PORTLAND CENTER FOR THE PERFORMING ARTS

Theatre Location:	222 SW Clay Street, Portland, OR 97201	
Mailing Address:	1111 SW Broadway, Portland, OR 97205	

Main Administrative Phone:	503-248-4335
Main Administrative Fax:	503-274-7490
Stage Door Phone:	503-274-6562
Backstage Pay Phone:	503-227-8744
Traveling Production Office Phone:	503-274-6561

THEATRE STAFF

Manager	Harriet Sherburne	503-274-6565
Booking	Lori Leyba-Kramer	503-274-6558
Operations	Don Scorby	503-274-6576

HOUSE CREW

Stage Supervisor	Steve Crick	503-796-6506

UNIONS

IATSE Local #28	John DiSciullo	503-295-2828

SEATING CAPACITY

Orchestra	1,858
Boxes	188
First Balcony	425
Second Balcony	529
Total:	**3,000**
pit (add'l)	42

BOX OFFICE

Computerized	
Box Office Manager	
Peggy Shaeffer	503-796-6513
Outside Ticket Agency	
Computerized	
Fastix	503- 224-0368
Ticketmaster	503-243-4655

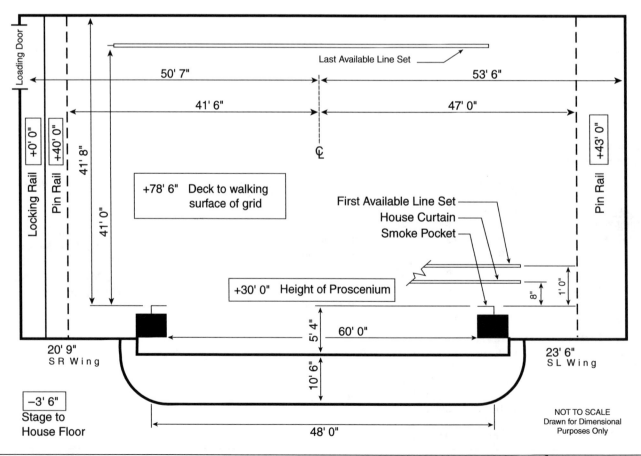

STAGE HOUSE

HOUSE CURTAIN
Operates as a guillotine or traveller from SR deck

RIGGING SYSTEM
Type:	Single purchase counter weight
Weight:	12,000 lbs available
Line sets:	76 sets at 6" o.c. with 6 lift lines per set
Arbors:	1,575 lb capacity
House Pipes:	74' long with 71' of travel from deck

Line sets are not moveable
Block & Falls are available 3:2 (2)
Chain hoists are not available
(90) spot wheels and 7,500' of hemp available

PERMANENT INSTALLATIONS OVER STAGE (FROM SMOKE POCKET)
None

PERMANENT INSTALLATIONS ON DECK
Ramp (1) into prop room located on SL side wall
Spiral staircase located in USR corner

ORCHESTRA PIT
Adjustable to 8' below stage level by hydraulic lift
Apron overhangs US wall of pit 8'0"
Pit lift is in (2) sections

BACKSTAGE

LOADING DOCK
Loading door(s):
10'0" high x 14'0" wide
Trucks load (2) side by side at same time
Dock is at truck level; load bars are suggested as truck access is sloped towards dock
Fork lift is not required
Sound/Props can load in FOH
Trailers cannot store on-site
Security at stage door

WARDROBE
Location: SR on 5th floor
Access: Direct from stage
(2) Washers (2) Dryers
Washer hookup available

DRESSING ROOMS
(2) Star, SR, stage level, t/s included, phone jack
(14) Small, SR, 2nd/ 3rd/ 4th/ 5th floors, t/s on same fl
(4) Chorus, SR, 2nd/ 3rd/ 4th/ 5th floors, t/s included
Additional production office available for company mgr

SOUND

CONSOLE
Yamaha PM 2000-32
32 inputs, 24 main outputs

SPEAKERS
House Cluster in proscenium
No speaker truss

COMMUNICATIONS
Chaos intercom with
(1) channel
Infrared sound system
Dressing room page system

ROAD CONSOLE
Located Center Orchestra
(16) seats required to be removed
Cable run from stage is 200'
Tie-in into house system with XLR connectors

REHEARSAL & STORAGE SPACE
Rehearsal: 38' x 45' located SL on 2nd fl; piano available
Storage: 30' x 30' located SL on stage level 18' x 80' located behind stage house

ELECTRICS

ROAD SERVICE POWER

Panel	Phase	Amp	Circuit Protection	Use	Location
A	3	600	fuse	dimmers	DSR on jump
B	3	800	fuse	dimmers	USR near lock rail
C	3	200	fuse	dimmers	DSL
D	3	100	fuse	sound	DSL in sound room
E	3	100	fuse	sound	DSL in sound room

Recommended location of touring dimmer racks: SR on deck
Hoist not required

FRONT OF HOUSE (BOX BOOM VALUES ARE PER SIDE)

Position	Pipe Width	Distance to Prosc.	House Circuits	Connector Type	FOH Transfer Circuits
1st Balc Rail	90'	90'	36	grd 20 amp stage pin	36
1st Cove Rail	16'	50'	15	grd 20 amp stage pin	15
2nd Cove Rail	18'	85'	18	grd 20 amp stage pin	18
Box Boom 1			8	grd 20 amp stage pin	8

Transfer circuits: grd 20 amp stage pin located in DSR dimmer room on jump

EQUIPMENT FOH (BOX BOOM VALUES ARE PER SIDE)

Position	Quantity	Wattage	Instrument	Removeable
1st Cove	18	1,000	6 x 16 Lekos	
2nd Cove	15	1,000	12° Lekos	

FOLLOWSPOTS
House Followspots:
(4) Lycian SuperArc 400 HTI; removeable

Followspot Booth:
(4) spots per booth;
165' throw to proscenium;
(8) 1Ø 30 amp breakers

DIMMERS
House console is Panache;
(53) Kliegel dimmers
House has programmable DMX control system
(1) dry run DMX station

STATE THEATRE CENTER FOR THE ARTS

YEAR BUILT: 1926   YEAR RENOVATED: 1990

Theatre Location: 453 Northampton Street, Easton, PA 18042

Main Administrative Phone:	610-258-7766
Main Administrative Fax:	610-258-2570
E-mail:	www.statetheatre.org
Website:	www.statetheatre.org
Stage Door Phone:	610-258-7766
Traveling Production Office Phone:	610-253-3880

THEATRE STAFF

Director, Operations	Glenn Gerchman	610-258-7766
Executive Director	Shelley Brown	610-258-7766

HOUSE CREW

Technical Director	Joe Livezey, Jr.	610-258-7766

SEATING CAPACITY

Boxes	16
Front Orchestra	544
Rear Orchestra	440
Loge	212
Balcony	288
Total:	**1,500**
pit (add'l)	0
wheelchair (add'l)	4-8
standing (add'l)	0

STAGE DIMENSIONS (FROM SMOKE POCKET)

Stage is 30'0" deep
Width from Center Line to SL is 34'0"
Width from Center Line to SR is 40'0"
Proscenium width is 48'0"
Proscenium height is 22'0"
Smoke pocket to apron edge is 3'0"
Orchestra pit exists

RIGGING

Grid Height:	50'
Type:	Double purchase counter weight
Weight:	10,000 lbs
Line sets:	27 sets at 10" o.c.
Arbors:	2,000 lb capacity
House Pipes:	53' long

LOADING DOCK

Loading door(s) are 8'0" high x 10'0" wide
Trucks load (1) at a time
Fork lift is not required and is not available

ELECTRICS

Total power available:
(1) 400A 3Ø DSR

FOLLOWSPOTS

House Followspots:
Color Arc 2000
Power in spot booth 20A

DIMMERS

(72) house dimmers
House has DMX control system
(1) dry run station(s) located
House Left Booth

SOUND

House has 400A dedicated
power located DSR
FOH mixing position in
Rear House Center
Sound console is available

WARNER THEATRE

AT: ERIE CIVIC CENTER COMPLEX   **YEAR BUILT: 1931**

Theatre Location: 811 State Street, Erie, PA 16501
Mailing Address: PO Box 6140, Erie, PA 16512-6140

Main Administrative Phone: 814-453-7117
Main Administrative Fax: 814-455-9931
E-mail: ecccasey@erie.net
Website: www.erieciviccenter.com

THEATRE STAFF
Managing Director   John "Casey" Wells   814-453-7117
Booking   John "Casey" Wells   814-453-7117
Marketing   Jennifer McKinney   814-453-7117
Operations   Barry Copple   814-453-7117
Group Sales   Jennifer McKinney   814-453-7117

HOUSE CREW
Stage Manager   Vinnie Marchant   814-456-1830

UNIONS
IATSE Local #113   Vinnie Marchant   814-456-1830
Music   Bill Fairgraves   814-454-0868

SEATING CAPACITY
Orchestra   1,782
Balcony   724
Total: **2,506**

BOX OFFICE
Computerized
Office Manager
  May Kavelman   814-453-7117

Outside Ticket Agency
Computerized
Ticketmaster
  Pat Lucas   412-323-1900

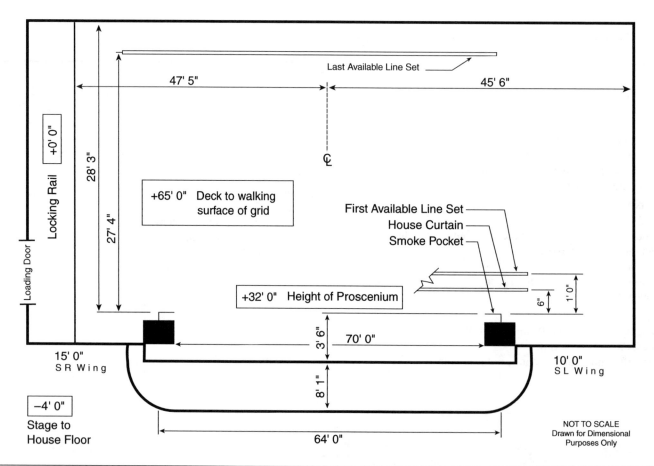

STAGE HOUSE

HOUSE CURTAIN
Operates as a guillotine from SR deck

RIGGING SYSTEM
Type:	Single purchase counter weight
Weight:	6,000 lbs available
Line sets:	32 sets at 3-6" o.c. with 5 lift lines per set
Arbors:	1,500 lb capacity
House Pipes:	60' long with 60' of travel from deck

Line sets are moveable
Block & Falls are available 3:2 (1)
400' of hemp available

PERMANENT INSTALLATIONS OVER STAGE (FROM SMOKE POCKET)
Orchestra shell (3) at 13'4", 21'4", 25'3"
Movie screen (1) at 10'8"
Electric bridge (1) at 6'8"

PERMANENT INSTALLATIONS ON DECK
Trap (1) 6'0" x 12'0" located USR
Pilasters (5) 1'8" wide x 0'6" deep located back wall

ORCHESTRA PIT
Nonadjustable at 4' below stage level
Apron overhangs US wall of pit 0'0"

BACKSTAGE

LOADING DOCK
Loading door(s):
    6'11" high x 4'8" wide
Trucks load (2) back to back at
    same time
Dock (loading door sill) is at
    street level
Fork lift is not required
Sound/Props can load in FOH
Lobby cannot be a work area
(10) Trailers can store on-site
Security at stage door

WARDROBE
Location: SR in Basement
Access: Trap in stage door USR
(1) Washer (1) Dryer

DRESSING ROOMS
(1) Star, SR, 2nd fl, t/s included
(9) Small, SR, +3 / +4 / +5, t/s
    included

SOUND

CONSOLE
No house console

SPEAKERS
Proscenium
No speaker truss

COMMUNICATIONS
David Clark intercom with
    (1) channel
FM system

ROAD CONSOLE
Located Rear House
(28) seats required to be
    removed
Cable run from stage is 100'
Tie-in into house system with
    XLR connectors

REHEARSAL & STORAGE SPACE
Rehearsal: 20' x 45' located
    in basement
Storage: None

ELECTRICS

ROAD SERVICE POWER

Panel	Phase	Amp	Circuit Protection	Use	Location
A	3	600	fuse	dimmers	DSR proscenium wall
B	3	200	fuse	extra	DSR proscenium wall
C	3	200	fuse	extra	DSR proscenium wall
D	3	100	fuse	sound	DSL proscneium wall

Recommended location of touring dimmer racks: SR on deck

FRONT OF HOUSE (BOX BOOM VALUES ARE PER SIDE)

Position	Pipe Width	Distance to Prosc.	House Circuits	Connector Type	FOH Transfer Circuits
1st Balc Rail	60'	75'	2	grd 20 amp stage pin	0
Box Boom 1		60'	3	grd 20 amp stage pin	0

EQUIPMENT FOH (BOX BOOM VALUES ARE PER SIDE)

Position	Quantity	Wattage	Instrument	Removeable
Box Boom 1	9	1,000	Lekos	yes

FOLLOWSPOTS
House Followspots:
    (2) HMI Satellite Long
    Throws; removeable

Followspot Booth:
    (3) spots per booth;
    125' throw to proscenium;
    (4) 1Ø 30 amp breakers

DIMMERS
No lighting console
No dimmers
No DMX control system

HERSHEY THEATRE

Theatre Location: East Caracas Avenue, Hershey, PA 17033
Mailing Address: PO Box 395, Hershey, PA 17033
Management Company: Hershey Educational & Cultural Center
                                PO Box 395, Hershey, PA 17033

Main Administrative Phone: 717-534-3411
Main Administrative Fax: 717-534-2350
Backstage Pay Phone: 717-534-9804

THEATRE STAFF
  Executive Director   Susan Fowler   717-534-3411
  Booking   Susan Fowler   717-534-3411
  Marketing   Diane Paul   717-534-3415
  Group Sales   Diane Paul   717-534-3415

HOUSE CREW
  Stage Manager   Marlin Urlich, Jr.   717-534-3418
  Sound   John Bosak   717-236-6000

UNIONS
  IATSE Local #98   Tim Staver   717-534-3895
  Musical Contractor   Ray Miller   717-534-2052

SEATING CAPACITY
  Orchestra   1,144
  Loge   122
  Balcony   638
  Total: **1,904**

BOX OFFICE
  Computerized
  Box Office Treasurer
    Millie Morris   717-534-3405

  Outside Ticket Agency
    None

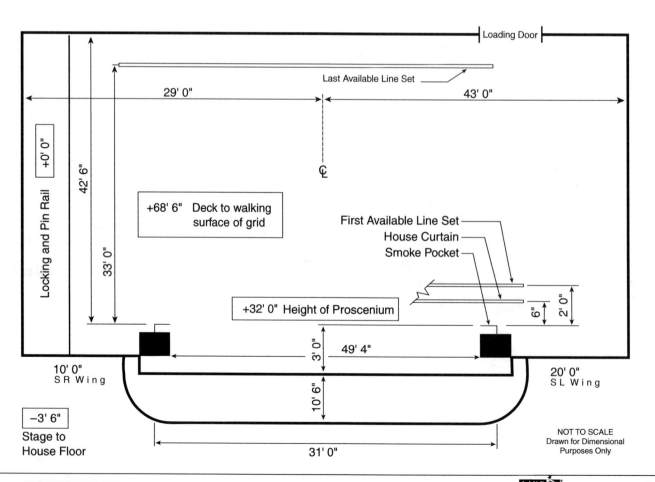

STAGE HOUSE

HOUSE CURTAIN
Operates as a traveler from SR deck; motorized

RIGGING SYSTEM
Type:	Single purchase counter weight
Weight:	11,000 lbs available
Line sets:	36 sets at 6" o.c. with 5 lift lines per set
Arbors:	790 lb capacity
House Pipes:	50' long with 64' of travel from deck

Line sets are not moveable
(50) spot wheels and 10,000' of hemp available

PERMANENT INSTALLATIONS OVER STAGE (FROM SMOKE POCKET)
Electric borders (5) at 6'0", 12'6", 19'6", 26'0", 32'0"
Movie screen (1) at 5'0"

PERMANENT INSTALLATIONS ON DECK
Lifts (3) in stage floor (1) 9'0" x 12'0" equipped with speaker tower; (2) 9'0" x 36'0" located CS

ORCHESTRA PIT
Adjustable to 10' below stage level by hydraulic lift
Pit has organ lift in SR corner

BACKSTAGE

LOADING DOCK
Loading door(s):
16'2" high x 11'0" wide
Trucks load (2) at a time; side by side
Dock (loading door sill) is at street level 4'0" above stage level; ramp down to stage is available
Fork lift is not required; Fork lift supplier: Hershey Park (717) 534-3895
Trailers can store (2) in back alley, (1) on street
Security at stage door

WARDROBE
Location: SR on stage level
Access: Direct from stage
(1) Washer (1) Dryer
No washer or dryer hookups

DRESSING ROOMS
(4) Star, SR, (1) stage level/ (3) 2nd fl, t/s included, phone jack
(8) Small, SR, (4) 3rd fl/ (4) 4th fl, t/s included, phone jack
(2) Chorus, (1) in basement, (1) on 5th fl, t/s included, phone jack
Elevator access for dressing rooms
Use dressing room for company mgr office

SOUND

CONSOLE
Yamaha PM 1800
24 inputs, 20 main outputs

SPEAKERS
House Cluster
Proscenium

COMMUNICATIONS
RTS intercom with (2) channels
Infrared sound system
Dressing room page system

ROAD CONSOLE
Located Rear House
No seats required to be removed
Cable run from stage is 100'
Tie-in into house system with XLR connectors

REHEARSAL & STORAGE SPACE
Rehearsal: None
Storage: 10' x 20' located USL on stage level

ELECTRICS

ROAD SERVICE POWER

Panel	Phase	Amp	Circuit Protection	Use	Location
A	3	400	fuse	dimmers	DSR in basement
B	3	200	fuse	extra	DSR in basement
C	1	400	fuse	extra	DSR in basement
D	1	400	fuse	sound	DSL in basement

Recommended location of touring dimmer racks: DSR in alcove
Hoist not required
Additional power is available for tour buses, generators, etc.

FRONT OF HOUSE (BOX BOOM VALUES ARE PER SIDE)

Position	Pipe Width	Distance to Prosc.	House Circuits	Connector Type	FOH Transfer Circuits
1st Balc Rail	50'	54'	48	grd 20 amp stage pin	48
Box Boom 1		30'	12	grd 20 amp stage pin	12
Box Boom 2		30'	12	grd 20 amp stage pin	12

Transfer circuits: grd 20 amp stage pin located DSR in basement

EQUIPMENT FOH (BOX BOOM VALUES ARE PER SIDE)

Position	Quantity	Wattage	Instrument	Removeable
1st Balc Rail	6	1,000	6 x 12	yes
1st Balc Rail	22	1,000	6 x 9	yes
Box Boom	24	1,000	30 Shakespeares	yes

FOLLOWSPOTS
House Followspots:
(3) Xenon Super Troupers; removeable

Followspot Booth:
(3) spots per booth;
130' throw to proscenium;
(5) 1Ø 20 amp breakers

DIMMERS
House console is TTI 2 scene;
(48) dimmers
House has programmable DMX control system
No dry run DMX

FISHER AUDITORIUM

AT: INDIANA UNIVERSITY OF PENNSYLVANIA

YEAR BUILT: 1938 **YEAR RENOVATED: 1987**

Theatre Location: 403 South Eleventh Street, Indiana, PA 15705
Management Company: Indiana University of Pennsylvania

Main Administrative Phone: 724-357-2548
Main Administrative Fax: 724-357-7899
E-mail: surtasky@grove.iup.edu
Website: www.iup.edu/fa/fisher.htmlx
Stage Door Phone: 724-357-1909

SEATING CAPACITY

Orchestra	1,118
Balcony	484
Total:	**1,602**
wheelchair (add'l)	2

THEATRE STAFF
Director CFA
   Public Events   Hank Knerr   724-357-2547
Asst. Director
   Student Activities   Frank DeStefano   724-357-2315
HOUSE CREW
Technical Director   David Surtasky   724-357-2548

STAGE DIMENSIONS (FROM SMOKE POCKET)
Stage is 39'0" deep
Width from Center Line to SL is 32'5"
Width from Center Line to SR is 42'0"
Proscenium width is 40'0"
Proscenium height is 22'0"
Smoke pocket to apron edge is 3'2"
Orchestra pit exists

RIGGING
Grid Height: 55'
Type: Single purchase counter weight
Weight: 8,000 lbs
Line sets: 30 sets at 12" o.c.
Arbors: 1,200 lb capacity
House Pipes: 52' long

LOADING DOCK
Loading door(s) are 10'0" high x 10'0" wide
Trucks load (1) at a time
Fork lift is not required and is not available

ELECTRICS
Total power available:
   (1) 600A 3Ø USC
   (1) 400A 3Ø DSR
FOLLOWSPOTS
House Followspots:
   (2) Ultra Arc II
No spot booth
DIMMERS
(186) house dimmers
No DMX control system

SOUND
No backstage power available
FOH mixing position in House Center
Sound console is available

ACADEMY OF MUSIC

YEAR BUILT: **1857**   YEAR RENOVATED: **1998**

Theatre Location: Broad & Locust Streets, Philadelphia, PA 19102

Main Administrative Phone: 215-893-1935
Main Administrative Fax: 215-893-1933
Stage Door Phone: 215-893-1938

THEATRE STAFF
  Manager   Hugh F. Walsh, Sr   215-893-1935
HOUSE CREW

                     James Gilroy   215-893-1947
                     Ralph Almadie   215-893-1943

SEATING CAPACITY
  Total: **2,835**

  wheelchair (add'l)   14

STAGE DIMENSIONS (FROM SMOKE POCKET)
  Stage is 70' deep
  Width from Center Line to SL is 45'
  Width from Center Line to SR is 45'
  Proscenium width is 48'
  Proscenium height is 30'
  Smoke pocket to apron edge is 6'3"
  Orchestra pit exists

RIGGING
  Data not provided

LOADING DOCK
  Data not provided

ELECTRICS
  Total power available: 3000A
    (4) panels 3Ø SL

FOLLOWSPOTS
  Power in spot booth 225A

DIMMERS
  (244) house dimmers
  House has DMX control system
  (3) dry run station(s) located
    SL/SR

SOUND
  Data not provided

ANNENBERG CENTER: ZELLERBACH THEATER

AT: UNIVERSITY OF PENNSYLVANIA, ANNENBERG CENTER FOR THE PERFORMING ARTS　　　**YEAR BUILT: 1970**　**YEAR RENOVATED: 1992**

Theatre Location:　　　3680 Walnut Street, Philadelphia , PA 19104

Main Administrative Phone:　　　215-898-6701
Main Administrative Fax:　　　215-898-7240
E-mail:　　　durkin@pobox.upenn.edu
Website:　　　http://www.libertynet.org/annctr
Stage Door Phone:　　　215-898-5359
Backstage Pay Phone:　　　215-222-9666
Traveling Production Office Phone:　　　215-898-6787

THEATRE STAFF
Managing Director　　Michael Rose　　215-898-5828
Booking　　Michael Rose　　215-898-5828
Marketing　　Judith Weiss　　215-898-6706
Group Sales　　Deborah Disbrow　　215-898-6683

HOUSE CREW
Technical Director　　Michael Durkin　　215-898-4953
Carpenter　　Jim Doherty　　215-898-5363
Electrician　　Joe Heppler　　215-898-5363
Sound　　Michael Durkin　　215-898-4953
Props　　Bill Hayes　　215-898-5363

UNIONS
IATSE #8　　Michael Barnes　　215-732-3316
Wardrobe #799　　John Davis　　215-546-4540

SEATING CAPACITY
Orchestra	710
Balcony	204
Total:	**914**

pit (add'l)　　56

BOX OFFICE
Computerized
Box Office Treasurer
　Catherine Borowyk　　215-898-5278

Outside Ticket Agency
None

Box office is promoter operated

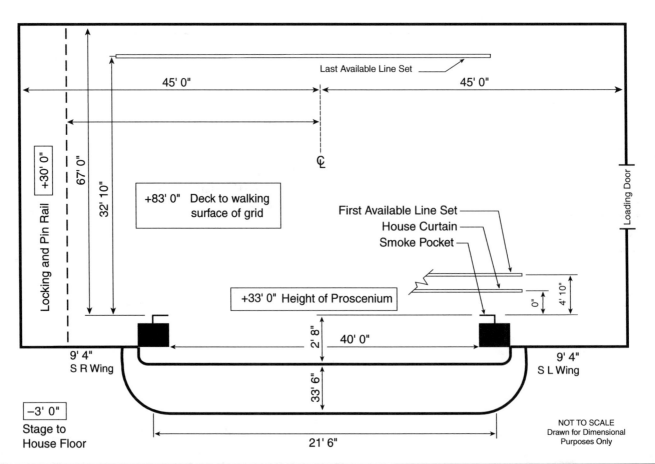

9' 4"
S R Wing

9' 4"
S L Wing

−3' 0"
Stage to
House Floor

+30' 0" Locking and Pin Rail

67' 0"

32' 10"

45' 0"

45' 0"

Last Available Line Set

+83' 0" Deck to walking surface of grid

First Available Line Set
House Curtain
Smoke Pocket

Loading Door

4' 10"

0"

+33' 0" Height of Proscenium

2' 8"

40' 0"

33' 6"

21' 6"

NOT TO SCALE
Drawn for Dimensional
Purposes Only

STAGE HOUSE

HOUSE CURTAIN
Operates as a guillotine from SR deck

RIGGING SYSTEM
Type:	Single purchase counter weight; Hemp System
Weight:	10,000 lbs available
Line sets:	46 sets at 7" o.c. with 7 lift lines per set
Arbors:	1,700 lb capacity
House Pipes:	60' long with 80' of travel from deck

Line sets are not moveable
Block & Falls are available
Chain hoists are not available
(40) spot wheels and 1,000' of hemp available

PERMANENT INSTALLATIONS OVER STAGE (FROM SMOKE POCKET)

Orchestra shells (12) portable
Electric Raceways (5) at 3'8", 10'1", 17'3", 22'2", 29'1"
Movie screen (1) at 12'5"
Electric pipes (6) at 3'8", 10'1", 17'3", 22'2", 29'1"
Hard portal (1) at 2'0" header, 2'9" legs
Cyclorama (1) at 32'1"
Fire curtain (1) at 0'0"

PERMANENT INSTALLATIONS ON DECK
Traps (25) 4'W x 8L
Hard Legs (1 set) 8'W x 35'H
Spiral stairs (1) 4'dia. x 80'h; 24'0" USR

ORCHESTRA PIT
Adjustable by hydraulic lift
Apron overhangs US wall of pit 0'0"
Pit lift is in (2) sections

BACKSTAGE

LOADING DOCK
Loading door(s):
(2) 27'0" high x 10'0" wide
Trucks load (1) at a time
Requires freight elevator to stage level, elevator: 7'6"w x 24' long x 12'h
Fork lift is not equired
Sound/Props can load in FOH
Lobby cannot be a work area
(2) Trailers can store on-site
Security can be arranged

WARDROBE
Location: Backstage in dressing room corridor
Access: Freight elevator/lobby elevator
(1) Washer (1) Dryer
Washer and dryer hookups available

DRESSING ROOMS
(4) Small, SL, stage level, t/s
(4) Chorus, SR, stage level, t/s
Elevator access for dressing rooms
Additional production office available for company mgr

SOUND

CONSOLE
Mackie 2408, located Rear House
24 inputs, 2 main outputs, 2 aux outs

SPEAKERS
House cluster
Proscenium
Portable
No speaker truss

COMMUNICATIONS
Clear Com intercom with (2) channels
Infrared sound system
Dressing room page system

ROAD CONSOLE
Located Rear House
13 seats required to be removed
Cable run from stage is 120'
Tie-in into house system with XLR connectors

REHEARSAL & STORAGE SPACE
Rehearsal:
28' x 18', stage level;
40' x 36', stage level;
40'x 40', +3 above stage,
Storage:
Scene dock, 55' x 35'
Shop area, 25' x 32'

ELECTRICS

ROAD SERVICE POWER

Panel	Phase	Amp	Circuit Protection	Use	Location
A-B	3	600	fuse	dimmers	USR
C	3	100	fuse	sound	DSL

Recommended location of touring dimmer racks: USR
Hoist not required
Additional power is available for tour buses, generators, etc.

FRONT OF HOUSE (BOX BOOM VALUES ARE PER SIDE)

Position	Pipe Width	Distance to Prosc.	House Circuits	Connector Type	FOH Transfer Circuits
2nd Cove		24'	14	grd 20 amp stage pin	
3rd Cove		38	24	grd 20 amp stage pin	
4th Cove		52'	38	grd 20 amp stage pin	
Box Boom 1		32'	16	grd 20 amp stage pin	
Balc Rail		30'	12	grd 20 amp stage pin	

Road truss: Rigging points available throughout; grid working height: +83'

EQUIPMENT FOH (BOX BOOM VALUES ARE PER SIDE)

Position	Quantity	Wattage	Instrument	Removeable
1st Balc Rail	14	1,000	8 x 9 Lekos	no
2nd Cove	12	1,000	10 x 12 Lekos	no
3rd Cove	24	1,000	10 x 12 Lekos	no
4th Cove	28	1,000	10 x 12 Lekos	no
Box Boom 1	8	1,000	10 x 12 Lekos	no

FOLLOWSPOTS
House Followspots:
(2) Ultra Arc; not removeable

Followspot Booth:
(None) spots per booth; throw to proscenium;
() Ø amp breakers

DIMMERS
Lighting console is Obsession II;
(192) Dual CD80 dimmers
House has programmable DMX control system
(1) dry run DMX station(s) located DSR proscenium wall

FORREST THEATRE

YEAR BUILT: 1928   YEAR RENOVATED: 1997

Theatre Location: 1114 Walnut Street, Philadelphia, PA 19107
Management Company: The Shubert Organization, Inc.
                          234 West 44th Street, New York NY 10036

Main Administrative Phone: 215-923-1515
Main Administrative Fax: 215-440-9223
Stage Door Phone: 215-627-8548

THEATRE STAFF
Manager	Mark Schweppe	215-923-1515
Booking Agent	Peter Entin	212-944-3700
Group Sales	Keith Bennett	215-923-1515

HOUSE CREW
Carpentry	John T. Callahan	215-923-1515
Electrics	Timothy Quigley	215-923-1515
Props	Frank Grandizio	215-923-1515

UNIONS
IATSE Local #8	Michael Barnes	215-732-3316
Wardrobe	John Davis	215-546-4540
Music	Joseph Ciccimaro	215-924-4056

SEATING CAPACITY
Orchestra	924
Boxes	16
Mezzanine	260
Balcony	639
Total:	**1,839**

pit (add'l)	16

BOX OFFICE
Computerized
Box Office Treasurer
   Regina Finnean   215-923-1515

Outside Ticket Agency
Computerized
Tele-Charge

                          800-447-7400

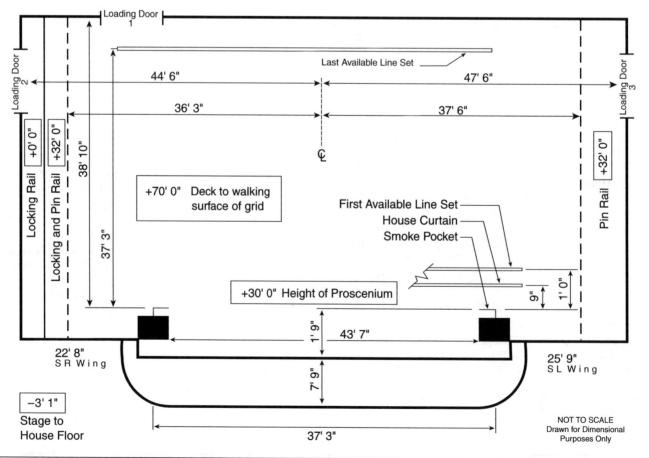

STAGE HOUSE

HOUSE CURTAIN
Operates as a guillotine from SR deck

RIGGING SYSTEM

Type:	Single purchase counter weight
Weight:	30,000 lbs available
Line sets:	77 sets at 6" o.c. with 4 lift lines per set
Arbors:	800 lb capacity
House Pipes:	48' long with 68' of travel from deck

Line sets are moveable
Block & Falls are available 2:1 (3); 3:2 (1)
(150) spot wheels and 15,000' of hemp available

PERMANENT INSTALLATIONS OVER STAGE (FROM SMOKE POCKET)
None

PERMANENT INSTALLATIONS ON DECK
Pilasters (3) 1'6" square against back wall
Traps in stage floor are on a sectional grid

ORCHESTRA PIT
Nonadjustable at 8' below stage level
Apron overhangs US wall of pit 5'0"

BACKSTAGE

LOADING DOCK
Loading door(s):
  1) 10' 0" high x 10'0" wide
  2) 8'7" high x 9'5" wide
  3) 8'0" high x 7'9" wide
Trucks load (3) at same time at
  separate docks
Docks, loading door sills,
  (3) are at street level; Door 3
  is 30" above stage level
  accessed by an alley; ramps
  down to stage are available

WARDROBE
Location: Separate building on
  2nd floor (see below)
Access: Elevator
(2) Washers (3) Dryers

DRESSING ROOMS
(1) Star, 1st fl, toilet included
(8) Small, 2nd & 3rd fls,
  toilet included, shower on
  same fl
(2) Chorus, 2nd & 3rd floors, t/s
  on same fl
Dressing rooms are located in a
  separate building behind stage
  accessed by an underground
  tunnel

SOUND

CONSOLE
No house console

SPEAKERS
Under Balcony
Speaker truss exists
Max allowable load 1,200 lbs

COMMUNICATIONS
No house intercom system
Infrared sound system
Dressing room page system

ROAD CONSOLE
Located Rear House
(13) seats required to be
  removed
Cable run from stage is 150'
Tie-in into house system with
  XLR connectors

REHEARSAL & STORAGE SPACE
Rehearsal: Large carpeted
  lounge; piano available
Storage: None

ELECTRICS

ROAD SERVICE POWER

Panel	Phase	Amp	Circuit Protection	Use	Location
A - F	3	400	breaker	dimmers	SL on jump
G	3	150	breaker	deck	SL side wall
H	3	150	breaker	deck	USR back wall
I	3	150	breaker	extra	DSR on jump
J	3	150	breaker	extra	DSL proscenium wall
K	3	100	breaker	sound	DSL on jump

Recommended location of touring dimmer racks: SL on jump
Hoist is required; house owns
Additional power is available for tour buses, generators, etc.

FRONT OF HOUSE (BOX BOOM VALUES ARE PER SIDE)

Position	Pipe Width	Distance to Prosc.	House Circuits	Connector Type	FOH Transfer Circuits
1st Balc Rail	58'	32'	48	grd 20 amp stage pin	48
Box Boom 1		20'	24	grd 20 amp stage pin	24
Box Boom 2		30'	24	grd 20 amp stage pin	24

Transfer circuits: grd 20 amp stage pin located SL on jump
Road truss: Holes in ceiling over house provide truss hanging position; pipe and rigging
  available

EQUIPMENT FOH (BOX BOOM VALUES ARE PER SIDE)
None

FOLLOWSPOTS
House Followspots:
  (3) Xenon Gladiator II

Followspot Booth:
  (3) spots per booth;
  90' throw to proscenium;
  3Ø 30 amp breakers

DIMMERS
No lighting console
No dimmers

MERRIAM THEATER

FORMERLY: THE SHUBERT THEATRE

YEAR BUILT: 1918 YEAR RENOVATED: 1994

Theatre Location: 250 S. Broad Street, Philadelphia, PA 19102
Management Company: Theatre League of Philadelphia

Main Administrative Phone: 215-732-5997
Main Administrative Fax: 215-732-1396

THEATRE STAFF
General Manager   DeVida Jenkins   215-732-5997
President/Booking   Sam L'Hommedieu   703-824-1525
Marketing   Kristina Lindsay   215-732-5997
Group Sales   Jim Weiner   215-732-1366

HOUSE CREW
Carpentry   Anthony Tortorice   215-735-1567
Electrics   Ken Pattinson
Sound   Michael Giaquinto
Props   Don Ogle

UNIONS
IATSE Local #8   Michael Barnes   215-732-3316
Wardrobe Local #799   John Davis   215-546-4540

SEATING CAPACITY
Orchestra   882
Balcony / Boxes   604
Family Circle / Boxes 304
Total: **1,790**

pit (add'l)   80

BOX OFFICE
Computerized
Treasurer
  Albert DeCola   215-732-6452

Outside Ticket Agency
None

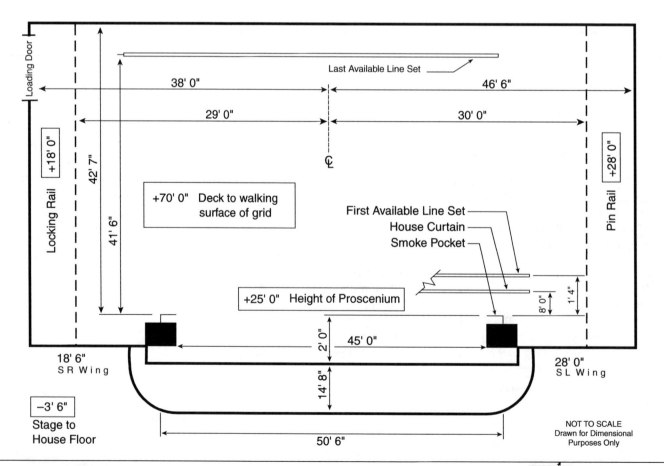

Locking Rail +18' 0"

Loading Door

Last Available Line Set

38' 0"   46' 6"

29' 0"   30' 0"

42' 7"

CL

+70' 0"   Deck to walking surface of grid

41' 6"

First Available Line Set
House Curtain
Smoke Pocket

Pin Rail +28' 0"

+25' 0"   Height of Proscenium

1' 4"
8' 0"

2' 0"

45' 0"

18' 6"
SR Wing

28' 0"
SL Wing

14' 8"

−3' 6"
Stage to
House Floor

50' 6"

NOT TO SCALE
Drawn for Dimensional
Purposes Only

STAGE HOUSE

HOUSE CURTAIN
Operates as a guillotine from SL deck

RIGGING SYSTEM

Type:	Single purchase counter weight
Weight:	60,000 lbs available
Line sets:	66 sets at 8" o.c. with lift lines as needed
Arbors:	800 lb capacity
House Pipes:	55' long with 65' of travel from deck.

Line sets are moveable
Block & Falls are available
Chain hoists are available as a rental; (4) one ton
(50) spot wheels and hemp available as needed

PERMANENT INSTALLATIONS OVER STAGE (FROM SMOKE POCKET)
M=Moveable with advance call
Orchestra shell (1) at 35' x 40'; M
Movie screen (1) at 20' x 20'; M
Traveller (1); M
Electric pipe at 6'; M
Cyclorama (1) as needed ; M
Fire curtain (1)
Fly SL for spot lines only (electric) 41'6" from center, 3'6" from smoke pocket; M

PERMANENT INSTALLATIONS ON DECK
Trap (42) in stage floor 4' x 4"
Stairs (2) 3 step ; M
Orchestra shell storage (1) 20' x 30', stored in old dressing rooms
Loading bridge (1) 8' x 38'

ORCHESTRA PIT
Adjustable to 6'6" below stage level by
Apron overhangs US wall of pit 6' 0"
Pit lift is SL in 24 sections; also Piano lift

BACKSTAGE

LOADING DOCK
Loading door(s):
  8'0" high x 8' 0" wide
Trucks load (2) at a time; back to back
Loading dock is street level, ramp down from truck
Sound/Props can load in FOH
Lobby can be a work area
Security at dock & stage door

WARDROBE
Location: Basement through trap in stage floor USL
Access: 1 - ton hoist to basement
(2) Washers (2) Dryers
Washer and dryer hookups available

DRESSING ROOMS
(2) Star, SR, stage level, t/s on same fl, phone jack
(1) Star, SR, +1, t/s on same fl, phone jack
(2) Small, SR, +1, t/s on same fl, phone jack
(2) Chorus, SR, +1, t/s on same fl, phone jack
Use dressing room for company manager office

SOUND

CONSOLE
Yamaha 24 Channel Mixer, located FOH
24 inputs

SPEAKERS
House Cluster
Proscenium
Portable
Speaker truss
Max allowable load 1,200 lbs

COMMUNICATIONS
Clear Com intercom with (2) channels
Dressing room page system

ROAD CONSOLE
Located Rear Orchestra
No seats required to be removed
Cable run from stage is 150'
Tie-in into house system with XLR connectors

REHEARSAL & STORAGE SPACE
Rehearsal: None
Storage: None

ELECTRICS

ROAD SERVICE POWER

Panel	Phase	Amp	Circuit Protection	Use	Location
A-B	3	1200	fuse	dimmers	SL
C	3	1200	fuse	dimmers	basement
D	3	100	breaker	sound	SL
E	3	100	fuse	sound	SR
F	3	100	breaker	extra	basement

Recommended location of touring dimmer racks: SL
Hoist not required
Additional power is available for tour buses, generators, etc.

FRONT OF HOUSE (BOX BOOM VALUES ARE PER SIDE)

Position	Pipe Width	Distance to Prosc.	House Circuits	Connector Type	FOH Transfer Circuits
1st Balc Rail	40'	47'	24	grd 20 amp stage pin	24
2nd Balc Rail	25'	65'	12	grd 20 amp stage pin	12
Box Boom 1	18'	26'	6	grd 20 amp stage pin	6

Transfer circuits: FOH 60 circuits DSL, grd 20 amp stage pin
Road truss: FOH for sound

EQUIPMENT FOH (BOX BOOM VALUES ARE PER SIDE)

Position	Quantity	Wattage	Instrument	Removeable
1st Balc Rail	12	1,000	6 par MFC / 11-20 Altman	yes
2nd Balc Rail	17	1,000	6 par MFC / 11-20 Altman	yes
Box Boom 1	12	1,000	30° Altman	yes

FOLLOWSPOTS
House Followspots:
  (3) Super Trouper; removeable
Followspot Booth:
  (4) spots per booth;
  150' throw to proscenium;
  (3) 3Ø amp breakers

DIMMERS
House console is Strand Pro Pallette; (288) LMI 2.4 dimmers
House has programmable DMX control system
(1) dry run DMX station(s)

WALNUT STREET THEATRE

YEAR BUILT: 1809   YEAR RENOVATED: 1969

Theatre Location: 825 Walnut Street, Philadelphia, PA 19107

Main Administrative Phone:	215-574-3550
Main Administrative Fax:	215-574-3598
E-mail:	wstmark@aol.com
Backstage Pay Phone:	215-627-9932
Traveling Production Office Phone:	215-574-3550 x577
Traveling Production Office Fax:	215-574-3598

SEATING CAPACITY

Orchestra	558
Mezzanine	510
VIP Booth	10
Total:	**1,078**
pit (add'l)	29
wheelchair (add'l)	12
standing (add'l)	0

THEATRE STAFF

General Manager	Mark D. Sylvester	215-574-3550
Booking	Mark D. Sylvester	215-574-3550

HOUSE CREW

Production Manager	Joseph Levy	215-574-3550 x574
Carpentry	Ed Neff	215-574-3550 x564
Electrics	Tom Douglass	215-574-3550 x561
Sound	Scott Smith	215-574-3550 x572
Props	Chuck Scott	215-574-3550 x564

STAGE DIMENSIONS (FROM SMOKE POCKET)

Stage is 41' deep
Width from Center Line to SL is 31'
Width from Center Line to SR is 31'
Proscenium width is 38'
Proscenium height is 24'
Smoke pocket to apron edge is 2'
Orchestra pit exists

RIGGING

Grid Height:	66'
Type:	Hemp System
Weight:	13,500 lbs
Line sets:	50 sets at 8" o.c. with 4 or 5 lift lines per set; moveable
House Pipes:	42' long with 48' & 64' of travel from deck

LOADING DOCK

Loading door(s) are 12'0" high x 8'0" wide
Trucks load (2) at same time
Fork lift is not required and is not available

ELECTRICS

Total power available:
800A 3Ø DSL side wall

FOLLOWSPOTS

House Followspots:
(2) Xenon Colortran Colorarc 2000
No power in spot booth
FOH transfer circuits per position: 24

DIMMERS

(153) house dimmers
House has DMX control system
No dry run station(s)

SOUND

House has 100A located DSL side wall
FOH mixing position in Mezzanine HR
Sound console is available, Crest

BENEDUM CENTER

YEAR BUILT: 1928   YEAR RENOVATED: 1987

Theatre Location: 719 Liberty Avenue, Pittsburgh, PA 15222

Main Administrative Phone:	412-456-2600
Main Administrative Fax:	412-456-2645
Website:	www.pgharts.org
Stage Door Phone:	412-456-2610
Backstage Pay Phone:	412-566-8373
Traveling Production Office Phone:	412-456-2625/7/8
Traveling Production Office Fax:	412-456-1385

THEATRE STAFF

Manager	Gene Ciavarra	412-456-2602
Booking	Gene Ciavarra	412-456-2602

HOUSE CREW

Technical Director	Berne Bloom	412-456-2635
Carpentry	Ken Brannigan Jr.	412-456-2600
Electrics	Will Dennis	412-456-2600
Sound	Chris Evans	412-456-2600

UNIONS

IATSE Local #3	Robert Brown	412-281-4568
Musical Contractor	Frank Ostrowski	412-885-1660

SEATING CAPACITY

Orchestra	1,264
Orchestra Pit	117
Director's Circle	300
First Tier	574
Second Tier	634
Total:	**2,889**

BOX OFFICE
Computerized
Ticket Sales Manager
  Al Rodibaugh   412-456-2693

Outside Ticket Agency
Computerized
Ticketmaster
  Al Rodibaugh   412-456-2693

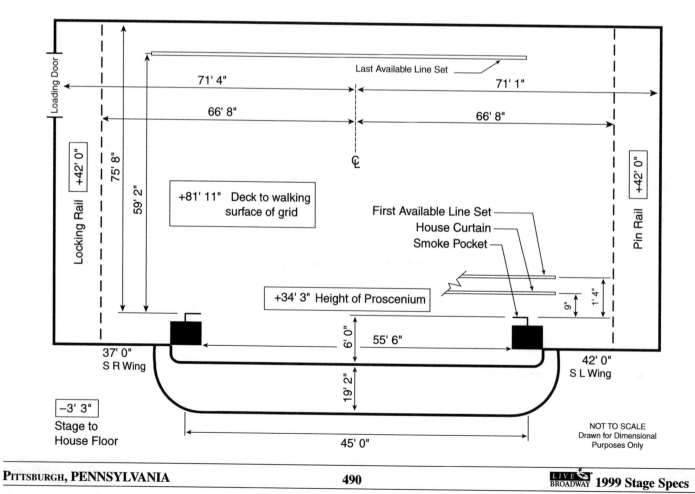

STAGE HOUSE

HOUSE CURTAIN
Operates as a traveller from SR deck; motorized

RIGGING SYSTEM
Type:	Single purchase counter weight; motorized
Weight:	85,500 lbs available
Line sets:	95 sets at 6" o.c. with 7 lift lines per set
Arbors:	2,000 lb capacity
House Pipes:	70' long with 71' of travel from deck

Line sets are moveable
Block & Falls are available 3:2 (1)
Chain hoists available; (4) one ton
(50) spot wheels and 5,000' of hemp available

PERMANENT INSTALLATIONS OVER STAGE (FROM SMOKE POCKET)
None

PERMANENT INSTALLATIONS ON DECK
Traps in stage floor are on a sectional grid and must be cut and restored

ORCHESTRA PIT
Adjustable to 9' below stage level by hydromechanical lift
Apron overhangs US wall of pit 5'0"
Pit lift is in (2) sections

BACKSTAGE

LOADING DOCK
Loading door(s):
1) 13'0" high x 7'4" wide
2) 10'0" high x 6'10" wide
Trucks load (2) at same time
Dock (1) loading door sill is ½" above street level; equipment is pushed from dock into 10' x 20' lift and lowered 5'6" down to stage level
Dock (2) sill is at street level 4'0" above stage level; ramp down to stage available; requires permit and/or police assistance
Trailers cannot store on-site
Security at stage door

WARDROBE
Location: Basement
Access: Freight Elevator
(2) Washers (3) Dryers
Washer and dryer hookups available

DRESSING ROOMS
(1) Star, SL, stage level, t/s included, phone jack
(12) Small, SL, stage level, t/s
(4) Chorus, SL, +2, -2, t/s
Elevator access for dressing rooms
Additional production office available for company mgr

SOUND

CONSOLE
Midas XL4, located House
48 inputs, 24 matrix outputs

SPEAKERS
House Cluster
Proscenium
Under Balcony
Portable
Speaker rigging points DS
Max available load 3,500 lbs

COMMUNICATIONS
Clear Com intercom with
(8) channels
Infrared sound system
Dressing room page system

ROAD CONSOLE
Located Rear House
Seats required to be removed, 3 rows deep, by 4' increments, center orchestra and rear
Cable run from stage is 250'
Tie-in into house system with XLR connectors

REHEARSAL & STORAGE SPACE
Rehearsal: (2) Studios, 59' x 56', 2nd/ 4th fl, prior arrangement required, fee for equipment
Storage: Very limited

ELECTRICS

ROAD SERVICE POWER

Panel	Phase	Amp	Circuit Protection	Use	Location
A-C	3	400	fuse	dimmers	SL Fly floor
D	3	100	fuse	sound	DSL
E	3	200	fuse	sound	DSL
F	3	200	fuse	winches	USR

Recommended location of touring dimmer racks: SL Fly floor or DSL with feeder cable
Hoist not required

FRONT OF HOUSE (BOX BOOM VALUES ARE PER SIDE)

Position	Pipe Width	Distance to Prosc.	House Circuits	Connector Type	FOH Transfer Circuits
1st Cove		160'	40	grd 20 amp stage pin	40
Balc Rail		50'	24	grd 20 amp stage pin	24
Box Boom 1		70'	18	grd 20 amp stage pin	18

Transfer circuits:Dimmers 1-175 @ transfer on SL Fly or DMX to D192 Colortran rack

EQUIPMENT FOH (BOX BOOM VALUES ARE PER SIDE)

Position	Quantity	Wattage	Instrument	Removeable
Balc Rail	24	575	ETC Zoom	yes
1st Cove	32	1,000	Colortran 5°	yes
Box Boom 1	18	1,000	Colortran 10°	yes

FOLLOWSPOTS
House Followspots:
(4) Xenon Super Troupers 2k; removeable

Followspot Booth:
(4) spots per booth;
162' throw to proscenium;
(4) 3Ø 30 amp breakers

DIMMERS
Lighting console is Obsession 1500;
(566) Colortran D192 dimmers
House has non-programmable DMX control system
(1) dry run DMX station(s), DSL and SL fly floor at transfer

BYHAM THEATER

FORMERLY: FULTON THEATRE AT: PITTSBURGH CULTURAL TRUST   **YEAR BUILT: 1903 RENOVATION ONGOING**

Theatre Location: 101 Sixth Street, Pittsburgh, PA 15222
Mailing Address: 125 Seventh Street, Suite 500
                         Pittsburgh, PA 15222
Management Company: Pittsburgh Cultural Trust
                         (mailing address as above)

Main Administrative Phone: 412-456-1350
Main Administrative Fax: 412-456-1365
Website: www.pgharts.org
Stage Door Phone: 412-456-1353

THEATRE STAFF
Theater Manager   David Nash   412-456-1376
Booking   Brenda Thompson   412-471-6070 x133
Marketing   Barry Colfelt   412-471-6070
Operations   David Nash   412-456-1376
Group Sales   Barry Colfelt   412-471-6070

HOUSE CREW
Production Manager   Marianne Montgomery 412-456-1371
Stage Technician   Sarah Higgins   412-456-1379

UNIONS
IATSE Local #3   Robert Brown   412-281-4568

SEATING CAPACITY
Orchestra   605
Lower Balcony   238
Upper Balcony   430
Total: **1,273**

pit (add'l)   32

BOX OFFICE
Computerized
Ticket Service Manager
  Al Rodibaugh   412-456-2693

Outside Ticket Agency
Ticketmaster
  Pat Lucas   412-323-1900

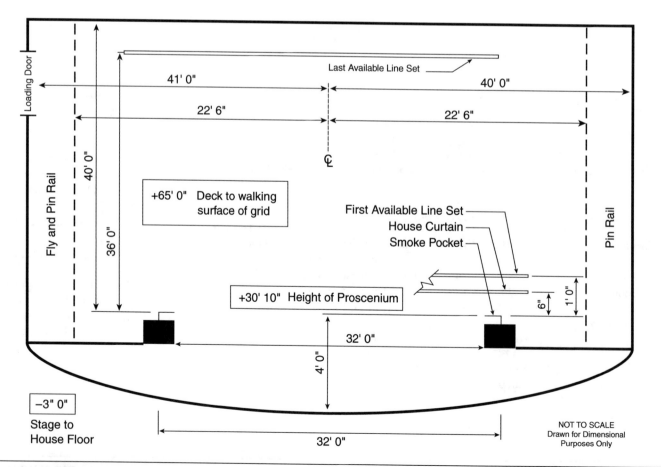

Loading Door

Fly and Pin Rail

Last Available Line Set

41' 0"   40' 0"

22' 6"   22' 6"

CL

40' 0"

+65' 0" Deck to walking surface of grid

36' 0"

First Available Line Set
House Curtain
Smoke Pocket

Pin Rail

+30' 10" Height of Proscenium

6"   1' 0"

32' 0"

4' 0"

−3" 0"
Stage to
House Floor

32' 0"

NOT TO SCALE
Drawn for Dimensional
Purposes Only

STAGE HOUSE

HOUSE CURTAIN
Operates as a guillotine from SL deck

RIGGING SYSTEM
Type:	Single purchase counter weight; motorized and Hemp System
Weight:	8,000 lbs available
Line sets:	58 sets at 6" o.c. with 3 lift lines per set
House Pipes:	42' long with 63' 5" of travel from deck

Line sets moveable
Block & Falls are available
Chain hoists available as a rental; (4) one ton
No spot wheels and 400' of hemp available
Grid slats are oak and run SL to SR;
    No bridling between grid beams

PERMANENT INSTALLATIONS OVER STAGE (FROM SMOKE POCKET)
M=Moveable with advance call
Movie screen (1) at 2'0", M
Traveller (1) at 30'0", M
Electric pipes(5) at 3'6", 10'6", 16'6", 25'0", 33'0", M
Dead spaces (10) at 6'0", 7'0', 8'6", 11'0", 19'0", 22'0", 23'6",
    27'0", 28'6", 32'0"
Cyclorama (1) at scrim 29'0", plastic 31'0", bounce 35'6", M
Catwalk (1) at 36'6"

PERMANENT INSTALLATIONS ON DECK
Traps in stage floor (2) 4' 0"x 6'6" and 4'9" x 6'6" located SR at loading door
Hard Legs (5 SL, 5 SR), 6'0"w x 31'0"h, 16' offstage of center line
Pilasters (4) on US wall
Stairs (2, SL and SR), SL:4' x 20 SR:5' x 8'
Radiators (2) on SL and SR walls

ORCHESTRA PIT
Adjustable to 9' below stage level
Apron overhangs US wall of pit 6'6"
Pit is manual; can hold 2 rows of seats

BACKSTAGE

LOADING DOCK
Loading door(s):
    16'0" high x 6'0" wide
Trucks load (1) at a time
Street is 5' below stage level
    42" x 12' ramp available to go from truck to stage
Fork lift is not required
Sound/Props can load in FOH
Lobby can be a work area
(1) Trailer can store on-site

WARDROBE
Location: 3rd fl at dressing rooms
Access: Stairs/chain motor
(1) Washer (1) Dryer
Washer and dryer hookups available

DRESSING ROOMS
(2) Small, SL, stage level, t/s included, phone jack
(2) Chorus, SL, +2, phone jack
(4) SL, 2nd fl, t/s on same fl, phone jack
Use dressing room for company mgr office

SOUND

CONSOLE
Soundcraft 8000, located Rear House Booth
40 inputs, 8 matrix outputs, 8 aux outputs

SPEAKERS
Proscenium
Under Balcony
Portable
(4) channels of monitor amplification available; all amplification QSC/Crest
No speaker truss

COMMUNICATIONS
Clear Com intercom with (4) channels

ROAD CONSOLE
Located Rear House box or Orchestra rows T/U/V
Number of seats required to be removed varies
Cable run from stage is 250'
Tie-in into house system with XLR connectors

REHEARSAL & STORAGE SPACE
Rehearsal: None at Byham, space available by arrangement with Benedum Center
Storage: 1) Security area FOH, 4' x 20' 2) Trap Room, 20' x 20'; 3) FOH 3rd fl, 16' x 30'

ELECTRICS

ROAD SERVICE POWER

Panel	Phase	Amp	Circuit Protection	Use	Location
A-B	3	400	fuse	dimmers	USL on side wall
C	3	400	fuse	dimmers/extra	USL on side wall
D	3	200	fuse	sound	USL on US wall

Panel D has an isolated ground separate from lighting system
Recommended location of touring dimmer racks: USL or MSL
Hoist not required

FRONT OF HOUSE (BOX BOOM VALUES ARE PER SIDE)

Position	Pipe Width	Distance to Prosc.	House Circuits	Connector Type	FOH Transfer Circuits
1st Balc Rail	32'	50'	8	ungrd 20 amp stage pin	8
Box Boom1		36'	14	ungrd 20 amp stage pin	14

Transfer circuits: ungrd 20 amp stage pin
Road truss: No front of house rigging points available

EQUIPMENT FOH (BOX BOOM VALUES ARE PER SIDE)

Position	Quantity	Wattage	Instrument	Removeable
1st Balc Rail	16	575	Source 4 19°	yes
Box Boom1	18	575	Source 4 19°	yes

FOLLOWSPOTS
House Followspots:
    (4) Colortran Colorarc 2000; removeable

Followspot Booth:
    (4) spots per booth;
    118' throw to proscenium;
    (4) 1Ø 30 amp breakers

DIMMERS
Lighting console is ETC Obsession 1500;
(184) 2.4 kw, (8) 6kw) ETC Sensor dimmers
House has programmable DMX control system
(2) dry run DMX station(s), DSL/DSR

HEINZ HALL FOR THE PERFORMING ARTS

YEAR BUILT: 1926   YEAR RENOVATED: 1995

Theatre Location: 600 Penn Avenue, Pittsburgh, PA 15222
Management Company: Pittsburgh Symphony Society, Inc.

Main Administrative Phone:	412-392-4843
Main Administrative Fax:	412-392-4910
Website:	www.pittsburghsymphony.org
Stage Door Phone:	412-392-4853
Backstage Pay Phone:	412-566-8342

SEATING CAPACITY

Orchestra	1,143
Boxes	20
Mezzanine	262
Balcony	1,236
Total:	**2,661**
pit (add'l)	65

THEATRE STAFF

Manager	Carl A. Mancuso	412-392-4843
Booking	Donna F. Saul	413-392-4844
Marketing	Heather Clark	412-392-4905
Operations	Donna F. Saul	412-392-4844
Group Sales	Aleta King	412-392-4833

HOUSE CREW

Technical Director	Rocky Esposito	412-392-4896
Electrics	Mike Karapandi	412-392-4896
Sound	Ray Clover	412-392-4858

UNIONS

IATSE Local #3	Bob Brown	412-281-4568
Wardrobe	Judy Cupp	724-733-3082
AFM	Frank Osterowski	412-563-6686

BOX OFFICE

Computerized
Assoc. Dir. Customer Service
   Aleta King   412-392-4833

Outside Ticket Agency
Computerized

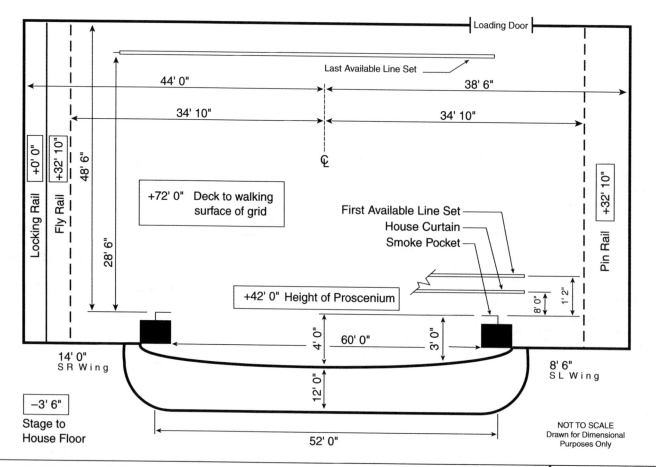

STAGE HOUSE

HOUSE CURTAIN
Operates as a guillotine from SR deck

RIGGING SYSTEM
Type:	Single purchase counter weight; motorized
Weight:	20,000 lbs available
Line sets:	46 sets at 6" o.c. with 4 lift lines per set
Arbors:	850 lb capacity
House Pipes:	56' long with 68' of travel from deck.

Line sets are moveable
Block & Falls are available
Chain hoists available as a rental, (2) one ton
(120) spot wheels and 20,000' of hemp available

PERMANENT INSTALLATIONS OVER STAGE (FROM SMOKE POCKET)
M=Moveable with advance call
Orchestra shells (16); M
Act curtain (1) at 5'1/2"

PERMANENT INSTALLATIONS ON DECK
Trap (2) in stage floor, 33" x 40", at 16' and 26'
Jumps (5) located above locking rail
Pilasters (2), 3' x 3', at 29'
Orchestra shell storage located on the US wall cave

ORCHESTRA PIT
Adjustable to 8' below stage level by hydraulic lift
Apron overhangs US wall of pit 16'
Pit lift is in (1) section

BACKSTAGE

LOADING DOCK
Loading door(s):
  9'3" high x 9'3" wide
Trucks load (2) at same time
Dock is at truck level; loading to stage thru separate loading bay to stage house
Fork lift is not required but available on site
Sound/Props can load in thru FOH
Lobby cannot be a work area
Security at dock & stage door

WARDROBE
Location: Rehearsal rooms
Access: Elevators and stairs
(2) Washers (2) Dryers
Washer and dryer hookups available

DRESSING ROOMS
(6) Star, behind stage, 2nd fl, t/s included, phone jack
(1) Small, SL, 5th fl, t/s included
(3) Chorus, SL, 2nd, 3rd & 4th fl, t/s on same fl

SOUND

CONSOLE
Yamaha 4000, located Rear House
32 inputs, 8 main outputs, 8 matrix outputs, 8 aux outputs

SPEAKERS
House Cluster
Proscenium
Under Balcony
Pit rail
No speaker truss

COMMUNICATIONS
Clear Com intercom with (4) channels
No infrared sound system
Dressing room page system

ROAD CONSOLE
Located Rear House
Cable run from stage is 115'
Tie in into house system with XLR connectors

REHEARSAL & STORAGE SPACE
Rehearsal: 40' x 52', on 4th fl, grand or upright piano
34' x 38', on 4th fl, grand or upright piano
Storage: Prop room, SL Hallway to dock area

ELECTRICS

ROAD SERVICE POWER

Panel	Phase	Amp	Circuit Protection	Use	Location
A	3	400	fuse	dimmers	SR
B	3	400	fuse	dimmers	SR
C	3	100	fuse	sound	SL
D	3	200	fuse	extra	dock

Recommended location of touring dimmer racks: SR
Hoist not required
Additional power is available for tour buses, generators, etc.

FRONT OF HOUSE (BOX BOOM VALUES ARE PER SIDE)

Position	Pipe Width	Distance to Prosc.	House Circuits	Connector Type	FOH Transfer Circuits
Box Boom 1		65'	16	grd 20 amp stage pin	16
1st Cove	40'	150'	24	grd 20 amp stage pin	24
Curtain Warmer			4	grd 20 amp stage pin	4

Transfer circuits: grd 20 amp stage pin; all FOH can be transferred

EQUIPMENT FOH (BOX BOOM VALUES ARE PER SIDE)

Position	Quantity	Wattage	Instrument	Removeable
1st Cove Rail	36	575	ETC 10 (Iris)	yes
Box Boom 1	24	575	ETC 19 (Iris)	yes

FOLLOWSPOTS
House Followspots:
  (2) Super Troupers (2500 watts) ; removeable
  (1) Gladiator (2500 watts); removeable
  (1) Super Trouper (1750 watts); removeable

Followspot Booth:
  (4) spots per booth;
  150' throw to proscenium;
  (4) 3Ø 150 amp breakers

DIMMERS
House console is ETC Obsession;
  (288) Strand 2.4 dimmers
No DMX control system

SCRANTON CULTURAL CENTER

AT: THE MASONIC TEMPLE

YEAR BUILT: 1927

Theatre Location: 420 N Washington Avenue, Scranton, PA 18503

Main Administrative Phone: 570-346-7369
Main Administrative Fax: 570-346-7365

THEATRE STAFF
Executive Director   Jo Ann Fremiotti   570-346-7369
Booking   Robert Sanchez   570-346-7369
Operations   Robert Sanchez   570-346-7369
Group Sales   Melissa Duffy   570-346-7369

HOUSE CREW
Technical Director   Jamie Kurtz   570-346-7369

UNIONS
IATSE Local #329   Eugene Ellis, Sr.   See Technical Dir

SEATING CAPACITY
Orchestra   1,004
Boxes   12
Mezzanine   282
Balcony   324
Total: **1,622**

pit
wheelchair
standing (add'l)

BOX OFFICE
Computerized
Box Office Manager
Melissa Duffy   570-344-1111

Outside Ticket Agency
None

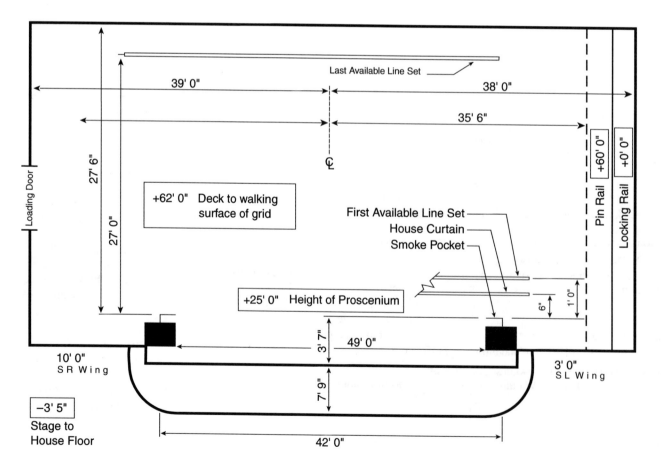

Last Available Line Set

39' 0"   38' 0"

35' 6"

27' 6"

Loading Door

27' 0"

+62' 0" Deck to walking surface of grid

℄

+60' 0"   Pin Rail
+0' 0"   Locking Rail

First Available Line Set
House Curtain
Smoke Pocket

1' 0"
6"

+25' 0" Height of Proscenium

10' 0"
SR Wing

3' 7"   49' 0"

3' 0"
SL Wing

7' 9"

−3' 5"
Stage to
House Floor

42' 0"

NOT TO SCALE
Drawn for Dimensional
Purposes Only

STAGE HOUSE

HOUSE CURTAIN
Operates as a guillotine or traveller from SL deck

RIGGING SYSTEM
Type:	Single purchase counter weight
Weight:	13,000 lbs available
Line sets:	64 sets at 5" o.c. with 4 lift lines per set
Arbors:	750 lb capacity
House Pipes:	52' long with 56' of travel from deck

Line sets are not moveable
Block & Falls are available 2:1 (1)
Chain hoists are not available
(20) spot wheels

PERMANENT INSTALLATIONS OVER STAGE (FROM SMOKE POCKET)
Electric borders (4) at 4'0", 8'0", 12'0", 16'0"

PERMANENT INSTALLATIONS ON DECK
Traps (36) in stage floor, 3'6" x 6'0", located on grid
Drilling, nailing or screwing into floor is not permitted

ORCHESTRA PIT
Nonadjustable at 6' below stage level
Apron overhangs US wall of pit 2'3"

BACKSTAGE

LOADING DOCK
Loading door(s):
10'0" high x 12'0" wide
Trucks load (2) at same time
Dock is at truck level and is equipped with electric leveler
Sound/Props cannot load in FOH

WARDROBE
Location: Basement
Access: Direct from stage
Washer and dryer hookups available

DRESSING ROOMS
(2) Star, SR, -1, t/s included
(8) Small, -1, t/s included
(2) Chorus, SL, -1, t/s included

SOUND

CONSOLE
Altec Lansing
8 inputs, 2 main outputs

SPEAKERS
Proscenium
Under Balcony
No speaker truss

COMMUNICATIONS
No intercom system

ROAD CONSOLE
Located Rear House
No seats required to be removed
Cable run from stage is 92'
Tie-in into house system with XLR connectors

REHEARSAL & STORAGE SPACE
Rehearsal: 60' x 100' located in basement
Storage: 60' x 107' located in basement

ELECTRICS

ROAD SERVICE POWER

Panel	Phase	Amp	Circuit Protection	Use	Location
A	3		fuse	dimmers	DSR
B	1	400	fuse	sound	DSL

Recommended location of touring dimmer racks: SR on deck
Hoist not required

FRONT OF HOUSE (BOX BOOM VALUES ARE PER SIDE)

Position	Pipe Width	Distance to Prosc.	House Circuits	Connector Type	FOH Transfer Circuits
1st Balc Rail	30'	50'	0		0
Box Boom 1		40'	0		0

EQUIPMENT FOH (BOX BOOM VALUES ARE PER SIDE)
None

FOLLOWSPOTS
House Followspots:
(2) Xenon Super Trouper 2k; removeable
(1) Xenon Trouper; removeable

Followspot Booth:
(2) spots per booth;
102' throw to proscenium;
1Ø 200 amp breakers

DIMMERS
Lighting console is Expression;
(72) ETC dimmers
House has DMX control system

EISENHOWER AUDITORIUM

AKA: MILTON S. EISENHOWER AUDITORIUM AT: PENN STATE UNIVERSITY   **YEAR BUILT: 1974**

Theatre Location: Penn State University
                           Shortlidge Road, University Park, PA 16802-2108
Management Company: Center for the Performing Arts
                           Penn State University- Eisenhower Auditorium
                           University Park, PA 16802-2108

Main Administrative Phone: 814-863-0388
Main Administrative Fax: 814-863-7218
Website: www.cpa.psu.edu
Stage Door Phone: 814-865-4333
Traveling Production Office Phone: 814-865-1025

THEATRE STAFF
Director   Joe Jefcoat   814-863-0388
General Manager   David W. Will   814-863-5733
Marketing   Tracy Noll   814-865-8722
Group Sales   Christine Johnston   814-863-0255

HOUSE CREW
Production Coordinator Gretchen Walker   814-863-7102

UNIONS
IATSE Local #636   Susan Kelley   814-238-0986

SEATING CAPACITY
Orchestra   1,641
Grand Tier   479
Balcony   369
Total: **2,489**

pit (add'l)   96
wheelchair (add'l)   10
standing   0

BOX OFFICE
Computerized
Box Office Manager
  Heather Storm   814-863-0255

Outside Ticket Agency
None

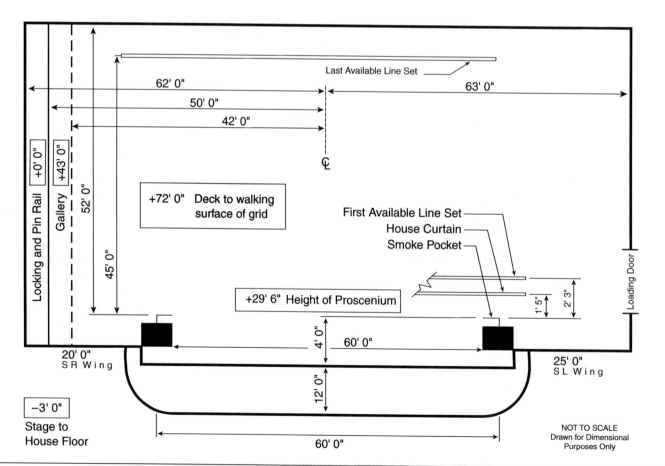

UNIVERSITY PARK, PENNSYLVANIA

LIVE BROADWAY 1999 Stage Specs

STAGE HOUSE

HOUSE CURTAIN
Operates as a traveller from SR deck

RIGGING SYSTEM
Type:	Single purchase counter weight
Weight:	7,500 lbs available
Line sets:	53 sets at 8-12" o.c. with 7 lift lines per set
Arbors:	1,400 lb capacity
House Pipes:	76' long with 68' of travel from deck

Line sets are not moveable
Block & Falls are available
Chain hoists are not available
(16) spot wheels and 3,600' of hemp available

PERMANENT INSTALLATIONS OVER STAGE (FROM SMOKE POCKET)
Orchestra shells (5) at 6'1", 13'4", 20'4", 27' 2", 34'5"
Movie screen (1) at 15' 0"
Traveller (1) at 1'3"
Electric Pipe (12) at 2'4", 2'10", 3'7", 4'6", 10'7", 16'4", 17'9", 23'1", 24'2", 30'6", 38'6", 39'10"
Cyclorama (1) at 44' 9"

PERMANENT INSTALLATIONS ON DECK
Orchestra shell storage (2) at 8'0" x 30'0", located SR/SL, DS of proscenium

ORCHESTRA PIT
Adjustable to 17' below stage level by hydraulic lift
Apron overhangs US wall of pit 8'0"
Pit lift is in (1) section
Pit prevents house to stage access - prearrangement required if access is necessary

BACKSTAGE

LOADING DOCK
Loading door(s):
    (2) 12'0" high x 12'0" wide
Trucks load (3) at same time
Dock height 3'10"
Fork lift is not required
(3) Trailers can store on-site
Security at dock & stage door

WARDROBE
Location: Basement
Access: Freight elevator
(2) Washers (2) Dryers
No washer or dryer hookups

DRESSING ROOMS
(4) Star, SR, stage level, t/s
(2) Chorus, SR/SL, -1, t/s
Additional production office available for company mgr

SOUND

CONSOLE
Mackie Designs, located Rear Orchestra
32 inputs, 2 main outputs, 8 aux outputs

SPEAKERS
House Cluster
Portable

COMMUNICATIONS
Clear Com intercom with (2) channels
Infrared sound system
Dressing room page system

ROAD CONSOLE
Located Rear Orchestra
No seats required to be removed
Cable run from stage is 110'
Tie-in into house system with XLR connectors

REHEARSAL & STORAGE SPACE
Rehearsal: None
Storage: Receiving area, SL, 30' x 20'
Basement, DSL, 60' x 15'

ELECTRICS

ROAD SERVICE POWER

Panel	Phase	Amp	Circuit Protection	Use	Location
A	3	1200	fuse	dimmers	SL
B	3	100	fuse	sound	SL

Recommended location of touring dimmer racks: SL
Hoist is not required
Additional power is available for tour buses, generators, etc.

FRONT OF HOUSE (BOX BOOM VALUES ARE PER SIDE)

Position	Pipe Width	Distance to Prosc.	House Circuits	Connector Type	FOH Transfer Circuits
1st Cove	72'	40'	18	grd 20 amp stage pin	18
2nd Cove	76'	52'	18	grd 20 amp stage pin	18
Box Boom 1		35'	8	grd 20 amp stage pin	8
Box Boom 2	12'	48'	8	grd 20 amp stage pin	8

Transfer circuits: grd 20 amp stage pin

EQUIPMENT FOH (BOX BOOM VALUES ARE PER SIDE)

Position	Quantity	Wattage	Instrument	Removeable
1st Balc Rail	24	575	6-15° Century Ellipsoidal	yes
2nd Balc Rail	34	1,000	14" Kleigl Ellipsoidal	yes
Box Boom 1	8	575	6-15° Century Ellipsoidal	yes
Box Boom 2	6	1,000	10" Kleigl Ellipsoidal	yes

FOLLOWSPOTS
House Followspots:
    (2) Strong Xenon Super Troupers; not removeable

Followspot Booth:
    (2) spots per booth;
    135' throw to proscenium;
    (2) 1Ø 50 amp breakers

DIMMERS
House lighting console is Prestar-96 channel control;
(96) Century SCR 12k dimmers

F.M. KIRBY CENTER FOR THE PERFORMING ARTS

YEAR BUILT: 1938   YEAR RENOVATED: 1986

Theatre Location: 71 Public Square, Wilkes-Barre, PA 18701
Mailing Address: PO Box 486, Wilkes-Barre, PA 18703-0486

Main Administrative Phone: 717-823-4599
Main Administrative Fax: 717-823-4890
E-mail: kirby@tl.infl.net
Website: www.kirbycenter.org
Traveling Production Office Phone: 717-821-2728

SEATING CAPACITY

Orchestra	1,191
Mezzanine	168
Balcony	457
Total:	**1,816**
pit (add'l)	32
wheelchair (add'l)	10

THEATRE STAFF

Facility Director	John Cardoni	717-823-4599
Administrative Dir.	Debbie Schonfeld	717-823-4599

HOUSE CREW

Facility Director	John Cardoni	717-823-4599

STAGE DIMENSIONS (FROM SMOKE POCKET)

Stage is 26'6" deep
Width from Center Line to SL is 33'8"
Width from Center Line to SR is 34'6"
Proscenium width is 48'0"
Proscenium height is 31'0"
Smoke pocket to apron edge is 3'3"
Orchestra pit exists

RIGGING

Grid Height:	68'
Type:	Double purchase counter weight
Weight:	48,000 lbs
Line sets:	38 sets at 8" o.c.
Arbors:	2,000 lb capacity
House Pipes:	52' long

LOADING DOCK

Loading door(s) are 10'0" high x 10'0" wide
Trucks load (2) at same time
Fork lift is not required and is available

ELECTRICS

Total power available:
(1) 600A 3Ø DSL prosc wall
(1) 200A 3Ø DSL prosc wall
(1) 100A 3Ø USL wall

FOLLOWSPOTS

House Followspots:
Xenon Super Trouper
Power in spot booth (2) 50A

DIMMERS

(228) house dimmers
House has DMX control system
(2) dry run station(s) located
Rear Orchestra

SOUND

House has 200A 3Ø dedi-
cated power located DSL
FOH mixing position in
Rear Orchestra Center
No sound console available

COMMUNITY ARTS CENTER

YEAR BUILT: 1928   YEAR RENOVATED: 1993

			SEATING CAPACITY	
Theatre Location:	220 West Fouth Street, Williamsport, PA 17701		Orchestra	1,190
			Loge	294
Main Administrative Phone:	717-327-7650		Balcony	674
Main Administrative Fax:	717-327-7663		**Total:**	**2,158**
E-mail:	gslaton@pct.edu			
Website:	www.pct.edu/commarts			
Backstage Pay Phone:	717-322-9513		pit (add'l)	50

THEATRE STAFF

Executive Director	Gram Slaton	717-327-7653
Booking	Gram Slaton	717-327-7653

HOUSE CREW

Building Manager	Ed Ploy, Jr.	717-327-7655

STAGE DIMENSIONS (FROM SMOKE POCKET)
Stage is 34'3" deep
Width from Center Line to SL is 32'3"
Width from Center Line to SR is 35'2"
Proscenium width is 48'0"
Proscenium height is 27'0"
Smoke pocket to apron edge is 5'0"
Orchestra pit exists

RIGGING
Grid Height: 63'9"
Type: Single purchase counter weight
Weight: 45,000 lbs
Line sets: 44 sets at 8" o.c.
Arbors: 800 lb capacity
House Pipes: 54' long

LOADING DOCK
Loading door(s) are 13'4" high x 7'0" wide
Trucks load (1) at a time
Fork lift is not required and is not available

ELECTRICS
Total power available:
(1) 400A 3Ø DSR
(1) 200A 3Ø DSR
(1) 100A 3Ø DSR

FOLLOWSPOTS
House Followspots:
(3) Alt Explorer 1200w HMI
Power in spot booth (1) 20A

DIMMERS
(400) house dimmers
House has DMX control system
(3) dry run station(s) located DSR

SOUND
House has 200A & 100A dedicated power located DSR
FOH mixing position in Rear Orchestra
Sound console is available

PROVIDENCE PERFORMING ARTS CENTER

YEAR BUILT: 1928   YEAR RENOVATED: 1996

Theatre Location: 220 Weybosset Street, Providence, RI 02903

Main Administrative Phone:	401-421-2997
Main Administrative Fax:	401-421-5767
Website:	www.ppacri.org
Stage Door Phone:	401-621-8012
Traveling Production Office Phone:	401-421-2125

THEATRE STAFF

President	J. 'Lynn' Singleton	401-421-2997
General Manager	Alan Chille	401-421-2997
Booking	Norbert Mongeon	401-421-2997
Marketing	P.J. Prokop	401-421-2997
Operations	Nick Beradinelli	401-421-2997

HOUSE CREW

Technical Director	Bill Brackett	401-421-2997
Carpentry	Barry Gay	401-421-2997
Electrics	Dick Goins	401-421-2997
Sound	Peter Archambault	401-421-2997
Props	Peter Vecchio	401-421-2997

UNIONS

IATSE Local #23	Richard Moore	401-421-2997
Wardrobe Local #831	Fran Howe	401-421-2997

SEATING CAPACITY

Orchestra	1,954
Loge	250
First Balcony	452
Second Balcony	539
Total:	**3,195**

pit (add'l)	30
wheelchair (incl.)	31
standing	0

BOX OFFICE

Computerized
Director of Ticketing
   Donna Santos   401-421-2787

Outside Ticket Agency
   Ticketmaster

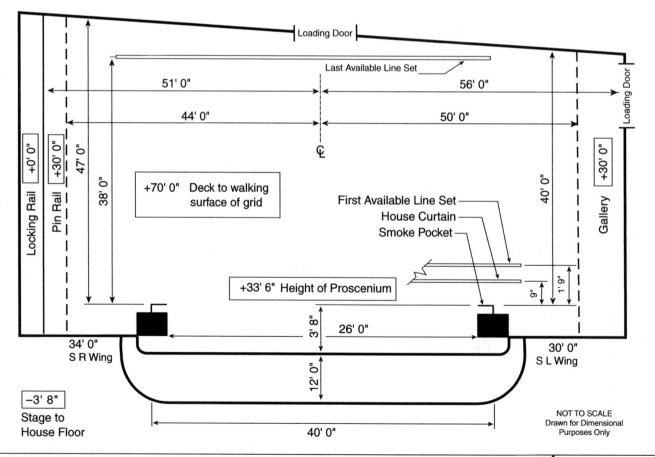

STAGE HOUSE

HOUSE CURTAIN
Operates as a guillotine from SR fly floor or deck

RIGGING SYSTEM
Type: Single purchase counter weight
Weight: 60,000 lbs available
Line sets: 68 sets at 6" o.c. with 7 lift lines per set
Arbors: 2,000 lb capacity
House Pipes: 66' long with 68'6" of travel from deck
Line sets are moveable
Block & Falls are not available
Chain hoists are not available
(70) spot wheels and 7,000' of hemp available

PERMANENT INSTALLATIONS OVER STAGE (FROM SMOKE POCKET)
None

PERMANENT INSTALLATIONS ON DECK
Jumps (2)

ORCHESTRA PIT
Adjustable to 8' below stage level by electric motor
   turnscrew
Apron overhangs US wall of pit 0'0"
Pit lift is in (1) section; Organ lift SR

BACKSTAGE

LOADING DOCK
Loading door(s):
   (2) @ 10'0" high x 8'0" wide
Trucks load (3) at same time
Both doors are stage/street level
Sound/Props can load in FOH
Lobby can be a work area
(1) Trailer can store on-site
Security at dock & stage door

WARDROBE
Location: Substage
Access: Freight elevator
(2) Washers (2) Dryers
Washer and dryer hookups
   available

DRESSING ROOMS
(3) Star, SL, stage level, t/s
   included, phone jack
(1) Star, SL, stage level, t/s
   included
(2) Small, SL, stage level, t/s
   included, phone jack
(2) Small, SL, stage level, t/s
   included
(2) Chorus, -1, t/s included
Elevator access for dressing
   rooms
Additional production office
   available for company mgr

SOUND

CONSOLE
Soundcraft K-3, located FOH
38 inputs, 16 main outputs

SPEAKERS
House Cluster
Proscenium
Under Balcony
Front fills
No speaker truss

COMMUNICATIONS
Clear Com intercom with
   (2) channels
Infrared sound system
Dressing room page system

ROAD CONSOLE
Located Rear Orchestra
No seats required to be
   removed
Cable run from stage is 150'
Tic-in into house system with
   XLR connectors

REHEARSAL & STORAGE SPACE
Rehearsal: None
Storage: None

ELECTRICS

ROAD SERVICE POWER

Panel	Phase	Amp	Circuit Protection	Use	Location
A	3	400	breaker	dimmers	DSR
B	3	200	breaker	dimmers	DSR
C	3	100	breaker	extra	DSR
D	3	200	breaker	sound	DSL

Recommended location of touring dimmer racks: DSR
Hoist not required

FRONT OF HOUSE (BOX BOOM VALUES ARE PER SIDE)

Position	Pipe Width	Distance to Prosc.	House Circuits	Connector Type	FOH Transfer Circuits
1st Balc Rail	40'	80'	24	grd 20 amp stage pin	24
Box Boom 1		90'	12	grd 20 amp stage pin	12

Transfer circuits: grd 20 amp stage pin

EQUIPMENT FOH (BOX BOOM VALUES ARE PER SIDE)

Position	Quantity	Wattage	Instrument	Removeable
Box Boom 1	6	1,000	6 x 16 Lekos	yes

FOLLOWSPOTS
House Followspots:
   (3) Strong Xenon Super
   Trouper II 2k ; removeable

Followspot Booth:
   (4) spots per booth;
   165' throw to proscenium;
   (4) 3Ø 30 amp breakers

DIMMERS
House has lighting console
   (36) Applied Electronics
   dimmers
No DMX control system

GAILLARD MUNICIPAL AUDITORIUM

Theatre Location: 77 Calhoun Street, Charleston, SC 29403
Management Company: City of Charleston

Main Administrative Phone: 843-577-7400
Main Administrative Fax: 843-724-7389

THEATRE STAFF
Director   Cam Patterson   843-577-7400
Booking   Cam Patterson   843-577-7400

HOUSE CREW
House Steward   Robert Albers   843-766-1730

UNIONS
IATSE Local #333 Scotty Haskell   843-795-7228

SEATING CAPACITY
Orchestra   1,619
Mezzanine   424
Balcony   689
Total: **2,732**

BOX OFFICE
Computerized
Box Office Manager
  Randal Davis   843-577-7400

Outside Ticket Agency
Computerized
  SCAT   843-577-4500

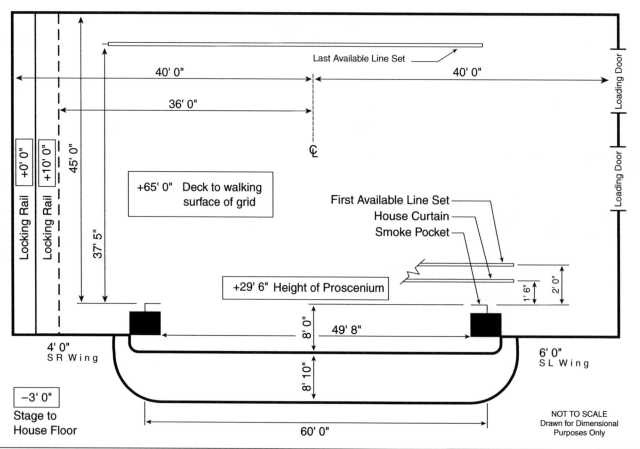

STAGE HOUSE

HOUSE CURTAIN
Operates as a traveller from SL deck

RIGGING SYSTEM
Type:	Double purchase counter weight
Weight:	30,000 lbs available
Line sets:	50 sets at 6" o.c. with 6 lift lines per set
Arbors:	2,000 lb capacity
House Pipes:	59' long with 60' of travel from deck

Line sets are not moveable

PERMANENT INSTALLATIONS OVER STAGE (FROM SMOKE POCKET)
Orchestra shells (4) at 5'3", 12'0", 21'0", 29'10"

PERMANENT INSTALLATIONS ON DECK
Traps (8) in stage floor 3'0" x 7'8" located DSR & DSL
Pilasters (3) 8'0" wide x 2'0" deep against back wall located at CS & 27'0" SR & SL of center
Orchestra shell stores on back wall, 7'0" deep

ORCHESTRA PIT
Nonadjustable at 8' below stage level
Apron overhangs US wall of pit 10'0"

BACKSTAGE

LOADING DOCK
Loading door(s):
  (2) 16'0" high x 12'0" wide
Trucks load (2) at same time
Fork lift is not required
Sound/Props cannot load in FOH
Trailers can store on-site
Security at stage door

WARDROBE
Location: SR Green Room on stage level
Access: Direct from stage
No Washers   No Dryers
Washer and dryer hookups available

DRESSING ROOMS
(5) Star, SR, 2nd fl, t/s included, phone jack
(2) Chorus, SR, basement, t/s included, phone jack
Additional production office available for company mgr

SOUND

CONSOLE
Altec
12 inputs, 4 main outputs

SPEAKERS
House Cluster
Under Balcony
Holes in ceiling over house provide truss hanging position
No pipe or rigging available

COMMUNICATIONS
Clear Com intercom with (2) channels
Infrared sound system
Dressing room page system

ROAD CONSOLE
Located HL
(30) seats required to be removed
Cable run from stage is 100'
Tie-in into house system with XLR connectors

REHEARSAL & STORAGE SPACE
Rehearsal: None
Storage: None

ELECTRICS

ROAD SERVICE POWER

Panel	Phase	Amp	Circuit Protection	Use	Location
A	3	400	fuse	dimmers	DSL side wall
B	3	400	fuse	sound	DSL side wall
C	3	200	breaker	extra	DSL room
D	3	60	fuse	extra	SR Green Room

Recommended location of touring dimmer racks: SL on deck
Hoist not required

FRONT OF HOUSE (BOX BOOM VALUES ARE PER SIDE)

Position	Pipe Width	Distance to Prosc.	House Circuits	Connector Type	FOH Transfer Circuits
1st Balc Rail	60'	50'	24	grd 20 amp stage pin	24
1st Cove	60'	50'	18	grd 20 amp stage pin	18
Torm		1'	16	grd 20 amp stage pin	16

Transfer circuits:grd 20 amp stage pin located on DSL side wall

EQUIPMENT FOH (BOX BOOM VALUES ARE PER SIDE)
None

FOLLOWSPOTS
House Followspots:
  (3) Altman 1200 HMI

Followspot Booth:
  (3) spots per booth;
  150' throw to proscenium;
  3Ø 100 amp breakers

DIMMERS
House lighting console is Microvision;
(260) LMI dimmers
House has programmable DMX control system
No dry run DMX station(s)

THE TOWNSHIP

YEAR BUILT: 1929   YEAR RENOVATED: 1998

Theatre Location: 1703 Taylor Street, Columbia, SC 29201
Mailing Address: PO Box 1088, Columbia, SC 29202

Main Administrative Phone: 803-252-2032
Main Administrative Fax: 803-779-2208

THEATRE STAFF
Executive Director   Marshall P. Perry   803-252-2032

HOUSE CREW
Stage Manager   Andrew Hackney   803-252-2037

SEATING CAPACITY

Orchestra	988
First Balcony (Box Seats)	1,036
Second Balcony	788
Gallery	388
Total:	**3,199**
pit (add'l)	40
wheelchair (add'l)	28
standing (add'l)	0

STAGE DIMENSIONS (FROM SMOKE POCKET)
Stage is 35'0" deep
Width from Center Line to SL is 25'0"
Width from Center Line to SR is 25'0"
Proscenium width is 50'0"
Proscenium height is 35'0"
Smoke pocket to apron edge is 3'0"
Orchestra pit exists

RIGGING
Grid Height:	70'
Type:	Single purchase counter weight
Weight:	990 lbs
Line sets:	20 sets at 12" o.c.
Arbors:	1,000 lb capacity
House Pipes:	60' long

LOADING DOCK
Loading door(s) are 10'0" high x 7'0" wide
Trucks load (1) at a time
Fork lift is not required and is available

ELECTRICS
Total power available:
(1) 800A 3Ø SR
(1) 800A 3Ø SL

FOLLOWSPOTS
House Followspots:
Lycian 1.2K
Power in spot booth 300A

DIMMERS
(196) house dimmers
No DMX control system

SOUND
House has 800A dedicated
power located USL
FOH mixing position in
Orchestra
No sound console available

PEACE CENTER FOR THE PERFORMING ARTS

Theatre Location: 101 West Broad Street, Greenville, SC 29615

Main Administrative Phone: 864-467-3030
Main Administrative Fax: 864-467-3040
E-mail: *(first initial last name)*@peacecenter.org
Website: www.peacecenter.org

THEATRE STAFF
  Executive Director   Megan Riegel   864-467-3030 x203
  Director of Marketing   Janet Roberson   864-467-3030 x203
  Dir. of Operations   Mark Loigman   864-467-3030 x204
  Box Office Manager   Sandy Hammond   864-467-3000

HOUSE CREW
  Technical Director   Mark Hurlburt   864-467-3008 x244
  Production Manager   Dirk Holleman   864-467-3008 x291
  Carpentry   Jeff Johnson   864-467-3008 x295
  Electrics   Mike Brown   864-467-3008 x296
  Sound   Doug Anderson   864-467-3008 x292

UNIONS
  IATSE   Gene Coffey   864-901-1219

SEATING CAPACITY

Orchestra	1,027
Founders Circle	438
Balcony	482
Boxes	80
Total:	**2,096**
pit	60
wheelchair	9

BOX OFFICE
  Computerized
  Box Office Manager
    Brian Haimbach
    864-467-3000 x218

  Outside Ticket Agency
    None

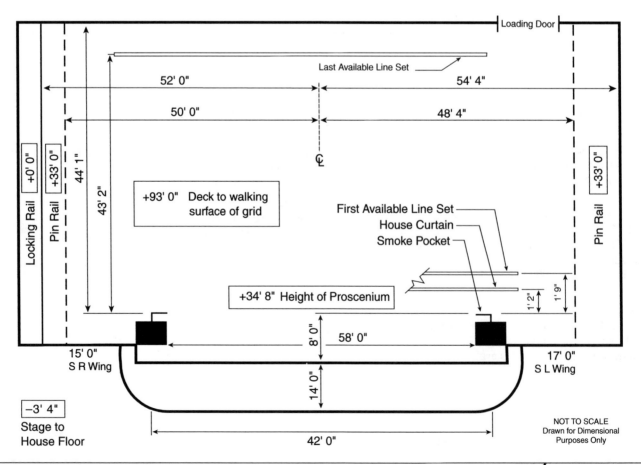

STAGE HOUSE

HOUSE CURTAIN
Operates as a guillotine from SR deck

RIGGING SYSTEM
Type:	Single purchase counter weight
Weight:	20,000 lbs available
Line sets:	58 sets at 7" o.c. with 7 lift lines per set
Arbors:	1,000 lb capacity
House Pipes:	74' long with 90' of travel from deck

Line sets are moveable
Block & Falls are available
Chain hoists are available
(30) spot wheels and 2,500' of hemp available

PERMANENT INSTALLATIONS OVER STAGE (FROM SMOKE POCKET)
M=Moveable with advance call
Orchestra shell (2) at 8'2", 19'10"
Electric pipe (4) at 1'6", 2'0", 14'7", 23'0"; M
Dead spaces (2) orchestra shells
Cyclorama (1); M
Fire curtain (1) at proscenium

PERMANENT INSTALLATIONS ON DECK
Stairs (2) DSL & DSR
Orchestra shell storage (1) USL
Loading bridge (1) SR + 90'

ORCHESTRA PIT
Adjustable to 12'6" below stage level by hydraulic lift
Apron overhangs US wall of pit 8'0"
Pit lift is in (1) section

BACKSTAGE

LOADING DOCK
Loading door(s):
   12'0" high x 10'0" wide
Trucks load (2) at same time
Fork lift is not required; House owns
Sound/Props can load in FOH
Lobby cannot be a work area
(8) Trailers can store on-site
Security at dock & stage door

WARDROBE
Location: Backstage dressing room hallway
Access: at stage level
(2) Washers (3) Dryers
Washer and dryer hookups available

DRESSING ROOMS
(1) Star, SL, stage level, t/s included, phone jack
(5) Small, stage level, t/s on same fl
(2) Chorus, stage level, t/s included
Additional production office available for company mgr

SOUND

CONSOLE
Midas XL 200, located HR
56 inputs, 3 main outputs, 8 matrix outputs, 2 aux outputs

SPEAKERS
House Cluster
Portable
No speaker truss

COMMUNICATIONS
Clear Com intercom with (3) channels
Infrared sound system
Dressing room page system

ROAD CONSOLE
Located HR
No seats required to be removed
Cable run from stage is 80'
Tie-in into house system with XLR connectors

REHEARSAL & STORAGE SPACE
Rehearsal: SR - mirrors and piano available
Storage: None

ELECTRICS

ROAD SERVICE POWER

Panel	Phase	Amp	Circuit Protection	Use	Location
A-B	3	400	breaker	dimmers	USR
C	3	300	breaker	sound	SL
D-E	3	200	breaker	utility	USR

Recommended location of touring dimmer racks: SR
Hoist not required
Additional power is available for tour buses, generators, etc.

FRONT OF HOUSE (BOX BOOM VALUES ARE PER SIDE)

Position	Pipe Width	Distance to Prosc.	House Circuits	Connector Type	FOH Transfer Circuits
Prosc. bridge	58'		37	grd 20 amp stage pin	37
Catwalk 2	65'	41'	37	grd 20 amp stage pin	37
Catwalk 3	65'	45'	37	grd 20 amp stage pin	37
1st Balc Rail		85'	8	grd 20 amp stage pin	8
Box Boom 1			13	grd 20 amp stage pin	13

EQUIPMENT FOH (BOX BOOM VALUES ARE PER SIDE)

Position	Quantity	Wattage	Instrument	Removeable
1st Cove	30	1,000	8 x 13 Lekos	yes
2nd Cove	30	1,000	10 x 23 Lekos	yes
Box Boom 1	16	1,000	6 x 12 Lekos	yes

FOLLOWSPOTS
House Followspots:
   (2)Xenon Super Trouper 2k; not removeable
   (2) Gladiators 2k; not removeable

Followspot Booth:
   (4) spots per booth;
   (4) 2Ø 30 amp breakers

DIMMERS
Lighting console is ETC Expression 3;
   (384) 2.4k Strand Century dimmers
House has programmable DMX control system
(1) dry run DMX station(s)

CROOK & CHASE THEATER

FORMERLY: THE GATLIN BROTHERS THEATRE **AT:** FANTASY HARBOUR   **YEAR BUILT: 1994   YEAR RENOVATED: 1999**

Theatre Location: 2901 Fantasy Way, Myrtle Beach, SC 29579
Management Company: Grand Strand Theater Productions, LLC

Main Administrative Phone: 843-236-5229
Main Administrative Fax: 843-236-3373
Stage Door Phone: 843-236-6112

THEATRE STAFF
President   C. Bailey, Jr.   843-236-6113
Booking   C. Bailey, Jr.   843-236-6113
Marketing   L.H. McCoy   843-236-5227
Operations   Bonita Lloyd   843-236-6581
Group Sales   843-236-5036

HOUSE CREW
Technical Director   Mike Cook   843-236-6112
Stage Manager   Ron Carpenter   843-236-6622
Electrics   Hans Shoop   843-236-6112
Sound   Larry "Les" Stock   843-236-6112

SEATING CAPACITY
Orchestra   973
Mezzanine   998
Total: **1,971**

wheelchair (add'l)   55

BOX OFFICE
Computerized
Box Office Manager
  Jason Aiesi   843-236-8022

Outside Ticket Agency
  None

Box office is promoter operated

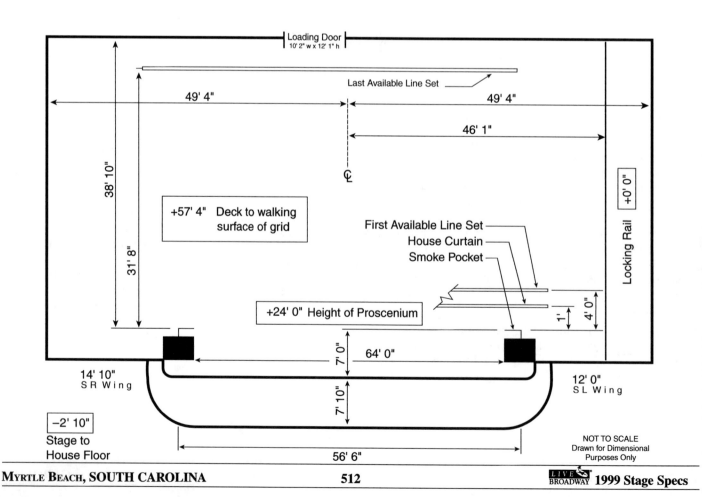

STAGE HOUSE

HOUSE CURTAIN
Operates as a guillotine or traveller from SL deck

RIGGING SYSTEM
Type:	Single purchase counter weight
Weight:	40,000 lbs available
Line sets:	40 sets at 8" o.c. with 7 lift lines per set
House Pipes:	76' long with 53' of travel from deck

Line sets are moveable
Block & Falls are not available
Chain hoists are not available
(1) spot wheel

PERMANENT INSTALLATIONS OVER STAGE (FROM SMOKE POCKET)
M=Moveable with advance call
Movie screen (1) at 15'0" x 20'0" at 0'4" from smoke pocket; M
Traveller (1) at 5'9" and 31'0"; M
Fire curtain (1)
Catwalk (3) at 27'0", 54'0", 77'0"

PERMANENT INSTALLATIONS ON DECK
Traps in stage door (2) 3'10" x 3' 10"
Hard legs (2) 24'0" high x 4'0" wide

ORCHESTRA PIT
Nonadjustable at 6' below stage level
Apron overhangs US wall of pit 0'0"

BACKSTAGE

LOADING DOCK
Loading door(s):
  12'1" high x 10'2" wide
Trucks load (2) at same time
Ground level; need ramps;
  partial cover above door
Fork lift is not required
Sound/Props can load in FOH
(10) Trailers can store on-site

WARDROBE
Location: Off USR
Access: 10' x 10' roll-up door
  & standard door
(2) Washers (3) Dryers
No washer or dryer hookups

DRESSING ROOMS
(5) Star, SL/SR, stage level, t/s included, phone jack
(2) Small, SR, stage level, t/s included, phone jack
(3) Chorus, SR, stage level, t/s included
Use dressing room for company mgr office

SOUND

CONSOLE
Soundcraft Vienna II, located Center House
36 mono, 4 stereo inputs,
  3 main outputs, 8 matrix
  outputs, 8 aux outputs
Mackie: 24inputs, 2main
  outputs, 6 aux outputs

SPEAKERS
House Cluster
No speaker truss
Main three clusters on
  motors, zones dead hung

COMMUNICATIONS
Clear Com intercom with
  (3) channels
Infrared sound system
Dressing room page system

ROAD CONSOLE
Located Center
(6) seats required to be
  removed
Cable run from stage is 130'
Tie-in into house system with
  XLR connectors

REHEARSAL & STORAGE SPACE
Rehearsal: None
Storage: None

ELECTRICS

ROAD SERVICE POWER
Panel	Phase	Amp	Circuit Protection	Use	Location
A	3	400	breaker	dimmers	DSL
B	3	400	breaker	dimmers	USL
C	3	100	breaker	sound	DSL
D	3	200	breaker	extra	Outside dock door
E	3	100	breaker	extra	Outside dock door

Recommended location of touring dimmer racks: SL
Hoist not required
Additional power is available for tour buses, generators, etc.

FRONT OF HOUSE (BOX BOOM VALUES ARE PER SIDE)
Position	Pipe Width	Distance to Prosc.	House Circuits	Connector Type	FOH Transfer Circuits
1st Catwalk		27'	32	grd 20 amp stage pin	0
2nd Catwalk		54'	20	grd 20 amp stage pin	0

Transfer circuits: DMX input DSR

EQUIPMENT FOH (BOX BOOM VALUES ARE PER SIDE)
Position	Quantity	Wattage	Instrument	Removeable
1st Catwalk	4	1,000	Leko/Par 64	yes
2nd Catwalk	6	1,000	Leko/Par 64	yes

FOLLOWSPOTS
House Followspots:
  (3) Lycian, Super Arc 400
  long throw; removeable

Followspot Booth:
  (3) spots per booth;
  120' throw to proscenium;
  (3) 1Ø 20 amp breakers

DIMMERS
Lighting console is Avo
  Sapphire;
(192) ETC Sensor dimmers
House has programmable
  DMX control system
(1) dry run DMX station

PALACE THEATER AT MYRTLE BEACH

AKA: BROADWAY AT THE BEACH   **YEAR BUILT: 1995**

Theatre Location: 1420 Celebrity Circle, Myrtle Beach, SC 29577

SEATING CAPACITY	
Floor	1,400
Mezzanine	1,200
Total:	**2,600**

Main Administrative Phone:	843-448-9224
Main Administrative Fax:	843-626-9659
Stage Door Phone:	843-448-9924
Traveling Production Office Phone:	843-444-9212
Traveling Production Office Fax:	843-444-9023

THEATRE STAFF

Producer and General Manager	Richard Akins	843-448-9224

HOUSE CREW

	Dan Laveglia	843-448-9224 x245
Stage Operations	Steve Sweet	843-448-9224 x127
Electrics	Scott Sanchez	843-448-9224 x128

STAGE DIMENSIONS (FROM SMOKE POCKET)

Stage is 41'4" deep
Width from Center Line to SL is 58'9"
Width from Center Line to SR is 58'9"
Proscenium width is 63'10"
Proscenium height is 30'0"
Smoke pocket to apron edge is 10'0"
No orchestra pit

RIGGING

Grid Height:	70'
Type:	Single purchase counter weight
Weight:	42,000 lbs
Line sets:	37 sets at 8" o.c.
Arbors:	2,000 lb capacity
House Pipes:	75' long

LOADING DOCK

Loading door(s) are 12'0" high x 12'0" wide
Trucks load (3) at same time
Fork lift is not required and is not available

ELECTRICS

Total power available:
    (1) 600A 3Ø SR
    (2) 200A 3Ø SR
    (2) 100A 3Ø SR

FOLLOWSPOTS

House Followspots:
    Lycian 1275/1.2k
No power in spot booth

DIMMERS

(288) house dimmers
House has DMX control system
(3) dry run station(s) located
    Dimmer rooms

SOUND

House has 100A dedicated
    power located SR
FOH mixing position in
    Center Orchestra
Sound console is available

RUSHMORE PLAZA CIVIC CENTER FINE ARTS THEATRE

YEAR BUILT: **1976**

Theatre Location: 444 Mt. Rushmore Road N., Rapid City, SD 57701

Main Administrative Phone: 605-394-4115
Main Administrative Fax: 605-394-4119
E-mail: civicctr@rapidnet.com
Website: www.gotmine.com

THEATRE STAFF

Stage Manager   Susan Ripple   605-394-9115
Event Coordinator   Ronda Oman   605-394-9115

SEATING CAPACITY

Main Floor	1,000
Balcony	800
Total:	**1,800**
pit (add'l)	0
wheelchair (add'l)	0
standing (add'l)	0

STAGE DIMENSIONS (FROM SMOKE POCKET)

Stage is 45'0" deep
Width from Center Line to SL is 45'0"
Width from Center Line to SR is 45'0"
Proscenium width is 55'6"
Proscenium height is 24'0"
Smoke pocket to apron edge is 8'0"
Orchestra pit exists

RIGGING

Grid Height:	68'8"
Type:	Single purchase counter weight
Weight:	10,000 lbs
Line sets:	60 sets at 6" o.c.
Arbors:	2,000 lb capacity
House Pipes:	65' long

LOADING DOCK

Loading door(s) are 20'0" high x 15'0" wide
Trucks load (1) at a time
Fork lift is not required

ELECTRICS

Total power available:
  (2) 800A 3Ø SL
  (1) 100A 3Ø SL

FOLLOWSPOTS

House Followspots:
  Carbon Super Troupers
Power in spot booth (2) 30A

DIMMERS

(100) house dimmers
No DMX control system
No dry run station(s)

SOUND

House has undedicated
  power located SL
FOH mixing position in
  Rear House Center
Sound console is available

MEMORIAL AUDITORIUM

AKA: SOLDIERS AND SAILORS MEMORIAL AUDITORIUM

YEAR BUILT: 1924   **YEAR RENOVATED: 1991**

Theatre Location: 399 McCallie Avenue, Chattanooga, TN 37402
Management Company: City of Chatanooga

Main Administrative Phone: 423-757-5156
Main Administrative Fax: 423-757-5326
E-mail: johnson-david@mail.chattanooga.gov
Website: www.chattanooga.gov/showplaces
Backstage Pay Phone: 423-757-0905/06
Traveling Production Office Phone: (4) Lines available

SEATING CAPACITY

Front Orchestra	1,309
Rear Orchestra	1,028
Boxes	32
Lower Balcony	1,166
Upper Balcony	331
Total:	**3,866**
pit (add'l)	48

BOX OFFICE
Computerized
Box Office Manager
   Sandra Coulter   423-757-5156

THEATRE STAFF
Manager	David Johnson	423-757-5156
Booking	David Johnson	423-757-5156
Marketing	Donna Landry	423-757-5156
Group Sales	Sandra Coulter	423-757-5156

HOUSE CREW
Technical Director	Mickey Hipp	423-757-5156

UNIONS
IATSE Local #140	Chris Keene	423-894-6738
Music	Bob Watkins	423-266-5912

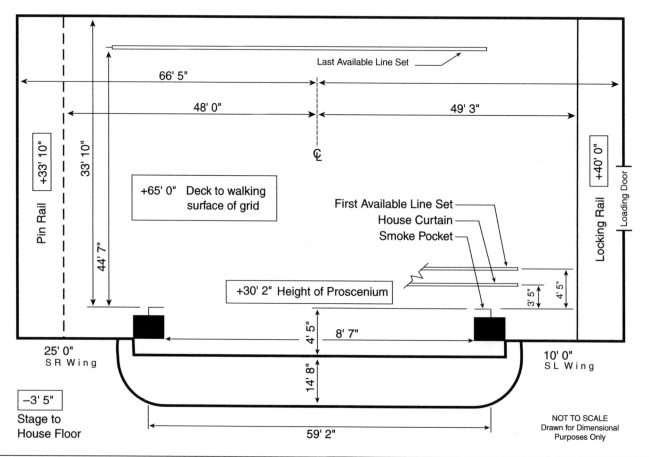

STAGE HOUSE

House Curtain
Operates as a guillotine or traveller from SL deck

Rigging System
Type:	Single and double purchase counter weight; Hemp system
Weight:	100,000 lbs available
Line sets:	39 sets with 7 lift lines per set (double)
	13 sets with 7 lift lines per set (single)
Arbors:	3,500 lb capacity
House Pipes:	73'6" long

Line sets moveable
(40) spot wheels and 10,000' of hemp available
Hemp sets are operated from SR fly floor

Permanent Installations Over Stage (from smoke pocket)
Electric raceways (4) at 6'4", 16'8", 26'1", 37'1"

Permanent Installations On Deck
None

Orchestra Pit
Adjustable by hydraulic lift from basement to stage level
Apron overhangs US wall of pit 0' 0"

BACKSTAGE

Loading Dock
Loading door(s):
    12'0" high x 10'0" wide
Dock is 42" high
(2) Trailers can store on-site
Security at dock & stage door

Wardrobe
Location: Basement
Access: Elevator or stairs
(1) Washer (1) Dryer
Washer and dryer hookups available

Dressing Rooms
(4) Star, basement, t/s, phone jack
(4) Chorus, basement, t/s
Elevator access for dressing rooms
Additional production office available for company mgr

SOUND

Console
Yamaha PM1800-24
24 inputs, 4 matrix outputs, 6 aux outputs

Speakers
House Cluster
Under Balcony

Communications
Clear Com intercom
Audex hearing impaired system
Dressing room page system

Road Console
Located Orchestra, left of center
Cable run from stage is 86'

Rehearsal & Storage Space
Rehearsal: 29' x 21', located basement level
Storage: None

ELECTRICS

Road Service Power

Panel	Phase	Amp	Circuit Protection	Use	Location
A-B	3	400	fuse	dimmers	DSR
C	3	200	fuse	dimmers	DSR
D	3	150	fuse	sound	DSL

Recommended location of touring dimmer racks: SR on deck
No additional power for buses

Front Of House (box boom values are per side)

Position	Pipe Width	Distance to Prosc.	House Circuits	Connector Type	FOH Transfer Circuits
Catwalk 1	76'	62'	32	grd 20 amp stage pin	2
Catwalk 2	76'	45'	25	grd 20 amp stage pin	2
Box Boom 1		21'	8	grd 20 amp stage pin	
Box Boom 2		37'	8	grd 20 amp stage pin	

Transfer circuits: grd 20 amp stage pin located on DSR proscenium wall
Road truss: FOH patch circuits located DSR

Equipment FOH (box boom values are per side)
None

Followspots
House Followspots:
    (4) Xenon Super Troupers; not removeable

Dimmers
Lighting console is Strand Light Palette, Strand LBM; (385) Strand dimmers
House has programmable DMX control system
(4) dry run DMX station(s) located right, left, catwalk, cockpit

TIVOLI THEATRE

AKA: MEMORIAL AUDITORIUM

YEAR BUILT: 1921   **YEAR RENOVATED: 1987**

Theatre Location: 709 Broad Street, Chattanooga, TN 37402
Mailing Address: 399 McCallie Ave., Chattanooga, TN 37402
Management Company: City of Chattanooga (mailing address as above)

Main Administrative Phone: 423-757-5156
Main Administrative Fax: 423-757-5326
E-mail: johnson-david@mail.chatanooga.gov
Website: www.chatanooga.gov/showplaces
Traveling Production Office Phone: 2 available lines

THEATRE STAFF
Manager	David Johnson	423-757-5156
Booking	David Johnson	423-757-5156
Marketing	Donna Landry	423-757-5156
Group Sales	Sandra Coulter	423-757-5156

HOUSE CREW
Technical Director	Ken Dolberry	423-757-5457

UNIONS
IATSE Local #140	Chris Keene	423-894-6738
Music	Bob Watkins	423-266-5912

SEATING CAPACITY
Orchestra	1,012
Boxes	48
Loge	78
Balcony	624
Total:	**1,762**
pit (add'l)	104

BOX OFFICE
Computerized
Box Office Manager
Sandra Coulter   423-757-5156

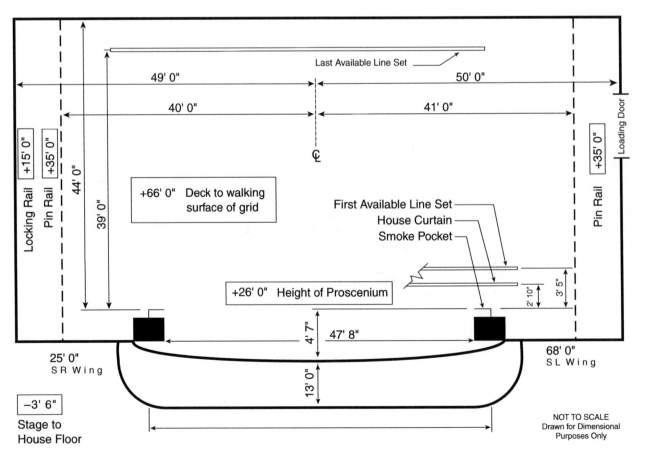

STAGE HOUSE

HOUSE CURTAIN
Operates as a guillotine or traveller from SR deck

RIGGING SYSTEM
Type:	Double purchase counter weight
Weight:	100,000 lbs available
Line sets:	40 sets at 7" o.c. with 6 lift lines per set
Arbors:	2,500 lb capacity
House Pipes:	63' long with 65' of travel from deck

Line sets are moveable
Block & Falls are available
(40) spot wheels and 10,000' of hemp available

PERMANENT INSTALLATIONS OVER STAGE (FROM SMOKE POCKET)
M=Moveable with advance call
Orchestra shell (3) at 8'1", 20'4", 34'4"; M
Electric raceways (4) at 5'9", 15'8", 23'3", 31'5"
Traveller (1) at 17'5"

PERMANENT INSTALLATIONS ON DECK
None

ORCHESTRA PIT
Adjustable to 9' below stage level by hydraulic lift
Apron overhangs US wall of pit 8' 4"
Pit lift is in (1) section

BACKSTAGE

LOADING DOCK
Loading door(s):
  10'0" high x 8'2" wide
Trucks load (2) side by side at same time
Fork lift is not required
Sound/Props cannot load in FOH
(2) Trailers can store on-site
Security at dock & stage door

WARDROBE
Location: Basement
Access: Elevator

DRESSING ROOMS
(4) Star, SL, stage, t/s included, phone jack
(2) Chorus, SL, stage, t/s included
Elevator access for dressing rooms
Additional production office available for company mgr

SOUND

CONSOLE
Ramsa WRA616, located Balcony
16 inputs, 2 main outputs, 2 aux outputs

SPEAKERS
House Cluster
Under Balcony
Portable
No speaker truss

COMMUNICATIONS
Clear Com intercom with (1) channel
Infrared sound system
Dressing room page system

ROAD CONSOLE
Located Rear Orchestra right under Balcony
No seats required to be removed
Cable run from stage is 100'
Tie-in into house system with XLR connectors

REHEARSAL & STORAGE SPACE
Rehearsal: 31' x 60' located +2, piano available
Storage: 42' x 30' located SL on stage level

ELECTRICS

ROAD SERVICE POWER
Panel	Phase	Amp	Circuit Protection	Use	Location
A-B	3	400	fuse	dimmers	SR
C	3	200	fuse	sound	SR
D-F	3	400	breaker	extra	SL basement
G	3	200	fuse	extra	SL

Hoist not required
Additional power is available for tour buses, generators, etc.

FRONT OF HOUSE (BOX BOOM VALUES ARE PER SIDE)
Position	Pipe Width	Distance to Prosc.	House Circuits	Connector Type	FOH Transfer Circuits
Box Boom 1		45'	20	grd 20 amp stage pin	20
Dome Catwalk		67'	20	grd 20 amp stage pin	20

Transfer circuits: grd 20 amp stage pin

EQUIPMENT FOH (BOX BOOM VALUES ARE PER SIDE)
None

FOLLOWSPOTS
House Followspots:
  (2) Xenon Super Troupers; not removeable

Followspot Booth:
  (2) spots per booth;
  100' throw to proscenium;
  (4) 3Ø 50 amp breakers

DIMMERS
Lighting console is Prestige 3000;
(350) Strand dimmers
House has programmable DMX control system
(3) dry run DMX station(s), Balcony, booth, pit

KNOXVILLE CIVIC AUDITORIUM

AT: **KNOXVILLE CIVIC AUDITORIUM & COLISEUM**   **YEAR BUILT: 1961**

Theatre Location: 500 East Church Avenue, Knoxville, TN 37915
Mailing Address: PO Box 2603, Knoxville, TN 37901

Main Administrative Phone: 423-544-5399
Main Administrative Fax: 423-544-5386
E-mail: kivey@ci.knoxville.tn.us
Stage Door Phone: 423-544-5399 X270

THEATRE STAFF
  Director   Bob Poke   423-544-5399
  Booking   Ken Ivey   423-544-5399
HOUSE CREW
  Stage Manager   David Scruggs   423-544-5399
UNIONS
  IATSE Local #197 Donald Scruggs   423-531-0319
  Wardrobe   Jean Wright   423-584-8123
  Music   Al Curtis   423-544-5399

SEATING CAPACITY
  Orchestra   1,300
  Balcony   1,100
  Total   **2,400**

  pit (add'l)   96
  wheelchair (incl.)   8

BOX OFFICE
  Computerized
  Box Office Manager
    Charlotte Bounds   423-544-5388

  Outside Ticket Agency
  Computerized
  Tickets Unlimited
    Mike Connor   423-494-0123

  Box office is promoter operated

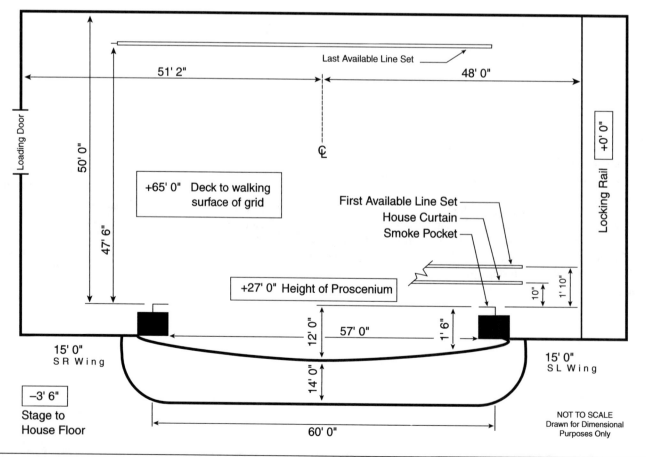

+65' 0"   Deck to walking
          surface of grid

51' 2"   48' 0"

Last Available Line Set

First Available Line Set
House Curtain
Smoke Pocket

Locking Rail   +0' 0"

Loading Door

50' 0"

47' 6"

+27' 0" Height of Proscenium

12' 0"   57' 0"   1' 6"

14' 0"

10"   1' 10"

15' 0"
S R Wing

15' 0"
S L Wing

−3' 6"
Stage to
House Floor

60' 0"

NOT TO SCALE
Drawn for Dimensional
Purposes Only

STAGE HOUSE

HOUSE CURTAIN
Operates as a guillotine or traveller from SR fly floor or deck

RIGGING SYSTEM
Type: Single purchase counter weight
Weight: 11,000 lbs available
Line sets: 59 sets at 8" o.c. with 50 lift lines per set
Arbors: 650 lb capacity
House Pipes: 70' long with 61' of travel from deck
Line sets are moveable
Chain hoists are available as a rental
1,200' of hemp available

PERMANENT INSTALLATIONS OVER STAGE (FROM SMOKE POCKET)
M=Moveable with advance call
Traveller (3) 0'18", 12'0", 20'0"; M

PERMANENT INSTALLATIONS ON DECK
Electric jump (1) 4'0" deep, SR

ORCHESTRA PIT
Adjustable to 8' below stage level by manual lift
Apron overhangs US wall of pit 9'0"

BACKSTAGE

LOADING DOCK
Loading door(s):
10'0" high x 11'7" wide
Trucks load (2) side-by-side at same time
Dock is at truck level; loading to stage thru separate scenery dock
Fork lift is not required
Sound/Props cannot load in FOH
Lobby cannot be a work area
(2) Trailers can store on-site
Security at dock & stage door

WARDROBE
Location: Basement
Access: Elevator
Washer and dryer hookups available

DRESSING ROOMS
(4) Star, SL, +½/ -½, t/s included
(4) Small, SL, +½/ -½, t/s included
(2) Chorus, basement, t/s included
Phone jacks can be installed upon request
Additional production office available for company mgr

SOUND

CONSOLE
Custom
16 inputs, 4 main outputs

SPEAKERS
House Cluster

COMMUNICATIONS
Clear Com intercom with (2) channels
Dressing room page system

ROAD CONSOLE
Located Rear House
No seats required to be removed
Cable run from stage is 150'
Tie-in into house system with XLR connectors

REHEARSAL & STORAGE SPACE
Rehearsal: 52' x 90' located in adjacent building
Storage: 70' x 159' located in adjacent building

ELECTRICS

ROAD SERVICE POWER

Panel	Phase	Amp	Circuit Protection	Use	Location
A	3	100	breaker	sound	SR
B	3	800	breaker	extra	USR

Recommended location of touring dimmer racks: SR
Hoist not required

FRONT OF HOUSE (BOX BOOM VALUES ARE PER SIDE)

Position	Pipe Width	Distance to Prosc.	House Circuits	Connector Type	FOH Transfer Circuits
1st Balc Rail	32'	85'	16	ungrd 20 amp stage pin	16
1st Cove	70'	59'	28	ungrd 20 amp stage pin	0

Transfer circuits: ungrd 20 amp stage pin located on DSR side wall
Road truss: Pipe width of 1st Balc Rail is comprised of (16) 2'0" long windows

EQUIPMENT FOH (BOX BOOM VALUES ARE PER SIDE)

Position	Quantity	Wattage	Instrument	Removeable
1st Cove	20	1,000	Colortran Zoom	yes

FOLLOWSPOTS
House Followspots:
None

Followspot Booth:
(3) spots per booth;
136' throw to proscenium;
3Ø 100 amp breakers
Additional followspot location in balcony

DIMMERS
No lighting console
No dimmers
No DMX control system

THE ORPHEUM THEATRE

YEAR BUILT: 1928   YEAR RENOVATED: 1997

Theatre Location: 203 South Main, Memphis, TN 38103
Mailing Address: PO Box 3370, Memphis, TN 38173

Main Administrative Phone: 901-525-7800
Main Administrative Fax: 901-526-0829
E-mail: orpheumtn@aol.com
Website: www.orpheum-memphis.com
Backstage Pay Phone: 901-578-8964

THEATRE STAFF
President   Pat Halloran   901-525-7800
Booking   Pat Halloran   901-525-7800
Marketing   Tracy Ingle   901-525-7800
Operations   Paulette Smithers 901-525-7800
Group Sales   Susan Parsons   901-525-7800

HOUSE CREW
Technical Director   Richard Reinach   901-525-7800 x286
Stage Manager   Charles Veach   901-525-7800 x286

UNIONS
IATSE Local #69   Bill Klyce   901-377-4836
Wardrobe Local #825   Jackie Hicks   901-272-1171
Music   Bill Flores   901-683-3193

SEATING CAPACITY
Orchestra   1,264
Mezzanine   314
Grand Tier   141
Balcony   400
Galleries   319
Total: **2,438**

wheelchair (add'l)   15

BOX OFFICE
Computerized
Director Patron Services
  Teresa Ward   901-525-7800 x222

Outside Ticket Agency
Computerized
Ticket Hubb   901-725-HUBB

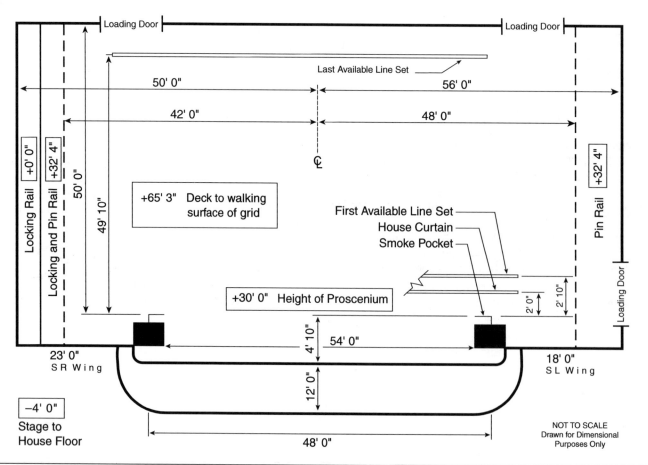

+65' 3"   Deck to walking surface of grid

+30' 0"   Height of Proscenium

First Available Line Set
House Curtain
Smoke Pocket

Last Available Line Set

Loading Door

Locking Rail   +0' 0"
Locking and Pin Rail   +32' 4"
Pin Rail   +32' 4"
Loading Door

50' 0"   56' 0"
42' 0"   48' 0"
50' 0"
49' 10"

23' 0"
SR Wing
18' 0"
SL Wing

4' 10"
54' 0"
12' 0"

2' 0"
2' 10"

−4' 0"
Stage to House Floor

48' 0"

NOT TO SCALE
Drawn for Dimensional
Purposes Only

STAGE HOUSE

HOUSE CURTAIN
Operates as a guillotine or traveller from SR fly floor or deck

RIGGING SYSTEM
Type:	Single purchase counter weight
Weight:	40,000 lbs available
Line sets:	90 sets at 6" o.c. with 6 lift lines per set
Arbors:	1,200 lb capacity
House Pipes:	73' long with 61' of travel from deck

Line sets are moveable
Block & Falls are not available
Chain hoists are available as a rental; (2) one ton
(50) spot wheels and 2,000' of hemp available

PERMANENT INSTALLATIONS OVER STAGE (FROM SMOKE POCKET)
M=Moveable with advance call
Electric Raceways (3) at 6'4", 13'4", 21'0"; M
Movie Screen (1) distance varies; M
Traveller (1) at 2'4"; M
Cyclorama (1) distance varies; M
Fire Curtain (1)

PERMANENT INSTALLATIONS ON DECK
None

ORCHESTRA PIT
Adjustable to 12' below stage level by hydraulic lift
Apron overhangs US wall of pit 13'0"
Pit lift is SL in (1) section
Organ lift SR

BACKSTAGE

LOADING DOCK
Loading door(s): (3) doors each 11'4" high x 9'4" wide
Trucks load (3) at same time
Fork lift is not required
Sound/Props can load in FOH
Lobby can be a work area
(3) Trailers can store on-site
Security at stage door

WARDROBE
Location: +1 above stage
Access: Freight elevator in loading dock
2 Washer(s) 3 Dryer(s)
Washer and dryer hookups available

DRESSING ROOMS
(1) Star, SR, stage level, t/s included, phone jacks
(5) Small, SL/SR, +1/-1, t/s included, phone jacks
(6) Chorus, SL/SR, +1, t/s included, phone jacks
Elevator access for dressing rooms
Use dressing room for company manager office

SOUND

CONSOLE
Soundcraft K2, located Rear Center
32 inputs, 3 main outputs, 4 matrix outputs, 8 aux outputs

SPEAKERS
House Cluster
Under Balcony
Portable
Speaker truss
Max allowable load 2,000 lbs
No pipe / rigging available

COMMUNICATIONS
Clear Com intercom with (2) channels
Infrared sound system
Dressing room page system

ROAD CONSOLE
Located Rear Center
No seats required to be removed
Cable run from stage is 95'
Tie-in into house system with XLR connectors

REHEARSAL & STORAGE SPACE
Rehearsal: 40' x 40', USL, Sprung floor
Storage: Loading dock, 40' x 40', USR

ELECTRICS

ROAD SERVICE POWER

Panel	Phase	Amp	Circuit Protection	Use	Location
A-C	3	400	fuse	dimmers	DSR
D-E	3	400	breaker	extra	USR
F-G	3	400	breaker	extra	USL
H	3	200	breaker	sound	Mid SL (isolated)

Recommended location of touring dimmer racks: DSR
Hoist not required

FRONT OF HOUSE (BOX BOOM VALUES ARE PER SIDE)

Position	Pipe Width	Distance to Prosc.	House Circuits	Connector Type	FOH Transfer Circuits
1st Balc Rail	50'	65'	30	grd 20 amp stage pin	30
1st Cove	50'	120'	24	grd 20 amp stage pin	24
Box Boom 1		30'	12	grd 20 amp stage pin	12

Transfer circuits: grd 20 amp stage pin

EQUIPMENT FOH (BOX BOOM VALUES ARE PER SIDE)

Position	Quantity	Wattage	Instrument	Removeable
1st Cove	10	1,000	10 x 23	
Box Boom 1	24	1,000	6 x 16	yes

FOLLOWSPOTS
House Followspots:
(3) Strong Xenon Super Troupers; not removeable

Followspot Booth:
(4) spots per booth;
125' throw to proscenium;
(4) 1Ø 30 amp breakers

DIMMERS
House console is ETC Obsession 1536; 297 Strand / ETC dimmers
House has non-programmable DMX control system

ANDREW JACKSON HALL

AT: TENNESSEE PERFORMING ARTS CENTER

YEAR BUILT: 1980   YEAR RENOVATED: 1997

Theatre Location: 505 Deaderick Street, Nashville, TN 37219
Management Company: Tennessee Performing Arts Center
                     Management Corporation
                     505 Deaderick Street, Nashville, TN 37219

Main Administrative Phone: 615-782-4000
Main Administrative Fax: 615-782-4001
Website: www.tpac.org
Stage Door Phone: 615-782-4038

THEATRE STAFF
President & CEO   Steven Greil   615-782-4021
Booking   Thomas K. Baker   615-782-4026
Marketing   Kathleen O'Brien   615-782-4027
Operations   Eric Swartz   615-782-4043
Group Sales   Nancy Malone   615-782-4046

HOUSE CREW
Technical Director   Jonathan Hutchins   615-782-4054
Electrics   Chris Wilson   615-782-4075
Sound   John Sanders   615-782-4083

UNIONS
IATSE Local #46   Mark Kirqcofe   615-885-1058
Wardrobe Local #915   Faye Cole   615-889-6358

SEATING CAPACITY
Orchestra	1,058
Grand Tier	760
Loge	220
Mezzanine	360
Total:	**2,398**

pit (add'l)	44
wheelchair (add'l)	20

BOX OFFICE
Computerized
Box Office Manager
  Mary I. Whitaker   615-782-4070

Outside Ticket Agency
Computerized
Ticketmaster
  Christi Dortch   615-782-4062

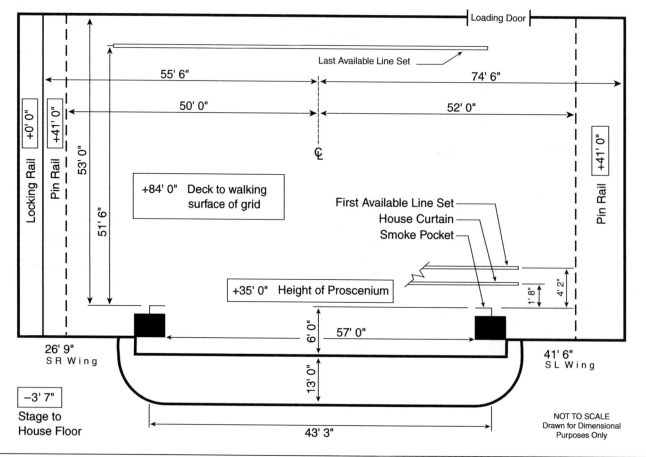

STAGE HOUSE

HOUSE CURTAIN
Operates as a guillotine from SR deck

RIGGING SYSTEM
Type:	Single purchase counter weight
Weight:	24,000 lbs available
Line sets:	68 sets at 6" o.c. with 7 lift lines per set
Arbors:	1,250 lb capacity
House Pipes:	76' long with 77' of travel from deck

Line sets are not moveable
Block & Falls are not available
Chain hoists available as a rental; (2) one ton
(40) spot wheels and 4000' of hemp available

PERMANENT INSTALLATIONS OVER STAGE (FROM SMOKE POCKET)
M=Moveable with advance call
Orchestra shell (4) at 5'4", 16'3", 26'2", 37'1"
Traveller (2) line at 35'9", 49'0"; M
Electric pipe (10) at 6'0", 7'6", 15'0", 17'0", 23'1", 24'6", 32'0", 33'1", 40'6", 42'0"
Cyclorama (1) at 48'3"

PERMANENT INSTALLATIONS ON DECK
Orchestra shell (12) 35' deep x 10' wide, located storage bay DSL wall

ORCHESTRA PIT
Adjustable to 25' below stage level by hydraulic lift
Apron overhangs US wall of pit 6' 0"
Pit lift is in (1) section

BACKSTAGE

LOADING DOCK
Loading door(s):
 16'0 high x 15'0" wide
Trucks load (2) at same time
Dock is on a 7° upgrade
Fork lift is not required
Sound/Props can load in FOH
Lobby cannot be a work area
Trailers cannot store on-site
Security at dock & stage door

WARDROBE
Location: Dressing room level, -1 below stage
Access: Elevator
(3) Washers (3) Dryers
Washer and dryer hookups available

DRESSING ROOMS
(1) Star, SR/SL, -1, t/s included, phone jack
(7) Small, SR/SL, -1, t/s included, phone jack
(4) Chorus, SR/SL, -2, t/s included, phone jack
Elevator access for dressing rooms
Additional production office available for company mgr

SOUND

CONSOLE
Yamaha PM 3500, located Orchestra
44-4 inputs, 4-stereo/4mono outputs, 8 aux outputs

SPEAKERS
House Cluster
Proscenium
Under Balcony
Portable
Delay system
No speaker truss

COMMUNICATIONS
Clear Com intercom with (2) channels
Infrared sound system
Dressing room page system

ROAD CONSOLE
Located Rear House
No seats required to be removed
Cable run from stage is 250'
Tie-in into house system with World Win W4 connectors

REHEARSAL & STORAGE SPACE
Rehearsal: 37' x 46', located -2, mirrors, piano, chairs, prior arrangement required
Storage: 46' x 36', store light & sound; Shop, 36' x 86', located +2, elevator access

ELECTRICS

ROAD SERVICE POWER

Panel	Phase	Amp	Circuit Protection	Use	Location
A-C	3	400	fuse	dimmers	SR Alcove
D	3	200	fuse	sound	SL Alcove

Recommended location of touring dimmer racks: SR Alcove
Hoist not required
Additional power is available for tour buses, generators, etc.

FRONT OF HOUSE (BOX BOOM VALUES ARE PER SIDE)

Position	Pipe Width	Distance to Prosc.	House Circuits	Connector Type	FOH Transfer Circuits
Bridge	57'	6'	52	grd 20 amp stage pin	17
1st Cove	70'	39'	52	grd 20 amp stage pin	17
2nd Cove	70'	67'	49	grd 20 amp stage pin	17
Box Boom 1		39'	12	grd 20 amp stage pin	12

Transfer circuits: Road circuits - pin plug males terminate in SR alcove
Road truss: Limited point availability DS of proscenium

EQUIPMENT FOH (BOX BOOM VALUES ARE PER SIDE)

Position	Quantity	Wattage	Instrument	Removeable
1st Cove	12	1,000	Berkey 6" Zooms	yes
Box Boom 1	20	1,000	Berkey 01 Strand 6" Zooms	yes

FOLLOWSPOTS
House Followspots:
(3) Strong Super Trouper Xenon 2k; not removeable
(4) Strong Gladiators Xenon 3k; not removeable

Followspot Booth:
(3) spots per booth;
125' throw to proscenium;
(3) 2Ø 30 amp breakers

DIMMERS
Lighting console is Strand LP90;
(477) Strand Series 600 dimmers
House has programmable DMX control system
(1) dry run DMX station(s)

JAMES K. POLK THEATRE

AT: TENNESSEE PERFORMING ARTS CENTER   YEAR BUILT: **1980**

Theatre Location: 505 Deaderick Street, Nashville, TN 37219
Management Company: Tennessee Performing Arts Center Management Corp.

Main Administrative Phone: 615-782-4000
Main Administrative Fax: 615-782-4001
Website: www.tpac.org

THEATRE STAFF
CEO & President   Steven Greil   615-782-4000
VP Event Services   Thomas K. Baker   615-782-4000

HOUSE CREW
Technical Director   Eric Swartz   615-782-4000

SEATING CAPACITY
Orchestra	617
Grand Tier	382
Total:	**999**
pit (add'l)	44
wheelchair (add'l)	12
standing (add'l)	0

STAGE DIMENSIONS (FROM SMOKE POCKET)
Stage is 50'0" deep
Width from Center Line to SL is 45'0"
Width from Center Line to SR is 42'6"
Proscenium width is 46'11"
Proscenium height is 30'0"
Smoke pocket to apron edge is 11'11"

RIGGING
Grid Height: 70'
Type: Combination purchase counter weight
Weight: 10,000 lbs
Line sets: 55 sets at 6" o.c.
Arbors: 1,200 lb capacity
House Pipes: 63' long

LOADING DOCK
Loading door(s) are 16'3" high x 12'3" wide
Trucks load (2) at same time
Fork lift is not required and is not available

ELECTRICS
Total power available:
    800A 3Ø SR alcove

FOLLOWSPOTS
House Followspots:
    Super Trouper 1k
Power in spot booth 150A
FOH transfer circuits: 16

DIMMERS
(237) house dimmers
House has DMX control system
(1) dry run station(s) located SR
    alcove

SOUND
House has 100A 3Ø
    undedicated power located
    loading dock
FOH mixing position in
    Rear House Right
Sound console is available

ABILENE CIVIC CENTER

YEAR BUILT: 1970

Theatre Location:	1100 N. 6th St., Abilene, TX 79601	
Mailing Address:	PO Box 60, Abilene, TX 79604	
Main Administrative Phone:	915-676-6211	
Main Administrative Fax:	915-676-6343	
Website:	www.abilenetx.com/civiccenter/toc.html	
Stage Door Phone:	915-738-8085	
Traveling Production Office Phone:	915-738-8085	

SEATING CAPACITY

Orchestra	1,465
Lower Balcony	397
Upper Balcony	270
Total:	**2,132**
pit (add'l)	90
wheelchair (add'l)	6

THEATRE STAFF

Manager	Audrey Perry	915-676-6210
Event Coordinator	Bill Henderson	915-676-6432

HOUSE CREW

Technical Coordinator	Phillip Engel	915-676-6211

STAGE DIMENSIONS (FROM SMOKE POCKET)
Stage is 60' deep
Width from Center Line to SL is 30'
Width from Center Line to SR is 30'
Proscenium width is 60'
Proscenium height is 22'
Smoke pocket to apron edge is 9'
Orchestra pit exists

RIGGING
Grid Height:	62'
Type:	Combination purchase counter weight
Weight:	40,000 lbs
Line sets:	39 sets at 6-12" o.c.
Arbors:	1,200 lb capacity
House Pipes:	62' long

LOADING DOCK
Loading door(s) are 14'0" high x 12'0" wide
Trucks load (1) at a time
Fork lift is not required and is not available
Loading dock is stage level

ELECTRICS
Total power available:
  (2) 400A 3Ø SL basement

FOLLOWSPOTS
House Followspots:
  Xenon Strong Super Trouper
Power in spot booth
  (2) 30A / (2) 20A

DIMMERS
(108) house dimmers
House has DMX control system
(1) dry run station(s) located
  Spot Booth

SOUND
House has (4) 30A
  undedicated power located
  SL
FOH mixing position in
  Upper Balcony
Sound console is available

BASS CONCERT HALL

AT: UNIVERSITY OF TEXAS AT AUSTIN PERFORMING ARTS CENTER   YEAR BUILT: 1981

Theatre Location: 23rd Street & East Campus Dr., Austin, TX 78705
Mailing Address: PO Box 7818, Austin, TX 78713

Main Administrative Phone: 512-471-2787
Main Administrative Fax: 512-471-3636
E-mail: ctanner@mail.utexas.edu
                                    pebbles@mail.utexas.edu
                                    conradhaden@mail.utexas.edu
Website: www.utexas.edu/cofa/pac
Stage Door Phone: 512-471-0621
Backstage Pay Phone: 512-477-0405

THEATRE STAFF

Director	Pebbles Wadsworth	512-471-1394
Booking	Neil Barclay	512-475-7149
Marketing	Bruce Hartman	512-471-0634
Operations	Alva Hascall	512-471-0665
Group Sales	Melissa Goodson	512-471-0648

HOUSE CREW

Technical Coordinator	Conrad Haden	512-471-0614
PSM	Rachel Durkin	512-471-0638
Electrics	Jeff Ellinger	512-471-0675
Sound	Bill Haddad	512-471-7120

UNIONS

IATSE Local #205	Mary Nelson	512-371-1217

SEATING CAPACITY

Orchestra	1,636
First Balcony	629
Second Balcony	607
Total:	**2,872**
pit (add'l)	97
wheelchair (add'l)	40

BOX OFFICE
Computerized
Ticket Office Manager
  Joan Dennis   512-471-0333

Outside Ticket Agency
Computerized
  Ticketmaster   512-471-0333

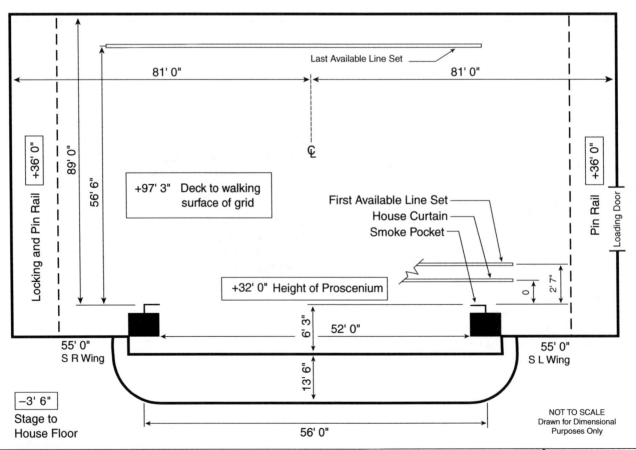

STAGE HOUSE

HOUSE CURTAIN
Operates as a guillotine from SL or SR deck

RIGGING SYSTEM
Type:	Double purchase counter weight
Weight:	72,000 lbs available
Line sets:	71 sets at 6" o.c. with 6 lift lines per set
Arbors:	2,000 lb capacity
House Pipes:	56' long with 90' of travel from deck

Line sets are moveable
Block & Falls are available
Chain hoists are available as a rental
(100) spot wheels and 8,000' of hemp available

PERMANENT INSTALLATIONS OVER STAGE (FROM SMOKE POCKET)
Orchestra shell (4) at 6'3", 17'6", 25'6", 34'0"
Electric raceways (8) at 14'0", 15'0", 23'6", 24'6", 32'6", 41'6", 47'0", 52'6"
Electric bridge (1) at 5'6"
Electric pipe (2) at 4'0", 33'6"
Cyclorama (1) at 48'0"

PERMANENT INSTALLATIONS ON DECK
None

ORCHESTRA PIT
Adjustable to 25' below stage level by hydraulic lift
Apron overhangs US wall of pit 10'0"
Pit lift is in (2) sections

BACKSTAGE

LOADING DOCK
Loading door(s):
    13'10" high x 23'10" wide
Trucks load (2) at same time
3'6" above ground, steep drive leading to dock
Fork lift is not required
Sound/Props can load in FOH
(1) Trailer can store on-site
Security at dock & stage door

WARDROBE
Location: One level below stage
Access: Elevator and stairs
(1) Washer (1) Dryer
Washer and dryer hookups available

DRESSING ROOMS
(4) Star, SL, +1/ +2, t/s included
(4) Small, SL, -1, t/s included
(2) Chorus, SL, +1/ +2, t/s included
Elevator access for dressing rooms
Additional production office available for company mgr

SOUND

CONSOLE
Yamaha PM 4000, located 1st Balcony
48 inputs, 2 main outputs, 8 matrix outputs, 12 aux outputs

SPEAKERS
House Cluster
Portable
Under seat
Speaker truss exists
Max available load 3,000 lbs per point

COMMUNICATIONS
RTS intercom with (6) channels
Dressing room page system

ROAD CONSOLE
Located Center or Rear Orchestra
(16) seats required to be removed
Cable run from stage is 250'
Tie-in into house system with XLR connectors

REHEARSAL & STORAGE SPACE
Rehearsal: 3rd floor, mirrored wall, 6' piano available
Storage: None

ELECTRICS

ROAD SERVICE POWER
Panel	Phase	Amp	Circuit Protection	Use	Location
A	3	400	fuse	sound	SL
B-D	3	400	fuse	extra/dimmers	SL

Recommended location of touring dimmer racks: SL
Hoist not required
Additional power is available for tour buses, generators, etc.

FRONT OF HOUSE (BOX BOOM VALUES ARE PER SIDE)
Position	Pipe Width	Distance to Prosc.	House Circuits	Connector Type	FOH Transfer Circuits
1st Cove	70'	80'	20	grd 20 amp stage pin	0
2nd Cove	86'	140'	20	grd 20 amp stage pin	0
Box Boom 1		52'	10	grd 20 amp stage pin	0
Box Boom 2		64'	10	grd 20 amp stage pin	0

Road truss: Grid over stage with non-removable orchestra shells, motorized light bridges and side ladders; ante-prosecenium hanging points should be discussed with stage carpenter: 30,000 lb max

EQUIPMENT FOH (BOX BOOM VALUES ARE PER SIDE)
Position	Quantity	Wattage	Instrument	Removeable
1st Balc Rail	20	1,000	Source4 19°	yes
1st Cove	6	1,000	Berkey 10°	yes
2nd Cove	10	1,000	Berkey 5°	yes
Box Boom 1	8	1,000	Berkey 10°	yes

FOLLOWSPOTS
House Followspots:
    (2) Xenon Super Trouper 2k; not removeable

Followspot Booth:
    (2) spots per booth;
    140' throw to proscenium;
    (4) 3Ø 30 amp breakers

DIMMERS
Lighting console is ETC Expression;
    (540) Kleigl R80 dimmers
House has programmable DMX control system
(2) dry run DMX station(s)

RUDDER AUDITORIUM

AT: TEXAS A&M UNIVERSITY

YEAR BUILT: 1973

Theatre Location: Joe Routt Blvd
Texas A&M University, College Station, TX 77844

Main Administrative Phone: 409-845-8903
Main Administrative Fax: 409-845-7312
Backstage Pay Phone: 409-846-9836

THEATRE STAFF

Theatre Manager   Bill Bielamowicz   409-845-8903
Executive Director   Anne Black   409-845-1661

HOUSE CREW

Technical Manager   John Whittemore   409-845-8903

SEATING CAPACITY

Orchestra	1,500
Balcony	1,000
Total:	**2,500**
pit (add'l)	0
wheelchair (add'l)	20
standing (add'l)	0

STAGE DIMENSIONS (FROM SMOKE POCKET)

Stage is 50'0" deep
Width from Center Line to SL is 56'0"
Width from Center Line to SR is 59'0"
Proscenium width is 60'0"
Proscenium height is 28'0"
Smoke pocket to apron edge is 3'0"
Orchestra pit exists

RIGGING

Grid Height:	68'
Type:	Single purchase counter weight
Weight:	24,000 lbs
Line sets:	56 sets at 8" o.c.
Arbors:	2,000 lb capacity
House Pipes:	80' long

LOADING DOCK

Loading door(s) are 9'8" high x 12'6" wide
Trucks load (2) at same time
Fork lift is not required and is not available

ELECTRICS

Total power available:
(1) 400A 3Ø USL
(1) 400A 3Ø DSL

FOLLOWSPOTS

House Followspots:
Xenon Super Trouper
Power in spot booth (3) 30A

DIMMERS

(60) house dimmers
House has DMX control system
(2) dry run station(s) located
DSL

SOUND

House has 100A 3Ø
undedicated power located
DSR
FOH mixing position in
Rear House
Sound console is available

BAYFRONT PLAZA AUDITORIUM

AT: BAYFRONT PLAZA CONVENTION CENTER　　　　　　　　**YEAR BUILT: 1978**

Theatre Location:	1901 N. Shoreline Dr., Corpus Christi, TX 78401	
Mailing Address:	PO Box 9277, Corpus Christi, TX 78469-9277	

Main Administrative Phone:	512-883-8543
Main Administrative Fax:	512-883-0788
E-mail:	bayfront@davlin.net
Website:	www.bayfront@davlin.net

SEATING CAPACITY

Orchestra	824
Graand Tier	981
Balcony	714
Total:	**2,526**

THEATRE STAFF

Convention Center Mgr.	John B. Meyer	512-883-8543
Scheduling Coordinator	Terri Caroona	512-883-8543

HOUSE CREW

Business Agent	Danny Vaughan	512-994-1672

STAGE DIMENSIONS (FROM SMOKE POCKET)
Stage is 45'0" deep
Width from Center Line to SL is 59'0"
Width from Center Line to SR is 37'0"
Proscenium width is 48'0"
Proscenium height is 29'0"
Smoke pocket to apron edge is 7'0"
Orchestra pit exists

RIGGING

Grid Height:	90'
Type:	Single purchase counter weight
Line sets:	41 sets at 6-12" o.c.
Arbors:	1,000 lb capacity
House Pipes:	48' long

LOADING DOCK
Loading door(s) are 20'0" high x 20'0" wide
Trucks load (2) at same time
Fork lift is not required and is not available

ELECTRICS
Total power available:
(3) 400A 3Ø SR

FOLLOWSPOTS
House Followspots:
LMI x3
No power in spot booth
FOH transfer circuits per
position: 0

DIMMERS
No house dimmers
House has DMX control system
(1) dry run station(s) located
light booth

SOUND
House has 1,200A 3Ø
undedicated power located
SR
FOH mixing position in
House Left
Sound console is available

THE MAJESTIC THEATRE

YEAR BUILT: 1921   YEAR RENOVATED: 1982

Theatre Location:	1925 Elm Street - Suite 300, Dallas, TX 75201-4516	
Management Company:	DSM Management Group, Inc.	
	PO Box 150188, Dallas, TX 75315-0188	

Main Administrative Phone:	214-565-1116
Main Administrative Fax:	214-565-0071
Website:	www.dallassummermusicals.org
Backstage Pay Phone:	214-220-9961

SEATING CAPACITY

Main Floor	723
Balcony	611
Mezzanine	255
Loges	24
Total:	**1,613**
pit (add'l)	35
wheelchair (incl)	10

THEATRE STAFF

Director	Michael A. Jenkins	214-421-5678
Booking	Nancy Marshall	214-421-5678
Marketing	Paulette Hopkins	214-421-5678

HOUSE CREW

Production Manager	LeeAnn Weller	214-421-5678 x113
Electrics	Ron Brooks	214-880-0137

UNIONS

IATSE Local #127	Jim Aman	214-742-4741
Wardrobe Local #803	Pat Neumann	214-443-1017
Music Local #72-147	John Osborne	214-827-2933

BOX OFFICE

Computerized
Box Office Manager
   Debbie Irvin   214-691-7200 x101

Outside Ticket Agency
Computerized
Ticketmaster   214-733-8000

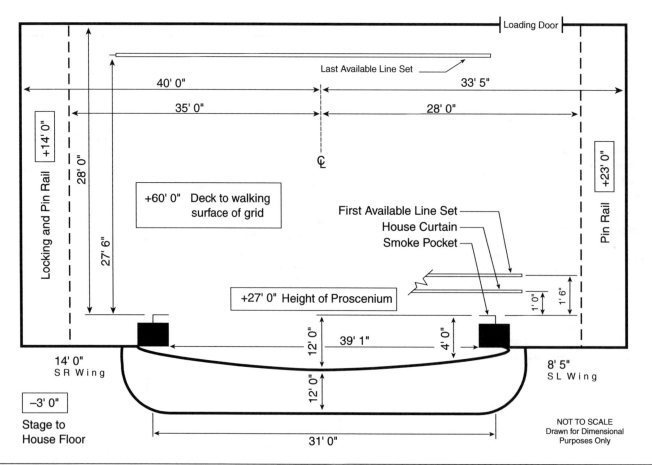

STAGE HOUSE

HOUSE CURTAIN
Operates as a guillotine or traveller from SR deck

RIGGING SYSTEM
Type: Single purchase counter weight
Weight: 40,000 lbs available
Line sets: 34 sets at 6" o.c. with 5 lift lines per set
Arbors: 1,000 lb capacity
House Pipes: 50' long with 58' of travel from deck
Line sets are moveable
Block & Falls are not available
Chain hoists are not available
(25) spot wheels and 3,000' of hemp available

PERMANENT INSTALLATIONS OVER STAGE (FROM SMOKE POCKET)
Electric Raceways (5) at 4'0", 11'6", 17'0", 22'0", 23'0"
Fire curtain (1) 0'0"

PERMANENT INSTALLATIONS ON DECK
Trap (1) in stage floor 3'6" located USL in wings
Pilasters (3) 16" located against back wall

ORCHESTRA PIT
Nonadjustable at 7' below stage level
Apron overhangs US wall of pit 8'0"
Must rent pianos, music stands and lights from outside
   source or supply your own

BACKSTAGE

LOADING DOCK
Loading door(s):
   9'6" high x 8'9" wide
Trucks load (2) back to back at
   same time
Loading door sill is at street
   level above stage level. Ramp
   down to stage level is in-
   stalled.
Fork lift is required; Supplier -
   Strawn 972-278-1372
Sound/Props cannot load in
   FOH
No trailers can store on-site
Security at stage door

WARDROBE
Location: Basement
Access: Via trap in floor USL
(1) Washer (1) Dryer
Washer hookups available

DRESSING ROOMS
(2) Star, SL, stage level, t/s
   included, phone jack
(12) Small, SL, 2nd/ 3rd fl, t/s
   included
(2) Chorus, SL, -1, -2, t/s
   included, phone jack
Use dressing room for company
   mgr office

SOUND

CONSOLE
TAC B-2
28 inputs

SPEAKERS
House Cluster
Proscenium
Under Balcony
No speaker truss

COMMUNICATIONS
Clear Com intercom with
   (1) channel
Infrared sound system
Dressing room page system

ROAD CONSOLE
Located Rear House center
Number of seats required to
   be removed varies
Cable run from stage is 150'
Tie-in into house system with
   XLR connectors

REHEARSAL & STORAGE SPACE
Rehearsal: 24' x 44' located
   in lobby basement has
   mirrors, dance floor, barres,
   must rent pianos
Storage: None

ELECTRICS

ROAD SERVICE POWER

Panel	Phase	Amp	Circuit Protection	Use	Location
A	3	400	breaker	dimmers	DSR
B	3	400	breaker	sound	DSR

FRONT OF HOUSE (BOX BOOM VALUES ARE PER SIDE)

Position	Pipe Width	Distance to Prosc.	House Circuits	Connector Type	FOH Transfer Circuits
1st Cove	30'	85'	24	grd 20 amp stage pin	24
Box Boom 1	48'	60'	10	grd 20 amp stage pin	10

Transfer circuits: grd 20 amp stage pin; located DSR

EQUIPMENT FOH (BOX BOOM VALUES ARE PER SIDE
Equipment available:
8" Fresnels, Altman 6 x 4.5, 6 x 9, 6 x 16 + striplights and footlights etc., all equipment
grd 20 amp stage pin

FOLLOWSPOTS
House Followspots:
   (2) HMI Short Throws;
   removeable

Followspot Booth:
   (2) spots per booth;
   120' throw to proscenium;
   3Ø 60 amp breakers

DIMMERS
No DMX control system

MUSIC HALL AT FAIR PARK

YEAR BUILT: 1925   YEAR RENOVATED: 1972

Theatre Location: 909 First Ave @ Parry, Dallas, TX 75210
Management Company: DSM Management Group, Inc.
                           PO Box 150188, Dallas, TX 75315-0188

Main Administrative Phone: 214-565-1116
Main Administrative Fax: 214-565-0071
Website: www.dallassummermusicals.org
Backstage Pay Phone: 214-428-9247

SEATING CAPACITY
  Orchestra   1,749
  Balcony   1,671
  Total: **3,420**

BOX OFFICE
  Outside Ticket Agency
  Ticketmaster   214-373-8000

THEATRE STAFF
  President/Managing Dir.   Michael Jenkins   214-421-5678 x105
  Booking   Nancy Marshall   214-565-1116
  Marketing   Paulette Hopkins   214-421-5678 x104

HOUSE CREW
  Production Manager   Leeann Weller   214-421-5678
  Carpentry   Stuart Hale   214-426-2907
  Electrics   Bill Bingham   214-421-5678 x117

UNIONS
  IATSE Local #127   Jim Aman   214-742-4741
  Wardrobe Local #803   Pat Neumann   214-443-1017
  Music Local #72-147   John Osborne   214-827-2933

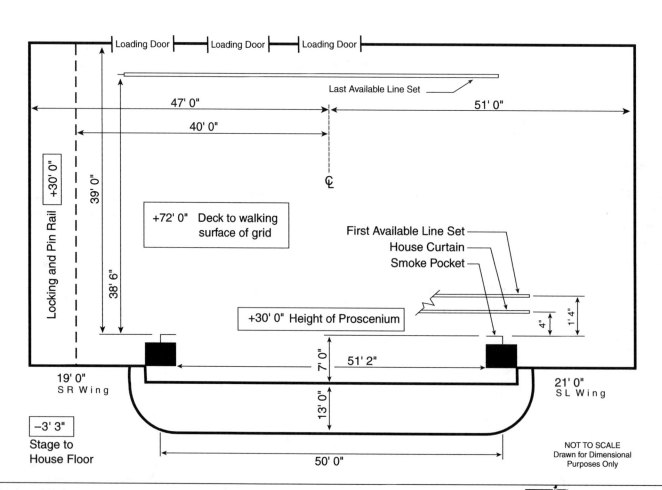

STAGE HOUSE

HOUSE CURTAIN
Operates as a guillotine from SR deck

RIGGING SYSTEM
Type:	Combination purchase counterweight
Weight:	30,000 lbs available
Line sets:	65 sets at 6" o.c. with 7' lift lines per set
Arbors:	1,000 lb capacity
House Pipes:	67' long with 68' of travel from deck

Line sets are moveable
Block & Falls are available 3:2 (4)
(100) spot wheels and 8,000' of hemp available

PERMANENT INSTALLATIONS OVER STAGE (FROM SMOKE POCKET)
Electric raceways (4) at 5'3", 15' 6", 21' 11", 29' 2"
Fire curtain (1) at smoke pocket

PERMANENT INSTALLATIONS ON DECK
Traps (1) in stage floor 3'0" x 2'4"; located DSC

ORCHESTRA PIT
Adjustable to 9' below stage level by hydraulic lift
Apron overhangs US wall of pit 20'0"
Must supply own pianos, music stands and lights or rent
from an outside source

BACKSTAGE

LOADING DOCK
(3) Loading door(s) each:
12'0" high x 10'0" wide
Trucks load (2) side by side at
same time
Doors 1 & 2 are at truck level
equipped with electric
levelers; Door 3 is at truck
level equipped with concrete
ramp up to stage loading to
stage thru separate receiving
area
Fork lift is not required
Sound/Props can load in FOH
(5) Trailers can store on-site
Security at stage door

WARDROBE
Location: SL
Access: Stage level
(1) Washer (1) Dryer
Washer and dryer hookups
available

DRESSING ROOMS
(6) Star, SL/ SR, stage level, t/s
included
(8) Small, SL/ SR, 2nd fl, t/s on
same fl
(4) Chorus, SL/ SR, stage level,
2nd fl, t/s included
Use dressing room for company
mgr office

SOUND

CONSOLE
Custom
10 inputs, 3 main outputs

SPEAKERS
House Cluster
Under Balcony

COMMUNICATIONS
Clear Com intercom with
(2) channels
Infrared sound system
Dressing room page system

ROAD CONSOLE
Located Center
(12) seats required to be
removed
Cable run from stage is 100'
Tie-in into house system with
XLR connectors

REHEARSAL & STORAGE SPACE
Rehearsal: 20' x 36' located
SL on 2nd floor, mirrors,
dance floor, must rent
piano
Storage: 44' x 58' located US
in receiving area

ELECTRICS

ROAD SERVICE POWER

Panel	Phase	Amp	Circuit Protection	Use	Location
A-B	3	600	breaker	dimmers	SR
C	3	225	breaker	extra	SL
D	3	225	breaker	sound	SL

Recommended location of touring dimmer racks: SR on deck
Hoist not required

FRONT OF HOUSE (BOX BOOM VALUES ARE PER SIDE)

Position	Pipe Width	Distance to Prosc.	House Circuits	Connector Type	FOH Transfer Circuits
1st Cove		70'	40	grd 20 amp stage pin	40
1st Balc Rail		100'	38	grd 20 amp stage pin	38
Slots #3		60'	10	grd 20 amp stage pin	10
Slots #2		60'	9	grd 20 amp stage pin	9
Slots #1		60'	9	grd 20 amp stage pin	9

Transfer circuits: grd 20 amp stage pin located DSR on procenium wall

EQUIPMENT FOH (BOX BOOM VALUES ARE PER SIDE)
None

FOLLOWSPOTS
House Followspots:
(3) Xenon Super Troupers
1600w; removeable

Followspot Booth:
(4) spots per booth;
175' throw to proscenium;
(6) 1Ø 20 amp breakers

DIMMERS
No lighting console
No dimmers
No DMX control system

ABRAHAM CHAVEZ THEATRE

AT: EL PASO CONVENTION & PERFORMING ARTS CENTER   **YEAR BUILT: 1974   YEAR RENOVATED: 1996**

Theatre Location: 1 Civic Center Plaza on Sante Fe Street
                           El Paso, TX 79901
Management Company: Leisure Management International
                           Eleven Greenway Plaza, Suite 3000
                           Houston, TX 77046-1105

Main Administrative Phone:	915-534-0646/0611
Main Administrative Fax:	915-532-2963
Backstage Pay Phone:	915-532-9702
Traveling Production Office Phone:	915-534-0620

THEATRE STAFF

Interim Manager	Esther Portillo	915-534-0646
Booking	Esther Portillo	915-534-0646
Marketing	Esther Portillo	915-534-0646
Operations	Diane Heath	915-534-0611
Groups	Esther Portillo	915-534-0646

UNIONS

IATSE Local #153	Paul Enger	915-544-6818

SEATING CAPACITY

Orchestra	955
Grand Tier	1,068
Balcony	395
Total:	**2,418**

pit (add'l)	78
wheelchair (add'l)	20

BOX OFFICE
Outside Ticket Agency
Ticketmaster
Becky Loya   915-532-4661

Box office is promoter operated

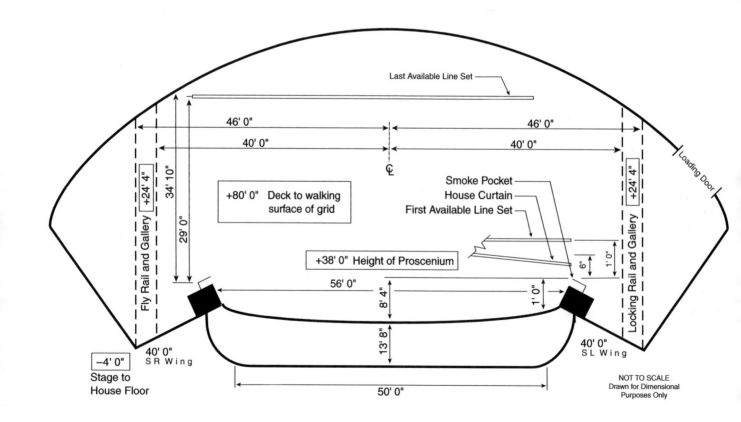

STAGE HOUSE

HOUSE CURTAIN
Operates as a guillotine/traveller from SL fly floor or deck
Curved act curtain, concave to audience

RIGGING SYSTEM
Type: Double purchase counter weight; Motorized
Weight: 15,000 lbs available
Line sets: 28 sets at various inches o.c. with 5 lift lines per set
Arbors: 2,000 lb capacity
House Pipes: 56' long with 75' of travel from deck
Line sets are moveable
Block & Falls are not available
Chain hoists available as rentals; (16) one ton, (2) half ton
(30) spot wheels and 3,500' of hemp available

PERMANENT INSTALLATIONS OVER STAGE
M=Moveable with advance call
Orchestra shell (1) at 7'2"; M
Electric raceways (2) at 2'9", 25'3"
Traveller (1) at 26'6"; M
Electric pipe (2) at 2'9", 25'3"; M
Cyclorama (1) at 29'5"; M

PERMANENT INSTALLATIONS ON DECK
Trap (1) in stage floor 3'0" x 7'0" located center of arc
Piano box (1) 5'd x 10'w x 4'h located SR

ORCHESTRA PIT
Adjustable to 14' below stage level by hydraulic lift
Pit lift is in (1) section

BACKSTAGE

LOADING DOCK
Loading door(s):
9'1" high x 12'0" wide
Trucks load (2) at same time
Park tractor at right angle to trailer, as trailer extends into street
Fork lift is not required
Sound/Props can load in FOH
Lobby can be a work area
Many trailers can store on-site
Security at dock & stage door

WARDROBE
Location: At stage door
Access: Street level, 5 steps to stage
(1) Washer (1) Dryer
Washer and dryer hookups available

DRESSING ROOMS
(2) Star, SR, stage, toilet/shower/phone jack
(8) Small, SR/SL, stage, toilet/shower
(2) Chorus, SR/SL, +1, toilet/shower
Elevator access for dressing rooms
Use dressing room for company mgr office

SOUND

CONSOLE
Electro Voice Tapco Series 2 located in Booth HR
20 inputs, 4 main outputs

SPEAKERS
House Cluster
Speaker truss does not exist

COMMUNICATIONS
Clear Com intercom with (1) channel
Infrared sound system
Dressing room page system

ROAD CONSOLE
Located HR
No seats required to be removed
Cable run from stage is 200'
Tie-in into house system with XLR connectors

REHEARSAL & STORAGE SPACE
Rehearsal: None
Storage:
Loading dock, 49' x 23'

ELECTRICS

ROAD SERVICE POWER

Panel	Phase	Amp	Circuit Protection	Use	Location
A	3	400	breaker	dimmers	SL
B	3	400	breaker	extra	SL
C	3	400	breaker	sound	SL

Recommended location of touring dimmer racks: SR
Hoist is not required
Additional power is available for tour buses, generators, etc.

FRONT OF HOUSE (BOX BOOM VALUES ARE PER SIDE)

Position	Pipe Width	Distance to Prosc.	House Circuits	Connector Type	FOH Transfer Circuits
1st Balc Rail	80'	50'10"	32	20 amp twistlock	32
2nd Balc Rail	80'	69'2'	24	20 amp twistlock	24

Transfer circuits: Male pin

EQUIPMENT FOH (BOX BOOM VALUES ARE PER SIDE)
None

FOLLOWSPOTS
House Followspots:
(4) Ultra Arc 400; removeable

Followspot Booth:
UNDER RENOVATION

DIMMERS
Lighting console is Datacue II;
(60) SCR 3k, 6k, 12k dimmers
No DMX control system

JOHN F. KENNEDY THEATRE

AT: FORT WORTH CONVENTION CENTER

YEAR BUILT: 1968

Theatre Location: 1111 Houston St., Fort Worth, TX 76102

Main Administrative Phone:		817-884-2222
Main Administrative Fax:		817-884-2323
Stage Door Phone:		817-884-2253
Backstage Pay Phone:		817-335-0025

THEATRE STAFF
Executive Director	Melvin Morgan	817-884-2200
Booking	Amber Godard	817-884-2203

HOUSE CREW
Stage Manager	Jerry Dawson	817-884-2252

UNIONS
IATSE Local #126	Sarge Hill	817-451-5479
Wardrobe	Kathy Gentry	817-834-3183

SEATING CAPACITY
Main Floor	1,965
Balcony	1,010
Total:	**2,975**

BOX OFFICE
Box office is promoter operated

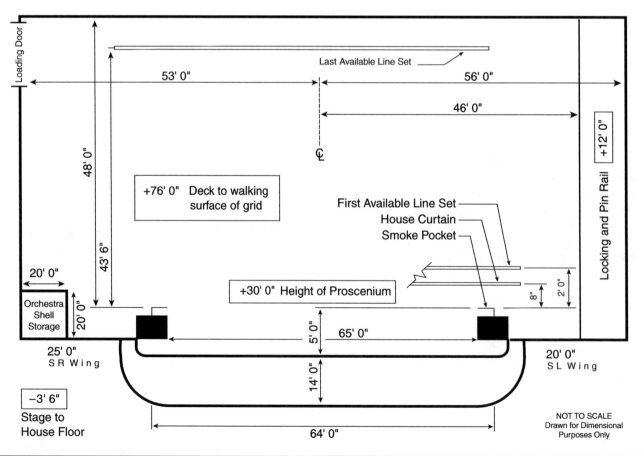

Last Available Line Set

53' 0"   56' 0"

46' 0"

+12' 0"

Locking and Pin Rail

CL

48' 0"

+76' 0" Deck to walking surface of grid

First Available Line Set
House Curtain
Smoke Pocket

43' 6"

+30' 0" Height of Proscenium

8"   2' 0"

20' 0"

Orchestra Shell Storage

20' 0"

5' 0"   65' 0"

25' 0"
SR Wing

20' 0"
SL Wing

14' 0"

−3' 6"
Stage to House Floor

64' 0"

NOT TO SCALE
Drawn for Dimensional Purposes Only

STAGE HOUSE

HOUSE CURTAIN
Operates as a guillotine or traveller from SL fly floor or deck

RIGGING SYSTEM
Type: Single purchase counter weight
Weight: 18,000 lbs available
Line sets: 69 sets at 6" o.c. with 7 lift lines per set
Arbors: 1,000 lb capacity
House Pipes: 74' long with 70' of travel from deck
Line sets are not moveable
Block & Falls are not available
Chain hoists available as a rental; (4) half ton
(30) spot wheels and 2,500' of hemp available

PERMANENT INSTALLATIONS OVER STAGE (FROM SMOKE POCKET)
M=Moveable with advance call
Orchestra shells (3) at 7'3", 16'9", 26'9"
Electric borders (5) at 7'9", 10'9", 19'3", 28'3", 37'3"; M
Traveller (3) at 8'9", 21'3", 35'9"; M
Electric bridge (1) at 4'4"
Electric pipe (1) at 14'9"
Hard portal (1) at 2'0"
Cyclorama (1) at 44'3"; M
Fire curtain (1)

PERMANENT INSTALLATIONS ON DECK
Trap (3) in stage floor located USC
Hard legs (2)
Loading bridge (2)

ORCHESTRA PIT
Adjustable to 16' below stage level by hydraulic lift
Apron overhangs US wall of pit 0'0"
Pit lift is in (1) section

BACKSTAGE

LOADING DOCK
Loading door(s):
     12'0" high x 14'0" wide
Trucks load (1) at a time
Street level, loading thru separate loading area, load bars are suggested as truck access is sloped toward dock
Fork lift is not required: House owns
Sound/Props cannot load in FOH
Security at dock

WARDROBE
Location: SL
Access: Direct from stage
(1) Washer   (1) Dryer
Washer and dryer hookups available

DRESSING ROOMS
(7) Small, SL / SL, stage level, t/s included
(3) Chorus, SL, behind stage, stage level, t/s included
Use dressing room for company mgr office

SOUND

CONSOLE
Located SL
24 inputs, 8 main outputs, 6 aux outputs

SPEAKERS
House Cluster
Proscenium
No speaker truss

COMMUNICATIONS
Clear Com intercom with (2) channels
Dressing room page system

ROAD CONSOLE
Located Rear House
No seats required to be removed
Cable run from stage is 200'
Tie-in into house system with XLR connectors

REHEARSAL & STORAGE SPACE
Rehearsal: None
Storage: 20' x 30' SR, loading area

ELECTRICS

ROAD SERVICE POWER

Panel	Phase	Amp	Circuit Protection	Use	Location
A	3	400	fuses	dimmers	SR
B	3	400	fuses	extra	SR
C	3	400	fuses	sound	SR

Recommended location of touring dimmer racks: SR
Hoist not required
Additional power is available for tour buses, generators, etc.

FRONT OF HOUSE (BOX BOOM VALUES ARE PER SIDE)

Position	Pipe Width	Distance to Prosc.	House Circuits	Connector Type	FOH Transfer Circuits
1st Balc Rail	60	77'	24	grd 20 amp stage pin	0
Cove	70	28'	24	grd 20 amp stage pin	0

EQUIPMENT FOH (BOX BOOM VALUES ARE PER SIDE)

Position	Quantity	Wattage	Instrument	Removable
1st Balc Rail	24	750	6 x 16 Lekos	yes
1st Cove	24	750	6 x 16 Lekos	yes
Box Boom 1	16	750	6 x 9 Lekos	yes

FOLLOWSPOTS
House Followspots:
     (2) Xenon Super Troupers; removeable
     (2) Carbon Arc Super Troupers; removeable

Followspot Booth:
     (4) spots per booth;
     138' throw to proscenium;
     (6) 3Ø 200 amp breakers

DIMMERS
Lighting console is Colortran Compact Elite;
(385) Colortran dimmers
No DMX control system

WILL ROGERS AUDITORIUM

AT: WILL ROGERS MEMORIAL CENTER   **YEAR BUILT: 1936**

Theatre Location: 3401 West Lancaster, Fort Worth, TX 76107-3078
Mailing Address: One Amon Carter Square, Fort Worth, TX 76107-3078

Main Administrative Phone: 817-871-8150
Main Administrative Fax: 817-871-8170
E-mail: jacksop@ci.fortworth.tx.us
Stage Door Phone: 817-871-8166

THEATRE STAFF
Public Events Mgr.   Pam Jackson   817-871-8150

HOUSE CREW
Stage Supervisor   Ronnie Rambin   817-871-8166

UNIONS
IATSE Local #126   Sargent Hill   817-451-5479

SEATING CAPACITY
Orchestra	1,820
Balcony Box	158
Balcony	878
Total:	**2,856**
pit (add'l)	30
wheelchair (incl)	24

BOX OFFICE
Outside Ticket Agency
Computerized
Ticketmaster
  Cindy Chu   214-750-7400
Dillard's
  Lori Foreman   217-284-6693

Box office is promoter operated

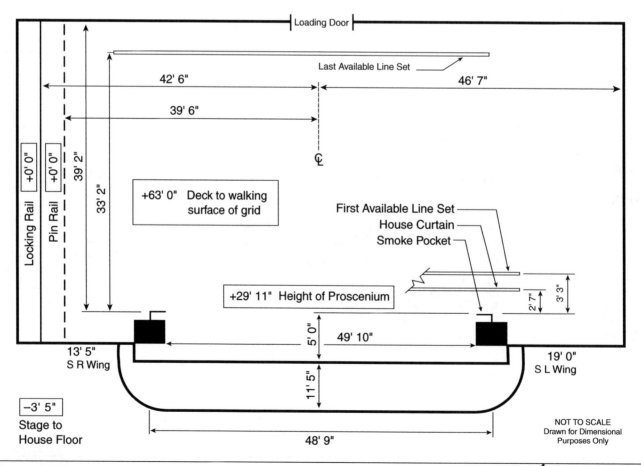

STAGE HOUSE

HOUSE CURTAIN
Operates as a guillotine or traveller from SR deck

RIGGING SYSTEM
Type:	Single purchase counter weight
Weight:	19,000 lbs available
Line sets:	42 sets at 7" o.c. with 7 lift lines per set
Arbors:	2,000 lb capacity
House Pipes:	70' long with 59' of travel from deck

Line sets are moveable
Block & Falls are not available
Chain hoists are not available
(3) rigging points over pit

PERMANENT INSTALLATIONS OVER STAGE (FROM SMOKE POCKET)
M=Moveable with advance call
Traveller (1) at 16'0"; M
Fire curtain (1) fits in smoke pocket
Blackout drop (1) at 34'5"; M

PERMANENT INSTALLATIONS ON DECK
Loading bridge (1) 5' x 35' located SR against wall above fly rail

ORCHESTRA PIT
Nonadjustable at 4'4" below stage level
Apron overhangs US wall of pit 2'0"

BACKSTAGE

LOADING DOCK
Loading door(s):
19'10" high x 7'7" wide
Trucks load (4) side by side at same time
Loading dock is ground/stage level; truck ramp and/or forklifts required
Forklift: House can furnish if notified
Sound/Props cannot load in FOH
(2) Trailers can store on-site

WARDROBE
Location: Basement
Access: Stairs USR & SL
(1) Washer (1) Dryer
Washer and dryer hookups available

DRESSING ROOMS
(4) Small, SR, stage level, t/s included, phone jacks
(6) Small, SL/SR, stage level, t/s included
(2) Chorus, basement, t/s included
Use dressing room for company mgr office

SOUND

CONSOLE
Soundcraft 400 Portable
24 inputs, 2 main outputs, 4 aux outputs

SPEAKERS
Portable
No speaker truss
Lighting truss can be used for balcony fills

COMMUNICATIONS
Clear Com intercom with (2) channels

ROAD CONSOLE
Located Rear House
(12) seats required to be removed
Cable run from stage is 150'

REHEARSAL & STORAGE SPACE
Rehearsal: None
Storage: None

ELECTRICS

ROAD SERVICE POWER

Panel	Phase	Amp	Circuit Protection	Use	Location
A	3	400	fuse	dimmers	USR
B	3	400	fuse	sound	DSR
C-D	1	60		extra	SL in basement
E	1	60		extra	SL in basement

Recommended location of touring dimmer racks: SR or SL
Hoist not required
Additional power is available for tour buses, generators, etc.

FRONT OF HOUSE (BOX BOOM VALUES ARE PER SIDE)
None
Road truss: Grid height 63'0"; grid block used; 10 rigging pipes in house

EQUIPMENT FOH (BOX BOOM VALUES ARE PER SIDE)
None
Moveable tomcat truss on winches mac load cap 2,000 lbs; (30 circuits on truss

FOLLOWSPOTS
House Followspots:
(1) Xenon Super Trouper 1600; removeable
(2) Xenon Super Trouper 2k; removeable

Followspot Booth:
(3) spots per booth;
130' throw to proscenium;
(3) 1Ø 30 amp breakers

DIMMERS
Lighting console is ETC Expression;
(209) ETC Sensor 2.4k dimmers
House has programmable DMX control system
(4) dry run DMX station(s), DSR, DSL, FOH, spot booth

THE GRAND 1894 OPERA HOUSE

YEAR BUILT: 1894 YEAR RENOVATED: 1976

Theatre Location: 2020 Post Office Street, Galveston, TX 77550

Main Administrative Phone:	409-763-7173	
Main Administrative Fax:	409-763-1068	
E-mail:	wwndstrom@thegrand.com	
Website:	www.thegrand.com	
Backstage Pay Phone:	409-763-9863	
Traveling Production Office Phone:	409-766-1546	

THEATRE STAFF

Executive Director	Maureen M. Patton	409-763-7173
Booking	Maureen M. Patton	409-763-7173

HOUSE CREW

Stage Manager	William Lindstrom	409-763-7173

SEATING CAPACITY

Orchestra	503
Mezzanine	264
Grand Tier	201
Box Seats	40
Total:	**1,008**
pit (add'l)	32
wheelchair (add'l)	6
standing (add'l)	34

STAGE DIMENSIONS (FROM SMOKE POCKET)
Stage is 36'0" deep
Width from Center Line to SL is 36'6"
Width from Center Line to SR is 36'6"
Proscenium width is 38'0"
Proscenium height is 27'0"
Smoke pocket to apron edge is 4'0"
Orchestra pit exists

RIGGING

Grid Height:	59'
Type:	Double purchase counter weight
Weight:	15,000 lbs
Line sets:	39 sets at 9" o.c.
Arbors:	1,500 lb capacity
House Pipes:	42' long

LOADING DOCK
Loading door(s) are 9'0"high x 8'5"wide
Trucks load (2) at same time
Fork lift is not required and is not available

ELECTRICS
Total power available:
  (3) 400A 3Ø SR

FOLLOWSPOTS
House Followspots:
  Xenon1600w
No power in spot booth

DIMMERS
(184) house dimmers
House has DMX control system

SOUND
House has dedicated power
  located SR
FOH mixing position in
  Rear Orchestra
Sound console is available

THE BROWN THEATER

AT: THE WORTHAM THEATER CENTER AKA: THE ALICE AND GEORGE BROWN THEATER

Theatre Location: 510 Preston, Houston, TX 77002
Management Company: Wortham Center Operating Company (Backstage only)
510 Preston, Suite 201, Houston, TX

Main Administrative Phone: 713-237-1439
Main Administrative Fax: 713-237-9313
Stage Door Phone: 713-250-3657

THEATRE STAFF
Manager — Michael Williams — 713-237-1439
Booking — Redu Richarson — 713-237-1439

HOUSE CREW
Crew Chief — Derwood Freitag — 713-238-9690
Carpentry — Mike Grawl — 713-238-9685
Electrics — Ron Ellis — 713-238-9686
Sound — Dan Nordby — 713-238-9688
Props — Hank Graff — 713-238-9687

UNIONS
IATSE Local #51 — Tom Sprague — 713-229-8277
Wardrobe Local #279 — Pat Padilla — 713-520-5021

SEATING CAPACITY

Orchestra	1,217
First Balcony	414
Founder's Boxes	124
Loge Boxes	148
Grand Tier	444
Total:	**2,347**
pit (incl.)	70
wheelchair (incl)	22

BOX OFFICE
Box Office Treasurer
Michael Mullis — 713-227-6796

Outside Ticket Agency
Computerized
TicketMaster — 713-629-3711

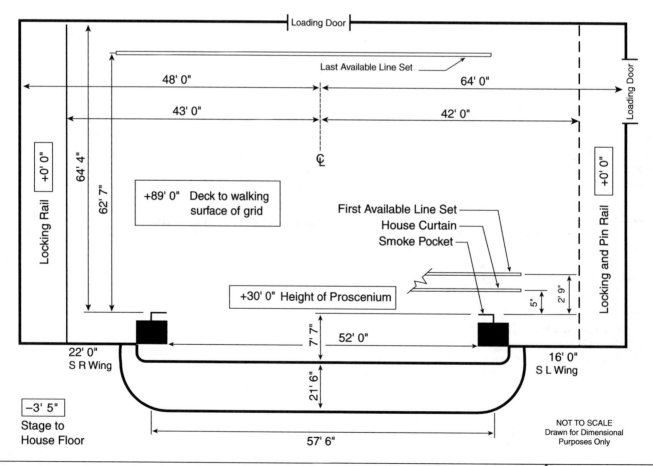

STAGE HOUSE

HOUSE CURTAIN
Operates as a guillotine or traveller from SL deck; motorized

RIGGING SYSTEM
Type: Single purchase counter weight; motorized
Weight: 120,000 lbs. available
Arbors: 1,500 lb. capacity
Line sets are not moveable
Block & Falls are not available
Chain hoists are not available

PERMANENT INSTALLATIONS OVER STAGE
None

PERMANENT INSTALLATIONS ON DECK
Trap (48) in stage floor 4' x 7'

ORCHESTRA PIT
Adjustable to 9'6' below stage level by hydraulic lift
Pit lift is in (1) section

BACKSTAGE

LOADING DOCK
Loading door(s):
    1) 22'0" high x 70'0" wide
    2) 40'0" high x 40'0" wide
Trucks load (2) at same time

WARDROBE
Location: Basement
Access: Freight elevator 18' x 34'
(1) Washer (1) Dryer
No washer or dryer hookups for outside equipment

DRESSING ROOMS
(3) Star, stage level, t/s
(9) Small, stage level/ -1, t/s
(4) Chorus, -1, t/s

SOUND

CONSOLE
Soundcraft 500B

SPEAKERS
Data not provided

COMMUNICATIONS
Clear Com intercom with (8) channels

ROAD CONSOLE
Located Rear House
Cable run from stage is 250'

ELECTRICS

ROAD SERVICE POWER

Panel	Phase	Amp	Circuit Protection	Use	Location
A-D	3	400	fuse	dimmers	DSR proscenium
E	3	60	fuse	sound	USL mid wall
F	3	200	fuse	sound	Loading dock
G	3	200	fuse	sound	Loading dock

Recommended location of touring dimmer racks: 40' offstage SR

FRONT OF HOUSE (BOX BOOM VALUES ARE PER SIDE)

Position	Pipe Width	Distance to Prosc.	House Circuits	Connector Type	FOH Transfer Circuits
1st Balc Rail	30'	70'	16	grd 20 amp stage pin	16
1st Cove	80'	66'	8	grd 20 amp stage pin	8
2nd Cove	80'	84'	14	grd 20 amp stage pin	14
3rd Cove	80'	102'	30	grd 20 amp stage pin	30
4th Cove	80'	120'	30	grd 20 amp stage pin	30
Box Boom 1		50'	10	grd 20 amp stage pin	10
Box Boom 2		20'	8	grd 20 amp stage pin	8
Box Boom 3			20	grd 20 amp stage pin	20

EQUIPMENT FOH (BOX BOOM VALUES ARE PER SIDE)

Position			Fixture		Transfer
1st Balc Rail	7	1,000	Altman 6 x 16		yes
1st Cove	16	1,000	Strand 6 x 16		yes
2nd Cove	24	1,000	Strand 8 x 13		yes
3rd Cove	36	1,000	Strand 10 x 23		yes
4th Cove	44	1,000	Strand 10 x 23		yes
Box Boom 1	10	1,000	Strand 6 x 22/ 6 x 16		yes
Box Boom 2	8	1,000	15° to 4° Zooms		yes
Box Boom 3	34	1,000	Strand 6 x 22/ 6 x 16		yes

All FOH circuits can transfer, panel located 40' SR of proscenium

FOLLOWSPOTS
House Followspots:
    (4) Strong Xenon 2k; removeable

Followspot Booth:
    (4) spots per booth;
    136 throw to proscenium;
    (4) 3Ø 60 amp breakers

DIMMERS
Lighting console is Obsession;
(15) Strand CD80 dimmers

CULLEN THEATER

AT: WORTHAM THEATER CENTER   AKA: THE LILLIE AND ROY CULLEN THEATER   YEAR BUILT: 1987

Theatre Location: 510 Preston, Houston, TX 77002

Main Administrative Phone: 713-237-1439
Main Administrative Fax: 713-237-9313
Stage Door Phone: 713-250-3657

THEATRE STAFF
  Manager   Michael Williams   713-237-1439
  Booking   Reda Richardson   713-237-1439
HOUSE CREW
  Carpentry   Mike Grawl   713-237-9685
  Electrics   Ron Ellis   713-238-9686
  Sound   Dan Nordby   713-238-9388
  Props   Hank Graff   713-238-9687
UNIONS
  IATSE Local #51   Tom Sprague   713-229-8277
  Wardrobe Local #279 Pat Padilla   713-520-5021

SEATING CAPACITY
  Orchestra   628
  Mezzanine   411
  Total: **1,039**

  pit (add'l)   35
  wheelchair (add'l)   16

BOX OFFICE
  Computerized
  Box Office Treasurer
    Michael Mollis   713-227-2787

  Outside Ticket Agency
  Computerized
  Ticketmaster

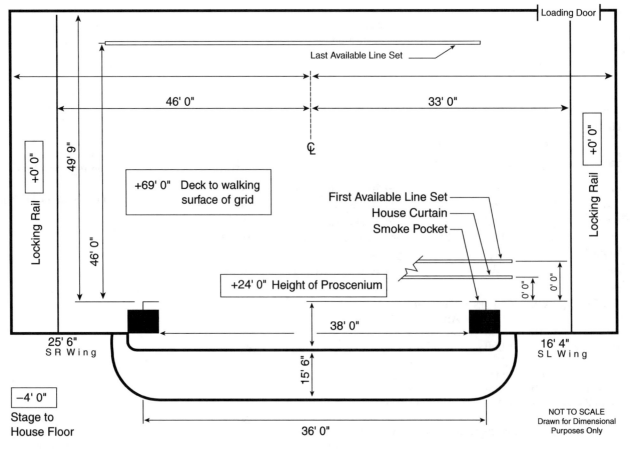

STAGE HOUSE

HOUSE CURTAIN
Operates as a guillotine or traveller from SL deck

RIGGING SYSTEM
Type:	Single purchase counter weight
Weight:	100,000 lbs available
Line sets:	94 sets
Arbors:	1,500 lb capacity
House Pipes:	48' long with 66' of travel from deck

Line sets are not moveable
Block & Falls are not available

PERMANENT INSTALLATIONS OVER STAGE (FROM SMOKE POCKET)
None

PERMANENT INSTALLATIONS ON DECK
Traps (16) @ 4' x 7'

ORCHESTRA PIT
Adjustable to 20' below stage level by hydraulic lift
Apron overhangs US wall of pit 5'0"
Pit lift is in (2) sections

BACKSTAGE

LOADING DOCK
Loading door(s):
    20'0" high x 20'0" wide
Trucks load (2) at same time
40' is the longest piece of pipe
    that can come out of a truck
Forklift is not required
Trailers cannot store on-site
Sound/Props cannot load in
    FOH
Lobby cannot be a work area

WARDROBE
Location: Basement
Access: Freight elevator
    18' x 34'
(1) Washer (1) Dryer
No washer or dryer hookups

DRESSING ROOMS
(3) Star, SL, stage level
(3) Small, -1
(1) Chorus, -1

SOUND

CONSOLE
Soundcraft 500B

SPEAKERS
House Cluster
No speaker truss

COMMUNICATIONS
Clear Com intercom with
    (8) channels
Infrared sound system
Dressing room page system

ROAD CONSOLE
Located Rear House
Cable run from stage is 200'

REHEARSAL & STORAGE SPACE
Rehearsal: 55' x 55', located
    in basement, piano, mirror,
    dance floor
Storage: None

ELECTRICS

ROAD SERVICE POWER

Panel	Phase	Amp	Circuit Protection	Use	Location
A-B	(2) 3	400	fuse	dimmers	USR wall
C	1	60	fuse	sound	USR wall

Recommended location of touring dimmer racks: DSR

FRONT OF HOUSE (BOX BOOM VALUES ARE PER SIDE)

Position	Pipe Width	Distance to Prosc.	House Circuits	Connector Type	FOH Transfer Circuits
1st Cove	80'	45'	20	grd 20 amp stage pin	DSR wall
2nd Cove	80'	65'	24	grd 20 amp stage pin	DSR wall
3rd Cove	80'	85'	24	grd 20 amp stage pin	DSR wall
Box Boom 1			12	grd 20 amp stage pin	DSR wall

Transfer circuits: all FOH circuits can transfer; transfer panel located SR

EQUIPMENT FOH (BOX BOOM VALUES ARE PER SIDE)

Position	Quantity	Wattage	Instrument	Removeable
1st Cove	24	1,000	Strand 6 x 16	yes
2nd Cove	12	1,000	Strand 6 x 22/ 8 x 13	yes
3rd Cove	24	1,000	Strand 8 x 13	yes

FOLLOWSPOTS
House Followspots:
    (3) Strong Xenon 2k;
    removeable

Followspot Booth:
    (3) spots per booth;
    108' throw to proscenium;
    (3) 4Ø 60 amp breakers

DIMMERS
Lighting console is Obses-
    sion;
(20) Strand CD 80s
    dimmers
House has programmable
    DMX control system

JONES HALL FOR THE PERFORMING ARTS

YEAR BUILT: 1966   YEAR RENOVATED: 1996

Theatre Location: 615 Louisiana, Houston, TX 77002
Mailing Address: PO Box 61469, Houston, TX 77208
Management Company: City of Houston
                        PO Box 61469, Houston, TX 77208

Main Administrative Phone: 713-227-3974
Main Administrative Fax: 713-228-9629
Stage Door Phone: 713-238-2384

THEATRE STAFF
Manager   Vivian Montejano   713-227-3974
Booking   Virginia Oxford   713-227-3974

HOUSE CREW
Technical Director   Charles Purchase   713-229-0029

SEATING CAPACITY

Orchestra	1,525
Mezzanine	326
Boxes	106
Grand Tier	180
Balcony	608
Total	**2,745**
pit (add'l)	108
wheelchair (add'l)	29
standing (add'l)	30

BOX OFFICE
Outside Ticket Agency
Houston Ticket Center
713-227-2787

Box office is promoter operated

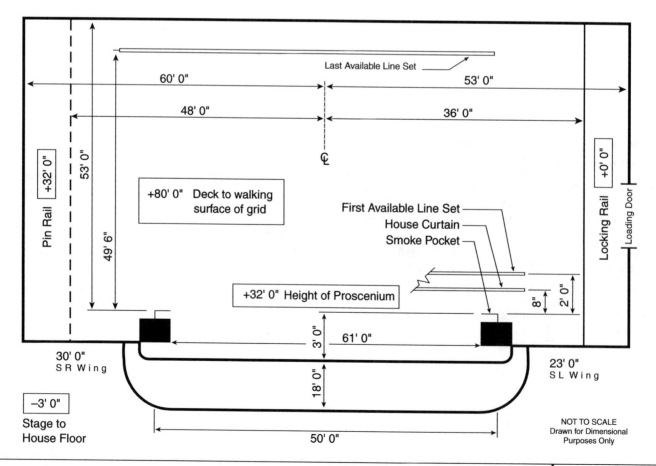

Last Available Line Set

60' 0"   53' 0"
48' 0"   36' 0"

53' 0"

Pin Rail   +32' 0"   Locking Rail   +0' 0"   Loading Door

+80' 0"   Deck to walking surface of grid

49' 6"

First Available Line Set
House Curtain
Smoke Pocket

+32' 0" Height of Proscenium

8"   2' 0"

3' 0"   61' 0"

30' 0"
S R Wing

18' 0"

23' 0"
S L Wing

−3' 0"
Stage to
House Floor

50' 0"

NOT TO SCALE
Drawn for Dimensional
Purposes Only

STAGE HOUSE

HOUSE CURTAIN

Operates as a guillotine or traveller from SR fly floor or deck

RIGGING SYSTEM

Type:	Double purchase counter weight
Weight:	26,000 lbs available
Line sets:	67 sets at 8" o.c. with 5 lift lines per set
Arbors:	1,200/1,800 lb capacity
House Pipes:	70' long with 77' of travel from deck

Line sets are not moveable
Block & Falls are not available
Chain hoists are not available
(50) spot wheels

PERMANENT INSTALLATIONS OVER STAGE (FROM SMOKE POCKET)

Orchestra shells (3) at 10'4", 24'4", 34'8"
Hard portal - hard teaser at 1'11"

PERMANENT INSTALLATIONS ON DECK

None

ORCHESTRA PIT

Adjustable to 15' below stage level by hydraulic lift
Apron overhangs US wall of pit 3'0"
Pit lift is in (2) sections

BACKSTAGE

LOADING DOCK

Loading door(s):
    14'0" high x 8'0" wide
Trucks load (2) at same time
Short loading dock; trailers must be dropped during peak traffic times.
Fork lift is not required
Sound/Props can load in FOH
Lobby cannot be a work area
Security at stage door

WARDROBE

Location: +1 above stage
Access: Freight elevators and stairs.
(2) Washers (2) Dryers
Washer and dryer hookups available

DRESSING ROOMS

(4) Star, SL, stage level, t/s included
(4) Small, SL, +2, t/s included
(5) Chorus, SL, +3, t/s included
Elevator access for dressing rooms
Use dressing room for company mgr office

SOUND

CONSOLE

TAC Scorpon, located Booth
24 inputs, 2 main outputs, 8 matrix outputs, 8 aux outputs

SPEAKERS

House Cluster
Under Balcony
No speaker truss

COMMUNICATIONS

Clear Com intercom with (2) channels
Infrared sound system
Dressing room page system

ROAD CONSOLE

Located Guest mix position on mezzanine crossover
No seats required to be removed
Cable run from stage is 150'
Tie-in into house system with XLR connectors

REHEARSAL & STORAGE SPACE

Rehearsal: 50' x 60', basement, wall mirror and barre
Storage: None

ELECTRICS

ROAD SERVICE POWER

Panel	Phase	Amp	Circuit Protection	Use	Location
A-C	3	400		dimmers/extra	SR
D	3	200		sound	SL

Recommended location of touring dimmer racks: SR

FRONT OF HOUSE (BOX BOOM VALUES ARE PER SIDE)

Position	Pipe Width	Distance to Prosc.	House Circuits	Connector Type	FOH Transfer Circuits
Cove		50'	24	ungrd 20 amp stage pin	24
Box Boom 1		40'	12	ungrd 20 amp stage pin	12

Transfer circuits: ungrd 20 amp stage pin

EQUIPMENT FOH (BOX BOOM VALUES ARE PER SIDE)

Position	Quantity	Wattage	Instrument	Removeable
1st Cove Rail	20	1,000	12	yes
Box Boom 1	22	1,000	20	yes

FOLLOWSPOTS

House Followspots:
    (4) Strong Xenon Trouper; removeable

(3) Followspot Booths:
    (1) spot in booth;
    50' throw to proscenium;
    (1) 1Ø 60 amp breakers

    (1) spot in booth;
    50' throw to proscenium;
    (1) 1Ø 60 amp breakers

    (2) spots in booth;
    125' throw to proscenium;
    (2) 1Ø 60 amp breakers

DIMMERS

Lighting console is LP 90;
(60) CD 80 6k/12k dimmers

LUBBOCK MUNICIPAL AUDITORIUM

YEAR BUILT: 1956   YEAR RENOVATED: 1980

Theatre Location: 2720 6th Street, Lubbock, TX 79409
Mailing Address: 1501 6th Street, Lubbock, TX 79401
Management Company: City of Lubbock
                          1501 6th Street, Lubbock, TX 79401

Main Administrative Phone: 806-775-2242
Main Administrative Fax: 806-775-3240
Website: www.lmcc.c1.lubbock.tx.us

THEATRE STAFF
  Building Manager   Vicki Key   806-775-2236
  Operations   Jesse Herrera   806-775-2260
HOUSE CREW
  Technical Coordinator John James   806-775-2258
UNIONS
  IATSE Local #903   Becky Burt   806-775-2264

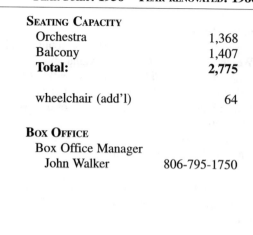

SEATING CAPACITY
  Orchestra   1,368
  Balcony   1,407
  Total: **2,775**

  wheelchair (add'l)   64

BOX OFFICE
  Box Office Manager
    John Walker   806-795-1750

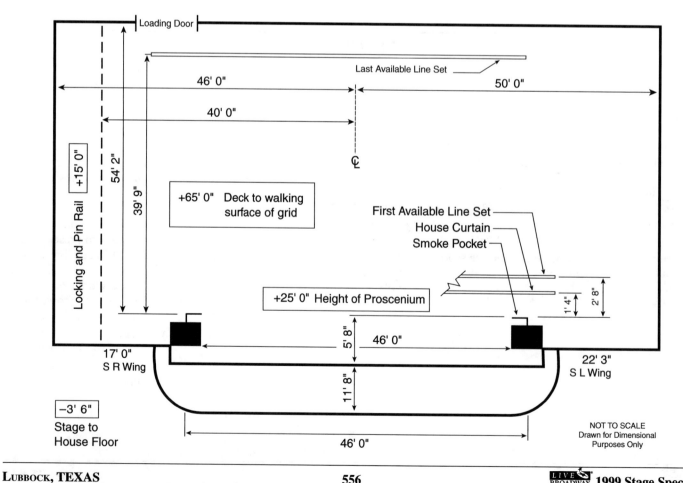

STAGE HOUSE

HOUSE CURTAIN
Operates as a guillotine from SR fly floor
Operates as a traveller from SR deck

RIGGING SYSTEM
Type: Single purchase counter weight
Weight: 10,000 lbs available
Line sets: 38 sets at 8-18" o.c. with 5 lift lines per set
Arbors: 750 lb capacity
House Pipes: 68' long with 54' of travel from deck
Line sets are not moveable
Block & Falls are not available
Chain hoists are not available
(4) spot wheels and 600' of hemp available

PERMANENT INSTALLATIONS OVER STAGE (FROM SMOKE POCKET)
Electric Raceways (5) at 5'0", 13'6", 21'6", 29'10", 35'10"
Electric bridge (1) at 5'0"

PERMANENT INSTALLATIONS ON DECK
Stairs (2) DSR/DSL
Electric bridges (1) on 1st electric
PA System (1) 0'20" x 0'20" x 0'25", located on DSR proscenium wall

ORCHESTRA PIT
Nonadjustable at 6'6" below stage level
Apron overhangs US wall of pit 2'6"
Pit is open (no cover) with curved railing

BACKSTAGE

LOADING DOCK
Loading door(s):
14'0"high x 10'0"wide
Trucks load (1) at a time
Fork lift is required - John James 806-775-2258
Sound/Props can load in FOH
Lobby can be a work area
No security

WARDROBE
Location: Property Room 10'x 50'
No Washers No Dryers
Washer and dryer hookups available

DRESSING ROOMS
(1) Star, SR, stage level, t/s included
(2) Star, SR/SL, stage level, t/s on same fl
(4) Small, (2) SL, (2) SR, +1, t/s on same fl
(2) Chorus, SL/SR, +1, t/s included
Use dressing room for company mgr office

SOUND

CONSOLE
Soundcraft, located Rear Orchestra
32 inputs, 2 main outputs, 2 aux outputs

SPEAKERS
Proscenium
Under Balcony
In balcony delays
No speaker truss

COMMUNICATIONS
Clear Com intercom with (2) channels
UHF phonic ear system
Dressing room page system

ROAD CONSOLE
Located Center Orchestra
No seats required to be removed
Cable run from stage is 130'
Tie-in into house system with XLR connectors

REHEARSAL & STORAGE SPACE
Rehearsal: None
Storage: None

ELECTRICS

ROAD SERVICE POWER

Panel	Phase	Amp	Circuit Protection	Use	Location
A	3	400	fuse	dimmers	SR
B	3	200	fuse	sound	SR

Recommended location of touring dimmer racks: SR
Hoist not required
Additional power is available for tour buses, generators, etc.

FRONT OF HOUSE (BOX BOOM VALUES ARE PER SIDE)

Position	Pipe Width	Distance to Prosc.	House Circuits	Connector Type	FOH Transfer Circuits
1st Cove	70'	35'	19	20 amp new twistlock	19

Transfer circuits: DMX Connectors

EQUIPMENT FOH (BOX BOOM VALUES ARE PER SIDE)

Position	Quantity	Wattage	Instrument	Removeable
1st Cove	19	1,000	10 x 10	yes

FOLLOWSPOTS
House Followspots:
(2) Strong Xenon Super Troupers; removeable

Followspot Booth:
(2) spots per booth;
140' throw to proscenium;
(2) 1Ø 30 amp breakers

DIMMERS
Lighting console is ETC;
(128) ETC Sensor dimmers
House has programmable DMX control system
(2) dry run DMX station(s), SL/SR

LUTCHER THEATER

YEAR BUILT: **1980**   YEAR RENOVATED: **1998**

Theatre Location:	707 W. Main, Orange, TX 77630	
Mailing Address:	PO Box 2310, Orange, TX 77631-2310	

Main Administrative Phone:	409-886-5535
Main Administrative Fax:	409-886-5537
E-mail:	lutcher @ exp.net
Website:	www.lutcher.org
Backstage Pay Phone:	409-886-8709

SEATING CAPACITY

Orchestra	870
Lower Balcony	282
Upper Balcony	294
Total:	**1,446**
pit (add'l)	28
wheelchair (add'l)	10
standing (add'l)	0

THEATRE STAFF

Managing Director	Jim Clark	409-886-5535

HOUSE CREW

Technical Director	Ben Meadows	409-886-5534

STAGE DIMENSIONS (FROM SMOKE POCKET)
Stage is 35'10" deep
Width from Center Line to SL is 43'6"
Width from Center Line to SR is 41'6"
Proscenium width is 45'0"
Proscenium height is 30'0"
Smoke pocket to apron edge is 4'0"
Orchestra pit exists

RIGGING
Grid Height:	27'
Type:	Single purchase counter weight
Weight:	10,000 lbs
Line sets:	42 sets at 9" o.c.
Arbors:	1,500 lb capacity
House Pipes:	61' long

LOADING DOCK
Loading door(s) are 16'0" high x 9'0" wide
Trucks load (3) at same time
Fork lift is not required and is not available

ELECTRICS
Total power available:
(1) 400A 3Ø SL
(1) 200A 3Ø SL

FOLLOWSPOTS
House Followspots:
Lycian 1275
Power in spot booth 20A

DIMMERS
(170) house dimmers
House has DMX control system
No dry run station(s)

SOUND
House has 100A dedicated
  power located SL
FOH mixing position in
  Rear House Left
Sound console is available

LILA COCKRELL THEATER

AT: **HENRY B. GONZALES CONVENTION CENTER**   **YEAR BUILT: 1968   YEAR RENOVATED: 1989**

Theatre Location: 200 E. Market St., San Antonio, TX 78205
Mailing Address: PO Box 1809, San Antonio, TX 78296
Management Company: City of San Antonio

Main Administrative Phone: 210-207-8500
Main Administrative Fax: 210-223-1495
Backstage Pay Phone: 210-225-9485

THEATRE STAFF
Booking Manager   Tillie Rheiner   210-207-8509

HOUSE CREW
Technical Supervisor Terry Price   210-207-8564

SEATING CAPACITY

First Floor	1,426
Mezzanine	631
Balcony	470
Total:	**2,527**

STAGE DIMENSIONS (FROM SMOKE POCKET)
Stage is 60'0" deep
Width from Center Line to SL is 60'0"
Width from Center Line to SR is 56'0"
Proscenium width is 55'8"
Proscenium height is 30'0"
Smoke pocket to apron edge is 5'6"
Orchestra pit exists

RIGGING
Grid Height: 80'
Type: Single purchase counter weight
Weight: 1,200 lbs
Line sets: 74 sets at 6" o.c.
Arbors: 1,000 lb capacity
House Pipes: 64' long

LOADING DOCK
Loading door(s) are 16'0" high x 16'0" wide
Trucks load (2) at same time
Fork lift is available

ELECTRICS
Total power available:
   (3) 400A 3Ø SL

FOLLOWSPOTS
House Followspots:
   Lycian
Power in spot booth (4) 220 volt
   circuits
FOH transfer circuits per
   position: 0

DIMMERS
(279) house dimmers
House has DMX control system
(1) dry run station(s) located
   Mezzanine

SOUND
House has dedicated power
   located SR
FOH mixing position in
   Rear Orchestra
Sound console is available

MAJESTIC THEATRE

YEAR BUILT: 1929   YEAR RENOVATED: 1989

Theatre Location: 230 East Houston Street, San Antonio, TX 78205
Mailing Address: P.O.Box 390, San Antonio, TX 78292
Management Company: Arts Center Enterprises,Inc.
                                      208 East Houston, San Antonio, TX 78205

Main Administrative Phone: 210-226-5700
Main Administrative Fax: 210-226-3377

SEATING CAPACITY
Orchestra	1,488
Mezzanine	456
Balcony	319
Total:	**2,263**
wheelchair (add'l)	50

THEATRE STAFF
General Manager	Marks Chowning	210-226-5700
Booking	Jeff Daniels	210-226-5700
Marketing	Jean Landers	210-226-5700
Operations	Mel Ellenwood	210-226-5700
Group Sales	Sherrie Villani	210-829-5460

HOUSE CREW
Technical Director	Haynes Knight	210-226-5700

UNIONS
IATSE Local #76	Ray Sewell	210-223-3911
Wardrobe Local #76	Ray Sewell	210-223-3911
Music	Julio Dominguez	210-226-5700

BOX OFFICE
Computerized
Box Office Manager
  Kevin Stephenson   210-226-3333

Outside Ticket Agency
Computerized
  Ticketmaster   210-224-9600

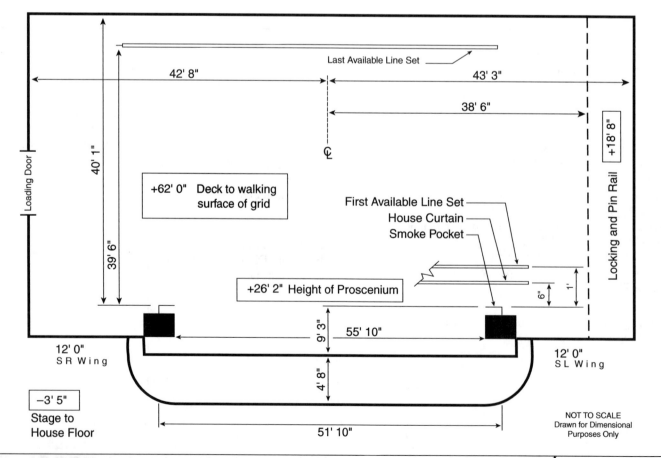

- 42' 8"
- 43' 3"
- Last Available Line Set
- 38' 6"
- +18' 8"
- 40' 1"
- Loading Door
- +62' 0" Deck to walking surface of grid
- First Available Line Set
- House Curtain
- Smoke Pocket
- Locking and Pin Rail
- 39' 6"
- +26' 2" Height of Proscenium
- 6"
- 1"
- 9' 3"
- 55' 10"
- 12' 0"
  SR Wing
- 12' 0"
  SL Wing
- 4' 8"
- −3' 5"
  Stage to House Floor
- 51' 10"
- NOT TO SCALE
  Drawn for Dimensional Purposes Only

STAGE HOUSE

HOUSE CURTAIN
Operates as a guillotine from SL fly floor
Operates as a traveller from SL deck

RIGGING SYSTEM
Type:	Combination purchase counter weight
Weight:	35,000 lbs available
Line sets:	61 sets at 6" o.c. with 5 lift lines per set
Arbors:	750 lb capacity
House Pipes:	60' long with 58' of travel from deck

Line sets are moveable
Chain hoists available as a rental; (2) one ton
(50) spot wheels and 5,000' of hemp available

PERMANENT INSTALLATIONS OVER STAGE (FROM SMOKE POCKET)
None

PERMANENT INSTALLATIONS ON DECK
Trap (1) in stage floor, 2' 0" x 3'0", located DSC

ORCHESTRA PIT
Nonadjustable at 13' below stage level
Apron overhangs US wall of pit 9' 0"

BACKSTAGE

LOADING DOCK
Loading door(s):
10'6" high x 8'6" wide
Trucks load (2) back to back at same time
Fork lift is not required
Sound/Props can load in FOH
(2) Trailers can store on-site
Security at stage door

WARDROBE
Location: Basement
Access: Elevator USL
(2) Washers (2) Dryers
Washer and dryer hookups available

DRESSING ROOMS
(2) Star, SR, -1, t/s included
(2) Star, SL, -1, t/s included
(2) Chorus, SL, -1, t/s included
Elevator access for dressing rooms
Additional production office available for company mgr

SOUND

CONSOLE
Crest, located FOH
40 inputs, 2 main outputs, 2 matrix outputs, 8 aux outputs

SPEAKERS
House Cluster
No speaker truss

COMMUNICATIONS
Clear Com intercom with (2) channels
Infrared sound system
Dressing room page system

ROAD CONSOLE
Located Center House right
No seats required to be removed
Cable run from stage is 100'
Tie-in into house system with XLR connectors

REHEARSAL & STORAGE SPACE
Rehearsal: None
Storage: None

ELECTRICS

ROAD SERVICE POWER

Panel	Phase	Amp	Circuit Protection	Use	Location
A	3	400	fuse	dimmers	SL side wall
B	3	400	fuse	extra	SL side wall
C	3	400	fuse	sound	SR side wall
D	3	200	fuse		basement

Recommended location of touring dimmer racks: SL
Hoist not required

FRONT OF HOUSE (BOX BOOM VALUES ARE PER SIDE)

Position	Pipe Width	Distance to Prosc.	House Circuits	Connector Type	FOH Transfer Circuits
1st Balc Rail	60'	40'	22	grd 20 amp stage pin	0
2nd Balc Rail	60'	90'	15	grd 20 amp stage pin	0
Box Boom 1		90'	15	grd 20 amp stage pin	0

EQUIPMENT FOH (BOX BOOM VALUES ARE PER SIDE)
None

FOLLOWSPOTS
House Followspots:
(2) Strong Super Trouper 2k; removeable
(1) Carbon Arc Trouper; removeable

Followspot Booth:
(4) spots per booth;
135' throw to proscenium;
(4) 1Ø 50 amp breakers

DIMMERS
Lighting console is Colortran Scenemaster 60; Colortran dimmers
House has programmable DMX control system
(2) dry run DMX station(s), SL, FOH mix position

WICHITA FALLS MEMORIAL AUDITORIUM

AKA: MEMORIAL AUDITORIUM

YEAR BUILT: 1927   YEAR RENOVATED: 1997

Theatre Location:	1300 Seventh Street, Wichita Falls, TX 76301
Mailing Address:	PO Box 1431, Wichita Falls, TX 76307
Management Company:	City of Wichita Falls (mailing address as above)

Main Administrative Phone:	940-716-5506
Main Administrative Fax:	940-716-5509
Stage Door Phone:	940-761-8878

THEATRE STAFF

Auditorium Manager	Don Burkman	940-716-5506

HOUSE CREW

Stagehand Manager	Richard Lehman	940-592-9753

SEATING CAPACITY

Lower Floor	1,400
First Balcony	692
Second Balcony	625
Total:	**2,717**
pit (add'l)	80
wheelchair (add'l)	12
standing (add'l)	0

STAGE DIMENSIONS (FROM SMOKE POCKET)

Stage is 35'0" deep
Width from Center Line to SL is 50'0"
Width from Center Line to SR is 50'0"
Proscenium width is 60'0"
Proscenium height is 25'0"
Smoke pocket to apron edge is 4'0"
Orchestra pit exists

RIGGING

Grid Height:	67'
Type:	Double purchase counter weight
Weight:	4,000 lbs
Line sets:	32 sets at 8" o.c.
Arbors:	400 lb capacity
House Pipes:	60' long

LOADING DOCK

Loading door(s) are 7'10" high x 8'0" wide
Trucks load (2) at same time
Fork lift is not required and is not available

ELECTRICS

Total power available:
400A 3Ø
200A 3Ø

FOLLOWSPOTS

House Followspots:
Carbon Arc
Super Troupers
Power in spot booth (4) 20A

DIMMERS

(12) house dimmers
No DMX control system

SOUND

House has 220A dedicated power located SL
FOH mixing position is below Balcony & behind seats
Sound console is available

CAPITOL THEATRE

AT: SALT LAKE FINE ARTS DIVISION

YEAR BUILT: 1913 YEAR RENOVATED: 1976

Theatre Location: 50 W. 200th South, Salt Lake City, UT 84101
Management Company: Salt Lake County Fine Arts

Main Administrative Phone: 801-323-6800
Main Administrative Fax: 801-538-2272
Website: www.arttix.org
Stage Door Phone: 801-323-6854
Backstage Pay Phone: 801-323-6850

THEATRE STAFF
Director   Marian Iwasaki   801-323-6800
Operations   John Stasco   801-323-6840

HOUSE CREW
Technical Director David Barber   801-323-6842
Stage Manager   Douglas W. Morgan 801-323-6897

UNIONS
IATSE Local #99   Steve Rood   801-359-0513

SEATING CAPACITY

Orchestra	1,083
Boxes	34
Grand Tier	92
Mezzanine	477
Balcony	241
Total	**1,927**

BOX OFFICE
Computerized
Box Office Manager
  Mark Chambers   801-323-6823

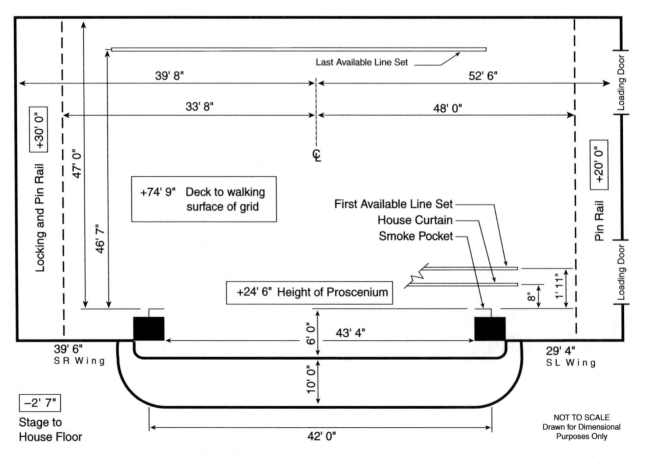

Last Available Line Set

39' 8"   52' 6"

33' 8"   48' 0"

Locking and Pin Rail   +30' 0"

Pin Rail   +20' 0"

Loading Door

47' 0"

+74' 9" Deck to walking surface of grid

46' 7"

First Available Line Set
House Curtain
Smoke Pocket

1' 11"
8"

+24' 6" Height of Proscenium

6' 0"   43' 4"

39' 6"
SR Wing

29' 4"
SL Wing

10' 0"

−2' 7"
Stage to House Floor

42' 0"

NOT TO SCALE
Drawn for Dimensional
Purposes Only

STAGE HOUSE

House Curtain
Operates as a guillotine from SL deck

Rigging System
Type:	Single purchase counter weight
Weight:	118,000 lbs available
Line sets:	66 sets at 8" o.c. with 7 lift lines per set
Arbors:	1,800 lb capacity
House Pipes:	60' long with 70' of travel from deck

Line sets are not moveable

Block & Falls are available 2:1 (1)

(50) spot wheels and 10,000 of hemp available

Permanent Installations Over Stage (from smoke pocket)
None

Permanent Installations On Deck
None

Orchestra Pit
Adjustable to 8' below stage level by hydraulic lift

Apron overhangs US wall of pit 3'6"

Pit lift is in (2) sections

BACKSTAGE

Loading Dock
Loading door(s):
1) 15'0" high x 10'2" wide
2) 13'0" high x 9'0" wide

Trucks load (2) at same time via separate docks

Dock 1) At street level, loading to stage thru separate loading area

Dock 2) At truck level, stage level +1 with 8,000 lb capacity freight elevator 13' high x 9' wide x 10'deep

Fork lift is required; house owns

Sound/Props can load in FOH

Lobby can be a work area

Security at dock & stage door

Wardrobe
Location: Basement

Access: Elevator

(3) Washers (3) Dryers

No washer or dryer hookups

Dressing Rooms
(5) Star, SL, -1, t/s included

(2) Small, SL, -1, toilet on same fl

(2) Chorus, -1, t/s included

Elevator access for dressing rooms

Additional production office available for company mgr

SOUND

Console
Midas

Speakers
House Cluster

Under Balcony

No speaker truss

Communications
Clear-Com intercom with (1) channel

No infrared sound system

Dressing room page system

Road Console
Located Rear

(43) seats required to be removed

Cable run from stage is 100'

Tie-in into house system with XLR connectors

Rehearsal & Storage Space
Rehearsal: 3 studios

Storage: None

ELECTRICS

Road Service Power

Panel	Phase	Amp	Circuit Protection	Use	Location
A	3	400	fuse	dimmers	SL side wall
B	3	400	fuse	sound	SL side wall
C	3	400	fuse	extra	SL side wall
D	3	200	fuse	sound	SL side wall

Recommended location of touring dimmer racks: SL on deck

Hoist provided but not required

Front Of House (box boom values are per side)

Position	Pipe Width	Distance to Prosc.	House Circuits	Connector Type	FOH Transfer Circuits
1st Balc Rail	30'	48'	27	grd 20 amp stage pin	27
1st Cove	40'	101'	10	grd 20 amp stage pin	10
Box Boom 1		55'	12	grd 20 amp stage pin	12
Box Boom 2		64'	12	grd 20 amp stage pin	12

Transfer circuits: grd 20 amp stage pin located on SL side wall

Road truss: Pipe width of cove position is comprised of short windows

Equipment FOH (box boom values are per side)

Position	Quantity	Wattage	Instrument	Removeable
1st Cove	12	1,500	Berkey 12°	no

Followspots
House Followspots:
(3) Xenon Super Troupers; removeable

Followspot Booth:
(4) spots per booth;
120' throw to proscenium;
(4) 3Ø 200 amp breakers

Dimmers
Lighting console is ETC Obsession;
(438) ETC Sensor dimmers

House has programmable DMX control system

(2) dry run DMX station(s)

KINGSBURY HALL

YEAR BUILT: 1930   YEAR RENOVATED: 1996

Theatre Location: 180 South 1400 East, Salt Lake City, UT 84112
Mailing Address: 1395 East President's Circle, Rm 190
                        Salt Lake City, UT 84112-0040

Main Administrative Phone: 801-581-6261
Main Administrative Fax: 801-585-5464
Website: www.kingsburyhall.org
Stage Door Phone: 801-581-6584
Traveling Production Office Phone: 801-582-8984
Traveling Production Office Fax: 801-582-2917

THEATRE STAFF
General Manager   Greg Geilmann   801-581-6965
Booking   Lynda Christensen   801-581-6261

HOUSE CREW
Stage Manager   Randy Rasmussen   801-581-6584

UNIONS
IATSE #99   Steve Rudd   801-359-0513
Wardrobe #99   Steve Rudd   801-359-0513
Music #104   801-486-0713

SEATING CAPACITY
Orchestra   1,030
Loge   153
Balcony   730
Total: **1,913**

pit (add'l)   64
wheelchair (add'l)   14

BOX OFFICE
Computerized
Box Office Manager
  Will Christensen   801-581-5645

Outside Ticket Agency
Computerized
Art Tiks
  Mark Chambers   801-323-6823

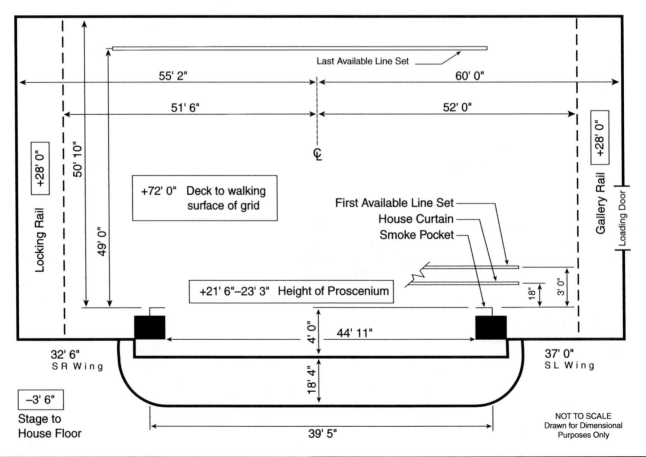

STAGE HOUSE

HOUSE CURTAIN
Operates as a guillotine from SL deck

RIGGING SYSTEM
Type:	Single purchase counter weight
Weight:	26,000 lbs available
Line sets:	72 sets at 6" o.c. with 8 lift lines per set
Arbors:	1,500 lb capacity
House Pipes:	70' long with 70' of travel from deck

Line sets are moveable
Block & Falls are not available
Chain hoists are not available
(30) spot wheels and 2,500' of hemp available

PERMANENT INSTALLATIONS OVER STAGE (FROM SMOKE POCKET)
M=Moveable with advance call
Electric Raceways (6) at 2'0", 9'4", 16'4", 23'4", 30'0", 37'0";M
Movie screen (1) at 3'4";M
Cyclorama (1) at 40'6"
Fire curtain (1) at 1'11"

PERMANENT INSTALLATIONS ON DECK
Loading bridge (2) at SR

ORCHESTRA PIT
Adjustable by hydraulic lift
Apron overhangs US wall of pit 0' 0"
Pit lift is in (2) sections
SL/SR portable apron platforms for speaker stacks or removable for more orchestra pit

BACKSTAGE

LOADING DOCK
Loading door(s):
16'0" high x 20'0" wide
Trucks load (2) at same time
Dock Address:
1375 East 100 South
Sound/Props can load in FOH
Lobby cannot be a work area
(1) Trailer can store on-site
Security at stage door

WARDROBE
Location: Under stage
Access: SL stairs
(2) Washers (2) Dryers
Washer and dryer hookups available

DRESSING ROOMS
(2) Star, SL, stage level, t/s included, phone jack
(4) Chorus, SL/CS/SR, -1, t/s included
Elevator access for dressing rooms
Additional production office available for company mgr

SOUND

CONSOLE
(2) Allen Heath
SL: 12 inputs, L R Center main outputs, 4 matrix outputs, 6 aux outputs
FOH/SR: 12 inputs, L R Center main outputs, 4 matrix outputs, 6 aux outputs

SPEAKERS
House Cluster
Proscenium
Under Balcony
No speaker truss
Max available load 4 points @ 750 lbs each

COMMUNICATIONS
Clear Com intercom with (1) channel
Infrared sound system
Dressing room page system

ROAD CONSOLE
Located Rear House left
(18) seats required to be removed
Cable run from stage is 100'
Tie-in into house system with XLR connectors

REHEARSAL & STORAGE SPACE
Rehearsal: 50' x 44', located -2, piano, mirror
Storage: 10' x 20', located -2

ELECTRICS

ROAD SERVICE POWER

Panel	Phase	Amp	Circuit Protection	Use	Location
A-C	3	600	breaker	dimmers	SL
D	3	200	breaker	sound	SL
E	3	100	breaker	extra	SL

Recommended location of touring dimmer racks: SL
Additional power is available for tour buses, generators, etc.

FRONT OF HOUSE (BOX BOOM VALUES ARE PER SIDE)

Position	Pipe Width	Distance to Prosc.	House Circuits	Connector Type	FOH Transfer Circuits
1st Cove	40'	46'	33	grd 20 amp stage pin	SL
2nd Cove	40'	59'	24	grd 20 amp stage pin	SL
Box Boom 1		56'	12	grd 20 amp stage pin	SL

Transfer circuits: grd 20 amp stage pin
Road truss: 8 FOH hanging points rated at 750 lbs each

EQUIPMENT FOH (BOX BOOM VALUES ARE PER SIDE)

Position	Quantity	Wattage	Instrument	Removeable
1st Balc Rail	17	575	Source 4 26°	yes
1st Cove	8	575	Source 4 19°	yes
2nd Cove	17	575	Source 4 19°	yes
Box Boom 1	10	575	Source 4 26°	yes

FOLLOWSPOTS
House Followspots:
(2) Lycian 1.2k; removeable

Followspot Booth:
(3) spots per booth; 102' throw to proscenium;
(3) 1Ø 20 amp breakers

DIMMERS
Lighting console is Expression 3X;
(512) sensor dimmers
House has programmable DMX control system
(4) dry run DMX station(s)

CHRYSLER HALL

AKA: SCOPE CENTER AT: NORFOLK CULTURAL AND CONVENTION CENTER   **YEAR BUILT: 1972**

Theatre Location:	201 East Brambleton Ave., Norfolk, VA 23510
Mailing Address:	PO Box 1808, Norfolk, VA 23501

Main Administrative Phone:	757-664-6464
Main Administrative Fax:	757-664-6990
E-mail:	plasako@norfolkscope.com
Website:	http://www.norfolkscope.com
Stage Door Phone:	757-664-6976
Backstage Pay Phone:	757-625-9195

SEATING CAPACITY

Orchestra	1,362
Dress Circle	412
Balcony	583
Total:	**2,357**
pit (add'l)	138
wheelchair (add'l)	8

BOX OFFICE
Computerized
Box Office Manager
Emily Sharpless   757-664-6964

THEATRE STAFF

Director	W.H. Luther	757-664-6953
Booking	Mary Collins	757-664-6958
Marketing	Cynthia Carter-West	757-664-6957
Operations	Roger Phelps	757-664-6967
Group Sales	Cynthia-Carter West	757-664-6957

HOUSE CREW

Production Manager	Paul Lasakow	757-664-6973

UNIONS
Contact theatre management

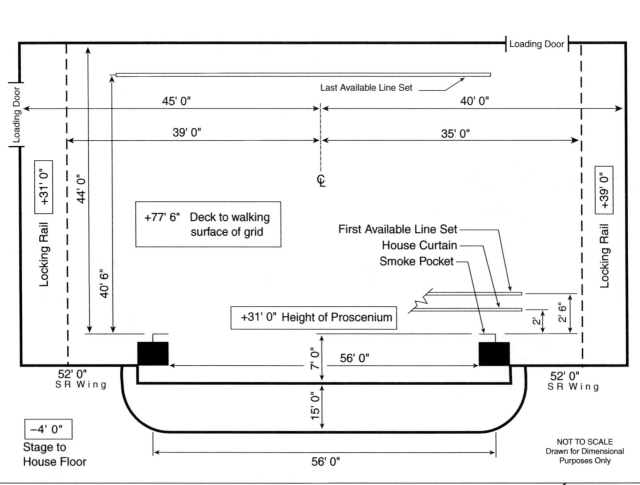

STAGE HOUSE

HOUSE CURTAIN
Operates as a guillotine from SR deck; motorized or manual
Operates as a manual traveller from SR deck

RIGGING SYSTEM
Type:	Double purchase counter weight
Weight:	70,000 lbs available
Line sets:	60 sets at 6 o.c. with 7 lift lines per set
Arbors:	3,000 lb capacity
House Pipes:	60' long with 68' of travel from deck

Line sets are moveable
Block & Falls are not available
Chain hoists are not available
(20) spot wheels and 5,000' of hemp available

PERMANENT INSTALLATIONS OVER STAGE (FROM SMOKE POCKET)
M=Moveable with advance call
Orchestra shell (7) 6'6", 6'6", 14'6", 14'6", 22'0", 30'6", 40'0"; M
Movie screen (1) at 43'0"; M
Traveller (3) at 2'0", 11'0", 36'0"; M
Cyclorama (1) at 41'0"; M
Fire curtain 0'0"

PERMANENT INSTALLATIONS ON DECK
None

ORCHESTRA PIT
Adjustable to 25' below stage level by hydraulic lift
Apron overhangs US wall of pit 4'0"
Pit lift is in (1) section

BACKSTAGE

LOADING DOCK
Loading door(s):
　12'0" high x 13'6" wide
Trucks load (1) at a time
Fork lift is not required
Sound/Props can load in FOH
Lobby can be a work area
Trailers cannot store on-site
Security at stage door

WARDROBE
Location: Basement
Access: Elevator/Freight elevator
(1) Washer (1) Dryer
Washer and dryer hookups available

DRESSING ROOMS
(1) Star, SR, stage level, t/s, phone jack
(7) Small, SR, -1, t/s
(3) Chorus, SR, -1/ +1, t/s
Elevator access for dressing rooms
Additional production office available for company mgr

SOUND

CONSOLE
Soundcraft 200SR, located in booth
24 inputs, 2 main outputs, 4 aux outputs

SPEAKERS
Under Balcony
Portable
Ambient resonance enhancement system in place & optional
No speaker truss

COMMUNICATIONS
Clear Com intercom with (1) channel
Infrared sound system

ROAD CONSOLE
Located Rear Center under balcony
Some seats required to be removed
Cable run from stage is 150'
Tie-in into house system with ¼" TRS connectors

REHEARSAL & STORAGE SPACE
Rehearsal: 40' x 40' in basement, piano at extra charge
Storage: None

ELECTRICS

ROAD SERVICE POWER

Panel	Phase	Amp	Circuit Protection	Use	Location
A-C	3	400	fuse	dimmers	USR
D	3	200	fuse	sound	USR
E	3	100	fuse	sound	USC
F	3	100	fuse	sound	DSL
G	3	200	fuse	extra	loading dock

A-C on transformer 1, D-G, on transformer 2
Recommended location of touring dimmer racks: USR
Hoist not required

FRONT OF HOUSE (BOX BOOM VALUES ARE PER SIDE)

Position	Pipe Width	Distance to Prosc.	House Circuits	Connector Type	FOH Transfer Circuits
Balc Rail	48'	89'	23	grd 20 amp stage pin	17
2nd Cove	70'	28'	26	grd 20 amp stage pin	9
3rd Cove	70'	45'	18	grd 20 amp stage pin	0
Box Boom 1		14'	6	grd 20 amp stage pin	4
Box Boom 2		14'	6	grd 20 amp stage pin	4

Transfer circuits: stage pin, 2 conductor no ground
Road truss: FOH truss points 4'-6' DS of proscenium; Standard phantom steel above apron; 2nd cove max 12 instruments; 3rd cove max 24 instruments; 1st cove unusable; All coves 50% obstructed

EQUIPMENT FOH (BOX BOOM VALUES ARE PER SIDE)

Position	Quantity	Wattage	Instrument	Removeable
3rd Cove	8	1,000	6 x 16	yes

FOLLOWSPOTS
House Followspots:
　(3) Xenon Super Troupers; removeable

Followspot Booth:
　(4) spots per booth;
　125' throw to proscenium;
　(4) 3Ø 20 amp breakers

DIMMERS
Lighting console is ETC Express 125;
(136) ENR dimmers
House has programmable DMX control system
(2) dry run DMX station(s)

CARPENTER CENTER FOR THE PERFORMING ARTS

YEAR BUILT: 1928   YEAR RENOVATED: 1983

Theatre Location: 600 E Grace Street, Richmond, VA 23219

Main Administrative Phone:	804-225-9000
Main Administrative Fax:	804-649-7402
E-mail:	103300.356@compuserve.com
Website:	www.chp2001.com/carpentercenter
Stage Door Phone:	804-649-0468
Backstage Pay Phone:	804-648-9339
Traveling Production Office Phone:	804-649-3683
Traveling Production Office Fax:	804-649-3684

SEATING CAPACITY

Orchestra	891
Loge	260
First Dress Circle	509
Second Dress Circle	279
Total:	**1,939**
pit (add'l)	62
wheelchair (add'l)	16
standing (add'l)	26

THEATRE STAFF

Executive Director	Joel D. Katz	804-649-0444
Booking	Joel D. Katz	804-649-0444
Operations	Joe Yarbrough	804-649-0467

HOUSE CREW

Technical Director	Joe Yarbrough	804-649-0467
Carpentry	Wilbur King	
Electrics	Mike Johnson	
Sound	Darryl Ransome	

UNIONS

IATSE Local #87	John Fulwider	804-264-8900

BOX OFFICE

Computerized
Box Office Manager
  Craig Mize   804-649-0588

Outside Ticket Agency
Computerized
Ticketmaster
  Sara Jacki   800-927-9266

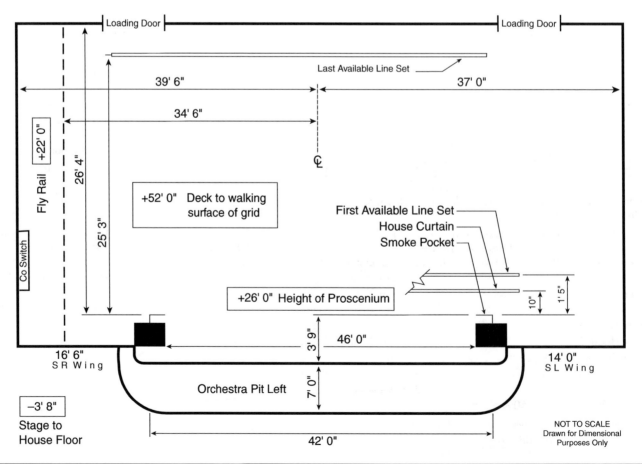

STAGE HOUSE

House Curtain
Operates as a guillotine from SR deck

Rigging System
Type:	Hydraulic vertilift system
Weight:	49,500 lbs available
Line sets:	33 sets at 6" o.c. with 5 lift lines per set
Arbors:	1,500 lb capacity
House Pipes:	57' long with 51' of travel from deck

Line sets are not moveable
Block & Falls are not available
Chain hoists are not available
(0) spot wheels and 500' of hemp available
Orchestra shell ceiling attached to light bridges

Permanent Installations Over Stage (from smoke pocket)
Orchestra shells (4) attached to light bridges,
Orchestra shell arms (10) 5 ea. (towers) stored SL & SR
Electric bridge (4) at 4'0", 10'0", 15'8", 21'6"
Cyclorama (1) at 26'4"
Fire curtain (1) at 0'2"

Permanent Installations On Deck
None

Orchestra Pit
Adjustable to 11' below stage level by hydraulic lift
Apron overhangs US wall of pit 3'3"
Pit lift is in (1) section

BACKSTAGE

Loading Dock
Loading door(s):
  (2) 7'11" high x 6'5" wide
Trucks load (1) at a time
Fork lift is not required
Sound/Props can load in FOH
Lobby can be a work area
(1) Trailer can store on-site
Security at dock & stage door

Wardrobe
Location: Green Room in
  basement below stage
Access: Orchestra pit elevator
(1) Washer (1) Dryer
Washer and dryer hookups
  available

Dressing Rooms
(1) Star, SR, stage level, t/s
  included, phone jack
(7) Small, SL, -1/+1/+2, t/s on
  same floor
(2) Chorus, SL, -1, t/s on same
  floor
Additional production office
  available for company mgr

SOUND

Console
Audio Arts
32 inputs, 4 aux outputs

Speakers
House Cluster
Under Balcony
Portable
No speaker truss

Communications
Clear Com intercom with
  (2) channels
Infrared sound system
Dressing room page system

Road Console
Located Rear Orchestra
No seats required to be
  removed
Cable run from stage is 100'
Tie-in into house system with
  XLR connectors

Rehearsal & Storage Space
Rehearsal: None
Storage: None

ELECTRICS

Road Service Power

Panel	Phase	Amp	Circuit Protection	Use	Location
A	3	800	fuse	dimmers	SR side wall
B	3	100	fuse	ssound	SR in basement

Recommended location of touring dimmer racks: SR in wing
Hoist not required or provided
Additional power is available for tour buses, generators, etc.

Front Of House (box boom values are per side)

Position	Pipe Width	Distance to Prosc.	House Circuits	Connector Type	FOH Transfer Circuits
1st Cove	100'	80'	30	grd 20 amp stage pin	30
Box Boom 1		40	12	grd 20 amp stage pin	12
Balc Rail	20	60	9	grd 20 amp stage pin	9

Transfer circuits: grd 20 amp stage pin
Road truss: cannot hang truss in FOH, -only above stage behind proscenium

Equipment FOH (box boom values are per side)

Position	Quantity	Wattage	Instrument	Removeable
1st Cove	12	1,000	Lekos	no
Box Boom 1	30	1,000	Lekos	no
Box Boom 2	12	1,000	Lekos	no

Followspots
House Followspots:
  (2) Super Troupers

Followspot Booth:
  (4) spots per booth;
  120' throw to proscenium;
  1Ø 100 amp breakers

Dimmers
Lighting console is Impression;
  (288) Colortran dimmers
No DMX control system
House is CMX

RICHMOND'S LANDMARK THEATER

FORMERLY: THE MOSQUE AKA: LANDMARK THEATER

YEAR BUILT: **1927** YEAR RENOVATED: **1995**

Theatre Location: 6 North Laurel Street, Richmond, VA 23220
Management Company: City of Richmond

Main Administrative Phone: 804-780-8226
Main Administrative Fax: 804-780-6101
Stage Door Phone: 804-780-8492

THEATRE STAFF
Marketing Audrey M. Booth 804-780-8226
Booking Audrey M. Booth 804-780-8226

HOUSE CREW
Electrics Kenny Fulwider 804-780-8492

SEATING CAPACITY
Orchestra	1,434
Grand Tier	880
Front and Rear Balconies	1,197
Boxes	54
Pit	51
Total:	**3,616**

STAGE DIMENSIONS (FROM SMOKE POCKET)
Stage is 22'1" deep;
Width from Center Line to SL is 43'6"
Width from Center Line to SR is 43'6"
Proscenium width is 69'9"
Proscenium height is 30'0"
Smoke pocket to apron edge is 2'3"
Orchestra pit exists

RIGGING
Grid Height: 60'
Type: Double purchase counter weight
Line sets: 42 sets
House Pipes: 70' with 55' of travel from deck long
6 FOH rigging points available; Hoist is not required

LOADING DOCK
Loading door(s):
(3) 15'7" high x 10'0" wide
(1) 10'3" high x 9'9" wide
Fork lift is not required

ELECTRICS
Total power available:
600A 3Ø SL

FOLLOWSPOTS
House Followspots:
(2) Explorer HMI long
throws; removeable

DIMMERS
Lighting console is Expression
2x
(60) house dimmers, Kleigl
House has programmable DMX
control system
(2) dry run station(s)

SOUND
Undedicated power
Sound console is available

ROANOKE CIVIC CENTER AUDITORIUM

Theatre Location: 710 Williamson Road, Roanoke, VA 24106-2000
Mailing Address: PO Box 13005, Roanoke, VA 24030-3005

Main Administrative Phone: 540-853-2241
Main Administrative Fax: 540-853-2748
Stage Door Phone: 540-345-9263

THEATRE STAFF

Civic Center Manager	Jim Evans	540-853-2241
Booking	Vivian Nelson	540-853-2241
Marketing	Robyn Schon	540-853-2241
Operations	Bill Johnson	540-853-2241
Group Sales	Robyn Schon	540-853-2241

HOUSE CREW

Stage Manager	Jim Nelson	540-362-5164
Carpentry	Paul Morris	540-853-2241
Electrics	Mike Jay	540-853-2241
Electrics	Randolph Patton	540-853-2241

UNIONS

IATSE Local # 55	Jim Nelson	540-362-5164

SEATING CAPACITY

Orchestra	1,563
Loge	295
Balcony	520
Total:	**2,378**
pit (add'l)	80

BOX OFFICE

Computerized
Box Office Manager
Judy Jennings   540-981-1201

Outside Ticket Agency
Computerized
Ticketmaster
Sara Rowan   757-518-5500

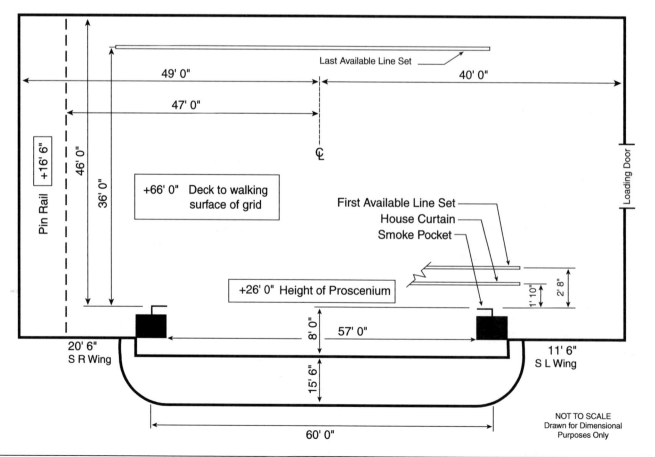

Last Available Line Set

49' 0"   40' 0"

47' 0"

46' 0"

Pin Rail +16' 6"

36' 0"

+66' 0" Deck to walking surface of grid

CL

First Available Line Set
House Curtain
Smoke Pocket

1' 10"   2' 8"

+26' 0" Height of Proscenium

Loading Door

8' 0"   57' 0"

20' 6"
S R Wing

11' 6"
S L Wing

15' 6"

60' 0"

NOT TO SCALE
Drawn for Dimensional
Purposes Only

STAGE HOUSE

House Curtain
Operates as a guillotine or traveller from SR deck

Rigging System
Type:	Single purchase counter weight
Weight:	10,000 lbs available
Line sets:	44 sets
Arbors:	1,000 lb capacity
House Pipes:	60' long

Chain hoists are available as a rental

Permanent Installations Over Stage (from smoke pocket)
M=Moveable with advance call
Movie Screen (1) at 10'0"; M
Traveller (1) Mid stage at Line 27; M
Electric Pipe (2) at line set #5 and #43

Permanent Installations On Deck
Loading bridge (1) located SR grid
Adjustable proscenium (1)

Orchestra Pit
Adjustable by hydraulic lift
Apron overhangs US wall of pit 4'4"
Pit lift is in (1) section
Piano Lift at Center Line

BACKSTAGE

Loading Dock
Loading door(s):
  9'8" high x 10'0" wide
Trucks load (2) at same time
Located SL, stage level
Fork lift is not required; House owns
Sound/Props cannot load in FOH
Lobby cannot be a work area
Many trailers can store on-site
Security at dock & stage door

Wardrobe
Location: Rear stage walkaround
(1) Washer (1) Dryer
No washer or dryer hookups

Dressing Rooms
(5) Small, SR, stage level, t/s
(2) Chorus, SR, stage level, t/s
Additional production office available for company mgr

Rehearsal & Storage Space
Rehearsal:
Storage:

SOUND

Console
Soundcraft 200 Delta 24 x 4 x 2, located Rear House
12 inputs, 1 main output

Speakers
House Cluster
No speaker truss

Communications
Clear Com intercom

Road Console
Located Rear House
No seats required to be removed
Cable run from stage is 216'
Tie-in into house system with XLR connectors

ELECTRICS

Road Service Power

Panel	Phase	Amp	Circuit Protection	Use	Location
A-C	3	400	breaker	extra	SL

Recommended location of touring dimmer racks: SL
Hoist not provided and not required
Additional power is available for tour buses, generators, etc.

Front Of House (box boom values are per side)

Position	Pipe Width	Distance to Prosc.	House Circuits	Connector Type	FOH Transfer Circuits
1st Balc Rail		30'	8	20 amp twistlock	
1st Cove		64'	18	20 amp twistlock	
2nd Cove		80'	18	20 amp twistlock	
Box Boom 1		4'	8	20 amp twistlock	

Transfer circuits: Twistlock to stage pin

Equipment FOH (box boom values are per side)

Position	Quantity	Wattage	Instrument	Removeable
1st Balc Rail	12	1,000	Major	yes
2nd Balc Rail	12	1,000	Major	yes
2nd Cove	8	750	Lekos	yes

Followspots
House Followspots:
(2) Strong Xenon Super Troupers; not removeable

Followspot Booth:
None

Dimmers
Lighting console is ETC Insight - 108 channels;
(70) dimmers
No DMX control system

THE 5TH AVENUE THEATRE

YEAR BUILT: 1926   YEAR RENOVATED: 1980

Theatre Location:	1308 5th Avenue, Seattle, WA 98101
Mailing Address:	1326 5th Avenue, 2nd Floor, Skinner Building
	Seattle, WA 98101

Main Administrative Phone:	206-625-1418
Main Administrative Fax:	206-292-9610
Website:	www.5thavenuetheatre.org
Stage Door Phone:	206-625-1418 x227
Backstage Pay Phone:	206-223-9073

THEATRE STAFF

Managing Director	Marilynn Sheldon	206-625-1418
Booking	Sharon Burke	206-625-1418
Marketing	Tracey Wickersham	206-625-1418
Group Sales	Beth Bowman	206-625-1418

HOUSE CREW

Technical Director	Cathy Johnstone	206-625-1418 x224
Carpentry	Dale Lane	206-625-1418 x223
Electrics	Candy Solie	206-625-1418 x236
Sound	Chris Tapping	206-625-1418 x222
Props	Kevin Bryce	206-625-1418 x234

UNIONS

IATSE Local #15	Sean Callahan	206-441-1515
Wardrobe Local #987	Benita Hyder	206-443-9354
Music In house	Sterling Tinsley	206-625-1418 x217

SEATING CAPACITY

Orchestra	1,231
Grand Tier	345
Middle Balcony	338
Upper Balcony	128
Side Balcony	73
Total:	**2,115**
pit (add'l)	42
wheelchair (incl.)	24

BOX OFFICE

Computerized
Box Office Treasurer

Peggy Busteed	206-625-1418

Outside Ticket Agency
Computerized
Ticketmaster

Scott Menefee	206-292-5400

Box office is promoter operated

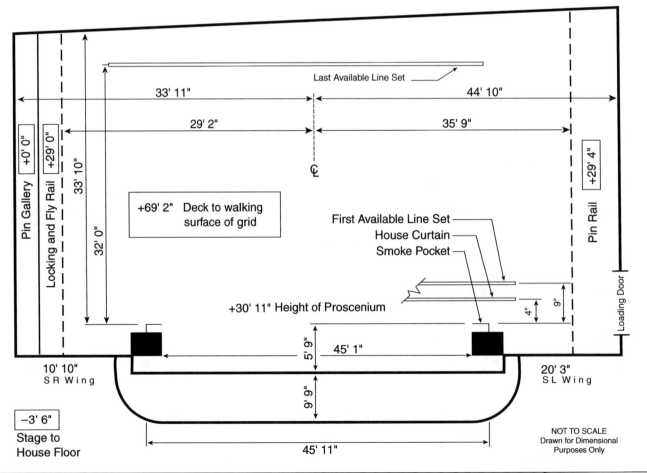

STAGE HOUSE

HOUSE CURTAIN
Operates as a guillotine from SR deck

RIGGING SYSTEM
Type:	Single purchase counter weight
Weight:	50,000 lbs available
Line sets:	55 sets at 6" o.c. with 5 lift lines per set
Arbors:	2,000 lb capacity
House Pipes:	52' long with 67' of travel from deck

Line sets are moveable
Block & Falls are available 3:2(4)
Chain hoists are available; (3) one ton, (5) half ton
(100) spot wheels and 10,000' of hemp available

PERMANENT INSTALLATIONS OVER STAGE (FROM SMOKE POCKET)
None

PERMANENT INSTALLATIONS ON DECK
Jump (1) 26'5" to steel SR, from DS wall to US wall
Electric Jump (1) 26'9" to steel SL, from DS wall to US wall
Pilasters (3) 1'x11"x11"/2@ 1'8" x 1'10" x 1'8" at 33'7" to smoke pocket
Stairs (1) 2'8" x 2'4" at 30'7" on SR
Loading bridge (1) 56'9" to steel SR, from DS wall to DS wall

ORCHESTRA PIT
Nonadjustable at 6' 11" below stage level
Apron overhangs US wall of pit 2'1"

BACKSTAGE

LOADING DOCK
Loading door(s):
  20'0"high x 8'7"wide
Trucks load (2) back to back at same time
Alley is raked; Load-in restrictions on trucks over 30' long between 7- 9am and 4-6pm on downtown streets
Fork lift is not required
Sound/Props can load in FOH
Lobby can be a work area
Trailers cannot store on-site
Security at stage door

WARDROBE
Location: Backstage, + 1 above stage
Access: Stairs/freight elevator (3'4" x 5'8" - 6'11" h)
(2) Washers (2) Dryers
No washer or dryer hookups

DRESSING ROOMS
(2) Star, behind stage, +1, t/s included, phone jack
(7) Small, behind stage, +1, t/s on same fl
(2) Chorus, behind stage, +1, t/s on same fl
Use dressing room for company mgr office

SOUND

CONSOLE
Yamaha PM 4000, located Rear House
44 mono/ 8 stereo inputs, 8 group/2 stereo main outputs, 8 matrix outputs, 12 aux outputs

SPEAKERS
House Cluster
Proscenium
Under Balcony
Upper balcony
No speaker truss

COMMUNICATIONS
Clearcom intercom with (4) channels
Infrared sound system
Dressing room page system

ROAD CONSOLE
Located Rear House
(10) seats required to be removed
Cable run from stage is 250'
Tie-in into house system with XLR connectors

REHEARSAL & STORAGE SPACE
Rehearsal: None
Storage: None

ELECTRICS

ROAD SERVICE POWER

Panel	Phase	Amp	Circuit Protection	Use	Location
A	3	400	breaker	dimmers	SL jump
B-C	3	400	breaker	extra	SL jump
D	3	200	breaker	extra	SR
E	3	200	breaker	sound	SL

Recommended location of touring dimmer racks: SL jump
Hoist required and provided

FRONT OF HOUSE (BOX BOOM VALUES ARE PER SIDE)

Position	Pipe Width	Distance to Prosc.	House Circuits	Connector Type	FOH Transfer Circuits
1st Balc Rail	45'	70'	33	grd 20 amp stage pin	30
Box Boom 1		44'	12	grd 20 amp stage pin	12
Box Boom		64'	12	grd 20 amp stage pin	12

Transfer circuits: grd 20 amp stage pin

EQUIPMENT FOH (BOX BOOM VALUES ARE PER SIDE)

Position	Quantity	Wattage	Instrument	Removeable
1st Balc Rail	20	575	5419D	yes
Box Boom 2	20	575	5419D	yes

FOLLOWSPOTS
House Followspots:
  (3) Strong Gladiators Xenon 3000; removeable

Followspot Booth:
  (3) spots per booth;
  175' throw to proscenium;
  (3) 1Ø 30 amp breakers

DIMMERS
Lighting console is ETC Obsession;
(512) IPS dimmers
No DMX control system
(0) dry run DMX station(s)

PARAMOUNT THEATRE

YEAR BUILT: 1927   YEAR RENOVATED: 1994

Theatre Location: 901 Pine Street, Seattle, WA 98101
Mailing Address: 907 Pine Street #905, Seattle, WA 98101
Management Company: Seattle Landmark Association (mailing address as above)

Main Administrative Phone: 206-467-5510
Main Administrative Fax: 206-682-4837
E-mail: soldout@theparamount.com
Website: www.theparamount.com
Stage Door Phone: 206-467-5510 x128
Backstage Pay Phone: 206-812-2744
Traveling Production Office Phone: 206-812-1430
Traveling Production Office Fax: 206-812-1433

THEATRE STAFF
Executive Director   John Donevant   206-812-3310
Executive Producer   Josh LaBelle   206-812-3319
Marketing   Michael Miller   206-812-3303
Operations   David Allen   206-812-3313
Group Sales   Danielle Olsen   206-812-3308

HOUSE CREW
Technical Director   Michael Miles   206-953-9900
Carpentry   Michael Miles   206-953-9900
Electrics   Jeff Payne   206-365-3169
Sound   Mark Anderson
Props   Joe Poole

UNIONS
IATSE Local #15   Sean Sallahan   206-441-1515
Wardrobe Local #887   Delia MulHolland   206-527-7647
Music Local #76-493   Douglas J. Soloman 206-324-0102

SEATING CAPACITY
Orchestra   1523
First Mezzanine   414
Second Mezzanine   444
Upper Balcony   422
Total: **2,803**

pit (add'l)   36

BOX OFFICE
Computerized
Manager
  Debbie Miles   206-812-1111

Outside Ticket Agency
Computerized
Ticket Master   206-628-0888

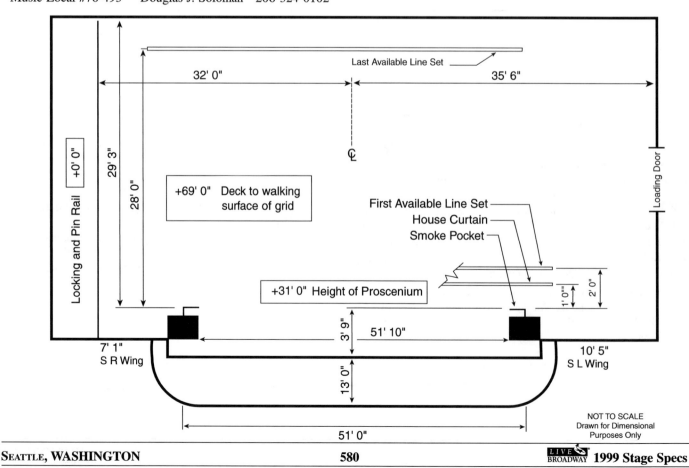

NOT TO SCALE
Drawn for Dimensional
Purposes Only

STAGE HOUSE

HOUSE CURTAIN
Operates as a guillotine from SL deck
Operates as a traveller from SR deck

RIGGING SYSTEM
Type:	Single purchase counter weight
Weight:	77,000 lbs available
Line sets:	66 sets at 8" o.c
Arbors:	1,460 lb capacity
House Pipes:	55' long with 62'6" of travel from deck

Line sets are moveable
Block & Falls are not available
Chain hoists are not available
(77) spot wheels and 2,000' of hemp available

PERMANENT INSTALLATIONS OVER STAGE (FROM SMOKE POCKET)
None

PERMANENT INSTALLATIONS ON DECK
None

ORCHESTRA PIT
Adjustable to below stage level by electric motor turnscrew
Apron overhangs US wall of pit 1'0"
Pit lift is in (2) sections
Pit has organ lift

BACKSTAGE

LOADING DOCK
Loading door(s):
    13'0" high x 8'0" wide
Trucks load (2) at same time
Fork lift is not required
Sound/Props can load in FOH
Lobby can be a work area
(3) Trailers can store on-site
Security at dock & stage door

WARDROBE
Location: Basement
Access: Passenger elevator/
    stairwell
(3) Washers (3) Dryers
No washer or dryer hookups

DRESSING ROOMS
(1) Star, SL, +3, t/s included,
    phone jack
(6) Small, SL, +3, t/s included,
    phone jack
(2) Chorus, SL, +4, +5, t/s
    included, phone jack
Elevator access for dressing
    rooms
Additional production office
    available for company mgr

SOUND

CONSOLE
Yamaha P7 4,000
44 Mono/ 4stereo inputs,
    2 main outputs, 8 matrix
    outputs, 16 aux outputs

SPEAKERS
House Cluster
Proscenium
Under Balcony
No speaker truss

COMMUNICATIONS
Clear Com intercom with
    (8) channels
Infrared sound system
Dressing room page system

ROAD CONSOLE
Located Rear House
No seats required to be
    removed
Cable run from stage is 120'
Tie-in into house system with
    XLR connectors

REHEARSAL & STORAGE SPACE
Rehearsal: None
Storage: None

ELECTRICS

ROAD SERVICE POWER
Panel	Phase	Amp	Circuit Protection	Use	Location
A-C	3	400	fuse	dimmers	DSL
D	3	200	fuse	sound	DSL
E	3	200	fuse	extra	USR
F	3	200	fuse	extra	Grid
G	3	200	fuse	extra	Loading Dock

Recommended location of touring dimmer racks: SL
Hoist not required
Additional power is available for tour buses, generators, etc.

FRONT OF HOUSE (BOX BOOM VALUES ARE PER SIDE)
Position	Pipe Width	Distance to Prosc.	House Circuits	Connector Type	FOH Transfer Circuits
1st Balc Rail	60'	47'	21	grd 20 amp stage pin	21
Box Boom 1		57'	18	grd 20 amp stage pin	18

EQUIPMENT FOH (BOX BOOM VALUES ARE PER SIDE)
Position	Quantity	Wattage	Instrument	Removeable
1st Balc Rail	6	575	Source 4	yes
Box Boom 1	12	575	Source 4	yes
Box Boom 2	12	575	Source 4	yes

FOLLOWSPOTS
House Followspots:
    (4) Lycian 1290 XLT;
    removeable

(1) Followspot Booth:
    (4) spots in booth;
    149' throw to proscenium;
    (4) 1Ø 30 amp breakers

(2) Additional followspot
    locations each with:
    86' throw to proscenium;
    (1) 1Ø 30 amp breakers

DIMMERS
House console is ETC
    Obsession;
    (340) ETC Sensor dimmers
House has programmable
    DMX control system
(12) dry run DMX station(s).

SEATTLE CENTER OPERA HOUSE

AKA: OPERA HOUSE AT: SEATTLE CENTER

Theatre Location: Seattle Center, Seattle, WA 98109
Mailing Address: 305 Harrison Street, Seattle , WA 98109

Main Administrative Phone: 206-684-7330
Main Administrative Fax: 206-684-7342

THEATRE STAFF
Manager   Shelley Sink   206-684-7207
Booking   206-684-7202

HOUSE CREW
Technical Director Carolyn MacLean 206-233-7012
Carpentry   Gary Hess   206-684-7006
Electrics   Marty Pavloff   206-233-7026

SEATING CAPACITY
Main Floor	1,723
First Balcony	660
Second Balcony	694
Total:	**3,077**
pit (add'l)	0
wheelchair (incl.)	31
standing	0

STAGE DIMENSIONS (FROM SMOKE POCKET)
Stage is 70'0" deep
Width from Center Line to SL is 54'0"
Width from Center Line to SR is 50'0"
Proscenium width is 60'0"
Proscenium height is 30'0"
Smoke pocket to apron edge is 8'0"
Orchestra pit exists

RIGGING
Grid Height: 85'
Type: Single purchase counter weight
Line sets: 100 sets at 6" o.c.
Arbors: 1,600 lb capacity
House Pipes: 68' long

LOADING DOCK
Loading door(s) are 15'6"high x 7'6"wide
Trucks load (2) at same time
Fork lift is not required

ELECTRICS
Total power available:
  (1) 600A 3Ø DSR
  (2) 50A 3Ø USC

FOLLOWSPOTS
House Followspots:
  Lycian XLT Throws
Power in spot booth (4) 50A

DIMMERS
(542) house dimmers
House has DMX control system
(6) dry run station(s) located
  Bridge balcony rail
  Main floor spot booth

SOUND
House has 600A dedicated
  power located DSL
FOH mixing position in
  Rear House
Sound console is available

SPOKANE OPERA HOUSE

AT: SPOKANE CENTER   YEAR BUILT: 1974

Theatre Location: 334 West Spokane Falls Boulevard, Spokane, WA 99201
Management Company: City of Spokane

Main Administrative Phone: 509-353-6500
Main Administrative Fax: 509-353-6511
E-mail: spokanecenter@spokanecity.org
Stage Door Phone: 509-353-6518
Backstage Pay Phone: 509-747-9773
Traveling Production Office Phone: 509-353-6519
Traveling Production Office Fax: 509-353-6520

SEATING CAPACITY
Orchestra   1,803
Terrace   476
Balcony   345
Total: **2,264**

pit (add'l)   76
wheelchair (add'l)   30

Note: Continental seating, no center aisle

THEATRE STAFF
Director   Mike Kobluk   509-353-6500
Booking   Maxey Adams   509-353-6500

HOUSE CREW
Technical Manager   Jay Nordling   509-353-6516

UNIONS
IATSE Local #93   Leroy Frengle   509-208-683-3507
Wardrobe Local #93   Leroy Frengle   509-208-683-3507
AFM Local #105   Jimmy Nixon   509-328-5253

BOX OFFICE
Computerized
Manager
  Jack Lucas   509-459-6100

Outside Ticket Agency
Computerized
  G & B Select-A-Seat 509-325-7328

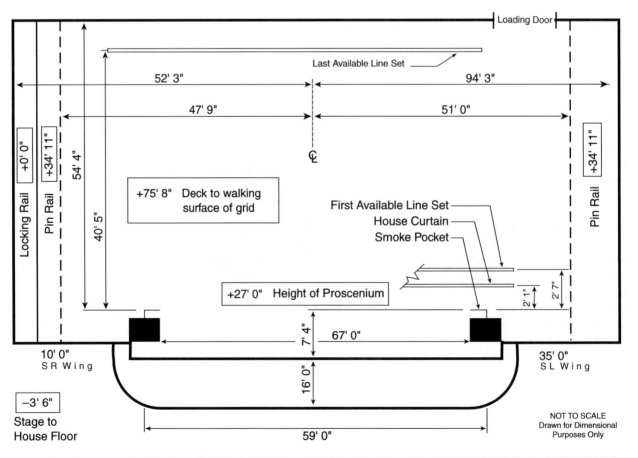

STAGE HOUSE

HOUSE CURTAIN
Operates as a traveller from SR deck
#1 pipe DS of traveller can be hung as guillotine

RIGGING SYSTEM
Type: Single purchase counter weight
Weight: 10,000 lbs available
Line sets: 76 sets at 6" o.c. with 7 lift lines per set
Arbors: 1,500 lb capacity
House Pipes: 72' long with 71' of travel from deck
Line sets are moveable
Block & Falls are available 3:2 (2)
Chain hoists are available; (6) one ton, (2) half ton
(20) spot wheels and 6,000' of hemp available

PERMANENT INSTALLATIONS OVER STAGE (FROM SMOKE POCKET)
M=Moveable with advance call
Orchestra shell (4) at 6'5", 13'11", 20'11, 27'11"; M
Electric borders (3) at 5'5", 12'11", 26'11"
Electric raceways (1) at 4'5"
Movie screen (2) at (1) 20' x 20' front, (1) 20' x 60' rear; M
Traveller (2) at 1 Brown 2'1", 1 Orange 6'11"
Electric pipe (1) at 4'5"
Fire curtain (1) at 0'
Catwalk (1) at 54' US   +35' high
Pinrail (1) SL & SR, +35' high

PERMANENT INSTALLATIONS ON DECK
Jumps (1) 10' x 55'
Orchestra shell storage (6) 20' x 20', 30' USL / 30' DSL
Loading bridge (2)

ORCHESTRA PIT
Adjustable to 15' below stage level by hydraulic lift
Apron overhangs US wall of pit 6'0"; Pit lift is in (1) section

BACKSTAGE

LOADING DOCK
Loading door(s):
  12'0" high x 18'0' wide
Trucks load (2) at same time
Tight backing across busy one-way street
Fork lift (small); house owns
Sound/Props cannot load in FOH
(2) Trailers can store on-site
Security at stage door

WARDROBE
Location: 2nd floor
Access: Cases winched to second floor
(2) Washers (2) Dryers
Washer and dryer hookups available

DRESSING ROOMS
(2) Star, SR, stage level, t/s included, phone jack
(2) Small, SR, stage level, t/s included, phone jack
(2) Chorus, SR, +1, t/s on same fl, phone jack
(1) Chorus, SR, +2
Additional production office available for company mgr

SOUND

CONSOLE
Crest Century GTX, located HR Terrace
52 inputs, 8 matrix outputs, 4 aux outputs

SPEAKERS
House Cluster
Proscenium
No speaker truss
No hanging points DS of proscenium

COMMUNICATIONS
Clear Com intercom with (2) channels
Infrared sound system
Dressing room page system

ROAD CONSOLE
Located Rear HR
No seats required to be removed
Cable run from stage is 275'
Tie-in into house system with XLR connectors

REHEARSAL & STORAGE SPACE
Rehearsal: Music Room, 50' x 50' in SL basement; piano available, prior arrangements/ rental required
Storage: Off SL, 1600 sq ft, empty case strorage only

ELECTRICS

ROAD SERVICE POWER

Panel	Phase	Amp	Circuit Protection	Use	Location
A-B	3	400	fuse	dimmers	DSR
C	3	100	fuse	sound	USL loading dock
D	3	100	fuse	extra	USL loading dock

USL dock is 100' from stage
Recommended location of touring dimmer racks: DSR
Hoist not required
Additional power is available for tour buses, generators, etc.

FRONT OF HOUSE (BOX BOOM VALUES ARE PER SIDE)

Position	Pipe Width	Distance to Prosc.	House Circuits	Connector Type	FOH Transfer Circuits
1st Balc Rail	60'	100'	20	grd 20 amp stage pin	20
2nd Balc Rail	30'	105'	8	grd 20 amp stage pin	8
Box Boom 1		70'	8	grd 20 amp stage pin	8
1st Catwalk	70'	2'	10	grd 20 amp stage pin	10
2nd Catwalk	70'	50'	26	grd 20 amp stage pin	26
3rd Catwalk	70'	20'	26	grd 20 amp stage pin	26

Transfer circuits: grd 20 amp stage pin
Road truss: No hanging positions DS of proscenium or in FOH

EQUIPMENT FOH (BOX BOOM VALUES ARE PER SIDE)

Position	Quantity	Wattage	Instrument	Removeable
Box Boom 1	26	1,000	10°	yes
2nd Catwalk	8	1,000	10°	yes
3rd Catwalk	26	1,000	10°	yes

FOLLOWSPOTS
House Followspots:
  (3) Lycian 1278; removeable

Followspot Booth:
  (3) spots per booth;
  118' throw to proscenium;
  (3) 1Ø 60 amp breakers
  (2) 1Ø 30 amp breakers

DIMMERS
Lighting console is Strand Light Board M;
(96) Strand dimmers

CAPITOL MUSIC HALL

YEAR BUILT: **1929**   YEAR RENOVATED: **1977**

Theatre Location: 1015 Main Street, Wheeling, WV 26003

Main Administrative Phone: 304-232-1170 x 731
Main Administrative Fax: 304-234-0067
E-mail: jamboree@hgo.net
Website: www.jamboreensa.com
Backstage Pay Phone: 304-232-9198
Traveling Production Office Fax: 304-234-0069

SEATING CAPACITY

Preferred	738
Reserved	1,134
Balcony	534
Total:	**2,442**
pit (add'l)	36

THEATRE STAFF
Theatre Manager   Paula Anderson   304-232-1170
General Manager   Larry Anderson   304-232-1170

HOUSE CREW
Production Manager   Tom Beck   304-242-6134

STAGE DIMENSIONS (FROM SMOKE POCKET)
Stage is 36'0" deep
Width from Center Line to SL is 32'0"
Width from Center Line to SR is 29'9"
Proscenium width is 43'6"
Proscenium height is 29'10"
Smoke pocket to apron edge is 3'0"
Orchestra pit exists

RIGGING
Grid Height:	64'
Type:	Single purchase counter weight
Weight:	4,000 lbs
Line sets:	30 sets at 12" o.c.
Arbors:	350 lb capacity
House Pipes:	45' long

LOADING DOCK
Loading door(s) are 7'7" high x 9'2" wide
Trucks load (1) at a time
Fork lift is not required and is not available

ELECTRICS
Total power available:
(4) 400A 3Ø SR
(1) 400A 1Ø SR

FOLLOWSPOTS
House Followspots:
Carbon Arc
Power in spot booth 100A

DIMMERS
(92) house dimmers
House has DMX control system
(2) dry run station(s) located
SR / FOH Right

SOUND
House has 400A 1Ø
undedicated power located
SR
FOH mixing position in
Rear House Right
Sound console is available

WEIDNER CENTER FOR THE PERFORMING ARTS

AT: UNIVERSITY OF WISCONSIN GREEN BAY

YEAR BUILT: **1993**   YEAR RENOVATED: **1998**

Theatre Location: 2430 Nicolet Drive, Green Bay, WI 54311-7001

Main Administrative Phone:	920-465-2726
Main Administrative Fax:	920-465-2619
E-mail:	weidner@uwgb.edu
Website:	www.uwgb.edu/~wiedner
Stage Door Phone:	920-465-2739
Backstage Pay Phone:	920-465-5927

THEATRE STAFF

Executive Director	Tom Gabbard	920-465-2906
Booking	Linda Erwin	920-465-2691
Marketing	Sherri Valitchka	920-465-2768
Group Sales	Ryan Brzozowski	920-465-2217

HOUSE CREW

Production Manager	Scott Conklin	920-465-2739
Electrics	Mark Schneider	920-465-2953
Sound	Brock Neverman	920-465-2759

UNIONS

IATSE Local #470	Steve Dedow	920-688-5030
Music Local #205	Lovell Ives	920-469-0402

SEATING CAPACITY

Orchestra	1,209
Mezzanine and Boxes	360
Balcony and Boxes	452
Total :	**2,021**
pit (incl.)	104
wheelchair (incl.)	10
standing (add'l)	42

BOX OFFICE

Computerized
Dir of Guest Services
  David Green   920-465-2217

Outside Ticket Agency
None

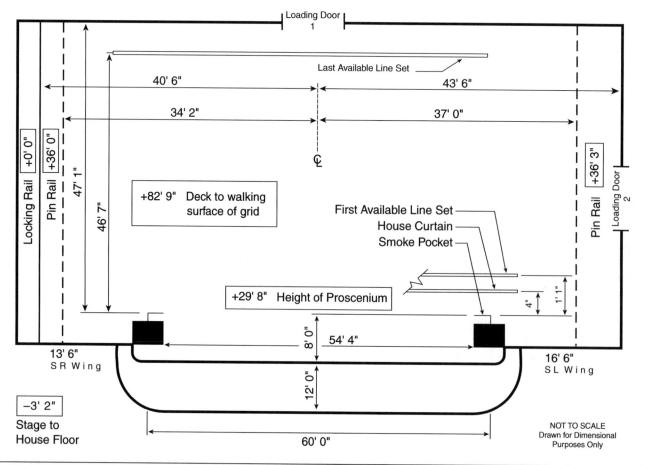

STAGE HOUSE

HOUSE CURTAIN
Operates as a guillotine from SR deck

RIGGING SYSTEM
Type:	Single purchase counter weight
Weight:	80,000 lbs available
Line sets:	86 sets at 6" o.c. with 6 lift lines per set
Arbors:	1,200 lb capacity
House Pipes:	63' long with 80' of travel from deck

Line sets are not moveable
Block & Falls are not available
Chain hoists are not available
(50) spot wheels and 500' of hemp available

PERMANENT INSTALLATIONS OVER STAGE (FROM SMOKE POCKET)
Orchestra shell (2) at 3'1", 10'7"
Fire curtain (1)

PERMANENT INSTALLATIONS ON DECK
HVAC Duct (2) 9'0" x 12'0" located USL/USR

ORCHESTRA PIT
Adjustable to 14'8" below stage level by electric motor turnscrew
Apron overhangs US wall of pit 9'4"
Pit lift is in (2) sections

BACKSTAGE

LOADING DOCK
Loading door(s) to stage:
  14'0" high x 14'0" wide
  28'0" high x 20'0" wide
(3) Dock doors from loading dock to loading area:
  (2) 9'10" high x 7'10" wide;
  (1) 9'10" high x 8'5" wide
Trucks load (3) at same time
Fork lift is not required
Sound/Props cannot load in FOH
(10) Trailers can store on-site

WARDROBE
Location: Basement
Access: Elevator/Stairs
(3) Washers (3) Dryers
Washer and dryer hookups available

DRESSING ROOMS
(2) Star, SL, stage level, t/s included, phone jack
(5) Small, basement, t/s included, phone jack
(2) Chorus, basement, t/s included
Elevator access for dressing rooms
Additional production office available for company mgr

SOUND

CONSOLE
Soundcraft Theatre Venue II, located Center House
40 inputs, 2 main outputs, 10 matrix outputs, 6 aux outputs

SPEAKERS
House Cluster
Proscenium
Under Balcony
Balc Cluster
No speaker truss

COMMUNICATIONS
Clear Com intercom with (4) channels
Infrared sound system
Dressing room page system

ROAD CONSOLE
Located Center House, 150' cable run from stage ; or Rear HR, 250' cable run
(18-24) seats required to be removed
Tie-in into house system with XLR connectors

REHEARSAL & STORAGE SPACE
Rehearsal: 1) Fort Howard, 45'x 54', piano available
2) Studio, 34' x 34', piano, mirrors, sprung floor
Storage: SL, 40' x 23'; Dock 92' x 22'

ELECTRICS

ROAD SERVICE POWER

Panel	Phase	Amp	Circuit Protection	Use	Location
A-F	3	400	fuse	extra	USL
G	3	200	fuse	extra	USL
H	3	100	fuse	extra	DSR
I	3	100	fuse	sound	DSL
J	3	100	fuse		grid

Recommended location of touring dimmer racks: SL on deck
Hoist not required

FRONT OF HOUSE (BOX BOOM VALUES ARE PER SIDE)

Position	Pipe Width	Distance to Prosc.	House Circuits	Connector Type	FOH Transfer Circuits
1st Cove	60'	60'	32	grd 20 amp stage pin	32
2nd Cove	60'	92	30	grd 20 amp stage pin	30
Mezz Rail	40'	110'	16	grd 20 amp stage pin	16
Box Boom 1		0'	10	grd 20 amp stage pin	10
Box Boom 2		37'	10	grd 20 amp stage pin	10

Transfer circuits: DMX control

EQUIPMENT FOH (BOX BOOM VALUES ARE PER SIDE)

Position	Quantity	Wattage	Instrument	Removeable
1st Cove	20	1,000	6 x 16	yes
2nd Cove	20	1,000	6 x 22	yes
Box Boom 1	6	1,000	6 x 12	yes
Box Boom 2	14	1,000	6 x 16	yes

FOLLOWSPOTS
House Followspots:
  (4) Xenon Super Trouper 2k; not removeable
  (2) Lycian Midget 2k; removeable

Followspot Booth:
  (4) spots per booth;
  150' throw to proscenium;
  (4) 1Ø 30 amp breakers

DIMMERS
Lighting console is ETC Insight 3/ Concept 500;
(372) L86 2.4k dimmers
House has programmable DMX control system
(2) dry run DMX station(s), SL Booth

OSCAR MAYER THEATRE

AT: MADISON CIVIC CENTER

YEAR BUILT: 1928 YEAR RENOVATED: 1980

Theatre Location: 211 State St., Madison, WI 53703

Main Administrative Phone: 608-266-6550
Main Administrative Fax: 608-266-4864
E-mail: civiccenter@ci.madison.wi.us
Website: www.ci.madison.wi.us/cvcenter/index
Backstage Pay Phone: 608-256-9631

THEATRE STAFF
  Director   Robert D'Angelo   608-266-6550
  Booking   Robert D'Angelo   608-266-6550
  Marketing   Anna Hahm   608-266-6550
HOUSE CREW
  Technical Director   Steve Schroeder   608-267-7978
UNIONS
  IATSE Local # 251   Gary Cleven   608-221-0003

SEATING CAPACITY
  Orchestra   1,137
  Mezzanine   400
  Circle   198
  Gallery   356
  Total: **2,091**

  pit (add'l)   126
  wheelchair (add'l)   21

BOX OFFICE
  Computerized
  Ticket Office Manager
    Anne Scott   608-266-6550

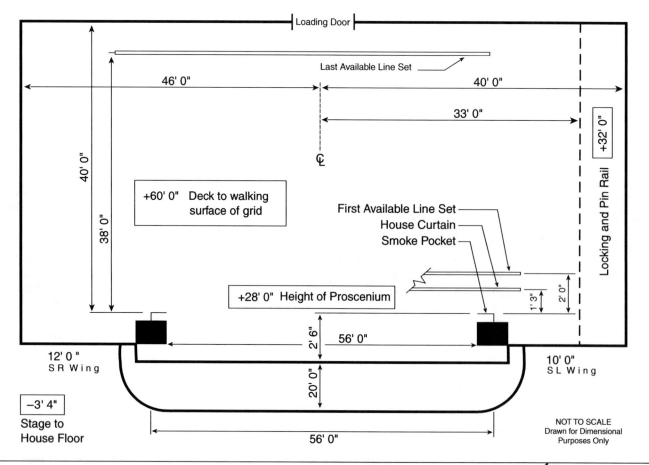

Loading Door

Last Available Line Set

46' 0"   40' 0"

33' 0"

+32' 0"

40' 0"

CL

+60' 0" Deck to walking surface of grid

38' 0"

First Available Line Set
House Curtain
Smoke Pocket

Locking and Pin Rail

1' 3"   2' 0"

+28' 0" Height of Proscenium

2' 6"   56' 0"

12' 0"
SR Wing

10' 0"
SL Wing

20' 0"

−3' 4"
Stage to
House Floor

56' 0"

NOT TO SCALE
Drawn for Dimensional
Purposes Only

STAGE HOUSE

HOUSE CURTAIN
Operates as a guillotine from SL deck

RIGGING SYSTEM
Type:	Combination purchase counter weight
Weight:	42,000 lbs available
Line sets:	60 sets at 6" o.c. with 5 lift lines per set
Arbors:	700 & 1,000 lb capacity
House Pipes:	58' long with 58' of travel from deck

Line sets are moveable

Block & Falls are available 2:1 (5); 3:2 (2)

(100) spot wheels and 5,000' of hemp available

1,500 lbs of sand available

PERMANENT INSTALLATIONS OVER STAGE (FROM SMOKE POCKET)
M=Moveable with advance call

Electric Border (1) at 3'6"; M

Orchestra shells (3) at 11'3", 21'3", 30'6"; M

Movie screen (1) at 6'9"; M

PERMANENT INSTALLATIONS ON DECK
Spiral staircase & platform 15'6" x 10'6" in USR corner

Traps (20) in stage floor 4'0" x 4'0" are on a sectional grid

ORCHESTRA PIT
Adjustable to 20' below stage level by hydraulic lift

Apron overhangs US wall of pit 2'6"

Pit lift is in (1) section

BACKSTAGE

LOADING DOCK
Loading door(s):
 9'6" high x 7'5" wide

Trucks load (1) at a time

Dock (loading door sill) is at street level one floor below stage; loading to stage thru trap room and up on orchestra lift

Forklift: House owns

Sound/Props cannot load in FOH

(6) Trailers can store on-site

Security at stage door

WARDROBE
Location: SL Green Room on stage level

Access: Direct from stage

(1) Washer (1) Dryer

DRESSING ROOMS
(2) Star, SL, stage level, t/s included, phone jack

(2) Chorus, basement, t/s included, phone jack

SOUND

CONSOLE
Midas XL 200

40 mono/4stereo inputs, 8 matrix outputs, 8 aux outputs

SPEAKERS
House Cluster

Proscenium

Under Balcony

COMMUNICATIONS
Clear Com intercom with (2) channels

AM hearing impaired system

Dressing room page system

ROAD CONSOLE
Located Center House left

(12) seats required to be removed

Cable run from stage is 40'

Tie-in into house system with XLR connectors

REHEARSAL & STORAGE SPACE
Rehearsal: 30' x 60' triangular room located SL on 3rd floor

Storage: Trap room below stage, 20' x 60'

ELECTRICS

ROAD SERVICE POWER
Panel	Phase	Amp	Circuit Protection	Use	Location
A	3	400	fuse	dimmers	DSL proscenium wall
B	3	400	fuse	extra	DSL proscenium wall
C	3	400	fuse	extra	DSL proscenium wall
D	3	60	fuse	sound	DSL proscenium wall
E	3	60	fuse	sound	DSR proscenium wall

Recommended location of touring dimmer racks: SL on deck

FRONT OF HOUSE (BOX BOOM VALUES ARE PER SIDE)
Position	Pipe Width	Distance to Prosc.	House Circuits	Connector Type	FOH Transfer Circuits
1st Balc Rail	60'	38'	20	grd 20 amp stage pin	20
1st Cove	60'	96'	28	grd 20 amp stage pin	28
Box Boom 1		55'	10	grd 20 amp stage pin	10
Box Boom 2		75'	10	grd 20 amp stage pin	10

Transfer circuits: grd 20 amp stage pin located on DSL proscenium wall

EQUIPMENT FOH (BOX BOOM VALUES ARE PER SIDE)
Position	Quantity	Wattage	Instrument	Removeable
1st Cove	16	1,000	8 x 13 Lekos	yes
1st Cove	16	2,000	12" Lekos	yes
Box Boom 1	8	1,000	6 x 16 Lekos	yes
Box Boom 1	6	1,000	6 x 12 Lekos	yes
Box Boom 2	8	1,000	8 x 13 Lekos	yes

FOLLOWSPOTS
House Followspots:
 (2) Xenon Super Troupers; removeable

(2) Followspot Booths each:
 (2) spots per booth;
 104' throw to proscenium;
 (2) 3Ø 50 amp breakers

DIMMERS
Lighting console is ETC Insight 2X;
 (82) & (24) Portable Strand Century dimmers

House has non-programmable DMX control system

WISCONSIN UNION THEATER

AT: UNIVERSITY OF WISCONSIN-MADISON

YEAR BUILT: **1939**   YEAR RENOVATED: **1997**

Theatre Location: 800 Langdon Street, Madison, WI 53706
Management Company: University of Wisconsin-Madison

Main Administrative Phone: 608-262-2202
Main Administrative Fax: 608-265-5084
E-mail: jpschaef@fucstaff.wisc.edu
Website: www.wisc.edu/union/mu/muarts/wut/wut.html
Stage Door Phone: 608-262-2202

SEATING CAPACITY

Orchestra	387
Mezzanine	225
Balcony	650
Total:	**1,262**
pit (add'l)	38
wheelchair (add'l)	4
standing (add'l)	0

THEATRE STAFF
Director   Michael Goldberg   608-262-2202
Assistant Director Rauel LaBreche   608-262-1771

HOUSE CREW
Technical Director   James P. Schaefer   608-262-1949

STAGE DIMENSIONS (FROM SMOKE POCKET)

Stage is 30' deep

Width from Center Line to SL is 38'
Width from Center Line to SR is 36'
Proscenium width is 36'
Proscenium height is 23'7"
Smoke pocket to apron edge is 3'
Orchestra pit exists

RIGGING
Grid Height: 70'
Type: Single purchase counter weight
Weight: 20,000 lbs
Line sets: 39 sets at 8" o.c.
Arbors: 600 lb capacity
House Pipes: 40' long
15 spot wheels and 1200' of hemp

LOADING DOCK
Loading door(s) are 12'0" high x 9'0" wide
Trucks load (2) at same time
 Forklift is not available

ELECTRICS
Total power available:

(1) 400A 3Ø DSR wall
(2) 400A 3Ø DSL wall
(3) 100A 3Ø DSL wall

FOLLOWSPOTS
House Followspots:
 (2) Superstar Lycian 1.2k
 Rental
Power in spot booth (3) 50A

DIMMERS
(320) house dimmers
House has DMX control
 system
(6) dry run station(s) located
 throughout

SOUND
House has 100A 3Ø located

DS wall
FOH mixing position in
 Rear Orchestra
Sound console is available

RIVERSIDE THEATRE

YEAR BUILT: **1908**   YEAR RENOVATED: **1988**

Theatre Location: 116 W Wisconsin, Milwaukee, WI 53203

Main Administrative Phone: 414-224-3000
Main Administrative Fax: 414-224-3019
Stage Door Phone: 414-224-3019
Traveling Production Office Phone: 414-224-3008
Traveling Production Office Fax: 414-224-3009

THEATRE STAFF
  General Manager   Van Johnson   414-224-3000
  Booking   Van Johnson   414-224-3000
HOUSE CREW
  Stage Manager   Kirt Holzhauer   414-224-3015
  Electrics   Rick Grilli   414-224-3015

SEATING CAPACITY

Main Floor	1,352
Mezzanine	540
First Balcony	318
Second Balcony	271
Box Seats	32
Total:	**2,513**
pit (add'l)	36
wheelchair (add'l)	20

BOX OFFICE
Computerized
Box Office Manager
  Anna Vanlow   414-224-3000

Outside Ticket Agency
Computerized
Ticketmaster
  Susie Martin   414-272-7272

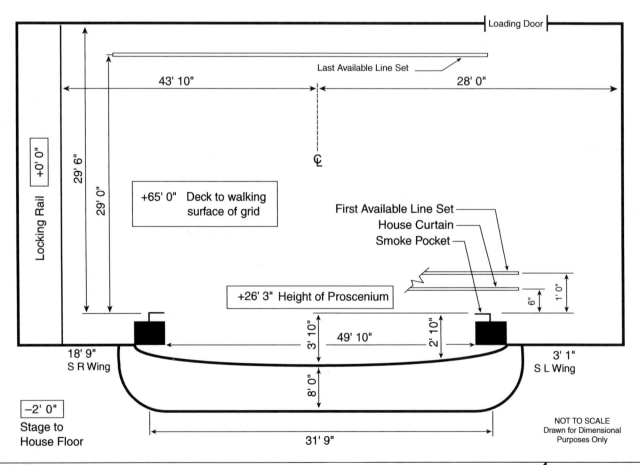

STAGE HOUSE

HOUSE CURTAIN
Operates as a guillotine or traveller from SR deck

RIGGING SYSTEM
Type:	Single purchase counter weight
Weight:	7,000 lbs available
Line sets:	48 sets with 4 lift lines per set
Arbors:	2,500 lb capacity
House Pipes:	49'9" long with 63' of travel from deck

Line sets are moveable
Block & Falls are not available
Chain hoists are not available
(0) spot wheels and 500' of hemp available
(4) points in house DS of proscenium 2-lights, 2-sound

PERMANENT INSTALLATIONS OVER STAGE (FROM SMOKE POCKET)
Electric borders (4) moveable
Electric raceways (4) at 3'0", 9'8", 16'8", 25'2"
Electric pipe (4)
Fire curtain (1)

PERMANENT INSTALLATIONS ON DECK
Hard legs (4)
Stairs (2)
Radiators (2)
Loading bridge (1)

ORCHESTRA PIT
Adjustable to 6' below stage level by manual lift
Apron overhangs US wall of pit 6'0"
Pit lift is in (18) sections

BACKSTAGE

LOADING DOCK
Loading door(s):
9'9" high x 7'8" wide
Trucks load (1) at a time
Fork lift is not required
Sound/Props can load in through FOH
Lobby can be used as a work area
(1) Trailer can store on-site; with permit
Security at dock

WARDROBE
Location: Basement
Access: Elevator
(1) Washer (1) Dryer
Washer and dryer hookups available

DRESSING ROOMS
(2) Star, SL, +2/+3, t/s included, phone jack
(4) Chorus, SL, +4/+5/+6/+7, t/s included
Elevator access for dressing rooms
Additional production office available for company mgr

SOUND

CONSOLE
No house console

SPEAKERS
House Cluster
No speaker truss

COMMUNICATIONS
Clear Com intercom with (2) channels
Infrared sound system

ROAD CONSOLE
Located Rear House
No seats required to be removed
Cable run from stage is 150'
Tie-in into house system with XLR connectors

REHEARSAL & STORAGE SPACE
Rehearsal: None
Storage: Basement

ELECTRICS

ROAD SERVICE POWER

Panel	Phase	Amp	Circuit Protection	Use	Location
A	3	200	fuse	sound	DSR in basement
B	3	400	fuse	dimmers	DSR in basement
C	3	600	fuse	dimmers	DSR in basement
D	3	60	fuse	extra	SL

Recommended location of touring dimmer racks: SR
Hoist not required

FRONT OF HOUSE (BOX BOOM VALUES ARE PER SIDE)

Position	Pipe Width	Distance to Prosc.	House Circuits	Connector Type	FOH Transfer Circuits
1st Balc Rail	50'	60'	28	grd 20 amp stage pin	28
Box Boom 1			8	grd 20 amp stage pin	8

EQUIPMENT FOH (BOX BOOM VALUES ARE PER SIDE)

Position	Quantity	Wattage	Instrument	Removeable
1st Balc Rail	8	1,000	Ellipsoidal 6 x 12	yes
2nd Balc Rail	13	1,000	Ellipsoidal 6 x 16	yes
Box Boom 1	8	1,000	Ellipsoidal 10 x 22	yes

FOLLOWSPOTS
House Followspots:
(2) Xenon Super Trouper 2k; removeable

Followspot Booth:
(3) spots per booth;
150' throw to proscenium;
(3) 1Ø 100 amp breakers

DIMMERS
Lighting console is Aud Roleacle;
(50) Light Pallette dimmers
No DMX control system
(0) dry run DMX station(s)

UIHLEIN HALL

AT: MARCUS CENTER FOR THE PERFORMING ARTS

YEAR BUILT: 1969   YEAR RENOVATED: 1997

Theatre Location: 929 North Water Street, Milwaukee, WI 53202

Main Administrative Phone: 414-273-7121
Main Administrative Fax: 414-273-5480
Website: www.milwaukeearts.org

THEATRE STAFF
Managing Director	Tom Gergerich	414-273-7121
Booking	Jerold Fox	414-273-7121
Marketing	Chris Stravinski	414-273-7121
Operations	Kathy Bialzik	414-273-7121
Group Sales	Carol Chapin	414-273-7121

HOUSE CREW
Technical Director	Eric Zaun	414-273-7121
Carpentry	Bob Jaeger	414-273-7121
Electrics	Bill Olsen	414-273-7121
Sound	Tim Kraetsch	414-273-7121

UNIONS
IATSE Local #18	Terry Little	414-272-3540
Wardrobe Local #777	Beverly Jaeger	414-782-4117
Music Local #8	Lori Babinec	414-363-2642

SEATING CAPACITY
Orchestra	1,297
Boxes	120
Side Loge	140
Center Loge	536
Balcony	208
Total:	**2,301**

pit (incl)	117
wheelchair (add'l)	4

Box Office
Computerized
Box Office Manager
   Jim Doyle   414-273-7121 x305

Outside Ticket Agency
Computerized
   Ticketmaster

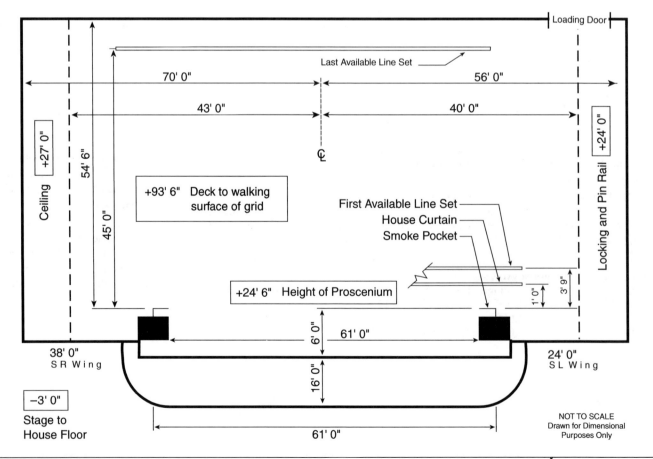

STAGE HOUSE

HOUSE CURTAIN
Operates as a guillotine or traveller from SL fly floor or deck

RIGGING SYSTEM
Type:	Double purchase counter weight
Weight:	35,000 lbs available
Line sets:	56 sets at 8" o.c. with 5 lift lines per set
Arbors:	1,800 lb capacity
House Pipes:	63' long with 90' of travel from deck

Line sets are moveable
Block & Falls are available
Chain hoists are available as rental; (3) one ton
(25) spot wheels and 5,000' of hemp available

PERMANENT INSTALLATIONS OVER STAGE (FROM SMOKE POCKET)
M=Moveable with advance call
Traveller (2) at 19'4", 33'5"; M
Electric bridge (3) at 3'2", 15'3", 26'6"; M
Electric pipe (1) 36'9"; M
Hard portal (1) at 2'2"; M

PERMANENT INSTALLATIONS ON DECK
Orchestra shed stores 1'0" off back wall

ORCHESTRA PIT
Adjustable to 8'6" below stage level by hydraulic lift
Apron overhangs US wall of pit 8'0"
Pit lift is in (2) sections

BACKSTAGE

LOADING DOCK
Loading door(s):
9'0" high x 10'4" wide
Trucks load (2) at same time
Hydraulic dock leveler; 2% grade; dock is 30' from stage loading door
Fork lift is not required
Sound/Props can load in FOH
Lobby cannot be a work area
No trailers can store on-site
Security at dock & stage door

WARDROBE
Location: Basement
Access: Elevator
(2) Washers (2) Dryers
Washer and dryer hookups available

DRESSING ROOMS
(2) Star, SL, stage level, t/s included, phone jack
(9) Small, SL, +1/ +2, t/s included
(2) Chorus, SL/ SR, -1, t/s included
Additional production office available for company mgr

SOUND

CONSOLE
Crest Century GTX located Rear House in booth
46 inputs, main outputs, 8 matrix outputs, 8 aux outputs

SPEAKERS
House Cluster
Proscenium
Under Balcony
Portable
Stage lip
No speaker truss

COMMUNICATIONS
Clear Com intercom with (2) channels
Infrared sound system
Dressing room page system

ROAD CONSOLE
Located House Left
Some seats required to be removed
Cable run from stage is 175'
Tie-in into house system with XLR connectors

REHEARSAL & STORAGE SPACE
Rehearsal: (2) 35' x 35' on 4th fl, must reserve, equipment available
Storage: None

ELECTRICS

ROAD SERVICE POWER
Panel	Phase	Amp	Circuit Protection	Use	Location
A - C	3	400	breaker	dimmers	DSL
D	3	200	breaker	extra	DSL
E	3	200	breaker	extra	DSR
F	3	200	breaker	sound	DSR
G	3	100			Dock

Sound on conditioned shielded isolation transformer
Recommended location of touring dimmer racks: DSL
Hoist not required
Additional power is available for tour buses, generators, etc.

FRONT OF HOUSE (BOX BOOM VALUES ARE PER SIDE)
Position	Pipe Width	Distance to Prosc.	House Circuits	Connector Type	FOH Transfer Circuits
Balc Rail	58'	84'	18	grd 20 amp stage pin	18
Side Rails	45'	80'/55'	32	twistlock	23
Box Boom 1	22'	35'	18	twistlock	0

Transfer circuits: (64) grd 20 amp stage pin

EQUIPMENT FOH (BOX BOOM VALUES ARE PER SIDE)
Position	Quantity	Wattage	Instrument	Removeable
Balc Rail	24	1,000	Source 4 10°/Strand 13°	no
Balc Rail	64	1,000	Strand 13° & 9°	no
Box Boom 1	20	1,000	Altman Zoom Leko	no

FOLLOWSPOTS
House Followspots:
(2) Strong Xenon Super Trouper 2k; not removeable

Followspot Booth:
(1) spots per booth;
110' throw to proscenium;
(1) 1Ø 20 amp breakers

DIMMERS
Lighting console is Strand Light Palette 90;
(446) CD80 dimmers
House has programmable DMX control system
(1) dry run DMX station

CHEYENNE CIVIC CENTER

Year built: **1981**   Year renovated: **1997**

Theatre Location: 2101 O'Niel Avenue, Cheyenne, WY 82001

Main Administrative Phone:	307-637-6364
Main Administrative Fax:	307-637-6365
Backstage Pay Phone:	307-637-6371
Traveling Production Office Phone:	307-638-4307
Traveling Production Office Fax:	307-638-4309

Theatre Staff
Director	Dru Rohla	307-637-6364
Booking	Dru Rohla	307-637-6364
Marketing	Dru Rohla	307-637-6364

House Crew
Technical Director	Dennis Madigan	307-637-6369

Unions
IATSE	Call Civic Center for info

Seating Capacity
Orchestra	578
Loge	478
Balcony	434
Total:	**1,490**
pit	0
wheelchair (add'l)	8
standing	0

Box Office
Hard Ticket
Box Office Manager
Joan Dorr	307-637-6363

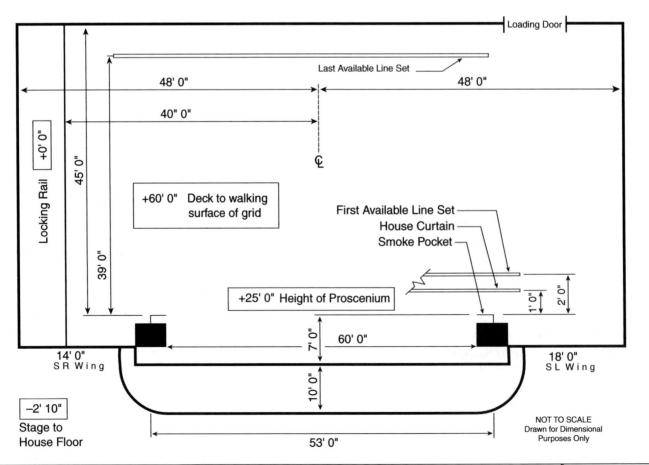

STAGE HOUSE

HOUSE CURTAIN
Operates as a guillotine or traveller from SR deck

RIGGING SYSTEM
Type:	Single purchase counter weight
Weight:	28,000 lbs available
Line sets:	36 sets at 12" o.c. with 9 lift lines per set
Arbors:	800 lb capacity
House Pipes:	80' long with 50' of travel from deck

Line sets are not moveable
Block & Falls are not available
Chain hoists are not available
(0) spot wheels and 500' of hemp available

PERMANENT INSTALLATIONS OVER STAGE (FROM SMOKE POCKET)
M=Moveable with advance call
Orchestra shells (4) at 5'6",15'8",25'6",29'3"
Electric Raceways (4) at 4'3",13'0",24'0",35'3"
Movie screen (1) at 14'11"; M
Traveller (4) at 1'0",16'11",27'3",37'10"; M
Cyclorama (1) at 38'10"; M
Fire curtain (1) at 0'4"

PERMANENT INSTALLATIONS ON DECK
Stairs (1), 6'0" in diameter; DSL corner
Orchestra shell storage (6), 5'0" x 20'0"; far USL corner

ORCHESTRA PIT
Adjustable to 5'10" below stage level by hydraulic lift
Apron overhangs US wall of pit 5'0"
Pit lift is in (3) sections
Pit can be be positioned at stage level or 5'10"; depths in between require platforming

BACKSTAGE

LOADING DOCK
Loading door(s):
  12'0" high x 12'0" wide
Trucks load (1) at a time
Fork lift is required; house owns
Sound/Props cannot load in FOH
Lobby cannot be a work area
(1) Trailer can store on-site at door; (6-8) can store in parking lot

WARDROBE
Location: Use dressing room or Green room
No Washers No Dryers
Washer and dryer hookups available

DRESSING ROOMS
(4) Small, stage level, t/s
(2) Chorus, stage level, t/s, phone jack

SOUND

CONSOLE
Megas Sountracks, located Rear Balcony
24 inputs, 2 main outputs, 8 matrix outputs

SPEAKERS
House Cluster
Under Balcony
Portable
No speaker truss

COMMUNICATIONS
Clear Com intercom with (2) channels
Radio listening device
Dressing room page system

ROAD CONSOLE
Located Rear Orchestra
No seats required to be removed
Cable run from stage is 100'
Tie-in into house system with XLR connectors
Space shared with handicap seating area

REHEARSAL & STORAGE SPACE
Rehearsal: 45' x 48', below stage; piano, barres, sprung wood floor
Storage: Loading Bay, 20' x 30', USL

ELECTRICS

ROAD SERVICE POWER

Panel	Phase	Amp	Circuit Protection Use	Location
A	3	400	fuse	USR
B	3	400	fuse	USR

Recommended location of touring dimmer racks: SR
Hoist not required

FRONT OF HOUSE (BOX BOOM VALUES ARE PER SIDE)

Position	Pipe Width	Distance to Prosc.	House Circuits	Connector Type	FOH Transfer Circuits
Cove	80'	62'	50	grd 20 amp stage pin	0
Box Beams	20'	50'	8	grd 20 amp stage pin	0

Road truss: No truss hang points DS of proscenium

EQUIPMENT FOH (BOX BOOM VALUES ARE PER SIDE)

Position	Quantity	Wattage	Instrument	Removeable
1st Cove Rail	42	1,000	ERS 8x11	yes

FOLLOWSPOTS
House Followspots:
  (2) Super Trouper Carbon; not removeable
  (2) Super Trouper Xenon 2k; not removeable

(2) Followspot Booths:
  (2) spots per booth;
  120' throw to proscenium;
  (2) 1Ø 20 amp breakers

DIMMERS
Lighting console is Kliegl Performer IV;
  (45) Kliegl P82 dimmers
House has programmable DMX control system
(1) dry run DMX station(s), SR

SOUTHERN ALBERTA JUBILEE AUDITORIUM

Theatre Location: 1415 14th Avenue NW
Calgary, AB T2N 1M4 CANADA

Main Administrative Phone: 403-297-8000
Main Administrative Fax: 403-297-3818

THEATRE STAFF
Manager   Michael W. Denscombe   403-297-8023
Booking   Gerri Goulet   403-297-8022
Operations   Dierdre Hancock   403-297-8018

HOUSE CREW
Technical Coordinator   Rick Packer   403-297-8044

UNIONS
IATSE Local #212   403-250-2199

SEATING CAPACITY

Orchestra	1,252
First Balcony	837
Second Balcony	624
Total:	**2,713**
wheelchair (add'l)	22

BOX OFFICE
Ticketmaster

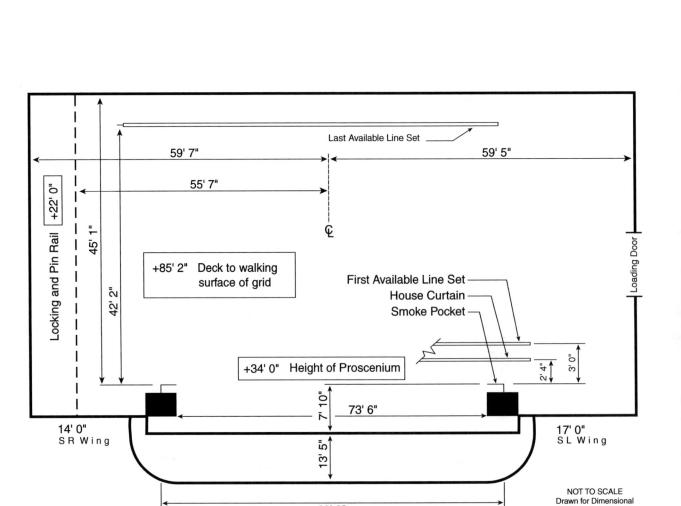

Last Available Line Set

59' 7"

55' 7"

59' 5"

C̶L

+22' 0"

Locking and Pin Rail

45' 1"

+85' 2" Deck to walking surface of grid

42' 2"

First Available Line Set
House Curtain
Smoke Pocket

Loading Door

2' 4" 3' 0"

+34' 0" Height of Proscenium

7' 10" 73' 6"

14' 0"
S R Wing

17' 0"
S L Wing

13' 5"

69' 8"

NOT TO SCALE
Drawn for Dimensional
Purposes Only

STAGE HOUSE

HOUSE CURTAIN
Operates as a guillotine or traveller from SR deck; motorized

RIGGING SYSTEM
Type:	Single purchase counter weight
Weight:	30,000 lbs available
Line sets:	54 sets at various o.c. with 9 lift lines per set
Arbors:	2,000 lb capacity
House Pipes:	84' long with 70' of travel from deck

Line sets are moveable
Block & Falls are available 3:2 (2)
Chain hoists are available; (5) one ton

PERMANENT INSTALLATIONS OVER STAGE (FROM SMOKE POCKET)
Electric bridges (2) at 4'9", 22'0" (24" wide)
Electric borders (2) at 13'0", 32'0"
Travellers (3) at 9'5", 24'3", 37'2"
Movie screen (1) at 10'10"

PERMANENT INSTALLATIONS ON DECK
Traps in stage floor are on sectional grid and must be cut
Trap (1) in stage floor 3'0" x 2'0" located DSC
Pilasters (6) against back wall
A/C duct (1) at 4'0" x 5'0" located on SL side wall
Patch panel (1) at 4'6" x 11'0" located on USL side wall
Electric bridge - located SR & SL approx. 50'0" from center

ORCHESTRA PIT
Adjustable to 7' below stage level by hydraulic lift
Apron overhangs US wall of pit 6'10"
Pit lift is in (2) sections

BACKSTAGE

LOADING DOCK
Loading door(s):
  8'10" high x 6'10" wide
Trucks load (3) at same time
Fork lift is not required
Sound/Props cannot load in FOH
Trailers cannot store on-site
Security at dock & stage door

WARDROBE
Location: SR on stage level
Access: Direct from stage
(2) Washers (2) Dryers
Washer and dryer hookups available

DRESSING ROOMS
(2) Star, SR, stage level, t/s included
(4) Small, SR, stage level, t/s included
(4) Chorus, SL/ SR, stage level/ -1, t/s included

SOUND

CONSOLE
Midas XL3-40, located 1st Balcony
40 inputs, 2 main outputs, 16 matrix outputs

SPEAKERS
House Cluster
Portable
No speaker truss

COMMUNICATIONS
Clear Com intercom with (8) channels
Infrared sound system
Dressing room page system

ROAD CONSOLE
Located Rear House
3 rows of seats required to be removed
Cable run from stage is 150'
Tie-in into house system with XLR connectors

REHEARSAL & STORAGE SPACE
Rehearsal: 56' x 38' located SR on 2nd fl, piano available; prior arrangements required
Storage: Various sizes & locations

ELECTRICS

ROAD SERVICE POWER
Panel	Phase	Amp	Circuit Protection	Use	Location
A	3	400	fuse	dimmers	USR back wall
B	3	400	fuse	extra	USL back wall
C	3	100	fuse	sound	DSL proscenium wall
D-E	3	600	fuse	dimmers	USL/USR
F-H	3	200	fuse	extra	USL/USR/SR proscenium wall
I	3	400	fuse	extra	DSL proscenium wall

Recommended location of touring dimmer racks: SR on deck
Additional power is available for tour buses, generators, etc.

FRONT OF HOUSE (BOX BOOM VALUES ARE PER SIDE)
Position	Pipe Width	Distance to Prosc.	House Circuits	Connector Type	FOH Transfer Circuits
2nd Balc Rail	120'	100'	10	20 amp old twistlock	0
2nd Cove	85'	50'	10	20 amp old twistlock	0
3rd Cove	90'	58'	12	20 amp old twistlock	0
4th Cove	95'	65'	30	20 amp old twistlock	0
5th Cove	105'	75'	8	20 amp old twistlock	0
Box Boom 1		14'	14	20 amp old twistlock	0

1st Cove position usually ineffective and is located orchestra pit
Box Boom positions are comprised of an upper & lower slot

EQUIPMENT FOH (BOX BOOM VALUES ARE PER SIDE)
Position	Quantity	Wattage	Instrument	Removeable
2nd Balc Rail	20	1,000	6 x 12 Lekos	yes
2nd Cove	10	2,000	8 x 21 Lekos	yes
3rd Cove	12	2,000	8 x 21 Lekos	yes
4th Cove	20	1,000	8 x 14 Lekos	yes
5th Cove	8		Source 4 10°	yes

FOLLOWSPOTS
House Followspots:
  (4) Xenon Super Trouper; removeable

Followspot Booth:
  (1) spots per booth;
  110' throw to proscenium;
  (4) 1Ø 30 amp breakers

DIMMERS
House console is Strand Century;
(960) Strand CD80 dimmers
House has programmable DMX control system

NORTHERN ALBERTA JUBILEE AUDITORIUM

Theatre Location:	87th Avenue & 114th Street	
	Edmonton, AB T5J 0K5 CANADA	
Mailing Address:	11455-87 Avenue	
	Edmonton, AB T6G 2T2 CANADA	

Main Administrative Phone: 403-427-2760
Main Administrative Fax: 403-422-3750
Stage Door Phone: 403-427-2760 x29

THEATRE STAFF
  Facility Manager   Marsha Regensburg   403-427-6009
  Booking   Marsha Regensburg   403-427-6009
HOUSE CREW
  Stage Manager   Tim Williamson   403-427-5933
  Electrics   Gregg Ingram   403-427-6437
  Sound   Roy Fraser   403-427-6519
UNIONS
  IATSE Local #210   Malcolm Kerr   403-423-1863

SEATING CAPACITY
  Orchestra   1,252
  First Balcony   790
  Second Balcony   636
  Total: **2,678**

  wheelchair (add'l)   22

BOX OFFICE
  Outside Ticket Agency
  Computerized
  TicketMaster   403-451-8000

Box office is promoter operated

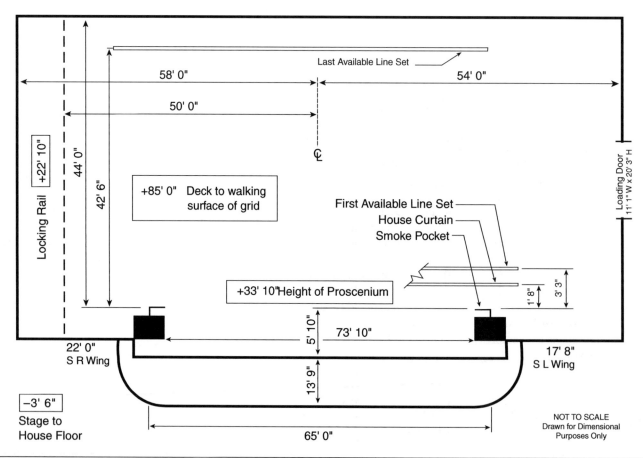

STAGE HOUSE

HOUSE CURTAIN
Operates as a guillotine or traveller from SR deck

RIGGING SYSTEM
Type: Single purchase counter weight
Weight: 27,500 lbs available
Line sets: 62 sets at 8" o.c. with 9 lift lines per set
Arbors: 1,500 lb capacity
House Pipes: 84' long with 67' of travel from deck
Line sets are moveable
(40) spot wheels and 1,500' of hemp available

PERMANENT INSTALLATIONS OVER STAGE (FROM SMOKE POCKET)
Main curtain truss (1) at 1'8"

PERMANENT INSTALLATIONS ON DECK
Traps (40) in stage floor 6'6" x 1'6" on a sectional grid
Trap (1) DSC for Les Mis/Phantom

ORCHESTRA PIT
Adjustable to 7' below stage level by hydraulic lift
Apron overhangs US wall of pit 7'0"
Pit has piano lift in SL corner

BACKSTAGE

LOADING DOCK
Loading door(s):
10'1" high x 9'8" wide
Trucks load (3) at same time, side by side
Docks (3) are at truck level; equipped with electric leveller; loading to stage thru separate scene shop

WARDROBE
Location: USR on stage level
Access: Direct from stage
(2) Washers (2) Dryers
Washer and dryer hookups available

DRESSING ROOMS
(2) Star, SR, stage level, t/s included, phone jack
(4) Small, SR, stage level, t/s included, phone jack
(4) Chorus, USL, (2) stage level, SR; (2) in basement, t/s included, phone jack

SOUND

CONSOLE
Rupert Neve Custom located Rear 1st Balcony
24 inputs, 8 main outputs, 8 matrix outputs, 2 aux outputs

SPEAKERS
House Cluster
Proscenium
Holes in ceiling over house provide truss hanging position; pipe and rigging unavailable
No speaker truss

COMMUNICATIONS
Clear Com intercom with (4) channels
Infrared sound system
Dressing room page system

ROAD CONSOLE
Located House Rear
No seats required to be removed
Cable run from stage is 200'
Tie in into house system with XLR connectors

REHEARSAL & STORAGE SPACE
Rehearsal: 50' x 60' SR on 2nd floor, piano available; prior arrangement required
Storage: 24' x 60' SR Shop

ELECTRICS

ROAD SERVICE POWER

Panel	Phase	Amp	Circuit Protection	Use	Location
A	3	400	fuse	dimmers	USR back wall
B	3	400	fuse	extra	USL back wall
C	3	100	breaker	sound	DSL proscenium wall
D	3	600	fuse		USR back wall
E-G	3	200	breaker		DSR / USR / USL
H	3	400	fuse		DSL

Recommended location of touring dimmer racks: SR on deck

FRONT OF HOUSE (BOX BOOM VALUES ARE PER SIDE)

Position	Pipe Width	Distance to Prosc.	House Circuits	Connector Type	FOH Transfer Circuits
1st Balc Rail	30'	95'	24	grd 20 amp stage pin	0
2nd Balc Rail	90'	120'	20	grd 20 amp stage pin	0
1st Cove	90'	42'	24	grd 20 amp stage pin	0
2nd Cove	78'	52'	20	grd 20 amp stage pin	0
3rd Cove	85'	61'	20	grd 20 amp stage pin	0
4th Cove	90'	80'	20	grd 20 amp stage pin	0
5th Cove	90'	80'	20	grd 20 amp stage pin	0
Box Boom 1		40'	24	grd 20 amp stage pin	0

EQUIPMENT FOH (BOX BOOM VALUES ARE PER SIDE)

Position	Quantity	Wattage	Instrument	Removeable
2nd Balc Rail	20	1,000	Parellishere	yes
1st-5th Cove	76	2k/1k	Various Lekos	yes
Box Boom 1	18	1k/575	6 x 16 Lekos	yes

FOLLOWSPOTS
House Followspots:
(3) Strong Carbon Arc Super Troupers; not removeable
(4) Strong Super Trouper II; removeable

Followspot Booths
(1) Booth with:
(4) spots in booth;
72' throw to proscenium;
(6) 3Ø 20 amp breakers

(3) Booths with:
(1) spot per booth;
143' throw to proscenium;
(1) 1Ø 30 amp breakers

DIMMERS
House console is Strand 550;
(800) Strand CD 80 dimmers
House has programmable DMX control system
(4) dry run DMX station(s)

FORD CENTER FOR THE PERFORMING ARTS

Year built: 1995

Theatre Location: 777 Homer Street, Vancouver, BC V6B 2W1 CANADA
Management Company: Livent, Inc.
165 Avenue Road, Toronto, ON M5R 3S4 CANADA

Main Administrative Phone: 604-602-0616
Main Administrative Fax: 604-602-0617
Stage Door Phone: 604-602-0616
Backstage Pay Phone: 604-683-9318

THEATRE STAFF
General Manager   Bill MacDonald-Kerr 604-334-7650
SR VP Touring   Bill Conner   416-324-5727
Dir Publicity/Promos   Janet Mitchell   604-847-2803
Operations Mgr   Bill Nelson   604-602-0616
Sales Manager   Wendy Worthwood   604-844-2802

HOUSE CREW
Sr. Technical Dir   Peter W. Lamb   416-324-5476
Carpentry   Don Underhill
Electrics   Nik VonSchulmann
Sound   Allen Sherst
Props   Brian Heath

UNIONS
IATSE Local #118   604-685-9553
Wardrobe Local #118   604-685-9553

SEATING CAPACITY
Orchestra   1,089
Dress Orchestra   363
Balcony   382
Total: **1,834**

wheelchair   6

BOX OFFICE
Computerized
Box Office Manager
  Heather Thomas   604-331-7617

Outside Ticket Agency
Computerized
Ticketmaster
  Peter Jackson   604-682-8455

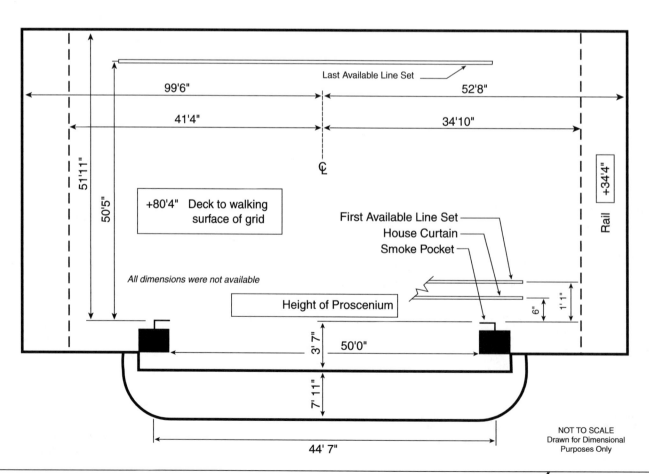

+80'4" Deck to walking surface of grid

All dimensions were not available

Height of Proscenium

Last Available Line Set

First Available Line Set
House Curtain
Smoke Pocket

NOT TO SCALE
Drawn for Dimensional
Purposes Only

STAGE HOUSE

HOUSE CURTAIN
No house curtain

RIGGING SYSTEM
Type:	Combination purchase counter weight
Weight:	96,000 lbs available
Line sets:	87 sets at 7" o.c. with 7 lift lines per set
Arbors:	1,650 lb capacity
House Pipes:	65' long with 74' of travel from deck

Line sets are moveable
Block & Falls are not available
Chain hoists are not available
(100) spot wheels and 12,000' of hemp available
4 motorized FOH line sets

PERMANENT INSTALLATIONS OVER STAGE (FROM SMOKE POCKET)
Fire Curtain (1) at 3"

PERMANENT INSTALLATIONS ON DECK
Traps (70) in stage floor 4' x 8'
Electric jump (1)
Loading bridge (2)
Heating duct (2) at 3' 6" located USL corner/ stage elev. grid

ORCHESTRA PIT
Nonadjustable to 9' below stage level
Apron overhangs US wall of pit 6' 9"
Removable pit rail

BACKSTAGE

LOADING DOCK
Loading door(s):
  12'0" high x 23'0" wide
Trucks load (1) at a time
One truck at a time - 90° turn to stage, portable loading dock to be placed in lane for loading
Sound/Props can load in FOH
Lobby can be a work area
Security at stage door

WARDROBE
Location: -1 below stage, SR
(4) Washers (4) Dryers
Washer and dryer hookups available

DRESSING ROOMS
Star, SL, -1, t/s, phone jack
Chorus, SL, -1, t/s, phone jacks
(2) Star, SL, -1, t/s, phone jack
(5) Small, SL, -1, t/s, phone jack
Chorus, SR, -1, t/s, phone jack
Additional production office available for company mgr

SOUND

CONSOLE
No house console available

SPEAKERS
Under Balcony
No speaker truss

COMMUNICATIONS
No intercom system
Dressing room page system

ROAD CONSOLE
Located Rear Orchestra
Cable run from stage is 150'
Tie-in into house system

REHEARSAL & STORAGE SPACE
Rehearsal: None
Storage: Trap room, 40' x 24'

ELECTRICS

ROAD SERVICE POWER

Panel	Phase	Amp	Circuit Protection	Use	Location
A	3	200	breaker	sound	USR Deck
B	3	100	breaker	utility	USR Grid
C	3	100	breaker	utility	FOH Grid
D	3	400	breaker	sound	SR Trap room
E	3	200	breaker	utility	SR Trap room
F-J	3	400	breaker	LX	SL jump

Recommended location of touring dimmer racks: SL jump
Hoist is provided

FRONT OF HOUSE (BOX BOOM VALUES ARE PER SIDE)

Position	Pipe Width	Distance to Prosc.	House Circuits	Connector Type	FOH Transfer Circuits
1st Balc Rail		63'		grd 20 amp stage pin	38
2nd Balc Rail		65'		grd 20 amp stage pin	24
1st Cove		26'		grd 20 amp stage pin	42
2nd Cove		44'		grd 20 amp stage pin	44
FOH Grid				grd 20 amp stage pin	110
Box Boom 1				grd 20 amp stage pin	34

Transfer circuits: grd 20 amp stage pin

EQUIPMENT FOH (BOX BOOM VALUES ARE PER SIDE)
None

FOLLOWSPOTS
House Followspots:
  (2) Xenon Super Troupers; removeable

Followspot Booth:
  (3) spots per booth;
  77' throw to proscenium;
  (3) 1Ø 30 amp breakers

DIMMERS
No lighting console
No dimmers

QUEEN ELIZABETH THEATRE

AKA: VANCOUVER CIVIC THEATRE   YEAR BUILT: 1959   YEAR RENOVATED: 1997

Theatre Location: 649 Cambie Street, Vancouver, BC V6B 2P1 CANADA
Management Company: Vancouver Civic Theatres - City of Vancouver

Main Administrative Phone:	604-665-3050
Main Administrative Fax:	604-665-3001
E-mail:	rae_ackerman@city.vancouver.bc.ca
Website:	www.city.vancouver.bc.ca/theatres
Stage Door Phone:	604-665-3050
Traveling Production Office Phone:	604-665-3044

SEATING CAPACITY

Orchestra	1,171
Mezzanine	556
Dress Circle	312
Balcony	666
Total:	**2,705**
pit (add'l)	210
wheelchair (add'l)	14

THEATRE STAFF

Director	Rae Ackerman	604-665-3020
Booking	Sandra Walton	604-665-3028
Operations	Andis Celms	604-665-3021
Group Sales	Diane MacDonald	604-665-3025

HOUSE CREW

Technical Director	Miles Muir	604-665-3043
Carpentry	Mike Glower	604-665-3024
Electrics	John Ellis	604-665-3032
Sound	Ken Gould	604-665-3458

UNIONS

IATSE Local #118	Bob Bancroft	604-685-9553
Wardrobe Local #118	Bob Bancroft	604-685-9553

BOX OFFICE

Outside Ticket Agency
Computerized
Ticketmaster   604-682-8455

Box office is promoter operated

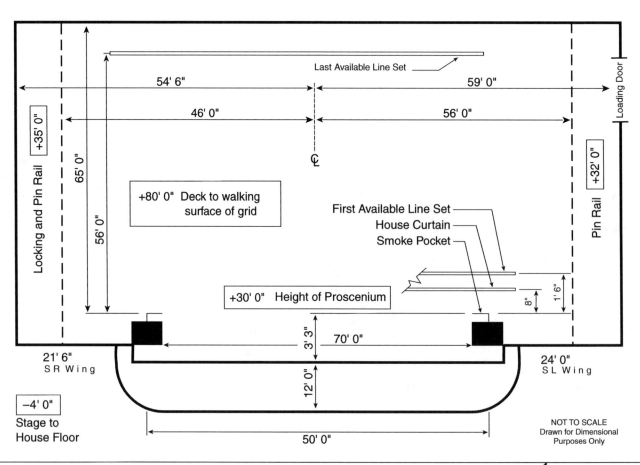

STAGE HOUSE

HOUSE CURTAIN
Operates as a guillotine or traveller from SR fly floor or deck

RIGGING SYSTEM
Type:	Single purchase counter weight
Weight:	32,000 lbs available
Line sets:	76 sets at 8" o.c. with 7 lift lines per set
Arbors:	1,300 lb capacity
House Pipes:	80' long with 6' of travel from deck

Line sets are moveable
Block & Falls are available
Chain hoists are not available
(30) spot wheels available

PERMANENT INSTALLATIONS OVER STAGE (FROM SMOKE POCKET)
M=Moveable with advance call
Electric Borders (2); M
Movie screen (1); M
Traveller (3); M
Cyclorama (1); M
Fire curtain (1) at 0'6" from proscenium wall

PERMANENT INSTALLATIONS ON DECK
Loading bridge (1) 66'0" x 6'0", DS proscenium wall to US wall SR

ORCHESTRA PIT
Adjustable below stage level by hydraulic lift
Apron overhangs US wall of pit 6'6"
Pit lift is in (5) sections

BACKSTAGE

LOADING DOCK
Loading door(s):
  16'0" high x 8'0" wide
Trucks load (2) at same time
Fork lift is not required
Sound/Props can load in FOH
Lobby cannot be a work area
Security at dock & stage door

WARDROBE
Location: Below stage
Access: By stairs and freight elevator
(1) Washer (1) Dryer
Washer and dryer hookups available

DRESSING ROOMS
(8) Star or Small, SR, stage level, t/s included, phone jacks
(2) Chorus, SR, -1, t/s included
Additional production office available for company mgr

SOUND

CONSOLE
Soundcraft 800B, located FOH
24 inputs, 2 main outputs, 8 matrix outputs, 8 aux outputs

SPEAKERS
House Cluster
Proscenium
Under Balcony
  Above balcony
No speaker truss

COMMUNICATIONS
Clear Com intercom with (4) channels
Infrared sound / hearing assist system
Dressing room page system

ROAD CONSOLE
Located Orchestra Center rows 24 & 25
(10 - 30) seats required to be removed
Cable run from stage is 114'
Tie-in into house system with XLR connectors

REHEARSAL & STORAGE SPACE
Rehearsal: (2) below stage
  33' x 56', piano & mirrors
  20'0" x 42'6" Green Room
Storage: Freight area 30' x 20', located below stage

ELECTRICS

ROAD SERVICE POWER

Panel	Phase	Amp	Circuit Protection	Use	Location
A	3	600	fuse	dimmers	USR (breakdown DSR)
B	3	600	fuse	dimmers	USL
C	3	200	fuse	sound	DSL
D	3	200	fuse	extra	loading dock

Recommended location of touring dimmer racks: DSR
Hoist not required
Additional power is available for tour buses, generators, etc.

FRONT OF HOUSE (BOX BOOM VALUES ARE PER SIDE)

Position	Pipe Width	Distance to Prosc.	House Circuits	Connector Type	FOH Transfer Circuits
1st Balc Rail	52'	80'	16	grd 20 amp stage pin	16
1st Cove	38'	24'	20	grd 20 amp stage pin	20
2nd Cove	29'	50'	12	grd 20 amp stage pin	12
Box Boom 1		30'	4	grd 20 amp stage pin	0
Balc Wings	6'	90'	6	grd 20 amp stage pin	6

Transfer circuits: Handled through use of DMX 5R interface
Road truss: (4) FOH points available; call for info

EQUIPMENT FOH (BOX BOOM VALUES ARE PER SIDE)

Position	Quantity	Wattage	Instrument	Removeable
1st Balc Rail	20	750	Altman 6 x 12	yes
1st Cove	6	1000	Lekos 8 x 16	yes
2nd Cove	12	1000	Lekos 8 x 22	yes

FOLLOWSPOTS
House Followspots:
  (4) Lycian 1290 XLT-2k Xenon; removeable

Followspot Booth:
  (4) spots per booth;
  140' throw to proscenium;
  (4) 1Ø 30 amp breakers

DIMMERS
House console is AVAB VLC; (536) 2k;
  5k dimmers
House has programmable DMX control system
(2) dry run DMX station(s)

CENTENNIAL CONCERT HALL

YEAR BUILT: 1970

Theatre Location: 555 Main Street, Winnipeg, MB R3B 1C3 CANADA
Management Company: Manitoba Centennial Centre Corporation

Main Administrative Phone: 204-956-1360
Main Administrative Fax: 204-944-1390
Stage Door Phone: 204-957-0826
Backstage Pay Phone: 204-942-9008
Traveling Production Office Phone: 204-942-1475

THEATRE STAFF
Executive Director   John C. Walton   204-956-1360
Booking   John C. Walton   204-956-1360

HOUSE CREW
Stage Manager   Vic Fontaine   204-956-1367
Electrics   Ray Lemieux   204-956-1367
Sound   Len Dalman   204-956-1367

UNIONS
IATSE Local #63   Wayne Docking   204-338-2423

SEATING CAPACITY

Orchestra	1,523
First Balcony	335
Second Balcony	341
Loges	106
Total:	**2,305**
wheelchair (add'l)	16

BOX OFFICE
Outside Ticket Agency
Select-A-Seat   204-780-7328
Ticketmaster   204-958-6800

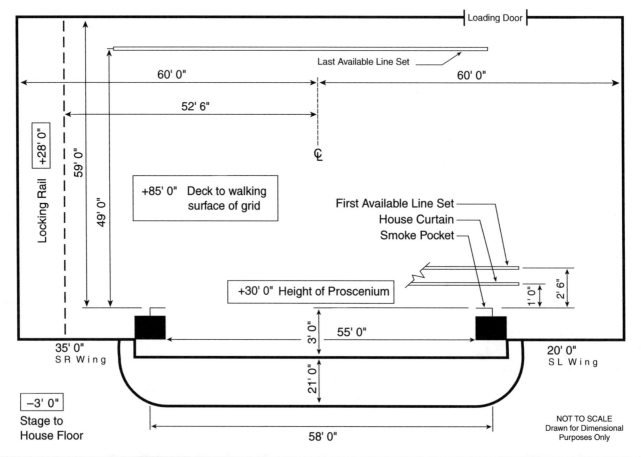

Loading Door

Last Available Line Set

60' 0"   60' 0"

52' 6"

℄

Locking Rail   +28' 0"

59' 0"

49' 0"

+85' 0" Deck to walking
             surface of grid

First Available Line Set
House Curtain
Smoke Pocket

+30' 0" Height of Proscenium

2' 6"
1' 0"

3' 0"   55' 0"

35' 0"
S R Wing

20' 0"
S L Wing

21' 0"

−3' 0"
Stage to
House Floor

58' 0"

NOT TO SCALE
Drawn for Dimensional
Purposes Only

STAGE HOUSE

HOUSE CURTAIN
Operates as a guillotine from SR fly floor
Operates as a traveller from SR deck

RIGGING SYSTEM
Type: Single purchase counter weight
Weight: 30,000 lbs available
Line sets: 55 sets at 9" o.c. with 5 lift lines per set
Arbors: 1,500 lb capacity
House Pipes: 72' long with 80' of travel from deck
Line sets are moveable
(18) spot wheels and 200 of hemp available

PERMANENT INSTALLATIONS OVER STAGE (FROM SMOKE POCKET)
M=Moveable with advance call
Electric bridges (3) at 3'8", 17'0", 37'8"
Movie screen (1), at 9'2"; M
Travellers (2), at 7'10", 28'8"; M

PERMANENT INSTALLATIONS ON DECK
None

ORCHESTRA PIT
Adjustable to to 21' below stage level by hydraulic lift
Apron overhangs US wall of pit 0'0"
Pit lift is in (2) sections

BACKSTAGE

LOADING DOCK
Loading door(s):
   12'0" high x 10'0" wide
Trucks load (2) side by side at same time
Dock is at truck level: loading to stage thru separate receiving area.
Fork lift is not required
Sound/Props can load in FOH
Lobby can be a work area
(1) Trailer can store on-site
Security at dock & stage door

WARDROBE
Location: SR on 3rd floor
Access: Freight elevator
(1) Washer (1) Dryer
No washer or dryer hookups

DRESSING ROOMS
(2) Star, SR, stage level, t/s
(6) Small, SR, 3rd fl, t/s
(3) Small, SR, stage level, t/s
(2) Chorus, 3rd fl, t/s
Elevator access for dressing rooms
Additional production office available for company mgr

SOUND

CONSOLE
Ramsa WR 5852
52 inputs, 8 main outputs

SPEAKERS
House Cluster

COMMUNICATIONS
Clear Com intercom with (1) channel
FM Hearing augmentation device
Dressing room page system

ROAD CONSOLE
Located Rear House
No seats required to be removed
Cable run from stage is 150'
Tie-in into house system with XLR connectors

REHEARSAL & STORAGE SPACE
Rehearsal: 34' x 56' , located behind stage on stage level piano available; prior arrangement required
Storage: 15' x 30', located SL on stage level

ELECTRICS

ROAD SERVICE POWER

Panel	Phase	Amp	Circuit Protection	Use	Location
A	3	400	breaker	dimmers	DSR in alcove
B	3	400	breaker	sound	DSR in alcove
C	3	400	breaker	extra	DSR in alcove

Recommended location of touring dimmer racks: SR on deck
Hoist not required
Additional power is available for tour buses, generators, etc.

FRONT OF HOUSE (BOX BOOM VALUES ARE PER SIDE)

Position	Pipe Width	Distance to Prosc.	House Circuits	Connector Type	FOH Transfer Circuits
1st Cove	60'	55'	24	20 amp new twistlock	24
2nd Cove	60'	80'	12	20 amp new twistlock	12
Box Boom 1		15"	8	20 amp new twistlock	8

Transfer circuits: 20 amp old twistlock located DSR in alcove

EQUIPMENT FOH (BOX BOOM VALUES ARE PER SIDE)
None

FOLLOWSPOTS
House Followspots:
(3) Xenon Super Trouper; removeable

Followspot Booth:
(3) spots per booth;
125' throw to proscenium;
(3) 3Ø 25 amp breakers

DIMMERS
Lighting console is ETC Obsession;
(456) Strand Century CD80 dimmers
House has programmable DMX control system
(3) dry run DMX station(s)

THE CENTRE IN THE SQUARE

AKA: RAFFI ARMENIAN THEATRE   **YEAR BUILT: 1979**

Theatre Location: 101 Queen Street North
                         Kitchener, ON N2H 6P7 CANADA
Mailing Address: PO Box 2187, Kitchener, ON N2H 6M1 CANADA

Main Administrative Phone: 519-578-5660
Main Administrative Fax: 519-578-9230
Website: www.centre-square.com

SEATING CAPACITY

Orchestra	1,089
Downstage Lift	136
Mezzanine	325
Balcony	219
Loges	70
Boxes	64
Total:	**1,903**
pit (add'l)	112
wheelchair (add'l)	32

THEATRE STAFF

General Manager	Jamie Grant	519-578-5660 x238
Marketing	Marlene Batchelor	519-578-5660 x212
Operations	Betty Dwyer	519-578-5660 x247

HOUSE CREW

Crew Chief	Bob Luffman	519-578-5660 x 210
Carpentry	Steve Cassaubon	519-578-5660 x 294
Electrics	Karl Wylie	519-578-5660 x223
Sound	Bob Luffman	519-578-5660 x210
Props	Terry Hynes	519-578-5660 x249

UNIONS

IATSE Local #357	Larry Miller	519-746-7474

BOX OFFICE
Computerized
Box Office Manager
  Bill Nuhn   519-578-5660 x213

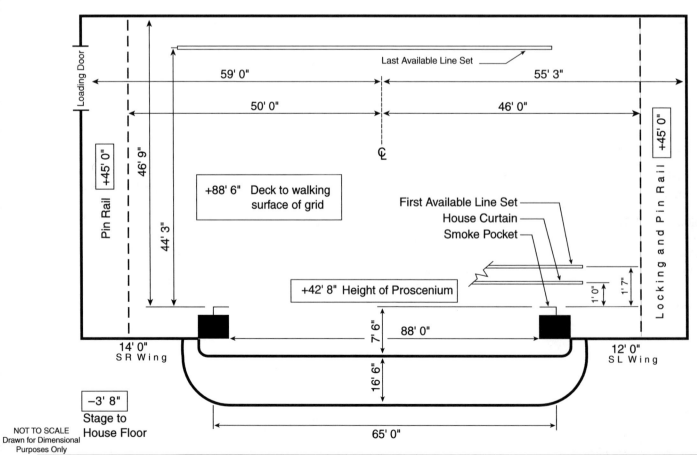

+88' 6" Deck to walking surface of grid

+42' 8" Height of Proscenium

Last Available Line Set

First Available Line Set
House Curtain
Smoke Pocket

Pin Rail   +45' 0"
Locking and Pin Rail   +45' 0"
+45' 0"

Loading Door

59' 0"   55' 3"
50' 0"   46' 0"
46' 9"
44' 3"
7' 6"
88' 0"
16' 6"
65' 0"
1' 0"
1' 7"

14' 0"
SR Wing

12' 0"
SL Wing

−3' 8"
Stage to House Floor

NOT TO SCALE
Drawn for Dimensional Purposes Only

STAGE HOUSE

HOUSE CURTAIN
Operates as a traveller from SR deck; motorized
Variable speed slow to start opening

RIGGING SYSTEM
Type:	Combination purchase counter weight
Weight:	31,000 lbs available
Line sets:	52 sets at 9" o.c. with 7 lift lines per set
Arbors:	1,500 lb capacity
House Pipes:	60' long with 88' of travel from deck

Line sets are moveable
Block & Falls are available, 3:2 (2)
Chain hoists are available; (1) one ton
(30) spot wheels and 5,000' of hemp available

PERMANENT INSTALLATIONS OVER STAGE (FROM SMOKE POCKET)
M=Moveable with advance call
Traveller (2); M
Electric pipe (1) at 3'1"
Dead spaces (4)
Cyclorama (1); M
Fire Curtain

PERMANENT INSTALLATIONS ON DECK
None

ORCHESTRA PIT
Adjustable to 8' below stage level by electric motor turnscrew
Apron overhangs US wall of pit 6'0"
Pit lift is in (2) sections

BACKSTAGE

LOADING DOCK
Loading door(s):
  12'6" high x 10'0" wide
Trucks load (3) at same time
Dock is at truck level and equipped with manual levelers
Fork lift is not required
Sound/Props can load in FOH
Lobby can be a work area
(1) Trailer can store on-site
Security at stage door

WARDROBE
Location: Basement
Access: Freight elevator
(1) Washer (1) Dryer
Washer and dryer hookups available

DRESSING ROOMS
(4) Star, SR, stage level, t/s
(3) Small, SR/SL, stage level/ basement, t/s
(3) Chorus, basement, t/s
Additional production office available for company mgr

SOUND

CONSOLE
CADAC, located Center
40 inputs, 12 main outputs, 12 matrix outputs, 8 aux outputs

SPEAKERS
House Cluster
Proscenium
Portable
No speaker truss

COMMUNICATIONS
Clear Com intercom with (8) channels
Infrared sound system
Dressing room page system

ROAD CONSOLE
Located Rear House next to house console
(16) seats required to be removed
Cable run from stage is 60' and 110'
Tie-in into house system with XLR connectors

REHEARSAL & STORAGE SPACE
Rehearsal: 60' x 60', SR, stage level, piano available, prior arrangement required
Storage: 31' x 45', USC behind stage

ELECTRICS

ROAD SERVICE POWER

Panel	Phase	Amp	Circuit Protection Use	Location
A	3	400	sound	DSL
B	3	400	dimmers	SR
C	3	400	extra	SR
D	3	60	extra	DSL
E	3	60	extra	SR
F	3	200	extra	USC
G	3	60	extra	Loading dock
H	3	60	extra	US

Recommended location of touring dimmer racks: SR
Hoist not required

FRONT OF HOUSE (BOX BOOM VALUES ARE PER SIDE)

Position	Pipe Width	Distance to Prosc.	House Circuits	Connector Type	FOH Transfer Circuits
2nd Cove	75'	60'	36	20 amp twistlock	36
Canopy	65'	100'	36	20 amp twistlock	36
Balc Rail	12'	90'	16	20 amp twistlock	16
Side Towers		varies	48	20 amp twistlock	48

Transfer circuits: grd 20 amp stage pin

EQUIPMENT FOH (BOX BOOM VALUES ARE PER SIDE)

Position	Quantity	Wattage	Instrument	Removeable
Balc Rail	36	1,000	8" Zoom	yes
1st Cove	9	575	Source 4 10°	yes
2nd Cove	36	575	Source 4 19°	yes

FOLLOWSPOTS
House Followspots:
  (2) Strong Xenon Super Trouper 1k; not removeable

(2) Followspot Booths:
  (1) spot per booth;
  110' throw to proscenium;
  (4) 1Ø 30 amp breakers

  (1) spot per booth;
  110' throw to proscenium;
  (3) 1Ø 20 amp breakers

DIMMERS
Lighting console is Colortran Medallion;
(420) dimmers
House has DMX control system
(3) dry run DMX station(s): SR, sound cockpit, lighting and recording booth

NATIONAL ARTS CENTRE: OPERA STAGE

Year built: 1969

Theatre Location: 53 Elgin Street, Ottawa, ON K1P 5W1 CANADA
Mailing Address: PO Box 1534 Station B, Ottawa, ON K1P 5W1 CANADA

Main Administrative Phone: 613-947-7000
Main Administrative Fax: 613-996-9578
E-mail: sdeneau@nac-cna.ca
Website: www.nac-cna.ca
Stage Door Phone: 613-947-7000 x666
Traveling Production Office Phone: 613-947-7000 x444

THEATRE STAFF

Director and CEO	John Cripton	613-947-7000 x200
Booking	Simone Deneau	613-947-7000 x220
Marketing	Heather Moore	613-947-7000 x307
Group Sales	Denise Goulet	613-947-7000 x278

HOUSE CREW

Technical Director	Charles Cotton	613-947-7000 x242
Carpentry	Kasey Krzyzanowski	613-947-7000 x448
Electrics	Ron Colpaart	613-947-7000 x449
Sound	Robert Allan	613-947-7000 x447
Props	Tim McGahey	613-947-7000 x446

UNIONS

IATSE Local #471	Mark Hollingworth	613-947-7000 x450
Wardrobe Local #890	Linda DuFresne	613-725-2765
Music Local #180	Peter Webster	613-947-7000 x435

SEATING CAPACITY

Orchestra	1,149
Boxes	188
Balcony	265
Mezzanine	265
Amphitheatre	265
Total:	**2,132**
pit (add'l)	193
wheelchair (add'l)	6
standing (add'l)	10

BOX OFFICE

Box Office Supervisor
Denise Goulet 613-947-7000 x278

Outside Ticket Agency
Ticketmaster

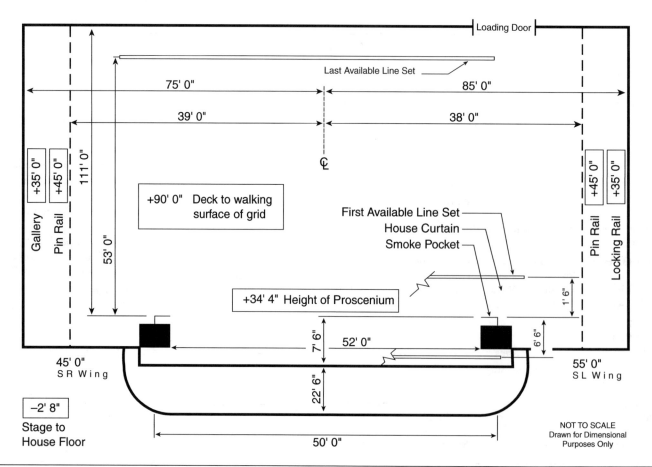

STAGE HOUSE

HOUSE CURTAIN
Operates as a guillotine from SR deck; also Festoons

RIGGING SYSTEM
Type:	Double purchase counter weight
Weight:	90,000 lbs available
Line sets:	85 sets at 6" o.c. with 5 lift lines per set
Arbors:	2,000 lb capacity
House Pipes:	55' long with 87' of travel from deck

Line sets are not moveable
Block & Falls are available
Chain hoists are not available
(100) spot wheels and 20,000' of hemp available
Pipes can be extended 5' SR/SL

PERMANENT INSTALLATIONS OVER STAGE (FROM SMOKE POCKET)
M=Moveable with advance call
Orchestra shells (4) at 4'6", 6'11", 18'0", 29'0"; M
Electric borders (2) at 12'6", 45'0"; M
Electric bridge (1) at 1'3", 3'9"
Scoop bar (1) at 40'0"
Fire curtain (1) -3"

PERMANENT INSTALLATIONS ON DECK
Traps in stage floor (77) 4'0" x 8'0" at 1'0" DS of pocket
Orchestra shell storage (14) 5'0" deep x 7'0" wide x 29'0" height USL
Adjustable proscenium (1)
Adjustable portal (1)

ORCHESTRA PIT
Adjustable to 18' below stage level by hydraulic lift
Apron overhangs US wall of pit 4'3"
Pit lift is in (4) sections

BACKSTAGE

LOADING DOCK
Loading door(s):
  9'0" high x 12'0" wide
Trucks load (2) at same time
Dock is at truck level accessed by long tunnel
Fork lift is not required
Sound/Props cannot load in FOH
Lobby cannot be a work area
Trailers cannot store on-site
Security at dock & stage door

WARDROBE
Location: Dressing room corridor
Access: Loading dock or stage door
(2) Washers (5) Dryers
No washer or dryer hookups

DRESSING ROOMS
(1) Star, SR, stage level, t/s included, phone jack
(6) Small, SR, stage level, t/s included, phone jack
(3) Chorus, SR, stage level, t/s, included
Additional production office available for company mgr

SOUND

CONSOLE
Midas XL-464, located Rear House
48 inputs, 8 matrix outputs, 16 mono aux outputs

SPEAKERS
House Cluster
Proscenium
Portable
No speaker truss

COMMUNICATIONS
Clear Com intercom with (4) channels
Infrared sound system
Dressing room page system

ROAD CONSOLE
Located Rear Orchestra
(8) seats required to be removed
Cable run from stage is 150'
Tie-in into house system with XLR connectors
Only house operator may operate house console

REHEARSAL & STORAGE SPACE
Rehearsal: (2) areas
  50' x 50' and 30' x 30' located SR on stage level, barres, mirrors and piano, prior arrangement required
Storage: None

ELECTRICS

ROAD SERVICE POWER

Panel	Phase	Amp	Circuit Protection	Use	Location
A	3	800	fuse	dimmers	DSL proscenium wall
B-C	3	600	fuse	extra	DSL proscenium wall
D-E	3	400	fuse	extra	DSL proscenium wall
F	3	100	fuse	sound	DSL proscenium wall

Recommended location of touring dimmer racks: SL on deck
Hoist not required
Additional power is available for tour buses, generators, etc.

FRONT OF HOUSE (BOX BOOM VALUES ARE PER SIDE)
Transfer circuits: New twistlock circuits connected to house instruments
Road truss: Trusses have been spotted in the past

EQUIPMENT FOH (BOX BOOM VALUES ARE PER SIDE)

Position	Quantity	Wattage	Instrument	Removeable
1st Balc Rail	40	2,000	Neithammer 9°	no
1st Cove	16	1,000	Neithammer 17°	no
Box Boom 1	16	575	ETC Source 26°	no
Box Boom 2	16	1,000	Berkey 20° Iris	no

FOLLOWSPOTS
House Followspots:
  (4) Super Trouper Carbon Arc; removeable

Followspot Booth:
  (4) spots per booth;
  120' throw to proscenium;
  (4) 1Ø 50 amp breakers

DIMMERS
Lighting console is Avab-Panther VLC;
(756) Avab DD11 dimmers
House has programmable DMX control system
(1) dry run DMX station

THUNDER BAY COMMUNITY AUDITORIUM

YEAR BUILT: 1985

Theatre Location:	450 Beverly Street, Thunder Bay, ON P7B 5E8 CANADA	
Mailing Address:	PO Box 2209, Thunder Bay, ON P7B 5E8 CANADA	

SEATING CAPACITY

Main Floor Orchestra	951
Mezzanine	289
Balcony	271
Total:	**1,511**

Main Administrative Phone:	807-343-2314
Main Administrative Fax:	807-345-8977
Stage Door Phone:	807-343-2311
Traveling Production Office Phone:	807-343-2340

THEATRE STAFF

General Manager	Clint Kuschak	807-343-2308
Executive Assistant	Elaine Mackenzie	807-343-2314

HOUSE CREW

Manager	Tony Ouwehand	807-343-2319
Sound	Rob Jardine	807-343-2318
Electrics	Joe Szabo	807-343-2317

STAGE DIMENSIONS (FROM SMOKE POCKET)

Stage is 50'0" deep
Width from Center Line to SL is 41'0"
Width from Center Line to SR is 44'0"
Proscenium width is 70'6"
Proscenium height is 39'6"
Smoke pocket to apron edge is 5'6"
Orchestra pit exists

RIGGING

Grid Height:	80"
Type:	Single purchase counter weight
Weight:	1,200 lbs
Line sets:	52 sets
House Pipes:	70' long

LOADING DOCK

Loading door(s) are 8'10" high x 7'3"wide
Trucks load (2) at same time
Fork lift is not required and is not available

ELECTRICS

Total power available:
(2) 400A 3Ø SR
(1) 100A 3Ø SR

FOLLOWSPOTS

House Followspots:
Xenon Super Trouper
Power in spot booth

DIMMERS

(361) house dimmers
House has DMX control system
(2) dry run station(s) located SR

SOUND

House has 200A dedicated
power located SR wall
FOH mixing position in
Rear Orchestra
Sound console is available

ELGIN THEATRE

Year built: 1913   Year renovated: 1988

Theatre Location: 189 Yonge Street, Toronto, ON M5B 1M4 CANADA

Main Administrative Phone: 416-314-2901
Main Administrative Fax: 416-314-3583
E-mail: zehr@heritagefdn.on.ca
Website: www.heritagefdn.on.ca
StageDoor Phone: 416-314-3718

Theatre Staff
  General Manager   Richard Mortimer   416-314-2870
  Marketing   Arnie Lappin   416-314-2874
House Crew
  Director of Production Howard Thornely   416-314-2884
Unions
  IATSE Local #58   Bill Hamilton   416-364-5565
  Wardrobe BA   Diane Luckett-Reilly 416-461-3903

Seating Capacity
  Orchestra   909
  Boxes   48
  Mezzanine   342
  Balcony   262
  Total: **1,561**

Box Office
  Box Office Manager
    Paul MacFarlane   416-314-2883

  Outside Ticket Agency
    Ticket Master   416-872-5555

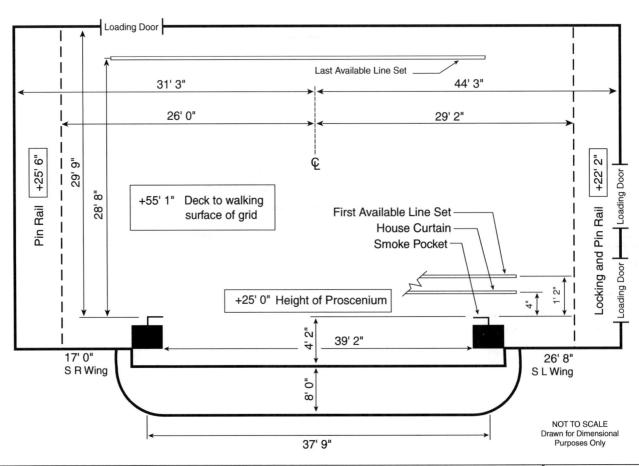

STAGE HOUSE

HOUSE CURTAIN
Operates as a guillotine from SL fly floor

RIGGING SYSTEM
Type:	Double purchase counter weight
Weight:	80,000 lbs available
Line sets:	54 sets at 6" o.c. with 5 lift lines per set
Arbors:	1,500 lb capacity
House Pipes:	48' long with 52' of travel from deck

Line sets are not moveable
(60) spot wheels and 3,600' of hemp available

PERMANENT INSTALLATIONS OVER STAGE (FROM SMOKE POCKET)
None

PERMANENT INSTALLATIONS ON DECK
Traps in stage floor are on sectional grid

ORCHESTRA PIT
Adjustable to 9' below stage level by hydraulic lift
Apron overhangs US wall of pit 11'9"
Additional 4'0" of pit is available extending towards house

BACKSTAGE

LOADING DOCK
Loading door(s):
   (1) 16'0" high x 5'0" wide
   (2) 13'6" high x 10'0" wide
   (3) 8'0" high x 4'0" wide
Trucks load (1) at a time
Dock (loading door sill) is at street level; loading to stage thru separate receiving room
Fork lift is required; must rent
Trailers can store on-site
Security at dock & stage door

WARDROBE
Location: USL on 3rd floor
Access: Freight elevator
(2) Washers (2) Dryers

DRESSING ROOMS
(1) Star, USL, 2nd fl, t/s included
(5) Small, 2nd fl/ 3rd fl, t/s included
(2) Chorus, USL, 3rd fl, t/s included

SOUND

CONSOLE
No house console

SPEAKERS
Holes in ceiling over house provide truss hanging position; winches available
Pipe and rigging unavailable

COMMUNICATIONS
Clear Com intercom with (4) channels
Radio listening device
Dressing room page system

ROAD CONSOLE
Located Rear House
No seats required to be removed
Cable run from stage is 120'

REHEARSAL & STORAGE SPACE
Rehearsal: 50' x 50' located on 4th fl; piano available; prior arrangement required
Storage: None

ELECTRICS

ROAD SERVICE POWER

Panel	Phase	Amp	Circuit Protection	Use	Location
A-B	3	400	breaker	dimmers	SL in basement
C-D	3	400	breaker	extra	SL in basement
E	3	200	breaker	sound	SR side wall
F	3	200	breaker	extra	SL side wall

Recommended location of touring dimmer racks: SL on deck or in basement

FRONT OF HOUSE (BOX BOOM VALUES ARE PER SIDE)

Position	Pipe Width	Distance to Prosc.	House Circuits	Connector Type	FOH Transfer Circuits
Truss	40'	26'	54	grd 20 amp stage pin	54
1st Balc Rail	92'	45'	30	grd 20 amp stage pin	30
1st Cove	50'	77'	31	grd 20 amp stage pin	31
Box Boom 1		8'	15	grd 20 amp stage pin	15
Box Boom 2		12'	6	grd 20 amp stage pin	6
Box Boom 3		30'	4	grd 20 amp stage pin	4
Box Boom 4		34'	6	grd 20 amp stage pin	6

Transfer circuits: grd 20 amp stage pin located SL in basement

EQUIPMENT FOH (BOX BOOM VALUES ARE PER SIDE)
None

FOLLOWSPOTS
House Followspots:
   (2) Xenon Super Troupers; removeable

Followspot Booth:
   (2) spots per booth;
   102' throw to proscenium;
   (2) 3Ø 30 amp breakers
   (2) 3Ø 20 amp breakers

DIMMERS
House has (72) Strand CD-80 dimmers
No DMX control system

FORD CENTRE FOR THE PERFORMING ARTS

YEAR BUILT: 1993

Theatre Location: 5040 Yonge Street, Toronto, ON M2N 6R8 CANADA

Main Administrative Phone:	416-733-9388
Main Administrative Fax:	416-733-9478
Stage Door Phone:	416-733-9388

SEATING CAPACITY

Orchestra	1,104
Dress Circle	236
Balcony	476
Total:	**1,816**

pit (add'l)	30
wheelchair	varies

THEATRE STAFF

General Manager	Terry Kealey	416-733-9388
Operations Manager	Albert Ruscich	416-733-9388
FOH Manager	Steven Fishman	416-733-9388

HOUSE CREW

Technical Director	Charles Kaiser	416-733-9388
Carpentry	Michael Maskell	416-733-9388
Electrics	John Beirne	416-733-9388
Sound	Rick Crowley	416-733-9388
Props	T. Eric Hastings	416-733-9388

UNIONS

IATSE Local #58	Bill Hamilton	416-364-5565
Wardrobe Local #822	Diane Luckett-Reilly	416-461-3903
Music T.M.A.	Moe Kofman	416-484-8241

BOX OFFICE

Computerized
Manager
  Martha Gall   416-733-9388

Outside Ticket Agency
Computerized
Ticketmaster
  Vesna Grujic   416-345-9200 x5235

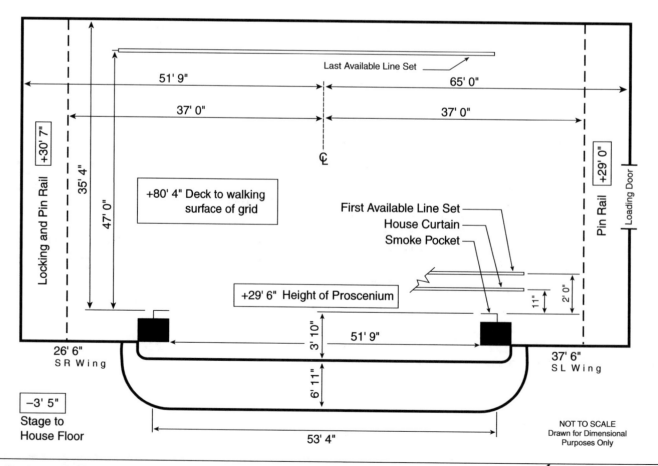

STAGE HOUSE

House Curtain
Operates as a guillotine or traveller from SR fly floor

Rigging System
Type:	Single purchase counter weight
Weight:	67,000 lbs available
Line sets:	77 sets at 7.5" o.c. with 7 lift lines per set
Arbors:	1,500 lb capacity
House Pipes:	67' long with 79'6" of travel from deck

Line sets are moveable
Block & Falls are available
Chain hoists are available; (2) one ton
(75) spot wheels and 500' of hemp available

Permanent Installations Over Stage (from smoke pocket)
None

Permanent Installations On Deck
Traps in stage floor cut as needed
Electric jump (1) at 7'8" x 55' 4" located SL

Orchestra Pit
Adjustable to 19' 7" below stage level by electric motor turnscrew
Apron overhangs US wall of pit 8'3"
Pit lift is in (2) sections

BACKSTAGE

Loading Dock
Loading door(s):
   (3) 9'8" high x 8'1" wide
Trucks load (3) at same time
Dock has slight incline down towards loading doors, dock height is 3'7"
Forklift is not required
Sound/Props can load in FOH
Lobby cannot be a work area
(2) Trailers can store on-site
Security at dock & stage door

Wardrobe
Location: SR at stage level
Access: Via backstage hallway
(4) Washers (5) Dryers
No washer or dryer hookups

Dressing Rooms
(2) Star, t/s, phone jacks
(6) Small, t/s, phone jacks
(3) Chorus, t/s, phone jacks
Additional production office available for company mgr

SOUND

Console
None

Speakers
Under Balcony
Truss can be hung on FOH lines; rigging required

Communications
Clear Com intercom
Infrared sound system
Dressing room page system

Road Console
Located Rear Orchestra center
Cable run from stage is 200'
Tie-in into house system with XLR connectors
Runs from trap room thru proscenium to mix position

Rehearsal & Storage Space
Rehearsal: SR upper level , 62' x 45', piano, mirrors, chairs, stands, sprung floor, prior arrangement required
Storage: None

ELECTRICS

Road Service Power

Panel	Phase	Amp	Circuit Protection Use	Location
A	3	400	fuse	SL proscenium wall
B	3	200	fuse	SL proscenium wall
C-D	3	100	fuse	SL proscenium wall
E	3	60	fuse	SL proscenium wall
F	3	50	fuse	SL proscenium wall
G-H	3	30	fuse	SL proscenium wall
I-L	3	400	fuse	SL proscenium wall
L-M	3	200	fuse	SL proscenium wall
N	3	100	fuse	USR

Recommended location of touring dimmer racks: SL Wing
Hoist is provided
Additional power is available for tour buses, generators, etc.

Front Of House (box boom values are per side)

Position	Pipe Width	Distance to Prosc.	House Circuits	Connector Type	FOH Transfer Circuits
Balc. Rail	77'	74'	0	none	0
1st Cove	48'	47'	0	none	0
2nd Cove	62'	74'	0	none	0

Equipment FOH (box boom values are per side)
None

Followspots
House Followspots:
   (3) Super Troupers;
   removeable

Followspot Booth:
   (3) spots per booth;
   90' throw to proscenium;
   (4) 3Ø 30 amp breakers

Dimmers
No lighting console
No dimmers
No DMX control system

HUMMINGBIRD CENTRE FOR THE PERFORMING ARTS

FORMERLY: O'KEEFE CENTER FOR THE PERFORMING ARTS   YEAR BUILT: 1960

Theatre Location: One Front Street East, Toronto, ON M5E 1B2 CANADA

Main Administrative Phone:	416-393-7474
Main Administrative Fax:	416-393-7454
Stage Door Phone:	416-393-7474 x215
Backstage Pay Phone:	416-869-9106
Traveling Production Office Phone:	416-393-7479
Traveling Production Office Fax:	416-393-7490

THEATRE STAFF

General Manager	Elizabeth Bradley	416-393-7474
Booking	Marianne Woods	416-393-7466
Marketing	Mary Ann Farrell	416-393-7461
Group Sales	Kelly Smith	416-393-7463

HOUSE CREW

Carpentry	Tom McLean	416-393-7468
Electrics	Tom Taylor	416-393-7440
Sound	Ross Tuskey	416-393-7439
Props	Roger Read	416-393-7441

UNIONS

IATSE Local #58	Bill Hamilton	416-364-5565
Wardrobe Local #822	Diane Luckett-Reilly	416-461-3903
AFM	Dave Woods	416-225-5447

SEATING CAPACITY

Front Orchestra	1,244
Mid Orchestra	496
Rear Orchestra	384
Mezzanine	256
Balcony	787
Total:	**3,167**

pit (add'l)	56
wheelchair (add'l)	16
standing (add'l)	52

BOX OFFICE
Computerized
Box Office Manager
  Heather Ledyit   416-393-7452

Outside Ticket Agency
Computerized
Ticketmaster
  Bruce Morrison   416-345-9200

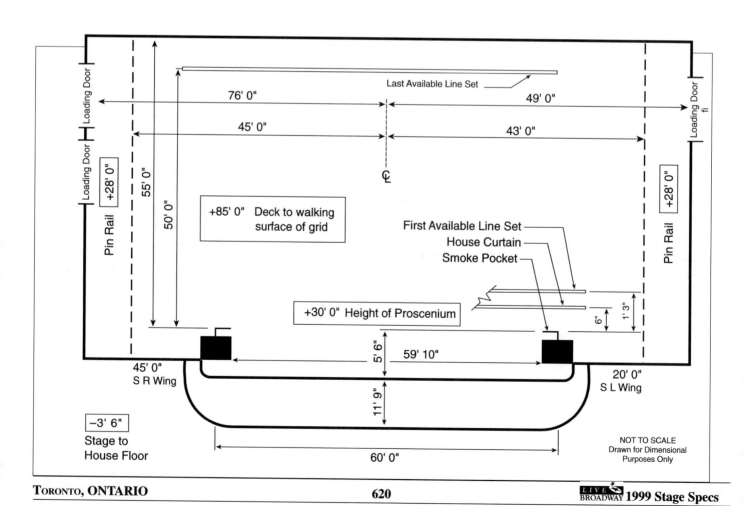

STAGE HOUSE

HOUSE CURTAIN
Operates as a guillotine from SL deck; motorized

RIGGING SYSTEM
Type:	Single purchase counter weight
Weight:	40,000 lbs available
Line sets:	74 sets at 6" o.c. with 6 lift lines per set
Arbors:	1,200 lb capacity
House Pipes:	60' long with 75' of travel from deck

Line sets are not moveable
Block & Falls are available 2:1 (4)
Chain hoists are not available
(130) spot wheels and 30,000' of hemp available
5 motorized line sets

PERMANENT INSTALLATIONS OVER STAGE (FROM SMOKE POCKET)
Electric borders (1) at 2'0"

PERMANENT INSTALLATIONS ON DECK
Electric bridge (1) 75' x 2'6", 2' US

ORCHESTRA PIT
Adjustable to 20' below stage level by electric motor
    turnscrew
Apron overhangs US wall of pit 12'0"
Pit lift is in (1) section

BACKSTAGE

LOADING DOCK
Loading door(s):
    1) 13'6" high x 12'6" wide
    2) 13'6" high x 12'6" wide
    3) 8'0" high x 8'0" wide
Trucks load (3) at same time
Downtown location - street
    parking not available for
    extended periods of time
Fork lift is required; House
    owns
Sound/Props cannot load in
    FOH
Trailers cannot store on-site
Security at stage door

WARDROBE
Location: SL on 2nd fl
Access: Elevator
(2) Washers (2) Dryers
Washer and dryer hookups
    available

DRESSING ROOMS
(8) Star, SL, stage level, t/s
    included
(6) Chorus, SL, +2, t/s included
Elevator access for dressing
    rooms
Additional production office
    available for company mgr

SOUND

CONSOLE
Cadac located
    Rear Orchestra
32 inputs, 10 main outputs,
    6 aux outputs

SPEAKERS
House Cluster
Proscenium
Under Balcony

COMMUNICATIONS
Clear Com intercom with
    (4) channels
Infrared sound system
Dressing room page system

ROAD CONSOLE
Located Rear Orchestra
Seats must be removed
Cable run from stage is 275'
Tie-in into house system with
    XLR connectors

REHEARSAL & STORAGE SPACE
Rehearsal: 40' x 60' off SL,
    stage level, mirrors, barres,
    piano
Storage: None

ELECTRICS

ROAD SERVICE POWER

Panel	Phase	Amp	Circuit Protection	Use	Location
A-E	3	400	breaker	dimmers	DSR proscenium wall
F	1	100	breaker	sound	DSL proscenium wall
G	3	100	breaker	winches	DSR proscenium wall
H-I	3	100	breaker	extra	DSR proscenium wall

Recommended location of touring dimmer racks: SR on deck   Hoist not required

FRONT OF HOUSE (BOX BOOM VALUES ARE PER SIDE)

Position	Pipe Width	Distance to Prosc.	House Circuits	Connector Type	FOH Transfer Circuits
1st Balc Rail	60'	90'	30	20 amp old twistlock	28
1st Cove	70'	35'	24	20 amp old twistlock	24
2nd Cove	70'	48'	24	20 amp old twistlock	24
Box Boom 1		2'	9	20 amp old twistlock	6
Box Boom 2		7'	9	20 amp old twistlock	6
Box Boom 3		11'	9	20 amp old twistlock	6

Transfer circuits: grd 20 amp stage pin located on DSR proscenium wall

EQUIPMENT FOH (BOX BOOM VALUES ARE PER SIDE)

Position	Quantity	Wattage	Instrument	Removeable
1st Balc Rail	24	1,000	8 x 13 Lekos	
1st Cove	30	1,000	8 x 13 Lekos	
2nd Cove	28	1,000	8 x 13 Lekos	
Box Boom 1	4	1,000	8 x 13 Lekos	
Box Boom 2	9	1,000	8 x 13 Lekos	
Box Boom 3	9	1,000	8 x 13 Lekos	

FOLLOWSPOTS
House Followspots:
    (4) Xenon Super Troupers;
    removeable

Followspot Booth:
    (4) spots per booth;
    145' throw to proscenium;
    (4) 3Ø 60 amp breakers

DIMMERS
Lighting console is Light
    Pallette 90
No DMX control system

MASSEY HALL

Theatre Location:	178 Victoria Street, Toronto , ON M5B 1T7
Mailing Address:	60 Simcoe Street, Toronto, ON M5J 2H5

Main Administrative Phone:	416-363-7624
Main Administrative Fax:	416-363-5290
Website:	www.masseyhall.com
Backstage Pay Phone:	416-363-7730

SEATING CAPACITY

Main Floor	1,050
Balcony	943
Gallery	764
Total:	**2,757**

pit (add'l)	0
wheelchair (add'l)	0
standing (add'l)	0

THEATRE STAFF

House Manager	Nancy Beaton	416-363-7624
Booking	Lillian Thalheimer	416-593-4822

HOUSE CREW

Production Manager	Yvette Drumgold	416-593-4822 x353
Electrics	Michael Murphy	416-363-7624 x224

STAGE DIMENSIONS (FROM SMOKE POCKET)
Stage is 35'0" deep
Width from Center Line to SL is 30'0"
Width from Center Line to SR is 30'0"
No orchestra pit

RIGGING
Data not provided

LOADING DOCK
Loading door(s) are 7'7" high x 4'2" wide
Trucks load (1) at a time
Fork lift is not required and is not available
Street level loading through front door of building

ELECTRICS
Total power available:
(2) 400A 3Ø SR
(1) 200A 3Ø SL

FOLLOWSPOTS
House Followspots:
Lycian Arc
Power in spot booth
Additional spot in every booth

DIMMERS
(48) house dimmers
House has DMX control system
(2) dry run station(s) located
SR / SL

SOUND
House has 200A 3Ø dedicated power located SL
FOH mixing position in House Left
No sound console available

PANTAGES THEATRE

AT: AT&T CENTRE FOR THE PERFORMING ARTS

YEAR BUILT: 1920   YEAR RENOVATED: 1989

Theatre Location: 244 Victoria Street, Toronto, ON M5B 1V8
Management Company: Livent Inc.
                                165 Avenue Road, Toronto, ON M5R 3S4

Main Administrative Phone: 416-362-3218
Main Administrative Fax: 416-362-0985
Website: www.livent.com
Stage Door Phone: 416-362-3218

THEATRE STAFF
General Manager   Lori-Anne Rzic   416-362-3218
Booking   Kim Loftus   416-362-3218
Marketing   Livent Inc.   416-324-5800
Operations   Eugene Zenger   416-362-3218
Group Sales   Livent Inc.   416-324-5800

HOUSE CREW
Sr. Technical Director   Peter W. Lamb   416-324-5476
Carpentry   Frank A. Galle   416-362-3218 x210
Electrics   Bill Asselstine   416-362-3218 x212
Sound   Jim Thibeau   416-362-3218 x212
Props   R. Paul Axford   416-362-3218

UNIONS
IATSE Local #58   William Hamilton   416-364-5565
Wardrobe Local #822   Diane Luckett Reilly 416-461-3903
Music TMA   Moe Kofman   416-484-8241

SEATING CAPACITY
Orchestra	1,100
Balcony	1169
Total:	**2,269**
wheelchair (add'l)	14

BOX OFFICE
Computerized
Box Office Manager   416-362-3218

Outside Ticket Agency
Computerized
Ticketmaster   416-872-2222

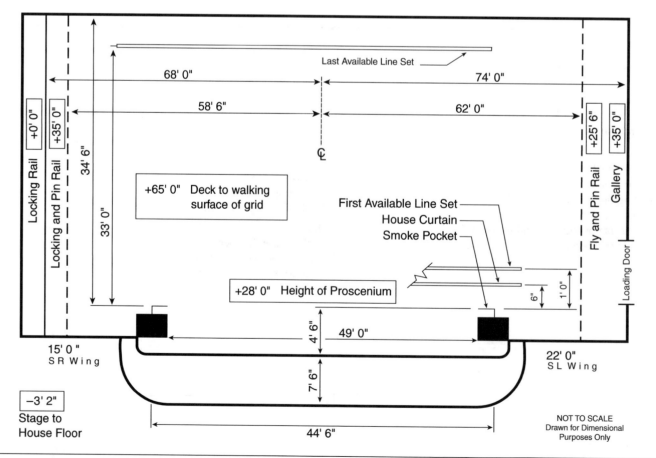

Last Available Line Set

68' 0"   74' 0"

58' 6"   62' 0"

CL

Locking Rail   +0' 0"

Locking and Pin Rail   +35' 0"

34' 6"

33' 0"

+65' 0"   Deck to walking surface of grid

First Available Line Set
House Curtain
Smoke Pocket

+25' 6"   Fly and Pin Rail
+35' 0"   Gallery

Loading Door

6"

1' 0"

+28' 0"   Height of Proscenium

4' 6"   49' 0"

15' 0"
S R Wing

7' 6"

22' 0"
S L Wing

−3' 2"
Stage to
House Floor

44' 6"

NOT TO SCALE
Drawn for Dimensional
Purposes Only

STAGE HOUSE

HOUSE CURTAIN
Operates as a guillotine from SR deck

RIGGING SYSTEM
Type:	Single purchase counter weight
Weight:	25,000 lbs available
Line sets:	61 sets at 6" o.c. with 7 lift lines per set
Arbors:	1,800 lb capacity
House Pipes:	57' long with 61' of travel from deck

Line sets are not moveable
Block & Falls are available
Chain hoists are available
(75) spot wheels and 2,400' of hemp available

PERMANENT INSTALLATIONS OVER STAGE (FROM SMOKE POCKET)
Fire curtain (1) at DS in pocket

PERMANENT INSTALLATIONS ON DECK
Trap (70) in stage floor 4'0" x 8'0", centered
Jump (1)

ORCHESTRA PIT
Adjustable to 9'0" below stage level by electric motor turnscrew
Apron overhangs US wall of pit 6'4"
Pit lift is in (1) section

BACKSTAGE

LOADING DOCK
Loading door(s):
    11'6" high x 11'6" wide
Trucks load (2) at same time
Located in very busy laneway, no ramp on site
Fork lift is not required
Sound/Props can load in FOH
Lobby can be a work area
Trailers cannot store on-site
Security at dock & stage door

WARDROBE
Location: Basement
Access: Stage door
(3) Washers (3) Dryers
Washer and dryer hookups available

DRESSING ROOMS
(2) Star, SL, -1, t/s included, phone jack
(4) Small, SL, -1, t/s included, phone jack
(3) Chorus, SL / SR, -1, t/s included
Elevator access for dressing rooms
Additional production office available for company mgr

SOUND

CONSOLE
No house console

SPEAKERS
True road house situation, bring what you need for FOH + monitors
Have motor available to hang center cluster (max 1 ton load)
Pipe and rigging available

COMMUNICATIONS
Clear Com intercom with (4) channels
Infrared sound system
Dressing room page system

ROAD CONSOLE
Located Rear Orchestra
(6) seats required to be removed
Cable run from stage is 200'

REHEARSAL & STORAGE SPACE
Rehearsal: None
Storage: None

ELECTRICS

ROAD SERVICE POWER

Panel	Phase	Amp	Circuit Protection	Use	Location
A-D	3	400	breaker	dimmers	dimmer loft SL
E	3	200	fuse	dimmers	USL
F	3	400	breaker	extra	Transformer room
G-H	1	100	fuse	sound	sound room
I	3	60	fuse	motors	dimmer loft SL
J	3	20	breaker	motors	USR

Recommended location of touring dimmer racks: Dimmer loft SL or SL wings
Hoist is required and provided

FRONT OF HOUSE (BOX BOOM VALUES ARE PER SIDE)

Position	Pipe Width	Distance to Prosc.	House Circuits	Connector Type	FOH Transfer Circuits
1st Balc Rail	90'	60'	36	grd 20 amp stagepin	18
1st Cove	28'	80'	18	grd 20 amp stagepin	36
Box Boom 1	12'	15'	12	grd 20 amp stagepin	12
Box Boom 2	12'	40'	12	grd 20 amp stagepin	12
Bridge	20'	65'	12	grd 20 amp stagepin	12

Transfer circuits: grd 20 amp stage pin
Road truss: There are (2) points for a light weight truss appox 6' DS from the proscenium

EQUIPMENT FOH (BOX BOOM VALUES ARE PER SIDE)

Position	Quantity	Wattage	Instrument	Removeable
1st Balc Rail	19	varies	Lekos	yes
1st Cove	30	1,000	6 x 22	yes
Box Boom 1	10	1,000	Lekos	yes
Box Boom 2	12	1,000	6 x 16 Lekos	yes
Lighting	14	1,000	Lekos	yes

FOLLOWSPOTS
House Followspots:
    (2) Xenon Super Trouper 2k; removeable

Followspot Booth:
    (2) spots per booth;
    145' throw to proscenium;
    (3) 1Ø 30 amp breakers

DIMMERS
House lighting console is Strand Light Pallette 3;
(456) Strand CD80 dimmers
No DMX control system

PRINCESS OF WALES

YEAR BUILT: 1993

Theatre Location: 300 King Street West, Toronto, ON M5V 1H9 CANADA
Management Company: Mirvish Productions
266 King Street West, Toronto, ON M5V 1H9 CANADA

Main Administrative Phone: 416-593-0351
Main Administrative Fax: 416-593-9221
E-mail: swhitham@mirvish.com
Website: www.onstagenow.com
Stage Door Phone: 416-351-9011
Traveling Production Office Phone: 416-351-9011

THEATRE STAFF
Theatre Manager   Ron Jacobson   416-593-0351
Executive Producer   Brian Sewell   416-593-0351
Technical Producer   John Wilbur   416-593-0351
Marketing   John Karastamatis   416-593-0351
Group Sales   Judi Pressman   416-461-2503

HOUSE CREW
Production Manager   Scot Whitham   416-593-0351
Carpentry   Grant Milligan   416-351-9011
Electrics   Ron Montgomery, Jr   416-351-9011
Props   Gerry Fava   416-351-9011

UNIONS
IATSE Local #58   Bill Hamilton   416-364-5565
Wardrobe Local #822   Diane Luckett-Reilly 416-461-3903
Music Local #149   Bobby Hariot   416-421-1020
Wigs Local #800   Rhonda Collins   416-536-3620

SEATING CAPACITY
Orchestra   1,032
Dress Circle   500
Balcony   500
Total: **2,032**

BOX OFFICE
Computerized

Outside Ticket Agency
Computerized
TicketKing   416-872-1212

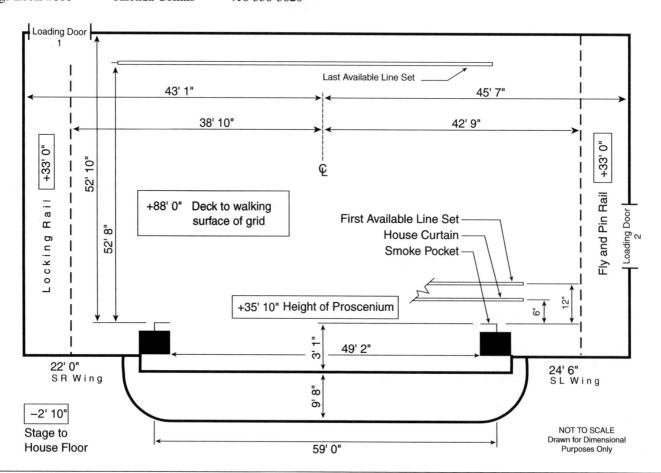

STAGE HOUSE

HOUSE CURTAIN
Operates as a guillotine from SR fly floor
May be installed on any line set or removed

RIGGING SYSTEM
Type: Single purchase counter weight and Hemp system
Weight: 32,000 lbs available
Line sets: 104 sets at 6" o.c. with 7 lift lines per set
Arbors: 1,350 lb capacity
House Pipes: 66' long with 82' of travel from deck
Line sets are not moveable
Block & Falls are not available
Chain hoists are available as rental; (12) one ton, (3) half ton
(74) spot wheels and 10,000' of hemp available

PERMANENT INSTALLATIONS OVER STAGE (FROM SMOKE POCKET)
Hard portal (1) at 2'0" DS of smoke, in front of proscenium

PERMANENT INSTALLATIONS ON DECK
Traps (4) - 3DS, 1CS, 3'3" square
Jumps (2), at loading floors SR
Electric jump (1), at fly floor for electric spot lines SL
Hard legs (1), on travelers 2' US from smoke pocket
Stairs (2), DR and DL
Adjustable proscenium (1), DS of concrete proscenium
Adjustable portal (1), DS of concrete proscenium

ORCHESTRA PIT
Nonadjustable at 10'0" below stage level
Apron overhangs US wall of pit 0'0"

BACKSTAGE

LOADING DOCK
Loading door(s):
1) 19'3" high x 18'0" wide
2) 8'0" high x 9'10" wide
Trucks load (2) at same time
Door #1 difficult back in for long tractors; must proceed wrong way on one-way street; police assistance required; recommend short yard tractor rental
Sound/Props can load in FOH
Lobby can be a work area
Trailers cannot store on-site
Security at stage door

WARDROBE
Location: Understage-trap room is used as wardrobe room
Access: Stairs SL/SR, Elevator
(3) Washers (3) Dryers
No washer or dryer hookups

DRESSING ROOMS
(2) Star, stage level, t/s included, phn jack
(1) Small, stage level, phn jack
(2) Small, trap level, (1) with t/s included
(3) Chorus, trap level, t/s included
Elevator access for dressing rms
Additional production office available for company mgr

SOUND

CONSOLE
No house console

SPEAKERS
Under balcony speakers are used as delay system and are self contained; only program feed
No speaker truss

COMMUNICATIONS
Clear Com intercom with (4) channels
Infrared sound system
Dressing room page system

ROAD CONSOLE
No seats required to be removed
Cable run from stage is 250'

REHEARSAL & STORAGE SPACE
Rehearsal: None
Storage: None

ELECTRICS

ROAD SERVICE POWER

Panel	Phase	Amp	Circuit Protection	Use	Location
A-C	3	400	fuse	dimmers	dimmer room
D-F	3	400	fuse	dimmers	USL
G-I	3	200	fuse	sound	trap rm DSL, Pros wall DSR

Recommended location of touring dimmer racks: USL
Hoist is required and provided

FRONT OF HOUSE (BOX BOOM VALUES ARE PER SIDE)

Position	Pipe Width	Distance to Prosc.	House Circuits	Connector Type	FOH Transfer Circuits
1st Balc Rail	52'	64'	0	grd 20 amp stage pin	
1st Cove			20	grd 20 amp stage pin	20
Under Booth	72'	52'	20	grd 20 amp stage pin	20

Transfer circuits: (234) stage pin house circuits in various locations in FOH; accessed in dimmer room off USL

EQUIPMENT FOH (BOX BOOM VALUES ARE PER SIDE)
None

FOLLOWSPOTS
House Followspots:
None

Followspot Booth:
(3) spots per booth;
99' throw to proscenium;
(3) 3Ø 30 amp breakers

DIMMERS
No lighting console
No dimmers
No DMX control system

ROY THOMSON HALL

AT: THE CORPORATION OF MASSEY HALL & ROY THOMSON HALL   YEAR BUILT: 1982

Theatre Location: 60 Simcoe Street, Toronto, ON M5J 2H5 CANADA

Main Administrative Phone: 416-593-4224
Main Administrative Fax: 416-593-4224
Website: www.roythomson.com
Stage Door Phone: 416-593-4822 x375

SEATING CAPACITY

Main Floor	1,095
Mezzanine	789
Balcony	428
Total:	**2,812**
wheelchair (add'l)	26

THEATRE STAFF

President & CEO	Charles S. Cutts	416-593-4822 x323
Booking	Lillian Thalheimer	416-593-4822 x353

HOUSE CREW

Production Manager	Yvette Drumgold	416-593-4822 x353

STAGE DIMENSIONS (FROM SMOKE POCKET)
Stage is 36'0" deep
Width from Center Line to SL is 28'0"
Width from Center Line to SR is 28'0"
No orchestra pit

RIGGING
Type: None
Line sets: 3 sets at 17' o.c.

LOADING DOCK
Loading door(s) are 8'5" high x 8'0" wide
Trucks load (1) at a time
Fork lift is not required and is not available

ELECTRICS
Total power available:
(2) 100A 3Ø SL
(1) 200A 3Ø SL
(1) 400A 3Ø SR

FOLLOWSPOTS
House Followspots:
Xenon Gladiator
Power in spot booth

DIMMERS
(208) house dimmers
House has DMX control system
(3) dry run station(s) located
SR / SL

SOUND
House has 100A dedicated
power located SL
FOH mixing position in
Rear House Right
Sound console is available

ROYAL ALEXANDRA THEATRE

YEAR BUILT: 1907   YEAR RENOVATED: 1963

Theatre Location: 260 King Street West, Toronto, ON M5V 1H9 CANADA
Management Company: Mirvish Productions
                          266 King Street West, Toronto, ON M5V 1H9 CANADA

Main Administrative Phone: 416-593-0351
Main Administrative Fax: 416-593-9221
E-mail: swhitham@mirvish.com
Website: www.onstagenow.com
Stage Door Phone: 416-593-1840
Traveling Production Office Phone: 416-593-1840 x751

THEATRE STAFF
Theatre Manager   Ron Jacobson   416-593-0351
Executive Producer   Brian Sewell   416-593-0351
Marketing   John Karastamatis   416-593-0351
Group Sales   Judi Pressman   416-461-2503

HOUSE CREW
Production Manager   Scot Whitham   416-593-0351
Carpentry   Michael Puhacz   416-593-1840
Electrics   John Still   416-593-1840
Props   Warren Hudson   416-593-1840

UNIONS
IATSE Local #58   Bill Hamilton   416-364-5565
Wardrobe Local #822   Diane Luckett-Reilly   416-461-3903
Music Local #149   Bobby Hariot   416-421-1020
Wigs Local #800   Rhonda Collins   416-536-3620

SEATING CAPACITY
Orchestra   673
Boxes   44
1st Balcony   400
2nd Balcony   380
Total: **1,497**

BOX OFFICE
James Aldridge   416-872-1212

Outside Ticket Agency
Computerized
Ticket King
  James Aldridge   416-872-1212

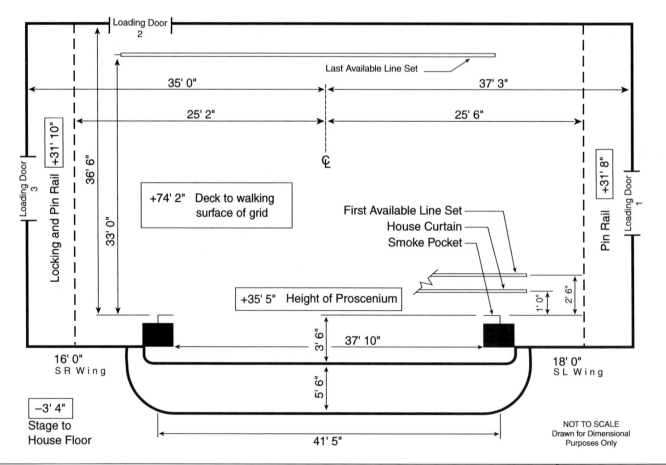

STAGE HOUSE

HOUSE CURTAIN
Operates as a guillotine from fly floor

RIGGING SYSTEM
Type:	Single purchase counter weight
Weight:	15,000 lbs available
Line sets:	57 sets at 6" o.c. with 5 lift lines per set
Arbors:	1,250 lb capacity
House Pipes:	48' long with 70' of travel from deck

Line sets are moveable
Block & Falls are available
Chain hoists are not available
(30) spot wheels and 0' of hemp available

PERMANENT INSTALLATIONS OVER STAGE (FROM SMOKE POCKET)
Dead spaces (2) at 11'9" and 26'3" over stage

PERMANENT INSTALLATIONS ON DECK
Trap (2) in stage floor 2'0" x 3'0" DSC & 3'0" x 6'0" USC
Electric Jump located on DSL & DSR proscenium walls - 7'0" high

ORCHESTRA PIT
Nonadjustable at 8' below stage level
Apron overhangs US wall of pit 12'5"

BACKSTAGE

LOADING DOCK
Loading door(s):
1) 18'0" high x 8'0" wide
2) 13'0" high x 5'0" wide
3) 13'0" high x 5'0" wide
Trucks load (2), at separate docks at same time
2 docks (loading door sills) are at street level 4' above stage level - 3'11" wide permanent concrete ramp to stage available
Fork lift is required; Masterlift (416) 671-8449
Sound/Props cannot load in FOH
Trailers cannot store on-site
Security at dock & stage door

WARDROBE
Location: Basement
Access: Trap in stage floor
(2) Washers (2) Dryers
No washer or dryer hookups

DRESSING ROOMS
(3) Star, behind stage, stage level, t/s included, phone jack
(14) Small, behind stage, +3/+4, t/s on same fl
(7) Chorus, behind stage, +2/+3/ +4, t/s on same fl
Additional production office available for company mgr

SOUND

CONSOLE
No house console

SPEAKERS
No speaker truss

COMMUNICATIONS
Clear Com intercom with (2) channels
Infrared sound system
Dressing room page system

ROAD CONSOLE
Located Rear House or upper box HR
(24) seats required to be removed
Cable run from stage is 150'

REHEARSAL & STORAGE SPACE
Rehearsal: None
Storage: 26' x 40' located in basement

ELECTRICS

ROAD SERVICE POWER
Panel	Phase	Amp	Circuit Protection	Use	Location
A-B	3	400	fuse	dimmers	DSL
C	3	400	fuse	extra	basement
D	3	200	fuse	sound	basement

Recommended location of touring dimmer racks: SL loading aisle

FRONT OF HOUSE (BOX BOOM VALUES ARE PER SIDE)
Position	Pipe Width	Distance to Prosc.	House Circuits	Connector Type	FOH Transfer Circuits
Truss	35'	25'	42	grd 20 amp stagepin	42
1st Balc Rail	64'	39'	20	grd 20 amp stagepin	20
2nd Balc Rail	43'	50'	50	grd 20 amp stagepin	20
Box Boom 1		14'	8	grd 20 amp stagepin	8
Box Boom 2		20'	8	grd 20 amp stagepin	8

Transfer circuits: grd 20 amp stage pin located in SL loading aisle

EQUIPMENT FOH (BOX BOOM VALUES ARE PER SIDE)
None

FOLLOWSPOTS
House Followspots:
None

Followspot Booth:
(3) spots per booth;
80' throw to proscenium;
1Ø 70 amp breakers

DIMMERS
No lighting console
No dimmers
No DMX control system

ST. LAWRENCE CENTER FOR THE ARTS: BLUMA APPEL

AT: ST. LAWRENCE CENTRE FOR THE ARTS   **YEAR BUILT: 1969**   **YEAR RENOVATED: 1984**

Theatre Location: 27 Front Street East, Toronto, ON M5E 1B4 CANADA
Management Company: St. Lawrence Centre for the Arts

Main Administrative Phone: 416-366-1656
Main Administrative Fax: 416-947-1387
E-mail: program@stlc.com
Website: www.stlc.com
Stage Door Phone: 416-366-1656 x244

SEATING CAPACITY	
Orchestra	531
Dress Circle	319
Boxes	26
Total:	**876**
pit (incl)	49
wheelchair (incl)	16

THEATRE STAFF

General Manager	David Wallett	416-366-1656 x224
Booking	Randy T. Leslie	416-366-1656 x260
Operations	Scott Lawrence	416-366-1656 x256

HOUSE CREW

Electrics	Chris Root	416-366-1656 x249

BOX OFFICE
Computerized
Box Office Manager
     Pauline Friesen   416-366-1656 x239

Outside Ticket Agency
     None

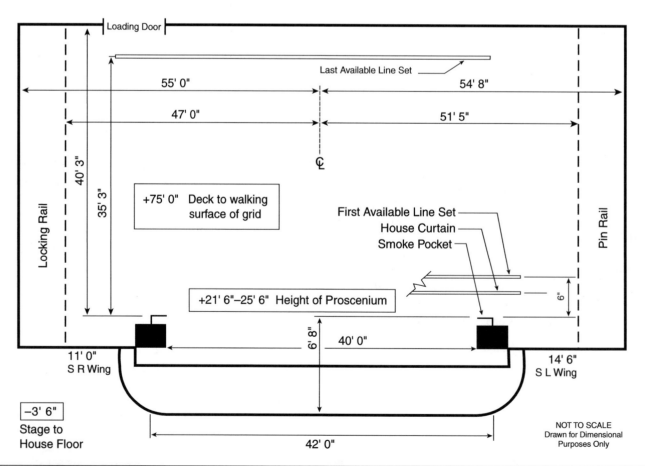

Loading Door

55' 0"   54' 8"
Last Available Line Set

47' 0"   51' 5"

+75' 0" Deck to walking surface of grid

First Available Line Set
House Curtain
Smoke Pocket

40' 3"
35' 3"

Locking Rail   Pin Rail

+21' 6"–25' 6" Height of Proscenium

6"

6' 8"   40' 0"

11' 0"
S R Wing

14' 6"
S L Wing

–3' 6"
Stage to House Floor

42' 0"

NOT TO SCALE
Drawn for Dimensional
Purposes Only

STAGE HOUSE

HOUSE CURTAIN
No house curtain

RIGGING SYSTEM
Type:	Combination purchase counter weight
Line sets:	69 sets at 6" o.c. with 7 lift lines per set
Arbors:	1,170 lb capacity
House Pipes:	70' long with 70' of travel from deck

Line sets are not moveable
Block & Falls are available
Chain hoists are not available
(36) spot wheels and 3,000' of hemp available

PERMANENT INSTALLATIONS OVER STAGE (FROM SMOKE POCKET)
M=Moveable with advance call
Electric raceway (1) at 2'0"; M
Traveller (1); M
Electric pipe (1) at 2'0"; M
Dead spaces (1) at 2'6"
Hard portal (1) at 1'0"
Fire curtain (1) at 0'6"

PERMANENT INSTALLATIONS ON DECK
Traps (48) 3'9" x 4'0" each

ORCHESTRA PIT
Adjustable to 8'6" below stage level by electric motor
  turnscrew
Apron overhangs US wall of pit 0'0"

BACKSTAGE

LOADING DOCK
Loading door(s):
  10'0" high x 10'0" wide
Trucks load (1) at a time
Public alleyway, sideways
  approach to loading doors
Fork lift is not required
Sound/Props can load in FOH
Lobby can be a work area
Trailers cannot store on-site
Security at stage door

WARDROBE
Location: Dressing room
  corridor
Access: Stairs
(2) Washers (2) Dryers
No washer or dryer hookups

DRESSING ROOMS
(7) Small, -1, t/s included
(2) Chorus, -1, t/s included,
  phone jack
Additional production office
  available for company mgr

SOUND

CONSOLE
Allen Heath

SPEAKERS
House Cluster
Proscenium
Under Balcony
Portable
No speaker truss

COMMUNICATIONS
Clear Com intercom with
  (2) channels
Infrared sound system
Dressing room page system

ROAD CONSOLE
Located Rear House right
(20) seats required to be
  removed
Cable run from stage is 150'

REHEARSAL & STORAGE SPACE
Rehearsal: 30' x 52' x 9'9"
  located in basement,
  mirrors, piano, linoleum on
  sprung floor
Storage: None

ELECTRICS

ROAD SERVICE POWER
None

FRONT OF HOUSE (BOX BOOM VALUES ARE PER SIDE)

Position	Pipe Width	Distance to Prosc.	House Circuits	Connector Type	FOH Transfer Circuits
Chandelier			70	20 amp twistlock	0
1st Cove		30'		20 amp twistlock	0
2nd Cove		45'		20 amp twistlock	0
3rd Cove		70'		20 amp twistlock	0
Box Boom 1		30'	18	20 amp twistlock	0
Box Boom 2		45'	18	20 amp twistlock	0
Box Boom 3		70'	18	20 amp twistlock	0

EQUIPMENT FOH (BOX BOOM VALUES ARE PER SIDE)

Position	Quantity	Wattage	Instrument	Removeable
1st Cove	34	1,000	Berkey Zoom	yes
2nd Cove	34	1,000	Berkey	yes
Box Boom 1	18	1,000	Berkey	yes

FOLLOWSPOTS
House Followspots:
  (2) Strong Xenon Super
  Trouper; not removeable

Followspot Booth:
  (2) spots per booth;
  85' throw to proscenium

DIMMERS
Lighting console is Strand
  530;
(350) EC Quads dimmers
House has programmable
  DMX control system
(1) dry run DMX station, SL

WINTER GARDEN THEATRE

YEAR BUILT: 1914   **YEAR RENOVATED: 1989**

Theatre Location: 189 Yonge Street, Toronto, ON M5B 1M4 CANADA

Main Administrative Phone: 416-314-2901
Main Administrative Fax: 416-314-3583
E-mail: zehr@heritagefdn.on.ca
Website: www.heritagefdn.on.ca
Stage Door Phone: 416-314-3718

THEATRE STAFF
  General Manager   Richard Mortimer   416-314-2870
  Marketing   Arnie Lappin   416-314-2874
HOUSE CREW
  Director of Production   Howard Thornley   416-314-2894
UNIONS
  IATSE Local #58   Bill Hamilton   416-364-5565
  Wardrobe   Diane Luckett-Reilly 416-461-3903

SEATING CAPACITY
  Orchestra   514
  Boxes   84
  Mezzanine   172
  Balcony   222
  Total: **992**

BOX OFFICE
  Box Office Manager
    Paul MacFarlane   416-314-2883

  Outside Ticket Agency
    Ticketmaster   416-872-5555

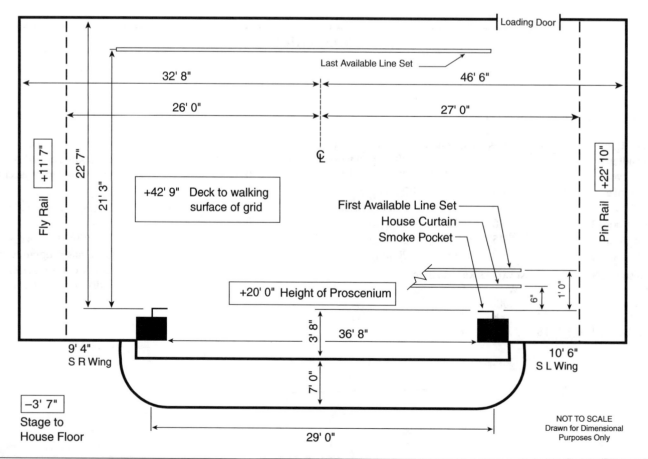

STAGE HOUSE

HOUSE CURTAIN
Operates as a guillotine from SR fly floor

RIGGING SYSTEM
Type:	Hemp System
Weight:	2,250 lbs available
Line sets:	22 sets at 8" o.c. with 5 lift lines per set
Line sets:	500 lb capacity; motorized lines sets (10) are available interspersed in hemp sets (1,000 lb capacity)
House Pipes:	40' long with 40' of travel from deck

Line sets are moveable
Block & Falls are available
(150) spot wheels and 1,800' of hemp available

PERMANENT INSTALLATIONS OVER STAGE (FROM SMOKE POCKET)
None

PERMANENT INSTALLATIONS ON DECK
Jumps located on DSR & DSL prosenium wall - 11'0" high

ORCHESTRA PIT
Nonadjustable at 7' below stage level
Extension over pit is available

BACKSTAGE

LOADING DOCK
Loading door(s):
8'0" high x 8'0" wide
Trucks load (1) at a time
Dock, loading door sill, is at street level 6 floors below stage level accessed by 18' high x 8' wide x 12' long freight elevator with 8,000 lb capacity

WARDROBE
Location: USL behind stage on stage level
Access: Freight elevator
(2) Washers (2) Dryers

DRESSING ROOMS
(2) Star, USR, stage level, t/s included
(4) Small, (2) USR/(2) behind stage, t/s included
(2) Chorus, USR, behind stage, t/s included

SOUND

CONSOLE
Allen & Heath SR 416
16 inputs, 4 main outputs

SPEAKERS
House Cluster

COMMUNICATIONS
Clear Com intercom with (2) channels
FM hearing augmentation system
Dressing room page system

ROAD CONSOLE
Located Rear House
No seats required to be removed
Cable run from stage is 100'
Tie in into house system with XLR connectors

REHEARSAL & STORAGE SPACE
Rehearsal: 50' x 50' located behind stage on 5th fl, piano available; prior arrangement required
Storage: 20' x 20' located behind stage

ELECTRICS

ROAD SERVICE POWER

Panel	Phase	Amp	Circuit Protection	Use	Location
A	3	400	breaker	dimmers	SR off fly floor
B	3	400	breaker	extra	SR off fly floor
C	3	100	breaker	sound	USL back wall
D	3	60	breaker	extra	USR side wall

Recommended location of touring dimmer racks: SR dimmer room off fly floor
Hoist required but not provided

FRONT OF HOUSE (BOX BOOM VALUES ARE PER SIDE)

Position	Pipe Width	Distance to Prosc.	House Circuits	Connector Type	FOH Transfer Circuits
1st Balc Rail	80'	40'	30	grd 20 amp stage pin	30
Box Boom 1		8'	12	grd 20 amp stage pin	12
Box Boom 2		12'	6	grd 20 amp stage pin	6
Box Boom 3		40'	8	grd 20 amp stage pin	8

Transfer circuits: grd 20 amp stage pin located in SR dimmer room off fly floor
Road truss: Additional FOH hanging positions are comprised of (4) 34' long pipes running at right angle to front of stage located over house each with (16) circuits

EQUIPMENT FOH (BOX BOOM VALUES ARE PER SIDE)
None

FOLLOWSPOTS
House Followspots:
None

Followspot Booth:
(2) spots per booth;
84' throw to proscenium;
(2) 1Ø 30 amp breakers
(2) 1Ø 20 amp breakers

DIMMERS
Lighting console is Strand 36 Channel Matrix;
(72) CD80 dimmers

THEATRE MAISONNEUVE

AT: Societe de la Place des Arts de Montreal   **Year built: 1967**

Theatre Location: 1410 St-Urbain, Montreal, QC H2X 1Y9
Mailing Address: 260 De Maisonneuve Ouest, Montreal, QC H2X 1Y9

Main Administrative Phone: 514-285-4200
Main Administrative Fax: 514-285-1968
E-mail: info@pda.qc.ca
Website: www.pda.qc.ca
Stage Door Phone: 514-285-4204
Backstage Pay Phone: 514-285-4347
Traveling Production Office Phone: 514-285-4300
Traveling Production Office Fax: 514-285-2354

Theatre Staff
Director General   France Fortin   514-285-4213
Booking   Isabelle Beaupre   514-285-4360
Marketing   Danielle Champagne   514-285-4271
Operations   Guy Primeau   514-285-4348

House Crew
Technical Director   Luc Gendron   514-285-4362
Carpentry   Daniel Desjardins   514-285-4295
Electrics   Pierre Desrochers   514-285-4341
Sound   Rejean Drolet   514-285-5317
Props   Jean-Claude Bergevin 514-285-4353

Unions
IATSE Local #56   Glenn Woo   514-844-7233
Wardrobe Local #863   Pierre A. Marcoux   514-837-9887

Seating Capacity
Parterre   819
Corbeille   339
Balcony   295
Total: **1,453**

pit (incl)   58

Box Office
Computerized
Director
  Andree Dubuc   514-285-4245

Outside Ticket Agency
Computerized
Admission
  Andree Dubuc   514-790-1245

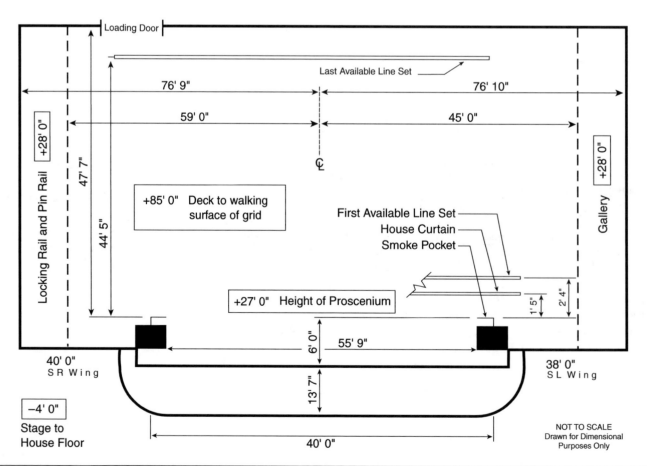

STAGE HOUSE

HOUSE CURTAIN
Operates as a guillotine from SR deck; motorized

RIGGING SYSTEM
Type:	Double purchase counter weight
Weight:	50,000 lbs available
Line sets:	72 sets at 8" o.c. with 5 lift lines per set
Arbors:	1,150 lb capacity
House Pipes:	70' long with 80' of travel from deck

Line sets are not moveable
Block & Falls are available 2:1 (4)
Chain hoists are not available
(50) spot wheels and 10,000' of hemp available

PERMANENT INSTALLATIONS OVER STAGE (FROM SMOKE POCKET)
Orchestra shells (3) at 4'0", 11'6", 20'6"
Movie screen (1), at 12'8"
Travelers (2) at 17'7", 31'5"
Electric bridge (1) at 4'7" (70" wide)
Scoop bar (1) at 38'0"
Cyclorama (1) at 44'5"

PERMANENT INSTALLATIONS ON DECK
None

ORCHESTRA PIT
Adjustable to 15' below stage level by hydraulic lift
Apron overhangs US wall of pit 4'0"
Pit lift is in (2) sections

BACKSTAGE

LOADING DOCK
Loading door(s):
9'10" high x 9'9" wide
Trucks load (2) side by side at same time
Dock is at street level, 2 floors below stage, accessed by 11' high x 11' wide x 25' long freight elevator
Fork lift is not required
Sound/Props cannot load in FOH
(2) Trailers can store on-site
Security at dock & stage door

WARDROBE
Location: USR on stage level
Access: Direct from stage
(1) Washer (1) Dryer

DRESSING ROOMS
(1) Star, behind stage, stage level, t/s included, phone jack
(9) Small, behind stage, stage level / -1, t/s included
(2) Chorus, behind stage, +2 / +3, t/s included
Elevator access for dressing rooms
Additional production office available for company mgr

SOUND

CONSOLE
Soundcraft Vienna II, located Rear House
40 inputs, 2 main outputs, 8 aux outputs

SPEAKERS
House Cluster
Proscenium
Under Balcony
Speaker truss exists
Max available load 1,000 lbs each side

COMMUNICATIONS
Clear Com intercom with (2) channels
Dressing room page system

ROAD CONSOLE
Located Rear House
(6) seats required to be removed
Cable run from stage is 150'
Tie-in into house system with XLR connectors

REHEARSAL & STORAGE SPACE
Rehearsal: Various areas exist for rehearsal; piano available; prior arrangement required
Storage: 20' x 15' at SR, one level below stage

ELECTRICS

ROAD SERVICE POWER
Panel	Phase	Amp	Circuit Protection	Use	Location
A	3	400	breaker	dimmers	SL
B	3	100	breaker	sound	SL

Recommended location of touring dimmer racks: SL on deck
Hoist not required

FRONT OF HOUSE (BOX BOOM VALUES ARE PER SIDE)
Position	Pipe Width	Distance to Prosc.	House Circuits	Connector Type	FOH Transfer Circuits
1st Cove	70'	30'	22	grd 20 amp stage pin	0
2nd Cove	70'	56'	22	grd 20 amp stage pin	0
Truss	50'	2'	18	grd 20 amp stage pin	0
Term 1		6'	8	grd 20 amp stage pin	0
Term 2			16	grd 20 amp stage pin	0

EQUIPMENT FOH (BOX BOOM VALUES ARE PER SIDE)
Position	Quantity	Wattage	Instrument	Removeable
1st Cove	18	1,000	6 x 16 Lekos	no
2nd Cove	24	2,000	8 x 9 Lekos	no
Truss	24	1,000	6 x 12 Par/Lekos	no
Term 1	8	1,000	Source 4 19°	no
Term 2	8	1,000	Source 4 26°	no

FOLLOWSPOTS
House Followspots:
(2) Xenon Super Trouper 1k; not removeable

Followspot Booth:
(2) spots per booth;
110' throw to proscenium;
1Ø 100 amp breakers

DIMMERS
Lighting console is Kliegl
House has own dimmers
Manual Control (separated from board)
House has programmable DMX control system,
Plugging stations SL/SR going to board

SHIRLEY BELL THEATRE

AT: SASKATCHEWAN CENTRE OF THE ARTS FORMERLY: CENTENNIAL THEATRE   YEAR BUILT: **1970**   YEAR RENOVATED: **1998**

Theatre Location: 200 Lakeshore Drive, Regina, SK S4P 3V7

Main Administrative Phone: 306-565-4500
Main Administrative Fax: 306-565-4567
E-mail: centre.arts@sk.symatico.ca
Stage Door Phone: 306-565-4515
Traveling Production Office Phone: 306-585-8833
Traveling Production Office Fax: 306-585-8834

THEATRE STAFF
Executive Director   Jim McCrum   306-565-4500
Theatre Services Mgr   Neil Donnelly   306-565-4567

HOUSE CREW
Operations Manager   Jerry Simko   306-565-4519
Carpentry   David Stettner   306-565-4529
Electrics   Harvey Volhoffer   306-565-4500

SEATING CAPACITY
Orchestra	1,143
Grand Circle	268
Second Balcony	264
Third Balcony	250
Private Suites	10
Total:	**1,935**
pit (add'l)	92
wheelchair (add'l)	6

STAGE DIMENSIONS (FROM SMOKE POCKET)
Stage is 59'9" deep
Width from Center Line to SL is 85'8"
Width from Center Line to SR is 85'8"
Proscenium width is 35'0"
Proscenium height is 30'0"
Smoke pocket to apron edge is 6'0"
Orchestra pit exists

RIGGING
Type:	Double purchase counter weight
Weight:	20,000 lbs
Line sets:	60 sets at 8" o.c.
Arbors:	950 lb capacity
House Pipes:	75' long

LOADING DOCK
Loading door(s) are 15'0" high x 12'0" wide
Trucks load (3) at same time
Fork lift is not required and is available

ELECTRICS
Total power available:
    (3) 400A 3Ø SR
    (1) 200A 3Ø SL

FOLLOWSPOTS
House Followspots:
    Xenon Super Trouper
Power in spot booth
FOH transfer circuits: 10

DIMMERS
(300) house dimmers
House has DMX control system
(2) dry run station(s) located
    SR / FOH

SOUND
House has dedicated power
FOH mixing position in
    Rear Orchestra
Sound console is available

THEATRES UNDER RENOVATION

Civic Center Music Hall
201 Channing Square
Oklahoma City, OK 73102
Contact: James Brown
Phone: 405-733-7960
Capacity: 2,500
Scheduled to reopen: March, 2001

Morris Performing Arts Center
Formerly: Morris Civic Auditorium,
211 North Michigan Street
South Bend, IN 46601
Contact: Denise Chambers
Phone: 219-235-5901
Fax: 219-235-5945
Capacity: 2,464
Scheduled to reopen: November 5, 1999

Music Hall,
Houston, TX
will re-open as
Hobby Center for the Performing Arts
Contact: Bud Franks, President/CEO
           Houston Music Hall Foundation
Phone: 713-227-2001
Fax: 713-227-2021
Capacity: 2,650
Scheduled to reopen: January, 2002

Radio City Music Hall
1260 Avenue of the Americas
New York, NY 10020
Phone: 212-632-4000
Capacity: 5,874 (1990)
Scheduled to reopen: Fall, 1999

Vanderburgh Auditorium
715 Locust Street
Evansville, IN 47708
Phone: 812-435-5770
Capacity: 2,500
Scheduled to reopen: 2001

THEATRES: ALPHABETICAL INDEX

THEATRE	CITY, STATE	PAGE
Abilene Civic Center	Abilene, TX	531
Abraham Chavez Theatre	El Paso, TX	542
Academy of Music	Philadelphia, PA	481
Adler Theatre	Davenport, IA	208
Ahmanson Theatre	Los Angeles, CA	40
Alabama Theatre, The	Birmingham, AL	3
Alaska Center for the Performing Arts		
see Evangeline Atwood Concert Hall		10
Alberta Bair Theater	Billings, MT	296
Alice and George Brown Theater	Houston, TX	
see Brown Theater, The		550
Allen Theatre	Cleveland, OH	434
Alvin Theatre		
see Neil Simon Theatre		380
Ambassador Theatre	New York, NY	332
Andrew Jackson Hall	Nashville, TN	526
Annenberg Center for the Performing Arts	Philadelphia, PA	482
Arie Crown Theatre	Chicago, IL	166
Arlene Schnitzer Concert Hall	Portland, OR	468
Aronoff Center for the Arts		
see Proctor & Gamble Hall		432
Assembly Hall	Champaign, IL	164
AT&T Centre for the Performing Arts		
see Pantages Theatre		624
Atlanta Civic Center Theater	Atlanta, GA	150
Auditorium Center	Rochester, NY	404
Auditorium Theatre	Chicago, IL	168
Auditorium Theatre	Denver, CO	82
Augusta Richmond County Civic Center Complex		
see William Bell Auditorium		154
Au-Rene Theatre		
see Broward Center for the Performing Arts		112
Aycock Auditorium	Greensboro, NC	423
B.F. Moss's Colony Theatre		
see Broadway Theatre		340
Barbara B. Mann Performing Arts Hall	Fort Myers, FL	116
Barrymore Theatre		
see Ethel Barrymore Theatre		348
Bass Concert Hall	Austin, TX	532
Bayfront Center		
see Mahaffey Theater for the Performing Arts		138
Bayfront Plaza Auditorium	Corpus Christi, TX	537
Belasco Theatre	New York, NY	334
Bell Auditorium		
see William Bell Auditorium		154
Benedum Center	Pittsburgh, PA	490
Billy Rose		
see Nederlander Theater		378
Birmingham-Jefferson Concert Hall	Birmingham, AL	4
Blaisdell Center		
see Neal S. Blaisdell Center Concert Hall		158
Blockbuster-Sony Music Entertainment Centre	Camden, NJ	309
Blumenthal Center: Belk Theater	Charlotte, NC	418
Bob Carr Performing Arts Center	Orlando, FL	130
Bob Hope Cultural Center		
see McCallum Theatre for the Performing Arts, The		55
Boise State University		
see Morrison Center for the Performing Arts		160
Booth Theatre	New York, NY	336
Braden Auditorium	Normal, IL	185
Briar Street Theater	Chicago, IL	171
Broadhurst Theatre	New York, NY	338
Broadway at the Beach *see Palace Theater at Myrtle Beach*		515
Broadway Theatre	New York, NY	340
Brooklyn Academy of Music: Majestic Theater	Brooklyn, NY	325
Brooklyn Academy of Music: Opera House	Brooklyn, NY	326
Brooks Atkinson Theatre	New York, NY	342
Broome County Forum Theatre	Binghamton, NY	323
Broward Center for the Performing Arts	Fort Lauderdale, FL	112
Brown Theater, The	Houston, TX	550
Brown Theatre	Louisville, KY	224
Bushnell, The	Hartford, CT	88
Butler University		
see Clowes Memorial Hall		200
Byham Theater	Pittsburgh, PA	492
Capitol Music Hall	Wheeling, WV	587
Capitol Theatre	Columbus, OH	444
Capitol Theatre	Salt Lake City, UT	566
Carol Morsani Hall		
see Tampa Bay Performing Arts Center		144
Carpenter Center for the Performing Arts	Richmond, VA	572
Cashman Theatre	Las Vegas, NV	302
Centennial Concert Hall	Winnipeg, MB	608
Centennial Hall	Tucson, AZ	18
Centennial Theatre	Regina, SK	
see Shirley Bell Theatre		639
Centre in the Square, The	Kitchener, ON	610
Centroplex Theatre for Performing Arts	Baton Rouge, LA	230
Centroplex	Orlando, FL	
see Bob Carr Performing Arts Center		130
Cerritos Center for the Performing Arts	Cerritos, CA	28
Chanin's 46th Street Theatre		
see Richard Rodgers Theatre		386
Chapman Music Hall	Tulsa, OK	464
Charlotte Performing Arts Center		
see Blumenthal Center: Belk Theater		418
Chester Fritz Auditorium	Grand Forks, ND	431
Cheyenne Civic Center	Cheyenne, WY	598
Chicago Theatre	Chicago, IL	172
Christopher Cohan Performing Arts Center		
see Harman Hall		75
Chrysler Hall	Norfolk, VA	570
City Center	New York, NY	344
City of Sacramento Convention Center		
see Sacramento Community Center Theatre		58
Civic Auditorium		
see Fred Kavli Theatre for the Performing Arts		76
Civic Center Music Hall (Renovation)	Oklahoma City, OK	640
Civic Center of Greater Des Moines	Des Moines, IA	210

THEATRE	CITY, STATE	PAGE	THEATRE	CITY, STATE	PAGE
Civic Center			Ford Centre for the Performing		
see Abraham Chavez Theatre		542	Arts	Toronto, ON	618
Civic Opera House	Chicago, IL	174	Forrest Theatre	Philadelphia, PA	484
Classic Center Theatre, The	Athens, GA	149	Fort Worth Convention Center		
Clemens Center Powers			see John F. Kennedy Theatre		544
Theatre	Elmira, NY	331	Fox Theatre	Detroit, MI	260
Cleveland Convention Center			Fox Theatre	Saint Louis, MO	290
see Music Hall		437	Fox Theatre, The	Atlanta, GA	152
Clowes Memorial Hall	Indianapolis, IN	200	Foxwoods Casino: The		
Colonial Theatre, The	Boston, MA	244	Fox Theatre	Mashantucket, CT	91
Community Arts Center	Williamsport, PA	503	Francis Pew Hayes Hall		
Coral Springs City Centre	Coral Springs, FL	111	see Philharmonic Center of the Arts		128
Cort Theatre	New York, NY	346	Fred Kavli Theatre for the		
Crook & Chase Theatre	Myrtle Beach, SC	512	Performing Arts	Thousand Oaks, CA	76
Crouse Performance Hall	Lima, OH	459	Fresno Convention Center		
Crouse-Hinds Concert Theatre	Syracuse, NY	408	see Saroyan Theatre		34
Cullen Theater	Houston, TX	552	Fulton Theater		
Curran Theatre	San Francisco, CA	64	see Byham Theater		492
Denver Performing Arts Complex			Gaillard Municipal Auditorium	Charleston, SC	506
see Auditorium Theatre		82	Gatlin Brothers Theatre, The		
Denver Performing Arts Complex			see Crook & Chase Theatre		512
see Temple Hoyne Buell Theatre		84	Geary Theatre	San Francisco, CA	66
Detroit Opera House	Detroit, MI	256	Gershwin Theatre	New York, NY	354
Devos Hall	Grand Rapids, MI	268	Golden Gate Theatre	San Francisco, CA	68
Duluth Entertainment			Grady Gammage Memorial		
Convention Center	Duluth, MN	272	Auditorium	Tempe, AZ	16
Edison Community College			Grand 1894 Opera House, The	Galveston, TX	549
see Barbara B. Mann Performing Arts Hall		116	Grand Center		
Eisenhower Auditorium	University Park, PA	498	see Devos Hall		268
Eisenhower Hall Theatre	West Point, NY	414	Greensboro Coliseum Complex		
Eisenhower Theatre	Washington, DC	100	see War Memorial Auditorium		424
El Paso Convention & Performing Arts Center			Gusman Center for the		
see Abraham Chavez Theatre		542	Performing Arts	Miami, FL	125
Elgin Theatre	Toronto, ON	616	Hammons Hall	Springfield, MO	294
Embassy Theatre	Fort Wayne, IN	196	Hancher Auditorium	Iowa City, IA	212
Emens Auditorium	Muncie, IN	204	Harman Hall	San Luis Obispo, CA	75
Erie Civic Center Complex			Harms Theater		
see Warner Theatre		474	see John Harms Center for the Arts		311
Ervin J. Nutter Center	Dayton, OH	453	Hartford Theatre Los Angeles		
Ethel Barrymore Theatre	New York, NY	348	see James W. Doolittle Theatre		44
Eugene O'Neill Theatre	New York, NY	350	Heinz Hall for the		
Evangeline Atwood Concert			Performing Arts	Pittsburgh, PA	494
Hall	Anchorage, AK	10	Helen Hayes Theatre	New York, NY	356
F.M. Kirby Center for the			Henry B. Gonzales Convention Center		
Performing Arts	Wilkes-Barre, PA	501	see Lila Cockrell Theater		561
Fabulous Fox, The			Henry Fonda Theatre	Los Angeles, CA	42
see Fox Theatre		290	Hershey Theatre	Hershey, PA	476
Fantasy Harbour			Heymann Performing		
see Crook & Chase Theatre		512	Arts Center	Lafayette, LA	232
Fifth 5th Avenue Theatre, The	Seattle, WA	578	Historic State Theatre	Minneapolis, MN	274
Fisher Auditorium	Indiana, PA	479	Hult Center for the		
			Performing Arts	Eugene, OR	466
Fisher Theatre	Detroit, MI	258	Hummingbird Centre for the		
Fitzgerald Theatre, The	St. Paul, MN	280	Performing Arts	Toronto, ON	620
Flint Center for the Performing			Ike Hall		
Arts	Cupertino, CA	33	see Eisenhower Hall Theatre		414
Florida Theatre	Jacksonville, FL	118	Illinois State University		
Ford Center for the Performing			see Braden Auditorium		185
Arts	New York, NY	352	Imperial Theatre	New York, NY	358
Ford Center for the Performing			Indiana University Auditorium	Bloomington, IN	194
Arts, Oriental Theatre	Chicago, IL	176	Indiana University of Pennsylvania		
Ford Centre for the			see Fisher Auditorium		479
Performing Arts	Vancouver, BC	604	Iowa State University		
			see Stephens Auditorium		207

THEATRE	CITY, STATE	PAGE	THEATRE	CITY, STATE	PAGE
Jackie Gleason Theater of Performing Arts, The	Miami Beach, FL	126	Longacre Theatre	New York, NY	362
Jackson Hall			Louisville Palace Theatre	Louisville, KY	228
see *Andrew Jackson Hall*		526	Lowell Memorial Auditorium	Lowell, MA	253
Jackson Municipal Auditorium:			Lubbock Municipal Auditorium	Lubbock, TX	556
Thalia Maria Hall	Jackson, MS	285	Lunt-Fontanne Theater	New York, NY	364
Jacksonville Civic Auditorium			Lutcher Theater	Orange, TX	559
see *Moran Theater*		120	Lyceum Theatre	New York, NY	366
James K. Polk Theatre	Nashville, TN	529	Lyric Opera House	Baltimore, MD	240
James W. Doolittle Theatre	Los Angeles, CA	44	Macauley Theatre		
James W. Miller Auditorium	Kalamazoo, MI	270	see *Brown Theatre*		224
John F. Kennedy Center for the Performing Arts, The			Macky Auditorium Concert Hall	Boulder, CO	79
see *Eisenhower Theatre*		100	Macomb Center for the Performing Arts	Clinton Township, MI	255
John F. Kennedy Center for the Performing Arts, The			Madison Civic Center		
see *Opera House*		104	see *Oscar Mayer Theatre*		590
John F. Kennedy Theatre	Fort Worth, TX	544	Madison Square Garden		
John Golden Theatre	New York, NY	360	see *Theater at Madison Square Garden, The*		394
John Harms Center for the Arts	Englewood, NJ	311	Mahaffey Theater for the Performing Arts	Saint Petersburg, FL	138
Johnny Mercer Theatre	Savannah, GA	156	Majestic Theatre	New York, NY	368
Jones Hall for the Performing Arts	Houston, TX	554	Majestic Theatre	San Antonio, TX	562
Juanita K. Hammons Hall			Majestic Theatre, The	Dallas, TX	538
see *Hammons Hall*		294	Marcus Center for the Performing Arts		
Kansas City Convention & Entertainment Centers			see *Uihlein Hall*		596
see *Municipal Auditorium Music Hall*		286	Marquis Theatre	New York, NY	370
Kansas City University			Martin Beck Theatre	New York, NY	372
see *McCain Auditorium*		219	Masonic Temple Theatre	Detroit, MI	262
Kennedy Center			Masonic Temple, The		
see *Eisenhower Theatre*		100	see *Scranton Cultural Center*		496
Kennedy Center			Massey Hall	Toronto, ON	623
see *Opera House*		104	McCain Auditorium	Manhattan, KS	219
Kentucky Center for the Performing Arts	Louisville, KY	226	McCallum Theatre for the Performing Arts, The	Palm Desert, CA	55
Kingsbury Hall	Salt Lake City, UT	568	Memorial Auditorium		
Kirby Center			see *Tivoli Theatre*		520
see *F.M. Kirby Center for the Performing Arts*		501	Memorial Auditorium	Chattanooga, TN	518
Knoxville Civic Auditorium	Knoxville, TN	522	Memorial Auditorium		
Krannert Center for the Performing Arts			see *Wichita Falls Memorial Auditorium*		565
see *Tryon Festival Theatre*		193	Memorial Hall		
Kravis Center			see *Montgomery County's Memorial Hall*		454
see *Raymond F. Kravis Center for the Performing Arts*		146	Memorial Union		
Lakeland Center, The			see *Wisconsin Union Theater*		593
see *Youkey Theatre at the Lakeland Center*		123	Merriam Theatre	Philadelphia, PA	486
Lakeside Center\McCormick Place			Michigan State University		
see *Arie Crown Theatre*		166	see *Wharton Center for Performing Arts*		266
Landmark Theater			Milton S. Eisenhower Auditorium		
see *Richmond's Landmark Theater*		575	see *Eisenhower Auditorium*		498
Landmark Theatre			Minskoff Theatre	New York, NY	374
see *Syracuse Area Landmark Theatre*		411	Mobile Civic Center Theatre	Mobile, AL	8
Leon County Civic Center			Monroe Civic Center Theatre	Monroe, LA	235
see *Tallahassee: Leon County Civic Center*		142	Montgomery County's Memorial Hall	Dayton, OH	454
Lexington Opera House			Moran Theater	Jacksonville, FL	120
see *Opera House in Lexington, The*		222	Morris A. Mechanic Theatre	Baltimore, MD	242
Lied Center for Performing Arts	Lincoln, NE	298	Morris Performing Arts Center (Renovation)	South Bend, IN	640
Lied Center	Lawrence, KS	216	Morrison Center for the Performing Arts	Boise, ID	160
Lila Cockrell Theater	San Antonio, TX	561	Mosque, The		
Lillie and Roy Cullen Theater			see *Richmond's Landmark Theater*		575
see *Cullen Theater*		552	Municipal Auditorium		
Lincoln Center Theater			Music Hall	Kansas City, MO	286
see *Vivian Beaumont Theater*		398	MUNY, The	Saint Louis, MO	292
Lincoln Center	Fort Collins, CO	87	Murat Theatre	Indianapolis, IN	202
Little Theatre					
see *Helen Hayes Theatre*		356			
Long Beach Convention Center					
see *Terrace Theatre*		38			

THEATRE	CITY, STATE	PAGE	THEATRE	CITY, STATE	PAGE
Music Box Theatre	New York, NY	376	Paramount Theater		
Music Center of Los Angeles			see Theater at Madison Square Garden, The		394
see Ahmanson Theatre		40	Paramount Theatre	Oakland, CA	53
Music Hall (Renovation)	Houston, TX	640	Paramount Theatre	Seattle, WA	580
Music Hall at Fair Park	Dallas, TX	540	Parker Playhouse	Fort Lauderdale, FL	114
Music Hall Center for the			Pasadena Civic Auditorium	Pasadena, CA	56
Performing Arts	Detroit, MI	265	Peace Center for the		
Music Hall	Cleveland, OH	437	Performing Arts	Greenville, SC	510
Music Hall	Tucson, AZ	20	Penn State University		
National Arts Centre:			see Eisenhower Auditorium		498
Opera Stage	Ottawa, ON	612	Peoria Civic Center Theatre	Peoria, IL	186
National Theatre	Washington, DC	102	Philharmonic Center of		
Neal S. Blaisdell Center			the Arts	Naples, FL	128
Concert Hall	Honolulu, HI	158	Phoenix Civic Plaza		
Nederlander Theater	New York, NY	378	see Symphony Hall		12
Neil Simon Theatre	New York, NY	380	Pikes Peak Center	Colorado Springs, CO	80
New Brunswick Cultural Center			Pioneer Center for the		
see State Theatre New Brunswick		313	Performing Arts	Reno, NV	304
New Jersey Performing Arts Center			Pittsburgh Cultural Trust		
see Prudential Hall		314	see Byham Theater		492
New Mexico State University			Place des Arts		
see Pan American Center		319	see Theatre Maisonneuve		636
Norfolk Cultural and Convention Center			Playhouse Square Center		
see Chrysler Hall		570	see Ohio Theatre		438
North Carolina Blumenthal Performing Arts Center			Playhouse Square Center		
see Blumenthal Center: Belk Theater		418	see Allen Theatre		434
Northern Alberta Jubilee			Playhouse Theatre, The	Wilmington, DE	98
Auditorium	Edmonton, AB	602	Plymouth Theatre	New York, NY	384
Nutter Center			Polk Theatre		
see Ervin J. Nutter Center		453	see James K. Polk Theatre		529
Ohio Theatre	Cleveland, OH	438	Popejoy Hall	Albuquerque, NM	316
Ohio Theatre	Columbus, OH	446	Portland Center for the Performing Arts		
O'Keefe Centre for the Performing Arts			see Arlene Schnitzer Concert Hall		468
see Hummingbird Centre for the Performing Arts		620	Portland Center for the Performing Arts		
Olympia Theater			see Portland Civic Auditorium		470
see Gusman Center for the Performing Arts		125	Portland Civic Auditorium	Portland, OR	470
On Center Complex			Princess of Wales	Toronto, ON	626
see Crouse-Hinds Concert Theatre		408	Probst Theatre		
Opera House in Lexington, The	Lexington, KY	222	see Fred Kavli Theatre for the Performing Arts		76
Opera House	Washington, DC	104	Proctor & Gamble Hall	Cincinnati, OH	432
Opera House: Seattle Center			Proctor's Theatre	Schenectady, NY	406
see Seattle Center Opera House		583	Providence Performing		
Orange County Performing			Arts Center	Providence, RI	504
Arts Center	Costa Mesa, CA	30	Prudential Hall	Newark, NJ	314
Ordway Music Theatre			Queen Elizabeth Theatre	Vancouver, BC	606
Main Hall	St. Paul, MN	282	Radio City Music Hall		
Oriental Theatre			(Renovation)	New York, NY	640
see Ford Center for the Performing Arts, Oriental Theatre		176	Raffi Armenian Theatre		
Orpheum Theatre	Minneapolis, MN	276	see Centre in the Square, The		610
Orpheum Theatre	Omaha, NE	300	Raleigh Convention and Conference Center Complex		
Orpheum Theatre	San Francisco, CA	70	see Raleigh Memorial Auditorium		426
Orpheum Theatre, The	Memphis, TN	524	Raleigh Memorial Auditorium	Raleigh, NC	426
Oscar Mayer Theatre	Madison, WI	590	Raymond F. Kravis Center		
Ovens Auditorium	Charlotte, NC	420	for the Performing Arts	West Palm Beach, FL	146
Palace Theater at Myrtle Beach	Myrtle Beach, SC	515	Rich Forum, The		
Palace Theater, The	Chicago, IL	179	see Truglia Theatre		96
Palace Theatre	Albany, NY	321	Richard B. Baumgardner Center for the Performing Arts		
Palace Theatre	Cleveland, OH	440	see Ruth Eckerd Hall		108
Palace Theatre	Columbus, OH	448	Richard Rodgers Theatre	New York, NY	386
Palace Theatre	Stamford, CT	94	Richmond's Landmark Theater	Richmond, VA	575
Palace Theatre, The	New York, NY	382	Riffe Center		
Pan American Center	Las Cruces, NM	319	see Capitol Theatre		444
Pantages Theatre	Los Angeles, CA	46	Ritz Theatre		
Pantages Theatre	Toronto, ON	624	see Walter Kerr Theatre		400
Paramount Arts Centre	Aurora, IL	163			

THEATRE	CITY, STATE	PAGE	THEATRE	CITY, STATE	PAGE
River Center			Southern Alberta Jubilee		
see Adler Theatre		208	Auditorium	Calgary, AB	600
Riverside Theatre	Milwaukee, WI	594	Southern Theatre	Columbus, OH	450
Roanoke Civic Center			Southwest Missouri State University		
Auditorium	Roanoke, VA	576	*see Hammons Hall*		294
Robinson Center Music Hall	Little Rock, AR	24	Spokane Center		
Rose State Performing Arts			*see Spokane Opera House*		584
Theatre	Midwest City, OK	462	Spokane Opera House	Spokane, WA	584
Rosemont Theatre	Rosemont, IL	188	Spreckels Theatre	San Diego, CA	62
Roy Thomson Hall	Toronto, ON	629	Stamford Center for the Arts		
Royal Alexandra Theatre	Toronto, ON	630	*see Palace Theatre*		94
Royal George Theatre	Chicago, IL	181	Stamford Center for the Arts		
Royal Poinciana Playhouse	Palm Beach, FL	134	*see Truglia Theatre*		96
Royale Theatre	New York, NY	388	Stanley Performing Arts Center	Utica, NY	412
Rudder Auditorium	College Station, TX	535	Starlight Theatre	Kansas City, MO	288
Rushmore Plaza Civic Center			State Theatre Center for the		
Fine Arts Theatre	Rapid City, SD	517	Arts	Easton, PA	473
Ruth Eckerd Hall	Clearwater, FL	108	State Theatre New Brunswick	New Brunswick, NJ	313
Sacramento Community			State Theatre	Cleveland, OH	442
Center Theatre	Sacramento, CA	58	Stephens Auditorium	Ames, IA	207
Saenger Theatre	New Orleans, LA	236	Stevens Center	Winston-Salem, NC	429
Saenger Theatre	Pensacola, FL	137	Stranahan Theater and Great		
St. James Theatre	New York, NY	390	Hall	Toledo, OH	460
St. Lawrence Centre for the			Strand Theatre of Shreveport	Shreveport, LA	238
Arts: Bluma Appel Theatre	Toronto, ON	632	Symphony Hall	Phoenix, AZ	12
Salt Lake Fine Arts Division			Syracuse Area Landmark		
see Capitol Theatre		566	Theatre	Syracuse, NY	411
San Diego Civic Theatre	San Diego, CA	60	T.B. Sheldon Auditorium Theatre		
San Jose Center for the			*see Sheldon Performing Arts Theatre*		279
Performing Arts	San Jose, CA	72	Tallahassee: Leon County		
Sangamon Auditorium	Springfield, IL	190	Civic Center	Tallahassee, FL	142
Saroyan Theatre	Fresno, CA	34	Tampa Bay Performing Arts		
Saskatchewan Centre of the Arts			Center	Tampa, FL	144
see Shirley Bell Theatre		639	Temple Hoyne Buell Theatre	Denver, CO	84
Savannah Civic Center			Tennessee Performing Arts Center		
see Johnny Mercer Theatre		156	*see Andrew Jackson Hall*		526
Scope Center			Tennessee Performing Arts Center		
see Chrysler Hall		570	*see James K. Polk Theatre*		529
Scottish Rite Auditorium	Fort Wayne, IN	199	Terrace Theatre	Long Beach, CA	38
Scottsdale Center for the Arts	Scottsdale, AZ	14	Texas A & M University		
Scranton Cultural Center	Scranton, PA	496	*see Rudder Auditorium*		535
Seattle Center Opera House	Seattle, WA	583	Thalia Maria Hall		
Segerstrom Hall			*see Jackson Municipal Auditorium: Thalia Maria Hall*		285
see Orange County Performing Arts Center		30	Theater at Madison Square		
Shea's Performing Arts Center	Buffalo, NY	328	Garden, The	New York, NY	394
Sheldon Performing Arts			Theatre Maisonneuve	Montreal, QC	636
Theatre	Red Wing, MN	279	Theatre Masque		
Shirley Bell Theatre	Regina, SK	639	*see John Golden Theatre*		360
Shubert Performing Arts			Thousand Oaks Civic Arts Plaza		
Center, The	New Haven, CT	92	*see Fred Kavli Theatre for the Performing Arts*		76
Shubert Theatre	Boston, MA	246	Thunder Bay Community		
Shubert Theatre	Chicago, IL	182	Auditorium	Thunder Bay, ON	615
Shubert Theatre	Los Angeles, CA	48	Times-Union Center for the Performing Arts		
Shubert Theatre	New York, NY	392	*see Moran Theater*		120
Shubert Theatre			Tivoli Theatre	Chattanooga, TN	520
see Merriam Theatre		486	Toledo Masonic Auditorium		
Silva Concert Hall			*see Stranahan Theater and Great Hall*		460
see Hult Center for the Performing Arts		466	Topeka Performing Arts Center	Topeka, KS	221
Sioux City Municipal			Township, The	Columbia, SC	509
Auditorium	Sioux City, IA	215	Trafalgar *see Nederlander Theater*		378
Societe de la Place des Arts de Montreal			Tremont Street Theatre, The		
see Theatre Maisonneuve		636	*see Wilbur Theatre*		250
Soldiers and Sailors Memorial Auditorium			Truglia Theatre	Stamford, CT	96
see Memorial Auditorium		518	Taj Mahal	Atlantic City, NJ	307
			Tryon Festival Theatre	Urbana, IL	193

THEATRE	CITY, STATE	PAGE	THEATRE	CITY, STATE	PAGE
Tucson Convention Center			Western Michigan University		
see Music Hall		20	*see James W. Miller Auditorium*		270
Tulsa Performing Arts Center			Wharton Center for		
see Chapman Music Hall		464	Performing Arts	East Lansing, MI	266
Tupperware Center Theatre	Orlando, FL	132	Whitney Hall		
Uihlein Hall	Milwaukee, WI	596	*see Kentucky Center for the Performing Arts*		226
University of Arizona			Wichita Falls Memorial		
see Centennial Hall		18	Auditorium	Wichita Falls, TX	565
University of Colorado			Wilbur Theatre	Boston, MA	250
see Macky Auditorium Concert Hall		79	Will Rogers Auditorium	Fort Worth, TX	546
University of Illinois			William Bell Auditorium	Augusta, GA	154
see Assembly Hall		164	Wilshire Theatre	Beverly Hills, CA	26
University of Illinois at Springfield			Wiltern Theatre	Los Angeles, CA	51
see Sangamon Auditorium		190	Winter Garden Theatre	New York, NY	402
University of Iowa			Winter Garden Theatre	Toronto, ON	634
see Hancher Auditorium		212	Wisconsin Union Theater	Madison, WI	593
University of Kansas			World Theatre, The		
see Lied Center		216	*see Fitzgerald Theatre, The*		280
University of Nebraska			Wortham Theater Center		
see Lied Center for Performing Arts		298	*see Brown Theater, The*		550
University of New Mexico, Center for the Arts			Wortham Theater Center		
see Popejoy Hall		316	*see Cullen Theater*		552
University of North Carolina at Greensboro			Youkey Theatre at the		
see Aycock Auditorium		423	Lakeland Center	Lakeland, FL	123
University of North Dakota			Zellerbach Theater		
see Chester Fritz Auditorium		431	*see Annenberg Center for the Performing Arts*		482
University of Pennsylvania					
see Annenberg Center for the Performing Arts		482			
University of Texas at Austin Performing Arts Center					
see Bass Concert Hall		532			
University of Wisconsin, Green Bay					
see Weidner Center for the Performing Arts		588			
University of Wisconsin, Madison					
see Wisconsin Union Theater		593			
Uris Theatre					
see Gershwin Theatre		354			
Van Wezel Performing Arts					
Hall	Sarasota, FL	140			
Vancouver Civic Theatre					
see Queen Elizabeth Theatre		606			
Vanderburgh Auditorium					
(Renovation)	Evansville, IN	640			
Velma S. Morrison Center for the Performing Arts, The					
see Morrison Center for the Performing Arts		160			
Veterans Memorial Civic and Convention Center					
see Crouse Performance Hall		459			
Victoria Theatre	Dayton, OH	456			
Virginia Theatre	New York, NY	396			
Vivian Beaumont Theater	New York, NY	398			
Von Braun Center	Huntsville, AL	6			
W.L. Lyons Brown Theatre					
see Brown Theatre		224			
Walnut Street Theatre	Philadelphia, PA	489			
Walter Kerr Theatre	New York, NY	400			
Walton Arts Center	Fayetteville, AR	23			
Wang Center for the					
Performing Arts	Boston, MA	248			
War Memorial Auditorium	Greensboro, NC	424			
Warner Theatre	Erie, PA	474			
Warner Theatre	Washington, DC	106			
Warnors Theatre	Fresno, CA	36			
Weidner Center for the					
Performing Arts	Green Bay, WI	588			
Westbury Music Fair	Westbury, NY	417			

THEATRES: GEOGRAPHICAL INDEX

UNITED STATES THEATRES

STATE, CITY	THEATRE	PAGE	STATE, CITY	THEATRE	PAGE
ALABAMA			CO Denver	Temple Hoyne Buell Theatre	84
AL Birmingham	Alabama Theatre, The	3	CO Fort Collins	Lincoln Center	87
AL Birmingham	Birmingham-Jefferson Concert Hall	4	**CONNECTICUT**		
AL Huntsville	Von Braun Center	6	CT Hartford	Bushnell, The	88
AL Mobile	Mobile Civic Center Theatre	8	CT Mashantucket	Foxwoods Casino: The Fox Theatre	91
ALASKA			CT New Haven	Shubert Performing Arts Center, The	92
AK Anchorage	Evangeline Atwood Concert Hall	10	CT Stamford	Palace Theatre	94
ARIZONA			CT Stamford	Truglia Theatre	96
AZ Phoenix	Symphony Hall	12	**DELAWARE**		
AZ Scottsdale	Scottsdale Center for the Arts	14	DE Wilmington	Playhouse Theatre, The	98
AZ Tempe	Grady Gammage Memorial Auditorium	16	**DISTRICT OF COLUMBIA**		
AZ Tucson	Centennial Hall	18	DC Washington	Eisenhower Theatre	100
AZ Tucson	Music Hall	20	DC Washington	National Theatre	102
ARKANSAS			DC Washington	Opera House	104
AR Fayetteville	Walton Arts Center	23	DC Washington	Warner Theatre	106
AR Little Rock	Robinson Center Music Hall	24	**FLORIDA**		
			FL Clearwater	Ruth Eckerd Hall	108
CALIFORNIA			FL Coral Springs	Coral Springs City Centre	111
CA Beverly Hills	Wilshire Theatre	26	FL Fort Lauderdale	Broward Center for the Performing Arts	112
CA Cerritos	Cerritos Center for the Performing Arts	28	FL Fort Lauderdale	Parker Playhouse	114
CA Costa Mesa	Orange County Performing Arts Center	30	FL Fort Myers	Barbara B. Mann Performing Arts Hall	116
CA Cupertino	Flint Center for the Performing Arts	33	FL Jacksonville	Florida Theatre	118
CA Fresno	Saroyan Theatre	34	FL Jacksonville	Moran Theater	120
CA Fresno	Warnors Theatre	36	FL Lakeland	Youkey Theatre at the Lakeland Center	123
CA Long Beach	Terrace Theatre	38	FL Miami	Gusman Center for the Performing Arts	125
CA Los Angeles	Ahmanson Theatre	40	FL Miami Beach	Jackie Gleason Theater of Performing Arts, The	126
CA Los Angeles	Henry Fonda Theatre	42	FL Naples	Philharmonic Center of the Arts	128
CA Los Angeles	James W. Doolittle Theatre	44	FL Orlando	Bob Carr Performing Arts Center	130
CA Los Angeles	Pantages Theatre	46	FL Orlando	Tupperware Center Theatre	132
CA Los Angeles	Shubert Theatre	48	FL Palm Beach	Royal Poinciana Playhouse	134
CA Los Angeles	Wiltern Theatre	51	FL Pensacola	Saenger Theatre	137
CA Oakland	Paramount Theatre	53	FL St. Petersburg	Mahaffey Theater for the Performing Arts	138
CA Palm Desert	McCallum Theatre for the Performing Arts, The	55	FL Sarasota	Van Wezel Performing Arts Hall	140
CA Pasadena	Pasadena Civic Auditorium	56	FL Tallahassee	Tallahassee: Leon County Civic Center	142
CA Sacramento	Sacramento Community Center Theatre	58	FL Tampa	Tampa Bay Performing Arts Center	144
CA San Diego	San Diego Civic Theatre	60	FL West Palm Beach	Raymond F. Kravis Center for the Performing Arts	146
CA San Diego	Spreckels Theatre	62	**GEORGIA**		
CA San Francisco	Curran Theatre	64	GA Athens	Classic Center Theatre	149
CA San Francisco	Geary Theatre	66	GA Atlanta	Atlanta Civic Center Theater	150
CA San Francisco	Golden Gate Theatre	68	GA Atlanta	Fox Theatre, The	152
CA San Francisco	Orpheum Theatre	70	GA Augusta	William Bell Auditorium	154
CA San Jose	San Jose Center for the Performing Arts	72	GA Savannah	Johnny Mercer Theatre	156
CA San Luis Obispo	Harman Hall	75			
CA Thousand Oaks	Fred Kavli Theatre for the Performing Arts	76			
COLORADO					
CO Boulder	Macky Auditorium Concert Hall	79			
CO Colorado Springs	Pikes Peak Center	80			
CO Denver	Auditorium Theatre	82			

HAWAII

HI Honolulu   Neal S. Blaisdell Center
Concert Hall   158

IDAHO

ID Boise   Morrison Center for the
Performing Arts   160

ILLINOIS

IL Aurora   Paramount Arts Centre   163
IL Champaign   Assembly Hall   164
IL Chicago   Arie Crown Theatre   166
IL Chicago   Auditorium Theatre   168
IL Chicago   Briar Street Theater   171
IL Chicago   Chicago Theatre   172
IL Chicago   Civic Opera House   174
IL Chicago   Ford Center for the Perform-
ing Arts, Oriental Theatre   176
IL Chicago   Palace Theater, The   179
IL Chicago   Royal George Theatre   181
IL Chicago   Shubert Theatre   182
IL Normal   Braden Auditorium   185
IL Peoria   Peoria Civic Center
Theatre   186
IL Rosemont   Rosemont Theatre   188
IL Springfield   Sangamon Auditorium   190
IL Urbana   Tryon Festival Theatre   193

INDIANA

IN Bloomington   Indiana University
Auditorium   194
IN Fort Wayne   Embassy Theatre   196
IN Fort Wayne   Scottish Rite Auditorium   199
IN Indianapolis   Clowes Memorial Hall   200
IN Indianapolis   Murat Theatre   202
IN Muncie   Emens Auditorium   204

IOWA

IA Ames   Stephens Auditorium   207
IA Davenport   Adler Theatre   208
IA Des Moines   Civic Center of Greater
Des Moines   210
IA Iowa City   Hancher Auditorium   212
IA Sioux City   Sioux City Municipal
Auditorium   215

KANSAS

KS Lawrence   Lied Center   216
KS Manhattan   McCain Auditorium   219
KS Topeka   Topeka Performing Arts
Center   221

KENTUCKY

KY Lexington   Opera House in
Lexington, The   222
KY Louisville   Brown Theatre   224
KY Louisville   Kentucky Center for the
Performing Arts   226
KY Louisville   Louisville Palace Theatre   228

LOUISIANA

LA Baton Rouge   Centroplex Theatre for
Performing Arts   230
LA Lafayette   Heymann Performing Arts
Center   232
LA Monroe   Monroe Civic Center
Theatre   235
LA New Orleans   Saenger Theatre   236
LA Shreveport   Strand Theatre of
Shreveport   238

MARYLAND

MD Baltimore   Lyric Opera House   240
MD Baltimore   Morris A. Mechanic
Theatre   242

MASSACHUSETTS

MA Boston   Colonial Theatre, The   244
MA Boston   Shubert Theatre   246
MA Boston   Wang Center for the
Performing Arts   248
MA Boston   Wilbur Theatre   250
MA Lowell   Lowell Memorial
Auditorium   253

MICHIGAN

MI Clinton Township   Macomb Center for the
Performing Arts   255
MI Detroit   Detroit Opera House   256
MI Detroit   Fisher Theatre   258
MI Detroit   Fox Theatre   260
MI Detroit   Masonic Temple Theatre   262
MI Detroit   Music Hall Center for the
Performing Arts   265
MI East Lansing   Wharton Center for
Performing Arts   266
MI Grand Rapids   Devos Hall   268
MI Kalamazoo   James W. Miller
Auditorium   270

MINNESOTA

MN Duluth   Duluth Entertainment
Convention Center   272
MN Minneapolis   Historic State Theatre   274
MN Minneapolis   Orpheum Theatre   276
MN Red Wing   Sheldon Performing Arts
Theatre   279
MN St. Paul   Fitzgerald Theatre, The   280
MN St. Paul   Ordway Music Theatre
Main Hall   282

MISSISSIPPI

MS Jackson   Jackson Municipal Auditorium: Thalia Maria Hall   285

MISSOURI

MO Kansas City   Municipal Auditorium
Music Hall   286
MO Kansas City   Starlight Theatre   288
MO Saint Louis   Fox Theatre   290
MO Saint Louis   MUNY, The   292
MO Springfield   Hammons Hall   294

MONTANA

MT Billings   Alberta Bair Theater   296

NEBRASKA

NE Lincoln   Lied Center for
Performing Arts   298
NE Omaha   Orpheum Theatre   300

NEVADA

NV Las Vegas   Cashman Theatre   302
NV Reno   Pioneer Center for the
Performing Arts   304

NEW JERSEY

NJ Atlantic City   Trump Taj Mahal   307
NJ Camden   Blockbuster-Sony Music
Entertainment Centre   309
NJ Englewood   John Harms Center for the
Arts   311
NJ New Brunswick   State Theatre New
Brunswick   313
NJ Newark   Prudential Hall   314

NEW MEXICO

NM Albuquerque   Popejoy Hall   316
NM Las Cruces   Pan American Center   319

NEW YORK

NY	Albany	Palace Theatre	321
NY	Binghamton	Broome County Forum Theatre	323
NY	Brooklyn	Brooklyn Academy of Music: Majestic Theater	325
NY	Brooklyn	Brooklyn Academy of Music: Opera House	326
NY	Buffalo	Shea's Performing Arts Center	328
NY	Elmira	Clemens Center Powers Theatre	331
NY	New York	Ambassador Theatre	332
NY	New York	Belasco Theatre	334
NY	New York	Booth Theatre	336
NY	New York	Broadhurst Theatre	338
NY	New York	Broadway Theatre	340
NY	New York	Brooks Atkinson Theatre	342
NY	New York	City Center	344
NY	New York	Cort Theatre	346
NY	New York	Ethel Barrymore Theatre	348
NY	New York	Eugene O'Neill Theatre	350
NY	New York	Ford Center for the Performing Arts	352
NY	New York	Gershwin Theatre	354
NY	New York	Helen Hayes Theatre	356
NY	New York	Imperial Theatre	358
NY	New York	John Golden Theatre	360
NY	New York	Longacre Theatre	362
NY	New York	Lunt-Fontanne Theater	364
NY	New York	Lyceum Theatre	366
NY	New York	Majestic Theatre	368
NY	New York	Marquis Theatre	370
NY	New York	Martin Beck Theatre	372
NY	New York	Minskoff Theatre	374
NY	New York	Music Box Theatre	376
NY	New York	Nederlander Theater	378
NY	New York	Neil Simon Theatre	380
NY	New York	Palace Theatre, The	382
NY	New York	Plymouth Theatre	384
NY	New York	Richard Rodgers Theatre	386
NY	New York	Royale Theatre	388
NY	New York	Saint James Theatre	390
NY	New York	Shubert Theatre	392
NY	New York	Theater at Madison Square Garden, The	394
NY	New York	Virginia Theatre	396
NY	New York	Vivian Beaumont Theater	398
NY	New York	Walter Kerr Theatre	400
NY	New York	Winter Garden Theatre	402
NY	Rochester	Auditorium Center	404
NY	Schenectady	Proctor's Theatre	406
NY	Syracuse	Crouse-Hinds Concert Theatre	408
NY	Syracuse	Syracuse Area Landmark Theatre	411
NY	Utica	Stanley Performing Arts Center	412
NY	West Point	Eisenhower Hall Theatre	414
NY	Westbury	Westbury Music Fair	417

NORTH CAROLINA

NC	Charlotte	Blumenthal Center: Belk Theater	418
NC	Charlotte	Ovens Auditorium	420
NC	Greensboro	Aycock Auditorium	423
NC	Greensboro	War Memorial Auditorium	424
NC	Raleigh	Raleigh Memorial Auditorium	426
NC	Winston-Salem	Stevens Center	429

NORTH DAKOTA

ND	Grand Forks	Chester Fritz Auditorium	431

OHIO

OH	Cincinnati	Proctor & Gamble Hall	432
OH	Cleveland	Allen Theatre	434
OH	Cleveland	Music Hall	437
OH	Cleveland	Ohio Theatre	438
OH	Cleveland	Palace Theatre	440
OH	Cleveland	State Theatre	442
OH	Columbus	Capitol Theatre	444
OH	Columbus	Ohio Theatre	446
OH	Columbus	Palace Theatre	448
OH	Columbus	Southern Theatre	450
OH	Dayton	Ervin J. Nutter Center	453
OH	Dayton	Montgomery County's Memorial Hall	454
OH	Dayton	Victoria Theatre	456
OH	Lima	Crouse Performance Hall	459
OH	Toledo	Stranahan Theater and Great Hall	460

OKLAHOMA

OK	Midwest City	Rose State Performing Arts Theatre	462
OK	Tulsa	Chapman Music Hall	464

OREGON

OR	Eugene	Hult Center for the Performing Arts	466
OR	Portland	Arlene Schnitzer Concert Hall	468
OR	Portland	Portland Civic Auditorium	470

PENNSYLVANIA

PA	Easton	State Theatre Center for the Arts	473
PA	Erie	Warner Theatre	474
PA	Hershey	Hershey Theatre	476
PA	Indiana	Fisher Auditorium	479
PA	Philadelphia	Academy of Music	481
PA	Philadelphia	Annenberg Center for the Performing Arts	482
PA	Philadelphia	Forrest Theatre	484
PA	Philadelphia	Merriam Theatre	486
PA	Philadelphia	Walnut Street Theatre	489
PA	Pittsburgh	Benedum Center	490
PA	Pittsburgh	Byham Theater	492
PA	Pittsburgh	Heinz Hall for the Performing Arts	494
PA	Scranton	Scranton Cultural Center	496
PA	University Park	Eisenhower Auditorium	498
PA	Wilkes-Barre	F.M. Kirby Center for the Performing Arts	501
PA	Williamsport	Community Arts Center	503

RHODE ISLAND

RI	Providence	Providence Performing Arts Center	504

SOUTH CAROLINA

SC	Charleston	Gaillard Municipal Auditorium	506

SC Columbia	Township, The	509
SC Greenville	Peace Center for the Performing Arts	510
SC Myrtle Beach	Crook & Chase Theatre	512
SC Myrtle Beach	Palace Theater at Myrtle Beach	515
SOUTH DAKOTA		
SD Rapid City	Rushmore Plaza Civic Center Fine Arts Theatre	517
TENNESSEE		
TN Chattanooga	Memorial Auditorium	518
TN Chattanooga	Tivoli Theatre	520
TN Knoxville	Knoxville Civic Auditorium	522
TN Memphis	Orpheum Theatre, The	524
TN Nashville	Andrew Jackson Hall	526
TN Nashville	James K. Polk Theatre	529
TEXAS		
TX Abilene	Abilene Civic Center	531
TX Austin	Bass Concert Hall	532
TX College Station	Rudder Auditorium	535
TX Corpus Christi	Bayfront Plaza Auditorium	537
TX Dallas	Majestic Theatre, The	538
TX Dallas	Music Hall at Fair Park	540
TX El Paso	Abraham Chavez Theatre	542
TX Fort Worth	John F. Kennedy Theatre	544
TX Fort Worth	Will Rogers Auditorium	546
TX Galveston	Grand 1894 Opera House	549
TX Houston	Brown Theater, The	550
TX Houston	Cullen Theater	552
TX Houston	Jones Hall for the Performing Arts	554
TX Lubbock	Lubbock Municipal Auditorium	556
TX Orange	Lutcher Theater	559
TX San Antonio	Lila Cockrell Theater	561
TX San Antonio	Majestic Theatre	562
TX Wichita Falls	Wichita Falls Memorial Auditorium	565
UTAH		
UT Salt Lake City	Capitol Theatre	566
UT Salt Lake City	Kingsbury Hall	568
VIRGINIA		
VA Norfolk	Chrysler Hall	570
VA Richmond	Carpenter Center for the Performing Arts	572
VA Richmond	Richmond's Landmark Theater	575
VA Roanoke	Roanoke Civic Center Auditorium	576
WASHINGTON		
WA Seattle	5th Avenue Theatre, The	578
WA Seattle	Paramount Theatre	580
WA Seattle	Seattle Center Opera House	583
WA Spokane	Spokane Opera House	584
WEST VIRGINIA		
WV Wheeling	Capitol Music Hall	587
WISCONSIN		
WI Green Bay	Weidner Center for the 0Performing Arts	588
WI Madison	Oscar Mayer Theatre	590
WI Madison	Wisconsin Union Theater	593
WI Milwaukee	Riverside Theatre	594
WI Milwaukee	Uihlein Hall	596
WYOMING		
WY Cheyenne	Cheyenne Civic Center	598

CANADIAN THEATRES

ALBERTA		
AB Calgary	Southern Alberta Jubilee Auditorium	600
AB Edmonton	Northern Alberta Jubilee Auditorium	602
BRITISH COLUMBIA		
BC Vancouver	Ford Centre for the Performing Arts	604
BC Vancouver	Queen Elizabeth Theatre	606
MANITOBA		
MB Winnipeg	Centennial Concert Hall	608
ONTARIO		
ON Kitchener	Centre in the Square, The	610
ON Ottawa	National Arts Centre: Opera Stage	612
ON Thunder Bay	Thunder Bay Community Auditorium	615
ON Toronto	Elgin Theatre	616
ON Toronto	Ford Centre for the Performing Arts	618
ON Toronto	Hummingbird Centre for the Performing Arts	620
ON Toronto	Massey Hall	623
ON Toronto	Pantages Theatre	624
ON Toronto	Princess of Wales	626
ON Toronto	Roy Thomson Hall	629
ON Toronto	Royal Alexandra Theatre	630
ON Toronto	Saint Lawrence Centre for the Arts: Bluma Appel Theatre	632
ON Toronto	Winter Garden Theatre	634
QUEBEC		
QC Montreal	Theatre Maisonneuve	636
SASKATCHEWAN		
SK Regina	Shirley Bell Theatre	639

THEATRES: CAPACITY INDEX

CAPACITY	THEATRE	CITY/STATE	PAGE
13,000	Pan American Center	Las Cruces, NM	319
12,192	Ervin J. Nutter Center	Dayton, OH	453
10,053	MUNY, The	St. Louis, MO	292
7,860	Starlight Theatre	Kansas City, MO	288
6,590	Blockbuster-Sony Music Entertainment Centre	Camden, NJ	309
5,610	Theater at Madison Square Garden, The	New York, NY	394
4,679	Fox Theatre	Detroit, MI	260
4,645	Sioux City Municipal Auditorium	Sioux City, IA	215
4,591	Atlanta Civic Center Theater	Atlanta, GA	150
4,518	Fox Theatre, The	Atlanta, GA	152
4,404	Masonic Temple Theatre	Detroit, MI	262
4,335	Eisenhower Hall Theatre	West Point, NY	414
4,300	Rosemont Theatre	Rosemont, IL	188
4,249	Arie Crown Theatre	Chicago, IL	166
4,100	Fox Theatre	St. Louis, MO	290
3,866	Memorial Auditorium	Chattanooga, TN	518
3,661	Auditorium Theatre	Chicago, IL	168
3,646	Assembly Hall	Champaign, IL	164
3,616	Richmond's Landmark Theater	Richmond, VA	575
3,611	Wang Center for the Performing Arts	Boston, MA	248
3,563	Civic Opera House	Chicago, IL	174
3,497	James W. Miller Auditorium	Kalamazoo, MI	270
3,457	Braden Auditorium	Normal, IL	185
3,444	Chicago Theatre	Chicago, IL	172
3,420	Music Hall at Fair Park	Dallas, TX	540
3,375	Emens Auditorium	Muncie, IN	204
3,216	Indiana University Auditorium	Bloomington, IN	194
3,200	Township, The	Columbia, SC	509
3,195	Providence Performing Arts Center	Providence, RI	504
3,183	Shea's Performing Arts Center	Buffalo, NY	328
3,167	Hummingbird Centre for the Performing Arts	Toronto, ON	620
3,098	State Theatre	Cleveland, OH	442
3,077	Seattle Center Opera House	Seattle, WA	583
3,000	Music Hall	Cleveland, OH	437
3,000	Portland Civic Auditorium	Portland, OR	470
2,992	Paramount Theatre	Oakland, CA	53
2,975	John F. Kennedy Theatre	Fort Worth, TX	544
2,945	Stanley Performing Arts Center	Utica, NY	412
2,938	Terrace Theatre	Long Beach, CA	38
2,936	Orange County Performing Arts Center	Costa Mesa, CA	30
2,931	Pasadena Civic Auditorium	Pasadena, CA	56
2,929	Grady Gammage Memorial Auditorium	Tempe, AZ	16
2,922	Syracuse Area Landmark Theatre	Syracuse, NY	411
2,896	San Diego Civic Theatre	San Diego, CA	60
2,889	Benedum Center	Pittsburgh, PA	490
2,872	Bass Concert Hall	Austin, TX	532
2,856	Will Rogers Auditorium	Fort Worth, TX	546
2,844	Lowell Memorial Auditorium	Lowell, MA	253
2,842	Prudential Hall	Newark, NJ	314
2,838	Temple Hoyne Buell Theatre	Denver, CO	84
2,835	Academy of Music	Philadelphia, PA	481
2,827	Palace Theatre	Columbus, OH	448
2,824	Moran Theater	Jacksonville, FL	120
2,812	Roy Thomson Hall	Toronto, ON	629
2,807	Orpheum Theatre	Omaha, NE	300
2,807	Palace Theatre	Albany, NY	321
2,803	Paramount Theatre	Seattle, WA	580
2,798	Birmingham-Jefferson Concert Hall	Birmingham, AL	4
2,779	Ohio Theatre	Columbus, OH	446
2,776	Arlene Schnitzer Concert Hall	Portland, OR	468
2,775	Lubbock Municipal Auditorium	Lubbock, TX	556
2,760	Bushnell, The	Hartford, CT	88
2,757	Massey Hall	Toronto, ON	623
2,753	City Center	New York, NY	344
2,745	Jones Hall for the Performing Arts	Houston, TX	554
2,742	Westbury Music Fair	Westbury, NY	417
2,741	Saenger Theatre	New Orleans, LA	236
2,736	Detroit Opera House	Detroit, MI	256
2,732	Gaillard Municipal Auditorium	Charleston, SC	506
2,717	Wichita Falls Memorial Auditorium	Wichita Falls, TX	565
2,713	Southern Alberta Jubilee Auditorium	Calgary, AB	600
2,705	Jackie Gleason Theater of Performing Arts	Miami Beach, FL	126
2,705	Queen Elizabeth Theatre	Vancouver, BC	606
2,700	Proctor's Theatre	Schenectady, NY	406
2,690	William Bell Auditorium	Augusta, GA	154
2,678	Northern Alberta Jubilee Auditorium	Edmonton, AB	602
2,673	Pantages Theatre	Los Angeles, CA	46
2,666	Palace Theatre	Cleveland, OH	440
2,661	Heinz Hall for the Performing Arts	Pittsburgh, PA	494
2,655	Proctor & Gamble Hall	Cincinnati, OH	432
2,653	Civic Center of Greater Des Moines	Des Moines, IA	210
2,623	Louisville Palace Theatre	Louisville, KY	228

2,622	Topeka Performing Arts Center	Topeka, KS	221
2,609	Robinson Center Music Hall	Little Rock, AR	24
2,609	Stephens Auditorium	Ames, IA	207
2,603	Ovens Auditorium	Charlotte, NC	420
2,600	Palace Theater at Myrtle Beach	Myrtle Beach, SC	515
2,579	San Jose Center for the Performing Arts	San Jose, CA	72
2,574	Broward Center for the Performing Arts	Fort Lauderdale, FL	112
2,537	Lyric Opera House	Baltimore, MD	240
2,533	Hancher Auditorium	Iowa City, IA	212
2,527	Auditorium Center	Rochester, NY	404
2,527	Lila Cockrell Theater	San Antonio, TX	561
2,526	Bayfront Plaza Auditorium	Corpus Christi, TX	537
2,526	Orpheum Theatre	Minneapolis, MN	276
2,524	Johnny Mercer Theatre	Savannah, GA	156
2,517	Murat Theatre	Indianapolis, IN	202
2,513	Riverside Theatre	Milwaukee, WI	594
2,506	Warner Theatre	Erie, PA	474
2,501	Montgomery County's Memorial Hall	Dayton, OH	454
2,500	Rudder Auditorium	College Station, TX	535
2,500	Tampa Bay Performing Arts Center	Tampa, FL	144
2,498	Symphony Hall	Phoenix, AZ	12
2,490	Tallahassee: Leon County Civic Center	Tallahassee, FL	142
2,489	Eisenhower Auditorium	University Park, PA	498
2,465	Brown Theater, The	Houston, TX	550
2,458	Roanoke Civic Center Auditorium	Roanoke, VA	576
2,456	Centennial Hall	Tucson, AZ	18
2,452	Allen Theatre	Cleveland, OH	434
2,442	Capitol Music Hall	Wheeling, WV	587
2,440	Bob Carr Performing Arts Center	Orlando, FL	130
2,438	Orpheum Theatre, The	Memphis, TN	524
2,427	Hult Center for the Performing Arts	Eugene, OR	466
2,425	Embassy Theatre	Fort Wayne, IN	196
2,418	Abraham Chavez Theatre	El Paso, TX	542
2,406	Flint Center for the Performing Arts	Cupertino, CA	33
2,406	Kentucky Center for the Performing Arts	Louisville, KY	226
2,400	Knoxville Civic Auditorium	Knoxville, TN	522
2,398	Andrew Jackson Hall	Nashville, TN	526
2,391	Municipal Auditorium Music Hall	Kansas City, MO	286
2,381	Wharton Center for Performing Arts	East Lansing, MI	266
2,376	War Memorial Auditorium	Greensboro, NC	424
2,370	Devos Hall	Grand Rapids, MI	268
2,367	Chapman Music Hall	Tulsa, OK	464
2,367	Duluth Entertainment Convention Center	Duluth, MN	272
2,362	Jackson Municipal Auditorium: Thalia Maria Hall	Jackson, MS	285
2,357	Chrysler Hall	Norfolk, VA	570
2,353	Saroyan Theatre	Fresno, CA	34
2,352	Adler Theatre	Davenport, IA	208
2,343	Aycock Auditorium	Greensboro, NC	423
2,337	Stranahan Theater and Great Hall	Toledo, OH	460
2,336	Palace Theater, The	Chicago, IL	179
2,326	Chester Fritz Auditorium	Grand Forks, ND	431
2,326	Sacramento Community Center Theatre	Sacramento, CA	58
2,305	Centennial Concert Hall	Winnipeg, MB	608
2,304	Golden Gate Theatre	San Francisco, CA	68
2,301	Uihlein Hall	Milwaukee, WI	596
2,286	Wiltern Theatre	Los Angeles, CA	51
2,277	Music Hall	Tucson, AZ	20
2,277	Raleigh Memorial Auditorium	Raleigh, NC	426
2,269	Pantages Theatre	Toronto, ON	624
2,264	Spokane Opera House	Spokane, WA	584
2,263	Majestic Theatre	San Antonio, TX	562
2,249	Ford Center for the Performing Arts, Oriental Theatre	Chicago, IL	176
2,230	Heymann Performing Arts Center	Lafayette, LA	232
2,220	Hammons Hall	Springfield, MO	294
2,210	Lied Center for Performing Arts	Lincoln, NE	298
2,203	Orpheum Theatre	San Francisco, CA	70
2,200	Alabama Theatre, The	Birmingham, AL	3
2,189	Raymond F. Kravis Center for the Performing Arts	West Palm Beach, FL	146
2,186	Youkey Theatre at the Lakeland Center	Lakeland, FL	123
2,177	Peoria Civic Center Theatre	Peoria, IL	186
2,173	Monroe Civic Center Theatre	Monroe, LA	235
2,164	Warnors Theatre	Fresno, CA	36
2,158	Community Arts Center	Williamsport, PA	503
2,155	Brooklyn Academy of Music: Opera House	Brooklyn, NY	326
2,153	Von Braun Center	Huntsville, AL	6
2,147	Scottish Rite Auditorium	Fort Wayne, IN	199
2,146	Opera House	Washington, DC	104
2,135	Historic State Theatre	Minneapolis, MN	274
2,133	Ahmanson Theatre	Los Angeles, CA	40
2,132	Abilene Civic Center	Abilene, TX	531
2,132	National Arts Centre: Opera Stage	Ottawa, ON	612
2,117	Crouse-Hinds Concert Theatre	Syracuse, NY	408
2,115	5th Avenue Theatre	Seattle, WA	578
2,113	Shubert Theatre	Los Angeles, CA	48
2,112	Ruth Eckerd Hall	Clearwater, FL	108
2,106	Clowes Memorial Hall	Indianapolis, IN	200
2,097	Blumenthal Center: Belk Theater	Charlotte, NC	418
2,096	Peace Center for the Performing Arts	Greenville, SC	510
2,091	Oscar Mayer Theatre	Madison, WI	590
2,089	Fisher Theatre	Detroit, MI	258
2,065	Auditorium Theatre	Denver, CO	82
2,053	Classic Center Theatre	Athens, GA	149

2,047	Macky Auditorium Concert Hall	Boulder, CO	79
2,032	Princess of Wales	Toronto, ON	626
2,030	Morrison Center for the Performing Arts	Boise, ID	160
2,024	Evangeline Atwood Concert Hall	Anchorage, AK	10
2,021	Weidner Center for the Performing Arts	Green Bay, WI	588
2,017	Neal S. Blaisdell Center Concert Hall	Honolulu, HI	158
2,008	Shubert Theatre	Chicago, IL	182
2,000	Tupperware Center Theatre	Orlando, FL	132
1,971	Crook & Chase Theatre	Myrtle Beach, SC	512
1,971	Pikes Peak Center	Colorado Springs, CO	80
1,952	Sangamon Auditorium	Springfield, IL	190
1,950	Popejoy Hall	Albuquerque, NM	316
1,944	Lied Center	Lawrence, KS	216
1,942	Cashman Theatre	Las Vegas, NV	302
1,939	Carpenter Center for the Performing Arts	Richmond, VA	572
1,937	Mobile Civic Center Theatre	Mobile, AL	8
1,935	Shirley Bell Theatre	Regina, SK	639
1,933	Gershwin Theatre	New York, NY	354
1,927	Capitol Theatre	Salt Lake City, UT	566
1,914	Florida Theatre	Jacksonville, FL	118
1,913	Kingsbury Hall	Salt Lake City, UT	568
1,908	Mahaffey Theater for the Performing Arts	Saint Petersburg, FL	138
1,907	Ordway Music Theatre Main Hall	St. Paul, MN	282
1,904	Hershey Theatre	Hershey, PA	476
1,903	Centre in the Square, The	Kitchener, ON	610
1,897	Centroplex Theatre for Performing Arts	Baton Rouge, LA	230
1,888	Paramount Arts Centre	Aurora, IL	163
1,868	Wilshire Theatre	Beverly Hills, CA	26
1,839	Forrest Theatre	Philadelphia, PA	484
1,834	Ford Centre for the Performing Arts	Vancouver, BC	604
1,821	Ford Center for the Performing Arts	New York, NY	352
1,816	F.M. Kirby Center for the Performing Arts	Wilkes-Barre, PA	501
1,816	Ford Centre for the Performing Arts	Toronto, ON	618
1,802	Saenger Theatre	Pensacola, FL	137
1,800	Rushmore Plaza Civic Center Fine Arts Theatre	Rapid City, SD	517
1,798	Warner Theatre	Washington, DC	106
1,793	State Theatre New Brunswick	New Brunswick, NJ	313
1,790	Merriam Theatre	Philadelphia, PA	486
1,764	Broadway Theatre	New York, NY	340
1,762	Tivoli Theatre	Chattanooga, TN	520
1,753	Barbara B. Mann Performing Arts Hall	Fort Myers, FL	116
1,752	McCain Auditorium	Manhattan, KS	219
1,740	Palace Theatre, The	New York, NY	382
1,728	Fred Kavli Theatre for the Performing Arts	Thousand Oaks, CA	76
1,713	Curran Theatre	San Francisco, CA	64
1,710	Minskoff Theatre	New York, NY	374
1,709	Gusman Center for the Performing Arts	Miami, FL	125
1,707	Saint James Theatre	New York, NY	390
1,707	Van Wezel Performing Arts Hall	Sarasota, FL	140
1,706	Music Hall Center for the Performing Arts	Detroit, MI	265
1,705	Colonial Theatre, The	Boston, MA	244
1,697	Crouse Performance Hall	Lima, OH	459
1,669	National Theatre	Washington, DC	102
1,649	Shubert Performing Arts Center, The	New Haven, CT	92
1,645	Majestic Theatre	New York, NY	368
1,636	Strand Theatre of Shreveport	Shreveport, LA	238
1,622	Scranton Cultural Center	Scranton, PA	496
1,613	Majestic Theatre, The	Dallas, TX	538
1,608	Clemens Center Powers Theatre	Elmira, NY	331
1,602	Fisher Auditorium	Indiana, PA	479
1,582	Marquis Theatre	New York, NY	370
1,580	Palace Theatre	Stamford, CT	94
1,564	Morris A. Mechanic Theatre	Baltimore, MD	242
1,561	Elgin Theatre	Toronto, ON	616
1,538	Shubert Theatre	Boston, MA	246
1,519	Broome County Forum Theatre	Binghamton, NY	323
1,513	Winter Garden Theatre	New York, NY	402
1,511	Thunder Bay Community Auditorium	Thunder Bay, ON	615
1,500	Pioneer Center for the Performing Arts	Reno, NV	304
1,500	State Theatre Center for the Arts	Easton, PA	473
1,497	Royal Alexandra Theatre	Toronto, ON	630
1,492	Lunt-Fontanne Theater	New York, NY	364
1,490	Cheyenne Civic Center	Cheyenne, WY	598
1,471	Foxwoods Casino: The Fox Theatre	Mashantucket, CT	91
1,466	Spreckels Theatre	San Diego, CA	62
1,453	Theatre Maisonneuve	Montreal, QC	636
1,449	Shubert Theatre	New York, NY	392
1,446	Lutcher Theater	Orange, TX	559
1,438	Coral Springs City Centre	Coral Springs, FL	111
1,437	Martin Beck Theatre	New York, NY	372
1,431	Cerritos Center for the Performing Arts	Cerritos, CA	28
1,418	Alberta Bair Theater	Billings, MT	296
1,417	Imperial Theatre	New York, NY	358
1,405	Rose State Performing Arts Theatre	Oklahoma City, OK	462
1,401	Brown Theatre	Louisville, KY	224
1,380	Stevens Center	Winston-Salem, NC	429
1,377	John Harms Center for the Arts	Englewood, NJ	311
1,368	Richard Rodgers Theatre	New York, NY	386
1,316	Neil Simon Theatre	New York, NY	380
1,282	Harman Hall	San Luis Obispo, CA	75
1,275	Virginia Theatre	New York, NY	396
1,273	Byham Theater	Pittsburgh, PA	492

1,262	Wisconsin Union Theater	Madison, WI	593
1,251	Playhouse Theatre, The	Wilmington, DE	98
1,223	Wilbur Theatre	Boston, MA	250
1,217	Macomb Center for the Performing Arts	Clinton Township, MI	255
1,201	Walton Arts Center	Fayetteville, AR	23
1,200	Parker Playhouse	Fort Lauderdale, FL	114
1,198	Philharmonic Center of the Arts	Naples, FL	128
1,194	Trump Taj Mahal	Atlantic City, NJ	307
1,182	Nederlander Theater	New York, NY	378
1,180	Lincoln Center	Fort Collins, CO	87
1,156	Broadhurst Theatre	New York, NY	338
1,139	Victoria Theatre	Dayton, OH	456
1,129	McCallum Theatre for the Performing Arts	Palm Desert, CA	55
1,108	Eugene O'Neill Theatre	New York, NY	350
1,100	Eisenhower Theatre	Washington, DC	100
1,096	Ethel Barrymore Theatre	New York, NY	348
1,088	Ambassador	New York, NY	332
1,083	Cort Theatre	New York, NY	346
1,079	Longacre Theatre	New York, NY	362
1,078	Walnut Street Theatre	Philadelphia, PA	489
1,073	Vivian Beaumont Theater	New York, NY	398
1,048	Royale Theatre	New York, NY	388
1,044	Brooks Atkinson Theatre	New York, NY	342
1,039	Cullen Theater	Houston, TX	552
1,037	Plymouth Theatre	New York, NY	384
1,029	Geary Theatre	San Francisco, CA	66
1,010	Music Box Theatre	New York, NY	376
1,008	Fitzgerald Theatre, The	St. Paul, MN	280
1,008	Grand 1894 Opera House, The	Galveston, TX	549
1,005	Ohio Theatre	Cleveland, OH	438
999	James K. Polk Theatre	Nashville, TN	529
993	Belasco Theatre	New York, NY	334
992	Winter Garden Theatre	Toronto, ON	634
978	Opera House in Lexington, The	Lexington, KY	222
953	James W. Doolittle Theatre	Los Angeles, CA	44
947	Walter Kerr Theatre	New York, NY	400
929	Tryon Festival Theatre	Urbana, IL	193
914	Annenberg Center for the Performing Arts	Philadelphia, PA	482
913	Lyceum Theatre	New York, NY	366
909	Southern Theatre	Columbus, OH	450
893	Brooklyn Academy of Music: Majestic Theater	Brooklyn, NY	325
878	Royal Poinciana Playhouse	Palm Beach, FL	134
876	Saint Lawrence Centre for the Arts: Bluma Appel Theatre	Toronto, ON	632
863	Henry Fonda Theatre	Los Angeles, CA	42
851	Capitol Theatre	Columbus, OH	444
805	John Golden Theatre	New York, NY	360
773	Scottsdale Center for the Arts	Scottsdale, AZ	14
767	Booth Theatre	New York, NY	336
711	Truglia Theatre	Stamford, CT	96
625	Briar Street Theater	Chicago, IL	171
597	Helen Hayes Theatre	New York, NY	356
475	Sheldon Performing Arts Theatre	Red Wing, MN	279
452	Royal George Theatre Civic Center Music Hall	Chicago, IL	181

PRESENTERS: GUIDE BY NAME

Judith Allen
North Carolina Blumenthal Center
PO Box 37322
Charlotte, NC 28237
704-333-4686 / 704-376-2289 F

Bob Alwine
The Ordway Music Theatre
345 Washington St.
Saint Paul, MN 55102
651-282-3000 / 651-224-5319 F

Ronald Andrew
Eagle Eye Entertainment, Inc.
1220 Yonge St. Ste 300
Toronto, ON CANADA M4T 1W1
416-960-7617 / 416-922-9877 F

Leland Ball
Sacramento Broadway Series
1510 J St Ste 200
Sacramento, CA 95814
916-446-5880 x137 / 916-446-1370 F

John W. Ballard
MagicWorks West
419 East 100 South
Salt Lake City, UT 84111
810-355-2200 / 801-355-2236 F

Rick Barr
Pasadena Civic Auditorium
300 E. Green St.
Pasadena, CA 91101
626-793-2122 / 626-793-8014 F

Alice Bernstein
Brooklyn Academy of Music
30 Lafayette Ave
Brooklyn, NY 11217
718-636-4195 / 718-636-4126 F

James Binger
Jujamcyn Theaters
80 South 8th St.
Minneapolis, MN 55402
612-341-3500 / 612-341-3501 F

Suzanne Bizer
The Shubert Theatre
22 W Monroe St Ste 600
Chicago, IL 60603
312-977-1701 / 312-977-1740 F

Paul Blake
The Municipal Theatre Association of St.
Louis (The Muny)
c/o GFI Productions, 31 Alston Place
Montecito, CA 93108
805-969-9631 / 805-969-7517 F

Elizabeth Bradley
Hummingbird Centre for the Performing Arts
1 Front St East
Toronto, ON M5E 1B2
416-393-7474 / 416-393-7454 F

Michael J. Brand
Baltimore Center for the Performing Arts
One North Charles St.
Baltimore, MD 21201
410-625-4230 / 410-625-4250 F

Bradley L. Broecker
Broadway Series Management Group, Inc.
611 W Main St
Louisville, KY 40202
502-584-7469 x221 / 502-584-2901 F

Carol R. Brown
The Pittsburgh Cultural Trust
125 Seventh St Ste 500
Pittsburgh, PA 15222-3411
412-471-6070 / 412-471-6917 F

Steven C. Callahan
Lincoln Center Theater
150 West 65th St
New York, NY 10023
212-501-3223 / 212-873-0761 F

Cynthia Carter-West
Chrysler Hall
PO Box 1808
Norfolk, VA 23501
757-664-6957 / 757-664-6990 F

Jeff Chelesvig
The Civic Center of Greater Des Moines
221 Walnut St
Des Moines, IA 50309-2104
515-243-0766 / 515-243-1179 F

Marks Chowning
San Antonio, TX
210-226-3333 / 210-226-3377 F

Geoff Cohen
Madison Square Garden
Two Penn Plaza
New York, NY 10121
212-465-6653 / 212-465-6420 f

Bill Conner
Livent, Inc.
165 Avenue Rd.
Toronto, ON M5R 2H7
416-324-5459 / 416-324-5702 F

R. Malcolm Cumming
The Broadway Theatre Guild
111 Lyon St. NW, ste 900
Grand Rapids, MI 49503-2487
616-752-2107 / 616-752-2500 F

Judith Daykin
City Center
130 West 56th St., 9th Fl.
New York, NY 10019
212-247-0430 / 212-246-9778 F

Patricia Dill
The Playhouse Theatre, Du Pont Building
10th & Market Streets
Wilmington, DE 19801
302-774-2215 / 302-594-1437 F

Mark Edelman
Theatre League, Inc.
301 W 13th St Ste 100
Kansas City, MO 64105
816-421-1801 / 816-421-1803 F

Douglas C. Evans
The Bushnell Memorial Hall
166 Capitol Ave Box 260898
Hartford, CT 06106-1621
860-987-6000 / 860-987-6002 F

Patrick Fagan
Shea's Performing Arts Center
646 Main St
Buffalo, NY 14202
716-847-1410 / 716-842-0968 F

David R. Fay
Fox Theatre
527 N. Grand Blvd.
St. Louis, MO 63103
314-534-1678 / 314-534-8702 F

Julie Ann Ferguson
Atlanta, GA
404-876-4300 / 404-872-0663 F

Michael Forst
Best of Broadway
1801 E Fifth St Ste 203
Charlotte, NC 28204
704-377-0071 / 704-377-0074 F

Susan R. Fowler
Hershey Theatre
PO Box 395, 15 E Caracas Ave
Hershey, PA 17033
717-534-3411 / 717-533-2882 F

Tom Gabbard
Weidner Center for the Performing Arts
2420 Nicolet Dr.
Green Bay, WI 54311-7001
920-465-2906 / 920-465-2619 F

Tom Gergerich
Marcus Center for the Performing Arts
929 N. Water St.
Milwaukee, WI 53202-5480
414-273-7121 / 414-273-5480 F

Elissa Getto
Cincinnati Association for the Performing
Arts
650 Walnut St
Cincinnati, OH 45202
513-721-3344 / 513-977-4150 F

Steven J. Greil
Tennessee Performing Arts Center
505 Deaderick St 3rd floor
Nashville, TN 37219
615-782-4021 / 615-782-4001 F

Pat Halloran
Orpheum Theatre
PO Box 3370
Memphis, TN 38173-0370
901-525-7800 / 901-526-0829 F

Michael Hardy
Kentucky Center for the Performing Arts
5 Riverfront Plaza, 501 West Main St
Louisville, KY 40202
502-562-0146 / 502-562-0105 F

Carole Shorenstein Hays
Shorenstein Hays Nederlander
1182 Market St., Ste. 320
San Francisco, CA 94102
415-551-2075 / 415-431-5052 F

Stephanie S. Hughley
New Jersey Performing Arts Center
1 Center St., 3rd Fl
Newark, NJ 07102
973-642-8989 / 973-648-6724 F

Atanas Ilitch
Olympia Entertainment/Fox Theatre/
The Young Production Group
2211 Woodward Ave.
Detroit, MI 48201
313-596-3200 / 313-983-6049 F

Joe Jefcoat
Penn State's Center for the Performing Arts
Eisenhower Auditorium
University Park, PA 16802
814-863-0388 / 814-863-7218 F

Michael Jenkins
Dallas Summer Musicals, Inc.
PO Box 710336
Dallas, TX 75371
214-421-0662 / 214-428-4526 F

Colleen Jennings-Roggensack
Arizona State University
ASU Public Events/PO Box 870205
Tempe, AZ 85287-0205
602-965-5062 / 602-965-7663 F

Jujamcyn Theaters
246 West 44th Street
New York, NY 10036
212-840-8181 / 212-768-1095 F

Jan Kallish
Auditorium Theatre Council
50 E. Congress Pkwy
Chicago, IL 60605
312-431-2391 / 312-341-9668 F

Van Kaplan
Pittsburgh Civic Light Opera
719 Liberty Ave
Pittsburgh, PA 15222-3504
412-281-3973 / 412-281-5339 F

John Dale Kennedy
Sangamon Auditorium, PAC 397
University of Illinois at Springfield
PO BOX 19243
Springfield, IL 62794-9243
217-206-6150 / 217-206-7279 F

Susie Krajsa
PACE Theatrical Group, Inc.
100 S. Biscayne Blvd., Ste 1200
Miami, FL 33133
305-379-2700 / 305-379-5901 F

Fred Krohn
c/o Historic State and Orpheum Theatres,
Theatre Live! Inc.
805 Hennepin Ave
Minneapolis, MN 55403
612-373-5600 / 612-339-4146 F

Elise J. Kushigian
Clowes Memorial Hall of Butler University
4600 Sunset Ave
Indianapolis, IN 46208-3845
317-940-9620 / 317-940-9820 F

Mick Levitt
Chicago, IL
312-573-1173 / 312-573-1177 F

Robert Lewis
Broadway Theatre League of Utica, Inc.
259 Genesee St
Utica, NY 13501
315-724-7196 / 315-724-1227 F

Sam L'Hommedieu
5203 Leesburg Pike Ste 1302
Falls Church, VA 22041
703-824-1525 / 703-824-1542 F

Alan N. Lichtenstein
Masonic Temple Theatre
500 Temple Ave
Detroit, MI 48201
313-832-5900 / 313-832-1047 F

Mark Light
Victoria Theatre Association
138 North Main St
Dayton, OH 45402
937-228-7591 / 937-449-5068 F

Judith Lisi
Tampa Bay Performing Arts Center
PO Box 518
Tampa, FL 33601-0518
813-222-1000 / 813-222-1057 F

Carl A. Mancuso
Heinz Hall for the Performing Arts
600 Penn Ave
Pittsburgh, PA 15222
412-392-4843 / 412-392-4910 F

Jerry Mandell
Orange County Performing Arts Center/PACE
Costa Mesa, CA
714-556-2121 / 714-556-7807 F

Christopher B. Manos
Theatre of the Stars, Inc.
PO Box 11748
Atlanta, GA 30355
404-252-8960 / 404-252-1460 F

Hoyt (Toby) Mattox
Society for the Performing Arts
615 Louisiana St
Houston, TX 77002
713-227-5134 / 713-223-8301 F

Kevin McCollum
The Ordway Music Theatre
345 Washington St.
Saint Paul, MN 55102
651-282-3000 / 651-224-5319 F

William A. Mitchell
Van Wezel Performing Arts Hall
777 North Tamiami Trail
Sarasota, FL 34236
941-955-7676 x223 / 941-951-1449 F

Arnold Mittelman
Coconut Grove Playhouse
3500 Main Highway
Miami, FL 33133
305-442-2662 / 305-444-6437 F

Paul Morer
The Little Theatre Group
240 West 44th St
New York, NY 10036
212-944-9457 / 212-302-3584 F

Richard Mortimer
Elgin & Winter Garden Theatre
189 Yonge St.
Toronto, ON M5B1M4
416-314-2871 / 416-314-3583 F

Scott Nederlander
Nederlander Enterprises
231 S. Old Woodward
Birmingham, MI 48009
248-644-3240 / 248-644-3408 F

The Nederlander Organization
810 Seventh Avenue
New York, NY 10019
212-262-2400 / 212-265-5558 F

Edgar Neiss
Fox Theatre
660 Peachtree St NE
Atlanta, GA 30365
404-881-2114 / 404-872-2972 F

Mark Nerenhausen
The Broward Center for the Performing Arts
201 Southwest Fifth Avenue
Fort Lauderdale, FL 33312
954-468-3299 / 954-462-3541 F

Albert Nocciolino
NAC Enterprises, Ltd.
PO Box 1921
Binghamton, NY 13902
607-772-1391 / 607-723-1211 F

Judith O'Dea Morr
Orange County Peforming Arts Center
600 Town Center Dr.
Costa Mesa, CA 92626
714-556-2121 x223 / 714-755-7807 F

Richard F. Pardy
c/o Lexington Center Corporation
430 W Vine St
Lexington, KY 40505
606-233-4567 / 606-253-2718 F

Larry Payton
Celebrity Attractions
8321 E 61st St Ste 202
Tulsa, OK 74133-1911
918-254-1069 / 918-254-8050 F

Jon B. Platt
American Artists, Inc.
120 Boylston St., Ste 502
Boston, MA 02116
617-451-2345 / 617-451-2434 F

Linda Bryant Potenza
The Broward Center for the Performing Arts
201 SW 5th Ave
Fort Lauderdale, FL 33312
954-468-3295 / 954-462-3541 F

Dennis M. Reagan
The Municipal Theatre Association of
St. Louis
Forest Park
St. Louis, MO 63112-1098
314-361-1900 x305 / 314-361-0009 F

Megan Riegel
Peace Center for the Performing Arts
101 W Broad St
Greenville, SC 29601
864-467-3030 / 864-467-3040 F

Bryan L. Rives
Indiana University Auditorium
1211 E 7th St
Bloomington, IN 47405
812-855-9528 / 812-855-4244 F

Robert M. Rohlf
Starlight Theatre
4600 Starlight Rd
Kansas City, MO 64132
816-333-9481 x110 / 816-361-6398 F

Milton A. Russos
FCCJ Artist Series
501 W State Street
Jacksonville, FL 32202
904-632-3373 / 904-632-3266 F

John E. Scott
Tulsa Performing Arts Center
110 E Second St
Tulsa, OK 74103
918-596-7122 / 918-596-7144 F

Beau Segal
Oakdale Theatre
Wallingford, CT
203-949-7700 / 203-284-1816 F

Kenneth F. Shaw
The Civic Opera House
20 N. Wacker Dr., Ste 860
Chicago, IL 60606-2806
312-419-0033 / 312-419-2806 F

James Sheeley
Jujamcyn Productions
12 South Sixth St., Ste 720
Minneapolis, MN 55402
612-373-0541 / 612-373-0544 F

Marilynn Sheldon
Fifth Avenue Theatre Association
1308 Fifth Ave
Seattle, WA 98101
206-625-1418 / 206-292-9610 F

The Shubert Organization
234 West 44th St.
New York, NY 10036
212-944-3700 / 212-944-3841 F

J. Lynn Singleton
Providence Performing Arts Center
220 Weybosset St
Providence, RI 02903
401-421-2997 / 401-421-5767 F

Richard D. Snyder
James W. Miller Auditorium
Western Michigan University
Kalamazoo, MI 49008
616-387-2311 / 616-387-2317 F

Ron Spencer
Tallahassee - Leon County Civic Center
PO Box 10604
Tallahassee, FL 32302
850-487-1691 / 850-222-6947 F

Gideon Toeplitz
Pittsburgh, PA
412-392-4800 / 412-392-4909 F

Steve Traxler
JAM Productions, LTD.
207 W. Goethe
Chicago, IL 60610
312-266-6262 / 312-266-9568 F

Kevin Ullestad
University of Illinois Assembly Hall
PO Box 1790
Champaign, IL 61820
217-333-2423 / 217-244-8888 F

Gina Vernaci
Playhouse Square Foundation
1501 Euclid Ave., Ste 200
Cleveland, OH 44115
216-348-5290 / 216-771-3974 F

Pebbles Wadsworth
Austin, TX
512-471-1196 / 512-471-3636 F

Randy Weeks
Denver Center Attractions
1245 Champa St
Denver, CO 80204
303-446-4800 / 303-572-8011 F

Caroline Werth
The Shubert Performing Arts Center
247 College St
New Haven, CT 06510
203-624-1825 / 203-789-2286 F

Lawrence J. Wilker
Kennedy Center for the Performing Arts
2700 F St NW
Washington, DC 20566-0011
202-416-8010 / 202-416-8205 F

William Wright
Wharton Center for the Performing Arts
Michigan State University
East Lansing, MI 48824
517-353-1982 / 517-353-5329 F

William A. Yost
Eisenhower Hall Theatre
Bldg. 655
West Point, NY 10996-1593
914-938-2782 / 914-446-5302 F

Greg Young
Olympia Entertainment/Fox Theatre/
The Young Production Group
2211 Woodward Ave.
Detroit, MI 48201
313-596-3200 / 313-596-3259 F

PRESENTERS: GUIDE BY MARKET
UNITED STATES

Alabama

Birmingham	Michael Forst	Best of Broadway
Huntsville	Michael Forst	Best of Broadway
Mobile	Michael Forst	Best of Broadway

Alaska

Anchorage	Ronald Andrew	Eagle Eye Entertainment

Arizona

Tempe	Colleen Jennings-Roggensack	
		Arizona State University and Pace Theatrical Group

Arkansas

Little Rock	Larry Payton	Celebrity Attractions

California

Beverly Hills		The Nederlander Organization
Costa Mesa	Jerry Mandell	Orange County Performing Arts Center and PACE Theatrical Group
Costa Mesa	Judith O'Dea Morr	Orange County Peforming Arts Center
Los Angeles		The Nederlander Organization
Los Angeles		The Shubert Organization
Montecito	Paul Blake	The Municipal Theatre Association of St. Louis (The Muny)
Pasadena	Rick Barr	Pasadena Civic Auditorium
Sacramento	Leland Ball	Sacramento Broadway Series
San Francisco	Carole Shorenstein Hays	
		Shorenstein Hays Nederlander

Colorado

Colorado Sprgs	John W. Ballard	MagicWorks West
Denver	Randy Weeks	Denver Center Attractions

Connecticut

Hartford	Douglas C. Evans	The Bushnell Memorial Hall
New Haven	Caroline Werth	The Shubert Performing Arts Center
Wallingford	Beau Segal	Oakdale Theatre

Delaware

Wilmington	Patricia Dill	The Playhouse Theatre, Du Pont Building

D.C.

Washington	Lawrence J. Wilker	Kennedy Center for the Performing Arts
Washington		The Shubert Organization

Florida

Coral Springs	J. Lynn Singleton	Professional Facilities Management
Ft. Lauderdale	Mark Nerenhausen Linda Bryant Potenza	Florida Theatrical Association, The Broward Center for the Performing Arts and PTG-Florida
Ft. Myers	J. Lynn Singleton	Professional Facilities Management
Jacksonville	Milton A. Russos	FCCJ Artist Series and PACE Theatrical Group
Miami	Arnold Mittelman	Coconut Grove Playhouse
Miami Beach	Susie Krajsa	Florida Theatrical Association and PTG-Florida
Orlando		Florida Theatrical Association and PTG-Florida
Palm Beach		Florida Theatrical Association and PTG-Florida
Sarasota	William A. Mitchell	Van Wezel Performing Arts Hall
Tallahassee	Ron Spencer	Tallahassee - Leon County Civic Center
Tampa	Judith Lisi	Tampa Bay Performing Arts Center, Florida Theatrical Association and PTG Florida

Georgia

Atlanta	Christopher B. Manos	Theatre of the Stars, Inc.
Atlanta	Edgar Neiss	Fox Theatre
Atlanta	Julie Ann Ferguson	PACE Theatrical Group
Savannah	Michael Forst	Best of Broadway

Hawaii

Honolulu	Ronald Andrew	Eagle Eye Entertainment

Idaho

Boise	John W. Ballard	MagicWorks West

Illinois

Champaign	Kevin Ullestad	University of Illinois Assembly Hall
Chicago	Mick Levitt	Fox Associates and Pace Theatrical Group
Chicago	Jan Kallish	Auditorium Theatre Council
Chicago	Kenneth F. Shaw	The Civic Opera House
Chicago	Bill Conner	Livent, Inc.
Chicago	Steve Traxler	JAM Productions, Ltd.
Chicago	Suzanne Bizer	The Shubert Theatre
Springfield	John Dale Kennedy	Sangamon Auditorium

Indiana

Bloomington	Bryan L. Rives	Indiana University Auditorium
Indianapolis	Elise J. Kushigian	Clowes Memorial Hall of Butler University
Indianapolis	Bradley L. Broecker	Broadway Series Management Group

Iowa

Des Moines	Jeff Chelesvig	The Civic Center of Greater Des Moines

Kansas

Wichita	John W. Ballard	MagicWorks West

Kentucky

Lexington	Richard F. Pardy	Lexington Center Corporation
Louisville	Bradley L. Broecker	Broadway Series Management Group, Inc.
Louisville	Michael Hardy	Kentucky Center for the Performing Arts

Louisiana

Baton Rouge	Michael Forst	Best of Broadway
New Orleans		PACE Theatrical Group

Maryland

Baltimore	Michael J. Brand	Jujamcyn Productions Company and The Baltimore Center for the Performing Arts

Massachusetts

Boston	Jon B. Platt	American Artists, Inc.
Boston		The Shubert Organization

Michigan

Detroit	Atanas Ilitch	Olympia Entertainment/Fox Theatre/The Young Production Group
Detroit	Alan N. Lichtenstein	Masonic Temple Theatre
Detroit	Scott Nederlander	Nederlander Organization
Detroit	Greg Young	Olympia Entertainment/Fox Theatre/The Young Production Group
East Lansing	William Wright	Wharton Center for the Performing Arts
Grand Rapids	R. Malcolm Cumming	The Broadway Theatre Guild
Kalamazoo	Richard D. Snyder	James W. Miller Auditorium

Minnesota
Minneapolis — James Binger — Jujamcyn Theaters
Minneapolis — Michael J. Brand — Jujamcyn Productions Company
Minneapolis — Fred Krohn — Historic State and Orpheum Theatres, Theatre Live! Inc.
Minneapolis — James Sheeley — Jujamcyn Productions
St. Paul — Bob Alwine — The Ordway Music Theatre
St. Paul — Kevin McCollum — The Ordway Music Theatre

Missouri
Kansas City — Mark Edelman — Theatre League, Inc.
Kansas City — Robert M. Rohlf — Starlight Theatre
St. Louis — David R. Fay — Fox Theatre
St. Louis — Dennis M. Reagan — The Municipal Theatre Association of St. Louis
Springfield — Larry Payton — Celebrity Attractions

Nebraska
Omaha — Michael J. Brand — Jujamcyn Productions Company

New Jersey
Newark — Stephanie S. Hughley — New Jersey Performing Arts Center

New Mexico
Albuquerque — John W. Ballard — MagicWorks West

New York
Binghamton — Albert Nocciolino — NAC Enterprises, Ltd.
Brooklyn — Alice Bernstein — Brooklyn Academy of Music
Buffalo — Albert Nocciolino — NAC Enterprises, Ltd.
Buffalo — Patrick Fagan — Shea's Performing Arts Center
New York — Judith Daykin — City Center
New York — Jujamcyn Theaters
New York — Lincoln Center Theater
New York — The Little Theatre Group
New York — Bill Conner — Livent, Inc.
New York — Geoff Cohen — Madison Square Garden
New York — The Nederlander Organization
New York — The Shubert Organization
Rochester — Albert Nocciolino — NAC Enterprises, Ltd.
Syracuse — Albert Nocciolino — NAC Enterprises, Ltd.
Utica — Robert Lewis — Broadway Theatre League of Utica, Inc.
West Point — William A. Yost — Eisenhower Hall Theatre

North Carolina
Charlotte — Judith Allen — North Carolina Blumenthal Center
Charlotte — Michael Forst — Best of Broadway
Greensboro — Michael Forst — Best of Broadway
Raleigh — Michael Forst — Best of Broadway

Ohio
Cincinnati — Elissa Getto — Cincinnati Association for the Performing Arts
Cincinnati — Bradley L. Broecker — Broadway Series Management Group
Cleveland — Gina Vernaci — Playhouse Square Foundation
Columbus — Bradley L. Broecker — Broadway Series Management Group
Dayton — Mark Light — Victoria Theatre Association
Toledo — Mark Edelman — Theatre League, Inc.

Oklahoma
Oklahoma City — Larry Payton — Celebrity Attractions
Tulsa — Larry Payton — Celebrity Attractions
Tulsa — John E. Scott — Tulsa Performing Arts Center

Oregon
Eugene — John W. Ballard — MagicWorks West
Portland — Michael J. Brand — The Portland Opera and Jujamcyn Productions Company

Pennsylvania
Hershey — Susan R. Fowler — Hershey Theatre
Philadelphia — Sam L'Hommedieu
Philadelphia — The Shubert Organization

Pittsburgh — Carol Brown & Gideon Toeplitz — The Pittsburgh Cultural Trust, The Symphony Society and PACE Theatrical Group
Pittsburgh — Van Kaplan — Pittsburgh Civic Light Opera
Pittsburgh — Carl A. Mancuso — Heinz Hall for the Performing Arts
Scranton — Albert Nocciolino — NAC Enterprises, Ltd.
University Park — Joe Jefcoat — Penn State's Center for the Performing Arts

Rhode Island
Providence — J. Lynn Singleton — Providence Performing Arts Center

South Carolina
Greenville — Megan Riegel — Peace Center for the Performing Arts
Myrtle Beach — Michael Forst — Best of Broadway

Tennessee
Memphis — Pat Halloran — Orpheum Theatre
Nashville — Steven J. Greil — Tennessee Performing Arts Center and PACE Theatrical Group

Texas
Austin — Pebbles Wadsworth — University of Texas and PACE Theatrical Group
Dallas — Michael Jenkins — Dallas Summer Musicals and PACE Theatrical Group
Houston — Hoyt (Toby) Mattox — Society for the Performing Arts and PACE Theatrical Group
San Antonio — Marks Chowning — The Majestic Theatre and PACE Theatrical Group
Lubbock — Larry Payton — Celebrity Attractions
Wichita Falls — Larry Payton — Celebrity Attractions

Utah
Salt Lake City — John W. Ballard — MagicWorks West

Virginia
Norfolk — Cynthia Carter-West — Chrysler Hall
Roanoke — Michael Forst — Best of Broadway

Washington
Seattle — Marilynn Sheldon — Fifth Avenue Theatre Association
Seattle — The Seattle Landmark Association and PACE Theatrical Group

Wisconsin
Green Bay — Tom Gabbard — Weidner Center for the Performing Arts
Milwaukee — Tom Gergerich — Marcus Center for the Performing Arts

CANADA

Alberta
Calgary — Ronald Andrew — Eagle Eye Entertainment
Edmonton — Ronald Andrew — Eagle Eye Entertainment

British Columbia
Vancouver — Livent
Vancouver — Ronald Andrew — Eagle Eye Entertainment

Manitoba
Winnipeg — Ronald Andrew — Eagle Eye Entertainment

Ontario
Hamilton — Ronald Andrew — Eagle Eye Entertainment
Ottawa — Ronald Andrew — Eagle Eye Entertainment
Toronto — Ronald Andrew — Eagle Eye Entertainment, Inc.
Toronto — Elizabeth Bradley — The Hummingbird Centre for the Performing Arts
Toronto — Bill Conner — Livent, Inc.
Toronto — Richard Mortimer — Elgin & Winter Garden Theatres

Saskatchewan
Regina — Ronald Andrew — Eagle Eye Entertainment
Saskatoon — Ronald Andrew — Eagle Eye Entertainment

United States Mileage Chart
and
Map

UNITED STATES MILEAGE CHART

	Albany, NY	Albuquerque, NM	Amarillo, TX	Atlanta, GA	Austin, TX	Baltimore, MD	Billings, MT	Birmingham, AL	Boise, ID	Boston, MA	Brownsville, TX	Buffalo, NY	Charleston, SC	Charleston, WV	Charlotte, NC	Chicago, IL	Cincinnati, OH	Cleveland, OH	Columbia, SC	Columbus, OH	Dallas, TX	Daytona Beach, FL	Denver, CO	Des Moines, IA	Detroit, MI	El Paso, TX	Fargo, ND	Fort Lauderdale, FL	Fort Wayne, IN	Fort Worth, TX	Grand Rapids, MI	Greensboro, NC	Hartford, CT	Houston, TX	Indianapolis, IN	Jackson, MS	Jacksonville, FL	Kansas City, MO	Knoxville, TN	Las Vegas, NV	Lincoln, NE	Little Rock, AK
Albany, NY	0	2125	1825	1007	1882	332	2073	1112	2601	170	2007	292	932	639	795	795	729	496	823	657	1679	1209	1853	1193	690	2327	1463	1403	705	1682	710	661	106	1825	836	1320	1111	1279	836	2609	1336	1370
Albuquerque, NM	2125	0	300	1387	716	1881	1022	1260	970	2214	988	1801	1695	1583	1628	1346	1394	1606	1598	1468	673	1716	446	1013	1537	267	1314	1953	1410	632	1491	1677	2084	870	1289	1087	1678	811	1407	576	837	883
Amarillo, TX	1825	300	0	1087	485	1581	1037	965	1235	1914	784	1501	1517	1304	1338	1046	1094	1306	1298	1168	363	1467	454	806	1289	508	999	1670	1109	344	1191	1377	1822	608	989	787	1378	552	1107	876	596	607
Atlanta, GA	1007	1387	1087	0	884	669	1804	160	2252	1068	1175	912	300	495	251	695	438	692	211	543	805	446	1401	924	726	1453	1364	681	612	837	749	348	969	816	543	397	329	810	204	1947	1013	540
Austin, TX	1882	716	485	884	0	1550	1449	793	1716	1930	331	1566	1247	1251	1237	1100	1127	1371	1095	1233	203	1158	1009	897	1330	583	1333	1326	1200	192	1288	1281	1867	162	1111	519	1057	680	1051	1297	851	520
Baltimore, MD	332	1881	1581	669	1550	0	1875	804	2416	409	1825	352	567	339	430	697	510	355	513	405	1347	876	1692	997	511	1997	1339	1036	550	1379	624	346	308	1409	584	1006	770	1078	503	2408	1192	1037
Billings, MT	2073	1022	1037	1804	1449	1875	0	1759	586	2232	1771	1857	2222	1762	2027	1214	1479	1662	2075	1654	1395	2173	579	959	1579	1284	625	2466	1405	1406	1396	1958	2169	1739	1400	1743	2227	1078	1723	1060	836	1439
Birmingham, AL	1112	1260	965	160	793	804	1759	0	2101	1267	1065	941	460	539	411	669	468	722	359	584	637	505	1370	838	721	1304	1311	764	610	702	739	493	1058	676	497	251	472	724	255	1822	953	394
Boise, ID	2601	970	1235	2252	1716	2416	586	2101	0	2794	1921	2271	2503	2246	2408	1777	1983	2058	2289	2069	1610	2576	870	1402	2020	1241	1245	2820	1871	1598	1917	2408	2652	1854	1890	2091	2579	1476	2022	662	1205	1781
Boston, MA	170	2214	1914	1068	1930	409	2232	1267	2794	0	2255	454	989	728	828	965	875	632	928	738	1727	1257	1953	1305	795	2376	1623	1492	847	1761	908	739	105	1878	933	1395	1167	1435	871	2765	1500	1472
Brownsville, TX	2007	988	784	1175	331	1825	1909	1065	1921	2255	0	1865	1500	1479	1426	1430	1426	1670	1360	1533	526	1353	1251	1184	1694	806	1601	1542	1455	518	1585	1480	2094	357	1427	791	1264	1008	1320	1573	1216	819
Buffalo, NY	292	1801	1501	912	1566	352	1857	941	2271	454	1865	0	947	430	666	543	438	195	822	333	1363	1069	1602	867	366	2011	1185	1400	381	1395	419	641	397	1492	512	1119	1068	1007	671	2254	1057	1046
Charleston, SC	932	1695	1517	300	1247	567	2222	460	2503	989	1500	947	0	479	203	912	628	750	113	670	1164	351	1743	1185	874	1729	1557	586	740	1116	959	271	867	1027	743	702	248	1135	368	2247	1287	814
Charleston, WV	639	1583	1304	495	1251	339	1762	539	2246	728	1479	430	479	0	276	469	178	284	376	156	1134	726	1377	761	371	1672	1126	1004	284	1056	457	227	662	1246	328	790	676	777	284	2119	960	707
Charlotte, NC	795	1628	1338	251	1237	430	2027	411	2408	828	1426	666	203	276	0	738	446	543	100	453	1054	469	1548	1029	607	1710	1414	721	602	1061	791	89	763	1053	551	640	413	940	219	2173	1151	743
Chicago, IL	795	1346	1046	695	1100	697	1214	669	1777	965	1430	543	912	469	738	0	291	348	794	340	932	1096	1037	357	284	1435	649	1348	159	945	178	729	875	1160	186	762	999	543	537	1749	527	675
Cincinnati, OH	729	1394	1094	438	1127	510	1479	468	1983	875	1426	438	628	178	446	291	0	249	502	105	924	861	1199	583	260	1472	940	1086	184	956	357	458	746	1053	105	680	786	591	246	1921	715	608
Cleveland, OH	496	1606	1306	692	1371	355	1662	722	2058	632	1670	195	750	284	543	348	249	0	627	138	1168	952	1407	672	171	1716	997	1232	211	1200	284	486	539	1297	317	924	908	803	489	2059	867	851
Columbia, SC	823	1598	1298	211	1095	513	2075	359	2289	928	1360	822	113	376	100	794	502	627	0	513	1032	381	1616	1126	745	1668	1446	622	671	1057	858	188	836	1066	625	610	290	1025	267	2162	1199	759
Columbus, OH	657	1469	1168	543	1233	405	1654	584	2069	738	1533	333	670	156	453	340	105	138	513	0	1030	901	1270	657	195	1540	989	1126	150	1062	311	381	641	1159	179	786	850	665	351	1995	776	713
Dallas, TX	1679	673	363	805	203	1347	1395	637	1610	1727	526	1363	1164	1134	1054	932	924	1168	1032	1030	0	1123	806	714	1203	648	1131	1097	1030	33	1110	1122	1664	243	908	422	1005	511	820	1249	648	317
Daytona Beach, FL	1209	1716	1467	446	1158	876	2173	505	2576	1257	1353	1069	351	726	469	1096	883	952	381	901	1123	0	1823	1329	1103	1728	1714	227	1006	1126	1143	551	1138	952	880	688	97	1209	603	2316	1401	904
Denver, CO	1853	446	454	1401	1009	1692	579	1370	870	1953	1251	1602	1743	1377	1548	1037	1199	1407	1616	1270	806	1823	0	695	1321	705	915	2067	1186	773	1201	1621	1988	1060	1091	1246	1779	608	1341	743	507	992
Des Moines, IA	1193	1013	806	924	897	997	959	838	1402	1305	1184	867	1185	761	1029	357	583	672	1126	657	714	1329	695	0	600	1114	475	1581	516	747	502	1028	1283	930	478	846	1270	203	821	1399	203	562
Detroit, MI	690	1537	1289	726	1330	511	1579	721	2020	795	1694	366	874	371	607	284	260	171	745	195	1203	1103	1321	600	0	1701	922	1346	170	1240	162	567	701	1304	293	923	1046	791	506	2011	819	850
El Paso, TX	2327	267	508	1453	583	1997	1274	1304	1241	2376	806	2011	1729	1672	1710	1435	1372	1716	1668	1540	648	1728	705	1114	1701	0	1460	1869	1573	609	1554	1783	2263	743	1460	1070	1626	915	1488	722	946	960
Fargo, ND	1463	1314	999	1364	1333	1339	625	1311	1245	1625	1601	1185	1557	1126	1414	649	940	997	1446	989	1131	1714	915	475	922	1460	0	2007	808	1072	827	1412	1531	1334	835	1335	1704	609	1195	1535	451	1091
Fort Lauderdale, FL	1435	1953	1670	681	1326	1036	2466	764	2820	1492	1542	1400	586	1004	721	1348	1086	1232	622	1126	1097	227	2067	1581	1346	1869	2007	0	1271	1129	1342	786	1403	1191	1232	883	332	1459	860	2530	1670	1184
Fort Wayne, IN	705	1410	1109	612	1200	550	1405	610	1871	847	1455	381	740	284	602	159	184	219	671	150	1030	1006	1186	516	170	1573	808	1271	0	1053	172	551	768	1176	122	784	929	648	430	1878	686	711
Fort Worth, TX	1682	632	344	837	192	1379	1406	702	1598	1761	518	1395	1116	1056	1061	945	956	1200	1057	1062	33	1126	773	747	1236	609	1072	1129	1053	0	1121	1154	1696	264	912	446	1037	513	853	1203	648	349
Grand Rapids, MI	710	1491	1191	749	1288	624	1396	739	1917	908	1585	419	959	457	791	178	357	284	858	311	1110	1143	1201	502	162	1554	827	1342	172	1121	0	707	794	1196	263	957	1071	638	573	1889	699	799
Greensboro, NC	661	1677	1377	348	1281	346	1958	493	2408	739	1480	641	271	227	89	729	458	486	188	381	1122	551	1621	1028	567	1783	1412	786	551	1154	707	0	650	1167	563	770	483	1013	283	2237	1202	778
Hartford	106	2084	1822	969	1867	308	2169	1058	2652	105	2044	397	867	662	763	875	746	539	836	641	1664	1138	1988	1283	701	2263	1531	1403	768	1696	794	650	0	1773	805	1306	1071	1297	841	2675	1378	1344
Houston, TX	1825	870	608	816	162	1409	1639	676	1854	1878	357	1492	1027	1246	1053	1160	1053	1297	1066	1159	243	952	1060	930	1304	743	1334	1191	1176	264	1196	1167	1773	0	1041	406	891	754	922	1468	892	446
Indianapolis, IN	836	1289	989	543	1111	584	1400	497	1890	933	1427	512	743	328	551	186	105	317	625	179	908	880	1091	478	293	1460	835	1232	122	912	263	563	805	1041	0	681	867	486	351	1816	673	608
Jackson, MS	1320	1087	787	397	519	1006	1743	251	2091	1395	991	1119	702	790	640	762	680	924	610	786	422	688	1246	846	923	1070	1335	883	784	446	957	770	1306	406	681	0	591	716	506	1650	874	251
Jacksonville, FL	1111	1678	1378	329	1057	770	2227	472	2579	1167	1264	1068	248	676	413	999	786	908	290	850	1005	97	1779	1270	1046	1626	1704	332	929	1037	1071	483	1071	891	867	591	0	1110	555	2238	1321	843
Kansas City, MO	1279	811	552	810	680	1078	1078	724	1476	1435	1008	1007	1135	777	940	543	591	803	1025	665	511	1209	608	203	791	916	609	1459	648	513	638	1013	1297	754	486	716	1110	0	752	1345	211	409
Knoxville, TN	836	1407	1107	204	1051	503	1723	255	2022	871	1320	671	368	284	219	537	246	489	267	351	820	603	1341	821	506	1488	1195	860	430	872	573	283	841	922	351	506	555	752	0	1983	944	523
Las Vegas, NV	2609	576	876	1947	1297	2408	1060	1822	662	2765	1573	2254	2247	2119	2173	1749	1921	2059	2162	1995	1249	2316	743	1399	2011	722	1535	2530	1878	1203	1889	2237	2675	1468	1816	1650	2238	1345	1983	0	1224	1483
Lincoln, NE	1386	837	596	1013	851	1192	836	953	1205	1500	1216	1057	1287	960	1151	527	802	867	1199	776	648	1401	507	203	819	946	451	1670	686	648	699	1202	1378	892	673	874	1321	211	944	1224	0	616
Little Rock, AK	1370	883	607	540	520	1207	1439	394	1781	1472	819	1046	814	707	743	675	608	851	759	713	317	904	992	562	850	960	1091	1184	711	349	799	778	1344	446	608	251	843	409	523	1483	616	0
Los Angeles, CA	2911	823	1095	2197	1410	2676	1254	2067	837	2993	1678	2587	2521	2394	2617	1989	2164	2392	2426	2254	1401	2407	1009	1654	2270	818	1844	2704	2137	1361	2148	2478	2829	1581	2075	1880	2402	1589	2201	275	1476	1678
Louisville, KY	868	1332	1041	421	1127	602	1550	373	1908	976	1372	543	608	258	438	300	105	349	494	211	819	801	1127	591	365	1467	949	1078	222	851	373	462	867	948	129	575	729	519	246	1861	730	502
Memphis, TN	1232	1021	721	397	658	900	1557	239	1833	1379	957	908	689	653	604	551	469	713	612	575	455	749	1151	599	712	1103	1224	989	592	487	690	640	1209	584	470	211	697	470	385	1581	647	138
Miami, FL	1439	1994	1694	665	1338	1095	2710	788	2860	1516	1580	1524	630	1046	745	1338	1086	1264	658	1210	1321	259	2131	1582	1386	1958	1986	24	1326	1353	1356	810	1427	1207	1208	907	356	1475	859	2570	1673	1208
Milwaukee, WI	933	1443	1143	784	1203	794	1143	766	1777	1078	1530	640	1032	566	835	92	388	445	891	448	1013	1180	1070	365	389	1528	576	1443	256	1059	275	826	948	1155	283	884	1067	568	643	1752	560	772
Minneapolis, MN	1215	1256	1062	1105	1120	1105	812	1088	1488	1362	1456	948	1316	874	1143	405	696	753	1276	753	1013	1458	956	251	698	1520	244	1723	564	1001	583	1135	1257	1266	591	1123	1376	459	932	1630	409	881
Mobile, AL	1322	1265	965	340	656	990	1854	269	2343	1379	851	1184	607	825	575	908	745	989	555	834	592	502	1372	954	988	1236	1413	705	839	624	1006	681	1290	478	749	178	413	819	449	1841	1039	430
Montgomery, AL	1178	1345	1042	164	804	833	1836	93	2346	1232	1041	1076	464	632	405	762	561	815	379	707	677	458	1412	1311	814	1325	1521	671	686	701	819	512	1133	709	590	255	379	867	348	2015	975	470
Nashville, TN	993	1232	932	243	869	688	1640	195	2059	1062	1168	722	576	458	399	474	283	527	458	389	666	639	1167	712	536	1314	1136	900	385	698	534	429	973	795	302	422	592	590	174	1792	770	349
New Orleans, LA	1453	1187	875	493	535	1136	1820	352	2191	1526	730	1273	727	891	721	925	820	1078	701	940	530	632	1323	978	1077	1127	1494	843	916	519	1071	810	1436	367	857	193	551	857	607	1800	1114	430
New York City, NY	146	1995	1695	855	1728	201	1926	1019	2571	203	2002	390	786	524	625	794	628	446	715	551	1525	1054	1775	1070	620	2173	1450	1289	691	1557	706	561	101	1679	730	1192	957	1192	771	2520	1274	1235
Norfolk, VA	505	1905	1632	551	1403	237	2098	711	2551	660	1735	569	454	369	341	851	681	493	412	559	1359	702	1800	1202	711	1998	1581	964	709	1382	802	227	471	1362	669	948	632	1179	412	2534	1354	1025
Oakland, CA	2982	1134	1430	2488	1786	2864	1218	2321	671	3124	2034	2745	2788	2600	2755	2098	2317	2498	2703	2391	1803	2831	1223	1742	2350	1194	1870	3041	2257	1723	2308	2809	2909	1957	2212	2270	2771	1799	2509	582	1604	1984
Oklahoma City, OK	1523	559	267	863	414	1322	1168	701	1451	1659	680	1242	1176	1031	1069	804	835	1047	1091	909	211	1257	660	576	1030	708	989	1481	852	210	932	1118	1546	454	730	575	1181	373	847	1119	433	324
Omaha, NE	1308	905	754	989	847	1143	904	904	1274	1443	1249	1005	1303	899	1135	464	721	824	1283	795	693	1402	559	146	726	1256	464	1604	634	634	640	1208	1321	949	616	914	1305	195	930	1249	57	690
Orlando, FL	1249	1751	1451	446	1142	917	2277	545	2695	1297	2034	1306	401	814	559	1127	892	1046	440	997	1078	81	1896	1363	1143	1735	1826	208	1059	1110	1188	648	1208	964	989	697	138	1266	665	2311	1452	965
Philadelphia, PA	251	1922	1622	766	1630	97	2051	880	2488	327	1954	397	688	517	522	757	559	430	627	460	1427	914	1762	998	585	2075	1370	1127	604	1459	672	438	220	1581	624	1094	859	1134	646	2449	1260	1110
Phoenix, AZ	2512	446	746	1810	1030	2311	1220	1700	1022	2644	1289	2269	2222	2045	2061	1776	1808	2045	2025	1907	1013	2101	802	1497	2019	438	1791	2244	1831	983	1906	2099	2523	1110	1719	1500	2100	1277	1845	284	1236	1379
Pittsburgh, PA	471	1654	1354	712	1412	245	1681	778	2203	584	1713	219	778	211	504	470	291	128	572	186	1209	859	1475	770	304	1833	1112	1216	336	1241	397	438	486	1345	349	965	882	851	515	2181	965	899
Portland, Or	2869	1378	1636	2763	2059	2765	867	2571	439	3149	2468	2677	2952	2615	2757	2140	2474	2416	2972	2478	2051	3018	1283	1816	2368	1661	1484	3204	2299	2003	2251	2823	2877	2369	2335	2518	3042	1809	2550	991	1641	2270
Providence, RI	178	2156	1856	1027	1898	356	2238	1189	2701	41	2222	454	956	699	785	924	790	600	888	713	1695	1201	1961	1256	746	2335	1566	1459	799	1727	859	706	73	1849	892	1362	1127	1378	935	2683	1451	1395
Raleigh, NC	656	1759	1459	397	1355	324	2273	557	2560	713	1506	721	300	297	162	802	540	559	215	453	1152	559	1694	1123	643	1800	1485	794	603	1184	754	73	624	1233	635	815	486	1086	356	2319	1263	851
Reno, NV	2763	1056	1345	2411	1775	2562	1021	2363	404	2871	2068	2433	2765	2407	2570	1897	2221	2238	2626	2295	1731	2758	1030	1606	2190	1183	1660	3008	2056	1608	2067	2591	2749	1932	2116	2143	2716	1606	2363	478	1411	1986
Richmond, VA	482	1833	1533	527	1463	155	1655	699	2594	544	1646	552	462	251	280	341	356	583	390	498	1313	713	1904	1293	609	2023	1481	946	635	1333	722	191	455	2291	907	946	693	1205	440	2406	1249	963
Rochester, NY	219	1857	1557	1015	1623	300	1922	965	2352	381	1891	81	871	495	689	608	502	268	789	397	1420	1176	1637	932	424	2036	1249	1410	464	1452	499	600	324	1555	551	1183	1102	1062	710	2371	1135	1111
Saint Louis, MO	1028	1054	754	588	806	827	1381	539	1727	1184	1216	747	884	544	689	292	340	552	737	414	641	956	859	377	585	1238	872	1208	369	898	437	762	1030	835	251	495	859	251	497	1581	462	422
Saint Paul, MN	1215	1362	1062	1105	1120	1095	812	1118	1398	892	1565	948	1316	870	1143	405	696	753	1320	745	1013	1458	956	251	698	1541	244	1753	564	987	583	1138	1257	1266	591	1160	1376	459	951	1630	408	881
Salt Lake City, UT	2290	621	1324	1900	1341	2051	579	1825	349	2417	1775	1922	2254	1896	2059	1386	1710	1727	2115	1711	1287	2283	519	1085	1679	892	1172	2578	1527	1184	1556	2059	2238	1460	1605	1742	2286	1095	1766	413	900	1054
San Antonio, TX	1986	684	530	965	81	1646	1600	895	1709	2052	300	1638	1371	1419	1272	1208	1208	1443	1180	1305	284	1175	975	1022	1500	576	1402	1378	1269	283	1353	1321	1965	203	1200	649	1086	795	1150	1273	916	592
San Diego, CA	2855	787	1078	2174	1313	2714	1309	2043	1010	2992	1574	2613	2505	2402	2423	2335	2193	2334	2389	2277	1369	2418	1054	1760	2419	721	1934	2621	2189	1332	2269	2457	2944	1484	2067	1783	2329	1627	2269	349	1573	1743
San Francisco, CA	2966	1135	1296	2477	1776	2765	1239	2371	595	3133	2044	2403	2923	2616	2756	2108	2329	2408	2738	2461	1865	2827	1233	1832	2360	1184	1886	3073	2304	1735	2318	2740	3019	1947	2224	2183	2781	1869	2549	592	1614	1994
Seattle, WA	2855	1500	1805	2656	2157	2685	815	2475	524	2961	2521	2531	2960	2748	2765	2043	2334	2336	2971	2408	2203	3070	1371	1889	2299	1775	1440	3882	2202	2071	2221	2773	2918	2498	2229	2585	3090	1884	2553	1209	1636	2320
Shreveport, LA	1599	868	568	624	340	1229	1691	474	1912	1618	644	1265	945	899	885	916	826	1070	833	592	196	903	1112	827	1069	844	1229	1144	909	228	1018	937	1519	271	827	223	814	624	729	1468	727	219
Spokane, WA	2652	1346	1563	2367	1981	2417	541	2469	369	2693	2359	2263	2700	2503	2505	1775	2066	2068	2572	2115	1978	2811	1095	1556	2020	1666	1166	3014	1921	1978	1941	2503	2650	2222	1961	2205	2822	1727	2298	1119	1460	2092
Tallahassee, FL	1249	1508	1208	268	899	932	2306	302	2512	1312	1094	1155	364	868	559	957	706	949	408	828	835	259	1727	1216	957	1492	1598	462	871	867	1022	608	1223	721	818	421	170	1045	584	2068	1227	679
Tampa, FL	1281	1759	1459	476	1150	949	2143	553	2763	1329	1345	1346	479	903	584	1143	908	1091	497	1013	1086	141	1858	1460	1200	1743	1849	268	1092	1118	1219	673	1240	972	1069	672	195	1296	730	2319	1477	958
Toledo, OH	633	1526	1220	641	1315	454	1557	673	2020	742	1622	309	973	284	533	243	203	114	683	138	1112	1063	1272	567	65	1699	885	1289	105	1144	170	516	624	1249	243	876	989	717	449	1954	762	803
Tuscon, AZ	2442	486	656	1785	908	2246	1342	1621	1144	2571	1176	2166	2100	2039	1913	1711	1750	1971	2080	1833	964	1999	835	1484	1938	316	1897	2271	1783	932	1856	2059	2433	1079	1668	1378	2010	1281	1755	389	1246	1257
Tulsa, OK	1409	674	336	803	462	1208	1293	636	2020	1532	835	1128	1103	941	989	673	721	933	1018	795	259	1156	714	471	916	788	972	1409	738	305	818	1037	1411	504	616	510	1167	283	782	1224	416	259
Washington, DC	378	1864	1564	630	1509	41	2006	781	2441	430	1787	429	559	299	334	697	478	341	498	418	1306	802	1654	1054	506	1954	1322	1062	531	1338	608	309	341	1220	551	965	730	1046	554	2376	1184	832
West Palm Beach, FL	1396	1938	1638	632	1329	1046	2736	702	2942	1426	1524	1443	568	982	673	1289	1063	1192	586	1146	1265	195	2157	1646	1305	1922	2028	41	1157	1297	1476	737	1339	1151	1176	851	284	1052	806	2498	1598	1101
Youngstown, OH	462	1632	1346	719	1368	298	1632	738	2090	568	1695	190	709	251	502	413	275	74	561	170	1193	986	1421	737	239	1804	1038	1219	275	1225	340	482	470	1322	341	949	958	843	521	2124	923	876

UNITED STATES MILEAGE CHART

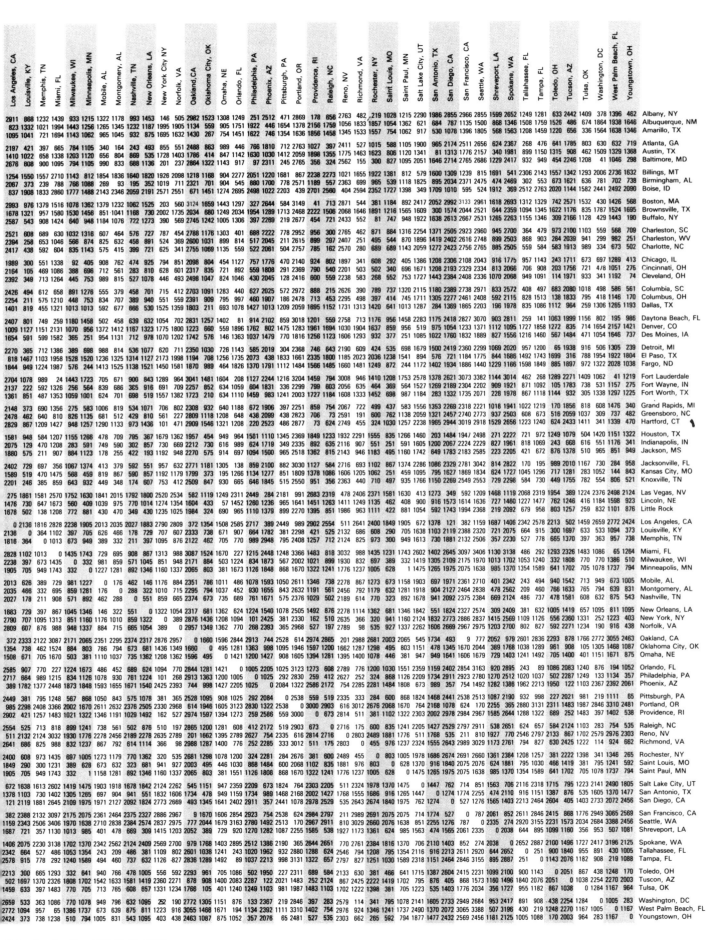

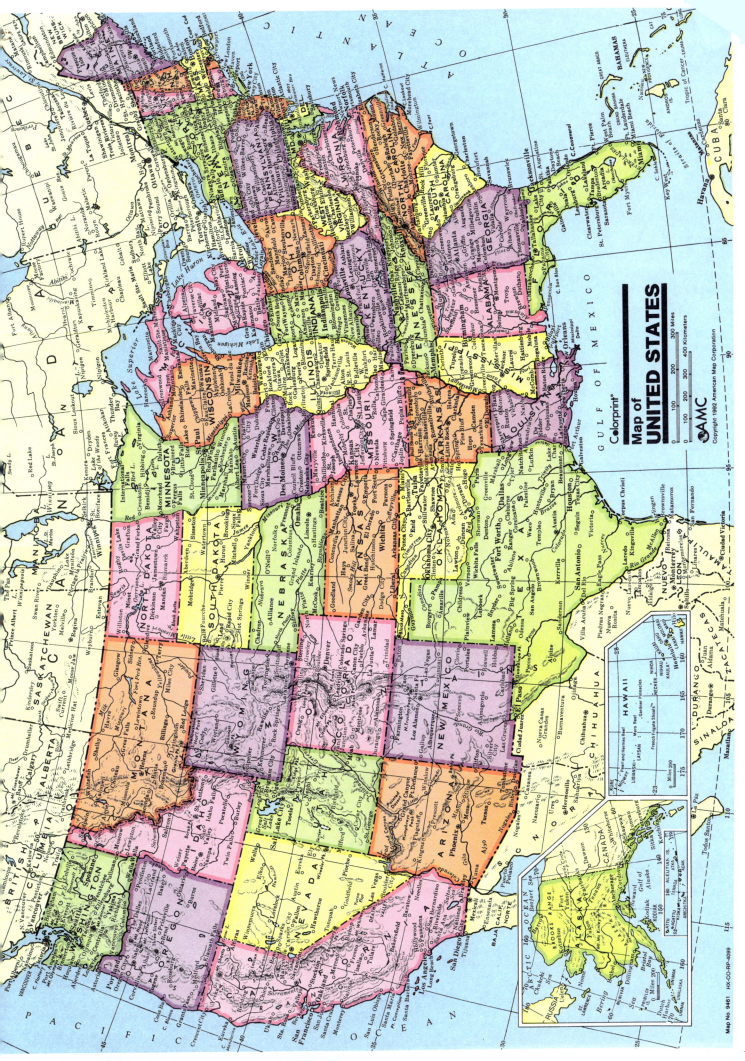

Colorprint®

Map of
UNITED STATES

AMC

Copyright 1992 American Map Corporation

Map No. 9461   HX-CO-RP-4099